Business Law Today

Text & Summarized Cases

Custom Edition for LAW 1101

Roger Leroy Miller

D1223851

CENGAGE
Learning

Australia • Brazil • Japan • Korea • Mexico • Singapore • Spain • United Kingdom • United States

Business Law Today: Text & Summarized Cases, Custom Edition for LAW 1101

Business Law Today: Text & Summarized Cases, Eleventh Edition
Roger Leroy Miller

© 2017 Cengage Learning. All rights reserved.

For product information and technology assistance, contact us at
Cengage Learning Customer & Sales Support, 1-800-354-9706

For permission to use material from this text or product,
submit all requests online at **cengage.com/permissions**
Further permissions questions can be emailed to
permissionrequest@cengage.com

This book contains select works from existing Cengage Learning resources and was produced by Cengage Learning Custom Solutions for collegiate use. As such, those adopting and/or contributing to this work are responsible for editorial content accuracy, continuity and completeness.

Compilation © 2016 Cengage Learning

ISBN: 978-1-337-03596-5

Cengage Learning
20 Channel Center Street
Boston, MA 02210
USA

Cengage Learning is a leading provider of customized learning solutions with office locations around the globe, including Singapore, the United Kingdom, Australia, Mexico, Brazil, and Japan. Locate your local office at:
www.international.cengage.com/region.

Cengage Learning products are represented in Canada by Nelson Education, Ltd.

For your lifelong learning solutions, visit **www.cengage.com/custom.**

Visit our corporate website at **www.cengage.com.**

Printed at CLDPC, USA, 06-18

Brief Contents

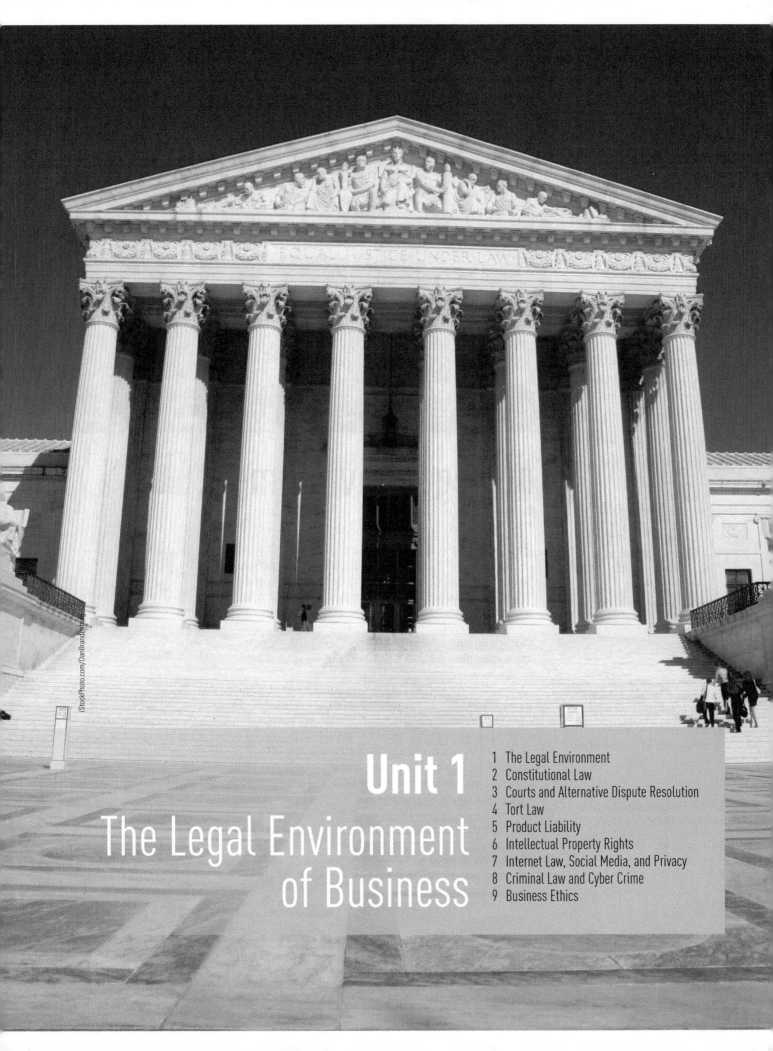

Unit 1
The Legal Environment of Business

1

iStockPhoto.com/Feverpitched

CHAPTER OUTLINE

- Business Activities and the Legal Environment
- Sources of American Law
- Common Law Tradition
- Classifications of Law

LEARNING OBJECTIVES

The five Learning Objectives below are designed to help improve your understanding of the chapter. After reading this chapter, you should be able to answer the following questions:

1. What are four primary sources of law in the United States?

2. What is the common law tradition?

3. What is a precedent? When might a court depart from precedent?

4. What is the difference between remedies at law and remedies in equity?

5. What are some important differences between civil law and criminal law?

Law A body of enforceable rules governing relationships among individuals and between individuals and their society.

The Legal Environment

In the chapter-opening quotation, Clarence Darrow asserts that law should be created to serve the public. Because you are part of that public, the law is important to you. In particular, those entering the world of business will find themselves subject to numerous laws and government regulations. A basic knowledge of these laws and regulations is beneficial—if not essential—to anyone contemplating a successful career in today's business environment.

Although the law has various definitions, all of them are based on the general observation that **law** consists of *enforceable rules governing relationships among individuals and between individuals and their society.* In some societies, these enforceable rules consist of unwritten principles of behavior. In other societies, they are set forth in ancient or contemporary law codes. In the United States, our rules consist of written laws and court decisions created by modern legislative and judicial bodies. Regardless of how such rules are created, they all have one feature in common: *they establish rights, duties, and privileges that are consistent with the values and beliefs of a society or its ruling group.*

In this introductory chapter, we look first at an important question for any student reading this text: How do business law and the legal environment affect business decision making? Next, we describe the basic sources of American law, the common law tradition, and some schools of legal thought. We conclude the chapter with a discussion of some general classifications of law.

> "Laws should be like clothes. They should be made to fit the people they are meant to serve."
>
> **CLARENCE DARROW**
> 1857–1938
> (AMERICAN LAWYER)

1–1 Business Activities and the Legal Environment

Laws and government regulations affect almost all business activities—from hiring and firing decisions to workplace safety, the manufacturing and marketing of products, business financing, and more. To make good business decisions, businesspersons need to understand the laws and regulations governing these activities.

Realize also that in today's business world, simply being aware of what conduct can lead to legal **liability** is not enough. Businesspersons must develop critical thinking and legal reasoning skills so that they can evaluate how various laws might apply to a given situation and determine the best course of action. Businesspersons are also pressured to make ethical decisions. Thus, the study of business law necessarily involves an ethical dimension.

Liability The state of being legally responsible (liable) for something, such as a debt or obligation.

1–1a Many Different Laws May Affect a Single Business Transaction

As you will note, each chapter in this text covers a specific area of the law and shows how the legal rules in that area affect business activities. Although compartmentalizing the law in this fashion facilitates learning, it does not indicate the extent to which many different laws may apply to just one transaction. Exhibit 1–1 illustrates the various areas of the law that may influence business decision making.

EXAMPLE 1.1 When Mark Zuckerberg started Facebook as a Harvard student, he probably did not imagine all the legal challenges his company would face as a result of his business decisions.

- Shortly after Facebook was launched, others claimed that Zuckerberg had stolen their ideas for a social networking site. Their claims involved alleged theft of intellectual property (see Chapter 6), fraudulent misrepresentation (see Chapter 13), partnership law (see Chapter 27), and securities law (see Chapter 30). Facebook ultimately paid a significant amount ($65 million) to settle those claims out of court.
- By 2015, Facebook had been sued repeatedly for violating users' privacy (such as by disseminating private information to third parties for commercial purposes—see Chapters 4 and 7). In 2012 and 2014, lawsuits were filed against Facebook for violating users' privacy (and federal laws) by tracking their Web site usage and by scanning private messages for purposes of data mining and user profiling. Also in 2014, a suit was filed in Europe against Facebook alleging violations of EU laws governing privacy and data use.

Mark Zuckerberg, founder of Facebook, has faced numerous legal challenges. These include privacy issues and the alleged theft of intellectual property. Can large Internet firms completely avoid such legal problems?

- Facebook's business decisions have come under scrutiny by federal regulators, such as the Federal Trade Commission (FTC) and the Securities and Exchange Commission (SEC). The company settled a complaint filed by the FTC alleging that Facebook failed to keep "friends" lists and other user information private. ■

A key to avoiding business disputes is to think ahead when starting or running a business or entering a contract. Learn what you can about the laws pertaining to that specific enterprise or transaction. Have some idea of the legal ramifications of your business decisions, and seek the advice of a licensed attorney. When you need to choose an attorney, obtain recommendations from friends, relatives, or business associates who have had long-standing relationships with their attorneys.

PREVENTING LEGAL DISPUTES

Exhibit 1–1 **Areas of the Law That May Affect Business Decision Making**

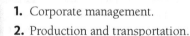

Contracts

Courts and
Court Procedures

Sales

Professional
Liability

Negotiable
Instruments

Business
Organizations

**Business
Decision
Making**

Creditors'
Rights

Agency

Intellectual
Property

Torts

E-Commerce

Product
Liability

1–1b Linking Business Law to the Six Functional Fields of Business

In all likelihood, you are taking a business law or legal environment course because you intend to enter the business world, though some of you may plan to become attorneys. Many of you are taking other business school courses and may therefore be familiar with the functional fields of business listed below:

1. Corporate management.
2. Production and transportation.
3. Marketing.
4. Research and development.
5. Accounting and finance.
6. Human resource management.

Why is basic knowledge of business law and the legal environment so important today?

One of our goals in this text is to show how legal concepts can be useful for managers and businesspersons, whether their activities focus on management, marketing, accounting, or some other field. To that end, numerous chapters, including this chapter, conclude with a special feature called "*Linking Business Law to* [one of the six functional fields of business]." The link between business law and accounting is so significant that we discuss it in detail in Chapter 33.

1–1c The Role of the Law in a Small Business

Some of you may end up working in a small business or even owning and running one. The small business owner/operator is the most general of managers. When you seek additional

Exhibit 1–2 Linking Business Law to the Management of a Small Business

Business Organization
What is the most appropriate business organizational form,
and what type of personal liability does it entail?

Taxation
How will the small business be taxed, and are there ways to reduce those taxes?

Intellectual Property
Does the small business have any patents or other intellectual
property that needs to be protected, and if so, what steps should the firm take?

Administrative Law
What types of government regulations apply to the
business, and what must the firm do to comply with them?

Employment
Does the business need an employment manual,
and does management have to explicitly inform employees of their rights?

Contracts, Sales, and Leases
Will the firm be regularly entering into contracts with others,
and if so, should it hire an attorney to review those contracts?

Accounting
Do the financial statements created by an accountant need to be verified for accuracy?

Finance
What are appropriate and legal ways to raise
additional capital so that the business can grow?

financing, you become a finance manager. When you "go over the books" with your book-keeper, you become an accountant. When you decide on a new advertising campaign, you are suddenly the marketing manager. When you hire employees and determine their salaries and benefits, you become a human resources manager.

Just as the functional fields of business are linked to the law, so too are all of the different managerial roles that a small-business owner/operator must perform. Exhibit 1–2 shows some of the legal issues that may arise as part of the management of a small business. Large businesses face most of these issues, too.

1–2 Sources of American Law

There are numerous sources of American law. **Primary sources of law**, or sources that establish the law, include the following:

Primary Source of Law A document that establishes the law on a particular issue, such as a constitution, a statute, an administrative rule, or a court decision.

- The U.S. Constitution and the constitutions of the various states.
- Statutory law—including laws passed by Congress, state legislatures, and local governing bodies.
- Regulations created by administrative agencies, such as the federal Food and Drug Administration.
- Case law (court decisions).

We describe each of these important primary sources of law in the following pages. (See the appendix at the end of this chapter for a discussion of how to find statutes, regulations, and case law.)

Secondary sources of law are books and articles that summarize and clarify the primary sources of law. Legal encyclopedias, compilations (such as *Restatements of the Law,* which summarize court decisions on a particular topic), official comments to statutes, treatises, articles in law reviews published by law schools, and articles in other legal journals are examples of secondary sources of law. Courts often refer to secondary sources of law for guidance in interpreting and applying the primary sources of law discussed here.

Secondary Source of Law A publication that summarizes or interprets the law, such as a legal encyclopedia, a legal treatise, or an article in a law review.

1–2a **Constitutional Law**

The federal government and the states have written constitutions that set forth the general organization, powers, and limits of their respective governments. **Constitutional law,** which deals with the fundamental principles by which the government exercises its authority, is the law as expressed in these constitutions.

The U.S. Constitution is the basis of all law in the United States. It provides a framework for statutes and regulations, and thus is the supreme law of the land. A law in violation of the U.S. Constitution, if challenged, will be declared unconstitutional and will not be enforced, no matter what its source. Because of its paramount importance in the American legal system, we discuss the U.S. Constitution at length in Chapter 2 and present its complete text in Appendix B.

The Tenth Amendment to the U.S. Constitution reserves to the states all powers not granted to the federal government. Each state in the union has its own constitution. Unless it conflicts with the U.S. Constitution or a federal law, a state constitution is supreme within that state's borders.

Constitutional Law The body of law derived from the U.S. Constitution and the constitutions of the various states.

1–2b **Statutory Law**

Laws enacted by legislative bodies at any level of government, such as the statutes passed by Congress or by state legislatures, make up the body of law generally referred to as **statutory law.** When a legislature passes a statute, that statute ultimately is included in the federal code of laws or the relevant state code of laws.

Whenever a particular statute is mentioned in this text, we usually provide a footnote showing its **citation** (a reference to a publication in which a legal authority—such as a statute or a court decision—or other source can be found). In the appendix following this chapter, we explain how you can use these citations to find statutory law.

Statutory law also includes local **ordinances**—regulations passed by municipal or county governing units to deal with matters not covered by federal or state law. Ordinances commonly have to do with city or county land use (zoning ordinances), building and safety codes, and other matters affecting only the local governing unit.

A federal statute, of course, applies to all states. A state statute, in contrast, applies only within the state's borders. State laws thus may vary from state to state. No federal statute may violate the U.S. Constitution, and no state statute or local ordinance may violate the U.S. Constitution or the relevant state constitution.

Statutory Law The body of law enacted by legislative bodies (as opposed to constitutional law, administrative law, or case law).

Citation A reference to a publication in which a legal authority—such as a statute or a court decision—or other source can be found.

Ordinance A regulation enacted by a city or county legislative body that becomes part of that state's statutory law.

Uniform Laws During the 1800s, the differences among state laws frequently created difficulties for businesspersons conducting trade and commerce among the states. To counter these problems, a group of legal scholars and lawyers formed the National Conference of Commissioners on Uniform State Laws (NCCUSL, online at **www.uniformlaws.org**) in 1892 to draft **uniform laws** ("model statutes") for the states to consider adopting. The NCCUSL still exists today and continues to issue uniform laws.

Each state has the option of adopting or rejecting a uniform law. *Only if a state legislature adopts a uniform law does that law become part of the statutory law of that state.* Furthermore, a state legislature may choose to adopt only part of a uniform law or to rewrite the sections that are adopted. Hence, even though many states may have adopted a uniform law, those laws may not be entirely "uniform."

Uniform Law A model law developed by the National Conference of Commissioners on Uniform State Laws for the states to consider enacting into statute.

The Uniform Commercial Code (UCC) One of the most important uniform acts is the Uniform Commercial Code (UCC), which was created through the joint efforts of the NCCUSL and the American Law Institute.[1] The UCC was first issued in 1952 and has been adopted in all fifty states,[2] the District of Columbia, and the Virgin Islands.

The UCC facilitates commerce among the states by providing a uniform, yet flexible, set of rules governing commercial transactions. Because of its importance in the area of commercial law, we cite the UCC frequently in this text. We also present excerpts of the UCC in Appendix C. From time to time, the NCCUSL revises the articles contained in the UCC and submits the revised versions to the states for adoption.

1-2c Administrative Law

Another important source of American law is **administrative law,** which consists of the rules, orders, and decisions of administrative agencies. An **administrative agency** is a federal, state, or local government agency established to perform a specific function.

Rules issued by various administrative agencies affect almost every aspect of a business's operations. Regulations govern a business's capital structure and financing, its hiring and firing procedures, its relations with employees and unions, and the way it manufactures and markets its products. (See the *Linking Business Law to Management* feature at the end of this chapter.)

Administrative Law The body of law created by administrative agencies in order to carry out their duties and responsibilities.

Administrative Agency A federal or state government agency created by the legislature to perform a specific function, such as to make and enforce rules pertaining to the environment.

Federal Agencies At the national level, numerous *executive agencies* exist within the cabinet departments of the executive branch. The Food and Drug Administration, for example, is an agency within the U.S. Department of Health and Human Services. Executive agencies are subject to the authority of the president, who has the power to appoint and remove their officers.

There are also major *independent regulatory agencies* at the federal level, including the Federal Trade Commission, the Securities and Exchange Commission, and the Federal Communications Commission. The president's power is less pronounced in regard to independent agencies, whose officers serve for fixed terms and cannot be removed without just cause.

State and Local Agencies There are administrative agencies at the state and local levels as well. Commonly, a state agency (such as a state pollution-control agency) is created as a parallel to a federal agency (such as the Environmental Protection Agency).

Just as federal statutes take precedence over conflicting state statutes, so do federal agency regulations take precedence over conflicting state regulations. Because the rules of state and local agencies vary widely, we focus here exclusively on federal administrative law.

Agency Creation Because Congress cannot possibly oversee the actual implementation of all the laws it enacts, it delegates such tasks to agencies. Congress creates an administrative

"Laws and institutions, like clocks, must occasionally be cleaned, wound up, and set to true time."

HENRY WARD BEECHER
1813–1887
(AMERICAN CLERGYMAN AND ABOLITIONIST)

---

1. This institute was formed in the 1920s and consists of practicing attorneys, legal scholars, and judges.
2. Louisiana has adopted only Articles 1, 3, 4, 5, 7, 8, and 9.

Which federal agency oversees worker safety?

Enabling Legislation A statute enacted by Congress that authorizes the creation of an administrative agency and specifies the name, composition, purpose, and powers of the agency being created.

Adjudicate To render a judicial decision. Adjudication is the trial-like proceeding in which an administrative law judge hears and resolves disputes involving an administrative agency's regulations.

Administrative Process The procedure used by administrative agencies in administering the law.

Rulemaking The process by which an administrative agency formally adopts a new regulation or amends an old one.

Legislative Rule An administrative agency rule that carries the same weight as a congressionally enacted statute.

Interpretive Rule A nonbinding rule or policy statement issued by an administrative agency that explains how it interprets and intends to apply the statutes it enforces.

agency by enacting **enabling legislation,** which specifies the name, composition, purpose, and powers of the agency being created.

EXAMPLE 1.2 The Federal Trade Commission (FTC) was created in 1914 by the Federal Trade Commission Act.[3] This act prohibits unfair and deceptive trade practices. It also describes the procedures the agency must follow to charge persons or organizations with violations of the act, and it provides for judicial review (review by the courts) of agency orders.

Other portions of the act grant the agency powers to "make rules and regulations for the purpose of carrying out the Act," and to conduct investigations of business practices. In addition, the FTC can obtain reports from interstate corporations concerning their business practices, investigate possible violations of the act, publish findings of its investigations, and recommend new legislation. The act also empowers the FTC to hold trial-like hearings and to **adjudicate** (resolve judicially) certain kinds of disputes involving its regulations. ∎

Note that the powers granted to the FTC incorporate functions associated with the legislative branch of government (rulemaking), the executive branch (investigation and enforcement), and the judicial branch (adjudication). Taken together, these functions constitute the **administrative process,** which is the administration of law by administrative agencies. The administrative process involves rulemaking, enforcement, and adjudication.

Rulemaking A major function of an administrative agency is **rulemaking**—formulating new regulations. When Congress enacts an agency's enabling legislation, it confers the power to make **legislative rules,** or substantive rules, which are legally binding on all businesses.

The Administrative Procedure Act (APA)[4] imposes strict procedural requirements that agencies must follow in legislative rulemaking and other functions. **EXAMPLE 1.3** The Occupational Safety and Health Act authorized the Occupational Safety and Health Administration (OSHA) to develop and issue rules governing safety in the workplace. When OSHA wants to formulate rules regarding safety in the steel industry, it has to follow specific procedures outlined by the APA. ∎

Legislative Rules. Legislative rulemaking under the APA typically involves the following three steps (referred to as *notice-and-comment rulemaking*).

1. *Notice of the proposed rulemaking.* The notice must be published in the *Federal Register,* a daily publication of the U.S. government.

2. *A comment period.* The agency must allow ample time for interested parties to comment in writing on the proposed rule. The agency takes these comments into consideration when drafting the final version of the regulation.

3. *The final rule.* Once the agency has drafted the final rule, it is published in the *Federal Register.* (See the appendix at the end of this chapter for an explanation of how to find agency regulations.)

Interpretive Rules. Administrative agencies also issue **interpretive rules** that are not legally binding but simply indicate how an agency plans to interpret and enforce its statutory authority. The APA does not apply to interpretive rulemaking. **EXAMPLE 1.4** The Equal Employment Opportunity Commission periodically issues interpretive rules indicating how it plans to interpret the provisions of certain statutes, such as the Americans with Disabilities Act. These informal rules provide enforcement guidelines for agency officials. ∎

Enforcement and Investigation Agencies often enforce their own rules and have both investigatory and prosecutorial powers. Agencies investigate a wide range of activities, including coal mining, automobile manufacturing, and the industrial discharge of pollutants into the environment.

---

3. 15 U.S.C. Sections 45–58.
4. 5 U.S.C. Sections 551–706.

In an investigation, an agency can request that individuals or organizations hand over specified books, papers, electronic records, or other documents. In addition, agencies may conduct on-site inspections, although a search warrant is normally required for such inspections.[5] Sometimes, a search of a home, an office, or a factory is the only means of obtaining evidence needed to prove a regulatory violation.

After investigating a suspected rule violation, an agency may decide to take action against an individual or a business. Most administrative actions are resolved through negotiated settlement at their initial stages without the need for formal adjudication. If a settlement cannot be reached, though, the agency may issue a formal complaint and proceed to adjudication.

Adjudication   Agency adjudication involves a trial-like hearing before an **administrative law judge (ALJ)**. Hearing procedures vary widely from agency to agency. After the hearing, the ALJ renders a decision in the case. The ALJ can fine the charged party or prohibit the party from carrying on some specified activity.

Either the agency or the charged party may appeal the ALJ's decision to the commission or board that governs the agency. If the party fails to get relief there, appeal can be made to a federal court. Courts give significant weight (deference) to an agency's judgment and interpretation of its rules, though, and typically uphold the ALJ's decision unless it is unreasonable. If neither side appeals the case, the ALJ's decision becomes final.

Do administrative agencies exercise too much authority? Administrative agencies, such as the Federal Trade Commission, combine in a single governmental entity functions normally divided among the three branches of government. They create rules, conduct investigations, and prosecute and pass judgment on violators. Yet administrative agencies' powers often go unchecked by the other branches. Some businesspersons have suggested that it is unethical for agencies—which are not even mentioned in the U.S. Constitution—to wield so many powers.

Although agency rulemaking must comply with the requirements of the Administrative Procedure Act (APA), the act applies only to legislative, not interpretive, rulemaking. In addition, the APA is largely procedural and aimed at preventing arbitrariness. It does little to ensure that the rules passed by agencies are fair or correct—or even cost effective. On those rare occasions when an agency's ruling is challenged and later reviewed by a court, the court cannot reverse the agency's decision unless the agency exceeded its authority or acted arbitrarily. Courts typically are reluctant to second-guess an agency's rules, interpretations, and decisions. Moreover, once an agency has final regulations in place, it is difficult to revoke or alter them.

Administrative Law Judge (ALJ) One who presides over an administrative agency hearing and has the power to administer oaths, take testimony, rule on questions of evidence, and make determinations of fact.

ETHICAL ISSUE

1–2d Case Law and Common Law Doctrines

The rules of law announced in court decisions constitute another basic source of American law. These rules of law include *interpretations* of constitutional provisions, of statutes enacted by legislatures, and of regulations created by administrative agencies. Today, this body of judge-made law is referred to as **case law.** Case law—the doctrines and principles announced in cases—governs all areas not covered by statutory law or administrative law and is part of our common law tradition. We look at the origins and characteristics of the common law tradition in some detail in the pages that follow.

Case Law The rules of law announced in court decisions. Case law interprets statutes, regulations, constitutional provisions, and other case law.

1–3 Common Law Tradition

Because of our colonial heritage, much American law is based on the English legal system. Knowledge of this tradition is crucial to understanding our legal system today because judges in the United States still apply common law principles when deciding cases.

LEARNING OBJECTIVE 2

What is the common law tradition?

---

5. In some heavily regulated industries, such as the sale of firearms or liquor, agencies can conduct searches without obtaining a warrant.

1–3a Early English Courts

After the Normans conquered England in 1066, William the Conqueror and his successors began the process of unifying the country under their rule. One of the means they used to do this was the establishment of the king's courts, or *curiae regis*. Before the Norman Conquest, disputes had been settled according to the local legal customs and traditions in various regions of the country. The king's courts sought to establish a uniform set of rules for the country as a whole. What evolved in these courts was the beginning of the **common law**—a body of general rules that applied throughout the entire English realm. Eventually, the common law tradition became part of the heritage of all nations that were once British colonies, including the United States.

Courts developed the common law rules from the principles underlying judges' decisions in actual legal controversies. Judges attempted to be consistent, and whenever possible, they based their decisions on the principles suggested by earlier cases. They sought to decide similar cases in a similar way and considered new cases with care because they knew that their decisions would make new law. Each interpretation became part of the law on the subject and served as a legal **precedent**—that is, a court decision that furnished an example or authority for deciding subsequent cases involving identical or similar legal principles or facts.

In the early years of the common law, there was no single place or publication where court opinions, or written decisions, could be found. Beginning in the late thirteenth and early fourteenth centuries, however, portions of significant decisions from each year were gathered together and recorded in *Year Books*. The *Year Books* were useful references for lawyers and judges. In the sixteenth century, the *Year Books* were discontinued, and other reports of cases became available. (See the appendix to this chapter for a discussion of how cases are reported, or published, in the United States today.)

1–3b *Stare Decisis*

The practice of deciding new cases with reference to former decisions, or precedents, eventually became a cornerstone of the English and U.S. judicial systems. The practice forms a doctrine called *stare decisis*[6] ("to stand on decided cases").

The Importance of Precedents in Judicial Decision Making
Under the doctrine of *stare decisis*, judges are obligated to follow the precedents established within their jurisdictions. (The term *jurisdiction* refers to a geographic area in which a court or courts have the power to apply the law—see Chapter 3.) Once a court has set forth a principle of law as being applicable to a certain set of facts, that court must apply the principle in future cases involving similar facts. Courts of lower rank (within the same jurisdiction) must do likewise. Thus, *stare decisis* has two aspects:

1. A court should not overturn its own precedents unless there is a strong reason to do so.

2. Decisions made by a higher court are binding on lower courts.

Controlling precedents in a *jurisdiction* are referred to as binding authorities. A **binding authority** is any source of law that a court must follow when deciding a case. Binding authorities include constitutions, statutes, and regulations that govern the issue being decided, as well as court decisions that are controlling precedents within the jurisdiction. United States Supreme Court case decisions, no matter how old, remain controlling until they are overruled by a subsequent decision of the Supreme Court, by a constitutional amendment, or by congressional legislation.

Stare Decisis and Legal Stability
The doctrine of *stare decisis* helps the courts to be more efficient because if other courts have carefully reasoned through a similar case, their legal

---

6. Pronounced stahr-ee dih-si-sis.

Common Law The body of law developed from custom or judicial decisions in English and U.S. courts, not attributable to a legislature.

Precedent A court decision that furnishes an example or authority for deciding subsequent cases involving identical or similar facts.

LEARNING OBJECTIVE 3
What is a precedent? When might a court depart from precedent?

Stare Decisis A common law doctrine under which judges are obligated to follow the precedents established in prior decisions.

Binding Authority Any source of law that a court *must* follow when deciding a case.

KNOW THIS
Courts normally must follow the rules set forth by higher courts in deciding cases with similar fact patterns.

reasoning and opinions can serve as guides. *Stare decisis* also makes the law more stable and predictable. If the law on a given subject is well settled, someone bringing a case to court can usually rely on the court to make a decision based on what the law has been.

Departures from Precedent Although courts are obligated to follow precedents, sometimes a court will depart from the rule of precedent. If a court decides that a precedent is simply incorrect or that technological or social changes have rendered the precedent inapplicable, the court may rule contrary to the precedent. Cases that overturn precedent often receive a great deal of publicity.

Why would this scene not have been likely before 1954?

CASE EXAMPLE 1.5 In *Brown v. Board of Education of Topeka*,[7] the United States Supreme Court expressly overturned precedent when it concluded that separate educational facilities for whites and blacks, which had been upheld as constitutional in numerous previous cases,[8] were inherently unequal. The Supreme Court's departure from precedent in the *Brown* decision received a tremendous amount of publicity as people began to realize the ramifications of this change in the law. ■

When There Is No Precedent At times, a case may raise issues that have not been raised before in that jurisdiction, so the court has no precedents on which to base its decision. Technological advances such as the one discussed in this chapter's *Adapting the Law to the Online Environment* feature often raise new legal issues, for example.

When deciding such cases, called "cases of first impression," courts often look at precedents established in other jurisdictions for guidance. Precedents from other jurisdictions, because they are not binding on the court, are referred to as **persuasive authorities.** A court may also consider other factors, including legal principles and policies underlying previous court decisions or existing statutes, fairness, social values and customs, public policy, and data and concepts drawn from the social sciences.

1-3c Equitable Remedies and Courts of Equity

A **remedy** is the means given to a party to enforce a right or to compensate for the violation of a right. **EXAMPLE 1.6** Elena is injured because of Rowan's wrongdoing. If Elena files a lawsuit and is successful, a court can order Rowan to compensate Elena for the harm by paying her a certain amount. The compensation is Elena's remedy. ■

The kinds of remedies available in the early king's courts of England were severely restricted. If one person wronged another, the king's courts could award either money or property, including land, as compensation. These courts became known as *courts of law,* and the remedies were called *remedies at law.* Even though this system introduced uniformity in the settling of disputes, when a person wanted a remedy other than economic compensation, the courts of law could do nothing, so "no remedy, no right."

Remedies in Equity *Equity* is a branch of law—founded on notions of justice and fair dealing—that seeks to supply a remedy when no adequate remedy at law is available. When individuals could not obtain an adequate remedy in a court of law, they petitioned the king for relief. Most of these petitions were referred to the *chancellor,* an adviser to the king who had the power to grant new and unique remedies. Eventually, formal chancery courts, or *courts of equity,* were established. The remedies granted by the chancery courts were called *remedies in equity*.

Plaintiffs (those bringing lawsuits) had to specify whether they were bringing an "action at law" or an "action in equity," and they chose their courts accordingly. **EXAMPLE 1.7** A plaintiff

Persuasive Authority Any legal authority or source of law that a court may look to for guidance but need not follow when making its decision.

Remedy The relief given to an innocent party to enforce a right or compensate for the violation of a right.

Plaintiff One who initiates a lawsuit.

LEARNING OBJECTIVE 4

What is the difference between remedies at law and remedies in equity?

---

7. 347 U.S. 483, 74 S.Ct. 686, 98 L.Ed. 873 (1954).
8. See *Plessy v. Ferguson*, 163 U.S. 537, 16 S.Ct. 1138, 41 L.Ed. 256 (1896).

ADAPTING THE LAW TO THE **ONLINE** ENVIRONMENT

Can New Laws Prevent People from Wearing Google Glass?

Google Glass is a wearable computer. Basically, it's a Bluetooth-enabled, hands-free device that allows wearers to take photos and videos, surf the Internet, and do other things through voice commands. For the most part, Google Glass devices have been sold to consumers. One result has been legal problems, including problems involving privacy issues, safety while driving, and movie pirating.

Invasion of Privacy?

Privacy advocates point out that it is much easier to film or photograph others secretly with wearable video technology than with cameras or even cell phones. The more people use wearable video technology, the greater the problem will become. The so-called sacred precincts of private life will increasingly be violated. This issue came up over a hundred years ago with the creation of low-cost cameras. Initially, there were widespread bans on cameras at beaches.[a] Today, numerous bars and restaurants are banning Google Glass. Corporations are concerned that employees wearing Google Glass can more easily photograph documents that reveal trade secrets.

What about facial recognition software in Google Glass? Such an application could allow anyone to get personal information about another person just by looking at the person through a Google Glass headset. Even Congress has made inquiries about this possibility. In response, Google announced

Under what circumstances could a user of Google Glass be violating the right to privacy of others?

that it would not allow facial recognition applications on Glass.

In any event, the doctrine of a reasonable expectation of privacy is going to be challenged because of Google Glass. If Glass is ubiquitous, can any of us have a reasonable expectation of privacy when we are in public places?

Driving While Watching

When a San Diego policeman pulled over a motorist for speeding, she was also cited for "driving with a monitor visible to driver." California law prohibits in-vehicle video displays that are visible to the vehicles' drivers.[b] The charge was thrown out because of a lack of evidence that the device was in operation at the time of the purported offense.

A number of states have introduced legislation that would restrict the use of Google Glass while driving. All such legislation specifies the prohibited activity as "using" wearable devices, such as Google Glass. William & Mary law professor Adam Gershowitz argues

that such driving bans are unenforceable. A police officer has no way of knowing whether a passing driver was *using,* as opposed to simply *wearing,* Google Glass.

The Pirated Movie Problem

Pirated movies offered free on the Internet have greatly affected revenues for movie production companies and movie theaters. Not surprisingly, movie theater owners are on the lookout for camouflaged, hand-held cameras during screenings of movies. When an AMC theater in Columbus, Ohio, noticed a customer wearing a Google Glass device, it contacted the Motion Picture Association of America (MPAA), which then contacted the federal Department of Homeland Security. An hour into the movie, the Glass wearer was removed from the theater by Immigration and Customs Enforcement (ICE) officers. He was released when an officer connected his Glass to a computer, which showed that no video of the movie had been taken.

Both the MPAA and the AMC theater chain stated that wearing "devices with recording capabilities is not appropriate at movie theaters." Note, though, that any restrictions on Google Glass and similar wearable devices will be more difficult to enforce as more individuals use prescription lenses in such devices.

<hr>

CRITICAL THINKING

- What benefits could wearers of Google Glass obtain from using facial recognition technology?

<hr>

a. Samuel D. Warren and Louis D. Brandeis, "The Right to Privacy," *Harvard Law Review* 4 (December 15, 1890): 193–220.

b. California Vehicle Code Section 27602.

<hr>

Defendant One against whom a lawsuit is brought or the accused person in a criminal proceeding.

might ask a court of equity to order the **defendant** (the person against whom a lawsuit is brought) to perform within the terms of a contract. A court of law could not issue such an order because its remedies were limited to the payment of money or property as compensation for damages.

A court of equity, however, could issue a decree for *specific performance*—an order to perform what was promised. A court of equity could also issue an *injunction,* directing a party to do or refrain from doing a particular act. In certain cases, a court of equity could allow for the *rescission* (cancellation) of the contract, thereby returning the parties to the positions that they held prior to the contract's formation. ■ Equitable remedies will be discussed in greater detail in the chapters covering contracts.

The Merging of Law and Equity Today, in most states, the courts of law and equity have merged, and thus the distinction between the two courts has largely disappeared. A plaintiff may now request both legal and equitable remedies in the same action, and the trial court judge may grant either form—or both forms—of relief.

The distinction between legal and equitable remedies remains significant, however, because a court normally will grant an equitable remedy only when the remedy at law (monetary damages) is inadequate. To request the proper remedy, a businessperson (or her or his attorney) must know what remedies are available for the specific kinds of harms suffered. Exhibit 1–3 summarizes the procedural differences (applicable in most states) between an action at law and an action in equity.

Equitable Principles and Maxims Over time, the courts have developed a number of **equitable principles and maxims** that provide guidance in deciding whether plaintiffs should be granted equitable relief. Because of their importance, both historically and in our judicial system today, these principles and maxims are set forth in this chapter's *Landmark in the Law* feature.

1-3d Schools of Legal Thought

How judges apply the law to specific cases, including disputes relating to the business world, depends on their philosophical approaches to law, among other things. The study of law, often referred to as **jurisprudence,** includes learning about different schools of legal thought and discovering how each school's approach to law can affect judicial decision making.

The Natural Law School Those who adhere to the **natural law** theory believe that a higher, or universal, law exists that applies to all human beings and that written laws should imitate these inherent principles. If a written law is unjust, then it is not a true (natural) law and need not be obeyed.

The natural law tradition is one of the oldest and most significant schools of jurisprudence. It dates back to the days of the Greek philosopher Aristotle (384–322 B.C.E.), who distinguished between natural law and the laws governing a particular nation. According to Aristotle, natural law applies universally to all humankind.

The notion that people have "natural rights" stems from the natural law tradition. Those who claim that certain nations, such as China and North Korea, are depriving many of their citizens of their human rights are implicitly appealing to a higher law that has universal applicability.

The question of the universality of basic human rights also comes into play in the context of international business operations. For instance, U.S. companies that have operations abroad

Equitable Principles and Maxims General propositions or principles of law that have to do with fairness (equity).

Jurisprudence The science or philosophy of law.

Natural Law The oldest school of legal thought, based on the belief that the legal system should reflect universal ("higher") moral and ethical principles that are inherent in human nature.

Exhibit 1–3 Procedural Differences between an Action at Law and an Action in Equity

PROCEDURE	ACTION AT LAW	ACTION IN EQUITY
Initiation of lawsuit	By filing a complaint	By filing a petition
Decision	By jury or judge	By judge (no jury)
Result	Judgment	Decree
Remedy	Monetary damages	Injunction, specific performance, or rescission

often hire foreign workers as employees. Should the same laws that protect U.S. employees apply to these foreign employees? This question is rooted implicitly in a concept of universal rights that has its origins in the natural law tradition.

Legal Positivism

Legal Positivism A school of legal thought centered on the assumption that there is no law higher than the laws created by a national government. Laws must be obeyed, even if they are unjust, to prevent anarchy.

Legal Positivism In contrast, *positive,* or national, law (the written law of a given society at a particular point in time) applies only to the citizens of that nation or society. Those who adhere to **legal positivism** believe that there can be no higher law than a nation's positive law.

According to the positivist school, there is no such thing as "natural rights." Rather, human rights exist solely because of laws. If the laws are not enforced, anarchy will result. Thus, whether a law is morally "bad" or "good" is irrelevant. The law is the law and must be obeyed until it is changed—in an orderly manner through a legitimate lawmaking process.

A judge with positivist leanings probably would be more inclined to defer to an existing law than would a judge who adheres to the natural law tradition.

The Historical School

Historical School A school of legal thought that looks to the past to determine what the principles of contemporary law should be.

The Historical School The **historical school** of legal thought emphasizes the evolutionary process of law by concentrating on the origin and history of the legal system. This school looks to the past to discover what the principles of contemporary law should be. The legal doctrines that have withstood the passage of time—those that have worked in the past—are deemed best suited for shaping present laws. Hence, law derives its legitimacy and authority from adhering to the standards that historical development has shown to be workable.

Followers of the historical school are more likely than those of other schools to adhere strictly to decisions made in past cases.

LANDMARK IN THE LAW — Equitable Principles and Maxims

In medieval England, courts of equity were expected to use discretion in supplementing the common law. Even today, when the same court can award both legal and equitable remedies, it must exercise discretion. Students of business law should know that courts often invoke equitable principles and maxims when making their decisions. Here are some of the most significant equitable principles and maxims:

1. *Whoever seeks equity must do equity.* (Anyone who wishes to be treated fairly must treat others fairly.)

2. *Where there is equal equity, the law must prevail.* (The law will determine the outcome of a controversy in which the merits of both sides are equal.)

3. *One seeking the aid of an equity court must come to the court with clean hands.* (Plaintiffs must have acted fairly and honestly.)

4. *Equity will not suffer a wrong to be without a remedy.* (Equitable relief will be awarded when there is a right to relief and there is no adequate remedy at law.)

5. *Equity regards substance rather than form.* (Equity is more concerned with fairness and justice than with legal technicalities.)

6. *Equity aids the vigilant, not those who rest on their rights.* (Equity will not help those who neglect their rights for an unreasonable period of time.)

The last maxim has come to be known as the *equitable doctrine of laches.* The doctrine arose to encourage people to bring lawsuits while the evidence was fresh. If they failed to do so, they would not be allowed to bring a lawsuit. What constitutes a reasonable time, of course, varies according to the circumstances of the case.

Time periods for different types of cases are now usually fixed by *statutes of limitations*—that is, statutes that set the maximum time period during which a certain action can be brought. After the time allowed under a statute of limitations has expired, no action can be brought, no matter how strong the case was originally.

APPLICATION TO TODAY'S WORLD *The equitable maxims listed here underlie many of the legal rules and principles that are commonly applied by the courts today—and that you will read about in this book. For instance, in the contracts materials you will read about the doctrine of promissory estoppel. Under this doctrine, a person who has reasonably and substantially relied on the promise of another may be able to obtain some measure of recovery, even though no enforceable contract exists. The court will estop (bar) the one making the promise from asserting the lack of a valid contract as a defense. The rationale underlying the doctrine of promissory estoppel is similar to that expressed in the fourth and fifth maxims listed.*

Legal Realism In the 1920s and 1930s, a number of jurists and scholars, known as *legal realists,* rebelled against the historical approach to law. **Legal realism** is based on the idea that law is just one of many institutions in society and that it is shaped by social forces and needs. This school reasons that because the law is a human enterprise, judges should look beyond the law and take social and economic realities into account when deciding cases.

Legal realists also believe that the law can never be applied with total uniformity. Given that judges are human beings with unique experiences, personalities, value systems, and intellects, different judges will obviously bring different reasoning processes to the same case. Female judges, for instance, might be more inclined than male judges to consider whether a decision might have a negative impact on the employment of women or minorities.

Legal Realism A school of legal thought that holds that the law is only one factor to be considered when deciding cases and that social and economic circumstances should also be taken into account.

1-4 Classifications of Law

The law may be broken down according to several classification systems. One classification system divides law into **substantive law** (all laws that define, describe, regulate, and create legal rights and obligations) and **procedural law** (all laws that establish the methods of enforcing the rights established by substantive law).

EXAMPLE 1.8 A state law that provides employees with the right to workers' compensation benefits for any on-the-job injuries they sustain is a substantive law because it creates legal rights (workers' compensation laws will be discussed in Chapter 24). Procedural laws, in contrast, establish the method by which an employee must notify the employer about an on-the-job injury, prove the injury, and periodically submit additional proof to continue receiving workers' compensation benefits. Note that a law concerning workers' compensation may contain both substantive and procedural provisions. ▪

Another classification system divides law into federal law and state law. Still another system distinguishes between private law (dealing with relationships between persons) and public law (addressing the relationship between persons and their governments). Frequently, people use the term **cyberlaw** to refer to the emerging body of law that governs transactions conducted via the Internet, but cyberlaw is not really a classification of law. Rather, it is an informal term used to describe traditional legal principles that have been modified and adapted to fit situations that are unique to the online world. Throughout this book, you will read about how the law is evolving to govern specific legal issues that arise in the online context.

Substantive Law Law that defines, describes, regulates, and creates legal rights and obligations.

Procedural Law Law that establishes the methods of enforcing the rights established by substantive law.

Cyberlaw An informal term used to refer to all laws governing electronic communications and transactions, particularly those conducted via the Internet.

1-4a Civil Law and Criminal Law

Civil law spells out the rights and duties that exist between persons and between persons and their governments. It also specifies the relief available when a person's rights are violated. Typically, in a civil case, a private party sues another private party to make sure that the other party complies with a duty or pays for the damage caused by the failure to comply with a duty. **EXAMPLE 1.9** If a seller fails to perform a contract with a buyer, the buyer may bring a lawsuit against the seller. The purpose of the lawsuit will be either to compel the seller to perform as promised or, more commonly, to obtain monetary damages for the seller's failure to perform. ▪ The government can also bring civil lawsuits against private parties in many situations.

Much of the law that we discuss in this text—including contract law and tort law—is civil law. Note that *civil law* is not the same as a *civil law system.* As you will read shortly, a **civil law system** is a legal system based on a written code of laws. (See this chapter's *Beyond Our Borders* feature for a discussion of the different legal systems used in other nations.)

Criminal law has to do with wrongs committed against society for which society demands redress. Criminal acts are proscribed by local, state, or federal government statutes. Thus, criminal defendants are prosecuted by public officials, such as a district attorney (D.A.), on behalf of the state, not by their victims or other private parties.

Whereas in a civil case the object is to obtain a remedy (such as monetary damages) to compensate the injured party, in a criminal case the object is to punish the wrongdoer in an

Civil Law The branch of law dealing with the definition and enforcement of all private or public rights, as opposed to criminal matters.

LEARNING OBJECTIVE 5

What are some important differences between civil law and criminal law?

Civil Law System A system of law derived from Roman law that is based on codified laws (rather than on case precedents).

Criminal Law The branch of law that defines and punishes wrongful actions committed against the public.

attempt to deter others from similar actions. Penalties for violations of criminal statutes consist of fines and/or imprisonment—and, in some cases, death.

1–4b National and International Law

Although the focus of this book is U.S. business law, increasingly businesspersons in this country engage in transactions that extend beyond our national borders. In these situations,

BEYOND OUR BORDERS

National Law Systems

Despite their varying cultures and customs, almost all countries have laws governing torts, contracts, employment, and other areas. Two types of legal systems predominate around the globe today. One is the common law system of England and the United States, which we have discussed elsewhere. The other system is based on Roman civil law, or "code law," which relies on the legal principles enacted into law by a legislature or governing body.

Civil Law Systems

Although national law systems share many commonalities, they also have distinct differences. In a *civil law system*, the primary source of law is a statutory code, and case precedents are not judicially binding, as they normally are in a common law system. Although judges in a civil law system commonly refer to previous decisions as sources

of legal guidance, those decisions are not binding precedents (*stare decisis* does not apply).

Common Law and Civil Law Systems Today

Exhibit 1–4 lists some countries that follow either the common law system or the civil law system. Generally, countries that were once colonies of Great Britain have retained their English common law heritage. The civil law system, which is used in most continental European nations, has been retained in the countries that were once colonies of those nations. In the United States, the state of Louisiana, because of its historical ties to France, has in part a civil law system, as do Haiti, Québec, and Scotland.

Islamic Legal Systems

A third, less prevalent legal system is common in Islamic countries, where the law is often influenced by *sharia,* the religious law

of Islam. Islam is both a religion and a way of life. *Sharia* is a comprehensive code of principles that governs the public and private lives of Islamic persons and directs many aspects of their day-to-day lives, including politics, economics, banking, business law, contract law, and social issues.

Although *sharia* affects the legal codes of many Muslim countries, the extent of its impact and its interpretation vary widely. In some Middle Eastern nations, aspects of *sharia* have been codified in modern legal codes and are enforced by national judicial systems.

CRITICAL THINKING

■ Does the civil law system offer any advantages over the common law system, or vice versa? Explain.

Exhibit 1–4 The Legal Systems of Selected Nations

CIVIL LAW		COMMON LAW	
Argentina	Indonesia	Australia	Nigeria
Austria	Iran	Bangladesh	Singapore
Brazil	Italy	Canada	United Kingdom
Chile	Japan	Ghana	United States
China	Mexico	India	Zambia
Egypt	Poland	Israel	
Finland	South Korea	Jamaica	
France	Sweden	Kenya	
Germany	Tunisia	Malaysia	
Greece	Venezuela	New Zealand	

the laws of other nations or the laws governing relationships among nations may come into play. For this reason, those who pursue a career in business today should have an understanding of the global legal environment (discussed further in Chapter 16).

National Law The law of a particular nation, such as the United States or Sweden, is **national law.** National law, of course, varies from country to country because each country's law reflects the interests, customs, activities, and values that are unique to that nation's culture. Even though the laws and legal systems of various countries differ substantially, broad similarities do exist.

International Law In contrast to national law, international law applies to more than one nation. **International law** can be defined as a body of written and unwritten laws observed by independent nations and governing the acts of individuals as well as governments. It is a mixture of rules and constraints derived from a variety of sources, including the laws of individual nations, customs developed among nations, and international treaties and organizations. Each nation is motivated not only by the need to be the final authority over its own affairs, but also by the desire to benefit economically from trade and harmonious relations with other nations. In essence, international law is the result of centuries-old attempts to strike a balance between these competing needs.

    The key difference between national law and international law is that government authorities can enforce national law. If a nation violates an international law, however, enforcement is up to other countries or international organizations, which may or may not choose to act. If persuasive tactics fail, the only option is to take coercive actions against the violating nation. Coercive actions range from the severance of diplomatic relations and boycotts to, as a last resort, war. We will examine the laws governing international business transactions in later chapters (including the chapter on international law and the chapters covering contracts for the sale and lease of goods).

National Law Law that pertains to a particular nation (as opposed to international law).

International Law The law that governs relations among nations.

Reviewing . . . The Legal Environment

Suppose that the California legislature passes a law that severely restricts carbon dioxide emissions of automobiles in that state. A group of automobile manufacturers files a suit against the state of California to prevent enforcement of the law. The automakers claim that a federal law already sets fuel economy standards nationwide and that these standards are essentially the same as carbon dioxide emission standards. According to the automobile manufacturers, it is unfair to allow California to impose more stringent regulations than those set by the federal law. Using the information presented in the chapter, answer the following questions.

1. Who are the parties (the plaintiffs and the defendant) in this lawsuit?

2. Are the plaintiffs seeking a legal remedy or an equitable remedy? Why?

3. What is the primary source of the law that is at issue here?

4. Read through the appendix that follows this chapter, and then answer the following question: Where would you look to find the relevant California and federal laws?

DEBATE THIS

■ Under the doctrine of *stare decisis,* courts are obligated to follow the precedents established in their jurisdiction unless there is a compelling reason not to do so. Should U.S. courts continue to adhere to this common law principle, given that our government now regulates so many areas by statute?

LINKING BUSINESS LAW TO CORPORATE MANAGEMENT

Dealing with Administrative Law

Whether you work for a large corporation or own a small business, you will be dealing with multiple aspects of administrative law. All federal, state, and local government administrative agencies create rules that have the force of law. As a manager, you probably will need to pay more attention to administrative rules and regulations than to laws passed by local, state, and federal legislatures.

Federal versus State and Local Agency Regulations

The three levels of government create three levels of rules and regulations though their respective administrative agencies. At the federal level, these include the Food and Drug Administration, the Equal Employment Opportunity Commission, and the Occupational Safety and Health Administration. Similar agencies govern business activities at the state level.

As a manager, you will have to learn about agency regulations that pertain to your business activities. It will be up to you,

as a manager or small-business owner, to discern which of those regulations are most important and could create the most liability if you violate them.

When Should You Participate in the Rulemaking Process?

All federal agencies and many state agencies invite public comments on proposed rules. Suppose that you manage a large construction company and your state occupational safety agency proposes a new rule requiring every employee on a construction site to wear hearing protection. You believe that the rule will lead to a *less* safe environment because your employees will not be able to communicate easily with one another.

Should you spend time offering comments to the agency? As an efficient manager, you make a trade-off calculation. First, you determine the value of the time that you would spend attempting to prevent or at least alter the proposed rule. Then you compare this implicit cost with your estimate of the potential benefits your company would receive if the rule is *not* put into place.

Be Prepared for Investigations

All administrative agencies have investigatory powers. Agencies' investigators usually

have the power to search business premises, although normally they first have to obtain a search warrant. As a manager, you often have the choice of cooperating with agency investigators or providing just the minimum amount of assistance. If your business is routinely investigated, you will often opt for cooperation. In contrast, if your business is rarely investigated, you may decide that the on-site proposed inspection is overreaching. Then you must contact your company's attorney for advice on how to proceed.

If an administrative agency cites you for a regulatory violation, you will probably negotiate a settlement with the agency rather than take your case before an administrative law judge. Again, as a manager, you have to weigh the cost of the negotiated settlement with the potential cost of fighting the enforcement action.

CRITICAL THINKING

- Why are owner/operators of small businesses at a disadvantage relative to large corporations when they attempt to decipher complex regulations that apply to their businesses?

Key Terms

adjudicate 8

administrative agency 7

administrative law 7

administrative law judge (ALJ) 9

administrative process 8

binding authority 10

case law 9

citation 6

civil law 15

civil law system 15

common law 10

concurring opinion 28

constitutional law 6

criminal law 15

cyberlaw 15

defendant 12

dissenting opinion 28

enabling legislation 8

equitable principles and maxims 13

historical school 14

international law 17

interpretive rule 8

jurisprudence 13

law 2

legal positivism 14

legal realism 15

legislative rule 8

liability 3

majority opinion 28

national law 17

natural law 13

ordinance 6

per curiam opinion 28

persuasive authority 11

plaintiff 11

plurality opinion 28

precedent 10

primary source of law 5

procedural law 15

remedy 11

rulemaking 8

secondary source of law 6

stare decisis 10

statutory law 6

substantive law 15

uniform law 7

Chapter Summary: The Legal Environment

Sources of American Law	**1.** *Constitutional law*—The law as expressed in the U.S. Constitution and the various state constitutions. The U.S. Constitution is the supreme law of the land. State constitutions are supreme within state borders to the extent that they do not violate the U.S. Constitution or a federal law. **2.** *Statutory law*—Laws or ordinances created by federal, state, and local legislatures and governing bodies. None of these laws can violate the U.S. Constitution or the relevant state constitutions. Uniform laws, when adopted by a state legislature, become statutory law in that state. **3.** *Administrative law*—The rules, orders, and decisions of federal or state government administrative agencies. Federal administrative agencies are created by enabling legislation enacted by the U.S. Congress. Agency functions include rulemaking, investigation and enforcement, and adjudication. **4.** *Case law and common law doctrines*—Judge-made law, including interpretations of constitutional provisions, of statutes enacted by legislatures, and of regulations created by administrative agencies. The common law—the doctrines and principles embodied in case law—governs all areas not covered by statutory law or administrative law.

Common Law Tradition	**1.** *Common law*—Law that originated in medieval England with the creation of the king's courts, or *curiae regis*, and the development of a body of rules that were common to (or applied in) all regions of the country.
	
	2. *Stare decisis*—A doctrine under which judges "stand on decided cases"—or follow the rule of precedent—in deciding cases. *Stare decisis* is the cornerstone of the common law tradition.
	
	3. *Remedies*—A remedy is the means by which a court enforces a right or compensates for a violation of a right. Courts typically grant legal remedies (monetary damages) but may also grant equitable remedies (specific performance, injunction, or rescission) when the legal remedy is inadequate or unavailable.
	
	4. *Schools of legal thought*—Judges' decision making is influenced by their philosophy of law. The following are four important schools of legal thought, or legal philosophies:
	  a. Natural law tradition—One of the oldest and most significant schools of legal thought. Those who believe in natural law hold that there is a universal law applicable to all human beings and that this law is of a higher order than positive, or conventional, law.
	  b. Legal positivism—A school of legal thought centered on the assumption that there is no law higher than the laws created by the government. Laws must be obeyed, even if they are unjust, to prevent anarchy.
	  c. Historical school—A school of legal thought that stresses the evolutionary nature of law and looks to doctrines that have withstood the passage of time for guidance in shaping present laws.
	  d. Legal realism—A school of legal thought that generally advocates a less abstract and more realistic approach to the law. This approach takes into account customary practices and the circumstances in which transactions take place.

Classifications of Law	The law may be broken down according to several classification systems, such as substantive or procedural law, federal or state law, and private or public law. Two broad classifications are civil and criminal law, and national and international law. Cyberlaw is not really a classification of law but a term that refers to the growing body of case and statutory law that applies to Internet transactions.

Issue Spotters

1. The First Amendment to the U.S. Constitution provides protection for the free exercise of religion. A state legislature enacts a law that outlaws all religions that do not derive from the Judeo-Christian tradition. Is this law valid within that state? Why or why not? (See *Sources of American Law*.)

2. Apples & Oranges Corporation learns that a federal administrative agency is considering a rule that will have a negative impact on the firm's ability to do business. Does the firm have any opportunity to express its opinion about the pending rule? Explain. (See *Sources of American Law*.)

—Check your answers to the *Issue Spotters* against the answers provided in Appendix D at the end of this text.

Learning Objectives Check

1. What are four primary sources of law in the United States?
2. What is the common law tradition?
3. What is a precedent? When might a court depart from precedent?
4. What is the difference between remedies at law and remedies in equity?
5. What are some important differences between civil law and criminal law?
   —Answers to the even-numbered *Learning Objectives Check* questions can be found in Appendix E at the end of this text.

Business Scenarios and Case Problems

1–1. Binding versus Persuasive Authority. A county court in Illinois is deciding a case involving an issue that has never been addressed before in that state's courts. The Iowa Supreme Court, however, recently decided a case involving a very similar fact pattern. Is the Illinois court obligated to follow the Iowa Supreme Court's decision on the issue? If the United States Supreme Court had decided a similar case, would that decision be binding on the Illinois court? Explain. (See *Common Law Tradition.*)

1–2. Remedies. Arthur Rabe is suing Xavier Sanchez for breaching a contract in which Sanchez promised to sell Rabe a Van Gogh painting for $150,000. (See *Common Law Tradition.*)

1. In this lawsuit, who is the plaintiff, and who is the defendant?
2. If Rabe wants Sanchez to perform the contract as promised, what remedy should Rabe seek?
3. Suppose that Rabe wants to cancel the contract because Sanchez fraudulently misrepresented the painting as an original Van Gogh when in fact it is a copy. In this situation, what remedy should Rabe seek?
4. Will the remedy Rabe seeks in either situation be a remedy at law or a remedy in equity?
5. Suppose that the court finds in Rabe's favor and grants one of these remedies. Sanchez then appeals the decision to a higher court. Read through the subsection entitled "Parties to Lawsuits" in the appendix following this chapter. On appeal, which party in the Rabe-Sanchez case will be the appellant (or petitioner), and which party will be the appellee (or respondent)?

1–3. Philosophy of Law. After World War II ended in 1945, an international tribunal of judges convened at Nuremberg, Germany. The judges convicted several Nazi war criminals of "crimes against humanity." Assuming that the Nazis who were convicted had not disobeyed any law of their country and had merely been following their government's (Hitler's) orders, what law had they violated? Explain. (See *Common Law Tradition.*)

1–4. Spotlight on AOL—Common Law. AOL, LLC, mistakenly made public the personal information of 650,000 of its members. The members filed a suit, alleging violations of

California law. AOL asked the court to dismiss the suit on the basis of a "forum-selection" clause in its member agreement that designates Virginia courts as the place where member disputes will be tried. Under a decision of the United States Supreme Court, a forum-selection clause is unenforceable "if enforcement would contravene a strong public policy of the forum in which suit is brought." California has declared in other cases that the AOL clause contravenes a strong public policy. If the court applies the doctrine of *stare decisis,* will it dismiss the suit? Explain. [*Doe 1 v. AOL, LLC,* 552 F.3d 1077 (9th Cir. 2009)] (See *Common Law Tradition.*)

1–5. Business Case Problem with Sample Answer—Law around the World. Karen Goldberg's husband was killed in a terrorist bombing in Israel. She filed a suit in a U.S. federal court against UBS AG, a Switzerland-based global financial services company. She claimed that UBS aided in her husband's killing because it provided services to the terrorists. UBS argued that the case should be transferred to another country. Like many nations, the United States has a common law system. Other nations have civil law systems. What are the key differences between these systems? [*Goldberg v. UBS AG,* 690 F.Supp.2d 92 (E.D.N.Y. 2010)] (See *Classifications of Law.*)

—For a sample answer to Problem 1–5, go to Appendix F at the end of this text.

1–6. Reading Citations. Assume that you want to read the court's entire opinion in the case of *Baker v. Premo,* 268 Or.App. 406, 342 P.3d 142 (2015). Read the section entitled "Finding Case Law" in the appendix that follows this chapter, and then explain specifically where you would find the court's opinion. (See *Finding Case Law.*)

1–7. A Question of Ethics—Stare Decisis. On July 5, 1884, Dudley, Stephens, and Brooks—"all able-bodied English seamen"—and a teenage English boy were cast adrift in a lifeboat following a storm at sea. They had no water with them in the boat, and all they had for sustenance were two one-pound tins of turnips. On July 24, Dudley proposed that one of the four in the lifeboat be sacrificed to save the others. Stephens agreed with Dudley, but Brooks refused to consent—and the boy was never asked for his opinion. On July 25, Dudley killed the boy, and the three men then fed on the boy's body and blood. Four days later, the men were rescued by a passing vessel. They were taken to England and tried for the murder of the boy. If the men had not fed on the boy's body, they would probably have died of starvation within the four-day period. The boy, who was in a much weaker condition, would likely have died before the rest. [*Regina v. Dudley and Stephens*, 14 Q.B.D. (Queen's Bench Division, England) 273 (1884)] (See *Common Law Tradition*.)

1. The basic question in this case is whether the survivors should be subject to penalties under English criminal law, given the men's unusual circumstances. You be the judge and decide the issue. Give the reasons for your decision.

2. Should judges ever have the power to look beyond the written "letter of the law" in making their decisions? Why or why not?

Critical Thinking and Writing Assignments

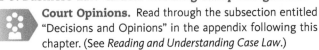

1–8. Business Law Writing. John's company is involved in a lawsuit with a customer, Beth. John argues that for fifty years higher courts in that state have decided cases involving circumstances similar to his case in a way that indicates he can expect a ruling in his company's favor. Write at least one paragraph discussing whether this is a valid argument. Write another paragraph discussing whether the judge in this case must rule as those other judges did, and why. (See *Common Law Tradition*.)

1–9. Business Law Critical Thinking Group Assignment—Court Opinions. Read through the subsection entitled "Decisions and Opinions" in the appendix following this chapter. (See *Reading and Understanding Case Law*.)

1. One group will explain the difference between a concurring opinion and a majority opinion.

2. Another group will outline the difference between a concurring opinion and a dissenting opinion.

3. A third group will explain why judges and justices write concurring and dissenting opinions, given that these opinions will not affect the outcome of the case at hand, which has already been decided by majority vote.

Appendix to Chapter 1

Finding and Analyzing the Law

This text includes numerous references, or *citations,* to primary sources of law—federal and state statutes, the U.S. Constitution and state constitutions, regulations issued by administrative agencies, and court cases. A citation identifies the publication in which a legal authority—such as a statute or court decision—can be found. In this appendix, we explain how you can use citations to find primary sources of law. Note that in addition to being published in sets of books, as described next, most federal and state laws and case decisions are available online.

Finding Statutory and Administrative Law

When Congress passes laws, they are collected in a publication titled *United States Statutes at Large.* When state legislatures pass laws, they are collected in similar state publications. Most frequently, however, laws are referred to in their codified form—that is, the form in which they appear in the federal and state codes. In these codes, laws are compiled by subject.

United States Code

The *United States Code* (U.S.C.) arranges all existing federal laws of a public and permanent nature by subject. Each of the fifty subjects into which the U.S.C. arranges the laws is given a title and a title number. For example, laws relating to commerce and trade are collected in "Title 15, Commerce and Trade." Titles are subdivided by sections.

A citation to the U.S.C. includes title and section numbers. Thus, a reference to "15 U.S.C. Section 1" means that the statute can be found in Section 1 of Title 15. ("Section" may be designated by the symbol §, and "Sections" by §§.) In addition to the print publication of the U.S.C., the federal government also provides a searchable online database of the *United States Code* at **www.gpo.gov** (click on "Libraries" and then "Core Documents of Our Democracy" to find the *United States Code*).

Commercial publications of these laws are available and are widely used. For example, Thomson Reuters publishes the *United States Code Annotated* (U.S.C.A.). The U.S.C.A. contains the complete text of laws included in the U.S.C., notes of court decisions that interpret and apply specific sections of the statutes, and the text of presidential proclamations and executive orders. The U.S.C.A. also includes research aids, such as cross-references to related statutes, historical notes, and other references. A citation to the U.S.C.A. is similar to a citation to the U.S.C.: "15 U.S.C.A. Section 1."

State Codes

State codes follow the U.S.C. pattern of arranging laws by subject. The state codes may be called codes, revisions, compilations, consolidations, general statutes, or statutes, depending on the state.

In some codes, subjects are designated by number. In others, they are designated by name. For example, "13 Pennsylvania Consolidated Statutes Section 1101" means that the statute can be found in Title 13, Section 1101, of the Pennsylvania code. "California Commercial Code Section 1101" means the statute can be found in Section 1101 under the subject heading

"Commercial Code" of the California code. Abbreviations may be used. For example, "13 Pennsylvania Consolidated Statutes Section 1101" may be abbreviated "13 Pa. C.S. § 1101," and "California Commercial Code Section 1101" may be abbreviated "Cal. Com. Code § 1101."

Administrative Rules

Rules and regulations adopted by federal administrative agencies are initially published in the *Federal Register,* a daily publication of the U.S. government. Later, they are incorporated into the *Code of Federal Regulations* (C.F.R.).

Like the U.S.C., the C.F.R. is divided into fifty titles. Rules within each title are assigned section numbers. A full citation to the C.F.R. includes title and section numbers. For example, a reference to "17 C.F.R. Section 230.504" means that the rule can be found in Section 230.504 of Title 17.

Finding Case Law

Before discussing the case reporting system, we need to look briefly at the court system. There are two types of courts in the United States: federal courts and state courts.

Both the federal and state court systems consist of several levels, or tiers, of courts. *Trial courts,* in which evidence is presented and testimony is given, are on the bottom tier (which also includes lower courts handling specialized issues). Decisions from a trial court can be appealed to a higher court, which commonly is an intermediate *court of appeals,* or an *appellate court.* Decisions from these intermediate courts of appeals may be appealed to an even higher court, such as a state supreme court or the United States Supreme Court.

State Court Decisions

Most state trial court decisions are not published (except in New York and a few other states, which publish selected trial court opinions). Decisions from state trial courts are typically filed in the office of the clerk of the court, where the decisions are available for public inspection. (Increasingly, they can be found online as well.)

Written decisions of the appellate, or reviewing, courts, however, are published and distributed (in print and online). As you will note, most of the state court cases presented in this book are from state appellate courts. The reported appellate decisions are published in volumes called *reports* or *reporters,* which are numbered consecutively. State appellate court decisions are found in the state reporters of that particular state. Official reports are published by the state, whereas unofficial reports are published by nongovernment entities.

Regional Reporters State court opinions appear in regional units of West's National Reporter System, published by Thomson Reuters. Most lawyers and libraries have these reporters because they report cases more quickly and are distributed more widely than the state-published reports. In fact, many states have eliminated their own reporters in favor of West's National Reporter System.

The National Reporter System divides the states into the following geographic areas: *Atlantic* (A., A.2d, or A.3d), *North Eastern* (N.E. or N.E.2d), *North Western* (N.W. or N.W.2d), *Pacific* (P., P.2d, or P.3d), *South Eastern* (S.E. or S.E.2d), *South Western* (S.W., S.W.2d, or S.W.3d), and *Southern* (So., So.2d, or So.3d). (The *2d* and *3d* in the abbreviations refer to *Second Series* and *Third Series,* respectively.) The states included in each of these regional divisions are indicated in Exhibit 1A–1, which illustrates West's National Reporter System.

Case Citations After appellate decisions have been published, they are normally referred to (cited) by the name of the case and the volume, name, and page number of the reporter(s) in which the opinion can be found. The citation first lists information from the state's official

Exhibit 1A–1 West's National Reporter System—Regional/Federal

Regional Reporters	Coverage Beginning	Coverage
Atlantic Reporter (A., A.2d, or A.3d)	1885	Connecticut, Delaware, District of Columbia, Maine, Maryland, New Hampshire, New Jersey, Pennsylvania, Rhode Island, and Vermont.
North Eastern Reporter (N.E. or N.E.2d)	1885	Illinois, Indiana, Massachusetts, New York, and Ohio.
North Western Reporter (N.W. or N.W.2d)	1879	Iowa, Michigan, Minnesota, Nebraska, North Dakota, South Dakota, and Wisconsin.
Pacific Reporter (P., P.2d, or P.3d)	1883	Alaska, Arizona, California, Colorado, Hawaii, Idaho, Kansas, Montana, Nevada, New Mexico, Oklahoma, Oregon, Utah, Washington, and Wyoming.
South Eastern Reporter (S.E. or S.E.2d)	1887	Georgia, North Carolina, South Carolina, Virginia, and West Virginia.
South Western Reporter (S.W., S.W.2d, or S.W.3d)	1886	Arkansas, Kentucky, Missouri, Tennessee, and Texas.
Southern Reporter (So., So.2d, or So.3d)	1887	Alabama, Florida, Louisiana, and Mississippi.
Federal Reporters		
Federal Reporter (F., F.2d, or F.3d)	1880	U.S. Circuit Courts from 1880 to 1912; U.S. Commerce Court from 1911 to 1913; U.S. District Courts from 1880 to 1932; U.S. Court of Claims (now called U.S. Court of Federal Claims) from 1929 to 1932 and since 1960; U.S. Courts of Appeals since 1891; U.S. Court of Customs and Patent Appeals since 1929; U.S. Emergency Court of Appeals since 1943.
Federal Supplement (F.Supp., F.Supp.2d, or F.Supp.3d)	1932	U.S. Court of Claims from 1932 to 1960; U.S. District Courts since 1932; U.S. Customs Court since 1956.
Federal Rules Decisions (F.R.D.)	1939	U.S. District Courts involving the Federal Rules of Civil Procedure since 1939 and Federal Rules of Criminal Procedure since 1946.
Supreme Court Reporter (S.Ct.)	1882	United States Supreme Court since the October term of 1882.
Bankruptcy Reporter (Bankr.)	1980	Bankruptcy decisions of U.S. Bankruptcy Courts, U.S. District Courts, U.S. Courts of Appeals, and the United States Supreme Court.
Military Justice Reporter (M.J.)	1978	U.S. Court of Military Appeals and Courts of Military Review for the Army, Navy, Air Force, and Coast Guard.

NATIONAL REPORTER SYSTEM MAP

Legend:
- Pacific
- North Western
- South Western
- North Eastern
- Atlantic
- South Eastern
- Southern

reporter (if different from West's National Reporter System), then the *National Reporter,* and then any other selected reporter. (Citing a reporter by volume number, name, and page number, in that order, is common to all citations.) When more than one reporter is cited for the same case, each reference is called a *parallel citation.*

Note that some states have adopted a "public domain citation system" that uses a somewhat different format for the citation. For example, in Ohio, an Ohio court decision might be designated "2015-Ohio-620," meaning that the decision was the 620th decision issued by the Ohio Supreme Court in 2015. Parallel citations to the *Ohio Appellate Court Reporter* and the *North Eastern Reporter* are included after the public domain citation.

Consider the following citation: *Brody v. Brody,* 315 Conn. 300, 105 A.3d 887 (2015). We see that the opinion in this case can be found in Volume 315 of the official *Connecticut Reports,* on page 300. The parallel citation is to Volume 105 of the *Atlantic Reporter, Third Series,* page 877.

When we present opinions in this text (starting in Chapter 2), in addition to the reporter, we give the name of the court hearing the case and the year of the court's decision. Sample citations to state court decisions are listed and explained in Exhibit 1A–2.

Federal Court Decisions

Federal district (trial) court decisions are published unofficially in the *Federal Supplement* (F.Supp., F.Supp.2d, or F.Supp.3d), and opinions from the circuit courts of appeals (federal reviewing courts) are reported unofficially in the *Federal Reporter* (F., F.2d, or F.3d). Cases concerning federal bankruptcy law are published unofficially in West's *Bankruptcy Reporter* (Bankr. or B.R.).

The official edition of United States Supreme Court decisions is the *United States Reports* (U.S.), which is published by the federal government. Unofficial editions of Supreme Court cases include West's *Supreme Court Reporter* (S.Ct.) and the *Lawyers' Edition of the Supreme Court Reports* (L.Ed. or L.Ed.2d). Sample citations for federal court decisions are also listed and explained in Exhibit 1A–2.

Unpublished Opinions

Many court opinions that are not yet published or that are not intended for publication can be accessed through Westlaw® (abbreviated in citations as "WL"), an online legal database. When no citation to a published reporter is available for cases cited in this text, we give the WL citation (such as 2015 WL 687700, which means it was case number 687700 decided in the year 2015).

Sometimes, both in this text and in other legal sources, you will see blanks left in a citation. This occurs when the decision will be published, but the particular volume number or page number is not yet available.

Old Cases

On a few occasions, this text cites opinions from old, classic cases dating to the nineteenth century or earlier. Some of these cases are from the English courts. The citations to these cases may not conform to the descriptions given above.

Reading and Understanding Case Law

The cases in this text have been condensed from the full text of the courts' opinions and paraphrased by the authors. For those wishing to review court cases for future research projects or to gain additional legal information, the following sections will provide useful insights into how to read and understand case law.

Exhibit 1A–2 How to Read Citations

STATE COURTS

290 Neb. 167, __ N.W.2d __ (2015)[a]

> *N.W.* is the abbreviation for the publication of state court decisions rendered in the *North Western Reporter* of West's National Reporter System. *2d* indicates that this case was included in the *Second Series* of that reporter. The blank lines in this citation (or any other citation) indicate that the appropriate volume of the case reporter has not yet been published and no page number is available.

> *Neb.* is an abbreviation for *Nebraska Reports,* Nebraska's official reports of the decisions of its highest court, the Nebraska Supreme Court.

233 Cal.App.4th 1285, 183 Cal.Rptr.3d 427 (2015)

> *Cal.Rptr.* is the abbreviation for the unofficial reports—titled *California Reporter—* of the decisions of California courts.

124 A.D.3d 536, 998 N.Y.S.2d 628 (2015)

> *N.Y.S.* is the abbreviation for the unofficial reports—titled *New York Supplement*—of the decisions of New York courts.

> *A.D.* is the abbreviation for *Appellate Division*, which hears appeals from the New York Supreme Court—the state's general trial court. The New York Court of Appeals is the state's highest court, analogous to other states' supreme courts.

___ Ga.App. ___, 767 S.E.2d 517 (2015)

> *Ga.App.* is the abbreviation for *Georgia Appeals Reports,* Georgia's official reports of the decisions of its court of appeals.

FEDERAL COURTS

___ U.S. ___, 135 S.Ct. 785, 190 L.Ed.2d 656 (2015)

> *L.Ed.* is an abbreviation for *Lawyers' Edition of the Supreme Court Reports*, an unofficial edition of decisions of the United States Supreme Court.

> *S.Ct.* is the abbreviation for West's unofficial reports—titled *Supreme Court Reporter*—of decisions of the United States Supreme Court.

> *U.S.* is the abbreviation for *United States Reports*, the official edition of the decisions of the United States Supreme Court.

a. The case names have been deleted from these citations to emphasize the publications. It should be kept in mind, however, that the name of a case is as important as the specific page numbers in the volumes in which it is found. If a citation is incorrect, the correct citation may be found in a publication's index of case names. In addition to providing a check on errors in citations, the date of a case is important because the value of a recent case as an authority is likely to be greater than that of older cases from the same court.

Exhibit 1A–2 How to Read Citations

FEDERAL COURTS (Continued)

775 F.3d 1172 (9th Cir. 2015)

> *9th Cir.* is an abbreviation denoting that this case was decided in the U.S. Court of Appeals for the Ninth Circuit.

___ F.Supp.3d ___ 2015 WL 273140 (N.D.Cal. 2015)

> *N.D.Cal.* is an abbreviation indicating that the U.S. District Court for the Northern District of California decided this case.

WESTLAW® CITATIONS[b]

2015 WL 358246

> *WL* is an abbreviation for Westlaw. The number 2015 is the year of the document that can be found with this citation in the Westlaw database. The number 358246 is a number assigned to a specific document. A higher number indicates that a document was added to the Westlaw database later in the year.

STATUTORY AND OTHER CITATIONS

18 U.S.C. Section 1961(1)(A)

> *U.S.C.* denotes *United States Code*, the codification of *United States Statutes at Large.* The number 18 refers to the statute's U.S.C. title number and 1961 to its section number within that title. The number 1 in parentheses refers to a subsection within the section, and the letter A in parentheses to a subsection within the subsection.

UCC 2–206(1)(b)

> *UCC* is an abbreviation for *Uniform Commercial Code.* The first number 2 is a reference to an article of the UCC, and 206 to a section within that article. The number 1 in parentheses refers to a subsection within the section, and the letter b in parentheses to a subsection within the subsection.

Restatement (Third) of Torts, Section 6

> *Restatement (Third) of Torts* refers to the third edition of the American Law Institute's *Restatement of the Law of Torts.* The number 6 refers to a specific section.

17 C.F.R. Section 230.505

> *C.F.R.* is an abbreviation for *Code of Federal Regulations*, a compilation of federal administrative regulations. The number 17 designates the regulation's title number, and 230.505 designates a specific section within that title.

b. Many court decisions that are not yet published or that are not intended for publication can be accessed through Westlaw, an online legal database.

Case Titles and Terminology

The title of a case, such as *Adams v. Jones*, indicates the names of the parties to the lawsuit. The *v.* in the case title stands for *versus*, which means "against." In the trial court, Adams was the plaintiff—the person who filed the suit. Jones was the defendant.

If the case is appealed, however, the appellate court will sometimes place the name of the party appealing the decision first, so the case may be called *Jones v. Adams*. Because some reviewing courts retain the trial court order of names, it is often impossible to distinguish the plaintiff from the defendant in the title of a reported appellate court decision. You must carefully read the facts of each case to identify the parties.

The following terms and phrases are frequently encountered in court opinions and legal publications. Because it is important to understand what these terms and phrases mean, we define and discuss them here.

Parties to Lawsuits As mentioned, the party initiating a lawsuit is referred to as the *plaintiff or petitioner*, depending on the nature of the action, and the party against whom a lawsuit is brought is the *defendant* or *respondent*. Lawsuits frequently involve more than one plaintiff and/or defendant.

When a case is appealed from the original court or jurisdiction to another court or jurisdiction, the party appealing the case is called the *appellant*. The *appellee* is the party against whom the appeal is taken. (In some appellate courts, the party appealing a case is referred to as the *petitioner,* and the party against whom the suit is brought or appealed is called the *respondent.*)

Judges and Justices The terms *judge* and *justice* are usually synonymous and are used to refer to the judges in various courts. All members of the United States Supreme Court, for example, are referred to as justices. Justice is the formal title usually given to judges of appellate courts, although this is not always the case. In New York, a justice is a judge of the trial court (which is called the Supreme Court), and a member of the Court of Appeals (the state's highest court) is called a judge. The term *justice* is commonly abbreviated to J., and *justices* to JJ. A Supreme Court case might refer to Justice Sotomayor as Sotomayor, J., or to Chief Justice Roberts as Roberts, C.J.

Decisions and Opinions Most decisions reached by reviewing, or appellate, courts are explained in written *opinions*. The opinion contains the court's reasons for its decision, the rules of law that apply, and the judgment. You may encounter several types of opinions as you read appellate cases, including the following:

- When all the judges (or justices) agree, a *unanimous opinion* is written for the entire court.
- When there is not unanimous agreement, a **majority opinion** is generally written. It outlines the views of the majority of the judges deciding the case.
- A judge who agrees (concurs) with the majority opinion as to the result but not as to the legal reasoning often writes a **concurring opinion.** In it, the judge sets out the reasoning that he or she considers correct.
- A **dissenting opinion** presents the views of one or more judges who disagree with the majority view. (See the *Business Case Study with Dissenting Opinion* that concludes each unit in this text for an example of a dissenting opinion.)
- Sometimes, no single position is fully supported by a majority of the judges deciding a case. In this situation, we may have a **plurality opinion.** This is the opinion that has the support of the largest number of judges, but the group in agreement is less than a majority.
- Finally, a court occasionally issues a ***per curiam*** **opinion** (*per curiam* is Latin for "of the court"), which does not indicate which judge wrote the opinion.

Majority Opinion A court opinion that represents the views of the majority (more than half) of the judges or justices deciding the case.

Concurring Opinion A court opinion by one or more judges or justices who agree with the majority but want to make or emphasize a point that was not made or emphasized in the majority's opinion.

Dissenting Opinion A court opinion that presents the views of one or more judges or justices who disagree with the majority's decision.

Plurality Opinion A court opinion that is joined by the largest number of the judges or justices hearing the case, but less than half of the total number.

***Per Curiam* Opinion** A court opinion that does not indicate which judge or justice authored the opinion.

A Sample Court Case

Knowing how to read and analyze a court opinion is an essential step in undertaking accurate legal research. A further step is "briefing," or summarizing, the case. Legal researchers routinely brief cases by reducing the texts of the opinions to their essential elements. Instructions on how to brief a case are given in Appendix A.

The cases within this text have already been analyzed and briefed by the authors, and the essential aspects of each case are presented in a convenient format consisting of four sections: *Facts, Issue, Decision,* and *Reason.* This format is illustrated in the sample court case in Exhibit 1A–3, which has been annotated to explain the kind of information that is contained in each section.

In the remaining chapters of this book, the basic format is often expanded to include special introductory sections. Each case is also followed by a question or section that is designed to enhance your analysis. *Critical Thinking* sections present a question about some issue raised by the case. *Why Is This Case Important?* sections explain the significance of the case. *What If the Facts Were Different?* questions alter the facts slightly and ask you to consider how this would change the outcome. A section entitled *Impact of This Case on Today's Law* concludes each of the *Classic Cases* that appear throughout the text to indicate the significance of the case for today's legal landscape.

The case we present in Exhibit 1A–3 is an actual case that the United States Court of Appeals for the Ninth Circuit decided in 2015. Michael Davis, a former professional football player, and other football players, sued Electronic Arts, Inc., the maker of a video game that replicated the players' physical characteristics. The players alleged a violation of their "right of publicity" (a tort discussed in Chapter 4). One of the issues before the court was whether Electronic Arts' use of the players' likenesses in the video game was protected under the First Amendment to the U.S. Constitution (see Chapter 2).

EXHIBIT 1A–3 A SAMPLE COURT CASE

1

Davis v. Electronic Arts, Inc.

United States Court of Appeals, Ninth Circuit, 775 F.3d 1172 (2015).

2 **3**

FACTS Electronic Arts, Inc. (EA) makes and sells the video game *Madden NFL,* which allows users to play virtual games between National Football League (NFL) teams, both current and "historic." EA's artists create avatars of the players, each of whom is identifiable by position, years in the NFL, height, weight, skin tone, and skill.

EA pays a fee to use the likenesses of current players, but not to use the likenesses of former players on the historic teams. Those **4** players filed a suit in a federal district court against EA, alleging a violation of their "right of publicity"—the right to control the use of one's likeness and prevent another from using it for commercial purposes without consent.

EA filed a motion to strike the complaint. The court denied the motion. EA appealed to the U.S. Court of Appeals for the Ninth Circuit, arguing that its use of the likenesses is protected under the First Amendment to the U.S. Constitution as an incidental use.

ISSUE Are the players likely to prevail against EA's defense of inci-**5** dental use?

DECISION Yes. The U.S. Court of Appeals for the Ninth Circuit **6** affirmed the lower court's denial of EA's motion. The appellate

court held that EA's use of the players' likenesses is not incidental "because it is central to EA's main commercial purpose."

REASON Video games are protected under the First Amendment, because like books and movies, "video games communicate ideas— **7** and even social messages." A number of factors establish an incidental use. These include the uniqueness and significance of the use's contribution to the work's commercial purpose. Here, "the former players' likenesses have unique value and contribute to the commercial value of *Madden NFL*" as indicated by the lengths to which EA goes to achieve realism in representing the players.

Other factors are the relationship of the use to the purpose of the work, and the prominence of, in this case, the likenesses. "The former players' likenesses are featured prominently in a manner that is substantially related to the main purpose and subject of *Madden NFL*—to create an accurate virtual simulation of an NFL game."

CRITICAL THINKING—Political Consideration *Why is the inci-* **8** *dental use of a person's likeness without his or her consent permitted?*

Review of Sample Court Case

1 The name of the case is *Davis v. Electronic Arts, Inc.* The lead plaintiff is Michael Davis, a former professional football player whose physical characteristics were replicated in a video game produced by Electronic Arts, Inc., the defendant.

2 The court deciding this case is the United States Court of Appeals for the Ninth Circuit.

3 The case citation includes a citation to the official *Federal Reporter, Third Series.* The case can be found in Volume 775 of the *Federal Reporter, Third Series,* beginning on page 1172.

4 The *Facts* section identifies the plaintiffs and the defendant, describes the events leading up to this suit, and what the plaintiffs sought to obtain by bringing this action. Because this is a case before an appellate court, the ruling of the lower court is also included here.

5 The *Issue* section presents the central issue (or issues) to be decided by the court. In this case, the court is to determine the likelihood of the success of the plaintiffs' case in light of the defendant's asserted defense. Most cases concern more than one issue, but the author of this textbook has edited each case to focus on just one issue.

6 The *Decision* section, as the term indicates, contains the court's decision on the issue or issues before the court. The decision reflects the opinion of the judge, or the majority of the judges or justices, hearing the case. In this particular case, the court reversed the lower court's judgment. Decisions by appellate courts are frequently phrased in reference to the lower court's decision. That is, the appellate court may "affirm" the lower court's ruling or "reverse" it. In either situation, the appellate court may "remand," or send back, the case for further proceedings.

7 The *Reason* section indicates what relevant laws and judicial principles were applied in forming the particular conclusion arrived at in the case at bar ("before the court"). In this case, the principle concerned a defense under the First Amendment to the U.S. Constitution to a charge that the defendant violated the plaintiffs' right of publicity. The court determined that the defense was not established in the circumstances of this case.

8 The *Critical Thinking—Political Consideration* section raises a question to be considered in relation to the case just presented. Here the question involves a "political" consideration. In other cases presented in this text, the "consideration" may involve a cultural, environmental, ethical, international, legal, social, or technological consideration.

iStockPhoto.com/Alina555

3

Courts and Alternative Dispute Resolution

LEARNING OBJECTIVES

The five Learning Objectives *below are designed to help improve your understanding of the chapter. After reading this chapter, you should be able to answer the following questions:*

1. What is judicial review? How and when was the power of judicial review established?

2. How are the courts applying traditional jurisdictional concepts to cases involving internet transactions?

3. What is the difference between the focus of a trial court and an appellate court?

4. What is discovery, and how does electronic discovery differ from traditional discovery?

5. What are three alternative methods of resolving disputes?

"An eye for an eye will make the whole world blind."

MAHATMA GANDHI
1869–1948
(INDIAN POLITICAL AND SPIRITUAL LEADER)

Every society needs to have an established method for resolving disputes. Without one, as Mahatma Gandhi implied in the chapter-opening quotation, the biblical "eye for an eye" would lead to anarchy. This is particularly true in the business world—almost every businessperson will face a lawsuit at some time in his or her career. For this reason, anyone involved in business needs to have an understanding of court systems in the United States, as well as the various methods of dispute resolution that can be pursued outside the courts.

In this chapter, after examining the judiciary's overall role in the American governmental system, we discuss some basic requirements that must be met before a party may bring a lawsuit before a particular court. We then look at the court systems of the United States in some detail and, to clarify judicial procedures, follow a hypothetical case through a state court system. We also touch upon a current controversy involving the introduction of some Islamic law into certain U.S. courts.

Throughout this chapter, we indicate how court doctrines and procedures are being adapted to the needs of a cyber age. The chapter concludes with an overview of some alternative methods of settling disputes, including online dispute resolution.

3-1 The Judiciary's Role in American Government

The body of American law includes the federal and state constitutions, statutes passed by legislative bodies, administrative law, and the case decisions and legal principles that form the common law. These laws would be meaningless, however, without the courts to interpret and apply them. This is the essential role of the judiciary—the courts—in the American governmental system: to interpret and apply the law.

3-1a Judicial Review

As the branch of government entrusted with interpreting the laws, the judiciary can decide, among other things, whether the laws or actions of the other two branches are constitutional. The process for making such a determination is known as **judicial review.**

The power of judicial review enables the judicial branch to act as a check on the other two branches of government, in line with the checks-and-balances system established by the U.S. Constitution. (Today, nearly all nations with constitutional democracies, including Canada, France, and Germany, have some form of judicial review.)

Judicial Review The process by which a court decides on the constitutionality of legislative enactments and actions of the executive branch.

3-1b The Origins of Judicial Review in the United States

The U.S. Constitution does not mention judicial review (although many constitutional scholars believe that the founders intended the judiciary to have this power). How was the doctrine of judicial review established? See this chapter's *Landmark in the Law* feature for the answer.

3-2 Basic Judicial Requirements

Before a court can hear a lawsuit, certain requirements must first be met. These requirements relate to jurisdiction, venue, and standing to sue. We examine each of these important concepts here.

James Madison (1751–1836) was Thomas Jefferson's secretary of state at the time of the case that established the power of judicial review. What is judicial review?

3-2a Jurisdiction

In Latin, *juris* means "law," and *diction* means "to speak." Thus, "the power to speak the law" is the literal meaning of the term **jurisdiction.** Before any court can hear a case, it must have jurisdiction over the person or company against whom the suit is brought (the defendant) or over the property involved in the suit. The court must also have jurisdiction over the subject matter of the dispute.

Jurisdiction The authority of a court to hear and decide a specific case.

Jurisdiction over Persons or Property   Generally, a court with jurisdiction over a particular geographic area can exercise personal jurisdiction (*in personam* jurisdiction) over any person or business that resides in that area. A state trial court, for instance, normally has jurisdictional authority over residents (including businesses) in a particular area of the state, such as a county or district. A state's highest court (often called the state supreme court)[1] has jurisdiction over all residents of that state.

A court can also exercise jurisdiction over property that is located within its boundaries. This kind of jurisdiction is known as *in rem* jurisdiction, or "jurisdiction over the thing." **EXAMPLE 3.1** A dispute arises over the ownership of a boat in dry dock in Fort Lauderdale, Florida. The boat is owned by an Ohio resident, over whom a Florida court normally cannot exercise personal jurisdiction. The other party to the dispute is a resident of Nebraska.

(Image credit, vertical text:) Library of Congress Prints and Photographs Division

---

1. As will be discussed shortly, a state's highest court is frequently referred to as the state supreme court, but there are exceptions. For example, in New York, the supreme court is a trial court.

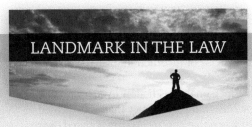

LANDMARK IN THE LAW

Marbury v. Madison (1803)

The power of judicial review was established in the Supreme Court's decision in the case of *Marbury v. Madison*.[a] Although the decision is widely viewed as a cornerstone of constitutional law, the case had its origins in early U.S. politics. When Thomas Jefferson defeated the incumbent president, John Adams, in the presidential elections of 1800, Adams feared the Jeffersonians' antipathy toward business and toward a strong national government. Adams thus rushed to "pack" the judiciary with loyal Federalists (those who believed in a strong national government) by appointing what came to be called "midnight judges" just before he left office. But Adams's secretary of state (John Marshall) was able to deliver only forty-two of the fifty-nine judicial appointment letters by the time Jefferson took over as president. Jefferson refused to order his secretary of state, James Madison, to deliver the remaining commissions.

MARSHALL'S DILEMMA William Marbury and three others to whom the commissions had not been delivered sought a writ of *mandamus* (an order directing a government official to fulfill a duty) from the United States Supreme Court, as authorized by the Judiciary Act in 1789. As fate would have it, John Marshall had just been appointed as chief justice of the Supreme Court. Marshall faced a dilemma: If he ordered the commissions delivered, the new secretary of state (Madison) could simply refuse to deliver them—and the Court had no way to compel him to act. At the same time, if Marshall simply allowed the new administration to do as it wished, the Court's power would be severely eroded.

MARSHALL'S DECISION Marshall masterfully fashioned his decision to enlarge the power of the Supreme Court by affirming the Court's power of judicial review. He stated, "It is emphatically the province and duty of the Judicial Department to say what the law is. . . . If two laws conflict with each other, the Courts must decide on the operation of each. . . . [I]f both [a] law and the Constitution apply to a particular case, . . . the Court must determine which of these conflicting rules governs the case."

Marshall's decision did not require anyone to do anything. He concluded that the highest court did not have the power to issue a writ of *mandamus* in this particular case. Although the Judiciary Act specified that the Supreme Court could issue writs of *mandamus* as part of its original jurisdiction, Article III of the Constitution, which spelled out the Court's original jurisdiction, did not mention such writs. Because Congress did not have the right to expand the Supreme Court's jurisdiction, this section of the Judiciary Act was unconstitutional—and thus void. The *Marbury* decision stands to this day as a judicial and political masterpiece.

APPLICATION TO TODAY'S WORLD *Since the* Marbury v. Madison *decision, the power of judicial review has remained unchallenged and today is exercised by both federal and state courts. If the courts did not have the power of judicial review, the constitutionality of Congress's acts could not be challenged in court—a congressional statute would remain law unless changed by Congress. The courts of other countries that have adopted a constitutional democracy often cite this decision as a justification for judicial review.*

---

a. 5 U.S. (1 Cranch) 137, 2 L.Ed. 60 (1803).

In this situation, a lawsuit concerning the boat could be brought in a Florida state court on the basis of the court's *in rem* jurisdiction. ■

Long Arm Statutes. Under the authority of a state **long arm statute,** a court can exercise personal jurisdiction over certain out-of-state defendants based on activities that took place within the state. Before exercising long arm jurisdiction over a nonresident, however, the court must be convinced that the defendant had sufficient contacts, or *minimum contacts,* with the state to justify the jurisdiction.[2] Generally, this means that the defendant must have enough of a connection to the state for the judge to conclude that it is fair for the state to exercise power over the defendant.

If an out-of-state defendant caused an automobile accident or sold defective goods within the state, for instance, a court will usually find that minimum contacts exist to exercise jurisdiction over that defendant. **CASE EXAMPLE 3.2** After an Xbox game system caught fire in Bonnie Broquet's home in Texas and caused substantial personal injuries, Broquet filed a lawsuit in a Texas court against Ji-Haw Industrial Company, a nonresident company that made

Long Arm Statute A state statute that permits a state to exercise jurisdiction over nonresident defendants.

---

2. The minimum-contacts standard was established in *International Shoe Co. v. State of Washington,* 326 U.S. 310, 66 S.Ct. 154, 90 L.Ed. 95 (1945).

Suppose that a young gamer is injured because Microsoft's Xbox, shown above, released an electrical shock. Whom can the parents sue?

the Xbox components. Broquet alleged that Ji-Haw's components were defective and had caused the fire. Ji-Haw argued that the Texas court lacked jurisdiction over it, but a state appellate court held that the Texas long arm statute authorized the exercise of jurisdiction over the out-of-state defendant.[3] ▨

Similarly, a state may exercise personal jurisdiction over a nonresident defendant who is sued for breaching a contract that was formed within the state. This is true even when that contract was negotiated over the phone or through correspondence.

Corporate Contacts. Because corporations are considered legal persons, courts use the same principles to determine whether it is fair to exercise jurisdiction over a corporation. A corporation normally is subject to personal jurisdiction in the state in which it is incorporated, has its principal office, and is doing business. Courts apply the minimum-contacts test to determine if they can exercise jurisdiction over out-of-state corporations.

The minimum-contacts requirement is usually met if the corporation advertises or sells its products within the state, or places its goods into the "stream of commerce" with the intent that the goods be sold in the state. **EXAMPLE 3.3** A business is incorporated under the laws of Maine but has a branch office and manufacturing plant in Georgia. The corporation also advertises and sells its products in Georgia. These activities would likely constitute sufficient contacts with the state of Georgia to allow a Georgia court to exercise jurisdiction over the corporation. ▨

Some corporations do not sell or advertise products or place any goods in the stream of commerce. Determining what constitutes minimum contacts in these situations can be more difficult. **CASE EXAMPLE 3.4** Independence Plating Corporation is a New Jersey corporation that provides metal-coating services. Its only office and all of its personnel are located in New Jersey, and it does not advertise out of state. Independence had a long-standing business relationship with Southern Prestige Industries, Inc., a North Carolina company. Eventually, Southern Prestige filed suit in North Carolina against Independence for defective workmanship. Independence argued that North Carolina did not have jurisdiction over it, but the court held that Independence had sufficient minimum contacts with the state to justify jurisdiction. The two parties had exchanged thirty-two separate purchase orders in a period of less than twelve months.[4] ▨

Jurisdiction over Subject Matter
Jurisdiction over subject matter is a limitation on the types of cases a court can hear. In both the federal and state court systems, there are courts of *general* (unlimited) *jurisdiction* and courts of *limited jurisdiction*. An example of a court of general jurisdiction is a state trial court or a federal district court.

An example of a state court of limited jurisdiction is a probate court. **Probate courts** are state courts that handle only matters relating to the transfer of a person's assets and obligations after that person's death, including matters relating to the custody and guardianship of children. An example of a federal court of limited subject-matter jurisdiction is a bankruptcy court. **Bankruptcy courts** handle only bankruptcy proceedings, which are governed by federal bankruptcy law.

A court's jurisdiction over subject matter is usually defined in the statute or constitution creating the court. In both the federal and state court systems, a court's subject-matter jurisdiction can be limited by any of the following:

Probate Court A state court of limited jurisdiction that conducts proceedings relating to the settlement of a deceased person's estate.

Bankruptcy Court A federal court of limited jurisdiction that handles only bankruptcy proceedings, which are governed by federal bankruptcy law.

---

3. *Ji-Haw Industrial Co. v. Broquet,* 2008 WL 441822 (Tex.App.—San Antonio 2008).
4. *Southern Prestige Industries, Inc. v. Independence Plating Corp.,* 690 S.E.2d 768 (N.C.App. 2010).

1. The subject of the lawsuit.

2. The sum in controversy.

3. Whether the case involves a felony (a more serious type of crime) or a misdemeanor (a less serious type of crime).

4. Whether the proceeding is a trial or an appeal.

Original and Appellate Jurisdiction

The distinction between courts of original jurisdiction and courts of appellate jurisdiction normally lies in whether the case is being heard for the first time. Courts having original jurisdiction are courts of the first instance, or trial courts—that is, courts in which lawsuits begin, trials take place, and evidence is presented. In the federal court system, the *district courts* are trial courts. In the various state court systems, the trial courts are known by various names, as will be discussed shortly.

The key point here is that any court having original jurisdiction is normally known as a trial court. Courts having appellate jurisdiction act as reviewing courts, or appellate courts. In general, cases can be brought before appellate courts only on appeal from an order or a judgment of a trial court or other lower court.

Jurisdiction of the Federal Courts

Because the federal government is a government of limited powers, the jurisdiction of the federal courts is limited. Federal courts have subject-matter jurisdiction in two situations.

Federal Questions. Article III of the U.S. Constitution establishes the boundaries of federal judicial power. Section 2 of Article III states that "[t]he judicial Power shall extend to all Cases, in Law and Equity, arising under this Constitution, the Laws of the United States, and Treaties made, or which shall be made, under their Authority." This clause means that whenever a plaintiff's cause of action is based, at least in part, on the U.S. Constitution, a treaty, or a federal law, then a **federal question** arises, and the federal courts have jurisdiction.

Any lawsuit involving a federal question, such as a person's rights under the U.S. Constitution, can originate in a federal court. Note that in a case based on a federal question, a federal court will apply federal law.

Diversity of Citizenship. Federal district courts can also exercise original jurisdiction over cases involving **diversity of citizenship.** The most common type of diversity jurisdiction requires *both* of the following: [5]

1. The plaintiff and defendant must be residents of different states.

2. The dollar amount in controversy must exceed $75,000.

For purposes of diversity jurisdiction, a corporation is a citizen of both the state in which it is incorporated and the state in which its principal place of business is located. A case involving diversity of citizenship can be filed in the appropriate federal district court. If the case starts in a state court, it can sometimes be transferred, or "removed," to a federal court. A large percentage of the cases filed in federal courts each year are based on diversity of citizenship.

As noted, a federal court will apply federal law in cases involving federal questions. In a case based on diversity of citizenship, in contrast, a federal court will apply the relevant state law (which is often the law of the state in which the court sits).

CASE EXAMPLE 3.5 Kelley Mala, a U.S. citizen of the Virgin Islands, was driving his powerboat near St. Thomas, Virgin Islands. He stopped at Crown Bay Marina to buy gas, and asked a Crown Bay attendant to watch his boat while the pump was running and he paid the cashier. Although the attendant turned off the pump, it malfunctioned. Gas overflowed and spilled

Federal Question
A question that pertains to the U.S. Constitution, an act of Congress, or a treaty and provides a basis for federal jurisdiction in a case.

Diversity of Citizenship
A basis for federal court jurisdiction over a lawsuit between citizens of different states or a lawsuit involving a U.S. citizen and a citizen of a different country.

---

5. Diversity jurisdiction also exists in cases between (1) a foreign country and citizens of a state or of different states and (2) citizens of a state and citizens or subjects of a foreign country. These bases for diversity jurisdiction are less commonly used.

If a marina employee commits a negligent act while servicing a boat owned by someone whose legal residence is nearby, can the injured boat owner have the case removed to a federal court?

Concurrent Jurisdiction
Jurisdiction that exists when two different courts have the power to hear a case.

Exclusive Jurisdiction
Jurisdiction that exists when a case can be heard only in a particular court or type of court.

into Mala's boat and the water. Mala cleaned the gas off his boat with soap and water that the attendant provided. When he left the dock, his engine caught fire and exploded, severely burning him and destroying the boat.

Mala sued the marina for negligence in a federal district court in the Virgin Islands. He alleged that the court had diversity jurisdiction and requested a jury trial. (A plaintiff in a maritime case does not have a right to a jury trial unless the court has diversity jurisdiction.) The court found that Crown Bay—like the plaintiff—was a citizen of the Virgin Islands, and therefore, the court did not have diversity jurisdiction. A federal appellate court affirmed this decision. Mala had to sue the marina under admiralty law (law governing transportation on the seas and ocean waters) and did not have a right to a jury trial.[6]

Exclusive versus Concurrent Jurisdiction When both federal and state courts have the power to hear a case, as is true in lawsuits involving diversity of citizenship, **concurrent jurisdiction** exists. When cases can be tried only in federal courts or only in state courts, **exclusive jurisdiction** exists.

Federal courts have exclusive jurisdiction in cases involving federal crimes, bankruptcy, most patent and copyright claims, suits against the United States, and some areas of admiralty law. State courts also have exclusive jurisdiction over certain subject matter—for instance, divorce and adoption.

When concurrent jurisdiction exists, a party may bring a suit in either a federal court or a state court. A number of factors can affect the decision of whether to litigate in a federal or a state court, such as the availability of different remedies, the distance to the respective courthouses, or the experience or reputation of a particular judge.

A resident of a state other than the one with jurisdiction might also choose a federal court over a state court if he or she is concerned that a state court might be biased against an out-of-state plaintiff. In contrast, a plaintiff might choose to litigate in a state court if it has a reputation for awarding substantial amounts of damages or if the judge is perceived as being pro-plaintiff. The concepts of exclusive and concurrent jurisdiction are illustrated in Exhibit 3–1.

3–2b Jurisdiction in Cyberspace

The Internet's capacity to bypass political and geographic boundaries undercuts the traditional basis on which courts assert personal jurisdiction. As already discussed, for a court to compel a defendant to come before it, there must be at least minimum contacts—the presence of a salesperson within the state, for example. Today, however, courts frequently have to decide what constitutes sufficient minimum contacts when a defendant's only connection to a jurisdiction is through an ad on a Web site.

The "Sliding-Scale" Standard The courts have developed a standard—called a "sliding-scale" standard—for determining when the exercise of jurisdiction over an out-of-state defendant is proper. The sliding-scale standard identifies three types of Internet business contacts and outlines the following rules for jurisdiction:

LEARNING OBJECTIVE 2

How are the courts applying traditional jurisdictional concepts to cases involving Internet transactions?

---

6. *Mala v. Crown Bay Marina, Inc.*, 704 F.3d 239 (2013).

Exhibit 3-1 Exclusive and Concurrent Jurisdiction

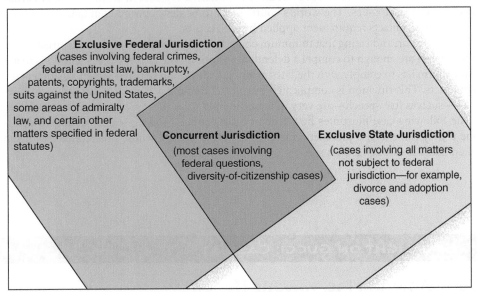

Exclusive Federal Jurisdiction
(cases involving federal crimes, federal antitrust law, bankruptcy, patents, copyrights, trademarks, suits against the United States, some areas of admiralty law, and certain other matters specified in federal statutes)

Concurrent Jurisdiction
(most cases involving federal questions, diversity-of-citizenship cases)

Exclusive State Jurisdiction
(cases involving all matters not subject to federal jurisdiction—for example, divorce and adoption cases)

1. When the defendant conducts *substantial business* over the Internet (such as contracts and sales), jurisdiction is proper. This is true whether the business is conducted with traditional computers, smartphones, or other means of Internet access.

2. When there is *some interactivity* through a Web site, jurisdiction may be proper, depending on the circumstances. Even a single contact can be sufficient to satisfy the minimum-contacts requirement in certain situations.

3. When a defendant merely engages in *passive advertising* on the Web, jurisdiction is never proper.[7]

   CASE EXAMPLE 3.6 A Louisiana resident, Daniel Crummey, purchased a used recreational vehicle (RV) from sellers in Texas after viewing photos of it on eBay. The sellers' statements on eBay claimed that "everything works great on this RV and will provide comfort and dependability for years to come. This RV will go to Alaska and back without problems!"

   Crummey picked up the RV in Texas, but on the drive home, the RV quit working. He filed a suit in Louisiana against the sellers alleging that the vehicle was defective, but the sellers claimed that the Louisiana court lacked jurisdiction. Because the sellers regularly used eBay to market and sell vehicles to remote parties and had sold this RV to a Louisiana buyer, the court found that jurisdiction was proper.[8] ■

iStockPhoto.com/RICH1

If you purchase a used RV outside your home state through an announcement on eBay, can you bring suit in your own state against the seller who lives in another state? Why or why not?

Those of you with an entrepreneurial spirit may be eager to establish Web sites to promote products and solicit orders. Be aware, however, that you can be sued in states in which you have *never* been physically present if you have had sufficient contacts with residents of those states over the Internet. Before you create a Web site that is the least bit interactive, you need to consult an attorney to find out whether you will be subjecting yourself to jurisdiction in every state. Becoming informed about the extent of your potential exposure to lawsuits in various locations is an important part of preventing litigation.

PREVENTING LEGAL DISPUTES

---

7. For a leading case on this issue, see *Zippo Manufacturing Co. v. Zippo Dot Com, Inc.*, 952 F.Supp. 1119 (W.D.Pa. 1997).
8. *Crummey v. Morgan*, 965 So.2d 497 (La.App.1 Cir. 2007). But note that a single sale on eBay does not necessarily confer jurisdiction. Jurisdiction depends on whether the seller regularly uses eBay as a means for doing business with remote buyers. See *Boschetto v. Hansing*, 539 F.3d 1011 (9th Cir. 2008).

International Jurisdictional Issues

Because the Internet is global in scope, it raises international jurisdictional issues. The world's courts seem to be developing a standard that echoes the minimum-contacts requirement applied by U.S. courts.

Most courts are indicating that minimum contacts—doing business within the jurisdiction, for instance—are enough to compel a defendant to appear. The effect of this standard is that a business firm has to comply with the laws in any jurisdiction in which it targets customers for its products. This situation is complicated by the fact that many countries' laws on particular issues—such as free speech—are very different from U.S. laws.

The following case illustrates how federal courts apply a sliding-scale standard to determine if they can exercise jurisdiction over a foreign defendant whose only contact with the United States is through a Web site.

SPOTLIGHT ON GUCCI: CASE 3.1

Gucci America, Inc. v. Wang Huoqing

United States District Court, Northern District of California, 2011 WL 30972 (2011).

COMPANY PROFILE *Gucci America, Inc., a New York corporation headquartered in New York City, is part of Gucci Group, a global fashion firm with offices in China, France, Great Britain, Italy, and Japan. Gucci makes and sells high-quality luxury goods, including footwear, belts, sunglasses, handbags, wallets, jewelry, fragrances, and children's clothing. In connection with its products, Gucci uses twenty-one federally registered trademarks. Gucci also operates a number of boutiques, some of which are located in California.*

Gucci luxury leather products are often counterfeited. Can Gucci sue an Asian company in the United States, nonetheless?

FACTS Wang Huoqing, a resident of the People's Republic of China, operates numerous Web sites. When Gucci discovered that Huoqing's Web sites were selling counterfeit goods—products that carried Gucci's trademarks but were not genuine Gucci articles—it hired a private investigator in San Jose, California, to buy goods from the Web sites. The investigator purchased a wallet that was labeled Gucci but was counterfeit.

Gucci filed a trademark infringement lawsuit against Huoqing in a federal district court in California seeking damages and an injunction to prevent further infringement. Huoqing was notified of the lawsuit via e-mail, but did not appear in court. Gucci asked the court to enter a default judgment—that is, a judgment entered when the defendant fails to appear. The court first had to determine whether it had personal jurisdiction over Huoqing based on the Internet sales.

ISSUE Could a U.S. federal court exercise personal jurisdiction over a resident of China whose only contact with the United States was through an interactive Web site that advertised and sold counterfeit goods?

DECISION Yes. The U.S. District Court for the Northern District of California held that it had personal jurisdiction over the foreign defendant, Huoqing. The court entered a default judgment against Huoqing and granted Gucci an injunction.

REASON The court reasoned that the due process clause allows a federal court to exercise jurisdiction over a defendant who has had sufficient minimum contacts with the court's forum—the place where the court exercises jurisdiction. Specifically, jurisdiction exists when (1) the nonresident defendant engages in some act or transaction with the forum "by which he purposefully avails himself of the privilege of conducting activities in the forum, thereby invoking the benefits and protections of its laws; (2) the claim must be one which arises out of or results from the defendant's forum-related activities; and (3) exercise of jurisdiction must be reasonable."

To determine whether Huoqing had purposefully conducted business activities in California, the court used a sliding-scale analysis. Under this analysis, passive Web sites do not create sufficient contacts for such a finding, but interactive sites may do so. Huoqing's Web sites were fully interactive. In addition, Gucci presented evidence that Huoqing had advertised and sold the counterfeited goods within the court's district, and that he had made one actual sale within the district—the sale to Gucci's private investigator.

WHAT IF THE FACTS WERE DIFFERENT? *Suppose that Gucci had not presented evidence that Huoqing made one actual sale through his Web site to a resident (the private investigator) of the court's district. Would the court still have found that it had personal jurisdiction over Huoqing? Why or why not?*

3-2c Venue

Jurisdiction has to do with whether a court has authority to hear a case involving specific persons, property, or subject matter. **Venue**[9] is concerned with the most appropriate physical location for a trial. Two state courts (or two federal courts) may have the authority to exercise jurisdiction over a case, but it may be more appropriate or convenient to hear the case in one court than in the other.

Basically, the concept of venue reflects the policy that a court trying a suit should be in the geographic neighborhood (usually the county) where the incident leading to the lawsuit occurred or where the parties involved in the lawsuit reside. Venue in a civil case typically is where the defendant resides, whereas venue in a criminal case normally is where the crime occurred. Pretrial publicity or other factors, though, may require a change of venue to another community, especially in criminal cases when the defendant's right to a fair and impartial jury has been impaired.

EXAMPLE 3.7 Police raid a compound of religious polygamists in Texas and remove many children from the ranch. Authorities suspect that some of the children were being sexually and physically abused. The raid receives a great deal of media attention, and the people living in nearby towns are likely influenced by this publicity. In this situation, if the government files criminal charges against a member of the religious sect, that individual may request—and will probably receive—a change of venue to another location. ■

Note that venue has lost some significance in today's world because of the Internet and 24/7 news reporting. Courts now rarely grant requests for a change of venue. Because everyone has instant access to the same information about a purported crime, courts reason that no community is more or less informed about the matter or prejudiced for or against the defendant.

Venue The geographic district in which a legal action is tried and from which the jury is selected.

3-2d Standing to Sue

Before a person can bring a lawsuit before a court, the party must have **standing to sue,** or a sufficient "stake" in the matter to justify seeking relief through the court system. In other words, to have standing, a party must have a legally protected and tangible interest at stake in the litigation.

The party bringing the lawsuit must have suffered a harm, or have been threatened by a harm, as a result of the action about which she or he has complained. At times, a person can have standing to sue on behalf of another person, such as a minor (child) or a mentally incompetent person. Standing to sue also requires that the controversy at issue be a **justiciable**[10] **controversy**—a controversy that is real and substantial, as opposed to hypothetical or academic.

CASE EXAMPLE 3.8 Harold Wagner obtained a loan through M.S.T. Mortgage Group to buy a house in Texas. After the sale, M.S.T. transferred its interest in the loan to another lender, which assigned it to another lender, as is common in the mortgage industry. Eventually, when Wagner failed to make the loan payments, CitiMortgage, Inc., notified him that it was going to foreclose on the property and sell the house. Wagner filed a lawsuit claiming that the lenders had improperly assigned the mortgage loan. In 2014, a federal district court ruled that Wagner lacked standing to contest the assignment. Under Texas law, only the parties directly involved in an assignment can challenge its validity. In this case, the assignment was between two lenders and did not directly involve Wagner.[11] ■

Standing to Sue The legal requirement that an individual must have a sufficient stake in a controversy before he or she can bring a lawsuit.

Justiciable Controversy A controversy that is not hypothetical or academic but real and substantial; a requirement that must be satisfied before a court will hear a case.

---

9. Pronounced *ven*-yoo.
10. Pronounced jus-*tish*-uh-bul.
11. *Wagner v. CitiMortgage, Inc.*, 995 F.Supp.2d 621 (N.D.Tex. 2014).

3-3 The State and Federal Court Systems

As mentioned earlier in this chapter, each state has its own court system. Additionally, there is a system of federal courts. Even though there are fifty-two court systems—one for each of the fifty states, one for the District of Columbia, and a federal system—similarities abound. Exhibit 3–2 illustrates the basic organizational structure characteristic of the court systems in many states. The exhibit also shows how the federal court system is structured.

Keep in mind that the federal courts are not superior to the state courts. They are simply an independent system of courts, which derives its authority from Article III, Sections 1 and 2, of the U.S. Constitution. We turn now to an examination of these court systems, beginning with the state courts.

3-3a The State Court Systems

Typically, a state court system will include several levels, or tiers, of courts. As indicated in Exhibit 3–2, state courts may include (1) trial courts of limited jurisdiction, (2) trial courts of general jurisdiction, (3) appellate courts, and (4) the state's highest court (often called the state supreme court).

Generally, any person who is a party to a lawsuit has the opportunity to plead the case before a trial court and then, if he or she loses, before at least one level of appellate court. If the case involves a federal statute or a federal constitutional issue, the decision of a state supreme court on that issue may be further appealed to the United States Supreme Court. (See this chapter's *Managerial Strategy* feature for a discussion of how state budget cuts are making it more difficult to bring cases in some state courts.)

Trial Courts Trial courts are courts in which trials are held and testimony taken. State trial courts have either general or limited jurisdiction. Trial courts that have general jurisdiction as to subject matter may be called county, district, superior, or circuit courts.[12] The jurisdiction

---

12. The name in Ohio is court of common pleas, and the name in New York is supreme court.

Exhibit 3–2 The State and Federal Court Systems

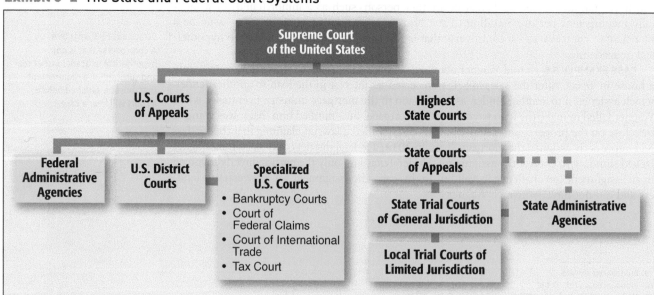

MANAGERIAL STRATEGY

Budget Cuts for State Courts Can Affect Businesses

Management Faces a Legal Issue

In the United States, businesses use the courts far more than anyone else. Most civil court cases involve a business suing another business for breach of contract or fraud, for instance. Additionally, when one company fails to pay another company for products or services, the unpaid company often turns to the court system. If that firm does not have ready access to the courts, its financial stability can be put at risk.

According to the National Center for State Courts, since 2009 forty-one state legislatures have reduced their state court services to the public as a result of budget restrictions. Many state courts have laid off staff members, delayed filling vacancies, and reduced hours of operation. California's courts have experienced the steepest cuts—nearly $1 billion since 2009. Texas has also experienced large cuts in court funding.

What the Courts Say

Today, the value of a company's intellectual property, such as its copyrights and patents, often exceeds the value of its physical property. Not surprisingly, disputes over intellectual property have grown in number and importance. As a result of the court budget cuts, these disputes also take longer to resolve. In California, for example, a typical patent lawsuit used to last twelve months. That same lawsuit now might take three to five years.

If an intellectual property case goes on to an appellate court, three or four more years typically pass before the dispute is resolved. In fact, the United States Supreme Court heard a case in 2014 involving a trademark dispute that had been in the courts for more than sixteen years.[a]

Other types of lawsuits are also taking longer to conclude. Now attorneys must tell businesses to consider not only the cost of bringing a lawsuit, but also the length of time involved. The longer the litigation lasts, the larger the legal bills and the greater the drain on company employees' time. During the years that a lawsuit can take, some businesses find that they cannot expand or hire new employees, and they are reluctant to spend funds on additional marketing and advertising. In fact, it is not unusual for a company to win its case but end up going out of business. As a result of putting its business on hold for years, the company becomes insolvent.

MANAGERIAL IMPLICATIONS

Many investors are reluctant to invest in a company that is the object of a patent or copyright lawsuit because they fear that if the company loses, it may lose the rights to its most valuable asset. Consequently, when litigation drags on for years, investors may abandon a company even though it is otherwise healthy. As a result, the company suffers.

Facing long delays in litigation with potential negative effects on their companies, business managers have become more reluctant to bring lawsuits, even when their cases clearly have merit. In Alabama, for instance, the number of civil cases filed has dropped by more than a third in the last few years. Before bringing a lawsuit, a manager must now take into account the possibility of long delays in resolving the case—delays that must figure into the cost-benefit analysis for undertaking litigation. Managers can no longer stand on principle because they know that they are right and that they will win a lawsuit. They have to look at the bigger picture, which includes substantial court delays.

---

a. *B&B Hardware Inc. v. Hargis Industries, Inc.*, __ U.S. __, 135 S.Ct. 696, 190 L.Ed.2d 386 (2014).

---

of these courts is often determined by the size of the county in which the court sits. State trial courts of general jurisdiction have jurisdiction over a wide variety of subjects, including both civil disputes and criminal prosecutions. (In some states, trial courts of general jurisdiction may hear appeals from courts of limited jurisdiction.)

Some courts of limited jurisdiction are called special inferior trial courts or minor judiciary courts. **Small claims courts** are inferior trial courts that hear only civil cases involving claims of less than a certain amount, such as $5,000 (the amount varies from state to state). Suits brought in small claims courts are generally conducted informally, and lawyers are not required (in a few states, lawyers are not even allowed). Another example of an inferior trial court is a local municipal court that hears mainly traffic cases. Decisions of small claims courts and municipal courts may sometimes be appealed to a state trial court of general jurisdiction.

Other courts of limited jurisdiction as to subject matter include domestic relations or family courts, which handle primarily divorce actions and child-custody disputes, and probate courts, as mentioned earlier. A few states have even established Islamic law courts, which are

Small Claims Court A special court in which parties can litigate small claims without an attorney.

Can a U.S. court ever use the Qur'an as a basis for reaching a decision?

Question of Fact In a lawsuit, an issue that involves only disputed facts, and not what the law is on a given point.

courts of limited jurisdiction that serve the American Muslim community. (See this chapter's *Beyond Our Borders* feature for a discussion of the rise of Islamic law courts.)

Appellate, or Reviewing, Courts Every state has at least one court of appeals (appellate court, or reviewing court), which may be an intermediate appellate court or the state's highest court. About three-fourths of the states have intermediate appellate courts. Generally, courts of appeals do not conduct new trials, in which evidence is submitted and witnesses are examined. Rather, an appellate court panel of three or more judges reviews the record of the case on appeal, which includes a transcript of the trial proceedings, and determines whether the trial court committed an error.

Focus on Questions of Law. Appellate courts generally focus on questions of law, not questions of fact. A **question of fact** deals with what really happened in regard to the dispute being tried—such as whether a party

BEYOND OUR BORDERS

Islamic Law Courts Abroad and at Home

Islamic law is one of the world's three most common legal systems, along with civil law and common law systems. In most Islamic countries, the law is based on *sharia,* a system of law derived from the Qur'an and the sayings and doings of Muhammad and his companions. Today, many non-Islamic countries are establishing Islamic courts for their Muslim citizens.

Islamic Law in Britain, Canada, and Belgium

For several years, Great Britain has had councils that arbitrate disputes between British Muslims involving child custody, property, employment, and housing. These councils do not deal with criminal law or with any civil issues that would put *sharia* in direct conflict with British statutory law. Most Islamic law cases involve marriage or divorce. Starting in 2008, Britain officially sanctioned the authority of *sharia* judges to rule on divorce and financial disputes of Muslim couples. Britain now has eighty-five officially recognized *sharia* courts that have the full power

of equivalent courts within the traditional British judicial system.

In Ontario, Canada, a group of Canadian Muslims established a judicial tribunal using *sharia.* To date, this tribunal has resolved only marital disagreements and some other civil disputes. Under Ontario law, the regular judicial system must uphold such agreements as long as they are voluntary and negotiated through an arbitrator. Any agreements that violate Canada's Charter of Rights and Freedoms will not be upheld.

In 2011, Belgium established its first *sharia* court. This court handles primarily family law disputes for Muslim immigrants in Belgium.

Islamic Law Courts in the United States

The use of Islamic courts in the United States has been somewhat controversial. The legality of arbitration clauses that require disputes to be settled in Islamic courts has been upheld by regular state courts in some states, including Minnesota and Texas. In some other states, however, there has been a public backlash against the use of Islamic courts.

For instance, in Detroit, Michigan, which has a large American Muslim population, a controversy erupted over the community's attempt to establish Islamic courts. Legislators in Michigan and many other states started introducing bills to limit consideration of foreign or religious laws in state court decisions. Voters in Oklahoma enacted a referendum banning courts from considering *sharia* law, but the ban was later held to be unconstitutional.[a] Legislation enacted in Arizona, Kansas, Louisiana, North Carolina, Oklahoma, South Dakota, and Tennessee bans judicial consideration of foreign law. (These laws do not explicitly mention Islamic, or *sharia,* law, because that might be ruled unconstitutional.)

CRITICAL THINKING

■ One of the arguments against allowing *sharia* courts in the United States is that we would no longer have a common legal framework within our society. Do you agree or disagree? Why?

a. *Awad v. Zirax,* 670 F.3d 1111 (10th Cir. 2012). A lower court later issued a permanent injunction to prevent the ban from being enforced. *Awad v. Zirax,* 966 F.Supp.2d 1198 (2013).

actually burned a flag. A **question of law** concerns the application or interpretation of the law—such as whether flag-burning is a form of speech protected by the First Amendment to the U.S. Constitution. Only a judge, not a jury, can rule on questions of law.

Defer to the Trial Court's Findings of Fact. Appellate courts normally defer (yield or give weight) to a trial court's findings on questions of fact, because the trial court judge and jury were in a better position to evaluate testimony. The trial court could directly observe witnesses' gestures, demeanor, and nonverbal behavior during the trial. At the appellate level, the judges review the written transcript of the trial, which does not include these nonverbal elements.

An appellate court will challenge a trial court's finding of fact only when the finding is clearly erroneous (that is, when it is contrary to the evidence presented at trial or when no evidence was presented to support the finding). **EXAMPLE 3.9** A jury concludes that a manufacturer's product harmed the plaintiff, but no evidence was submitted to the court to support that conclusion. In this situation, the appellate court will hold that the trial court's decision was erroneous. ■ The options exercised by appellate courts will be discussed further later in this chapter.

Highest State Courts

The highest appellate court in a state is usually called the supreme court but may be called by some other name. For example, in both New York and Maryland, the highest state court is called the court of appeals. The decisions of each state's highest court are final on all questions of state law. Only when issues of federal law are involved can a decision made by a state's highest court be overruled by the United States Supreme Court.

3–3b The Federal Court System

The federal court system is basically a three-tiered model consisting of (1) U.S. district courts (trial courts of general jurisdiction) and various courts of limited jurisdiction, (2) U.S. courts of appeals (intermediate courts of appeals), and (3) the United States Supreme Court.

Unlike state court judges, who are usually elected, federal court judges—including the justices of the Supreme Court—are appointed by the president of the United States and confirmed by the U.S. Senate. Under Article III, federal judges "hold their offices during Good Behavior." In essence, this means that federal judges receive lifetime appointments.

U.S. District Courts

At the federal level, the equivalent of a state trial court of general jurisdiction is the district court. There is at least one federal district court in every state. The number of judicial districts can vary over time, primarily owing to population changes and corresponding caseloads. Today, there are ninety-four federal judicial districts.

U.S. district courts have original jurisdiction in federal matters. Federal cases typically originate in district courts. Federal courts with original, but special (or limited), jurisdiction include the bankruptcy courts and others that were shown in Exhibit 3–2.

U.S. Courts of Appeals

In the federal court system, there are thirteen U.S. courts of appeals—also referred to as U.S. circuit courts of appeals. The federal courts of appeals for twelve of the circuits, including the U.S. Court of Appeals for the District of Columbia Circuit, hear appeals from the federal district courts located within their respective judicial circuits.

Question of Law In a lawsuit, an issue involving the application or interpretation of a law.

LEARNING OBJECTIVE 3
What is the difference between the focus of a trial court and an appellate court?

KNOW THIS
The decisions of a state's highest court are final on questions of state law.

Trial decisions are normally determined by juries. Under what types of circumstances might an appellate court reverse a jury's decision?

The Court of Appeals for the Thirteenth Circuit is called the Federal Circuit. It has national appellate jurisdiction over certain types of cases, such as cases involving patent law and cases in which the U.S. government is a defendant.

The decisions of the circuit courts of appeals are final in most cases, but appeal to the United States Supreme Court is possible. Exhibit 3–3 shows the geographic boundaries of the U.S. circuit courts of appeals and the boundaries of the U.S. district courts within each circuit.

The United States Supreme Court The highest level of the three-tiered model of the federal court system is the United States Supreme Court. According to Article III of the U.S. Constitution, there is only one national Supreme Court. All other courts in the federal system are considered "inferior." Congress is empowered to create inferior courts as it deems necessary. The inferior courts that Congress has created include the second tier in our model—the U.S. courts of appeals—as well as the district courts and any other courts of limited, or specialized, jurisdiction.

The United States Supreme Court consists of nine justices. Although the Supreme Court has original, or trial, jurisdiction in rare instances (set forth in Article III, Section 2), most of its work is as an appeals court. The Supreme Court can review any case decided by any of the federal courts of appeals, and it also has appellate authority over some cases decided in the state courts.

Appeals to the Supreme Court. To bring a case before the Supreme Court, a party requests that the Court issue a writ of *certiorari*. A **writ of *certiorari***[13] is an order issued by the Supreme

Writ of *Certiorari* A writ from a higher court asking a lower court for the record of a case.

_____

13. Pronounced sur-shee-uh-*rah*-ree.

Exhibit 3–3 Boundaries of the U.S. Courts of Appeals and U.S. District Courts

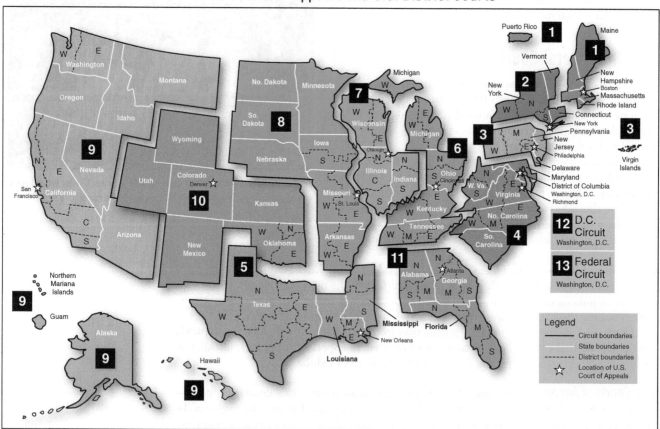

Source: Administrative Office of the United States Courts.

Court to a lower court requiring that court to send the record of the case for review. Under the **rule of four,** the Court will not issue a writ unless at least four of the nine justices approve.

Whether the Court will issue a writ of *certiorari* is entirely within its discretion. The Court is not required to issue one, and most petitions for writs are denied. (Although thousands of cases are filed with the Supreme Court each year, it hears, on average, fewer than one hundred of these cases.)[14] A denial is not a decision on the merits of a case, nor does it indicate agreement with the lower court's opinion. Furthermore, a denial of the writ has no value as a precedent.

Petitions Granted by the Court. Typically, the Court grants petitions when cases raise important constitutional questions or when the lower courts are issuing conflicting decisions on a significant issue. The justices, however, never explain their reasons for hearing certain cases and not others, so it is difficult to predict which type of case the Court might select.

How much weight should Supreme Court justices give to arguments made in *amicus* briefs? Parties not directly involved in a case before the United States Supreme Court are allowed to file friend-of-the-court (*amicus curiae*) briefs. Important, headline-making cases sometimes elicit eighty or more *amicus* briefs. Supreme Court justices often rely on these briefs to buttress their opinions. Law professor Allison Orr Larsen found that over a recent five-term period, the Court's opinions cited factual assertions from *amicus* briefs 124 times.[15]

Critics of the justices' use of *amicus* briefs for factual information, including Larsen, argue that such "information" can be highly unreliable and even outright incorrect. After all, in the age of the Internet, almost anyone can become an "expert." Some recent Supreme Court opinions have cited facts from *amicus* briefs that were backed up only by blog posts or e-mails. Furthermore, some studies presented in *amicus* briefs were paid for by the groups providing the briefs and published only on the Internet. In spite of these problems, Supreme Court justices are increasingly citing *amicus* briefs for statements of fact, rather than citing underlying factual sources and their authority, prompting Justice Antonin Scalia to argue that "Supreme Court briefs are an inappropriate place to develop the key facts in a case."

ETHICAL ISSUE

Rule of Four A rule of the United States Supreme Court under which the Court will not issue a writ of *certiorari* unless at least four justices approve of the decision to issue the writ.

No. _____

IN THE
SUPREME COURT OF THE UNITED STATES

METRO-GOLDWYN-MAYER STUDIOS, INC., ET AL.,
Petitioners,

v.

GROKSTER, LTD., ET AL,

Respondent.

ON PETITION FOR A WRIT OF CERTIORARI TO
THE UNITED STATES COURT OF APPEALS FOR
THE NINTH CIRCUIT

BRIEF AMICUS CURIAE FOR RECORDING
ARTISTS' COALITION
AND DON HENLEY, GLEN FREY, JOE WALSH,
TIMOTHY B. SCHMIT ("THE EAGLES"), KIX
BROOKS & RONNIE DUNN ("BROOKS & DUNN"),
NATALIE MAINES, MARTIE MAGUIRE, EMILY
ROBISON ("THE DIXIE CHICKS"), BONNIE RAITT,
SHERYL CROW, PHIL VASSER, "MYA" HARRISON,
KENNETH "BABYFACE" EDMONDS, BILL
KREUTZMAN & MICKY HART (OF "THE
GRATEFUL DEAD"), JIMMY BUFFETT, PATTY
LOVELESS, STEVIE NICKS (OF "FLEETWOOD
MAC"), AND GAVIN ROSSDALE (OF "BUSH")
IN SUPPORT OF PETITIONERS

Library of Congress

This *amicus* brief was filed on behalf of many well-known recording artists. Are there any rules concerning the quality of the research or facts presented in such briefs?

"Lawsuit: A machine which you go into as a pig and come out of as a sausage."

AMBROSE BIERCE
1842–1914
(AMERICAN JOURNALIST)

3-4 Following a State Court Case

To illustrate the procedures that would be followed in a civil lawsuit brought in a state court, we present a hypothetical case and follow it through the state court system. The case involves an automobile accident in which Kevin Anderson, driving a Lexus, struck Lisa Marconi, driving a Hyundai Genesis. The accident occurred at the intersection of Wilshire Boulevard and Rodeo Drive in Beverly Hills, California. Marconi suffered personal injuries and incurred medical and hospital expenses as a result, as well as lost wages for four months. Anderson and Marconi are unable to agree on a settlement, and Marconi sues Anderson. Marconi is the plaintiff, and Anderson is the defendant. Both are represented by lawyers.

During each phase of the **litigation** (the process of working a lawsuit through the court system), Marconi and Anderson will have to observe strict procedural requirements. A large body of law—procedural law—establishes the rules and standards for determining disputes in courts.

Procedural rules are very complex, and they vary from court to court and from state to state. In addition to the various sets of rules for state courts, the federal courts have their own rules of procedure. Additionally, the applicable procedures will depend on whether the case is

Litigation The process of resolving a dispute through the court system.

---

14. From the mid-1950s through the early 1990s, the United States Supreme Court reviewed more cases per year than it has in the last few years. In the Court's 1982–1983 term, for example, the Court issued opinions in 151 cases. In contrast, in its 2014–2015 term, the Court issued opinions in only 76 cases.
15. Allison Orr Larsen, "The Trouble with *Amicus* Facts," *Virginia Law Review* 100 (December 2014).

a civil or criminal proceeding. Generally, the Marconi-Anderson civil lawsuit will involve the procedures discussed in the following subsections. Keep in mind that attempts to settle the case may be ongoing throughout the trial.

3–4a The Pleadings

The complaint and answer (and the counterclaim and reply)—all of which are discussed here—taken together are called the **pleadings.** The pleadings inform each party of the other's claims and specify the issues (disputed questions) involved in the case. The style and form of the pleadings may be quite different in different states.

Pleadings Statements by the plaintiff and the defendant that detail the facts, charges, and defenses of a case.

The Plaintiff's Complaint Marconi's suit against Anderson commences when her lawyer files a **complaint** with the appropriate court. The complaint contains statements alleging:

Complaint The pleading made by a plaintiff alleging wrongdoing on the part of the defendant. When filed with a court, the complaint initiates a lawsuit.

1. The facts necessary for the court to take *jurisdiction*.

2. A brief summary of the *facts* necessary to show that the plaintiff is entitled to relief (a remedy).[16]

3. A statement of the *remedy* the plaintiff is seeking.

Complaints may be lengthy or brief, depending on the complexity of the case and the rules of the jurisdiction.

Service of Process Before the court can exercise personal jurisdiction over the defendant (Anderson)—in effect, before the lawsuit can begin—the court must have proof that the defendant was notified of the lawsuit. Formally notifying the defendant of a lawsuit is called **service of process.** The plaintiff must deliver, or serve, a copy of the complaint and a **summons** (a notice requiring the defendant to appear in court and answer the complaint) to the defendant.

Service of Process The delivery of the complaint and summons to a defendant.

Summons A document informing a defendant that a legal action has been commenced against her or him and that the defendant must appear in court on a certain date to answer the plaintiff's complaint.

The summons notifies Anderson that he must file an answer to the complaint within a specified time period (twenty days in the federal courts) or suffer a default judgment against him. A **default judgment** in Marconi's favor would mean that she would be awarded the damages alleged in her complaint because Anderson failed to respond to the allegations. In our legal system, no case can proceed to trial unless the plaintiff can prove that he or she has properly served the defendant.

Default Judgment A judgment entered by a court against a defendant who has failed to appear in court to answer or defend against the plaintiff's claim.

How service of process occurs depends on the rules of the court or jurisdiction in which the lawsuit is brought. Usually, the server hands the summons and complaint to the defendant personally or leaves it at the defendant's residence or place of business. In some states, process can be served by mail if the defendant consents (accepts service). When the defendant cannot be reached, special rules provide for alternative means of service, such as publishing a notice in the local newspaper or serving process via e-mail.

The Defendant's Answer The defendant's **answer** either admits the statements or allegations set forth in the complaint or denies them and outlines any defenses that the defendant may have. If Anderson admits to all of Marconi's allegations in his answer, the court will enter a judgment for Marconi. If Anderson denies any of Marconi's allegations, the litigation will go forward.

Answer Procedurally, a defendant's response to the plaintiff's complaint.

Anderson can deny Marconi's allegations and set forth his own claim that Marconi was negligent and therefore owes him compensation for the damage to his Lexus. This is appropriately called a **counterclaim.** If Anderson files a counterclaim, Marconi will have to answer it with a pleading, normally called a **reply,** which has the same characteristics as an answer.

Counterclaim A claim made by a defendant in a civil lawsuit against the plaintiff. In effect, the defendant is suing the plaintiff.

Reply Procedurally, a plaintiff's response to a defendant's answer.

---

16. The factual allegations in a complaint must be enough to raise a right to relief above the speculative level. They must plausibly suggest that the plaintiff is entitled to a remedy. See *Bell Atlantic Corp. v. Twombly,* 550 U.S. 544, 127 S.Ct. 1955, 167 L.Ed.2d 929 (2007).

Anderson can also admit the truth of Marconi's complaint but raise new facts that may result in dismissal of the action. This is called raising an *affirmative defense*. For example, Anderson could assert that Marconi was driving negligently at the time of the accident and thus was partially responsible for her own injuries. In some states, a plaintiff's contributory negligence operates as a complete defense, whereas in others it simply reduces the amount of damages that Marconi can recover (see Chapter 4).

Motion to Dismiss   A *motion* is a procedural request submitted to the court by an attorney on behalf of her or his client. A **motion to dismiss** requests the court to dismiss the case for stated reasons. Grounds for dismissal of a case include improper delivery of the complaint and summons, improper venue, and the plaintiff's failure to state a claim for which a court could grant relief. For instance, suppose that Marconi had suffered no injuries or losses as a result of Anderson's negligence. In that situation, Anderson could move to have the case dismissed because Marconi would not have stated a claim for which relief could be granted.

If the judge grants the motion to dismiss, the plaintiff generally is given time to file an amended complaint. If the judge denies the motion, the suit will go forward, and the defendant must then file an answer. Note that if Marconi wishes to discontinue the suit because, for example, an out-of-court settlement has been reached, she can likewise move for dismissal. The court can also dismiss the case on its own motion.

CASE EXAMPLE 3.10   Espresso Disposition Corporation 1 entered into a contract with Santana Sales & Marketing Group, Inc. The agreement included a mandatory *forum-selection clause*—which was a provision designating that any disputes arising under the contract would be decided by a court in Illinois. When Santana Sales filed a lawsuit against Espresso in a Florida state court, Espresso filed a motion to dismiss based on the agreement's forum selection clause. Santana claimed that the forum-selection clause had been a mistake. The court denied Espresso's motion to dismiss. Espresso appealed. A state intermediate appellate court reversed the trial court's denial of Espresso's motion to dismiss and remanded the case to the lower court for the entry of an order of dismissal.[17] ▪

3–4b Pretrial Motions

Either party may attempt to get the case dismissed before trial through the use of various pretrial motions. We have already mentioned the motion to dismiss. Two other important pretrial motions are the motion for judgment on the pleadings and the motion for summary judgment.

At the close of the pleadings, either party may make a **motion for judgment on the pleadings,** or on the merits of the case. The judge will grant the motion only when there is no dispute over the facts of the case and the sole issue to be resolved is a question of law. In deciding on the motion, the judge may consider only the evidence contained in the pleadings.

In contrast, in a **motion for summary judgment,** the court may consider evidence outside the pleadings, such as sworn statements (affidavits) by parties or witnesses, or other documents relating to the case. Either party can make a motion for summary judgment. Like the motion for judgment on the pleadings, a motion for summary judgment will be granted only if there are no genuine questions of fact and the sole question is a question of law.

3–4c Discovery

Before a trial begins, each party can use a number of procedural devices to obtain information and gather evidence about the case from the other party or from third parties. The process of obtaining such information is known as **discovery.** Discovery includes gaining access to witnesses, documents, records, and other types of evidence.

Motion to Dismiss   A pleading in which a defendant admits the facts as alleged by the plaintiff but asserts that the plaintiff's claim to state a cause of action has no basis in law.

Motion for Judgment on the Pleadings   A motion by either party to a lawsuit at the close of the pleadings requesting the court to decide the issue solely on the pleadings without proceeding to trial. The motion will be granted only if no facts are in dispute.

Motion for Summary Judgment   A motion requesting the court to enter a judgment without proceeding to trial. The motion can be based on evidence outside the pleadings and will be granted only if no facts are in dispute.

LEARNING OBJECTIVE 4

What is discovery, and how does electronic discovery differ from traditional discovery?

Discovery   A method by which the opposing parties obtain information from each other to prepare for trial.

---

17. *Espresso Disposition Corp. 1 v. Santana Sales & Marketing Group, Inc.,* 105 So.3d 592 (Fla.App. 3 Dist. 2013).

The Federal Rules of Civil Procedure and similar rules in the states set forth the guidelines for discovery. Generally, discovery is allowed regarding any matter that is not privileged and is relevant to the claim or defense of any party. Discovery rules also attempt to protect witnesses and parties from undue harassment and to safeguard privileged or confidential material from being disclosed.

If a discovery request involves privileged or confidential business information, a court can deny the request and can limit the scope of discovery in a number of ways. For instance, a court can require the party to submit the materials to the judge in a sealed envelope so that the judge can decide if they should be disclosed to the opposing party.

Discovery prevents surprises at trial by giving parties access to evidence that might otherwise be hidden. This allows both parties to learn what to expect during a trial before they reach the courtroom. Discovery also serves to narrow the issues so that trial time is spent on the main questions in the case. The following case shows how vital discovery can be to the outcome of litigation.

CASE 3.2

Brothers v. Winstead

Supreme Court of Mississippi, 129 So.3d 906 (2014).

FACTS Phillips Brothers, LP (limited partnership), Harry Simmons, and Ray Winstead were the owners of Kilby Brake Fisheries, LLC (limited liability company), a catfish farm in Mississippi. For nearly eight years, Winstead operated a hatchery for the firm. During this time, the hatchery had only two profitable years. Consequently, Winstead was fired. He filed a suit in a Mississippi state court against Kilby Brake and its other owners, alleging a "freeze-out." (A freeze-out occurs when a majority of the owners of a firm exclude other owners from certain benefits of participating in the firm.)

The defendants filed a counterclaim of theft. To support this claim, the defendants asked the court to allow them to obtain documents from Winstead regarding his finances, particularly income from his Winstead Cattle Company. The court refused this request. A jury awarded Winstead more than $1.7 million, and the defendants appealed.

ISSUE Were the defendants entitled to discovery of information concerning Winstead's finances to seek evidence to support their claims?

DECISION Yes. The Mississippi Supreme Court reversed the lower court's decision to deny discovery of information on Winstead's outside finances and remanded the case for a new trial.

Why was Winstead fired from his catfish hatchery position?

iStockPhoto.com/J.Leeuwtie

REASON The state supreme court noted several factors in explaining its reasoning. Winstead testified that Winstead Cattle Company did no business—it was "simply his hunting camp." But during discovery, Winstead provided tax returns that showed substantial income from the company.

Other documents showed income from sales of "cattle" to a fish farmer named Scott Kiker, which did not appear on Winstead's tax returns. Kilby Brake contended that this income represented sales of Kilby Brake fish, not cattle. Kiker testified that he received a load of fish from Kilby Brake, sold the fish, and gave Winstead a commission without paying Kilby Brake.

Winstead countered that he often acted as a "middleman" between a farmer in need of fish and another with fish for sale, taking a commission on the deal. Further discovery of information on Winstead's financial dealings could reveal whether he was selling fish from Kilby Brake and disguising these sales on his tax returns.

CRITICAL THINKING—Ethical Consideration *Does Winstead have an ethical duty to comply with the defendants' discovery request? Discuss.*

Depositions and Interrogatories

Deposition The testimony of a party to a lawsuit or a witness taken under oath before a trial.

Discovery can involve the use of depositions, interrogatories, or both. A **deposition** is sworn testimony by a party to the lawsuit or any witness. The person being deposed (the deponent) answers questions asked by the attorneys, and the questions and answers are recorded by an authorized court official and sworn to and signed by the deponent. (Occasionally, written depositions are taken when witnesses are unable to appear in person.) The answers given to depositions will, of course, help the attorneys prepare for the trial. They can also be used in court to impeach (challenge the credibility of) a party or a witness who changes her or his testimony at the trial. In addition, a witness's deposition can be used as testimony if he or she is not available for the trial.

Interrogatories are written questions for which written answers are prepared and then signed under oath. The main difference between interrogatories and written depositions is that interrogatories are directed to a party to the lawsuit (the plaintiff or the defendant), not to a witness, and the party can prepare answers with the aid of an attorney. In addition, the scope of interrogatories is broader because parties are obligated to answer the questions, even if that means disclosing information from their records and files.

> **Interrogatories** A series of written questions for which written answers are prepared by a party to a lawsuit, usually with the assistance of the party's attorney, and then signed under oath.

Note that, as with discovery requests, a court can impose sanctions on a party who fails to answer interrogatories. **CASE EXAMPLE 3.11** Computer Task Group, Inc. (CTG), sued a former employee, William Brotby, for violating the terms of his employment agreement. During discovery, Brotby refused to respond fully to CTG's interrogatories. He gave contradictory answers, made frivolous objections, filed baseless motions, and never disclosed all the information that CTG sought. The court ordered Brotby to comply with discovery requests five times. Nevertheless, Brotby continued to make excuses and changed his story repeatedly, making it impossible for CTG to establish basic facts with any certainty. Eventually, CTG requested and the court granted a default judgment against Brotby based on his failure to cooperate.[18] ▪

Requests for Other Information
A party can serve a written request on the other party for an admission of the truth on matters relating to the trial. Any matter admitted under such a request is conclusively established for the trial. For instance, Marconi can ask Anderson to admit that he was driving at a speed of forty-five miles an hour. A request for admission saves time at trial because the parties will not have to spend time proving facts on which they already agree.

A party can also gain access to documents and other items not in her or his possession in order to inspect and examine them. Likewise, a party can gain "entry upon land" to inspect the premises. Anderson's attorney, for instance, normally can gain permission to inspect and photocopy Marconi's car repair bills.

When the physical or mental condition of one party is in question, the opposing party can ask the court to order a physical or mental examination, but the court will do so only if the need for the information outweighs the right to privacy of the person to be examined. If the court issues the order, the opposing party can obtain the results of the examination.

Electronic Discovery
Any relevant material, including information stored electronically, can be the object of a discovery request. The federal rules and most state rules now specifically allow all parties to obtain electronic "data compilations." Electronic evidence, or **e-evidence,** includes all types of computer-generated or electronically recorded information. This might include e-mail, voice mail, tweets, blogs, social media posts, and spreadsheets, as well as documents and other data stored on computers.

> **E-Evidence** A type of evidence that consists of computer-generated or electronically recorded information.

E-evidence can reveal significant facts that are not discoverable by other means. Computers, smartphones, cameras, and other devices automatically record certain information about files—such as who created a file and when, and who accessed, modified, or transmitted it—on their hard drives. This information is called **metadata,** which can be thought of as "data about data." Metadata can be obtained only from the file in its electronic format—not from printed-out versions.

> **Metadata** Data that are automatically recorded by electronic devices and provide information about who created a file and when, and who accessed, modified, or transmitted the file on their hard drives. Can be described as data about data.

EXAMPLE 3.12 In 2012, John McAfee, the programmer responsible for creating McAfee antivirus software, was wanted for questioning in the murder of his neighbor in Belize. McAfee

---

18. *Computer Task Group, Inc. v. Brotby,* 364 F.3d 1112 (9th Cir. 2004).

left Belize and was on the run from police, but he allowed a journalist to come with him and photograph him. When the journalist posted photos of McAfee online, some metadata were attached to a photo. The police used the metadata to pinpoint the latitude and longitude of the image and subsequently arrested McAfee in Guatemala. ■

E-Discovery Procedures. The Federal Rules of Civil Procedure deal specifically with the preservation, retrieval, and production of electronic data. Although parties may still use traditional means, such as interrogatories and depositions, to find out about the e-evidence, they must usually hire an expert to retrieve evidence in its electronic format. The expert uses software to reconstruct e-mail exchanges and establish who knew what and when they knew it. The expert can even recover files that the user thought had been deleted from a computer.

Advantages and Disadvantages. E-discovery has significant advantages over paper discovery. Back-up copies of documents and e-mail can provide useful—and often quite damaging—information about how a particular matter progressed over several weeks or months. E-discovery can uncover the proverbial smoking gun that will win the lawsuit, but it is also time consuming and expensive, especially when lawsuits involve large firms with multiple offices. Many companies have found it challenging to fulfill their duty to preserve electronic evidence from a vast number of sources. Failure to do so, however, can lead to sanctions and even force companies to agree to settlements that are not in their best interests.[19]

3-4d Pretrial Conference

Either party or the court can request a pretrial conference, or hearing. Usually, the hearing consists of an informal discussion between the judge and the opposing attorneys after discovery has taken place. The purpose of the hearing is to explore the possibility of a settlement without trial and, if this is not possible, to identify the matters that are in dispute and to plan the course of the trial.

3-4e Jury Selection

A trial can be held with or without a jury. The Seventh Amendment to the U.S. Constitution guarantees the right to a jury trial for cases in *federal* courts when the amount in controversy exceeds $20, but this guarantee does not apply to state courts. Most states have similar guarantees in their own constitutions (although the threshold dollar amount is higher than $20). The right to a trial by jury does not have to be exercised, and many cases are tried without a jury. In most states and in federal courts, one of the parties must request a jury in a civil case, or the judge presumes that the parties waive the right.

Before a jury trial commences, a jury must be selected. The jury selection process is known as *voir dire*.[20] During *voir dire* in most jurisdictions, attorneys for the plaintiff and the defendant ask prospective jurors oral questions to determine whether a potential jury member is biased or has any connection with a party to the action or with a prospective witness. In some jurisdictions, the judge may do all or part of the questioning based on written questions submitted by counsel for the parties.

During *voir dire*, a party may challenge a prospective juror *peremptorily*—that is, ask that an individual not be sworn in as a juror without providing any reason. Alternatively, a party may challenge a prospective juror *for cause*—that is, provide a reason why an individual should not be sworn in as a juror. If the judge grants the challenge, the individual is asked to step down. A prospective juror may not be excluded from the jury by the use of discriminatory challenges, however, such as those based on racial criteria or gender.

---

19. See, for example, *E. I. Du Pont de Nemours & Co. v. Kolon Industries, Inc.*, 803 F.Supp.2d 469 (E.D.Va. 2011); and *In re Intel Corp. Microprocessor Antitrust Litigation*, 2008 WL 2310288 (D.Del. 2008).
20. Pronounced vwahr *deehr*.

> "The judicial system is the most expensive machine ever invented for finding out what happened and what to do about it."
>
> **IRVING R. KAUFMAN**
> 1910–1992
> (AMERICAN JURIST)

KNOW THIS
Picking the "right" jury is often an important aspect of litigation strategy, and a number of firms now specialize in jury-selection consulting services.

Voir Dire An important part of the jury selection process in which the attorneys question prospective jurors about their backgrounds, attitudes, and biases to ascertain whether they can be impartial jurors.

3–4f At the Trial

Once the trial begins, it follows the specific procedures discussed next.

Opening Arguments and Examination of Witnesses

At the beginning of the trial, the attorneys present their opening arguments, setting forth the facts that they expect to prove during the trial. Then the plaintiff's case is presented. In our hypothetical case, Marconi's lawyer would introduce evidence (relevant documents, exhibits, and the testimony of witnesses) to support Marconi's position. The defendant has the opportunity to challenge any evidence introduced and to cross-examine any of the plaintiff's witnesses.

At the end of the plaintiff's case, the defendant's attorney has the opportunity to ask the judge to direct a verdict for the defendant on the ground that the plaintiff has presented no evidence that would justify the granting of the plaintiff's remedy. This is called a **motion for a directed verdict** (known in federal courts as a *motion for judgment as a matter of law*).

If the motion is not granted (it seldom is granted), the defendant's attorney then presents the evidence and witnesses for the defendant's case. At the conclusion of the defendant's case, the defendant's attorney has another opportunity to make a motion for a directed verdict. The plaintiff's attorney can challenge any evidence introduced and cross-examine the defendant's witnesses.

Motion for a Directed Verdict A motion for the judge to take the decision out of the hands of the jury and to direct a verdict for the party making the motion on the ground that the other party has not produced sufficient evidence to support her or his claim.

Closing Arguments and Awards

After the defense concludes its presentation, the attorneys present their closing arguments, each urging a verdict in favor of her or his client. The judge instructs the jury in the law that applies to the case (these instructions are often called *charges*), and the jury retires to the jury room to deliberate a verdict. Typically, jurors are instructed that they must decide the case based only on the information that they learned during the trial. But today, jurors may be tempted to conduct their own investigation of the case using wireless devices—as discussed in this chapter's *Adapting the Law to the Online Environment* feature.

In the Marconi-Anderson case, the jury will not only decide for the plaintiff or for the defendant but, if it finds for the plaintiff, will also decide on the amount of the **award** (the compensation to be paid to her).

Award The monetary compensation given to a party at the end of a trial or other proceeding.

3–4g Posttrial Motions

After the jury has rendered its verdict, either party may make a posttrial motion. If Marconi wins and Anderson's attorney has previously moved for a directed verdict, Anderson's attorney may make a **motion for judgment *n.o.v.*** (from the Latin *non obstante veredicto*, which means "notwithstanding the verdict"—called a *motion for judgment as a matter of law* in the federal courts). Such a motion will be granted only if the jury's verdict was unreasonable and erroneous. If the judge grants the motion, the jury's verdict will be set aside, and a judgment will be entered in favor of the opposite party (Anderson).

Alternatively, Anderson could make a **motion for a new trial,** asking the judge to set aside the adverse verdict and to hold a new trial. The motion will be granted if, after looking at all the evidence, the judge is convinced that the jury was in error but does not feel that it is appropriate to grant judgment for the other side. A judge can also grant a new trial on the basis of newly discovered evidence, misconduct by the participants or the jury during the trial, or error by the judge.

Motion for Judgment *n.o.v.* A motion requesting the court to grant judgment in favor of the party making the motion on the ground that the jury's verdict against him or her was unreasonable and erroneous.

Motion for a New Trial A motion asserting that the trial was so fundamentally flawed (because of error, newly discovered evidence, prejudice, or another reason) that a new trial is necessary to prevent a miscarriage of justice.

3–4h The Appeal

Assume here that any posttrial motion is denied and that Anderson appeals the case. (If Marconi wins but receives a smaller monetary award than she sought, she can appeal also.) Keep in mind, though, that a party cannot appeal a trial court's decision simply because he or she is dissatisfied with the outcome of the trial.

ADAPTING THE LAW TO THE **ONLINE** ENVIRONMENT
Jurors' Use of Wireless Devices and the Internet

One former juror, fresh from trial, complained that the members of the courtroom work group had not provided the jury with enough information to render a fair verdict. "We felt deeply frustrated at our inability to fill those gaps in our knowledge," he added. Until recently, frustrated jury members lacked the means to carry out their own investigations in court. Today, however, jurors with smartphones and tablets can easily access news stories and online research tools. With these wireless devices, they can look up legal terms, blog and tweet about their experiences, and sometimes even try to contact other participants in the trial through "friend" requests on social media Web sites such as Facebook.

What Jurors Are Not Supposed to Learn Outside the Courtroom

Jurors are generally not supposed to obtain background information about the parties to a case or about case events. And certainly, they are prohibited from obtaining outside information about the attorneys, judges, and witnesses they encounter in the courtroom.

In one case, the judge explicitly instructed the jurors that they were not to "use any electronic device or media, such as a telephone, cellphone, smartphone, iPhone, BlackBerry, computer; the Internet, any Internet service, or any text or instant messaging service; or Internet chat room, blog, or Web site, such as Facebook, MySpace, YouTube, or Twitter

How easy is it for judges to prevent Web information searches by jurors during a trial?

to communicate to anyone any information in this case or to conduct any research about this case" until after the verdict. When a juror did do Internet research, and that fact came to light during an appeal of the verdict, the appellate court required a new trial.[a]

In another case, a juror used the Internet to access information about the defendant's past criminal history. Again, the verdict was appealed, and the appellate court stated, "Because there is a reasonable possibility that the extrinsic information acquired by the juror influenced the verdict, we reverse and remand for a new trial."[b]

---

a. *Baird v. Owczarek,* 93 A.3d 1222, Del.Supr. (2014).
b. *State v. Johnson,* 177 Wash.App. 1035, 2013 WL 6092149 (2013).

Legislators Are Reacting

In response to widespread mistrials stemming from jurors' use of wireless devices and the Internet, some states have passed legislation to address the problem. California amended its Code of Civil Procedure to require that all trial courts admonish jurors "that the prohibition on research, dissemination of information, and conversation applies to all forms of electronic and wireless communication." Any juror may be found guilty of a misdemeanor for "willful disobedience ... of a court admonishment related to the prohibition on any form of communication or research about the case, including all forms of electronic or wireless communication or research."[c]

CRITICAL THINKING

- The Sixth Amendment guarantees the accused a right of trial by an "impartial jury." How does the use of wireless devices in the courtroom or research on the Internet threaten this right?

---

c. California Statutes 2011, Chapter 181, as cited in *Steiner v. Superior Court,* 220 Cal.App.4th 1479, 164 Cal.Rptr. 3d 155, Cal.App. 2 Dist. (2013). This law amended the California Code of Civil Procedure, Section 166, to make it contempt of court for a juror to disobey the judge and use wireless devices to perform research about a case.

A party must have legitimate grounds to file an appeal. In other words, he or she must be able to claim that the lower court committed an error. If Anderson has grounds to appeal the case, a notice of appeal must be filed with the clerk of the trial court within a prescribed time. Anderson now becomes the appellant, or petitioner, and Marconi becomes the appellee, or respondent.

Filing the Appeal Anderson's attorney files the record on appeal with the appellate court. The record includes the pleadings, the trial transcript, the judge's rulings on motions made by the parties, and other trial-related documents. Anderson's attorney will also provide the reviewing court with a condensation of the record, known as an *abstract,* and a brief. The **brief** is a formal legal document outlining the facts and issues of the case, the judge's rulings or jury's findings that should be reversed or modified, the applicable law, and arguments on Anderson's behalf (citing applicable statutes and relevant cases as precedents).

Brief A written summary or statement prepared by one side in a lawsuit to explain its case to the judge.

Marconi's attorney will file an answering brief. Anderson's attorney can file a reply to Marconi's brief, although it is not required. The reviewing court then considers the case.

Appellate Review As explained earlier, a court of appeals does not hear evidence. Instead, the court reviews the record for errors of law. Its decision concerning a case is based on the record on appeal, the abstracts, and the attorneys' briefs. The attorneys can present oral arguments, after which the case is taken under advisement.

After reviewing a case, an appellate court has the following options:

1. The court can *affirm* the trial court's decision.

2. The court can *reverse* the trial court's judgment if it concludes that the trial court erred or that the jury did not receive proper instructions.

3. The appellate court can *remand* (send back) the case to the trial court for further proceedings consistent with its opinion on the matter.

4. The court might also affirm or reverse a decision *in part.* For instance, the court might affirm the jury's finding that Anderson was negligent but remand the case for further proceedings on another issue (such as the extent of Marconi's damages).

5. An appellate court can also *modify* a lower court's decision. If the appellate court decides that the jury awarded an excessive amount in damages, for instance, the court might reduce the award to a more appropriate, or fairer, amount.

Do parties to a trial decision always have a right to appeal that decision?

Appeal to a Higher Appellate Court If the reviewing court is an intermediate appellate court, the losing party may decide to appeal to the state supreme court (the highest state court). Such a petition corresponds to a petition for a writ of *certiorari* from the United States Supreme Court. Although the losing party has a right to ask (petition) a higher court to review the case, the party does not have a right to have the case heard by the higher appellate court.

Appellate courts normally have discretionary power and can accept or reject an appeal. Like the United States Supreme Court, state supreme courts generally deny most appeals. If the appeal is granted, new briefs must be filed before the state supreme court, and the attorneys may be allowed or requested to present oral arguments. Like the intermediate appellate court, the supreme court may reverse or affirm the appellate court's decision or remand the case. At this point, the case typically has reached its end (unless a federal question is at issue and one of the parties has legitimate grounds to seek review by a federal appellate court).

3–4i Enforcing the Judgment

The uncertainties of the litigation process are compounded by the lack of guarantees that any judgment will be enforceable. Even if a plaintiff wins an award of damages in court, the defendant may not have sufficient assets or insurance to cover that amount. Usually, one of the factors considered before a lawsuit is initiated is whether the defendant will be able to pay the damages sought, should the plaintiff win the case.

3-5 Courts Online

Most courts today have sites on the Web. Of course, each court decides what to make available at its site. Some courts display only the names of court personnel and office phone numbers. Others add court rules and forms. Many appellate court sites include judicial decisions, although the decisions may remain online for only a limited time. In addition, in some states, including California and Florida, court clerks offer information about the court's **docket** (its schedule of cases to be heard) and other searchable databases online.

Appellate court decisions are often posted online immediately after they are rendered. Recent decisions of the U.S. courts of appeals, for instance, are available online at their Web sites. The United States Supreme Court also has an official Web site and publishes its opinions there immediately after they are announced to the public. In fact, even decisions that are designated as "unpublished" opinions by the appellate courts are usually published (posted) online.

Docket The list of cases entered on a court's calendar and thus scheduled to be heard by the court.

3-5a Electronic Filing

A number of state and federal courts now allow parties to file litigation-related documents with the courts via the Internet or other electronic means. In fact, the federal court system has implemented its electronic filing system, Case Management/Electronic Case Files (CM/ECF), in nearly all federal courts. The system is available in federal district, appellate, and bankruptcy courts, as well as the U.S. Court of International Trade and the U.S. Court of Federal Claims. More than 33 million cases are on the CM/ECF system. Access to the electronic documents filed on CM/ECF is available through a system called PACER (Public Access to Court Electronic Records), which is a service of the U.S. courts.

A majority of the states have some form of electronic filing, although often it is not yet available in state appellate courts. Some states, including Arizona, California, Colorado, Delaware, Mississippi, New Jersey, New York, and Nevada, offer statewide e-filing systems. Generally, when electronic filing is made available, it is optional. Nonetheless, some state courts have now made e-filing mandatory in certain types of disputes, such as complex civil litigation.

3-5b Cyber Courts and Proceedings

Eventually, litigants may be able to use cyber courts, in which judicial proceedings take place only on the Internet. The parties to a case could meet online to make their arguments and present their evidence. Cyber proceedings might use e-mail submissions, video cameras, designated chat rooms, closed sites, or other Internet and social media facilities. The promise of these virtual proceedings is greater efficiency and lower costs.

Electronic courtroom projects have already been developed in some federal and state courts. The state of Michigan has cyber courts that hear cases involving technology issues and high-tech businesses. Other states that have introduced cyber courts include California, Delaware, Louisiana, and North Carolina. Wisconsin has a rule authorizing the use of video-conferencing in both civil and criminal trials, at the discretion of the trial court.[21] The Federal Rules of Civil Procedure also authorizes video conferencing, and some federal bankruptcy courts offer online chatting at their Web sites.

3-6 Alternative Dispute Resolution

Litigation is expensive. It is also time consuming. Because of the backlog of cases pending in many courts, several years may pass before a case is actually tried. For these and other

---

21. Wisconsin Statute Section 751.12.

reasons, more and more businesspersons are turning to **alternative dispute resolution (ADR)** as a means of settling their disputes.

The great advantage of ADR is its flexibility. Methods of ADR range from the parties sitting down together and attempting to work out their differences to multinational corporations agreeing to resolve a dispute through a formal hearing before a panel of experts. Normally, the parties themselves can control how they will attempt to settle their dispute, what procedures will be used, whether a neutral third party will be present or make a decision, and whether that decision will be legally binding or nonbinding.

Today, more than 90 percent of cases are settled before trial through some form of ADR. Indeed, most states either require or encourage parties to undertake ADR prior to trial. Many federal courts have instituted ADR programs as well. In the following pages, we examine the basic forms of ADR. Keep in mind, though, that new methods of ADR—and new combinations of existing methods—are constantly being devised and employed.

3–6a Negotiation

The simplest form of ADR is **negotiation,** in which the parties attempt to settle their dispute informally, with or without attorneys to represent them. Attorneys frequently advise their clients to negotiate a settlement voluntarily before they proceed to trial. Parties may even try to negotiate a settlement during a trial or after the trial but before an appeal. Negotiation traditionally involves just the parties themselves and (typically) their attorneys. The attorneys, though, are advocates—they are obligated to put their clients' interests first.

3–6b Mediation

In **mediation,** a neutral third party acts as a mediator and works with both sides in the dispute to facilitate a resolution. The mediator talks with the parties separately as well as jointly and emphasizes their points of agreement in an attempt to help them evaluate their options. Although the mediator may propose a solution (called a *mediator's proposal*), he or she does not make a decision resolving the matter. States that require parties to undergo ADR before trial often offer mediation as one of the ADR options or (as in Florida) the only option.

One of the biggest advantages of mediation is that it is not as adversarial as litigation. In a trial, the parties "do battle" with each other in the courtroom, trying to prove each other wrong, while the judge is usually a passive observer. In mediation, the mediator takes an active role and attempts to bring the parties together so that they can come to a mutually satisfactory resolution. The mediation process tends to reduce the hostility between the disputants, allowing them to resume their former relationship without bad feelings. For this reason, mediation is often the preferred form of ADR for disputes involving business partners, employers and employees, or other parties involved in long-term relationships.

EXAMPLE 3.13 Two business partners, Mark Shalen and Charles Rowe, have a dispute over how the profits of their firm should be distributed. If the dispute is litigated, Shalen and Rowe will be adversaries, and their respective attorneys will emphasize how the parties' positions differ, not what they have in common. In contrast, if the dispute is mediated, the mediator will emphasize the common ground shared by Shalen and Rowe and help them work toward agreement. The two men can work out the distribution of profits without damaging their continuing relationship as partners. ■

3–6c Arbitration

In **arbitration,** a more formal method of ADR, an arbitrator (a neutral third party or a panel of experts) hears a dispute and imposes a resolution on the parties. Arbitration differs from other forms of ADR in that the third party hearing the dispute makes a decision for the parties. Exhibit 3–4 outlines the basic differences among the three traditional forms of ADR.

Alternative Dispute Resolution (ADR) The resolution of disputes in ways other than those involved in the traditional judicial process, such as negotiation, mediation, and arbitration.

Negotiation A process in which parties attempt to settle their dispute informally, with or without attorneys to represent them.

Mediation A method of settling disputes outside the courts by using the services of a neutral third party, who acts as a communicating agent between the parties and assists them in negotiating a settlement.

Arbitration The settling of a dispute by submitting it to a disinterested third party (other than a court), who renders a decision.

Exhibit 3–4 Basic Differences in the Traditional Forms of Alternative Dispute Resolution

TYPE OF ADR	DESCRIPTION	NEUTRAL THIRD PARTY PRESENT?	WHO DECIDES THE RESOLUTION?
Negotiation	The parties meet informally with or without their attorneys and attempt to agree on a resolution.	No	The parties themselves reach a resolution.
Mediation	A neutral third party meets with the parties and emphasizes points of agreement to help them resolve their dispute.	Yes	The parties decide the resolution, but the mediator may suggest or propose a resolution.
Arbitration	The parties present their arguments and evidence before an arbitrator at a hearing, and the arbitrator renders a decision resolving the parties' dispute.	Yes	The arbitrator imposes a resolution on the parties that may be either binding or nonbinding.

What are the steps in a typical arbitration proceeding?

Usually, the parties in arbitration agree that the third party's decision will be *legally binding,* although the parties can also agree to *nonbinding* arbitration. (Arbitration that is mandated by the courts often is nonbinding.) In nonbinding arbitration, the parties can go forward with a lawsuit if they do not agree with the arbitrator's decision.

In some respects, formal arbitration resembles a trial, although usually the procedural rules are much less restrictive than those governing litigation. In the typical arbitration, the parties present opening arguments and ask for specific remedies. Both sides present evidence and may call and examine witnesses. The arbitrator then renders a decision.

The Arbitrator's Decision

The arbitrator's decision is called an *award.* It is usually the final word on the matter. Although the parties may appeal an arbitrator's decision, a court's review of the decision will be much more restricted in scope than an appellate court's review of a trial court's decision. The general view is that because the parties were free to frame the issues and set the powers of the arbitrator at the outset, they cannot complain about the results. A court will set aside an award only in the event of one of the following:

1. The arbitrator's conduct or "bad faith" substantially prejudiced the rights of one of the parties.
2. The award violates an established public policy.
3. The arbitrator exceeded her or his powers—that is, arbitrated issues that the parties did not agree to submit to arbitration.

Arbitration Clauses

Just about any commercial matter can be submitted to arbitration. Parties can agree to arbitrate a dispute after it arises. Frequently, though, parties include an **arbitration clause** in a contract. The clause provides that any dispute that arises under the contract will be resolved through arbitration rather than through the court system.

Arbitration Statutes

Most states have statutes (often based in part on the Uniform Arbitration Act) under which arbitration clauses will be enforced. Some state statutes compel arbitration of certain types of disputes, such as those involving public employees. At the federal level, the Federal Arbitration Act (FAA) enforces arbitration clauses in contracts involving maritime activity and interstate commerce (though its applicability to employment contracts has been controversial, as discussed later). Because of the breadth of the commerce clause, arbitration agreements involving transactions only slightly connected to the flow of interstate commerce may fall under the FAA.

Arbitration Clause A clause in a contract that provides that, in the event of a dispute, the parties will submit the dispute to arbitration rather than litigate the dispute in court.

CASE EXAMPLE 3.14 Buckeye Check Cashing, Inc., cashes personal checks for consumers in Florida. Buckeye would agree to delay submitting a consumer's check for payment if the consumer paid a "finance charge." For each transaction, the consumer signed an agreement that included an arbitration clause. A group of consumers filed a lawsuit claiming that Buckeye was charging an illegally high rate of interest in violation of state law. Buckeye filed a motion to compel arbitration, which the trial court denied, and the case was appealed.

The plaintiffs argued that the entire contract—including the arbitration clause—was illegal and therefore arbitration was not required. The United States Supreme Court found that the arbitration provision was *severable,* or capable of being separated, from the rest of the contract. The Court held that when the challenge is to the validity of a contract as a whole, and not specifically to an arbitration clause within the contract, an arbitrator must resolve the dispute. Even if the contract itself later proves to be unenforceable, arbitration will still be required because the FAA established a national policy favoring arbitration and that policy extends to both federal and state courts.[22]

The Issue of Arbitrability

The terms of an arbitration agreement can limit the types of disputes that the parties agree to arbitrate. Disputes can arise, however, when the parties do not specify limits or when the parties disagree on whether a particular matter is covered by their arbitration agreement.

When one party files a lawsuit to compel arbitration, it is up to the court to resolve the issue of *arbitrability.* That is, the court must decide whether the matter is one that must be resolved through arbitration. If the court finds that the subject matter in controversy is covered by the agreement to arbitrate, then it may compel arbitration. Usually, a court will allow the claim to be arbitrated if the court finds that the relevant statute (the state arbitration statute or the FAA) does not exclude such claims.

No party, however, will be ordered to submit a particular dispute to arbitration unless the court is convinced that the party has consented to do so. Additionally, the courts will not compel arbitration if it is clear that the arbitration rules and procedures are inherently unfair to one of the parties.

Mandatory Arbitration in the Employment Context

A significant question for businesspersons has concerned mandatory arbitration clauses in employment contracts. Many employees claim they are at a disadvantage when they are forced, as a condition of being hired, to agree to arbitrate all disputes and thus waive their rights under statutes designed to protect employees. The United States Supreme Court, however, has held that mandatory arbitration clauses in employment contracts are generally enforceable.

CASE EXAMPLE 3.15 In a landmark decision, *Gilmer v. Interstate/Johnson Lane Corp.,*[23] the Supreme Court held that a claim brought under a federal statute prohibiting age discrimination could be subject to arbitration. The Court concluded that the employee had waived his right to sue when he agreed, as part of a required registration application to be a securities representative with the New York Stock Exchange, to arbitrate "any dispute, claim, or controversy" relating to his employment.

Since the *Gilmer* decision, some courts have refused to enforce one-sided arbitration clauses. Employment-related agreements often require the parties to split the costs of arbitration, but some courts have overturned those provisions when an individual worker lacked the ability to pay.[24]

In the following case, the court considered the effect of an arbitration clause included in an employment application.

---

22. *Buckeye Check Cashing, Inc. v. Cardegna,* 546 U.S. 440, 126 S.Ct. 1204, 163 L.Ed.2d 1038 (2006).

23. 500 U.S. 20, 111 S.Ct. 1647, 114 L.Ed.2d 26 (1991).

24. See, for example, *Macias v. Excel Building Services, LLC,* 767 F.Supp.2d 1002 (N.D.Cal. 2011), citing *Davis v. O'Melveny & Myers, LLC,* 485 F.3d 1066 (9th Cir. 2007), and *Nagrampa v. MailCoups, Inc.,* 469 F.3d 1257 (9th Cir. 2006).

CASE 3.3

Cruise v. Kroger Co.

Court of Appeal of California, Second District, Division 3, 233 Cal.App.4th 390, 183 Cal.Rptr.3d 17 (2015).

FACTS Stephanie Cruise applied for a job with Kroger Co.'s Compton Creamery & Deli Kitchen. The application contained a clause requiring arbitration of "employment-related disputes" and referred to the company's arbitration policy. Cruise was hired. Four years later, she was fired. Cruise filed a suit in a California state court against Kroger, alleging employment discrimination—retaliation, sexual harassment, sexual and racial discrimination, and failure to investigate and prevent harassment and retaliation—as well as wrongful termination in violation of public policy, intentional infliction of emotional distress, and defamation. Kroger filed a motion to compel arbitration and provided the court with an undated four-page arbitration policy. Because the company could not prove that the policy was in effect when Cruise signed the employment application, the court held that there was no proof of a written agreement to arbitrate and denied the motion. Kroger appealed.

ISSUE Is an arbitration clause in an employment agreement sufficient to establish an agreement to arbitrate?

DECISION Yes. The state intermediate appellate court reversed the lower court's denial of Kroger's motion to compel arbitration with directions to grant the motion.

When does an employee have to submit to arbitration for employment-related disputes?

REASON The appellate court concluded that the arbitration clause in the employment application established that the parties had agreed to arbitrate their "employment-related disputes." The employment application was signed by Cruise. The arbitration clause, which was initialed by Cruise separately, stated that "any Employee who wishes to initiate or participate in formal proceedings to resolve any Covered Disputes must submit the claims or disputes to final and binding arbitration in accordance with the Policy." The court reasoned that this "language eliminates any argument the parties did not agree to arbitrate their employment-related disputes." Kroger's inability to prove the precise terms of the arbitration policy did not disprove the existence of the arbitration agreement. The court also concluded that all of Cruise's claims were employment-related disputes that fell within the meaning of the arbitration agreement.

CRITICAL THINKING—Legal Consideration *In the circumstances of this case, what procedures should govern the arbitration? Discuss.*

3–6d Other Types of ADR

The three forms of ADR just discussed are the oldest and traditionally the most commonly used. In addition, a variety of newer types of ADR have emerged, including those described here.

1. In *early neutral case evaluation,* the parties select a neutral third party (generally an expert in the subject matter of the dispute) and then explain their respective positions to that person. The case evaluator assesses the strengths and weaknesses of each party's claims.

2. In a *mini-trial,* each party's attorney briefly argues the party's case before the other party and a panel of representatives from each side who have the authority to settle the dispute. Typically, a neutral third party (usually an expert in the area being disputed) acts as an adviser. If the parties fail to reach an agreement, the adviser renders an opinion as to how a court would likely decide the issue.

Summary Jury Trial (SJT)
A method of settling disputes by holding a trial in which the jury's verdict is not binding but instead guides the parties toward reaching an agreement during the mandatory negotiations that immediately follow.

3. Numerous federal courts now hold **summary jury trials,** in which the parties present their arguments and evidence and the jury renders a verdict. The jury's verdict is not binding, but it does act as a guide to both sides in reaching an agreement during the mandatory negotiations that immediately follow the trial.

3-6e Providers of ADR Services

ADR services are provided by both government agencies and private organizations. A major provider of ADR services is the American Arbitration Association (AAA), which handles more than 200,000 claims a year in its numerous offices worldwide. Most of the largest U.S. law firms are members of this nonprofit association. Cases brought before the AAA are heard by an expert or a panel of experts in the area relating to the dispute and are usually settled quickly. The AAA has a special team devoted to resolving large, complex disputes across a wide range of industries.

Hundreds of for-profit firms around the country also provide various dispute-resolution services. Typically, these firms hire retired judges to conduct arbitration hearings or otherwise assist parties in settling their disputes. The judges follow procedures similar to those of the federal courts and use similar rules. Usually, each party to the dispute pays a filing fee and a designated fee for a hearing session or conference.

3-6f Online Dispute Resolution

An increasing number of companies and organizations offer dispute-resolution services using the Internet. The settlement of disputes in these online forums is known as **online dispute resolution (ODR)**. The disputes have most commonly involved disagreements over the rights to domain names or over the quality of goods sold via the Internet, including goods sold through Internet auction sites.

Online Dispute Resolution (ODR) The resolution of disputes with the assistance of organizations that offer dispute-resolution services via the Internet.

Rules being developed in online forums may ultimately become a code of conduct for everyone who does business in cyberspace. Most online forums do not automatically apply the law of any specific jurisdiction. Instead, results are often based on general, universal legal principles. As with most offline methods of dispute resolution, any party may appeal to a court at any time.

ODR may be best suited for resolving small- to medium-sized business liability claims, which may not be worth the expense of litigation or traditional ADR. In addition, some local governments are using ODR to resolve claims. **EXAMPLE 3.16** New York City has used Cybersettle.com to resolve auto accident, sidewalk, and other personal-injury claims made against the city. Parties with complaints submit their demands, and the city submits its offers confidentially online. If an offer exceeds a demand, the claimant keeps half the difference as a bonus. ■

Reviewing . . . Courts and Alternative Dispute Resolution

Stan Garner resides in Illinois and promotes boxing matches for SuperSports, Inc., an Illinois corporation. Garner created the promotional concept of the "Ages" fights—a series of three boxing matches pitting an older fighter (George Foreman) against a younger fighter, such as John Ruiz or Riddick Bowe. The concept included titles for each of the three fights ("Challenge of the Ages," "Battle of the Ages," and "Fight of the Ages"), as well as promotional epithets to characterize the two fighters ("the Foreman Factor").

Garner contacted George Foreman and his manager, who both reside in Texas, to sell the idea, and they arranged a meeting at Caesar's Palace in Las Vegas, Nevada. At some point in the negotiations, Foreman's manager signed a nondisclosure agreement prohibiting him from disclosing Garner's promotional concepts unless they signed a contract. Nevertheless, after negotiations between Garner and Foreman fell through, Foreman used Garner's "Battle of the Ages" concept to promote a subsequent fight. Garner filed a lawsuit against Foreman and his manager in a federal district court in Illinois, alleging breach of contract. Using the information presented in the chapter, answer the following questions.

Continues

1. On what basis might the federal district court in Illinois exercise jurisdiction in this case?
2. Does the federal district court have original or appellate jurisdiction?
3. Suppose that Garner had filed his action in an Illinois state court. Could an Illinois state court have exercised personal jurisdiction over Foreman or his manager? Why or why not?
4. What if Garner had filed his action in a Nevada state court? Would that court have had personal jurisdiction over Foreman or his manager? Explain.

DEBATE THIS

■ In this age of the Internet, when people communicate via e-mail, tweets, social media, and Skype, is the concept of jurisdiction losing its meaning?

Key Terms

alternative dispute resolution (ADR) 79
answer 70
arbitration 79
arbitration clause 80
award 75
bankruptcy court 58
brief 77
complaint 70
concurrent jurisdiction 60
counterclaim 70
default judgment 70
deposition 72
discovery 71
diversity of citizenship 59
docket 78
e-evidence 73
exclusive jurisdiction 60

federal question 59
interrogatories 73
judicial review 56
jurisdiction 56
justiciable controversy 63
litigation 69
long arm statute 57
mediation 79
metadata 73
motion for a directed verdict 75
motion for a new trial 75
motion for judgment *n.o.v.* 75
motion for judgment on the pleadings 71
motion for summary judgment 71
motion to dismiss 71
negotiation 79

online dispute resolution (ODR) 83
pleadings 70
probate court 58
question of fact 66
question of law 67
reply 70
rule of four 69
service of process 70
small claims court 65
standing to sue 63
summary jury trial (SJT) 82
summons 70
venue 63
voir dire 74
writ of *certiorari* 68

Chapter Summary: Courts and Alternative Dispute Resolution

The Judiciary's Role in American Government	The role of the judiciary—the courts—in the American governmental system is to interpret and apply the law. Through the process of judicial review—determining the constitutionality of laws—the judicial branch acts as a check on the executive and legislative branches of government.

Basic Judicial Requirements	1. *Jurisdiction*—Before a court can hear a case, it must have jurisdiction over the person against whom the suit is brought or the property involved in the suit, as well as jurisdiction over the subject matter.
	  a. Limited versus general jurisdiction—Limited jurisdiction exists when a court is limited to a specific subject matter, such as probate or divorce. General jurisdiction exists when a court can hear any kind of case.
	  b. Original versus appellate jurisdiction—Original jurisdiction exists when courts have authority to hear a case for the first time (trial courts). Appellate jurisdiction is exercised by courts of appeals, or reviewing courts, which generally do not have original jurisdiction.
	  c. Federal jurisdiction—Arises (1) when a federal question is involved (when the plaintiff's cause of action is based, at least in part, on the U.S. Constitution, a treaty, or a federal law) or (2) when a case involves diversity of citizenship (citizens of different states, for example) and the amount in controversy exceeds $75,000.
	  d. Concurrent versus exclusive jurisdiction—Concurrent jurisdiction exists when two different courts have authority to hear the same case. Exclusive jurisdiction exists when only state courts or only federal courts have authority to hear a case.
	2. *Jurisdiction in cyberspace*—Because the Internet does not have physical boundaries, traditional jurisdictional concepts have been difficult to apply in cases involving activities conducted via the Web. Gradually, the courts are developing standards to use in determining when jurisdiction over a Web site owner or operator located in another state is proper.
	3. *Venue*—Venue has to do with the most appropriate location for a trial, which is usually the geographic area where the event leading to the dispute took place or where the parties reside.
	4. *Standing to sue*—A requirement that a party must have a legally protected and tangible interest at stake sufficient to justify seeking relief through the court system. The controversy at issue must also be a justiciable controversy—one that is real and substantial, as opposed to hypothetical or academic.

The State and Federal Court Systems	1. *Trial courts*—Courts of original jurisdiction, in which legal actions are initiated.
	  a. State—Courts of general jurisdiction can hear any case. Courts of limited jurisdiction include domestic relations courts, probate courts, traffic courts, and small claims courts.
	  b. Federal—The federal district court is the equivalent of the state trial court. Federal courts of limited jurisdiction include the U.S. Tax Court, the U.S. Bankruptcy Court, and the U.S. Court of Federal Claims.
	2. *Intermediate appellate courts*—Courts of appeals, or reviewing courts, which generally do not have original jurisdiction. Many states have intermediate appellate courts. In the federal court system, the U.S. circuit courts of appeals are the intermediate appellate courts.
	3. *Supreme (highest) courts*—Each state has a supreme court, although it may be called by some other name. Appeal from the state supreme court to the United States Supreme Court is possible only if the case involves a federal question. The United States Supreme Court is the highest court in the federal court system and the final arbiter of the U.S. Constitution and federal law.

Following a State Court Case	Rules of procedure prescribe the way in which disputes are handled in the courts. Rules differ from court to court, and separate sets of rules exist for federal and state courts, as well as for criminal and civil cases. A civil court case in a state court would involve the following procedures:
	1. *The pleadings*—
	  a. Complaint—Filed by the plaintiff with the court to initiate the lawsuit. The complaint is served with a summons on the defendant.
	  b. Answer—A response to the complaint in which the defendant admits or denies the allegations made by the plaintiff. The answer may assert a counterclaim or an affirmative defense.
	  c. Motion to dismiss—A request to the court to dismiss the case for stated reasons, such as the plaintiff's failure to state a claim for which relief can be granted.
	2. *Pretrial motions (in addition to the motion to dismiss)*—
	  a. Motion for judgment on the pleadings—May be made by either party. It will be granted if the parties agree on the facts and the only question is how the law applies to the facts. The judge bases the decision solely on the pleadings.
	  b. Motion for summary judgment—May be made by either party. It will be granted if the parties agree on the facts and the sole question is a question of law. The judge can consider evidence outside the pleadings when evaluating the motion.

Continues

Following a State Court Case (Continued)	3. *Discovery*—The process of gathering evidence concerning the case. Discovery involves depositions (sworn testimony by a party to the lawsuit or any witness), interrogatories (written questions and answers to these questions made by parties to the action with the aid of their attorneys), and various requests (for admissions, documents, and medical examinations, for example). Discovery may also involve electronically recorded information, such as e-mail, voice mail, word-processing documents, and other data compilations. Although electronic discovery has significant advantages over paper discovery, it is also more time consuming and expensive and often requires the parties to hire experts.
	 4. *Pretrial conference*—Either party or the court can request a pretrial conference to identify the matters in dispute after discovery has taken place and to plan the course of the trial.
	 5. *Trial*—Following jury selection (*voir dire*), the trial begins with opening statements from both parties' attorneys. The following events then occur:
	   a. The plaintiff's introduction of evidence (including the testimony of witnesses) supporting the plaintiff's position. The defendant's attorney can challenge evidence and cross-examine witnesses.
	   b. The defendant's introduction of evidence (including the testimony of witnesses) supporting the defendant's position. The plaintiff's attorney can challenge evidence and cross-examine witnesses.
	   c. Closing arguments by the attorneys in favor of their respective clients, the judge's instructions to the jury, and the jury's verdict.
	 6. *Posttrial motions*—
	   a. Motion for judgment *n.o.v.* ("notwithstanding the verdict")—Will be granted if the judge is convinced that the jury was in error.
	   b. Motion for a new trial—Will be granted if the judge is convinced that the jury was in error. The motion can also be granted on the grounds of newly discovered evidence, misconduct by the participants during the trial, or error by the judge.
	 7. *Appeal*—Either party can appeal the trial court's judgment to an appropriate court of appeals. After reviewing the record on appeal, the abstracts, and the attorneys' briefs, the appellate court holds a hearing and renders its opinion.

Courts Online	A number of state and federal courts now allow parties to file litigation-related documents with the courts via the Internet or other electronic means. Nearly all of the federal appellate courts and bankruptcy courts and a majority of the federal district courts have implemented electronic filing systems. Almost every court now has a Web page offering information about the court and its procedures, and increasingly courts are publishing their opinions online. In the future, we may see cyber courts, in which all trial proceedings are conducted online.
Alternative Dispute Resolution	1. *Negotiation*—The parties come together, with or without attorneys to represent them, and try to reach a settlement without the involvement of a third party. 2. *Mediation*—The parties themselves reach an agreement with the help of a neutral third party, called a mediator. The mediator may propose a solution but does not make a decision resolving the matter. 3. *Arbitration*—The parties submit their dispute to a neutral third party, the arbitrator, who renders a decision. The decision may or may not be legally binding, depending on the circumstances. 4. *Other types of ADR*—These include assisted negotiation, early neutral case evaluation, mini-trials, and summary jury trials (SJTs). 5. *Providers of ADR services*—The leading nonprofit provider of ADR services is the American Arbitration Association. Hundreds of for-profit firms also provide ADR services. 6. *Online dispute resolution*—A number of organizations and firms are now offering negotiation, mediation, and arbitration services through online forums. These forums have been a practical alternative for the resolution of domain name disputes and e-commerce disputes in which the amount in controversy is relatively small.

Issue Spotters

1. At the trial, after Sue calls her witnesses, offers her evidence, and otherwise presents her side of the case, Tom has at least two choices between courses of action. Tom can call his first witness. What else might he do? (See *Following a State Court Case*.)

2. Sue contracts with Tom to deliver a quantity of computers to Sue's Computer Store. They disagree over the amount, the delivery date, the price, and the quality. Sue files a suit against Tom in a state court. Their state requires that their dispute be submitted to mediation or nonbinding arbitration. If the dispute is not resolved, or if either party disagrees with the decision of the mediator or arbitrator, will a court hear the case? Explain. (See *Alternative Dispute Resolution*.)

—**Check your answers to the *Issue Spotters* against the answers provided in Appendix D at the end of this text.**

Learning Objectives Check

1. What is judicial review? How and when was the power of judicial review established?

2. How are the courts applying traditional jurisdictional concepts to cases involving Internet transactions?

3. What is the difference between the focus of a trial court and an appellate court?

4. What is discovery, and how does electronic discovery differ from traditional discovery?

5. What are three alternative methods of resolving disputes?

—**Answers to the even-numbered *Learning Objectives Check* questions can be found in Appendix E at the end of this text.**

Business Scenarios and Case Problems

3–1. Standing to Sue. Jack and Maggie Turton bought a house in Jefferson County, Idaho, located directly across the street from a gravel pit. A few years later, the county converted the pit to a landfill. The landfill accepted many kinds of trash that cause harm to the environment, including major appliances, animal carcasses, containers with hazardous content warnings, leaking car batteries, and waste oil. The Turtons complained to the county, but the county did nothing. The Turtons then filed a lawsuit against the county alleging violations of federal environmental laws pertaining to groundwater contamination and other pollution. Do the Turtons have standing to sue? Why or why not? (See *Basic Judicial Requirements*.)

3–2. Discovery. Advance Technology Consultants, Inc. (ATC), contracted with RoadTrac, LLC, to provide software and client software systems for products using global positioning satellite (GPS) technology being developed by RoadTrac. RoadTrac agreed to provide ATC with hardware with which ATC's software would interface. Problems soon arose, however, and RoadTrac filed a lawsuit against ATC alleging breach of contract. During discovery, RoadTrac requested ATC's customer lists and marketing procedures. ATC objected to providing this information because RoadTrac and ATC had become competitors in the GPS industry. Should a party to a lawsuit have to hand over its confidential business secrets as part of a discovery request? Why or why not? What limitations might a court consider imposing before requiring ATC to produce this material? (See *Following a State Court Case*.)

3–3. Spotlight on the National Football League—Arbitration. Bruce Matthews played football for the Tennessee Titans. As part of his contract, he agreed to submit any dispute to arbitration. He also agreed that Tennessee law would determine all matters related to workers' compensation. After Matthews retired, he filed a workers' compensation claim in California. The arbitrator ruled that Matthews could pursue his claim in California but only under Tennessee law. Should the arbitrator's award be set aside? Explain. [*National Football League Players Association v. National Football League*

Management Council, 2011 WL 1137334 (S.D.Cal. 2011)] (See *Alternative Dispute Resolution*.)

3–4. Minimum Contacts. Seal Polymer Industries sold two freight containers of latex gloves to Med-Express, Inc., a company based in North Carolina. When Med-Express failed to pay the $104,000 owed for the gloves, Seal Polymer sued in an Illinois court and obtained a judgment against Med-Express. Med-Express argued that it did not have minimum contacts with Illinois and therefore the Illinois judgment based on personal jurisdiction was invalid. Med-Express stated that it was incorporated under North Carolina law, had its principal place of business in North Carolina, and therefore had no minimum contacts with Illinois. Was this statement alone sufficient to prevent the Illinois judgment from being collected against Med-Express in North Carolina? Why or why not? [*Seal Polymer Industries v. Med-Express, Inc.,* 725 S.E.2d 5 (N.C.App. 2012)] (See *Basic Judicial Requirements*.)

3–5. Arbitration. Horton Automatics and the Industrial Division of the Communications Workers of America—the union that represented Horton's workers—negotiated a collective bargaining agreement. If an employee's discharge for a workplace-rule violation was submitted to arbitration, the agreement limited the arbitrator to determining whether the rule was reasonable and whether the employee had violated it. When Horton discharged its employee Ruben de la Garza, the union appealed to arbitration. The arbitrator found that de la Garza had violated a reasonable safety rule, but "was not totally convinced" that Horton should have treated the violation more seriously than other rule violations. The arbitrator ordered de la Garza reinstated to his job. Can a court set aside this order from the arbitrator? Explain. [*Horton Automatics v. The Industrial Division of the Communications Workers of America, AFL-CIO,* __ F.3d __, 2013 WL 59204 (5th Cir. 2013)] (See *Alternative Dispute Resolution*.)

3–6. Business Case Problem with Sample Answer—Discovery. Jessica Lester died from injuries suffered in an auto accident caused by the driver of a truck owned by Allied Concrete Co. Jessica's widower, Isaiah, filed a suit against Allied for damages. The defendant requested copies of all of Isaiah's Facebook photos and other postings. Before responding, Isaiah "cleaned up" his Facebook page. Allied suspected that some of the items had been deleted, including a photo of Isaiah holding a beer can while wearing a T-shirt that declared "I [heart] hotmoms." Can this material be recovered? If so, how? What effect might Isaiah's "misconduct" have on the result in this case? Discuss. [*Allied Concrete Co. v. Lester,* 736 S.E.2d 699 (Va. 2013)] (See *Following a State Court Case.*)

—**For a sample answer to Problem 3–6, go to Appendix F at the end of this text.**

3–7. Electronic Filing. Betsy Faden worked for the U.S. Department of Veterans Affairs. Faden was removed from her position in April 2012 and was given until May 29 to appeal the removal decision. She submitted an appeal through the Merit Systems Protection Board's e-filing system seven days after the deadline. Ordered to show good cause for the delay, Faden testified that she had attempted to e-file the appeal while the board's system was down. The board acknowledged that its system had not been functioning on May 27, 28, and 29. Was Faden sufficiently diligent in ensuring a timely filing? Discuss. [*Faden v. Merit Systems Protection Board,* __ F.3d __, 2014 WL 163394 (Fed. Cir. 2014)] (See *Courts Online.*)

3–8. Corporate Contacts. LG Electronics, Inc., and nineteen other foreign companies participated in the global market for cathode ray tube (CRT) products, which were integrated as components in consumer goods, including television sets.

These goods were sold for many years in high volume in the United States, including the state of Washington. Later, the state filed a suit in a Washington state court against LG and the others, alleging a conspiracy to raise prices and set production levels in the market for CRTs in violation of a state consumer protection statute. The defendants filed a motion to dismiss the suit for lack of personal jurisdiction. Should this motion be granted? Explain. [*State of Washington v. LG Electronics, Inc.,* 341 P.3d 346 (Wash. App., Div. 1 2015)] (See *Basic Judicial Requirements.*)

3–9. A Question of Ethics—Agreement to Arbitrate. Nellie Lumpkin, who suffered from dementia, was admitted to the Picayune Convalescent Center, a nursing home. Because of her mental condition, her daughter, Beverly McDaniel, signed the admissions agreement. It included a clause requiring the parties to submit any dispute to arbitration. After Lumpkin left the center two years later, she filed a suit against Picayune to recover damages for mistreatment and malpractice. [*Covenant Health & Rehabilitation of Picayune, LP v. Lumpkin,* 23 So.3d 1092 (Miss. App. 2009)] (See *Alternative Dispute Resolution.*)

1. Is it ethical for this dispute—involving negligent medical care, not a breach of a commercial contract—to be forced into arbitration? Why or why not? Discuss whether medical facilities should be able to impose arbitration when there is generally no bargaining over such terms.

2. Should a person with limited mental capacity be held to the arbitration clause agreed to by her next of kin, who signed on her behalf? Why or why not?

Critical Thinking and Writing Assignments

3–10. Business Law Critical Thinking Group Assignment. Bento Cuisine is a lunch-cart business. It occupies a street corner in Texarkana, a city that straddles the border of Arkansas and Texas. Across the street—and across the state line, which runs down the middle of the street—is Rico's Tacos. The two businesses compete for customers. Recently, Bento has begun to suspect that Rico's is engaging in competitive behavior that is illegal. Bento's manager overheard several of Rico's employees discussing these competitive tactics while on a break at a nearby Starbucks. Bento files a lawsuit against

Rico's in a federal court based on diversity jurisdiction. (See *Basic Judicial Requirements* and *Following a State Court Case.*)

1. One group will determine whether Rico's could file a motion claiming that the federal court lacks jurisdiction over this dispute.

2. Another group will assume that the case goes to trial. Bento believes that it has both the law and the facts on its side. Nevertheless, at the end of the trial, the jury decides against Bento, and the judge issues a ruling in favor of Rico's. If Bento is unwilling to accept this result, what are its options?

corgarashu/ShutterStock.com

Tort Law

"Two wrongs do not make a right."

ENGLISH PROVERB

Most of us agree with the chapter-opening quotation—two wrongs do not make a right. In this chapter, we consider a particular type of wrongful actions called **torts** (the word *tort* is French for "wrong"). As you will see, torts form the basis for many lawsuits.

As noted in earlier chapters, part of doing business today is the risk of being involved in a lawsuit. The list of circumstances in which businesspersons can be sued is long and varied. A customer who is injured by a security guard at a business establishment, for instance, may sue the business owner. A person who slips and falls at a retail store may sue the company for negligence. Any time one party's allegedly wrongful conduct causes injury to another, an action may arise under the law of torts. Through tort law, society compensates those who have suffered injuries as a result of the wrongful conduct of others.

Many of the lawsuits brought by or against business firms are based on the tort theories discussed in this chapter and the next chapter, which covers product liability. In addition, Chapter 7 discusses how tort law applies to wrongful actions in the online environment.

4-1 The Basis of Tort Law

Two notions serve as the basis of all torts: wrongs and compensation. Tort law is designed to compensate those who have suffered a loss or injury due to another person's wrongful act. In a tort action, one person or group brings a personal suit against another person or group to obtain compensation (monetary damages) or other relief for the harm suffered.

LEARNING OBJECTIVES

The five Learning Objectives below are designed to help improve your understanding of the chapter. After reading this chapter, you should be able to answer the following questions:

1. What is the purpose of tort law? What types of damages are available in tort lawsuits?

2. What are two basic categories of torts?

3. What is defamation? Name two types of defamation.

4. Identify the four elements of negligence.

5. What is meant by strict liability? In what circumstances is strict liability applied?

Tort A wrongful act (other than a breach of contract) that results in harm or injury to another and leads to civil liability.

89

Damages A monetary award sought as a remedy for a breach of contract or a tortious action.

Compensatory Damages A monetary award equivalent to the actual value of injuries or damage sustained by the aggrieved party.

Special Damages In a tort case, an amount awarded to compensate the plaintiff for quantifiable monetary losses, such as medical expenses, property damage, and lost wages and benefits (now and in the future).

General Damages In a tort case, an amount awarded to compensate individuals for the nonmonetary aspects of the harm suffered, such as pain and suffering. Not available to companies.

Punitive Damages Monetary damages that may be awarded to a plaintiff to punish the defendant and deter similar conduct in the future.

Do tort lawsuits end up in civil or criminal courts?

4–1a The Purpose of Tort Law

Generally, the purpose of tort law is to provide remedies for the invasion of various *protected interests*. Society recognizes an interest in personal physical safety, and tort law provides remedies for acts that cause physical injury or interfere with physical security and freedom. Society also recognizes an interest in protecting property, and tort law provides remedies for acts that cause destruction of or damage to property.

Note that in legal usage, the singular *damage* is used to refer to harm or injury to persons or property. The plural **damages** is used to refer to monetary compensation for such harm or injury.

4–1b Damages Available in Tort Actions

Because the purpose of tort law is to compensate the injured party for the damage suffered, it is important to have a basic understanding of the types of damages that plaintiffs seek in tort actions.

Compensatory Damages Plaintiffs are awarded **compensatory damages** to compensate or reimburse them for actual losses. Thus, the goal is to make the plaintiffs whole and put them in the same position that they would have been in had the tort not occurred. Compensatory damages awards are often broken down into *special damages* and *general damages*.

Special damages compensate plaintiffs for quantifiable monetary losses, such as medical expenses, lost wages and benefits (now and in the future), extra costs, the loss of irreplaceable items, and the costs of repairing or replacing damaged property. **CASE EXAMPLE 4.1** Seaway Marine Transport operates the *Enterprise,* a large cargo ship with twenty-two hatches for storing coal. When the *Enterprise* moved into position to receive a load of coal on the shores of Lake Erie in Ohio, it struck a land-based coal-loading machine operated by Bessemer & Lake Erie Railroad Company. A federal court found Seaway liable for negligence and awarded $522,000 in special damages to compensate Bessemer for the cost of repairing the damage to the loading machine.[1] ■

General damages compensate individuals (not companies) for the nonmonetary aspects of the harm suffered, such as pain and suffering. A court might award general damages for physical or emotional pain and suffering, loss of companionship, loss of consortium (losing the emotional and physical benefits of a spousal relationship), disfigurement, loss of reputation, or loss or impairment of mental or physical capacity.

Punitive Damages Occasionally, the courts also award **punitive damages** in tort cases to punish the wrongdoers and deter others from similar wrongdoing. Punitive damages are appropriate only when the defendant's conduct was particularly egregious (flagrant) or reprehensible (blameworthy).

Thus, punitive damages are normally available mainly in intentional tort actions and only rarely in negligence lawsuits (*intentional torts* and *negligence* will be explained later in the chapter). They may be awarded, however, in suits involving *gross negligence,* which can be defined as an intentional failure to perform a manifest duty in reckless disregard of the effect on the life or property of another. (See this chapter's *Business Application* feature for steps businesses can take to avoid tort liability and the large damages awards that may go with it.)

Courts exercise great restraint in granting punitive damages to plaintiffs in tort actions because punitive damages are subject to the limitations imposed by the due process clause of the U.S. Constitution. The United States Supreme Court

---

1. *Bessemer & Lake Erie Railroad Co. v. Seaway Marine Transport*, 596 F.3d 357 (6th Cir. 2010).

has held that, when an award of punitive damages is grossly excessive, it furthers no legitimate purpose and violates due process requirements.[2] Consequently, an appellate court will sometimes reduce the amount of punitive damages awarded to a plaintiff because the amount was excessive and thereby violates the due process clause.

4-1c Tort Reform

Tort law performs a valuable function by enabling injured parties to obtain compensation. Nevertheless, critics contend that certain aspects of today's tort law encourage too many trivial and unfounded lawsuits, which clog the courts and add unnecessary costs. They say that damages awards are often excessive and bear little relationship to the actual damage suffered, which inspires more plaintiffs to file lawsuits. The result, in the critics' view, is a system that disproportionately rewards a few plaintiffs while imposing a "tort tax" on business and society as a whole. Among other consequences, physicians and hospitals order more tests than necessary in an effort to avoid medical malpractice suits, thereby adding to the nation's health-care costs.

"Do you have any picture books that could help a child understand tort reform?"

Types of Reform   The federal government and a number of states have begun to take some steps toward tort reform. Measures to reduce the number of tort cases include the following:

1. Limiting the amount of both punitive damages and general damages that can be awarded.

2. Capping the amount that attorneys can collect in *contingency fees* (attorneys' fees that are based on a percentage of the damages awarded to the client).

3. Requiring the losing party to pay both the plaintiff's and the defendant's expenses.

Federal Reform   At the federal level, the Class Action Fairness Act (CAFA)[3] shifted jurisdiction over large interstate tort and product liability class-action lawsuits from the state courts to the federal courts. (A *class action* is a lawsuit in which a large number of plaintiffs bring suit as a group. *Product liability* suits involve the manufacture, sale, and distribution of allegedly dangerous or defective goods.)

The CAFA prevents plaintiffs' attorneys from *forum shopping*—looking for a court based on whether the court is likely to provide a favorable judgment. Previously, multiple courts often had jurisdiction over class-action claims. Plaintiffs' attorneys naturally chose to bring suit in state courts that were known to be sympathetic to their clients' cause and predisposed to award large damages. Now, under the CAFA, state courts no longer have jurisdiction over class actions.

State Reform   At the state level, more than half of the states have placed caps ranging from $250,000 to $750,000 on noneconomic general damages (for example, pain and suffering), especially in medical malpractice suits. More than thirty states have limited punitive damages, with some imposing outright bans.

Note, though, that the highest courts in about half a dozen states have declared their states' damages caps to be unconstitutional. **CASE EXAMPLE 4.2** Naython Watts was born with disabling brain injuries caused by the negligence of physicians at Cox Medical Centers in Missouri. At the age of six, Naython could not walk, talk, or feed himself. He had the

KNOW THIS
Damage refers to harm or injury to persons or property. *Damages* is a legal term that refers to the monetary compensation awarded to a plaintiff who has suffered such harm or injury.

---

2. *State Farm Mutual Automobile Insurance Co. v. Campbell*, 538 U.S. 408, 123 S.Ct. 1513, 155 L.Ed.2d 585 (2003).
3. 28 U.S.C. Sections 1453, 1711–1715.

mental capacity of a two-year-old, suffered from seizures, and needed around-the-clock care. His mother, Deborah Watts, sued the medical center on his behalf. A jury awarded Watts $1.45 million in noneconomic damages, plus $3.37 million in future medical damages.

The trial court reduced the noneconomic damages award to $350,000—the statutory cap under Missouri's law. Watts appealed. Missouri's highest court struck down the state's damages cap, holding that it violated the state constitution's right to trial by jury. The court reasoned that the amount of damages is a fact for the jury to determine, and the legislature cannot place caps on jury awards independent of the facts of a case.[4] ■

4–1d Classifications of Torts

LEARNING OBJECTIVE 2
What are two basic categories of torts?

There are two broad classifications of torts: *intentional torts* and *unintentional torts* (torts involving negligence). Intentional torts result from the intentional violation of person or property (fault with intent). Negligence results from the breach of a duty to act reasonably (fault without intent). The classification of a particular tort depends largely on how the tort occurs (intentionally or negligently) and the surrounding circumstances.

4–1e Defenses

Even if a plaintiff proves all the elements of a tort, the defendant can raise a number of legally recognized **defenses**—reasons why the plaintiff should not obtain damages. The defenses available may vary depending on the specific tort involved.

A common defense to intentional torts against persons, for instance, is *consent*. When a person consents to the act that damages her or him, there is generally no liability. The most widely used defense in negligence actions is *comparative negligence* (discussed later in this chapter). A successful defense releases the defendant from partial or full liability for the tortious act.

Defense A reason offered by a defendant in an action or lawsuit as to why the plaintiff should not recover or establish what she or he seeks.

Most states also have a *statute of limitations* that establishes the time limit (often two years from the date of discovering the harm) within which a particular type of lawsuit can be filed. After that time period has run, the plaintiff can no longer file a claim.

4–2 Intentional Torts against Persons

Intentional Tort A wrongful act knowingly committed.

Tortfeasor One who commits a tort.

An **intentional tort,** as just mentioned, requires *intent.* The **tortfeasor** (the one committing the tort) must intend to commit an act, the consequences of which interfere with the personal or business interests of another in a way not permitted by law. An evil or harmful motive is not required—in fact, the person committing the action may even have a beneficial motive for committing what turns out to be a tortious act.

KNOW THIS
In intentional tort actions, the defendant must intend to commit the act, but need not have intended to cause harm to the plaintiff.

In tort law, intent means only that the person intended the consequences of his or her act or knew with substantial certainty that certain consequences would result from the act. The law generally assumes that individuals intend the *normal* consequences of their actions. Thus, forcefully pushing another—even if done in jest and without any evil motive—is an intentional tort if injury results, because the object of a strong push can ordinarily be expected to fall down.

Transferred Intent A legal principle under which a person who intends to harm one individual, but unintentionally harms a different individual, can be liable to the second victim for an intentional tort.

Intent can be transferred when a defendant intends to harm one individual, but unintentionally harms a different person. This is called **transferred intent.** `EXAMPLE 4.3` Alex swings a bat intending to hit Blake but misses and hits Carson instead. Carson can sue Alex for the tort of battery (discussed shortly) because Alex's intent to harm Blake can be transferred to Carson. ■

---

4. *Watts v. Lester E. Cox Medical Centers*, 376 S.W.3d 633 (Mo. 2012).

In this section, we discuss intentional torts against persons. These torts include assault and battery, false imprisonment, infliction of emotional distress, defamation, invasion of the right to privacy, appropriation, misrepresentation, abusive or frivolous litigation, and wrongful interference.

4-2a Assault and Battery

An **assault** is any intentional and unexcused threat of immediate harmful or offensive contact—words or acts that create in another person a reasonable apprehension of harmful contact. An assault can be completed even if there is no actual contact with the plaintiff, provided the defendant's conduct causes the plaintiff to have a reasonable apprehension of imminent harm. Tort law aims to protect individuals from having to expect harmful or offensive contact.

If the act that created the apprehension is *completed* and results in harm to the plaintiff, it is a **battery,** which is defined as an unexcused and harmful or offensive physical contact *intentionally* performed. **EXAMPLE 4.4** Ivan threatens Jean with a gun and then shoots her. The pointing of the gun at Jean is an assault. The firing of the gun (if the bullet hits Jean) is a battery. ■

The contact can be harmful, or it can be merely offensive (such as an unwelcome kiss). Physical injury need not occur. The contact can be made by the defendant or by some force set in motion by the defendant, such as a rock thrown by the defendant. Whether the contact is offensive or not is determined by the *reasonable person standard.*[5]

If the plaintiff shows that there was contact, and the jury (or judge, if there is no jury) agrees that the contact was offensive, the plaintiff has a right to compensation. A plaintiff may be compensated for the emotional harm resulting from a battery, as well as for physical harm. The defendant may raise a number of legally recognized defenses to justify his or her conduct, including self-defense and defense of others.

4-2b False Imprisonment

False imprisonment is the intentional confinement or restraint of another person's activities without justification. False imprisonment interferes with the freedom to move without restraint. The confinement can be accomplished through the use of physical barriers, physical restraint, or threats of physical force. Moral pressure or threats of future harm do not constitute false imprisonment. It is essential that the person under restraint does not wish to be restrained.

Businesspersons may face suits for false imprisonment after they have attempted to confine a suspected shoplifter for questioning. Under the "privilege to detain" granted to merchants in most states, a merchant can use *reasonable force* to detain or delay a person suspected of shoplifting the merchant's property. Although the details of the privilege vary from state to state, generally laws require that any detention be conducted in a *reasonable* manner and for only a *reasonable* length of time. Undue force or unreasonable detention can lead to liability for the business.

Cities and counties may also face lawsuits for false imprisonment if they detain individuals without reason. **CASE EXAMPLE 4.5** Police arrested Adetokunbo Shoyoye for an unpaid subway ticket and for a theft that had been committed by someone who had stolen his identity. A court ordered that he be released, but a county employee mistakenly confused Shoyoye's paperwork with that of another person, who was scheduled to be sent to state prison. As a result, instead of being released, Shoyoye was held in county jail for more than two weeks. Shoyoye later sued the county for false imprisonment and won.[6] ■

Assault Any word or action intended to make another person fearful of immediate physical harm—a reasonably believable threat.

Battery Physical contact with another that is unexcused, harmful or offensive, and intentionally performed.

Can cities and counties be sued for false imprisonment?

---

5. The reasonable person standard is an objective test of how a reasonable person would have acted under the same circumstances. See "The Duty of Care and Its Breach" later in this chapter.
6. *Shoyoye v. County of Los Angeles*, 203 Cal.App.4th 947, 137 Cal.Rptr.3d 839 (2012).

Actionable Capable of serving as the basis of a lawsuit. An actionable claim can be pursued in a lawsuit or other court action.

4-2c Intentional Infliction of Emotional Distress

The tort of *intentional infliction of emotional distress* can be defined as extreme and outrageous conduct resulting in severe emotional distress to another. To be **actionable** (capable of serving as the ground for a lawsuit), the conduct must be so extreme and outrageous that it exceeds the bounds of decency accepted by society.

Outrageous Conduct Courts in most jurisdictions are wary of emotional distress claims and confine them to truly outrageous behavior. Generally, repeated annoyances (such as those experienced by a person who is being stalked), coupled with threats, are sufficient to support a claim. Acts that cause indignity or annoyance alone usually are not enough. **EXAMPLE 4.6** A father attacks a man who has had consensual sexual relations with the father's nineteen-year-old daughter. The father handcuffs the man to a steel pole and threatens to kill him unless he leaves town immediately. The father's conduct may be sufficiently extreme and outrageous to be actionable as an intentional infliction of emotional distress. ■

Limited by the First Amendment When the outrageous conduct consists of speech about a public figure, the First Amendment's guarantee of freedom of speech limits emotional distress claims. **CASE EXAMPLE 4.7** *Hustler* magazine once printed a fake advertisement that showed a picture of the Reverend Jerry Falwell and described him as having lost his virginity to his mother in an outhouse while he was drunk. Falwell sued the magazine for intentional infliction of emotional distress and won, but the United States Supreme Court overturned the decision. The Court held that creators of parodies of public figures are protected under the First Amendment from claims of intentional infliction of emotional distress. (The Court applied the same standards that apply to public figures in defamation lawsuits, discussed next.)[7] ■

Is it legal to create a parody of a public figure, such as the Reverend Jerry Falwell?

Ron Galella/Getty Images

4-2d Defamation

As discussed in Chapter 2, the freedom of speech guaranteed by the First Amendment to the U.S. Constitution is not absolute. In interpreting the First Amendment, the courts must balance free speech rights against other strong social interests, including society's interest in preventing and redressing attacks on reputation. (Nations with fewer free speech protections have seen an increase in defamation lawsuits targeting U.S. citizens and journalists as defendants. See this chapter's *Beyond Our Borders* feature for a discussion of this trend.)

The tort of **defamation** involves wrongfully hurting a person's good reputation. The law has imposed a general duty on all persons to refrain from making false, defamatory statements of fact about others. Breaching this duty in writing or another permanent form (such as a digital recording) constitutes the tort of **libel.** Breaching the duty orally is the tort of **slander.** The tort of defamation also arises when a false statement of fact is made about a person's product, business, or legal ownership rights to property.

To establish defamation, a plaintiff normally must prove the following:

1. The defendant made a false statement of fact.

2. The statement was understood as being about the plaintiff and tended to harm the plaintiff's reputation.

3. The statement was published to at least one person other than the plaintiff.

4. In addition, if the plaintiff is a public figure, she or he must prove *actual malice.*

LEARNING OBJECTIVE 3

What is defamation? Name two types of defamation.

Defamation Anything published or publicly spoken that causes injury to another's good name, reputation, or character.

Libel Defamation in writing or another permanent form (such as a digital recording).

Slander Defamation in oral form.

---

7. *Hustler Magazine, Inc. v. Falwell*, 485 U.S. 46, 108 S.Ct. 876, 99 L.Ed.2d 41 (1988). For another example of how the courts protect parody, see *Busch v. Viacom International, Inc.,* 477 F.Supp.2d 764 (N.D.Tex. 2007), involving a fake endorsement of televangelist Pat Robertson's diet shake.

Statement of Fact Requirement Often at issue in defamation lawsuits (including online defamation, discussed in Chapter 7) is whether the defendant made a *statement of fact* or a *statement of opinion*.[8] Statements of opinion normally are not actionable because they are protected under the First Amendment. In other words, making a negative statement about another person is not defamation unless the statement is false and represents something as a fact (for example, "Lane cheats on his taxes") rather than a personal opinion (for example, "Lane is a jerk").

The Publication Requirement The basis of the tort of defamation is the publication of a statement or statements that hold an individual up to contempt, ridicule, or hatred. *Publication* here means that the defamatory statements are communicated to persons other than the defamed party.

> **EXAMPLE 4.8** If Thompson writes Andrews a private letter or text falsely accusing him of embezzling funds, the action does not constitute libel. If Peters falsely states that Gordon is dishonest and incompetent when no one else is around, the action does not constitute slander. In neither instance was the message communicated to a third party. ■

The courts have generally held that even dictating a letter to a secretary constitutes publication, although the publication may be privileged (as discussed shortly). If a third party overhears defamatory statements by chance, the courts usually hold that this also constitutes publication. Defamatory statements made via the Internet (in e-mail or posted on social media)

---

8. See, for example, *Lott v. Levitt*, 469 F.Supp.2d 575 (N.D.Ill. 2007).

BEYOND OUR BORDERS — "Libel Tourism"

As mentioned earlier, U.S. plaintiffs have sometimes engaged in forum shopping by trying to have their complaints heard by a particular state court that is likely to be sympathetic to their claims. *Libel tourism* is essentially forum shopping on an international scale. Rather than filing a defamation lawsuit in the United States, where the freedoms of speech and press are strongly protected, a plaintiff files it in a foreign jurisdiction where there is a greater chance of winning.

The Threat of Libel Tourism
Libel tourism can have a chilling effect on the speech of U.S. journalists and authors because the fear of liability in other nations may prevent them from freely discussing topics of profound public importance. Libel tourism might even increase the threat to our nation's security if it discourages authors from writing about persons who support or finance terrorism or other dangerous activities.

The threat of libel tourism captured media attention when Khalid bin Mahfouz, a Saudi Arabian businessman, sued U.S. resident Dr. Rachel Ehrenfeld in London, England. Ehrenfeld had written a book on terrorist financing that claimed Mahfouz financed Islamic terrorist groups. Mahfouz filed the case in England because English law assumes that the offending speech is false (libelous), and the author must prove that the speech is true in order to prevail. The English court took jurisdiction because twenty-three copies of the book had been sold online to residents of the United Kingdom.

Ehrenfeld did not go to England to defend herself, and the court entered a judgment of $225,000 against her. She then countersued Mahfouz in a U.S. court in an attempt to show that she was protected under the First Amendment and had not committed libel, but that case was dismissed for lack of jurisdiction.[a]

The U.S. Response
In response to the *Ehrenfeld* case, the New York state legislature enacted the Libel Terrorism Reform Act in 2008.[b] That act enables New York courts to assert jurisdiction over anyone who obtains a foreign libel judgment against a writer or publisher living in New York State. It also prevents courts from enforcing foreign libel judgments unless the foreign country provides free speech protection equal to or greater than that available in New York. In 2010, the federal government passed similar legislation that makes foreign libel judgments unenforceable in U.S. courts unless they are consistent with the First Amendment.[c]

CRITICAL THINKING

- Why do we need special legislation designed to control foreign libel claims against U.S. citizens? Explain.

---

a. *Ehrenfeld v. Mahfouz*, 518 F.3d 102 (2d Cir. 2008).

b. McKinney's Consolidated Laws of New York, Sections 302 and 5304.

c. Securing the Protection of our Enduring and Established Constitutional Heritage Act, 28 U.S.C. Sections 4101–4105.

are also actionable, as you will read in Chapter 7. Note further that anyone who republishes or repeats defamatory statements is liable even if that person reveals the source of the statements.

Damages for Libel   Once a defendant's liability for libel is established, general damages (defined earlier) are presumed as a matter of law. General damages are designed to compensate the plaintiff for nonspecific harms such as disgrace or dishonor in the eyes of the community, humiliation, injured reputation, and emotional distress—harms that are difficult to measure. In other words, to recover general damages in a libel case, the plaintiff need not prove that she or he was actually harmed in any specific way as a result of the libelous statement.

Damages for Slander   In contrast to cases alleging libel, in a case alleging slander, the plaintiff must prove *special damages* (defined earlier) to establish the defendant's liability. In other words, the plaintiff must show that the slanderous statement caused the plaintiff to suffer actual economic or monetary losses. Unless this initial hurdle of proving special damages is overcome, a plaintiff alleging slander normally cannot go forward with the suit and recover any damages. This requirement is imposed in cases involving slander because slanderous statements have a temporary quality. In contrast, a libelous (written) statement has the quality of permanence, can be circulated widely, especially through social media, and usually results from some degree of deliberation on the part of the author.

Exceptions to the burden of proving special damages in cases alleging slander are made for certain types of slanderous statements. If a false statement constitutes "slander *per se*," no proof of special damages is required for it to be actionable. The following four types of false utterances are considered to be slander *per se*:

1. A statement that another has a loathsome disease (historically, leprosy and sexually transmitted diseases, but now also including allegations of mental illness).

2. A statement that another has committed improprieties while engaging in a business, profession, or trade.

3. A statement that another has committed or has been imprisoned for a serious crime.

4. A statement that a person (usually only unmarried persons and sometimes only women) is unchaste or has engaged in serious sexual misconduct.

Defenses to Defamation   Truth is normally an absolute defense against a defamation charge. In other words, if the defendant in a defamation suit can prove that his or her allegedly defamatory statements were true, normally no tort has been committed.

Other defenses to defamation may exist if the statement is privileged or concerns a public figure. Note that the majority of defamation actions in the United States are filed in state courts, and the states may differ both in how they define defamation and in the particular defenses they allow, such as privilege (discussed shortly).

ETHICAL ISSUE

Can a person post online a criticism about a physician's "bedside manner" without being successfully sued for defamation?

When does an online criticism of a physician become defamation? Just as there are online rating sites for college professors, there are rating sites for practicing physicians. A posting at such a site formed the basis for a defamation lawsuit brought by neurologist Dr. David McKee.

McKee went to examine a patient who had been transferred from the intensive care unit (ICU) to a private room. In the room were family members of the patient, including his son. The patient's son later made the following post on a physician-rating Web site: "[Dr. McKee] seemed upset that my father had been moved [into a private room]. Never having met my father or his family, Dr. McKee said 'When you weren't in ICU, I had to spend time finding out if you transferred or died.' When we gaped at him, he said 'Well, 44 percent of hemorrhagic strokes dies within 30 days. I guess this is the better option.'" [9]

McKee filed suit for defamation but lost. The court found that all the statements made by the son were essentially true, and truth is a complete defense to a defamation action. In other words, true statements, however disparaging, are not actionable. Even the presence of minor inaccuracies of expression or detail does not render basically true statements false. As long as the "sting of the libelous charge is justified," defamation has not occurred.

Privileged Communications. In some circumstances, a person will not be liable for defamatory statements because she or he enjoys a **privilege,** or immunity. Privileged communications are of two types: absolute and qualified. [10] Only in judicial proceedings and certain government proceedings is an absolute privilege granted. Thus, statements made in a courtroom by attorneys and judges during a trial are absolutely privileged, as are statements made by government officials during legislative debate.

In other situations, a person will not be liable for defamatory statements because he or she has a *qualified,* or conditional, privilege. An employer's statements in written evaluations of employees are an example of a qualified privilege. Generally, if the statements are made in good faith and the publication is limited to those who have a legitimate interest in the communication, the statements fall within the area of qualified privilege. **EXAMPLE 4.9** Jorge worked at Facebook for five years and was being considered for a management position. His supervisor, Lydia, wrote a memo about Jorge's performance to those evaluating him for the management position. The memo contained certain negative statements. As long as Lydia honestly believed that what she wrote was true and limited her disclosure to company representatives, her statements would likely be protected by a qualified privilege. ■

Privilege A special right, advantage, or immunity that enables a person or a class of persons to avoid liability for defamation.

Public Figures. Politicians, entertainers, professional athletes, and other persons who are in the public eye are considered *public figures.* In general, public figures are considered fair game, and false and defamatory statements about them that appear in the media will not constitute defamation unless the statements are made with **actual malice.** [11] To be made with actual malice, a statement must be made *with either knowledge of its falsity or a reckless disregard of the truth.*

Statements about public figures, especially when made via a public medium, are usually related to matters of general interest. They are made about people who substantially affect all of us. Furthermore, public figures generally have some access to a public medium for answering disparaging (belittling) falsehoods about themselves, whereas private individuals do not. For these reasons, public figures have a greater burden of proof in defamation cases (they must prove actual malice) than do private individuals.

CASE EXAMPLE 4.10 *In Touch* magazine published a story about a former call girl who claimed to have slept with legendary soccer player David Beckham more than once. Beckham sued *In Touch* magazine for libel, seeking $25 million in damages. He said that he had never met the woman, had not cheated on his wife with her, and had not paid her for sex. After months of litigation, a federal district court dismissed the case because Beckham could not show that the magazine had acted with actual malice. Whether or not the statements in the article were accurate, there was no evidence that the defendants had made the statements with knowledge of their falsity or reckless disregard for the truth. [12] ■

Actual Malice The deliberate intent to cause harm that exists when a person makes a statement with either knowledge of its falsity or reckless disregard of the truth. Actual malice is required to establish defamation against public figures.

Helga Esteb/ShutterStock.com

A publication printed statements by a woman who claimed that she had slept with David Beckham on several occasions. In order for Beckham to prevail in a lawsuit against the publication for defamatory statements, what legal barrier must he overcome?

9. *McKee v. Laurion,* Supreme Court of Minnesota, 825 N.W.2d 725 (2013).

10. Note that the term *privileged communication* in this context is *not* the same as privileged communication between a professional, such as an attorney, and his or her client.

11. *New York Times Co. v. Sullivan,* 376 U.S. 254, 84 S.Ct. 710, 11 L.Ed.2d 686 (1964).

12. *Beckham v. Bauer Pub. Co., L.P.,* 2011 WL 977570 (2011).

4–2e Invasion of the Right to Privacy and Appropriation

A person has a right to solitude and freedom from prying public eyes—in other words, to privacy. As discussed in Chapter 2, the Supreme Court has held that a fundamental right to privacy is implied by various amendments to the U.S. Constitution. Some state constitutions also explicitly provide for privacy rights. In addition, a number of federal and state statutes have been enacted to protect individual rights in specific areas.

Tort law also safeguards these rights through the torts of *invasion of privacy* and *appropriation.* Generally, to sue successfully for an invasion of privacy, a person must have a reasonable expectation of privacy, and the invasion must be highly offensive. (See this chapter's *Adapting the Law to the Online Environment* feature for a discussion of how invasion of privacy claims can arise when someone posts pictures or videos taken with digital devices.)

ADAPTING THE LAW TO THE **ONLINE** ENVIRONMENT

Revenge Porn and Invasion of Privacy

Every digital device today takes photos and videos at virtually no cost. Software allows the recording of conversations via Skype. Many couples immortalize their "private moments" using such digital devices. One partner may take a racy "selfie" and send it as an attachment to a text message to the other partner, for example.

Occasionally, after a couple breaks off their relationship, one of them seeks a type of digital revenge. The result, called revenge porn, has been defined in the Cyber Civil Rights Initiative as "The online distribution of sexually explicit images of a non-consenting individual with the intent to humiliate that person." Until relatively recently, few states had criminal statutes that covered revenge porn. Therefore, victims have sued on the basis of (1) invasion of privacy, (2) public disclosure of private facts, and (3) intentional infliction of emotional distress.

It Is More Than Just Pictures and Videos

The most egregious form of revenge porn occurs when the perpetuator provides detailed information about the victim. Such information may include the victim's name,

Facebook page, address, and phone number, as well as the victim's workplace and children's names. This information, along with the sexually explicit photos and videos, are posted on hosting Web sites. Many such Web sites have been shut down, as was the case with IsAnybodyDown? and Texxxan.com. But others are still active, usually with offshore servers and foreign domain-name owners.

The Injurious Results of Revenge Porn

To be sure, victims of revenge porn suffer extreme embarrassment. They may also have their reputations ruined. Some have lost their jobs. A number of victims have been stalked in the physical world and harassed online and offline. When attempts at having offending photos removed from Web sites have failed, victims have changed their phone numbers and sometimes their names.

A Class Action Lawsuit

Hollie Toups, along with twenty-two other female plaintiffs, sued the domain name registrar and Web hosting company GoDaddy in a Texas court. Although GoDaddy did not create the defamatory and offensive material at issue, GoDaddy knew of the content and did not remove it. The plaintiffs asserted

causes of action "for intentional infliction of emotional distress," among other claims. Additionally, the plaintiffs argued that "by its knowing participation in these unlawful activities, GoDaddy has also committed the intentional Texas tort of invasion of privacy . . . as well as intrusion on Plaintiffs' right to seclusion, the public disclosure of their private facts, [and] the wrongful appropriation of their names and likenesses. . . ." GoDaddy sought to dismiss the case, and an appeals court eventually granted GoDaddy's motion to dismiss.[a]

Another Texas woman had better luck. In a jury trial in early 2014, she won a $500,000 award. The woman's ex-boyfriend had uploaded videos to YouTube and other sites. At the time she made the complaint, revenge porn was not a crime in Texas.

CRITICAL THINKING

- Should domain name hosting companies be liable for revenge porn?

---

a. *GoDaddy.com, LLC. v. Toups*, 429 S.W.3d 752, Tex. App—Beaumont (2014).

Invasion of Privacy Four acts qualify as an invasion of privacy:

1. *Intrusion into an individual's affairs or seclusion.* Invading someone's home or illegally searching someone's briefcase is an invasion of privacy. The tort has been held to extend to eavesdropping by wiretap, the unauthorized scanning of a bank account, compulsory blood testing, and window peeping. **EXAMPLE 4.11** A female sports reporter for ESPN is digitally videoed while naked through the peephole in the door of her hotel room. If she sues, she will likely win a lawsuit against the man who took the video and posted it on the Internet. ■

2. *False light.* Publication of information that places a person in a false light is also an invasion of privacy. For instance, writing a story about a person that attributes ideas and opinions not held by that person is an invasion of privacy. (Publishing such a story could involve the tort of defamation as well.) **EXAMPLE 4.12** An Arkansas newspaper prints an article with the headline "Special Delivery: World's oldest newspaper carrier, 101, quits because she's pregnant!" Next to the article is a picture of a ninety-six-year-old woman who is not the subject of the article (and not pregnant). If she sues the paper for invasion of privacy, she will probably win. ■

3. *Public disclosure of private facts.* This type of invasion of privacy occurs when a person publicly discloses private facts about an individual that an ordinary person would find objectionable or embarrassing. A newspaper account about a private citizen's sex life or financial affairs could be an actionable invasion of privacy, even if the information revealed is true, because it should not be a matter of public concern.

4. *Appropriation of identity.* Under the common law, using a person's name, picture, or other likeness for commercial purposes without permission is a tortious invasion of privacy. An individual's right to privacy normally includes the right to the exclusive use of her or his identity. **EXAMPLE 4.13** An advertising agency asks a singer with a distinctive voice and stage presence to do a marketing campaign for a new automobile. The singer rejects the offer. If the agency then uses someone who imitates the singer's voice and dance moves in the ad, this would be actionable as an appropriation of identity. ■

Appropriation Most states today have codified the common law tort of appropriation of identity in statutes that establish the distinct tort of **appropriation,** or right of publicity. States differ as to the degree of likeness that is required to impose liability for appropriation, however.

Some courts have held that even when an animated character in a video or a video game is made to look like an actual person, there are not enough similarities to constitute appropriation. **CASE EXAMPLE 4.14** The Naked Cowboy, Robert Burck, was a street entertainer in New York City who had achieved some fame performing for tourists. He performed wearing only a white cowboy hat, white cowboy boots, and white underwear and carrying a guitar strategically placed to give the illusion of nudity. Burck sued Mars, Inc., the maker of M&Ms candy, over a video it showed on billboards in Times Square that depicted a blue M&M dressed exactly like The Naked Cowboy. The court, however, held that the use of Burck's signature costume did not amount to appropriation.[13] ■

4-2f Fraudulent Misrepresentation

A misrepresentation leads another to believe in a condition that is different from the condition that actually exists. This is often accomplished through a false or incorrect statement. Although persons sometimes make misrepresentations accidentally because they are unaware of the existing facts, the tort of **fraudulent misrepresentation,** or fraud, involves *intentional* deceit for personal gain. The tort includes several elements:

---

13. *Burck v. Mars, Inc.,* 571 F.Supp.2d 446 (S.D.N.Y. 2008). Also see *Kirby v. Sega of America, Inc.,* 144 Cal.App.4th 47, 50 Cal.Rptr.3d 607 (2006).

Appropriation In tort law, the use by one person of another person's name, likeness, or other identifying characteristic without permission and for the benefit of the user.

iStockPhoto.com/anouchka

Under what circumstances, if any, could the use of the image of the Naked Cowboy in an ad constitute appropriation?

Fraudulent Misrepresentation Any misrepresentation, either by misstatement or by omission of a material fact, knowingly made with the intention of deceiving another and on which a reasonable person would and does rely to his or her detriment.

1. The misrepresentation of facts or conditions with knowledge that they are false or with reckless disregard for the truth.

2. An intent to induce another to rely on the misrepresentation.

3. Justifiable reliance by the deceived party.

4. Damage suffered as a result of the reliance.

5. A causal connection between the misrepresentation and the injury suffered.

Puffery A salesperson's exaggerated claims concerning the quality of property offered for sale. Such claims involve opinions rather than facts and are not legally binding promises or warranties.

For fraud to occur, more than mere **puffery,** or *seller's talk,* must be involved. Fraud exists only when a person represents as a fact something she or he knows is untrue. For example, it is fraud to claim that a roof does not leak when one knows it does. Facts are objectively ascertainable, whereas seller's talk is not. "I am the best accountant in town" is seller's talk because *best* is subjective. In the following case, the court considered each of the elements of fraud.

CASE 4.1

Revell v. Guido

New York Supreme Court, Appellate Division, Third Department, 124 A.D.3d 1006, __ N.Y.S.2d __ (2015).

FACTS Joseph Guido bought a parcel of land in Stillwater, New York, that contained nine rental houses. The houses shared a waste disposal system that was defective. Guido had a new septic system installed. When town officials discovered sewage on the property, Guido had the system partially replaced. Prospective buyers, including Danny Revell, were given a property information sheet that stated, "Septic system totally new—each field totally replaced." In response to a questionnaire from the buyers' bank, Guido denied any knowledge of environmental problems. A month after the buyers bought the houses, the septic system failed and required substantial remediation. The lender foreclosed on the property. The buyers filed a suit in a New York state court against Guido and his firm, Real Property Solutions, LLC, alleging fraud. A jury found fraud and awarded damages. The court issued a judgment in the plaintiffs' favor. The defendants appealed.

ISSUE Did the facts of the case and the plaintiffs' proof meet all of the requirements for establishing fraud?

DECISION Yes. The state intermediate appellate court affirmed the lower court's judgment in the plaintiffs' favor.

If a home seller claims that a new septic system was installed when it wasn't, does that constitute fraud?

REASON The court explained that to prove fraud, the plaintiffs had to establish that the defendants, with the intent to deceive, misrepresented a material fact that they knew to be false and on which the plaintiffs justifiably relied, incurring damages. The property's information sheet and Guido's responses to the environmental questionnaire misrepresented the facts. The septic system was not "totally new," and Guido knew that partially treated sewage had been discovered on the property. Guido's intent to deceive was shown by the "cavalier manner" in which he answered the questionnaire and his knowledge of the problems with the septic system. Because a visual inspection of the property did not reveal those problems, "one would assume that the system was working properly." The plaintiffs' reliance on the representation in the property information sheet was thus justified. The evidence of damages included "an abundance of receipts, invoices, billing statements and canceled checks" used by an accountant to calculate the amount.

CRITICAL THINKING—Legal Consideration *Financing for the purchase of the property was conditioned on the bank's review of Guido's answers to the environmental questionnaire. How could the court conclude that the plaintiffs justifiably relied on misrepresentations made to the bank? Explain.*

Statement of Fact versus Opinion Normally, the tort of misrepresentation or fraud occurs only when there is reliance on a *statement of fact.* Sometimes, however, the tort may involve reliance on a *statement of opinion* if the individual making the statement has a superior knowledge of the subject matter. For instance, when a lawyer makes a statement of opinion about the law in a state in which the lawyer is licensed to practice, a court would treat it as a statement of fact.

Negligent Misrepresentation Sometimes, a tort action can arise from misrepresentations that are made negligently rather than intentionally. The key difference between intentional and negligent misrepresentation is whether the person making the misrepresentation had actual knowledge of its falsity. Negligent misrepresentation requires only that the person making the statement or omission did not have a reasonable basis for believing its truthfulness.

Liability for negligent misrepresentation usually arises when the defendant who made the misrepresentation owed a duty of care to the plaintiff to supply correct information. Statements or omissions made by attorneys and accountants to their clients, for instance, can lead to liability for negligent misrepresentation.

4–2g Abusive or Frivolous Litigation

Tort law recognizes that people have a right not to be sued without a legally just and proper reason, and therefore it protects individuals from the misuse of litigation. Torts related to abusive litigation include malicious prosecution and abuse of process.

If a party initiates a lawsuit out of malice and without a legitimate legal reason, and ends up losing the suit, that party can be sued for *malicious prosecution. Abuse of process* can apply to any person using a legal process against another in an improper manner or to accomplish a purpose for which it was not designed.

The key difference between the torts of abuse of process and malicious prosecution is the level of proof required to succeed. Unlike malicious prosecution, abuse of process is not limited to prior litigation and does not require the plaintiff to prove malice. It can be based on the wrongful use of subpoenas, court orders to attach or seize real property, or other types of formal legal process.

4–2h Wrongful Interference

The torts known as **business torts** generally involve wrongful interference with another's business rights. Business torts involving wrongful interference are generally divided into two categories: wrongful interference with a contractual relationship and wrongful interference with a business relationship.

Business Tort Wrongful interference with another's business rights and relationships.

Wrongful Interference with a Contractual Relationship Three elements are necessary for wrongful interference with a contractual relationship to occur:

1. A valid, enforceable contract must exist between two parties.

2. A third party must know that this contract exists.

3. The third party must *intentionally* induce a party to breach the contract.

CASE EXAMPLE 4.15 A landmark case involved an opera singer, Johanna Wagner, who was under contract to sing for a man named Lumley for a specified period of years. A man named Gye, who knew of this contract, nonetheless "enticed" Wagner to refuse to carry out the agreement, and Wagner began to sing for Gye. Gye's action constituted a tort because it wrongfully interfered with the contractual relationship between Wagner and Lumley.[14] (Of course, Wagner's refusal to carry out the agreement also entitled Lumley to sue Wagner for breach of contract.) ■

The body of tort law relating to intentional interference with a contractual relationship has expanded greatly in recent years. In principle, any lawful contract can be the basis for an action of this type. The contract could be between a firm and its employees or a firm and its customers. Sometimes, for instance, a competitor draws away one of a firm's key employees. Only if the original employer can show that the competitor knew of the contract's existence, and intentionally induced the breach, can damages be recovered from the competitor.

GARWOOD & VOIGT Fine & Rare Books Maps & Prints

Opera singer Johanna Jachmann-Wagner is shown here in one of her many roles. She was under contract to sing for one person, but was enticed to break the contract and sing for someone else. Was a tort committed? If so, by whom?

---

14. *Lumley v. Gye*, 118 Eng.Rep. 749 (1853).

Wrongful Interference with a Business Relationship Businesspersons devise countless schemes to attract customers, but they are prohibited from unreasonably interfering with another's business in their attempts to gain a share of the market. There is a difference between *competitive methods* and *predatory behavior*—actions undertaken with the intention of unlawfully driving competitors completely out of the market. Attempting to attract customers in general is a legitimate business practice, whereas specifically targeting the customers of a competitor is more likely to be predatory.

EXAMPLE 4.16 A shopping mall contains two athletic shoe stores: Joe's and Ultimate Sport. Joe's cannot station an employee at the entrance of Ultimate Sport to divert customers by telling them that Joe's will beat Ultimate Sport's prices. This type of activity constitutes the tort of wrongful interference with a business relationship, which is commonly considered to be an unfair trade practice. If this activity were permitted, Joe's would reap the benefits of Ultimate Sport's advertising. ■

Defenses to Wrongful Interference A person will not be liable for the tort of wrongful interference with a contractual or business relationship if it can be shown that the interference was justified or permissible. Bona fide competitive behavior is a permissible interference even if it results in the breaking of a contract.

EXAMPLE 4.17 If Antonio's Meats advertises so effectively that it induces Sam's Restaurant to break its contract with Burke's Meat Company, Burke's will be unable to recover against Antonio's Meats on a wrongful interference theory. After all, the public policy that favors free competition in advertising outweighs any possible instability that such competitive activity might cause in contractual relations. ■

4-3 Intentional Torts against Property

Intentional torts against property include trespass to land, trespass to personal property, conversion, and disparagement of property. These torts are wrongful actions that interfere with individuals' legally recognized rights with regard to their land or personal property. The law distinguishes real property from personal property. *Real property* is land and things "permanently" attached to the land. *Personal property* consists of all other items, which are basically movable. Thus, a house and lot are real property, whereas the furniture inside the house is personal property. Cash and stocks and bonds are also personal property.

4-3a Trespass to Land

A **trespass to land** occurs anytime a person, without permission, does any of the following:

1. Enters onto, above, or below the surface of land that is owned by another.

2. Causes anything to enter onto land owned by another.

3. Remains on land owned by another or permits anything to remain on it.

Actual harm to the land is not an essential element of this tort, because the tort is designed to protect the right of an owner to exclusive possession.

Common types of trespass to land include walking or driving on another's land, shooting a gun over the land, and throwing rocks at a building that belongs to someone else. Another common form of trespass involves constructing a building so that part of it is on an adjoining landowner's property.

Establishing Trespass Before a person can be a trespasser, the real property owner (or other person in actual and exclusive possession of the property) must establish that person as a trespasser. For instance, "posted" trespass signs expressly establish as a trespasser a person

Trespass to Land Entry onto, above, or below the surface of land owned by another without the owner's permission or legal authorization.

who ignores these signs and enters onto the property. Any person who enters onto property to commit an illegal act (such as a thief entering a lumberyard at night to steal lumber) is established impliedly as a trespasser, without posted signs. In contrast, a guest in your home is not a trespasser unless she or he has been asked to leave but refuses.

Damages At common law, a trespasser is liable for any damage caused to the property and generally cannot hold the owner liable for injuries sustained on the premises. This common law rule is being abandoned in many jurisdictions in favor of a *reasonable duty of care* rule that varies depending on the status of the parties.

For instance, a landowner may have a duty to post a notice that guard dogs patrol the property. Also, if young children are likely to be attracted to the property by some object, such as a swimming pool or a sand pile, and are injured, the landowner may be held liable under the *attractive nuisance doctrine*. An owner can normally use reasonable force to remove a trespasser from the premises—or detain the trespasser for a reasonable time—without liability for damages, however.

Defenses against Trespass to Land One defense to a claim of trespass to land is to show that the trespass was warranted. This may occur, for instance, when the trespasser entered the property to assist someone in danger.

Another defense is for the trespasser to show that he or she had a license to come onto the land. A *licensee* is one who is invited (or allowed to enter) onto the property of another for the licensee's benefit. A person who enters another's property to read an electric meter, for example, is a licensee. When you purchase a ticket to attend a movie or sporting event, you are licensed to go onto the property of another to view that movie or event.

Note that licenses to enter are *revocable* by the property owner. If a property owner asks a meter reader to leave and the meter reader refuses to do so, the meter reader at that point becomes a trespasser.

4-3b Trespass to Personal Property

Whenever an individual wrongfully takes or harms the personal property of another or otherwise interferes with the lawful owner's possession of personal property, **trespass to personal property** (also called *trespass to chattels* or *trespass to personalty*[15]) occurs. In this context, harm means not only destruction of the property, but also anything that diminishes its value, condition, or quality.

Trespass to personal property involves intentional meddling with a possessory interest (the right to possess), including barring an owner's access to personal property. **EXAMPLE 4.18** Kelly takes Ryan's business law book as a practical joke and hides it so that Ryan is unable to find it for several days before the final examination. Here, Kelly has engaged in a trespass to personal property. (Kelly has also committed the tort of *conversion*—to be discussed next.) ▪

If it can be shown that trespass to personal property was warranted, then a complete defense exists. Most states, for example, allow automobile repair shops to retain a customer's car (under what is called an *artisan's lien*) when the customer refuses to pay for repairs already completed.

4-3c Conversion

Any act that deprives an owner of personal property or of the use of that property without the owner's permission and without just cause can constitute **conversion.** Even the taking of electronic records and data can form the basis of a conversion claim. Often, when conversion occurs, a trespass to personal property also occurs. The original taking of the personal property from the owner was a trespass, and wrongfully retaining the property is conversion.

Trespass to Personal Property Wrongfully taking or harming the personal property of another or otherwise interfering with the lawful owner's possession of personal property.

Conversion Wrongfully taking or retaining possession of an individual's personal property and placing it in the service of another.

---

15. Pronounced *per*-sun-ul-tee.

Conversion is the civil side of crimes related to theft, but it is not limited to theft. Even if the rightful owner consented to the initial taking of the property, so there was no theft or trespass, a failure to return the personal property may still be conversion. **EXAMPLE 4.19** Chen borrows Mark's iPad to use while traveling home from school for the holidays. When Chen returns to school, Mark asks for his iPad back. Chen tells Mark that she gave it to her little brother for Christmas. In this situation, Mark can sue Chen for conversion, and Chen will have to either return the iPad or pay damages equal to its replacement value. ■

Conversion can occur even when a person mistakenly believes that she or he was entitled to the goods. In other words, good intentions are not a defense against conversion. Someone who buys stolen goods, for instance, can be sued for conversion even if he or she did not know that the goods were stolen. If the true owner brings a tort action against the buyer, the buyer must either return the property to the owner or pay the owner the full value of the property (despite having already paid the purchase price to the thief).

In the following case, the court was asked to decide whether the tort of conversion was an appropriate cause of action for the misappropriation and use of a credit card.

> ### KNOW THIS
> It is the *intent* to do an act that is important in tort law, not the motive behind the intent.

CASE 4.2

Welco Electronics, Inc. v. Mora

Court of Appeal of California, Second District, 223 Cal.App.4th 202, 166 Cal.Rptr.3d 877 (2014).

FACTS Darrel Derouis, the president of Welco Electronics, Inc., hired a certified bookkeeper to help him "find where his money went." During the investigation, discrepancies in Welco's credit-card statements were discovered. Statements from the credit-card company contained charges to AQM Supplies—a company established by Nicholas Mora, who worked for Welco as a quality assurance manager. The credit-card charges to AQM, which totaled more than $375,000, did not appear on Welco's copies of the statements. At the time of the transactions, AQM had leased a portable credit-card terminal, and funds paid through the terminal were electronically deposited into Mora's bank account.

Welco filed a suit in a California state court against Mora, alleging conversion. Welco sought the value of the funds allegedly converted, as well as interest, expenses, punitive damages, and other costs. The court ruled in Welco's favor, and Mora appealed.

ISSUE Can the use of a company's credit card by an employee to obtain funds from the company constitute conversion?

DECISION Yes. A state intermediate appellate court affirmed the lower court's judgment.

How can a portable credit card terminal be used for conversion?
©iStock.com/iStockphoto.com

REASON In the words of the court, "The tort of conversion has been adapted to new property rights and modern means of commercial transactions." The court acknowledged that "historically, the tort of conversion was limited to tangible property and did not apply to intangible property," but added that "modern courts . . . have permitted conversion claims against intangible interests." The owner of a checking account, for instance, has an intangible property interest in his or her checks. Other examples of instruments representing intangible property rights include a savings account, an insurance policy, a company's customer list, and a stock certificate.

Credit card, debit card, and PayPal information may also be subject to conversion. The card or account information is similar to the intangible property interest in a check. The court reasoned that when Mora misappropriated Welco's credit card and used it, he took part of Welco's credit balance with the credit-card company. The result was an unauthorized transfer to Mora of Welco's property rights.

CRITICAL THINKING—E-Commerce Consideration *Can the appropriation of an Internet domain name constitute conversion? Explain.*

4–3d Disparagement of Property

> **Disparagement of Property** An economically injurious falsehood about another's product or property.

Disparagement of property occurs when economically injurious falsehoods are made about another's product or property, rather than about another's reputation (as in the tort of defamation). Disparagement of property is a general term for torts specifically referred to as *slander of quality* or *slander of title*.

Publication of false information about another's product, alleging that it is not what its seller claims, constitutes the tort of **slander of quality,** or **trade libel.** To establish trade libel, the plaintiff must prove that the improper publication caused a third party to refrain from dealing with the plaintiff and that the plaintiff sustained economic damages (such as lost profits) as a result. An improper publication may be both a slander of quality and defamation of character. For example, a statement that disparages the quality of a product may also, by implication, disparage the character of the person who would sell such a product.

Slander of Quality (Trade Libel) The publication of false information about another's product, alleging that it is not what its seller claims.

When a publication denies or casts doubt on another's legal ownership of property, and the property's owner suffers financial loss as a result, the tort of **slander of title** may exist. Usually, this is an intentional tort that occurs when someone knowingly publishes an untrue statement about property with the intent of discouraging a third party from dealing with the property's owner. For instance, a car dealer would have difficulty attracting customers after competitors published a notice that the dealer's stock consisted of stolen automobiles.

Slander of Title The publication of a statement that denies or casts doubt on another's legal ownership of property, causing financial loss to that property's owner.

4-4 Unintentional Torts (Negligence)

The tort of **negligence** occurs when someone suffers injury because of another's failure to live up to a required *duty of care.* In contrast to intentional torts, in torts involving negligence, the tortfeasor neither wishes to bring about the consequences of the act nor believes that they will occur. The actor's conduct merely creates a *risk* of such consequences. If no risk is created, there is no negligence. Moreover, the risk must be foreseeable—that is, it must be such that a reasonable person engaging in the same activity would anticipate the risk and guard against it. In determining what is reasonable conduct, courts consider the nature of the possible harm.

Negligence The failure to exercise the standard of care that a reasonable person would exercise in similar circumstances.

Many of the actions giving rise to the intentional torts discussed earlier in the chapter constitute negligence if the element of intent is missing (or cannot be proved). **EXAMPLE 4.20** Juan walks up to Maya and intentionally shoves her. Maya falls and breaks an arm as a result. In this situation, Juan has committed an intentional tort (assault and battery). If Juan carelessly bumps into Maya, however, and she falls and breaks an arm as a result, Juan's action will constitute negligence. In either situation, Juan has committed a tort. ■

LEARNING OBJECTIVE 4
Identify the four elements of negligence.

To succeed in a negligence action, the plaintiff must prove each of the following:

1. *Duty.* That the defendant owed a duty of care to the plaintiff.
2. *Breach.* That the defendant breached that duty.
3. *Causation.* That the defendant's breach caused the plaintiff's injury.
4. *Damages.* That the plaintiff suffered a legally recognizable injury.

We discuss each of these four elements of negligence next.

4-4a The Duty of Care and Its Breach

Central to the tort of negligence is the concept of a **duty of care.** The basic principle underlying the duty of care is that people in society are free to act as they please so long as their actions do not infringe on the interests of others. When someone fails to comply with the duty to exercise reasonable care, a potentially tortious act may result.

Duty of Care The duty of all persons, as established by tort law, to exercise a reasonable amount of care in their dealings with others. Failure to exercise due care, which is normally determined by the reasonable person standard, constitutes the tort of negligence.

Failure to live up to a standard of care may be an act (setting fire to a building) or an omission (neglecting to put out a campfire). It may be a careless act or a carefully performed but nevertheless dangerous act that results in injury. In determining whether the duty of care has been breached, courts consider several factors:

1. The nature of the act (whether it is outrageous or commonplace).
2. The manner in which the act was performed (cautiously versus heedlessly).
3. The nature of the injury (whether it is serious or slight).

Creating even a very slight risk of a dangerous explosion might be unreasonable, whereas creating a distinct possibility of someone's burning his or her fingers on a stove might be reasonable.

Reasonable Person Standard The standard of behavior expected of a hypothetical "reasonable person." It is the standard against which negligence is measured and that must be observed to avoid liability for negligence.

The Reasonable Person Standard

Tort law measures duty by the **reasonable person standard.** In determining whether a duty of care has been breached, the courts ask how a reasonable person would have acted in the same circumstances. The reasonable person standard is said to be (though in an absolute sense it cannot be) objective. It is not necessarily how a particular person *would* act. It is society's judgment on how people *should* act. If the so-called reasonable person existed, he or she would be careful, conscientious, even tempered, and honest.

The degree of care to be exercised varies, depending on the defendant's occupation or profession, her or his relationship with the plaintiff, and other factors. Generally, whether an action constitutes a breach of the duty of care is determined on a case-by-case basis. The outcome depends on how the judge (or jury, in a jury trial) decides a reasonable person in the position of the defendant would act in the particular circumstances of the case.

Note that the courts frequently use the reasonable person standard in other areas of law as well as in negligence cases. That individuals are required to exercise a reasonable standard of care in their activities is a pervasive concept in business law, and many of the issues discussed in subsequent chapters of this text have to do with this duty.

The Duty of Landowners

Landowners are expected to exercise reasonable care to protect persons coming onto their property from harm. In some jurisdictions, landowners are held to owe a duty to protect even trespassers against certain risks. Landowners who rent or lease premises to tenants are expected to exercise reasonable care to ensure that the tenants and their guests are not harmed in common areas, such as stairways, entryways, and laundry rooms.

"A little neglect may breed great mischief."

BENJAMIN FRANKLIN
1706–1790
(AMERICAN POLITICIAN AND INVENTOR)

Business Invitee A person, such as a customer or a client, who is invited onto business premises by the owner of those premises for business purposes.

Duty to Warn Business Invitees of Risks. Retailers and other firms that explicitly or implicitly invite persons to come onto their premises have a duty to exercise reasonable care to protect these **business invitees.** The duty normally requires storeowners to warn business invitees of foreseeable risks about which the owners knew or *should have known*.

EXAMPLE 4.21 Liz enters a supermarket, slips on a wet floor, and sustains injuries as a result. If there was no sign warning that the floor was wet when Liz slipped, the owner of the supermarket would be liable for damages. A court would hold that the business owner was negligent because the owner failed to exercise a reasonable degree of care in protecting the store's customers against foreseeable risks about which the owner knew or should have known. That a patron might slip on the wet floor and be injured was a foreseeable risk, and the owner should have taken care to avoid this risk or to warn the customer of it (by posting a sign or setting out orange cones, for example). ∎

The landowner also has a duty to discover and remove any hidden dangers that might injure a customer or other invitee. Store owners have a duty to protect customers from potentially slipping and injuring themselves on merchandise that has fallen off the shelves, for instance.

Does a "Wet Floor" sign relieve a restaurant owner from being held negligent if a customer slips?

Obvious Risks Are an Exception. Some risks, of course, are so obvious that the owner need not warn of them. For instance, a business owner does not need to warn customers to open a door before attempting to walk through it. Other risks, however, may seem obvious to a business owner but may not be so to someone else, such as a child. In addition, even if a risk is obvious, that does not necessarily excuse a business owner from the duty to protect customers from foreseeable harm.

CASE EXAMPLE 4.22 Giorgio's Grill in Hollywood, Florida, is a restaurant that becomes a nightclub after hours. At those times, traditionally—as the manager of Giorgio's knew—the staff and customers throw paper napkins into the air as the music plays. The napkins land on the floor, but no one picks them up. One night, Jane Izquierdo went to Giorgio's. Although she had been to the club on other occasions and knew about the napkin-throwing tradition, she slipped on a napkin and fell, breaking her leg. She sued Giorgio's for negligence but lost at trial because the jury found that the risk of slipping on the napkins was obvious. A state appellate court reversed, however, holding that the obviousness of a risk does not discharge a business owner's duty to its invitees to maintain the premises in a safe condition.[16] ■

It can be difficult to determine whether a risk is obvious. Because you can be held liable if you fail to discover hidden dangers on business premises that could cause injuries to customers, you should post warnings of any conceivable risks on the property. Be vigilant and frequently reassess potential hazards. Train your employees to be on the lookout for possibly dangerous conditions at all times and to notify a supervisor immediately if they notice something. Remember that a finding of liability in a single lawsuit can leave a small enterprise close to bankruptcy. To prevent potential negligence liability, make sure that your business premises are as safe as possible for all persons who might be there, including children, senior citizens, and individuals with disabilities.

PREVENTING LEGAL DISPUTES

The Duty of Professionals Persons who possess superior knowledge, skill, or training are held to a higher standard of care than others. Professionals—such as physicians, dentists, architects, engineers, accountants, and lawyers—are required to have a standard minimum level of special knowledge and ability. In determining what constitutes reasonable care, the law takes their training and expertise into account. Thus, an accountant's conduct is judged not by the reasonable person standard, but by the reasonable accountant standard.

If a professional violates her or his duty of care toward a client, the professional may be sued for **malpractice,** which is essentially professional negligence. For instance, a patient might sue a physician for *medical malpractice.* A client might sue an attorney for *legal malpractice.*

Malpractice Professional misconduct or the lack of the requisite degree of skill as a professional. Negligence on the part of a professional, such as a physician, is commonly referred to as malpractice.

4-4b Causation

Another element necessary in a negligence action is *causation.* If a person breaches a duty of care and someone suffers an injury, the wrongful act must have caused the harm for it to constitute the tort of negligence.

Courts Ask Two Questions In deciding whether there is causation, the court must address two questions:

1. *Is there causation in fact?* Did the injury occur because of the defendant's act, or would it have occurred anyway? If an injury would not have occurred without the defendant's act, then there is **causation in fact.**

   Causation in fact can usually be determined by the use of the *but for* test: "but for" the wrongful act, the injury would not have occurred. Theoretically, causation in fact is limitless. One could claim, for example, that "but for" the creation of the world, a particular injury would not have occurred. Thus, as a practical matter, the law has to establish limits, and it does so through the concept of proximate cause.

Causation in Fact An act or omission without which an event would not have occurred.

2. *Was the act the proximate cause of the injury?* **Proximate cause,** or legal cause, exists when the connection between an act and an injury is strong enough to justify imposing liability. Courts use proximate cause to limit the scope of the defendant's liability to a subset of the

Proximate Cause Legal cause. It exists when the connection between an act and an injury is strong enough to justify imposing liability.

---

16. *Izquierdo v. Gyroscope, Inc.,* 946 So.2d 115 (Fla.App. 2007).

Injuries from car accidents can cause handicaps that last a lifetime. Do such injuries satisfy the injury requirement for a finding of negligence?

total number of potential plaintiffs that might have been harmed by the defendant's actions.

EXAMPLE 4.23 Ackerman carelessly leaves a campfire burning. The fire not only burns down the forest but also sets off an explosion in a nearby chemical plant that spills chemicals into a river, killing all the fish for a hundred miles downstream and ruining the economy of a tourist resort. Should Ackerman be liable to the resort owners? To the tourists whose vacations were ruined? These are questions of proximate cause that a court must decide. ■

Both questions concerning causation must be answered in the affirmative for tort liability to arise. If a defendant's action constitutes causation in fact but a court decides that the action was not the proximate cause of the plaintiff's injury, the causation requirement has not been met—and the defendant normally will not be liable to the plaintiff.

KNOW THIS
Proximate cause can be thought of in terms of social policy. Should the defendant be made to bear the loss instead of the plaintiff?

Foreseeability Questions of proximate cause are linked to the concept of foreseeability. It would be unfair to impose liability on a defendant unless the defendant's actions created a foreseeable risk of injury. Probably the most cited case on proximate cause is the *Palsgraf* case, which is discussed in this chapter's *Landmark in the Law* feature. In determining the issue of proximate cause, the court addressed the following question: Does a defendant's duty of care extend only to those who may be injured as a result of a foreseeable risk, or does it also extend to a person whose injury could not reasonably have been foreseen?

LANDMARK IN THE LAW   *Palsgraf v. Long Island Railroad Co.* (1928)

In 1928, the New York Court of Appeals (that state's highest court) issued its decision in *Palsgraf v. Long Island Railroad Co.,*[a] a case that has become a landmark in negligence law and proximate cause.

THE FACTS OF THE CASE The plaintiff, Helen Palsgraf, was waiting for a train on a station platform. A man carrying a small package wrapped in newspaper was rushing to catch a train that had begun to move away from the platform. As the man attempted to jump aboard the moving train, he seemed unsteady and about to fall. A railroad guard on the train car reached forward to grab him, and another guard on the platform pushed him from behind to help him board the train. In the process, the man's package fell on the railroad tracks and exploded, because it contained fireworks. The repercussions of the

explosion caused scales at the other end of the train platform to fall on Palsgraf, who was injured as a result. She sued the railroad company for damages in a New York state court.

THE QUESTION OF PROXIMATE CAUSE At the trial, the jury found that the railroad guards were negligent in their conduct. On appeal, the question before the New York Court of Appeals was whether the conduct of the railroad guards was the proximate cause of Palsgraf's injuries. In other words, did the guards' duty of care extend to Palsgraf, who was outside the zone of danger and whose injury could not reasonably have been foreseen?

The court stated that the question of whether the guards were negligent *with respect to Palsgraf* depended on whether her injury was *reasonably foreseeable* by the railroad guards. Although the guards may have acted negligently with respect to the man boarding the train, this had no bearing on the question of their negligence with respect to Palsgraf. This was not a situation in which

a person committed an act so potentially harmful (for example, firing a gun at a building) that he or she would be held responsible for any harm that resulted. The court stated that here "there was nothing in the situation to suggest to the most cautious mind that the parcel wrapped in newspaper would spread wreckage through the station." The court thus concluded that the railroad guards were not negligent with respect to Palsgraf, because her injury was not reasonably foreseeable.

APPLICATION TO TODAY'S WORLD *The Palsgraf case established foreseeability as the test for proximate cause. Today, the courts continue to apply this test in determining proximate cause—and thus tort liability for injuries. Generally, if the victim of a harm or the consequences of a harm done are unforeseeable, there is no proximate cause. Note, though, that in the online environment, distinctions based on physical proximity, such as the "zone of danger" cited by the court in this case, are largely inapplicable.*

a. 248 N.Y. 339, 162 N.E. 99 (1928).

4-4c The Injury Requirement and Damages

For a tort to have been committed, the plaintiff must have suffered a *legally recognizable* injury. To recover damages (receive compensation), the plaintiff must have suffered some loss, harm, wrong, or invasion of a protected interest. If no harm or injury results from a given negligent action, there is nothing to compensate—and no tort exists. **EXAMPLE 4.24** If you carelessly bump into a passerby, who stumbles and falls as a result, you may be liable in tort if the passerby is injured in the fall. If the person is unharmed, however, there normally cannot be a suit for damages because no injury was suffered. ■

Essentially, the purpose of tort law is to compensate for legally recognized injuries resulting from wrongful acts. Thus, compensatory damages are the norm in negligence cases. As noted earlier, a court will award punitive damages only if the defendant's conduct was grossly negligent, reflecting an intentional failure to perform a duty with reckless disregard of the consequences to others.

4-4d Defenses to Negligence

Defendants often defend against negligence claims by asserting that the plaintiffs failed to prove the existence of one or more of the required elements for negligence. Additionally, there are three basic *affirmative* defenses in negligence cases (defenses that a defendant can use to avoid liability even if the facts are as the plaintiff states): (1) assumption of risk, (2) superseding cause, and (3) contributory and comparative negligence.

Assumption of Risk A plaintiff who voluntarily enters into a risky situation, knowing the risk involved, will not be allowed to recover. This is the defense of **assumption of risk,** which requires two elements:

1. Knowledge of the risk.
2. Voluntary assumption of the risk.

This defense is frequently asserted when a plaintiff is injured during recreational activities that involve known risk, such as skiing and skydiving. Courts do not apply the assumption of risk doctrine in certain situations, such as those involving emergencies, however.

Assumption of risk can apply not only to participants in sporting events, but to spectators and bystanders who are injured while attending those events. In the following *Spotlight Case,* the issue was whether a spectator at a baseball game voluntarily assumed the risk of being hit by an errant ball thrown while the players were warming up before the game.

> **Assumption of Risk** A defense to negligence that bars a plaintiff from recovering for injuries or damage suffered as a result of risks he or she knew of and voluntarily assumed.

SPOTLIGHT ON THE SEATTLE MARINERS: CASE 4.3

Taylor v. Baseball Club of Seattle, L.P.
Court of Appeals of Washington, 132 Wash.App. 32, 130 P.3d 835 (2006).

FACTS Delinda Middleton Taylor went to a Mariners baseball game at Safeco Field with her boyfriend and two minor sons. Their seats were four rows up from the field along the right field foul line. They arrived more than an hour before the game began so that they could see the players warm up and get their autographs. When she walked in, Taylor saw that Mariners pitcher Freddy Garcia was throwing a ball back

Many fans arrive at baseball games early so they can watch the players warm up.

Alan C. Heison/ShutterStock.com

and forth with José Mesa right in front of their seats. As Taylor stood in front of her seat, she looked away from the field, and a ball thrown by Mesa got past Garcia and struck her in the face, causing serious injuries. Taylor sued the Mariners for the allegedly negligent warm-up throw. The Mariners filed a motion for a summary judgment in which they argued that Taylor, a Mariners fan, was familiar with baseball

Continues

and the inherent risk of balls entering the stands, and therefore assumed the risk of her injury. The trial court granted the motion and dismissed Taylor's case. Taylor appealed.

ISSUE Was the risk of injury from an errant baseball thrown during pregame warm-up foreseeable to a reasonable person with Taylor's familiarity with baseball?

DECISION Yes. The state intermediate appellate court affirmed the lower court's judgment. Taylor, as a spectator in an unprotected area of seats, voluntarily undertook the risk associated with being hit by an errant baseball thrown during warm-ups before the start of the game.

REASON The court observed that there was substantial evidence that Taylor was familiar with the game. She was a seasoned Mariners fan, and both of her sons had played baseball for at least six years. "She attended many of her sons' baseball games, she witnessed balls entering the stands, she had watched Mariners' games both at the Kingdome [the Mariners' former stadium] and on television, and she knew that there was no screen protecting her seats, which were close to the field. In fact, as she walked to her seat she saw the players warming up and was excited about being in an unscreened area where her party might get autographs from the players and catch balls."

It was not legally relevant that the injury occurred during the pregame warm-up because "it is the normal, every-day practice at all levels of baseball for pitchers to warm up in the manner that led to this incident." The Mariners had satisfied their duty to protect spectators from balls entering the stands by providing a protective screen behind home plate. Taylor chose not to sit in the protected area and thus knowingly put herself at risk.

CRITICAL THINKING—Ethical Consideration *Would the result in this case have been different if Taylor's minor son, rather than Taylor herself, had been struck by the ball? Should courts apply the doctrine of assumption of risk to children? Discuss.*

Superseding Cause

Superseding Cause An unforeseeable intervening event may break the connection between a wrongful act and an injury to another. If so, the event acts as a *superseding cause*—that is, it relieves a defendant of liability for injuries caused by the intervening event.

EXAMPLE 4.25 While riding his bicycle, Derrick negligently hits Julie, who is walking on the sidewalk. As a result of the impact, Julie falls and fractures her hip. While she is waiting for help to arrive, a small plane crashes nearby and explodes, and some of the fiery debris hits her, causing her to sustain severe burns. Derrick will be liable for Julie's fractured hip because the risk of hitting her with his bicycle was foreseeable. Normally, though, Derrick will not be liable for the burns caused by the plane crash, because the risk of a plane's crashing nearby and injuring Julie was not foreseeable. ■

Contributory Negligence
A rule in tort law, used in only a few states, that completely bars the plaintiff from recovering any damages if the damage suffered is partly the plaintiff's own fault.

Contributory Negligence All individuals are expected to exercise a reasonable degree of care in looking out for themselves. In the past, under the common law doctrine of **contributory negligence,** a plaintiff who was also negligent (who failed to exercise a reasonable degree of care) could not recover anything from the defendant. Under this rule, no matter how insignificant the plaintiff's negligence was relative to the defendant's negligence, the plaintiff was precluded from recovering any damages. Today, only a few jurisdictions still follow this doctrine.

Comparative Negligence
A rule in tort law, used in the majority of states, that reduces the plaintiff's recovery in proportion to the plaintiff's degree of fault, rather than barring recovery completely.

Comparative Negligence In most states, the doctrine of contributory negligence has been replaced by a **comparative negligence** standard. Under this standard, both the plaintiff's and the defendant's negligence are computed, and the liability for damages is distributed accordingly.

Some jurisdictions have adopted a "pure" form of comparative negligence that allows a plaintiff to recover, even if the extent of his or her fault is greater than that of the defendant. For instance, if a plaintiff was 80 percent at fault and the defendant 20 percent at fault, the plaintiff may recover 20 percent of his or her damages.

Many states' comparative negligence statutes, however, contain a "50 percent" rule that prevents a plaintiff from recovering any damages if she or he was more than 50 percent at fault. Under this rule, a plaintiff who is 35 percent at fault could recover 65 percent of his or her damages, but a plaintiff who is 65 percent at fault could recover nothing.

4-4e Special Negligence Doctrines and Statutes

There are a number of special doctrines and statutes relating to negligence. We examine a few of them here.

Res Ipsa Loquitur Generally, in lawsuits involving negligence, the plaintiff has the burden of proving that the defendant was negligent. In certain situations, however, the courts may infer that negligence has occurred under the doctrine of ***res ipsa loquitur***[17] (meaning "the facts speak for themselves"). Then the burden of proof rests on the defendant to prove that she or he was *not* negligent. This doctrine is applied only when the event creating the damage or injury is one that ordinarily would occur only as a result of negligence.

CASE EXAMPLE 4.26 A kidney donor, Darnell Backus, sustained injuries to his cervical spine and to the muscles on the left side of his body as a result of the surgery to harvest his kidney. He sued the hospital and physicians involved in the transplant operation for damages. Backus asserted *res ipsa loquitor* because the injury was of the kind that ordinarily does not occur in the absence of someone's negligence. The burden of proof shifted to the defendants, and because they failed to show that they had *not* been negligent, Backus won.[18] ■

Negligence *Per Se* Certain conduct, whether it consists of an action or a failure to act, may be treated as **negligence *per se*** (*per se* means "in or of itself"). Negligence *per se* may occur if an individual violates a statute or ordinance and thereby causes the kind of harm that the statute was intended to prevent. The statute must clearly set out what standard of conduct is expected, when and where it is expected, and of whom it is expected. The standard of conduct required by the statute is the duty that the defendant owes to the plaintiff, and a violation of the statute is the breach of that duty.

CASE EXAMPLE 4.27 A Delaware statute states that anyone "who operates a motor vehicle and who fails to give full time and attention to the operation of the vehicle" is guilty of inattentive driving. Michael Moore was cited for inattentive driving after he collided with Debra Wright's car when he backed a truck out of a parking space. Moore paid the ticket, which meant that he pleaded guilty to violating the statute. The day after the accident, Wright began having back pain, which eventually required surgery. She sued Moore for damages, alleging negligence *per se*. The Delaware Supreme Court ruled that the inattentive driving statute set forth a sufficiently specific standard of conduct to warrant application of negligence *per se*.[19] ■

"Danger Invites Rescue" Doctrine Sometimes, a person who is trying to avoid harm—such as an individual who swerves to avoid a head-on collision with a drunk driver—ends up causing harm to another (such as a cyclist riding in the bike lane) as a result. In those situations, the original wrongdoer (the drunk driver in this scenario) is liable to anyone who is injured, even if the injury actually resulted from another person's attempt to escape harm.

The "danger invites rescue" doctrine extends the same protection to a person who is trying to rescue another from harm—the original wrongdoer is liable for injuries to an individual attempting a rescue. The idea is that rescuers should not be held liable for any damages, because they did not cause the danger and because danger invites rescue. Whether rescuers injure themselves, the person rescued, or a passer-by, the original wrongdoer will still be liable.

EXAMPLE 4.28 Ludley drives down a street but fails to see a stop sign because he is trying to quiet his squabbling children in the car's back seat. Salter, who is standing on the curb, realizes that Ludley is about to hit a pedestrian and runs into the street to push the pedestrian out of the way. If Ludley's vehicle hits Salter instead, Ludley will be liable for Salter's injury, as well as for any injuries the other pedestrian sustained. ■

---

17. Pronounced *rehz ihp*-suh *low*-kwuh-tuhr.
18. *Backus v. Kaleida Health*, 91 A.D.3d 1284, 937 N.Y.S.2d 773 (N.Y.A.D. 4 Dept. 2012).
19. *Wright v. Moore*, 931 A.2d 405 (Del.Supr. 2007).

Res Ipsa Loquitur A doctrine under which negligence may be inferred simply because an event occurred, if it is the type of event that would not occur in the absence of negligence. Literally, the term means "the facts speak for themselves."

Negligence *Per Se* An action or failure to act in violation of a statutory requirement.

Good Samaritan Statute
A state statute stipulating that persons who provide emergency services to, or rescue, someone in peril cannot be sued for negligence unless they act recklessly and cause further harm.

Dram Shop Act A state statute that imposes liability on the owners of bars and taverns, as well as those who serve alcoholic drinks to the public, for injuries resulting from accidents caused by intoxicated persons when the sellers or servers of alcoholic drinks contributed to the intoxication.

Good Samaritan Statutes Most states have enacted what are called **Good Samaritan statutes.**[20] Under these statutes, someone who is aided voluntarily by another cannot turn around and sue the "Good Samaritan" for negligence. These laws were passed largely to protect physicians and medical personnel who voluntarily render medical services in emergency situations to those in need, such as individuals hurt in car accidents.

Dram Shop Acts Many states have also passed **dram shop acts,**[21] under which a tavern owner or bartender may be held liable for injuries caused by a person who became intoxicated while drinking at the bar or who was already intoxicated when served by the bartender. Some states' statutes also impose liability on *social hosts* (persons hosting parties) for injuries caused by guests who became intoxicated at the hosts' homes. Under these statutes, it is unnecessary to prove that the tavern owner, bartender, or social host was negligent. **EXAMPLE 4.29** Selena hosts a Super Bowl party at which Raul, a minor, sneaks alcoholic drinks. Selena is potentially liable for damages resulting from Raul's drunk driving after the party. ■

4–5 Strict Liability

Strict Liability Liability regardless of fault, which is imposed on those engaged in abnormally dangerous activities, on persons who keep dangerous animals, and on manufacturers or sellers that introduce into commerce defective and unreasonably dangerous goods.

Another category of torts is called **strict liability,** or *liability without fault.* Intentional torts and torts of negligence involve acts that depart from a reasonable standard of care and cause injuries. Under the doctrine of strict liability, liability for injury is imposed for reasons other than fault.

4–5a Abnormally Dangerous Activities

Strict liability for damages proximately caused by an abnormally dangerous or exceptional activity is one application of this doctrine. Courts apply the doctrine of strict liability in such cases because of the extreme risk of the activity. For instance, even if blasting with dynamite is performed with all reasonable care, there is still a risk of injury. Because of the potential for harm, the person who is engaged in an abnormally dangerous activity—and benefits from it—is responsible for paying for any injuries caused by that activity. Although there is no fault, there is still responsibility because of the dangerous nature of the undertaking.

LEARNING OBJECTIVE 5

What is meant by strict liability? In what circumstances is strict liability applied?

4–5b Other Applications of Strict Liability

The strict liability principle is also applied in other situations. Persons who keep wild animals, for example, are strictly liable for any harm inflicted by the animals. In addition, an owner of domestic animals may be strictly liable for harm caused by those animals if the owner knew, or should have known, that the animals were dangerous or had a propensity to harm others.

A significant application of strict liability is in the area of *product liability*—liability of manufacturers and sellers for harmful or defective products—discussed in the next chapter. Liability here is a matter of social policy. Manufacturers and sellers can better bear the cost of injuries, and because they profit from making and selling the products, they should be responsible for the injuries the products cause.

---

20. These laws derive their name from the Good Samaritan story in the Bible. In the story, a traveler who had been robbed and beaten lay along the roadside, ignored by those passing by. Eventually, a man from the country of Samaria (the "Good Samaritan") stopped to render assistance to the injured person.

21. Historically, a *dram* was a small unit of liquid, and spirits were sold in drams. Thus, a dram shop was a place where liquor was sold in drams.

Reviewing . . . Tort Law

Elaine Sweeney went to Ragged Mountain Ski Resort in New Hampshire with a friend. Elaine went snow tubing down a run designed exclusively for snow tubers. No Ragged Mountain employees were present in the snow-tube area to instruct Elaine on the proper use of a snow tube. On her fourth run down the trail, Elaine crossed over the center line between snow-tube lanes, collided with another snow tuber, and was injured. Elaine filed a negligence action against Ragged Mountain seeking compensation for the injuries that she sustained. Two years earlier, the New Hampshire state legislature had enacted a statute that prohibited a person who participates in the sport of skiing from suing a ski-area operator for injuries caused by the risks inherent in skiing. Using the information presented in the chapter, answer the following questions.

1. What defense will Ragged Mountain probably assert?

2. The central question in this case is whether the state statute establishing that skiers assume the risks inherent in the sport applies to Elaine's suit. What would your decision be on this issue? Why?

3. Suppose that the court concludes that the statute applies only to skiing and not to snow tubing. Will Elaine's lawsuit be successful? Explain.

4. Now suppose that the jury concludes that Elaine was partly at fault for the accident. Under what theory might her damages be reduced in proportion to how much her actions contributed to the accident and her resulting injuries?

DEBATE THIS

- Each time a state legislature enacts a law that applies the assumption of risk doctrine to a particular sport, participants in that sport suffer.

BUSINESS APPLICATION

How Important Is Tort Liability to Business?*

Although there are more claims for breach of contract than for any other category of lawsuits, tort claims are also commonplace for businesses. Furthermore, the dollar amount of damages awarded in tort actions is typically much higher than the awards in contract claims.

Because of the potential for large damages awards for intentional and unintentional acts, businesspersons should take preventive measures to help them avoid tort liability. Remember that, for most torts, injured persons can bring actions against businesses as well as against individuals. In fact, if given a choice, a plaintiff often sues a business rather than an individual because the business is more likely to have "deep pockets" (the ability to pay large damages awards). Moreover, sometimes businesses

can be held liable for torts that do not apply to individuals.

The Extent of Business Negligence Liability

A business can be exposed to negligence liability in a wide variety of instances. Liability to business invitees is a clear example. A business that fails to warn invitees that its

---

* This *Business Application* is not meant to substitute for the services of an attorney who is licensed to practice law in your state.

Continues

floor is slippery after a rainstorm, or that its parking lot is icy after a snow, may be liable to an injured customer. Indeed, business owners can be liable for nearly any fall or other injury that occurs on business premises.

Even the hiring of employees can lead to negligence liability. For example, a business can be liable if it fails to do a criminal background check before hiring a person to supervise a child-care center when an investigation would have revealed that the person had previously been convicted of sexual assault. Failure to properly supervise or instruct employees can also lead to liability for a business.

Liability for Torts of Employees and Agents

A business can also be held liable for the negligence or intentional torts of its employees and agents. As you will learn in later chapters, a business is liable for the torts committed by an employee who is acting within the scope of his or her employment or an agent who is acting with the authority of the business. Therefore, if a sales agent commits fraud while acting within the scope of her or his employment, the business will be held liable.

CHECKLIST for Minimizing Business Tort Liability:

1. Constantly inspect the premises and look for areas where customers or employees might trip, slide, or fall. Take corrective action whenever you find a problem.

2. Train employees on the importance of periodic safety inspections and the procedures for reporting unsafe conditions.

3. Routinely maintain all business equipment (including vehicles).

4. Check with your liability insurance company for suggestions on improving the safety of your premises and operations.

5. Make sure that your general liability policy will adequately cover the potential exposure of the business, and reassess your coverage annually.

6. Review the background and qualifications of individuals you are considering hiring as employees or agents.

7. Investigate and review all negligence claims promptly. Most claims can be settled at a lower cost before a lawsuit is filed.

Key Terms

actionable 94
actual malice 97
appropriation 99
assault 93
assumption of risk 109
battery 93
business invitee 106
business tort 101
causation in fact 107
comparative negligence 110
compensatory damages 90
contributory negligence 110
conversion 103
damages 90
defamation 94

defense 92
disparagement of property 104
dram shop act 112
duty of care 105
fraudulent misrepresentation 99
general damages 90
Good Samaritan statute 112
intentional tort 92
libel 94
malpractice 107
negligence 105
negligence *per se* 111
privilege 97
proximate cause 107
puffery 100

punitive damages 90
reasonable person standard 106
res ipsa loquitur 111
slander 94
slander of quality (trade libel) 105
slander of title 105
special damages 90
strict liability 112
tort 89
tortfeasor 92
transferred intent 92
trespass to land 102
trespass to personal property 103

Chapter Summary: Tort Law

Intentional Torts against Persons	1. *Assault and battery*—An assault is an unexcused and intentional act that causes another person to be apprehensive of immediate harm. A battery is an assault that results in physical contact. 2. *False imprisonment*—The intentional confinement or restraint of another person's movement without justification. 3. *Intentional infliction of emotional distress*—An extreme and outrageous act, intentionally committed, that results in severe emotional distress to another. 4. *Defamation (libel or slander)*—A false statement of fact, not made under privilege, that is communicated to a third person and that causes damage to a person's reputation. For public figures, the plaintiff must also prove actual malice. 5. *Invasion of the right to privacy*—Includes four types: wrongful intrusion into a person's private activities; publication of information that places a person in a false light; disclosure of private facts that an ordinary person would find objectionable; and appropriation of identity, which involves the use of a person's name, likeness, or other identifying characteristic, without permission and for a commercial purpose. Most states have enacted statutes establishing appropriation of identity as the tort of *appropriation*, or right of publicity. Courts differ on the degree of likeness required. 6. *Misrepresentation (fraud)*—A false representation made by one party, through misstatement of facts or through conduct, with the intention of deceiving another and on which the other reasonably relies to his or her detriment. Negligent misrepresentation occurs when a person supplies information without having a reasonable basis for believing its truthfulness. 7. *Abusive or frivolous litigation*—A person who initiates a lawsuit out of malice and without probable cause, and loses the suit, can be sued for the tort of *malicious prosecution*. A person who uses a legal process against another improperly or to accomplish a purpose for which it was not designed can be sued for *abuse of process*. 8. *Wrongful interference*—The knowing, intentional interference by a third party with an enforceable contractual relationship or an established business relationship between other parties for the purpose of advancing the economic interests of the third party.
Intentional Torts against Property	1. *Trespass to land*—The invasion of another's real property without consent or privilege. 2. *Trespass to personal property*—Unlawfully damaging or interfering with the owner's right to use, possess, or enjoy her or his personal property. 3. *Conversion*—Wrongfully taking or using the personal property of another without permission. 4. *Disparagement of property*—Any economically injurious falsehood that is made about another's product or property. The term includes the torts of *slander of quality* and *slander of title*.

Unintentional Torts (Negligence)	1. *Negligence*—The careless performance of a legally required duty or the failure to perform a legally required act. A plaintiff must prove that a legal duty of care existed, that the defendant breached that duty, that the breach caused the plaintiff's injury, and that the plaintiff suffered a legally recognizable injury.
	2. *Defenses to negligence*—The basic affirmative defenses in negligence cases are assumption of risk, superseding cause, and contributory or comparative negligence.
	3. *Special negligence doctrines and statutes*—
	  a. *Res ipsa loquitur*—A doctrine under which a plaintiff need not prove negligence on the part of the defendant because "the facts speak for themselves."
	  b. Negligence *per se*—A type of negligence that may occur if a person violates a statute or an ordinance and the violation causes another to suffer the kind of injury that the statute or ordinance was intended to prevent.
	  c. Special negligence statutes—State statutes that prescribe duties and responsibilities in certain circumstances. Violation of these statutes will impose civil liability. Dram shop acts and Good Samaritan statutes are examples.

Strict Liability	Under the doctrine of strict liability, parties may be held liable, regardless of the degree of care exercised, for damages or injuries caused by their products or activities. Strict liability includes liability for harms caused by abnormally dangerous activities, by dangerous animals, and by defective products (product liability).

Issue Spotters

1. Jana leaves her truck's motor running while she enters a Kwik-Pik Store. The truck's transmission engages, and the vehicle crashes into a gas pump, starting a fire that spreads to a warehouse on the next block. The warehouse collapses, causing its billboard to fall and injure Lou, a bystander. Can Lou recover from Jana? Why or why not? (See *Negligence.*)

2. A water pipe bursts, flooding a Metal Fabrication Company utility room and tripping the circuit breakers on a panel in the room. Metal Fabrication contacts Nouri, a licensed electrician with five years' experience, to check the damage and turn the breakers back on. Without testing for short circuits, which Nouri knows that he should do, he tries to switch on a breaker. He is electrocuted, and his wife sues Metal Fabrication for damages, alleging negligence. What might the firm successfully claim in defense? (See *Negligence.*)

—**Check your answers to the *Issue Spotters* against the answers provided in Appendix D at the end of this text.**

Learning Objectives Check

1. What is the purpose of tort law? What types of damages are available in tort lawsuits?
2. What are two basic categories of torts?
3. What is defamation? Name two types of defamation.
4. Identify the four elements of negligence.
5. What is meant by strict liability? In what circumstances is strict liability applied?

—**Answers to the even-numbered *Learning Objectives Check* questions can be found in Appendix E at the end of this text.**

Business Scenarios and Case Problems

4–1. Liability to Business Invitees. Kim went to Ling's Market to pick up a few items for dinner. It was a stormy day, and the wind had blown water through the market's door each time it opened. As Kim entered through the door, she slipped and fell in the rainwater that had accumulated on the floor. The manager knew of the weather conditions but had not posted any sign to warn customers of the water hazard. Kim injured her back as a result of the fall and sued Ling's for damages. Can Ling's be held liable for negligence? Discuss. (See *Negligence.*)

4–2. Spotlight on Intentional Torts—Defamation. Sharon Yeagle was an assistant to the vice president of student affairs at Virginia Polytechnic Institute and State University (Virginia Tech). As part of her duties, Yeagle helped students participate in the Governor's Fellows Program. The *Collegiate Times,* Virginia Tech's student newspaper, published an article about the university's success in placing students in the program. The article's text surrounded a block quotation attributed to Yeagle with the phrase "Director of Butt Licking" under her name. Yeagle sued the *Collegiate Times* for defamation. She argued that the phrase implied the commission of sodomy and was therefore actionable. What is *Collegiate Times*'s defense to this claim? [*Yeagle v. Collegiate Times,* 497 S.E.2d 136 (Va. 1998)] (See *Intentional Torts against Persons.*)

4–3. Business Torts. Medtronic, Inc., is a medical technology company that competes for customers with St. Jude Medical S.C., Inc. James Hughes worked for Medtronic as a sales manager. His contract prohibited him from working for a competitor for one year after leaving Medtronic. Hughes sought a position as a sales director for St. Jude. St. Jude told Hughes that his contract with Medtronic was unenforceable and offered him a job. Hughes accepted. Medtronic filed a suit, alleging wrongful interference. Which type of interference was most likely the basis for this suit? Did it occur here? Explain. [*Medtronic, Inc. v. Hughes,* 2011 WL 134973 (Minn.App. 2011)] (See *Intentional Torts against Persons.*)

4–4. Intentional Infliction of Emotional Distress. While living in her home country of Tanzania, Sophia Kiwanuka signed an employment contract with Anne Margareth Bakilana, a Tanzanian living in Washington, D.C. Kiwanuka traveled to the United States to work as a babysitter and maid in Bakilana's house. When Kiwanuka arrived, Bakilana confiscated her passport, held her in isolation, and forced her to work long hours under threat of having her deported. Kiwanuka worked seven days a week without breaks and was subjected to regular verbal and psychological abuse by Bakilana. Kiwanuka filed a complaint against Bakilana for intentional infliction of emotional distress, among other claims. Bakilana argued that Kiwanuka's complaint should be dismissed because the allegations were insufficient to show outrageous intentional conduct that resulted in severe emotional distress. If you were the judge, in whose favor would you rule? Why? [*Kiwanuka v. Bakilana,* 844 F.Supp.2d 107 (D.D.C. 2012)] (See *Intentional Torts against Persons.*)

4–5. Business Case Problem with Sample Answer—Negligence. At the Weatherford Hotel in Flagstaff, Arizona, in Room 59, a balcony extends across thirty inches of the room's only window, leaving a twelve-inch gap with a three-story drop to the concrete below. A sign prohibits smoking in the room but invites guests to "step out onto the balcony" to smoke. Toni Lucario was a guest in Room 59 when she climbed out of the window and fell to her death. Patrick McMurtry, her estate's personal representative, filed a suit against the Weatherford. Did the hotel breach a duty of care to Lucario? What might the Weatherford assert in its defense? Explain. [*McMurtry v. Weatherford Hotel, Inc.,* 293 P.3d 520 (Ariz. App. 2013)] (See *Negligence.*)

—**For a sample answer to Problem 4–5, go to Appendix F at the end of this text.**

4–6. Negligence. Ronald Rawls and Zabian Bailey were in an auto accident in Bridgeport, Connecticut. Bailey rear-ended Rawls at a stoplight. Evidence showed it was more likely than not that Bailey failed to apply his brakes in time to avoid the collision, failed to turn his vehicle to avoid the collision, failed to keep his vehicle under control, and was inattentive to his surroundings. Rawls filed a suit in a Connecticut state court against his insurance company, Progressive Northern Insurance Co., to obtain benefits under an underinsured motorist clause, alleging that Bailey had been negligent. Could Rawls collect? Discuss. [*Rawls v. Progressive Northern Insurance* Co., 310 Conn. 768, 83 A.3d 576 (2014)] (See *Negligence.*)

4–7. Negligence. Charles Robison, an employee of West Star Transportation, Inc., was ordered to cover an unevenly loaded flatbed trailer with a 150-pound tarpaulin. The load included uncrated equipment and pallet crates of different heights, about thirteen feet off the ground at its highest point. While standing on the load, manipulating the tarpaulin without safety equipment or assistance, Robison fell headfirst and sustained a traumatic head injury. He filed a suit against West Star to recover for his injury. Was West Star "negligent in failing to provide a reasonably safe place to work," as Robison claimed? Explain. [*West Star Transportation, Inc. v. Robison,* __ S.W.3d __, 2015 WL 348594 (Tex.App.—Amarillo 2015)] (See *Unintentional Torts (Negligence).*)

4–8. A Question of Ethics—Wrongful Interference. White Plains Coat & Apron Co. and Cintas Corp. are competitors. White Plains had five-year exclusive contracts with some of its customers. As a result of Cintas's soliciting of business, dozens of White Plains' customers breached their contracts and entered into rental agreements with Cintas. White Plains filed a suit against Cintas, alleging wrongful interference. [*White Plains Coat & Apron Co. v. Cintas Corp.,* 8 N.Y.3d 422, 867 N.E.2d 381 (2007)] (See *Intentional Torts against Persons.*)

1. What are the two policies at odds in wrongful interference cases? When there is an existing contract, which of these interests should be accorded priority? Why?

2. Is a general interest in soliciting business for profit a sufficient defense to a claim of wrongful interference with a contractual relationship? What do you think? Why?

Critical Thinking and Writing Assignments

4–9. Business Law Critical Thinking Group Assignment. Donald and Gloria Bowden hosted a cookout at their home in South Carolina, inviting mostly business acquaintances. Justin Parks, who was nineteen years old, attended the party. Alcoholic beverages were available to all of the guests, even those who, like Parks, were between the ages of eighteen and twenty-one.

Parks consumed alcohol at the party and left with other guests. One of these guests detained Parks at the guest's home to give Parks time to "sober up." Parks then drove himself from this guest's home and was killed in a one-car accident. At the time of death, he had a blood alcohol content of 0.291 percent, which exceeded the state's limit for driving a motor vehicle.

Linda Marcum, Parks's mother, filed a suit in a South Carolina state court against the Bowdens and others, alleging negligence. (See *Negligence.*)

1. The first group will present arguments in favor of holding the social hosts liable in this situation.

2. The second group will formulate arguments against holding the social hosts liable based on principles in this chapter.

3. The states vary widely in assessing liability and imposing sanctions in the circumstances described in this problem. The third group will determine the reasons why courts do not treat social hosts the same as parents who serve alcoholic beverages to their underage children.

iStockPhoto.com/milanklusacek

5

CHAPTER OUTLINE

- Product Liability
- Strict Product Liability
- Defenses to Product Liability

LEARNING OBJECTIVES

The five Learning Objectives below are designed to help improve your understanding of the chapter. After reading this chapter, you should be able to answer the following questions:

1. Can a manufacturer be held liable to any person who suffers an injury proximately caused by the manufacturer's negligently made product?

2. What public policy assumptions underlie strict product liability?

3. What are the elements of a cause of action in strict product liability?

4. What are three types of product defects?

5. What defenses to liability can be raised in a product liability lawsuit?

Product Liability The legal liability of manufacturers, sellers, and lessors of goods for injuries or damage caused by the goods to consumers, users, or bystanders.

Product Liability

An area of tort law of particular importance to business-persons is product liability. As Warren Buffett implies in the chapter-opening quote, to be successful, a business cannot make too many mistakes. This is especially true for businesses that make or sell products. The manufacturers and sellers of products may incur product liability when product defects cause injury or property damage to consumers, users, or bystanders (people in the vicinity of the product when it fails).

Although multimillion-dollar product liability claims often involve big automakers, pharmaceutical companies, or tobacco companies, many businesses face potential liability. For instance, in the last few years, numerous reports have suggested that energy drinks, such as Monster, Red Bull, Rockstar, and 5-hour Energy, have serious adverse effects—especially on young people. Several individuals have been hospitalized, and some have even died, after consuming large amounts of energy drinks. The federal government has issued a report concerning the adverse effects of these products and is investigating their safety. Meanwhile, the producers of energy drinks are facing a number of product liability actions. For example, the parents of a teenage girl who died after consuming two Monster energy drinks have filed a lawsuit against Monster Beverage Corporation in California.

"You only have to do a very few things right in your life so long as you don't do too many things wrong."

WARREN BUFFETT
1930–PRESENT
(AMERICAN BUSINESSMAN AND THE MOST SUCCESSFUL INVESTOR IN THE TWENTIETH CENTURY)

5-1 Product Liability

Those who make, sell, or lease goods can be held liable for physical harm or property damage caused by those goods to a consumer, user, or bystander. This is called **product liability.**

Product liability claims may be based on the tort theories of negligence, fraudulent misrepresentation, and strict liability. We look here at product liability based on negligence and misrepresentation.

5–1a Negligence

Chapter 4 defined *negligence* as the failure to exercise the degree of care that a reasonable, prudent person would have exercised under the circumstances. If a manufacturer fails to exercise "due care" to make a product safe, a person who is injured by the product may sue the manufacturer for negligence.

To what extent are energy drink manufacturers responsible for injuries to those who consume large amounts of their products?

Due Care Must Be Exercised The manufacturer must exercise due care in all of the following areas:

1. Designing the product.
2. Selecting the materials.
3. Using the appropriate production process.
4. Assembling and testing the product.
5. Placing adequate warnings on the label to inform the user of dangers of which an ordinary person might not be aware.
6. Inspecting and testing any purchased components used in the final product.

Privity of Contract Not Required A product liability action based on negligence does not require privity of contract between the injured plaintiff and the defendant manufacturer. **Privity of contract** refers to the relationship that exists between the promisor and the promisee of a contract. Privity is the reason that normally only the parties to a contract can enforce that contract.

In the context of product liability law, privity is not required. A person who is injured by a defective product can bring a negligence suit even though he or she was not the one who actually purchased the product—and thus is not in privity. A manufacturer is liable for its failure to exercise due care to *any person* who sustains an injury proximately caused by a negligently made (defective) product.

Relative to the long history of the common law, this exception to the privity requirement is a fairly recent development, dating to the early part of the twentieth century. A leading case in this respect is *MacPherson v. Buick Motor Co.,* which is presented as this chapter's *Landmark in the Law* feature.

Privity of Contract The relationship that exists between the promisor and the promisee of a contract.

5–1b Misrepresentation

When a user or consumer is injured as a result of a manufacturer's or seller's fraudulent misrepresentation, the basis of liability may be the tort of fraud. In this situation, the misrepresentation must have been made knowingly or with reckless disregard for the facts. The intentional mislabeling of packaged cosmetics, for instance, or the intentional concealment of a product's defects constitutes fraudulent misrepresentation.

The misrepresentation must be of a material fact, and the seller must have intended to induce the buyer's reliance on the misrepresentation. Misrepresentation on a label or advertisement is enough to show the intent to induce reliance. Of course, to bring a lawsuit on this ground, the buyer must have relied on the misrepresentation.

LANDMARK IN THE LAW   *MacPherson v. Buick Motor Co.* (1916)

In the landmark case of *MacPherson v. Buick Motor Co.,*[a] the New York Court of Appeals—New York's highest court—considered the liability of a manufacturer that had failed to exercise reasonable care in manufacturing a finished product.

CASE BACKGROUND Donald MacPherson suffered injuries while riding in a Buick automobile that suddenly collapsed because one of the wheels was made of defective wood. The spokes crumbled into fragments, throwing MacPherson out of the vehicle and injuring him.

MacPherson had purchased the car from a Buick dealer, but he brought a lawsuit against the manufacturer, Buick Motor Company. Buick itself had not made the wheel but

had bought it from another manufacturer. There was evidence, though, that the defects could have been discovered by a reasonable inspection by Buick and that no such inspection had taken place. MacPherson charged Buick with negligence for putting a human life in imminent danger.

THE ISSUE BEFORE THE COURT AND THE COURT'S RULING The primary issue was whether Buick owed a duty of care to anyone except the immediate purchaser of the car—that is, the Buick dealer. In deciding the issue, Justice Benjamin Cardozo stated that "if the nature of a thing is such that it is reasonably certain to place life and limb in peril when negligently made, it is then a thing of danger. . . . If to the element of danger there is added knowledge that the thing will be used by persons other than the purchaser, and used without new tests, then, irrespective of contract, the manufacturer of this thing of danger is under a duty to make it carefully."

The court concluded that "beyond all question, the nature of an automobile gives warning of probable danger if its construction is defective. This automobile was designed to go 50 miles an hour. Unless its wheels were sound and strong, injury was almost certain." Although Buick itself had not manufactured the wheel, the court held that Buick had a duty to inspect the wheels and that Buick "was responsible for the finished product." Therefore, Buick was liable to MacPherson for the injuries he sustained when he was thrown from the car.

APPLICATION TO TODAY'S WORLD *This landmark decision was a significant step in creating the legal environment of the modern world. As often happens, technological developments necessitated changes in the law. Today, automobile manufacturers are commonly held liable when their negligence causes automobile users to be injured.*

---
a. 217 N.Y. 382, 111 N.E. 1050 (1916).

5-2 Strict Product Liability

LEARNING OBJECTIVE 2
What public policy assumptions underlie strict product liability?

Under the doctrine of strict liability, people may be liable for the results of their acts regardless of their intentions or their exercise of reasonable care. In addition, liability does not depend on privity of contract. The injured party does not have to be the buyer or a *third party beneficiary* (one for whose benefit a contract is made). In the 1960s, courts applied the doctrine of strict liability in several landmark cases involving manufactured goods, and this doctrine has since become a common method of holding manufacturers liable.

5-2a Strict Product Liability and Public Policy

The law imposes strict product liability as a matter of public policy. This public policy rests on a threefold assumption:

1. Consumers should be protected against unsafe products.
2. Manufacturers and distributors should not escape liability for faulty products simply because they are not in privity of contract with the ultimate user of those products.
3. Manufacturers, sellers, and lessors of products are generally in a better position than consumers to bear the costs associated with injuries caused by their products—costs that they can ultimately pass on to all consumers in the form of higher prices.

Development of the Doctrine California was the first state to impose strict product liability in tort on manufacturers. **CASE EXAMPLE 5.1** William Greenman was injured when his Shopsmith combination power tool threw off a piece of wood that struck him in the head. He sued the manufacturer, claiming that he had followed the product instructions and that the product must be defective.

In a landmark decision, *Greenman v. Yuba Power Products, Inc.*,[1] the California Supreme Court set out the reason for applying tort law rather than contract law in cases involving consumers who were injured by defective products. According to the *Greenman* court, the "purpose of such liability is to [e]nsure that the costs of injuries resulting from defective products are borne by the manufacturers . . . rather than by the injured persons who are powerless to protect themselves." ■ Today, the majority of states recognize strict product liability, although some state courts limit its application to situations involving personal injuries (rather than property damage).

If a power tool is defective and injures a user, does the user sue under contract law or tort law?

Statement of Public Policy The public policy concerning strict product liability may be expressed in a statute or in the common law. Sometimes, public policy may be revealed in a court's interpretation of a statute, as in the following *Spotlight Case*.

---

1. 59 Cal.2d 57, 377 P.2d 897, 27 Cal.Rptr. 697 (1962).

SPOTLIGHT ON INJURIES FROM VACCINATIONS: CASE 5.1

Bruesewitz v. Wyeth, LLC

Supreme Court of the United States, 562 U.S. 223, 131 S.Ct. 1068, 179 L.Ed.2d 1 (2011).

FACTS When Hannah Bruesewitz was six months old, her pediatrician administered a dose of the diphtheria, tetanus, and pertussis (DTP) vaccine according to the Centers for Disease Control and Prevention's recommended childhood immunization schedule. Within twenty-four hours, Hannah began to experience seizures. She suffered more than one hundred seizures during the next month. Her doctors diagnosed her with "residual seizure disorder" and "developmental delay."

Hannah's parents, Russell and Robalee Bruesewitz, filed a claim for relief in the U.S. Court of Federal Claims under the National Childhood Vaccine Injury Act (NCVIA). The NCVIA set up a no-fault compensation program for persons injured by vaccines. The claim was denied. The Bruesewitzes then filed a suit in a Pennsylvania state court against Wyeth, LLC, the maker of the vaccine, alleging strict product liability. The suit was moved to a federal district court. The court held that the claim was preempted by the NCVIA, which includes provisions protecting manufacturers from liability for "a vaccine's unavoidable, adverse side effects." A federal appellate court affirmed the district court's judgment. The Bruesewitzes appealed to the United States Supreme Court.

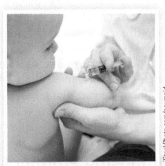

What happens when a vaccine causes adverse side effects?

ISSUE Was the Bruesewitzes' strict product liability claim against Wyeth for the injuries that their child suffered from vaccination preempted by the National Childhood Vaccine Injury Act?

DECISION Yes. The United States Supreme Court affirmed the lower court's judgment. The NCVIA preempted the Bruesewitzes' claim against Wyeth for injury to their daughter caused by the DTP vaccine's side effects.

REASON The Court reasoned that Congress enacted the NCVIA as a matter of public policy to stabilize the vaccine market and facilitate compensation. In the no-fault compensation program set up by the NCVIA, a person with a vaccine-related claim files a petition with the U.S. Court of Federal Claims. The court may award compensation for legal, medical, rehabilitation, counseling, special education, and vocational training expenses, as well as for diminished earning capacity, pain and suffering, and death. The awards are funded by a tax on the vaccine. In exchange for the "informal, efficient" compensation program, vaccine manufacturers that comply with the regulatory requirements are "immunized" from liability. The statute thus strikes a balance between paying victims harmed by vaccines and protecting the vaccine industry from collapsing under the costs of tort liability.

CRITICAL THINKING—Political Consideration *If the public wants to change the policy outlined in this case, which branch of the government—and at what level—should be lobbied to make the change? Explain.*

5–2b Requirements for Strict Product Liability

After the *Restatement (Second) of Torts* was issued in 1964, Section 402A became a widely accepted statement of how the doctrine of strict liability should be applied to sellers of goods. These sellers include manufacturers, processors, assemblers, packagers, bottlers, wholesalers, distributors, retailers, and lessors.

The bases for an action in strict liability that are set forth in Section 402A can be summarized as the following six requirements. Depending on the jurisdiction, if these requirements are met, a manufacturer's liability to an injured party can be almost unlimited.

1. The product must have been in a *defective condition* when the defendant sold it.
2. The defendant must normally be engaged in the *business of selling* (or otherwise distributing) that product.
3. The product must be *unreasonably dangerous* to the user or consumer because of its defective condition (in most states).
4. The plaintiff must incur *physical harm* to self or property by use or consumption of the product.
5. The defective condition must be the *proximate cause* of the injury or damage.
6. The *goods must not have been substantially changed* from the time the product was sold to the time the injury was sustained.

Proving a Defective Condition   Under these requirements, in any action against a manufacturer, seller, or lessor, the plaintiff does not have to show why or how the product became defective. The plaintiff does, however, have to prove that the product was defective at the time it left the seller or lessor and that this defective condition made it "unreasonably dangerous" to the user or consumer. (See this chapter's *Beyond Our Borders* feature for a discussion of how foreign suppliers were held liable for defective goods sold in the United States.)

Unless evidence can be presented that will support the conclusion that the product was defective when it was sold or leased, the plaintiff normally will not succeed. If the product was delivered in a safe condition and subsequent mishandling made it harmful to the user, the seller or lessor usually is not strictly liable.

Does a person injured by a defective air bag have to prove that it was defective when the car was manufactured?

iStockPhoto.com/nikkytok

BEYOND OUR BORDERS

Imposing Product Liability as Far Away as China

U.S. builders began using Chinese drywall in the construction of houses in 2003. By 2007, thousands of homes had been constructed with this product in Alabama, Florida, Louisiana, Mississippi, and a few other states. There was a problem, though—use of the Chinese drywall caused blackening and pitting of electrical wires. Homeowners began to notice an odor similar to rotten eggs in their houses. Air-conditioning units started failing, as did ceiling fans, alarm systems, refrigerators, and other appliances.

Numerous lawsuits were filed against the Chinese drywall manufacturers. The companies initially fought the claims but decided to settle when the number of lawsuits ran into the thousands. The estimated value of the settlement is between $800 million and $1 billion. It includes an uncapped fund to pay for repairs to about 4,500 homes and a separate fund capped at $30 million that will be used to pay for health problems stemming from the defective drywall.

CRITICAL THINKING

- Could U.S. companies that sold Chinese drywall to consumers also be held liable for damages? Why or why not?

Unreasonably Dangerous Products The *Restatement* recognizes that many products cannot possibly be made entirely safe for all uses. Thus, sellers or lessors of these products are held liable only when the products are *unreasonably* dangerous. A court may consider a product so defective as to be an **unreasonably dangerous product** in either of the following situations.

1. The product is dangerous beyond the expectation of the ordinary consumer.

2. A less dangerous alternative was economically feasible for the manufacturer, but the manufacturer failed to produce it.

As will be discussed next, a product may be unreasonably dangerous due to a design or manufacturing flaw or due to an inadequate warning.

If this Chinese-made drywall adversely affects electrical wiring, who has legal liability?

5-2c Product Defects—Restatement (Third) of Torts

The *Restatement (Third) of Torts: Products Liability* defines the three types of product defects that have traditionally been recognized in product liability law—manufacturing defects, design defects, and inadequate warnings.

Manufacturing Defects According to Section 2(a) of the *Restatement (Third) of Torts: Products Liability,* a product "contains a manufacturing defect when the product departs from its intended design even though all possible care was exercised in the preparation and marketing of the product." Basically, a manufacturing defect is a departure from design specifications that results in products that are physically flawed, damaged, or incorrectly assembled. A glass bottle that is made too thin, causing it to explode in a consumer's face, is an example of a product with a manufacturing defect.

Encouraging Higher Standards. Usually, manufacturing defects occur when a manufacturer fails to assemble, test, or check the quality of a product adequately. In fact, the idea behind holding defendants strictly liable for manufacturing defects is to encourage greater investment in product safety and stringent quality control standards.

Note that liability is imposed on a manufacturer (and on the wholesaler and retailer) regardless of whether the manufacturer's quality control efforts were "reasonable." For more information on how effective quality control procedures can help businesses reduce their potential legal liability for defective products, see the *Linking Business Law to Corporate Management* feature at the end of this chapter.

The Role of Expert Testimony. Cases involving allegations of a manufacturing defect are often decided based on the opinions and testimony of experts. **CASE EXAMPLE 5.2** Kevin Schmude purchased an eight-foot stepladder and used it to install radio-frequency shielding in a hospital room. While Schmude was standing on the ladder, it collapsed, and he was seriously injured. He filed a lawsuit against the ladder's maker, Tricam Industries, Inc., based on a manufacturing defect.

Experts testified that when the ladder was assembled during manufacturing, the preexisting holes in the top cap did not properly line up with the holes in the rear right rail and backing plate. As a result of the misalignment, the rear legs of the ladder were not securely fastened in place, causing the ladder to fail. A jury concluded that this manufacturing defect made the ladder unreasonably dangerous and awarded Schmude more than $677,000 in damages.[2] ◼

Unreasonably Dangerous Product A product that is so defective that it is dangerous beyond the expectation of an ordinary consumer or a product for which a less dangerous alternative was feasible but the manufacturer failed to produce it.

LEARNING OBJECTIVE 4
What are three types of product defects?

---

2. *Schmude v. Tricam Industries, Inc.,* 550 F.Supp.2d 846 (E.D.Wis. 2008).

Design Defects

Unlike a product with a manufacturing defect, a product with a design defect is made in conformity with the manufacturer's design specifications. Nevertheless, it results in injury to the user because the design itself is flawed. The product's design creates an unreasonable risk to the user. A product "is defective in design when the foreseeable risks of harm posed by the product could have been reduced or avoided by the adoption of a reasonable alternative design by the seller or other distributor, or a predecessor in the commercial chain of distribution, and the omission of the alternative design renders the product not reasonably safe."[3]

Test for Design Defects. To successfully assert a design defect, a plaintiff has to show that:

1. A reasonable alternative design was available.

2. As a result of the defendant's failure to adopt the alternative design, the product was not reasonably safe.

In other words, a manufacturer or other defendant is liable only when the harm was reasonably preventable.

CASE EXAMPLE 5.3 After Gillespie cut off several of his fingers while operating a table saw, he filed a lawsuit against the maker of the saw. Gillespie alleged that the blade guards on the saw were defectively designed. At trial, however, an expert testified that the alternative design for blade guards used for table saws could not have been used for the particular cut that Gillespie was performing at the time he was injured. The court found that Gillespie's claim must fail because there was no proof that the "better" design of guard would have prevented his injury.[4]

ETHICAL ISSUE

Is showing that a Taser caused the death of a victim sufficient under the doctrine of strict liability?

Can a Taser be considered unreasonably dangerous as designed? Taser International, Inc., located in Scottsdale, Arizona, provides nonlethal devices that police personnel can use to "stun" aggressors. When officer Jeremy Baird of the Moberly, Missouri, Police Department used a Taser device after a routine traffic stop, the victim fell to the ground, lost consciousness, and died two hours later. The victim's mother sued the city of Moberly and several police officers. That case was settled for $2.4 million.

The victim's mother then sued Taser International. The claim was that the company did not provide adequate warnings that using the device directly on the chest could lead to cardiac arrest. The lawsuit also argued that the Taser was defectively designed. A federal trial court dismissed the case.

On appeal, the reviewing court pointed out that the plaintiff would have had to prove that additional warnings on the use of the Taser "would have altered the behavior of the officers involved in the incident." But, concluded the court, there was "no dispute on this record that Officer Baird would not have read any additional warning Taser may have added about the cardiac danger" of its device. As to the defective design claim, the court noted that "under strict liability, a manufacturer is not intended to be an ensurer of any and all injuries caused by its products."[5] Just showing a link between the use of the Taser and the victim's injury was insufficient to establish strict liability.

Factors to Be Considered. According to the Official Comments accompanying the *Restatement (Third) of Torts*, a court can consider a broad range of factors in deciding claims of design defects. These factors include the magnitude and probability of the foreseeable risks, as well

---

3. *Restatement (Third) of Torts: Products Liability*, Section 2(b).
4. *Gillespie v. Sears, Roebuck & Co.*, 386 F.3d 21 (1st Cir. 2004).
5. *Bachtel v. Taser International, Inc.*, 747 F.3d 967 (2014). In contrast, see *Fontenot v. Taser International, Inc.*, 736 F.3d 318 (4th Cir. 2013).

as the relative advantages and disadvantages of the product as it was designed and as it alternatively could have been designed.

CASE EXAMPLE 5.4 Jodie Bullock smoked cigarettes manufactured by Philip Morris for forty-five years. When she was diagnosed with lung cancer, Bullock brought a product liability suit against Philip Morris. She presented evidence that by the late 1950s, scientists had proved that smoking caused lung cancer. Nonetheless, Philip Morris had publicly announced that there was no proof that smoking caused cancer and that "numerous scientists" questioned "the validity of the statistics."

At trial, the judge instructed the jury to consider the gravity of the danger posed by the design, as well as the likelihood that the danger would cause injury. The jury found that there was a defect in the design of the cigarettes and that they had been negligently designed, and awarded Bullock damages. A reviewing court affirmed the jury's verdict on appeal.[6] ■

Risk-Utility Analysis. Most courts engage in a risk-utility analysis, determining whether the risk of harm from the product as designed outweighs its utility to the user and to the public. The court in the following case reviewed whether the plaintiff had satisfied the risk-utility test.

---

6. *Bullock v. Philip Morris USA, Inc.,* 159 Cal.App.4th 655, 71 Cal.Rptr.3d 775 (2008). The California Court of Appeal subsequently upheld a punitive damages award of $13.8 million. See *Bullock v. Philip Morris USA, Inc.,* 198 Cal.App.4th 543, 131 Cal.Rptr.3d 382 (2011).

CASE 5.2

Riley v. Ford Motor Co.

Court of Appeals of South Carolina, 408 S.C. 1, 757 S.E.2d 422 (2014).

FACTS Jasper County Sheriff Benjamin Riley was driving his Ford F-150 pickup truck near Ehrhardt, South Carolina, when it collided with another vehicle. The impact caused Riley's truck to leave the road and roll over. The driver's door of the truck opened in the collision, and Riley was ejected and killed.

Riley's widow, Laura, as the representative of his estate, filed a product liability suit in a South Carolina state court against Ford Motor Company. The plaintiff alleged that the design of the door-latch system of the truck allowed the door to open in the collision. The court awarded the estate $900,000 in damages "because of the stature of Riley and what he's done in life, what he's contributed to his family." Ford appealed, arguing that the plaintiff had not proved the existence of a reasonable alternative design.

ISSUE Did the plaintiff prove the existence of a reasonable alternative design?

DECISION Yes. A state intermediate appellate court affirmed the lower court's ruling. Evidence showed that Ford knew of a reasonable alternative design for the truck's door-latch system. Ford was aware

How can a plaintiff prove that a truck's door latch was defectively designed?

Mark Scheuern/Alamy

of the safety problems presented by the current system (a rod-linkage system). After conducting a risk-utility analysis of a different system (a cable-linkage system), Ford had concluded that the alternative system was a "feasible, if not superior, alternative."

REASON To meet the risk-utility test, a plaintiff must show a reasonable alternative design for the product at issue. This involves showing that the manufacturer, after weighing costs and benefits, decided to use one design instead of another. In this case, the plaintiff presented evidence of Ford's own design for a cable-linkage door-latch system, which the manufacturer had used in earlier F-150 trucks. According to studies conducted by Ford, cable systems have several advantages over rod systems—"cable systems are easier for assembly plants to handle," "reduce cost and reduce operator dependence," "reduce complexity in service," and "are more robust to crash." The only disadvantage is that cable systems cost more than rod systems.

CRITICAL THINKING—Legal Environment Consideration *By what means did the plaintiff most likely discover the defendant's studies of an alternative design for the door-latch system?*

Consumer-Expectation Test. Instead of the risk-utility test, some courts apply the consumer-expectation test to determine whether a product's design was defective. Under this test, a product is unreasonably dangerous when it fails to perform in the manner that would reasonably be expected by an ordinary consumer.

CASE EXAMPLE 5.5 A representative from Wilson Sporting Goods Company gave Edwin Hickox an umpire's mask that was designed to be safer than other umpire's masks. The mask had a newly designed throat guard that angled forward instead of extending straight down. While Hickox was working as an umpire during a game and wearing the mask, he was was struck by a foul ball and injured. He suffered a concussion and damage to his inner ear, which caused permanent hearing loss. Hickox and his wife sued the manufacturer for product liability based on a defective design and won. A jury awarded $750,000 to Hickox and $25,000 to his wife. Wilson appealed.

The reviewing court affirmed the jury's verdict. The design was defective because "an ordinary consumer would have expected the mask to perform more safely than it did." The evidence presented to the jury had shown that Wilson's mask was more dangerous than comparable masks sold at the time. The new "masks could concentrate energy at the point of impact, rather than distribute energy evenly throughout the padded area of the mask," as an ordinary consumer would have expected a baseball mask to do.[7]

When is an umpire's mask defectively designed under the consumer-expectation test?

Inadequate Warnings A product may also be deemed defective because of inadequate instructions or warnings. A product will be considered defective "when the foreseeable risks of harm posed by the product could have been reduced or avoided by the provision of reasonable instructions or warnings by the seller or other distributor, or a predecessor in the commercial chain of distribution, and the omission of the instructions or warnings renders the product not reasonably safe."[8] Generally, a seller must also warn consumers of the harm that can result from the *foreseeable misuse* of its product.

Content of Warnings. Important factors for a court to consider include the risks of a product, the "content and comprehensibility" and "intensity of expression" of warnings and instructions, and the "characteristics of expected user groups."[9] Courts apply a "reasonableness" test to determine if the warnings adequately alert consumers to the product's risks. For instance, children will likely respond more readily to bright, bold, simple warning labels, while educated adults might need more detailed information. For more on tips on making sure a product's warnings are adequate, see this chapter's *Managerial Strategy* feature.

CASE EXAMPLE 5.6 Jeffrey Johnson was taken to the emergency room for an episode of atrial fibrillation, a heart rhythm disorder. Dr. David Hahn used a defibrillator manufactured by Medtronic, Inc., to deliver electric shocks to Johnson's heart. The defibrillator had synchronous and asynchronous modes, and it reverted to the asynchronous mode after each use. Hahn intended to deliver synchronized shocks, which required him to select the synchronous mode for each shock. Hahn did not read the device's instructions, which Medtronic had provided both in a manual and on the device itself. As a result, he delivered one synchronized shock, followed by twelve asynchronous shocks that endangered Johnson's life.

Johnson and his wife filed a product liability suit against Medtronic asserting that Medtronic had provided inadequate warnings about the defibrillator and that the device had a design defect. A Missouri appellate court held that the Johnsons could not pursue a claim based on the inadequacy of Medtronic's warnings, but they could pursue a claim alleging a design defect. The court reasoned that in some cases, "a manufacturer may be held liable

---

7. *Wilson Sporting Goods Co. v. Hickox,* 59 A.3d 1267 (D.C.App. 2013).
8. *Restatement (Third) of Torts: Products Liability,* Section 2(c).
9. *Restatement (Third) of Torts: Products Liability,* Section 2, Comment h.

iStockPhoto.com/StushD90

where it chooses to warn of the danger . . . rather than preclude the danger by design."[10]

Obvious Risks. There is no duty to warn about risks that are obvious or commonly known. Warnings about such risks do not add to the safety of a product and could even detract from it by making other warnings seem less significant. As will be discussed later in this chapter, the obviousness of a risk and a user's decision to proceed in the face of that risk may be a defense in a product liability suit based on an inadequate warning.

---

10. *Johnson v. Medtronic, Inc.*, 365 S.W.3d 226 (Mo.App. 2012).

When a physician misuses a defibrillator manufactured by Medtronic without reading its warning label, is Medtronic liable for inadequate warnings?

MANAGERIAL STRATEGY — When Is a Warning Legally Bulletproof?

Management Faces a Legal Issue

A company can develop and sell a perfectly manufactured and designed product, yet still face product liability lawsuits for defective warnings. A product may be defective because of inadequate instructions or warnings when the foreseeable risks of harm posed by the product could have been reduced by reasonable warnings offered by the seller or other distributor. Manufacturers and distributors have a duty to warn users of any hidden dangers of their products. Additionally, they have a duty to instruct users in how to use the product to avoid any dangers. Warnings generally must be clear and specific. They must also be conspicuous.

Not all manufacturers have to provide warnings, as pointed out in the text. People are expected to know that knives can cut fingers, for example, so a seller need not place a bright orange label on each knife sold reminding consumers of this danger. Most household products are generally safe when used as intended.

What the Courts Say

In a 2014 New Jersey case, an appeals court reviewed a product liability case against the manufacturer of a Razor A–type kick scooter. A ten-year-old boy was injured when he fell and struck his face on the scooter's handlebars. The padded end caps on the handlebars had deteriorated, and the boy's mother had thrown them away, exposing the handlebars' metal ends.

The boy and his mother sued, claiming that the manufacturer was required to provide a warning to prevent injuries of this type. The appellate court noted, however, that the plaintiffs were not able to claim that the Razor A was defective. "Lacking evidence that Razor A's end-cap design was defective, plaintiffs cannot show that Razor A had a duty to warn of such a defect, and therefore cannot make out their failure to warn claim."[a]

In another 2014 case, a woman suffered neurological disorders after taking a generic drug to treat her gastroesophageal reflux disease. Part of her complaint asserted strict liability for failure to warn. The plaintiff claimed that the manufacturer had not updated its label to indicate that usage should not exceed twelve weeks. The reviewing court reasoned that "The adequacy of the instructions . . . made no difference to the outcome . . . because [the plaintiff alleges that her prescribing physician] did not read those materials."[b]

In contrast, in a 2013 Massachusetts case, a family was awarded over $63 million in a lawsuit against Johnson & Johnson for defective warnings on bottles of children's Motrin. A seven-year-old girl lost 70 percent of her skin, experienced brain damage, and went blind after suffering a reaction to the drug. The drug did have a specific warning label that instructed consumers to stop taking the medication and contact a physician in the event of an allergic reaction. Nonetheless, Johnson & Johnson was found liable for failing to warn about the known risk of severe side effects.

MANAGERIAL IMPLICATIONS

Managers must be aware that whenever a product presents a danger, a warning is required. The seller, though, must know about the danger for the warning to be obligatory. In addition, the danger must not be obvious to a reasonable user. Here is where a manager's task may become difficult, because it is not always clear what would be obvious to a "reasonable user."

When product warnings are supplied, they must be obvious and easy to understand. Here, one issue to be considered is that of warning non-English-speaking users. Some manufacturers publish warnings in foreign languages and also use symbols to indicate dangers. One downside of excessive safety warnings is that so many warnings may be attached to a product that few consumers will bother to read any of them.

---

a. *Vann v. Toys R Us*, N.J.Super.A.D., 2014 WL3537937 (N.J.Sup. A.D. 2014).
b. *Brinkley v. Pfizer, Inc.*, 772 F.3d 1133 (8th Cir. 2014).

How many and what types of warnings against doing back flips on this trampoline must be affixed to eliminate the manufacturer's liability?

CASE EXAMPLE 5.7 Sixteen-year-old Gary Crosswhite failed in an attempt to do a back flip on a trampoline and was paralyzed as a result. The manufacturer had provided nine warning labels affixed to the trampoline, an instruction manual with safety warnings, and a placard to be attached to the entry ladder. Each advised users not to do flips on the trampoline. Crosswhite sued the manufacturer for inadequate warnings. The court found that the warnings were sufficient to make the risks obvious and insulate the manufacturer from liability for Crosswhite's injuries.[11]

Risks that may seem obvious to some users will not be obvious to all users. This is a particular problem when users are likely to be children. A young child may not be able to read or understand warning labels or comprehend the risk of certain activities. To avoid liability, the manufacturer would have to prove that the warnings it provided were adequate to make the risk of injury obvious to a young child.

State Laws and Constitutionality. An action alleging that a product is defective due to an inadequate label can be based on state law, but that law must not violate the U.S. Constitution. **CASE EXAMPLE 5.8** California once enacted a law imposing restrictions and a labeling requirement on the sale or rental of "violent video games" to minors. Although the video game industry had adopted a voluntary rating system for games, the legislators deemed those labels inadequate. The Video Software Dealers Association and the Entertainment Software Association immediately filed a suit in federal court to invalidate the law, and the law was struck down. The court found that the definition of a violent video game in California's law was unconstitutionally vague and violated the First Amendment's guarantee of freedom of speech.[12]

5–2d Market-Share Liability

Generally, in cases involving product liability, a plaintiff must prove that the defective product that caused her or his injury was made by a specific defendant. In a few situations, however, courts have dropped this requirement when a plaintiff cannot prove which of many distributors of a harmful product supplied the particular product that caused the injury. Under a theory of **market-share liability,** a court can hold each manufacturer responsible for a percentage of the plaintiff's damages that is equal to the percentage of its market share.

CASE EXAMPLE 5.9 Suffolk County Water Authority (SWCA) is a municipal water supplier in Suffolk County, New York. SWCA discovered the presence of a toxic chemical, perchlorethylene (PCE), used by dry cleaners and others in its local water. SWCA filed a product liability lawsuit against Dow Chemical Corporation and other companies that manufactured and distributed PCE. Dow filed a motion to dismiss the case for failure to state a claim, since SWCA could not identify each defendant whose allegedly defective product caused the water contamination.

A state trial court refused to dismiss the action, holding that SWCA's allegations were sufficient to invoke market-share liability. Under market-share liability, the burden of identification shifts to defendants if the plaintiff establishes a *prima facie* case on every element of the claim except identification of the specific defendant. (A *prima facie* case is one in which the plaintiff has presented sufficient evidence for the claim to go forward.)[13]

Courts in many jurisdictions do not recognize market-share liability, believing that it deviates too significantly from traditional legal principles. Jurisdictions that do recognize this theory of liability apply it only when it is difficult or impossible to determine which company made a particular product.

Market-Share Liability
A theory under which liability is shared among all firms that manufactured and distributed a particular product during a certain period of time. This form of liability sharing is used only when the specific source of the harmful product is unidentifiable.

---

11. *Crosswhite v. Jumpking, Inc.,* 411 F.Supp.2d 1228 (D.Or. 2006).

12. *Video Software Dealers Association v. Schwarzenegger,* 556 F.3d 950 (9th Cir. 2009); *Brown v. Entertainment Merchants Association,* __ U.S. __, 131 S.Ct. 2729, 180 L.Ed.2d 708 (2011).

13. *Suffolk County Water Authority v. Dow Chemical Co.,* 44 Misc.3d 569, 987 N.Y.S.2d 819 (N.Y.Sup. 2014).

5–2e Other Applications of Strict Liability

Almost all courts extend the strict liability of manufacturers and other sellers to injured bystanders. **EXAMPLE 5.10** A forklift that Trent is operating will not go into reverse, and as a result, it runs into a bystander. In this situation, the bystander can sue the manufacturer of the defective forklift under strict liability (and possibly bring a negligence action against the forklift operator as well). ■

Strict liability also applies to suppliers of component parts. **EXAMPLE 5.11** Toyota buys brake pads from a subcontractor and puts them in Corollas without changing their composition. If those pads are defective, both the supplier of the brake pads and Toyota will be held strictly liable for injuries caused by the defects. ■

5–3 Defenses to Product Liability

Defendants in product liability suits can raise a number of defenses. One defense, of course, is to show that there is no basis for the plaintiff's claim. For instance, in a product liability case based on negligence, if a defendant can show that the plaintiff has not met the requirements (such as causation) for an action in negligence, generally the defendant will not be liable. A defendant may also assert that the *statute of limitations* for a product liability claim has lapsed.[14]

In a case involving strict product liability, a defendant can claim that the plaintiff failed to meet one of the requirements. If the defendant establishes that goods were altered after they were sold, for instance, the defendant normally will not be held liable.

In the following case, a product's safety switch had been disabled before the plaintiff used the product.

---

14. Similar state statutes, called *statutes of repose*, place outer time limits on product liability actions.

CASE 5.3

Verost v. Mitsubishi Caterpillar Forklift America, Inc.

New York Supreme Court, Appellate Division, Fourth Department, 124 A.D.3d 1219, 1 N.Y.S.3d 589 (2015).

FACTS Drew Verost was employed at a manufacturing facility in Buffalo, New York, owned by Nuttall Gear, LLC. While operating a forklift at Nuttall's facility, Verost climbed out of the seat and attempted to engage a lever on the vehicle. As he stood on the front of the forklift and reached for the lever with his hand, he inadvertently stepped on the vehicle's gearshift. The activated gears caused part of the forklift to move backward, injuring Verost. He filed a suit in a New York state court against the forklift's maker, Mitsubishi Caterpillar Forklift America, Inc., and others, asserting claims in product liability. The defendants established that the vehicle had been manufactured with a safety switch that would have prevented the accident had it not been disabled after delivery to Nuttall. The court issued a summary judgment in the defendants' favor. Verost appealed.

Under what circumstances can a forklift manufacturer avoid product liability?

iStockPhoto.com/SimplyCreative Photography

ISSUE Is the modification of a product after its sale an effective defense against a claim of product liability?

DECISION Yes. The state intermediate appellate court affirmed the lower court's judgment in the product liability defendants' favor. To succeed in an action based on product liability, the goods at issue must not have been substantially changed from the time the product was sold to the time the injury was sustained.

REASON The forklift was made by Mitsubishi and sold new to Nuttall by Buffalo Lift Trucks, Inc., and Mullen Industrial Handling Corporation. The forklift had been made and delivered to Nuttall with a safety switch to render it inoperable if an operator was not in the driver's seat. At the time of Verost's accident, however, someone—"a third party"—had

Continues

intentionally disabled the safety switch so that the forklift still had power when the operator was not in the driver's seat. Seven of Nuttall's ten forklifts had disabled safety switches. Verost had asserted causes of action in product liability against Mitsubishi, Buffalo Lift, and Mullen. The appellate court concluded that the lower court had properly issued judgment in these defendants' favor. "A manufacturer, who has designed and produced a safe product, will not be liable for injuries resulting from substantial alterations or modifications of the product by a third party which render the product defective or otherwise unsafe."

CRITICAL THINKING—Legal Consideration *Could Verost succeed in an action against Nuttall alleging that the company's failure to maintain the forklift in a safe condition constituted negligence? Discuss.*

5–3a Preemption

LEARNING OBJECTIVE 5
What defenses to liability can be raised in a product liability lawsuit?

A defense that has been successfully raised by defendants in recent years is preemption—that government regulations preempt claims for product liability (see *Spotlight Case 5.1*, for example). An injured party may not be able to sue a manufacturer of defective products that are subject to comprehensive federal regulatory schemes.

Medical devices, for instance, are subject to extensive government regulation and undergo a rigorous premarket approval process. **CASE EXAMPLE 5.12** The United States Supreme Court decided in *Riegel v. Medtronic, Inc.*, that a man who was injured by an approved medical device (a balloon catheter) could not sue its maker for product liability. The Court reasoned that Congress had created a comprehensive scheme of federal safety oversight for medical devices. The U.S. Food and Drug Administration is required to review the design, labeling, and manufacturing of medical devices before they are marketed to make sure that they are safe and effective. Because premarket approval is a "rigorous process," it preempts all common law claims challenging the safety or effectiveness of a medical device that has been approved.[15]

Since the *Medtronic* decision, some courts have extended the preemption defense to other product liability actions. Other courts have been unwilling to deny an injured party relief simply because the federal government was supposed to ensure the product's safety.[16] Even the United States Supreme Court refused to extend the preemption defense to preclude a drug maker's liability in one subsequent case.[17]

5–3b Assumption of Risk

Under what circumstances can a tanning salon customer sue for injuries even though she or he signed a release?

Assumption of risk can sometimes be used as a defense in a product liability action. To establish such a defense, the defendant must show that (1) the plaintiff knew and appreciated the risk created by the product defect and (2) the plaintiff voluntarily assumed the risk, even though it was unreasonable to do so. (See Chapter 4 for a more detailed discussion of assumption of risk.)

Although assumption of the risk is a defense in product liability actions, some courts do not allow it to be used as a defense to strict product liability claims. **CASE EXAMPLE 5.13** When Savannah Boles became a customer of Executive Tans, she signed a contract. One clause stated that signers used the company's tanning booths at their own risk. It also released the manufacturer and others from liability for any injuries. Later, Boles's fingers were partially amputated when they came into contact with a tanning booth's fan. Boles sued the manufacturer, claiming strict product liability. The Colorado Supreme Court held that assumption of risk was not applicable because strict product liability is driven by public-policy considerations. The theory focuses on the nature of the product rather than the conduct of either the manufacturer or the person injured.[18]

15. *Riegel v. Medtronic, Inc.*, 552 U.S. 312, 128 S.Ct. 999, 169 L.Ed.2d 892 (2008).
16. See, for example, *McGuan v. Endovascular Technologies, Inc.*, 182 Cal.App.4th 974, 106 Cal.Rptr.3d 277 (2010), and *Paduano v. American Honda Motor Co.*, 169 Cal.App.4th 1453, 88 Cal.Rptr.3d 90 (2009).
17. *Wyeth v. Levine*, 555 U.S. 555, 129 S.Ct. 1187, 173 L.Ed.2d 51 (2009).
18. *Boles v. Sun Ergoline, Inc.*, 223 P.3d 724 (Co.Sup.Ct. 2010).

5-3c Product Misuse

Similar to the defense of voluntary assumption of risk is that of product misuse, which occurs when a product is used for a purpose for which it was not intended. The courts have severely limited this defense. Today, product misuse is recognized as a defense *only when the particular use was not reasonably foreseeable*. If the misuse is foreseeable, the seller must take measures to guard against it.

CASE EXAMPLE 5.14 David Stults developed "popcorn lung" (bronchiolitis obliterans) from consuming multiple bags of microwave popcorn daily for several years. When he filed suit against the manufacturers of the popcorn and butter flavorings, the defendants asked the court for a summary judgment in their favor. The court denied defendants' motion and found that a manufacturer has a duty to warn of dangers associated with reasonably foreseeable misuses of a product. If it is foreseeable that a person might consume several bags of the popcorn a day, then the manufacturer might have to warn users about the potential health risks associated with doing so.[19] ▪

5-3d Comparative Negligence (Fault)

Developments in the area of comparative negligence, or fault (discussed in the torts chapter), have also affected the doctrine of strict liability. Today, courts in many jurisdictions consider the negligent or intentional actions of both the plaintiff and the defendant when apportioning liability and awarding damages. A defendant may be able to limit at least some liability for injuries caused by a defective product if it can show that the plaintiff's misuse of the product contributed to the injuries.

When proved, comparative negligence differs from other defenses in that it does not completely absolve the defendant of liability. It can, however, reduce the amount of damages that will be awarded to the plaintiff. Note that some jurisdictions allow only intentional conduct to affect a plaintiff's recovery, whereas others allow ordinary negligence to be used as a defense to product liability.

CASE EXAMPLE 5.15 Dan Smith, a mechanic, was not wearing a hard hat at work when he was asked to start the diesel engine of an air compressor. Because the compressor was an older model, he had to prop open a door to start it. When the engine started, the door fell from its position and hit Smith's head. The injury caused him to suffer from seizures. Smith sued the manufacturer, claiming that the engine was defectively designed. The manufacturer contended that Smith had been negligent by failing to wear a hard hat and propping open the door in an unsafe manner. Smith argued that ordinary negligence could not be used as a defense in product liability cases. The court ruled that defendants can use the plaintiff's ordinary negligence to reduce their liability proportionately.[20] ▪

5-3e Commonly Known Dangers

As mentioned, the dangers associated with certain products (such as sharp knives and guns) are so commonly known that manufacturers need not warn users of those dangers. If a defendant succeeds in convincing the court that a plaintiff's injury resulted from a *commonly known danger,* the defendant normally will not be liable.

CASE EXAMPLE 5.16 In a classic example from 1957, Marguerite Jamieson was injured when an elastic exercise rope slipped off her foot and struck her in the eye, causing a detachment of the retina. Jamieson claimed that the manufacturer should be liable because it had failed to warn users that the exerciser might slip off a foot in such a manner.

---

19. *Stults v. International Flavors and Fragrances, Inc.,* 31 F.Supp.3d 1015 (N.D. Iowa 2014).
20. *Smith v. Ingersoll-Rand Co.,* 14 P.3d 990 (Alaska 2000). See also *Winschel v. Brown*, 171 P.3d 142 (Alaska 2007).

The court stated that to hold the manufacturer liable in these circumstances "would go beyond the reasonable dictates of justice in fixing the liabilities of manufacturers." After all, stated the court, "almost every physical object can be inherently dangerous or potentially dangerous in a sense. . . . A manufacturer cannot manufacture a knife that will not cut or a hammer that will not mash a thumb or a stove that will not burn a finger. The law does not require [manufacturers] to warn of such common dangers."[21]

5–3f Knowledgeable User

A related defense is the *knowledgeable user* defense. If a particular danger (such as electrical shock) is or should be commonly known by particular users of the product (such as electricians), the manufacturer of electrical equipment need not warn these users of the danger.

CASE EXAMPLE 5.17 The parents of a group of teenagers who had become overweight and developed health problems filed a product liability lawsuit against McDonald's. The plaintiffs claimed that the well-known fast-food chain should be held liable for failing to warn customers of the adverse health effects of eating its food products. The court rejected this claim, however, based on the knowledgeable user defense.

According to the court, it is well known that the food at McDonald's contains high levels of cholesterol, fat, salt, and sugar and is therefore unhealthful. The court's opinion, which thwarted numerous future lawsuits against fast-food restaurants, stated: "If consumers know (or reasonably should know) the potential ill health effects of eating at McDonald's, they cannot blame McDonald's if they, nonetheless, choose to satiate [satisfy] their appetite with a surfeit [excess] of supersized McDonald's products."[22]

5–3g Statutes of Limitations and Repose

Tolling Temporary suspension of the running of a prescribed time period, such as a statute of limitations.

Statute of Repose A statute that places outer time limits on product liability actions. Such statutes cut off absolutely the right to bring an action after a specified period of time following some event (often the product's manufacture or purchase) other than the occurrence of an injury.

As mentioned previously, statutes of limitations restrict the time within which an action may be brought. The statute of limitations for product liability cases varies according to state law. Usually, the injured party must bring a product liability claim within two to four years. Often, the running of the prescribed period is **tolled** (that is, suspended) until the party suffering an injury has discovered it or should have discovered it.

To ensure that sellers and manufacturers will not be left vulnerable to lawsuits indefinitely, many states have passed **statutes of repose**, which place outer time limits on product liability actions. For instance, a statute of repose may require that claims be brought within twelve years from the date of sale or manufacture of the defective product. If the plaintiff does not bring an action before the prescribed period expires, the seller cannot be held liable.

---

21. *Jamieson v. Woodward & Lothrop*, 247 F.2d 23, 101 D.C.App. 32 (1957).
22. *Pelman v. McDonald's Corp.*, 237 F.Supp.2d 512 (S.D.N.Y. 2003).

Reviewing . . . Product Liability

Shalene Kolchek bought a Great Lakes Spa from Val Porter, a dealer who was selling spas at the state fair. After Kolchek signed the contract, Porter handed her the manufacturer's paperwork and arranged for the spa to be delivered and installed for her. Three months later, Kolchek left her six-year-old daughter, Litisha, alone in the spa. While exploring the spa's hydromassage jets, Litisha got her index finger stuck in one of the jet holes.

Litisha yanked hard, injuring her finger, and then panicked and screamed for help. Kolchek was unable to remove Litisha's finger, and the local police and rescue team were called to assist. After a three-hour operation that included draining the spa, sawing out a section of the spa's plastic molding, and slicing the jet casing, Litisha's finger was freed. Following this procedure, the spa was no longer functional. Litisha was taken to the local emergency room, where she was told that a bone in her finger was broken in two places. Using the information presented in the chapter, answer the following questions.

1. Under which theories of product liability can Kolchek sue Porter to recover for Litisha's injuries?

2. Would privity of contract be required for Kolchek to succeed in a product liability action against Great Lakes? Explain.

3. For an action in strict product liability against Great Lakes, what six requirements must Kolchek meet?

4. What defenses to product liability might Porter or Great Lakes be able to assert?

DEBATE THIS

- All liability suits against tobacco companies for causing lung cancer should be thrown out of court now and forever.

LINKING BUSINESS LAW TO CORPORATE MANAGEMENT
Quality Control

In this chapter, you learned that manufacturing and design defects can give rise to liability. Although it is possible to minimize liability through various defenses to product liability claims, all businesspersons know that such defenses do not necessarily fend off expensive lawsuits.

The legal issues surrounding product liability relate directly to quality control. As all of your management courses will emphasize, quality control is a major issue facing managers in every organization. Companies that have cost-effective quality control systems produce products with fewer manufacturing and design defects. As a result, these companies incur fewer potential and actual product liability lawsuits.

Three Types of Quality Control

Most management systems involve three types of quality control—preventive, concurrent, and feedback. They apply at different stages of the manufacturing process: preventive quality control occurs before the process begins, concurrent control takes place during the process, and feedback control occurs after it is finished.

In a typical manufacturing process, for example, preventive quality control might involve inspecting raw materials before they are put into the production process. Once the process begins, measuring and monitoring devices constantly assess quality standards as part of a concurrent quality control system. When the standards are not being met, employees correct the problem.

Once the manufacturing is completed, the products undergo a final quality inspection as part of the feedback quality control system. Of course, there are economic limits to how complete the final inspection will be. A refrigerator can be tested for an hour, a day, or a year. Management faces a trade-off. The less the refrigerator is tested, the sooner it gets to market and the faster the company receives its payment. The shorter the testing period, however, the higher the probability of a defect that will cost the manufacturer.

Total Quality Management (TQM)

Some managers attempt to reduce product liability costs by relying on a concurrent quality control system known as total quality management (TQM). TQM is an organization-wide effort to infuse quality into every activity in a company through continuous improvement.

Quality circles are a popular TQM technique. These are groups of six to twelve employees who volunteer to meet regularly to discuss problems and how to solve them. In a continuous stream manufacturing process, for example, a quality circle might consist of workers from different phases in the production process. Quality circles force changes in the production process that affect workers who are actually on the production line.

Benchmarking is another technique used in TQM. In benchmarking, a company continuously measures its products against those of its toughest competitors or the industry leaders in order to identify areas for improvement. In the automobile industry, benchmarking enabled several Japanese firms to overtake U.S. automakers in terms of quality. Some argue that Toyota gained worldwide market share by effectively using this type of quality control management system.

Continues

Another TQM system is called *Six Sigma*. Motorola introduced the quality principles in this system in the late 1980s, but Six Sigma has now become a generic term for a quality control approach based on a five-step methodology: define, measure, analyze, improve, and control. Six Sigma controls emphasize discipline and a relentless attempt to achieve higher quality (and lower costs). A possible impediment to the institution of a Six Sigma program is that it requires a major commitment from top management because it may involve widespread changes throughout the entire organization.

CRITICAL THINKING

■ Quality control leads to fewer defective products and fewer lawsuits. Consequently, managers know that quality control is important to their company's long-term financial health. At the same time, the more quality control managers impose on their organization, the higher the average cost per unit of whatever is produced and sold. How does a manager decide how much quality control to undertake?

Key Terms

market-share liability 128
product liability 118

privity of contract 119
statute of repose 132

tolled 132
unreasonably dangerous product 123

Chapter Summary: Product Liability

Liability Based on Negligence	1. The manufacturer must use due care in designing the product, selecting materials, using the appropriate production process, assembling and testing the product, and placing adequate warnings on the label or product. 2. Privity of contract is not required. A manufacturer is liable for failure to exercise due care to any person who sustains an injury proximately caused by a negligently made (defective) product. 3. Fraudulent misrepresentation of a product may result in product liability based on the tort of fraud.
Strict Product Liability—Requirements	1. The defendant must have sold the product in a defective condition. 2. The defendant must normally be engaged in the business of selling that product. 3. The product must be unreasonably dangerous to the user or consumer because of its defective condition (in most states). 4. The plaintiff must incur physical harm to self or property by use or consumption of the product. 5. The defective condition must be the proximate cause of the injury or damage. 6. The goods must not have been substantially changed from the time the product was sold to the time the injury was sustained.
Strict Product Liability—Product Defects	A product may be defective in three basic ways: 1. In its manufacture. 2. In its design. 3. In the instructions or warnings that come with it.
Market-Share Liability	When plaintiffs cannot prove which of many distributors of a defective product supplied the particular product that caused the plaintiffs' injuries, some courts apply market-share liability. All firms that manufactured and distributed the harmful product during the period in question are then held liable for the plaintiffs' injuries in proportion to the firms' respective share of the market, as directed by the court.
Other Applications of Strict Liability	1. Manufacturers and other sellers are liable for harms suffered by bystanders as a result of defective products. 2. Suppliers of component parts are strictly liable for defective parts that, when incorporated into a product, cause injuries to users.
Defenses to Product Liability	1. *Preemption*—An injured party may not be able to sue the manufacturer of a product that is subject to comprehensive federal safety regulations, such as medical devices. 2. *Assumption of risk*—The user or consumer knew of the risk of harm and voluntarily assumed it. 3. *Product misuse*—The user or consumer misused the product in a way unforeseeable by the manufacturer. 4. *Comparative negligence*—Liability may be distributed between the plaintiff and the defendant under the doctrine of comparative negligence if the plaintiff's misuse of the product contributed to the risk of injury. 5. *Commonly known dangers*—If a defendant succeeds in convincing the court that a plaintiff's injury resulted from a commonly known danger, such as the danger associated with using a sharp knife, the defendant will not be liable. 6. *Knowledgeable user*—If a particular danger is or should be commonly known by particular users of the product, the manufacturer of the product need not warn these users of the danger.

Issue Spotters

1. Rim Corporation makes tire rims that it sells to Superior Vehicles, Inc., which installs them on cars. One set of rims is defective, which an inspection would reveal. Superior does not inspect the rims. The car with the defective rims is sold to Town Auto Sales, which sells the car to Uri. Soon, the car is in an accident caused by the defective rims, and Uri is injured. Is Superior Vehicles liable? Explain your answer. (See *Product Liability*.)

2. Bensing Company manufactures generic drugs for the treatment of heart disease. A federal law requires generic drug makers to use labels that are identical to the labels on brand-name versions of the drugs. Hunter Rothfus purchased Bensing's generic drugs in Ohio and wants to sue Bensing for defective labeling based on its failure to comply with Ohio state common law (rather than the federal labeling requirements). What defense might Bensing assert to avoid liability under state law? (See *Defenses to Product Liability*.)

—**Check your answers to the *Issue Spotters* against the answers provided in Appendix D at the end of this text.**

Learning Objectives Check

1. Can a manufacturer be held liable to any person who suffers an injury proximately caused by the manufacturer's negligently made product?

2. What public policy assumptions underlie strict product liability?

3. What are the elements of a cause of action in strict product liability?

4. What are three types of product defects?

5. What defenses to liability can be raised in a product liability lawsuit?

—**Answers to the even-numbered *Learning Objectives Check* questions can be found in Appendix E at the end of this text.**

Business Scenarios and Case Problems

5–1. Product Liability. Carmen buys a television set manufactured by AKI Electronics. She is going on vacation, so she takes the set to her mother's house for her mother to use. Because the set is defective, it explodes, causing considerable damage to her mother's house. Carmen's mother sues AKI for the damage to her house. Discuss the theories under which Carmen's mother can recover from AKI. (See *Product Liability*.)

5–2. Product Liability. Jason Clark, an experienced hunter, bought a paintball gun. Clark practiced with the gun and knew how to screw in the carbon dioxide cartridge, pump the gun, and use its safety and trigger. Although Clark was aware that he could purchase protective eyewear, he chose not to. Clark had taken gun safety courses and understood that it was "common sense" not to shoot anyone in the face. Clark's friend, Chris Wright, also owned a paintball gun and was similarly familiar with the gun's use and its risks.

Clark, Wright, and their friends played a game that involved shooting paintballs at cars whose occupants also had the guns. One night, while Clark and Wright were cruising with their guns, Wright shot at Clark's car, but hit Clark in the eye. Clark filed a product liability lawsuit against the manufacturer of Wright's paintball gun to recover for the injury. Clark claimed that the gun was defectively designed. During the trial, Wright testified that his gun "never malfunctioned." In whose favor should the court rule? Why? (See *Product Liability*.)

5–3. Defenses to Product Liability. Brandon Stroud was driving a golf car made by Textron, Inc. The golf car did not have lights, but Textron did not warn against using it on public roads at night. When Stroud attempted to cross a road at 8:30 P.M., his golf car was struck by a vehicle driven by Joseph Thornley. Stroud was killed. His estate filed a suit against Textron, alleging strict product liability and product liability based on negligence. The charge was that the golf car was defective and unreasonably dangerous. What defense might Textron assert? Explain. [*Moore v. Barony House Restaurant*, LLC, 382 S.C. 35, 674 S.E.2d 500 (S.C.App. 2009)] (See *Defenses to Product Liability*.)

5–4. Product Liability. Yun Tung Chow tried to unclog a floor drain in the kitchen of the restaurant where he worked. He used a drain cleaner called Lewis Red Devil Lye that contained crystalline sodium hydroxide. The product label said that users should wear eye protection, put one tablespoon of lye directly into the drain, and keep their faces away from the drain to avoid dangerous backsplash.

Not wearing eye protection, Chow mixed three spoonfuls of lye in a can and poured that mixture down the drain while bending over it. Liquid splashed back into his face, causing injury. He sued for product liability based on inadequate warnings and a design defect. The trial court granted summary judgment to the manufacturer. Chow appealed. An expert for Chow stated that the product was defective because it had a tendency to backsplash. Is that a convincing argument? Why or why not? [*Yun Tung Chow v. Reckitt & Coleman, Inc.*, 17 N.Y.3d 29, 950 N.E.2d 113 (2011)] (See *Product Liability*.)

5–5. Strict Product Liability. David Dobrovolny bought a new Ford F-350 pickup truck. A year later, the truck spontaneously caught fire in Dobrovolny's driveway. The truck was destroyed, but no other property was damaged, and no one was injured. Dobrovolny filed a suit in a Nebraska state court against Ford Motor Co. on a theory of strict product liability to recover the cost of the truck. Nebraska limits the application of strict product liability to situations involving personal injuries. Is Dobrovolny's claim likely to succeed? Why or why not? Is there another basis for liability on which he might recover? Explain. [*Dobrovolny v. Ford Motor Co.*, 281 Neb. 86, 793 N.W.2d 445 (2011)] (See *Strict Product Liability*.)

5–6. Product Misuse. Five-year-old Cheyenne Stark was riding in the backseat of her parents' Ford Taurus. Cheyenne was not sitting in a booster seat. Instead, she was using a seatbelt designed by Ford, but was wearing the shoulder belt behind her back. The car was involved in a collision. As a result, Cheyenne suffered a spinal cord injury and was paralyzed from the waist down. The family filed a suit against Ford Motor Co., alleging that the seatbelt was defectively designed. Could Ford successfully claim that Cheyenne had misused the seatbelt? Why or why not? [*Stark v. Ford Motor Co.*, 365 N.C. 468, 723 S.E.2d 753 (2012)] (See *Defenses to Product Liability*.)

5–7. Business Case Problem with Sample Answer— Product Liability. While driving on Interstate 40 in North Carolina, Carroll Jett became distracted by a texting system in the cab of his tractor-trailer truck. He smashed into several vehicles that were slowed or stopped in front of him, injuring Barbara and Michael Durkee and others. The injured motorists filed a suit in a federal district court against Geologic Solutions, Inc., the maker of the texting system, alleging product liability. Was the accident caused by Jett's inattention or the texting device? Should a manufacturer be required to design a product that is incapable of distracting a driver? Discuss. [*Durkee v. Geologic Solutions, Inc.*, 2013 WL 14717 (4th Cir. 2013)] (See *Product Liability*.)

—For a sample answer to Problem 5–7, go to Appendix F at the end of this text.

5–8. Strict Product Liability. Medicis Pharmaceutical Corp. makes Solodyn, a prescription oral antibiotic. Medicis warns physicians that "autoimmune syndromes, including drug-induced lupus-like syndrome," may be associated with use of the drug. Amanda Watts had chronic acne. Her physician prescribed Solodyn. Information included with the drug did not mention the risk of autoimmune disorders, and Watts was not otherwise advised of it. She was prescribed the drug twice, each time for twenty weeks. Later, she experienced debilitating joint pain and, after being hospitalized, was diagnosed with lupus. On what basis could Watts recover from Medicis in an action grounded in product liability? Explain. [*Watts v. Medicis Pharmaceutical Corp.*, 236 Ariz. 511, 342 P.3d 847 (2015)] (See *Strict Product Liability*.)

5–9. A Question of Ethics—Strict Product Liability. Susan Calles lived with her four daughters, Amanda (age 11), Victoria (age 5), and Jenna and Jillian (age 3). In March 1998, Calles bought an Aim N Flame utility lighter, which she stored on the top shelf of her kitchen cabinet. A trigger can ignite the Aim N Flame after an on/off switch is slid to the "on" position. On the night of March 31, Calles and Victoria left to get videos. Jenna and Jillian were in bed, and Amanda was watching television. Calles returned to find fire trucks and emergency vehicles around her home. Robert Finn, a fire investigator, determined that Jenna had started a fire using the lighter. Jillian suffered smoke inhalation, was hospitalized, and died on April 21. Calles filed a suit in an Illinois state court against Scripto-Tokai Corp., which distributed the Aim N Flame, and others. In her suit, which was grounded, in part, in strict liability claims, Calles alleged that the lighter was an "unreasonably dangerous product." Scripto filed a motion for summary judgment. [*Calles v. Scripto-Tokai Corp.*, 224 Ill.2d 247, 864 N.E.2d 249, 309 Ill.Dec. 383 (2007)] (See *Strict Product Liability*.)

1. A product is "unreasonably dangerous" when it is dangerous beyond the expectation of the ordinary consumer. Whose expectation—Calles's or Jenna's—applies here? Why? Does the lighter pass this test? Explain.

2. A product is also "unreasonably dangerous" when a less dangerous alternative was economically feasible for its maker, and the maker failed to produce it. Scripto contended that because its product was "simple" and the danger was

"obvious," it should not be liable under this test. Do you agree? Why or why not?

3. Calles presented evidence as to the likelihood and seriousness of injury from lighters that do not have child-safety devices. Scripto argued that the Aim N Flame is a useful, inexpensive, alternative source of fire and is safer than a match. Calles admitted that she was aware of the dangers presented by lighters in the hands of children. Scripto admitted that it had been a defendant in at least twenty-five suits for injuries that occurred under similar circumstances. With these factors in mind, how should the court rule? Why?

Critical Thinking and Writing Assignments

5–10. Business Law Critical Thinking Group Assignment.
Bret D'Auguste was an experienced skier when he rented equipment to ski at Hunter Mountain Ski Bowl in New York. When D'Auguste entered an extremely difficult trail, he noticed immediately that the surface consisted of ice with almost no snow. He tried to exit the steeply declining trail by making a sharp right turn, but in the attempt, his left ski snapped off. D'Auguste lost his balance, fell, and slid down the mountain, striking his face and head against a fence along the trail. According to a report by a rental shop employee, one of the bindings on D'Auguste's skis had a "cracked heel housing."

D'Auguste filed a lawsuit against the bindings' manufacturer on a theory of strict product liability. The manufacturer filed a motion for summary judgment. (See *Product Liability*.)

1. The first group will take the position of the manufacturer and develop an argument why the court should *grant* the summary judgment motion and dismiss the strict product liability claim.

2. The second group will take the position of D'Auguste and formulate a basis for why the court should *deny* the motion and allow the strict product liability claim.

iStockPhoto.com/Warchi

6

LEARNING OBJECTIVES

The five Learning Objectives *below are designed to help improve your understanding of the chapter. After reading this chapter, you should be able to answer the following questions:*

1. What is intellectual property?

2. Why is the protection of trademarks important?

3. How does the law protect patents?

4. What laws protect authors' rights in the works they create?

5. What are trade secrets, and what laws offer protection for this form of intellectual property?

Intellectual Property Property resulting from intellectual and creative processes.

LEARNING OBJECTIVE 1
What is intellectual property?

Intellectual Property Rights

Intellectual property is any property resulting from intellectual, creative processes—the products of an individual's mind, as suggested in the chapter-opening quotation. Although it is an abstract term for an abstract concept, intellectual property is nonetheless familiar to almost everyone. The apps for your iPhone, iPad, or Samsung Galaxy, the movies you see, and the music you listen to are all forms of intellectual property.

More than two hundred years ago, the framers of the U.S. Constitution recognized the importance of protecting creative works in Article I, Section 8 (see Appendix B). Statutory protection of these rights began in the 1940s and continues to evolve to meet the needs of modern society. In today's global economy, however, protecting intellectual property in one country is no longer sufficient. The United States is participating in various international agreements to secure ownership rights in intellectual property in other countries, as you will learn in this chapter.

Whether locally or globally, businesspersons have a vital need to protect their rights in intellectual property, which may be more valuable than their physical property, such as machines and buildings. Consider, for instance, the importance of intellectual property rights to technology companies, such as Apple, Inc., and Samsung Electronics Company. In today's world, intellectual property rights can be a company's most valuable assets, which is why Apple recently sued its rival Samsung. Apple claimed that Samsung's Galaxy line of mobile phones and tablets (those that run Google's Android software) copy the look, design, and user interface of Apple's iPhone and iPad. Although Apple is one of Samsung's biggest customers and buys many of its components from Samsung, Apple also needs to protect its iPhone and iPad revenues from competing Android products. You will read about the verdict in this case later in this chapter.

"My words and my ideas are my property, and I'll keep and protect them as surely as I do my stable of unicorns."

JAROD KINTZ
1982–PRESENT
(AMERICAN AUTHOR)

6-1 Trademarks

A **trademark** is a distinctive word, symbol, sound, or design that identifies the manufacturer as the source of particular goods and distinguishes its products from those made or sold by others. At common law, the person who used a symbol or mark to identify a business or product was protected in the use of that trademark. Clearly, if another company used the trademark, it could lead consumers to believe that its goods were made by the trademark owner. The law seeks to avoid this kind of confusion. (For information on how companies use trademarks and service marks, see the *Linking Business Law to Marketing* feature at the end of this chapter.)

In the following *Classic Case* concerning Coca-Cola, the defendants argued that the Coca-Cola trademark was not entitled to protection under the law because the term did not accurately represent the product.

Trademark A distinctive word, symbol, or design that identifies the manufacturer as the source of particular goods and distinguishes its products from those made or sold by others.

★★★ CLASSIC CASE 6.1 ★★★

Coca-Cola Co. v. Koke Co. of America
Supreme Court of the United States, 254 U.S. 143, 41 S.Ct. 113, 65 L.Ed. 189 (1920).

COMPANY PROFILE *John Pemberton, an Atlanta pharmacist, invented a caramel-colored, carbonated soft drink in 1886. His bookkeeper, Frank Robinson, named the beverage Coca-Cola after two of the ingredients, coca leaves and kola nuts. Asa Candler bought the Coca-Cola Company in 1891 and, within seven years, had made the soft drink available throughout the United States and in parts of Canada and Mexico as well. Candler continued to sell Coke aggressively and to open up new markets, reaching Europe before 1910. In doing so, however, he attracted numerous competitors, some of whom tried to capitalize directly on the Coke name.*

How is Coca-Cola protected?

Rob Wilson/ShutterStock.com

FACTS The Coca-Cola Company brought an action in a federal district court to enjoin (prevent) other beverage companies from using the names Koke and Dope for their products. The defendants contended that the Coca-Cola trademark was a fraudulent representation and that Coca-Cola was therefore not entitled to any help from the courts. By using the Coca-Cola name, the defendants alleged, the Coca-Cola Company represented that the beverage contained cocaine (from coca leaves). The district court granted the injunction, but the federal appellate court reversed. The Coca-Cola Company appealed to the United States Supreme Court.

ISSUE Did the marketing of products called Koke and Dope by the Koke Company of America and other firms constitute an infringement on Coca-Cola's trademark?

DECISION Yes for Koke, but no for Dope. The United States Supreme Court enjoined the competing beverage companies from calling their products Koke but not from calling their products Dope.

REASON The Court noted that before 1900 the Coca-Cola beverage had contained a small amount of cocaine. This ingredient had been deleted from the formula by 1906 at the latest, however, and the Coca-Cola Company had advertised to the public that no cocaine was present in its drink. The court emphasized that Coca-Cola was a widely popular drink "to be had at almost any soda fountain." Because of the public's widespread familiarity with Coca-Cola, the retention of the name (referring to coca leaves and kola nuts) was not misleading: "Coca-Cola probably means to most persons the plaintiff's familiar product to be had everywhere rather than a compound of particular substances." The name Coke was found to be so common a term for the trademarked product Coca-Cola that the defendants' use of the similar-sounding Koke as a name for their beverages was disallowed. The Court could find no reason to restrain the defendants from using the name Dope, however.

WHAT IF THE FACTS WERE DIFFERENT? *Suppose that Coca-Cola had been trying to make the public believe that its product contained cocaine. Would the result in the case likely have been different? Explain your answer.*

IMPACT OF THIS CASE ON TODAY'S LAW *In this early case, the United States Supreme Court made it clear that trademarks and trade names (and nicknames for those marks and names, such as "Coke" for "Coca-Cola") that are in common use receive protection under the common law. This holding is significant historically because it is the predecessor to the federal statute later passed to protect trademark rights (the Lanham Act of 1946, discussed next).*

6–1a Statutory Protection of Trademarks

Statutory protection of trademarks and related property is provided at the federal level by the Lanham Act of 1946.[1] The Lanham Act was enacted in part to protect manufacturers from losing business to rival companies that used confusingly similar trademarks. The Lanham Act incorporates the common law of trademarks and provides remedies for owners of trademarks who wish to enforce their claims in federal court. Many states also have trademark statutes.

Trademark Dilution In 1995, Congress amended the Lanham Act by passing the Federal Trademark Dilution Act,[2] which allowed trademark owners to bring suits in federal court for **trademark dilution.** In 2006, Congress further amended the law on trademark dilution by passing the Trademark Dilution Revision Act (TDRA).[3]

Under the TDRA, to state a claim for trademark dilution, a plaintiff must prove the following:

1. The plaintiff owns a famous mark that is distinctive.

2. The defendant has begun using a mark in commerce that allegedly is diluting the famous mark.

3. The similarity between the defendant's mark and the famous mark gives rise to an *association* between the marks.

4. The association is likely to impair the distinctiveness of the famous mark or harm its reputation.

Trademark dilution laws protect "distinctive" or "famous" trademarks (such as Rolls-Royce, McDonald's, Starbucks, and Apple) from certain unauthorized uses. Such a mark is protected even when the unauthorized use is on noncompeting goods or is unlikely to confuse. More than half of the states have also enacted trademark dilution laws.

The Marks Need Not Be Identical A famous mark may be diluted not only by the use of an *identical* mark but also by the use of a *similar* mark, provided that it reduces the value of the famous mark.[4] A similar mark is more likely to lessen the value of a famous mark when the companies using the marks provide related goods or compete against each other in the same market.

CASE EXAMPLE 6.1 When Samantha Lundberg opened Sambuck's Coffeehouse in Astoria, Oregon, she knew that Starbucks was one of the largest coffee chains in the nation. Starbucks Corporation filed a dilution lawsuit, and a federal court ruled that use of the Sambuck's mark constituted trademark dilution because it created confusion for consumers. Not only was there a "high degree" of similarity between the marks, but also both companies provided coffee-related services through stand-alone retail stores. Therefore, the use of the similar mark (Sambuck's) reduced the value of the famous mark (Starbucks).[5] ■

6–1b Trademark Registration

Trademarks may be registered with the state or with the federal government. To register for protection under federal trademark law, a person must file an application with the U.S. Patent and Trademark Office in Washington, D.C. A mark can be registered (1) if it is currently in commerce or (2) if the applicant intends to put it into commerce within six months.

In special circumstances, the six-month period can be extended by thirty months. Thus, the applicant would have a total of three years from the date of notice of trademark approval

---

Trademark Dilution The unauthorized use of a distinctive and famous mark in a way that impairs the mark's distinctiveness or harms its reputation.

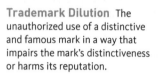

KNOW THIS

Trademark dilution laws protect the owners of distinctive marks from unauthorized uses even when the defendants' use involves noncompeting goods or is unlikely to cause confusion.

Why can't someone call its coffee shop "Sambuck's"?

iStockPhoto.com/borchee

---

1. 15 U.S.C. Sections 1051–1128.
2. 15 U.S.C. Section 1125.
3. Pub. L. No. 103-312, 120 Stat. 1730 (2006).
4. See *Moseley v. V Secret Catalogue, Inc.*, 537 U.S. 418, 123 S.Ct. 1115, 155 L.Ed.2d 1 (2003).
5. *Starbucks Corp. v. Lundberg*, 2005 WL 3183858 (D.Or. 2005).

to make use of the mark and to file the required use statement. Registration is postponed until the mark is actually used.

During this waiting period, an applicant can legally protect his or her trademark against a third party who has neither used the mark previously nor filed an application for it. Registration is renewable between the fifth and sixth years after the initial registration and every ten years thereafter (every twenty years for trademarks registered before 1990).

6–1c Trademark Infringement

Registration of a trademark with the U.S. Patent and Trademark Office gives notice on a nationwide basis that the trademark belongs exclusively to the registrant. The registrant is also allowed to use the symbol ® to indicate that the mark has been registered. Whenever that trademark is copied to a substantial degree or used in its entirety by another, intentionally or unintentionally, the trademark has been *infringed* (used without authorization).

When a trademark has been infringed, the owner has a cause of action against the infringer. To succeed in a lawsuit for trademark infringement, the owner must show that the defendant's use of the mark created a likelihood of confusion about the origin of the defendant's goods or services. The owner need not prove that the infringer acted intentionally or that the trademark was registered (although registration does provide proof of the date of inception of the trademark's use).

The most commonly granted remedy for trademark infringement is an *injunction* to prevent further infringement. Under the Lanham Act, a trademark owner that successfully proves infringement can recover actual damages, plus the profits that the infringer wrongfully received from the unauthorized use of the mark. A court can also order the destruction of any goods bearing the unauthorized trademark. In some situations, the trademark owner may also be able to recover attorneys' fees.

6–1d Distinctiveness of the Mark

A central objective of the Lanham Act is to reduce the likelihood that consumers will be confused by similar marks. For that reason, only those trademarks that are deemed sufficiently distinctive from all competing trademarks will be protected.

Strong Marks Fanciful, arbitrary, or suggestive trademarks are generally considered to be the most distinctive (strongest) trademarks. These marks receive automatic protection because they serve to identify a particular product's source, as opposed to describing the product itself.

Fanciful and Arbitrary Trademarks. Fanciful trademarks use invented words. Examples include *Xerox* for one company's copiers and *Google* for another company's search engine.

Arbitrary trademarks use common words that would not ordinarily be associated with the product, such as *Dutch Boy* as a name for paint. Even a single letter used in a particular style can be an arbitrary trademark. **CASE EXAMPLE 6.2** Sports entertainment company ESPN sued Quiksilver, Inc., a maker of youth-oriented clothing, alleging trademark infringement. ESPN claimed that Quiksilver had used on its clothing the stylized "X" mark that ESPN uses in connection with the "X Games" (competitions in extreme action sports).

Quiksilver filed counterclaims for trademark infringement and dilution, arguing that it had a long history of using the stylized X on its products. ESPN created the X Games in the mid-1990s, and Quiksilver has used the X mark since 1994. ESPN asked the court to dismiss Quiksilver's counterclaims, but the court refused, holding that the X on Quiksilver's clothing was clearly an arbitrary mark. The court found that the two Xs were "similar enough that a consumer might well confuse them." Therefore, Quicksilver could continue its claim for trademark infringement.[6] ▪

---

6. *ESPN, Inc. v. Quiksilver, Inc.*, 586 F.Supp.2d 219 (S.D.N.Y. 2008).

Suggestive Trademarks. Suggestive trademarks indicate something about a product's nature, quality, or characteristics without describing the product directly. For instance, "Blu-ray" is a suggestive mark that is associated with the high-quality, high-definition video contained on a particular optical data storage disc. Although blue-violet lasers are used to read blu-ray discs, the term *blu-ray* does not directly describe the disc.

Secondary Meaning

Descriptive terms, geographic terms, and personal names are not inherently distinctive and do not receive protection under the law until they acquire a secondary meaning. Whether a secondary meaning becomes attached to a term or name usually depends on how extensively the product is advertised, the market for the product, the number of sales, and other factors.

Health maintenance organization insurers exist in many states. If one is called Unity Health and another is called UnityPoint Health, is there a problem?

A secondary meaning may arise when customers begin to associate a specific term or phrase (such as *London Fog*) with specific trademarked items made by a particular company (coats with "London Fog" labels). **CASE EXAMPLE 6.3** Unity Health Plans Insurance Corporation has been a health maintenance organization (HMO) insurer in Wisconsin since 1955. In 2013, another health-care provider, Iowa Health System, began rebranding itself (changing its name and marketing) as UnityPoint Health. When the company expanded into Wisconsin, where Unity Health already had an established presence, Unity Health filed a trademark infringement suit in federal court.

The court found that Unity Health was a descriptive mark, and thus not inherently distinctive. But the court also held that the Unity Health mark had acquired a secondary meaning, largely because it had been used for so long and so exclusively by one health insurer in Wisconsin. It made no difference to the court that only one part of the mark (Unity) was common to both trademarks. To allow Iowa Health Systems to use the mark UnityPoint Health in Wisconsin would likely create confusion for consumers. Therefore, the court issued an injunction and blocked Iowa Health from using the trademark UnityPoint Health.[7]

Once a secondary meaning is attached to a term or name, a trademark is considered distinctive and is protected. Even a color can qualify for trademark protection, such as the color schemes used by four state university sports teams, including Ohio State University and Louisiana State University.[8]

Generic Terms

Generic terms that refer to an entire class of products, such as *bicycle* and *computer,* receive no protection, even if they acquire secondary meanings. A particularly thorny problem for a business arises when its trademark acquires generic use. For instance, *aspirin* and *thermos* were originally trademarked products, but today the words are used generically. Other trademarks that have acquired generic use include *escalator, trampoline, raisin bran, dry ice, lanolin, linoleum, nylon,* and *cornflakes.*

A trademark that is commonly used does not automatically become generic, though. **CASE EXAMPLE 6.4** In 2014, David Elliot and Chris Gillespie sought to register numerous domain names, including "googledisney.com" and "googlenewstvs.com." (A **domain name** is part of an Internet address, such as "cengage.com.") They were unable to register the names because all of them used the word *google,* a trademark of Google, Inc.

Elliot and Gillespie brought an action in federal court to have the Google trademark canceled because it had become a generic term. They argued that because most people now use *google* as a verb ("to google") when referring to searching the Internet with any search engine (not just Google), the term should no longer be protected. The court held that even if people do use the word *google* as a verb, it is still a protected trademark if consumers associate the noun with one company. The court concluded that "the primary significance of the word

Domain Name Part of an Internet address, such as "cengage .com."

---

7. *Unity Health Plans Insurance Co. v. Iowa Health System,* 995 F.Supp.2d 874 (W.D. Wis. 2014).
8. *Board of Supervisors of LA State University v. Smack Apparel Co.,* 438 F.Supp.2d 653 (2006).

google to a majority of the public who utilize Internet search engines is a designation of the Google search engine."[9]

6-1e Service, Certification, and Collective Marks

A **service mark** is essentially a trademark that is used to distinguish the services (rather than the products) of one person or company from those of another. For instance, each airline has a particular mark or symbol associated with its name. Titles and character names used in radio and television are frequently registered as service marks.

Other marks protected by law include certification marks and collective marks. A **certification mark** is used by one or more persons, other than the owner, to certify the region, materials, mode of manufacture, quality, or other characteristic of specific goods or services. Certification marks include such marks as "Good Housekeeping Seal of Approval" and "UL Tested."

When used by members of a cooperative, association, labor union, or other organization, a certification mark is referred to as a **collective mark.** **EXAMPLE 6.5** Collective marks appear at the end of a movie's credits to indicate the various associations and organizations that participated in making the movie. The labor union marks found on the tags of certain products are also collective marks. ▪

6-1f Trade Dress

The term **trade dress** refers to the image and overall appearance of a product. Trade dress is a broad concept that can include all or part of the total image or overall impression created by a product or its packaging. **EXAMPLE 6.6** The distinctive decor, menu, and style of service of a particular restaurant may be regarded as the restaurant's trade dress. Similarly, trade dress can include the layout and appearance of a mail-order catalogue, the use of a lighthouse as part of a golf hole, the fish shape of a cracker, or the G-shaped design of a Gucci watch. ▪

Basically, trade dress is subject to the same protection as trademarks. In cases involving trade dress infringement, as in trademark infringement cases, a major consideration is whether consumers are likely to be confused by the allegedly infringing use. **EXAMPLE 6.7** Converse makes All-Star shoes, which were the first shoes ever endorsed by a famous basketball player, Chuck Taylor. Nike, Inc., which now owns Converse, filed a suit against thirty-one companies, including Ralph Lauren, for manufacturing knock-off versions of these shoes. Nike claims that consumers are likely to be confused because the knock-offs use the same white rubber soles, rubber cap on the toes, canvas tops, and conspicuous stitching as used on All-Stars. In 2015, Ralph Lauren agreed to settle its dispute with Nike by destroying all remaining fake All-Stars and paying Nike an undisclosed sum. ▪

6-1g Counterfeit Goods

Counterfeit goods copy or otherwise imitate trademarked goods but are not genuine. The importation of goods bearing counterfeit trademarks poses a growing problem for U.S. businesses, consumers, and law enforcement. It is estimated that nearly 7 percent of the goods imported into the United States are counterfeit. In addition to having negative financial effects on legitimate businesses, sales of certain counterfeit goods, such as pharmaceuticals and nutritional supplements, can present serious public health risks.

Stop Counterfeiting in Manufactured Goods Act In 2006, Congress enacted the Stop Counterfeiting in Manufactured Goods Act[10] (SCMGA). The act made it a crime to intentionally

Service Mark A trademark that is used to distinguish the services (rather than the products) of one person or company from those of another.

Certification Mark A mark used by one or more persons, other than the owner, to certify the region, materials, mode of manufacture, quality, or other characteristic of specific goods or services.

Collective Mark A mark used by members of a cooperative, association, union, or other organization to certify the region, materials, mode of manufacture, quality, or other characteristic of specific goods or services.

Trade Dress The image and overall appearance of a product.

iStockPhoto.com/ANGELGILD

Can the layout and appearance of a restaurant chain's menu qualify as trade dress?

---

9. *Elliot v. Google Inc.*, ___ F.Supp.3d ___, 2014 WL 4470390 (D.Ariz. 2014).
10. Pub. L. No. 109-181 (2006), which amended 18 U.S.C. Sections 2318–2320.

traffic in, or attempt to traffic in, counterfeit goods or services, or to knowingly use a counterfeit mark on or in connection with goods or services.

Before this act went into effect, the law did not prohibit the creation or shipment of counterfeit labels that were not attached to products. Therefore, counterfeiters would make labels and packaging bearing a counterfeit trademark, ship the labels to another location, and then affix them to inferior products to deceive buyers. The SCMGA closed this loophole by making it a crime to traffic in counterfeit labels, stickers, packaging, and the like, whether or not they are attached to goods.

Penalties for Counterfeiting   Persons found guilty of violating the SCMGA may be fined up to $2 million or imprisoned for up to ten years (or more if they are repeat offenders). If a court finds that the statute was violated, it must order the defendant to forfeit the counterfeit products (which are then destroyed), as well as any property used in the commission of the crime. The defendant must also pay restitution to the trademark holder or victim in an amount equal to the victim's actual loss.

CASE EXAMPLE 6.7 Wajdi Beydoun pleaded guilty to conspiring to import cigarette-rolling papers from Mexico that were falsely marked as "Zig-Zags" and sell them in the United States. The defendant was sentenced to prison and ordered to pay $566,267 in restitution. On appeal, the court affirmed the prison sentence but ordered the trial court to reduce the amount of restitution because it exceeded the actual loss suffered by the legitimate sellers of Zig-Zag rolling papers.[11] ■

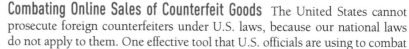

How easy is it to create fake Zig-Zag cigarette rolling papers? Is so doing a civil or criminal wrong?

Africa Studio/ShutterStock.com

Combating Online Sales of Counterfeit Goods   The United States cannot prosecute foreign counterfeiters under U.S. laws, because our national laws do not apply to them. One effective tool that U.S. officials are using to combat online sales of counterfeit goods is to obtain a court order to close down the domain names of Web sites that sell such goods.

EXAMPLE 6.8 In 2013, U.S. agents shut down 297 domain names on the Monday after Thanksgiving. (This so-called "Cyber Monday" is the online version of "Black Friday," the day after Thanksgiving, when the holiday shopping season begins.) Europol, an international organization, shut down 393 domain names. Of course, some criminal enterprises may continue selling counterfeit products under different domain names. Nevertheless, shutting down the Web sites, particularly on key shopping days, prevents some counterfeit goods from entering the United States. ■

6–1h Trade Names

Trade Name A name that a business uses to identify itself and its brand. A trade name is directly related to a business's reputation and goodwill and is protected under trademark law.

Trademarks apply to *products*. The term **trade name** refers to part or all of a *business's name,* whether the business is a sole proprietorship, a partnership, or a corporation. Generally, a trade name is directly related to a business and its goodwill.

A trade name may be protected as a trademark if the trade name is the same as the company's trademarked product—for instance, Coca-Cola. Unless it is also used as a trademark or service mark, a trade name cannot be registered with the federal government. Trade names are protected under the common law, but only if they are unusual or fancifully used. The word *Safeway,* for example, was sufficiently fanciful to obtain protection as a trade name for a grocery chain.

6–1i Licensing

License An agreement by the owner of intellectual property to permit another to use a trademark, copyright, patent, or trade secret for certain limited purposes.

One way to avoid litigation and still make use of another's trademark or other form of intellectual property is to obtain a license to do so. A **license** in this context is an agreement

---

11. *United States v. Beydoun,* 469 F.3d 102 (5th Cir. 2006).

permitting the use of a trademark, copyright, patent, or trade secret for certain limited purposes. The party that owns the intellectual property rights and issues the license is the *licensor,* and the party obtaining the license is the *licensee.*

A license grants only the rights expressly described in the license agreement. A licensor might, for instance, allow the licensee to use a trademark as part of its company or domain name, but not otherwise use the mark on any products or services. Disputes frequently arise over licensing agreements, particularly when the license involves Internet use.

PREVENTING LEGAL DISPUTES

Typically, license agreements are very detailed and should be carefully drafted. Consult with an attorney before signing any licensing contract to make sure that the wording of the contract is very clear as to what rights are or are not being conveyed. This safeguard can help you to avoid litigation. Moreover, to prevent misunderstandings over the scope of the rights being acquired in intellectual property, determine whether any other parties hold licenses to use the same intellectual property and the extent of those rights.

6-2 Patents

A **patent** is a grant from the government that gives an inventor the exclusive right to make, use, and sell an invention for a period of twenty years. Patents for designs, as opposed to inventions, are given for a fourteen-year period. The applicant must demonstrate to the satisfaction of the U.S. Patent and Trademark Office that the invention, discovery, process, or design is novel, useful, and not obvious in light of current technology.

Until recently, patent law in the United States differed from the laws of many other countries because the first person to invent a product or process obtained the patent rights, rather than the first person to file for a patent. It was often difficult to prove who invented an item first, however, which prompted Congress to change the system in 2011 by passing the America Invents Act.[12] Now, the first person to file an application for a patent on a product or process will receive patent protection. In addition, the law established a nine-month limit for challenging a patent on any ground.

The period of patent protection begins on the date when the patent application is filed, rather than when the patent is issued, which can sometimes be years later. After the patent period ends (either fourteen or twenty years later), the product or process enters the public domain, and anyone can make, sell, or use the invention without paying the patent holder.

Patent A property right granted by the federal government that gives an inventor an exclusive right to make, use, sell, or offer to sell an invention in the United States for a limited time.

LEARNING OBJECTIVE 3

How does the law protect patents?

6-2a Searchable Patent Databases

A significant development relating to patents is the availability online of the world's patent databases. The Web site of the U.S. Patent and Trademark Office (**www.uspto.gov**) provides searchable databases covering U.S. patents granted since 1976. The Web site of the European Patent Office (**www.epo.org**) provides online access to 50 million patent documents in more than seventy nations through a searchable network of databases.

Businesses use these searchable databases in many ways. Companies may conduct patent searches to list or inventory their patents, which are valuable assets. Patent searches also enable companies to study trends and patterns in a specific technology or to gather information about competitors in the industry.

United States Patent and Trademark Office

This is the home page of the U.S. Patent and Trademark Office. Is its database searchable?

---

12. The full title of this law is the Leahy-Smith America Invents Act, Pub. L. No. 112-29 (2011), which amended 35 U.S.C. Sections 1, 41, and 321.

6–2b What Is Patentable?

Under federal law, "[w]hoever invents or discovers any new and useful process, machine, manufacture, or composition of matter, or any new and useful improvement thereof, may obtain a patent therefor, subject to the conditions and requirements of this title."[13] Thus, to be patentable, an invention must be *novel, useful,* and *not obvious* in light of current technology.

Almost anything is patentable, except the laws of nature, natural phenomena, and abstract ideas (including algorithms[14]). Even artistic methods and works of art, certain business processes, and the structures of storylines are patentable, provided that they are novel and not obvious.[15]

Plants that are reproduced asexually (by means other than from seed), such as hybrid or genetically engineered plants, are patentable in the United States, as are genetically engineered (or cloned) microorganisms and animals. **CASE EXAMPLE 6.9** Monsanto, Inc., has sold its patented genetically modified (GM) seeds to farmers to help them achieve higher crop yields using fewer pesticides. Monsanto has required farmers who bought GM seeds to sign agreements promising to plant the seeds for only one crop and to pay a technology fee for each acre planted. To ensure compliance, seventy-five Monsanto employees are assigned to investigate and prosecute farmers who use the GM seeds illegally. Monsanto has filed lawsuits against nearly 150 farmers in the United States and has been awarded more than $15 million in damages (not including out-of-court settlement amounts).[16]

A patent application was rejected in the following case as obvious in light of previous patents. The applicant challenged the rejection. The court's decision turned on the meaning of the terms *wireless* and *streaming video.*

---

13. 35 U.S.C. 101.
14. An *algorithm* is a step-by-step procedure, formula, or set of instructions for accomplishing a specific task. An example is the set of rules used by a search engine to rank the listings contained within its index in response to a particular query.
15. For a United States Supreme Court case discussing the obviousness requirement, see *KSR International Co. v. Teleflex, Inc.,* 550 U.S. 398, 127 S.Ct. 1727, 167 L.Ed.2d 705 (2007). For a discussion of business process patents, see *In re Bilski,* 545 F3d 943 (Fed. Cir. 2008).
16. See, for example, *Monsanto Co. v. Bowman,* 657 F.3d 1341 (Fed.Cir. 2011); and *Monsanto Co. v. Scruggs,* 459 F.3d 1328 (2006).

CASE 6.2

In re Imes

United States Court of Appeals, Federal Circuit, 778 F.3d 1250 (2015).

FACTS Kevin Imes filed a patent application for a device that can send digital camera images and videos wirelessly over a network. The U.S. Patent and Trademark Office examiner rejected Imes's device as obvious based on earlier patents—the Schuetzle and Knowles patents. The Schuetzle patent protects a device that can transfer images to a computer via a removable memory card. The examiner concluded that this device was wireless because to transfer images, the card is removed from the camera and inserted into the computer. "In other words, no wire is utilized." The Knowles system allows a user to take multiple consecutive still images and queues them so that they can be serially transmitted as e-mail attachments. The examiner explained that "a continuous process of sending images is the equivalent of streaming video." The Patent Trial and

What constitutes a wireless transfer of data from a digital camera over a network?

Appeal Board affirmed the examiner's rejection of Imes's application. Imes appealed.

ISSUE Did the examiner misconstrue the terms *wireless* and *streaming video?*

DECISION Yes. The U.S. Court of Appeals for the Federal Circuit reversed the Patent Trial and Appeal Board's rejection of Imes's application and remanded the case.

REASON The court concluded that the examiner's construction of the term *wireless* to include communication via the metal contacts of a removable memory card and a computer is "inconsistent with the broadest reasonable interpretation" of the term. Imes's application used wireless "to refer to methods and devices that carry waves through atmospheric space, such as Bluetooth and various cellular protocols." The court found that this was the correct meaning of the term, and this construction did not support the examiner's rejection of Imes's application. As for the examiner's conclusion with respect to the Knowles patent, the court found no substantial evidence to support the examiner's determination that Knowles's system transmits streaming video. "Streaming video is the continuous transmission of video. A series of e-mails with attachments does not meet the definition of 'streaming' and still images do not meet the definition of 'video.'"

CRITICAL THINKING—Legal Consideration *How should an invention be described in a patent application—in broad terms, specific terms, or both? Discuss.*

6-2c Patent Infringement

If a firm makes, uses, or sells another's patented design, product, or process without the patent owner's permission, it commits the tort of patent infringement. Patent infringement may occur even though the patent owner has not put the patented product in commerce. Patent infringement may also occur even though not all features or parts of an invention are copied. (To infringe the patent on a process, however, all steps or their equivalent must be copied.) To read about an important issue in patent infringement today, see this chapter's *Adapting the Law to the Online Environment*.

Patent Infringement Suits and High-Tech Companies Obviously, companies that specialize in developing new technology stand to lose significant profits if someone "makes, uses, or sells" devices that incorporate their patented inventions. Because these firms are the holders of numerous patents, they are frequently involved in patent infringement lawsuits (as well as other types of intellectual property disputes).

A complication in many such lawsuits is their global scope. Many companies that make and sell electronics and computer software and hardware are based in foreign nations (for instance, Samsung Electronics Company is a Korean firm). Foreign firms can apply for and obtain U.S. patent protection on items that they sell within the United States, just as U.S. firms can obtain protection in foreign nations where they sell goods.

In the United States, however, the Supreme Court has narrowly construed patent infringement as it applies to exported software. As a general rule, under U.S. law, no patent infringement occurs when a patented product is made and sold in another country. **CASE EXAMPLE 6.10** AT&T Corporation holds a patent on a device used to digitally encode, compress, and process recorded speech. AT&T brought an infringement case against Microsoft Corporation, which admitted that its Windows operating system incorporated software code that infringed on AT&T's patent.

The case reached the United States Supreme Court on the question of whether Microsoft's liability extended to computers made in another country. The Court held that it did not. Microsoft was liable only for infringement in the United States and not for the Windows-based computers produced in foreign locations. The Court reasoned that Microsoft had not "supplied" the software for the computers but had only electronically transmitted a master copy, which the foreign manufacturers then copied and loaded onto the computers.[17] ■

Apple, Inc. v. Samsung Electronics Company Apple sued Samsung in federal court alleging that Samsung's Galaxy smartphones and tablets that use Google's HTC Android operating system infringe on Apple's patents. Apple has design patents that cover the devices' graphical user interface, shell, and screen and button design. Apple has also patented the way information is displayed on iPhones and other devices, the way windows pop open, and the way information is scaled and rotated.

> "To invent, you need a good imagination and a pile of junk."
>
> **THOMAS EDISON**
> 1847–1931
> (AMERICAN INVENTOR)

AT&T owns numerous patents, including one for digitally encoding, compressing, and processing recorded speech, which is used in Microsoft's Windows operating system. Is Microsoft liable for infringement of Windows-based computers produced outside the United States?

---

17. *Microsoft Corp. v. AT&T Corp.*, 550 U.S. 437, 127 S.Ct. 1746, 167 L.Ed.2d 737 (2007).

ADAPTING THE LAW TO THE ONLINE ENVIRONMENT
The Problem of Patent Trolls

In recent years, a huge number of patent infringement lawsuits have been filed against software and technology firms. Many patent cases involve companies defending real innovations, but some lawsuits are "shakedowns" by patent trolls.

Patent trolls—more formally called nonpracticing entities (NPEs) or patent assertion entities (PAEs)—are firms that do not make or sell products or services but are in the business of patent litigation. These firms buy patents and then try to enforce them against companies that *do* sell products or services, demanding licensing fees and threatening infringement lawsuits. Patent trolls usually target online businesses.

"I'm Going to Sue You Unless You Pay Me to Go Away"
Patent trolls literally bank on the fact that when threatened with infringement suits, most companies would rather pay to settle than engage in costly litigation, even if they believe they could win. Consider an example. Soverain Software, LLC, sued dozens of online retailers, including Amazon,

Avon, Home Depot, Macy's, Nordstrom, Kohl's, RadioShack, The Gap, and Victoria's Secret. Soverain claimed that it owned patents that covered nearly any use of online shopping-cart technology and that all these retailers had infringed on its patents. Amazon paid millions to settle with Soverain, as did most of the other defendants.

Interestingly, one online retailer, Newegg, Inc., refused to pay Soverain and ultimately won in court. In 2013, a federal appellate court held that the shopping-cart patent claim was invalid on the ground of obviousness because the technology for it already existed before Soverain obtained its patent.[a]

The Role of Software Patents
The patent troll problem is concentrated in software patents, which often include descriptions of what the software does rather than the computer code involved. Many software patents are vaguely worded and overly broad. In the United States, both the patent system and the courts have had

difficulty evaluating and protecting such patents.

As a result, nearly any business that uses basic technology can be a target of patent trolls. In fact, *more than 60 percent of all new patent cases* are filed by patent trolls. The firms most commonly targeted by patent trolls, however, are large technology companies, including AT&T, Google, Apple, Samsung, Amazon, and Verizon. In 2013 alone, "AT&T was sued for patent infringement by so-called patent trolls a startling 54 times—more than once a week."[b]

CRITICAL THINKING

- Some argue that the best way to stop patent trolls from taking advantage of the system would be to eliminate software patents completely and pass a law that makes software unpatentable. Would this be fair to software and technology companies? Why or why not?

---

a. *Soverain Software, LLC v. Newegg, Inc.,* 728 F.3d 1332 (Fed.Cir. 2013), *cert. denied,* 134 S.Ct. 910 (2014).

b. Roger Parloff, "Taking on the Patent Trolls," *Fortune,* February 27, 2014.

> "The patent system . . . added the fuel to the fire of genius."
>
> **ABRAHAM LINCOLN**
> 1809–1865
> (SIXTEENTH PRESIDENT OF THE UNITED STATES, 1861–1865)

In 2012, a jury issued a verdict in favor of Apple, finding that Samsung had willfully infringed five of Apple's patents. Although the jury awarded more than $1 billion in damages—one of the largest awards ever made in a patent case—a judge later ruled that part of the damages had been incorrectly calculated.[18] The case provided an important precedent for Apple in its legal battles against Android devices made by other companies worldwide. Nevertheless, litigation between Apple and Samsung over the current generation of smartphones and mobile devices has continued.

6–2d Remedies for Patent Infringement

If a patent is infringed, the patent holder may sue for relief in federal court. The patent holder can seek an injunction against the infringer and can also request damages for royalties and lost profits. (A royalty is a payment made to a patent or copyright holder for the privilege of using the patent or the copyrighted work.) In some cases, the court may grant the winning party

---

18. *Apple, Inc. v. Samsung Electronics Co., Ltd.,* 926 F.Supp.2d 1100 (N.D.Cal. 2013); and *Apple, Inc. v. Samsung Electronics Co., Ltd.,* 735 F.3d 1352 (2013).

reimbursement for attorneys' fees and costs. If the court determines that the infringement was willful, the court can triple the amount of damages awarded (treble damages).

In the past, permanent injunctions were routinely granted to prevent future infringement. Today, however, according to the United States Supreme Court, a patent holder must prove that it has suffered irreparable injury and that the public interest would not be *disserved* by a permanent injunction.[19] Thus, courts have the discretion to decide what is equitable in the circumstances and to consider the public interest rather than just the interests of the parties.

CASE EXAMPLE 6.11 Cordance Corporation developed some of the technology and software that automates Internet communications. Cordance sued Amazon.com, Inc., for patent infringement, claiming that Amazon's one-click purchasing interface infringed on one of Cordance's patents. After a jury found Amazon guilty of infringement, Cordance requested the court to issue a permanent injunction against Amazon's infringement or, alternatively, to order Amazon to pay Cordance an ongoing royalty.

The court refused to issue a permanent injunction, because Cordance had not proved that it would otherwise suffer irreparable harm. Cordance and Amazon were not direct competitors in the relevant market. Cordance had never sold or licensed the technology infringed by Amazon's one-click purchasing interface and had presented no market data or evidence to show how the infringement negatively affected Cordance. The court also refused to impose an ongoing royalty on Amazon.[20] ▪

6-3 Copyrights

A **copyright** is an intangible property right granted by federal statute to the author or originator of certain literary or artistic productions. The Copyright Act of 1976,[21] as amended, governs copyrights. Works created after January 1, 1978, are automatically given statutory copyright protection for the life of the author plus 70 years. For copyrights owned by publishing companies, the copyright expires 95 years from the date of publication or 120 years from the date of creation, whichever is first. For works by more than one author, the copyright expires 70 years after the death of the last surviving author.

CASE EXAMPLE 6.12 The popular character Sherlock Holmes originated in stories written by Arthur Conan Doyle and published from 1887 through 1927. Over the years, elements of the characters and stories created by Doyle have appeared in books, movies, and television series, including the recent *Elementary* on CBS and *Sherlock* on BBC. Before 2013, those who wished to use the copyrighted Sherlock material had to pay a licensing fee to Doyle's estate. Then, in 2013, the editors of a book of Holmes-related stories filed a lawsuit in federal court claiming that the basic Sherlock Holmes story elements introduced before 1923 should no longer be protected. The court agreed and ruled that these elements have entered the public domain—that is, the copyright has expired, and they can be used without permission.[22] ▪

Copyrights can be registered with the U.S. Copyright Office (**www.copyright.gov**) in Washington, D.C. Registration is not required, however. A copyright owner need not place a © or *Copr.* or *Copyright* on the work to have the work protected against infringement. Chances are that if somebody created it, somebody owns it.

Generally, copyright owners are protected against the following:

1. Reproduction of the work.
2. Development of derivative works.
3. Distribution of the work.
4. Public display of the work.

LEARNING OBJECTIVE 4
What laws protect authors' rights in the works they create?

Copyright The exclusive right of an author or originator of a literary or artistic production to publish, print, sell, or otherwise use that production for a statutory period of time.

KNOW THIS
A creative work that is not copyrightable may be protected by other intellectual property law.

---

19. *eBay, Inc. v. MercExchange, LLC*, 547 U.S. 388, 126 S.Ct. 1837, 164 L.Ed.2d 641 (2006).
20. *Cordance Corp. v. Amazon.com, Inc.*, 730 F.Supp.2d 333 (D.Del. 2010).
21. 17 U.S.C. Sections 101 *et seq.*
22. *Klinger v. Conan Doyle Estate, Ltd.*, 988 F.Supp.2d 879 (N.D.Ill. 2013).

Artist Shepard Fairey created a poster portrait of Barack Obama. It was clearly based on an Associated Press file photo taken by Manny Garcia. Did Fairey violate copyright law?

6–3a What Is Protected Expression?

Works that are copyrightable include books, records, films, artworks, architectural plans, menus, music videos, product packaging, and computer software. To be protected, a work must be "fixed in a durable medium" from which it can be perceived, reproduced, or communicated. As noted, protection is automatic, and registration is not required.

To obtain protection under the Copyright Act, a work must be original and fall into one of the following categories:

1. Literary works (including newspaper and magazine articles, computer and training manuals, catalogues, brochures, and print advertisements).

2. Musical works and accompanying words (including advertising jingles).

3. Dramatic works and accompanying music.

4. Pantomimes and choreographic works (including ballets and other forms of dance).

5. Pictorial, graphic, and sculptural works (including cartoons, maps, posters, statues, and even stuffed animals).

6. Motion pictures and other audiovisual works (including multimedia works).

7. Sound recordings.

8. Architectural works.

Section 102 Exclusions Generally, anything that is not an original expression will not qualify for copyright protection. Facts widely known to the public are not copyrightable. Page numbers are not copyrightable because they follow a sequence known to everyone. Mathematical calculations are not copyrightable.

In addition, it is not possible to copyright an idea. Section 102 of the Copyright Act specifically excludes copyright protection for any "idea, procedure, process, system, method of operation, concept, principle, or discovery, regardless of the form in which it is described, explained, illustrated, or embodied." Thus, others can freely use the underlying ideas or principles embodied in a work. What is copyrightable is the particular way in which an idea is *expressed*. Whenever an idea and an expression are inseparable, the expression cannot be copyrighted.

An idea and its expression, then, must be separable to be copyrightable. Thus, for the design of a useful item to be copyrightable, the sculptural features—that is, the way it looks—must be separate from its utilitarian (functional) purpose. In the following case, the court was asked to apply this principle.

CASE 6.3

Inhale, Inc. v. Starbuzz Tobacco, Inc.

United States Court of Appeals for the Ninth Circuit, 755 F.3d 1038 (2014).

FACTS A hookah is a device for smoking tobacco by filtering the smoke through water. The water is held in a container at the base of the hookah. Inhale, Inc., claimed to hold a registered copyright on a hookah that covered the shape of the hookah's water container. Inhale filed a suit in a federal district court against Starbuzz Tobacco, Inc., for copyright infringement, alleging that Starbuzz sold hookahs with water containers shaped exactly like the Inhale containers. The court determined that the shape

Is the shape of this hookah's water container copyrightable?

of the water container on Inhale's hookahs was not copyrightable and issued a summary judgment in Starbuzz's favor. Inhale appealed.

ISSUE Was Inhale's registered copyright infringed by Starbuzz's sale of hookahs with water containers identical in shape to Inhale's containers?

DECISION No. The U.S. Court of Appeals for the Ninth Circuit affirmed the lower court's judgment.

REASON The federal appellate court stated, "The shape of a container is not independent of the container's utilitarian function—to hold the contents within its shape—because the shape accomplishes the function." The water container on a hookah is a "useful article." Thus, the shape of the container is copyrightable only if it incorporates sculptural features that can be identified separately from the container's useful aspect. Inhale argued that the shape of its hookah water container was distinctive. In an earlier case involving bottle designs, the U.S. Copyright Office had reasoned that whether an item's shape is distinctive does not affect a determination of whether the item's sculptural features can be separated from the item's utility. With regard to Inhale's water container, "The shape of the alleged artistic features and of the useful article are one and the same." Thus, the shape of the water container on Inhale's hookahs was not copyrightable.

WHAT IF THE FACTS WERE DIFFERENT? *Suppose that Inhale had claimed a copyright in the design of a vodka bottle instead of a hookah. Would the result have been different? Why or why not?*

Compilations of Facts As mentioned, facts widely known to the public are not copyrightable. *Compilations* of facts, however, may be copyrightable. Under Section 103 of the Copyright Act, a compilation is a work formed by the collection and assembling of preexisting materials or of data that are selected, coordinated, or arranged in such a way that the resulting work as a whole constitutes an original work of authorship.

The key requirement for the copyrightability of a compilation is originality. The White Pages of a telephone directory do not qualify for copyright protection because they simply list names and telephone numbers alphabetically. The Yellow Pages of a directory can be copyrightable, provided that the information is selected, coordinated, or arranged in an original way. Similarly, a court held that a compilation of information about yachts listed for sale may qualify for copyright protection.[23]

6–3b Copyright Infringement

Whenever the form or expression of an idea is copied, an infringement of copyright occurs. The reproduction does not have to be exactly the same as the original, nor does it have to reproduce the original in its entirety. If a substantial part of the original is reproduced, copyright infringement has occurred.

Remedies for Copyright Infringement Those who infringe copyrights may be liable for damages or criminal penalties. These range from actual damages or statutory damages, imposed at the court's discretion, to criminal proceedings for willful violations. Actual damages are based on the harm caused to the copyright holder by the infringement, while statutory damages, not to exceed $150,000, are provided for under the Copyright Act. In addition, criminal proceedings may result in fines and/or imprisonment. In some instances, a court may grant an injunction against the infringer.

CASE EXAMPLE 6.13 Rusty Carroll operated an online term paper business, R2C2, Inc., that offered up to 300,000 research papers for sale on nine different Web sites. Individuals whose work was posted on these Web sites without their permission filed a lawsuit against Carroll for copyright infringement. Because Carroll repeatedly failed to comply with court orders regarding discovery, the court found that the copyright infringement was likely to continue unless an injunction was issued. The court therefore issued a permanent injunction prohibiting Carroll and R2C2 from selling any term paper without sworn documentary evidence that the paper's author had given permission.[24]

The "Fair Use" Exception An exception to liability for copyright infringement is made under the "fair use" doctrine. In certain circumstances, a person or organization can reproduce

"Don't worry about people stealing an idea. If it's original and it's any good, you'll have to ram it down their throats."

HOWARD AIKEN
1900–1973
(ENGINEER AND PIONEER IN COMPUTING)

---

23. *BUC International Corp. v. International Yacht Council, Ltd.*, 489 F.3d 1129 (11th Cir. 2007).
24. *Weidner v. Carroll*, 2010 WL 310310 (S.D.Ill. 2010).

copyrighted material without paying royalties. Section 107 of the Copyright Act provides as follows:

> [T]he fair use of a copyrighted work, including such use by reproduction in copies or phonorecords or by any other means specified by [Section 106 of the Copyright Act], for purposes such as criticism, comment, news reporting, teaching (including multiple copies for classroom use), scholarship, or research, is not an infringement of copyright. In determining whether the use made of a work in any particular case is a fair use the factors to be considered shall include—
>
> (1) the purpose and character of the use, including whether such use is of a commercial nature or is for nonprofit educational purposes;
> (2) the nature of the copyrighted work;
> (3) the amount and substantiality of the portion used in relation to the copyrighted work as a whole; and
> (4) the effect of the use upon the potential market for or value of the copyrighted work.

What Is Fair Use? Because the fair use guidelines are very broad, the courts determine whether a particular use is fair on a case-by-case basis. Thus, anyone reproducing copyrighted material may be committing a violation. In determining whether a use is fair, courts have often considered the fourth factor to be the most important.

Do makers of karaoke machines automatically have the right to reproduce printed lyrics?

CASE EXAMPLE 6.14 BMG Music Publishing, an owner of copyrighted music, granted a license to Leadsinger, Inc., a manufacturer of karaoke devices. The license gave Leadsinger permission to reproduce the sound recordings, but not to reprint the song lyrics. The lyrics, however, appeared at the bottom of a TV screen when the karaoke device was used.

BMG demanded that Leadsinger pay a "lyric reprint" fee and a "synchronization" fee for this use of the song lyrics. Leadsinger refused, claiming that its use of the lyrics was educational and thus did not constitute copyright infringement under the fair use exception. A federal appellate court disagreed. The court held that Leadsinger's display of the lyrics was not a fair use because it would negatively affect the value of the copyrighted work.[25] ■

ETHICAL ISSUE

Should fair use include the creation of a full-text searchable database of millions of books? Back in 2004, a number of research universities, in partnership with Google, Inc., agreed to digitize books from their libraries and create a repository for them. In 2008, the HathiTrust Digital Library was formed by eighty institutions, including the University of California at Berkeley, Cornell University, and the University of Michigan. As of 2012, the library contained some 10 million digitized works.

Not all authors whose works were represented in the library were happy with what they considered a violation of their intellectual property rights. After all, shouldn't copyright law protect authors (and publishers) from having Google, Inc., electronically scan their books without their permission? Google and the HathiTrust responded that there was no copyright violation. The library's main interest was preservation, and its full-text searchable database of the library's books was an aid to scholarship. It enabled researchers to find terms of interest in the digital volumes—not to read the volumes online. Search results yielded only page numbers where the terms could be found.

In 2011, a group of authors and authors' associations sued the HathiTrust and several associated entities for copyright infringement. The U.S. District Court for the Southern District of New York granted summary judgment in favor of the defendants.[26] On appeal, the reviewing court noted, "A fair use must not excessively damage the market for the original by providing the public with a substitute for that original work." But, the appellate court pointed out, the HathiTrust database "does not allow users to view any portion of the books they are search-

---

25. *Leadsinger, Inc. v. BMG Music Publishing*, 512 F.3d 522 (9th Cir. 2008).
26. *Authors Guild, Inc. v. HathiTrust*, 902 F.Supp.2d 445 (S.D.N.Y. 2012).

ing. Consequently, in providing this service, the [HathiTrust] does not add into circulation any new, human-readable copies of any books." Indeed, the court suggested that full-text searches might add to the value of copyrighted works.[27]

The First Sale Doctrine   Section 109(a) of the Copyright Act provides that "the owner of a particular copy or phonorecord lawfully made under [the Copyright Act], or any person authorized by such owner, is entitled, without the authority of the copyright owner, to sell or otherwise dispose of the possession of that copy or phonorecord." This rule is known as the first sale doctrine.

Under this doctrine, once a copyright owner sells or gives away a particular copy of a work, the copyright owner no longer has the right to control the distribution of that copy. **EXAMPLE 6.15** Miranda buys *The Hunger Games* by Suzanne Collins, a copyrighted book. She can legally sell the book to another person. ■

In 2012, the United States Supreme Court heard the appeal of a case involving the resale of textbooks on eBay. To read about the Court's decision in this important case, see this chapter's *Beyond Our Borders* feature.

---

27. *Authors Guild, Inc. v. HathiTrust*, 755 F.3d 87 (2d Cir. 2014).

BEYOND OUR BORDERS

The Resale of Textbooks Purchased Abroad

Students and professors alike complain about the high price of college textbooks. Some enterprising students have found that if they purchase textbooks printed abroad, they may save enough to justify the shipping charges. Textbook prices are lower in other countries because production costs are lower there and average incomes are also lower, so students are unable to pay higher prices.

A University Student Starts a Side Business

Supap Kirtsaeng, a citizen of Thailand, was a graduate student at the University of Southern California. He enlisted friends and family in Thailand to buy copies of textbooks there and ship them to him in the United States. Kirtsaeng resold the textbooks on eBay, where he eventually made about $100,000.

John Wiley & Sons, Inc., had printed eight of those textbooks in Asia. Wiley sued Kirtsaeng in federal district court for copyright

infringement. Kirtsaeng argued that Section 109(a) of the Copyright Act allows the first purchaser-owner of a book to sell it without the copyright owner's permission. But the trial court held in favor of Wiley, and that decision was affirmed on appeal.[a] The lower courts reasoned that the first sale doctrine in the Copyright Act refers specifically to works manufactured in the United States and should not apply to textbooks printed and sold abroad. Kirtsaeng appealed to the United States Supreme Court.

The Supreme Court Weighs In

Can a copy of a book or CD or DVD that was legally produced abroad, acquired abroad, and then imported into the United States be resold in the United States without the copyright owner's permission? That was the issue before the Supreme Court. The answer has implications not only for individuals but

also for discount sellers such as Costco and online businesses such as eBay and Google.

The Supreme Court ruled in Kirtsaeng's favor, reversing the appellate court's decision.[b] The Court held that the first sale doctrine applies even to goods purchased abroad. According to the Court, "the common-law history of the 'first-sale' doctrine . . . favors a non-geographical interpretation." The justices were clearly concerned about what might occur if the Court did not reverse the appellate court's decision. Allowing that decision to stand could have made it possible to "prevent a buyer from domestically selling or even giving away copies of a video game made in Japan."

CRITICAL THINKING

■ What options do textbook publishers face given this Supreme Court decision?

---

a. *John Wiley & Sons, Inc. v. Kirtsaeng*, 2009 WL 3364037 (S.D.N.Y. 2009); and *John Wiley & Sons, Inc. v. Kirtsaeng*, 654 F.3d 210 (2d Cir. 2011).

b. *Kirtsaeng v. John Wiley & Sons, Inc.*, ___ U.S. ___, 133 S.Ct. 1351, 185 L.Ed.2d 392 (2013).

6-3c Copyright Protection for Software

In 1980, Congress passed the Computer Software Copyright Act, which amended the Copyright Act to include computer programs in the list of creative works protected by federal copyright law. Generally, copyright protection extends to those parts of a computer program that can be read by humans, such as the high-level language of a source code. Protection also extends to the binary-language object code, which is readable only by the computer, and to such elements as the overall structure, sequence, and organization of a program.

Not all aspects of software are protected, however. Courts typically have not extended copyright protection to the "look and feel"—the general appearance, command structure, video images, menus, windows, and other screen displays—of computer programs. **EXAMPLE 6.16** MiTek develops a software program for laying out wood trusses (used in construction). A competing company comes out with a program that has similar elements, including the menu and submenu command structures. MiTek cannot successfully sue for copyright infringement, because the command structure of software is not protected. ■ Note that copying the "look and feel" of another's product may be a violation of trade dress or trademark laws, however.

As will be discussed in Chapter 7, technology has vastly increased the potential for copyright infringement via the Internet.

LEARNING OBJECTIVE 5

What are trade secrets, and what laws offer protection for this form of intellectual property?

Trade Secret A formula, device, idea, process, or other information used in a business that gives the owner a competitive advantage in the marketplace.

6-4   Trade Secrets

The law of trade secrets protects some business processes and information that are not or cannot be protected under patent, copyright, or trademark law. A **trade secret** is basically information of commercial value. A company's customer lists, plans, and research and development are trade secrets. Trade secrets may also include pricing information, marketing techniques, and production methods—anything that makes an individual company unique and that would have value to a competitor.

Unlike copyright and trademark protection, protection of trade secrets extends both to ideas and to their expression. (For this reason, and because there are no registration or filing requirements for trade secrets, trade secret protection may be well suited for software.) Of course, the secret formula, method, or other information must be disclosed to some persons, particularly to key employees. Businesses generally attempt to protect their trade secrets by having all employees who use the process or information agree in their contracts, or in confidentiality agreements, never to divulge it.

6-4a State and Federal Law on Trade Secrets

Under Section 757 of the *Restatement of Torts*, those who disclose or use another's trade secret, without authorization, are liable to that other party if either of the following is true:

1. They discovered the secret by improper means.

2. Their disclosure or use constitutes a breach of a duty owed to the other party.

Stealing of confidential business data by industrial espionage, as when a business taps into a competitor's computer, is a theft of trade secrets without any contractual violation and is actionable in itself.

Although trade secrets have long been protected under the common law, today most states' laws are based on the Uniform Trade Secrets Act, which has been adopted in forty-seven states. Additionally, the Economic Espionage Act made the theft of trade secrets a federal crime, as we will discuss in Chapter 8.

6-4b Trade Secrets in Cyberspace

Today's computer technology undercuts a business firm's ability to protect its confidential information, including trade secrets. For instance, a dishonest employee could e-mail trade secrets in a company's computer to a competitor or a future employer. If e-mail is not an option, the employee might walk out with the information on a flash pen drive.

Misusing a company's social media accounts is yet another way in which employees may appropriate trade secrets. **CASE EXAMPLE 6.17** Noah Kravitz worked for a company called Phone-Dog for four years as a product reviewer and video blogger. PhoneDog provided him with the Twitter account "@PhoneDog_Noah." Kravitz's popularity grew, and he had approximately 17,000 followers by the time he quit in 2010. PhoneDog requested that Kravitz stop using the Twitter account. Although Kravitz changed his handle to "@noahkravitz," he continued to use the account. PhoneDog subsequently sued Kravitz for misappropriation of trade secrets, among other things. Kravitz moved for a dismissal, but the court found that the complaint adequately stated a cause of action for misappropriation of trade secrets and allowed the suit to continue.[28]

For a summary of trade secrets and other forms of intellectual property, see Exhibit 6–1.

---

28. *PhoneDog v. Kravitz*, 2011 WL 5415612 (N.D.Cal. 2011).

Exhibit 6–1 Forms of Intellectual Property

	DEFINITION	HOW ACQUIRED	DURATION	REMEDY FOR INFRINGEMENT
Patent	A grant from the government that gives an inventor exclusive rights to an invention.	By filing a patent application with the U.S. Patent and Trademark Office and receiving its approval.	Twenty years from the date of the application; for design patents, fourteen years.	Monetary damages, including royalties and lost profits, plus attorneys' fees. Damages may be tripled for intentional infringement.
Copyright	The right of an author or originator of a literary or artistic work, or other production that falls within a specified category, to have the exclusive use of that work for a given period of time.	Automatic (once the work or creation is put in tangible form). Only the *expression* of an idea (and not the idea itself) can be protected by copyright.	For authors: the life of the author plus 70 years. For publishers: 95 years after the date of publication or 120 years after creation.	Actual damages plus profits received by the party who infringed *or* statutory damages under the Copyright Act, *plus* costs and attorneys' fees in either situation.
Trademark (service mark and trade dress)	Any distinctive word, name, symbol, or device (image or appearance), or combination thereof, that an entity uses to distinguish its goods or services from those of others. The owner has the exclusive right to use that mark or trade dress.	1. At common law, ownership created by use of the mark. 2. Registration with the appropriate federal or state office gives notice and is permitted if the mark is currently in use or will be within the next six months.	Unlimited, as long as it is in use. To continue notice by registration, the owner must renew by filing between the fifth and sixth years, and thereafter, every ten years.	1. Injunction prohibiting the future use of the mark. 2. Actual damages plus profits received by the party who infringed (can be increased under the Lanham Act). 3. Destruction of articles that infringed. 4. *Plus* costs and attorneys' fees.
Trade Secret	Any information that a business possesses and that gives the business an advantage over competitors (including formulas, lists, patterns, plans, processes, and programs).	Through the originality and development of the information and processes that constitute the business secret and are unknown to others.	Unlimited, so long as not revealed to others. Once revealed to others, it is no longer a trade secret.	Monetary damages for misappropriation (the Uniform Trade Secrets Act also permits punitive damages if willful), *plus* costs and attorneys' fees.

6-5 International Protections

For many years, the United States has been a party to various international agreements relating to intellectual property rights. For example, the Paris Convention of 1883, to which about 173 countries are signatory, allows parties in one country to file for patent and trademark protection in any of the other member countries. Other international agreements include the Berne Convention, the Trade-Related Aspects of Intellectual Property Rights (known as the TRIPS agreement), the Madrid Protocol, and the Anti-Counterfeiting Trade Agreement.

6-5a The Berne Convention

Under the Berne Convention of 1886, an international copyright agreement, if a U.S. citizen writes a book, every country that has signed the convention must recognize her or his copyright in the book. Also, if a citizen of a country that has not signed the convention first publishes a book in one of the 168 countries that have signed, all other countries that have signed the convention must recognize that author's copyright. Copyright notice is not needed to gain protection under the Berne Convention for works published after March 1, 1989.

In 2011, the European Union altered its copyright rules under the Berne Convention by agreeing to extend the period of royalty protection for musicians from fifty years to seventy years. This decision aids major record labels as well as performers and musicians. The profits of musicians and record companies have been shrinking in recent years because of the sharp decline in sales of compact discs and the rise in digital downloads (both legal and illegal).

6-5b The TRIPS Agreement

The Berne Convention and other international agreements have given some protection to intellectual property on a worldwide level. None of them, however, has been as significant and far reaching in scope as the TRIPS agreement.

Representatives from more than one hundred nations signed the TRIPS agreement in 1994. The agreement established, for the first time, standards for the international protection of intellectual property rights, including patents, trademarks, and copyrights for movies, computer programs, books, and music. The TRIPS agreement provides that each member country must include in its domestic laws broad intellectual property rights and effective remedies (including civil and criminal penalties) for violations of those rights.

Generally, the TRIPS agreement forbids member nations from discriminating against foreign owners of intellectual property rights in the administration, regulation, or adjudication of such rights. In other words, a member nation cannot give its own nationals (citizens) favorable treatment without offering the same treatment to nationals of all member countries. **EXAMPLE 6.18** A U.S. software manufacturer brings a suit for the infringement of intellectual property rights under Germany's national laws. Because Germany is a member of the TRIPS agreement, the U.S. manufacturer is entitled to receive the same treatment as a German manufacturer. ■

Each member nation must ensure that legal procedures are available for parties who wish to bring actions for infringement of intellectual property rights. Additionally, a related document established a mechanism for settling disputes among member nations.

6-5c The Madrid Protocol

In the past, one of the difficulties in protecting U.S. trademarks internationally was that it was time consuming and expensive to apply for trademark registration in foreign countries. The filing fees and procedures for trademark registration vary significantly among individual countries. The Madrid Protocol, which was signed into law in 2003, may help to resolve these problems.

The Madrid Protocol is an international treaty that has been signed by seventy-three countries. Under its provisions, a U.S. company wishing to register its trademark abroad can submit a single application and designate other member countries in which it would like to register the mark. The treaty was designed to reduce the costs of obtaining international trademark protection by more than 60 percent.

Although the Madrid Protocol may simplify and reduce the cost of trademark registration in foreign nations, it remains to be seen whether it will provide significant benefits to trademark owners. Even with an easier registration process, the question of whether member countries will enforce the law and protect the mark still remains.

6-5d The Anti-Counterfeiting Trade Agreement

In 2011, Australia, Canada, Japan, Korea, Morocco, New Zealand, Singapore, and the United States signed the Anti-Counterfeiting Trade Agreement (ACTA), an international treaty to combat global counterfeiting and piracy. The members of the European Union, Mexico, Switzerland, and other nations that support the ACTA are still developing domestic procedures to comply with its provisions. Once a nation has adopted appropriate procedures, it can ratify the treaty.

Provisions and Goals The goals of the treaty are to increase international cooperation, facilitate the best law enforcement practices, and provide a legal framework to combat counterfeiting. The treaty will have its own governing body.

The ACTA applies not only to counterfeit physical goods, such as medications, but also to pirated copyrighted works being distributed via the Internet. The idea is to create a new standard of enforcement for intellectual property rights that goes beyond the TRIPS agreement and encourages international cooperation and information sharing among signatory countries.

Border Searches Under ACTA, member nations are required to establish border measures that allow officials, on their own initiative, to search commercial shipments of imports and exports for counterfeit goods. The treaty neither requires nor prohibits random border searches of electronic devices, such as laptops and iPads, for infringing content.

If border authorities reasonably believe that any goods in transit are counterfeit, the treaty allows them to keep the suspect goods unless the owner proves that the items are authentic and noninfringing. The treaty allows member nations, in accordance with their own laws, to order online service providers to furnish information about (including the identity of) suspected trademark and copyright infringers.

Reviewing . . . Intellectual Property Rights

Two computer science majors, Trent and Xavier, have an idea for a new video game, which they propose to call "Hallowed." They form a business and begin developing their idea. Several months later, Trent and Xavier run into a problem with their design and consult with a friend, Brad, who is an expert in creating computer source codes. After the software is completed but before Hallowed is marketed, a video game called Halo 2 is released for both the Xbox and PlayStation 3 systems. Halo 2 uses source codes similar to those of Hallowed and imitates Hallowed's overall look and feel, although not all the features are alike. Using the information presented in the chapter, answer the following questions.

1. Would the name Hallowed receive protection as a trademark or as trade dress?

2. If Trent and Xavier had obtained a business process patent on Hallowed, would the release of Halo 2 infringe on their patent? Why or why not?

Continues

3. Based only on the facts presented above, could Trent and Xavier sue the makers of Halo 2 for copyright infringement? Why or why not?

4. Suppose that Trent and Xavier discover that Brad took the idea of Hallowed and sold it to the company that produced Halo 2. Which type of intellectual property issue does this raise?

DEBATE THIS

- Congress has amended the Copyright Act several times. Copyright holders now have protection for many decades. Was Congress justified in extending the copyright time periods? Why or why not?

LINKING BUSINESS LAW TO MARKETING
Trademarks and Service Marks

In your marketing courses, you have learned or will learn about the importance of trademarks. If you become a marketing manager, you will likely be involved in creating trademarks or service marks for your firm, protecting the firm's existing marks, and ensuring that the firm does not infringe on anyone else's marks.

The Broad Range of Trademarks and Service Marks

The courts have held that trademarks and service marks consist of much more than well-known brand names, such as Apple and Amazon. As a marketing manager, you will need to be aware that parts of a brand name or other forms of product identification may qualify for trademark protection.

- **Catchy phrases**—Certain brands have established phrases that are associated with the brands, such as Nike's "Just Do It!" Marketing managers for competing product should avoid using similar phrases

in their marketing programs. Note, though, that not all phrases can become part of a trademark or service mark. When a phrase is extremely common, the courts normally will not grant trademark or service mark protection to it.

- **Abbreviations**—The public sometimes abbreviates a well-known trademark. For example, Budweiser beer is known as Bud and Coca-Cola as Coke. Marketing managers should avoid using any name for a product or service that closely resembles a well-known abbreviation, such as Koke for a cola drink.

- **Shapes**—The shape of a brand name, a service mark, or a container can take on exclusivity if the shape clearly aids in product or service identification. For example, just about everyone throughout the world recognizes the shape of a Coca-Cola bottle. Marketing managers would do well to avoid using a similar shape for a new carbonated drink.

- **Ornamental colors**—Sometimes, color combinations can become part of a service mark or trademark. For example,

FedEx established its unique identity with the use of bright orange and purple. The courts have protected this color combination. The same holds for the black-and-copper color combination of Duracell batteries.

- **Ornamental designs**—Symbols and designs associated with a particular mark are normally protected. Marketing managers should not attempt to copy them. Levi's places a small tag on the left side of the rear pocket of its jeans. Cross uses a cutoff black cone on the top of its pens.

- **Sounds**—Sounds can also be protected. For example, the familiar roar of the Metro-Goldwyn-Mayer (MGM) lion is protected.

When to Protect Trademarks and Service Marks

Every business should register its logo as a trademark, and perhaps also its business name and Web site address, to provide the company with the highest level of protection. A trademark will discourage counterfeiting and will give your firm the advantage in the event of future infringement.

Once your company has established a trademark or a service mark, as a manager, you will have to decide how aggressively you wish to protect those marks. If you fail to protect them, your company faces the possibility that they will become generic. Remember that *aspirin, cellophane, thermos, dry ice, shredded wheat,* and many other familiar terms were once legally protected trademarks. Protecting exclusive rights to a mark can be expensive, however, so you will have to determine how much it is worth to your company to protect your rights. If you work in a small company, making major expenditures to protect your trademarks and service marks might not be cost-effective.

- The U.S. Patent and Trademark Office requires that a registered trademark or service mark be put into commercial use within three years after the application has been approved. Why do you think the federal government established this requirement?

Key Terms

certification mark 143

collective mark 143

copyright 149

domain name 142

intellectual property 138

license 144

patent 145

service mark 143

trade dress 143

trade name 144

trade secret 154

trademark 139

trademark dilution 140

Chapter Summary: Intellectual Property Rights

Trademarks	1. A *trademark* is a distinctive word, symbol, or design that identifies the manufacturer as the source of the goods and distinguishes its products from those made or sold by others. 2. The major federal statutes protecting trademarks and related property are the Lanham Act of 1946 and the Federal Trademark Dilution Act of 1995. Generally, to be protected, a trademark must be sufficiently distinctive from all competing trademarks. 3. *Trademark infringement* occurs when one party uses a mark that is the same as, or confusingly similar to, the protected trademark, service mark, trade name, or trade dress of another party without permission when marketing goods or services.
Patents	1. A *patent* is a grant from the government that gives an inventor the exclusive right to make, use, and sell an invention for a period of twenty years (fourteen years for a design patent) from the date when the application for a patent is filed. To be patentable, an invention (or a discovery, process, or design) must be genuine, novel, useful, and not obvious in light of current technology. Computer software may be patented. 2. Almost anything is patentable, except the laws of nature, natural phenomena, and abstract ideas (including algorithms). Even artistic methods and works of art, certain business processes, and the structures of storylines may be patentable. 3. *Patent infringement* occurs when someone uses or sells another's patented design, product, or process without the patent owner's permission. The patent holder can sue the infringer in federal court and request an injunction, but must prove irreparable injury to obtain a permanent injunction against the infringer. The patent holder can also request damages and attorneys' fees. If the infringement was willful, the court can grant treble damages.
Copyrights	1. A *copyright* is an intangible property right granted by federal statute to the author or originator of certain literary or artistic productions. The Copyright Act of 1976, as amended, governs copyrights. 2. *Copyright infringement* occurs whenever the form or expression of an idea is copied without the permission of the copyright holder. An exception applies if the copying is deemed a "fair use." 3. In 1980, Congress passed the Computer Software Copyright Act, which amended the Copyright Act to include computer programs in the list of creative works protected by federal copyright law.
Trade Secrets	*Trade secrets* include customer lists, plans, research and development, and pricing information. Trade secrets are protected under the common law and, in most states, under statutory law against misappropriation by competitors. The Economic Espionage Act made the theft of trade secrets a federal crime.
International Protections	Various international agreements provide international protection for intellectual property. A landmark agreement is the Trade-Related Aspects of Intellectual Property Rights (TRIPS) agreement, which provides for enforcement procedures in all countries signatory to the agreement.

Issue Spotters

1. Roslyn, a food buyer for Organic Cornucopia Food Company, decides to go into business for herself as Roslyn's Kitchen. She contacts Organic's suppliers, offering to buy their entire harvest for the next year. She also contacts Organic's customers, offering to sell her products for less than Organic. Has Roslyn violated any of the intellectual property rights discussed in this chapter? Explain. (See *Trade Secrets*.)

2. Global Products develops, patents, and markets software. World Copies, Inc., sells Global's software without the maker's permission. Is this patent infringement? If so, how might Global save the cost of suing World for infringement and at the same time profit from World's sales? (See *Patents*.)

—**Check your answers to the *Issue Spotters* against the answers provided in Appendix D at the end of this text.**

Learning Objectives Check

1. What is intellectual property?

2. Why is the protection of trademarks important?

3. How does the law protect patents?

4. What laws protect authors' rights in the works they create?

5. What are trade secrets, and what laws offer protection for this form of intellectual property?

—**Answers to the even-numbered *Learning Objectives Check* questions can be found in Appendix E at the end of this text.**

Business Scenarios and Case Problems

6–1. Patent Infringement. John and Andrew Doney invented a hard-bearing device for balancing rotors. Although they obtained a patent for their invention from the U.S. Patent and Trademark Office, it was never used as an automobile wheel balancer. Some time later, Exetron Corp. produced an automobile wheel balancer that used a hard-bearing device similar to the Doneys' device. Given that the Doneys had not used their device for automobile wheel balancing, does Exetron's use of a similar device infringe on the Doneys' patent? (See *Patents*.)

6–2. Fair Use. Professor Wise is teaching a summer seminar in business torts at State University. Several times during the course, he makes copies of relevant sections from business law texts and distributes them to his students. Wise does not realize that the daughter of one of the textbook authors is a member of his seminar. She tells her father about Wise's copying activities, which have taken place without her father's or his publisher's permission. Her father sues Wise for copyright infringement. Wise claims protection under the fair use doctrine. Who will prevail? Explain. (See *Copyrights*.)

6–3. Licensing. Redwin Wilchcombe composed, performed, and recorded a song called *Tha Weedman* at the request of Lil Jon, a member of Lil Jon & the East Side Boyz (LJESB), for LJESB's album *Kings of Crunk*. Wilchcombe was not paid, but was given credit on the album as a producer. After the album had sold two million copies, Wilchcombe filed a suit against LJESB, alleging copyright infringement. The defendants claimed that they had a license to use the song. Do the facts support this claim? Explain. [*Wilchcombe v. TeeVee Toons, Inc.*, 555 F.3d 949 (11th Cir. 2009)] (See *Copyrights*.)

6–4. Spotlight on Macy's—Copyright Infringement. United Fabrics International, Inc., bought a fabric design from an Italian designer and registered a copyright to the design with the U.S. Copyright Office. When Macy's, Inc., began selling garments with a similar design, United filed a copyright infringement suit against Macy's. Macy's argued that United did not own a valid copyright to the design and so could not claim infringement. Does United have to prove that the copyright is valid to establish infringement? Explain. [*United Fabrics International, Inc. v. C & J Wear, Inc.*, 630 F.3d 1255 (9th Cir. 2011)] (See *Copyrights*.)

6–5. Copyright Infringement. SilverEdge Systems Software hired Catherine Conrad to perform a singing telegram. SilverEdge arranged for James Bendewald to record Conrad's performance of her copyrighted song to post on the company's Web site. Conrad agreed to wear a microphone to assist in the recording, told Bendewald what to film, and asked for an additional fee only if SilverEdge used the video for a commercial purpose. Later, the company chose to post a video of a different performer's singing telegram instead. Conrad filed a suit in a federal district court against SilverEdge and Bendewald for copyright infringement. Are the defendants liable? Explain. [*Conrad v. Bendewald*, 2013 WL 310194 (7th Cir. 2013)] (See *Copyrights*.)

6–6. Business Case Problem with Sample Answer—Patents.
The U.S. Patent and Trademark Office (PTO) denied Raymond Gianelli's application for a patent for a "Rowing Machine"—an exercise machine on which a user *pulls* on handles to perform a rowing motion against a selected resistance. The PTO considered the device obvious in light of a previously patented "Chest Press Apparatus for Exercising Regions of the Upper Body"—an exercise machine on which a user *pushes* on handles to overcome a selected resistance. On what ground might this result be reversed on appeal? Discuss. [*In re Gianelli*, 739 F.3d 1375 (Fed. Cir. 2014)] (See *Patents*.)

—**For a sample answer to Problem 6–6, go to Appendix F at the end of this text.**

6–7. Patents. Rodney Klassen was employed by the U.S. Department of Agriculture (USDA). Without the USDA's authorization, Klassen gave Jim Ludy, a grape grower, plant material for two unreleased varieties of grapes. For almost two years, most of Ludy's plantings bore no usable fruit, none of the grapes were sold, and no plant material was given to any other person. The plantings were visible from publicly accessible roads, but none of the vines were labeled, and the variety could not be identified by simply viewing the vines. Under patent law, an applicant may not obtain a patent for an invention that is in public use more than one year before the date of the application. Could the USDA successfully apply for patents on the two varieties given to Ludy? Explain. [*Delano Farms Co. v. California Table Grape Commission*, __ F.3d __, 2015 WL 127317 (Fed.Cir. 2015)] (See *Patents*.)

6–8. A Question of Ethics—Copyright Infringement. Custom Copies, Inc., prepares and sells coursepacks, which contain compilations of readings for college courses. A teacher selects the readings and delivers a syllabus to the copy shop, which obtains the materials from a library, copies them, and binds the copies. Blackwell Publishing, Inc., which owns the copyright to some of the materials, filed a suit, alleging copyright infringement. [*Blackwell Publishing, Inc. v. Custom Copies, Inc.*, 2006 WL 1529503 (N.D.Fla. 2006)] (See *Copyrights*.)

1. Custom Copies argued, in part, that it did not "distribute" the coursepacks. Does a copy shop violate copyright law if it only copies materials for coursepacks? Does the fair use doctrine apply in these circumstances? Discuss.

2. What is the potential impact if copies of a book or journal are created and sold without the permission of, and the payment of royalties or a fee to, the copyright owner? Explain.

Critical Thinking and Writing Assignments

6–9. Case Analysis Question—Copyright Infringement. Go to Appendix G at the end of this text and examine the excerpt of Case No. 1, *Winstead v. Jackson*. Review and then brief the case, making sure that your brief answers the following questions. (See *Copyrights*.)

1. **Issue:** This case focused on an allegation of copyright infringement involving what parties and which creative works?

2. **Rule of Law:** What is the test for determining whether a creative work infringes the copyright of another work?

3. **Applying the Rule of Law:** How did the court determine whether the claim of copyright infringement was supported in this case?

4. **Conclusion:** Was the defendant liable for copyright infringement? Why or why not?

6–10. Business Law Critical Thinking Group Assignment.
After years of research, your company has developed a product that might revolutionize the green (environmentally conscious) building industry. The product is made from relatively inexpensive and widely available materials combined in a unique way that can substantially lower the heating and cooling costs of residential and commercial buildings. The company has registered the trademark it intends to use for the product and has filed a patent application with the U.S. Patent and Trademark Office. (See *Patents*.)

1. One group should provide three reasons why this product does or does not qualify for patent protection.

2. Another group should develop a four-step plan for how the company can best protect its intellectual property rights (trademark, trade secret, and patent) and prevent domestic and foreign competitors from producing counterfeit goods or cheap knockoffs.

3. Another group should list and explain three ways in which the company can utilize licensing.

8

iStockPhoto.com/mathieukor

LEARNING OBJECTIVES

The five Learning Objectives *below are designed to help improve your understanding of the chapter. After reading this chapter, you should be able to answer the following questions:*

1. What two elements normally must exist before a person can be held liable for a crime?

2. What are five broad categories of crimes? What is white-collar crime?

3. What defenses can be raised to avoid liability for criminal acts?

4. What constitutional safeguards exist to protect persons accused of crimes?

5. How has the Internet expanded opportunities for identity theft?

Criminal Law and Cyber Crime

The "crime problem" is of concern to all Americans, as suggested in the chapter-opening quotation. Not surprisingly, laws dealing with crime are an important part of the legal environment of business.

Society imposes a variety of sanctions to protect businesses from harm so that they can compete and flourish. These sanctions include damages for tortious conduct, damages for breach of contract, and various equitable remedies. Additional sanctions are imposed under criminal law. Many statutes regulating business provide for criminal as well as civil sanctions.

In this chapter, after explaining some essential differences between criminal law and civil law, we look at the elements that must be present for criminal liability to exist. We then examine various categories of crimes, the defenses that can be raised to avoid liability for criminal actions, constitutional safeguards for those accused of crimes, and the rules of criminal procedure.

We conclude with a discussion of crimes that occur in cyberspace, which are often called *cyber crimes*. Cyber attacks are becoming all too common—even e-mail and data of government agencies have been hacked. Many businesses have suffered cyber attacks as well. Smartphones are being infected by malicious software, which puts users' data at risk, as you will read in a feature later in this chapter.

"The crime problem is getting really serious. The other day, the Statue of Liberty had both hands up."

JAY LENO
1950–PRESENT
(AMERICAN COMEDIAN AND FORMER TELEVISION HOST)

8-1 Civil Law and Criminal Law

Remember from Chapter 1 that *civil law* spells out the duties that exist between persons or between persons and their governments. Criminal law, in contrast, has to do with crime.

A **crime** can be defined as a wrong against society proclaimed in a statute and, if committed, punishable by society through fines and/or imprisonment—and, in some cases, death.

Because crimes are *offenses against society* as a whole, they are prosecuted by a public official, such as a district attorney (D.A.) or an attorney general (AG), not by the crime victims. Once a crime has been reported, the D.A.'s office decides whether to file criminal charges and to what extent to pursue the prosecution or carry out additional investigation.

8-1a Key Differences between Civil Law and Criminal Law

Because the state has extensive resources at its disposal when prosecuting criminal cases, and because the sanctions can be so severe, there are numerous procedural safeguards to protect the rights of defendants. We look here at one of these safeguards—the higher burden of proof that applies in a criminal case—and at the sanctions imposed for criminal acts. Exhibit 8–1 summarizes these and other key differences between civil law and criminal law.

Burden of Proof
In a civil case, the plaintiff usually must prove his or her case by a *preponderance of the evidence.* Under this standard, the plaintiff must convince the court that, based on the evidence presented by both parties, it is more likely than not that the plaintiff's allegation is true.

In a criminal case, in contrast, the state must prove its case **beyond a reasonable doubt.** If the jury views the evidence in the case as reasonably permitting either a guilty or a not guilty verdict, then the jury's verdict must be *not* guilty. In other words, the prosecutor must prove beyond a reasonable doubt that the defendant has committed every essential element of the offense with which she or he is charged. If the jurors are not convinced of the defendant's guilt beyond a reasonable doubt, they must find the defendant not guilty.

Note also that in a criminal case, the jury's verdict normally must be unanimous—agreed to by all members of the jury—to convict the defendant.[1] In a civil trial by jury, in contrast, typically only three-fourths of the jurors need to agree.

Criminal Sanctions
The sanctions imposed on criminal wrongdoers are also harsher than those applied in civil cases. Remember that the purpose of tort law is to allow persons harmed by the wrongful acts of others to obtain compensation from the wrongdoer rather than to punish the wrongdoer.

In contrast, criminal sanctions are designed to punish those who commit crimes and to deter others from committing similar acts in the future. Criminal sanctions include fines as well as the much harsher penalty of the loss of liberty by incarceration in a jail or prison. The harshest criminal sanction is, of course, the death penalty.

---

1. Note that there are exceptions—a few states allow jury verdicts that are not unanimous. Arizona, for example, allows six of eight jurors to reach a verdict in criminal cases. Louisiana and Oregon have also relaxed the requirement of unanimous jury verdicts.

Exhibit 8–1 Key Differences between Civil Law and Criminal Law

ISSUE	CIVIL LAW	CRIMINAL LAW
Party who brings suit	The person who suffered harm.	The state.
Wrongful act	Causing harm to a person or to a person's property.	Violating a statute that prohibits some type of activity.
Burden of proof	Preponderance of the evidence.	Beyond a reasonable doubt.
Verdict	Three-fourths majority (typically).	Unanimous (almost always).
Remedy	Damages to compensate for the harm or a decree to achieve an equitable result.	Punishment (fine, imprisonment, or death).

8–1b Civil Liability for Criminal Acts

Some torts, such as assault and battery, provide a basis for a criminal prosecution as well as a tort action. **EXAMPLE 8.1** Carlos is walking down the street, minding his own business, when suddenly a person attacks him. In the ensuing struggle, the attacker stabs Carlos several times, seriously injuring him. A police officer restrains and arrests the wrongdoer. In this situation, the attacker may be subject both to criminal prosecution by the state and to a tort lawsuit brought by Carlos. ■ Exhibit 8–2 illustrates how the same act can result in both a tort action and a criminal action against the wrongdoer.

8–1c Classification of Crimes

Felony A crime—such as arson, murder, rape, or robbery—that carries the most severe sanctions, ranging from more than one year in a state or federal prison to the death penalty.

Depending on their degree of seriousness, crimes are classified as felonies or misdemeanors. **Felonies** are serious crimes punishable by death or by imprisonment for more than one year.[2] Many states also define several degrees of felony offenses and vary the punishment according to the degree.[3] For instance, most jurisdictions punish a burglary that involves forced entry

---

2. Federal law and most state laws use this definition, but there is some variation among states as to the length of imprisonment associated with a felony conviction.
3. Although the American Law Institute issued the Model Penal Code in 1962, it is not a uniform code, and each state has developed its own set of laws governing criminal acts. Thus, types of crimes and prescribed punishments may differ from one jurisdiction to another.

Exhibit 8–2 Tort Lawsuit and Criminal Prosecution for the Same Act

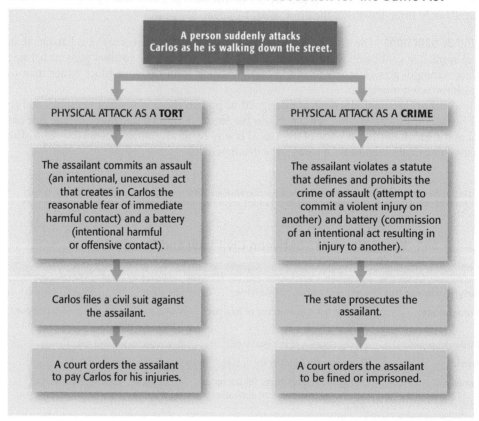

into a home at night more harshly than a burglary that involves breaking into a nonresidential building during the day.

Misdemeanors are less serious crimes, punishable by a fine or by confinement for up to a year. **Petty offenses** are minor violations, such as jaywalking or violations of building codes, considered to be a subset of misdemeanors. Even for petty offenses, however, a guilty party can be put in jail for a few days, fined, or both, depending on state or local law. Whether a crime is a felony or a misdemeanor can determine in which court the case is tried and, in some states, whether the defendant has a right to a jury trial.

8-2 Criminal Liability

Two elements normally must exist simultaneously for a person to be convicted of a crime: (1) the performance of a prohibited act and (2) a specified state of mind or intent on the part of the actor. Note that to establish criminal liability, there must be a *concurrence* between the act and the intent. In other words, these two elements must occur together.

8-2a The Criminal Act

Every criminal statute prohibits certain behavior. Most crimes require an act of *commission*. That is, a person must *do* something in order to be accused of a crime. In criminal law, a prohibited act is referred to as the **actus reus**,[4] or guilty act. In some situations, an act of *omission* can be a crime, but only when a person has a legal duty to perform the omitted act. For instance, failing to file a tax return is a crime of omission.

The *guilty act* requirement is based on one of the premises of criminal law—that a person is punished for harm done to society. For a crime to exist, the guilty act must cause some harm to a person or to property. Thinking about killing someone or about stealing a car may be wrong, but the thoughts do no harm until they are translated into action. Of course, a person can be punished for *attempting* murder or robbery, but normally only if he or she took substantial steps toward the criminal objective. Additionally, the person must have specifically intended to commit the crime to be convicted of an attempt.

8-2b State of Mind

A wrongful mental state *(mens rea)*[5] is generally required to establish criminal liability. The required mental state, or intent, is indicated in the applicable statute or law. Theft, for example, involves the guilty act of taking another person's property. The guilty mental state involves both the awareness that the property belongs to another and the intent to deprive the owner of it. A court can also find that the required mental state is present when a defendant's acts are reckless or criminally negligent.

Recklessness A defendant is *criminally reckless* if he or she consciously disregards a substantial and unjustifiable risk. **EXAMPLE 8.2** A fourteen-year-old New Jersey girl posts a Facebook message saying that she is going to launch a terrorist attack on her high school and asks if anyone wants to help. The police arrest the girl for the crime of making a terrorist threat, which requires the intent to commit an act of violence with "the intent to terrorize" or "in reckless disregard of the risk of causing" terror or inconvenience. Although the girl claims that she does not intend to cause harm, she can be prosecuted under the "reckless disregard" part of the statute. ■

Misdemeanor A lesser crime than a felony, punishable by a fine or incarceration in jail for up to one year.

Petty Offense The least serious kind of criminal offense, such as a traffic or building-code violation.

LEARNING OBJECTIVE 1
What two elements normally must exist before a person can be held liable for a crime?

Actus Reus A guilty (prohibited) act; one of the two essential elements required to establish criminal liability.

Mens Rea A wrongful mental state ("guilty mind"), or intent; one of the two essential elements required to establish criminal liability.

---

4. Pronounced *ak*-tuhs *ray*-uhs.
5. Pronounced *mehns ray*-uh.

Criminal Negligence

Criminal negligence occurs when the defendant takes an unjustified, substantial, and foreseeable risk that results in harm. A defendant can be negligent even if she or he was not actually aware of the risk but *should have been aware* of it.[6]

A homicide is classified as *involuntary manslaughter* when it results from an act of criminal negligence and there is no intent to kill. **EXAMPLE 8.3** Dr. Conrad Murray, the personal physician of pop star Michael Jackson, was convicted of involuntary manslaughter in 2011 for prescribing the drug that led to Jackson's sudden death in 2009. Murray had given Jackson propofol, a powerful anesthetic normally used in surgery, as a sleep aid on the night of his death, even though Murray knew that Jackson had already taken other sedatives. ■

Strict Liability and Overcriminalization

An increasing number of laws and regulations have imposed criminal sanctions for strict liability crimes—that is, offenses that do not require a wrongful mental state, or malice, to establish criminal liability.

Assume that you do not know that you are on federal lands. What doctrine makes you criminally liable for removing ancient arrowheads even without *mens rea*?

Federal Crimes. The federal criminal code now lists more than four thousand criminal offenses, many of which do not require a specific mental state. In addition, several hundred thousand federal rules can be enforced through criminal sanctions, and many of these rules do not require intent. See this chapter's *Managerial Strategy* feature for a discussion of how these laws and rules affect American businesspersons.

EXAMPLE 8.4 Eddie Leroy Anderson, a retired logger and former science teacher, and his son went digging for arrowheads near a campground in Idaho. They did not realize that they were on federal land and that it is a crime to take artifacts from federal land without a permit. Although the penalty could be as much as two years in prison, the father and son pleaded guilty and were sentenced to probation and a $1,500 fine each. ■

Strict liability crimes are often connected with environmental laws, laws aimed at combating illegal drugs, and other laws related to public health, safety, and welfare. Under federal law, for instance, tenants can be evicted from public housing if one of their relatives or guests used illegal drugs—regardless of whether the tenant knew or should have known about the drug activity.

State Crimes. Many states have also enacted laws that punish behavior as criminal without the need to show criminal intent. **EXAMPLE 8.5** In Arizona, a hunter who shoots an elk outside the area specified by the hunting permit has committed a crime. The hunter can be convicted of the crime regardless of her or his intent or knowledge of the law. ■

8-2c Corporate Criminal Liability

A *corporation* is a legal entity created under the laws of a state. At one time, it was thought that a corporation could not incur criminal liability because, although a corporation is a legal person, it can act only through its agents (corporate directors, officers, and employees). Therefore, the corporate entity itself could not "intend" to commit a crime. Over time, this view has changed. Obviously, corporations cannot be imprisoned, but they can be fined or denied certain legal privileges (such as necessary licenses).

Liability of the Corporate Entity

Today, corporations are normally liable for the crimes committed by their agents and employees within the course and scope of their employment.[7] For liability to be imposed, the prosecutor typically must show that the corporation could have prevented the act or that a supervisor within the corporation authorized or had knowledge of

---

6. Model Penal Code Section 2.02(2)(d).
7. See Model Penal Code Section 2.07.

MANAGERIAL STRATEGY

The Criminalization of American Business

Management Faces a Legal Issue

What do Bank of America, Citigroup, JPMorgan Chase, and Goldman Sachs have in common? All recently paid hefty fines for purportedly misleading investors about mortgage-backed securities. In fact, these companies paid the government a total of $50 billion in fines. The payments were made in lieu of criminal prosecutions.

Today, several hundred thousand federal rules that apply to businesses carry some form of criminal penalty. That's in addition to more than four thousand federal laws, many of which carry criminal sanctions for their violation. From 2000 to the beginning of 2015, about 2,200 corporations either were convicted or pleaded guilty to violating federal statutes or rules. More than 300 corporations reached so-called non-prosecution agreements, which typically involve multi-million- or multibillion-dollar fines. These numbers do not include fines paid to the Environmental Protection Agency or to the Fish and Wildlife Service.

According to law professors Margaret Lemos and Max Minzner, "Public enforcers often seek large monetary awards for self-interested reasons divorced from the public interest and deterrents. The incentives are strongest when enforcement agencies are permitted to retain all or some of the proceeds of enforcement."[a]

What the Courts Say

The first successful criminal conviction in a federal court against a company—The New York Central and Hudson River Railroad—was upheld by the Supreme Court in 1909 (the violation: cutting prices).[b] Many other successful convictions followed. One landmark case developed the *aggregation test,* now called the Doctrine of Collective Knowledge.[c] This test aggregates the omissions and acts of two or more persons in a corporation, thereby constructing an *actus reus* and a *mens rea* out of the conduct and knowledge of several individuals.

Not all government attempts at applying criminal law to corporations survive. In 2013, for example, Sentinel Offender Services, LLC, prevailed on appeal. There was no actual evidence to show that the company had acted with specific intent to commit theft by deception.[d]

_____

a. Margaret Lemos and Max Minzner, "For-Profit Public Enforcement," *Harvard Law Review* 127, January 17, 2014.

b. *New York Central and Hudson River Railroad v. United States,* 212 U.S. 481 (1909).

c. *U.S. v. Bank of New England,* 821 F.2d 844 (1987).

d. *McGee v. Sentinel Offender Services, LLC,* 719 F.3d 1236 (2013).

In 2014, the U.S. District Court for the Northern District of California in San Francisco indicted FedEx Corporation for purportedly illegally shipping prescription drugs ordered through Web sites.[e] FedEx has chosen to proceed to court. As suggested earlier, however, many companies choose to reach a settlement agreement with the government rather than fight criminal indictments.

Managers in a large corporation must make sure that the company retains sufficient documents to respond to potential regulatory requests. William Hubbard at the University of Chicago Law School estimates that a typical large company spends more than $40 million annually to do so. Managers also face the question of whether to agree to pay a large fine rather than to be indicted and proceed to trial. Most corporate managers choose the former option because they worry that a criminal indictment will harm their corporation's reputation, its profitability, and ultimately its existence.

_____

e. *United States of America v. FedEx Corporation, FedEx Express, Inc., and FedEx Corporate Services, Inc.,* July 17, 2014.

_____

the act. In addition, corporations can be criminally liable for failing to perform specific duties imposed by law (such as duties under environmental laws or securities laws).

CASE EXAMPLE 8.6 A prostitution ring, the Gold Club, was operating out of motels in West Virginia. A motel manager, who was also an officer in the corporation that owned the motels, gave discounted rates to Gold Club prostitutes, and they paid him in cash. The corporation received a portion of the funds generated by the Gold Club's illegal operations. At trial, the jury found that the corporation was criminally liable because a supervisor within the corporation—the motel manager—had knowledge of the prostitution and the corporation had allowed it to continue.[8]

_____

8. As a result of the convictions, the motel manager was sentenced to fifteen months in prison, and the corporation was ordered to forfeit the motel property. *United States v. Singh,* 518 F.3d 236 (4th Cir. 2008).

Corporations that operate underground storage tanks are responsible for any leaking gasoline. At what point does the responsible corporate officer doctrine make corporate officers criminally liable for continued leakages?

Liability of Corporate Officers and Directors Corporate directors and officers are personally liable for the crimes they commit, regardless of whether the crimes were committed for their personal benefit or on the corporation's behalf. Additionally, corporate directors and officers may be held liable for the actions of employees under their supervision. Under the *responsible corporate officer doctrine,* a court may impose criminal liability on a corporate officer regardless of whether she or he participated in, directed, or even knew about a given criminal violation.[9]

CASE EXAMPLE 8.7 The Roscoe family owned the Customer Company, which operated an underground storage tank that leaked gasoline. After the leak occurred, an employee, John Johnson, notified the state environmental agency, and the Roscoes hired an environmental services firm to clean up the spill. The clean-up did not occur immediately, however, and the state sent many notices to John Roscoe, a corporate officer, warning him that the company was violating federal and state environmental laws. Roscoe gave the letters to Johnson, who passed them on to the environmental services firm, but the spill was not cleaned up.

The state eventually filed criminal charges against the corporation and the Roscoes individually, and they were convicted. On appeal, the court affirmed the Roscoes' convictions under the responsible corporate officer doctrine. The Roscoes were in positions of responsibility, they had influence over the corporation's actions, and their failure to act constituted a violation of environmental laws.[10] ▪

PREVENTING LEGAL DISPUTES   **If you become a corporate officer or director at some point in your career, you will be potentially liable for the crimes of your subordinates.** Always be familiar with any criminal statutes relevant to the corporation's industry or trade. Also, make sure that corporate employees are trained in how to comply with the multitude of applicable rules, particularly environmental laws and health and safety regulations, which frequently involve criminal sanctions.

8-3 Types of Crimes

LEARNING OBJECTIVE 2

What are five broad categories of crimes? What is white-collar crime?

Federal, state, and local laws provide for the classification and punishment of hundreds of thousands of different criminal acts. Traditionally, though, crimes have been grouped into five broad categories: violent crime (crimes against persons), property crime, public order crime, white-collar crime, and organized crime. Many crimes may be committed in cyberspace. When crimes occur in the virtual world, we refer to them as cyber crimes, as discussed later in the chapter.

8-3a Violent Crime

Robbery The act of forcefully and unlawfully taking personal property of any value from another.

Certain crimes are called *violent crimes,* or crimes against persons, because they cause others to suffer harm or death. Murder is a violent crime. So, too, is sexual assault, or rape. **Robbery**—defined as the taking of cash, personal property, or any other article of value from a person by means of force or fear—is another violent crime. Typically, states have more severe penalties for *aggravated robbery*—robbery with the use of a deadly weapon.

Assault and battery, which were discussed in Chapter 4 in the context of tort law, are also classified as violent crimes. **EXAMPLE 8.8** Former rap star Flavor Flav (whose real name is William Drayton) was arrested in Las Vegas on assault and battery charges. During an argument with his fiancée, Drayton allegedly threw her to the ground and then grabbed two kitchen knives and chased her son. ▪

---

9. For a landmark case in this area, see *United States v. Park,* 421 U.S. 658, 95 S.Ct. 1903, 44 L.Ed.2d 489 (1975).

10. The Roscoes and the corporation were sentenced to pay penalties of $2,493,250. *People v. Roscoe,* 169 Cal.App.4th 829, 87 Cal. Rptr.3d 187 (3 Dist. 2008).

Each of these violent crimes is further classified by degree, depending on the circumstances surrounding the criminal act. These circumstances include the intent of the person committing the crime and whether a weapon was used. For crimes other than murder, the level of pain and suffering experienced by the victim is also a factor.

8–3b Property Crime

The most common type of criminal activity is property crime—crimes in which the goal of the offender is some form of economic gain or the damaging of property. Robbery is a form of property crime, as well as a violent crime, because the offender seeks to gain the property of another. We look here at a number of other crimes that fall within the general category of property crime.

Burglary Traditionally, **burglary** was defined under the common law as breaking and entering the dwelling of another at night with the intent to commit a felony. Originally, the definition was aimed at protecting an individual's home and its occupants. Most state statutes have eliminated some of the requirements found in the common law definition. The time of day at which the breaking and entering occurs, for example, is usually immaterial. State statutes frequently omit the element of breaking, and some states do not require that the building be a dwelling. When a deadly weapon is used in a burglary, the person can be charged with *aggravated burglary* and punished more severely.

The defendant in the following case challenged the sufficiency of the evidence to support his conviction for burglary.

> **Burglary** The unlawful entry or breaking into a building with the intent to commit a felony.

State of Minnesota v. Smith

Court of Appeals of Minnesota, 2015 WL 303643 (2015).

FACTS Over a Labor Day weekend in Rochester, Minnesota, two homes and the Rochester Tennis Center, a business, were burglarized. One day later, less than five blocks away, in Albert Smith's room at the Bell Tower Inn, cleaning personnel found a garbage bag containing a passport that belonged to the owner of one of the burglarized homes and documents that belonged to the business. The police arrested Smith. A search of a bag in his possession revealed other stolen items and burglary tools. Smith claimed that he had bought some of the items on Craigslist and had found the documents from the tennis center in a dumpster. Convicted of burglary in a Minnesota state court, Smith appealed.

ISSUE Was the evidence sufficient to support Smith's conviction for burglary?

DECISION Yes. A state intermediate appellate court affirmed Smith's conviction. The appellate court concluded that the circumstances "are consistent with guilt and inconsistent with any rational hypothesis except that of guilt."

REASON The burglarized homes and business were within a few blocks of Smith's hotel. The hotel manager saw Smith carrying a

When a person possesses property that was recently stolen, can a court infer that he or she engaged in burglary?

Sentry safe that had been stolen in one of the burglaries into the hotel. Only a few hours later, Smith was found in possession of property stolen in the burglaries. When arrested, he was carrying a bag that contained other stolen items and the burglary tools. The nature and assortment of the items "suggested that they came directly from the burglaries," illustrating Smith's guilt—the items looked like "the raw loot that a thief quickly grabbed and made off with." The time frame and the short distance between the hotel and the burglary locations were also consistent with a finding that Smith was the thief. The trial court found that Smith's claims as to how he came into possession of the items were not credible. The appellate court considered his claims "improbable" and concluded that "the only rational hypothesis that can be drawn from the proved circumstances is that Smith committed the burglaries."

CRITICAL THINKING—Social Consideration *Who is in the best position to evaluate the credibility of the evidence and the witnesses in a case? Why?*

Larceny The wrongful taking and carrying away of another person's personal property with the intent to permanently deprive the owner of the property.

Larceny

Under the common law, the crime of **larceny** involved the unlawful taking and carrying away of someone else's personal property with the intent to permanently deprive the owner of possession. Put simply, larceny is stealing, or theft. Whereas robbery involves force or fear, larceny does not. Therefore, picking pockets is larceny, not robbery. Similarly, an employee who takes company products and supplies home for personal use without authorization commits larceny.

Most states have expanded the definition of property that is subject to larceny statutes. Stealing computer programs may constitute larceny even though the "property" is not physical (see the discussion of computer crime later in this chapter). So, too, can the theft of natural gas or Internet and television cable service.

Obtaining Goods by False Pretenses

Obtaining goods by means of false pretenses is a form of theft that involves trickery or fraud, such as using someone else's credit-card number without permission to purchase an iPad. Statutes dealing with such illegal activities vary widely from state to state. They often apply not only to property, but also to services and cash.

CASE EXAMPLE 8.9 While Matthew Steffes was incarcerated, he devised a scheme to make free collect calls from prison. (A *collect call* is a telephone call in which the calling party places a call at the called party's expense.) Steffes had his friends and family members set up new phone number accounts by giving false information to AT&T. This information included fictitious business names, as well as personal identifying information stolen from a health-care clinic. Once a new phone number was working, Steffes made unlimited collect calls to it without paying the bill until AT&T eventually shut down the account. For nearly two years, Steffes used sixty fraudulently obtained phone numbers to make hundreds of collect calls. The loss to AT&T was more than $28,000.

Steffes was convicted in a state court of theft by fraud. He appealed, arguing that he had not made false representations to AT&T. The Wisconsin Supreme Court affirmed his conviction. The court held that Steffes had made false representations to AT&T by providing it with fictitious business names and stolen personal identifying information. He made these false representations so that he could make phone calls without paying for them, which deprived the company of its "property"—its electricity.[11] ■

Receiving Stolen Goods

It is a crime to receive goods that a person knows or should have known were stolen or illegally obtained. To be convicted, the recipient of such goods need not know the true identity of the owner or the thief, and need not have paid for the goods. All that is necessary is that the recipient knows or should have known that the goods were stolen, and intended to deprive the true owner of those goods.

Arson The intentional burning of a building.

If this fire was started to obtain insurance money, what type of crime was committed?

iStockPhoto.com/Burning building

Arson

The willful and malicious burning of a building (and, in some states, vehicles and other items of personal property) is the crime of **arson.** At common law, arson traditionally applied only to burning down another person's house. The law was designed to protect human life. Today, arson statutes have been extended to cover the destruction of any building, regardless of ownership, by fire or explosion.

Every state has a special statute that covers the act of burning a building for the purpose of collecting insurance. **EXAMPLE 8.10** Benton owns an insured apartment building that is falling apart. If he sets fire to it or pays someone else to do so, he is guilty not only of arson but also of defrauding the insurer, which is attempted larceny. ■ Of course, the insurer need not pay the claim when insurance fraud is proved.

---

11. *State of Wisconsin v. Steffes,* 347 Wis.2d 683, 832 N.W.2d 101 (2013).

Forgery The fraudulent making or altering of any writing (including electronic records) in a way that changes the legal rights and liabilities of another is **forgery**. EXAMPLE 8.11 Without authorization, Severson signs Bennett's name to the back of a check made out to Bennett and attempts to cash it. Severson has committed the crime of forgery. ■ Forgery also includes changing trademarks, falsifying public records, counterfeiting, and altering a legal document.

Forgery The fraudulent making or altering of any writing in a way that changes the legal rights and liabilities of another.

8–3c Public Order Crime

Historically, societies have always outlawed activities considered to be contrary to public values and morals. Today, the most common public order crimes include public drunkenness, prostitution, gambling, and illegal drug use. These crimes are sometimes referred to as victimless crimes because they normally harm only the offender. From a broader perspective, however, they are deemed detrimental to society as a whole because they may create an environment that gives rise to property and violent crimes.

EXAMPLE 8.12 A flight attendant observed a man and woman engaging in sex acts while on a flight to Las Vegas in 2013. A criminal complaint was filed, and the two defendants pleaded guilty in federal court to the public order crime of misdemeanor disorderly conduct. ■

8–3d White-Collar Crime

Crimes occurring in the business context are popularly referred to as *white-collar crimes,* although this is not an official legal term. Ordinarily, **white-collar crime** involves an illegal act or series of acts committed by an individual or business entity using some nonviolent means to obtain a personal or business advantage.

Usually, this kind of crime is committed in the course of a legitimate occupation. Corporate crimes fall into this category. In addition, certain property crimes, such as larceny and forgery, may also be white-collar crimes if they occur within the business context.

White-Collar Crime Nonviolent crime committed by individuals or corporations to obtain a personal or business advantage.

Embezzlement The fraudulent appropriation of funds or other property by a person who was entrusted with the funds or property.

Embezzlement When a person who is entrusted with another person's funds or property fraudulently appropriates it, **embezzlement** occurs. Embezzlement is not larceny, because the wrongdoer does not physically take the property from another's possession, and it is not robbery, because force or fear is not used.

Typically, embezzlement is carried out by an employee who steals funds. Banks are particularly prone to this problem, but embezzlement can occur in any firm. In a number of businesses, corporate officers or accountants have fraudulently converted funds for their own benefit and then "fixed" the books to cover up their crime. Embezzlement occurs whether the embezzler takes the funds directly from the victim or from a third person. If the financial officer of a corporation pockets checks from third parties that were given to her to deposit into the corporate account, she is embezzling.

Frequently, an embezzler takes relatively small amounts repeatedly over a long period. This might be done by underreporting income or deposits and embezzling the remaining amount or by creating fictitious persons or accounts and writing checks to them from the corporate account. An employer's failure to remit state withholding taxes that were collected from employee wages can also constitute embezzlement.

The intent to return embezzled property—or its actual return—is not a defense to the crime of embezzlement, as the following *Spotlight Case* illustrates.

Bernard Madoff (center) perpetuated the largest fraudulent investment scheme in modern history.

SPOTLIGHT ON WHITE-COLLAR CRIME: CASE 8.2

People v. Sisuphan

Court of Appeal of California, First District, 181 Cal.App.4th 800, 104 Cal.Rptr.3d 654 (2010).

FACTS Lou Sisuphan was the director of finance at a Toyota dealership. Sisuphan complained repeatedly to management about another employee, Ian McClelland. The general manager, Michael Christian, would not terminate McClelland "because he brought a lot of money into the dealership." To jeopardize McClelland's employment, Sisuphan took and kept an envelope containing a payment of nearly $30,000 from one of McClelland's customers that McClelland had tried to deposit in the company's safe. Later, Sisuphan told the dealership what he had done and returned the money, adding that he had "no intention of stealing the money." Christian fired Sisuphan the next day, and the district attorney later charged Sisuphan with embezzlement. After a jury trial, Sisuphan was found guilty. Sisuphan appealed.

ISSUE Did Sisuphan take the funds with the intent to defraud his employer?

DECISION Yes. The appellate court affirmed Sisuphan's conviction for embezzlement. Sisuphan had the required intent at the time he

A Toyota dealership employee committed embezzlement, but returned the funds. Is this a crime?

took the funds, and the evidence that he repaid the dealership was properly excluded.

REASON The court reasoned that evidence of repayment is admissible only if it shows that a defendant's intent at the time of the taking was not fraudulent. In determining whether Sisuphan's intent was fraudulent at the time of the taking, the main issue was not whether he intended to spend the funds that he had taken, but whether he intended to use the payment "for a purpose other than that for which the dealership entrusted it to him." Sisuphan's stated purpose was to get McClelland fired. Because this purpose was beyond the scope of his responsibility, it was "outside the trust afforded him by the dealership" and indicated fraudulent intent.

CRITICAL THINKING—Legal Consideration *Why was Sisuphan convicted of embezzlement instead of larceny? What is the difference between these two crimes?*

> "It was beautiful and simple as all truly great swindles are."
>
> **O. HENRY**
> 1862–1910
> (AMERICAN WRITER)

Mail and Wire Fraud One of the most potent weapons against white-collar criminals are the federal laws that prohibit mail fraud[12] and wire fraud.[13] These laws make it a federal crime to devise any scheme that uses the U.S. mail, commercial carriers (such as FedEx or UPS), or wire (including telegraph, telephone, television, e-mail, or online social media) with the intent to defraud the public. These laws are often applied when persons send advertisements via e-mail or social media with the intent to obtain cash or property by false pretenses.

CASE EXAMPLE 8.13 Cisco Systems, Inc., offers a warranty program to authorized resellers of Cisco parts. Iheanyi Frank Chinasa and Robert Kendrick Chambliss formulated a scheme to use this program to defraud Cisco by obtaining replacement parts to which they were not entitled. The two men sent numerous e-mails and Internet service requests to Cisco to convince the company to ship them new parts via commercial carriers. Ultimately, Chinasa and Chambliss were convicted of mail and wire fraud, as well as conspiracy to commit mail and wire fraud.[14] ■

The maximum penalty under these statutes is substantial. Persons convicted of mail or wire fraud may be imprisoned for up to twenty years and/or fined. If the violation affects a financial institution or involves fraud in connection with emergency disaster-relief funds, the violator may be fined up to $1 million, imprisoned for up to thirty years, or both.

---

12. The Mail Fraud Act of 1990, 18 U.S.C. Sections 1341–1342.
13. 18 U.S.C. Section 1343.
14. *United States v. Chinasa*, 789 F.Supp.2d 691 (E.D.Va. 2011).

Bribery The crime of bribery involves offering something of value to someone in an attempt to influence that person—who is usually, but not always, a public official—to act in a way that serves a private interest. Three types of bribery are considered crimes: bribery of public officials, commercial bribery, and bribery of foreign officials. As an element of the crime of bribery, intent must be present and proved. The bribe itself can be anything the recipient considers to be valuable. Realize that the *crime of bribery occurs when the bribe is offered*—it is not required that the bribe be accepted. *Accepting a bribe* is a separate crime.

Commercial bribery involves corrupt dealings between private persons or businesses. Typically, people make commercial bribes to obtain proprietary information, cover up an inferior product, or secure new business. Industrial espionage sometimes involves commercial bribes. **EXAMPLE 8.14** Kent works at the firm of Jacoby & Meyers. He offers to pay Laurel, an employee in a competing firm, if she will give him her firm's trade secrets and pricing schedules. Kent has committed commercial bribery. ■ So-called kickbacks, or payoffs for special favors or services, are a form of commercial bribery in some situations.

Bankruptcy Fraud Federal bankruptcy law allows individuals and businesses to be relieved of oppressive debt through bankruptcy proceedings. Numerous white-collar crimes may be committed during the many phases of a bankruptcy proceeding. A creditor may file a false claim against the debtor. Also, a debtor may attempt to protect assets from creditors by fraudulently transferring property to favored parties. For instance, a company-owned automobile may be "sold" at a bargain price to a trusted friend or relative. Closely related to the crime of fraudulently transferring property is the crime of fraudulently concealing property, such as hiding gold coins.

Theft of Trade Secrets Trade secrets constitute a form of intellectual property that can be extremely valuable for many businesses. The Economic Espionage Act[15] made the theft of trade secrets a federal crime. The act also made it a federal crime to buy or possess trade secrets of another person, knowing that the trade secrets were stolen or otherwise acquired without the owner's authorization.

Violations of the act can result in steep penalties. An individual who violates the act can be imprisoned for up to ten years and fined up to $500,000. A corporation or other organization can be fined up to $5 million. Additionally, any property acquired as a result of the violation, such as airplanes and automobiles, is subject to criminal forfeiture, or seizure by the government. Similarly, any property used in the commission of the violation, such as servers and other electronic devices, is subject to forfeiture. A theft of trade secrets conducted via the Internet, for instance, could result in the forfeiture of every computer or other device used to commit or facilitate the crime.

Insider Trading An individual who obtains "inside information" about the plans of a publicly listed corporation can often make stock-trading profits by purchasing or selling corporate securities based on the information. **Insider trading** is a violation of securities law and will be discussed more fully later in this text. Generally, the rule is that a person who possesses inside information and has a duty not to disclose it to outsiders may not profit from the purchase or sale of securities based on that information until the information is made available to the public.

Insider Trading The purchase or sale of securities on the basis of information that has not been made available to the public.

8–3e Organized Crime

As mentioned, white-collar crime takes place within the confines of the legitimate business world. *Organized crime,* in contrast, operates *illegitimately* by, among other things, providing illegal goods and services. For organized crime, the traditional markets in the past were

---

15. 18 U.S.C. Sections 1831–1839.

How do criminals launder money?

Money Laundering Engaging in financial transactions to conceal the identity, source, or destination of illegally gained funds.

gambling, prostitution, illegal narcotics, and loan sharking (lending at higher-than-legal interest rates), along with counterfeiting and credit-card scams. Today, organized crime is heavily involved in cyber crime.

Money Laundering Organized crime and other illegal activities generate many billions of dollars in profits each year from illegal drug transactions and, to a lesser extent, from racketeering, prostitution, and gambling. Under federal law, banks and other financial institutions are required to report currency transactions involving more than $10,000. Consequently, those who engage in illegal activities face difficulties when they try to deposit their cash profits from illegal transactions.

As an alternative to simply storing cash from illegal transactions in a safe-deposit box, wrongdoers and racketeers often launder their "dirty" money to make it "clean" by passing it through a legitimate business. **Money laundering** is engaging in financial transactions to conceal the identity, source, or destination of illegally gained funds.

EXAMPLE 8.15 Leo Harris, a successful drug dealer, becomes a partner with a restaurateur. Little by little, the restaurant shows increasing profits. As a partner in the restaurant, Harris is able to report the "profits" of the restaurant as legitimate income on which he pays federal and state taxes. He can then spend those funds without worrying that his lifestyle may exceed the level possible with his reported income. ■

The Racketeer Influenced and Corrupt Organizations Act To curb the entry of organized crime into the legitimate business world, Congress in 1970 enacted the Racketeer Influenced and Corrupt Organizations Act (RICO).[16] The statute makes it a federal crime to:

1. Use income obtained from racketeering activity to purchase any interest in an enterprise.

2. Acquire or maintain an interest in an enterprise through racketeering activity.

3. Conduct or participate in the affairs of an enterprise through racketeering activity.

4. Conspire to do any of the preceding activities.

Broad Application of RICO. The broad language of RICO has allowed it to be applied in cases that have little or nothing to do with organized crime. RICO incorporates by reference twenty-six separate types of federal crimes and nine types of state felonies.[17] If a person commits two of these offenses, he or she is guilty of "racketeering activity."

Under the criminal provisions of RICO, any individual found guilty is subject to a fine of up to $25,000 per violation, imprisonment for up to twenty years, or both. Additionally, any assets (property or cash) that were acquired as a result of the illegal activity or that were "involved in" or an "instrumentality of" the activity are subject to government forfeiture.

Civil Liability. In the event of a RICO violation, the government can seek not only criminal penalties but also civil penalties, such as the divestiture of a defendant's interest in a business (called forfeiture) or the dissolution of the business. (Divestiture refers to the taking of possession—or forfeiture—of the defendant's interest and its subsequent sale.)

Moreover, in some cases, the statute allows private individuals to sue violators and potentially to recover three times their actual losses (treble damages), plus attorneys' fees, for business injuries caused by a RICO violation. This is perhaps the most controversial aspect of RICO and one that continues to cause debate in the nation's federal courts. The prospect of receiving treble damages in civil RICO lawsuits has given plaintiffs a financial incentive to pursue businesses and employers for violations.

---

16. 18 U.S.C. Sections 1961–1968.
17. See 18 U.S.C. Section 1961(1)(A).

8-4 Defenses to Criminal Liability

Persons charged with crimes may be relieved of criminal liability if they can show that their criminal actions were justified under the circumstances. In certain circumstances, the law may also allow a person to be excused from criminal liability because she or he lacks the required mental state. We look at several of the defenses to criminal liability here.

Note that procedural violations, such as obtaining evidence without a valid search warrant, may also operate as defenses. Evidence obtained in violation of a defendant's constitutional rights normally may not be admitted in court. If the evidence is suppressed, then there may be no basis for prosecuting the defendant.

LEARNING OBJECTIVE 3
What defenses can be raised to avoid liability for criminal acts?

8-4a Justifiable Use of Force

Probably the best-known defense to criminal liability is **self-defense.** Other situations, however, also justify the use of force: the defense of one's dwelling, the defense of other property, and the prevention of a crime. In all of these situations, it is important to distinguish between deadly and nondeadly force. *Deadly force* is likely to result in death or serious bodily harm. *Nondeadly force* is force that reasonably appears necessary to prevent the imminent use of criminal force.

Generally speaking, people can use the amount of nondeadly force that seems necessary to protect themselves, their dwellings, or other property or to prevent the commission of a crime. Deadly force can be used in self-defense if the defender *reasonably believes* that imminent death or grievous bodily harm will otherwise result. In addition, normally the attacker must be using unlawful force, and the defender must not have initiated or provoked the attack.

Many states are expanding the situations in which the use of deadly force can be justified. Florida, for example, allows the use of deadly force to prevent the commission of a "forcible felony," including robbery, carjacking, and sexual battery.

Self-Defense The legally recognized privilege to do what is reasonably necessary to protect oneself, one's property, or someone else against injury by another.

8-4b Necessity

Sometimes, criminal defendants are relieved of liability if they can show that a criminal act was necessary to prevent an even greater harm. **EXAMPLE 8.16** Jake Trevor is a convicted felon and, as such, is legally prohibited from possessing a firearm. While he and his wife are in a convenience store, a man draws a gun, points it at the cashier, and demands all the cash. Afraid that the man will start shooting, Trevor grabs the gun and holds on to it until police arrive. In this situation, if Trevor is charged with possession of a firearm, he can assert the defense of necessity. ■

8-4c Insanity

A person who suffers from a mental illness may be incapable of the state of mind required to commit a crime. Thus, insanity can be a defense to a criminal charge. Note that an insanity defense does not allow a person to avoid imprisonment. It simply means that if the defendant successfully proves insanity, she or he will be placed in a mental institution.

EXAMPLE 8.17 James Holmes opened fire with an automatic weapon in a crowded Colorado movie theater during the screening of *The Dark Knight Rises*, killing twelve people and injuring more than fifty. Holmes had been a graduate student but had increasingly suffered from mental health problems and had left school. Before the incident, he had no criminal history. Holmes's attorneys asserted the defense of insanity in an attempt to avoid

If a person starts to suffer from mental health problems and opens fire inside a movie theater, can that person use the defense of insanity?

iStockPhoto.com/track5

a possible death penalty. If the defense is ultimately successful, Holmes will be confined to a mental institution rather than a prison. ■

The courts have had difficulty deciding what the test for legal insanity should be, and psychiatrists as well as lawyers are critical of the tests used. Almost all federal courts and some states use the relatively liberal substantial-capacity test set forth in the Model Penal Code:

> A person is not responsible for criminal conduct if at the time of such conduct as a result of mental disease or defect he [or she] lacks substantial capacity either to appreciate the wrongfulness of his [or her] conduct or to conform his [or her] conduct to the requirements of the law.

Some states use the *M'Naghten* test.[18] Under this test, a criminal defendant is not responsible if, at the time of the offense, he or she did not know the nature and quality of the act or did not know that the act was wrong. Other states use the irresistible-impulse test. A person operating under an irresistible impulse may know an act is wrong but cannot refrain from doing it.

Under any of these tests, proving insanity is extremely difficult. For this reason, the insanity defense is rarely used and usually is not successful.

8–4d Mistake

Everyone has heard the saying "ignorance of the law is no excuse." Ordinarily, ignorance of the law or a mistaken idea about what the law requires is not a valid defense. A *mistake of fact*, as opposed to a *mistake of law*, can excuse criminal responsibility if it negates the mental state necessary to commit a crime.

EXAMPLE 8.18 If Oliver Wheaton mistakenly walks off with Julie Tyson's briefcase because he thinks it is his, there is no crime. Theft requires knowledge that the property belongs to another. (If Wheaton's act causes Tyson to incur damages, however, she may sue him in a civil action for the tort of trespass to personal property or conversion.) ■

8–4e Duress

Duress Unlawful pressure brought to bear on a person, causing the person to perform an act that she or he would not otherwise perform.

Duress exists when the *wrongful threat* of one person induces another person to perform an act that she or he would not otherwise perform. In such a situation, duress is said to negate the mental state necessary to commit a crime because the defendant was forced or compelled to commit the act.

Duress can be used as a defense to most crimes except murder. The states vary in how duress is defined and what types of crimes it can excuse, however. Generally, to successfully assert duress as a defense, the defendant must reasonably believe that he or she is in immediate danger, and the jury (or judge) must conclude that the defendant's belief was reasonable.

8–4f Entrapment

Entrapment A defense in which a defendant claims that he or she was induced by a public official to commit a crime that he or she would otherwise not have committed.

Entrapment is a defense designed to prevent police officers or other government agents from enticing persons to commit crimes so that they can later be prosecuted for criminal acts. In the typical entrapment case, an undercover agent *suggests* that a crime be committed and pressures or induces an individual to commit it. The agent then arrests the individual for the crime.

For entrapment to succeed as a defense, both the suggestion and the inducement must take place. The defense is not intended to prevent law enforcement agents from ever setting a trap for an unwary criminal. Rather, its purpose is to prevent them from pushing the individual into a criminal act. The crucial issue is whether the person who committed a crime was predisposed to commit the illegal act or did so only because the agent induced it.

---

18. A rule derived from *M'Naghten's* Case, 8 Eng.Rep. 718 (1843).

8-4g Statute of Limitations

With some exceptions, such as for the crime of murder, statutes of limitations apply to crimes just as they do to civil wrongs. In other words, the state must initiate criminal prosecution within a certain number of years. If a criminal action is brought after the statutory time period has expired, the accused person can raise the statute of limitations as a defense.

The running of the time period in a statute of limitations may be *tolled*—that is, suspended or stopped temporarily—if the defendant is a minor or is not in the jurisdiction. When the defendant reaches the age of majority or returns to the jurisdiction, the statutory time period begins to run again.

8-4h Immunity

Accused persons are understandably reluctant to give information if it will be used to prosecute them, and they cannot be forced to do so. The privilege against **self-incrimination** is granted by the Fifth Amendment to the U.S. Constitution. The clause reads "nor shall [any person] be compelled in any criminal case to be a witness against himself."

When the state wishes to obtain information from a person accused of a crime, the state can grant *immunity* from prosecution or agree to prosecute for a less serious offense in exchange for the information. Once immunity is given, the person can no longer refuse to testify on Fifth Amendment grounds because he or she now has an absolute privilege against self-incrimination.

Often, a grant of immunity from prosecution for a serious crime is part of the **plea bargaining** between the defendant and the prosecuting attorney. The defendant may be convicted of a lesser offense, while the state uses the defendant's testimony to prosecute accomplices for serious crimes carrying heavy penalties.

Self-Incrimination Giving testimony in a trial or other legal proceeding that could expose the person testifying to criminal prosecution.

Plea Bargaining The process by which a criminal defendant and the prosecutor work out an agreement to dispose of the criminal case, subject to court approval.

8-5 Constitutional Safeguards and Criminal Procedures

Criminal law brings the power of the state, with all its resources, to bear against the individual. Criminal procedures are designed to protect the constitutional rights of individuals and to prevent the arbitrary use of power by the government.

The U.S. Constitution provides specific safeguards for those accused of crimes. Most of these safeguards protect individuals not only against federal government actions but also, by virtue of the due process clause of the Fourteenth Amendment, against state government actions. These protections are set forth in the Fourth, Fifth, Sixth, and Eighth Amendments.

LEARNING OBJECTIVE 4

What constitutional safeguards exist to protect persons accused of crimes?

Search Warrant An order granted by a public authority, such as a judge, that authorizes law enforcement personnel to search particular premises or property.

8-5a Fourth Amendment Protections

The Fourth Amendment protects the "right of the people to be secure in their persons, houses, papers, and effects." Before searching or seizing private property, law enforcement officers must obtain a **search warrant**—an order from a judge or other public official authorizing the search or seizure.

Advances in technology have allowed authorities to track phone calls and vehicle movements with greater ease and precision. The use of such technology can constitute a search within the meaning of the Fourth Amendment. **CASE EXAMPLE 8.19** Antoine Jones owned and operated a nightclub in the District of Columbia. Government agents suspected

Can these officers enter and search a dwelling without first obtaining a search warrant?

a katz/ShutterStock.com

that he was also trafficking in narcotics. As part of their investigation, agents obtained a warrant to attach a global positioning system (GPS) to Jones's wife's car, which Jones regularly used. The warrant authorized installation in the District of Columbia and within ten days, but agents installed the device on the eleventh day and in Maryland.

The agents then tracked the vehicle's movement for about a month, eventually arresting Jones for possession and intent to distribute cocaine. Jones was convicted. He appealed, arguing that the government did not have a valid warrant for the GPS tracking. The United States Supreme Court held that the attachment of a GPS tracking device to a suspect's vehicle does constitute a Fourth Amendment search. The Court did not rule on whether the search in this case was unreasonable, however, and allowed Jones's conviction to stand.[19] ■

Probable Cause

Probable Cause Reasonable grounds for believing that a search should be conducted or that a person should be arrested.

To obtain a search warrant, law enforcement officers must convince a judge that they have reasonable grounds, or **probable cause,** to believe a search will reveal a specific illegality. Probable cause requires the officers to have trustworthy evidence that would convince a reasonable person that the proposed search or seizure is more likely justified than not.

Furthermore, the Fourth Amendment prohibits general warrants. It requires a particular description of what is to be searched or seized. General searches through a person's belongings are impermissible. The search cannot extend beyond what is described in the warrant. Although search warrants require specificity, if a search warrant is issued for a person's residence, items in that residence may be searched even if they do not belong to that individual.

Because of the strong governmental interest in protecting the public, a warrant normally is not required for seizures of spoiled or contaminated food. Nor are warrants required for searches of businesses in such highly regulated industries as liquor, guns, and strip mining.

Reasonable Expectation of Privacy

The Fourth Amendment protects only against searches that violate a person's *reasonable expectation of privacy*. A reasonable expectation of privacy exists if (1) the individual actually expects privacy, and (2) the person's expectation is one that society as a whole would think is legitimate.

The issue before the court in the following case was whether a defendant had a reasonable expectation of privacy in cell phone texts stored in the account of another person.

---

19. *United States v. Jones,* __ U.S. __, 132 S.Ct. 945, 181 L.Ed.2d 911 (2012).

State of Oklahoma v. Marcum

Court of Criminal Appeals of Oklahoma, 319 P.3d 681 (2014).

FACTS Angela Marcum, a drug court coordinator associated with a county court in Oklahoma, was romantically involved with James Miller, an assistant district attorney in the same county. When Miller learned that state officials were "in town" investigating suspected embezzlement, he quickly sent Marcum text messages from his personal phone. She sent messages back. The state obtained a search warrant and collected the records of the messages from U.S. Cellular, Miller's phone company. Later, the state charged Marcum

Is there an absolute right to privacy for text messages?

Prodakszyn/ShutterStock.com

with obstructing the investigation and offered in evidence the messages obtained pursuant to the search warrant. Marcum filed a motion to suppress the records, which the court granted. The state appealed.

ISSUE Does an individual who has exchanged text messages with another person have a reasonable expectation of privacy in those messages when they reside in the other person's account records at the telephone company?

DECISION No. A state intermediate appellate court reversed the ruling of the lower court. The case was reversed and remanded for further proceedings.

REASON According to the court, "Once the messages were both transmitted and received, the expectation of privacy was lost." When Marcum sent texts to Miller's phone, it was similar to mailing a letter—there is no expectation of privacy in the letter once it is delivered. Similarly, a caller cannot claim that a voice mail message, once it has been left and the recipient has played it, is private. In all of these situations, the individual's expectation of privacy in the communication is "defeated" by the decision to transmit a message to an electronic device that could be in anybody's possession. An individual has no reasonable expectation of privacy in the text messages or cell phone account records of another person when the individual does not have a possessory interest in the phone and the warrant is directed to a third party (here, U.S. Cellular).

CRITICAL THINKING—Technological Consideration *If Miller and Marcum had used smartphones and U.S. Cellular had stored its records in the "cloud," would the outcome likely have been different? Explain.*

8–5b Fifth Amendment Protections

The Fifth Amendment offers significant protections for accused persons. One is the guarantee that no one can be deprived of "life, liberty, or property without due process of law." Two other important Fifth Amendment provisions protect persons against double jeopardy and self-incrimination.

Due Process of Law Remember that *due process of law* has both procedural and substantive aspects. Procedural due process requirements underlie criminal procedures. The law must be carried out in a fair and orderly way. In criminal cases, due process means that defendants should have an opportunity to object to the charges against them before a fair, neutral decision maker, such as a judge. Defendants must also be given the opportunity to confront and cross-examine witnesses and accusers and to present their own witnesses.

Double Jeopardy The Fifth Amendment also protects persons from **double jeopardy** (being tried twice for the same criminal offense). The prohibition against double jeopardy means that once a criminal defendant is acquitted (found "not guilty") of a particular crime, the government may not retry him or her for the same crime.

The prohibition against double jeopardy does not preclude the crime victim from bringing a civil suit against that same defendant to recover damages, however. In other words, a person found "not guilty" of assault and battery in a state criminal case can be sued for damages by the victim in a civil tort case.

Additionally, a state's prosecution of a crime will not prevent a separate federal prosecution relating to the same activity (and vice versa), provided the activity can be classified as a different crime. **CASE EXAMPLE 8.20** Professional football player Michael Vick was convicted in federal court for operating a dogfighting ring and sentenced to serve twenty-three months in federal prison. A year later, Virginia, the state where the crime took place, filed its own charges against Vick for dogfighting. He pleaded guilty to those charges and received a *suspended sentence* (meaning that the judge reserved the option of imposing a sentence later if circumstances warranted it).[20] ▪

Self-Incrimination As explained earlier, the Fifth Amendment grants a privilege against self-incrimination. Thus, in any criminal proceeding, an accused person cannot be compelled to give testimony that might subject her or him to criminal prosecution.

The Fifth Amendment's guarantee against self-incrimination extends only to natural persons. Because a corporation is a legal entity and not a natural person, the privilege against

Double Jeopardy The Fifth Amendment requirement that prohibits a person from being tried twice for the same criminal offense.

KNOW THIS
The Fifth Amendment protection against self-incrimination does not cover partnerships or corporations.

---

20. See *United States v. Kizeart*, 2010 WL 3768023 (S.D.Ill. 2010) for a discussion of the Michael Vick dogfighting case.

self-incrimination does not apply to it. Similarly, the business records of a partnership do not receive Fifth Amendment protection. When a partnership is required to produce these records, it must do so even if the information incriminates the persons who constitute the business entity.

ETHICAL ISSUE

Should police be able to force you to unlock your cell phone? Modern cell phones can store countless pages of text, thousands of pictures, and hundreds of videos. Such data can remain on a cell phone for years. Also, since the advent of the "cloud," much of the data viewable on a cell phone is stored on a remote server. Should police nonetheless be able to force you to unlock your phone? Or does this practice violate the Fifth Amendment protection against self-incrimination?

A Virginia circuit court judge ruled that police officers cannot force criminal suspects to divulge cell phone passwords. They can, however, force suspects to use their fingerprints to unlock the phones. The judge argued that biometric information from a fingerprint lies outside the protection of the Fifth Amendment. In the judge's view, giving police a fingerprint is similar to providing a DNA or handwriting sample, which the law permits.[21]

At about the same time, in *Riley v. California*,[22] the United States Supreme Court unanimously held that warrantless search and seizure of digital contents of a cell phone during an arrest is unconstitutional. Chief Justice John Roberts stated, "The fact that technology now allows for an individual to carry [the privacies of life] in his hand does not make the information any less worthy of the protection for which the Founders fought."

8–5c Protections under the Sixth and Eighth Amendments

The Sixth Amendment guarantees several important rights for criminal defendants: the right to a speedy trial, the right to a jury trial, the right to a public trial, the right to confront witnesses, and the right to counsel. The Sixth Amendment right to counsel is one of the rights of which a suspect must be advised when he or she is arrested. In many cases, a statement that a criminal suspect makes in the absence of counsel is not admissible at trial unless the suspect has knowingly and voluntarily waived this right.

The Eighth Amendment prohibits excessive bail and fines, as well as cruel and unusual punishment. Under this amendment, prison officials are required to provide humane conditions of confinement, including adequate food, clothing, shelter, and medical care. If a prisoner has a serious medical problem, for instance, and a correctional officer is deliberately indifferent to it, a court could find that the prisoner's Eighth Amendment rights have been violated. Critics of the death penalty claim that it constitutes cruel and unusual punishment.[23]

8–5d The Exclusionary Rule and the *Miranda* Rule

Two other procedural protections for criminal defendants are the exclusionary rule and the *Miranda* rule.

Exclusionary Rule A rule that prevents evidence that is obtained illegally or without a proper search warrant from being admissible in court.

The Exclusionary Rule   Under what is known as the **exclusionary rule,** any evidence obtained in violation of the constitutional rights spelled out in the Fourth, Fifth, and Sixth Amendments generally is not admissible at trial. All evidence derived from the illegally obtained evidence is known as the "fruit of the poisonous tree," and such evidence normally must also be excluded from the trial proceedings. For instance, if a confession is obtained after an illegal arrest, the arrest is the "poisonous tree," and the confession, if "tainted" by the arrest, is the "fruit."

---

21. *Commonwealth of Virginia v. David Charles Baust*, Case No. CR14-1439, 2nd Judicial Circuit, Virginia, October 28, 2014.
22. 573 U.S. ___, 134 S.Ct. 2473, 189 L.Ed.2d 430 (2014).
23. For an example of a case challenging the constitutionality of the death penalty, see *Baze v. Rees*, 553 U.S. 535, 128 S.Ct. 1520, 170 L.Ed.2d 420 (2008).

The purpose of the exclusionary rule is to deter police from conducting warrantless searches and engaging in other misconduct. The rule can sometimes lead to injustice, however. If evidence of a defendant's guilt was obtained improperly (without a valid search warrant, for instance), it normally cannot be used against the defendant in court.

The *Miranda* Rule   In *Miranda v. Arizona,* a case decided in 1966, the United States Supreme Court established the rule that individuals who are arrested must be informed of certain constitutional rights. Suspects must be informed of their Fifth Amendment right to remain silent and their Sixth Amendment right to counsel. If the arresting officers fail to inform a criminal suspect of these constitutional rights, any statements the suspect makes normally will not be admissible in court. Because of its importance in criminal procedure, the *Miranda* case is presented as this chapter's *Landmark in the Law* feature.

Exceptions to the *Miranda* Rule   Although the Supreme Court's *Miranda* ruling was controversial, the decision has survived attempts by Congress to overrule it. Over time, however, the Supreme Court has made a number of exceptions to the *Miranda* ruling. For instance, the Court has recognized a "public safety" exception that allows certain statements to be admitted even if the defendant was not given *Miranda* warnings. A defendant's statements that reveal the location of a weapon would be admissible under this exception. Additionally, a suspect must unequivocally and assertively ask to exercise her or his right to counsel in order to stop police questioning. Saying, "Maybe I should talk to a lawyer" during an interrogation after being taken into custody is not enough.

LANDMARK IN THE LAW   *Miranda v. Arizona* (1966)

The United States Supreme Court's decision in *Miranda v. Arizona*[a] has been cited in more court decisions than any other case in the history of U.S law. Through television shows and other media, the case has also become familiar to most of the adult population in the United States.

The case arose after Ernesto Miranda was arrested in his home on March 13, 1963, for the kidnapping and rape of an eighteen-year-old woman. Miranda was taken to a police station in Phoenix, Arizona, and questioned by two police officers. Two hours later, the officers emerged from the interrogation room with a written confession signed by Miranda.

RULINGS BY THE LOWER COURTS The confession was admitted into evidence at the trial, and Miranda was convicted and sentenced to prison for twenty to thirty years.

Miranda appealed his conviction, claiming that he had not been informed of his constitutional rights. He did not assert that he was innocent of the crime or that his confession was false or made under duress. He claimed only that he would not have confessed if he had been advised of his right to remain silent and to have an attorney.

The Supreme Court of Arizona held that Miranda's constitutional rights had not been violated and affirmed his conviction. In its decision, the court emphasized that Miranda had not specifically requested an attorney.

THE SUPREME COURT'S DECISION The *Miranda* case was subsequently consolidated with three other cases involving similar issues and reviewed by the United States Supreme Court. In its decision, the Court stated that whenever an individual is taken into custody, "the following measures are required: He must be warned prior to any questioning that he has the right to remain silent, that anything he says can be used against him in a court of law, that he has the right to the presence of an attorney, and that

if he cannot afford an attorney one will be appointed for him prior to any questioning if he so desires." If the accused waives his or her rights to remain silent and to have counsel present, the government must be able to demonstrate that the waiver was made knowingly, intelligently, and voluntarily.

APPLICATION TO TODAY'S WORLD *Today, both on television and in the real world, police officers routinely advise suspects of their "Miranda rights" on arrest. When Ernesto Miranda himself was later murdered, the suspected murderer was "read his Miranda rights." Interestingly, this decision has also had ramifications for criminal procedure in Great Britain. British police officers are required, when making arrests, to inform suspects, "You do not have to say anything. But if you do not mention now something which you later use in your defense, the court may decide that your failure to mention it now strengthens the case against you. A record will be made of everything you say, and it may be given in evidence if you are brought to trial."*

---

a. 384 U.S. 436, 86 S.Ct. 1602, 16 L.Ed.2d 694 (1966).

8-5e Criminal Process

As mentioned, as a result of the effort to safeguard the rights of the individual against the state, a criminal prosecution differs from a civil case in several respects. Exhibit 8–3 summarizes the major procedural steps in processing a criminal case. Here, we discuss three phases of the criminal process—arrest, indictment or information, and trial—in more detail.

Arrest Before a warrant for arrest can be issued, there must be probable cause to believe that the individual in question has committed a crime. As discussed earlier, *probable cause* can be defined as a substantial likelihood that the person has committed or is about to commit a crime. Note that probable cause involves a likelihood, not just a possibility. An arrest can be made without a warrant if there is no time to get one, but the action of the arresting officer is still judged by the standard of probable cause.

Indictment or Information Individuals must be formally charged with having committed specific crimes before they can be brought to trial. If issued by a grand jury, this charge is called an **indictment**.[24] A **grand jury** usually consists of more jurors than the ordinary trial jury. A grand jury does not determine the guilt or innocence of an accused party. Rather, its function is to hear the state's evidence and to determine whether a reasonable basis (probable cause) exists for believing that a crime has been committed and that a trial ought to be held.

Usually, grand juries are used in cases involving serious crimes, such as murder. For lesser crimes, an individual may be formally charged with a crime by what is called an **information,** or criminal complaint. An information will be issued by a government prosecutor if the prosecutor determines that there is sufficient evidence to justify bringing the individual to trial.

Trial At a criminal trial, the accused person does not have to prove anything. The entire burden of proof is on the prosecutor (the state). As mentioned earlier, the prosecution must show that, based on all the evidence presented, the defendant's guilt is established *beyond a reasonable doubt.*

If there is a reasonable doubt as to whether a criminal defendant committed the crime with which she or he has been charged, then the verdict must be "not guilty." A verdict of "not guilty" is not the same as stating that the defendant is innocent. It merely means that not enough evidence was properly presented to the court to prove guilt beyond a reasonable doubt.

Courts have complex rules about what types of evidence may be presented and how the evidence may be brought out in criminal cases. These rules are designed to ensure that evidence in trials is relevant, reliable, and not prejudicial toward the defendant.

8-5f Federal Sentencing Guidelines

The Sentencing Reform Act of 1984 created the U.S. Sentencing Commission to develop standardizing sentences for *federal* crimes. The commission's guidelines established a range of possible penalties for each federal crime. Originally, the guidelines were mandatory. That is, the judge was required to select a sentence from within the set range and was not allowed to deviate from it.

Problems with Constitutionality In 2005, the United States Supreme Court held that certain provisions of the federal sentencing guidelines were unconstitutional. **CASE EXAMPLE 8.21** Freddie Booker was arrested with 92.5 grams of crack cocaine in his possession. Booker admitted to police that he had sold an additional 566 grams of crack cocaine, but he was never charged with, or tried for, possession of this additional quantity. Nevertheless, under the

---

Indictment A formal charge by a grand jury that there is probable cause to believe that a named person has committed a crime.

Grand Jury A group of citizens who decide, after hearing the state's evidence, whether a reasonable basis (probable cause) exists for believing that a crime has been committed and that a trial ought to be held.

Information A formal accusation or complaint (without an indictment) issued in certain types of actions (usually criminal actions involving lesser crimes) by a government prosecutor.

How have federal sentencing guidelines for crack cocaine changed?

Kevin L. Chesson/ShutterStock.com

---

24. Pronounced in-*dyte*-ment.

Exhibit 8–3 Major Procedural Steps in a Criminal Case

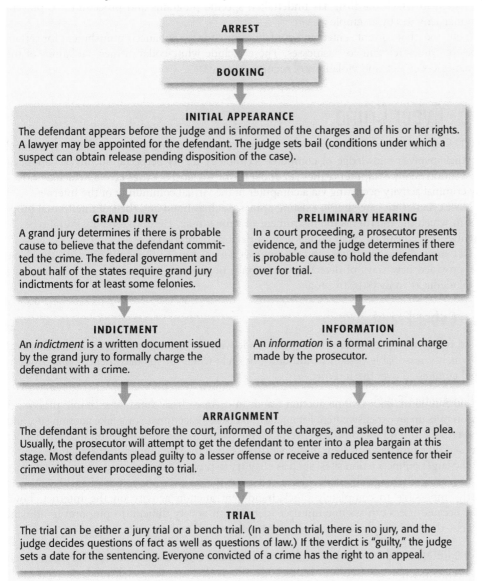

ARREST

BOOKING

INITIAL APPEARANCE
The defendant appears before the judge and is informed of the charges and of his or her rights. A lawyer may be appointed for the defendant. The judge sets bail (conditions under which a suspect can obtain release pending disposition of the case).

GRAND JURY
A grand jury determines if there is probable cause to believe that the defendant committed the crime. The federal government and about half of the states require grand jury indictments for at least some felonies.

PRELIMINARY HEARING
In a court proceeding, a prosecutor presents evidence, and the judge determines if there is probable cause to hold the defendant over for trial.

INDICTMENT
An *indictment* is a written document issued by the grand jury to formally charge the defendant with a crime.

INFORMATION
An *information* is a formal criminal charge made by the prosecutor.

ARRAIGNMENT
The defendant is brought before the court, informed of the charges, and asked to enter a plea. Usually, the prosecutor will attempt to get the defendant to enter into a plea bargain at this stage. Most defendants plead guilty to a lesser offense or receive a reduced sentence for their crime without ever proceeding to trial.

TRIAL
The trial can be either a jury trial or a bench trial. (In a bench trial, there is no jury, and the judge decides questions of fact as well as questions of law.) If the verdict is "guilty," the judge sets a date for the sentencing. Everyone convicted of a crime has the right to an appeal.

federal sentencing guidelines the judge was required to sentence Booker to twenty-two years in prison. The Court ruled that this sentence was unconstitutional because a jury did not find beyond a reasonable doubt that Booker had possessed the additional 566 grams of crack.[25] ■

Essentially, the Court's ruling changed the federal sentencing guidelines from mandatory to advisory. Depending on the circumstances of the case, a federal trial judge may now depart from the guidelines if she or he believes that it is reasonable to do so.

Factors in Determining the Sentence
The sentencing judge must take into account the various sentencing factors that apply to an individual defendant before concluding that a particular sentence is reasonable. When the defendant is a business firm, these factors include the

---

25. *United States v. Booker,* 543 U.S. 220, 125 S.Ct. 738, 160 L.Ed.2d 621 (2005).

"In school, every period ends with a bell. Every sentence ends with a period. Every crime ends with a sentence."

STEVEN WRIGHT
1955–PRESENT
(AMERICAN COMEDIAN)

Computer Crime Any violation of criminal law that involves knowledge of computer technology for its perpetration, investigation, or prosecution.

Cyber Crime A crime that occurs in the online environment.

Cyber Fraud Any misrepresentation knowingly made over the Internet with the intention of deceiving another for the purpose of obtaining property or funds.

company's history of past violations, management's cooperation with federal investigators, and the extent to which the firm has undertaken specific programs and procedures to prevent criminal activities by its employees.

Note, too, that current sentencing guidelines provide for enhanced punishment for certain types of crimes relevant to businesses. These include white-collar crimes, violations of the Sarbanes-Oxley Act, and violations of securities laws.[26]

8–6 Cyber Crime

The U.S. Department of Justice broadly defines **computer crime** as any violation of criminal law that involves knowledge of computer technology for its perpetration, investigation, or prosecution. Many computer crimes fall under the broad label of **cyber crime,** which describes any criminal activity occurring via a computer in the virtual community of the Internet.

Most cyber crimes are simply existing crimes, such as fraud and theft of intellectual property, in which the Internet is the instrument of wrongdoing. Here we look at several types of activities that constitute cyber crimes against persons or property.

Of course, just as computers and the Internet have expanded the scope of crime, they have also provided new ways of detecting and combatting crime. For instance, police are using social media as an investigative tool.

8–6a Cyber Fraud

Fraud is any misrepresentation knowingly made with the intention of deceiving another and on which a reasonable person would and does rely to her or his detriment. **Cyber fraud** is fraud committed over the Internet.

Online Auction Fraud Online auction fraud, in its most basic form, is a simple process. A person puts up an expensive item for auction, on either a legitimate or a fake auction site, and then refuses to send the product after receiving payment. Or, as a variation, the wrongdoer may send the purchaser an item that is worth less than the one offered in the auction.

The larger online auction sites, such as eBay, try to protect consumers against such schemes by providing warnings about deceptive sellers or offering various forms of insurance. It is nearly impossible to completely block fraudulent auction activity on the Internet, however. Because users can assume multiple identities, it is very difficult to pinpoint fraudulent sellers—they will simply change their screen names with each auction.

Online Retail Fraud Somewhat similar to online auction fraud is online retail fraud, in which consumers pay directly (without bidding) for items that are never delivered. As with other forms of online fraud, it is difficult to determine the actual extent of online sales fraud, but anecdotal evidence suggests that it is a substantial problem.

CASE EXAMPLE 8.22 Jeremy Jaynes grossed more than $750,000 per week selling nonexistent or worthless products such as "penny stock pickers" and "Internet history erasers." By the time he was arrested, he had amassed an estimated $24 million from his various fraudulent schemes.[27] ■

8–6b Cyber Theft

In cyberspace, thieves are not subject to the physical limitations of the "real" world. A thief can steal data stored in a networked computer with Internet access from anywhere on the globe.

---

26. The sentencing guidelines were amended in 2003, as required under the Sarbanes-Oxley Act, to impose stiffer penalties for corporate securities fraud.

27. *Jaynes v. Commonwealth of Virginia*, 276 Va. 443, 666 S.E.2d 303 (2008).

Only the speed of the connection and the thief's computer equipment limit the quantity of data that can be stolen.

Identity Theft Not surprisingly, there has been a marked increase in identity theft in recent years. **Identity theft** occurs when the wrongdoer steals a form of identification—such as a name, date of birth, or Social Security number—and uses the information to access and steal the victim's financial resources. This crime existed to a certain extent before the widespread use of the Internet. Thieves would rifle through garbage, for example, to find credit-card or bank account numbers and then use those numbers to purchase goods or to withdraw funds from the victims' accounts.

The Internet has provided even easier access to private data. Frequent Web surfers surrender a wealth of information about themselves without knowing it. Most Web sites use "cookies" to collect data on those who visit their sites. Web browsers often store information such as the consumer's name and e-mail address. In addition, every time a purchase is made online, the item is linked to the purchaser's name.

Phishing In a distinct form of identity theft known as **phishing,** the perpetrators "fish" for financial data and passwords from consumers by posing as a legitimate business such as a bank or credit-card company. The "phisher" sends an e-mail asking the recipient to "update" or "confirm" vital information, often with the threat that an account or some other service will be discontinued if the information is not provided. Once the unsuspecting individual enters the information, the phisher can sell it or use it to masquerade as that person or to drain his or her bank or credit account.

EXAMPLE 8.23 Customers of Wells Fargo Bank receive official-looking e-mails telling them to enter personal information in an online form to complete mandatory installation of a new Internet security certificate. But the Web site is bogus. When the customers complete the forms, their computers are infected and funnel their data to a computer server. The cyber criminals then sell the data. ■

Employment Fraud Cyber criminals also look for victims at online job-posting sites. Claiming to be an employment officer in a well-known company, the criminal sends bogus e-mails to job seekers. The message asks the unsuspecting job seeker to reveal enough information to allow for identity theft.

EXAMPLE 8.24 The job site Monster.com once asked 4.5 million users to change their passwords. Cyber thieves had broken into its databases and stolen user identities, passwords, and other data in one of Britain's largest cyber theft cases. ■

Credit-Card Numbers Companies take risks by storing their online customers' credit-card numbers. Although the consumer can make a purchase more quickly without entering a lengthy card number, the electronic warehouses that store the numbers are targets for cyber thieves.

EXAMPLE 8.25 In 2013, a security breach at Target Corporation exposed the personal information of 70 million Target customers. Hackers stole credit- and debit-card numbers and debit-card PINs from the embedded code on the magnetic strips of the cards, as well as customers' names, addresses, and phone numbers. JPMorgan Chase Bank, the world's largest issuer of credit cards, had to replace 2 million credit and debit cards as a result of the breach. ■

Stolen credit-card numbers are much more likely to hurt merchants and credit-card issuers (such as banks) than consumers. In most situations, the legitimate holders of credit cards are not held responsible for the costs of purchases made with a stolen number.

8-6c Hacking

A **hacker** is someone who uses one computer, smartphone, or other device to break into another. The danger posed by hackers has increased significantly because of **botnets,** or

---

Identity Theft The illegal use of someone else's personal information to access the victim's financial resources.

LEARNING OBJECTIVE 5
How has the Internet expanded opportunities for identity theft?

Phishing A form of identity theft in which the perpetrator sends e-mails purporting to be from legitimate businesses to induce recipients to reveal their personal financial data, passwords, or other information.

Hacker A person who uses computers to gain unauthorized access to data.

Botnet A network of compromised computers connected to the Internet that can be used to generate spam, relay viruses, or cause servers to fail.

Not far from Moscow's Red Square, Russian hackers are outside the jurisdiction of U.S. authorities. Why?

Malware Malicious software programs, such as viruses and worms, that are designed to cause harm to a computer, network, or other device.

Worm A software program that automatically replicates itself over a network but does not alter files and is usually invisible to the user until it has consumed system resources.

Virus A software program that can replicate itself over a network and spread from one device to another, altering files and interfering with normal operations.

networks of computers that have been appropriated by hackers without the knowledge of their owners. A hacker may secretly install a program on thousands, if not millions, of personal computer "robots," or "bots." To read about a group of well-known hackers in Russia, see this chapter's *Beyond Our Borders* feature.

EXAMPLE 8.26 When a hacker broke into Sony Corporation's Play-Station 3 video gaming and entertainment networks, the company had to temporarily shut down its online services. This single hacking incident affected more than 100 million online accounts that provide gaming, chat, and music streaming services. ▪

Malware Botnets are one form of **malware,** a term that refers to any program that is harmful to a computer or, by extension, its user. A **worm,** for example, is a software program that is capable of reproducing itself as it spreads from one computer to the next.

EXAMPLE 8.27 Within three weeks, the computer worm called Conflicker spread to more than a million personal computers around the world. It was transmitted to some computers through the use of Facebook and Twitter. This worm also infected servers and devices plugged into infected computers via USB ports, such as iPods, iPhones, iPads, and USB flash drives. ▪

A **virus,** another form of malware, is also able to reproduce itself, but must be attached to an "infested" host file to travel from one computer network to another. For example, hackers are now capable of corrupting banner ads that use Adobe's Flash Player. When an Internet user clicks on the banner ad, a virus is installed.

Worms and viruses can be programmed to perform a number of functions, such as prompting host computers to continually "crash" and reboot, or to otherwise infect the system. For a discussion of how malware is changing the criminal landscape and even affecting smartphones, see this chapter's *Adapting the Law to the Online Environment* feature.

Service-Based Hacking A recent trend in business computer applications is the use of "software as a service." Instead of buying software to install on a computer, the user connects to

BEYOND OUR BORDERS   Hackers Hide in Plain Sight in Russia

According to the security software company Symantec, few Internet users and businesses have completely avoided computer crime. Consumers alone lose about $120 billion a year worldwide to cyber fraud and hacking. In recent years, Russia has become a haven for hackers.

The KoobFace Gang
A group of at least five men who live comfortably in St. Petersburg, Russia, started hacking a few years ago—and are still at it.

Calling themselves KoobFace, they created a system of illegal botnets that includes 800,000 infected personal computers. Via this system, they have succeeded in using the KoobFace worm to infiltrate Facebook accounts. The KoobFace gang continues to make $2 million to $5 million a year from this venture. KoobFace is considered a pioneer in the criminal exploitation of social networks.

Knowing the Perpetrators Does Not Lead to Convictions
Authorities worldwide know the identities of the members of KoobFace, yet so far none of them has been charged with a crime. No

law enforcement agencies have even confirmed that the group is under investigation. Because Western law officials do not have the resources to tackle even well-known hackers, the Russians hackers are free to continue their activities. It is not surprising that Russia has gained a reputation as a "hacker haven."

CRITICAL THINKING

▪ Why might it be difficult for U.S. authorities to ever investigate the KoobFace gang?

ADAPTING THE LAW TO THE **ONLINE** ENVIRONMENT
Malware Is Changing the Criminal Landscape

Recent statistics show that the number of bank robberies occurring annually is on the decline. Criminals have learned that it is easier, less risky, and more profitable to steal via the Internet. Advances in the speed and use of the Internet have fostered the growth of a relatively new criminal industry that uses malware to conduct espionage and profit from crime.

Who Are the Creators of Malware?

While any teenager can buy prepackaged hacking software on the Internet, the malware that businesses and governments are worried about is much more sophisticated. They are concerned about malware that can be used for international diplomatic espionage and industrial espionage. Evidence indicates that this malware is most often developed by so-called cyber mercenaries. According to Steve Sachs of the cyber security firm FireEye, "There are entire little villages dedicated to malware in Russia, villages in China, very sophisticated, very organized, very well-funded."

Flame Malware

Perhaps the most sophisticated global malware has been labeled Flame. Flame was discovered in 2012, although experts believe that it had been lying dormant in thousands of computers worldwide for at least five years. Flame can record screen shots, keyboard strokes, network traffic, and audio. It can also record Skype conversations. It can even turn infected computers into Bluetooth beacons, which can then attempt to download contact information from nearby Bluetooth-enabled devices.

The Malware Can Infect Smartphones

Many smartphone owners are unaware that their phones can be infected with Flame malware or variants of it without their knowledge. The information that is hacked from smartphones can then be sent to a series of command-and-control servers and ultimately to members of international criminal gangs.

Once a computer or smartphone is infected with this malware, all information in the device can be transferred. Additionally, files can be deleted, and files that have been erased can be resurrected. The malware has been responsible for the theft of e-mail databases from Microsoft's e-mail program Outlook and has even captured e-mail from remote servers.[a]

Businesses Are Worried

Until recently, most attacks involved diplomatic espionage, but cyber technicians at large business enterprises are now worried that industrial espionage may be taking place as well. In fact, an extensive hacking operation was uncovered in 2013 that was linked to a Chinese military unit (the "Comment Crew"). The wide-ranging cyber attacks involved the theft of hundreds of terabytes of data and intellectual property of more than 140 corporations in twenty different industries. The goal of the attacks was to help Chinese companies better compete against U.S. and other foreign firms.[b]

CRITICAL THINKING

■ What entities might pay "cyber mercenaries" to create some of the malware described in this feature?

a. Mark Stevens, *"CWI Cryptanalyst Discovers New Cryptographic Attack Variant in Flame Spy Malware,"* June 7, 2012, www.cwi.nl/news/2012.

b. David E. Sanger, David Barboza, and Nicole Perlroth, *"Chinese Army Unit Is Seen as Tied to Hacking Against U.S.,"* www.nytimes.com/2013.

Web-based software. The user can then write e-mails, edit spreadsheets, and the like using a Web browser.

Cyber criminals have adapted this method and now offer "crimeware as a service." A would-be thief no longer has to be a computer hacker to create a botnet or steal banking information and credit-card numbers. He or she can rent the online services of cyber criminals to do the work for a small price. The thief can even target individual groups, such as U.S. physicians or British attorneys. (For some tips on protecting a company against hackers, see the *Business Application* at the end of this chapter.)

> "A hacker does for love what others would not do for money."
>
> **LAURA CREIGHTON**
> (COMPUTER PROGRAMMER AND ENTREPRENEUR)

8-6d Cyberterrorism

Cyberterrorists, as well as hackers, may target businesses. The goals of a hacking operation might include a wholesale theft of data, such as a merchant's customer files, or the monitoring of a computer to discover a business firm's plans and transactions. A cyberterrorist might also want to insert false codes or data into a computer. For instance, the processing control system of a food manufacturer could be changed to alter the levels of ingredients so that consumers of the food would become ill.

A cyberterrorist attack on a major financial institution, such as the New York Stock Exchange or a large bank, could leave securities or money markets in flux and seriously affect the daily lives of millions of citizens. Similarly, any prolonged disruption of computer, cable, satellite, or telecommunications systems due to the actions of expert hackers would have serious repercussions on business operations—and national security—on a global level.

8-6e Prosecution of Cyber Crime

Cyber crime has raised new issues in the investigation of crimes and the prosecution of offenders. Determining the "location" of a cyber crime and identifying a criminal in cyberspace are two significant challenges for law enforcement.

Jurisdiction and Identification Challenges A threshold issue is, of course, jurisdiction. Jurisdiction is normally based on physical geography, as discussed previously, and each state and nation has jurisdiction over crimes committed within its boundaries. But geographic boundaries simply do not apply in cyberspace. A person who commits an act against a business in California, where the act is a cyber crime, might never have set foot in California but might instead reside in, say, Canada, where the act may not be a crime.

Identifying the wrongdoer can also be difficult. Cyber criminals do not leave physical traces, such as fingerprints or DNA samples, as evidence of their crimes. Even electronic "footprints" (digital evidence) can be hard to find and follow. For instance, e-mail can be sent through a remailer, an online service that guarantees that a message cannot be traced to its source.

For these reasons, laws written to protect physical property are often difficult to apply in cyberspace. Nonetheless, governments at both the state and the federal level have taken significant steps toward controlling cyber crime, both by applying existing criminal statutes and by enacting new laws that specifically address wrongs committed in cyberspace. California, for instance, which has the highest identity theft rate in the nation, has established an eCrime unit to investigate and prosecute cyber crimes. Other states, including Florida, Louisiana, and Texas, also have special law enforcement units that focus solely on Internet crimes.

The Computer Fraud and Abuse Act Perhaps the most significant federal statute specifically addressing cyber crime is the Counterfeit Access Device and Computer Fraud and Abuse Act.[28] This act is commonly known as the Computer Fraud and Abuse Act, or CFAA.

Among other things, the CFAA provides that a person who accesses a computer online, without authority, to obtain classified, restricted, or protected data (or attempts to do so) is subject to criminal prosecution. Such data could include financial and credit records, medical records, legal files, military and national security files, and other confidential information in government or private computers. The crime has two elements: accessing a computer without authority and taking the data.

This theft is a felony if it is committed for a commercial purpose or for private financial gain, or if the value of the stolen information exceeds $5,000. Penalties include fines and imprisonment for up to twenty years. A victim of computer theft can also bring a civil suit against the violator to obtain damages, an injunction, and other relief.

---

28. 18 U.S.C. Section 1030.

Reviewing . . . Criminal Law and Cyber Crime

Edward Hanousek worked for Pacific & Arctic Railway and Navigation Company (P&A) as a roadmaster of the White Pass & Yukon Railroad in Alaska. As an officer of the corporation, Hanousek was responsible "for every detail of the safe and efficient maintenance and construction of track, structures, and marine facilities of the entire railroad," including special projects. One project was a rock quarry, known as "6-mile," above the Skagway River. Next to the quarry, and just beneath the surface, ran a high-pressure oil pipeline owned by Pacific & Arctic Pipeline, Inc., P&A's sister company. When the quarry's backhoe operator punctured the pipeline, an estimated 1,000 to 5,000 gallons of oil were discharged into the river. Hanousek was charged with negligently discharging a harmful quantity of oil into a navigable water of the United States in violation of the criminal provisions of the Clean Water Act (CWA). Using the information presented in the chapter, answer the following questions.

1. Did Hanousek have the required mental state *(mens rea)* to be convicted of a crime? Why or why not?

2. Which theory discussed in the chapter would enable a court to hold Hanousek criminally liable for violating the statute regardless of whether he participated in, directed, or even knew about the specific violation?

3. Could the quarry's backhoe operator who punctured the pipeline also be charged with a crime in this situation? Explain.

4. Suppose that, at trial, Hanousek argued that he could not be convicted because he was not aware of the requirements of the CWA. Would this defense be successful? Why or why not?

DEBATE THIS

- Because of overcriminalization, particularly by the federal government, Americans may be breaking the law regularly without knowing it. Should Congress rescind many of the more than four thousand federal crimes now on the books?

BUSINESS APPLICATION

Protecting Your Company against Hacking of Its Bank Accounts*

Each year, conventional, old-fashioned crooks rob banks to the tune of about $50 million. In contrast, every year cyber-crooks steal billions of dollars from the bank accounts of small and mid-size companies in Europe and the United States. Why? The reason is that small businesses tend to be lax in protecting themselves from hackers. They keep their accounts in community or regional banks, have only rudimentary security measures, and usually fail to hire an on-site cyber security expert.

You May Not Receive Compensation for Your Losses

Many small-business owners believe that if their bank accounts are hacked and disappear, their banks will reimburse them. That is not always the case, however. Just ask Mark Patterson, the owner of Patco Construction in Stanford, Maryland. He lost more than $350,000 to cyberthieves. When People's United Bank would not agree to a settlement, Patterson sued, claiming that the bank should have monitored his account. So far,

---

* This *Business Application* is not meant to substitute for the services of an attorney who is licensed to practice law in your state.

Continues

federal judges have agreed with the bank—that its protections were "commercially reasonable," which is the only standard that banks have to follow.

Insurance May Not Be the Answer
Similarly, small-business owners often think that their regular insurance policy will cover cyber losses at their local banks. In reality, unless there is a specific "rider" to a business's insurance policy, its bank accounts are not covered. Thus, even though your insurance company will reimburse you if thieves break in and steal your machines and network servers, it may not have to reimburse you if cybercrooks break into your bank account.

CHECKLIST for Preventing Cyberthefts of Your Bank Accounts:

1. Meet with your bank managers and discuss what you can do to protect your company's bank accounts.

2. Have your company sign up for identity-theft-protection services. Many large banks provide these.

3. Change your company's passwords frequently. Always use long, complicated passwords.

4. Instruct your employees never to reply to unknown e-mail requests, particularly if they ask for any information about the company.

5. Have a computer expert test the firewalls safeguarding your internal computer network.

Key Terms

actus reus 187
arson 192
beyond a reasonable doubt 185
botnet 207
burglary 191
computer crime 206
crime 185
cyber crime 206
cyber fraud 206
double jeopardy 201
duress 198
embezzlement 193
entrapment 198

exclusionary rule 202
felony 186
forgery 193
grand jury 204
hacker 207
identity theft 207
indictment 204
information 204
insider trading 195
larceny 192
malware 208
mens rea 187
misdemeanor 187

money laundering 196
petty offense 187
phishing 207
plea bargaining 199
probable cause 200
robbery 190
search warrant 199
self-defense 197
self-incrimination 199
virus 208
white-collar crime 193
worm 208

Chapter Summary: Criminal Law and Cyber Crime

Civil Law and Criminal Law	1. *Civil law*—Spells out the duties that exist between persons or between persons and their governments, excluding the duty not to commit crimes. 2. *Criminal law*—Has to do with crimes, which are wrongs against society proclaimed in statutes and, if committed, punishable by society through fines and/or imprisonment—and, in some cases, death. Because crimes are *offenses against society as a whole*, they are prosecuted by a public official, not by the victims. 3. *Key differences*—An important difference between civil and criminal law is that the standard of proof is higher in criminal cases (see Exhibit 8–1 for other differences between civil and criminal law). 4. *Civil liability for criminal acts*—A criminal act may give rise to both criminal liability and tort liability (see Exhibit 8–2 for an example of criminal and tort liability for the same act). 5. *Classification of crimes*—Crimes may also be classified according to their degree of seriousness. Felonies are serious crimes usually punishable by death or by imprisonment for more than one year. Misdemeanors are less serious crimes punishable by fines or by confinement for up to one year.
Criminal Liability	1. *Guilty act*—In general, some form of harmful act must be committed for a crime to exist. 2. *Intent*—An intent to commit a crime, or a wrongful mental state, is generally required for a crime to exist.

Types of Crimes	1. *Violent crimes*—Violent crimes are those that cause others to suffer harm or death, including murder, assault and battery, sexual assault (rape), and robbery. 2. *Property crimes*—Property crimes are the most common form of crime. The offender's goal is to obtain some economic gain or to damage property. This category includes burglary, larceny, obtaining goods by false pretenses, receiving stolen property, arson, and forgery. 3. *Public order crimes*—Public order crimes are acts, such as public drunkenness, prostitution, gambling, and illegal drug use, that a statute has established are contrary to public values and morals. 4. *White-collar crimes*—White-collar crimes are illegal acts committed by a person or business using nonviolent means to obtain a personal or business advantage. Usually, such crimes are committed in the course of a legitimate occupation. Examples include embezzlement, mail and wire fraud, bribery, bankruptcy fraud, theft of trade secrets, and insider trading. 5. *Organized crimes*—Organized crime is a form of crime conducted by groups operating illegitimately to satisfy the public's demand for illegal goods and services (such as gambling or illegal narcotics). This category of crime also includes money laundering and racketeering (RICO) violations.
Defenses to Criminal Liability	Defenses to criminal liability include justifiable use of force, necessity, insanity, mistake, duress, entrapment, and the statute of limitations. Also, in some cases defendants may be relieved of criminal liability, at least in part, if they are given immunity.
Criminal Procedures	1. *Fourth Amendment*—Provides protection against unreasonable searches and seizures and requires that probable cause exist before a warrant for a search or an arrest can be issued. 2. *Fifth Amendment*—Requires due process of law, prohibits double jeopardy, and protects against self-incrimination. 3. *Sixth Amendment*—Guarantees a speedy trial, a trial by jury, a public trial, the right to confront witnesses, and the right to counsel. 4. *Eighth Amendment*—Prohibits excessive bail and fines, and cruel and unusual punishment. 5. *Exclusionary rule*—A criminal procedural rule that prohibits the introduction at trial of all evidence obtained in violation of constitutional rights, as well as any evidence derived from the illegally obtained evidence. 6. *Miranda rule*—A rule set forth by the Supreme Court in *Miranda v. Arizona* holding that individuals who are arrested must be informed of certain constitutional rights, including their right to counsel. 7. *Criminal process*—Procedures governing arrest, indictment, and trial for a crime are designed to safeguard the rights of the individual against the government (see Exhibit 8–3). 8. *Sentencing guidelines*—The federal government has established sentencing laws or guidelines, which are no longer mandatory but provide a range of penalties for each federal crime.
Cyber Crime	1. *Cyber fraud*—Occurs when misrepresentations are knowingly made over the Internet to deceive another. Two widely reported forms are online auction fraud and online retail fraud. 2. *Cyber theft*—In cyberspace, thieves can steal data from anywhere in the world. Identity theft is made easier by the fact that many e-businesses store information such as consumers' names, e-mail addresses, and credit-card numbers. Phishing and employment fraud are variations of identity theft. 3. *Hacking*—A hacker is a person who uses one computer to break into another. Malware is any program that is harmful to a computer or, by extension, a computer user. Worms and viruses are examples. 4. *Cyberterrorism*—Cyberterrorists aim to cause serious problems for computer systems. A cyberterrorist attack on a major U.S. financial institution or telecommunications system could have serious repercussions, including jeopardizing national security. 5. *Prosecution of cyber crime*—Prosecuting cyber crime is more difficult than prosecuting traditional crime. Identifying the wrongdoer is complicated, and jurisdictional issues may arise. A significant federal statute addressing cyber crime is the computer fraud and abuse act.

Issue Spotters

1. Daisy takes her roommate's credit card, intending to charge expenses that she incurs on a vacation. Her first stop is a gas station, where she uses the card to pay for gas. With respect to the gas station, has she committed a crime? If so, what is it? (See *Types of Crimes*.)
2. Without permission, Ben downloads consumer credit files from a computer belonging to Consumer Credit Agency. He then sells the data to Dawn. Has Ben committed a crime? If so, what is it? (See *Cyber Crime*.)

—**Check your answers to the *Issue Spotters* against the answers provided in Appendix D at the end of this text.**

Learning Objectives Check

1. What two elements normally must exist before a person can be held liable for a crime?
2. What are five broad categories of crimes? What is white-collar crime?
3. What defenses can be raised to avoid liability for criminal acts?
4. What constitutional safeguards exist to protect persons accused of crimes?
5. How has the Internet expanded opportunities for identity theft?
   —**Answers to the even-numbered *Learning Objectives Check* questions can be found in Appendix E at the end of this text.**

Business Scenarios and Case Problems

8–1. Types of Cyber Crimes. The following situations are similar, but each represents a variation of a particular crime. Identify the crime and point out the differences in the variations. (See *Cyber Crime.*)

1. Chen, posing fraudulently as Diamond Credit Card Co., sends an e-mail to Emily, stating that the company has observed suspicious activity in her account and has frozen the account. The e-mail asks her to reregister her credit-card number and password to reopen the account.
2. Claiming falsely to be Big Buy Retail Finance Co., Conner sends an e-mail to Dino, asking him to confirm or update his personal security information to prevent his Big Buy account from being discontinued.
3. Felicia posts her résumé on GotWork.com, an online job-posting site, seeking a position in business and managerial finance and accounting. Hayden, who misrepresents himself as an employment officer with International Bank & Commerce Corp., sends her an e-mail asking for more personal information.

8–2. Cyber Scam. Kayla, a student at Learnwell University, owes $20,000 in unpaid tuition. If Kayla does not pay the tuition, Learnwell will not allow her to graduate. To obtain the funds to pay the debt, she sends e-mails to people that she does not know asking them for financial help to send her child, who has a disability, to a special school. In reality, Kayla has no children. Is this a crime? If so, which one? (See *Cyber Crime.*)

8–3. Search. Charles Byrd was in a minimum-security county jail awaiting trial. A team of sheriff's deputies wearing T-shirts and jeans took Byrd and several other inmates into a room for a strip search without any apparent justification. Byrd was ordered to remove all his clothing except his boxer shorts. A female deputy searched Byrd while several male deputies watched. One of the male deputies videotaped the search. Byrd filed a suit against the sheriff's department. Did the search violate Byrd's rights? Discuss. [*Byrd v. Maricopa County Sheriff's Department*, 629 F.3d. 1135 (9th Cir. 2011)] (See *Criminal Procedures.*)

8–4. Credit- and Debit-Card Theft. Jacqueline Barden was shopping for school clothes with her children when her purse and automobile were taken. In Barden's purse were her car keys, credit and debit cards for herself and her children, as well as the children's Social Security cards and birth certificates needed for enrollment at school. Immediately after the purse and car were stolen, Rebecca Mary Turner attempted to use Barden's credit card at a local Exxon gas station, but the card was declined. The gas station attendant recognized Turner because she had previously written bad checks and used credit cards that did not belong to her.

Turner was later arrested while attempting to use one of Barden's checks to pay for merchandise at a Walmart—where the clerk also recognized Turner from prior criminal activity. Turner claimed that she had not stolen Barden's purse or car, and that a friend had told her he had some checks and credit cards and asked her to try using them at Walmart. Turner was convicted at trial. She appealed, claiming that there was insufficient evidence that she committed credit- and debit-card theft. Was the evidence sufficient to uphold her conviction? Why or why not? [*Turner v. State of Arkansas*, 2012 Ark.App. 150 (2012)] (See *Types of Crimes.*)

8–5. Business Case Problem with Sample Answer— Criminal Liability. During the morning rush hour, David Green threw bottles and plates from a twenty-sixth-floor hotel balcony overlooking Seventh Avenue in New York City. A video of the incident also showed him doing cartwheels while holding a beer bottle and sprinting toward the balcony while holding a glass steadily in his hand. When he saw police on the street below and on the roof of the building across the street, he suspended his antics but resumed tossing objects off the balcony after the police left. He later admitted that he could recall what he had done, but claimed to have been intoxicated and said his only purpose was to amuse himself and his friends. Did Green have the mental state required to establish criminal liability? Discuss. [*State of New York v. Green*, 104 A.D.3d 126, 958 N.Y.S.2d 138 (1 Dept. 2013)] (See *Criminal Liability.*)

—**For a sample answer to Problem 8–5, go to Appendix F at the end of this text.**

8–6. White-Collar Crime. Matthew Simpson and others created and operated a series of corporate entities to defraud telecommunications companies, creditors, credit reporting agencies, and others. Through these entities, Simpson and his confederates used routing codes and spoofing services to make long-distance calls appear to be local. They stole other firms' network capacity and diverted payments to themselves. They leased goods and services without paying for them. To hide their association with their corporate entities and with each other, they used false identities, addresses, and credit histories, and issued false bills, invoices, financial statements, and credit references. Did these acts constitute mail and wire fraud? Discuss. [*United States v. Simpson,* 741 F.3d 539 (5th Cir. 2014)] (See *Types of Crimes.*)

8–7. Defenses to Criminal Liability. George Castro told Ambrosio Medrano that a bribe to a certain corrupt Los Angeles County official would buy a contract with the county hospitals. To share in the deal, Medrano recruited Gustavo Buenrostro. In turn, Buenrostro contacted his friend James Barta, the owner of Sav–Rx, which provides prescription benefit management services. Barta was asked to pay a "finder's fee" to Castro. He did not pay, even after frequent e-mails and calls with deadlines and ultimatums delivered over a period of months. Eventually, Barta wrote Castro a Sav–Rx check for $6,500, saying that it was to help his friend Buenrostro. Castro was an FBI agent, and the county official and contract were fictional. Barta was charged with conspiracy to commit bribery. At trial, the government conceded that Barta was not predisposed to commit the crime. Could he be absolved of the charge on a defense of entrapment? Explain. [*United States v. Barta,* __ F.3d __, 2015 WL 350672 (7th Cir. 2015)] (See *Defenses to Criminal Liability.*)

8–8. A Question of Ethics—Criminal Process. Gary Peters fraudulently told an undocumented immigrant that Peters could help him obtain lawful status. Peters said that he knew immigration officials and asked for money to aid the process. The victim paid Peters at least $25,000 in wire transfers and checks. Peters had others call the victim, falsely represent that they were agents with the U.S. Department of Homeland Security, and induce continued payments. He threatened to contact authorities to detain or deport the victim and his wife. Peters was convicted in a federal district court of wire fraud. [*United States v. Peters,* __ F.3d __, 2015 WL 120637 (11th Cir. 2015)] (See *Constitutional Safeguards and Criminal Procedures.*)

1. Peters had previously committed theft and fraud. The court stated, "This is the person he is. He steals from his relatives. He steals from his business partner. He steals from immigrants. He steals from anybody he comes into contact with." What does Peters's conduct indicate about his ethics?

2. Peters's attorney argued that his client's criminal history was partially due to "difficult personal times" caused by divorce, illness, and job loss. Despite this claim, Peters was sentenced to forty-eight months imprisonment, which exceeded the federal sentencing guidelines but was less than the statutory maximum of twenty years. Was this sentence too harsh or too lenient? Discuss.

Critical Thinking and Writing Assignments

8–9. Critical Legal Thinking. Ray steals a purse from an unattended car at a gas station. Because the purse contains money and a handgun, Ray is convicted of grand theft of property (cash) and grand theft of a firearm. On appeal, Ray claims that he is not guilty of grand theft of a firearm because he did not know that the purse contained a gun. Can Ray be convicted of grand theft of a firearm even though he did not know that the gun was in the purse? Explain. (See *Types of Crimes.*)

8–10. Business Law Critical Thinking Group Assignment. Cyber crime costs consumers millions of dollars every year. It costs businesses, including banks and other credit-card issuers, even more. Nonetheless, when cyber criminals are caught and convicted, they are rarely ordered to pay restitution or sentenced to long prison terms. (See *Cyber Crime.*)

1. One group should argue that stiffer sentences would reduce the amount of cyber crime.

2. A second group should determine how businesspersons can best protect themselves from cyber crime and avoid the associated costs.

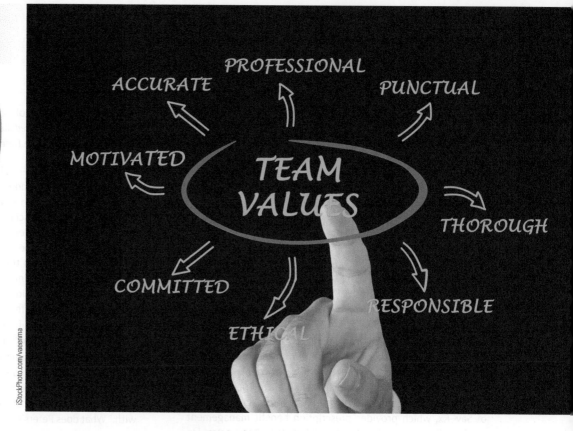

9

LEARNING OBJECTIVES

The five Learning Objectives *below are designed to help improve your understanding of the chapter. After reading this chapter, you should be able to answer the following questions:*

1. What is business ethics, and why is it important?

2. How do duty-based ethical standards differ from outcome-based ethical standards?

3. What are five steps that a businessperson can take to evaluate whether his or her actions are ethical?

4. How can business leaders encourage their companies to act ethically?

5. What types of ethical issues might arise in the context of international business transactions?

Ethics Moral principles and values applied to social behavior.

Business Ethics

One of the most complex issues that businesspersons and corporations face is ethics. Ethics is not as clearly defined as the law. To be sure, some ethical scandals arise from illegal conduct, such as when corporate executives trade stock based on inside information (information that has not become public). Others, though, involve activities that are legal but ethically questionable. For instance, in 2014 it was discovered that more than three hundred corporations (many from the United States) had entered into secret agreements that allowed them to funnel cash into Luxembourg to avoid paying billions in taxes. Although there is nothing wrong with minimizing tax liability, dodging taxes completely may have ethical implications.

As the chapter-opening quotation states, "New occasions teach new duties." The ethics scandals of the last several years have taught everyone that business ethics cannot be taken lightly. Ethical behavior, or the lack of it, can have a substantial impact on a firm's finances and reputation. How businesspersons should act and whose interests they should consider—those of the firm, its executives, its employees, its shareholders, and more—are the focus of this chapter on business ethics.

> "New occasions teach new duties."
>
> **JAMES RUSSELL LOWELL**
> 1819–1891
> (AMERICAN EDITOR, POET, AND DIPLOMAT)

9–1 Business Ethics

At the most basic level, the study of **ethics** is the study of what constitutes right or wrong behavior. It is the branch of philosophy that focuses on morality and the way in which moral principles are derived and applied to one's conduct in daily life. Ethics has to do with questions relating to the fairness, justness, rightness, or wrongness of an action.

The study of **business ethics** typically looks at the decisions businesses make and whether those decisions are right or wrong. It has to do with how businesspersons apply moral and ethical principles in making their decisions. Those who study business ethics also evaluate what duties and responsibilities exist or should exist for businesses.

Business Ethics The application of moral and ethical principles in a business context.

9–1a Why Is Studying Business Ethics Important?

Over the last two hundred years, the public perception of the corporation has changed from an entity that primarily generates revenues for its owners to an entity that participates in society as a corporate citizen. Originally, the only goal or duty of a corporation was to maximize profits. Although many people today may view this idea as greedy or inhumane, the rationale for the profit-maximization theory is still valid.

LEARNING OBJECTIVE 1
What is business ethics, and why is it important?

Profit Maximization as a Goal In theory, if all firms strictly adhere to the goal of profit maximization, resources flow to where they are most highly valued by society. Corporations can focus on their strengths. Other entities that are better suited to deal with social problems and perform charitable acts can specialize in those activities. The government, through taxes and other financial allocations, can shift resources to those other entities to perform public services. Thus, profit maximization can lead to the most efficient allocation of scarce resources.

The Rise of Corporate Citizenship Over the years, many people became dissatisfied with profit-maximization theory. Investors and others began to look beyond profits and dividends and to consider the **triple bottom line**—a corporation's profits, its impact on people, and its impact on the planet. Magazines and Web sites began to rank companies based on their environmental impacts and their ethical decisions (or lack thereof). The corporation came to be viewed as a "citizen" that was expected to participate in bettering communities and society. Even so, many still believe that corporations are fundamentally money-making entities that should have no responsibility other than profit maximization.

Triple Bottom Line A measure that includes a corporation's profits, its impact on people, and its impact on the planet.

9–1b The Importance of Ethics in Making Business Decisions

Whether one believes in profit-maximization theory or corporate citizenship, ethics is important in making business decisions. Corporations should strive to be "good citizens." When making decisions, a business should evaluate each of the following:

1. The legal implications of each decision.
2. The public relations impact.
3. The safety risks for consumers and employees.
4. The financial implications.

This four-part analysis will assist the firm in making decisions that not only maximize profits but also reflect good corporate citizenship.

"It's easy to make a buck. It's a lot tougher to make a difference."

TOM BROKAW
1940–PRESENT
(AMERICAN TELEVISION JOURNALIST)

Short-Run versus Long-Run Profit Maximization In attempting to maximize profits, corporate executives and employees have to distinguish between *short-run* and *long-run* profit maximization. In the short run, a company may increase its profits by continuing to sell a product, even though it knows that the product is defective. In the long run, though, because of lawsuits, large settlements, and bad publicity, such unethical conduct will cause profits to suffer. Thus, business ethics is consistent only with long-run profit maximization. An overemphasis on short-term profit maximization is the most common reason that ethical problems occur in business.

CASE EXAMPLE 9.1 When the powerful narcotic painkiller OxyContin was first marketed, its manufacturer, Purdue Pharma, claimed that it was unlikely to lead to drug addiction or

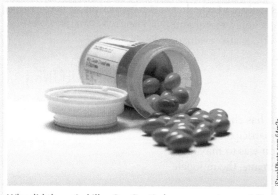

Why did the pain killer OxyContin become controversial?

abuse. Internal company documents later showed that the company's executives knew that OxyContin could be addictive, but kept this risk a secret to boost sales and maximize short-term profits.

Subsequently, Purdue Pharma and three former executives pleaded guilty to criminal charges that they had misled regulators, patients, and physicians about OxyContin's risks of addiction. Purdue Pharma agreed to pay $600 million in fines and other payments. The three former executives agreed to pay $34.5 million in fines and were barred from doing business with federal health programs for fifteen years. Thus, the company's focus on maximizing profits in the short run led to unethical conduct that hurt profits in the long run.[1] ▪

The Internet Can Ruin Reputations   In the past, negative information or opinions about a company might remain hidden. Now, however, cyberspace provides a forum in which disgruntled employees, unhappy consumers, and special interest groups can post derogatory remarks. Thus, the Internet has increased the potential for a major corporation (or other business) to suffer damage to its reputation or loss of profits through negative publicity.

Walmart and Nike have been frequent targets for advocacy groups that believe those corporations exploit their workers. Although these assertions may be unfounded or exaggerated, the courts generally have refused to consider them *defamatory* (defamation was discussed in the torts chapter). Most courts regard online attacks as expressions of opinion, a form of speech protected by the First Amendment. Even so, corporations often incur considerable expense in running marketing campaigns to counteract bad publicity, and they may face legal costs if the allegations lead to litigation.

Image Is Everything   Business ethics relates to the purposes of a business and how that business achieves those purposes. These factors, in turn, involve the business's image and the impacts that the business has on the environment, customers, suppliers, employees, and the global economy. Unethical corporate decision making can negatively affect suppliers, consumers, the community, and society as a whole. It can also harm the reputation of the company and the individuals who run it. Hence, an in-depth understanding of business ethics is important to the long-run viability of any corporation today.

9–1c The Relationship of Law and Ethics

The law does not codify all ethical requirements. Because the law cannot make all our ethical decisions for us, compliance with the law is not always sufficient to determine "right" behavior.

Legal Requirements   Laws have to be general enough to apply in a variety of circumstances. Laws are broad in their purpose and their scope. They prohibit or require certain actions to prevent significant harm to society. When two competing companies secretly agree to set prices on products, for instance, society suffers harm—typically, the companies will charge higher prices than they could if they continued to compete. This harm has negative consequences for the economy, and so

"Have you noticed ethics creeping into some of these deals lately?"

---

1. *United States v. Purdue Frederick Co.*, 495 F.Supp.2d 569 (W.D.Va. 2007).

colliding to set prices is an illegal activity. Similarly, when a company is preparing to issue stock, the law requires certain disclosures to potential investors.

The Moral Minimum   Compliance with the law is sometimes called the **moral minimum.** In other words, those who merely comply with the law are acting at the lowest ethical level society will tolerate. The following case illustrates some consequences of a businessperson's failure to meet the moral minimum.

Moral Minimum The minimum level of ethical behavior expected by society, which is usually defined as compliance with the law.

CASE 9.1

Scott v. Carpanzano
United States Court of Appeals, Fifth Circuit, 2014 WL 274493 (2014).

FACTS Rick Scott deposited $2 million in an escrow account maintained by a company owned by Salvatore Carpanzano. Immediately after the deposit was made, in violation of the escrow agreement, the funds were withdrawn. When Scott was unable to recover his money, he filed a suit against Salvatore Carpanzano and others, including Carmela Carpanzano, Salvatore's daughter. In the complaint, Scott made no allegations of acts or knowledge on Carmela's part, and Carmela denied that she was involved in her father's business or the Scott transaction.

Salvatore failed to cooperate with discovery, did not respond to attempts to contact him by certified letters and other means, refused to make an appearance in court, and did not finalize a settlement negotiated between the parties' attorneys. Carmela indicated that she was relying on her father to protect her interests in the lawsuit. The court issued a judgment for more than $6 million in Scott's favor, finding that the defendants had willfully defaulted—that is, intentionally failed to respond to the litigation. The defendants appealed to the U.S. Court of Appeals for the Fifth Circuit.

ISSUE Did the defendants willfully default and thereby justify the judgment against them?

Why is certified mail used?

DECISION Yes, as to Salvatore. No, as to Carmela. The federal appellate court affirmed the judgment against Salvatore, but reversed the decision against Carmela.

REASON Salvatore failed almost entirely to participate in the litigation in any way. In particular, he did not cooperate with discovery, respond to attempts to communicate with him, appear in court, or finalize his attorneys' negotiated settlement. This intentional failure to respond constituted a willful default. In contrast, Carmela did not willfully default. Rather, she relied on her father to protect her interests in the lawsuit. As for her liability, Scott's complaint made no allegations of acts or knowledge on her part, and she denied that she was involved in her father's business or the Scott transaction. "Even if Scott were able to prove the entirety of the . . . complaint, we fail to see how it would justify a judgment . . . against Ms. Carpanzano."

CRITICAL THINKING—Ethical Consideration *Are Salvatore's actions likely to affect his business's ability to profit in the long run? Discuss.*

Ethical Requirements   The study of ethics goes beyond legal requirements to evaluate what is right for society. Businesspersons thus must remember that an action that is legal is not necessarily ethical. For instance, a company's refusal to negotiate liability claims for alleged injuries because of a faulty product is legal. But it may not be ethical if the reason the business refused to negotiate was to increase the injured party's legal costs and force the person to drop a legitimate claim.

Ethics and Private Company Codes of Ethics   Most companies attempt to link ethics and law through the creation of internal codes of ethics. (We present the code of ethics of Costco Wholesale Corporation as an example in the appendix following this chapter.) Company codes are not laws. Instead, they are rules that the company sets forth and that it can also enforce (by terminating an employee who does not follow them, for instance). Codes of conduct typically outline the company's policies on particular issues and indicate how employees are expected to act.

"Never let your sense of morals prevent you from doing what is right."

ISAAC ASIMOV
1920–1992
(RUSSIAN-BORN WRITER AND SCIENTIST)

EXAMPLE 9.2 Google's code of conduct starts with the motto "Don't be evil." The code then makes general statements about how Google promotes integrity, mutual respect, and the highest standard of ethical business conduct. Google's code also provides specific rules on a number of issues, such as privacy, drugs and alcohol, conflicts of interest, co-worker relationships, and confidentiality—it even has a dog policy. The company takes a stand against employment discrimination that goes further than the law requires. It prohibits discrimination based on sexual orientation, gender identity or expression, and veteran status. ■

Numerous industries have also developed codes of ethics. The American Institute of Certified Public Accountants (AICPA) has a comprehensive Code of Professional Conduct for the ethical practicing of accounting. The American Bar Association has model rules of professional conduct for attorneys, and the American Nurses Association has a code of ethics that applies to nurses. These codes can give guidance to decision makers facing ethical questions. Violation of a code may result in discipline of an employee or sanctions against a company from the industry organization. Remember, though, that these internal codes are not laws, so their effectiveness is determined by the commitment of the industry or company leadership to enforcing the codes.

Ethics and "Gray Areas" of the Law

Because it is often highly subjective and subject to change over time without any sort of formal process, ethics is less certain than law. But the law can also be uncertain. Numerous "gray areas" in the law make it difficult to predict with certainty how a court will apply a given law to a particular action. In addition, laws frequently change.

Such uncertainty can make decision making difficult, especially when a law requires a court to determine what is "foreseeable" or "reasonable" in a particular situation. Because a business has no way of predicting how a specific court will decide these issues, decision makers need to proceed with caution. In such situations, it is helpful to evaluate an action and its consequences from an ethical perspective. A company that can show it acted ethically, responsibly, and in good faith (honestly) has a better chance of succeeding in a dispute than one that cannot make such a showing.

In the following case, the court considered whether an employer's response to complaints about harassment against one of its employees warranted a large penalty against the employer.

CASE 9.2

May v. Chrysler Group, LLC

United States Court of Appeals, Seventh Circuit, 716 F.3d 963 (2013).

FACTS For three years, Otto May, Jr., a pipefitter at a Chrysler Group, LLC, plant in Illinois, was the target of more than fifty racist, homophobic, and anti-Semitic messages and graffiti. He received death threats, his bike and car tires were punctured, and someone poured sugar into the gas tank of his car. May complained to Chrysler. In response, the employer documented the complaints and began an investigation. Records were checked to determine who was in the building when the incidents occurred, and the graffiti handwriting was examined. The company reminded its workers that employee harassment was not acceptable. The harassers

What other ways can employees be harassed?

Ike Hayden/ShutterStock.com

were never caught, but the incidents became fewer and eventually stopped.

May filed a suit against Chrysler in a federal district court for hostile-work-environment harassment. A jury awarded May $709,000 in compensatory damages and $3.5 million in punitive damages. When the judge overturned the punitive damages award, May appealed.

ISSUE Were the steps Chrysler took to stop and prevent the harassment against May sufficient to protect the company from an assessment of punitive damages?

DECISION Yes. The U.S. Court of Appeals for the Seventh Circuit affirmed the lower court's judgment.

REASON In a case involving charges of hostile-work-environment harassment, an employer must act with malice or reckless indifference to an employee's federally protected rights to support an award of punitive damages. Here, Chrysler did not act with malice or reckless indifference to May's federally protected rights. Instead, the company used several strategies to stop and prevent the harassment. These steps included an increased security presence and anti-harassment training for its employees. Supervisors met with their workers to review Chrysler's anti-harassment policy. A protocol was implemented to document the incidents, take photos, clean up graffiti, and interview witnesses. Management also increased its presence with area walk-throughs. Graffiti handwriting was analyzed.

Ultimately, Chrysler's actions had a positive effect because the harassment gradually decreased in frequency and finally ceased completely. In short, Chrysler could have done more to prevent the harassment against May, but the company did not act with malice or reckless indifference. Thus, the $3.5 million punitive damages award was overturned.

CRITICAL THINKING—Ethical Consideration *Does an organization have an ethical obligation to secure a safe and harassment-free workplace for its employees? Discuss.*

9–2 Business Ethics and Social Media

Although most people may think of social media—Facebook, Instagram, Twitter, Google+, and the like—simply as ways to communicate rapidly, businesses face ethical issues with respect to these same social media platforms.

9–2a Hiring Procedures

In the past, to learn about a prospective employee, an employer would often ask the candidate's former employers for references. Today, employers may also conduct Internet searches to discover what job candidates have posted on their Facebook pages, blogs, and tweets. Many people, however, believe that judging a job candidate based on what she or he does outside the work environment is unethical. Among other things, these critics say that researching candidates' social media posts invades their privacy.

Sometimes, too, the opposite situation occurs, and job candidates are rejected because they *do not* participate in social media. Given that the vast majority of younger people do use social media, some employers have decided that the failure to do so raises a red flag. Some might consider an employer's discriminating against a person for not using social media to be unethical as well.

9–2b Discussion of Work-Related Issues

Americans often discuss work-related issues on social media. Numerous companies have provided strict guidelines to inform their employees about what is appropriate and inappropriate when they make posts on their own or others' social media accounts. A number of companies have fired employees for such activities as criticizing other employees or managers through social media outlets. Until recently, such disciplinary measures were considered ethical and legal. Today, the situation has changed.

The Government Acts A recent ruling by the National Labor Relations Board (NLRB, the federal agency that investigates unfair labor practices) has made some social media guidelines illegal. **EXAMPLE 9.3** Costco's social media policy specified that its employees should not make statements that would damage the company, harm another person's reputation, or violate the company's policies. Employees who violated these rules were subject to discipline and could be fired.

In 2012, the NLRB ruled that Costco's social media policy violated federal labor law, which protects employees' right to engage in "concerted activities." Employees can freely associate

Why did the National Labor Relations Board rule against Costco's social media policy?

with each other and have conversations about common workplace issues without employer interference. This right extends to social media posts. Therefore, Costco cannot broadly prohibit its employees from criticizing the company or co-workers, supervisors, or managers via social media. ■

The Ethical Responsibilities of Employees The discussion in this chapter focuses on business ethics, but employee ethics is also an important issue. Is it ethical for employees to make negative posts in social media about other employees or, more commonly, about managers? After all, disgruntled employees may exaggerate the negative qualities of managers they dislike. These negative comments reflect badly on the managers, who often are reluctant to respond to the criticism via social media.

Some may consider the NLRB decision outlined in *Example 9.3* to be too lenient toward employees and too strict toward management. There is likely to be an ongoing debate about how to balance employees' right to free expression against employers' right to prevent inaccurate, negative statements from being spread across the Internet.

9–3 Approaches to Ethical Reasoning

iStockPhoto.com/slobo

Ethical Reasoning A reasoning process in which an individual links his or her moral convictions or ethical standards to the situation at hand.

Duty-based Ethics An ethical philosophy rooted in the idea that every person has certain duties to others, including both humans and the planet. Those duties may be derived from religious principles or from other philosophical reasoning.

Outcome-based Ethics An ethical philosophy that focuses on the impacts of a decision on society or on key stakeholders.

As Dean Krehmeyer, executive director of the Business Roundtable's Institute for Corporate Ethics, once said, "Evidence strongly suggests being ethical—doing the right thing—pays." Even if ethics "pays," though, instilling ethical business decision making into the fabric of a business organization is no small task. How do business decision makers decide whether a given action is the "right" one for their firms? What ethical standards should be applied?

Broadly speaking, **ethical reasoning**—the application of morals and ethics to a situation—applies to businesses just as it does to individuals. As businesses make decisions, they must analyze the alternatives in a variety of ways, one of which is from an ethical perspective. In analyzing alternatives in this way, businesses may take one of two approaches, which we discuss next.

Generally, the study of ethics is divided into two major categories—duty-based ethics and outcome-based ethics. **Duty-based ethics** is rooted in the idea that every person has certain duties to others, including humans and the planet. Those duties may be derived from religious principles or from other philosophical reasoning. **Outcome-based ethics** focuses on the impacts of a decision on society or on key *stakeholders*.

9–3a Duty-Based Ethics

Duty-based ethics focuses on the obligations of the corporation. It deals with standards for behavior that traditionally were derived from revealed truths, religious authorities, or philosophical reasoning. These standards involve concepts of right and wrong, duties owed, and rights to be protected. Corporations today often describe these values or duties in their mission statements or strategic plans. Some companies base their statements on a nonreligious rationale. Others still derive their values from religious doctrine.

Religious Ethical Principles Nearly every religion has principles or beliefs about how one should treat others. In the Judeo-Christian tradition, which is the dominant religious tradition in the United States, the Ten Commandments of the Old Testament establish these fundamental rules for moral action. The principles of the Muslim faith are set out in the Qur'an, and Hindus find their principles in the four Vedas.

Religious rules generally are absolute with respect to the behavior of their adherents. For instance, the commandment "Thou shalt not steal" is an absolute mandate for a person who believes that the Ten Commandments reflect revealed truth. Even a benevolent motive for stealing (such as Robin Hood's) cannot justify the act, because the act itself is inherently immoral and thus wrong.

For businesses, religious principles can be a unifying force for employees or a rallying point to increase employee motivation. They can also present problems, however, because different owners, suppliers, employees, and customers may have different religious backgrounds. Taking an action based on religious principles, especially when those principles address socially or politically controversial topics, can lead to negative publicity and even to protests or boycotts.

EXAMPLE 9.4 In 2012, the chief operating officer of the Chick-fil-A restaurant chain made several statements about the company's commitment to supporting traditional marriage. After that, it became public knowledge that Chick-fil-A had made donations to Christian organizations perceived to be opposed to same-sex marriage. Supporters of same-sex marriage held support rallies to gain media attention, and some politicians denounced Chick-fil-A's position and said that they would block expansion of the company in their cities. Eventually, Chick-fil-A issued a statement saying that it had stopped giving donations to any organization that promotes discrimination in any way. Chick-fil-A no longer sponsors charities that discriminate against same-sex couples or persons who identify as gay, lesbian, bisexual, or transgendered. ■

The Principle of Rights

Another view of duty-based ethics focuses on basic rights. The principle that human beings have certain fundamental rights (to life, freedom, and the pursuit of happiness, for example) is deeply embedded in Western culture. As discussed in Chapter 1, the natural law tradition embraces the concept that certain actions (such as killing another person) are morally wrong because they are contrary to nature (the natural desire to continue living).

Those who adhere to the **principle of rights,** or "rights theory," believe that a key factor in determining whether a business decision is ethical is how that decision affects the rights of others. These others include the firm's owners, its employees, the consumers of its products or services, its suppliers, the community in which it does business, and society as a whole.

Conflicting Rights. A potential dilemma for those who support rights theory is that they may disagree on which rights are most important. When considering all those affected by a business decision to downsize a firm, for instance, how much weight should be given to employees relative to shareholders? Which employees should be laid off first—those with the highest salaries or those who have worked for the firm for a shorter time (and have less seniority)? How should the firm weigh the rights of customers relative to the community, or of employees relative to society as a whole?

Resolving Conflicts. In general, rights theorists believe that whichever right is stronger in a particular circumstance takes precedence. **EXAMPLE 9.5** Murray Chemical Corporation has to decide whether to keep a chemical plant in Utah open, thereby saving the jobs of a hundred and fifty workers, or shut it down. Closing the plant will prevent the contamination of a river with pollutants that would endanger the health of tens of thousands of people. In this situation, a rights theorist can easily choose which group to favor because the value of the right to health and well-being is obviously stronger than the basic right to work. (Not all choices are so clear-cut, however.) ■

Kantian Ethical Principles

Duty-based ethical standards may be derived solely from philosophical reasoning. The German philosopher Immanuel Kant (1724–1804) identified some general guiding principles for moral behavior based on what he thought to be the fundamental nature of human beings. Kant believed that human beings are qualitatively different from

> "When I do good, I feel good. When I do bad, I feel bad. And that's my religion."
>
> **ABRAHAM LINCOLN**
> 1809–1865
> (SIXTEENTH PRESIDENT OF THE UNITED STATES, 1861–1865)

Principle of Rights The belief that human beings have certain fundamental rights. Whether an action or decision is ethical depends on how it affects the rights of various groups, such as owners, employees, consumers, suppliers, the community, and society.

other physical objects and are endowed with moral integrity and the capacity to reason and conduct their affairs rationally.

People Are Not a Means to an End. Based on his view of human beings, Kant said that when people are treated merely as a means to an end, they are being treated as the equivalent of objects and are being denied their basic humanity. For instance, a manager who treats subordinates as mere profit-making tools is less likely to retain motivated and loyal employees than a manager who respects his or her subordinates. Management research has shown that employees who feel empowered to share their thoughts, opinions, and solutions to problems are happier and more productive.

The Categorical Imperative. When a business makes unethical decisions, it often rationalizes its action by saying that the company is "just one small part" of the problem or that its decision would have "only a small impact." A central theme in Kantian ethics is that individuals should evaluate their actions in light of the consequences that would follow if everyone in society acted in the same way. This **categorical imperative** can be applied to any action.

Categorical Imperative
An ethical guideline developed by Immanuel Kant under which an action is evaluated in terms of what would happen if everybody else in the same situation, or category, acted the same way.

EXAMPLE 9.6 CHS Fertilizer is deciding whether to invest in expensive equipment that will decrease profits but will also reduce pollution from its factories. If CHS has adopted Kant's categorical imperative, the decision makers will consider the consequences if every company invested in the equipment (or if no company did so). If the result would make the world a better place (less polluted), CHS's decision would be clear. ∎

How might a company use Kant's categorical imperative to decide whether to voluntarily reduce pollution?

iStockPhoto.com/mr_morton

9–3b Outcome-Based Ethics: Utilitarianism

In contrast to duty-based ethics, outcome-based ethics focuses on the consequences of an action, not on the nature of the action itself or on any set of preestablished moral values or religious beliefs. Outcome-based ethics looks at the impacts of a decision in an attempt to maximize benefits and minimize harms.

The premier philosophical theory for outcome-based decision making is **utilitarianism**, a philosophical theory developed by Jeremy Bentham (1748–1832) and modified by John Stuart Mill (1806–1873)—both British philosophers. "The greatest good for the greatest number" is a paraphrase of the major premise of the utilitarian approach to ethics.

Utilitarianism An approach to ethical reasoning in which an action is evaluated in terms of its consequences for those whom it will affect. A "good" action is one that results in the greatest good for the greatest number of people.

Cost-Benefit Analysis
A decision-making technique that involves weighing the costs of a given action against the benefits of that action.

Cost-Benefit Analysis Under a utilitarian model of ethics, an action is morally correct, or "right," when, among the people it affects, it produces the greatest amount of good for the greatest number (or creates the least amount of harm). When an action affects the majority adversely, it is morally wrong. Applying the utilitarian theory thus requires the following steps:

1. A determination of which individuals will be affected by the action in question.

2. A **cost-benefit analysis,** which involves an assessment of the negative and positive effects of alternative actions on these individuals.

3. A choice among alternative actions that will produce maximum societal utility (the greatest positive net benefits for the greatest number of individuals).

For instance, assume that expanding a factory would provide hundreds of jobs but generate pollution that could endanger the lives of thousands of people. A utilitarian analysis would find that not endangering the lives of thousands creates greater good than providing jobs for hundreds.

Problems with the Utilitarian Approach There are problems with a strict utilitarian analysis. In some situations, an action that produces the greatest good for the most people may not seem to be the most ethical. **EXAMPLE 9.7** Phazim Company is producing a drug that will cure a disease in 95 percent of patients, but the other 5 percent will experience agonizing side effects and a horrible, painful death. A quick utilitarian analysis would suggest that the drug should be produced and marketed because the majority of patients will benefit. Many people, however, have significant concerns about manufacturing a drug that will cause serious harm to anyone. ■

9-3c Corporate Social Responsibility

In pairing duty-based concepts with outcome-based concepts, strategists and theorists developed the idea of the corporate citizen. **Corporate social responsibility (CSR)** combines a commitment to good citizenship with a commitment to making ethical decisions, improving society, and minimizing environmental impact.

CSR is a relatively new concept in the history of business, but a concept that becomes more important every year. CSR is not imposed on corporations by law. Nevertheless, it does involve a commitment to self-regulation that takes into account not only the text of the law, but also the intent of the law, ethical norms, and global standards. A survey of U.S. executives undertaken by the Boston College Center for Corporate Citizenship found that more than 70 percent of those polled agreed that corporate citizenship must be treated as a priority. More than 60 percent said that good corporate citizenship had added to their companies' profits.

CSR can be a highly successful strategy for companies, but corporate decision makers must not lose track of the two descriptors in the title: *corporate* and *social*. The company must link the responsibility of citizenship with the strategy and key principles of the business. Incorporating both the social and the corporate components of CSR and making ethical decisions can help companies grow and prosper.

The Social Aspects of CSR Because business controls so much of the wealth and power in this country, business has a responsibility to use that wealth and power in socially beneficial ways. Thus, the social aspect of CSR requires that corporations demonstrate that they are promoting goals that society deems worthwhile and are moving toward solutions to social problems.

Companies may be judged on how much they donate to social causes, as well as how they conduct their operations with respect to employment discrimination, human rights, environmental concerns, and similar issues. Some corporations publish annual social responsibility reports, which may also be called corporate sustainability (referring to the capacity to endure) or citizenship reports.

EXAMPLE 9.8 The software company Symantec Corporation issues corporate responsibility reports to demonstrate its focus on critical environmental, social, and governance issues. In its 2014 report, Symantec pointed out that 88 percent of facilities it owns or leases on a long-term basis are certified as environmentally friendly by the LEED (Leadership in Energy and Environmental Design) program. Certification requires the achievement of high standards for energy efficiency, material usage in construction, and other environmental qualities. ■

The Corporate Aspects of CSR Arguably, any socially responsible activity will benefit a corporation. A corporation may see an increase in goodwill in the local community for creating a park, for instance. Corporations that are viewed as good citizens may see increases in sales.

At times, the benefit may not be immediate. Constructing a new plant that meets the high LEED standards may cost more initially. Nevertheless, over the life of the building, the savings in maintenance and utilities costs may more than make up for the extra cost of construction.

Corporate Social Responsibility (CSR) The idea that corporations can and should act ethically and be accountable to society for their actions.

Bill Gates, co-founder of Microsoft, and his wife run the Bill and Melinda Gates Foundation. How do their actions relate to corporate social responsibility?

iStockPhoto.com/EdStock

Surveys of college students about to enter the job market confirm that many young people are looking for socially responsible employers. Socially responsible activities may cost a corporation now, but may lead to more impressive, and more committed, employees. Corporations that engage in meaningful social activities retain workers longer, particularly younger ones.

Corporate responsibility is most successful when a company undertakes activities that are significant and related to its business operations. **EXAMPLE 9.9** In an effort to help curb childhood obesity, the Walt Disney Company began issuing strict nutritional standards for all products advertised through its media outlets. In addition to focusing on a major social issue, the initiative was intended to clarify Disney's mission and values, as well as enhance its reputation as a trustworthy, family-friendly company. The initiative was praised by many commentators and politicians and is expected to increase Disney's revenues in the long term. ■

ETHICAL ISSUE

Can outsourcing lead to violations of corporate social responsibility norms? Outsourcing occurs when a domestic company, such as Apple, Nike, or Walmart, has its goods or services produced abroad. Many U.S. companies have manufacturing plants or customer service call centers in other countries, and others outsource information technology tasks.

Companies that are not careful about the social responsibility aspects of outsourcing may find themselves in trouble. Nike provides a classic example. Throughout the 1990s, Nike faced protests accusing it of outsourcing to foreign companies that paid "slave" wages and used other abusive practices—protests that eventually tarnished Nike's reputation. Nike at first attempted to counter complaints about poor working conditions in its outsourced Indonesian plants by creating a factory code of conduct, with little effect.

Then, in 1999, Nike created the Fair Labor Association, a nonprofit group that independently monitors conditions in the factories of Nike and other companies abroad. Over the next several years, the company performed six hundred factory audits. By 2005, Nike had become the first in the industry to publish a complete list of factories that it used for outsourcing. The company now provides audit data as part of its corporate social responsibility reports. These efforts to be socially responsible have helped Nike to rebuild its reputation.

Stakeholders Groups that are affected by corporate decisions. Stakeholders include employees, customers, creditors, suppliers, and the community in which the corporation operates.

Stakeholders

One view of CSR stresses that corporations have a duty not just to shareholders, but also to other groups affected by corporate decisions—called **stakeholders**. The rationale for this "stakeholder view" is that, in some circumstances, one or more of these other groups may have a greater stake in company decisions than shareholders do.

Under this approach, a corporation considers the impact of its decisions on its employees, customers, creditors, suppliers, and the community in which it operates. Stakeholders could also include advocacy groups such as environmental groups and animal rights groups. To avoid making a decision that may be perceived as unethical and result in negative publicity or protests, a corporation should consider the impact of its decision on the stakeholders. The most difficult aspect of the stakeholder analysis is determining which group's interests should receive greater weight if the interests conflict.

Stakeholder-sensitive decisions can take many forms. For instance, during the last recession, layoffs numbered in the millions. Nonetheless, some corporations succeeded in reducing labor costs without layoffs. To avoid slashing their workforces, these employers turned to alternatives such as (1) four-day workweeks, (2) unpaid vacations and voluntary furloughs, (3) wage freezes, (4) pension cuts, and (5) flexible work schedules. Some companies asked their workers to accept wage cuts to prevent layoffs, and the workers agreed. Companies finding alternatives to layoffs included Dell (extended unpaid holidays), Cisco Systems (four-day end-of-year shutdowns), Motorola (salary cuts), and Honda (voluntary unpaid vacation time).

Why do companies such as Nike have to worry about outsourcing their manufacturing operations?

iStockPhoto.com/skodonnell

9-4 Making Ethical Business Decisions

Even if officers, directors, and others in a company want to make ethical decisions, it is not always clear what is ethical in a given situation. Thinking beyond things that are easily measured, such as profits, can be challenging. It may seem that considering the personal impacts of decisions on employees, shareholders, customers, and even the community requires too much subjectivity. But this subjective component of decision making has a potentially great influence on a company's profits.

Companies once considered leaders in their industry, such as Enron and the worldwide accounting firm Arthur Andersen, were brought down by the unethical behavior of a few. A two-hundred-year-old British investment banking firm, Barings Bank, was destroyed by the actions of one employee and a few of his friends. Clearly, ensuring that all employees get on the ethical business decision-making "bandwagon" is crucial in today's fast-paced world.

Individuals entering the global corporate community, even in entry-level positions, must be prepared to make hard decisions. Sometimes, there is no "good" answer to the questions that arise. Therefore, it is important to have tools to help in the decision-making process and a framework for organizing those tools.

9-4a A Systematic Approach

Organizing ethical concerns and issues and approaching them systematically can help a businessperson eliminate some alternatives and identify the strengths and weaknesses of the remaining alternatives. Ethics consultant Leonard H. Bucklin of Corporate-Ethics.US™ has devised a procedure that he calls Business Process Pragmatism™ to help in this process. It involves five steps:

> **LEARNING OBJECTIVE 3**
> What are five steps that a businessperson can take to evaluate whether his or her actions are ethical?

Step 1: Inquiry. First, the decision maker must understand the problem. This step involves identifying the parties involved (the stakeholders) and collecting the relevant facts. Once the ethical problem or problems are clarified, the decision maker lists any relevant legal and ethical principles that will guide the decision.

Step 2: Discussion. In this step, the decision maker lists possible actions. The ultimate goals for the decision are determined, and each option is evaluated using the laws and ethical principles listed in Step 1.

Step 3: Decision. In this step, those participating in the decision making work together to craft a consensus decision or consensus plan of action for the corporation.

Step 4: Justification. In this step, the decision maker articulates the reasons for the proposed action or series of actions. Generally these reasons should come from the analysis done in Step 3. This step essentially results in documentation to be shared with stakeholders explaining why the proposal is an ethical solution to the problem.

Step 5: Evaluation. This final step occurs once the decision has been made and implemented. The solution should be analyzed to determine if it was effective. The results of this evaluation may be used in making future decisions.

9-4b The Importance of Ethical Leadership

Talking about ethical business decision making is meaningless if management does not set standards. Furthermore, managers must apply the same standards to themselves as they do to the company's employees. See this chapter's *Adapting the Law to the Online Environment* feature for a discussion of an ethical dilemma that has arisen from increased demands on employees to stay digitally connected to the workplace after work hours.

ADAPTING THE LAW TO THE ONLINE ENVIRONMENT
Should Employees Have a "Right of Disconnecting"?

Almost all jobs today involve digital technology, whether it be e-mails, Internet access, or smartphone use. Most employees, when interviewed, say that digital technology increases their productivity and flexibility. The downside is what some call an "electronic leash"—employees are constantly connected and therefore end up working when they are not "at work." Over one-third of full-time workers, for example, say that they frequently check e-mails outside normal working hours.

**Do Workers Have
the Right to Disconnect?**
Because the boundaries between being "at work" and being "at leisure" can be so hazy, some labor unions in other countries have attempted to pass rules that allow employees to disconnect from e-mail and other work-related digital communication during nonworking hours. For example, a French labor union representing high-tech workers signed an agreement with a large business association recognizing a "right of disconnecting."

In Germany, Volkswagen and BMW no longer forward e-mail to staff from company servers after the end of the working day. Other German firms have declared that workers are not expected to check e-mail on weekends and holidays. The government

is considering legislating such restrictions nationwide.

**The Thorny Issue of Overtime
and the Fair Labor Standards Act**
Payment for overtime work is strictly regulated under the Fair Labor Standards Act (FLSA). According to the Supreme Court, in this context, *work* is "physical or mental exertion (whether burdensome or not) controlled or required by the employer and pursued necessarily for the benefit of the employer and his business."[a] This definition was extended to off-duty work if such work is an "integral and indispensible part of [employees'] activities."[b]

Today's modern digital connectivity raises issues about the definition of *work*. Employees at several major companies, including Black & Decker, T-Mobile, and Verizon, have sued for unpaid overtime related to smartphone use. In another case, a police sergeant has sued the city of Chicago claiming that he

should have been paid overtime for hours spent using his personal digital assistant (PDA).[c] The police department issues PDAs to officers and requires them to respond to work-related text messages, e-mails, and voice mails not only while on duty, but also while off duty. Off-duty responses are not compensated by the city.

**Not All Employees Demand
the "Right to Disconnect"**
According to a Gallup tracking poll in 2014, 79 percent of full-time employees had either strongly positive or somewhat positive views of using computers, e-mail, tablets, and smartphones to work remotely outside of normal business hours. According to the same poll, 17 percent of them report "better overall lives" because of constant online connectivity with their work. Finally, working remotely after business hours apparently does not necessarily result in additional work-related stress.

CRITICAL THINKING

- From an ethical point of view, is there any difference between calling subordinates during off hours for work-related questions and sending them e-mails or text messages?

a. *Tennessee Coal, Iron & R. Co. v. Muscoda Local No. 123,* 321 U.S. 590, 64 S.Ct. 698, 8 L.Ed. 949 (1944). Although Congress later passed a statute that superseded the holding in this case, the statute gave the courts broad authority to interpret the FLSA's definition of work. 29 U.S.C. Section 251(a). See *Integrity Staffing Solutions, Inc. v. Busk,* __ U.S. __, 135 S.Ct. 513, 190 L.Ed.2d 410 (2014).

b. *Steiner v. Mitchell,* 350 U.S. 247, 76 S.Ct. 330, 100 L.Ed. 267 (1956).

c. *Allen v. City of Chicago,* 2014 WL 5461856 (N.D.Ill 2014).

KNOW THIS
One of the best ways to encourage good business ethics at a workplace is to take immediate corrective action in response to any unethical conduct.

Attitude of Top Management One of the most important ways to create and maintain an ethical workplace is for top management to demonstrate its commitment to ethical decision making. A manager who is not totally committed to an ethical workplace rarely succeeds in creating one. Management's behavior, more than anything else, sets the ethical tone of a firm. Employees take their cues from management. **EXAMPLE 9.10** Devon, a BioTek employee, observes his manager cheating on her expense account. Later, when Devon is promoted to a managerial position, he "pads" his expense account as well, knowing that he is unlikely to face sanctions for doing so. ■

Managers who set unrealistic production or sales goals increase the probability that employees will act unethically. If a sales quota can be met only through high-pressure, unethical sales tactics, employees will try to act "in the best interest of the company" and will continue to behave unethically.

A manager who looks the other way when she or he knows about an employee's unethical behavior also sets an example—one indicating that ethical transgressions will be accepted. Managers have found that discharging even one employee for ethical reasons has a tremendous impact as a deterrent to unethical behavior in the workplace. This is true even if the company has a written code of ethics. If management does not enforce the company code, the code is essentially nonexistent.

The administration of a university may have had this concept in mind in the following case when it applied the school's professionalism standard to a student who had engaged in serious misconduct.

> "What you do speaks so loudly that I cannot hear what you say."
>
> **RALPH WALDO EMERSON**
> 1803–1882
> (AMERICAN ESSAYIST AND POET)

CASE 9.3

Al-Dabagh v. Case Western Reserve University

United States Court of Appeals, Sixth Circuit, 777 F.3d 355 (2015).

FACTS The curriculum at Case Western Reserve University School of Medicine identifies nine "core competencies." At the top of the list is professionalism, which includes "ethical, honest, responsible and reliable behavior." The university's Committee on Students determines whether a student has met the professionalism requirements. Amir Al-Dabagh enrolled at the school and did well academically. But he sexually harassed fellow students, often asked an instructor not to mark him late for class, received complaints from hospital staff about his demeanor, and was convicted of driving while intoxicated. The Committee on Students unanimously refused to certify him for graduation and dismissed him from the university. He filed a suit in a federal district court against Case Western, alleging a breach of good faith and fair dealing. The court ordered the school to issue a diploma. Case Western appealed.

ISSUE Should a court defer to a university's determination that a student lacks the professionalism required to graduate?

DECISION Yes. The U.S. Court of Appeals for the Sixth Circuit reversed the lower court's order to issue a diploma. The appellate court found nothing to indicate that Case Western had

Under what circumstances can a medical school withhold a diploma from one of its students?

"impermissible motives," acted in bad faith, or dealt unfairly with Al-Dabagh.

REASON The Committee on Students' refusal to approve Al-Dabagh for graduation was an academic judgment. The court explained that it would overturn such a decision only if it substantially departed from accepted academic norms. There was nothing to indicate that such a departure occurred in Al-Dabagh's case. The plaintiff argued that the committee's decision was a "punitive disciplinary measure" unrelated to academics. But Case Western placed a high value on professionalism in the school's *academic* curriculum. Al-Dabagh also argued that the university defined professionalism too broadly and that it should be linked only to test scores and similar academic performance. "That is not how we see it or for that matter how the medical school sees it. . . . Our own standards indicate that professionalism does not end at the courtroom door. Why should hospitals operate any differently?"

WHAT IF THE FACTS WERE DIFFERENT? *Suppose that Case Western had tolerated Al-Dabagh's conduct and awarded him a diploma. What impact might that have had on other students at the school? Why?*

Misbehavior of Owners and Managers Business owners and managers sometimes take more active roles in fostering unethical and illegal conduct. This may indicate to their co-owners, co-managers, employees, and others that unethical business behavior will be tolerated. Business owners' misbehavior can have negative consequences for themselves and their business. Not only can a court sanction the owners and managers, but it can also issue an injunction that prevents them from engaging in similar patterns of conduct in the future.

Ethics Training for Employees For an ethical code to be effective, its provisions must be clearly communicated to employees. Most large companies have implemented ethics training programs, in which managers discuss with employees on a face-to-face basis the firm's policies

LEARNING OBJECTIVE 4

How can business leaders encourage their companies to act ethically?

and the importance of ethical conduct. Smaller firms should also offer some form of ethics training to employees. If a firm is accused of an ethics violation, the court will consider the presence or absence of such training in evaluating the firm's conduct.

Some firms hold periodic ethics seminars during which employees can openly discuss any ethical problems that they may be experiencing and learn how the firm's ethical policies apply to those specific problems. Other companies require their managers to meet individually with employees and grade them on their ethical (or unethical) behavior.

PREVENTING LEGAL DISPUTES

To avoid disputes over ethical violations in your company, you should first create a written ethical code that is expressed in clear and understandable language. The code should establish specific procedures that employees can follow if they have questions or complaints. It should assure employees that their jobs will be secure and that they will not face reprisals if they do file a complaint. A well-written code might also include examples to clarify what the company considers to be acceptable and unacceptable conduct. You should also hold periodic training meetings so that you can explain to employees face to face why ethics is important to the company. If your company does business internationally, you might also communicate the code to firms in your supply chain and make sure they follow your ethics policies.

Companies can comply with the Sarbanes-Oxley Act by using a Web-based system, such as NAVEX Global, that allows employees to report suspected unethical accounting practices.

iStockPhoto.com/Squaredpixels

The Sarbanes-Oxley Act and Web-Based Reporting Systems Congress enacted the Sarbanes-Oxley Act[2] to help reduce corporate fraud and unethical management decisions. The act requires companies to set up confidential systems so that employees and others can "raise red flags" about suspected illegal or unethical auditing and accounting practices.

Some companies have implemented online reporting systems to accomplish this goal. In one such system, employees can click on an icon on their computers that anonymously links them with NAVEX Global, an organization based in Oregon. Through NAVEX Global, employees can report suspicious accounting practices, sexual harassment, and other possibly unethical behavior. NAVEX, in turn, alerts management personnel or the audit committee at the designated company to the possible problem.

9-5 Global Business Ethics

> "If you are uncertain about an issue, it's useful to ask yourself, 'Would I be absolutely comfortable for my actions to be disclosed on the front page of my hometown newspaper?'"
>
> **WARREN E. BUFFETT**
> 1930–PRESENT
> (AMERICAN BUSINESSPERSON AND PHILANTHROPIST)

Given the various cultures and religions throughout the world, it is not surprising that conflicts in ethics frequently arise between foreign and U.S. businesspersons. For instance, in certain countries, the consumption of alcohol is forbidden for religious reasons. Under such circumstances, it would be considered unethical for a U.S. businessperson to start a business that produces alcohol and to employ local workers in alcohol production.

We look here at how laws governing workers in other countries, particularly developing countries, have created some especially difficult ethical problems for U.S. sellers of goods manufactured in foreign countries. We also examine some of the ethical ramifications of laws prohibiting U.S. businesspersons from bribing foreign officials to obtain favorable business contracts.

---

2. 15 U.S.C. Sections 7201 *et seq.*

9–5a Monitoring the Employment Practices of Foreign Suppliers

Many businesses contract with companies in developing nations to produce goods, such as shoes and clothing, because the wage rates in those nations are significantly lower than wages in the United States. Yet what if a foreign company exploits its workers—by hiring women and children at below-minimum-wage rates, for instance, or by requiring its employees to work long hours in a workplace full of health hazards? What if the company's supervisors routinely engage in workplace conduct that is offensive to women? What if plants that are operated abroad routinely violate labor and environmental standards?

Many high-tech companies rely heavily on foreign suppliers for components and assembly. Some of these foreign suppliers engage in unethical practices, which can reflect on the companies that deal with them. **EXAMPLE 9.11** Pegatron Corporation, a company based in China, manufactures and supplies parts to Apple, Inc., for iPads and other Apple products. After an explosion at a Pegatron factory in Shanghai, allegations surfaced that the conditions at the factory violated labor and environmental standards. Similar allegations were made about other Apple suppliers.

Apple started to evaluate practices at companies in its supply chain and to communicate its ethics policies to them. Its audits revealed numerous violations. Apple released a list of its suppliers for the first time and issued a lengthy "Supplier Responsibility Report" detailing supplier practices. Numerous facilities had withheld worker pay as a disciplinary measure. Some had falsified pay records and forced workers to use machines without safeguards. Others had engaged in unsafe environmental practices, such as dumping wastewater on neighboring farms. Apple terminated its relationship with one supplier and turned over its findings to the Fair Labor Association for further inquiry. ■

Given today's global communications network, few companies can assume that their actions in other nations will go unnoticed by "corporate watch" groups that discover and publicize unethical corporate behavior. As a result, U.S. businesses today usually take steps to avoid such adverse publicity—either by refusing to deal with certain suppliers or by arranging to monitor their suppliers' workplaces to make sure that the employees are not being mistreated.

9–5b The Foreign Corrupt Practices Act

Another ethical problem in international business dealings has to do with the legitimacy of certain "side" payments to government officials. In the United States, most contracts are formed within the private sector. In many countries, however, government regulation and control over trade and industry are much more extensive than in the United States, so government officials make the decisions on most major construction and manufacturing contracts. Side payments to government officials in exchange for favorable business contracts are not unusual in such countries where they are not considered to be unethical. In the past, U.S. corporations doing business in these countries largely followed the dictum "When in Rome, do as the Romans do."

In the 1970s, however, large side payments by U.S. corporations to foreign representatives for the purpose of securing advantageous international trade contracts led to a number of scandals. In response, Congress passed the Foreign Corrupt Practices Act[3] (FCPA), which prohibits U.S. businesspersons from bribing foreign officials to secure advantageous contracts. (See this chapter's *Beyond Our Borders* feature for a discussion of Mexico's anticorruption law.)

Prohibition against the Bribery of Foreign Officials The first part of the FCPA applies to all U.S. companies and their directors, officers, shareholders, employees, and agents. This part

"Never doubt that a small group of committed citizens can change the world; indeed, it is the only thing that ever has."

Margaret Mead
1901–1978
(American anthropologist)

---

3. 15 US.C. Sections 78 dd-1 *et seq.*

BEYOND OUR BORDERS

Bribery and the Foreign Corrupt Practices Act

Many countries have followed in the footsteps of the United States by passing anticorruption laws, some of which are similar to our Foreign Corrupt Practices Act. Nevertheless, some countries are still not diligent in weeding out corruption—of government officials, for instance.

Mexico Faces a Corruption Issue

Recently, Mexico passed an anticorruption law that prevents hospital administrators from approving contracts. Medical device supplier Orthofix International NV, based in Texas, faced a problem after passage of the new law. It wanted to continue providing bone-repair products to Mexico. It therefore bribed regional government officials instead of hospital administrators. Over several years, Orthofix paid more than $300,000 in bribes to Mexican officials to retain government health-care contracts. Employees at Orthofix called these bribes "chocolates." The contracts generated almost $8.7 million in revenues for the company.

The Bribing Process

Before the anticorruption law was enacted, Orthofix's Mexican subsidiary, Promeca, regularly offered cash and gifts, such as vacation packages, televisions, and laptops, to hospital employees in order to secure sales contracts. These employees then submitted falsified receipts for imaginary expenses such as meals and new car tires. When the bribes became too large to hide in this manner, Promeca's employees falsely attributed the payments to promotional and training expenses. After the new law was passed, Mexico formed a special national committee to approve medical contracts. Promeca employees then simply bribed committee members to ensure that the company was awarded the contracts.

No Compliance Policy or Training to Prevent Violations

As it turned out, Orthofix did not provide any training in how to prevent violations of the Foreign Corrupt Practices Act or have a compliance policy in place in Mexico. Orthofix did create a code of ethics and antibribery training materials, but they were distributed only in English. When Orthofix managers found out about Promeca's overbudget expenses, they questioned the amounts, but initially took no further steps.

The U.S. Government Investigates

Sometime after Orthofix learned of the payments, it self-reported them to the U.S. Securities and Exchange Commission (SEC). After negotiations with the SEC, Orthofix agreed to terminate the Promeca executives who had engaged in the bribery and to end Promeca's operations. Orthofix required mandatory training for all employees and strengthened its auditing of company payments. In addition, the company paid more than $7 million in penalties.

CRITICAL THINKING

- Managers are potentially responsible for all actions of their foreign subsidiaries, whether or not they knew of the illegal conduct. Taking that fact into account, what actions should Orthofix's upper management have taken before this corruption scandal came to light?

---

prohibits the bribery of officials of foreign governments if the purpose of the payment is to induce the officials to act in their official capacity to provide business opportunities.

The FCPA does not prohibit payment of substantial sums to minor officials whose duties are ministerial. A ministerial action is a routine activity, such as the processing of paperwork, that involves little or no discretion. These payments are often referred to as "grease," or facilitating payments. They are meant to accelerate the performance of administrative services that might otherwise be carried out at a slow pace. Thus, for instance, if a firm makes a payment to a minor official to speed up an import licensing process, the firm has not violated the FCPA.

Generally, the act, as amended, permits payments to foreign officials if such payments are lawful within the foreign country. In addition, the act does not prohibit payments to private foreign companies or other third parties unless the U.S. firm knows that the payments will be passed on to a foreign government in violation of the FCPA.

Business firms that violate the FCPA may be fined up to $2 million. Individual officers or directors who violate the act may be fined up to $100,000 (the fine cannot be paid by the company) and may be imprisoned for up to five years.

Accounting Requirements In the past, bribes were often concealed in corporate financial records. Thus, the second part of the FCPA is directed toward accountants. All companies must keep detailed records that "accurately and fairly" reflect the company's financial activities. In addition, all companies must have an accounting system that provides "reasonable assurance" that all transactions entered into by the company are accounted for and legal. These requirements assist in detecting illegal bribes. The FCPA further prohibits any person from making false statements to accountants or false entries in any record or account.

Reviewing . . . Business Ethics

James Stilton is the chief executive officer (CEO) of RightLiving, Inc., a company that buys life insurance policies at a discount from terminally ill persons and sells the policies to investors. RightLiving pays the terminally ill patients a percentage of the future death benefit (usually 65 percent) and then sells the policies to investors for 85 percent of the value of the future benefit. The patients receive the cash to use for medical and other expenses, the investors are "guaranteed" a positive return on their investment, and RightLiving profits on the difference between the purchase and sale prices. Stilton is aware that some sick patients may obtain insurance policies through fraud (by not revealing the illness on the insurance application). An insurance company that discovers such fraud will cancel the policy and refuse to pay. Stilton believes that most of the policies he has purchased are legitimate, but he knows that some probably are not. Using the information presented in this chapter, answer the following questions.

1. Would a person who adheres to the principle of rights consider it ethical for Stilton not to disclose the potential risk of cancellation to investors? Why or why not?

2. Using Immanuel Kant's categorical imperative, are the actions of RightLiving ethical? Why or why not?

3. Under the theory of utilitarianism, are Stilton's actions ethical? Why or why not? Will it make a difference in this analysis if most of the policies are legitimate and valid rather than fraudulently procured and void?

4. Using the Business Process Pragmatism™ steps discussed in this chapter, discuss the decision process Stilton should use in deciding whether to disclose the risk of fraudulent policies to potential investors.

DEBATE THIS

- Executives in large corporations are ultimately rewarded if their companies do well, particularly as evidenced by rising stock prices. Consequently, shouldn't we just let those who run corporations decide what level of negative side effects is "acceptable" for their companies' products?

LINKING BUSINESS LAW TO ACCOUNTING AND FINANCE
Managing a Company's Reputation

In business school, all of you must take basic accounting courses. Accounting generally is associated with developing balance sheets and profit-and-loss statements, but it can also be used as a support system to provide information that can help managers do their jobs correctly. Enter managerial accounting, which involves the provision of accounting information for a company's internal use. Managerial accounting is used within a company for planning, controlling, and decision making.

Increasingly, managerial accounting is also being used to *manage corporate reputations*. To this end, more than 2,500 multinationals now release to the public large quantities of managerial accounting information.

Continues

Internal Reports Designed for External Scrutiny

Some large companies refer to the managerial accounting information that they release to the public as their corporate sustainability reports. Dow Chemical Company, for example, issues its Global Reporting Initiative Sustainability Report annually. So does Waste Management, Inc., which calls its report "The Color of Our World."

Other corporations call their published documents social responsibility reports. The Hitachi Group releases an Annual Corporate Social Responsibility Report, which outlines its environmental strategy, including its attempts to reduce carbon dioxide emissions (so-called greenhouse gases). The Hitachi Group also has Web pages dedicated to its CSR initiatives and includes reports outlining its environmental strategies, its human rights policies, and its commitment to diversity.

A smaller number of multinationals provide what they call citizenship reports. Citigroup, ExxonMobil, and FedEx release annual Citizenship Reports. General Electric (GE) calls its yearly citizenship report "Sustainable Growth." GE's emphasis is on energy and climate change, demographics, growth markets, and financial markets. The company also has a Web site that provides detailed performance metrics (**www.gesustainability .com**).

Why Use Managerial Accounting to Manage Reputations?

We live in an age of information. Any news about a corporation, whether positive or negative, will be known throughout the world almost immediately given the 24/7 cable and online news networks, social media, and Internet bloggers. Consequently, corporations want to manage their reputations by preparing and releasing the news that the public, their shareholders, and government officials will receive. In a world in which corporations are often blamed for anything bad that happens, corporations are finding that managerial accounting information can provide a useful counterweight. To this end, some corporations have combined their social responsibility reports with their traditional financial accounting information. When a corporation's reputation is on the line, its future is at stake.

CRITICAL THINKING

■ Valuable company resources are used to create and publish corporate social responsibility reports. Under what circumstances can a corporation justify such expenditures?

Key Terms

Chapter Summary: Business Ethics

Business Ethics	1. *Business ethics*—Business ethics focuses on how moral and ethical principles are applied in the business context. 2. *Short-run versus long-run profit maximization*—One of the most pervasive reasons why ethical breaches occur in the business world is the focus on short-term profit maximization. Only long-run profit maximization is consistent with business ethics. 3. *The moral minimum and ethics*—Lawful behavior is the moral minimum. The law has its limits, though, and some actions may be legal but not ethical. The study of ethics goes beyond legal requirements to evaluate what is right for society. 4. *Ethical codes*—Most large firms have internal ethical codes. Many industry associations also have codes of ethics for their members. 5. *Ethics and "gray areas"*—It may be difficult to predict whether particular actions are legal, given changes in the laws regulating business and "gray areas" in the law. In such cases, a company that can show it acted ethically has a better chance of succeeding in a dispute.
Business Ethics and Social Media	Employers today may conduct Internet searches to see what job candidates have posted on social media. Employers may also look at, but not interfere with, the social media posts of their employees. Many companies have explicit policies regarding the use of social media by workers, but employers must be careful when considering disciplinary action for violations of these policies.

Approaches to Ethical Reasoning	1. *Duty-based ethics*—Ethics based on religious beliefs; philosophical reasoning, such as that of Immanuel Kant; and the basic rights of human beings (the principle of rights). A potential problem for those who support this approach is deciding which rights are more important in a given situation. Management constantly faces ethical conflicts and trade-offs when considering all those affected by a business decision. 2. *Outcome-based ethics (utilitarianism)*—Ethics based on philosophical reasoning, such as that of Jeremy Bentham and John Stuart Mill. Applying this theory requires a cost-benefit analysis, weighing the negative effects against the positive and deciding which course of action produces the better outcome. 3. *Corporate social responsibility*—A number of theories based on the idea that corporations can and should act ethically and be accountable to society for their actions. These include the stakeholder approach and corporate citizenship.
Making Ethical Business Decisions	Making ethical business decisions is crucial in today's legal environment. Doing the right thing pays off in the long run, both by increasing profits and by avoiding negative publicity. Management must take the lead in establishing an ethical workplace.
Global Business Ethics	Businesses must take account of the many cultural, religious, and legal differences among nations. Notable differences relate to employment laws governing workplace conditions and the practice of giving side payments to foreign officials to secure favorable contracts.

Issue Spotters

1. Acme Corporation decides to respond to what it sees as a moral obligation to correct for past discrimination by adjusting pay differences among its employees. Does this raise an ethical conflict between Acme and its employees? Between Acme and its shareholders? Explain your answers. (See *Making Ethical Business Decisions*.)

2. Delta Tools, Inc., markets a product that under some circumstances is capable of seriously injuring consumers. Does Delta have an ethical duty to remove this product from the market, even if the injuries result only from misuse? Why or why not? (See *Approaches to Ethical Reasoning*.)

   —**Check your answers to the *Issue Spotters* against the answers provided in Appendix D at the end of this text.**

Learning Objectives Check

1. What is business ethics, and why is it important?

2. How do duty-based ethical standards differ from outcome-based ethical standards?

3. What are five steps that a businessperson can take to evaluate whether his or her actions are ethical?

4. How can business leaders encourage their companies to act ethically?

5. What types of ethical issues might arise in the context of international business transactions?

   —**Answers to the even-numbered *Learning Objectives Check* questions can be found in Appendix E at the end of this text.**

Business Scenarios and Case Problems

9–1. Business Ethics. Jason Trevor owns a commercial bakery in Blakely, Georgia, that produces a variety of goods sold in grocery stores. Trevor is required by law to perform internal tests on food produced at his plant to check for contamination. On three occasions, tests of food products containing peanut butter were positive for salmonella contamination. Trevor was not required to report the results to U.S. Food and Drug Administration officials, however, so he did not. Instead, Trevor instructed his employees to simply repeat the tests until the results were negative. Meanwhile, the products that had originally tested positive for salmonella were eventually shipped out to retailers. Five people who ate Trevor's baked goods that year became seriously ill, and one person died from a salmonella infection.

Even though Trevor's conduct was legal, was it unethical for him to sell goods that had once tested positive for salmonella? Why or why not? (See *Business Ethics*.)

9–2. Ethical Conduct. Internet giant Zoidle, a U.S. company, generated sales of £2.5 billion in the United Kingdom in 2013 (approximately $4 billion in U.S. dollars). Its net profits before taxes on these sales were £200 million, and it paid £6 million in corporate tax, resulting in a tax rate of 3 percent. The corporate tax rate in the United Kingdom is between 20 percent and 24 percent.

The CEO of Zoidle held a press conference stating that he was proud of his company for taking advantage of tax loopholes and for sheltering profits in other nations to avoid paying taxes. He called this practice "capitalism at its finest." He further stated that it would be unethical for Zoidle not to take advantage of loopholes and that it would be verging on illegal to tell shareholders that the company paid more taxes than it had to pay because it felt that it should.

Zoidle receives significant benefits for doing business in the United Kingdom, including tremendous sales tax exemptions and some property tax breaks. The United Kingdom relies on the corporate income tax to provide services to the poor and to help run the agency that regulates corporations. Is it ethical for Zoidle to avoid paying taxes? Why or why not? (See *Business Ethics*.)

9–3. Spotlight on Pfizer—Corporate Social Responsibility.

Methamphetamine (meth) is an addictive drug made chiefly in small toxic labs (STLs) in homes, tents, barns, and hotel rooms. The manufacturing process is dangerous, often resulting in explosions, burns, and toxic fumes. Government entities spend time and resources to find and destroy STLs, imprison meth dealers and users, treat addicts, and provide services for affected families.

Meth cannot be made without ingredients that are also used in cold and allergy medications. Arkansas has one of the highest numbers of STLs in the United States. To recoup the costs of fighting the meth epidemic, twenty counties in Arkansas filed a suit against Pfizer, Inc., which makes cold and allergy medications. What is Pfizer's ethical responsibility here, and to whom is it owed? Why? [*Ashley County, Arkansas v. Pfizer, Inc.,* 552 F.3d 659 (8th Cir. 2009)] (See *Approaches to Ethical Reasoning*.)

9–4. Business Case Problem with Sample Answer—Online

Privacy. Facebook, Inc., launched a program called "Beacon" that automatically updated the profiles of users on Facebook's social networking site when those users had any activity on Beacon "partner" sites. For example, one partner site was Blockbuster.com. When a user rented or purchased a movie through Blockbuster.com, the user's Facebook profile would be updated to share the purchase. The Beacon program was set up as a default setting, so users never consented to the program, but they could opt out. What are the ethical implications of an opt-in program versus an opt-out program in social media? [*Lane v. Facebook, Inc.,* 696 F.3d 811 (9th Cir. 2011)] (See *Business Ethics and Social Media.*)

—**For a sample answer to Problem 9–4, go to Appendix F at the end of this text.**

9–5. Business Ethics.
Mark Ramun worked as a manager for Allied Erecting and Dismantling Co., where he had a tense relationship with his father, who was Allied's president. After more than ten years, Mark left Allied, taking 15,000 pages of Allied's documents on DVDs and CDs, which constituted trade secrets. Later, he joined Allied's competitor, Genesis Equipment &

Manufacturing, Inc. Genesis soon developed a piece of equipment that incorporated elements of Allied equipment. How might business ethics have been violated in these circumstances? Discuss. [*Allied Erecting and Dismantling Co. v. Genesis Equipment & Manufacturing, Inc.,* 2013 WL 85907 (6th Cir. 2013)] (See *Making Ethical Business Decisions.*)

9–6. Business Ethics.
Stephen Glass made himself infamous as a dishonest journalist by fabricating material for more than forty articles for *The New Republic* magazine and other publications. He also fabricated supporting materials to delude *The New Republic*'s fact checkers. At the time, he was a law student at Georgetown University. Once suspicions were aroused, Glass tried to avoid detection. Later, Glass applied for admission to the California bar. The California Supreme Court denied his application, citing "numerous instances of dishonesty and disingenuousness" during his "rehabilitation" following the exposure of his misdeeds. How do these circumstances underscore the importance of ethics? Discuss. [*In re Glass,* 58 Cal.4th 500, 316 P.3d 1199 (2014)] (See *Business Ethics*.)

9–7. Business Ethics.
Operating out of an apartment in Secane, Pennsylvania, Hratch Ilanjian convinced Vicken Setrakian, the president of Kenset Corp., that he was an international businessman who could help Kenset turn around its business in the Middle East. At Ilanjian's insistence, Setrakian provided confidential business documents. Claiming that they had an agreement, Ilanjian demanded full, immediate payment and threatened to disclose the confidential information to a Kenset supplier if payment was not forthcoming. Kenset denied that they had a contract and filed a suit in a federal district court against Ilanjian, seeking return of the documents. During discovery, Ilanjian was uncooperative. Who behaved unethically in these circumstances? Explain. [*Kenset Corp. v. Ilanjian,* __ F.3d __, 2015 WL 344046 (3d Cir. 2015)] (See *Business Ethics.*)

9–8. A Question of Ethics—Consumer Rights.
Best Buy, a national electronics retailer, offered a credit card that allowed users to earn "reward points" that could be redeemed for discounts on Best Buy goods. After reading a newspaper advertisement for the card, Gary Davis applied for, and was given, a credit card. As part of the application process, he visited a Web page containing Frequently Asked Questions as well as terms and conditions for the card. He clicked on a button affirming that he understood the terms and conditions. When Davis received his card, it came with seven brochures about the card and the reward point program. As he read the brochures, he discovered that a $59 annual fee would be charged for the card. Davis went back to the Web pages he had visited and found a statement that the card "may" have an annual fee. Davis sued, claiming that the company did not adequately disclose the fee. [*Davis v. HSBC Bank Nevada, N.A.,* 691 F.3d 1152 (9th Cir. 2012)] (See *Business Ethics.*)

1. Online applications frequently have click-on buttons or check boxes for consumers to acknowledge that they have read and understand the terms and conditions of applications or purchases. Often, the terms and conditions go on for so long that they cannot all be seen on one screen, and users must scroll to view the entire document. Is it unethical for companies to put terms and conditions, especially terms that may cost the consumer money, in an electronic document that is too long to read on one screen? Why or why not? Does this differ from having a consumer sign a hard-copy document with terms and conditions printed on it? Why or why not?

2. The Truth-in-Lending Act requires that credit terms be clearly and conspicuously disclosed in application materials. Assuming that the Best Buy credit-card materials had sufficient legal disclosures, discuss the ethical aspects of businesses strictly following the language of the law compared with following the intent of the law.

Critical Thinking and Writing Assignments

9–9. Business Law Writing. Assume that you are a high-level manager for a shoe manufacturer. You know that your firm could increase its profit margin by producing shoes in Indonesia, where you could hire women for $100 a month to assemble them. You also know that human rights advocates recently accused a competing shoe manufacturer of engaging in exploitative labor practices because the manufacturer sold shoes made by Indonesian women for similarly low wages. You personally do not believe that paying $100 a month to Indonesian women is unethical because you know that in their country, $100 a month is a better-than-average wage rate. Write one page explaining whether you would have the shoes manufactured in Indonesia and make higher profits for the company or avoid the risk of negative publicity and its potential adverse consequences for the firm's reputation. Are there other alternatives? Discuss fully. (See *Global Business Ethics*.)

9–10. Business Law Critical Thinking Group Assignment. Pfizer, Inc., developed a new antibiotic called Trovan (trovafloxacinmesylate). Tests showed that in animals Trovan had life-threatening side effects, including joint disease, abnormal cartilage growth, liver damage, and a degenerative bone condition. Several years later, an epidemic of bacterial meningitis swept across Nigeria. Pfizer sent three U.S. physicians to test Trovan on children who were patients in Nigeria's Infectious Disease Hospital. Pfizer did not obtain the patients' consent, alert them to the risks, or tell them that Médecins Sans Frontières (Doctors without Borders) was providing an effective conventional treatment at the same site. Eleven children died in the experiment, and others were left blind, deaf, paralyzed, or brain damaged. Rabi Abdullahi and other Nigerian children filed a suit in a U.S. federal court against Pfizer, alleging a violation of a customary international law norm prohibiting involuntary medical experimentation on humans. (See *Global Business Ethics.*)

1. One group should use the principles of ethical reasoning discussed in this chapter to develop three arguments concerning how Pfizer's conduct was a violation of ethical standards.

2. A second group should take a pro-Pfizer position and argue that the company did not violate any ethical standards (and counter the first group).

3. A third group should come up with proposals for what Pfizer might have done differently to avert the consequences.

Appendix to Chapter 9

COSTCO CODE OF ETHICS
By Jim Sinegal

OBEY THE LAW

The law is irrefutable! Absent a moral imperative to challenge a law, we must conduct our business in total compliance with the laws of every community where we do business.

- Comply with all statutes.
- Cooperate with authorities.
- Respect all public officials and their positions.
- Avoid all conflict of interest issues with public officials.
- Comply with all disclosure and reporting requirements.
- Comply with safety and security standards for all products sold.
- Exceed ecological standards required in every community where we do business.
- Comply with all applicable wage and hour laws.
- Comply with all applicable anti-trust laws.
- Protect "inside information" that has not been released to the general public.

TAKE CARE OF OUR MEMBERS

The member is our key to success. If we don't keep our members happy, little else that we do will make a difference.

- Provide top-quality products at the best prices in the market.
- Provide a safe shopping environment in our warehouses.
- Provide only products that meet applicable safety and health standards.
- Sell only products from manufacturers who comply with "truth in advertising/packaging" standards.
- Provide our members with a 100% satisfaction guaranteed warranty on every product and service we sell, including their membership fee.
- Assure our members that every product we sell is authentic in make and in representation of performance.
- Make our shopping environment a pleasant experience by making our members feel welcome as our guests.
- Provide products to our members that will be ecologically sensitive.

> Our member is our reason for being. If they fail to show up, we cannot survive. Our members have extended a "trust" to Costco by virtue of paying a fee to shop with us. We can't let them down or they will simply go away. We must always operate in the following manner when dealing with our members:
> Rule #1 – The member is always right.
> Rule #2 – In the event the member is ever wrong, refer to rule #1.
>
> There are plenty of shopping alternatives for our members. We will succeed only if we do not violate the trust they have extended to us. We must be committed at every level of our company, with every once of energy and grain of creativity we have, to constantly strive to "bring goods to market at a lower price."

> **If we do these four things throughout our organization, we will realize our ultimate goal, which is to REWARD OUR SHAREHOLDERS.**

TAKE CARE OF OUR EMPLOYEES

To claim "people are our most important asset" is true and an understatement. Each employee has been hired for a very important job. Jobs such as stocking the shelves, ringing members' orders, buying products, and paying our bills are jobs we would all choose to perform because of their importance. The employees hired to perform these jobs are performing as management's "alter egos." Every employee, whether they are in a Costco warehouse, or whether they work in the regional or corporate offices, is a Costco ambassador trained to give our members professional, courteous treatment.

Today we have warehouse managers who were once stockers and callers, and vice presidents who were once in clerical positions for Costco. We believe that Costco's future executive officers are currently working in our warehouses, depots, buying offices, and accounting departments, as well as in our home offices.

To that end, we are committed to these principles:

- Provide a safe work environment.
- Pay a fair wage.
- Make every job challenging, but make it fun!
- Consider the loss of any employee as a failure on the part of the company and a loss to the organization.
- Teach our people how to do their jobs and how to improve personally and professionally.
- Promote from within the company to achieve the goal of a minimum of 80% of management positions being filled by current employees.
- Create an "open door" attitude at all levels of the company that is dedicated to "fairness and listening."

RESPECT OUR VENDORS

Our vendors are our partners in business and for us to prosper as a company, they must prosper with us. It is important that our vendors understand that we will be tough negotiators, but fair in our treatment of them.

- Treat all vendors and their representatives as you would expect to be treated if visiting their places of business.
- Pay all bills within the allocated time frame.
- Honor all commitments.
- Protect all vendor property assigned to Costco as though it were our own.
- Always be thoughtful and candid in negotiations.
- Provide a careful review process with at least two levels of authorization before terminating business with an existing vendor of more than two years.
- Do not accept gratuities of any kind from a vendor.

> These guidelines are exactly that - guidelines, some common sense rules for the conduct of our business. Intended to simplify our jobs, not complicate our lives, these guidelines will not answer every question or solve every problem. At the core of our philosophy as a company must be the implicit understanding that not one of us is required to lie or cheat on behalf of PriceCostco. In fact, dishonest conduct will not be tolerated. To do any less would be unfair to the overwhelming majority of our employees who support and respect Costco's commitment to ethical business conduct.
>
> If your are ever in doubt as to what course of action to take on a business matter that is open to varying ethical interpretations, take the high road and do what is right.
>
> If you want our help, we are always available for advice and counsel. That's our job and we welcome your questions or comments.
>
> Our continued success depends on you. We thank each of you for your contribution to our past success and for the high standards you have insisted upon in our company.

"Truth in advertising/packaging" legal standards are part of the statutes and regulations dealing with consumer law.	Accepting "gratuities" from a vendor might be interpreted as accepting a bribe. This can be a crime. In an international context, a bribe can be a violation of the Foreign Corrupt Practices Act.
If the company did not provide products that comply with safety and health standards, it could be held liable in civil suits on legal grounds that are classified as torts.	If the company fails to honor one of its commitments, it may be sued for breach of contract.
Disclosure of "inside information" that constitutes *trade secrets* could subject an employee to civil liability or criminal prosecution.	Failing to pay bills when they become due could subject the company to the creditors' remedies. The company might even be forced into involuntary bankruptcy.
Antitrust laws apply to illegal restraints of trade—an agreement between competitors to set prices, for example, or an attempt by one company to control an entire market.	Promotions and other benefits of employment cannot be granted or withheld on the basis of discrimination. Employment discrimination is against the law.
Failure to comply with "ecological" standards could be a violation of environmental laws.	Safety standards for the work environment are governed by the Occupational Safety and Health Act and other statutes.

Unit One—Business Case Study with Dissenting Opinion

Central Radio Co. v. City of Norfolk, Virginia

In the chapter on constitutional law, we reviewed the meaning and some of the boundaries of the freedom of speech under the First Amendment to the U.S. Constitution. A democratic form of government cannot survive unless people can express their political opinions and criticize government actions. This is an important value in our democracy. Thus, a law that regulates the content of speech is subject to strict scrutiny by the courts. But expression can be subject to reasonable restrictions. A law that regulates the time, place, and manner of speech, rather than its content, and is intended to fulfill a government's obligation to protect its citizens is subject to a lesser standard of review.

In this business case study, we examine *Central Radio Co. v. City of Norfolk, Virginia,*[1] a recent decision focusing on whether a city's sign ordinance was content neutral and whether the ordinance's restrictions and exemptions could survive scrutiny.

This sign protests the taking of Central Radio Company property. Can the city successfully argue that it's too big?

CASE BACKGROUND

In Norfolk, Virginia, the Norfolk Redevelopment and Housing Authority initiated proceedings to take and transfer the property of Central Radio Company to Old Dominion University.

In response, Central Radio hung a 375-square-foot banner on the side of the company's building. The banner depicted an American flag, Central Radio's logo, and a red circle with a slash across the words "Eminent Domain Abuse," and included a message that read "50 YEARS ON THIS STREET/ 78 YEARS IN NORFOLK/ 100 WORKERS/ THREATENED BY/ EMINENT DOMAIN!"

The city cited Central Radio for violating the size restrictions in the city's sign code. Central Radio filed a suit in a federal district court against the city, alleging that the restrictions were unconstitutional. The court ruled in the city's favor. Central Radio appealed this decision to the U.S. Court of Appeals for the Fourth Circuit.

MAJORITY OPINION

BARBARA MILANO KEENAN, Circuit Judge.

* * * *

The core component of the plaintiffs' challenge to the sign code is their argument that the sign code constitutes a content-based restriction on speech, both facially [on its face] and as applied, that cannot survive strict scrutiny.

* * * *

In evaluating the content neutrality of a municipal sign ordinance, *our principal inquiry is whether the government has adopted a regulation of speech because of disagreement with the message it conveys.* * * * A regulation is not a content-based regulation of speech if (1) the regulation is not a regulation of speech, but rather a regulation of the places where some speech may occur; (2) the regulation was not

adopted because of disagreement with the message the speech conveys; or (3) the government's interests in the regulation are unrelated to the content of the affected speech. [Emphasis added.]

* * * *

* * * The City generally allows signs regardless of the message displayed, and simply restricts the time, place, or manner of their location. Exemptions to those restrictions may have an incidental effect on some speakers or messages, but such exemptions do not convert the sign code into a content-based restriction on speech when the exemptions bear a reasonable relationship to the City's asserted interests.

* * * These exemptions do not differentiate between content based on the ideas or views expressed. By exempting the flags or emblems of governmental or religious organizations from reasonable size restrictions, the City has not indicated any preference for a particular governmental or religious speaker or message, and the sign code exerts only an incidental effect on the flags or emblems of other organizations. Also, by exempting works of art that are noncommercial in character, the City has not favored certain artistic messages over others. Given the City's clear content-neutral purpose and the absence of a more specific inquiry in the sign code regarding the content of the regulated signs, we conclude that the sign code is a content-neutral regulation of speech.

* * * *

Because the sign code is content-neutral, we evaluate its constitutionality under intermediate scrutiny. Under this level of deference, a content-neutral regulation is valid if it furthers a substantial government interest, is narrowly tailored to further that interest, and leaves open ample alternative channels of communication. [Emphasis added.]

Initially, we observe that the sign code was enacted to promote the City's physical appearance and to reduce the distractions,

1. 776 F.3d 229 (4th Cir. 2015).

Continues

obstructions and hazards to pedestrian and auto traffic. Such concerns for aesthetics and traffic safety undoubtedly are substantial government interests. Moreover, * * * Central Radio's banner affected those interests * * *. The banner was sufficiently large to be seen from a distance of three city blocks, and * * * passing motorists reacted to the banner by honking their horns, yelling things in support, and waving.

Next, we conclude that the sign code is narrowly tailored because it does not burden substantially more speech than is necessary to further the government's legitimate interests. Instead, the sign code's size and location restrictions demonstrate that the City has carefully calculated the costs and benefits associated with the burden on speech * * *. Such restrictions do no more than eliminate the exact source of the evil [that] the ordinance sought to remedy.

Finally, unlike an outright ban on speech, the sign code leaves open ample alternative channels of communication by generally permitting the display of signs subject only to size and location restrictions.

It is undisputed here that the plaintiffs' 375-square-foot banner would comport with the City's sign code if the banner were reduced to a size of 60 square feet. * * * Such an alternative [is] adequate * * *. Accordingly, because the City's content-neutral sign code satisfies intermediate scrutiny both facially and as applied to the plaintiffs' display, we agree with the district court's holding that the sign code satisfies the constitutional requirements of the First Amendment.

DISSENTING OPINION

GREGORY, Circuit Judge, dissenting:

* * * *

I would apply a content-based test to the City's Sign Code. * * * In a case like this, involving political speech against the heaviest hand of government attempting to seize its citizen's land, we must ensure a reasonable fit between the City's asserted interests in aesthetics and traffic safety, and the Code's exemptions for government and religious emblems and flags.

I disagree that the City has demonstrated this reasonable fit. Why is it that the symbols and text of a government flag do not affect aesthetics or traffic safety and escape regulation, whereas a picture of a flag does negatively affect these interests and must be subjected to size and location restrictions? I see no reason in such a distinction. * * * I find no * * * justification [for the exemptions on the basis of aesthetics and safety concerns] where the City's regulatory scheme perpetually disadvantages dissidents like Central Radio.

Furthermore, the City has not adequately demonstrated that its adoption of the Code and its exemptions was unrelated to disagreement with a particular message. Although the City maintains this is the case, it references only the Purpose Statement within the Code as support. * * * The mere assertion of a content-neutral purpose is not enough to save a law which, on its face, discriminates based on content. Even if a party need not come forward with voluminous evidence justifying a regulation, surely it must do something more than simply point to a content-neutral justification written into the law's preface. * * * The city [could show] that its legislative interests were unrelated to the ordinance's content distinctions through legislative findings, policy statements, and testimony of [city] officials. I find no such showing in this record.

This case implicates some of the most important values at the heart of our democracy: political speech challenging the government's seizure of private property—exactly the kind of taking that our Fifth Amendment protects against. If a citizen cannot speak out against the king taking her land, I fear we abandon a core protection of our Constitution's First Amendment. Here, Central Radio spoke out against the king * * *. It may be that the Code passes the heightened scrutiny of a content-based inquiry. But to stop short without subjecting the regulation to a more rigorous examination does a disservice to our cherished constitutional right to freedom of speech.

QUESTIONS FOR ANALYSIS

1. ***Law.*** *How did the majority in this case respond to the issue framed at the beginning of this feature? What was the reasoning behind the response?*

2. ***Law.*** *Did the dissent agree or disagree with the test that the majority applied to the statute at the center of this case? Why?*

3. ***Ethics.*** *Does a party that "speaks out against the king" have an ethical obligation to comply with a law that regulates the time, place, and manner of that speech?*

4. ***Technological Dimension.*** *How should the Internet's "ample alternative channels of communication" affect a court's decision about a government's regulation of signs?*

5. ***Implications for the Business Owner.*** *What is the significance of the outcome in this case to a business?*

Unit One—Business Scenario

CompTac, Inc., which is headquartered in San Francisco, California, is one of the leading software manufacturers in the United States. The company invests millions of dollars to research and develop new software applications and computer games that are sold worldwide. It also has a large service department and takes great pains to offer its customers excellent support services.

1. **Jurisdiction.** CompTac routinely purchases some of the materials necessary to produce its computer games from a New York firm, Electrotex, Inc. A dispute arises between the two firms, and CompTac wants to sue Electrotex for breach of contract. Can CompTac bring the suit in a California state court? Can CompTac bring the suit in a federal court? Explain.

2. **Negligence.** A customer at one of CompTac's retail stores stumbles over a crate in the parking lot and breaks her leg. Just moments earlier, the crate had fallen off a CompTac truck that was delivering goods from a CompTac warehouse to the store. The customer sues CompTac, alleging negligence. Will she succeed in her suit? Why or why not?

3. **Wrongful Interference.** Roban Electronics, a software manufacturer and one of CompTac's major competitors, has been trying to convince one of CompTac's key employees, Jim Baxter, to come to work for Roban. Roban knows that Baxter has a written employment contract with CompTac, which Baxter would breach if he left CompTac before the contract expired. Baxter goes to work for Roban, and the departure of its key employee causes CompTac to suffer substantial losses due to delays in completing new software. Can CompTac sue Roban to recoup some of these losses? If so, on what ground?

4. **Cyber Crime.** One of CompTac's employees in its accounting division, Alan Green, has a gambling problem. To repay a gambling debt of $10,000, Green decides to "borrow" from CompTac to cover the debt. Using his knowledge of CompTac account numbers, Green electronically transfers $10,000 from a CompTac account into his personal checking account. A week later, he is luckier at gambling and uses the same electronic procedures to transfer funds from his personal checking account back to the CompTac account. Has Green committed any crimes? If so, what are they?

5. **Ethical Decision Making.** One of CompTac's best-selling products is a computer game that includes some extremely violent actions. Groups of parents, educators, and consumer activists have bombarded CompTac with letters and e-mail messages calling on the company to stop selling the product. CompTac executives are concerned about the public outcry, but at the same time, they realize that the game is CompTac's major source of profits. If it ceased marketing the game, the company could go bankrupt. If you were a CompTac decision maker, what would your decision be in this situation? How would you justify your decision from an ethical perspective?

6. **Intellectual Property.** CompTac wants to sell one of its best-selling software programs to An Phat Company, a firm located in Ho Chi Minh City, Vietnam. CompTac is concerned, however, that after an initial purchase, An Phat will duplicate the software without permission (and in violation of U.S. copyright laws) and sell the illegal bootleg software to other firms in Vietnam. How can CompTac protect its software from being pirated by An Phat Company?

7. **Social Media.** CompTac seeks to hire fourteen new employees. Its human resources (HR) department asks all candidates during their interview to disclose their social media passwords so that the company can access their social media accounts. Is it legal for employers to ask prospective employees for their social media passwords? Explain. If CompTac does not ask for passwords, can it legally look at a person's online posts when evaluating whether to hire or fire the person?

iStockPhoto.com/Tramino

Unit One—Group Project

Constitutional Law. Assume that your group makes decisions for an automaker that sells cars in every state and that each state has slightly different consumer protection statutes.

1. One group will list two underlying reasons why there is a strong presumption against preemption.

2. One group will evaluate the truth or falsity of the majority's conclusion that "as long as a state's regulation does not require a manufacturer to provide a fuel estimate different from the EPA fuel economy estimate," there is no preemption.

3. Another group will develop the dissent's argument that a presumption against preemption is not triggered when the state regulates in an area where there has been a "history of significant federal presence."

10

iStockPhoto.com/eyescar

LEARNING OBJECTIVES

The five Learning Objectives *below are designed to help improve your understanding of the chapter. After reading this chapter, you should be able to answer the following questions:*

1. What is a contract? What is the objective theory of contracts?

2. What are the four basic elements necessary to the formation of a valid contract?

3. What is the difference between express and implied contracts?

4. How does a void contract differ from a voidable contract? What is an unenforceable contract?

5. What rules guide the courts in interpreting contracts?

Promise A declaration that binds a person who makes it (the promisor) to do or not to do a certain act.

Promisor A person who makes a promise.

Promisee A person to whom a promise is made.

Nature and Classification

As Ralph Waldo Emerson observed in the chapter-opening quotation, people tend to act in their own self-interest, and this influences the terms they seek in their contracts. Contract law must therefore provide rules to determine which contract terms will be enforced.

A contract is based on a **promise**—a declaration by a person (the **promisor**) that binds the person to do or not to do a certain act. As a result, the person to whom the promise is made (the **promisee**) has a right to expect or demand that something either will or will not happen in the future.

Like other types of law, contract law reflects our social values, interests, and expectations at a given point in time. It shows, for example, what kinds of promises our society thinks should be legally binding. It distinguishes between promises that create only moral obligations (such as a promise to take a friend to lunch) and promises that are legally binding (such as a promise to pay for merchandise purchased).

Increasingly, contracts are formed online. While some believe that we need a new body of law to cover e-contracts, others point out that we can apply existing contract law quite easily. Through the following chapters, you will see how contract law can be used to resolve online disputes. For instance, in this chapter you will read about the validity of the *disclaimers* that are often seen on e-mails.

> "All sensible people are selfish, and nature is tugging at every contract to make the terms of it fair."
>
> **RALPH WALDO EMERSON**
> 1803–1882
> (AMERICAN POET)

10-1 An Overview of Contract Law

Before we look at the numerous rules that courts use to determine whether a particular promise will be enforced, it is necessary to understand some fundamental concepts of contract law. In this section, we describe the sources and general function of contract law and introduce the objective theory of contracts.

10-1a Sources of Contract Law

The common law governs all contracts except when it has been modified or replaced by statutory law, such as the Uniform Commercial Code (UCC), or by administrative agency regulations. Contracts relating to services, real estate, employment, and insurance, for example, generally are governed by the common law of contracts.

Contracts for the sale and lease of goods, however, are governed by the UCC—to the extent that the UCC has modified general contract law. The relationship between general contract law and the law governing sales and leases of goods will be explored in detail in the next unit. In the discussion of general contract law that follows, we indicate in footnotes the areas in which the UCC has significantly altered common law contract principles.

House purchases always are completed with explicit contracts. Why?

10-1b The Function of Contracts

No aspect of modern life is entirely free of contractual relationships. You acquire rights and obligations, for instance, when you borrow funds, buy or lease a house, obtain insurance, form a business, or purchase goods or services. Contract law is designed to provide stability and predictability for both buyers and sellers in the marketplace by assuring the parties to these private agreements that the promises they make will be enforceable.

To be sure, when they make an agreement, a promisor and a promisee may decide to honor it for various reasons other than the existence of contract law. Clearly, many promises are kept because the parties involved feel a moral obligation to keep a promise or because keeping a promise is in their mutual self-interest. Nevertheless, in business agreements, the rules of contract law are often followed to avoid potential disputes.

By supplying procedures for enforcing private agreements, contract law provides an essential condition for the existence of a market economy. Without a legal framework of reasonably assured expectations within which to make long-run plans, businesspersons would be able to rely only on the good faith of others. Duty and good faith are usually sufficient to obtain compliance with a promise. When price changes or adverse economic factors make compliance costly, however, these elements may not be enough. Contract law is necessary to ensure compliance with a promise or to entitle the innocent party to some form of relief.

LEARNING OBJECTIVE 1

What is a contract? What is the objective theory of contracts?

10-1c Definition of a Contract

A **contract** is an agreement that can be enforced in court. It is formed by two or more parties who agree to perform or to refrain from performing some act now or in the future.

Generally, contract disputes arise when there is a promise of future performance. If the contractual promise is not fulfilled, the party who made it is subject to the sanctions of a court. That party may be required to pay damages for failing to perform the contractual promise. In a few instances, the party may be required to perform the promised act.

Contract A set of promises constituting an agreement between parties, giving each a legal duty to the other and the right to seek a remedy for the breach of the promises or duties.

10-1d The Objective Theory of Contracts

In determining whether a contract has been formed, the element of intent is of prime importance. In contract law, intent is determined by what is referred to as the **objective theory of contracts.** Under this theory, a party's intention to enter into a contract is judged by outward, objective facts as interpreted by a *reasonable person,* rather than by the party's secret, subjective intentions.

Objective Theory of Contracts The view that contracting parties shall only be bound by terms that can be objectively inferred from promises made.

Objective facts include (1) what the party said when entering into the contract, (2) how the party acted or appeared, and (3) the circumstances surrounding the transaction. As will be discussed later in this chapter, in the section on express versus implied contracts, intent to form a contract may be manifested by conduct, as well as by words, oral or written.

A party may have many reasons for entering into an agreement—obtaining real property, goods, or services, for example, and profiting from the deal. Any of these purposes may provide motivation for performing the contract. In the following case, however, one party failed to perform and claimed that he had not intended to enter into the contract when he signed it.

CASE 10.1

Pan Handle Realty, LLC v. Olins

Appellate Court of Connecticut, 140 Conn.App. 556, 59 A.3d 842 (2013).

FACTS Pan Handle Realty, LLC, built a luxury home in Westport, Connecticut. Robert Olins proposed to lease the property. Pan Handle forwarded a draft of a lease to Olins. On January 17, the parties met and negotiated changes to the lease's terms. After the final draft of the lease was signed, Olins gave Pan Handle a check for $138,000, which was the amount of the annual rent. Olins said that he planned to move into the home on January 28. Before that date, according to the lease, Pan Handle was to remove all furnishings from the property.

On January 27, Pan Handle's bank notified the company that Olins had stopped payment on the rental check. Olins then told Pan Handle that he was "unable to pursue any further interest in the property." Pan Handle made substantial efforts to find a new tenant but was unable to do so. Consequently, Pan Handle filed a lawsuit in a Connecticut state court against Olins, alleging that he had breached the lease. The court found in Pan Handle's favor and awarded damages in the amount of $138,000 in unpaid rent, plus $8,000 in utility fees, interest, and attorneys' fees. Olins appealed.

ISSUE Did Olins and Pan Handle intend to be bound by the agreement when they signed the lease?

DECISION Yes. The state intermediate appellate court affirmed the lower court's judgment.

REASON The objective fact—as supported by the evidence—was that the parties intended to be bound by the lease when they signed

Under what circumstances can a property owner prevail when a prospective lessee "backs out" of a lease agreement?

iStockPhoto.com/Franck-Boston

it. Olins contended that because material terms of the lease were still being negotiated there was no "meeting of the minds," which is required to form a contract. As the reviewing court noted, "If there has been a misunderstanding between the parties, or a misapprehension by one or both so that their minds have never met, no contract has been entered into by them and the court will not make for them a contract which they themselves did not make."

Here, though, Olins and a representative of Pan Handle made revisions and signed the final draft of the lease. In addition, Olins tendered a check, on which he noted payment for a one-year lease of the premises. Olins's "apparent unilateral change of heart regarding the lease agreement does not negate the parties' prior meeting of the minds that occurred at the time the lease was executed." Thus, "the lease agreement was a valid and binding contract which the defendant . . . breached."

The court also upheld the lower court's measure of damages, stating that "the unpaid rent . . . may be used by the court in computing the losses suffered" by Pan Handle because of Olins's breach. The company should be placed in the same position it would have been in had the contract been fully performed.

CRITICAL THINKING—Legal Consideration *How did the objective theory of contracts affect the result in this case? Explain.*

10-2 Elements of a Contract

The many topics that will be discussed in the following chapters on contract law require an understanding of the basic elements of a valid contract and the way in which a contract is created. Also important is an understanding of the types of circumstances in which even legally valid contracts will not be enforced.

10–2a Requirements of a Valid Contract

The following list briefly describes the four requirements that must be met for a valid contract to exist.

1. *Agreement.* An agreement to form a contract includes an *offer* and an *acceptance.* One party must offer to enter into a legal agreement, and another party must accept the terms of the offer.

2. *Consideration.* Any promises made by the parties must be supported by legally sufficient and bargained-for consideration (something of value received or promised to convince a person to make a deal).

3. *Contractual capacity.* Both parties entering into the contract must have the contractual capacity to do so. The law must recognize them as possessing characteristics that qualify them as competent parties.

4. *Legality.* The contract's purpose must be to accomplish some goal that is legal and not against public policy.

If any of these elements is lacking, no contract will have been formed. Each item will be explained more fully in subsequent chapters.

> **LEARNING OBJECTIVE 2**
> What are the four basic elements necessary to the formation of a valid contract?

10–2b Defenses to the Enforceability of a Contract

Even if all of the requirements listed above are satisfied, a contract may be unenforceable if the following requirements are not met.

1. *Voluntary consent.* The consent of both parties must be voluntary. For instance, if a contract was formed as a result of fraud, mistake, or duress (coercion), the contract may not be enforceable.

2. *Form.* The contract must be in whatever form the law requires. Some contracts must be in writing to be enforceable.

These requirements typically are raised as *defenses* to the enforceability of an otherwise valid contract.

10–3 Types of Contracts

There are many types of contracts. They may be categorized based on legal distinctions as to their *formation, performance,* and *enforceability.*

10–3a Contract Formation

Contracts may be classified based on how and when they are formed. Exhibit 10–1 shows three such classifications, and the following subsections explain them in greater detail.

Bilateral versus Unilateral Contracts Every contract involves at least two parties. The **offeror** is the party making the offer (promising to do or not to do something). The **offeree** is the party to whom the offer is made. A contract is classified as *bilateral* or *unilateral* depending on what the offeree must do to accept the offer and bind the offeror to a contract.

Bilateral Contracts. If the offeree can accept simply by promising to perform, the contract is a **bilateral contract.** Hence, a bilateral contract is a "promise for a promise." An example of a bilateral contract is a contract in which one person agrees to buy another person's automobile for a specified price. No performance, such as the payment of funds or delivery of goods, need take place for a bilateral contract to be formed. The contract comes into existence at the moment the promises are exchanged.

Offeror A person who makes an offer.

Offeree A person to whom an offer is made.

Bilateral Contract A type of contract that arises when a promise is given in exchange for a return promise.

Exhibit 10–1 Classifications Based on Contract Formation

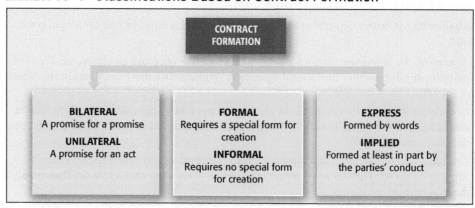

CONTRACT FORMATION

BILATERAL
A promise for a promise

UNILATERAL
A promise for an act

FORMAL
Requires a special form for creation

INFORMAL
Requires no special form for creation

EXPRESS
Formed by words

IMPLIED
Formed at least in part by the parties' conduct

EXAMPLE 10.1 Javier offers to buy Ann's smartphone for $200. Javier tells Ann that he will give her the cash for the phone on the following Friday, when he gets paid. Ann accepts Javier's offer and promises to give him the phone when he pays her on Friday. Javier and Ann have formed a bilateral contract. ■

Unilateral Contracts.   If the offer is phrased so that the offeree can accept only by completing the contract performance, the contract is a **unilateral contract.** Hence, a unilateral contract is a "promise for an act." In other words, the contract is formed not at the moment when promises are exchanged but rather when the contract is *performed.*

> **Unilateral Contract** A type of contract that results when an offer can be accepted only by the offeree's performance.

EXAMPLE 10.2 Reese says to Kay, "If you drive my car from New York to Los Angeles, I'll give you $1,000." Only on Kay's completion of the act—bringing the car to Los Angeles—does she fully accept Reese's offer to pay $1,000. If she chooses not to accept the offer to drive the car to Los Angeles, there are no legal consequences. ■

Contests, lotteries, and other competitions offering prizes are also examples of offers for unilateral contracts. If a person complies with the rules of the contest—such as by submitting the right lottery number at the right place and time—a unilateral contract is formed. The organization offering the prize is then bound to a contract to perform as promised in the offer. If the person fails to comply with the contest rules, however, no binding contract is formed.

ETHICAL ISSUE

Does a "You break it, you buy it" sign create a unilateral contract? It is not unusual to see posted in retail stores signs that say, "You break it, you buy it." The implication, of course, is that you are legally obligated to buy something if you break it while inspecting it prior to a potential purchase. This "rule" is often known as the "Pottery Barn Rule," even though that retailer has no such rule.

Some argue that posted signs of this nature create unilateral contracts. It is difficult to prove the validity of such contracts, however. After all, for a contract to be formed, the accepting party has to demonstrate acceptance of the terms purposed. Few courts would uphold the notion that every customer agrees to every proposition posted on the walls of retail establishments. Moreover, where is the consideration? That is, what does the retailer give customers in return for their acceptance of a unilateral contract that says, "You break it, you buy it"?

Consider also that every customer in a retail establishment is an *invitee.* Consequently, the retailer accepts the risk that customers may accidentally damage items on display, regardless of posted warnings. Simply stating that once a customer reads a sign and chooses to continue shopping constitutes an acceptance is not only legally problematic, it is ethically bothersome. Merchants cannot transfer the risk of breakage to customers just by posting notices.

Revocation of Offers for Unilateral Contracts. A problem arises in unilateral contracts when the promisor attempts to *revoke* (cancel) the offer after the promisee has begun performance but before the act has been completed. **EXAMPLE 10.3** Seiko offers to buy Jin's sailboat, moored in San Francisco, on delivery of the boat to Seiko's dock in Newport Beach, three hundred miles south of San Francisco. Jin rigs the boat and sets sail. Shortly before his arrival at Newport Beach, Jin receives a message from Seiko withdrawing her offer. Was the offer terminated? ■

What is the so-called Pottery Barn Rule?

In contract law, offers are normally *revocable* (capable of being taken back, or canceled) until accepted. Thus, under the traditional view of unilateral contracts, in *Example 10.3,* Seiko's revocation would terminate the offer. Because Seiko's offer was to form a unilateral contract, only Jin's delivery of the sailboat at her dock would have been an acceptance.

Because of the harsh effect on the offeree of the revocation of an offer to form a unilateral contract, the modern-day view is different. Today, once performance has been *substantially* undertaken, the offeror cannot revoke the offer. Thus, in *Example 10.3,* even though Jin has not yet accepted the offer by complete performance, Seiko is prohibited from revoking it. Jin can deliver the boat and bind Seiko to the contract.

Formal versus Informal Contracts Another classification system divides contracts into formal contracts and informal contracts. **Formal contracts** are contracts that require a special form or method of creation (formation) to be enforceable.[1] One example is *negotiable instruments,* which include checks, drafts, promissory notes, and certificates of deposit. Negotiable instruments are formal contracts because, under the Uniform Commercial Code, a special form and language are required to create them. *Letters of credit,* which are frequently used in international sales contracts, are another type of formal contract.

Formal Contract An agreement that by law requires a specific form for its validity.

Informal contracts (also called *simple contracts*) include all other contracts. No special form is required (except for certain types of contracts that must be in writing). The contracts are usually based on their substance rather than their form. Typically, though, businesspersons put their contracts in writing to ensure that there is some proof of a contract's existence should problems arise.

Informal Contract A contract that does not require a specific form or method of creation to be valid.

LEARNING OBJECTIVE 3
What is the difference between express and implied contracts?

Express versus Implied Contracts Contracts may also be categorized as express or implied. In an **express contract,** the terms of the agreement are fully and explicitly stated in words, oral or written. A signed lease for an apartment or a house is an express written contract. If a classmate accepts your offer to sell your textbooks from last semester for $100, an express oral contract has been made.

A contract that is implied from the conduct of the parties is called an **implied contract** (or sometimes an *implied-in-fact contract*). This type of contract differs from an express contract in that the *conduct* of the parties, rather than their words, creates and defines at least some of the terms of the contract. For an implied contract to arise, certain requirements must be met.

Express Contract A contract in which the terms of the agreement are stated in words, oral or written.

Implied Contract A contract formed in whole or in part from the conduct of the parties.

Requirements for Implied Contracts. Normally, if the following conditions exist, a court will hold that an implied contract was formed:

1. The plaintiff furnished some service or property.

2. The plaintiff expected to be paid for that service or property, and the defendant knew or should have known that payment was expected.

3. The defendant had a chance to reject the services or property and did not.

---

1. See *Restatement (Second) of Contracts*, Section 6. Remember that *Restatements of the Law* are books that summarize court decisions on a particular topic and that courts often refer to for guidance.

EXAMPLE 10.4 Oleg, a small-business owner, needs an accountant to complete his tax return. He drops by a local accountant's office, explains his situation to the accountant, and learns what fees she charges. The next day, he returns and gives the receptionist all of the necessary documents to complete his tax return. Then he walks out without saying anything further. In this situation, Oleg has entered into an implied contract to pay the accountant the usual fees for her services. The contract is implied because of Oleg's conduct and hers. She expects to be paid for completing the tax return, and by bringing in the records she will need to do the job, Oleg has implied an intent to pay her. ■

Mixed Contracts with Express and Implied Terms. Note that a contract can be a mixture of an express contract and an implied contract. In other words, a contract may contain some express terms, while others are implied. During the construction of a home, for instance, the homeowner often asks the builder to make changes in the original specifications.

CASE EXAMPLE 10.5 Lamar Hopkins hired Uhrhahn Construction & Design, Inc., for several projects in the construction of his home. For each project, the parties signed a written contract that was based on a cost estimate and specifications and that required changes to the agreement to be in writing. While the work was in progress, however, Hopkins repeatedly asked Uhrhahn to deviate from the contract specifications, which Uhrhahn did. None of these requests was made in writing.

Under what circumstances can an owner be liable for additional costs due to a request for a change in materials even though no written contract modification was created?

One day, Hopkins asked Uhrhahn to use Durisol blocks instead of the cinder blocks specified in the original contract, indicating that the cost would be the same. Uhrhahn used the Durisol blocks but demanded extra payment when it became clear that the Durisol blocks were more complicated to install. Although Hopkins had paid for the other orally requested deviations from the contract, he refused to pay Uhrhahn for the substitution of the Durisol blocks. Uhrhahn sued for breach of contract. The court found that Hopkins, through his conduct, had waived the provision requiring written contract modification and created an implied contract to pay the extra cost of installing the Durisol blocks.[2] ■

Among other implied terms, all contracts include an implied covenant of good faith and fair dealing. This implied term requires the parties to perform in accord with the contract and the parties' reasonable expectations under it. In the following case, the plaintiff claimed that the defendant had breached both the express terms of the parties' contract and the implied covenant of good faith and fair dealing.

---

2. *Uhrhahn Construction & Design, Inc. v. Hopkins,* 179 P.3d 808 (Utah App. 2008).

CASE 10.2

Vukanovich v. Kine

Court of Appeals of Oregon, 342 P.3d 1075 (2015).

FACTS Mark Vukanovich and Larry Kine agreed under a "Letter of Understanding" to work together to buy a certain parcel of real property in Eugene, Oregon, from Umpqua Bank. They expressly agreed to develop the property and to split the cost and profits equally. Vukanovich shared confidential financial information with Kine that he would not otherwise have shared. The bank agreed to accept

Can a "letter of understanding" bind partners to a joint offer for real estate?

$1.6 million for the property, and a closing date was set. Kine then said that he no longer wanted to pursue the deal with Vukanovich or to buy the property. The closing did not occur. A month later, without Vukanovich's knowledge, Kine made a new offer to buy the property. At about the same time, Vukanovich made his own new offer. The bank accepted Kine's offer. Vukanovich filed a suit in an

Oregon state court against Kine, alleging breach of contract. The jury returned a verdict in favor of Vukanovich, awarding him $686,000 on the breach of contract claim and other damages, but the court entered a judgment in favor of Kine. Vukanovich appealed.

ISSUE Was the evidence sufficient to support Vukanovich's claim for breach?

DECISION Yes. A state intermediate appellate court reinstated the jury verdict. "The record contains sufficient evidence permitting the jury to find" that Kine had breached both the express terms of the parties' contract and the implied covenant of good faith and fair dealing.

REASON Vukanovich, Kine, and the bank had agreed on a price for the property and set a closing date, but Kine had refused to close and had then repudiated the agreement with Vukanovich. There was

evidence that Kine had lied about his reasons for not closing and that he had subsequently used confidential information given to him by Vukanovich to devise his new offer to buy the property. Kine argued that his separate attempt to buy the property was not a breach of his agreement with Vukanovich because it occurred after that deal had ended. The court explained that it was Kine's "refusal to complete the purchase of the property with plaintiff, his surreptitious use of the information that plaintiff had provided him to devise a more favorable transaction for himself . . . , and his lies to plaintiff about his reasons for not closing the deal" that constituted the breach. These actions had caused the parties' joint effort to fail and damaged Vukanovich by cutting him out of an ownership interest in the property and the profits generated by that property.

CRITICAL THINKING—Economic Consideration *What did the amount of the jury's award of $686,000 in damages represent? Explain.*

10–3b Contract Performance

Contracts are also classified according to their state of performance. A contract that has been fully performed on both sides is called an **executed contract.** A contract that has not been fully performed by the parties is called an **executory contract.** If one party has fully performed but the other has not, the contract is said to be executed on the one side and executory on the other, but the contract is still classified as executory.

    EXAMPLE 10.6 Jackson, Inc., agreed to buy ten tons of coal from the Northern Coal Company. Northern has delivered the coal to Jackson's steel mill, but Jackson has not yet paid. At this point, the contract is executed on the part of Northern and executory on Jackson's part. After Jackson pays Northern, the contract will be executed on both sides. ■

Executed Contract A contract that has been fully performed by both parties.

Executory Contract A contract that has not yet been fully performed.

10–3c Contract Enforceability

A **valid contract** has the four elements necessary to entitle at least one of the parties to enforce it in court. Those elements, as mentioned earlier, consist of (1) an agreement (offer and acceptance), (2) supported by legally sufficient consideration, (3) made by parties who have the legal capacity to enter into the contract, and (4) for a legal purpose.

    As you can see in Exhibit 10–2, valid contracts may be enforceable, voidable, or unenforceable. Additionally, a contract may be referred to as a *void contract*. We look next at the meaning of the terms *voidable, unenforceable,* and *void* in relation to contract enforceability.

Voidable Contracts A **voidable contract** is a valid contract but one that can be avoided at the option of one or both of the parties. The party having the option can elect either to avoid any duty to perform or to *ratify* (make valid) the contract. If the contract is avoided, both parties are released from it. If it is ratified, both parties must fully perform their respective legal obligations.

    As a general rule, for instance, contracts made by minors are voidable at the option of the minor (as will be discussed in the chapter covering capacity). Additionally, contracts entered into under fraudulent conditions are voidable at the option of the defrauded party. Contracts entered into under legally defined duress or undue influence are also voidable (as you will learn in the chapter on contract defenses).

LEARNING OBJECTIVE 4

How does a void contract differ from a voidable contract? What is an unenforceable contract?

Valid Contract A contract that results when the elements necessary for contract formation (agreement, consideration, capacity, and legality) are present.

Voidable Contract A contract that may be legally avoided at the option of one or both of the parties.

Exhibit 10-2 Enforceable, Voidable, Unenforceable, and Void Contracts

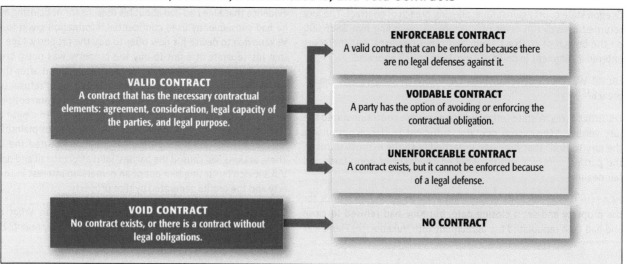

Unenforceable Contract
A valid contract rendered unenforceable by some statute or law.

Unenforceable Contracts An **unenforceable contract** is one that cannot be enforced because of certain legal defenses against it. It is not unenforceable because a party failed to satisfy a legal requirement of the contract. Rather, it is a valid contract rendered unenforceable by some statute or law. For instance, some contracts must be in writing. If they are not, they will not be enforceable except in certain exceptional circumstances.

Void Contract A contract having no legal force or binding effect.

Void Contracts A **void contract** is no contract at all. The terms *void* and *contract* are contradictory. None of the parties has any legal obligations if a contract is void. A contract can be void because one of the parties was previously determined by a court to be mentally incompetent, for instance, or because the purpose of the contract was illegal (such as a contract to burn down a building).

10-4 Quasi Contracts

Quasi Contract An obligation or contract imposed by law (a court), in the absence of an agreement, to prevent the unjust enrichment of one party.

Express contracts and implied contracts are actual or true contracts formed by the words or actions of the parties. **Quasi contracts,** or contracts *implied in law,* are not actual contracts. They are not true contracts because they do not arise from any agreement, express or implied, between the parties themselves. Rather, they are fictional contracts that courts can impose on the parties "as if" the parties had entered into an actual contract. (The word *quasi* is Latin for "as if.")

Quasi contracts are equitable rather than legal contracts. Usually, they are imposed to avoid the *unjust enrichment* of one party at the expense of another. The doctrine of unjust enrichment is based on the theory that individuals should not be allowed to profit or enrich themselves inequitably at the expense of others. **CASE EXAMPLE 10.7** Seawest Services Association operated a water distribution system that served homes inside a housing development (full members) and some homes located outside the subdivision (limited members). Both full and limited members paid water bills and assessments for work performed on the water system when necessary.

The Copenhavers purchased a home outside the housing development. They did not have an express contract with Seawest, but they paid water bills for eight years and paid one $3,950 assessment for water system upgrades. After a dispute arose, the Copenhavers refused to pay their water bills and assessments. Seawest sued. The court found that the Copenhavers had a quasi contract with Seawest and were liable. The Copenhavers had enjoyed the benefits of Seawest's water services and even paid for them prior to their dispute. In addition, "the Copenhavers would be unjustly enriched if they could retain benefits provided by Seawest without paying for them."[3] ■

When the court imposes a quasi contract, a plaintiff may recover in *quantum meruit*,[4] a Latin phrase meaning "as much as he or she deserves." *Quantum meruit* essentially describes the extent of compensation owed under a quasi contract.

Quantum Meruit A Latin phrase meaning "as much as he or she deserves." The expression describes the extent of compensation owed under a quasi contract.

10-4a Limitations on Quasi-Contractual Recovery

Although quasi contracts exist to prevent unjust enrichment, in some situations, the party who obtains a benefit is not liable for its fair value. Basically, a party who has conferred a benefit on someone else unnecessarily or as a result of misconduct or negligence cannot invoke the doctrine of quasi contract. The enrichment in those situations will not be considered "unjust."

Also, even when it can be shown that a party received some benefit, it is not necessarily sufficient to prove unjust enrichment. **CASE EXAMPLE 10.8** Qwest Wireless, LLC, provided wireless phone services in Arizona and thirteen other states. Qwest marketed and sold handset insurance to its wireless customers, although it did not have a license to sell insurance in Arizona or in any other state. Patrick and Vicki Van Zanen sued Qwest in a federal court for unjust enrichment based on its receipt of sales commissions for the insurance.

The court agreed that Qwest had violated the insurance-licensing statute, but found that the sales commissions did not constitute unjust enrichment because the customers had, in fact, received the handset insurance. Also, Qwest had not retained a benefit (the commissions) without paying for it (providing insurance). Therefore, Qwest had not been unjustly enriched.[5] ■

10-4b When an Actual Contract Exists

The doctrine of quasi contract generally cannot be used when an actual contract covers the area in controversy. In this situation, a remedy already exists if a party is unjustly enriched because the other fails to perform. The nonbreaching party can sue the breaching party for breach of contract.

EXAMPLE 10.9 Lopez contracts with Cameron to deliver a furnace to a building owned by Grant. Lopez delivers the furnace, but Cameron never pays Lopez. Grant has been unjustly enriched in this situation, to be sure. Nevertheless, Lopez cannot recover from Grant in quasi contract, because Lopez has an actual contract with Cameron. Lopez already has a remedy—he can sue for breach of contract to recover the price of the furnace from Cameron. In this situation, the court does not need to impose a quasi contract to achieve justice. ■

If you buy smartphone insurance from a company that is not licensed to sell this insurance in your state, has that company obtained unjust enrichment? Why or why not?

10-5 Interpretation of Contracts

Parties may sometimes agree that a contract has been formed but disagree on its meaning or legal effect. One reason that this may happen is the technical legal terminology traditionally used in contracts, sometimes referred to as *legalese*. Today, many contracts are written in

---

3. *Seawest Services Association v. Copenhaver*, 166 Wash.App. 1006 (2012).
4. Pronounced *kwahn*-tuhm *mehr*-oo-wit.
5. *Van Zanen v. Qwest Wireless, LLC*, 522 F.3d 1127 (10th Cir. 2008).

"plain," nontechnical language. Even then, though, a dispute may arise over the meaning of a contract simply because the rights or obligations under the contract are not expressed clearly—no matter how "plain" the language used.

In this section, we look at some common law rules of contract interpretation. These rules provide the courts with guidelines for deciding disputes over how contract terms or provisions should be interpreted. Exhibit 10–3 provides a brief graphic summary of how these rules are applied.

PREVENTING LEGAL DISPUTES

To avoid disputes over contract interpretation, make sure your intentions are clearly expressed in your contracts. Careful drafting of contracts not only helps prevent potential disputes over the meaning of terms but may also be crucial if the firm brings a lawsuit or needs to defend against a lawsuit for breach of contract. By using simple, clear language and avoiding legalese, you can take a major step toward avoiding contract disputes.

10–5a Plain Language Laws

The federal government and a majority of the states have enacted *plain language laws* to regulate legal writing and eliminate legalese. All federal agencies are required to use plain language in most of their forms and written communications. Plain language requirements have been extended to agency rulemaking as well. States frequently have plain language laws that apply to consumer contracts—contracts made primarily for personal, family, or household purposes. The legal profession has also moved toward plain English, and court rules in many jurisdictions require attorneys to use plain language in court documents.

KNOW THIS

No one can avoid contractual obligations by claiming that she or he did not read the contract. A contract normally is interpreted as if each party had read every word carefully.

10–5b The Plain Meaning Rule

When a contract's language is clear and unequivocal, a court will enforce it according to its obvious terms. The meaning of the terms must be determined from *the face of the instrument*—from the written document alone. This is sometimes referred to as the *plain meaning rule*. The words—and their plain, ordinary meanings—determine the intent of the parties at the time they entered into the contract. A court is bound to give effect to the contract according to this intent.

Exhibit 10–3 Rules of Contract Interpretation

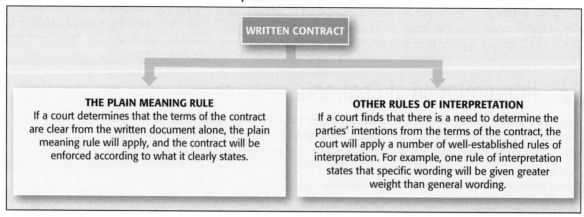

WRITTEN CONTRACT

THE PLAIN MEANING RULE
If a court determines that the terms of the contract are clear from the written document alone, the plain meaning rule will apply, and the contract will be enforced according to what it clearly states.

OTHER RULES OF INTERPRETATION
If a court finds that there is a need to determine the parties' intentions from the terms of the contract, the court will apply a number of well-established rules of interpretation. For example, one rule of interpretation states that specific wording will be given greater weight than general wording.

Ambiguity What if a contract's language is not clear and unequivocal? A court will consider a contract to be unclear, or ambiguous, in the following situations:

1. When the intent of the parties cannot be determined from its language.

2. When it lacks a provision on a disputed issue.

3. When a term is susceptible to more than one interpretation.

4. When there is uncertainty about a provision.

Extrinsic Evidence If a contract term is ambiguous, a court may interpret the ambiguity against the party who drafted the contract term, as discussed shortly. Sometimes, too, a court may consider **extrinsic evidence**—evidence not contained in the document itself—in interpreting ambiguous contract terms. Such evidence may include the testimony of the parties, additional agreements or communications, or other information relevant to determining the parties' intent.

The admissibility of extrinsic evidence can significantly affect the court's interpretation of ambiguous contractual provisions and thus the outcome of litigation. But when the contract is clear and unambiguous, a court normally cannot consider evidence outside the contract. The following *Spotlight Case* illustrates these points.

Extrinsic Evidence
Any evidence not contained in the contract itself, which may include the testimony of the parties, additional agreements or communications, or other information relevant to determining the parties' intent.

SPOTLIGHT ON COLUMBIA PICTURES: CASE 10.3

Wagner v. Columbia Pictures Industries, Inc.

California Court of Appeal, Second District, 146 Cal.App.4th 586, 52 Cal.Rptr.3d 898 (2007).

FACTS Actor Robert Wagner entered into an agreement with Spelling-Goldberg Productions (SGP) "relating to *Charlie's Angels* (herein called the 'series')." The contract entitled Wagner to 50 percent of the net profits that SGP received from broadcasting the series and from all ancillary, music, and subsidiary rights in connection with the series. SGP hired Ivan Goff and Ben Roberts to write the series, under a contract subject to the Writers Guild of America Minimum Basic Agreement (MBA).[a] The MBA stipulated that the writer of a television show retains the right to make and market films based on the material, subject to the producer's right to buy this right if the writer decides to sell it within five years.

Actor Robert Wagner had the rights to the TV series, Charlie's Angels.

The first *Charlie's Angels* episode aired in 1976. In 1982, SGP sold its rights to the series to Columbia Pictures Industries, Inc. Thirteen years later, Columbia bought the movie rights to the material from Goff's and Roberts's heirs. In 2000 and 2003, Columbia produced and distributed two *Charlie's Angels* movies. Wagner filed a suit in a California state court against Columbia, claiming a share of the profits from the films. The court granted Columbia's motion for summary judgment. Wagner appealed to a state intermediate appellate court.

ISSUE Did the language of Wagner's contract with SGP entitle Columbia to all of the profits from the two *Charlie's Angels* movies?

DECISION Yes. The state intermediate appellate court affirmed the lower court's judgment.

REASON Wagner offered evidence to show that a previous contract with SGP involving a property titled *Love Song* had been intended to give him half of the net profits that SGP received from the property from all sources without limitation as to source or time. Wagner argued that because the profits provision in the *Charlie's Angels* agreement used identical language, the provision should be interpreted to give him the same share. The court stated that an "agreement is the writing itself." Extrinsic evidence is not admissible "to show intention independent of an unambiguous written instrument." The court reasoned that even if the parties intended Wagner to share in the profits from all sources, "they did not say so in their contract." Under the language of the contract, Wagner was not entitled to share in the profits from the exercise of the movie rights to *Charlie's Angels* if those rights were acquired separately. SGP did not acquire the movie rights to *Charlie's Angels* by exercising this right within the five-year period. Columbia obtained those rights separately more than five years later.

CRITICAL THINKING—Legal Consideration *How might the result in this case have been different if the court had allowed Wagner's extrinsic evidence of the prior contract regarding* Love Song *to be used as evidence in this dispute?*

---

a. The Writers Guild of America is an association of screen and television writers that negotiates industry-wide agreements with motion picture and television producers to cover the rights of its members.

LEARNING OBJECTIVE 5
What rules guide the courts in interpreting contracts?

10-5c Other Rules of Interpretation

Generally, as mentioned, a court will interpret contract language to give effect to the parties' intent *as expressed in the contract*. This is the primary purpose of the rules of interpretation—to determine the parties' intent from the language used in their agreement and to give effect to that intent. A court normally will not make or remake a contract, nor will it normally interpret the language according to what the parties *claim* their intent was when they made the contract.

Rules the Courts Use The courts use the following rules in interpreting contractual terms:

1. Insofar as possible, a reasonable, lawful, and effective meaning will be given to all of a contract's terms.

2. A contract will be interpreted as a whole. Individual, specific clauses will be considered subordinate to the contract's general intent. All writings that are a part of the same transaction will be interpreted together.

3. Terms that were the subject of separate negotiation will be given greater consideration than standardized terms and terms that were not negotiated separately.

4. A word will be given its ordinary, commonly accepted meaning, and a technical word or term will be given its technical meaning, unless the parties clearly intended something else.

5. Specific and exact wording will be given greater consideration than general language.

6. Written or typewritten terms prevail over preprinted terms.

7. Because a contract should be drafted in clear and unambiguous language, a party that uses ambiguous expressions is held to be responsible for the ambiguities. Thus, when the language has more than one meaning, it will be interpreted *against* the party that drafted the contract.

8. Evidence of *trade usage, prior dealing,* and *course of performance* may be admitted to clarify the meaning of an ambiguously worded contract. (We will define and discuss these terms in the chapter on sales and lease contracts.)

> "The difference between the right word and the almost right word is the difference between lightning and a lightning bug."
>
> **MARK TWAIN**
> 1835–1910
> (AMERICAN AUTHOR AND HUMORIST)

Express Terms Usually Given Most Weight In situations in which trade usage, prior dealing, and course of performance come into play, the courts observe certain priorities in interpreting contracts. Express terms (terms expressly stated in the contract) are given the greatest weight, followed by course of performance, course of dealing, and custom and usage of trade—in that order. When considering custom and usage, a court will look at the trade customs and usage common to the particular business or industry and to the locale in which the contract was made or is to be performed.

CASE EXAMPLE 10.10 Jessica Robbins bought a house in Tennessee. U.S. Bank financed the purchase, and Tennessee Farmers Mutual Insurance Company issued the homeowner's insurance policy. The policy included a clause that promised payment to the bank for losses unless the loss was due to an "increase in hazard" about which the bank knew but did not tell the insurer. When Robbins fell behind on her mortgage payments, the bank started foreclosure proceedings. No one told the insurer. Robbins filed for bankruptcy, which postponed foreclosure.

Meanwhile, the house was destroyed in a fire. The bank filed a claim under the policy, but the insurer refused to pay on the ground that it had not been told by the bank of an "increase in hazard"—the foreclosure. The bank then filed a lawsuit. The court found that the plain meaning of the words "increase in hazard" in the policy referred to physical conditions on the property that posed a risk, not to events such as foreclosure. Thus, the bank was not required to notify the insurer under the terms of the policy, and the lack of notice did not invalidate the coverage.[6]

---

6. *U.S. Bank, N.A. v. Tennessee Farmers Mutual Insurance Co.,* 277 S.W.3d 381 (Tenn.Sup.Ct. 2009).

Reviewing . . . Nature and Classification

Mitsui Bank hired Ross Duncan as a branch manager in one of its Southern California locations. At that time, Duncan received an employee handbook informing him that Mitsui would review his performance and salary level annually. In 2015, Mitsui decided to create a new lending program to help financially troubled businesses stay afloat. It hired Duncan as the credit development officer (CDO) and gave him a written compensation plan. Duncan's compensation was to be based on the new program's success and involved a bonus and commissions based on new loans and sales volume. The written plan also stated, "This compensation plan will be reviewed and potentially amended after one year and will be subject to such review and amendment annually thereafter."

Duncan's efforts as CDO were successful, and the business-lending program he developed grew to represent 25 percent of Mitsui's business in 2016 and 40 percent by 2017. Nevertheless, Mitsui refused to give Duncan a raise in 2016. Mitsui also amended Duncan's compensation plan to significantly reduce his compensation and to change his performance evaluation schedule to every six months. When he had still not received a raise by 2017, Duncan resigned as CDO and filed a lawsuit claiming breach of contract. Using the information presented in the chapter, answer the following questions.

1. What are the four requirements of a valid contract?

2. Did Duncan have a valid contract with Mitsui for employment as credit development officer? If so, was it a bilateral or a unilateral contract?

3. What are the requirements of an implied contract?

4. Can Duncan establish an implied contract based on the employment manual or the written compensation plan? Why or why not?

DEBATE THIS

- Companies should be able to make or break employment contracts whenever and however they wish.

Key Terms

bilateral contract 247
contract 245
executed contract 251
executory contract 251
express contract 249
extrinsic evidence 255
formal contract 249
implied contract 249

informal contract 249
objective theory of contracts 245
offeree 247
offeror 247
promise 244
promisee 244
promisor 244
quantum meruit 253

quasi contract 252
unenforceable contract 252
unilateral contract 248
valid contract 251
void contract 252
voidable contract 251

Chapter Summary: Nature and Classification

An Overview of Contract Law	1. *Sources of contract law*—The common law governs all contracts except when it has been modified or replaced by statutory law, such as the Uniform Commercial Code (UCC), or by administrative agency regulations. The UCC governs contracts for the sale or lease of goods. 2. *The function of contracts*—Contract law establishes what kinds of promises will be legally binding and supplies procedures for enforcing legally binding promises, or agreements. 3. *Definition of a contract*—A contract is an agreement that can be enforced in court. It is formed by two or more competent parties who agree to perform or to refrain from performing some act now or in the future. 4. *Objective theory of contracts*—In contract law, intent is determined by objective facts, not by the personal or subjective intent, or belief, of a party.
Elements of a Contract	1. *Requirements of a valid contract*—The four requirements of a valid contract are agreement, consideration, contractual capacity, and legality. 2. *Defenses to the enforceability of a contract*—Even if the four requirements of a valid contract are met, a contract may be unenforceable if it lacks voluntary consent or is not in the required form.
Types of Contracts	1. *Bilateral*—A promise for a promise. 2. *Unilateral*—A promise for an act (acceptance is the completed or substantial performance of the contract by the offeree). 3. *Formal*—Requires a special form for contract formation. 4. *Informal*—Requires no special form for contract formation. 5. *Express*—Formed by words (oral, written, or a combination). 6. *Implied*—Formed at least in part by the conduct of the parties. 7. *Executed*—A fully performed contract. 8. *Executory*—A contract not yet fully performed. 9. *Valid*—A contract that has the four necessary contractual elements of agreement, consideration, capacity, and legality. 10. *Voidable*—A contract in which a party has the option of avoiding or enforcing the contractual obligation. 11. *Unenforceable*—A valid contract that cannot be enforced because of a legal defense. 12. *Void*—No contract exists, or there is a contract without legal obligations.
Quasi Contracts	A quasi contract, or a contract implied in law, is a contract that is imposed by law to prevent unjust enrichment.
Interpretation of Contracts	Increasingly, plain language laws require contracts to be written in plain language so that the terms are clear and understandable to the parties. Under the plain meaning rule, a court will enforce the contract according to its plain terms, the meaning of which must be determined from the written document alone. Other rules applied by the courts when interpreting contracts are set out in Exhibit 10–3.

Issue Spotters

1. Kerin sends a letter to Joli telling her that he has a book to sell at a certain price. Joli signs and returns the letter. When Kerin delivers the book, Joli sends it back, claiming that they do not have a contract. Kerin claims they do. What standard determines whether these parties have a contract? (See *An Overview of Contract Law*.)

2. Dyna tells Ed that she will pay him $1,000 to set fire to her store so that she can collect under a fire insurance policy. Ed sets fire to the store, but Dyna refuses to pay. Can Ed recover? Why or why not? (See *Types of Contracts*.)

—**Check your answers to the *Issue Spotters* against the answers provided in Appendix D at the end of this text.**

Learning Objectives Check

1. What is a contract? What is the objective theory of contracts?

2. What are the four basic elements necessary to the formation of a valid contract?

3. What is the difference between express and implied contracts?

4. How does a void contract differ from a voidable contract? What is an unenforceable contract?

5. What rules guide the courts in interpreting contracts?

—**Answers to the even-numbered *Learning Objectives Check* questions can be found in Appendix E at the end of this text.**

Business Scenarios and Case Problems

10–1. Unilateral Contract. Rocky Mountain Races, Inc., sponsors the "Pioneer Trail Ultramarathon," with an advertised first prize of $10,000. The rules require the competitors to run 100 miles from the floor of Blackwater Canyon to the top of Pinnacle Mountain. The rules also provide that Rocky reserves the right to change the terms of the race at any time. Monica enters the race and is declared the winner. Rocky offers her a prize of $1,000 instead of $10,000. Did Rocky and Monica have a contract? Explain. (See *Types of Contracts*.)

10–2. Implied Contract. Janine was hospitalized with severe abdominal pain and placed in an intensive care unit. Her doctor told hospital personnel to order around-the-clock nursing care for Janine. At the hospital's request, a nursing services firm, Nursing Services Unlimited, provided two weeks of in-hospital care and, after Janine was sent home, two additional weeks of at-home care. During the at-home period of care, Janine was fully aware that she was receiving the benefit of the nursing services. Nursing Services later billed Janine $4,000 for the nursing care, but Janine refused to pay on the ground that she had never contracted for the services, either orally or in writing. In view of the fact that no express contract was ever formed, can Nursing Services recover the $4,000 from Janine? If so, under what legal theory? Discuss. (See *Types of Contracts*.)

10–3. Contract Classification. For employment with the Firestorm Smokejumpers—a crew of elite paratroopers who parachute into dangerous situations to fight fires—applicants must complete a series of tests. The crew chief sends the most qualified applicants a letter stating that they will be admitted to Firestorm's training sessions if they pass a medical exam. Jake Kurzyniec receives the letter and passes the exam, but a new crew chief changes the selection process and rejects him. Is there a contract between Kurzyniec and Firestorm? If there is a contract, what type of contract is it? (See *Types of Contracts*.)

10–4. Spotlight on Taco Bell—Implied Contract. Thomas Rinks and Joseph Shields developed Psycho Chihuahua, a caricature of a Chihuahua dog with a "do-not-back-down" attitude. They promoted and marketed the character through their company, Wrench, LLC. Ed Alfaro and Rudy Pollak, representatives of Taco Bell Corp., learned of Psycho Chihuahua and met with Rinks and Shields to talk about using the character as a Taco Bell "icon." Wrench sent artwork, merchandise, and marketing ideas to Alfaro, who promoted the character within Taco Bell. Alfaro asked Wrench to propose terms for Taco Bell's use of Psycho Chihuahua. Taco Bell did not accept Wrench's terms, but Alfaro continued to promote the character within the company.

Meanwhile, Taco Bell hired a new advertising agency, which proposed an advertising campaign involving a Chihuahua. When Alfaro learned of this proposal, he sent the Psycho Chihuahua materials to the agency. Taco Bell made a Chihuahua the focus of its marketing but paid nothing to Wrench. Wrench filed a suit against Taco Bell in a federal court claiming that it had an implied contract with Taco Bell and that Taco Bell breached that contract. Do these facts satisfy the requirements for an implied contract? Why or why not? [*Wrench, LLC. v. Taco Bell Corp.*, 256 F.3d 446 (6th Cir. 2001), *cert. denied*, 534 U.S. 1114, 122 S.Ct. 921, 151 L.Ed.2d 805 (2002)] (See *Types of Contracts*.)

10–5. Quasi Contract. Kim Panenka asked to borrow $4,750 from her sister, Kris, to make a mortgage payment. Kris deposited a check for that amount into Kim's bank account. Hours later, Kim asked to borrow another $1,100. Kris took a cash advance on her credit card and deposited this amount into Kim's account. When Kim did not repay Kris, the sister filed a suit, arguing that she had "loaned" Kim the money. Can the court impose a contract between the sisters? Explain. [*Panenka v. Panenka*, 331 Wis.2d 731, 795 N.W.2d 493 (2011)] (See *Quasi Contracts*.)

10–6. Business Case Problem with Sample Answer—Quasi Contract. Robert Gutkowski, a sports marketing expert, met with George Steinbrenner, the owner of the New York Yankees, many times to discuss the Yankees Entertainment and Sports Network (YES). Gutkowski was paid as a consultant. Later, he filed a suit, seeking an ownership share in YES. There was no written contract for the share, but he claimed that there were discussions about him being a part owner. Does Gutkowski have a valid claim for payment? Discuss. [*Gutkowski v. Steinbrenner*, 680 F.Supp.2d 602 (S.D.N.Y. 2010)] (See *Quasi Contracts*.)

—**For a sample answer to Problem 10–6, go to Appendix F at the end of this text.**

10–7. Implied Contracts. Ralph Ramsey insured his car with Allstate Insurance Co. He also owned a house on which he maintained a homeowner's insurance policy with Allstate. Bank of America had a mortgage on the house and paid the insurance premiums on the homeowner's policy from Ralph's account. After Ralph died, Allstate canceled the car insurance. Ralph's son Douglas inherited the house. The bank continued to pay the premiums on the homeowner's policy, but from Douglas's account, and Allstate continued to renew the insurance. When a fire destroyed the house, Allstate denied coverage, however, claiming that the policy was still in Ralph's name. Douglas filed a suit in a federal district court against the insurer. Was Allstate liable under the homeowner's policy? Explain. [*Ramsey* *v. Allstate Insurance Co.,* 2013 WL 467327 (6th Cir. 2013)] (See *Types of Contracts.*)

10–8. Quasi Contracts. Lawrence M. Clarke, Inc., was the general contractor for construction of a portion of a sanitary sewer system in Billings, Michigan. Clarke accepted Kim Draeger's proposal to do the work for a certain price. Draeger arranged with two subcontractors to work on the project. The work provided by Draeger and the subcontractors proved unsatisfactory. All of the work fell under Draeger's contract with Clarke. Clarke filed a suit in a Michigan state court against Draeger, seeking to recover damages on a theory of quasi contract. The court awarded Clarke $900,000 in damages on that theory. A state intermediate appellate court reversed this award. Why? [*Lawrence M. Clarke, Inc. v. Draeger,* __ N.W.2d __, 2015 WL 205182 (Mich.App. 2015)] (See *Quasi Contracts.*)

10–9. A Question of Ethics—Unilateral Contracts. International Business Machines Corp. (IBM) hired Niels Jensen as a software sales representative. According to the brochure on IBM's "Sales Incentive Plan" (SIP), "the more you sell, the more earnings for you." The brochure also stated that "the SIP program does not constitute a promise by IBM. IBM reserves the right to modify the program at any time." Jensen was given a "quota letter" that said he would be paid $75,000 as a base salary and, if he attained his quota, an additional $75,000 as incentive pay. Jensen closed a deal worth more than $24 million to IBM. When IBM paid him less than $500,000 as a commission, Jensen filed a suit. He argued that the SIP was a unilateral offer that became a binding contract when he closed the sale. [*Jensen v. International Business Machines Corp.,* 454 F.3d 382 (4th Cir. 2006)] (See *Types of Contracts.*)

1. Would it be fair to the employer for the court to hold that the SIP brochure and the quota letter created a unilateral contract if IBM did not *intend* to create such a contract? Would it be fair to the employee to hold that *no* contract was created? Explain.

2. The "Sales Incentives" section of IBM's brochure included a clause providing that "management will decide if an adjustment to the payment is appropriate" when an employee closes a large transaction. Does this affect your answers to the above questions? From an ethical perspective, would it be fair to hold that a contract exists despite this statement? Explain.

Critical Thinking and Writing Assignments

10–10. Business Law Critical Thinking Group Assignment. Review the basic requirements for a valid contract listed at the beginning of this chapter. Now consider the relationship entered into when a student enrolls in a college or university. (See *Elements of A Contract.*)

1. One group should analyze and discuss whether a contract has been formed between the student and the college or university.

2. A second group should assume that there is a contract and explain whether it is bilateral or unilateral.

11

Agreement

LEARNING OBJECTIVES

The five Learning Objectives *below are designed to help improve your understanding of the chapter. After reading this chapter, you should be able to answer the following questions:*

1. What elements are necessary for an effective offer? What are some examples of nonoffers?

2. In what circumstances will an offer be irrevocable?

3. What are the elements that are necessary for an effective acceptance?

4. How do shrink-wrap and click-on agreements differ from other contracts? How have traditional laws been applied to these agreements?

5. What is the Uniform Electronic Transactions Act? What are some of the major provisions of this act?

"It is necessity that makes laws."

VOLTAIRE
1694–1778
(FRENCH INTELLECTUAL AND WRITER)

Voltaire's statement that it is "necessity that makes laws" is certainly true in regard to contracts. In the last chapter, we pointed out that promises and agreements, and the knowledge that some of those promises and agreements will be legally enforced, are essential to civilized society. The homes we live in, the food we eat, the clothes we wear, and the cars we drive—all of these have been purchased through implicit or explicit contractual agreements. The common law of contracts has developed over time to meet society's need to know with certainty what kinds of promises will be enforced and at what point a valid and binding contract is formed.

For a contract to be valid and enforceable, the requirements listed in the previous chapter must be met. In this chapter, we look closely at the first of these requirements, *agreement.* Agreement is required to form a contract, regardless of whether the contract is formed by exchanging paper documents or by exchanging electronic messages online. We discuss online offers and acceptances and examine some laws that have been created to apply to electronic contracts, or *e-contracts,* in the latter part of the chapter. Can a person's e-mails or instant messages create an enforceable agreement? You will read more on this topic in a feature in this chapter.

11–1 Agreement

An essential element for contract formation is **agreement**—the parties must agree on the terms of the contract. Ordinarily, agreement is evidenced by two events: an *offer* and an *acceptance.* One party offers a certain bargain to another party, who then accepts that bargain.

Agreement A mutual understanding or meeting of the minds between two or more individuals regarding the terms of a contract.

261

Because words often fail to convey the precise meaning intended in such bargaining, the law of contracts generally adheres to the *objective theory of contracts,* as discussed in the preceding chapter. Under this theory, a party's words and conduct are held to mean whatever a reasonable person in the other party's position would think they meant.

11–1a Requirements of the Offer

Offer A promise or commitment to perform or refrain from performing some specified act in the future.

An **offer** is a promise or commitment to perform or refrain from performing some specified act in the future. The party making an offer is called the *offeror,* and the party to whom the offer is made is called the *offeree.*

Three elements are necessary for an offer to be effective:

1. There must be a serious, objective intention by the offeror.

2. The terms of the offer must be reasonably certain, or definite, so that the parties and the court can ascertain the terms of the contract.

3. The offer must be communicated to the offeree.

Once an effective offer has been made, the offeree's acceptance of that offer creates a legally binding contract (providing the other essential elements for a valid and enforceable contract are present).

LEARNING OBJECTIVE 1
What elements are necessary for an effective offer? What are some examples of nonoffers?

Intention   The first requirement for an effective offer is serious, objective intent on the part of the offeror. Intent is not determined by the *subjective* intentions, beliefs, or assumptions of the offeror. Rather, it is determined by what a reasonable person in the offeree's position would conclude that the offeror's words and actions meant. Offers made in obvious anger, jest, or undue excitement do not meet the requirement of serious, objective intent. Because these offers are not effective, an offeree's acceptance does not create an agreement.

EXAMPLE 11.1 You ride to school each day with Spencer in his new automobile, which has a market value of $25,000. One cold morning, the car will not start. Spencer yells in anger, "I'll sell this car to anyone for $500!" You drop $500 in his lap. A reasonable person—taking into consideration Spencer's frustration and the obvious difference in value between the car's market price and the purchase price—would realize that Spencer's offer was not made with serious and objective intent. Therefore, no agreement is formed. ■

The concept of intent can be further clarified through an examination of the types of statements that are *not* offers. We look at these expressions and statements in the subsections that follow. In the *Classic Case* presented next, the court considered whether an offer made "after a few drinks" met the serious-intent requirement.

★★★ CLASSIC CASE 11.1 ★★★

Lucy v. Zehmer

Supreme Court of Appeals of Virginia, 196 Va. 493, 84 S.E.2d 516 (1954).

FACTS W. O. Lucy and A. H. Zehmer had known each other for fifteen to twenty years. For some time, Lucy had wanted to buy Zehmer's farm, but Zehmer had always said that he was not interested in selling. One night, Lucy stopped in to visit with the Zehmers at a restaurant they operated. Lucy said to Zehmer, "I bet you wouldn't take $50,000 for that place." Zehmer replied, "Yes, I would, too; you wouldn't give fifty." Throughout the evening, the conversation

Can an intoxicated person's offer to sell his farm for a specific price meet the serious-intent requirement?

returned to the sale of the farm. All the while, the parties were drinking whiskey.

Eventually, Zehmer wrote up an agreement on the back of a restaurant check for the sale of the farm, and he asked his wife, Ida, to sign it—which she did. When Lucy brought an action in a Virginia state court to enforce the agreement, Zehmer argued that he had been "high as a Georgia pine" at the time and that the offer had been made in jest: "two doggoned drunks bluffing to see who could talk the biggest and say the most." Lucy claimed that he had not been intoxicated and did not think Zehmer had been, either, given the way Zehmer handled the transaction. The trial court ruled in favor of the Zehmers, and Lucy appealed.

ISSUE Did the agreement meet the serious-intent requirement despite the claim of intoxication?

DECISION Yes. The agreement to sell the farm was binding.

REASON The court held that the evidence given about the nature of the conversation, the appearance and completeness of the agreement, and the signing all tended to show that a serious business transaction, not a casual jest, was intended. The court had to look into the objective meaning of the Zehmers' words and acts: "An agreement or mutual assent is of course essential to a valid contract, but the law imputes to a person an intention corresponding to the reasonable meaning of his words and acts. If his words and acts, judged by a reasonable standard, manifest an intention to agree, it is immaterial what may be the real but unexpressed state of mind."

WHAT IF THE FACTS WERE DIFFERENT? *Suppose that after Lucy signed the agreement, he decided he did not want the farm after all, and that Zehmer sued Lucy to perform the contract. Would this change in the facts alter the court's decision that Lucy and Zehmer had created an enforceable contract? Why or why not?*

IMPACT OF THIS CASE ON TODAY'S LAW *This is a classic case in contract law because it so clearly illustrates the objective theory of contracts with respect to determining whether an offer was intended. Today, the courts continue to apply the objective theory of contracts and routinely cite the* Lucy v. Zehmer *decision as a significant precedent in this area.*

Expressions of Opinion. An expression of opinion is not an offer. It does not demonstrate an intention to enter into a binding agreement. **CASE EXAMPLE 11.2** Hawkins took his son to McGee, a physician, and asked McGee to operate on the son's hand. McGee said that the boy would be in the hospital three or four days and that the hand would *probably* heal a few days later. The son's hand did not heal for a month, but nonetheless the father did not win a suit for breach of contract. The court held that McGee did not make an offer to heal the son's hand in three or four days. He merely expressed an opinion as to when the hand would heal.[1]

Statements of Future Intent. A statement of an *intention* to do something in the future is not an offer. **EXAMPLE 11.3** If Samir says, "I *plan* to sell my stock in Novation, Inc., for $150 per share," no contract is created if John "accepts" and gives Samir $150 per share for the stock. Samir has merely expressed his intention to enter into a future contract for the sale of the stock. If John accepts and hands over the $150 per share, no contract is formed, because a reasonable person would conclude that Samir was only *thinking about* selling his stock, not *promising* to sell it.

Preliminary Negotiations. A request or invitation to negotiate is not an offer. It only expresses a willingness to discuss the possibility of entering into a contract. Examples are statements such as "Will you sell Forest Acres?" and "I wouldn't sell my car for less than $8,000." A reasonable person would not conclude that such statements indicated an intention to enter into binding obligations.

A similar situation arises when the government or a private firm invites contractors to submit bids to do construction work. The *invitation* to submit bids is not an offer, and a contractor does not bind the government or private firm by submitting a bid. (The bids that the contractors submit are offers, however, and the government or private firm can bind the contractor by accepting the bid.)

Advertisements, Catalogues, and Circulars. In general, advertisements, catalogues, price lists, and circular letters (meant for the general public) are treated as invitations to negotiate, not as offers to form a contract.[2] This applies whether the publications appear in traditional media or online.

KNOW THIS
An opinion is not an offer and not a contract term. Goods or services can be "pèrfect" in one party's opinion and "poor" in another's.

---

1. *Hawkins v. McGee*, 84 N.H. 114, 146 A. 641 (1929).
2. *Restatement (Second) of Contracts*, Section 26, Comment b.

CASE EXAMPLE 11.4 An ad on *Science*NOW's Web site asked for "news tips." Erik Trell, a professor and physician, submitted a manuscript in which he claimed to have solved a famous mathematical problem. When *Science*NOW did not publish his solution, Trell filed a lawsuit for breach of contract. He claimed that *Science*NOW's ad was an offer, which he had accepted by submitting his manuscript. The court dismissed Trell's suit, holding that an ad is only an invitation for offers, and not an offer itself. Hence, responses to an ad are not acceptances—instead, the responses are the offers. Thus, Trell's submission of the manuscript for publication was the offer, which *Science*NOW did not accept.[3] ▦

Price lists are another form of invitation to negotiate or trade. A seller's price list is not an offer to sell at that price. It merely invites the buyer to offer to buy at that price. In fact, the seller usually puts "prices subject to change" on the price list. Only in rare circumstances will a price quotation be construed as an offer.

Although most advertisements and the like are treated as invitations to negotiate, an advertisement can occasionally be an offer. In some situations, courts have construed advertisements to be offers because the ads contained definite terms that invited acceptance (such as an ad offering a reward for the return of a lost dog).

When a contractor submits a bid proposal, is that proposal binding on the entity to whom the bid was addressed?

KNOW THIS
Advertisements are not binding, but they cannot be deceptive.

Agreements to Agree. In the past, agreements to agree—that is, agreements to agree to the material terms of a contract at some future date—were not considered to be binding contracts. The modern view, however, is that agreements to agree may be enforceable agreements (contracts) if it is clear that the parties intended to be bound by the agreements. In other words, today the emphasis is on the parties' intent rather than on form.

CASE EXAMPLE 11.5 After a customer nearly drowned on a water ride at one of its amusement parks, Six Flags, Inc., filed a lawsuit against the manufacturer that had designed the ride. The manufacturer claimed that the parties did not have a binding contract but had only engaged in preliminary negotiations that were never formalized into a contract to construct the ride.

The court, however, held that a faxed document specifying the details of the ride, along with the parties' subsequent actions (having begun construction and written notes on the faxed document), was sufficient to show an intent to be bound. Because of the court's finding, the manufacturer was required to provide insurance for the water ride at Six Flags, and its insurer was required to defend Six Flags in the personal-injury lawsuit that arose out of the incident.[4] ▦

Preliminary Agreements. Increasingly, the courts are holding that a preliminary agreement constitutes a binding contract if the parties have agreed on all essential terms and no disputed issues remain to be resolved.[5] In contrast, if the parties agree on certain major terms but leave other terms open for further negotiation, a preliminary agreement is binding only in the sense that the parties have committed themselves to negotiate the undecided terms in good faith in an effort to reach a final agreement.

In the following *Spotlight Case,* one party claimed that an agreement formed via e-mail was binding, while the other party claimed that it was merely an agreement to agree or to work out the terms of a settlement in the future.

---

3. *Trell v. American Association for the Advancement of Science*, 2007 WL 1500497 (W.D.N.Y. 2007).

4. *Six Flags, Inc. v. Steadfast Insurance Co.*, 474 F.Supp.2d 201 (D.Mass. 2007).

5. See, for example, *Tractebel Energy Marketing, Inc. v. AEP Power Marketing, Inc.*, 487 F.3d 89 (2d Cir. 2007); and *Barrand v. Whataburger, Inc.*, 214 S.W.3d 122 (Tex.App.—Corpus Christi 2006).

SPOTLIGHT ON AMAZON.COM: CASE 11.2

Basis Technology Corp. v. Amazon.com, Inc.

Appeals Court of Massachusetts, 71 Mass.App.Ct. 29, 878 N.E.2d 952 (2008).

FACTS Basis Technology Corporation created software and provided technical services for a Japanese-language Web site operated by Amazon.com, Inc. The agreement between the two companies allowed for separately negotiated contracts for additional services that Basis might provide to Amazon. Later, Basis sued Amazon for various claims, including failure to pay for services not included in the original agreement. During the trial, the two parties appeared to reach an agreement to settle out of court via a series of e-mail exchanges outlining the settlement. When Amazon reneged, Basis served a motion to enforce the proposed settlement. The trial judge entered a judgment against Amazon, which appealed.

ISSUE Did the agreement that Amazon entered into with Basis via e-mail constitute a binding settlement contract?

DECISION Yes. The Appeals Court of Massachusetts affirmed the trial court's finding that Amazon intended to be bound by the terms of the e-mail exchanges.

Can Amazon.com, Inc., be held to an agreement arrived at via e-mail exchanges?

REASON The court examined the evidence consisting of e-mails between the two parties. It pointed out that in open court and on the record, counsel had "reported the result of the settlement without specification of the terms." Amazon claimed that the e-mail terms were incomplete and were not definite enough to form an agreement. The court noted, however, that "provisions are not ambiguous simply because the parties have developed different interpretations of them." In the exchange of e-mails, the essential business terms were indeed resolved. Afterward, the parties were simply proceeding to record the settlement terms, not to create them. The e-mails constituted a complete and unambiguous statement of the parties' desire to be bound by the settlement terms.

WHAT IF THE FACTS WERE DIFFERENT? *Assume that, instead of exchanging e-mails, the attorneys for both sides had had a phone conversation that included all of the terms to which they actually agreed in their e-mail exchanges. Would the court have ruled differently? Why or why not?*

To avoid potential legal disputes, be cautious when drafting a memorandum that outlines a preliminary agreement or understanding with another party. If all the major terms are included, a court might hold that the agreement is binding even though you intended it to be only a tentative agreement. One way to avoid being bound is to include in the writing the points of disagreement, as well as the points on which you and the other party agree. Alternatively, you can add a disclaimer to the memorandum stating that, although you anticipate entering a contract in the future, neither party intends to be legally bound to the terms included in the memorandum. That way, the other party cannot claim that you have already reached an agreement on all essential terms.

PREVENTING LEGAL DISPUTES

Definiteness The second requirement for an effective offer involves the definiteness of its terms. An offer must have reasonably definite terms so that a court can determine if a breach has occurred and give an appropriate remedy.[6] The specific terms required depend, of course, on the type of contract. Generally, a contract must include the following terms, either expressed in the contract or capable of being reasonably inferred from it:

1. The identification of the parties.

2. The identification of the object or subject matter of the contract (also the quantity, when appropriate), including the work to be performed, with specific identification of such items as goods, services, and land.

---

6. *Restatement (Second) of Contracts*, Section 33. The UCC has relaxed the requirements regarding the definiteness of terms in contracts for the sale of goods. See UCC 2–204(3).

3. The consideration to be paid.

4. The time of payment, delivery, or performance.

An offer may invite an acceptance to be worded in such specific terms that the contract is made definite. **EXAMPLE 11.6** Nintendo of America, Inc., contacts your Play 2 Win Games store and offers to sell "from one to twenty-five Nintendo 3DS gaming systems for $75 each. State number desired in acceptance." You agree to buy twenty systems. Because the quantity is specified in the acceptance, the terms are definite, and the contract is enforceable. ■

Communication A third requirement for an effective offer is communication—the offer must be communicated to the offeree. **EXAMPLE 11.7** Tolson advertises a reward for the return of her lost cat. Dirk, not knowing of the reward, finds the cat and returns it to Tolson. Ordinarily, Dirk cannot recover the reward, because an essential element of a reward contract is that the one who claims the reward must have known it was offered. A few states would allow recovery of the reward, but not on contract principles. Dirk would be allowed to recover on the basis that it would be unfair to deny him the reward just because he did not know about it. ■

11–1b Termination of the Offer

The communication of an effective offer to an offeree gives the offeree the power to transform the offer into a binding, legal obligation (a contract) by an acceptance. This power of acceptance does not continue forever, though. It can be terminated by either the *action of the parties* or by *operation of law.* Termination by the action of the parties can involve a revocation by the offeror or a rejection or counteroffer by the offeree.

Termination by Action of the Offeror The offeror's act of withdrawing an offer is referred to as **revocation.** Unless an offer is irrevocable, the offeror usually can revoke the offer (even if he or she has promised to keep it open), as long as the revocation is communicated to the offeree before the offeree accepts.

Revocation may be accomplished by an express repudiation of the offer (such as "I withdraw my previous offer of October 17") or by the performance of acts that are inconsistent with the existence of the offer and that are made known to the offeree. **EXAMPLE 11.8** Misha offers to sell some land to Gary. A month passes, and Gary, who has not accepted the offer, learns that Misha has sold the property to Liam. Because Misha's sale of the land to Liam is inconsistent with the continued existence of the offer to Gary, the offer to Gary is effectively revoked. ■

The general rule followed by most states is that a revocation becomes effective when the offeree or the offeree's *agent* (a person acting on behalf of the offeree) actually receives it. Therefore, a statement of revocation sent via FedEx on April 1 and delivered at the offeree's residence or place of business on April 2 becomes effective on April 2.

Termination by Action of the Offeree If the offeree rejects the offer, either by words or by conduct, the offer is terminated. Any subsequent attempt by the offeree to accept will be construed as a new offer, giving the original offeror (now the offeree) the power of acceptance.

Like a revocation, a rejection is effective only when it is actually received by the offeror or the offeror's agent. **EXAMPLE 11.9** Goldfinch Farms offers to sell specialty Maitake mushrooms to a Japanese buyer, Kinoko Foods. If Kinoko rejects the offer by sending a letter via U.S. mail, the rejection will not be effective (and the offer will not be terminated) until Goldfinch receives the letter. ■

Inquiries about an Offer. Merely inquiring about an offer does not constitute rejection. **EXAMPLE 11.10** Your friend offers to buy your Inkling digital pen for $100. You respond, "Is that your best offer?" A reasonable person would conclude that you have not rejected the offer but have merely made an inquiry. You could still accept and bind your friend to the $100 price. ■

Counteroffers. A **counteroffer** is a rejection of the original offer and the simultaneous making of a new offer. EXAMPLE 11.11 Burke offers to sell his home to Lang for $270,000. Lang responds, "Your price is too high. I'll offer to purchase your house for $250,000." Lang's response is a counteroffer because it rejects Burke's offer to sell at $270,000 and creates a new offer by Lang to purchase the home at a price of $250,000. ■

At common law, the **mirror image rule** requires that the offeree's acceptance match the offeror's offer exactly. In other words, the terms of the acceptance must "mirror" those of the offer. If the acceptance materially changes or adds to the terms of the original offer, it will be considered not an acceptance but a counteroffer—which, of course, need not be accepted. The original offeror can, however, accept the terms of the counteroffer and create a valid contract.[7]

Termination by Operation of Law
The power of the offeree to transform the offer into a binding, legal obligation can be terminated by operation of law through the occurrence of any of the following events:

1. Lapse of time.

2. Destruction of the specific subject matter of the offer.

3. Death or incompetence of the offeror or the offeree.

4. Supervening illegality of the proposed contract.

Lapse of Time. An offer terminates automatically by law when the period of time *specified in the offer* has passed. If the offer states that it will be left open until a particular date, then the offer will terminate at midnight on that day. If the offer states that it will be left open for a number of days, this time period normally begins to run when the offer is actually *received* by the offeree, not when it is formed or sent.

If the offer does not specify a time for acceptance, the offer terminates at the end of a *reasonable* period of time. A reasonable period of time is determined by the subject matter of the contract, business and market conditions, and other relevant circumstances. An offer to sell farm produce, for instance, will terminate sooner than an offer to sell farm equipment because produce is perishable and subject to greater fluctuations in market value.

Destruction, Death, or Illegality. An offer is automatically terminated if the specific subject matter of the offer (such as a smartphone or a house) is destroyed before the offer is accepted. An offeree's power of acceptance is also terminated when the offeror or offeree dies or becomes legally incapacitated, *unless the offer is irrevocable.* Finally, a statute or court decision that makes an offer illegal automatically terminates the offer.

Irrevocable Offers
Although most offers are revocable, some can be made irrevocable. Increasingly, courts refuse to allow an offeror to revoke an offer when the offeree has changed position because of justifiable reliance on the offer (under the doctrine of *promissory estoppel*). In some circumstances, "firm offers" made by merchants may also be considered irrevocable.

Another form of irrevocable offer is an option contract. An **option contract** is created when an offeror promises to hold an offer open for a specified period of time in return for a payment (consideration) given by the offeree. An option contract takes away the offeror's power to revoke an offer for the period of time specified in the option. If no time is specified, then a reasonable period of time is implied.

Option contracts are frequently used in conjunction with the sale of real estate. EXAMPLE 11.12 Tyrell agrees to lease a house from Jackson, the property owner. The lease contract includes a clause stating that Tyrell is paying an additional $15,000 for an option to purchase the property within a specified period of time. If Tyrell decides not to purchase the house after

---

7. The mirror image rule has been greatly modified in regard to sales contracts. Section 2–207 of the UCC provides that a contract is formed if the offeree makes a definite expression of acceptance (such as signing the form in the appropriate location), even though the terms of the acceptance modify or add to the terms of the original offer.

Counteroffer An offeree's response to an offer in which the offeree rejects the original offer and at the same time makes a new offer.

Mirror Image Rule A common law rule that requires that the terms of the offeree's acceptance adhere exactly to the terms of the offeror's offer for a valid contract to be formed.

KNOW THIS
When an offer is rejected, it is terminated.

LEARNING OBJECTIVE 2
In what circumstances will an offer be irrevocable?

Option Contract A contract under which the offeror cannot revoke the offer for a stipulated time period (because the offeree has given consideration for the offer to remain open).

LEARNING OBJECTIVE 3

What are the elements that are necessary for an effective acceptance?

Acceptance The act of voluntarily agreeing, through words or conduct, to the terms of an offer, thereby creating a contract.

the specified period has lapsed, he loses the $15,000, and Jackson is free to sell the property to another buyer. ■

11–1c Acceptance

An **acceptance** is a voluntary act by the offeree that shows assent, or agreement, to the terms of an offer. The offeree's act may consist of words or conduct. The acceptance must be unequivocal and must be communicated to the offeror. Generally, only the person to whom the offer is made or that person's agent can accept the offer and create a binding contract. (See this chapter's *Adapting the Law to the Online Environment* feature for a discussion of how parties can sometimes inadvertently accept a contract via e-mail or instant messages.)

ADAPTING THE LAW TO THE ONLINE ENVIRONMENT
Can Your E-Mails or Instant Messages Create a Valid Contract?

Instant messaging and e-mailing are among the most common forms of informal communication. Not surprisingly, parties considering an agreement often exchange offers and counteroffers via e-mail (and, to a lesser extent, instant messaging). The parties may believe that these informal electronic exchanges are for negotiation purposes only. But such communications can lead to the formation of valid contracts.

E-mails and Settlements

After automobile accidents, the parties' attorneys sometimes exchange e-mails as part of the negotiation process. Consider the case of John Forcelli, who claimed that he had been injured in an accident by a vehicle owned by Gelco Corporation. Forcelli commenced litigation. While the litigation was progressing, a representative of Gelco's insurer offered Forcelli's attorneys a $230,000 settlement. The attorneys orally accepted the offer on behalf of Forcelli. The insurance company's representative sent an e-mail message confirming the terms of the settlement, and Forcelli signed a notarized release.

A few days later, however, a New York trial court issued an order granting a motion for summary judgment in favor of Gelco and dismissing Forcelli's claims. Gelco then tried to reject the settlement, claiming that the e-mail message did not constitute a binding written settlement agreement. A New York trial court ruled against Gelco, and an appeal followed.

The reviewing court upheld the trial court's finding. The e-mail contained all the necessary elements of contractual agreement.[a]

"Accidental" Contracts via E-mail

When a series of e-mails signal intent to be bound, a contract may be formed, even though some language in the e-mails may be careless or accidental. Even if a party later claims to have had unstated objections to the terms, the e-mails will prevail. What matters is whether a court determines that it is reasonable for the receiving party to believe that there is an agreement.

Indeed, e-mail contracting has become so common that only unusually strange circumstances will cause a court to reject such contracts.[b] Furthermore, under the Uniform Electronic Transactions Act, a contract "may not be denied legal effect solely because an electronic record was used in its formation." Most states have adopted this act, at least in part, as you will read later in this chapter.

Instant Messaging Can Create Valid Contract Modifications

Like e-mail exchanges, instant messaging conversations between individuals in the process of negotiations can result in the formation (or modification) of a contract. One case involved

an online marketing service, CX Digital Media, Inc., which provides clients with advertising referrals from its network of affiliates.

CX Digital charges a fee for its services based on number of referrals. One of its clients was Smoking Everywhere, Inc., a seller of electronic cigarettes. While the two companies were negotiating a change in contract terms via instant messaging, the issue of the maximum number of referrals per day came up. A CX Digital employee sent an instant message to a Smoking Everywhere executive asking about the maximum number. The executive responded, "NO LIMIT," and CX Digital's employee replied, "awesome!"

After that, CX Digital referred a higher volume of sales leads than previously. Smoking Everywhere refused to pay for these additional referrals, claiming that the instant messaging chat did not constitute an enforceable modification of the initial contract. At trial, CX Digital prevailed. Smoking Everywhere had to pay more than $1 million for the additional sales leads.[c]

CRITICAL THINKING

■ How can a company structure e-mail negotiations to avoid "accidentally" forming a contract?

---

a. *Forcelli v. Gelco Corporation*, 109 A.D.3d 244, 972 N.Y.S.2d 570 (2013).

b. See, for example, *Beastie Boys v. Monster Energy Co.*, 983 F.Supp.2d 338 (S.D.N.Y. 2013).

c. *CX Digital Media, Inc. v. Smoking Everywhere, Inc.*, 2011 WL 1102782 (S.D.Fla. 2011).

Unequivocal Acceptance To exercise the power of acceptance effectively, the offeree must accept unequivocally. This is the mirror image rule previously discussed. If the acceptance is subject to new conditions or if the terms of the acceptance materially change the original offer, the acceptance may be deemed a counteroffer that implicitly rejects the original offer.[8]

Certain terms included in an acceptance will not change the offer sufficiently to constitute rejection. **EXAMPLE 11.13** In response to an art dealer's offer to sell a painting, the offeree, Ashton Gibbs, replies, "I accept. Please send a written contract." Gibbs is requesting a written contract but is not making it a condition for acceptance. Therefore, the acceptance is effective without the written contract. In contrast, if Gibbs replies, "I accept *if* you send a written contract," the acceptance is expressly conditioned on the request for a writing, and the statement is not an acceptance but a counteroffer. (Notice how important each word is!) ■

Whether an offeree's conduct was sufficient to show acceptance of the terms of an offer was the issue at the center of the following case.

An art dealer offers to sell the painting on the front left of this photo. In response, a collector sends an e-mail in which she says "I accept your offer; please send a written contract." Is her acceptance effective?

---

8. As noted in footnote 7, in regard to sales contracts, the UCC provides that an acceptance may still be effective even if some terms are added. The new terms are simply treated as proposals for additions to the contract, unless both parties are merchants. If the parties are merchants, the additional terms (with some exceptions) become part of the contract [UCC 2–207(2)].

CASE 11.3

Brown v. Lagrange Development Corp.

Court of Appeals of Ohio, Sixth District, Lucas County, __ Ohio App.3d __, __ N.E.3d __, 2015 Ohio 133 (2015).

FACTS Lagrange Development Corp. is a non-profit corporation that acquires and rehabilitates real property in Toledo, Ohio. Sonja Brown presented Lagrange with a written offer to buy a house at 52 Rockingham Avenue for $79,900. Lagrange's executive director, Terry Glazer, penciled in modifications to the offer—an increased purchase price of $84,200 and a later date for acceptance. Glazer initialed the changes and signed the document.

Brown initialed the date change but not the price increase, and did not sign the revised document. Brown then applied for and obtained a mortgage, agreed to the closing, and received a deed. Later, Brown filed a suit in an Ohio state court against Lagrange, claiming that she had not agreed to the proposed changes. The court found the modified terms to be a counteroffer, which Brown had accepted by performance. Brown appealed.

ISSUE Was Brown's conduct sufficient to constitute acceptance of Lagrange's counteroffer?

DECISION Yes. A state intermediate appellate court affirmed the judgment of the lower court. Although Brown did not sign the counteroffer, her subsequent conduct showed that she had accepted it.

Under what circumstances are modifications to a real estate contract part of the final bargain?

REASON The appellate court acknowledged that Glazer revised Brown's offer by changing material terms—the price and the closing date. Glazer initialed the changes and signed the document. On receipt of this document, Brown initialed only the date change. This alone was not enough to show acceptance of Lagrange's counteroffer. Brown's subsequent conduct, however, indicated an intent to accept it. She faxed the document with a loan application to obtain a mortgage. Later, she agreed to close the sale on the terms set out in the revised contract and accepted a deed. The court explained that it is not necessary for all of the parties to a contract to sign it for a valid contract to exist. An offeree can accept by performance. "Generally conduct sufficient to show agreement, including performance, constitutes acceptance of an offer." Here, Lagrange's counteroffer did not restrict the manner of acceptance, and Brown accepted its terms by performance.

CRITICAL THINKING—Social Consideration *How should an offeree indicate a definite lack of consent to a counteroffer?*

Silence as Acceptance

Ordinarily, silence cannot constitute acceptance, even if the offeror states, "By your silence and inaction, you will be deemed to have accepted this offer." This general rule applies because an offeree should not be put under a burden of liability to act affirmatively in order to reject an offer. No consideration—that is, nothing of value—has passed to the offeree to impose such a liability.

In some instances, however, the offeree does have a duty to speak. If so, his or her silence or inaction will operate as an acceptance. Silence may be an acceptance when an offeree takes the benefit of offered services even though he or she had an opportunity to reject them and knew that they were offered with the expectation of compensation.

EXAMPLE 11.14 Juan earns extra income by washing store windows. Juan taps on the window of a store, catches the attention of the store's manager, and points to the window and raises his cleaner, signaling that he will be washing the window. The manager does nothing to stop him. Here, the store manager's silence constitutes an acceptance, and an implied contract is created. The store is bound to pay a reasonable value for Juan's work. ■

Silence can also operate as an acceptance when the offeree has had prior dealings with the offeror. If a merchant, for instance, routinely receives shipments from a supplier and in the past has always notified the supplier when defective goods were rejected, then silence constitutes acceptance. Also, if a buyer solicits an offer specifying that certain terms and conditions are acceptable, and the seller makes the offer in response to the solicitation, the buyer has a duty to reject—that is, a duty to tell the seller that the offer is not acceptable. Failure to reject (silence) will operate as an acceptance.

Communication of Acceptance

Whether the offeror must be notified of the acceptance depends on the nature of the contract. In a unilateral contract, the full performance of some act is called for. Acceptance is usually evident, and notification is therefore unnecessary (unless the law requires it or the offeror asks for it). In a bilateral contract, in contrast, communication of acceptance is necessary, because acceptance is in the form of a promise. The bilateral contract is formed when the promise is made rather than when the act is performed.

CASE EXAMPLE 11.15 Powerhouse Custom Homes, Inc., owed $95,260.42 to 84 Lumber Company under a credit agreement. When Powerhouse failed to pay, 84 Lumber filed a suit to collect. During mediation, the parties agreed to a deadline for objections to whatever agreement they might reach. If there were no objections, the agreement would be binding.

Powerhouse then offered to pay less than the amount owed, but 84 Lumber did not respond. Powerhouse argued that 84 Lumber had accepted the offer by not objecting to it within the deadline. The court ruled in 84 Lumber's favor for the entire amount of the debt. To form a contract, an offer must be accepted unequivocally. Powerhouse made an offer, but 84 Lumber did not communicate acceptance. Therefore, the parties did not reach an agreement on settlement.[9] ■

Mode and Timeliness of Acceptance

Acceptance in bilateral contracts must be timely. The general rule is that acceptance in a bilateral contract is timely if it is made before the offer is terminated. Problems may arise, though, when the parties involved are not dealing face to face. In such situations, the offeree should use an authorized mode of communication.

The Mailbox Rule. Acceptance takes effect, and thus completes formation of the contract, at the time the offeree sends or delivers the acceptance via the mode of communication expressly or impliedly authorized by the offeror. This is the so-called **mailbox rule,** also called the *deposited acceptance rule,* which the majority of courts follow. Under this rule, if the authorized mode of communication is the mail, then an acceptance becomes valid when it is dispatched (placed in the control of the U.S. Postal Service)—not when it is received by the offeror. (Note,

---

KNOW THIS

A bilateral contract is a promise for a promise, and a unilateral contract is performance for a promise.

Mailbox Rule A common law rule that acceptance takes effect, and thus completes formation of the contract, at the time the offeree sends or delivers the acceptance via the communication mode expressly or impliedly authorized by the offeror.

---

9. *Powerhouse Custom Homes, Inc. v. 84 Lumber Co.,* 307 Ga.App. 605, 705 S.E.2d 704 (2011).

however, that if the offer stipulates when acceptance will be effective, then the offer will not be effective until the time specified.)

The mailbox rule does not apply to instantaneous forms of communication, such as when the parties are dealing face to face, by phone, by fax, and usually by e-mail. Under the Uniform Electronic Transactions Act (UETA—discussed later in this chapter), e-mail is considered sent when it either leaves the sender's control or is received by the recipient. This rule, which takes the place of the mailbox rule if the parties have agreed to conduct transactions electronically, allows an e-mail acceptance to become effective when sent.

Authorized Means of Communication. A means of communicating acceptance can be expressly authorized by the offeror or impliedly authorized by the facts and circumstances of the situation. An acceptance sent by means not expressly or impliedly authorized normally is not effective until it is received by the offeror.

When an offeror specifies how acceptance should be made, such as by overnight delivery, the contract is not formed unless the offeree uses that mode of acceptance. Both the offeror and the offeree are bound in contract the moment the specified means of acceptance is employed. **EXAMPLE 11.16** Motorola Mobility, Inc., offers to sell 144 Atrix 4G smartphones and 72 Lapdocks to Call Me Plus phone stores. The offer states that Call Me Plus must accept the offer via FedEx overnight delivery. The acceptance is effective (and a binding contract is formed) the moment that Call Me Plus gives the overnight envelope containing the acceptance to the FedEx driver. ■

If the offeror does not expressly authorize a certain mode of acceptance, then acceptance can be made by *any reasonable means*.[10] Courts look at the prevailing business usages and the surrounding circumstances to determine whether the mode of acceptance used was reasonable. Usually, the offeror's choice of a particular means in making the offer implies that the offeree can use the *same or a faster* means for acceptance. **EXAMPLE 11.17** If the offer is made via Priority U.S. mail, it would be reasonable to accept the offer via Priority mail or by a faster method, such as signed scanned documents sent as attachments via e-mail or overnight delivery. ■

Substitute Method of Acceptance. Sometimes, the offeror authorizes a particular method of acceptance, but the offeree accepts by a different means. In that situation, the acceptance may still be effective if the substituted method serves the same purpose as the authorized means. Acceptance by a substitute method is not effective on dispatch, though. No contract will be formed until the acceptance is received by the offeror. **EXAMPLE 11.18** Bennion's offer specifies acceptance via FedEx overnight delivery but the offeree accepts instead by overnight delivery from UPS. The substitute method of acceptance will still be effective, but not until the offeror (Bennion) receives it from UPS. ■

11-2 E-Contracts

Numerous contracts are formed online. Electronic contracts, or **e-contracts,** must meet the same basic requirements (agreement, consideration, contractual capacity, and legality) as paper contracts. Disputes concerning e-contracts, however, tend to center on contract terms and whether the parties voluntarily agreed to those terms.

E-Contract A contract that is formed electronically.

Online contracts may be formed not only for the sale of goods and services but also for *licensing*. The "sale" of software generally involves a license, or a right to use the software, rather than the passage of title (ownership rights) from the seller to the buyer. **EXAMPLE 11.19** Lauren wants to obtain software that will allow her to work on spreadsheets on her smartphone.

---

10. Note that UCC 2–206(1)(a) states specifically that an acceptance of an offer for the sale of goods can be made by any medium that is *reasonable* under the circumstances.

She goes online and purchases GridMagic. During the transaction, she has to click on several on-screen "I agree" boxes to indicate that she understands that she is purchasing only the right to use the software, not ownership rights. After she agrees to these terms (the licensing agreement), she can download the software. ■

As you read through the following subsections, keep in mind that although we typically refer to the offeror and the offeree as a *seller* and a *buyer,* in many online transactions these parties would be more accurately described as a *licensor* and a *licensee.*

11–2a Online Offers

Sellers doing business via the Internet can protect themselves against contract disputes and legal liability by creating offers that clearly spell out the terms that will govern their transactions if the offers are accepted. All important terms should be conspicuous and easy to view.

Do online "I agree" click-ons validate software licensing agreements?

Displaying the Offer   The seller's Web site should include a hypertext link to a page containing the full contract so that potential buyers are made aware of the terms to which they are assenting. The contract generally must be displayed online in a readable format such as in a twelve-point typeface. All provisions should be reasonably clear.

EXAMPLE 11.20   Netquip sells a variety of heavy equipment, such as trucks and trailers, online at its Web site. Because Netquip's pricing schedule is very complex, the schedule must be fully provided and explained on the Web site. In addition, the terms of the sale (such as any warranties and the refund policy) must be fully disclosed. ■

Provisions to Include   An important rule to keep in mind is that the offeror (seller) controls the offer and thus the resulting contract. The seller should therefore anticipate the terms she or he wants to include in a contract and provide for them in the offer. In some instances, a standardized contract form may suffice. At a minimum, an online offer should include the following provisions:

1. *Acceptance of terms.* A clause that clearly indicates what constitutes the buyer's agreement to the terms of the offer, such as a box containing the words "I accept" that the buyer can click on to indicate acceptance. (Mechanisms for accepting online offers will be discussed in detail later in this chapter.)

2. *Payment.* A provision specifying how payment for the goods (including any applicable taxes) must be made.

3. *Return policy.* A statement of the seller's refund and return policies.

4. *Disclaimer.* Disclaimers of liability for certain uses of the goods. For example, an online seller of business forms may add a disclaimer that the seller does not accept responsibility for the buyer's reliance on the forms rather than on an attorney's advice.

5. *Limitation on remedies.* A provision specifying the remedies available to the buyer if the goods are found to be defective or if the contract is otherwise breached. Any limitation of remedies should be clearly spelled out.

6. *Privacy policy.* A statement indicating how the seller will use the information gathered about the buyer. (See the *Linking Business Law to Marketing* feature at the end of this chapter for a discussion of how the information may be used.)

7. *Dispute resolution.* Provisions relating to dispute settlement, such as an arbitration clause.

Dispute-Settlement Provisions   Online offers frequently include provisions relating to dispute settlement. For instance, the offer might include an arbitration clause specifying that any dispute arising under the contract will be arbitrated in a designated forum.

"If two men agree on everything, you can be sure one of them is doing the thinking."

LYNDON BAINES JOHNSON
1908–1973
(THIRTY-SIXTH PRESIDENT OF THE UNITED STATES, 1963–1969)

CASE EXAMPLE 11.21 Scott Rosendahl enrolled in an online college, Ashford University. He claimed that the school's adviser had told him that Ashford offered one of the cheapest undergraduate degree programs in the country. In fact, it did not. Rosendahl later sued the school, claiming that it had violated false advertising laws and had engaged in fraud and negligent misrepresentation. The university argued that the enrollment agreement clearly contained a requirement that all disputes be arbitrated. Rosendahl, like other students, had electronically assented to this agreement when he enrolled. Ashford presented the online application forms to the court, and the court dismissed Rosendahl's lawsuit. Rosendahl had agreed to arbitrate any disputes he had with Ashford.[11] ▪

Forum-Selection Clause. Many online contracts also contain a **forum-selection clause** indicating the forum, or location (such as a court or jurisdiction), for the resolution of any dispute arising under the contract. As discussed in the chapter on courts, significant jurisdictional issues may occur when parties are at a great distance, as they often are when they form contracts via the Internet. A forum-selection clause will help to avert future jurisdictional problems and also help to ensure that the seller will not be required to appear in court in a distant state.

CASE EXAMPLE 11.22 Before advertisers can place ads through Google, Inc., they must agree to certain terms that are displayed in an online window. These terms include a forum-selection clause, which provides that any dispute is to be "adjudicated in Santa Clara County, California." Lawrence Feldman, who advertised through Google, complained that he was overcharged and filed a lawsuit against Google in a federal district court in Pennsylvania. The court held that Feldman had agreed to the forum-selection clause in Google's online contract and transferred the case to a court in Santa Clara County.[12] ▪

Choice-of Law Clause. Some online contracts may also include a *choice-of-law clause* specifying that any dispute arising out of the contract will be settled in accordance with the law of a particular jurisdiction, such as a state or country. Choice-of-law clauses are particularly common in international contracts, but they may also appear in e-contracts to specify which state's laws will govern in the United States.

11–2b Online Acceptances

The *Restatement (Second) of Contracts*—a compilation of common law contract principles—states that parties may agree to a contract "by written or spoken words or by other action or by failure to act."[13] The Uniform Commercial Code (UCC), which governs sales contracts, has a similar provision. Section 2–204 of the UCC states that any contract for the sale of goods "may be made in any manner sufficient to show agreement, including conduct by both parties which recognizes the existence of such a contract." The courts have used these provisions in determining what constitutes an online acceptance.

Click-On Agreements The courts have concluded that the act of clicking on a box labeled "I accept" or "I agree" can indicate acceptance of an online offer. The agreement resulting from such an acceptance is often called a **click-on agreement** (sometimes, *click-on license* or *click-wrap agreement*). Exhibit 11–1 shows a portion of a click-on agreement that accompanies a software package.

Generally, the law does not require that the parties have read all of the terms in a contract for it to be effective. Therefore, clicking on a box that states "I agree" to certain terms can be enough to bind a party to these terms. The terms may be contained on a Web site through which the buyer is obtaining goods or services, or they may appear on the screen of

Forum-Selection Clause A provision in a contract designating the court, jurisdiction, or tribunal that will decide any disputes arising under the contract.

Click-On Agreement An agreement that arises when an online buyer clicks on "I agree" or otherwise indicates her or his assent to be bound by the terms of an offer.

---

11. *Rosendahl v. Bridgepoint Education, Inc.*, 2012 WL 667049 (S.D.Cal. 2012).
12. *Feldman v. Google, Inc.*, 513 F.Supp.2d 229 (E.D.Pa. 2007).
13. *Restatement (Second) of Contracts*, Section 19.

Exhibit 11–1 A Click-On Agreement

This exhibit illustrates an online offer to form a contract. To accept the offer, the user simply scrolls down the page and clicks on the "I Accept" button.

> **Type the characters you see in the picture**
>
> Picture: XJXM2GeN
>
> The picture contains 8 characters.
>
> Characters: _____
>
> **Review and accept the agreements**
>
> - Microsoft service agreement
> - Microsoft online privacy statement
>
> To accept the terms of service, click **I accept**. Clicking "I accept" means that you agree to the terms of the Microsoft service agreement and privacy statement. You understand that you are creating credentials that you can use on other Windows Live ID sites and services, you agree to receive required notices from Microsoft electronically, and you agree to receive targeted advertisements and periodic member e-mails. If you do not agree to these terms, click Cancel.

LEARNING OBJECTIVE 4

How do shrink-wrap and click-on agreements differ from other contracts? How have traditional laws been applied to these agreements?

Shrink-Wrap Agreement
An agreement whose terms are expressed in a document located inside a box in which goods (usually software) are packaged.

a computer, smartphone, or other device when software is downloaded from the Internet.

CASE EXAMPLE 11.23 The "Terms of Use" that govern Facebook users' accounts include a forum-selection clause that provides for the resolution of all disputes in a court in Santa Clara County. To sign up for a Facebook account, a person must click on a box indicating that he or she has agreed to this term.

Mustafa Fteja was an active user of facebook.com when his account was disabled. He sued Facebook in a federal court in New York, claiming that it had disabled his Facebook page without justification and for discriminatory reasons. Facebook filed a motion to transfer the case to California under the forum-selection clause. The court found that the clause in Facebook's online contract was binding and transferred the case. When Fteja clicked on the button to accept the contract terms, he agreed to resolve all disputes with Facebook in Santa Clara County, California.[14]

Shrink-Wrap Agreements A **shrink-wrap agreement** (or *shrink-wrap license*) is an agreement whose terms are expressed inside a box in which goods are packaged. (The term *shrink-wrap* refers to the plastic that covers the box.) Usually, the party who opens the box is told that she or he agrees to the terms by keeping the goods. Similarly, when the purchaser opens a software package, he or she agrees to abide by the terms of the limited license agreement.

EXAMPLE 11.24 Arial orders a new iMac from Big Dog Electronics, which ships it to her. Along with the iMac, the box contains an agreement setting forth the terms of the sale, including what remedies are available. The document also states that Arial's retention of the iMac for longer than thirty days will be construed as an acceptance of the terms.

In most instances, a shrink-wrap agreement is not between a retailer and a buyer, but is between the manufacturer of the hardware or software and the ultimate buyer-user of the product. The terms generally concern warranties, remedies, and other issues associated with the use of the product.

Shrink-Wrap Agreements and Enforceable Contract Terms. In some cases, the courts have enforced the terms of shrink-wrap agreements in the same way as the terms of other contracts. These courts have reasoned that by including the terms with the product, the seller proposed a contract that the buyer could accept by using the product after having an opportunity to read the terms. Thus, a buyer's failure to object to terms contained within a shrink-wrapped software package may constitute an acceptance of the terms by conduct.

Shrink-Wrap Terms That May Not Be Enforced. Sometimes, courts have refused to enforce certain terms included in shrink-wrap agreements because the buyer did not expressly consent to them. An important factor is when the parties form their contract.

Suppose that a buyer orders a product over the telephone. If the contract is formed at that time and the seller does not mention terms such as an arbitration clause or a forum-selection clause, clearly the buyer has not expressly agreed to these terms. If the clauses are then included in a shrink-wrap agreement, a court may conclude that those terms were only proposals for additional terms, and not part of the original contract. After all, the buyer did not discover them until *after* the contract was formed.

---

14. *Fteja v. Facebook, Inc.*, 841 F.Supp.2d 829 (S.D.N.Y. 2012).

Is it fair to enforce shrink-wrap and click-wrap terms that buyers were not aware of at the time they agreed to a purchase? Most people realize that if they sign a written contract without reading it, they can be held to its terms. But are most people aware that they can be legally bound by a host of conditions included in the packaging of electronics and software, not to mention the music, movies, and software they download from the Web? Simply by buying and keeping the latest electronic gadgets, we enter into binding contracts with the manufacturers that include rather one-sided terms. The terms may be unfair, but the law says we are bound by them.

For instance, just by installing or downloading certain software, users routinely agree to allow the companies to install tracking software on their computers. Moreover, many software programs—including some that are designed to combat *malware* (harmful programs, as discussed in the criminal law chapter)—automatically delete files from users' hard drives. Consumers and businesspersons are often unaware of these consequences, and yet by buying and installing the software, they have agreed that they will not hold the manufacturer liable.

Browse-Wrap Terms Like the terms of a click-on agreement, **browse-wrap terms** can occur in a transaction conducted over the Internet. Unlike a click-on agreement, however, browse-wrap terms do not require the buyer or user to assent to the terms before, say, downloading or using certain software. In other words, a person can install the software without clicking "I agree" to the terms of a license. Browse-wrap terms are often unenforceable because they do not satisfy the agreement requirement of contract formation.[15]

Browse-Wrap Term A term or condition of use that is presented when an online buyer downloads a product but to which the buyer does not have to agree before installing or using the product.

11–2c Federal Law on E-Signatures and E-Documents

An **e-signature** has been defined as "an electronic sound, symbol, or process attached to or logically associated with a record and executed or adopted by a person with the intent to sign the record."[16] Electronic documents can be signed in a number of ways. Thus, e-signatures include encrypted digital signatures, names (intended as signatures) at the ends of e-mail messages, and "clicks" on a Web page if the clicks include some means of identification.

E-Signature An electronic sound, symbol, or process attached to or logically associated with a record and adopted by a person with the intent to sign the record.

The E-SIGN Act In 2000, Congress enacted the Electronic Signatures in Global and National Commerce Act (E-SIGN Act).[17] The E-SIGN Act provides that no contract, record, or signature may be "denied legal effect" solely because it is in electronic form.

Under the act, an electronic signature is as valid as a signature on paper, and an e-document can be as enforceable as a paper one. For an e-signature to be enforceable, however, the contracting parties must have agreed to use electronic signatures. For an electronic document to be valid, it must be in a form that can be retained and accurately reproduced.

The E-SIGN Act does not apply to all types of documents. Contracts and documents that are exempt include court papers, divorce decrees, evictions, foreclosures, health-insurance terminations, prenuptial agreements, and wills. Also, the only agreements governed by the UCC that fall under this law are those covered by Articles 2 and 2A and UCC 1–107 and 1–206. Despite these limitations, the E-SIGN Act significantly expanded contracting online.

Why are many e-signatures binding today?

The FACT Act Another federal law, The Fair and Accurate Credit Transactions (FACT) Act,[18] was passed in 2003 to combat identity theft. One provision of the FACT Act involves how credit-card receipts should be handled. In the case of online transactions, these receipts take the form of e-documents. See this chapter's *Managerial Strategy* feature for more details on how the FACT Act's provisions may affect online transactions.

---

15. See, for example, *Jesmer v. Retail Magic, Inc.*, 863 N.Y.S.2d 737 (2008).
16. This definition is from the Uniform Electronic Transactions Act.
17. 15 U.S.C. Sections 7001 *et seq.*
18. 15 U.S.C. Section 1681 *et seq.*

MANAGERIAL STRATEGY   E-Mailed Credit Card Receipts

Management Faces a Legal Issue

As more and more sales transactions take place on the Internet, retailers continue to face new issues in online selling. One such issue involves credit-card receipts. Merchants who print out paper receipts must follow strict guidelines. Under the Fair and Accurate Credit Transaction (FACT) Act, merchants may print only the last five digits of a credit or debit card number and may not print the card's expiration date on any receipt provided to the cardholder at the point of sale.

This prohibition, the so-called truncation requirement, applies only to receipts that are "electronically printed." Congress did not indicate exactly what it meant by "electronically printed," however. Internet retailers thus have faced the legal issue of whether online receipts are subject to the FACT Act's truncation requirement.

What the Courts Say

The question, then, is whether a Web screen shot or an e-mailed sale confirmation counts as a receipt under the FACT Act. The courts that have examined this issue have generally concluded that the FACT Act's truncation requirement does not apply to e-mailed credit-card receipts.[a]

One case involved the online sale of contact lenses by a popular telephone and online retailer. The plaintiff was a customer who received an e-mail confirmation that included his credit card's expiration date. He sued the company for violating the FACT Act's truncation requirement. The court ruled in favor of the defendant, noting that the legislative history of the FACT Act clearly shows that Congress intended this law to apply to physical, printed-paper receipts. The court reasoned that the act "makes no use of terms like 'Internet' or 'e-mail' that would signal an intent to reach paperless receipts transmitted to the consumer via e-mail."[b]

MANAGERIAL IMPLICATIONS

Online retailers appear not to be subject to the FACT Act's truncation requirement for credit-card receipts sent via the Internet. Nonetheless, sensible online retailers might wish to conform to the act's provisions simply as a good business practice, to keep customers content and to protect customers' personal information. After all, hackers can sometimes illegally access Web sites and e-mail correspondence.

---

a. See, for example, *Bormes v. U.S.*, 759 F.3d 793 (7th Cir. 2014); and *Simonoff v. Expedia, Inc.*, 643 F.3d 1202 (9th Cir. 2011).

b. *Shlahtichman v. 1-800 Contacts, Inc.*, 615 F.3d 794 (7th Cir. 2010), *cert. denied*, 131 S.Ct. 1007, 178 L.Ed.2d 828 (2011).

11–2d Partnering Agreements

One way that online sellers and buyers can prevent disputes over signatures in their e-contracts, as well as disputes over the terms and conditions of those contracts, is to form partnering agreements. In a **partnering agreement,** a seller and a buyer who frequently do business with each other agree in advance on the terms and conditions that will apply to all transactions subsequently conducted electronically. The partnering agreement can also establish special access and identification codes to be used by the parties when transacting business electronically.

A partnering agreement reduces the likelihood that disputes will arise under the contract because the buyer and the seller have agreed in advance to the terms and conditions that will accompany each sale. Furthermore, if a dispute does arise, a court or arbitration forum will be able to refer to the partnering agreement when determining the parties' intent.

> **Partnering Agreement** An agreement between a seller and a buyer who frequently do business with each other concerning the terms and conditions that will apply to all subsequently formed electronic contracts.

11–3 The Uniform Electronic Transactions Act

> **LEARNING OBJECTIVE 5**
>
> What is the Uniform Electronic Transactions Act? What are some of the major provisions of this act?

Although most states have laws governing e-signatures and other aspects of electronic transactions, these laws vary. To create more uniformity among the states, in 1999 the National Conference of Commissioners on Uniform State Laws and the American Law Institute promulgated the Uniform Electronic Transactions Act (UETA). The UETA has been adopted, at least in part, by forty-eight states.

The primary purpose of the UETA is to remove barriers to e-commerce by giving the same legal effect to electronic records and signatures as is given to paper documents and signatures. The UETA broadly defines an *e-signature* as "an electronic sound, symbol, or process attached to or logically associated with a record and executed or adopted by a person with the intent to sign the record."[19] A **record** is "information that is inscribed on a tangible medium or that is stored in an electronic or other medium and is retrievable in perceivable [visual] form."[20]

Record Information that is either inscribed on a tangible medium or stored in an electronic or other medium and is retrievable.

11–3a The Scope and Applicability of the UETA

The UETA does not create new rules for electronic contracts. Rather, it establishes that records, signatures, and contracts may not be denied enforceability solely due to their electronic form.

The UETA does not apply to all writings and signatures. It covers only electronic records and electronic signatures *relating to a transaction*. A *transaction* is defined as an interaction between two or more parties relating to business, commercial, or governmental activities.[21] The act specifically does not apply to wills or testamentary trusts or to transactions governed by the UCC (other than those covered by Articles 2 and 2A).[22] In addition, the provisions of the UETA allow the states to exclude its application to other areas of law.

11–3b The Federal E-SIGN Act and the UETA

Congress passed the E-SIGN Act in 2000, a year after the UETA was presented to the states for adoption. Thus, a significant issue was to what extent the federal E-SIGN Act preempted the UETA as adopted by the states.

The E-SIGN Act[23] explicitly provides that if a state has enacted the uniform version of the UETA, it is not preempted by the E-SIGN Act. In other words, if the state has enacted the UETA without modification, state law will govern.

The problem is that many states have enacted nonuniform (modified) versions of the UETA, largely for the purpose of excluding other areas of state law from the UETA's terms. The E-SIGN Act specifies that those exclusions will be preempted to the extent that they are inconsistent with the E-SIGN Act's provisions.

The E-SIGN Act explicitly allows the states to enact alternative requirements for the use of electronic records or electronic signatures. Generally, however, the requirements must be consistent with the provisions of the E-SIGN Act, and the state must not give greater legal status or effect to one specific type of technology. Additionally, if a state enacts alternative requirements *after* the E-SIGN Act was adopted, the state law must specifically refer to the E-SIGN Act.

The relationship between the E-SIGN Act and the UETA is illustrated in Exhibit 11–2.

11–3c Highlights of the UETA

The UETA will not apply to a transaction unless the parties have agreed to conduct transactions by electronic means. The agreement may be explicit, or it may be implied by the conduct of the parties and the surrounding circumstances.[24] It may be reasonable, for example, to infer that a person who gives out a business card with an e-mail address on it has consented to transact business electronically.[25] Agreement may also be inferred from a letter or other writing, as well as from verbal communication. Furthermore, a person who has previously agreed

---

19. UETA 102(8).
20. UETA 102(15).
21. UETA 2(12) and 3.
22. UETA 3(b).
23. 15 U.S.C. Section 7002(2)(A)(i).
24. UETA 5(b).
25. UETA 5, Comment 4B.

Exhibit 11–2 The E-SIGN Act and the UETA

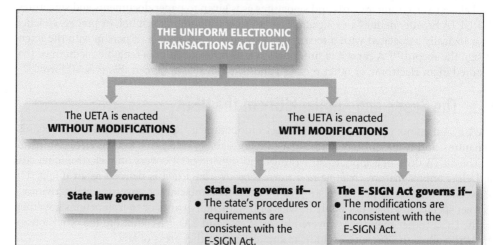

THE UNIFORM ELECTRONIC TRANSACTIONS ACT (UETA)

The UETA is enacted **WITHOUT MODIFICATIONS**

The UETA is enacted **WITH MODIFICATIONS**

State law governs

State law governs if—
- The state's procedures or requirements are consistent with the E-SIGN Act.
- The state does not give priority to one type of technology.
- The state law was enacted after the E-SIGN Act and refers to it.

The E-SIGN Act governs if—
- The modifications are inconsistent with the E-SIGN Act.

to an electronic transaction can withdraw his or her consent and refuse to conduct further business electronically.

Attribution Under the UETA, if an electronic record or signature is the act of a particular person, the record or signature may be attributed to that person. If a person types her or his name at the bottom of an e-mail purchase order, for instance, that name will qualify as a "signature" and be attributed to the person whose name appears.

In some contexts, a record may have legal effect even if no one has signed it. **EXAMPLE 11.25** J. P. Darby sends a fax to Corina Scott. The fax contains a letterhead identifying Darby as the sender, but Darby's signature does not appear on the faxed document. Depending on the circumstances, the fax may be attributed to Darby. ■

If an agreement is sent on letterhead stationery, does it need to be signed to be a valid acceptance?

Authorized Signatures The UETA contains no express provisions about what constitutes fraud or whether an agent is authorized to enter a contract. Under the UETA, other state laws control if any issues relating to agency, authority, forgery, or contract formation arise. If existing state law requires a document to be notarized, the electronic signature of a notary public or other person authorized to verify signatures satisfies this requirement.

The Effect of Errors The UETA encourages, but does not require, the use of security procedures (such as encryption) to verify changes to electronic documents and to correct errors. If the parties have agreed to a security procedure and one party does not detect an error because he or she did not follow the procedure, the conforming party can legally avoid the effect of the change or error. To avoid the effect of errors, a party must promptly notify the other party of the error and of her or his intent not to be bound by the error. In addition, the party must take reasonable steps to return any benefit received. Parties cannot avoid a transaction if they have benefited.

Timing An electronic record is considered *sent* when it is properly directed to the intended recipient in a form readable by the recipient's computer system. Once the electronic record leaves the control of the sender or comes under the control of the recipient, the UETA deems it to have been sent. An electronic record is considered *received* when it enters the recipient's processing system in a readable form—*even if no individual is aware of its receipt.*

Reviewing . . . Agreement

Ted and Betty Hyatt live in California, a state that has extensive statutory protection for consumers. The Hyatts decided to buy a computer so that they could use e-mail to stay in touch with their grandchildren, who live in another state. Over the phone, they ordered a computer from CompuEdge, Inc. When the box arrived, it was sealed with a brightly colored sticker warning that the terms enclosed within the box would govern the sale unless the recipient returned the computer within thirty days. Among those terms was a clause that required any disputes to be resolved in Tennessee state courts.

The Hyatts then signed up for Internet service through CyberTool, an Internet service provider. They downloaded CyberTool's software and clicked on the "quick install" box, which allowed them to bypass CyberTool's "Terms of Service" page. It was possible to read this page by scrolling to the next screen, but the Hyatts did not realize this. The terms included a clause stating that all disputes were to be submitted to a Virginia state court. As soon as the Hyatts attempted to e-mail their grandchildren, they experienced problems using CyberTool's e-mail service, which continually stated that the network was busy. They also were unable to receive the photos sent by their grandchildren.

Using the information presented in the chapter, answer the following questions.

1. Did the Hyatts accept the list of contract terms included in the computer box? Why or why not? What is this type of e-contract called?

2. What type of agreement did the Hyatts form with CyberTool?

3. Suppose that the Hyatts experienced trouble with the computer's components after they had used the computer for two months. What factors would a court consider in deciding whether to enforce the forum-selection clause? Would a court be likely to enforce the clause in this contract? Why or why not?

4. Are the Hyatts bound by the contract terms specified on CyberTool's "Terms of Service" page, though they did not read these terms? Which of the required elements for contract formation might the Hyatts claim were lacking? How might a court rule on this issue?

DEBATE THIS

■ The terms and conditions in click-on agreements are so long and detailed that no one ever reads the agreements. Therefore, the act of clicking on "Yes, I agree" is not really an acceptance.

LINKING BUSINESS LAW TO MARKETING
Customer Relationship Management

As you learned in this chapter, increasingly the contracting process is moving online. Large and small e-commerce Web sites offer to sell millions of goods and services. The vast amount of data collected from online shoppers has pushed *customer relationship management (CRM)* to the fore. CRM is a marketing strategy that allows companies to acquire information about customers' wants, needs, and behaviors. The companies can then use that information to build customer relationships and loyalty. The focus of CRM is understanding customers as individuals rather than simply as a group of consumers. As Exhibit 11–3 shows, CRM is a closed system that uses feedback from customers to build relationships with those customers.

Two Examples—Netflix and Amazon

If you are a customer of Netflix.com, you choose Blu-ray discs and DVDs that are sent to you by mail or streamed online based on your individual tastes and preferences. Netflix asks you to rate movies that you have rented (or seen in theaters) on a scale of one to five stars. Using a computer algorithm, Netflix then creates an individualized rating system that predicts how you will rate other movies. As you rate more movies, the system's predictions become more accurate. By applying your individual rating system to movies you have not seen, Netflix is able to suggest movies that you might like.

Amazon.com uses similar technology to recommend books and music that you might wish to buy. Amazon sends out numerous "personalized" e-mails to its customers with suggestions based on those customers' individual buying habits.

Thus, CRM allows both Netflix and Amazon to focus their marketing efforts. Such focused efforts are much more effective than the typical shotgun approach used in spam advertising on the Internet.

CRM in Online versus Traditional Companies

For online companies such as Amazon and Netflix, all customer information has some value because the cost of obtaining it, analyzing it, and utilizing it is so small. In contrast, traditional companies often must use a much more costly process to obtain data for CRM. An automobile company, for example, obtains customer information from a variety of sources, including dealers, customer surveys, online inquiries, and the like. Integrating, storing, and managing such information generally makes CRM much more expensive for traditional companies than for online companies.

- Online companies such as Amazon not only target individual customers but also utilize each customer's buying habits to create generalized marketing campaigns. Might any privacy issues arise as an online company creates a database to be used for generalized marketing campaigns?

Exhibit 11–3 A Customer Relationship Management Cycle

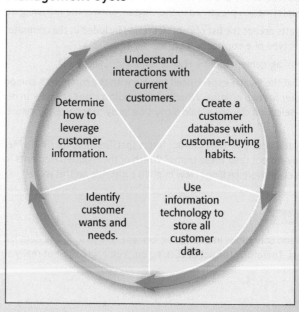

Understand interactions with current customers.

Create a customer database with customer-buying habits.

Use information technology to store all customer data.

Identify customer wants and needs.

Determine how to leverage customer information.

Key Terms

Chapter Summary: Agreement

Requirements of the Offer	1. *Intent*—There must be a serious, objective intention by the offeror to become bound by the offer. Nonoffer situations include (a) expressions of opinion; (b) statements of future intent; (c) preliminary negotiations; (d) generally, advertisements, catalogues, price lists, and circulars; and (e) traditionally, agreements to agree in the future. 2. *Definiteness*—The terms of the offer must be sufficiently definite to be ascertainable by the parties or by a court. 3. *Communication*—The offer must be communicated to the offeree.

Termination of the Offer	1. *By action of the parties*—
	  a. Revocation—Unless the offer is irrevocable, it can be revoked at any time before acceptance without liability. Revocation is not effective until received by the offeree or the offeree's agent. Some offers, such as a merchant's firm offer and option contracts, are irrevocable.
	  b. Rejection—Accomplished by words or actions that demonstrate a clear intent not to accept the offer. A rejection is not effective until it is received by the offeror or the offeror's agent.
	  c. Counteroffer—A rejection of the original offer and the making of a new offer.
	2. *By operation of law*—
	  a. Lapse of time—The offer terminates (1) at the end of the time period specified in the offer or (2) if no time period is stated in the offer, at the end of a reasonable time period.
	  b. Destruction of the specific subject matter of the offer—Automatically terminates the offer.
	  c. Death or incompetence of the offeror or offeree—Terminates the offer unless the offer is irrevocable.
	  d. Illegality—Supervening illegality terminates the offer.

Acceptance	1. Can be made only by the offeree or the offeree's agent. 2. Must be unequivocal. Under the common law (mirror image rule), if new terms or conditions are added to the acceptance, it will be considered a counteroffer. 3. Acceptance of a unilateral offer is effective on full performance of the requested act. Generally, no communication is necessary. 4. Except in a few situations, an offeree's silence does not constitute an acceptance. 5. Acceptance of a bilateral offer can be communicated by the offeree by any authorized mode of communication and is effective on dispatch. If the offeror does not specify the mode of communication, acceptance can be made by any reasonable means. Usually, the same means used by the offeror or a faster means can be used.
Online Offers	The terms of contract offers presented via the Internet should be as inclusive as the terms in an offer made in a written (paper) document. The offer should be displayed in an easily readable format and should include some mechanism, such as an "I agree" or "I accept" box, by which the customer may accept the offer. Because jurisdictional issues frequently arise with online transactions, the offer should include dispute-settlement provisions, as well as a forum-selection clause.

Online Acceptances	1. *Click-on agreement*—
	  a. Definition—An agreement created when a buyer, completing an online transaction, is required to indicate her or his assent to be bound by the terms of an offer by clicking on a box that says, for example, "I agree." The terms of the agreement may appear on the Web site through which the buyer is obtaining goods or services, or they may appear on a computer screen when software is downloaded.
	  b. Enforceability—The courts have enforced click-on agreements, holding that by clicking on "I agree," the offeree has indicated acceptance by conduct. In contrast, browse-wrap terms, which do not require any action to indicate agreement, may not be enforced on the ground that the user is not made aware that he or she is entering into a contract.
	2. *Shrink-wrap agreement*—
	  a. Definition—An agreement whose terms are expressed inside a box in which goods are packaged. The party who opens the box is informed that, by keeping the goods, he or she agrees to the terms of the shrink-wrap agreement.
	  b. Enforceability—The courts have often enforced shrink-wrap agreements. A court may deem a shrink-wrap agreement unenforceable, however, if the buyer learns of the shrink-wrap terms after the parties entered into the agreement.

Continues

E-Signatures	1. *Definition*—The Uniform Electronic Transactions Act (UETA) defines an e-signature as "an electronic sound, symbol, or process attached to or logically associated with a record and executed or adopted by a person with the intent to sign the record." E-signatures may include encrypted digital signatures, names at the ends of e-mail messages, and clicks on a Web page. 2. *Federal law on e-signatures and e-documents*—The Electronic Signatures in Global and National Commerce Act (E-SIGN Act) of 2000 gave validity to e-signatures by providing that no contract, record, or signature may be "denied legal effect" solely because it is in an electronic form.
The Uniform Electronic Transactions Act (UETA)	The Uniform Electronic Transactions Act (UETA) has been adopted, at least in part, by most states, to create rules to support the enforcement of e-contracts. Under the UETA, contracts entered into online, as well as other documents, are presumed to be valid. The UETA does not apply to certain transactions governed by the UCC or to wills or testamentary trusts.

Issue Spotters

1. Fidelity Corporation offers to hire Ron to replace Monica, who has given Fidelity a month's notice of her intent to leave the company. Fidelity gives Ron a week to decide whether to accept. Two days later, Monica decides not to leave and signs an employment contract with Fidelity for another year. The next day, Monica tells Ron of the new contract. Ron immediately faxes a formal letter of acceptance to Fidelity. Do Fidelity and Ron have a contract? Why or why not? (See *Agreement*.)

2. Applied Products, Inc., does business with Beltway Distributors, Inc., online. Under the Uniform Electronic Transactions Act, what determines the effect of the electronic documents evidencing the parties' deal? Is a party's "signature" necessary? Explain. (See *The Uniform Electronic Transactions Act*.)

   —**Check your answers to the *Issue Spotters* against the answers provided in Appendix D at the end of this text.**

Learning Objectives Check

1. What elements are necessary for an effective offer? What are some examples of nonoffers?

2. In what circumstances will an offer be irrevocable?

3. What are the elements that are necessary for an effective acceptance?

4. How do shrink-wrap and click-on agreements differ from other contracts? How have traditional laws been applied to these agreements?

5. What is the Uniform Electronic Transactions Act? What are some of the major provisions of this act?

   —**Answers to the even-numbered *Learning Objectives Check* questions can be found in Appendix E at the end of this text.**

Business Scenarios and Case Problems

11–1. Agreement. Ball writes to Sullivan and inquires how much Sullivan is asking for a specific forty-acre tract of land Sullivan owns. Ball then receives a letter from Sullivan stating, "I will not take less than $60,000 for the forty-acre tract as specified." Ball immediately sends Sullivan a fax stating, "I accept your offer for $60,000 for the forty-acre tract as specified." Discuss whether Ball can hold Sullivan to a contract for sale of the land. (See *Agreement*.)

11–2. Shrink-Wrap Agreements. TracFone Wireless, Inc., sells phones and wireless service. The phones are sold for less than their cost, and TracFone recoups this loss by selling prepaid airtime for their use on its network. Software in the phones prohibits their use on other networks. The phones are sold subject to the condition that the buyer agrees "not to tamper with or alter the software." This condition is printed on the packaging. Bequator Corp. bought at least 18,616 of the phones, disabled the software so that they could be used on other networks, and resold them. Is Bequator liable for breach of contract? Explain. [*TracFone Wireless, Inc. v. Bequator Corp.*, __ F.Supp.2d __ (S.D.Fla. 2011)] (See *E-Contracts*.)

11–3. Spotlight on Crime Stoppers—Communication. The Baton Rouge Crime Stoppers (BCS) offered a reward for information about the "South Louisiana Serial Killer." The information was to be provided via a hotline. Dianne Alexander had survived an attack by a person suspected of being the killer. She identified a suspect in a police photo lineup and later sought to collect the reward. BCS refused to pay because she had not provided information via the hotline. Did

Alexander comply with the terms of the offer? Explain. [*Alexander v. Lafayette Crime Stoppers, Inc.*, 38 So.3d 282 (La.App. 3 Dist. 2010)] (See *Agreement.*)

11–4. Business Case Problem with Sample Answer—Online Acceptances. Heather Reasonover opted to try Internet service from Clearwire Corp. Clearwire sent her a confirmation e-mail that included a link to its Web site. Clearwire also sent her a modem. In the enclosed written materials, at the bottom of a page, in small type was the Web site URL. When Reasonover plugged in the modem, an "I accept terms" box appeared. Without clicking on the box, Reasonover quit the page. A clause in Clearwire's "Terms of Service," accessible only through its Web site, required its subscribers to submit any dispute to arbitration. Is Reasonover bound to this clause? Why or why not? [*Kwan v. Clearwire Corp.*, 2012 WL 32380 (W.D.Wash. 2012)] (See *E-Contracts.*)

—**For a sample answer to Problem 11–4, go to Appendix F at the end of this text.**

11–5. Acceptance. Judy Olsen, Kristy Johnston, and their mother, Joyce Johnston, owned seventy-eight acres of real property on Eagle Creek in Meagher County, Montana. When Joyce died, she left her interest in the property to Kristy. Kristy wrote to Judy, offering to buy Judy's interest or to sell her own interest to Judy. She requested that Judy "please respond to Bruce Townsend." In a letter to Kristy—not to Bruce—Judy accepted the offer to buy Kristy's interest in the property. By that time, however, Kristy had offered to sell her interest to their brother, Dave, and he had accepted. Did Judy and Kristy have an enforceable binding contract, entitling Judy to specific performance? Or did Kristy's offer so limit its acceptance to one exclusive mode that Judy's reply was not effective? Discuss. [*Olsen v. Johnston*, 368 Mont. 347, 301 P.3d 791 (Mont. 2013)] (See *Agreement.*)

11–6. Agreement. Amy Kemper was seriously injured when her motorcycle was struck by a vehicle driven by Christopher Brown. Kemper's attorney wrote to Statewide Claims Services, the administrator for Brown's insurer, asking for "all the insurance money that Mr. Brown had under his insurance policy." In exchange, the letter indicated that Kemper would sign a "limited release" on Brown's liability, provided that it did not include any language requiring her to reimburse Brown or his insurance company for any of their incurred costs. Statewide then sent a check and release form to Kemper, but the release demanded that Kemper "place money in an escrow account in regards to any and all liens pending." Kemper refused the demand, claiming that Statewide's response was a counteroffer rather than an unequivocal acceptance of the settlement offer. Did Statewide and Kemper have an enforceable agreement? Discuss. [*Kemper v. Brown*, 754 S.E.2d 141 (Ga.App. 2014)] (See *Agreement.*)

11–7. Requirements of the Offer. Technical Consumer Products, Inc. (TCP) makes and distributes energy-efficient lighting products. Emily Bahr was TCP's district sales manager in Minnesota, North Dakota, and South Dakota when the company announced the details of a bonus plan. A district sales manager who achieved 100 percent year-over-year sales growth and a 42 percent gross margin would earn 200 percent of his or her base salary as a bonus. TCP retained absolute discretion to modify the plan. Bahr's base salary was $42,500. Her final sales results for the year showed 113 percent year-over-year sales growth and a 42 percent gross margin. She anticipated a bonus of $85,945, but TCP could not afford to pay the bonuses as planned, and Bahr received only $34,229. In response to Bahr's claim for breach of contract, TCP argued that the bonus plan was too indefinite to be an offer. Is TCP correct? Explain. [*Bahr v. Technical Consumer Products, Inc.*, __ F.3d __, 2015 WL 527468 (6th Cir. 2015)] (See *Agreement.*)

11–8. A Question of Ethics—Dispute-Settlement Provisions. Dewayne Hubbert, Elden Craft, Chris Grout, and Rhonda Byington bought computers from Dell Corp. through its Web site. Before buying, Hubbert and the others configured their own computers. To make a purchase, each buyer completed forms on five Web pages. On each page, Dell's "Terms and Conditions of Sale" were accessible by clicking on a blue hyperlink. A statement on three of the pages read, "All sales are subject to Dell's Term[s] and Conditions of Sale," but a buyer was not required to click an assent to the terms to complete a purchase. The terms were also printed on the backs of the invoices and on separate documents contained in the shipping boxes with the computers. Among those terms was a "Binding Arbitration" clause.

The computers contained Pentium 4 microprocessors, which Dell advertised as the fastest, most powerful Intel Pentium processor available at that time. Hubbert and the others filed a suit in an Illinois state court against Dell, alleging that this marketing was false, misleading, and deceptive. The plaintiffs claimed that the Pentium 4 microprocessor was slower and less powerful, and provided less performance, than either a Pentium III or an AMD Athlon, and at a greater cost. Dell asked the court to compel arbitration. [*Hubbert v. Dell Corp.*, 359 Ill. App.3d 976, 835 N.E.2d 113, 296 Ill.Dec. 258 (5 Dist. 2005)] (See *E-Contracts.*)

1. Should the court enforce the arbitration clause in this case? If you were the judge, how would you rule on this issue?

2. In your opinion, do shrink-wrap, click-on, and browse-wrap terms impose too great a burden on purchasers? Why or why not?

3. An ongoing complaint about shrink-wrap, click-on, and browse-wrap terms is that sellers (often large corporations) draft them and buyers (typically individual consumers) do not read them. Should purchasers be bound in contract by terms that they have not even read? Why or why not?

Critical Thinking and Writing Assignments

11–9. Case Analysis Question. Go to Appendix G at the end of this text and examine the excerpt of Case No. 2, *Gyabaah v. RivLab Transportation Corp.* Review and then brief the case, making sure that your brief answers the following questions. (See *Agreement*.)

1. **Issue:** The dispute between the parties to this case centered on what agreement and asked which question?

2. **Rule of Law:** What rule concerning the existence of a contract did the court apply in this case?

3. **Applying the Rule of Law:** How did the language in the parties' agreement and its context affect the application of the rule of law?

4. **Conclusion:** Why did the court conclude that the parties in this case were not bound by the settlement and release documents signed by Gyabaah?

11–10. Business Law Critical Thinking Group Assignment. To download a specific app to your smartphone or tablet device, you usually have to check a box indicating that you agree to the company's terms and conditions. Most individuals do so without ever reading those terms and conditions. Print out a specific set of terms and conditions from a downloaded app to use in this assignment. All group members should print out the same set of terms and conditions. (See *E-Contracts*.)

1. One group will determine which of these terms and conditions are favorable to the company.

2. Another group will determine which of these terms and conditions could conceivably be favorable to the individual.

3. A third group will determine which terms and conditions, on net, favor the company too much.

CHAPTER OUTLINE

- Consideration
- Promissory Estoppel
- Contractual Capacity
- Legality
- The Effect of Illegality

Consideration, Capacity, and Legality

"Liberty of contract is not an absolute concept. It is relative to many conditions of time and place and circumstance."

BENJAMIN CARDOZO
1870–1938
(ASSOCIATE JUSTICE OF THE UNITED STATES SUPREME COURT, 1932–1938)

LEARNING OBJECTIVES

The five Learning Objectives *below are designed to help improve your understanding of the chapter. After reading this chapter, you should be able to answer the following questions:*

1. What is consideration? What is required for consideration to be legally sufficient?

2. In what circumstances might a promise be enforced despite a lack of consideration?

3. Does a minor have the capacity to enter into an enforceable contract? What does it mean to disaffirm a contract?

4. Under what circumstances will a covenant not to compete be enforced? When will such covenants not be enforced?

5. What is an exculpatory clause? In what circumstances might exculpatory clauses be enforced? When will they not be enforced?

Courts generally want contracts to be enforceable, and much of the law is devoted to aiding the enforceability of contracts. Before a court will enforce a contractual promise, however, it must be convinced that there was some exchange of consideration underlying the bargain.

Furthermore, as indicated in the chapter-opening quotation, "liberty of contract" is not absolute. In other words, not all people can make legally binding contracts at all times. Contracts entered into by persons lacking the capacity to do so may be voidable. Similarly, contracts calling for the performance of an illegal act are illegal and thus void—they are not contracts at all.

In this chapter, we first examine the requirement of consideration and then look at contractual capacity and legality. As more commerce is done online, the issues of consideration, capacity, and legality have become the subject of many disputes. In covenants not to compete, for instance, what constitutes a reasonable time period in the online environment? This is among current topics you will read about in this chapter.

12-1 Consideration

In any legal system, some promises will be enforced, and other promises will not be enforced. The simple fact that a party has made a promise does not necessarily mean that the promise is enforceable.

Consideration The value given in return for a promise or performance in a contractual agreement.

Forbearance The act of refraining from an action that one has a legal right to undertake.

When you ask someone to paint your garage, what is the consideration?

"Understanding does not necessarily mean agreement."

HOWARD VERNON
1918–1992
(AMERICAN AUTHOR)

Under the common law, a primary basis for the enforcement of promises is consideration. **Consideration** usually is defined as the value given in return for a promise. Often, consideration is broken down into two parts: (1) something of *legally sufficient value* must be given in exchange for the promise, and (2) there must be a *bargained-for exchange*.

12–1a Legally Sufficient Value

To be legally sufficient, consideration must be something of value in the eyes of the law. The "something of legally sufficient value" may consist of any of the following:

1. A promise to do something that one has no prior legal duty to do (to pay on receipt of certain goods, for example).

2. The performance of an action that one is otherwise not obligated to undertake (such as providing accounting services).

3. The refraining from an action that one has a legal right to undertake (called a **forbearance**).

Consideration in bilateral contracts normally consists of a promise in return for a promise. In a contract for the sale of goods, for instance, the seller promises to ship specific goods to the buyer, and the buyer promises to pay for those goods when they are received. Each of these promises constitutes consideration for the contract.

In contrast, unilateral contracts involve a promise in return for a performance. **EXAMPLE 12.1** Anita says to her neighbor, "If you paint my garage, I will pay you $800." Anita's neighbor paints the garage. The act of painting the garage is the consideration that creates Anita's contractual obligation to pay her neighbor $800. ■

What if, in return for a promise to pay, a person refrains from pursuing harmful habits, such as the use of tobacco and alcohol? Does such forbearance create consideration for the contract? This was the issue in the 1891 case *Hamer v. Sidway*, which we present as this chapter's *Landmark in the Law* feature.

12–1b Bargained-for Exchange

The second element of consideration is that it must provide the basis for the bargain struck between the contracting parties. The item of value must be given or promised by the promisor (offeror) in return for the promisee's promise or performance.

This element of bargained-for exchange distinguishes contracts from gifts. **EXAMPLE 12.2** Sheng-Li says to his son, "In consideration of the fact that you are not as wealthy as your brothers, I will pay you $5,000." The fact that the word *consideration* is used does not, by itself, mean that consideration has been given. Indeed, Sheng-Li's promise is not enforceable, because the son need not do anything to receive the $5,000 promised. Because the son does not need to give Sheng-Li something of legal value in return for his promise, there is no bargained-for exchange. Rather, Sheng-Li has simply stated his motive for giving his son a gift. ■

12–1c Adequacy of Consideration

Adequacy of consideration involves "how much" consideration is given. Essentially, adequacy of consideration concerns the fairness of the bargain.

The General Rule　On the surface, when the items exchanged are of unequal value, fairness would appear to be an issue. In general, however, a court will not question the adequacy of consideration based solely on the comparative value of the things exchanged.

Under the doctrine of freedom of contract, courts leave it up to the parties to decide what something is worth, and parties are usually free to bargain as they wish. If people could sue

iStockPhoto.com/JodiJacobson

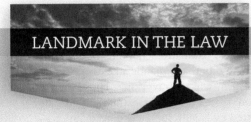

LANDMARK IN THE LAW

Hamer v. Sidway (1891)

In *Hamer v. Sidway*,[a] the issue before the court arose from a contract created in 1869 between William Story, Sr., and his nephew, William Story II. The uncle promised his nephew that if the nephew refrained from drinking alcohol, using tobacco, and playing billiards and cards for money until he reached the age of twenty-one, the uncle would pay him $5,000 (about $75,000 in today's dollars). The nephew, who indulged occasionally in all of these "vices," agreed to refrain from them and did so for the next six years.

Following his twenty-first birthday in 1875, the nephew wrote to his uncle that he had performed his part of the bargain and was thus entitled to the promised $5,000 (plus interest). A few days later, the

a. 124 N.Y. 538, 27 N.E. 256 (1891).

uncle wrote the nephew a letter stating, "[Y]ou shall have the five thousand dollars, as I promised you." The uncle said that the money was in the bank and that the nephew could "consider this money on interest."

THE ISSUE OF CONSIDERATION The nephew left the money in the care of his uncle, who held it for the next twelve years. When the uncle died in 1887, however, the executor of the uncle's estate refused to pay the $5,000 (plus interest) claim brought by Hamer, a third party to whom the promise had been *assigned*. (The law allows parties to assign, or transfer, rights in contracts to third parties.) The executor, Sidway, contended that the contract was invalid because there was insufficient consideration to support it. The uncle had received nothing, and the nephew had actually benefited by fulfilling the uncle's wishes. Therefore, no contract existed.

THE COURT'S CONCLUSION Although a lower court upheld Sidway's position, the

New York Court of Appeals reversed and ruled in favor of the plaintiff, Hamer. "The promisee used tobacco, occasionally drank liquor, and he had a legal right to do so," the court stated. "That right he abandoned for a period of years upon the strength of the promise of the testator [one who makes a will] that for such forbearance he would give him $5,000. We need not speculate on the effort which may have been required to give up the use of those stimulants. It is sufficient that he restricted his lawful freedom of action within certain prescribed limits upon the faith of his uncle's agreement."

APPLICATION TO TODAY'S WORLD *Although this case was decided more than a century ago, the principles enunciated by the court remain applicable to contracts formed today, including online contracts. For a contract to be valid and binding, consideration must be given, and that consideration must be something of legally sufficient value.*

merely because they had entered into an unwise contract, the courts would be overloaded with frivolous suits.

In short, the determination of whether consideration exists does not depend on the values of the things exchanged. Something need not be of direct economic or financial value to be considered legally sufficient consideration. In many situations, the exchange of promises and potential benefits is deemed to be sufficient consideration.

When Voluntary Consent May Be Lacking Occasionally, an exception may be made to the general rule just discussed. A large disparity in the amount or value of the consideration exchanged may raise a red flag for a court to look more closely at the bargain. Shockingly inadequate consideration can indicate that fraud, duress, or undue influence was involved. Judges are uneasy about enforcing unequal bargains, and it is their task to make certain that there was not some defect in the contract's formation that negated voluntary consent.

12-1d Agreements That Lack Consideration

Sometimes, one or both of the parties to a contract may think that they have exchanged consideration when in fact they have not. Here, we look at some situations in which the parties' promises or actions do not qualify as contractual consideration.

Preexisting Duty Under most circumstances, a promise to do what one already has a legal duty to do does not constitute legally sufficient consideration. A sheriff, for example, cannot

KNOW THIS
A consumer's signature on a contract does not always guarantee that the contract will be enforced. The contract must also comply with state and federal consumer protection laws.

collect a reward for information leading to the capture of a criminal if the sheriff already has a legal duty to capture the criminal.

Likewise, if a party is already bound by contract to perform a certain duty, that duty cannot serve as consideration for a second contract. **EXAMPLE 12.3** Bauman-Bache, Inc., begins construction on a seven-story office building and after three months demands an extra $75,000 on its contract. If the extra $75,000 is not paid, the firm will stop working. The owner of the land, finding no one else to complete construction, agrees to pay the extra $75,000. The agreement is not enforceable because it is not supported by legally sufficient consideration—Bauman-Bache had a preexisting contractual duty to complete the building. ■

Unforeseen Difficulties. The preexisting duty rule is intended to prevent extortion and the so-called holdup game. Nonetheless, if, during performance of a contract, extraordinary difficulties arise that were totally unforeseen at the time the contract was formed, a court may allow an exception to the rule. The key is whether the court finds that the modification is fair and equitable in view of circumstances not anticipated by the parties when the contract was made.[1]

Are there circumstances under which a contractor, who has performed cement work, can legally demand a payment amount that is greater than what was stated in the contract?

Suppose that in *Example 12.3*, Bauman-Bache asked for the extra $75,000 because it encountered a rock formation that no one knew existed. Suppose, too, that the landowner agreed to pay the extra amount to excavate the rock. In this situation, if the court finds that it is fair to do so, it may enforce the agreement. If rock formations are common in the area, however, the court may determine that the contractor should have known of the risk. In that situation, the court may choose to apply the preexisting duty rule and prevent Bauman-Bache from obtaining the extra $75,000.

Rescission and New Contract. The law recognizes that two parties can mutually agree to rescind, or cancel, their contract, at least to the extent that it is *executory* (still to be carried out). **Rescission**[2] is the unmaking of a contract so as to return the parties to the positions they occupied before the contract was made.

Rescission A remedy whereby a contract is canceled and the parties are returned to the positions they occupied before the contract was made.

Sometimes, parties rescind a contract and make a new contract at the same time. When this occurs, it is often difficult to determine whether there was consideration for the new contract or whether the parties had a preexisting duty under the previous contract. If a court finds there was a preexisting duty, then the new contract will be invalid because there was no consideration.

Past Consideration Promises made in return for actions or events that have already taken place are unenforceable. These promises lack consideration in that the element of bargained-for exchange is missing. In short, you can bargain for something to take place now or in the future but not for something that has already taken place. Therefore, **past consideration** is no consideration.

Past Consideration An act that takes place before a contract is made and that ordinarily, by itself, cannot later be consideration with respect to that contract.

CASE EXAMPLE 12.4 Jamil Blackmon became friends with Allen Iverson when Iverson was a high school student who showed tremendous promise as an athlete. Blackmon suggested that Iverson use "The Answer" as a nickname in the league tournaments, and said that Iverson would be "The Answer" to the National Basketball Association's declining attendance. Later, Iverson said that he would give Blackmon 25 percent of any proceeds from the merchandising of products that used "The Answer" as a logo or a slogan. Because Iverson's promise was made in return for past consideration (Blackmon's earlier suggestion), it was unenforceable. In effect, Iverson stated his intention to give Blackmon a gift.[3] ■

---

1. *Restatement (Second) of Contracts*, Section 73.
2. Pronounced reh-*sih*-zhen.
3. *Blackmon v. Iverson*, 324 F.Supp.2d 602 (E.D.Pa. 2003).

Illusory Promises If the terms of the contract express such uncertainty of performance that the promisor has not definitely promised to do anything, the promise is said to be *illusory*—without consideration and unenforceable. EXAMPLE 12.5 The president of Tuscan Corporation says to his employees, "All of you have worked hard, and if profits remain high, a 10 percent bonus at the end of the year will be given—if management thinks it is warranted." This is an *illusory promise,* or no promise at all, because performance depends solely on the discretion of the president (the management). There is no bargained-for consideration. The statement declares merely that management may or may not do something in the future. ■

Option-to-cancel clauses in contracts for specified time periods sometimes present problems because of illusory promises. EXAMPLE 12.6 Abe contracts to hire Chris for one year at $5,000 per month, reserving the right to cancel the contract at any time. On close examination of these words, you can see that Abe has not actually agreed to hire Chris, as Abe can cancel without liability before Chris starts performance. Abe has not given up the opportunity of hiring someone else. This contract is therefore illusory.

But if, instead, Abe reserves the right to cancel the contract at any time *after* Chris has begun performance by giving Chris *thirty days' notice,* the promise is not illusory. Abe, by saying that he will give Chris thirty days' notice, is relinquishing the opportunity (legal right) to hire someone else instead of Chris for a thirty-day period. If Chris works for one month and Abe then gives him thirty days' notice, Chris has an enforceable claim for two months' salary ($10,000). ■

12-1e Settlement of Claims

Businesspersons and others often enter into contracts to settle legal claims. It is important to understand the nature of the consideration given in these settlement agreements, or contracts. Commonly used settlement agreements include the *accord and satisfaction,* the *release,* and the *covenant not to sue.*

Accord and Satisfaction In an **accord and satisfaction,** a debtor offers to pay, and a creditor accepts, a lesser amount than the creditor originally claimed was owed. The *accord* is the agreement. In the accord, one party undertakes to give or perform, and the other to accept, in satisfaction of a claim, something other than that on which the parties originally agreed. *Satisfaction* is the performance (usually payment) that takes place after the accord is executed.

A basic rule governing such agreements is that there can be no satisfaction unless there is first an accord. In addition, for accord and satisfaction to occur, the amount of the debt *must be in dispute.*

Liquidated Debts. If a debt is *liquidated,* accord and satisfaction cannot take place. A **liquidated debt** is one whose amount has been ascertained, fixed, agreed on, settled, or exactly determined. EXAMPLE 12.7 Barbara Kwan signs an installment loan contract with her banker. In the contract, Kwan agrees to pay a specified rate of interest on a specified amount of borrowed funds at monthly intervals for two years. Because both parties know the precise amount of the total obligation, it is a liquidated debt. ■

In the majority of states, a creditor's acceptance of a lesser sum than the entire amount of a liquidated debt is not satisfaction, and the balance of the debt is still legally owed. The reason for this rule is that the debtor has given no consideration to satisfy the obligation of paying the balance to the creditor. The debtor has a preexisting legal obligation to pay the entire debt. (Of course, even with liquidated debts, creditors often do negotiate debt settlement agreements with debtors for a lesser amount than was originally owed. Creditors sometimes even forgive or write off a liquidated debt as uncollectable.)

Unliquidated Debts. An **unliquidated debt** is the opposite of a liquidated debt. The amount of the debt is *not* settled, fixed, agreed on, ascertained, or determined, and reasonable persons

Accord and Satisfaction
A common means of settling a disputed claim, whereby a debtor offers to pay a lesser amount than the creditor purports to be owed.

Liquidated Debt A debt whose amount has been ascertained, fixed, agreed on, settled, or exactly determined.

KNOW THIS
Even with liquidated debts, creditors will often enter into settlement agreements that allow debtors to pay a lesser amount than was originally owed.

Unliquidated Debt A debt that is uncertain in amount.

may differ over the amount owed. In these circumstances, acceptance of payment of the lesser sum operates as a satisfaction, or discharge, of the debt because there is valid consideration. The parties give up a legal right to contest the amount in dispute.

Release **Release** An agreement in which one party gives up the right to pursue a legal claim against another party.

Release

A **release** is a contract in which one party forfeits the right to pursue a legal claim against the other party. It bars any further recovery beyond the terms stated in the release.

A release will generally be binding if it meets the following requirements:

1. The agreement is made in good faith.

2. The release contract is in a signed writing (required in many states).

3. The contract is accompanied by consideration.[4]

A person involved in an automobile accident may be asked to sign a release. Clearly, the person is better off knowing the extent of his or her injuries or damages before signing. **EXAMPLE 12.8** Kara's car is damaged in an accident caused by Raoul's negligence. Raoul offers to give Kara $3,000 if she will release him from further liability resulting from the accident. Kara agrees and signs the release.

If Kara later discovers that the repairs will cost $4,200, she cannot recover the additional amount from Raoul. Kara is limited to the $3,000 specified in the release because a valid contract was formed. Kara and Raoul both voluntarily agreed to the terms in a signed writing, and sufficient consideration was present. The consideration was the legal right to recover damages that Kara forfeited should her damages be more than $3,000, in exchange for Raoul's promise to give her $3,000. ■

Covenant Not to Sue An agreement to substitute a contractual obligation for some other type of legal action based on a valid claim.

Covenant Not to Sue

Unlike a release, a **covenant not to sue** does not always prevent further recovery. The parties simply substitute a contractual obligation for some other type of legal action based on a valid claim. Suppose in *Example 12.8* that Kara agrees not to sue Raoul for damages in a tort action if he will pay for the damage to her car. If Raoul fails to pay, Kara can bring an action for breach of contract.

As the following *Spotlight Case* illustrates, a covenant not to sue can form the basis for a dismissal of the claims of either party to the covenant.

Is it possible to limit one's liability after a car accident?

---

4. Under the Uniform Commercial Code (UCC), a written, signed waiver by an aggrieved party discharges any further liability for a breach, even without consideration.

SPOTLIGHT ON NIKE: CASE 12.1

Already, LLC v. Nike, Inc.

Supreme Court of the United States, __ U.S. __, 133 S.Ct. 721, 184 L.Ed.2d 553 (2013).

COMPANY PROFILE *Bill Bowerman was a track coach at the University of Oregon, and Phil Knight was an accountant in Portland, Oregon, who had been a track athlete on Bowerman's team. In 1964, the two men shook hands, pledged $500 each, and formed Blue Ribbon Sports to distribute athletic footwear manufactured by a Japanese company. A decade later, Blue Ribbon became Nike, Inc., adopted the familiar "Swoosh" logo, and began marketing shoes of its own design. Today, Nike's markets are global. In 2014, it reported revenue of over $27*

Will a plaintiff's covenant not to sue prevent the defendant from pursuing a counterclaim against the plaintiff?

billion. Nike is the official sponsor of the National Football League in the United States, as well as other athletes and sports teams around the world. Nike continues to design, make, and sell innovative footwear, including a line known as Air Force 1s.

FACTS Nike, Inc., designs, makes, and sells athletic footwear, including a line of shoes known as "Air Force 1." Already, LLC, also designs and markets athletic footwear, including the "Sugar" and "Soulja Boy" lines. Nike filed a suit in a federal district court against Already, alleging that Soulja Boys and Sugars infringed the Air Force 1 trademark. Already filed a counterclaim, contending that the Air Force 1 trademark was invalid.

While the suit was pending, Nike issued a covenant not to sue, promising not to raise any trademark claims against Already based on Already's existing footwear designs or any future Already designs that constituted a "colorable imitation" of Already's current products. Nike then filed a motion to dismiss its own claims and to dismiss Already's counterclaim. Already opposed the dismissal of its counterclaim, but the court granted Nike's motion. The U.S. Court of Appeals for the Second Circuit affirmed. Already appealed to the United States Supreme Court.

ISSUE Did Nike's covenant not to sue Already over the Air Force 1 trademark prevent Already from suing to establish that Nike's trademark was invalid?

DECISION Yes. The United States Supreme Court affirmed the judgment of the lower courts. Under the covenant not to sue, Nike could

not file a trademark infringement claim against Already, and Already could not assert that Nike's trademark was invalid.

REASON The Supreme Court looked at the wording of the covenant not to sue to determine whether Already's counterclaim was *moot*. (A matter is moot if it involves no actual controversy for the court to decide, and federal courts will dismiss moot cases.) Nike had unconditionally and irrevocably promised not to assert any trademark infringement claims against Already relating to the mark used on any of Already's current footwear products and similar future designs. Under the covenant's broad language, the Court noted, "It is hard to imagine a scenario that would potentially infringe Nike's trademark and yet not fall under the covenant." Therefore, further litigation of the trademark dispute was unnecessary, and dismissal was proper.

CRITICAL THINKING—Economic Consideration *Why would any party agree to a covenant not to sue?*

12-2 Promissory Estoppel

Sometimes, individuals rely on promises, and their reliance may form a basis for a court to infer contract rights and duties. Under the doctrine of **promissory estoppel** (also called *detrimental reliance*), a person who has reasonably and substantially relied on the promise of another can obtain some measure of recovery. Promissory estoppel allows a party to recover on a promise even though it was made *without consideration*. Under this doctrine, a court may enforce an otherwise unenforceable promise to avoid an injustice that would otherwise result.

Promissory Estoppel
A doctrine that can be used to enforce a promise when the promisee has justifiably relied on the promise and when justice will be better served by enforcing the promise.

12-2a Requirements to Establish Promissory Estoppel

For the doctrine of promissory estoppel to be applied, the following elements are required:

1. There must be a clear and definite promise.
2. The promisor should have expected that the promisee would rely on the promise.
3. The promisee reasonably relied on the promise by acting or refraining from some act.
4. The promisee's reliance was definite and resulted in substantial detriment.
5. Enforcement of the promise is necessary to avoid injustice.

If these requirements are met, a promise may be enforced even though it is not supported by consideration. In essence, the promisor (the offeror) will be **estopped** (barred or prevented) from asserting lack of consideration as a defense.

Promissory estoppel is similar in some ways to the doctrine of quasi contract that was discussed in a previous chapter. In both situations, a court is acting in the interests of equity and imposes contract obligations on the parties to prevent unfairness even though no actual contract exists. The difference is that with quasi contract, no promise was made at all. In contrast, with promissory estoppel, an otherwise unenforceable promise was made and relied on.

LEARNING OBJECTIVE 2
In what circumstances might a promise be enforced despite a lack of consideration?

Estopped Barred, impeded, or precluded.

12–2b Application of Promissory Estoppel

Promissory estoppel was originally applied to situations involving gifts (I promise to pay you $1,000 a week so that you will not have to work) and donations to charities (I promise to contribute $50,000 a year to the All Saints orphanage). Later, courts began to apply the doctrine in other situations, including business transactions, employment relationships, and disputes among family members.

CASE EXAMPLE 12.9 Jeffrey and Kathryn Dow own 125 acres of land in Corinth, Maine. The Dows regarded the land as their children's heritage, and the subject of the children's living on the land was often discussed within the family.

With the Dows' permission, their daughter Teresa installed a mobile home and built a garage on the land. After Teresa married Jarrod Harvey, the Dows agreed to finance the construction of a house on the land for the couple. When Jarrod died in a motorcycle accident, however, Teresa financed the house with his life insurance proceeds. The construction cost about $200,000.

Teresa then asked her parents for a deed to the property so that she could obtain a mortgage. They refused. Teresa sued her parents based on promissory estoppel. Maine's highest court ruled in Teresa's favor. The court reasoned that the Dows' support and encouragement of their daughter's construction of a house on the land "conclusively demonstrated" their intent to transfer it. For years, they had made general promises to convey the land to their children, including Teresa. Teresa had reasonably relied on their promise in financing construction of the house to her detriment ($200,000). The court concluded that enforcing the promise was the only way to avoid injustice in this situation.[5] ■

When must a property owner transfer a deed to his or her child?

12–3 Contractual Capacity

Contractual capacity is the legal ability to enter into a contractual relationship. Courts generally presume the existence of contractual capacity, but in some situations, capacity is lacking or may be questionable. A person who has been determined by a court to be mentally incompetent, for instance, cannot form a legally binding contract. In other situations, a party may have the capacity to enter into a valid contract but may also have the right to avoid liability under it. For instance, minors—or *infants,* as they are commonly referred to in the law—usually are not legally bound by contracts.

In this section, we look at the effect of youth, intoxication, and mental incompetence on contractual capacity.

Contractual Capacity The capacity required by the law for a party who enters into a contract to be bound by that contract.

12–3a Minors

Today, in almost all states, the **age of majority** (when a person is no longer a minor) for contractual purposes is eighteen years.[6] In addition, some states provide for the termination of minority on marriage.

Minority status may also be terminated by a minor's **emancipation,** which occurs when a child's parent or legal guardian relinquishes the legal right to exercise control over the child. Normally, minors who leave home to support themselves are considered emancipated. Several jurisdictions permit minors to petition a court for emancipation. For business purposes, a minor may petition a court to be treated as an adult.

The general rule is that a minor can enter into any contract that an adult can, provided that the contract is not one prohibited by law for minors (such as a contract involving the sale of alcoholic beverages or tobacco products). A contract entered into by a minor, however, is

Age of Majority The age (eighteen in most states) at which a person, formerly a minor, is recognized by law as an adult and is legally responsible for his or her actions.

Emancipation In regard to minors, the act of being freed from parental control.

---

5. *Harvey v. Dow,* 2011 ME 4, 11 A.3d 303 (2011).
6. The age of majority may still be twenty-one for other purposes, such as the purchase and consumption of alcohol.

voidable at the option of that minor, subject to certain exceptions (to be discussed shortly). To exercise the option to avoid a contract, a minor need only manifest (clearly show) an intention not to be bound by it. The minor "avoids" the contract by disaffirming it.

Disaffirmance   The legal avoidance, or setting aside, of a contractual obligation is referred to as **disaffirmance.** To disaffirm, a minor must express, through words or conduct, his or her intent not to be bound to the contract. The minor must disaffirm the entire contract, not merely a portion of it. For instance, a minor cannot decide to keep part of the goods purchased under a contract and return the remaining goods.

CASE EXAMPLE 12.10 Fifteen-year-old Morgan Kelly was a cadet in her high school's Navy Junior Reserve Officer Training Corps. As part of the program, she visited the U.S. Marine Corps training facility at Camp Lejeune, North Carolina. To enter the camp, she was required to sign a waiver that exempted the Marines from liability for any injuries arising from her visit. While participating in activities on the camp's confidence-building course, Kelly fell from the "Slide for Life" and suffered serious injuries. She filed a suit to recover her medical costs. The Marines asserted that Kelly could not recover because she had signed the waiver of liability. The court ruled in Kelly's favor. Liability waivers are generally enforceable contracts, but a minor can avoid a contract by disaffirming it. In this case, Kelly disaffirmed the waiver when she filed her suit to recover for the cost of her injuries.[7] ■

Note that an adult who enters into a contract with a minor cannot avoid his or her contractual duties on the ground that the minor can do so. Unless the minor exercises the option to disaffirm the contract, the adult party normally is bound by it.

The question in the following case was whether a minor had effectively disaffirmed an agreement to arbitrate with her employer.

LEARNING OBJECTIVE 3

Does a minor have the capacity to enter into an enforceable contract? What does it mean to disaffirm a contract?

Disaffirmance The legal avoidance, or setting aside, of a contractual obligation.

---

7. *Kelly v. United States*, 809 F.Supp.2d 429 (E.D.N.C. 2011).

CASE 12.2

PAK Foods Houston, LLC v. Garcia
Court of Appeals of Texas, Houston (14th District), 433 S.W.3d 171 (2014).

FACTS S.L., a sixteen-year-old minor, worked at a KFC Restaurant operated by PAK Foods Houston, LLC. PAK Foods' policy was to resolve any dispute with an employee through arbitration. At the employer's request, S.L. signed an acknowledgement of this policy. S.L. was injured on the job and subsequently terminated her employment. S.L.'s mother, Marissa Garcia, filed a suit on S.L.'s behalf in a Texas state court against PAK Foods to recover the medical expenses for the injury. PAK Foods filed a motion to compel arbitration. The court denied the motion. "To the extent any agreement to arbitrate existed between S.L. and PAK Foods Houston, LLC, S.L. voided such agreement by filing this suit." PAK Foods appealed.

ISSUE Did S.L. disaffirm the agreement to arbitrate?

DECISION Yes. A state intermediate appellate court affirmed the decision of the lower court. A minor may disaffirm a contract at his or her option. S.L. opted to disaffirm the agreement to arbitrate.

REASON In Texas, the age of majority is eighteen years. S.L. was a sixteen-year-old minor when she signed the arbitration agreement,

When minors sign employment agreements with fast-food restaurants, how can they disaffirm those agreements?

iStockPhoto.com/zokara

and she was a minor throughout the time she was employed by PAK Foods. A contract entered into by a minor may be disaffirmed or ratified after the minor reaches the age of majority at his or her option. PAK Foods argued that S.L. had not signed an employment contract and had not notified PAK Foods that she was disaffirming the arbitration agreement. The appellate court held that "these distinctions do not alter the settled law that a minor may void a contract at her election." In response to PAK Foods's motion to compel arbitration, S.L. and her mother stated that "as S.L.'s disaffirmance of the Arbitration Agreement has manifestly occurred with her termination of employment and election to file suit, she cannot be bound by the terms of the Arbitration Agreement." This response was "a definitive disaffirmance of any agreement to arbitrate."

CRITICAL THINKING—Legal Consideration *Could PAK Foods successfully contend that S.L.'s minority does not bar enforcement of the arbitration agreement because medical expenses are necessaries? Discuss.*

Disaffirmance within a Reasonable Time. A contract can ordinarily be disaffirmed at any time during minority[8] or for a reasonable time after the minor reaches the age of majority. What constitutes a "reasonable" time may vary. If an individual fails to disaffirm an executed contract within a reasonable time after reaching the age of majority, a court will likely hold that the contract has been ratified (*ratification* will be discussed shortly).

A Minor's Obligations on Disaffirmance. All states' laws permit minors to disaffirm contracts (with certain exceptions), including executed contracts. However, state laws differ on the extent of a minor's obligations on disaffirmance.

Courts in most states hold that the minor need only return the goods (or other consideration) subject to the contract, provided the goods are in the minor's possession or control. Even if the minor returns damaged goods, the minor often is entitled to disaffirm the contract and obtain a refund of the purchase price.

A growing number of states place an additional duty on the minor to restore the adult party to the position she or he held before the contract was made. These courts may hold a minor responsible for damage, ordinary wear and tear, and depreciation of goods that the minor used prior to disaffirmance. **EXAMPLE 12.11** Sixteen-year-old Jay Dodd buys a truck for $5,900 from a used-car dealer. The truck develops mechanical problems nine months later, but Dodd continues to drive it until the engine blows up and the truck stops running. Dodd then disaffirms the contract and attempts to return the truck to the dealer for a refund of the full purchase price. In states that hold minors responsible for damage, Dodd can still disaffirm the contract, but he may only recover the depreciated value—not the purchase price—of the truck. ■

If a minor buys a pickup truck, doesn't maintain it such that the engine explodes, can that minor obtain a full-purchase-price refund?

Necessaries Necessities required for life, such as food, shelter, clothing, and medical attention.

Ratification The acceptance or confirmation of an act or agreement that gives legal force to an obligation that previously was not enforceable.

Exceptions to a Minor's Right to Disaffirm

State courts and legislatures have carved out several exceptions to the minor's right to disaffirm. Some contracts, such as marriage contracts and contracts to enlist in the armed services, cannot be avoided. These exceptions are made for reasons of public policy.

In addition, although ordinarily minors can disaffirm contracts even when they have misrepresented their age, a growing number of states have enacted laws to prohibit disaffirmance in such situations. Other states prohibit disaffirmance by minors who misrepresented their age while engaged in business as adults.

Finally, a minor who enters into a contract for necessaries may disaffirm the contract but remains liable for the reasonable value of the goods. **Necessaries** include whatever is reasonably needed to maintain the minor's standard of living. In general, food, clothing, shelter, and medical services are necessaries. What is a necessary for one minor, however, may be a luxury for another, depending on the minors' customary living standard.

Ratification

In contract law, **ratification** is the act of accepting and giving legal force to an obligation that previously was not enforceable. A minor who has reached the age of majority can ratify a contract expressly or impliedly. *Express* ratification occurs when the individual, on reaching the age of majority, states orally or in writing that she or he intends to be bound by the contract. *Implied* ratification takes place when the minor, on reaching the age of majority, behaves in a manner inconsistent with disaffirmance.

EXAMPLE 12.12 Lin enters into a contract to sell her laptop to Andrew, a minor. Andrew does not disaffirm the contract. If, on reaching the age of majority, he writes a letter to Lin stating that he still agrees to buy the laptop, he has expressly ratified the contract. If, instead, Andrew takes possession of the laptop as a minor and continues to use it well after reaching the age of majority, he has impliedly ratified the contract. ■

If a minor fails to disaffirm a contract within a reasonable time after reaching the age of majority, then a court must determine whether the conduct constitutes implied ratification or

---

8. In some states, however, a minor who enters into a contract for the sale of land cannot disaffirm the contract until she or he reaches the age of majority.

disaffirmance. Generally, courts presume that executed contracts (fully performed) are ratified and that executor contracts (not yet fully performed by both parties) are disaffirmed.

Parents' Liability As a general rule, parents are not liable for the contracts made by minor children acting on their own, except contracts for necessaries, which the parents are legally required to provide. This is why businesses ordinarily require parents to cosign any contract made with a minor. The parents then become personally obligated to perform the conditions of the contract, even if their child avoids liability.

12–3b Intoxicated Persons

Intoxication is a condition in which a person's normal capacity to act or think is inhibited by alcohol or some other drug. A contract entered into by an intoxicated person can be either voidable or valid (and thus enforceable). If the person was sufficiently intoxicated to lack mental capacity, then the transaction may be voidable at the option of the intoxicated person, even if the intoxication was purely voluntary. If, despite intoxication, the person understood the legal consequences of the agreement, the contract is enforceable.

Courts look at objective indications of the intoxicated person's condition to determine if he or she possessed or lacked the required capacity. It is difficult to prove that a person's judgment was so severely impaired that he or she could not comprehend the legal consequences of entering into a contract. Therefore, courts rarely permit contracts to be avoided due to intoxication.

12–3c Mentally Incompetent Persons

Contracts made by mentally incompetent persons can be void, voidable, or valid. If a court has previously determined that a person is mentally incompetent and has appointed a guardian to represent the person, any contract made by that person is *void*—no contract exists. Only the guardian can enter into a binding contract on behalf of the mentally incompetent person.

If a court has not previously judged a person to be mentally incompetent but the person was incompetent at the time the contract was formed, the contract is *voidable* in most states. A contract is voidable if the person did not know that he or she was entering into the contract or lacked the mental capacity to comprehend its nature, purpose, and consequences. In such situations, the contract is voidable (or can be ratified) at the option of the mentally incompetent person but not at the option of the other party.

EXAMPLE 12.13 Larry agrees to sell his stock in Google, Inc., to Sergey for substantially less than its market value. At the time of the deal, Larry is confused about the purpose and details of the transaction, but he has not been declared incompetent. Nonetheless, if a court finds that Larry did not understand the nature and consequences of the contract due to a lack of mental capacity, he can avoid the sale. ■

A contract entered into by a mentally ill person (whom a court has not previously declared incompetent) may also be *valid* if the person had capacity *at the time the contract was formed*. Some people who are incompetent due to age or illness have *lucid intervals*—temporary periods of sufficient intelligence, judgment, and will. During such intervals, they will be considered to have legal capacity to enter into contracts in the majority of states.

12–4 Legality

Legality is the fourth requirement for a valid contract to exist. For a contract to be valid and enforceable, it must be formed for a legal purpose. A contract to do something that is prohibited by federal or state statutory law is illegal and, as such, is void from the outset and thus unenforceable. Additionally, a contract to commit a tortious act (such as engage in fraudulent misrepresentation) or to commit an action that is contrary to public policy is illegal and unenforceable.

12–4a Contracts Contrary to Statute

Statutes often prescribe the terms of contracts. Some statutes set forth rules specifying which terms and clauses may be included in certain contracts and which are prohibited. Others prohibit certain contracts on the basis of their subject matter, the status of the contracting parties, or other factors. Next, we examine several ways in which contracts may be contrary to statute.

Contracts to Commit a Crime Any contract to commit a crime is in violation of a statute. Thus, a contract to sell illegal drugs in violation of criminal laws is unenforceable, as is a contract to hide a corporation's violation of the Dodd-Frank Wall Street Reform and Consumer Protection Act. Similarly, a contract to smuggle undocumented workers from another country into the United States for an employer is illegal, as is a contract to dump hazardous waste in violation of environmental laws.

Sometimes, the object or performance of a contract is rendered illegal by statute *after* the contract has been formed. In that situation, the contract is considered discharged (terminated) by law.

Usury Almost every state has a statute that sets the maximum rate of interest that can be charged for different types of transactions, including ordinary loans. A lender who makes a loan at an interest rate above the lawful maximum commits **usury.**

Usury Charging an illegal rate of interest.

Although usurious contracts are illegal, most states simply limit the interest that the lender may collect on the contract to the lawful maximum interest rate in that state. In a few states, the lender can recover the principal amount of the loan but no interest. In addition, states can make exceptions to facilitate business transactions. For instance, many states exempt corporate loans from the usury laws, and nearly all states allow higher interest rate loans for borrowers who could not otherwise obtain loans.

Gambling Gambling is the creation of risk for the purpose of assuming it. Traditionally, the states have deemed gambling contracts illegal and thus void. Today, many states allow (and regulate) certain forms of gambling, such as horse racing, video poker machines, and charity-sponsored bingo. In addition, nearly all states allow state-operated lotteries and gambling on Native American reservations. Even in states that permit certain types of gambling, though, courts often find that gambling contracts are illegal.

CASE EXAMPLE 12.14 Video poker machines are legal in Louisiana, but their use requires the approval of the state video gaming commission. Gaming Venture, Inc., did not obtain this approval before agreeing with Tastee Restaurant Corporation to install poker machines in some of its restaurants. For this reason, when Tastee allegedly reneged on the deal by refusing to install poker machines, a state court held that their agreement was an illegal gambling contract and therefore void.[9] ▪

Licensing Statutes All states require members of certain professions—including physicians, lawyers, real estate brokers, accountants, architects, electricians, and stockbrokers—to have licenses. Some licenses are obtained only after extensive schooling and examinations, which indicate to the public that a special skill has been acquired. Others require only that the person obtaining the license be of good moral character and pay a fee.

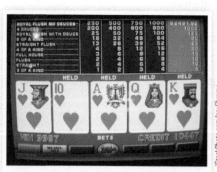

Can any video poker vending machine distributor install such machines without a permit?

iStockPhoto.com/spxChrome

---

9. *Gaming Venture, Inc. v. Tastee Restaurant Corp.,* 996 So.2d 515 (La.App. 5 Cir. 2008).

Whether a contract with an unlicensed person is legal and enforceable depends on the purpose of the licensing statute. If the statute's purpose is to protect the public from unauthorized practitioners, then a contract involving an unlicensed practitioner generally is illegal and unenforceable. If the purpose is merely to raise government revenues, however, a contract with an unlicensed person may be enforced (and the unlicensed practitioner fined).

CASE EXAMPLE 12.15 The United Arab Emirates (UAE) held a competition for the design of a new embassy in Washington, D.C. Elena Sturdza—an architect licensed in Maryland but not in the District of Columbia—won. Sturdza and the UAE exchanged proposals, but the UAE stopped communicating with her before the parties had signed a contract. Later, Sturdza learned that the UAE had contracted with a District of Columbia architect to use another design. She filed a suit against the UAE for breach of contract.

Sturdza argued that the licensing statute should not apply to architects who submit plans in international architectural design competitions. The court held, however, that licensing requirements are necessary to ensure the safety of those who work in and visit buildings in the District of Columbia, as well as the safety of neighboring buildings. Because Sturdza was not a licensed architect in the District of Columbia, she could not recover on a contract to perform architectural services there.[10]

12-4b Contracts Contrary to Public Policy

Although contracts involve private parties, some are not enforceable because of the negative impact they would have on society. These contracts are said to be *contrary to public policy*. Examples include a contract to commit an immoral act, such as selling a child, and a contract that prohibits marriage (such as a contract to pay someone not to marry one's daughter). Business contracts that may be contrary to public policy include contracts in restraint of trade and unconscionable contracts or clauses.

Contracts in Restraint of Trade The United States has a strong public policy favoring competition in the economy. Thus, contracts in restraint of trade (anticompetitive agreements) generally are unenforceable because they are contrary to public policy. Typically, such contracts also violate one or more federal or state antitrust laws.

An exception is recognized when the restraint is reasonable and is an ancillary (secondary, or subordinate) part of the contract. Such restraints often are included in contracts for the sale of an ongoing business and employment contracts.

Covenants Not to Compete and the Sale of an Ongoing Business. Many contracts involve a type of restraint called a **covenant not to compete,** or a restrictive covenant (promise). A covenant not to compete may be created when a merchant who sells a store agrees not to open a new store in a certain geographic area surrounding the old store. Such an agreement enables the seller to sell, and the purchaser to buy, the goodwill and reputation of an ongoing business without having to worry that the seller will open a competing business a block away. Provided the restrictive covenant is reasonable and is an ancillary part of the sale of an ongoing business, it is enforceable.

Covenants Not to Compete in Employment Contracts. Sometimes, agreements not to compete are included in **employment contracts.** People in middle-level and upper-level management positions commonly agree not to work for competitors and not to start a competing business for a specified period of time after terminating employment.

Such agreements are generally legal in most states so long as the specified period of time (of restraint) is not excessive in duration and the geographic restriction is reasonable. To be reasonable, a restriction on competition must protect a legitimate business interest and must

LEARNING OBJECTIVE 4
Under what circumstances will a covenant not to compete be enforced? When will such covenants not be enforced?

Covenant Not to Compete A contractual promise of one party to refrain from conducting business similar to that of another party for a certain period of time and within a specified geographical area.

Employment Contract A contract between an employer and an employee in which the terms and conditions of employment are stated.

---

10. *Sturdza v. United Arab Emirates,* 11 A.3d 251 (D.C.App. 2011).

not be any greater than necessary to protect that interest. What constitutes a reasonable time period may be different in the online environment than in conventional employment contracts. Because the geographical restrictions apply worldwide, the time restrictions may be shorter.

CASE EXAMPLE 12.16 An insurance firm in New York City, Brown & Brown, Inc., hired Theresa Johnson to perform actuarial analysis. On her first day of work, Johnson was asked to sign a nonsolicitation covenant, which prohibited her from soliciting or servicing any of Brown's clients for two years after the termination of her employment. Less than five years later, when Johnson's employment with Brown was terminated, she went to work for Lawley Benefits Group, LLC. Brown sued to enforce the covenant. A state appellate court ruled that the covenant was overly broad and unenforceable because it attempted to restrict Johnson from working for any of Brown's clients, without regard to whether she had had a relationship with those clients.[11]

ETHICAL ISSUE

Are expansive noncompete agreements reducing worker mobility? You would probably expect workers to be asked to sign noncompete agreements that prevented them from, say, taking proprietary software code to a competitor. But would you expect a sandwich chain to require a worker to sign a noncompete agreement related to sandwich making? In the past, such agreements would not have been upheld in court. Today, they increasingly are. James Bessen, a writer for *The Atlantic,* estimates that the number of lawsuits over noncompete agreements and trade secrets has nearly tripled since 2000.

Employees in high-tech firms seem to be the most affected. They often sign noncompete agreements that "freeze" them out of their industry for two years after they leave a high-tech employer, forcing them to seek jobs in other industries where they cannot use key skills and knowledge. The result is that noncompete agreements tend to limit job opportunities for highly skilled workers. In other words, job mobility may be suffering from overly expansive noncompete agreements.

Enforcement Problems. The laws governing the enforceability of covenants not to compete vary significantly from state to state. California prohibits the enforcement of all covenants not to compete. In some states, such as Texas, such a covenant will not be enforced unless the employee has received some benefit in return for signing the noncompete agreement. This is true even if the covenant is reasonable as to time and area. If the employee receives no benefit, the covenant will be deemed void.

Reformation. Occasionally, depending on the jurisdiction, courts will *reform* covenants not to compete. If a covenant is found to be unreasonable in time or geographic area, the court may convert the terms into reasonable ones and then enforce the reformed covenant. This presents a problem, however, in that the judge has implicitly become a party to the contract. Consequently, courts usually resort to contract **reformation** only when necessary to prevent undue burdens or hardships.

Reformation A court-ordered correction of a written contract so that it reflects the true intentions of the parties.

PREVENTING LEGAL DISPUTES

A business clearly has a legitimate interest in having employees sign covenants not to compete and in preventing them from using the valuable skills and training provided by the business for the benefit of a competitor. The problem is that these covenants frequently lead to litigation. Moreover, it is difficult to predict what a court will consider reasonable in a given situation. Therefore, you need to be aware of the difficulties in enforcing noncompete agreements. Seek the advice of counsel in the relevant jurisdiction when drafting covenants not to compete. Avoid overreaching in terms of time and geographic restrictions, particularly if you are the manager of a high-tech or Web-based company. Consider using

---

11. *Brown & Brown, Inc. v. Johnson,* 980 N.Y.S.2d 631 (2014).

noncompete clauses only for key employees and, if necessary, offer them some compensation (consideration) for signing the agreement. If an employee signed a noncompete clause when he or she was hired, be sure to discuss the meaning of that clause and your expectations with the employee at the time of termination.

Unconscionable Contracts or Clauses

Ordinarily, a court does not look at the fairness or equity of a contract, or, as discussed earlier, inquire into the adequacy of consideration. Persons are assumed to be reasonably intelligent, and the courts will not come to their aid just because they have made unwise or foolish bargains.

In certain circumstances, however, bargains are so oppressive that the courts relieve innocent parties of part or all of their duties. Such bargains are deemed **unconscionable**[12] because they are so unscrupulous or grossly unfair as to be "void of conscience."

The Uniform Commercial Code (UCC) incorporates the concept of unconscionability in its provisions with regard to the sale and lease of goods.[13] A contract can be unconscionable on either procedural or substantive grounds, as discussed in the following subsections and illustrated graphically in Exhibit 12–1.

Procedural Unconscionability. Procedural unconscionability often involves inconspicuous print, unintelligible language ("legalese"), or the lack of an opportunity to read the contract or ask questions about its meaning. This type of unconscionability typically arises when a party's lack of knowledge or understanding of the contract terms deprive him or her of any meaningful choice.

Procedural unconscionability can also occur when there is such a disparity in bargaining power between the two parties that the weaker party's consent is not voluntary. This type of situation often involves an **adhesion contract,** which is a standard-form contract written

> **Unconscionable (Contract or Clause)** A contract or clause that is void on the basis of public policy because one party was forced to accept terms that are unfairly burdensome and that unfairly benefit the other party.

> **Adhesion Contract** A standard-form contract in which the stronger party dictates the terms.

---

12. Pronounced un-*kon*-shun-uh-bul.
13. See UCC 2–302 and 2–719.

Exhibit 12–1 Unconscionability

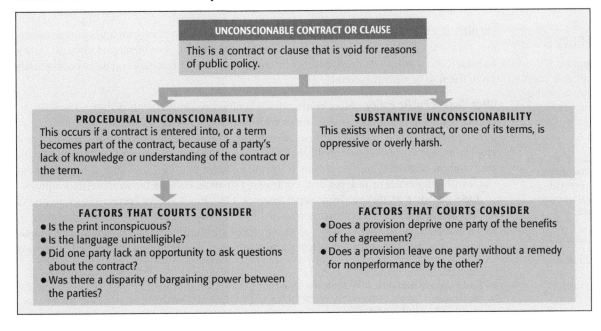

| UNCONSCIONABLE CONTRACT OR CLAUSE |
| This is a contract or clause that is void for reasons of public policy. |

PROCEDURAL UNCONSCIONABILITY
This occurs if a contract is entered into, or a term becomes part of the contract, because of a party's lack of knowledge or understanding of the contract or the term.

SUBSTANTIVE UNCONSCIONABILITY
This exists when a contract, or one of its terms, is oppressive or overly harsh.

FACTORS THAT COURTS CONSIDER
- Is the print inconspicuous?
- Is the language unintelligible?
- Did one party lack an opportunity to ask questions about the contract?
- Was there a disparity of bargaining power between the parties?

FACTORS THAT COURTS CONSIDER
- Does a provision deprive one party of the benefits of the agreement?
- Does a provision leave one party without a remedy for nonperformance by the other?

exclusively by one party (the dominant party) and presented to the other (the adhering party) on a take-it-or-leave-it basis. In other words, the adhering party (usually a buyer or borrower) has no opportunity to negotiate the terms of the contract. Not all adhesion contracts are unconscionable, only those that unreasonably favor the drafter.

CASE EXAMPLE 12.17 Roberto Basulto and Raquel Gonzalez responded to an ad they saw on Spanish-language television sponsored by Potamkin Dodge. Because the two men did not speak or read English, which Potamkin's staff knew, the deal was transacted in Spanish. Potamkin's staff explained the English-language purchase contract, but did not explain an accompanying arbitration agreement, which limited the buyers' damages but did not limit the dealer's damages. Basulto and Gonzalez signed the contract to buy a Dodge Caravan but did not fill in all of the blanks on the form.

A dispute arose when Potamkin later filled in a lower trade-in allowance than the parties had agreed to and refused to change it. The buyers returned the van—having driven it a total of seven miles—and asked for a return of their trade-in vehicle, but it had been sold. The buyers sued Potamkin, which sought arbitration. The court refused to enforce the arbitration agreement on the ground that it was unconscionable. The agreement was written in English and was not explained to the buyers in any language. The buyers therefore had not been given a meaningful opportunity to understand the bargain.[14] ■

Substantive Unconscionability. Substantive unconscionability occurs when contracts, or portions of contracts, are oppressive or overly harsh. Courts generally focus on provisions that deprive one party of the benefits of the agreement or leave that party without remedy for nonperformance by the other.

In *Case Example 12.17,* the court held that the contract was substantively, as well as procedurally, unconscionable. The contract was substantively unconscionable because the buyers were limited to seeking damages of $5,000 or less from the dealer, while the dealer could seek a higher amount of damages.

Substantive unconscionability can arise in a wide variety of business contexts. For instance, a contract clause that gives the business entity unrestricted access to the courts but requires the other party to arbitrate any dispute with the firm may be unconscionable. Similarly, contracts drafted by cell phone providers and insurance companies have been struck down as substantively unconscionable when they included provisions that were overly harsh or one sided.[15]

LEARNING OBJECTIVE 5

What is an exculpatory clause? In what circumstances might exculpatory clauses be enforced? When will they not be enforced?

Exculpatory Clauses Often closely related to the concept of unconscionability are **exculpatory clauses,** which release a party from liability in the event of monetary or physical injury, *no matter who is at fault.* Indeed, courts sometimes refuse to enforce such clauses because they deem them to be unconscionable.

Exculpatory Clause A clause that releases a contractual party from liability in the event of monetary or physical injury, no matter who is at fault.

Often Violate Public Policy. Most courts view exculpatory clauses with disfavor. Exculpatory clauses found in rental agreements for commercial property are frequently held to be contrary to public policy, and such clauses are almost always unenforceable in residential property leases. Courts also usually hold that exculpatory clauses are against public policy in the employment context. Thus, employers frequently cannot enforce exculpatory clauses in contracts with employees or independent contractors to avoid liability for work-related injuries.

CASE EXAMPLE 12.18 Speedway SuperAmerica, LLC, hired Sebert Erwin to work in one of its convenience stores. The company required Erwin, who had an eighth-grade education, to sign a contract stating that he was not an employee and had no right to workers' compensation. The contract also included a clause under which Erwin promised not to hold Speedway

---

14. *Basulto v. Hialeah Automotive,* 141 So.3d 1145 (Fla. 2014).

15. See, for example, *Gatton v. T-Mobile USA, Inc.,* 152 Cal.App.4th 571, 61 Cal.Rptr.3d 344 (2007); and *Aul v. Golden Rule Insurance Co.,* 2007 WL 1695243 (Wis.App. 2007).

liable for anything that happened to him while working for the company. When Erwin was later injured on the job and sued Speedway for damages, the court held that the exculpatory clause was invalid because it was against public policy.[16] ▣

When Courts Will Enforce Exculpatory Clauses. Courts do enforce exculpatory clauses if they are reasonable, do not violate public policy, and do not protect parties from liability for intentional misconduct. The language used must not be ambiguous, and the parties must have been in relatively equal bargaining positions. See this chapter's *Managerial Strategy* feature for suggestions on drafting exculpatory clauses that will not be considered unconscionable.

Businesses such as health clubs, racetracks, amusement parks, skiing facilities, horse-rental operations, golf-cart concessions, and skydiving organizations frequently use exculpatory clauses to limit their liability for patrons' injuries. Because these services are not essential, the firms offering them are sometimes considered to have no relative advantage in bargaining strength, and anyone contracting for their services is considered to do so voluntarily. Courts also may enforce reasonable exculpatory clauses in loan documents, real estate contracts, and trust agreements.

In the following case, the court considered whether an exculpatory clause that released "any Event sponsors and their agents and employees" from liability for future negligence was ambiguous.

Can a convenience store company require its employees to sign contracts that state that those employees have no rights to workers' compensation?

---

16. *Speedway SuperAmerica, LLC v. Erwin*, 250 S.W.3d 339 (Ky. 2008).

CASE 12.3

Holmes v. Multimedia KSDK, Inc.

Missouri Court of Appeals, Eastern District, Division 2, 395 S.W.3d 557 (2013).

FACTS Colleen Holmes signed an entry form for the Susan G. Komen Race for the Cure to be held in June 2009 in St. Louis, Missouri. The form included a "RACE WAIVER AND RELEASE" clause under which Holmes agreed to release "any Event sponsors and their agents and employees . . . for any injury or damages" that Holmes might suffer in connection with her participation in the race. Among other causes, the release applied to injury or damages caused by "negligence of the [sponsors]."

Multimedia KSDK, Inc., was one of the race sponsors and also broadcasted the race. During the event, Holmes was injured when she tripped and fell over a Multimedia audiovisual box. Multimedia employees had placed the box on the ground without barricades or warnings of its presence. Holmes filed a suit in a Missouri state court against Multimedia, alleging negligence. The court entered a judgment in Multimedia's favor, and Holmes appealed.

ISSUE Did the exculpatory clause that Holmes signed clearly release Multimedia from liability for negligence?

DECISION Yes. The state intermediate appellate court affirmed the lower court's judgment in favor of Multimedia.

Is a waiver of negligence liability that appears on an entry form for a foot race enforceable?

REASON The appellate court held that the language used in the exculpatory clause clearly released all sponsors and their agents and employees without exclusion from liability for future negligence. The reviewing court was not persuaded by Holmes's argument that the language in the release was ambiguous "because it did not specifically name the individuals and entities released."

Further, "a release that releases claims against 'any and all persons' is unambiguous and enforceable . . . and it is not necessary that the release identify those persons by name or otherwise." The reviewing court noted that while public policy disfavors releases from liability for future negligence, it does not prohibit them. All that is necessary is "there must be no doubt that a reasonable person agreeing to an exculpatory clause actually understands what future claims he or she is waiving." Such was the situation here.

CRICITAL THINKING—Social Consideration *At the time Holmes signed the release, Multimedia had not yet become a sponsor of the event. Should this fact have rendered the clause unenforceable? Explain.*

Creating Liability Waivers That Are Not Unconscionable

Management Faces a Legal Issue

Blanket liability waivers that absolve a business from virtually every event, even those caused by the business's own negligence, are usually unenforceable because they are unconscionable. Exculpatory waivers are common, nonetheless. We observe such waivers in gym memberships, on ski lift tickets, on admissions tickets to sporting events, and in simple contracts for the use of campgrounds.

Typically, courts view liability waivers as voluntarily bargained for whether or not they have been read. Thus, a waiver included in the fine print on the back of an admission ticket or on an entry sign to a stadium may be upheld. In general, if such waivers are unambiguous and conspicuous, the assumption is that patrons have had a chance to read them and have accepted their terms.

What the Courts Say

Cases challenging liability waivers have been brought against sky diving operations, skiing operations, bobsledding operations, white-water rafting companies, and health clubs. For example, in *Bergin v. Wild Mountain, Inc.,*[a] an appellate court in Minnesota upheld a ski resort's liability waiver. In that case, the plaintiff hit a snowmaking mound, which was "an inherent risk of skiing." Before the accident, the plaintiff had stated that he knew "that an inherent risk of serious injury in downhill skiing was hitting snowmaking mounds." Furthermore, he had not rejected the season pass that contained the resort's exculpatory clause. Thus, the ski resort prevailed.

While most liability waivers have survived legal challenges, some have not. In *Bagley v. Mt. Bachelor, Inc.,*[b] the Supreme Court of Oregon ruled against a ski resort's "very broad" liability waiver. The case involved an 18-year-old, Myles Bagley, who was paralyzed from the waist down after a snowboarding accident at Mt. Bachelor ski resort. The season pass that Bagley signed included a liability waiver. The waiver stated that the signer agreed not to sue the resort for injury even if "caused by negligence."

Bagley argued that the resort had created a dangerous condition because of the way it had set up a particular ski jump. He sued for $21.5 million and eventually won the right to go forward with his lawsuit. The Oregon Supreme Court found that, for various reasons, enforcement of the release would have been unconscionable. "Because the release is unenforceable, genuine issues of fact exist that preclude summary judgment in defendant's favor."

MANAGERIAL IMPLICATIONS

Whether you manage a campground, a ski resort, a white-water rafting company, or any other enterprise that caters to those engaged in physical activity, you should make sure that any explicit liability waivers are not overly broad. That is, the waivers should not attempt to remove all liability for damages to the signing parties. For instance, waivers should not attempt to cover malicious or intentional acts by the company or its employees.

a. 2014 WL 996788 (Minn.App. 2014).
b. 356 Or. 543, 340 P.3d 27 (Or. Sup.Ct. 2014).

12–5 The Effect of Illegality

In general, an illegal contract is void—that is, the contract is deemed never to have existed, and the courts will not aid either party. In most illegal contracts, both parties are considered to be equally at fault—*in pari delicto.*[17] If the contract is executory (not yet fulfilled), neither party can enforce it. If it has been executed, neither party can recover damages.

The courts usually are not concerned if one wrongdoer in an illegal contract is unjustly enriched at the expense of the other. The main reason for this hands-off attitude is a belief that a plaintiff who has broken the law by entering into an illegal bargain should not be allowed to obtain help from the courts. Another justification is the hoped-for deterrent effect: a plaintiff who suffers a loss because of an illegal bargain will presumably be deterred from entering into similar illegal bargains in the future.

There are exceptions to the general rule that neither party to an illegal bargain can sue for breach and neither party can recover for performance rendered. We look at these exceptions here.

---

17. Pronounced in-*pah*-ree deh-*lick*-tow.

12-5a Justifiable Ignorance of the Facts

Sometimes, one of the parties to a contract has no reason to know that the contract is illegal and thus is relatively innocent. That party can often recover any benefits conferred in a partially executed contract. The courts will not enforce the contract but will allow the parties to return to their original positions.

A court may sometimes permit an innocent party who has fully performed under a contract to enforce the contract against the guilty party. **EXAMPLE 12.19** A trucking company contracts with Gillespie to carry crates filled with goods to a specific destination for a normal fee of $5,000. The trucker delivers the crates and later finds out that they contained illegal goods. Although the shipment, use, and sale of the goods are illegal under the law, the trucker, being an innocent party, can normally still legally collect the $5,000 from Gillespie. ■

12-5b Members of Protected Classes

When a statute is clearly designed to protect a certain class of people, a member of that class can enforce a contract in violation of the statute even though the other party cannot. **EXAMPLE 12.20** Statutes prohibit certain employees (such as flight attendants or pilots) from working more than a specified number of hours per month. An employee who is required to work more than the maximum can recover for those extra hours of service. ■

Other examples of statutes designed to protect a particular class of people are state statutes that regulate the sale of insurance. If an insurance company violates a statute when selling insurance, the purchaser can still enforce the policy and recover from the insurer.

12-5c Withdrawal from an Illegal Agreement

If the illegal part of a bargain has not yet been performed, the party rendering performance can withdraw from the contract and recover the performance or its value. **EXAMPLE 12.21** Marta and Andy decide to wager (illegally) on the outcome of a boxing match. Each deposits $1,000 with a stakeholder, who agrees to pay the winner of the bet. At this point, each party has performed part of the agreement. Before payment occurs, either party is entitled to withdraw from the agreement by giving notice to the stakeholder of his or her withdrawal. ■

12-5d Severable, or Divisible, Contracts

A contract that is *severable,* or divisible, consists of distinct parts that can be performed separately, with separate consideration provided for each part. With an *indivisible* contract, in contrast, complete performance by each party is essential, even if the contract contains a number of seemingly separate provisions.

If a contract is divisible into legal and illegal portions, a court may enforce the legal portion but not the illegal one, so long as the illegal portion does not affect the essence of the bargain. This approach is consistent with the basic policy of enforcing the legal intentions of the contracting parties whenever possible.

EXAMPLE 12.22 Cole signs an employment contract that is valid but includes an overly broad and thus illegal covenant not to compete. In that situation, a court might find the employment contract enforceable but reform the unreasonably broad covenant by converting its terms into reasonable ones. Alternatively, the court could declare the covenant illegal (and thus void) and enforce the remaining employment terms. ■

When two persons place an illegal bet on the outcome of a boxing match, can either withdraw from the wager?

12-5e Fraud, Duress, or Undue Influence

Often, one party to an illegal contract is more at fault than the other. When one party uses fraud, duress, or undue influence to induce the other party to enter into an agreement, the second party will be allowed to recover for the performance or its value.

Reviewing . . . Consideration, Capacity, and Legality

Renee Beaver started racing go-karts competitively in 2015, when she was fourteen. Many of the races required her to sign an exculpatory clause to participate. She or her parents regularly signed such clauses. In 2017, right before her birthday, Renee participated in the annual Elkhart Grand Prix, a series of races in Elkhart, Indiana. During the event in which she drove, a piece of foam padding used as a course barrier was torn from its base and ended up on the track. A portion of the padding struck Beaver in the head, and another portion was thrown into oncoming traffic, causing a multikart collision during which she sustained severe injuries. Beaver filed an action against the race organizers for negligence. The organizers could not locate the exculpatory clause that Beaver had supposedly signed. Race organizers argued that she must have signed one to enter the race, but even if she had not signed one, her actions showed her intent to be bound by its terms. Using the information presented in the chapter, answer the following questions.

1. Did Beaver have the contractual capacity to enter into a contract with an exculpatory clause? Why or why not?

2. Assuming that Beaver did, in fact, sign the exculpatory clause, did she later disaffirm or ratify the contract? Explain.

3. Now assume that Beaver had stated that she was eighteen years old at the time she signed the exculpatory clause. How might this affect her ability to disaffirm or ratify the contract?

4. Suppose Beaver can prove that she did not actually sign an exculpatory clause and this fact convinces race organizers to pursue a settlement. They offer to pay Beaver one-half of the amount that she is claiming in damages if she now signs a release of all claims. Because Beaver is young and the full effect of her injuries may not yet be clear, what other type of settlement agreement might she prefer? What is the consideration to support any settlement agreement that Beaver enters into with the race organizers?

DEBATE THIS

- After agreeing to an exculpatory clause or purchasing some item, minors often seek to avoid the contracts. Today's minors are far from naïve and should not be allowed to avoid their contractual obligations.

Key Terms

Chapter Summary: Consideration, Capacity, and Legality

Consideration	1. *Elements of consideration*—
	  a. Something of *legally sufficient value* must be given in exchange for a promise.
	  b. There must be a bargained-for exchange.
	2. *Legal sufficiency and adequacy of consideration*—Legal sufficiency means that something of legal value must be given in exchange for a promise. Adequacy relates to "how much" consideration is given and whether a fair bargain was reached. Courts will inquire into the adequacy of consideration only when fraud, undue influence, duress, or unconscionability may be involved.
	3. *Contracts that lack consideration*—Consideration is lacking in the following situations:
	  a. Preexisting duty—A promise to do what one already has a legal duty to do is not legally sufficient consideration for a new contract.
	  b. Past consideration—Actions or events that have already taken place do not constitute legally sufficient consideration.
	  c. Illusory promises—When the nature or extent of performance is too uncertain, the promise is rendered illusory (without consideration and unenforceable).
	4. *Settlement of claims*—Disputes may be settled by the following, which are enforceable provided there is consideration:
	  a. Accord and satisfaction—An *accord* is an agreement in which a debtor offers to pay a lesser amount than the creditor claims is owed. *Satisfaction* takes place when the accord is executed.
	  b. Release—An agreement in which, for consideration, a party forfeits the right to seek further recovery beyond the terms specified in the release.
	  c. Covenant not to sue—An agreement not to sue on a present, valid claim.

Promissory Estoppel	The equitable doctrine of promissory estoppel applies when a promisor should have expected a promise to induce definite and substantial action or forbearance by the promisee, and the promisee does act in reliance on the promise. Such a promise is binding, even though there is no consideration, if injustice can be avoided only by enforcement of the promise. Also known as the doctrine of *detrimental reliance*.

CONTRACTUAL CAPACITY

Minors	1. *General rule*—Contracts with minors are voidable at the option of the minor.
	2. *Disaffirmance*—The legal avoidance of a contractual obligation.
	  a. Disaffirmance can take place (in most states) at any time during minority and within a reasonable time after the minor has reached the age of majority.
	  b. The minor must disaffirm the entire contract, not just part of it.
	  c. When disaffirming executed contracts, the minor has a duty to return the received goods if they are still in the minor's control or (in some states) to pay their reasonable value.
	  d. A minor who has misrepresented her or his age will be denied the right to disaffirm by some courts.
	  e. A minor may disaffirm a contract for necessaries but remains liable for the reasonable value of the goods.
	3. *Ratification*—The acceptance, or affirmation, of a legal obligation.
	  a. Express ratification—Occurs when the minor, in writing or orally, explicitly assumes the obligations imposed by the contract.
	  b. Implied ratification—Occurs when the conduct of the minor is inconsistent with disaffirmance or when the minor fails to disaffirm an executed contract within a reasonable time after reaching the age of majority.
	4. *Parents' liability*—Generally, except for contracts for necessaries, parents are not liable for the contracts made by minor children acting on their own.
	5. *Emancipation*—Occurs when a child's parent or legal guardian relinquishes the legal right to exercise control over the child. Normally, minors who leave home to support themselves are considered emancipated. In some jurisdictions, minors are permitted to petition a court for emancipation.

Intoxicated Persons	1. A contract entered into by an intoxicated person is voidable at the option of the intoxicated person if the person was sufficiently intoxicated to lack mental capacity, even if the intoxication was voluntary. 2. A contract with an intoxicated person is enforceable if, despite being intoxicated, the person understood the legal consequences of entering into the contract.
Mentally Incompetent Persons	1. A contract made by a person previously judged by a court to be mentally incompetent is void. 2. A contract made by a person who is mentally incompetent, but has not been previously declared incompetent by a court, is voidable at the option of that person.

Continues

LEGALITY

Contracts Contrary to Statute	1. *Usury*—Usury occurs when a lender makes a loan at an interest rate above the lawful maximum, which varies from state to state. 2. *Gambling*—Gambling contracts that violate state statutes are deemed illegal and thus void. 3. *Licensing statutes*—Contracts entered into by persons who do not have a license, when one is required by statute, will not be enforceable unless the underlying purpose of the statute is to raise government revenues (and not to protect the public from unauthorized practitioners).
Contracts Contrary to Public Policy	1. *Contracts in restraint of trade*—Contracts to restrain free competition are illegal and prohibited by statutes. An exception is a *covenant not to compete*. Such covenants usually are enforced by the courts if the terms are secondary to a contract (such as a contract for the sale of a business or an employment contract) and are reasonable as to time and area of restraint. Courts tend to scrutinize covenants not to compete closely and, at times, may reform them if they are overly broad rather than declaring the entire covenant unenforceable. 2. *Unconscionable contracts and clauses*—When a contract or contract clause is so unfair that it is oppressive to one party, it may be deemed unconscionable. As such, it is illegal and cannot be enforced. 3. *Exculpatory clauses*—An exculpatory clause releases a party from liability in the event of monetary or physical injury, no matter who is at fault. In certain situations, exculpatory clauses may be contrary to public policy and thus unenforceable.

EFFECT OF ILLEGALITY

General Rule	In general, an illegal contract is void, and the courts will not aid either party when both parties are considered to be equally at fault *(in pari delicto)*. If the contract is executory, neither party can enforce it. If the contract is executed, neither party can recover damages.
Exceptions	Several exceptions exist to the general rule that neither party to an illegal bargain will be able to recover. In the following situations, the court may grant recovery: 1. *Justifiable ignorance of the facts*—When one party to the contract is relatively innocent. 2. *Members of protected classes*—When one party to the contract is a member of a group of persons protected by a particular statute. 3. *Withdrawal from an illegal agreement*—When either party seeks to recover consideration given for an illegal contract before the illegal act is performed. 4. *Severable, or divisible, contracts*—When the court can divide the contract into illegal and legal portions and the illegal portion is not essential to the bargain. 5. *Fraud, duress, or undue influence*—When one party was induced to enter into an illegal bargain through fraud, duress, or undue influence.

Issue Spotters

1. In September, Sharyn agrees to work for Totem Productions, Inc., at $500 a week for a year beginning January 1. In October, Sharyn is offered $600 a week for the same work by Umber Shows, Ltd. When Sharyn tells her boss at Totem about the other offer, he tears up their contract and agrees that Sharyn will be paid $575. Is the new contract binding? Explain. (See *Consideration*.)

2. Sun Airlines, Inc., prints on its tickets that it is not liable for any injury to a passenger caused by the airline's negligence. If the cause of an accident is found to be the airline's negligence, can it use the clause as a defense to liability? Why or why not? (See *Legality*.)

—Check your answers to the *Issue Spotters* against the answers provided in Appendix D at the end of this text.

Learning Objectives Check

1. What is consideration? What is required for consideration to be legally sufficient?

2. In what circumstances might a promise be enforced despite a lack of consideration?

3. Does a minor have the capacity to enter into an enforceable contract? What does it mean to disaffirm a contract?

4. Under what circumstances will a covenant not to compete be enforced? When will such covenants not be enforced?

5. What is an exculpatory clause? In what circumstances might exculpatory clauses be enforced? When will they not be enforced?

—Answers to the even-numbered *Learning Objectives Check* questions can be found in Appendix E at the end of this text.

Business Scenarios and Case Problems

12–1. Contracts by Minors. Kalen is a seventeen-year-old minor who has just graduated from high school. He is attending a university two hundred miles from home and has contracted to rent an apartment near the university for one year at $500 per month. He is working at a convenience store to earn enough income to be self-supporting. After living in the apartment and paying monthly rent for four months, he becomes involved in a dispute with his landlord. Kalen, still a minor, moves out and returns the key to the landlord. The landlord wants to hold Kalen liable for the balance of the payments due under the lease. Discuss fully Kalen's liability in this situation. (See *Contractual Capacity*.)

12–2. Disaffirmance. J.T., a minor, is a motocross competitor. At Monster Mountain MX Park, he signed a waiver of liability to "hold harmless the park for any loss due to negligence." Riding around the Monster Mountain track, J.T. rode over a blind jump, became airborne, and crashed into a tractor that he had not seen until he was in the air. To recover for his injuries, J.T. filed a suit against Monster Mountain, alleging negligence for its failure to remove the tractor from the track. Does the liability waiver bar this claim? Explain. [*J.T. v. Monster Mountain, LLC,* 754 F.Supp.2d 1323 (M.D.Ala. 2010)] (See *Contractual Capacity*.)

12–3. Business Case Problem with Sample Answer— Unconscionable Contracts or Clauses. Geographic Expeditions, Inc. (GeoEx), which guided climbs up Mount Kilimanjaro, required climbers to sign a release to participate in an expedition. The form required any disputes to be submitted to arbitration in San Francisco and limited damages to the cost of the trip. GeoEx told climbers that the terms were nonnegotiable and that other travel firms imposed the same terms. Jason Lhotka died on a GeoEx climb. His mother filed a suit against GeoEx. GeoEx sought arbitration. Was the arbitration clause unconscionable? Why or why not? [*Lhotka v. Geographic Expeditions, Inc.,* 181 Cal.App.4th 816, 104 Cal.Rptr.3d 844 (1 Dist. 2010)] (See *Legality*.)

—**For a sample answer to Problem 12–3, go to Appendix F at the end of this text.**

12–4. Mental Incompetence. Dorothy Drury suffered from dementia and chronic confusion. When she became unable to manage her own affairs, including decisions about medical and financial matters, her son Eddie arranged for her to move to an assisted living facility. During admission, she signed a residency agreement, which included an arbitration clause. After she sustained injuries in a fall at the facility, a suit was filed to recover damages. The facility asked the court to compel arbitration. Was Dorothy bound to the residency agreement? Discuss. [*Drury v. Assisted Living Concepts, Inc.,* 245 Or.App. 217, 262 P.3d 1162 (2011)] (See *Contractual Capacity*.)

12–5. Licensing Statutes. PEMS Co. International, Inc., agreed to find a buyer for Rupp Industries, Inc., for a commission of 2 percent of the purchase price, which was to be paid by the buyer. Using PEMS's services, an investment group bought Rupp for $20 million and changed its name to Temp-Air, Inc. PEMS asked Temp-Air to pay a commission on the sale. Temp-Air refused, arguing that PEMS had acted as a broker in the deal without a license. The applicable statute defines a broker as any person who deals with the sale of a business. If this statute was intended to protect the public, can PEMS collect its commission? Explain. [*PEMS Co. International, Inc. v. Temp-Air, Inc.,* __ N.W.2d __, 2011 WL 69098 (Minn.App. 2011)] (See *Legality*.)

12–6. Spotlight on Kansas City Chiefs—Consideration. On Brenda Sniezek's first day of work for the Kansas City Chiefs Football Club, she signed a document that purported to compel arbitration of any disputes that she might have with the Chiefs. In the document, Sniezek agreed to comply at all times with and be bound by the constitution and bylaws of the National Football League (NFL). She agreed to refer all disputes to the NFL commissioner for a binding decision and to release the Chiefs and others from any related claims. Nowhere in the document did the Chiefs agree to do anything. Was there consideration for the arbitration provision? Explain. [*Sniezek v. Kansas City Chiefs Football Club,* 402 S.W.3d 580 (Mo.App. W.D. 2013)] (See *Consideration*.)

12–7. Minors. D.V.G. (a minor) was injured in a one-car auto accident in Hoover, Alabama. The vehicle was covered by an insurance policy issued by Nationwide Mutual Insurance Co. Stan Brobston, D.V.G.'s attorney, accepted Nationwide's offer of $50,000 on D.V.G.'s behalf. Before the settlement could be submitted to an Alabama state court for approval, D.V.G. died from injuries received in a second, unrelated auto accident. Nationwide argued that it was not bound to the settlement because a minor lacks the capacity to contract and cannot enter into a binding settlement without court approval. Should Nationwide be bound to the settlement? Why or why not? [*Nationwide Mutual Insurance Co. v. Wood,* 121 So.3d 982 (Ala. 2013)] (See *Contractual Capacity*.)

12–8. Consideration. Citynet, LLC, established an employee incentive plan "to enable the Company to attract and retain experienced individuals." The plan provided that a participant who left Citynet's employment was entitled to "cash out" his or her entire vested balance. (When an employee's rights to a particular benefit become *vested,* they belong to that employee and cannot be taken away. The vested balance refers to the part of an account that goes with the employee if he or she leaves the company.) When Citynet employee Ray Toney terminated his employment, he asked to redeem his $87,000.48

vested balance. Citynet refused, citing a provision of the plan that limited redemptions to no more than 20 percent annually. Toney filed a suit in a West Virginia state court against Citynet, alleging breach of contract. Citynet argued that the plan was not a contract but a discretionary bonus over which Citynet had sole discretion. Was the plan a contract? If so, was it bilateral or unilateral, and what was the consideration? [*Citynet, LLC v. Toney*, __ W.Va. __, __ S.E.2d __, 2015 WL 591519 (2015)] (See *Consideration*.)

12–9. A Question of Ethics—Promissory Estoppel. Claudia Aceves borrowed $845,000 from U.S. Bank to buy a home. Less than two years into the loan, she could no longer afford the monthly payments. The bank notified her that it planned to foreclose on her home. (Foreclosure is a process that allows a lender to repossess and sell the property that secures a loan.) The bank offered to modify Aceves's mortgage if she would forgo bankruptcy. In reliance on the bank's promise, she agreed. Once she withdrew the filing, however, the bank foreclosed and began eviction proceedings. Aceves filed a suit against the bank for promissory estoppel. [*Aceves v. U.S. Bank, N.A.*, 192 Cal.App.4th 218, 120 Cal.Rptr.3d 507 (2 Dist. 2011)] (See *Promissory Estoppel*.)

1. Could Aceves succeed in her claim of promissory estoppel? Why or why not?
2. Did Aceves or U.S. Bank behave unethically? Discuss.

Critical Thinking and Writing Assignments

12–10. Business Law Critical Thinking Group Assignment. Melissa Faraj owns a lot and wants to build a house according to a particular set of plans and specifications. She solicits bids from building contractors and receives three bids: one from Carlton for $160,000, one from Feldberg for $158,000, and one from Siegel for $153,000. She accepts Siegel's bid. One month after beginning construction of the house, Siegel contacts Faraj and tells her that because of inflation and a recent price hike for materials, he will not finish the house unless Faraj agrees to pay an extra $13,000. Faraj reluctantly agrees to pay the additional sum. (See *Consideration*.)

1. One group will discuss whether a contractor can ever raise the price of completing construction based on inflation and the rising cost of materials.
2. A second group will assume that after the house is finished, Faraj refuses to pay the extra $13,000. The group will decide whether Faraj is legally required to pay this additional amount.
3. A third group will discuss what types of extraordinary difficulties could arise during construction that would justify a contractor's charging more than the original bid.

13

Defenses to Contract Enforceability

LEARNING OBJECTIVES

The five Learning Objectives *below are designed to help improve your understanding of the chapter. After reading this chapter, you should be able to answer the following questions:*

1. In what types of situations might voluntary consent to a contract's terms be lacking?

2. What is the difference between a unilateral and a bilateral mistake?

3. What are the elements of fraudulent misrepresentation?

4. What contracts must be in writing to be enforceable?

5. What is parol evidence? When is it admissible to clarify the terms of a written contract?

"Understanding is a two-way street."

ELEANOR ROOSEVELT
1884–1962
(FIRST LADY OF THE UNITED STATES, 1933–1945)

An otherwise valid contract may still be unenforceable if the parties have not genuinely agreed to its terms. The lack of voluntary consent is a *defense* to the enforcement of a contract. As Eleanor Roosevelt stated in the chapter-opening quotation, "Understanding is a two-way street." If one party does not voluntarily consent to the terms of a contract, then there is no genuine "meeting of the minds," and the law will not normally enforce the contract, as we discuss in the first part of this chapter.

A contract that is otherwise valid may also be unenforceable if it is not in the proper form. For instance, if a contract is required by law to be in writing and there is no written evidence of the contract, it may not be enforceable. In the second part of this chapter, we examine the kinds of contracts that require a writing under what is called the *Statute of Frauds*. The chapter concludes with a discussion of the parol evidence rule, under which courts determine the admissibility at trial of evidence extraneous (external) to written contracts.

13–1 Voluntary Consent

LEARNING OBJECTIVE 1

In what types of situations might voluntary consent to a contract's terms be lacking?

Voluntary consent (assent) may be lacking because of mistake, fraudulent misrepresentation, undue influence, or duress. Generally, a party who demonstrates that he or she did not genuinely agree to the terms of a contract can choose either to carry out the contract or to rescind (cancel) it and thus avoid the entire transaction. This is one reason why many contracts include definitions of important terms.

13–1a Mistakes

We all make mistakes, so it is not surprising that mistakes are made when contracts are created. In certain circumstances, contract law allows a contract to be avoided on the basis of mistake. It is important to distinguish between *mistakes of fact* and *mistakes of value or quality*. Only a mistake of fact may allow a contract to be avoided.

EXAMPLE 13.1 Paco buys a violin from Beverly for $250. Although the violin is very old, neither party believes that it is valuable. Later, however, an antiques dealer informs the parties that the violin is rare and worth thousands of dollars. Here, both parties were mistaken, but the mistake is a mistake of *value* rather than a mistake of *fact* that warrants contract rescission. Therefore, Beverly cannot rescind the contract. ■

Mistakes of fact occur in two forms—*unilateral* and *bilateral (mutual)*. A unilateral mistake is made by only one of the contracting parties, whereas a mutual mistake is made by both. We look at these two types of mistakes next and illustrate them graphically in Exhibit 13–1.

Unilateral Mistakes A **unilateral mistake** occurs when only one party is mistaken as to a *material fact*—that is, a fact important to the subject matter of the contract. Generally, a unilateral mistake does not give the mistaken party any right to relief from the contract. In other words, the contract normally is enforceable against the mistaken party.

EXAMPLE 13.2 Elena intends to sell her jet ski for $2,500. When she learns that Chin is interested in buying a used jet ski, she sends him an e-mail offering to sell the jet ski to him. When typing the e-mail, however, she mistakenly keys in the price of $1,500. Chin immediately sends Elena an e-mail reply accepting her offer. Even though Elena intended to sell her jet ski for $2,500, she has made a unilateral mistake and is bound by the contract to sell it to Chin for $1,500. ■

This rule has at least two exceptions.[1] The contract may not be enforceable in either of the following situations.

1. The *other* party to the contract knows or should have known that a mistake of fact was made.

2. The error was due to a substantial mathematical mistake in addition, subtraction, division, or multiplication and was made inadvertently and without gross (extreme)

---

1. The *Restatement (Second) of Contracts*, Section 153, liberalizes the general rule to take into account the modern trend of allowing avoidance in some circumstances even though only one party has been mistaken.

Unilateral Mistake A mistake that occurs when one party to a contract is mistaken as to a material fact.

LEARNING OBJECTIVE 2

What is the difference between a unilateral and a bilateral mistake?

iStockPhoto.com/MrPants

If this jet ski owner wants to sell it for one price, but mistakenly types in a lower price in her e-mail offer, is she bound by the lower price?

Exhibit 13–1 Mistakes of Fact

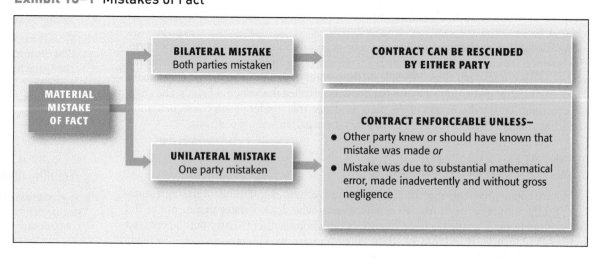

MATERIAL MISTAKE OF FACT

BILATERAL MISTAKE
Both parties mistaken

→ CONTRACT CAN BE RESCINDED BY EITHER PARTY

UNILATERAL MISTAKE
One party mistaken

→ CONTRACT ENFORCEABLE UNLESS—
- Other party knew or should have known that mistake was made *or*
- Mistake was due to substantial mathematical error, made inadvertently and without gross negligence

negligence. If, for instance, a contractor's bid was significantly low because he or she made a mistake in addition when totaling the estimated costs, any contract resulting from the bid normally may be rescinded.

In both situations, the mistake must still involve some material fact.

Bilateral (Mutual) Mistakes   A **bilateral mistake** is a "mutual misunderstanding concerning a basic assumption on which the contract was made."[2] When both parties are mistaken about the same material fact, the contract can be rescinded, or canceled, by either party. Note that, as with unilateral mistakes, the mistake must be about a material fact.

When a bilateral mistake occurs, normally the contract is voidable by the adversely affected party and can be rescinded. **CASE EXAMPLE 13.3** Coleman Holdings LP bought a parcel of real estate subject to setback restrictions imposed by a document entitled "Partial Release of Restrictions" that effectively precluded building a structure on the property. Lance and Joanne Eklund offered to buy the parcel from Coleman, intending to combine it with an adjacent parcel and build a home. Coleman gave the Eklunds a title report that referred to the "Partial Release of Restrictions," but they were not given a copy of the release.

Mistakenly believing that the document released restrictions on the property, the Eklunds did not investigate further. Meanwhile, Coleman mistakenly believed that the setback restrictions had been removed. After buying the property and discovering the restrictions, the Eklunds filed a suit in a Nevada state court against Coleman, seeking rescission of the sale. The court ordered the deal rescinded. The Nevada Supreme Court affirmed the order. "The parties made a mutual mistake in their mutual belief that the parcel had no setback restrictions."[3]

A word or term in a contract may be subject to more than one reasonable interpretation. If the parties to the contract attach materially different meanings to the term, their mutual misunderstanding may allow the contract to be rescinded. **CASE EXAMPLE 13.4** L&H Construction Company contracted with Circle Redmont, Inc., to make a cast-iron staircase and a glass flooring system. Redmont's original proposal was to "engineer, fabricate, and install" the staircase and flooring system, but installation was later dropped from the deal as a cost-cutting measure. The final contract stated that payment was due on "Supervision of Installation," although "install" appeared elsewhere in the contract. L&H insisted that installation was included and sued Redmont. The court found that the word *install* in the phrase "engineer, fabricate, and install" was the result of a mutual mistake. Both parties understood that Redmont would only supervise the installation, not perform it.[4]

13-1b Fraudulent Misrepresentation

Although fraud is a tort, the presence of fraud also affects the authenticity of the innocent party's consent to a contract. When an innocent party is fraudulently induced to enter into a contract, the contract usually can be avoided because that party has not *voluntarily* consented to the terms.[5] Normally, the innocent party can either rescind the contract and be restored to her or his original position or enforce the contract and seek damages for any harms resulting from the fraud.

Generally, fraudulent misrepresentation refers only to misrepresentation that is consciously false and is intended to mislead another. That is, the person making a fraudulent misrepresentation knows or believes that the assertion is false or knows that she or he does not have a basis (stated or implied) for the assertion.[6]

---

2. *Restatement (Second) of Contracts*, Section 152.
3. *Coleman Holdings Limited Partnership v. Eklund*, 2015 WL 428567 (Nev.Sup.Ct. 2015).
4. *L&H Construction Co. v. Circle Redmont, Inc.*, 55 So.3d 630 (Fla. 2011).
5. *Restatement (Second) of Contracts*, Sections 163 and 164.
6. *Restatement (Second) of Contracts*, Section 162.

When will the use of the word "install" in a contract be considered a mistake?

KNOW THIS
To collect damages in almost any lawsuit, there must be some sort of injury.

"If a man smiles all the time, he's probably selling something that doesn't work."

GEORGE CARLIN
1937–2008
(AMERICAN COMEDIAN)

Typically, fraud involves three elements:

1. A misrepresentation of a material fact must occur.
2. There must be an intent to deceive.
3. The innocent party must justifiably rely on the misrepresentation.

Additionally, to collect damages, a party must have been harmed as a result of the misrepresentation.

Misrepresentation Has Occurred The first element of proving fraud is to show that misrepresentation of a material fact has occurred. This misrepresentation can occur by words or actions. For instance, an art gallery owner's statement "This painting is a Picasso" is a misrepresentation of fact if the painting was done by another artist. Similarly, if a customer asks to see only Jasper Johns paintings and the owner immediately leads the customer over to paintings that were not done by Johns, the owner's actions can be a misrepresentation.

Misrepresentation by Conduct. Misrepresentation also occurs when a party takes specific action to conceal a fact that is material to the contract.[7] Therefore, if a seller, by her or his actions, prevents a buyer from learning of some fact that is material to the contract, the seller's behavior constitutes misrepresentation by conduct. It would also be misrepresentation by conduct for a seller to untruthfully deny knowledge of facts that are material to the contract when a buyer requests such information.

CASE EXAMPLE 13.5 Actor Tom Selleck contracted to purchase a horse named Zorro for his daughter from Dolores Cuenca. Cuenca acted as though Zorro were fit to ride in competitions, when in reality the horse was unfit for this use because of a medical condition. Selleck filed a lawsuit against Cuenca for wrongfully concealing the horse's condition, and a jury awarded Selleck more than $187,000 for Cuenca's misrepresentation by conduct.[8]

Statements of Opinion. Statements of opinion and representations of future facts (predictions) are generally not subject to claims of fraud. Statements such as "This land will be worth twice as much next year" and "This car will last for years and years" are statements of opinion, not fact. Contracting parties should recognize them as opinions and not rely on them. A fact is objective and verifiable, whereas an opinion is usually subject to debate. Therefore, a seller is allowed to use *puffery* to sell her or his goods without being liable for fraud.

Nevertheless, in certain situations, such as when a naïve purchaser relies on an opinion from an expert, the innocent party may be entitled to rescission or reformation. (Recall that reformation is an equitable remedy by which a court alters the terms of a contract to reflect the true intentions of the parties.)

CASE EXAMPLE 13.6 In a classic case, an instructor at an Arthur Murray dance school told Audrey Vokes, a widow without family, that she had the potential to become an accomplished dancer. The instructor sold her 2,302 hours of dancing lessons for a total amount of $31,090.45 (equivalent to $144,000 in 2016). When it became clear to Vokes that she did not, in fact, have the potential to be an excellent dancer, she sued the school for fraudulent misrepresentation. The court held that because the dance school had superior knowledge about a person's dance potential, the instructor's statements could be considered statements of fact rather than opinion.[9]

Misrepresentation of Law. Misrepresentation of law *ordinarily* does not entitle a party to be relieved of a contract. **EXAMPLE 13.7** Cameron has a parcel of property that she is trying to sell to Levi. Cameron knows that a local ordinance prohibits building anything higher than three stories on the property. Nonetheless, she tells Levi, "You can build a condominium one

---

7. *Restatement (Second) of Contracts*, Section 160.
8. *Selleck v. Cuenca*, Case No. GIN056909, North County of San Diego, California, decided September 9, 2009.
9. *Vokes v. Arthur Murray, Inc.*, 212 So.2d 906 (Fla.App. 1968).

hundred stories high if you want to." Levi buys the land and later discovers that Cameron's statement is false. Levi generally cannot avoid the contract, because under the common law, people are assumed to know state and local laws. ■

Exceptions to this rule occur when the misrepresenting party is in a profession known to require greater knowledge of the law than the average citizen possesses. For instance, if Cameron, in *Example 13.7*, had been a lawyer or a real estate broker, her willful misrepresentation of the area's zoning laws probably would have constituted fraud.

Misrepresentation by Silence. Ordinarily, neither party to a contract has a duty to come forward and disclose facts, and a contract normally will not be set aside because certain pertinent information has not been volunteered. **EXAMPLE 13.8** Jude is selling a car that has been in an accident and has been repaired. He does not need to volunteer this information to a potential buyer. If, however, the buyer asks him if the car has had extensive bodywork and he lies, Jude has committed fraudulent misrepresentation. ■

In general, if the seller knows of a serious potential problem that the buyer cannot reasonably be expected to discover, the seller may have a duty to speak. Normally, the seller must disclose only **latent defects**—that is, defects that could not readily be ascertained. Because a buyer of a house could easily discover the presence of termites through an inspection, for instance, termites may not qualify as a latent defect. Also, when the parties are in a *fiduciary relationship*—one of trust, such as partners, physician and patient, or attorney and client—there is a duty to disclose material facts. Failure to do so may constitute fraud.

> **Latent Defect** A defect that is not obvious or cannot readily be ascertained.

Intent to Deceive
The second element of fraud is knowledge on the part of the misrepresenting party that facts have been misrepresented. This element, usually called **scienter,**[10] or "guilty knowledge," generally signifies that there was an intent to deceive.

Scienter clearly exists if a party knows that a fact is not as stated. *Scienter* also exists if a party makes a statement that he or she believes not to be true or makes a statement recklessly, without regard to whether it is true or false. Finally, this element is met if a party says or implies that a statement is made on some basis, such as personal knowledge or personal investigation, when it is not.

> ***Scienter*** Knowledge on the part of a misrepresenting party that material facts have been falsely represented or omitted with an intent to deceive.

If you are selling your car, must you tell every potential buyer about any accidents in which that car was involved?

CASE EXAMPLE 13.9 Robert Sarvis applied for a position as a business law professor two weeks after his release from prison. On his résumé, he said that he had been a corporate president for fourteen years and had taught business law at another college. After he was hired, his probation officer alerted the school to Sarvis's criminal history. The school immediately fired him, and Sarvis sued for breach of his employment contract. The court concluded that by not disclosing his history, Sarvis had clearly exhibited an intent to deceive and that the school had justifiably relied on his misrepresentations. Therefore, the school could rescind Sarvis's employment contract.[11] ■

Innocent Misrepresentation. If a person makes a statement that she or he believes to be true but that actually misrepresents material facts, the person is guilty only of an **innocent misrepresentation,** not of fraud. When an innocent misrepresentation occurs, the aggrieved party can rescind the contract but usually cannot seek damages. **EXAMPLE 13.10** Parris tells Roberta that a tract of land contains 250 acres. Parris is mistaken—the tract contains only 215 acres—but Parris had no knowledge of the mistake. Roberta relies on the statement and contracts to buy the land. Even though the misrepresentation is innocent, Roberta can avoid the contract if the misrepresentation is material. ■

> **Innocent Misrepresentation** A misrepresentation that occurs when a person makes a false statement of fact that he or she believes is true.

Negligent Misrepresentation. Sometimes, a party will make a misrepresentation through carelessness, believing the statement is true. Such a misrepresentation may constitute **negligent misrepresentation** if the party did not exercise reasonable care in uncovering or disclosing the facts or did not use the skill and competence that her or his business or profession

> **Negligent Misrepresentation** A misrepresentation that occurs when a person makes a false statement of fact because he or she did not exercise reasonable care or use the skill and competence required by her or his business or profession.

---

10. Pronounced sy-*en*-ter.
11. *Sarvis v. Vermont State Colleges*, 172 Vt. 76, 772 A.2d 494 (2001).

requires. **EXAMPLE 13.11** Dirk, an operator of a weight scale, certifies the weight of Sneed's commodity. If Dirk knows that the scale's accuracy has not been checked for more than three years, his action may constitute negligent misrepresentation. ■

In almost all states, negligent misrepresentation is equal to *scienter*, or knowingly making a misrepresentation. In effect, negligent misrepresentation is treated as fraudulent misrepresentation, even though the misrepresentation was not purposeful. In negligent misrepresentation, culpable ignorance of the truth supplies the intention to mislead, even if the defendant can claim, "I didn't know."

Justifiable Reliance on the Misrepresentation The third element of fraud is reasonably justifiable reliance on the misrepresentation of fact. The deceived party must have a justifiable reason for relying on the misrepresentation. Also, the misrepresentation must be an important factor (but not necessarily the sole factor) in inducing the deceived party to enter into the contract.

Reliance is not justified if the innocent party knows the true facts or relies on obviously extravagant statements (such as, "this pickup truck will get fifty miles to the gallon"). The same rule applies to defects in property sold. If the defects would be obvious on inspection, the buyer cannot justifiably rely on the seller's representations. If the defects are hidden or latent, as previously discussed, however, the buyer is justified in relying on the seller's statements.

In the following case, the buyer of a car wash relied on the seller's representations that the property would be "appropriately winterized" to protect it from damage, but it was not. Was the buyer justified in relying on the seller's representations?

CASE 13.1

Cronkelton v. Guaranteed Construction Services, LLC

Court of Appeals of Ohio, Third District, 988 N.E.2d 656, 2013-Ohio-328 (2013).

FACTS A court appointed Patrick Shivley to be the receiver of a foreclosed car wash that was being sold in Bellefontaine, Ohio. (A receiver is an independent, impartial party appointed by a bankruptcy court to manage property in bankruptcy proceedings and dispose of it in an orderly manner for the benefit of the creditors.) The buyer, Clifford Cronkelton, inspected the car wash in November 2009. He knew that some equipment would have to be replaced, but he was concerned that the property needed to be winterized to protect it from damage. In phone calls and e-mails, Shivley assured him that the winterizing would be done.

Shivley contacted Guaranteed Construction Services, which hired Strayer Company to winterize the property. Strayer told Shivley that the only way to avoid problems was to leave the heat on at the car wash, but Shivley knew that the bank had shut off the heat because the property was not generating income. In March 2010, Shivley informed the bank of damage to the property caused by freezing. Shivley did not share this information with Cronkelton, who did not become aware of the damage until after he had bought the car wash in June.

Cronkelton filed a suit in an Ohio state court against Guaranteed and Shivley, asserting fraud. The jury returned a verdict in Cronkelton's favor, and he was awarded more than $140,000 in damages and attorneys' fees. The defendants appealed.

Is it reasonable for the buyer of a car wash to rely on the seller's statements that the property has been properly winterized?

John de la Bastide/ShutterStock.com

ISSUE Did Cronkelton justifiably rely on Shivley's representations that the car wash had been winterized?

DECISION Yes. A state intermediate appellate court affirmed the lower court's judgment in Cronkelton's favor.

REASON The reviewing court found that the jury verdict was supported by "competent, credible evidence" indicating that Cronkelton had reasonably relied on Shivley's representations. No one denied that the damage by freezing was open and obvious upon inspection and that Cronkelton could have inspected the property again before signing the purchase agreement. But Cronkelton testified that Shivley had guaranteed in an e-mail that everything had been taken care of. The jury's finding that Cronkelton had reasonably relied on Shivley's representations appeared justified.

As a receiver, Shivley had a fiduciary duty to take care of the assets under his control. "Under the circumstances of this case, Cronkelton had a reasonable basis to believe that Shivley, who was acting as an arm of the [bankruptcy] court, would take the promised steps to winterize the property."

CRITICAL THINKING—Legal Consideration *Did Shivley's misrepresentations rise to the level of fraud? Explain.*

If you are selling products or services, assume that all clients and customers are naïve and that they rely on your representations. Instruct employees to phrase their comments so that customers understand that any statements that are not factual are the employees' opinion. If someone asks a question that is beyond an employee's knowledge, it is better for the employee to say that he or she does not know than to guess and have the customer rely on a representation that turns out to be false. This can be particularly important when the questions concern topics such as compatibility or speed of electronic and digital goods, software, or related services.

PREVENTING
LEGAL
DISPUTES

Injury to the Innocent Party Most courts do not require a showing of harm in an action to rescind a contract. These courts hold that because rescission returns the parties to the positions they held before the contract was made, a showing of injury to the innocent party is unnecessary.

In contrast, to recover damages caused by fraud, proof of harm is universally required. The measure of damages is ordinarily equal to the property's value had it been delivered as represented, less the actual price paid for the property. (What if someone pretends to be someone else online? Can the victim of the hoax prove injury sufficient to recover for fraudulent misrepresentation? See this chapter's *Adapting the Law to the Online Environment* feature for a discussion of this topic.)

Because fraud actions necessarily involve wrongful conduct, courts may also award *punitive,* or *exemplary, damages,* which compensate a plaintiff over and above the amount of the actual loss. Because of the potential for punitive damages, which normally are not available in contract actions, plaintiffs often include a claim for fraudulent misrepresentation in their contract disputes.

In the following case, a real estate investor claimed that a seller's failure to disclose material facts about the property affected its value. The court had to determine not only if the seller's conduct constituted fraud, but also whether the fraud had caused harm to the property value.

CASE 13.2

Fazio v. Cypress/GR Houston I, LP

Court of Appeals of Texas, First District, 403 S.W.3d 390 (2013).

FACTS Peter Fazio began talks with Cypress/GR Houston I, LP, to buy retail property whose main tenant was a Garden Ridge store. In performing a background investigation, Fazio and his agents became concerned about Garden Ridge's financial health. Nevertheless, after being assured that Garden Ridge had a positive financial outlook, Fazio sent Cypress a letter of intent to buy the property for $7.67 million "[b]ased on the currently reported absolute net income of $805,040.00." Cypress then agreed to provide all information in its possession, but it failed to disclose the following:

1. A consultant for Garden Ridge had recently requested a $240,000 reduction in the annual rent as part of a restructuring of the company's real estate leases.

What does a rent-reduction request from a shopping mall's main tenant indicate?

iStockPhoto.com/jnatkin

2. Cypress's bank was so concerned about Garden Ridge's financial health that it had required a personal guaranty of the property's loan.

The parties entered into a purchase agreement, but Garden Ridge went into bankruptcy shortly after the deal closed. Fazio sued Cypress for fraud after he was forced to sell the property three years later for only $3.75 million. A jury found in Fazio's favor. Although the jury agreed that Cypress had failed to disclose a material fact, however, it determined that Fazio was not entitled to any damages. The jury concluded that no damages had been proximately caused by the fraud, because the fraud had not negatively affected the value of the property at the time it was sold to Fazio. The trial court entered a

Continues

judgment notwithstanding the verdict in favor of Cypress, and Fazio appealed.

ISSUE Was Fazio fraudulently induced to enter into the purchase agreement?

DECISION Yes. The appellate court affirmed the jury's verdict. Cypress's failure to disclose these facts constituted fraud. Fazio was not entitled to damages, however, because the misrepresentation had not negatively affected the property's value.

REASON There was sufficient evidence of fraud. Before the parties entered into the purchase agreement, Cypress had agreed to provide all information in its possession. Cypress knew that Fazio had been concerned about Garden Ridge's financial health and that he had based the purchase price on the anticipated income from the property. Moreover, a reasonable person in Fazio's position would have attached significance to Garden Ridge's recent request for a $240,000 rent reduction. The fact that Cypress had been required to provide a personal guaranty of the property's loan was also significant.

There are two measures of direct damages in a fraud case: out-of-pocket damages and benefit-of-the-bargain damages. Out-of-pocket damages measure the difference between the amount the buyer paid and the value of the property the buyer received. Benefit-of-the-bargain damages measure the difference between the value of the property as represented and the actual value of the property. Both measures are determined at the time of the sale, not "at some future time." Here, the jury received a number of instructions on determining the amount of damages and concluded that there were zero damages to Fazio at the time of the purchase agreement.

CRITICAL THINKING—Ethical Consideration *Was Cypress's conduct unethical? Why or why not?*

13–1c Undue Influence

Undue Influence Persuasion that is less than actual force but more than advice and that induces a person to act according to the will or purposes of the dominating party.

Undue influence arises from relationships in which one party can greatly influence another party, thus overcoming that party's free will. A contract entered into under excessive or undue influence lacks voluntary consent and is therefore voidable.[12]

One Party Dominates the Other In various types of relationships, one party may have an opportunity to dominate and unfairly influence another party. Minors and elderly people, for instance, are often under the influence of guardians (persons who are legally responsible for others). If a guardian induces a young or elderly ward (the person whom the guardian looks after) to enter into a contract that benefits the guardian, the guardian may have exerted undue influence. Undue influence can arise from a number of confidential or fiduciary relationships, including attorney-client, physician-patient, guardian-ward, parent-child, husband-wife, and trustee-beneficiary.

The essential feature of undue influence is that the party being taken advantage of does not exercise free will in entering into a contract. It is not enough that a person is elderly or suffers from some mental or physical impairment. There must be clear and convincing evidence that the person did not act out of her or his free will. Similarly, the existence of a fiduciary relationship alone is insufficient to prove undue influence.

A Presumption of Undue Influence in Certain Situations The dominant party in a fiduciary relationship must exercise the utmost good faith in dealing with the other party. When the dominant party benefits from the relationship, a presumption of undue influence may arise. Thus, when a contract enriches the dominant party in a fiduciary relationship, the court will often *presume* that the contract was made under undue influence.

EXAMPLE 13.12 Erik is the guardian for Kinsley, his ward. On her behalf, he enters into a contract from which he benefits financially. If Kinsley challenges the contract, the court will likely presume that the guardian has taken advantage of his ward. To rebut (refute) this presumption, Erik has to show that he made full disclosure to Kinsley and that consideration was present. He must also show that Kinsley received, if available, independent and competent

---

12. *Restatement (Second) of Contracts*, Section 177.

ADAPTING THE LAW TO THE **ONLINE** ENVIRONMENT

"Catfishing": Is That Online "Friend" for Real?

When you are communicating with a person you have met only online, how do you know who that person really is? After all, the person could turn out to be a "catfish."

The term *catfish* comes from a 2010 film of the same name about a fake online persona. According to a story told in the film, when live cod were shipped long distances, they were inactive, and their flesh became mushy. When catfish were added to the tanks, the cod swam around and stayed in good condition. At the end of the film, a character says of the creator of the fake persona, "There are those people who are catfish in life. And they keep you on your toes. They keep you guessing, they keep you thinking, they keep you fresh."

Catfishing Makes National Headlines

Catfishing made headlines when a popular Notre Dame football star supposedly fell victim to it in 2012. Linebacker Manti Te'o said that his girlfriend, Lennay Kekua, a student at Stanford, had died of leukemia after a near-fatal car accident. Although Kekua had Facebook and Twitter accounts and Te'o had communicated with her online and by telephone for several years, reporters could find no evidence of her existence. Te'o later claimed that he had been a victim of a catfishing hoax. Others suggested that his friends had created the persona and her tragic death to provide an inspirational story that would increase Te'o's chances of winning the Heisman trophy.

Is Online Fraudulent Misrepresentation Actionable?

Some victims of catfishing have turned to the courts, but they have had little success. A few have attempted to sue Internet service providers for allowing fake personas, but the courts have generally dismissed these suits.[a] Laws in some states make it a crime to impersonate someone online, but these laws generally do not apply to those who create totally fictional personas.

Attempts to recover damages for fraudulent misrepresentation have generally failed to meet the requirement that there must be proof of actual injury. For instance, Paula Bonhomme developed an online romantic relationship with a man called Jesse. Jesse was actually a woman named Janna St. James, who also communicated with Bonhomme using her own name and pretending to be a friend of Jesse's.

St. James created a host of fictional characters, including an ex-wife and a son, for Jesse. Bonhomme in turn sent gifts totaling more than $10,000 to Jesse and the other characters. After being told by St. James that Jesse had attempted suicide, Bonhomme suffered such emotional distress that she incurred more than $5,000 in bills for a therapist. Eventually, she was told that Jesse had died of liver cancer. When Bonhomme finally learned the truth, she suffered additional emotional distress, resulting in more expenses for a therapist and lost earnings due to her "affected mental state."

Although Bonhomme had incurred considerable expenses, the Illinois Supreme Court ruled that she could not bring a suit for fraudulent misrepresentation. The case involved a "purely personal relationship" without any "commercial, transactional, or regulatory component." Bonhomme and St. James "were not engaged in any kind of business dealings or bargaining." The truth of representations "made in the context of purely private personal relationships is simply not something the state regulates or in which the state possesses any kind of valid public policy interest."[b]

CRITICAL THINKING

- So far, victims of catfishing have had little success in the courts. Under what circumstances might a person be able to collect damages for fraudulent misrepresentation involving online impersonation?

---

a. See, for example, *Beckman v. Match.com*, 2013 WL 2355512 (D.Nev. 2013); and *Robinson v. Match.com, LLC*, 2012 WL 3263992 (N.D.Tex. 2012).

b. *Bonhomme v. St. James*, 970 N.E.2d 1 (Ill. 2012).

---

advice before completing the transaction. Unless the presumption can be rebutted, the contract will be rescinded. ∎

When is assent really assent? Musician Sly Stone, of the group Sly and the Family Stone, had numerous hits in the 1960s and 1970s. Then drug use apparently took its toll on the singer. By the 1980s, Stone was broke.

Along came a group that convinced the former star to sign a series of contracts. Stone became an employee and co-owner of Even St. Productions in 1989. He was to have received a portion of the royalties collected by the new company. Twenty years later, he was homeless. In 2010, Stone sued his business manager, his attorney, and the company for breach of contract.

ETHICAL ISSUE

An additional issue concerned whether he understood all of the complicated contracts that he was asked to sign. In other words, was there unambiguous assent?

In 2015, a Los Angeles Superior Court civil jury found in favor of Stone in his breach of contract lawsuit. The defendants argued that most of the royalties they had collected for him were used to pay off the millions that he owed to the Internal Revenue Service. They are appealing the verdict. Nevertheless, one of Stone's attorney's said, "This was an important verdict for people that are artists, entertainers, and music composers."

13-1d Duress

Agreement to the terms of a contract is not voluntary if one of the parties is *forced* into the agreement. The use of threats to force a party to enter into a contract constitutes *duress,*[13] as does the use of blackmail or extortion to induce consent. Duress is both a defense to the enforcement of a contract and a ground for rescission of a contract.

To establish duress, there must be proof of a threat to do something that the threatening party has no right to do. Generally, for duress to occur, the threatened act must be wrongful or illegal, and it must render the person who receives the threat incapable of exercising free will. A threat to exercise a legal right, such as the right to sue someone, ordinarily does not constitute duress.

13-2 The Writing Requirement

Statute of Frauds A state statute that requires certain types of contracts to be in writing to be enforceable.

Another defense to the enforceability of a contract is *form*—specifically, some contracts must be in writing. All states require certain types of contracts to be in writing or evidenced by a written memorandum or an electronic record. In addition, the party or parties against whom enforcement is sought must have signed the contract, unless certain exceptions apply (as discussed later in this chapter). In this text, we refer to these state statutes collectively as the **Statute of Frauds.**

The following types of contracts are said to fall "within" or "under" the Statute of Frauds and therefore require a writing:

1. Contracts involving interests in land.

2. Contracts that cannot *by their terms* be performed within one year from the day after the date of formation.

3. Collateral, or secondary, contracts, such as promises to answer for the debt or duty of another.

4. Promises made in consideration of marriage.

5. Under the Uniform Commercial Code, contracts for the sale of goods priced at $500 or more.

The actual name of the Statute of Frauds is misleading because it does not apply to fraud. Rather, in an effort to prevent fraud, the statute denies enforceability to certain contracts that do not comply with its requirements. The name derives from an English act passed in 1677 that was titled "An Act for the Prevention of Frauds and Perjuries."

13-2a Contracts Involving Interests in Land

A contract calling for the sale of land is not enforceable unless it is in writing or evidenced by a written memorandum. Land is *real property* and includes all physical objects that are

---

13. *Restatement (Second) of Contracts,* Sections 174 and 175.

permanently attached to the soil, such as buildings, fences, trees, and the soil itself. The Statute of Frauds operates as a defense to the enforcement of an oral contract for the sale of land. **EXAMPLE 13.13** Skylar contracts orally to sell his property in Fair Oaks to Beth. If he later decides not to sell, under most circumstances, Beth cannot enforce the contract. ■

The Statute of Frauds also requires written evidence of contracts for the transfer of other interests in land, such as mortgage agreements and leases. Similarly, an agreement that includes an option to purchase real property must be in writing for the option to be enforced.

13–2b The One-Year Rule

Contracts that cannot, *by their own terms,* be performed within one year *from the day after* the contract is formed must be in writing to be enforceable. The reason for this rule is that the parties' memory of their contract's terms is not likely to be reliable for longer than a year.

Time Period Starts the Day after the Contract Is Formed
The one-year period begins to run *the day after the contract is made.* **EXAMPLE 13.14** Superior University forms a contract with Kimi San stating that San will teach three courses in history during the coming academic year (September 15 through June 15). If the contract is formed in March, it must be in writing to be enforceable—because it cannot be performed within one year. If the contract is formed in July, in contrast, it will not have to be in writing to be enforceable—because it can be performed within one year. ■

Must Be Objectively Impossible to Perform within One Year
The test for determining whether an oral contract is enforceable under the one-year rule is whether performance is *possible* within one year from the day after the date of contract formation. It does not matter whether the agreement is *likely* to be performed during that period.

When performance of a contract is objectively impossible during the one-year period, the contract must be in writing to be enforceable. **EXAMPLE 13.15** A contract to provide five crops of tomatoes to be grown on a specific farm in Illinois would be objectively impossible to perform within one year. No farmer in Illinois can grow five crops of tomatoes in a single year. ■

If performance is possible within one year under the contract's terms, the contract does not fall under the Statute of Frauds and need not be in writing. **EXAMPLE 13.16** Janine enters into a contract to create a carving of President Barack Obama's face on a mountainside, similar to the carvings of other presidents' faces on Mount Rushmore. It is technically possible—although not very likely—that the contract could be performed within one year. (Mount Rushmore took over fourteen years to complete.) Therefore, Janine's contract need not be in writing to be enforceable. ■ Exhibit 13–2 graphically illustrates the one-year rule.

13–2c Collateral Promises

A **collateral promise,** or secondary promise, is one that is ancillary (subsidiary) to a principal transaction or primary contractual relationship. In other words, a collateral promise is one made by a third party to assume the debts or obligations of a primary party to a contract if that party does not perform. Any collateral promise of this nature falls under the Statute of Frauds and therefore must be in writing to be enforceable.

Primary versus Secondary Obligations
A direct party to a contract incurs a *primary obligation* under that contract. A contract in which a party assumes a primary obligation normally does not need to be in writing to be enforceable. **EXAMPLE 13.17** Nigel tells Dr. Lu, an orthodontist, that he will pay for the services provided for Nigel's niece. Because Nigel has assumed direct financial responsibility for his niece's debt, this is a primary obligation and need not be in writing to be enforceable. ■

> "A verbal contract isn't worth the paper it's written on."
>
> **SAMUEL GOLDWYN**
> 1879–1974
> (HOLLYWOOD MOTION PICTURE PRODUCER)

Collateral Promise
A secondary promise to a primary transaction, such as a promise made by one person to pay the debts of another if the latter fails to perform. A collateral promise normally must be in writing to be enforceable.

Exhibit 13–2 The One-Year Rule

Under the Statute of Frauds, contracts that by their terms are impossible to perform within one year from the day after the date of contract formation must be in writing to be enforceable. Put another way, if it is at all possible to perform an oral contract within one year from the day after the contract is made, the contract will fall outside the Statute of Frauds and be enforceable.

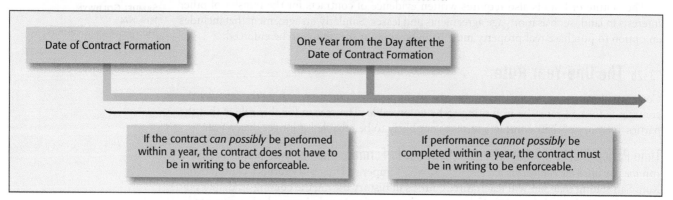

In contrast, a contract in which a party assumes a *secondary obligation* does have to be in writing to be enforceable. **EXAMPLE 13.18** Kareem's mother borrows $10,000 from the Medford Trust Company on a promissory note payable in six months. Kareem promises the bank officer handling the loan that he will pay the $10,000 *if his mother does not pay the loan on time.* Kareem, in this situation, becomes what is known as a *guarantor* on the loan. He is guaranteeing to the bank (the creditor) that he will pay the loan if his mother fails to do so. This kind of collateral promise must be in writing to be enforceable. ■

An Exception—The "Main Purpose" Rule An oral promise to answer for the debt of another is covered by the Statute of Frauds *unless* the guarantor's purpose in accepting secondary liability is to secure a personal benefit. Under the "main purpose" rule, this type of contract need not be in writing.[14] The assumption is that a court can infer from the circumstances of a case whether a "leading objective" of the promisor was to secure a personal benefit.

EXAMPLE 13.19 Carrie Braswell contracts with Custom Manufacturing Company to have some machines custom made for her factory. She promises Newform Supply, Custom's supplier, that if Newform continues to deliver the materials to Custom for the production of the custom-made machines, she will guarantee payment. This promise need not be in writing, even though the effect may be to pay the debt of another, because Braswell's main purpose is to secure a benefit for herself. ■

Another typical application of the main purpose doctrine occurs when one creditor guarantees a debtor's debt to another creditor to forestall litigation. The purpose is to allow the debtor to remain in business long enough to generate profits sufficient to pay *both* creditors. In this situation, the guaranty does not need to be in writing to be enforceable.

13-2d Promises Made in Consideration of Marriage

A unilateral promise to make a monetary payment or to give property in consideration of marriage must be in writing. **EXAMPLE 13.20** Evan promises to buy Celeste a house in Maui if she marries him. Celeste would need written evidence of Evan's promise to enforce it. ■

The same rule applies to **prenuptial agreements**—agreements made before marriage that define each partner's ownership rights in the other partner's property. **EXAMPLE 13.21** Before

Prenuptial Agreement An agreement made before marriage that defines each partner's ownership rights in the other partner's property. Prenuptial agreements must be in writing to be enforceable.

_____

14. *Restatement (Second) of Contracts*, Section 116.

marrying country singer Keith Urban, actress Nicole Kidman entered into a prenuptial agreement with him. Kidman agreed that if the couple divorced, she would pay Urban $640,000 for every year they had been married, unless Urban had begun to use drugs again. In that event, he would receive nothing. ■

13–2e Contracts for the Sale of Goods

The Uniform Commercial Code (UCC) includes Statute of Frauds provisions that require written evidence or an electronic record of a contract for the sale of goods priced at $500 or more. (This low threshold amount may be increased in the future.) A writing that will satisfy the UCC requirement need only state the quantity term (6,000 boxes of cotton gauze, for instance). The contract will not be enforceable for any quantity greater than that set forth in the writing.

Other agreed-on terms can be omitted or even stated imprecisely in the writing, as long as they adequately reflect both parties' intentions. The writing normally need not designate the buyer or the seller, the terms of payment, or the price. In addition, a written memorandum or series of communications (including e-mail) evidencing a contract will suffice, provided that the writing is signed by the party against whom enforcement is sought. (See this chapter's *Beyond Our Borders* feature to learn whether other countries have requirements similar to those in the Statute of Frauds.)

"Wallace, have you forgotten our prenuptial contract? No whistling!"

Henry Martin/The New Yorker Collection/Cartoonbank.com

13–2f Exceptions to the Statute of Frauds

Exceptions to the applicability of the Statute of Frauds are made in certain situations. We describe those situations here.

BEYOND OUR BORDERS

The Statute of Frauds and International Sales Contracts

The Convention on Contracts for the International Sale of Goods (CISG) provides rules that govern international sales contracts between citizens of countries that have ratified the convention (agreement). Article 11 of the CISG does not incorporate any Statute of Frauds provisions. Rather, it states that a "contract for sale need not be concluded in or evidenced by writing and is not subject to any other requirements as to form."

Article 11 accords with the legal customs of most nations, which no longer require contracts to meet certain formal or writing requirements to be enforceable. Ironically, even England, the nation that enacted the original Statute of Frauds in 1677, has repealed all of it except the provisions relating to collateral promises and to transfers of interests in land. Many other countries that once had such statutes have also repealed all or parts of them. Civil law countries, such as France, have never required certain types of contracts to be in writing. Obviously, without a writing requirement, contracts can take on any form.

CRITICAL THINKING

■ If a country does not have a Statute of Frauds and a dispute arises over an oral agreement, how can the parties substantiate their positions?

Partial Performance When a contract has been partially performed and the parties cannot be returned to their positions prior to the contract's formation, a court may grant *specific performance*. Specific performance is an equitable remedy that requires that a contract be performed according to its precise terms. The parties still must prove that an oral contract existed, of course.

In cases involving oral contracts for the transfer of interests in land, courts usually look at whether justice is better served by enforcing the oral contract when partial performance has taken place. For instance, if the purchaser has paid part of the price, taken possession, and made valuable improvements to the property, a court may grant specific performance.

In some states, mere reliance on certain types of oral contracts is enough to remove them from the Statute of Frauds. Under the UCC, an oral contract for goods priced at $500 or more is enforceable to the extent that a seller accepts payment or a buyer accepts delivery of the goods.[15]

CASE EXAMPLE 13.22 Pacific Fruit, Inc., exports cargo from Ecuador. NYKCool, based in Sweden, provides maritime transportation. NYKCool and Pacific entered into a written contract with a two-year duration, under which NYKCool agreed to transport weekly shipments of bananas from Ecuador to California and Japan.

At the end of the period, the parties agreed to extend the deal, but a new contract was never signed. The parties continued making weekly shipments for four more years until a dispute arose over unused cargo capacity and unpaid freight charges. An international arbitration panel found that Pacific Fruit was liable to NYKCool for $8.7 million for breach of contract. Pacific Fruit appealed, arguing that there was no contract in place. The court affirmed the award in favor of NYKCool. "The parties' substantial partial performance on the contract weighs strongly in favor of contract formation."[16] ■

Admissions If a party against whom enforcement of an oral contract is sought "admits" under oath that a contract for sale was made, the contract will be enforceable.[17] The party's admission can occur at any stage of the court proceedings, such as during a deposition or other discovery, pleadings, or testimony.

If a party admits a contract subject to the UCC, the contract is enforceable, but only to the extent of the quantity admitted.[18] **EXAMPLE 13.23** Rachel, the president of Bistro Corporation, admits under oath that an oral agreement was made with Commercial Kitchens, Inc., to buy certain equipment for $10,000. A court will enforce the agreement only to the extent admitted ($10,000), even if Commercial Kitchens claims that the agreement involved $20,000 worth of equipment. ■

Promissory Estoppel An oral contract that would otherwise be unenforceable under the Statute of Frauds may be enforced under the doctrine of *promissory estoppel*. Section 139 of the *Restatement (Second) of Contracts* provides that an oral promise can be enforceable, notwithstanding the Statute of Frauds, if the promisee has justifiably relied on the promise to his or her detriment. The promisee's reliance must have been foreseeable to the person making the promise, and enforcing the promise must be the only way to avoid injustice.

Note the similarities between promissory estoppel and the doctrine of partial performance discussed previously. Both require reasonable reliance and operate to estop, or prevent, a party from claiming that no contract exists.

Special Exceptions under the UCC Special exceptions to the applicability of the Statute of Frauds exist for sales contracts. Oral contracts for customized goods may be enforced in certain circumstances. Another exception has to do with oral contracts *between merchants* that

If a seller admits under oath that a contract was for only $10,000 of commercial kitchen equipment, does the buyer owe more if additional equipment was installed?

---

15. UCC 2–201(3)(c).

16. *NYKCool A.B. v. Pacific Fruit, Inc.,* 2013 WL 163621 (2d Cir. 2013). The initials *A.B.* stand for *Aktiebolag*, which is the Swedish term for "limited company."

17. *Restatement (Second) of Contracts*, Section 133.

18. UCC 2–201(3)(b).

have been confirmed in a written memorandum. We will examine this exception when we discuss the UCC's Statute of Frauds provisions.

Exhibit 13–3 graphically summarizes the types of contracts that fall under the Statute of Frauds and the various exceptions that apply.

13-3 Sufficiency of the Writing or Electronic Record

A written contract will satisfy the writing requirement of the Statute of Frauds, as will a written memorandum or an electronic record that evidences the agreement and is signed by the party against whom enforcement is sought. The signature need not be placed at the end of the document but can be anywhere in the writing. A signature can consist of a typed name or even just initials rather than the full name.

13-3a What Constitutes a Writing?

A writing can consist of any confirmation, invoice, sales slip, check, fax, or e-mail—or such items in combination. The written contract need not be contained in a single document to constitute an enforceable contract. One document may incorporate another document by expressly referring to it. Several documents may form a single contract if they are physically attached—such as by staple, paper clip, or glue—or even if they are only placed in the same envelope.

EXAMPLE 13.24 Simpson orally agrees to sell some land next to a shopping mall to Terro Properties. Simpson gives Terro an unsigned memo that contains a legal description of the property, and Terro gives Simpson an unsigned first draft of their contract. Simpson sends Terro a signed letter that refers to the memo and to the first and final drafts of the contract. Terro sends Simpson an unsigned copy of the final draft of the contract with a signed check stapled to it. Together, the documents can constitute a writing sufficient to satisfy the Statute of Frauds and bind both parties to the terms of the contract as evidenced by the writings. ■

13-3b What Must Be Contained in the Writing?

A memorandum or note evidencing an oral contract need only contain the essential terms of the contract, not every term. There must, of course, also be some indication that the parties

Exhibit 13–3 Contracts Subject to the Statute of Frauds

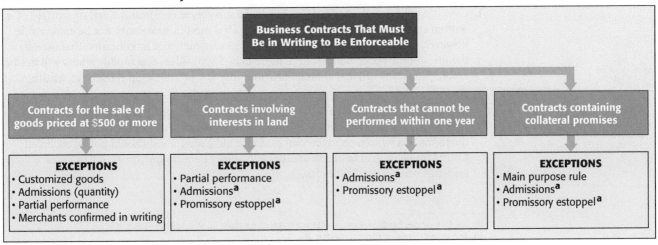

Business Contracts That Must Be in Writing to Be Enforceable			
Contracts for the sale of goods priced at $500 or more	**Contracts involving interests in land**	**Contracts that cannot be performed within one year**	**Contracts containing collateral promises**
EXCEPTIONS • Customized goods • Admissions (quantity) • Partial performance • Merchants confirmed in writing	**EXCEPTIONS** • Partial performance • Admissions[a] • Promissory estoppel[a]	**EXCEPTIONS** • Admissions[a] • Promissory estoppel[a]	**EXCEPTIONS** • Main purpose rule • Admissions[a] • Promissory estoppel[a]

a. In some states.

voluntarily agreed to the terms. As mentioned earlier, under the UCC, a writing evidencing a contract for the sale of goods need only state the quantity and be signed by the party against whom enforcement is sought.

Under most state laws, the writing must also name the parties and identify the subject matter, the consideration, and the essential terms with reasonable certainty. In addition, contracts for the sale of land usually must state the price and describe the property with sufficient clarity to allow these terms to be determined without reference to outside sources.[19]

Note that because only the party against whom enforcement is sought must have signed the writing, a contract may be enforceable by one of its parties but not by the other. **EXAMPLE 13.25** Rock orally agrees to buy Betty Devlin's lake house and lot for $350,000. Devlin writes Rock a letter confirming the sale by identifying the parties and the essential terms of the sales contract—price, method of payment, and legal address—and signs the letter. Devlin has made a written memorandum of the oral land contract. Because she signed the letter, she normally can be held to the oral contract by Rock. Devlin cannot enforce the agreement against Rock, however. Because he has not signed or entered into a written contract or memorandum, Rock can plead the Statute of Frauds as a defense. ■

13–4 The Parol Evidence Rule

LEARNING OBJECTIVE 5
What is parol evidence? When is it admissible to clarify the terms of a written contract?

Parol Evidence Rule A rule of contracts under which a court will not receive into evidence prior or contemporaneous external agreements that contradict the terms of the parties' written contract.

Sometimes, a written contract does not include—or contradicts—an oral understanding reached by the parties before or at the time of contracting. For instance, a landlord might tell a person who agrees to rent an apartment that she or he can have a cat, whereas the lease contract clearly states that no pets are allowed. In determining the outcome of such disputes, the courts look to a common law rule called the **parol evidence rule.**

Under this rule, if a court finds that a written contract represents the complete and final statement of the parties' agreement, then it will not allow either party to present parol evidence. *Parol evidence* is testimony or other evidence of communications between the parties that is not contained in the contract itself. Thus, a party normally cannot present evidence of the parties' "prior or contemporaneous agreements or negotiations" if that evidence contradicts or varies the terms of the parties' written contract.[20]

13–4a Exceptions to the Parol Evidence Rule

Because of the rigidity of the parol evidence rule, courts make several exceptions. These exceptions include the following:

1. *Contracts subsequently modified.* Evidence of a *subsequent modification* (oral or written) of a written contract can be introduced in court. Oral modifications may not be enforceable, however, if they come under the Statute of Frauds (such as a modification that increases the price of the goods being sold to more than $500). Also, oral modifications will not be enforceable if the original contract provides that any modification must be in writing.[21]

2. *Voidable or void contracts.* Oral evidence can be introduced in all cases to show that the contract was voidable or void (for example, induced by mistake, fraud, or misrepresentation). The reason is simple: if deception led one of the parties to agree to the terms of a written contract, oral evidence indicating fraud should not be excluded. Courts frown on bad faith and are quick to allow the introduction at trial of parol evidence when it establishes fraud.

---

19. See, for example, *Beneficial Homeowner Service Corporation v. Steele*, 30 Misc.3d 1208(A) (N.Y. 2011).
20. *Restatement (Second) of Contracts*, Section 213.
21. UCC 2–209(2), (3).

3. *Contracts containing ambiguous terms.* When the terms of a written contract are ambiguous, evidence is admissible to show the meaning of the terms. **CASE EXAMPLE 13.26** Pamela Watkins bought a home from Sandra Schexnider. Their agreement stated that Watkins would make payments on the mortgage until the note was paid in full, when "the house" would become hers. The agreement also stipulated that she would pay for insurance on "the property." The home was destroyed in a hurricane, and the insurance proceeds paid off the mortgage. Watkins claimed that she owned the land, but Schexnider argued that she had sold only the house. The court found that because "the house" term in the contract was ambiguous, parol evidence was admissible. The court concluded that the parties had intended to transfer ownership of both the house and the land, and ordered that title to the property be transferred to Watkins.[22] ■

4. *Incomplete contracts.* Evidence is admissible when the written contract is incomplete in that it lacks one or more of the essential terms. The courts allow evidence to "fill in the gaps" in the contract.

5. *Prior dealing, course of performance, or usage of trade.* Under the UCC, evidence can be introduced to explain or supplement a written contract by showing a prior dealing, course of performance, or usage of trade.[23] This is because when buyers and sellers deal with each other over extended periods of time, certain customary practices develop. These practices are often overlooked in the writing of the contract, so courts allow the introduction of evidence to show how the parties have acted in the past. Usage of trade—practices and customs generally followed in a particular industry—can also shed light on the meaning of certain contract provisions, and thus evidence of trade usage may be admissible.

6. *Contracts subject to an orally agreed-on condition precedent.* Sometimes the parties agree that a condition must be fulfilled before a party is required to perform the contract. This is called a *condition precedent.* If the parties have orally agreed on a condition precedent and the condition does not conflict with the terms of a written agreement, then a court may allow parol evidence to prove the oral condition. The parol evidence rule does not apply here because the existence of the entire written contract is subject to an orally agreed-on condition. Proof of the condition does not alter or modify the written terms but affects the *enforceability* of the written contract.

    EXAMPLE 13.27 A city leases property for an airport from a well-established helicopter business. The lease is renewable every five years. During the second five-year lease, a dispute arises, and the parties go to mediation. They enter into a settlement memorandum under which they agree to amend the lease agreement subject to the approval of the city council. The city amends the lease, but the helicopter business refuses to sign it, contending that the council has not given its approval. In this situation, the council's approval is a condition precedent to the formation of the settlement memorandum contract. Therefore, the parol evidence rule does not apply, and oral evidence is admissible to show that no agreement exists as to the terms of the settlement. ■

7. *Contracts with an obvious or gross clerical (or typographic) error.* When an *obvious* or *gross* clerical (or typographic) error exists that clearly would not represent the agreement of the parties, parol evidence is admissible to correct the error. **EXAMPLE 13.28** Davis agrees to lease office space from Stone Enterprises for $3,000 per month. The signed written lease provides for a monthly lease payment of $300 rather than the $3,000 agreed to by the parties. Because the error is obvious, Stone Enterprises would be allowed to admit parol evidence to correct the mistake. ■

In the following case, an appeals court considered whether the trial court should have admitted parol evidence regarding the terms of an apartment lease.

---

22. *Watkins v. Schexnider,* 31 So.3d 609 (La.App. 3 Cir. 2010).
23. UCC 1–205, 2–202.

KNOW THIS
The parol evidence rule and its exceptions relate to the rules concerning the *interpretation* of contracts.

Assume that a helicopter company agrees to lease property to the city. If a dispute arises, when does the parol evidence rule apply?

CASE 13.3

Frewil, LLC v. Price

Court of Appeals of South Carolina, __ S.C. __, __ S.E.2d __, 2015 WL 446558 (2015).

FACTS Madison Price and Carter Smith were planning to attend the College of Charleston in South Carolina. They contacted Frewil LLC about renting an apartment at the beginning of the fall semester. They asked if the apartment had a washer/dryer and dishwasher, and were told yes. The lease did not expressly state that the unit contained those appliances, but it provided that any overflow from a washing machine or dishwasher was the responsibility of the tenant and that the dishwasher had to be clean for a refund of the security deposit. When Price and Smith arrived to move in, the apartment had no washer/dryer or dishwasher and no connections for them. The students found housing elsewhere. Frewil filed a suit in a South Carolina state court against Price and Smith, claiming breach of contract. The defendants sought to introduce parol evidence to challenge Frewil's claim. The court denied the request and issued a judgment in Frewil's favor. Price and Smith appealed.

ISSUE Was parol evidence admissible to challenge Frewil's claim?

DECISION Yes. A state intermediate appellate court reversed the judgment of the lower court. "The lease was ambiguous thereby permitting the introduction of parol evidence."

If a lease is ambiguous about the existence of a washer and dryer, can parol evidence be introduced in a contract dispute?

iStockPhoto.com/RBOZUK

REASON The appellate court explained that when a contract is ambiguous, parol evidence is admissible to show the contract's "true meaning." A contract is ambiguous when it is subject to more than one reasonable interpretation, "expresses its purpose in an indefinite manner," or does not address a certain situation. In these instances, a court can review the circumstances at the time of contract formation to determine the parties' intent. In this case, the court held that the contract between Frewil and the students was subject to more than one interpretation. The lease did not state that the apartment contained a washer/dryer or a dishwasher, but it did make statements that referred to these appliances. Because the lease was ambiguous on this point, parol evidence was admissible to challenge Frewil's breach of contract claim.

CRITICAL THINKING—Economic Consideration *How does the parol evidence rule save time and money for the parties to a dispute and the court that hears it? Discuss.*

13–4b Integrated Contracts

Integrated Contract A written contract that constitutes the final expression of the parties' agreement. Evidence extraneous to the contract that contradicts or alters the meaning of the contract in any way is inadmissible.

In determining whether to allow parol evidence, courts consider whether the written contract is intended to be a complete and final statement of the terms of the agreement. If it is, the contract is referred to as an **integrated contract,** and extraneous evidence (evidence from outside the contract) is excluded.

EXAMPLE 13.29 TKTS, Inc., offers to sell Gwen season tickets to the Dallas Cowboys football games in Cowboys Stadium. Prices and seat locations are indicated in diagrams in a brochure that accompanies the offer. Gwen responds, listing her seat preference. TKTS sends her the tickets, along with a different diagram showing seat locations. Also enclosed is a document that reads, "This is the entire agreement of the parties," which Gwen signs and returns. When Gwen goes to the first game, she discovers that her seat is not where she expected, based on the brochure. Under the parol evidence rule, however, the brochure is not part of the parties' agreement. The document that Gwen signed was identified as the parties' entire contract. Therefore, she cannot introduce in court any evidence of prior negotiations or agreements that contradict or vary the contract's terms. ■

A contract can be either completely or partially integrated. If it contains all of the terms of the parties' agreement, then it is completely integrated. If it contains only some of the terms and not others, it is partially integrated. If the contract is only partially integrated, evidence of consistent additional terms is admissible to supplement the written agreement.[24] Note that

---

24. *Restatement (Second) of Contracts*, Section 216.

Exhibit 13–4 The Parol Evidence Rule

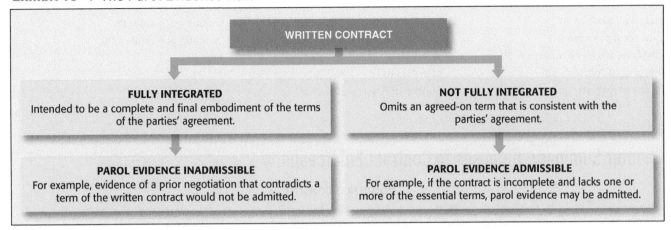

parol evidence is admitted only to add to the terms of a partially integrated contract. For both completely and partially integrated contracts, courts exclude any evidence that *contradicts* the writing.

Exhibit 13–4 illustrates the relationship between integrated contracts and the parol evidence rule.

Reviewing . . . Defenses to Contract Enforceability

Chelene had been a caregiver for Marta's elderly mother, Janis, for nine years. Shortly before Janis passed away, Chelene convinced her to buy Chelene's house for Marta. Janis died before the papers were signed, however. Four months later, Marta used her inheritance to buy Chelene's house without having it inspected. The house was built in the 1950s, and Chelene said it was in "perfect condition." Nevertheless, one year after the purchase, the basement started leaking. Marta had the paneling removed from the basement walls and discovered that the walls were bowed inward and cracked. Marta then had a civil engineer inspect the basement walls, and he found that the cracks had been caulked and painted over before the paneling was installed. He concluded that the "wall failure" had existed "for at least thirty years" and that the basement walls were "structurally unsound." Using the information presented in the chapter, answer the following questions.

1. Can Marta avoid the contract on the ground that both parties made a mistake about the condition of the house? Explain.

2. Can Marta sue Chelene for fraudulent misrepresentation? Why or why not? What element (or elements) might be lacking?

3. Now assume that Chelene knew that the basement walls were cracked and bowed and that she hired someone to install paneling before offering to sell the house. Did she have a duty to disclose this defect to Marta? Could a court find that Chelene's silence in this situation constituted misrepresentation? Explain.

4. Can Marta obtain rescission of the contract based on undue influence? If the sale to Janis had been completed before her death, could Janis have obtained rescission based on undue influence? Explain.

DEBATE THIS

- Many countries have eliminated the Statute of Frauds except for sales of real estate. The United States should do the same.

Key Terms

Chapter Summary: Defenses to Contract Enforceability

	VOLUNTARY CONSENT
Mistakes	1. *Unilateral*—Generally, the mistaken party is bound by the contract *unless* (a) the other party knows or should have known of the mistake or (b) the mistake is an inadvertent mathematical error—such as an error in addition or subtraction—committed without gross negligence. 2. *Bilateral (mutual)*—When both parties are mistaken about the same material fact, such as identity, either party can avoid the contract.
Fraudulent Misrepresentation	When fraud occurs, usually the innocent party can enforce or avoid the contract. The following elements are necessary to establish fraud: 1. A misrepresentation of a material fact must occur. 2. There must be an intent to deceive. 3. The innocent party must justifiably rely on the misrepresentation.
Undue Influence	Undue influence arises from special relationships, such as fiduciary relationships, in which one party's free will has been overcome by the undue influence exerted by the other party. Usually, the contract is voidable.
Duress	Duress is the tactic of forcing a party to enter a contract under the fear of a threat—for example, the threat of violence or serious economic loss. The party forced to enter the contract can rescind the contract.
	FORM

The Writing Requirement	1. *Applicability*—The following types of contracts fall under the Statute of Frauds and must be in writing to be enforceable:
	  a. Contracts involving interests in land, such as sales, leases, or mortgages.
	  b. Contracts that cannot by their terms be fully performed within one year from (the day after) the contract's formation.
	  c. Collateral promises, such as contracts made between a guarantor and a creditor whose terms make the guarantor secondarily liable. *Exception:* the "main purpose" rule.
	  d. Promises made in consideration of marriage, including promises to make a monetary payment or give property in consideration of a promise to marry and prenuptial agreements made in consideration of marriage.
	  e. Contracts for the sale of goods priced at $500 or more under the Statute of Frauds provision in Section 2–201 of the Uniform Commercial Code.
	2. *Exceptions*—Partial performance, admissions, and promissory estoppel.

Sufficiency of the Writing or Electronic Record	To constitute an enforceable contract under the Statute of Frauds, a writing must be signed by the party against whom enforcement is sought, name the parties, identify the subject matter, and state with reasonable certainty the essential terms of the contract. Under the UCC, a contract for a sale of goods is not enforceable beyond the quantity of goods shown in the contract.
The Parol Evidence Rule	The parol evidence rule prohibits the introduction at trial of evidence of the parties' prior or contemporaneous negotiations or agreements if this evidence contradicts or varies the terms of the parties' written contract. The written contract is assumed to be the complete embodiment of the parties' agreement. Because of the rigidity of the parol evidence rule, courts make a number of exceptions. For example, courts may allow parol evidence when a contract is void or voidable, contains ambiguous terms, or is incomplete.

Issue Spotters

1. In selling a house, Matt tells Ann that the wiring, fixtures, and appliances are of a certain quality. Matt knows nothing about the quality, but it is not as specified. Ann buys the house. On learning the true quality, Ann confronts Matt. He says he wasn't trying to fool her, he was only trying to make a sale. Can she rescind the deal? Why or why not? (See *Voluntary Consent*.)

2. My-T Quality Goods, Inc., and Nu! Sales Corporation orally agree to a deal. My-T's president has the essential terms written up on company letterhead stationery, and the memo is filed in My-T's office. If Nu! Sales later refuses to complete the transaction, is this memo a sufficient writing to enforce the contract against it? Explain your answer. (See *Sufficiency of the Writing or Electronic Record*.)

—**Check your answers to the *Issue Spotters* against the answers provided in Appendix D at the end of this text.**

Learning Objectives Check

1. In what types of situations might voluntary consent to a contract's terms be lacking?
2. What is the difference between a unilateral and a bilateral mistake?
3. What are the elements of fraudulent misrepresentation?
4. What contracts must be in writing to be enforceable?
5. What is parol evidence? When is it admissible to clarify the terms of a written contract?

—**Answers to the even-numbered *Learning Objectives Check* questions can be found in Appendix E at the end of this text.**

Business Scenarios and Case Problems

13–1. Voluntary Consent. Jerome is an elderly man who lives with his nephew, Philip. Jerome is totally dependent on Philip's support. Philip tells Jerome that unless Jerome transfers a tract of land he owns to Philip for a price 30 percent below market value, Philip will no longer support and take care of him. Jerome enters into the contract. Discuss fully whether Jerome can set aside this contract. (See *Voluntary Consent*.)

13–2. Statute of Frauds. Gemma promises a local hardware store that she will pay for a lawn mower that her brother is purchasing on credit if the brother fails to pay the debt. Must this promise be in writing to be enforceable? Why or why not? (See *The Writing Requirement*.)

13–3. Misrepresentation. Charter One Bank owned a fifteen-story commercial building. A fire inspector told Charter that the building's drinking-water and fire-suppression systems were linked, which violated building codes. Without disclosing this information, Charter sold the building to Northpoint Properties, Inc. Northpoint spent $280,000 to repair the water and fire-suppression systems and filed a suit against Charter One. Is the seller liable for not disclosing the building's defects? Discuss. [*Northpoint Properties, Inc. v. Charter One Bank*, 2011-Ohio-2512 (Ohio App. 8 Dist. 2011) (See *Voluntary Consent*.)

13–4. Statute of Frauds. Newmark & Co. Real Estate, Inc., contacted 2615 East 17 Street Realty, LLC, to lease certain real property on behalf of a client. Newmark e-mailed the landlord a separate agreement for the payment of Newmark's commission. The landlord e-mailed it back with a separate demand to pay the commission in installments. Newmark revised the agreement and e-mailed a final copy to the landlord. Do the parties have an agreement that qualifies as a writing under the Statute of Frauds? Explain. [*Newmark & Co. Real Estate, Inc. v. 2615 East 17 Street Realty, LLC*, 80 A.D.3d 476, 914 N.Y.S.2d 162 (1 Dept. 2011)] (See *Sufficiency of the Writing or Electronic Record*.)

13–5. The Parol Evidence Rule. Rimma Vaks and her husband, Steven Mangano, executed a written contract with Denise Ryan and Ryan Auction Co. to auction their furnishings. The six-page contract provided a detailed summary of the parties' agreement. It addressed the items to be auctioned, how reserve prices would be determined, and the amount of Ryan's commission. When a dispute arose between the parties, Vaks and Mangano sued Ryan for breach of contract. Vaks and Mangano asserted that, before they executed the contract, Ryan had made various oral representations that were inconsistent with the terms of their written agreement. Assuming that their written contract was valid, can Vaks and Mangano recover for breach of an oral contract? Why or why not? [*Vaks v. Ryan*, 2012 WL 194398 (Mass.App. 2012)] (See *The Parol Evidence Rule*.)

13–6. Promises Made in Consideration of Marriage. After twenty-nine years of marriage, Robert and Mary Lou Tuttle were divorced. They admitted in court that before they were married, they had signed a prenuptial agreement. They agreed that the agreement had stated that each would keep his or her own property and anything derived from that property. Robert came into the marriage owning farmland, while Mary Lou owned no real estate. During the marriage, ten different parcels of land, totaling about six hundred acres, were acquired, and two corporations, Tuttle Grain, Inc., and Tuttle Farms, Inc., were formed. A copy of the prenuptial agreement could not be found. Can the court enforce the agreement without a writing? Why or why not? [*In re Marriage of Tuttle*, 2013 WL 164035 (Ill. App. 5 Dist. 2013)] (See *The Writing Requirement*.)

13–7. Business Case Problem with Sample Answer— Fraudulent Misrepresentation. Joy Pervis and Brenda Pauley worked together as talent agents in Georgia. When Pervis "discovered" actress Dakota Fanning, Pervis sent Fanning's audition tape to Cindy Osbrink, a talent agent in California. Osbrink agreed to represent Fanning in California and to pay 3 percent of Osbrink's commissions to Pervis and Pauley, who agreed to split the payments equally. Six years later, Pervis told Pauley that their agreement with Osbrink had expired and there would be no more payments. Nevertheless, Pervis continued to receive payments from Osbrink. Each time Pauley asked about commissions, however, Pervis replied that she was not receiving any. Do these facts evidence fraud? Explain. [*In re Pervis*, 512 Bankr. 348 (N.D.Ga. 2014)] (See *Voluntary Consent*.)

—For a sample answer to Problem 13–7, go to Appendix F at the end of this text.

13–8. Promises Made in Consideration of Marriage. Before their marriage, Linda and Gerald Heiden executed a prenuptial agreement. The agreement provided that "no spouse shall have any right in the property of the other spouse, even in the event of the death of either party." The description of Gerald's separate property included a settlement from a personal injury suit. Twenty-four years later, Linda filed for divorce. The court ruled that the prenuptial agreement applied only in the event of death, not divorce, and entered a judgment that included a

property division and spousal support award. The ruling disparately favored Linda, whose monthly income with spousal support would be $4,467, leaving Gerald with only $1,116. Did the court interpret the Heidens' prenuptial agreement correctly? Discuss. [*Heiden v. Heiden*, 2015 WL 849006 (Mich.App. 2015)] (See *The Writing Requirement*.)

13–9. A Question of Ethics—Bilateral Mistake. On behalf of BRJM, LLC, Nicolas Kepple offered Howard Engelsen $210,000 for a parcel of land known as lot five on the north side of Barnes Road in Stonington, Connecticut. Engelsen's company, Output Systems, Inc., owned the land. Engelsen had the lot surveyed and obtained an appraisal. The appraiser valued the property at $277,000, after determining that it was 3 acres in size and thus could not be subdivided because it did not meet the town's minimum legal requirement of 3.7 acres for subdivision. Engelsen responded to Kepple's offer with a counteroffer of $230,000, which Kepple accepted. The parties signed a contract. When Engelsen refused to go through with the deal, BRJM filed a suit against Output, seeking specific performance and other relief. Output asserted the defense of mutual mistake on at least two grounds. [*BRJM, LLC v. Output Systems, Inc.*, 100 Conn.App. 143, 917 A.2d 605 (2007)] (See *Voluntary Consent*.)

1. In the counteroffer, Engelsen asked Kepple to remove from their contract a clause requiring written confirmation of the availability of a "free split," which meant that the property could be subdivided without the town's prior approval. Kepple agreed. After signing the contract, Kepple learned that the property was *not* entitled to a free split. Would this circumstance qualify as a mistake on which the *defendant* could avoid the contract? Why or why not?

2. After signing the contract, Engelsen obtained a second appraisal that established the size of lot five as 3.71 acres, which meant that it could be subdivided, and valued the property at $490,000. Can the defendant avoid the contract on the basis of a mistake in the first appraisal? Explain.

Critical Thinking and Writing Assignments

13–10. Business Law Critical Thinking Group Assignment. Jason Novell, doing business as Novell Associates, hired Barbara Meade as an independent contractor. The parties orally agreed on the terms of employment, including payment of a share of the company's income to Meade, but they did not put anything in writing. Two years later, Meade quit. Novell then told Meade that she was entitled to $9,602— 25 percent of the difference between the accounts receivable and the accounts payable as of Meade's last day of work. Meade disagreed and demanded more than $63,500—25 percent of the revenue from all invoices, less the cost of materials and outside processing, for each of the years that she had worked

for Novell. Meade filed a lawsuit against Novell for breach of contract. (See *The Writing Requirement*.)

1. The first group will evaluate whether the parties had an enforceable contract.

2. The second group will decide whether the parties' oral agreement falls within any exception to the Statute of Frauds.

3. The third group will discuss how the lawsuit would be affected if Novell admitted that the parties had an oral contract under which Meade was entitled to 25 percent of the difference between the accounts receivable and payable as of the day Meade quit.

14

Third Party Rights and Discharge

LEARNING OBJECTIVES

The five Learning Objectives *below are designed to help improve your understanding of the chapter. After reading this chapter, you should be able to answer the following questions:*

1. What is an assignment? What is the difference between an assignment and a delegation?

2. In what situations is the delegation of duties prohibited?

3. What factors indicate that a third party beneficiary is an intended beneficiary?

4. How are most contracts discharged?

5. When is a breach considered material, and what effect does that have on the other party's obligation to perform?

Privity of Contract The relationship that exists between the promisor and the promisee of a contract.

> "The laws of a state change with the changing times."
>
> **AESCHYLUS**
> 525–456 B.C.E.
> (GREEK DRAMATIST)

Once it has been determined that a valid and legally enforceable contract exists, attention can turn to the rights and duties of the parties to the contract. A contract is a private agreement between the parties who have entered into it, and traditionally these parties alone have rights and liabilities under the contract. This principle is referred to as **privity of contract**, and it establishes the basic principle that third parties have no rights in contracts to which they are not parties.

You may be convinced by now that for every rule of contract law, there is an exception. As times change, so must the laws, as indicated in the chapter-opening quotation. When justice cannot be served by adherence to a rule of law, exceptions to the rule must be made.

In this chapter, we look at some exceptions to the rule of privity of contract. These exceptions include *assignments, delegations,* and *third party beneficiary contracts.* We also examine how contractual obligations can be *discharged.* Normally, contract discharge is accomplished when both parties perform the acts promised in the contract. In the latter part of the chapter, we look at the degree of performance required to discharge a contractual obligation, as well as at some other ways that contract discharge can occur.

14-1 Assignments

In a bilateral contract, the two parties have corresponding rights and duties. One party has a *right* to require the other to perform some task, and the other has a *duty* to perform it.

331

Assignment The transfer to another of all or part of one's rights arising under a contract.

Sometimes, though, a party will transfer her or his rights under the contract to someone else. The transfer of contract *rights* to a third person is known as an **assignment.** (The transfer of contract duties is a *delegation,* as will be discussed later in this chapter.)

Assignments are important because they are often used in business financing. Lending institutions, such as banks, frequently assign the rights to receive payments under their loan contracts to other firms, which pay for those rights. Lenders that make *mortgage loans* (loans that enable prospective home buyers to purchase real estate), for instance, often assign their rights to collect the mortgage payments to a third party. Following an assignment, the home buyer is notified that future payments must be made to the third party, rather than to the original lender. Billions of dollars change hands daily in the business world in the form of assignments of rights in contracts. If it were not possible to transfer contractual rights, many businesses could not continue to operate.

14–1a Effect of an Assignment

Assignor A party who transfers (assigns) his or her rights under a contract to another party (the *assignee*).

Assignee A party to whom the rights under a contract are transferred, or assigned.

Obligee One to whom an obligation is owed.

Obligor One who owes an obligation to another.

In an assignment, the party assigning the rights to a third party is known as the **assignor,**[1] and the party receiving the rights is the **assignee.**[2] Other terms traditionally used to describe the parties in assignment relationships are **obligee** (the person to whom a duty, or obligation, is owed) and **obligor** (the person who is obligated to perform the duty). Exhibit 14–1 illustrates assignment relationships.

In general, an assignment can take any form, oral or written, although it is advisable to put all assignments in writing. Of course, assignments covered by the Statute of Frauds—such as an assignment of an interest in land—must be in writing to be enforceable. In addition, most states require contracts for the assignment of wages to be in writing.[3] There are other assignments that must be in writing as well.

---

1. Pronounced uh-*sye*-nore.
2. Pronounced uh-*sye*-*nee.*
3. See, for example, California Labor Code Section 300.

Exhibit 14–1 Assignment Relationships

In the assignment relationship illustrated here, Alex assigns his *rights* under a contract that he made with Brent to a third party, Carmen. Alex thus becomes the *assignor* and Carmen the *assignee* of the contractual rights. Brent, the *obligor,* now owes performance to Carmen instead of to Alex. Alex's original contract rights are extinguished after the assignment.

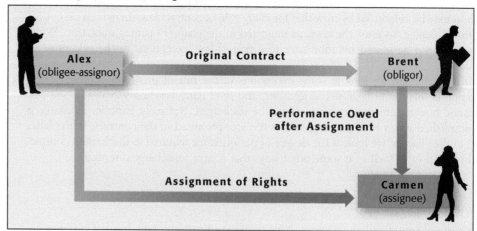

Extinguishes the Rights of the Assignor When rights under a contract are assigned unconditionally, the rights of the assignor are extinguished.[4] The assignee has a right to demand performance from the other original party to the contract, the obligor.

EXAMPLE 14.1 Brent (the obligor) owes Alex $1,000 under a contract in which Brent agreed to buy Alex's MacBook Pro laptop. Alex, the obligee, assigns to Carmen the right to receive the $1,000 (thus, Alex is the assignor). Here, a valid assignment of a debt exists. Carmen, the assignee, can enforce the contract against Brent, the obligor, if he fails to perform (pay the $1,000). ▪

Assignee Takes Rights Subject to Defenses The assignee obtains only those rights that the assignor originally had. In addition, the assignee's rights are subject to the defenses that the obligor has against the assignor.

EXAMPLE 14.2 In *Example 14.1,* Brent owes Alex $1,000 under a contract in which Brent agreed to buy Alex's laptop. Alex assigns his right to receive the $1,000 to Carmen. But Brent, in deciding to purchase the laptop, relied on Alex's fraudulent misrepresentation that the computer had sixteen megabytes of memory. When Brent discovers that the computer has only eight megabytes of memory, he tells Alex that he is going to return it and cancel the contract. Even though Alex has assigned his "right" to receive the $1,000 to Carmen, Brent need not pay Carmen the $1,000—Brent can raise the defense of Alex's fraudulent misrepresentation to avoid payment. ▪

14-1b Rights That Cannot Be Assigned

As a general rule, all rights can be assigned. Exceptions are made, however, in the following special circumstances.

When a Statute Expressly Prohibits Assignment If a statute expressly prohibits assignment, the right in question cannot be assigned. **EXAMPLE 14.3** Quincy is an employee of Specialty Travel, Inc. Specialty is an employer bound by workers' compensation statutes in this state, and thus Quincy is a covered employee. Quincy is injured on the job and begins to collect monthly workers' compensation checks. In need of a loan, Quincy borrows from Draper, offering to assign to Draper all of her future workers' compensation benefits. A state statute prohibits the assignment of *future* workers' compensation benefits, and thus such rights cannot be assigned. ▪

When a Contract Is Personal in Nature When a contract is for personal services, the rights under the contract normally cannot be assigned unless all that remains is a monetary payment.[5] **EXAMPLE 14.4** Anton signs a contract to be a tutor for Marisa's children. Marisa then attempts to assign to Roberto her right to Anton's services. Roberto cannot enforce the contract against Anton. Roberto's children may be more difficult to tutor than Marisa's. Thus, if Marisa could assign her rights to Anton's services to Roberto, it would change the nature of Anton's obligation. Because personal services are unique to the person rendering them, rights to receive personal services are likewise unique and cannot be assigned. ▪

When an Assignment Will Significantly Change the Risk or Duties of the Obligor A right cannot be assigned if assignment will significantly alter the risks or the duties of the obligor.[6] **EXAMPLE 14.5** Alex has a hotel, and to insure it, he takes out a policy with Northwest Insurance Company. The policy insures against fire, theft, floods, and vandalism. Alex attempts to assign the insurance policy to Carmen, who also owns a hotel.

Can the rights to receive piano lessons be assigned to another student?

---

4. *Restatement (Second) of Contracts,* Section 317.
5. *Restatement (Second) of Contracts,* Sections 317 and 318.
6. See Section 2–210(2) of the Uniform Commercial Code (UCC).

The assignment is ineffective because it may substantially alter the insurance company's duty of performance and the risk that the company undertakes. An insurance company evaluates the particular risk associated with a specific party and tailors its policy to fit that risk. If the policy were assigned to a third party, the insurance risk would be materially altered. ■

When the Contract Prohibits Assignment

If a contract stipulates that the right cannot be assigned, then *ordinarily* it cannot be assigned. This restraint operates only against the parties themselves. It does not prohibit an assignment by operation of law, such as an assignment pursuant to bankruptcy or death.

Whether an *antiassignment clause* is effective depends, in part, on how it is phrased. A contract that states that *any* assignment is void effectively prohibits any assignment. **EXAMPLE 14.6** Ramirez agrees to build a house for Lee. Their contract states "This contract cannot be assigned by Lee without Ramirez's consent. Any assignment without such consent renders the contract void." This antiassignment clause is effective, and Lee cannot assign her rights without obtaining Ramirez's consent. ■

The rule that a contract can prohibit assignments has several exceptions:

1. A contract cannot prevent an assignment of the right to receive funds. This exception exists to encourage the free flow of funds and credit in modern business settings.

2. The assignment of ownership rights in real estate often cannot be prohibited because such a prohibition is contrary to public policy in most states. Prohibitions of this kind are called restraints against **alienation** (the voluntary transfer of land ownership).

3. The assignment of negotiable instruments (such as checks and promissory notes) cannot be prohibited.

4. In a contract for the sale of goods, the right to receive damages for breach of contract or payment on an account may be assigned even though the sales contract prohibits such an assignment.[7]

The lease and purchase agreement in the following case contained an antiassignment clause. The court had to decide whether the clause was enforceable.

> **Alienation** The transfer of title to real property (which "alienates" the real property from the former owner).

---

7. UCC 2–210(2).

Bass-Fineberg Leasing, Inc. v. Modern Auto Sales, Inc.

Court of Appeals of Ohio, Ninth District, Medina County, __ Ohio App.3d __, __ N.E.3d __, 2015-Ohio-46 (2015).

FACTS Bass-Fineberg Leasing, Inc., leased a tour bus to Modern Auto Sales, Inc., and Michael Cipriani. The lease included an option to buy the bus. The lease prohibited Modern Auto and Cipriani from assigning their rights without Bass-Fineberg's written consent. Later, Cipriani left the bus with Anthony Allie at BVIP Limo Services, Ltd., for repairs. Modern Auto and Cipriani did not pay for the repairs. At the same time, they defaulted on the lease payments to Bass-Fineberg. While BVIP retained possession of the bus, Allie signed an agreement with Cipriani to buy it and to make an initial $5,000 payment to Bass-Fineberg. Bass-Fineberg filed an action in an Ohio

Can the rights to a leased tour bus be assigned?

iStockPhoto.com/mladn61

state court against Modern Auto, Cipriani, BVIP, and Allie to regain possession of the bus. The court ordered the bus returned to Bass-Fineberg and the $5,000 payment refunded to Allie. All of the parties appealed.

ISSUE Was the lease's antiassignment clause enforceable?

DECISION Yes. A state intermediate appellate court affirmed the lower court's order. The bus was to be returned to Bass-Fineberg and the $5,000 was to be refunded to Allie.

REASON An antiassignment clause can be enforceable when it clearly prohibits an assignment. Violation of an enforceable anti-assignment provision renders the resulting agreement void. The antiassignment clause in the lease between Bass-Fineberg and Modern Auto and Cipriani was clear—"MODERN AUTO AND CIPRIANI MAY NOT ASSIGN . . . [THEIR] RIGHTS . . . UNDER THIS LEASE . . . WITHOUT BASS-FINEBERG'S PRIOR WRITTEN CONSENT." Bass-Fineberg argued that under this clause, the contract between Cipriani and Allie was void, because Bass-Fineberg had not provided written consent. BVIP contended that if the contract was void, then BVIP should receive a refund of its $5,000 payment. The court agreed with both of these parties. The contract between Cipriani and Allie was void because Cipriani could not assign his rights under the lease without Bass-Fineberg's written consent. Because the contract was void, the parties were to be returned to their precontract status, which included a refund of the $5,000 payment.

CRITICAL THINKING—Economic Consideration *The repairs to the bus cost $1,341.50. Who should pay this amount? Why?*

14–1c Notice of Assignment

Once a valid assignment of rights has been made to a third party, the third party should notify the obligor of the assignment (for example, in Exhibit 14–1, Carmen should notify Brent). Giving notice is not legally necessary to establish the validity of the assignment because an assignment is effective immediately, whether or not notice is given. Two major problems arise, however, when notice of the assignment is *not* given to the obligor.

Priority Issues If the assignor assigns the same right to two different persons, the question arises as to which one has priority—that is, which one has the right to the performance by the obligor. The rule most often observed in the United States is that the first assignment in time is the first in right. Some states, though, follow the English rule, which basically gives priority to the first assignee who gives notice.

    EXAMPLE 14.7 Jason owes Alexis $5,000 under a contract. Alexis first assigns the claim to Louisa, who does not give notice to Jason. Then Alexis assigns it to Dorman, who notifies Jason. In most states, Louisa would have priority because the assignment to her was first in time. In some states, however, Dorman would have priority because he gave first notice. ∎

Potential for Discharge by Performance to the Wrong Party Until the obligor has notice of an assignment, the obligor can discharge his or her obligation by performance to the assignor, and this performance constitutes a discharge to the assignee. Once the obligor receives proper notice, only performance to the assignee can discharge the obligor's obligations.

    EXAMPLE 14.8 Recall that Alexis, the obligee in *Example 14.7,* assigned to Louisa her right to collect $5,000 from Jason, and Louisa did not give notice to Jason. What will happen if Jason later pays Alexis the $5,000? Although the assignment was valid, Jason's payment to Alexis will discharge the debt. Louisa's failure to notify Jason of the assignment will cause her to lose the right to collect the $5,000 from Jason. (Note that Louisa will still have a claim against Alexis for the $5,000.) If Louisa had given Jason notice of the assignment, Jason's payment to Alexis would not have discharged the debt. ∎

Providing notice of assignment, though not legally required, is one of the best ways to avoid potential legal disputes over assignments. Whether you are the assignee or the assignor, you should inform the obligor of the assignment. An assignee who does not give notice may lose the right to performance, but failure to notify the obligor may have repercussions for the assignor as well. If no notice is given and the obligor performs the duty for the assignor, the assignee can sue the assignor for breach of contract. Litigation may also ensue if the assignor has assigned a right to two different parties, as may happen when rights that overlap (such as rights to receive various profits from a given enterprise) are assigned.

PREVENTING LEGAL DISPUTES

14-2 Delegations

Just as a party can transfer rights to a third party through an assignment, a party can also transfer duties. Duties are not assigned, however. They are *delegated*. Normally, a **delegation of duties** does not relieve the party making the delegation (the **delegator**) of the obligation to perform in the event that the party to whom the duty has been delegated (the **delegatee**) fails to perform.

No special form is required to create a valid delegation of duties. As long as the delegator expresses an intention to make the delegation, it is effective. The delegator need not even use the word *delegate*.

14-2a Duties That Cannot Be Delegated

As a general rule, any duty can be delegated. This rule has some exceptions, however. Delegation is prohibited in the following circumstances:

1. When performance depends on the personal skill or talents of the obligor.

2. When special trust has been placed in the obligor.

3. When performance by a third party will vary materially from that expected by the obligee.

4. When the contract expressly prohibits delegation.

When the Duties Are Personal in Nature When special trust has been placed in the obligor or when performance depends on the obligor's personal skill or talents, contractual duties cannot be delegated. **EXAMPLE 14.9** O'Brien, who is impressed with Brodie's ability to perform veterinary surgery, contracts with Brodie to have her perform surgery on O'Brien's prize-winning stallion in July. Brodie later decides that she would rather spend the summer at the beach, so she delegates her duties under the contract to Lopez, who is also a competent veterinary surgeon. The delegation is not effective without O'Brien's consent, no matter how competent Lopez is, because the contract is for *personal* performance. ■

In contrast, nonpersonal duties may be delegated. Suppose that, in *Example 14.9*, Brodie contracts with O'Brien to pick up a large horse trailer and deliver it to O'Brien's property. Brodie delegates this duty to Lopez, who owns a towing business. This delegation is effective because the performance required is of a *routine* and *nonpersonal* nature.

When Performance by a Third Party Will Vary Materially from That Expected by the Obligee When performance by a third party will vary materially from that expected by the obligee under the contract, contractual duties cannot be delegated. **EXAMPLE 14.10** Jared, a wealthy investor, established the company Heaven Sent to provide grants of capital to struggling but potentially successful businesses. Jared contracted with Merilyn, whose judgment Jared trusted, to select the recipients of the grants. Later, Merilyn delegated this duty to Donald. Jared did not trust Donald's ability to select worthy recipients. This delegation is not effective because it materially alters Jared's expectations under the contract with Merilyn. ■

When the Contract Prohibits Delegation When the contract expressly prohibits delegation by including an *antidelegation clause,* the duties cannot be delegated. **EXAMPLE 14.11** Dakota Company has contracted with Belisario, a certified public accountant, to perform its audits. Because the contract prohibits delegation, Belisario cannot delegate the duty to perform the audits to another accountant—not even an accountant at the same firm. ■

14-2b Effect of a Delegation

If a delegation of duties is enforceable, the obligee (the one to whom performance is owed) must accept performance from the delegatee (the one to whom the duties are delegated). **EXAMPLE 14.12** Brent has a duty to pick up and deliver heavy construction machinery to Alex's

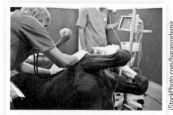

Under what circumstances may a veterinary surgeon delegate her duties to another veterinarian?

iStockPhoto.com/baranozdemir

property. Brent delegates his duty to Carmen. In this situation, Alex (the obligee) must accept performance from Carmen (the delegatee) because the delegation is effective. The obligee can legally refuse performance from the delegatee only if the duty is one that cannot be delegated. ■ Exhibit 14–2 graphically illustrates their delegation relationship.

As noted, a valid delegation of duties does not relieve the delegator of obligations under the contract.[8] Although there are many exceptions, the general rule today is that the obligee can sue both the delegatee and the delegator for failure to perform.

EXAMPLE 14.13 In the situation in *Example 14.12,* if Carmen (the delegatee) fails to perform, Brent (the delegator) is still liable to Alex (the obligee). The obligee can also hold the delegatee liable if the delegatee made a promise of performance that will directly benefit the obligee. In this situation, there is an "assumption of duty" on the part of the delegatee, and breach of this duty makes the delegatee liable to the obligee. For instance, if Carmen promised Brent, in a contract, to pick up and deliver the construction equipment to Alex's property but fails to do so, Alex can sue Brent, Carmen, or both. ■

14-2c "Assignment of All Rights"

Sometimes, a contract provides for an "assignment of all rights." This wording may create both an assignment of rights and a delegation of duties.[9] Typically, this situation occurs when general words are used, such as "I assign the contract" or "I assign all my rights under the contract." A court normally will construe such words as implying both an assignment of rights and a delegation of any duties of performance. Thus, the assignor remains liable if the assignee fails to perform the contractual obligations.

---

8. For a classic case on this issue, see *Crane Ice Cream Co. v. Terminal Freezing & Heating Co.,* 147 Md. 588, 128 A. 280 (1925).
9. See UCC 2–210(1), (4); and *Restatement (Second) of Contracts,* Section 328.

Exhibit 14–2 Delegation Relationships

In the delegation relationship illustrated here, Brent delegates his *duties* under a contract that he made with Alex to a third party, Carmen. Brent thus becomes the *delegator* and Carmen the *delegatee* of the contractual duties. Carmen now owes performance of the contractual duties to Alex. Note that a delegation of duties normally does not relieve the delegator (Brent) of liability if the delegatee (Carmen) fails to perform the contractual duties.

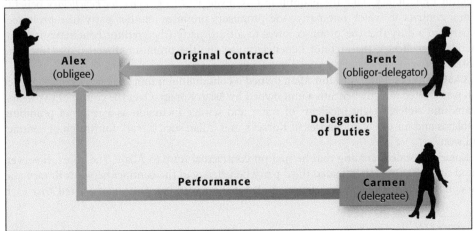

14-3 Third Party Beneficiaries

Third Party Beneficiary
One who is not a party to the contract but who stands to benefit from the contract's performance.

Intended Beneficiary A third party for whose benefit a contract is formed. An intended beneficiary can sue the promisor if the contract is breached.

Another exception to the doctrine of privity of contract may arise when a third party benefits from a contract between two other parties. This **third party beneficiary** may have rights in the contract. Note, though, that the law identifies two types of third party beneficiaries: *intended beneficiaries* and *incidental beneficiaries*. Only intended beneficiaries have legal rights in the contract.

An **intended beneficiary** is one for whose benefit the contract was made. That is, the original parties to the contract agreed when they made the contract that performance should be rendered to or directly benefit a third person. This type of third party beneficiary has legal rights and can sue the promisor directly for breach of the contract.

Who, though, is the promisor? After all, in bilateral contracts, both parties to the contract are promisors because both make promises that can be enforced.

14-3a Who Is the Promisor?

In third party beneficiary contracts, courts determine the identity of the promisor by asking which party made the promise that benefits the third party. That person is the promisor.

In effect, allowing the third party to sue the promisor directly circumvents the "middle person" (the promisee) and thus reduces the burden on the courts. Otherwise, the third party would sue the promisee, who would then sue the promisor. Indeed, at one time, this circuitous route was the rule. The reason was that the third party beneficiary was not a party to the contract and thus, under the doctrine of privity of contract, had no legal rights under the contract.

CASE EXAMPLE 14.14 The classic case that gave third party beneficiaries the right to bring a suit directly against a promisor was decided in 1859. The case involved three parties—Holly, Lawrence, and Fox. Holly had borrowed $300 from Lawrence. Shortly thereafter, Holly loaned $300 to Fox, who in return promised Holly that he would pay Holly's debt to Lawrence on the following day. When Lawrence failed to obtain the $300 from Fox, he sued Fox to recover the funds. The court had to decide whether Lawrence could sue Fox directly (rather than suing Holly). The court held that when "a promise [is] made for the benefit of another, he for whose benefit it is made may bring an action for its breach."[10] ■

14-3b Types of Intended Beneficiaries

Intended beneficiaries can be further classified as *creditor beneficiaries* or *donee beneficiaries*.

Creditor Beneficiary Like the plaintiff in *Case Example 14.14*, a *creditor beneficiary* benefits from a contract in which one party (the promisor) promises another party (the promisee) to perform a duty that the promisee owes to a third party (the creditor beneficiary). As an intended beneficiary, the creditor beneficiary can sue the promisor directly to enforce the contract.

CASE EXAMPLE 14.15 Autumn Allan owned a condominium unit in a Texas complex. Her unit was located directly beneath a unit owned by Aslan Koraev. Over the course of two years, Allan's unit suffered eight incidents of water and sewage incursion as a result of plumbing problems and misuse of appliances in Koraev's unit. Allan sued Koraev for breach of contract and won.

Koraev appealed, arguing that he had no contractual duty to Allan. The court, however, found that Allan was an intended third party beneficiary of the contract between Koraev and the condominium owners' association. Because the governing documents stated that each

---

10. *Lawrence v. Fox*, 20 N.Y. 268 (1859).

owner had to comply strictly with their provisions, failure to comply created grounds for an action by either the condominium association or an aggrieved (wronged) owner. Here, Allan was an aggrieved owner and could sue Koraev directly for his failure to perform his contractual duties to the condominium association.[11] ▪

Donee Beneficiary When a contract is made for the express purpose of giving a *gift* to a third party, the third party is a *donee beneficiary*. Like a creditor beneficiary, a donee beneficiary can sue the promisor directly to enforce the promise.[12]

The most common donee beneficiary contract is a life insurance contract. **EXAMPLE 14.16** Ang (the promisee) pays premiums to Standard Life, a life insurance company, and Standard Life (the promisor) promises to pay a certain amount on Ang's death to anyone Ang designates as a beneficiary. The designated beneficiary is a donee beneficiary under the life insurance policy and can enforce the promise made by the insurance company to pay her or him on Ang's death. ▪

14-3c When the Rights of an Intended Beneficiary Vest

An intended third party beneficiary cannot enforce a contract against the original parties until the third party's rights have *vested*, meaning that the rights have taken effect and cannot be taken away. Until these rights have vested, the original parties to the contract—the promisor and the promisee—can modify or rescind the contract without the consent of the third party.

When do the rights of third parties vest? Generally, the rights vest when one of the following occurs:

1. When the third party demonstrates express consent to the agreement, such as by sending a letter, a note, or an e-mail acknowledging awareness of, and consent to, a contract formed for her or his benefit.

2. When the third party materially alters his or her position in detrimental reliance on the contract, such as when a donee beneficiary contracts to have a home built in reliance on the receipt of funds promised to him or her in a donee beneficiary contract.

3. When the conditions for vesting are satisfied. For instance, the rights of a beneficiary under a life insurance policy vest when the insured person dies.

14-3d Incidental Beneficiaries

Sometimes, a third person receives a benefit from a contract even though that person's benefit is not the reason the contract was made. Such a person is known as an **incidental beneficiary.** Because the benefit is unintentional, an incidental beneficiary cannot sue to enforce the contract.

CASE EXAMPLE 14.17 Spectators at the infamous boxing match in which Mike Tyson was disqualified for biting his opponent's ear sued Tyson and the fight's promoters for a refund on the basis of breach of contract. The spectators claimed that they were third party beneficiaries of the contract between Tyson and the fight's promoters. The court, however, held that the spectators could not sue, because they were not in contractual privity with the defendants. Any benefits they received from the contract were incidental to the contract. According to the court, the spectators got what they paid for: "the right to view whatever event transpired."[13] ▪

When can a condominium owner directly sue another owner in the same building because of water and sewage incursion?

Incidental Beneficiary A third party who benefits from a contract even though the contract was not formed for that purpose. An incidental beneficiary has no rights in the contract and cannot sue to have it enforced.

11. *Allan v. Nersesova*, 307 S.W.3d 564 (Tx.App—Dallas 2010).
12. This principle was first enunciated in *Seaver v. Ransom*, 224 N.Y. 233, 120 N.E. 639 (1918).
13. *Castillo v. Tyson*, 268 A.D.2d 336, 701 N.Y.S.2d 423 (Sup.Ct.App.Div. 2000).

LEARNING OBJECTIVE 3

What factors indicate that a third party beneficiary is an intended beneficiary?

14–3e Identifying Intended versus Incidental Beneficiaries

In determining whether a party is an intended or an incidental beneficiary, the courts focus on the parties' intent, as expressed in the contract language and implied by the surrounding circumstances. Any beneficiary who is not deemed an intended beneficiary is considered incidental. Exhibit 14–3 graphically illustrates the distinction between intended and incidental beneficiaries.

Although no single test can embrace all possible situations, courts often apply the *reasonable person* test: Would a reasonable person in the position of the beneficiary believe that the promisee intended to confer on the beneficiary the right to enforce the contract? In addition, the presence of one or more of the following factors strongly indicates that the third party is an intended beneficiary of the contract:

1. Performance is rendered directly to the third party.

2. The third party has the right to control the details of performance.

3. The third party is expressly designated as a beneficiary in the contract.

CASE EXAMPLE 14.18 Neumann Homes, Inc., contracted to make public improvements for the Village of Antioch, Illinois. Neumann subcontracted the grading work required under the contract to Lake County Grading Company. The subcontractor completed the work but was not paid in full. When Neumann declared bankruptcy, the subcontractor filed a suit against the Village to recover, claiming to be a third party beneficiary of the contract between the Village and Neumann.

The court held in favor of the subcontractor. Under an Illinois statute, the Village was required to obtain a payment bond guaranteeing that a contractor would pay what was owed for the completion of any public works project. The court reasoned that this statute was intended to benefit subcontractors in public works contracts. Thus, it was reasonable for Lake County to believe that it was an intended third party beneficiary. Because the Village had failed to obtain a bond ensuring payment to subcontractors, Lake County could sue for breach of contract.[14] ▪

---

14. *Lake County Grading Co. v. Village of Antioch*, 2014 IL 115805, 19 N.E.3d 615 (Ill. Sup. 2014).

Exhibit 14–3 Third Party Beneficiaries

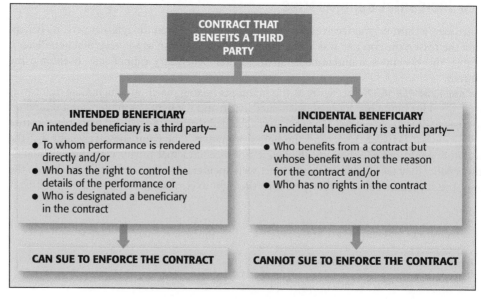

14-4 Contract Discharge

The most common way to **discharge,** or terminate, one's contractual duties is by the **performance** of those duties. The duty to perform under a contract may be *conditioned* on the occurrence or nonoccurrence of a certain event, or the duty may be *absolute.* As shown in Exhibit 14–4, in addition to performance, a contract can be discharged in numerous other ways, including discharge by agreement of the parties and discharge by operation of law.

14-4a Conditions of Performance

In most contracts, promises of performance are not expressly conditioned or qualified. Instead, they are *absolute promises.* They must be performed, or the party making the promise will be in breach of contract. **EXAMPLE 14.19** Paloma Enterprises contracts to sell a truckload of organic produce to Tran for $10,000. The parties' promises are unconditional: Paloma will deliver the produce to Tran, and Tran will pay $10,000 to Paloma. The payment does not have to be made if the produce is not delivered. ◼

In some situations, however, contractual promises are conditioned. A **condition** is a qualification in a contract based on a possible future event, the occurrence or nonoccurrence of which will trigger the performance of a legal obligation or terminate an existing obligation under a contract. If the condition is not satisfied, the obligations of the parties are discharged.

Three types of conditions can be present in any given contract: *conditions precedent, conditions subsequent,* and *concurrent conditions.*

Conditions Precedent   A condition that must be fulfilled before a party's promise becomes absolute is called a **condition precedent.** The condition precedes the absolute duty to perform. Life insurance contracts frequently specify that certain conditions, such as passing a physical examination, must be met before the insurance company will be obligated to perform under the contract.

Many contracts are conditioned on an independent appraisal of value. **EXAMPLE 14.20** Restoration Motors offers to buy Charlie's 1960 Cadillac limousine only if an expert appraiser estimates that it can be restored for less than a certain price. Thus, the parties' obligations are conditioned on the outcome of the appraisal. If the condition is not satisfied—that is, if the appraiser deems the cost to be significantly above that price—their obligations are discharged. ◼

Conditions Subsequent   When a condition operates to terminate a party's absolute promise to perform, it is called a **condition subsequent.** The condition follows, or is subsequent to, the absolute duty to perform. If the condition occurs, the party need not perform any further.

EXAMPLE 14.21 A law firm hires Julia Darby, a recent law school graduate. Their contract provides that the firm's obligation to continue employing Darby is discharged if she fails to pass the bar exam by her second attempt. This is a condition subsequent because a failure to pass the exam—and thus to obtain a license to practice law—will discharge a duty (employment) that has already arisen. ◼

Generally, conditions precedent are common, and conditions subsequent are rare. The *Restatement (Second) of Contracts* omits the terms *condition subsequent* and *condition precedent* and refers to both simply as "conditions."[15]

Concurrent Conditions   When each party's absolute duty to perform is conditioned on the other party's absolute duty to perform, **concurrent conditions** are present. These conditions

---

15. *Restatement (Second) of Contracts,* Section 224. Note that a plaintiff must prove a condition precedent, whereas the defendant normally proves a condition subsequent.

LEARNING OBJECTIVE 4
How are most contracts discharged?

Discharge The termination of an obligation, such as occurs when the parties to a contract have fully performed their contractual obligations.

Performance The fulfillment of one's duties under a contract—the normal way of discharging one's contractual obligations.

What is the most common way to discharge a contract for delivery of organic vegetables?

Condition A qualification, provision, or clause in a contractual agreement, the occurrence or nonoccurrence of which creates, suspends, or terminates the obligations of the contracting parties.

Condition Precedent A condition in a contract that must be met before a party's promise becomes absolute.

Condition Subsequent A condition in a contract that, if it occurs, operates to terminate a party's absolute promise to perform.

Concurrent Conditions Conditions that must occur or be performed at the same time—they are mutually dependent. No obligations arise until these conditions are simultaneously performed.

Exhibit 14–4 Contract Discharge

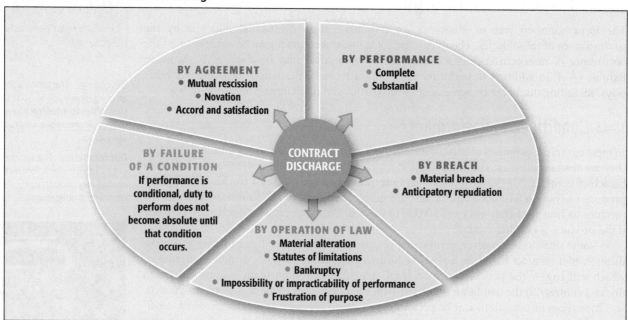

exist only when the parties expressly or impliedly are to perform their respective duties *simultaneously.*

EXAMPLE 14.22 If Janet Feibush promises to pay for goods when Hewlett-Packard delivers them, the parties' promises to perform are mutually dependent. Feibush's duty to pay for the goods does not become absolute until Hewlett-Packard either delivers or tenders the goods. Likewise, Hewlett-Packard's duty to deliver the goods does not become absolute until Feibush tenders or actually makes payment. Therefore, neither can recover from the other for breach without first tendering performance. ■

If HP agrees to sell and deliver goods to someone who agrees to pay for them, what are the concurrent conditions?

Tender An unconditional offer to perform an obligation by a person who is ready, willing, and able to do so.

14–4b Discharge by Performance

The contract comes to an end when both parties fulfill their respective duties by performing the acts they have promised. Performance can also be accomplished by tender. **Tender** is an unconditional offer to perform by a person who is ready, willing, and able to do so. Therefore, a seller who places goods at the disposal of a buyer has tendered delivery and can demand payment according to the terms of the agreement. A buyer who offers to pay for goods has tendered payment and can demand delivery of the goods.

Once performance has been tendered, the party making the tender has done everything possible to carry out the terms of the contract. If the other party then refuses to perform, the party making the tender can consider the duty discharged and sue for breach of contract.

Complete Performance When a party performs exactly as agreed, there is no question as to whether the contract has been performed. When a party's performance is perfect, it is said to be complete.

Normally, conditions expressly stated in the contract must fully occur in all aspects for complete performance (strict performance) of the contract to take place. Any deviation breaches the contract and discharges the other party's obligations to perform.

For instance, most construction contracts require the builder to meet certain specifications. If the specifications are conditions, complete performance is required to avoid material breach. (*Material breach* will be discussed shortly.) If the conditions are met, the other party to the contract must then fulfill her or his obligation to pay the builder.

If the parties to the contract did not expressly make the specifications a condition, however, and the builder fails to meet the specifications, performance is not complete. What effect does that failure have on the other party's obligation to pay? The answer is part of the doctrine of *substantial performance*.

Substantial Performance

A party who in good faith performs substantially all of the terms of a contract can enforce the contract against the other party under the doctrine of substantial performance. Note that good faith is required. Intentionally failing to comply with the terms is a breach of the contract.

The basic requirements for performance to qualify as substantial performance are as follows:

1. The party must have performed in good faith. Intentional failure to comply with the contract terms is a breach of the contract.

2. The performance must not vary greatly from the performance promised in the contract. An omission, variance, or defect in performance is considered minor if it can easily be remedied by compensation (monetary damages).

3. The performance must create substantially the same benefits as those promised in the contract.

Courts decide whether performance was substantial on a case-by-case basis, examining all of the facts of the particular situation. **CASE EXAMPLE 14.23** Wisconsin Electric Power Company (WEPCO) contracted with Union Pacific Railroad to transport coal to WEPCO from mines in Colorado. The contract required WEPCO to notify Union Pacific monthly of how many tons of coal (below a certain maximum) it wanted to have shipped the next month. Union Pacific was to make "good faith reasonable efforts" to meet the schedule.

The contract also required WEPCO to supply the railcars. When WEPCO did not supply railcars, Union Pacific used its own railcars and delivered 84 percent of the requested coal. After WEPCO sued for breach of contract, a federal court held that the delivery of 84 percent of the contracted amount constituted substantial performance.[16] ▪

Effect on Duty to Perform. If one party's performance is substantial, the other party's duty to perform—for instance, to make payment—remains absolute. (The party can, however, sue for damages due to the minor deviations.) In other words, the parties must continue performing under the contract. If performance is not substantial, there is a *material breach* (to be discussed shortly), and the nonbreaching party is excused from further performance.

Measure of Damages. Because substantial performance is not perfect, the other party is entitled to damages to compensate for the failure to comply with the contract. The measure of the damages is the cost to bring the object of the contract into compliance with its terms, if that cost is reasonable under the circumstances. If the cost is unreasonable, the measure of damages is the difference in value between the performance that was rendered and the performance that would have been rendered if the contract had been performed completely.

Performance to the Satisfaction of Another

Contracts often state that completed work must personally satisfy one of the parties or a third person. The question is whether this satisfaction becomes a condition precedent, requiring actual personal satisfaction or approval for discharge, or whether the test of satisfaction is performance that would satisfy a *reasonable person* (substantial performance).

Does Union Pacific Railroad have to deliver 100 percent of promised railcars of coal to an electric power company?

---

16. *Wisconsin Electric Power Co. v. Union Pacific Railroad Co.*, 557 F.3d 504 (7th Cir. 2009).

When the subject matter of the contract is *personal,* a contract to be performed to the satisfaction of one of the parties is conditioned, and performance must actually satisfy that party. For instance, contracts for portraits and works of art are considered personal. Therefore, only the personal satisfaction of the party fulfills the condition (unless a court finds that the party is expressing dissatisfaction to avoid payment or otherwise is not acting in good faith).

Most other contracts need be performed only to the satisfaction of a reasonable person unless they *expressly state otherwise.* When such contracts require performance to the satisfaction of a third party (such as, "to the satisfaction of Robert Ames, the supervising engineer"), the courts are divided. A majority of courts require the work to be satisfactory to a reasonable person. But some courts do require the personal satisfaction of the third party designated in the contract (here, Robert Ames). Again, the personal judgment must be made honestly, or the condition will be excused.

> **Breach of Contract** The failure, without legal excuse, of a promisor to perform the obligations of a contract.

Material Breach of Contract

A **breach of contract** is the nonperformance of a contractual duty. A breach is *material* when performance is not at least substantial.[17] If there is a material breach, the nonbreaching party is excused from the performance of contractual duties and can sue for damages caused by the breach.

If the breach is *minor* (not material), the nonbreaching party's duty to perform may sometimes be suspended until the breach is remedied, but the duty is not entirely excused. Once the minor breach is cured (corrected), the nonbreaching party must resume performance of the contractual obligations.

> **LEARNING OBJECTIVE 5**
> When is a breach considered material, and what effect does that have on the other party's obligation to perform?

Any breach entitles the nonbreaching party to sue for damages, but only a material breach discharges the nonbreaching party from the contract. The policy underlying these rules is that contracts should go forward when only minor problems occur, but that contracts should be terminated if major problems arise.[18] (Does changing the terms of a service contract on a social networking site constitute a breach of contract? See this chapter's *Adapting the Law to the Online Environment* feature for a look at this issue.)

Both parties in the following case were arguably in breach of their contract. The court had to determine which party's breach was material.

---

17. *Restatement (Second) of Contracts,* Section 241.
18. See UCC 2–612, which deals with installment contracts for the sale of goods.

CASE 14.2

Kohel v. Bergen Auto Enterprises, LLC

Superior Court of New Jersey, Appellate Division, 2013 WL 439970 (2013).

FACTS Marc and Bree Kohel agreed to buy a used 2009 Mazda from Bergen Auto Enterprises, LLC, doing business as Wayne Mazda, Inc. The Kohels were credited $7,000 as a trade-in for their 2005 Nissan Altima. They still owed about $8,000 on the Nissan, which Wayne Mazda agreed to pay. The Kohels took possession of the Mazda with temporary plates.

Sometime later, Wayne Mazda discovered that the Nissan was missing a vehicle identification number (VIN) tag. The dealer therefore refused to make the payment for the Nissan and also refused to give the Kohels permanent plates for the Mazda. The Kohels applied and paid for a replacement VIN tag for the Nissan, but Wayne

When is it considered a material breach for a car dealer to refuse to go through with a sale?

Mazda refused to take their calls on the matter and continued to refuse to supply permanent plates for the Mazda. The Kohels filed a complaint against the dealer in a New Jersey state court, alleging breach of contract. The court ruled in the plaintiffs' favor, and Wayne Mazda appealed.

ISSUE Was it a material breach of the contract for Wayne Mazda to refuse to go through with the sales agreement because the trade-in vehicle was missing a VIN tag?

DECISION Yes. A state intermediate appellate court affirmed the judgment in the Kohel's favor.

REASON While both parties were arguably in breach of their contract, "there is a material distinction in plaintiffs' conduct," which was unintentional, "and defendant's refusal to release the permanent plates for which the plaintiffs had paid." The Kohels had not been aware that their trade-in Nissan lacked a vehicle identification number (VIN) tag. Moreover, "defendant's representatives examined the car twice before accepting it in trade and did not notice the missing VIN tag until they took the car to an auction where they tried to sell it."

The reviewing court found that Wayne Mazda had acted only to maintain "leverage." The Kohels had applied and paid for a replacement VIN tag in an attempt to remedy the problem, but the owner of Wayne Mazda would not even take their calls to discuss the matter. Thus, the court concluded that Wayne Mazda had acted in an unreasonable manner, which was a material breach of the contract.

CRITICAL THINKING—Legal Consideration *What is a material breach of contract? When a material breach occurs, what are the non-breaching party's options?*

ADAPTING THE LAW TO THE **ONLINE** ENVIRONMENT
When Do Changes in Social Media Terms of Service Constitute a Breach of Contract?

Hundreds of millions of individuals use some form of social media. To do so, they must agree to certain terms of service.

The Terms of Service Are a Contract
Any time you use social media on the Internet or download an app for your mobile device, you must accept the associated terms of service. To be sure, users generally do not read these terms. They just click on "accept" and start using the social media platform or the app. Nonetheless, by clicking the "accept" button, each user is entering into a contract.

An Example: Instagram Changes Its Terms of Service
In 2012, to the consternation of many users, Instagram changed its terms of service to give it the right to transfer and otherwise use user content on the site, apparently without compensation to users. The new terms also limited users' ability to bring class-action lawsuits against Instagram, limited the damages they could recover to $100, and required arbitration of any disputes.

Lucy Funes, an Instagram user in California, filed a class-action lawsuit on behalf of herself and other users, claiming breach of contract and breach of the covenant of good faith and fair dealing that a contract implies.[a] Although Instagram subsequently modified the language that appeared to give it the right to use users' photos without compensation, it retained other controversial terms. They included the mandatory arbitration clause and a provision allowing it to place ads in conjunction with user content.

Instagram Seeks Dismissal of the Lawsuit
While Funes contended that Instagram had breached its contract by changing its terms of service, Instagram argued that Funes could not claim breach of contract. For one thing, she—and other users—had thirty days' notice before the new terms of service took effect. Because Funes continued to use her account after that thirty-day period, Instagram maintained that, in effect, she had agreed to the new terms. The courts ultimately agreed with Instagram and dismissed the lawsuit.

Instagram Changes Its Policies
For several years, Instagram has been using its revised terms of service agreement. As mentioned, it abandoned some of its previous changes and denied any intention to sell user content. In the terms of service, Instagram continues to state that it does "not claim ownership of any content user's post on or through the service."

Nonetheless, the terms state clearly that each user "hereby grants to Instagram a non-exclusive, fully paid and royalty-free, transferable, sublicensable, worldwide license to use content that the user posts." That means that Instagram can reassign the rights or relicense the work to any other party for free or for a fee. The user—anyone who posts on Instagram—need not be compensated or even given notice.

■ Instagram's current terms of service state, "We may not always identify paid services, sponsored content, or commercial communications as such." Is it ethical for Instagram to post advertisements without identifying them as advertisements? Discuss.

---

a. *Funes v. Instagram, Inc.*, 3:12-CV06482-WHA (N.D.Cal. 2012). See also *Rodriguez v. Instagram, LLC*, 2013 WL 3732883.

Is it a material breach of contract for a hospital to accept a donation and then refuse to honor part of its commitment? Country singer Garth Brooks was born in Yukon, Oklahoma, and has made generous contributions to charities in that town. When his mother, Colleen Brooks, died, he donated $500,000 to Integris Rural Health, Inc., in that town. Brooks believed that he and the hospital's president had agreed verbally that the donation would be used to build a new women's health center in Yukon, which would be named after his mother. Several years passed, but the health center was not built. Integris claimed that it intended to do something to honor Colleen Brooks but insisted that it had never promised to build a new health center. When Integris refused to return the $500,000, Garth Brooks sued for breach of contract.

Was the hospital's failure to build a women's health center and name it after Brooks's mother a material breach of the verbal contract between Brooks and hospital management? A jury in Rogers County, Oklahoma, thought so and awarded Brooks $500,000 in actual damages for breach of contract. The jury also awarded Brooks another $500,000 because it found the hospital guilty of reckless disregard and intentional malice.

Anticipatory Repudiation
An assertion or action by a party indicating that he or she will not perform a contractual obligation.

Anticipatory Repudiation of a Contract

Before either party to a contract has a duty to perform, one of the parties may refuse to perform her or his contractual obligations. This is called **anticipatory repudiation.**[19]

Repudiation Is a Material Breach. When anticipatory repudiation occurs, it is treated as a material breach of the contract, and the nonbreaching party is permitted to bring an action for damages immediately, even though the scheduled time for performance under the contract may still be in the future. Until the nonbreaching party treats this early repudiation as a breach, however, the breaching party can retract the anticipatory repudiation by proper notice and restore the parties to their original obligations.

An anticipatory repudiation is treated as a present, material breach for two reasons. First, the nonbreaching party should not be required to remain ready and willing to perform when the other party has already repudiated the contract. Second, the nonbreaching party should have the opportunity to seek a similar contract elsewhere. Indeed, that party may have the duty to do so to minimize his or her loss.

KNOW THIS
The risks that prices will fluctuate and values will change are ordinary business risks for which the law does not provide relief.

May Occur When Market Prices Fluctuate. Quite often, an anticipatory repudiation occurs when performance of the contract would be extremely unfavorable to one of the parties because of a sharp fluctuation in market prices.

EXAMPLE 14.24 Mobile X enters into an e-contract to manufacture and sell 100,000 smartphones to Best Com, a global telecommunications company. Delivery is to be made two months from the date of the contract. One month later, three inventory suppliers raise their prices to Mobile X. Because of these higher prices, Mobile X stands to lose $500,000 if it sells the smartphones to Best Com at the contract price. Mobile X immediately sends an e-mail to Best Com, stating that it cannot deliver the 100,000 phones at the contract price. Even though you may sympathize with Mobile X, its e-mail is an anticipatory repudiation of the contract. Best Com can treat the repudiation as a material breach and immediately pursue remedies, even though the contract delivery date is still a month away. ▪

14–4c Discharge by Agreement

Any contract can be discharged by agreement of the parties. The agreement can be contained in the original contract, or the parties can form a new contract for the express purpose of discharging the original contract.

---

19. *Restatement (Second) of Contracts*, Section 253; and UCC 2–610.

Discharge by Mutual Rescission As mentioned in previous chapters, rescission occurs when the parties cancel the contract and are returned to the positions they occupied prior to the contract's formation. For *mutual rescission* to take place, the parties must make another agreement that also satisfies the legal requirements for a contract—there must be an *offer,* an *acceptance,* and *consideration.* Ordinarily, if the parties agree to rescind the original contract, their promises not to perform those acts promised in the original contract will be legal consideration for the second contract.

Generally, a rescission agreement may be written or oral. Oral agreements to rescind most executory contracts (that neither party has performed) are enforceable even if the original agreement was in writing. A writing (or electronic record) is required to rescind a contract for the sale of goods under the Uniform Commercial Code when the contract requires a written rescission. Also, agreements to rescind contracts involving transfers of realty must be evidenced by a writing or record.

When one party has fully performed, an agreement to rescind the original contract usually is not enforceable unless additional consideration or restitution is made. Because the performing party has received no consideration for the promise to call off the original bargain, additional consideration is necessary.

Discharge by Novation The process of **novation** substitutes a third party for one of the original parties. Essentially, the parties to the original contract and one or more new parties get together and agree to the substitution. The requirements of a novation are as follows:

Novation The substitution, by agreement, of a new contract for an old one, with the rights under the old one being terminated.

1. A previous valid obligation.
2. An agreement by all of the parties to a new contract.
3. The extinguishing of the old obligation (discharge of the prior party).
4. A new, valid contract.

EXAMPLE 14.25 Union Corporation contracts to sell its pharmaceutical division to British Pharmaceuticals, Ltd. Before the transfer is completed, Union, British Pharmaceuticals, and a third company, Otis Chemicals, execute a new agreement to transfer all of British Pharmaceuticals' rights and duties in the transaction to Otis Chemicals. As long as the new contract is supported by consideration, the novation will discharge the original contract (between Union and British Pharmaceuticals) and replace it with the new contract (between Union and Otis Chemicals). ■

A novation expressly or impliedly revokes and discharges a prior contract. The parties involved may expressly state in the new contract that the old contract is now discharged. If the parties do not expressly discharge the old contract, it will be impliedly discharged if the new contract's terms are inconsistent with the old contract's terms.

Discharge by Accord and Satisfaction As explained in a previous chapter, in an *accord and satisfaction,* the parties agree to accept performance different from the performance originally promised. An *accord* is a contract to perform some act to satisfy an existing contractual duty that has not yet been discharged.[20] A *satisfaction* is the performance of the accord agreement. An accord and its satisfaction discharge the original contractual obligation.

Once the accord has been made, the original obligation is merely suspended until the accord agreement is fully performed. If it is not performed, the party to whom performance is owed can bring an action on the original obligation or for breach of the accord. **EXAMPLE 14.26** Shea obtains a judgment of $8,000 against Marla. Later, both parties agree that the judgment can be satisfied by Marla's transfer of her automobile to Shea. This agreement to accept the auto in lieu of $8,000 in cash is the accord. If Marla transfers her automobile to Shea, the accord agreement is fully performed, and the $8,000 debt is discharged. If Marla refuses to

---

20. *Restatement (Second) of Contracts,* Section 281.

"Law is a practical matter."

Roscoe Pound
1870–1964
(American jurist)

transfer her car, the accord is breached. Because the original obligation is merely suspended, Shea can sue to enforce the judgment for $8,000 in cash or bring an action for breach of the accord. ■

14-4d Discharge by Operation of Law

Under specified circumstances, contractual duties may be discharged by operation of law. These circumstances include material alteration of the contract, the running of the relevant statute of limitations, bankruptcy, and impossibility or impracticability of performance.

Material Alteration   To discourage parties from altering written contracts, the law allows an innocent party to be discharged from a contract that has been materially altered. If one party alters a material term of the contract—such as the quantity term or the price term—without the knowledge or consent of the other party, the party who was unaware of the alteration can treat the contract as discharged or terminated.

Statutes of Limitations   As mentioned earlier in this text, statutes of limitations limit the period during which a party can sue on a particular cause of action. After the applicable limitations period has passed, a suit can no longer be brought.

The period for bringing lawsuits for breach of oral contracts is usually two to three years, and for written contracts, four to five years. Lawsuits for breach of a contract for the sale of goods must be brought within four years after the cause of action has accrued. In their original contract, the parties can agree to reduce this four-year period to not less than one year. They cannot, however, agree to extend it beyond four years.

Bankruptcy   A proceeding in bankruptcy attempts to allocate the debtor's assets to the creditors in a fair and equitable fashion. Once the assets have been allocated, the debtor receives a *discharge in bankruptcy*. A discharge in bankruptcy ordinarily prevents the creditors from enforcing most of the debtor's contracts. Partial payment of a debt *after* discharge in bankruptcy will not revive the debt.

Impossibility of Performance   After a contract has been made, supervening events (such as a fire) may make performance impossible in an objective sense. This so-called **impossibility of performance** can discharge the contract.[21] The doctrine of impossibility of performance is applied only when the parties could not have reasonably foreseen, at the time the contract was formed, the event or events that rendered performance impossible.

Objective impossibility ("It cannot be done") must be distinguished from subjective impossibility ("I'm sorry, I personally cannot do it"). An example of subjective impossibility occurs when a party cannot deliver goods on time because of railcar shortages or cannot make payment on time because the bank is closed. In effect, the nonperforming party is saying, "It is impossible for *me* to perform," rather than "It is impossible for *anyone* to perform." Accordingly, such excuses do not discharge a contract, and the nonperforming party is normally held in breach of contract.

When Performance Is Impossible. Three basic types of situations may qualify as grounds for the discharge of contractual obligations based on impossibility of performance:[22]

1. *When a party whose personal performance is essential to the completion of the contract dies or becomes incapacitated prior to performance.* EXAMPLE 14.27 Fred, a famous dancer, contracts with Ethereal Dancing Guild to play a leading role in its new ballet. Before the ballet can be performed, Fred becomes ill and dies. His personal performance was essential to

Impossibility of Performance
A doctrine under which a party to a contract is relieved of his or her duty to perform when performance becomes objectively impossible or totally impracticable.

---

21. *Restatement (Second) of Contracts*, Section 261.
22. *Restatement (Second) of Contracts*, Sections 262–266; and UCC 2–615.

the completion of the contract. Thus, his death discharges the contract and his estate's liability for his nonperformance. ■

2. *When the specific subject matter of the contract is destroyed.* **EXAMPLE 14.28** A-1 Farm Equipment agrees to sell Gunther the green tractor on its lot and promises to have the tractor ready for Gunther to pick up on Saturday. On Friday night, however, a truck veers off the nearby highway and smashes into the tractor, destroying it beyond repair. Because the contract was for this specific tractor, A-1's performance is rendered impossible owing to the accident. ■

3. *When a change in the law renders performance illegal.* **EXAMPLE 14.29** Russo contracts with Playlist, Inc., to create a Web site through which users can post and share movies, music, and other forms of digital entertainment. Russo goes to work. Before the site is operational, however, Congress passes the No Online Piracy in Entertainment (NOPE) Act. The NOPE Act makes it illegal to operate a Web site on which copyrighted works are posted without the copyright owners' consent. In this situation, the contract is discharged by operation of law. The purpose of the contract has been rendered illegal, and contract performance is objectively impossible. ■

Can an agreement that prohibits personal contact between two parties affect the performance of contracts between one of these parties and the other party's business? That was the question before the court in the following case.

This dancer has a contract to dance the lead role in a famous ballet that will run for a month of performances. What happens if he breaks a leg before the shows start?

CASE 14.3

Kolodin v. Valenti

New York Supreme Court, Appellate Division, 115 A.D.3d 197, 979 N.Y.S.2d 587 (2014).

FACTS Hilary Kolodin, a jazz singer, was personally involved with John Valenti, the sole shareholder and president of Jayarvee, Inc. Jayarvee manages artists, produces recordings, and owns and operates a jazz club in New York City. Kolodin contracted professionally with Jayarvee for recording and management services. After Kolodin and Valenti's personal relationship deteriorated, Kolodin asked a New York state court to issue a temporary protection order against Valenti, alleging domestic abuse. The parties then agreed under a court-ordered stipulation to have no further contact with one another. The stipulation specified that "no contact shall include no third party contact, excepting counsel." Later, Kolodin filed a suit in a New York state court against Valenti, alleging breach of her Jayarvee contracts and seeking their rescission. The court declared the contracts between Kolodin and Jayarvee terminated. Valenti appealed.

ISSUE Did Kolodin and Valenti's stipulation render the performance of Kolodin's Jayarvee contracts objectively impossible?

DECISION Yes. A state intermediate appellate court affirmed the lower court's ruling. The court concluded that, "In undertaking to perform recording and management contracts, the eventuality that the parties would subsequently stipulate to forbid contact with one another could not have been foreseen or guarded against."

Can severe disagreement within a couple render a personal services contract impossible to perform?

REASON Impossibility excuses a party's performance when the destruction of the means of performance makes performance objectively impossible. But the impossibility must be created by an event that could not have been foreseen at the time of contract formation. In this case, the "no contact" stipulation between Kolodin and Valenti destroyed the means of performing Kolodin's contracts with Jayarvee. The contracts were for personal services and required "substantial and ongoing communication" between Kolodin and Jayarvee. Because Jayarvee is a small organization and Valenti oversees its daily operations, performance of the contracts would have required his input, thereby violating the stipulation. Even if the communication had been carried out only through the company's employees, the stipulation's ban on third party contact would have been violated. Furthermore, it was not foreseeable at the time the Jayarvee contracts were formed that Kolodin and Valenti would agree to have no contact with one another.

CRITICAL THINKING—Legal Environment Consideration *Should Kolodin's role in bringing about the "no contact" stipulation through her request for a protection order have rendered the doctrine of impossibility inapplicable? Explain.*

Temporary Impossibility. An occurrence or event that makes performance temporarily impossible operates to suspend performance until the impossibility ceases. Once the temporary event ends, the parties ordinarily must perform the contract as originally planned.

CASE EXAMPLE 14.30 On August 22, Keefe Hurwitz contracted to sell his home in Louisiana to Wesley and Gwendolyn Payne for $241,500. On August 26—just four days later—Hurricane Katrina made landfall and caused extensive damage to the house. The cost of repairs was estimated at $60,000. Hurwitz refused to pay for the repairs only to sell the property to the Paynes for the previously agreed-on price. The Paynes sued to enforce the contract. Hurwitz claimed that Hurricane Katrina had made it impossible for him to perform and had discharged his duties under the contract. The court ruled that Hurricane Katrina had caused only temporary impossibility. Therefore, Hurwitz had to pay for the necessary repairs and to perform the contract as written. He could not obtain a higher purchase price to offset the cost of the repairs.[23] ■

Sometimes, however, the lapse of time and the change in circumstances surrounding such a contract make it substantially more burdensome for the parties to perform the promised acts. In that situation, the contract may be discharged. **CASE EXAMPLE 14.31** In 1942, actor Gene Autry was drafted into the U.S. Army. Being drafted rendered his contract with a Hollywood movie company temporarily impossible to perform, and it was suspended until the end of World War II in 1945. When Autry got out of the army, the purchasing power of the dollar had declined so much that performance of the contract would have been substantially burdensome to him. Therefore, the contract was discharged.[24] ■

Commercial Impracticability

Courts may also excuse parties from their performance obligations when the performance becomes much more difficult or expensive than the parties originally contemplated. For someone to invoke the doctrine of **commercial impracticability** successfully, however, the anticipated performance must become *extremely difficult or costly*.[25] Furthermore, the added burden of performing *must not have been foreseeable by the parties when the contract was made*.

In one classic case, for instance, a court held that a contract could be discharged because a party would have to pay ten times more than the original estimate to excavate a certain amount of gravel.[26] In another case, a power failure during a wedding reception relieved the owner of a banquet hall from the duty to perform a contract.[27] (See this chapter's *Beyond Our Borders* feature for a discussion of Germany's approach to impracticability and impossibility of performance.)

Frustration of Purpose

Closely allied with the doctrine of commercial impracticability is the doctrine of **frustration of purpose.** In principle, a contract will be discharged if supervening circumstances make it impossible to attain the purpose both parties had in mind when making the contract. As with commercial impracticability, the supervening event must not have been foreseeable at the time of the contracting.[28]

There are some differences between the doctrines, however. Commercial impracticability usually involves an event that increases the cost or difficulty of performance. In contrast, frustration of purpose typically involves an event that decreases the value of what a party receives under the contract.

KNOW THIS
The doctrine of commercial impracticability does not provide relief from such events as ordinary price increases or easily predictable changes in the weather.

Commercial Impracticability
A doctrine that may excuse the duty to perform a contract when performance becomes much more difficult or costly due to forces that neither party could control or foresee at the time the contract was formed.

Frustration of Purpose
A court-created doctrine under which a party to a contract will be relieved of her or his duty to perform when the objective purpose for performance no longer exists due to reasons beyond that party's control.

---

23. *Payne v. Hurwitz*, 978 So.2d 1000 (La.App. 1st Cir. 2008).
24. *Autry v. Republic Productions*, 30 Cal.2d 144, 180 P.2d 888 (1947).
25. *Restatement (Second) of Contracts*, Section 264.
26. *Mineral Park Land Co. v. Howard*, 172 Cal. 289, 156 P. 458 (1916).
27. *Facto v. Panagis*, 390 N.J.Super. 227, 915 A.2d 59 (2007).
28. See, for example, *East Capitol View Community Development Corp. v. Robinson*, 941 A.2d 1036 (D.C.App. 2008).

BEYOND OUR BORDERS

Impossibility or Impracticability of Performance in Germany

In the United States, when a party alleges that contract performance is impossible or impracticable because of circumstances unforeseen at the time the contract was formed, a court will either discharge the party's contractual obligations or hold the party to the contract. In other words, if a court agrees that the contract is impossible or impracticable to perform, the remedy is to rescind (cancel) the contract. Under German law, however, a court may reform (adjust the terms of) a contract in light of economic developments. If an unforeseen event affects the foundation of the agreement, the court can alter the contract's terms to align with the parties' original expectations, thus making the contract fair to the parties.

CRITICAL THINKING

- When a contract becomes impossible or impracticable to perform, which remedy would a businessperson prefer—rescission or reformation? Why? Explain your answer.

Reviewing . . . Third Party Rights and Discharge

Val's Foods signs a contract to buy 1,500 pounds of basil from Sun Farms, a small organic herb grower, if an independent organization inspects the crop and certifies that it contains no pesticide or herbicide residue. Val's has a contract with several restaurant chains to supply pesto and intends to use Sun Farms' basil in the pesto to fulfill these contracts. When Sun Farms is preparing to harvest the basil, an unexpected hailstorm destroys half the crop. Sun Farms attempts to purchase additional basil from other farms, but it is late in the season, and the price is twice the normal market price. Sun Farms is too small to absorb this cost and immediately notifies Val's that it will not fulfill the contract. Using the information presented in the chapter, answer the following questions.

1. Suppose that Sun Farms supplies the basil that survived the storm but the basil does not pass the chemical-residue inspection. Which concept discussed in the chapter might allow Val's to refuse to perform the contract in this situation?

2. Under which legal theory or theories might Sun Farms claim that its obligation under the contract has been discharged by operation of law? Discuss fully.

3. Suppose that Sun Farms contacts every basil grower in the country and buys the last remaining chemical-free basil anywhere. Nevertheless, Sun Farms is able to ship only 1,475 pounds to Val's. Would this fulfill Sun Farms' obligations to Val's? Why or why not?

4. Now suppose that Sun Farms sells its operations to Happy Valley Farms. As part of the sale, all three parties agree that Happy Valley will provide the basil as stated under the original contract. What is this type of agreement called?

DEBATE THIS

- The doctrine of commercial impracticability should be abolished.

BUSINESS APPLICATION   Dealing with Third Party Rights*

Assignment of contractual rights and delegation of duties are common in the business world. As you have read in this chapter, third party rights and duties stem from the law on assignments, delegations, and third party beneficiaries. A business may at different times wish to assign or delegate its contractual rights, to prevent a third party from acquiring such rights, or to understand its own third party rights. In any of these situations, some familiarity with the law is essential.

The general rule is that any contractual right or duty can be assigned or delegated unless the assignment or delegation is prohibited by (1) the contract, (2) a statute, or (3) other limitations. Thus, one way to prevent assignment or delegation is to prohibit it when drafting the contract.

For example, a tenant under a long-term lease contract may wish to assign the lease to another party. To avoid such assignments, property owners often prohibit the assignment of the balance of a lease term unless the property owner's consent is obtained.

When a contract calls for the manufacture and sale of goods, the manufacturer may assign or delegate the production of such goods to a third party unless prohibited by the contract. Consequently, most purchase orders (contracts) have a clause that prohibits such assignments or delegations without the buyer's consent.

CHECKLIST for the Businessperson:

1. Determine whether you can assign or delegate your rights or duties under a contract to a third party.

2. If you can assign or delegate your contract rights or performance, attempt to determine your benefits and obligations, such as notice to customers, if you do make the assignment or delegation.

3. If you do not want your contract rights or duties to be assigned or delegated, insert a contract clause that prohibits assignment or delegation without your consent.

4. Whenever you might be a third party beneficiary to a contract, such as a creditor beneficiary, take steps to determine your rights.

---

* This *Business Application* is not meant to substitute for the services of an attorney who is licensed to practice law in your state.

Key Terms

Chapter Summary: Third Party Rights and Discharge

<table>
<tr><td colspan="2" align="center">**THIRD PARTY RIGHTS**</td></tr>
<tr>
<td>**Assignments**</td>
<td>

1. An assignment is the transfer of rights under a contract to a third party. The person assigning the rights is the *assignor*, and the party to whom the rights are assigned is the *assignee*. The assignee has a right to demand performance from the other original party to the contract, the *obligor*.
2. Generally, all rights can be assigned *unless:*
   a. A statute expressly prohibits assignment.
   b. The contract is for personal services.
   c. The assignment will materially alter the obligor's risk or duties.
   d. The contract prohibits assignment. (Exception: Contracts cannot generally prohibit assignment of the right to receive funds, of ownership rights in real property, of negotiable instruments, or of certain payments under a sales contract.)
3. The assignee should notify the obligor of the assignment. Although not legally required, notification avoids two potential problems:
   a. If the assignor assigns the same right to two different persons, the first assignment in time is generally the first in right, but in some states the first assignee to give notice takes priority.
   b. Until the obligor is notified of the assignment, the obligor can tender performance to the assignor. If the assignor accepts the performance, the obligor's duties under the contract are discharged without benefit to the assignee.

</td>
</tr>
<tr>
<td>**Delegations**</td>
<td>

1. A delegation is the transfer of duties under a contract to a third party (the *delegatee*), who then assumes the obligation of performing the contractual duties previously held by the one making the delegation (the *delegator*).
2. As a general rule, any duty can be delegated *unless:*
   a. Performance depends on the obligor's personal skills or talents, or special trust has been placed in the obligor.
   b. Performance by a third party will vary materially from that expected by the obligee.
   c. The contract prohibits delegation.
3. A valid delegation of duties does not relieve the delegator of obligations under the contract. If the delegatee fails to perform, the delegator is still liable to the obligee.
4. An "assignment of all rights" or an "assignment of the contract" is often construed to mean that both the rights and the duties arising under the contract are transferred to a third party.

</td>
</tr>
<tr>
<td>**Third Party Beneficiaries**</td>
<td>

A third party beneficiary contract is one made for the purpose of benefiting a third party.
1. *Intended beneficiary*—One for whose benefit a contract is created. When the promisor (the one making the contractual promise that benefits a third party) fails to perform as promised, the third party can sue the promisor directly. Types of third party beneficiaries are creditor and donee beneficiaries.
2. *Incidental beneficiary*—A third party who indirectly (incidentally) benefits from a contract but for whose benefit the contract was not specifically intended. Incidental beneficiaries have no rights to the benefits received and cannot sue to have the contract enforced.

</td>
</tr>
<tr><td colspan="2" align="center">**CONTRACT DISCHARGE**</td></tr>
<tr>
<td>**Conditions of Performance**</td>
<td>

Contract obligations may be subject to the following types of conditions:
1. *Condition precedent*—A condition that must be fulfilled before a party's promise becomes absolute.
2. *Condition subsequent*—A condition that, if it occurs, operates to terminate a party's absolute promise to perform.
3. *Concurrent conditions*—Conditions that must be performed simultaneously. Each party's absolute duty to perform is conditioned on the other party's absolute duty to perform.

</td>
</tr>
<tr>
<td>**Discharge by Performance**</td>
<td>

A contract may be discharged by complete (strict) performance or by substantial performance. In some instances, performance must be to the satisfaction of another. Totally inadequate performance constitutes a material breach of the contract. An anticipatory repudiation of a contract allows the other party to sue immediately for breach of contract.

</td>
</tr>
<tr>
<td>**Discharge by Agreement**</td>
<td>

Parties may agree to discharge their contractual obligations in several ways:
1. *By rescission*—The parties mutually agree to rescind (cancel) the contract.
2. *By novation*—A new party is substituted for one of the primary parties to a contract.
3. *By accord and satisfaction*—The parties agree to render and accept performance different from that on which they originally agreed.

</td>
</tr>
<tr>
<td>**Discharge by Operation of Law**</td>
<td>

Parties' obligations under contracts may be discharged by operation of law owing to one of the following:
1. Material alteration.
2. Statutes of limitations.
3. Bankruptcy.
4. Impossibility of performance.
5. Impracticability of performance.
6. Frustration of purpose.

</td>
</tr>
</table>

Issue Spotters

1. Eagle Company contracts to build a house for Frank. The contract states that "any assignment of this contract renders the contract void." After Eagle builds the house, but before Frank pays, Eagle assigns its right to payment to Good Credit Company. Can Good Credit enforce the contract against Frank? Why or why not? (See *Assignments*.)

2. Ready Foods contracts to buy two hundred carloads of frozen pizzas from Speedy Distributors. Before Ready or Speedy starts performing, can the parties call off the deal? What if Speedy has already shipped the pizzas? Explain your answers. (See *Contract Discharge*.)

—**Check your answers to the *Issue Spotters* against the answers provided in Appendix D at the end of this text.**

Learning Objectives Check

1. What is an assignment? What is the difference between an assignment and a delegation?

2. In what situations is the delegation of duties prohibited?

3. What factors indicate that a third party beneficiary is an intended beneficiary?

4. How are most contracts discharged?

5. When is a breach considered material, and what effect does that have on the other party's obligation to perform?

—**Answers to the even-numbered *Learning Objectives Check* questions can be found in Appendix E at the end of this text.**

Business Scenarios and Case Problems

14–1. Third Party Beneficiaries. Wilken owes Rivera $2,000. Howie promises Wilken that he will pay Rivera the $2,000 in return for Wilken's promise to give Howie's children guitar lessons. Is Rivera an intended beneficiary of the Howie-Wilken contract? Explain. (See *Third Party Beneficiaries.*)

14–2. Assignment. Aron, a college student, signs a one-year lease agreement that runs from September 1 to August 31. The lease agreement specifies that the lease cannot be assigned without the landlord's consent. In late May, Aron decides not to go to summer school and assigns the balance of the lease (three months) to a close friend, Erica. The landlord objects to the assignment and denies Erica access to the apartment. Aron claims that Erica is financially sound and should be allowed the full rights and privileges of an assignee. Discuss fully whether the landlord or Aron is correct. (See *Assignments.*)

14–3. Spotlight on Drug Testing—Third Party Beneficiaries. Bath Iron Works (BIW) offered a job to Thomas Devine, contingent on Devine's passing a drug test. The testing was conducted by NorDx, a subcontractor of Roche Biomedical Laboratories. When NorDx found that Devine's urinalysis showed the presence of opiates, a result confirmed by Roche, BIW refused to offer Devine permanent employment. Devine sued Roche, claiming that the ingestion of poppy seeds can lead to a positive result and that he had tested positive for opiates only because of his daily consumption of poppy seed muffins. Devine argued that he was a third party beneficiary of the contract between his employer (BIW) and NorDx (Roche). Was Devine an intended third party beneficiary of this contract? Why or why not? Do drug-testing labs have a duty to the employees they test to exercise reasonable care in conducting the tests? Explain. [*Devine v. Roche Biomedical Laboratories,* 659 A.2d 868 (Me. 1995)] (See *Third Party Beneficiaries.*)

14–4. Third Party Beneficiary. David and Sandra Dess contracted with Sirva Relocation, LLC, to assist in selling their home. In their contract, the Desses agreed to disclose all information about the property—information on which Sirva "and other prospective buyers may rely in deciding whether and on what terms to purchase the Property." The Kincaids contracted with Sirva to buy the house. After the closing, they discovered dampness in the walls, defective and rotten windows, mold, and other undisclosed problems. Can the Kincaids bring an action against the Desses for breach of their contract with Sirva? Why or why not? [*Kincaid v. Dess,* 298 P.3d 358 (2013)] (See *Third Party Beneficiaries.*)

14–5. Business Case Problem with Sample Answer—Material Breach. The Northeast Independent School District in Bexar County, Texas, hired STR Constructors, Ltd., to renovate a middle school. STR subcontracted the tile work in the school's kitchen to Newman Tile, Inc. (NTI). The project had already fallen behind schedule. As a result, STR allowed other workers to walk over and damage the newly installed tile before it had cured, forcing NTI to constantly redo its work. Despite NTI's requests for payment, STR remitted only half the amount due under their contract. When the school district refused to accept the kitchen, including the tile work, STR told NTI to quickly make the repairs. A week later, STR terminated their contract. Did STR breach the contract with NTI? Explain. [*STR Constructors, Ltd. v. Newman Tile, Inc.,* 395 S.W.3d 383 (Tex.App.—El Paso 2013)] (See *Contract Discharge.*)

—For a sample answer to Problem 14–5, go to Appendix F at the end of this text.

14–6. Conditions of Performance. Russ Wyant owned Humble Ranch in Perkins County, South Dakota. Edward Humble, whose parents had previously owned the ranch, was Wyant's uncle. Humble held a two-year option to buy the ranch. The option included specific conditions. Once it was exercised, the parties had thirty days to enter into a purchase agreement, and the seller could become the buyer's lender by matching the terms of the proposed financing. After the option was exercised, the parties engaged in lengthy negotiations, but Humble did not respond to Wyant's proposed purchase agreement nor advise him of available financing terms before the option expired. Six months later, Humble filed a suit against Wyant to enforce the option. Is Humble entitled to specific performance? Explain. [*Humble v. Wyant,* 843 N.W.2d 334 (S.Dak. 2014)] (See *Contract Discharge.*)

14–7. Discharge by Operation of Law. Dr. Jake Lambert signed an employment agreement with Baptist Health Services, Inc., to provide cardiothoracic-surgery services to Baptist Memorial Hospital–North Mississippi, Inc., in Oxford, Mississippi. Complaints about Lambert's behavior arose almost immediately. He was evaluated by a team of doctors and psychologists, who diagnosed him as suffering from obsessive-compulsive personality disorder and concluded that he was unfit to practice medicine. Based on this conclusion, the hospital suspended his staff privileges. Citing the suspension, Baptist Health Services claimed that Lambert had breached his employment contract. What is Lambert's best defense to this claim? Explain. [*Baptist Memorial Hospital–North Mississippi, Inc. v. Lambert,* 157 So.3d 109 (Miss.App. 2015)] (See *Contract Discharge.*)

14–8. A Question of Ethics—Assignment and Delegation. Premier Building & Development, Inc., entered a listing agreement giving Sunset Gold Realty, LLC, the exclusive right to find a tenant for some commercial property. The terms of the listing agreement stated that it was binding on both parties and "their * * * assigns." Premier Building did not own the property at the time, but had the option to purchase it. To secure financing for the project, Premier Building established a new company called Cobblestone Associates. Premier Building then bought the property and conveyed it to Cobblestone the same day. Meanwhile, Sunset Gold found a tenant for the property, and Cobblestone became the landlord. Cobblestone acknowledged its obligation to pay Sunset Gold for finding a tenant, but it later refused to pay Sunset Gold's commission. Sunset Gold then sued Premier Building and Cobblestone for breach of the listing agreement. [*Sunset Gold Realty, LLC v. Premier Building & Development, Inc.,* 133 Conn.App. 445, 36 A.3d 243 (2012)] (See *Assignments* and *Delegations.*)

1. Is Premier Building relieved of its contractual duties if it assigned the contract to Cobblestone? Why or why not?

2. Given that Sunset Gold performed its obligations under the listing agreement, did Cobblestone behave unethically in refusing to pay Sunset Gold's commission? Why or why not?

Critical Thinking and Writing Assignments

14–9. Critical Legal Thinking. The concept of substantial performance permits a party to be discharged from a contract even though the party has not fully performed her or his obligations according to the contract's terms. Is this fair? Why or why not? What policy interests are at issue here? (See *Contract Discharge.*)

14–10. Business Law Critical Thinking Group Assignment. ABC Clothiers, Inc., has a contract with John Taylor, owner of Taylor & Sons, a retailer, to deliver one thousand summer suits to Taylor's place of business on or before May 1. On April 1, John receives a letter from ABC informing him that ABC will not be able to make the delivery as scheduled. John is very upset, as he had planned a big ad campaign. (See *Contract Discharge.*)

1. The first group will discuss whether John Taylor can immediately sue ABC for breach of contract (on April 2).

2. Now suppose that John Taylor's son, Tom, tells his father that they cannot file a lawsuit until ABC actually fails to deliver the suits on May 1. The second group will decide who is correct, John or Tom.

3. Assume that Taylor & Sons can either file immediately or wait until ABC fails to deliver the goods. The third group will evaluate which course of action is better, given the circumstances.

iStockPhoto.com/BrianAJackson

15

LEARNING OBJECTIVES

The five Learning Objectives *below are designed to help improve your understanding of the chapter. After reading this chapter, you should be able to answer the following questions:*

1. What is the standard measure of compensatory damages when a contract is breached? How are damages computed differently in construction contracts?

2. What is the difference between compensatory damages and consequential damages? What are nominal damages, and when do courts award nominal damages?

3. Under what circumstances is the remedy of rescission and restitution available?

4. When do courts grant specific performance as a remedy?

5. What is a limitation-of-liability clause, and when will courts enforce it?

Breach and Remedies

Normally, people enter into contracts to secure some advantage. When it is no longer advantageous for a party to fulfill her or his contractual obligations, that party may *breach,* or fail to perform, the contract.[1] Once one party breaches the contract, the other party—the nonbreaching party—can choose one or more of several remedies.

A *remedy* is the relief provided to an innocent party when the other party has breached the contract. It is the means employed to enforce a right or to redress an injury. Although it may be an exaggeration to say there is a remedy for "everything" in life, as Cervantes claimed in in the chapter-opening quotation, there is a remedy available for nearly every contract breach.

The most common remedies available to a nonbreaching party under contract law include damages, rescission and restitution, specific performance, and reformation. Courts distinguish between *remedies at law* and *remedies in equity.* Today, the remedy at law is normally monetary damages. We discuss this remedy in the first part of the chapter. Equitable remedies include rescission and restitution, specific performance, and reformation, all of which we examine later in the chapter. Usually, a court will not award an equitable remedy unless the remedy at law is inadequate.

> "There's a remedy for everything except death."
>
> **MIGUEL DE CERVANTES**
> 1547–1616
> (SPANISH AUTHOR)

15-1 Damages

A breach of contract entitles the nonbreaching party to sue for monetary damages. As you have already learned, tort law damages are designed to compensate a party for harm

---

1. A *breach of contract* occurs when one party fails to perform part or all of the required duties under a contract. *Restatement (Second) of Contracts*, Section 235(2).

suffered as a result of another's wrongful act. In the context of contract law, damages are designed to compensate the nonbreaching party for the loss of the bargain. Often, courts say that innocent parties are to be placed in the position they would have occupied had the contract been fully performed.[2]

15-1a Types of Damages

There are basically four broad categories of damages:

1. Compensatory (to cover direct losses and costs).

2. Consequential (to cover indirect and foreseeable losses).

3. Punitive (to punish and deter wrongdoing).

4. Nominal (to recognize wrongdoing when no monetary loss is shown).

Compensatory and punitive damages were discussed in the context of tort law. Here, we look at these types of damages, as well as consequential and nominal damages, in the context of contract law.

Compensatory Damages Damages that compensate the nonbreaching party for the *loss of the bargain* are known as *compensatory damages*. These damages compensate the injured party only for damages actually sustained and proved to have arisen directly from the loss of the bargain caused by the breach of contract. They simply replace what was lost because of the wrong or damage, and, for this reason, are often said to "make the person whole."

Can an award of damages for a breach of contract elevate the nonbreaching party to a better position than he or she would have been in if the contract not been breached? That was the question in the following case.

---

2. *Restatement (Second) of Contracts*, Section 347.

CASE 15.1

Hallmark Cards, Inc. v. Murley

United States Court of Appeals, Eighth Circuit, 703 F.3d 456 (2013).

FACTS Janet Murley was the vice president of marketing at Hallmark Cards, Inc., until Hallmark eliminated her position as part of a corporate restructuring. As a vice president, Murley had access to Hallmark's confidential information, including its business plans, market research, and financial statements. In 2002, Murley and the company entered into a separation agreement. Murley agreed not to work in the greeting card or gift industry for a period of eighteen months and not to disclose any confidential information or retain any business records or documents relating to Hallmark. In exchange, Hallmark paid $735,000 to Murley as part of her severance package.

After the expiration of her noncompete agreement, Murley accepted a consulting position with Recycled Paper Greetings (RPG) for $125,000 and disclosed confidential Hallmark information to

When a former Hallmark employee breaches a term in her severance contract, how much can Hallmark recover as damages?

RPG. Hallmark filed a suit in a federal district court against Murley, alleging breach of contract. A jury returned a verdict in Hallmark's favor and awarded $860,000 in compensatory damages (the $735,000 severance payment and $125,000 that Murley received from RPG). Murley appealed.

ISSUE Can Hallmark (the nonbreaching party) obtain compensatory damages in an amount that is more than what it lost ($735,000) as a result of the breach?

DECISION No. The U.S. Court of Appeals for the Eighth District affirmed the judgment in Hallmark's favor but remanded the case to the lower court to reduce the award of damages. Hallmark was entitled to a return of the $735,000 severance it paid Murley, but not the $125,000 she earned from RPG.

Continues

REASON The federal appellate court noted that there was ample evidence that Murley retained and disclosed Hallmark's confidential materials to RPG, a competitor, in violation of the "terms and primary purpose" of the noncompete agreement. "A plaintiff may recover the benefit of his or her bargain as well as damages naturally and proximately caused by the breach and damages that could have been reasonably contemplated by the defendant at the time of the agreement." The court reasoned that by awarding Hallmark more than its $735,000 severance payment, the jury award placed Hallmark in a better position than it would find itself had Murley not breached the agreement. The jury's award of the $125,000 payment by RPG was, therefore, improper.

CRITICAL THINKING—Legal Consideration *What are compensatory damages? What is the standard measure of compensatory damages?*

LEARNING OBJECTIVE 1

What is the standard measure of compensatory damages when a contract is breached? How are damages computed differently in construction contracts?

Incidental Damages Damages that compensate for expenses directly incurred because of a breach of contract, such as those incurred to obtain performance from another source.

Under what circumstances will a court award monetary damages for a breached sale-of-land contract?

Standard Measure. The standard measure of compensatory damages is the difference between the value of the breaching party's promised performance under the contract and the value of her or his actual performance. This amount is reduced by any loss that the injured party has avoided.

EXAMPLE 15.1 Randall contracts to perform certain services exclusively for Hernandez during the month of March for $4,000. Hernandez cancels the contract and is in breach. Randall is able to find another job during March but can earn only $3,000. He can sue Hernandez for breach and recover $1,000 as compensatory damages. Randall can also recover from Hernandez the amount that he spent to find the other job. ■ Expenses that are directly incurred because of a breach of contract—such as those incurred to obtain performance from another source—are called **incidental damages**.

Note that the measure of compensatory damages often varies by type of contract. Certain types of contracts deserve special mention.

Sale of Goods. In a contract for the sale of goods, the usual measure of compensatory damages is the difference between the contract price and the market price.[3] **EXAMPLE 15.2** Medik Laboratories contracts to buy ten model UTS 400 network servers from Cal Industries for $4,000 each, but Cal Industries fails to deliver the servers. The market price of the servers at the time Medik learns of the breach is $4,500. Therefore, Medik's measure of damages is $5,000 (10 × $500), plus any incidental damages (expenses) caused by the breach. ■

Sometimes, the buyer breaches when the seller has not yet produced the goods. In that situation, compensatory damages normally equal the seller's lost profits on the sale, not the difference between the contract price and the market price.

Sale of Land. Ordinarily, because each parcel of land is unique, the remedy for a seller's breach of a contract for a sale of real estate is specific performance. The buyer is awarded the parcel of property for which he or she bargained (specific performance will be discussed more fully later in the chapter). The majority of states follow this rule.

A minority of states apply a different rule when the seller breaches a land-sale contract unintentionally (for instance, when the seller cannot deliver good title to the land for a reason he or she had previously been unaware of). In these states, a prospective buyer is limited to a refund of any down payment made plus any expenses incurred (such as fees for title searches, attorneys, and escrows). Thus, the minority rule effectively returns purchasers to the positions they occupied prior to the sale, rather than to give them the benefit of the bargain.

When the *buyer* is the party in breach, the measure of damages is typically the difference between the contract price and the market price of the land. The same measure is used when

---

3. This is the difference between the contract price and the market price at the time and place at which the goods were to be delivered or tendered. See Sections 2–708, 2–713, and 2–715(1) of the Uniform Commercial Code (UCC).

specific performance is not available (because the seller has sold the property to someone else, for instance).

Construction Contracts. The measure of damages in a building or construction contract depends on which party breaches and when the breach occurs.

1. *Breach by owner.* The owner may breach at three different stages—before performance has begun, during performance, or after performance has been completed. If the owner breaches *before performance has begun,* the contractor can recover only the profits that would have been made on the contract (that is, the total contract price less the cost of materials and labor). If the owner breaches *during performance,* the contractor can recover the profits plus the costs incurred in partially constructing the building. If the owner breaches *after construction has been completed,* the contractor can recover the entire contract price, plus interest.

2. *Breach by contractor.* When the contractor breaches the contract—either by failing to begin construction or by stopping work partway through the project—the measure of damages is the cost of completion. The cost of completion includes reasonable compensation for any delay in performance. If the contractor finishes late, the measure of damages is the loss of use.

3. *Breach by both owner and contractor.* When the performance of both parties—the construction contractor and the owner—falls short of what their contract required, the courts attempt to strike a fair balance in awarding damages.

CASE EXAMPLE 15.3 Jamison Well Drilling, Inc., contracted to drill a well for Ed Pfeifer for $4,130. Jamison drilled the well and installed a storage tank. The well did not comply with state health department requirements, however, and failed repeated tests for bacteria. The health department ordered the well to be abandoned and sealed. Pfeifer used the storage tank but paid Jamison nothing. Jamison filed a suit to recover. The court held that Jamison was entitled to $970 for the storage tank but was not entitled to the full contract price because the well was not usable.[4]

Exhibit 15–1 summarizes the rules for the measure of damages in breached construction contracts. The *Business Application* feature at the end of this chapter offers some suggestions on what to do if you cannot perform.

Consequential Damages Foreseeable damages that result from a party's breach of contract are called **consequential damages,** or *special damages.* They differ from compensatory damages in that they are caused by special circumstances beyond the contract itself. They flow

---

4. *Jamison Well Drilling, Inc. v. Pfeifer,* 2011-Ohio-521 (2011).

Exhibit 15–1 Measurement of Damages—Breach of Construction Contracts

PARTY IN BREACH	TIME OF BREACH	MEASUREMENT OF DAMAGES
Owner	Before construction has begun	Profits (contract price less cost of materials and labor)
Owner	During construction	Profits plus costs incurred up to time of breach
Owner	After construction is completed	Full contract price, plus interest
Contractor	Before construction has begun	Cost in excess of contract price to complete work
Contractor	Before construction is completed	Generally, all costs incurred by owner to complete

> "A long dispute means that both parties are wrong."
>
> **VOLTAIRE**
> 1694–1778
> (FRENCH AUTHOR)

Consequential Damages
Foreseeable damages that result from a party's breach of contract but are caused by special circumstances beyond the contract itself.

When a drilled water well fails bacteria testing, can the buyer of the drilling services keep the storage tank provided without paying for it?

KNOW THIS
To avoid the risk of consequential damages, a seller can limit the buyer's remedies via contract.

Nominal Damages A small monetary award (often one dollar) granted to a plaintiff when no actual damage was suffered.

Mitigation of Damages The requirement that a plaintiff do whatever is reasonable to minimize the damages caused by the defendant's breach of contract.

from the consequences, or results, of a breach. When a seller fails to deliver goods, knowing that the buyer is planning to use or resell those goods immediately, a court may award consequential damages for the loss of profits from the planned resale.

EXAMPLE 15.4 Mason contracts to buy a certain quantity of Quench, a specialty sports drink, from Nathan. Nathan knows that Mason has contracted with Ruthie to resell and ship the Quench within hours of its receipt. The beverage will then be sold to fans attending the Super Bowl. Nathan fails to deliver the Quench on time. Mason can recover the consequential damages—the loss of profits from the planned resale to Ruthie—caused by the nondelivery. (If Mason purchases Quench from another vendor, he can also recover compensatory damages for the difference between the contract price and the market price.) ■

For the nonbreaching party to recover consequential damages, the breaching party must know (or have reason to know) that special circumstances will cause the nonbreaching party to suffer an additional loss.[5] See this chapter's *Landmark in the Law* feature for a discussion of the nineteenth-century English case that established this rule on consequential damages.

Punitive Damages Punitive, or exemplary, damages, generally are not awarded in an action for breach of contract. Such damages have no legitimate place in contract law because they are, in essence, penalties, and a breach of contract is not unlawful in a criminal sense. A contract is simply a civil relationship between the parties. The law may compensate one party for the loss of the bargain—no more and no less. In a few situations, when a person's actions cause both a breach of contract and a tort, punitive damages may be available. Overall, though, punitive damages are almost never available in contract disputes.

Nominal Damages When no actual damage or financial loss results from a breach of contract and only a technical injury is involved, the court may award **nominal damages** to the innocent party. Nominal damages awards are often small, such as one dollar, but they do establish that the defendant acted wrongfully. Most lawsuits for nominal damages are brought as a matter of principle under the theory that a breach has occurred and some damages must be imposed regardless of actual loss.

EXAMPLE 15.5 Hernandez contracts to buy potatoes from Stanley at fifty cents a pound. Stanley breaches the contract and does not deliver the potatoes. Meanwhile, the price of potatoes falls. Hernandez is able to buy them in the open market at half the price he agreed to pay Stanley. Hernandez is clearly better off because of Stanley's breach. Thus, if Hernandez sues for breach of contract and wins, the court will likely award only nominal damages. ■

15–1b Mitigation of Damages

In most situations, when a breach of contract occurs, the injured party is held to a duty to mitigate, or reduce, the damages that he or she suffers. Under this doctrine of **mitigation of damages**, the required action depends on the nature of the situation.

Employment Contracts In the majority of states, a person whose employment has been wrongfully terminated has a duty to mitigate damages incurred because of the employer's breach of the employment contract. In other words, a wrongfully terminated employee has a duty to take a similar job if one is available.

If the employee fails to do this, the damages received will be equivalent to the person's former salary less the income he or she would have received in a similar job obtained by reasonable means. The employer has the burden of proving that such a job existed and that the employee could have been hired. Normally, a terminated employee is under no duty to take a job that is not of the same type and rank.

---

5. UCC 2–715(2).

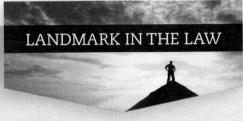

LANDMARK IN THE LAW

Hadley v. Baxendale (1854)

The rule that requires a breaching party to have notice of special ("consequential") circumstances that will result in additional loss to the nonbreaching party before consequential damages can be awarded was first enunciated in *Hadley v. Baxendale,*[a] a landmark case decided in 1854.

CASE BACKGROUND The case involved a broken crankshaft used in a flour mill run by the Hadley family in Gloucester, England. The crankshaft attached to the steam engine in the mill broke, and the shaft had to be sent to a foundry in Greenwich so that a new shaft could be made to fit the engine.

The Hadleys hired Baxendale, a common carrier, to transport the shaft from Gloucester to Greenwich. Baxendale received payment in advance and promised to deliver the shaft the following day. It was not delivered for several days, however. The Hadleys had no extra crankshaft on hand to use, so

they had to close the mill during those days. The Hadleys sued Baxendale to recover the profits they lost during that time. Baxendale contended that the loss of profits was "too remote."

In the mid-1800s, it was common knowledge that large mills, such as that run by the Hadleys, normally had more than one crankshaft in case the main one broke and had to be repaired. It is against this background that the parties presented their arguments on whether the damages resulting from the loss of profits while the crankshaft was out for repair were "too remote" to be recoverable.

THE ISSUE BEFORE THE COURT AND THE COURT'S RULING The crucial issue for the court was whether the Hadleys had informed the carrier, Baxendale, of the special circumstances surrounding the crankshaft's repair. Specifically, did Baxendale know at the time of the contract that the mill would have to shut down while the crankshaft was being repaired?

In the court's opinion, the only circumstances communicated by the Hadleys to Baxendale at the time the contract was

made were that the item to be transported was a broken crankshaft of a mill and that the Hadleys were the owners and operators of that mill. The court concluded that these circumstances did not reasonably indicate that the mill would have to stop operations if the delivery of the crankshaft was delayed.

APPLICATION TO TODAY'S WORLD *Today, the rule enunciated by the court in this case still applies. When damages are awarded, compensation is given only for those injuries that the defendant could reasonably have foreseen as a probable result of the usual course of events following a breach. If the alleged injury is outside the usual and foreseeable course of events, the plaintiff must show specifically that the defendant had reason to know the facts and foresee the injury.*

This rule applies to contracts in the online environment as well. For example, suppose that a Web merchant loses business (and profits) due to a computer system's failure. If the failure was caused by malfunctioning software, the merchant normally may recover the lost profits from the software maker if these consequential damages were foreseeable.

a. 9 Exch. 341, 156 Eng.Rep. 145 (1854).

EXAMPLE 15.6 Susan De La Concha works as a librarian at Brigham Young University. When she is fired, she claims that she was terminated in retaliation for filing an employment discrimination claim. Suppose that De La Concha succeeds in her employment discrimination claim but that Brigham Young can show that she has failed to take another librarian position when several comparable positions were available. Brigham Young can assert that she has failed to mitigate damages. In that situation, any compensation she is awarded for wrongful termination will be reduced by the amount she *could have obtained* from other employment. ■

Rental Agreements

Some states require a landlord to use reasonable means to find a new tenant if a tenant abandons the premises and fails to pay rent. If an acceptable tenant becomes available, the landlord is required to lease the premises to this tenant to mitigate the damages recoverable from the former tenant. The former tenant is still liable for the difference between the amount of the rent under the original lease and the rent received from the new tenant. If the landlord has not taken reasonable steps to find a new tenant, a court will likely reduce any award by the amount of rent the landlord could have received had he or she done so.

iStockPhoto.com/iphotoir

Assume that a librarian is wrongfully fired for filing an employment discrimination claim. Is she obligated to mitigate damages by taking another librarian position?

15–1c Liquidated Damages versus Penalties

Liquidated Damages
An amount, stipulated in a contract, that the parties to the contract believe to be a reasonable estimation of the damages that will occur in the event of a breach.

Penalty A contract clause that specifies a certain amount to be paid in the event of a default or breach of contract but is unenforceable because it is designed to punish the breaching party rather than to provide a reasonable estimate of damages.

A **liquidated damages** provision in a contract specifies that a certain dollar amount is to be paid in the event of a *future* default or breach of contract. (*Liquidated* means determined, settled, or fixed.)

Liquidated damages differ from penalties. Although a **penalty** also specifies a certain amount to be paid in the event of a default or breach of contract, it is designed to penalize the breaching party, not to make the innocent party whole. Liquidated damages provisions normally are enforceable. In contrast, if a court finds that a provision calls for a penalty, the agreement as to the amount will not be enforced, and recovery will be limited to actual damages.

Enforceability To determine whether a particular provision is for liquidated damages or a penalty, the court must answer two questions:

1. At the time the contract was formed, was it apparent that damages would be difficult to estimate in the event of a breach?

2. Was the amount set as damages a reasonable estimate and not excessive?[6]

If the answers to both questions are yes, the provision normally will be enforced. If either answer is no, the provision usually will not be enforced.

In the following *Spotlight Case,* the court had to decide whether a clause in a contract was an enforceable liquidated damages provision or an unenforceable penalty.

---

6. *Restatement (Second) of Contracts,* Section 356(1).

SPOTLIGHT ON LIQUIDATED DAMAGES: CASE 15.2

Kent State University v. Ford

Court of Appeals of Ohio, Eleventh District, Portage County, __ Ohio App.3d __, 26 N.E.3d 868, 2015 -Ohio- 41 (2015).

FACTS Gene Ford signed a five-year contract with Kent State University in Ohio to work as the head coach for the men's basketball team. The contract provided that if Ford quit before the end of the term, he would pay to the school liquidated damages in an amount equal to his salary ($300,000), multiplied by the number of years remaining on the contract. Laing Kennedy, Kent State's athletic director, told Ford that the contract would be renegotiated within a few years. Four years before the contract expired, however, Ford left Kent State and began to coach for Bradley University at an annual salary of $700,000. Kent State filed a suit in an Ohio state court against Ford, alleging breach of contract. The court enforced the liquidated damages clause and awarded the university $1.2 million. Ford appealed, arguing that the liquidated damages clause in his employment contract was an unenforceable penalty.

ISSUE Was the liquidated damages clause in Ford's contract enforceable?

DECISION Yes. A state intermediate appellate court affirmed the lower court's award. The clause was not a penalty. "There was justification for seeking liquidated damages to compensate for Kent State's losses" on Ford's breach.

If a college coach quits before the end of his contract, can the university recover liquidated damages?

Debby Wong/ShutterStock.com

REASON At the time the contract was entered into, determining the damages that would result from a breach was "difficult, if not impossible." The resignation of a head coach from a university's basketball team may cause a loss in ticket sales and a drop in community and alumni support for the team. The university's ability to recruit players may also be affected. Of course, a search for a new coach and coaching staff will be required. These effects are not easy to measure before they happen, especially considering that such results may be different at different times in a coach's tenure. Kennedy's statement that the contract would be renegotiated indicated that Kent State was interested in the stability of these factors. And in this case, "based on the record, . . . the damages were reasonable." The salary that Bradley was willing to pay Ford showed the cost to Kent State of finding a new coach with his skill and experience. "There was also an asserted decrease in ticket sales, costs associated with the trip for the coaching search, and additional potential sums that may be expended."

CRITICAL THINKING—Cultural Consideration *How does a college basketball team's record of wins and losses, and its ranking in its conference, support the court's decision in this case?*

Common Uses of Liquidated Damages Provisions Liquidated damages provisions are frequently used in construction contracts. For instance, a provision requiring a construction contractor to pay $300 for every day he or she is late in completing the project is a liquidated damages provision.

Such provisions are also common in contracts for the sale of goods.[7] In addition, contracts with entertainers and professional athletes often include liquidated damages provisions. **EXAMPLE 15.7** A television network settled its contract dispute with *Tonight Show* host Conan O'Brien for $33 million. The amount of the settlement was somewhat less than the $40 million O'Brien could have received under a liquidated damages clause in his contract. ■

15-2 Equitable Remedies

Sometimes, damages are an inadequate remedy for a breach of contract. In these situations, the nonbreaching party may ask the court for an equitable remedy. Equitable remedies include rescission and restitution, specific performance, and reformation.

15-2a Rescission and Restitution

As previously discussed, *rescission* is essentially an action to undo, or cancel, a contract—to return nonbreaching parties to the positions that they occupied prior to the transaction.[8] When fraud, mistake, duress, undue influence, lack of capacity, or failure of consideration is present, rescission is available. Rescission may also be available by statute.[9] The failure of one party to perform under a contract entitles the other party to rescind the contract. The rescinding party must give prompt notice to the breaching party.

Restitution To rescind a contract, both parties generally must make **restitution** to each other by returning goods, property, or funds previously conveyed.[10] If the property or goods can be returned, they must be. If the property or goods have been consumed, restitution must be made in an equivalent dollar amount. Essentially, restitution involves the recapture of a benefit conferred on the defendant that has unjustly enriched her or him.

EXAMPLE 15.8 Katie contracts with Mikhail to design a house for her. Katie pays Mikhail $9,000 and agrees to make two more payments of $9,000 (for a total of $27,000) as the design progresses. The next day, Mikhail calls Katie and tells her that he has taken a position with a large architectural firm in another state and cannot design the house. Katie decides to hire another architect that afternoon. Katie can obtain restitution of the $9,000. ■

Restitution Is Not Limited to Rescission Cases Restitution may be required when a contract is rescinded, but the right to restitution is not limited to rescission cases. Because an award of restitution basically returns something to its rightful owner, a party can seek restitution in actions for breach of contract, tort actions, and other types of actions.

For instance, restitution can be obtained when funds or property has been transferred by mistake or because of fraud or incapacity. Similarly, restitution might be available when there has been misconduct by a party with a special relationship with the other party. Even in

Why might television personality Conan O'Brien settle a contract dispute for less than that contract's liquidated damages clause?

LEARNING OBJECTIVE 3
Under what circumstances is the remedy of rescission and restitution available?

Restitution An equitable remedy under which a person is restored to his or her original position prior to loss or injury, or placed in the position he or she would have been in had the breach not occurred.

KNOW THIS
Restitution offers several advantages over traditional damages. First, restitution may be available in situations when damages cannot be proved or are difficult to prove. Second, restitution can be used to recover specific property. Third, restitution sometimes results in a greater overall award.

---

7. Section 2–718(1) of the UCC specifically authorizes the use of liquidated damages provisions.
8. The rescission discussed here refers to *unilateral* rescission, in which only one party wants to undo the contract. In *mutual* rescission, both parties agree to undo the contract. Mutual rescission discharges the contract, whereas unilateral rescission is generally available as a remedy for breach of contract.
9. Many states have laws that allow individuals who enter into "home solicitation contracts" to rescind these contracts within three business days for any reason. See, for example, California Civil Code Section 1689.5.
10. *Restatement (Second) of Contracts*, Section 370.

criminal cases, a court can order restitution of funds or property obtained through embezzlement, conversion, theft, or copyright infringement.

As mentioned, one of the bases that a court may use to order the rescission of a contract is fraud. That was the ground for the order of rescission in the following case.

CASE 15.3

Clara Wonjung Lee, DDS, Ltd. v. Robles

Appellate Court of Illinois, First District, 2014 WL 976776 (2014).

FACTS Clara Lee agreed to buy Rosalina Robles's dental practice and to lease her dental offices in Chicago, Illinois. The price was $267,000, with $133,500 allocated to goodwill—that is, the market value of the business's good reputation. After Lee took over the practice, *Chicago Magazine* and other local media revealed that Gary Kimmel, one of Robles's dentists, had illegally treated underage prostitutes in the practice's offices after hours. The media reported that Kimmel was under investigation by federal officials for this and other activities.

Lee filed a suit in an Illinois state court against Robles, seeking to rescind the contract. Lee alleged that Robles had deliberately withheld the information about Kimmel and that this information "adversely impacted the desirability and economic value of the practice." The court ruled in Lee's favor and awarded rescission and damages, which included the purchase price less Lee's unpaid rent and a portion of her income during her ownership of the practice. Robles appealed.

ISSUE Was Lee entitled to the rescission of her contract with Robles on the basis of fraud?

DECISION Yes. A state intermediate court affirmed the lower court's judgment awarding rescission and damages, finding that the holding

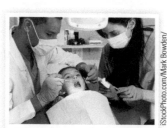

What determines the value of the reputation of a dental office?

"was consistent with the manifest weight of the evidence presented at trial."

REASON The parties' agreement for the sale of the dental practice required Robles to disclose "any material information," including actions by a "governmental agency that materially alters the desirability or economic potential of the assets." The testimony of Lee and a business appraiser at the trial indicated that information about Kimmel's activities "would have been material to a reasonable dentist's decision to purchase the practice." Robles knew about the federal investigation of Kimmel—both the Federal Bureau of Investigation and *Chicago Magazine* had interviewed her about Kimmel's activities. Robles, however, failed to disclose this information to Lee. The evidence showed that Robles's failure was "purposeful and not the result of any mistake or accident." Her "nondisclosure was designed to prevent [Lee] from gaining relevant information that may have caused [her] to not proceed with the sales transaction."

CRITICAL THINKING—Legal Consideration *When rescission is awarded, what is the measure of recovery? What did the recovery include in this case?*

15–2b Specific Performance

Specific Performance
An equitable remedy in which a court orders the parties to perform as promised in the contract. This remedy normally is granted only when the legal remedy (monetary damages) is inadequate.

The equitable remedy of **specific performance** calls for the performance of the act promised in the contract. This remedy is attractive to a nonbreaching party because it provides the exact bargain promised in the contract. It also avoids some of the problems inherent in a suit for monetary damages, such as collecting a judgment and arranging another contract. Moreover, the actual performance may be more valuable (to the promisee) than the monetary damages.

Normally, however, specific performance will not be granted unless the party's legal remedy (monetary damages) is inadequate.[11] For this reason, contracts for the sale of goods rarely qualify for specific performance. Monetary damages ordinarily are adequate in sales contracts because substantially identical goods can be bought or sold in the market. Only if the goods are unique will a court grant specific performance. For instance, paintings, sculptures, and

---

11. *Restatement (Second) of Contracts*, Section 359.

rare books and coins are often unique, and monetary damages will not enable a buyer to obtain substantially identical substitutes in the market.

LEARNING OBJECTIVE 4
When do courts grant specific performance as a remedy?

Sale of Land A court may grant specific performance to a buyer in an action for a breach of contract involving the sale of land. In this situation, the legal remedy of monetary damages may not compensate the buyer adequately because every parcel of land is unique. The same land in the same location obviously cannot be obtained elsewhere. Only when specific performance is unavailable (such as when the seller has sold the property to someone else) will damages be awarded instead.

CASE EXAMPLE 15.9 Howard Stainbrook entered into a contract to sell Trent Low forty acres of mostly timbered land for $45,000. Low agreed to pay for a survey of the property and other costs in addition to the price. He gave Stainbrook a check for $1,000 to show his intent to fulfill the contract. One month later, Stainbrook died. His son David became the executor of the estate. After he discovered that the timber on the property was worth more than $100,000, David asked Low to withdraw his offer to buy the forty acres. Low refused and filed a suit against David seeking specific performance of the contract. The court found that because Low had substantially performed his obligations under the contract and offered to perform the rest, he was entitled to specific performance.[12]

Contracts for Personal Services Contracts for personal services require one party to work personally for another party. Courts normally refuse to grant specific performance of personal-service contracts. One reason is that ordering a party to perform personal services against his or her will would amount to a type of involuntary servitude.[13]

Moreover, the courts do not want to monitor contracts for personal services, which usually require the exercise of personal judgment or talent. **EXAMPLE 15.10** Nicole contracts with a surgeon to remove a tumor on her brain. If he refuses to perform the surgery, the court will not compel him to perform (nor would Nicole want him to do so). A court cannot ensure meaningful performance in such a situation.[14]

If a contract is not deemed personal, the remedy at law of monetary damages may be adequate if a substantially identical service (for instance, lawn mowing) is available from other persons.

"Controversy equalizes fools and wise men— and the fools know it."

OLIVER WENDELL HOLMES
1809–1894
(AMERICAN AUTHOR)

15-2c Reformation

Reformation is an equitable remedy used when the parties have *imperfectly* expressed their agreement in writing. Reformation allows a court to rewrite the contract to reflect the parties' true intentions.

Fraud or Mutual Mistake Courts order reformation most often when fraud or mutual mistake is present. **EXAMPLE 15.11** If Carson contracts to buy a forklift from Yoshie but the written contract refers to a crane, a mutual mistake has occurred. Accordingly, a court could reform the contract so that the writing conforms to the parties' original intention as to which piece of equipment is being sold.

Written Contract Incorrectly States the Parties' Oral Agreement A court will also reform a contract when two parties enter into a binding oral contract but later make an error when they attempt to put the terms into writing. Usually, the court will allow into evidence the correct terms of the oral contract, thereby reforming the written contract.

What happens when a contract mistakenly specifies a crane instead of a forklift?

12. *Stainbrook v. Low*, 842 N.E.2d 386 (Ind.App. 2006).
13. Involuntary servitude, or slavery, is contrary to the public policy expressed in the Thirteenth Amendment to the U.S. Constitution.
14. Similarly, courts often refuse to order specific performance of construction contracts because courts are not set up to operate as construction supervisors or engineers.

Covenants Not to Compete Courts also may reform contracts involving written covenants not to compete, or restrictive covenants. Such covenants, as explained in an earlier chapter, are often included in contracts for the sale of ongoing businesses and in employment contracts. The agreements restrict the area and time in which one party can directly compete with the other party.

If a covenant not to compete is for a valid and legitimate purpose, but the area or time restraints are unreasonable, some courts will reform the restraints by making them reasonable and will then enforce the entire contract as reformed. Other courts will throw out the entire restrictive covenant as illegal. Thus, when businesspersons create restrictive covenants, they must make sure that the restrictions imposed are reasonable.

CASE EXAMPLE 15.12 Cardiac Study Center, Inc., a medical practice group, hired Dr. Robert Emerick. Later, Emerick became a shareholder of Cardiac and signed an agreement that included a covenant not to compete. The covenant stated that a physician who left the group promised not to practice competitively in the surrounding area for a period of five years. After Cardiac began receiving complaints from patients and other physicians about Emerick, it terminated his employment.

Emerick sued Cardiac, claiming that the covenant not to compete that he had signed was unreasonable and should be declared illegal. Ultimately, a state appellate court held that the covenant was both reasonable and enforceable. Cardiac had a legitimate interest in protecting its existing client base and prohibiting Emerick from taking its clients.[15] ■

Exhibit 15–2 graphically presents the remedies, including reformation, that are available to the nonbreaching party.

15-3 Recovery Based on Quasi Contract

In some situations, when no actual contract exists, a court may step in to prevent one party from being unjustly enriched at the expense of another party. As previously discussed, *quasi contract* is a legal theory under which an obligation is imposed in the absence of an agreement. A quasi contract is not a true contract but rather a fictional contract that is imposed on the parties to prevent unjust enrichment.

15. *Emerick v. Cardiac Study Center, Inc.,* 166 Wash.App. 1039 (2012).

Exhibit 15–2 Remedies for Breach of Contract

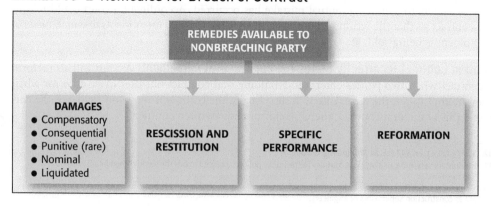

15–3a When Quasi Contract Is Used

Quasi contract allows a court to act as if a contract exists when there is no actual contract or agreement between the parties. Therefore, if the parties have entered into a contract concerning the matter in controversy, a court normally will not impose a quasi contract. A court can also use the doctrine when the parties entered into a contract, but it is unenforceable for some reason.

Quasi-contractual recovery is often granted when one party has partially performed under a contract that is unenforceable. Quasi contracts provide an alternative to suing for damages and allow the party to recover the reasonable value of the partial performance. Depending on the case, the amount of the recovery may be measured either by the benefit received or by the detriment suffered.

EXAMPLE 15.13 Ericson contracts to build two oil derricks for Petro Industries. The derricks are to be built over a period of three years, but the parties do not create a written contract. Therefore, the writing requirement will bar the enforcement of the contract.[16] After Ericson completes one derrick, Petro Industries informs him that it will not pay for the derrick. Ericson can sue Petro Industries under the theory of quasi contract. ■

15–3b The Requirements of Quasi Contract

To recover on a quasi contract theory, the party seeking recovery must show the following:

1. The party conferred a benefit on the other party.
2. The party conferred the benefit with the reasonable expectation of being paid.
3. The party did not act as a volunteer in conferring the benefit.
4. The party receiving the benefit would be unjustly enriched if allowed to retain the benefit without paying for it.

Applying these requirements to *Example 15.13,* Ericson can sue in quasi contract because all of the conditions for quasi-contractual recovery have been fulfilled. Ericson conferred a benefit on Petro Industries by building the oil derrick. Ericson built the derrick with the reasonable expectation of being paid. He did not intend to act as a volunteer. Petro Industries would be unjustly enriched if it was allowed to keep the derrick without paying Ericson for the work. Therefore, Ericson should be able to recover the reasonable value of the oil derrick that was built (under the theory of *quantum meruit*[17]—"as much as he or she deserves"). The reasonable value is ordinarily equal to the fair market value.

KNOW THIS
The function of a quasi contract is to impose a legal obligation on a party who made no actual promise.

iStockPhoto.com/shotbydave

Assume that it takes several years to build two oil derricks, but no written contract exists. If one is built, does the purchaser have to pay for it?

15–4 Contract Provisions Limiting Remedies

A contract may include provisions stating that no damages can be recovered for certain types of breaches or that damages will be limited to a maximum amount. A contract may also provide that the only remedy for breach is replacement, repair, or refund of the purchase price. In addition, a contract may provide that one party can seek injunctive relief if the other party breaches the contract. Provisions stating that no damages can be recovered are called *exculpatory clauses.* Provisions that affect the availability of certain remedies are called *limitation-of-liability clauses.*

---

16. Contracts that by their terms cannot be performed within one year from the day after the date of contract formation must be in writing to be enforceable under the Statute of Frauds.
17. Pronounced *kwahn*-tuhm *mehr*-oo-wuht.

ETHICAL ISSUE

Can contracts for mixed martial arts fighters limit a fighter's right to stop fighting? If you are a mixed martial arts champion, the highest-profile league to work for is the Ultimate Fighting Championship, or UFC. But a contract with UFC's parent company, Zuffa, LLC, includes numerous restrictions on your behavior.

The UFC's exclusivity clause, for instance, prevents you from competing in other mixed martial arts leagues. Another clause states that if you refuse a fight—or are injured or disabled—Zuffa can choose to extend the term of your contract. The term may be extended for any period when a fighter is unable or unwilling to compete or train for any reason. Zuffa can even retain the rights to a fighter who wants to retire from mixed martial arts.

You probably also signed an agreement that has a "champions clause." That means that if you become a champion, your contract with the UFC is automatically extended. If you get really famous, you do not even have rights to your likeness. You have signed those away to the UFC. So if a video game is based on your likeness, the UFC obtains the profits, and you do not. Therefore, you will have trouble negotiating with sponsors outside of the UFC, because you really do not own much of yourself to "sell."

A group of current and former mixed martial arts fighters have filed a lawsuit against Zuffa. They claim that these contract limitations are fundamentally unfair. Because the contracts prevent fighters from working with other promoters, profiting from individual marketing deals, and signing with outside sponsors, the suit alleges that the UFC is violating antitrust laws.

15–4a Sales Contracts

The Uniform Commercial Code (UCC) provides that remedies can be limited in a contract for the sale of goods. We will examine the UCC provisions on limitation-of-liability clauses again in the context of the remedies available on the breach of a contract for the sale or lease of goods.[18]

15–4b Enforceability of Limitation-of-Liability Clauses

LEARNING OBJECTIVE 5

What is a limitation-of-liability clause, and when will courts enforce it?

Whether a limitation-of-liability clause in a contract will be enforced depends on the type of breach that is excused by the provision. Clauses that normally will not be enforced include provisions excluding liability for fraudulent or intentional injury or for illegal acts or other violations of law. Clauses excluding liability for negligence may be enforced in certain situations, however. When an exculpatory clause for negligence is contained in a contract made between parties who have roughly equal bargaining positions, the clause usually will be enforced.

CASE EXAMPLE 15.14 Engineering Consulting Services, Ltd. (ECS), contracted with RSN Properties, Inc., a real estate developer, to perform soil studies for $2,200 and render an opinion on the use of septic systems in a residential subdivision being developed. A clause in the contract limited ECS's liability to RSN to the value of the engineering services or the sum of $50,000, whichever was greater.

ECS concluded that most of the lots were suitable for septic systems, so RSN proceeded with development. RSN constructed roads and water lines to the subdivision in reliance on ECS's conclusions, which turned out to be incorrect. RSN sued ECS for breach of contract and argued that the limitation-of-liability clause was against public policy and unenforceable. The court, however, enforced the limitation-of-liability clause as "a reasonable allocation of risks in an arm's-length business transaction."[19] ▪

---

18. UCC 2–719.
19. *RSN Properties, Inc. v. Engineering Consulting Services, Ltd.*, 301 Ga.App. 52, 686 S.E.2d 853 (2009).

Reviewing . . . Breach and Remedies

Kyle Bruno enters into a contract with X Entertainment to be a stuntman in a movie. Bruno is widely known as the best motorcycle stuntman in the business, and the movie, *Xtreme Riders,* has numerous scenes involving high-speed freestyle street-bike stunts. Filming is set to begin August 1 and end by December 1 so that the film can be released the following summer. Both parties to the contract have stipulated that the filming must end on time in order to capture the profits from the summer movie market.

The contract states that Bruno will be paid 10 percent of the net proceeds from the movie for his stunts. The contract also includes a liquidated damages provision, which specifies that if Bruno breaches the contract, he will owe X Entertainment $1 million. In addition, the contract includes a limitation-of-liability clause stating that if Bruno is injured during filming, X Entertainment's liability is limited to nominal damages. Using the information presented in the chapter, answer the following questions.

1. One day, while Bruno is preparing for a difficult stunt, he gets into an argument with the director and refuses to perform any stunts. Can X Entertainment seek specific performance of the contract? Why or why not?
2. Suppose that while performing a high-speed wheelie on a motorcycle, Bruno is injured by an intentionally reckless act of an X Entertainment employee. Will a court be likely to enforce the limitation-of-liability clause? Why or why not?
3. What factors would a court consider to determine if the $1 million liquidated damages clause is valid or is a penalty?
4. Suppose that there was no liquidated damages clause (or the court refused to enforce it) and X Entertainment breached the contract. The breach caused the release of the film to be delayed by many months. Could Bruno seek consequential (special) damages for lost profits from the summer movie market in that situation? Explain.

DEBATE THIS

- Courts should always uphold limitation-of-liability clauses, whether or not the two parties to the contract had equal bargaining power.

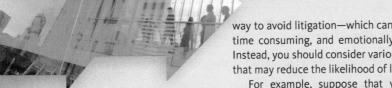

BUSINESS APPLICATION   What Do You Do When You Cannot Perform?*

Not every contract can be performed. If you are a contractor, you may take on a job that, for one reason or another, you cannot or do not wish to perform. Simply walking away from the job and hoping for the best normally is not the most effective way to avoid litigation—which can be costly, time consuming, and emotionally draining. Instead, you should consider various options that may reduce the likelihood of litigation.

For example, suppose that you are a building contractor and you sign a contract to build a home for the Andersons according to a set of plans that they provided. Performance is to begin on June 15. On June 1, Central Enterprises offers you a position that will pay you two and a half times as much net income as you could earn as an independent builder. To take the job, you have to start on June 15. You cannot be in two places at the same time, so to accept the new position, you must breach the contract with the Andersons.

---

* This *Business Application* is not meant to substitute for the services of an attorney who is licensed to practice law in your state.

Continues

Consider Your Options

What can you do in this situation? One option is to subcontract the work to another builder and oversee the work yourself to make sure it conforms to the contract. Another option is to negotiate with the Andersons for a release. You can offer to find another qualified builder who will build a house of the same quality at the same price. Alternatively, you can offer to pay any additional costs if another builder takes the job and is more expensive. In any event, this additional cost would be one measure of damages that a court would impose on you if the Andersons prevailed in a suit for breach of contract (in

addition to any costs the Andersons suffer as a result of the breach, such as costs due to the delay in construction). Thus, by making the offer, you might be able to avoid the expense of litigation—if the Andersons accept your offer.

Offers for Settlement

Often, parties are reluctant to propose compromise settlements because they fear that what they say will be used against them in court if litigation ensues. Generally, however, offers for settlement will not be admitted in court to prove that you are liable for a breach of contract (though they are at times

admissible to prove a party breached the duty of good faith).

CHECKLIST for When You Cannot Perform:

1. Consider a compromise.
2. Subcontract out the work and oversee it.
3. Offer to find an alternative contractor to fulfill your obligation.
4. Make a cash offer to "buy" a release from your contract. Work with an attorney in making the offer unless the amount involved is insignificant.

Key Terms

consequential damages 359
incidental damages 358
liquidated damages 362

mitigation of damages 360
nominal damages 360
penalty 362

restitution 363
specific performance 364

Chapter Summary: Breach and Remedies

	COMMON REMEDIES AVAILABLE TO NONBREACHING PARTY

Damages	The legal remedy designed to compensate the nonbreaching party for the loss of the bargain. The nonbreaching party frequently has a duty to *mitigate* (lessen or reduce) the damages suffered. There are four broad categories of damages. In addition, a contract may contain a provision for liquidated damages.
	1. *Compensatory damages*—Damages that compensate the nonbreaching party for injuries actually sustained and proved to have arisen directly from the loss of the bargain resulting from the breach of contract.
	   a. In breached contracts for the sale of goods, the usual measure of compensatory damages is the difference between the contract price and the market price.
	   b. In breached contracts for the sale of land, the measure of damages is ordinarily the same as in contracts for the sale of goods.
	   c. In breached construction contracts, the measure of damages depends on which party breaches and at what stage of construction the breach occurs.
	2. *Consequential damages*—Damages that result from special circumstances beyond the contract itself. The damages flow only from the consequences of a breach. For a party to recover consequential damages, the damages must be the foreseeable result of a breach of contract, and the breaching party must have known at the time the contract was formed that special circumstances existed that would cause the nonbreaching party to incur additional loss on breach of the contract. Also called *special damages*.
	3. *Punitive damages*—Damages awarded to punish the breaching party. Usually not awarded in an action for breach of contract unless a tort is involved.
	4. *Nominal damages*—Damages small in amount (such as one dollar) that are awarded when a breach has occurred but no actual injury has been suffered. Awarded only to establish that the defendant acted wrongfully.
	5. *Liquidated damages*—Damages specified in a contract as the amount to be paid to the nonbreaching party in the event the contract is breached. Clauses providing for liquidated damages are enforced if the damages were difficult to estimate at the time the contract was formed and if the amount stipulated is reasonable. If the amount is construed to be a penalty, the clause will not be enforced.

Rescission and Restitution	1. *Rescission*—A remedy whereby a contract is canceled and the parties are restored to the original positions that they occupied prior to the transaction. Available when fraud, a mistake, duress, or failure of consideration is present. The rescinding party must give prompt notice of the rescission to the breaching party. 2. *Restitution*—When a contract is rescinded, both parties must make restitution to each other by returning the goods, property, or funds previously conveyed. Restitution prevents the unjust enrichment of the parties.
Specific Performance	An equitable remedy calling for the performance of the act promised in the contract. This remedy is available only in special situations—such as those involving contracts for the sale of unique goods or land—when monetary damages would be an inadequate remedy. Specific performance is not available as a remedy for breached contracts for personal services.
Reformation	An equitable remedy allowing a contract to be "reformed," or rewritten, to reflect the parties' true intentions. Available when an agreement is imperfectly expressed in writing.
Recovery Based on Quasi Contract	An equitable theory imposed by the courts to obtain justice and prevent unjust enrichment in a situation in which no enforceable contract exists. The party seeking recovery must show the following: 1. A benefit was conferred on the other party. 2. The party conferring the benefit did so with the expectation of being paid. 3. The benefit was not volunteered. 4. The party receiving the benefit would be unjustly enriched if allowed to retain the benefit without paying for it.
CONTRACT DOCTRINES RELATING TO REMEDIES	
Contract Provisions Limiting Remedies	A contract may provide that no damages (or only a limited amount of damages) can be recovered in the event the contract is breached. Under the Uniform Commercial Code, remedies may be limited in contracts for the sale of goods. Clauses excluding liability for fraudulent or intentional injury or for illegal acts cannot be enforced. Clauses excluding liability for negligence may be enforced if both parties hold roughly equal bargaining power.

Issue Spotters

1. Greg contracts to build a storage shed for Haney. Haney pays Greg in advance, but Greg completes only half the work. Haney pays Ipswich $500 to finish the shed. If Haney sues Greg, what would be the measure of recovery? (See *Damages*.)

2. Lyle contracts to sell his ranch to Marley, who is to take possession on June 1. Lyle delays the transfer until August 1. Marley incurs expenses in providing for cattle that he bought for the ranch. When they made the contract, Lyle had no reason to know of the cattle. Is Lyle liable for Marley's expenses in providing for the cattle? Why or why not? (See *Damages*.)

—**Check your answers to the *Issue Spotters* against the answers provided in Appendix D at the end of this text.**

Learning Objectives Check

1. What is the standard measure of compensatory damages when a contract is breached? How are damages computed differently in construction contracts?

2. What is the difference between compensatory damages and consequential damages? What are nominal damages, and when do courts award nominal damages?

3. Under what circumstances is the remedy of rescission and restitution available?

4. When do courts grant specific performance as a remedy?

5. What is a limitation-of-liability clause, and when will courts enforce it?

—**Answers to the even-numbered *Learning Objectives Check* questions can be found in Appendix E at the end of this text.**

Business Scenarios and Case Problems

15–1. Liquidated Damages. Carnack contracts to sell his house and lot to Willard for $100,000. The terms of the contract call for Willard to make a deposit of 10 percent of the purchase price as a down payment. The terms further stipulate that if the buyer breaches the contract, Carnack will retain the deposit as liquidated damages. Willard makes the deposit, but because her expected financing of the $90,000 balance falls through, she breaches the contract. Two weeks later, Carnack sells the house and lot to Balkova for $105,000. Willard demands her $10,000 back, but Carnack refuses, claiming that Willard's breach and the contract terms entitle him to keep the deposit. Discuss who is correct. (See *Damages*.)

15–2. Mitigation of Damages. Lauren Barton, a single mother with three children, lived in Portland, Oregon. Cynthia VanHorn also lived in Oregon until she moved to New York City to open and operate an art gallery. VanHorn asked Barton to manage the gallery under a one-year contract for an annual salary of $72,000. To begin work, Barton relocated to New York. As part of the move, Barton transferred custody of her children to her husband, who lived in London, England. In accepting the job, Barton also forfeited her husband's alimony and child-support payments, including unpaid amounts of nearly $30,000.

Before Barton started work, VanHorn repudiated the contract. Unable to find employment for more than an annual salary of $25,000, Barton moved to London to be near her children. Barton filed a suit in an Oregon state court against VanHorn, seeking damages for breach of contract. Should the court hold, as VanHorn argued, that Barton did not take reasonable steps to mitigate her damages? Why or why not? (See *Damages*.)

15–3. Quasi Contract. Middleton Motors, Inc., a struggling Ford dealership in Wisconsin, sought managerial and financial assistance from Lindquist Ford, Inc., a successful Ford dealership in Iowa. While the two dealerships negotiated the terms for the services and a cash infusion, Lindquist sent Craig Miller, its general manager, to assume control of Middleton. After a year, the parties had not agreed on the terms, Lindquist had not invested any funds, Middleton had not made a profit, and Miller was fired without being paid. Can Miller recover pay for his time on a quasi-contract theory? Why or why not? Which of the quasi-contractual requirements is most likely to be disputed in this case? Why? [*Lindquist Ford, Inc. v. Middleton Motors, Inc.,* 557 F.3d 469 (7th Cir. 2009)] (See *Recovery Based on Quasi Contract*.)

15–4. Liquidated Damages versus Penalties. Planned Pethood Plus, Inc. (PPP), a veterinary clinic, borrowed $389,000 from KeyBank. The term of the loan was ten years. A "prepayment penalty" clause provided a formula to add an amount to the balance due if PPP offered to repay its loan early. The additional amount depended on the time of the prepayment. Such clauses are common in loan agreements. After one year, PPP offered to pay its loan. KeyBank applied the formula to add $40,525.92 to the balance due. Is this a penalty or liquidated damages? Explain. [*Planned Pethood Plus, Inc. v. KeyCorp, Inc.,* 228 P.3d 262 (Colo.App. 2010)] (See *Damages*.)

15–5. Measure of Damages. Before buying a house, Dean and Donna Testa hired Ground Systems, Inc. (GSI), to inspect the sewage and water disposal system. GSI reported a split system with a watertight septic tank, a wastewater tank, a distribution box, and a leach field. The Testas bought the house. Later, Dean saw that the system was not as GSI described—there was no distribution box or leach field, and there was only one tank, which was not watertight. The Testas arranged for the installation of a new system and sold the house. Assuming that GSI is liable for breach of contract, what is the measure of damages? [*Testa v. Ground Systems, Inc.,* 206 N.J. 330, 20 A.3d 435 (App. Div. 2011)] (See *Damages*.)

15–6. Business Case Problem with Sample Answer— Consequential Damages. After submitting the high bid at a foreclosure sale, David Simard entered into a contract to purchase real property in Maryland for $192,000. Simard defaulted (failed to pay) on the contract, so a state court ordered the property to be resold at Simard's expense, as required by state law. The property was then resold for $163,000, but the second purchaser also defaulted on his contract. The court then ordered a second resale, resulting in a final price of $130,000. Assuming that Simard is liable for consequential damages, what is the extent of his liability? Is he liable for losses and expenses related to the first resale? If so, is he also liable for losses and expenses related to the second resale? Why or why not? [*Burson v. Simard,* 35 A.3d 1154 (Md. 2012)] (See *Damages*.)

—For a sample answer to Problem 15–6, go to Appendix F at the end of this text.

15–7. Liquidated Damages. Cuesport Properties, LLC, sold a condominium in Anne Arundel County, Maryland, to Critical Developments, LLC. As part of the sale, Cuesport agreed to build a wall between Critical Developments' unit and an adjacent unit within thirty days of closing. If Cuesport failed to do so, it was to pay $126 per day until completion. This was an estimate of the amount of rent that Critical Developments would lose until the wall was finished and the unit could be rented. Actual damages were otherwise difficult to estimate at the time of the contract. The wall was built on time, but without a county permit, and it did not comply with the county building code. Critical Developments did not modify the wall to comply with the code until 260 days after the date of the contract deadline for completion of the wall. Does Cuesport have to pay Critical Developments $126 for each of the 260 days? Explain. [*Cuesport Properties, LLC v. Critical Developments, LLC,* 209 Md.App. 607, 61 A.3d 91 (2013)] (See *Damages*.)

15–8. Limitation-of-Liability Clauses. Mia Eriksson was a seventeen-year-old competitor in horseback-riding events. Her riding coach was Kristi Nunnink. Eriksson signed an agreement that released Nunnink from all liability except for damages caused by Nunnink's "direct, willful and wanton negligence." During an event at Galway Downs in Temecula, California, Eriksson's horse struck a hurdle. She fell from the horse and the horse fell on her, causing her death. Her parents, Karan and Stan Eriksson, filed a suit in a California state court against

Nunnink for wrongful death. Is the limitation-of-liability agreement that Eriksson signed likely to be enforced in her parents' case? If so, how would it affect their claim? Explain. [*Eriksson v. Nunnink,* 233 Cal.App.4th 708, 183 Cal.Rptr.3d 234 (4 Dist. 2015)] (See *Contract Provisions Limiting Remedies*.)

15–9. A Question of Ethics—Performance and Damages. On a weekday, Tamara Cohen, a real estate broker, showed a townhouse owned by Ray and Harriet Mayer to Jessica Seinfeld, the wife of comedian Jerry Seinfeld. On the weekend, when Cohen was unavailable because her religious beliefs prevented her from working, the Seinfelds revisited the townhouse on their own and agreed to buy it. The contract stated that the "buyers will pay buyer's real estate broker's fees." [*Cohen v. Seinfeld,* 15 Misc.3d 1118(A), 839 N.Y.S.2d 432 (Sup. 2007)] (See *Damages*.)

1. Is Cohen entitled to payment even though she was not available to show the townhouse to the Seinfelds on the weekend? Explain.

2. What obligation do parties involved in business deals owe to each other with respect to their religious beliefs? How might the situation in this case have been avoided?

Critical Thinking and Writing Assignments

15–10. Critical Legal Thinking. Review the discussion of the doctrine of mitigation of damages in this chapter. What are some of the advantages and disadvantages of this doctrine? (See *Damages*.)

15–11. Business Law Critical Thinking Group Assignment. Frances Morelli agreed to sell Judith Bucklin a house in Rhode Island for $177,000. The sale was supposed to be closed by September 1. The contract included a provision that "if Seller is unable to convey good, clear, insurable, and marketable title, Buyer shall have the option to: (a) accept such title as Seller is able to convey without reduction of the Purchase Price, or (b) cancel this Agreement and receive a return of all Deposits."

An examination of the public records revealed that the house did not have marketable title. Bucklin offered Morelli additional time to resolve the problem, and the closing did not occur as scheduled. Morelli decided that "the deal [was] over" and offered to return the deposit. Bucklin refused and, in mid-October, decided to exercise her option to accept the house without marketable title. She notified Morelli, who did not respond. She then filed a lawsuit against Morelli in a state court. (See *Equitable Remedies*.)

1. One group will discuss whether Morelli has breached the contract and will decide in whose favor the court should rule.

2. A second group will assume that Morelli did breach the contract and will determine what the appropriate remedy is in this situation.

Unit Two—Business Case Study with Dissenting Opinion

Braddock v. Braddock

Fraudulent misrepresentation is one of the conditions that may cause a contract to lack voluntary consent. For a misrepresentation to be fraudulent, it must misrepresent a present, material fact. A representation, or prediction, of a future fact does not qualify. The misrepresentation must be consciously false and intended to mislead an innocent party, who must justifiably rely on it. When an innocent party is fraudulently induced to enter into a contract, the party can rescind the contract and be restored to her or his original position or can enforce the contract and seek damages for injuries resulting from the fraud.

In this *Business Case Study with Dissenting Opinion*, we present *Braddock v. Braddock*,[1] a case involving an individual who gave up his career and relocated his home and family based on his cousin's representations about a newly formed entrepreneurial venture. The individual's position in the new enterprise was not what the cousin had told him it would be, however. Were the cousin's statements fraudulent? Or were they simply expressions of expectation—predictions of future possibilities—subject to contingencies that neither party could control?

iStockPhoto.com/kali9

Is it fraudulent to offer a relative a great job, requiring relocation, only to reduce substantially the quality of the promised job?

CASE BACKGROUND

David Braddock wanted to form a company, Broad Oak Energy, Inc. (BOE), to tap oil and gas reserves in Louisiana and Texas. He asked his cousin John, an investment banker in New York, to find an investor to provide BOE with $75 to $150 million and also asked John to come to work for BOE. David assured John that he would be BOE's chief financial officer (CFO) and land manager. He also told John that he would receive half as much stock in the company as would be issued to David, who would serve as the company's chief executive officer. John quit his job, agreed to accept a significantly reduced fee to find an investor for BOE, and moved his family to Texas. As a result of John's efforts, Warburg Pincus, LLC, agreed to provide $150 million in start-up capital.

Two weeks later, David told John that Warburg Pincus insisted that John not be made CFO or land manager. Instead, David offered him a substantially reduced position, that of landman. Surprised, John nevertheless cooperated. He signed "engagement agreements" to accept the lesser position as an "employee at will," subject to discharge for any reason at any time. Stress soon began to take a toll on his health, and he was granted a conditional medical leave of absence. The next month, BOE terminated his employment.

John filed a suit in a New York state court against David, asserting that these circumstances constituted fraud. The court dismissed the complaint. John appealed to a state intermediate appellate court.

MAJORITY OPINION

SAXE, J. [Judge]
* * * *

To plead a claim for [fraud], a plaintiff must assert the misrepresentation of a material fact, which was known by the defendant to be false

---

1. 60 A.D.3d 84, 871 N.Y.S.2d 68 (1 Dept. 2009).

and intended to be relied on when made, and that there was justifiable reliance and resulting injury. The complaint here sufficiently sets forth these elements. [Emphasis added.]
* * * *

[John's] allegations satisfy the particularity requirement for a fraud claim.
* * * *

* * * Since David and John are cousins, John's reliance on David's good faith may be found to be reasonable even where it might not be reasonable in the context of an arm's length transaction with a stranger. Family members stand in a fiduciary relationship [one of trust] toward one another in a co-owned business venture. * * * Under the circumstances alleged here, John had reason to believe that David would treat him, in their interaction, with good faith and integrity.
* * * *

The situation presented here should be distinguished from cases in which a plaintiff who was involved in a business deal claims that, in the original discussions of the deal, misrepresentations were made as to its terms but the falsity of those representations was revealed by the time the deal was executed. In such cases, the ultimate terms of the deal, if agreed upon, are all that the plaintiff is entitled to, and he will not be permitted to seek damages based upon the original misrepresentations, because he did not rely on them in electing to go through with the deal. Here, in contrast, John's subsequent execution of documents that fundamentally altered the originally promised terms of his position with the company was not merely an election to enter into the deal anyway. First of all, even before he executed * * * the agreements * * *, the deal was essentially under way, at least on his part, in that he had already sacrificed his former life and undertaken tasks to forward the venture, and he was no longer in a position to reject the offered terms or even to negotiate effectively. Indeed, when the allegations are understood in the context of an ongoing attempt by John to salvage something from his dashed expectations, the fact that he subsequently acceded to new and lesser terms should not justify holding * * * that he did not reasonably rely on his cousin's alleged misrepresentations and false assurances, to his own severe detriment.

If all these interactions had been between strangers conducting an arm's length business transaction, strict reliance on the signed written documents, to the exclusion of the parties' words and conduct, would be appropriate. But the expectation of the good faith of a family member in circumstances such as these may justify some reliance on assurances that are not incorporated into written documents drafted and executed later.

* * * *

Here, * * * the issues of material misrepresentation and reasonable reliance are not subject to summary disposition [settlement], and the fiduciary relationship between the parties, with its concomitant [associated] mutual obligation to act in good faith, makes John's reliance on David's assurances all the more reasonable.

* * * *

* * * Defendants' motion to dismiss the complaint for failure to state a cause of action * * * [is] denied * * * so as to reinstate the [plaintiffs' fraud] cause of action.

DISSENTING OPINION

LIPPMAN, P.J. [Presiding Judge], (DISSENTING).

* * * *

* * * It is, in essence, alleged that John's entire course of conduct in providing investment banking services for a discounted fee, giving up his lucrative New York employment as an investment banker and advisor, moving to Texas and agreeing to take the non-executive position with BOE from which he was eventually dismissed * * * was induced by David's * * * assurances.

* * * *

* * * At the time of David's nominal assurances, BOE was but an unfunded shell requiring for its viability an enormous infusion of capital. And, while John was confident of procuring financing for the venture, there had been, at the time, neither a commitment of funds nor even the emergence of a leading candidate to provide such a commitment. Moreover, John, in addition to being an experienced investment banker and financial consultant, was, by reason of his own prior professional involvement in oil and gas ventures and his extensive familial connections to the industry, particularly well aware of the risks such ventures entailed. * * * In these circumstances, * * * no promise of high executive-level employment in the company * * * could reasonably have been viewed as an "assurance" or a "guarantee." * * * What he now terms "assurances" and "guarantees" could have been reasonably understood as only expressions of expectation or intent, the realization of which would depend upon contingencies not within the power of the parties to foreseeably accommodate to their stated objectives.

* * * While he may have had a moral claim to rely upon his cousin even when objective circumstances counseled otherwise, there is no legal right to recovery in fraud that may be vindicated upon such a predicate.

Accordingly, I would affirm the dismissal of plaintiffs' fraud cause of action.

QUESTIONS FOR ANALYSIS

1. **Law.** What did the majority conclude on the issue before the court in this case? What reasoning supported this conclusion?

2. **Law.** On what important point did the dissent disagree with the majority, and why?

3. **Ethics.** How do you view David's statements and John's actions? Did David take unethical advantage of his cousin, luring him in bad faith? Was John too willing to rely on assurances concerning events that he should have known from experience might not occur? Discuss.

4. **Economic Dimensions.** What does this case indicate about employment and employment contracts?

5. **Implications for the Investor.** Why would an investor like Warburg Pincus not want someone like John in an executive role in an enterprise for which the investor was providing significant capital?

Unit Two—Business Scenario

iStock/Photo.com/mitza

Alberto Corelli offers to pay $2,500 to purchase a painting titled *Moonrise* from Tara Shelley, an artist whose works have been causing a stir in the art world. Shelley accepts Corelli's offer. Assuming that the contract has met all of the requirements for a valid contract, answer the following questions.

1. **Minors.** Corelli is a minor when he purchases the painting. Is the contract void? Is it voidable? What is the difference between these two conditions? A month after his eighteenth birthday, Corelli decides that he would rather have the $2,500 than the painting. He informs Shelley that he is disaffirming the contract and requests that Shelley return the $2,500 to him. When she refuses to do so, Corelli brings a court action to recover the $2,500. What will the court likely decide in this situation? Why?

Continues

2. **Statute of Frauds.** Both parties are adults, the contract is oral, and the painting is still in progress. Corelli pays Shelley the $2,500 in return for her promise to deliver the painting to his home when it is finished. A week later, after Shelley finishes the painting, a visitor to her gallery offers her $3,500 for it. Shelley sells the painting to the visitor and sends Corelli a signed letter explaining that she is "canceling" their contract for the sale of the *Moonrise* painting. Corelli sues Shelley to enforce the contract. Is the contract enforceable? Explain.

3. **Capacity.** Both parties are adults, and the contract, which is in writing, states that Corelli will pay Shelley the $2,500 the following day. In the meantime, Shelley allows Corelli to take the painting home with him. The next day, Corelli's son returns the painting to Shelley, stating that he is canceling the contract. He explains that his father has been behaving strangely lately, that he seems to be mentally incompetent at times, and that he clearly was not acting rationally when he bought the painting, which he could not afford. Is the contract enforceable? Discuss fully.

4. **Impossibility of Performance.** Both parties are adults, and the contract is in writing. The contract calls for Shelley to deliver the painting to Corelli's gallery in two weeks. Corelli has already arranged to sell the painting to a third party for $4,000 (a $1,500 profit), but it must be available for the third party in two weeks, or the sale will not go through. Shelley knows this but does not deliver the painting at the time promised. Corelli sues Shelley for $1,500 in damages. Shelley claims that performance was impossible because her mother fell seriously ill and required Shelley's care. Who will win this lawsuit, and why?

5. **Agreement in E-Contracts.** Both parties are adults. Shelley, on her Web site, offers to sell the painting for $2,500. Corelli accepts the offer by clicking on an "I accept" box on the computer screen displaying the offer. Among other terms, the online offer includes a forum-selection clause stating that any disputes under the contract are to be resolved by a court in California, the state in which Shelley lives. After Corelli receives the painting, he notices a smear of paint across the lower corner that was not visible in the digitized image that appeared on Shelley's Web site. Corelli calls Shelley, tells her about the smear, and says that he wants to cancel the contract and return the painting. When Shelley refuses to cooperate, Corelli sues her in a Texas state court, seeking to rescind the contract. Shelley claims that any suit against her must be filed in a California court in accordance with the forum-selection clause. Corelli maintains that the forum-selection clause is unconscionable and should not be enforced. What factors will the court consider in deciding this case? What will the court likely decide? Would it matter whether Corelli read the terms of the online offer before clicking on "I accept"?

Unit Two—Group Project

RiotGear, LLC, contracts with Standard Transit, Inc., to distribute RiotGear's Occupy Earth/Global Movement line of apparel to retail outlets for a certain price. RiotGear promises to donate a share of the proceeds from the sale of the Occupy Earth/Global Movement line to The Cause, a charitable organization dedicated to supporting those who seek social and economic change through protest. In reliance on the expected donation, The Cause contracts for medical and other supplies. Standard later increases the distribution cost, and RiotGear tells The Cause that there will be no donation.

1. While the goods are in transit, RiotGear receives this tweet from Standard: "Price increase of 99 percent or no delivery." RiotGear agrees and pays, but later sues Standard for the increase over the original price. The first group will identify the rule that a court would apply in this situation and decide whether RiotGear is entitled to the difference in price.

2. The second group will determine whether The Cause can enforce RiotGear's original promise despite the lack of consideration. What doctrine might a court apply in this situation, and what are the requirements to enforce a promise?

17

iStockPhoto.com/IS_imagesource

LEARNING OBJECTIVES

The five Learning Objectives *below are designed to help improve your understanding of the chapter. After reading this chapter, you should be able to answer the following questions:*

1. If a contract involves both goods and services, does the UCC apply?

2. In a sales contract, if an offeree includes additional or different terms in an acceptance, will a contract result? If so, what happens to these terms?

3. What exceptions to the writing requirements of the Statute of Frauds are provided in Article 2 and Article 2A of the UCC?

4. Risk of loss does not necessarily pass with title. If the parties to a contract do not expressly agree when risk passes and the goods are to be delivered without movement by the seller, when does risk pass?

5. What law governs contracts for the international sale of goods?

The Formation of Sales and Lease Contracts

When we turn to contracts for the sale and lease of goods, we move away from common law principles and into the area of statutory law. State statutory law governing sales and lease transactions is based on the Uniform Commercial Code (UCC), which has been adopted as law by all of the states.[1] (See this chapter's *Landmark in the Law* for more information on the UCC.)

"I am for free commerce with all nations."

GEORGE WASHINGTON
1732–1799
(FIRST PRESIDENT OF THE UNITED STATES, 1789–1797)

The chapter-opening quotation echoes a sentiment that most Americans believe—free commerce will benefit our nation. The Uniform Commercial Code (UCC) seeks to promote commerce. The goal of the UCC is to simplify and to streamline commercial transactions. The UCC allows parties to form sales and lease contracts, including those entered into online, without observing the same degree of formality used in forming other types of contracts. We open this chapter with a discussion of the UCC's Article 2 (on sales) and Article 2A (on leases) as a background to the topic of this chapter, which is the formation of contracts for the sale and lease of goods.

Today, businesses often engage in sales and lease transactions on a global scale. Therefore, we conclude the chapter with an examination of the United Nations Convention on Contracts for the International Sale of Goods (CISG), which governs international sales contracts. The CISG is a model uniform law that applies only when a nation has adopted it, just as the UCC applies only to the extent that it has been adopted by a state.

---

1. Louisiana has not adopted Articles 2 and 2A, however.

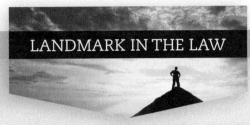

LANDMARK IN THE LAW   The Uniform Commercial Code

Of all the attempts to produce a uniform body of laws relating to commercial transactions in the United States, none has been as successful or comprehensive as the Uniform Commercial Code (UCC).

THE ORIGINS OF THE UCC The UCC was the brainchild of William A. Schnader, president of the National Conference of Commissioners on Uniform State Laws (NCCUSL). The drafting of the UCC began in 1945. The most significant individual involved in the project was its chief editor, Karl N. Llewellyn of the Columbia University Law School. Llewellyn's intellect, continuous efforts, and ability to compromise made the first version of the UCC—completed in 1949—a legal landmark. Over the next several years, the UCC was substantially accepted by almost every state in the nation.

COMPREHENSIVE COVERAGE The UCC attempts to provide a consistent, integrated framework of rules to deal with all phases ordinarily arising in a commercial sales or lease transaction. For example, consider the following events, all of which may occur during a single transaction:

1. *A contract for the sale or lease of goods is formed and executed.* Article 2 and Article 2A of the UCC provide rules governing all aspects of this transaction.

2. *The transaction may involve a payment—by check, electronic fund transfer, or other means.* Article 3 (on negotiable instruments), Article 4 (on bank deposits and collections), Article 4A (on fund transfers), and Article 5 (on letters of credit) cover this part of the transaction.

3. *The transaction may involve a bill of lading or a warehouse receipt that covers goods when they are shipped or stored.* Article 7 (on documents of title) deals with this subject.

4. *The transaction may involve a demand by the seller or lender for some form of security for the remaining balance owed.* Article 9 (on secured transactions) covers this part of the transaction.

PERIODIC CHANGES AND UPDATES Various articles and sections of the UCC are periodically changed or supplemented to clarify certain rules or to establish new rules when changes in business customs render the existing UCC provisions inapplicable.

For instance, when leases of goods in the commercial context became important, Article 2A governing leases was added to the UCC. To clarify the rights of parties to commercial fund transfers, particularly electronic fund transfers, Article 4A was issued. Articles 3 and 4, on negotiable instruments and banking relationships, have undergone significant revisions. Because of other changes in business and in the law, the NCCUSL recommended the repeal of Article 6 (on bulk transfers) and offered a revised Article 6 to those states that preferred not to repeal it. The NCCUSL also substantially revised Article 9 on secured transactions, and the revised Article 9 has been adopted by all of the states.

APPLICATION TO TODAY'S WORLD *By periodically revising the UCC's articles, the NCCUSL has been able to adapt its provisions to changing business customs and practices. UCC provisions governing sales and lease contracts have also been extended to contracts formed in the online environment.*

17-1 The Scope of Articles 2 and 2A

Article 2 of the UCC sets forth the requirements for *sales contracts,* as well as the duties and obligations of the parties involved in the sales contract. Article 2A covers similar issues for *lease contracts.* Bear in mind, however, that the parties to sales or lease contracts are free to agree to terms different from those stated in the UCC.

17-1a Article 2—Sales

Article 2 of the UCC governs **sales contracts,** or contracts for the sale of goods. To facilitate commercial transactions, Article 2 modifies some of the common law contract requirements that were discussed in previous chapters.

To the extent that it has not been modified by the UCC, however, the common law of contracts also applies to sales contracts. In other words, the common law requirements for a valid contract—agreement, consideration, capacity, and legality—are also applicable to sales contracts.

In general, the rule is that when a UCC provision addresses a certain issue, the UCC governs, but when the UCC is silent, the common law governs. The relationship between general contract law and the law governing sales of goods is illustrated in Exhibit 17–1.

Sales Contract A contract for the sale of goods.

Exhibit 17–1 The Law Governing Contracts

This exhibit graphically illustrates the relationship between general contract law and statutory law (UCC Articles 2 and 2A) governing contracts for the sale and lease of goods. Sales contracts are not governed exclusively by Article 2 of the UCC but are also governed by general contract law whenever it is relevant and has not been modified by the UCC.

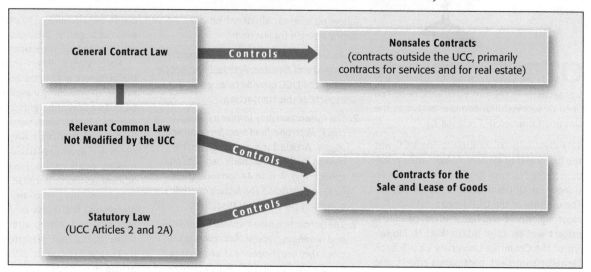

In regard to Article 2, keep two points in mind.

1. Article 2 deals with the sale of *goods*. It does not deal with real property (real estate), services, or intangible property such as stocks and bonds. Thus, if the subject matter of a dispute is goods, the UCC governs. If it is real estate or services, the common law applies.

2. In some situations, the rules can vary depending on whether the buyer or the seller is a *merchant*.

Sale The passing of title to property from the seller to the buyer for a price.

What Is a Sale? The UCC defines a **sale** as "the passing of title [evidence of ownership rights] from the seller to the buyer for a price" [UCC 2–106(1)]. The price may be payable in cash (or its equivalent) or in other goods or services. (For a discussion of whether states can impose taxes on online sales, see this chapter's *Adapting the Law to the Online Environment* feature.)

In the following case, the court was asked to determine who owned the "personal property" damaged in a fire. How did the UCC's definition of a sale affect the answer to that question?

CASE 17.1

Nautilus Insurance Co. v. Cheran Investments LLC

Court of Appeals of Nebraska, 2014 WL 292809 (2014).

FACTS Under a contract with Cheran Investments, LLC, Blasini, Inc., agreed to buy the business assets of the Attic Bar & Grill in Omaha, Nebraska. The contract required Blasini to make a down payment and monthly payments until the price was fully paid. Blasini obtained insurance on the property from Nautilus Insurance Co. Less than three years later, a fire damaged the "personal property" (the business assets, such as furniture and equipment) in the Attic. Because

Who carries the risk of loss and personal property at a bar?

the purchase price had not yet been fully paid, Nautilus filed an action in a Nebraska state court against several defendants, including Cheran, to determine who was entitled to the insurance proceeds for the damage. The court concluded that Blasini had "failed to consummate the purchase agreement" and declared Cheran the owner of the personal property. Blasini appealed, arguing that title to the Attic's assets had passed at the time of the sale.

ISSUE Did the sale of the Attic's assets pass title to those goods to Blasini?

DECISION Yes. A state intermediate appellate court reversed the lower court's ruling. When the contract for the sale of the Attic's assets was formed, title to the assets passed to Blasini, which became the owner. The appellate court remanded the case to the lower court, however, to determine whether Blasini had breached the contract.

REASON The sale of the personal property in the Attic involved "goods," and thus the agreement for their sale was subject to the UCC. All of the items designated in the agreement were movable, and no real estate, intellectual property, or goodwill was transferred under the agreement. Blasini entered into a contract to buy the assets of the bar and grill and agreed to assume its operation. Under UCC 2–401, title to the goods passed to Blasini at the time the agreement was made. No physical delivery was necessary because Blasini was to assume the operation of the Attic, which is where the goods were located. "Therefore, irrespective of whether Blasini paid the purchase price . . . , Blasini became the owner of the property in the purchase agreement."

WHAT IF THE FACTS WERE DIFFERENT? *Suppose that Blasini had made no payments under the contract for the sale of the Attic's assets. How should that circumstance affect the distribution of the insurance proceeds?*

What Are Goods?

To be characterized as a *good,* the item of property must be *tangible,* and it must be *movable.* **Tangible property** has physical existence—it can be touched or seen. **Intangible property**—such as corporate stocks and bonds, patents and copyrights, and ordinary contract rights—has only conceptual existence and thus does not come under Article 2. A *movable* item can be carried from place to place.

Goods Associated with Real Estate.

Because real estate cannot be carried from place to place, it is excluded from Article 2. Goods *associated* with real estate often fall within the scope of Article 2, however [UCC 2–107]. For instance, a contract for the sale of minerals, oil, or natural gas is a contract for the sale of goods if *severance, or separation, is to be made by the seller.* In contrast, a contract for the sale of growing crops or timber to be cut is a contract for the sale of goods *regardless of who severs them from the land.*

Goods and Services Combined.

When contracts involve a combination of goods and services, courts generally use the **predominant-factor test** to determine whether a contract is primarily for the sale of goods or for the sale of services. If a court decides that a mixed contract is primarily a goods contract, *any* dispute, even a dispute over the services portion, will be decided under the UCC.

CASE EXAMPLE 17.1 Gene and Martha Jannusch agreed to sell Festival Foods, a concessions business, to Lindsey and Louann Naffziger for a price of $150,000. The deal included a truck, a trailer, freezers, roasters, chairs, tables, a fountain service, signs, and lighting. The Naffzigers paid $10,000 down with the balance to come from a bank loan. They took possession of the equipment and began to use it immediately in Festival Foods operations at various events.

After six events, the Naffzigers returned the truck and all the equipment and wanted out of the deal because the business did not generate as much income as they expected. The Jannusches sued the Naffzigers for the balance due on the purchase price, claiming that the Naffzigers could no longer reject the goods under the UCC. The Naffzigers claimed that the UCC did not apply because the deal primarily involved the sale of a business rather than the sale of goods.

The court found that the UCC governed under the predominant-factor test. The primary value of the contract was in the goods, not the value of the business. The parties had agreed on the essential terms of the contract (such as the price). Thus, a contract had been formed, and the Naffzigers had breached it. The Naffzigers had taken possession of the business and had no right to return it.[2]

Tangible Property Property that has physical existence and can be distinguished by the senses of touch and sight.

Intangible Property Property that cannot be seen or touched but exists only conceptually, such as corporate stocks. Such property is not governed by Article 2 of the UCC.

LEARNING OBJECTIVE 1
If a contract involves both goods and services, does the UCC apply?

Predominant-Factor Test A test courts use to determine whether a contract is primarily for the sale of goods or for the sale of services.

If a couple buys a concessions business that includes a truck, trailer, and tables and chairs, would this purchase be a sale of goods or services?

---

2. *Jannusch v. Naffziger,* 379 Ill.App.3d 381, 883 N.E.2d 711 (2008).

ADAPTING THE LAW TO THE ONLINE ENVIRONMENT
Taxing Web Purchases

In 1992, the United States Supreme Court ruled that an individual state cannot compel an out-of-state business that lacks a substantial physical presence within that state to collect and remit state taxes.[a] Although Congress has the power to pass legislation requiring out-of-state corporations to collect and remit state sales taxes, it has not yet done so. Thus, only online retailers that also have a physical presence within a state must collect state taxes on any Web sales made to residents of that state. (State residents are supposed to self-report their purchases and pay use taxes to the state, which they rarely do.)

Redefining Physical Presence

Several states have found a way to collect taxes on Internet sales made to state residents by out-of-state corporations. These states have simply redefined *physical presence*. In 2008, New York changed its tax laws in this manner. Now, an online retailer that pays any party within New York to solicit business for its products is considered to have a physical presence in the state and must collect state taxes. Since then, at least seventeen other states have made similar changes in an effort to increase their revenues by collecting sales tax from online retailers.

These new laws are often called "Amazon tax" laws because they are aimed largely at

Amazon.com. Nevertheless, they affect all online sellers, especially those that pay affiliates to direct traffic to their Web sites. The laws allow states to tax online commerce even though, to date, Congress has explicitly chosen not to tax Internet sales.

Local Governments Sue Online Travel Companies

Travelocity, Priceline.com, Hotels.com, and Orbitz.com are online travel companies (OTCs) that offer, among other things, hotel booking services. By 2016, more than twenty-five cities, including Atlanta, Charleston, Philadelphia, and San Antonio, had filed suits claiming that the OTCs owed taxes on hotel reservations that they had booked. All of the cities involved in the suits impose a hotel occupancy tax, which is essentially a sales tax.

Initially, some cities won their cases, but more recently, cities have been losing in court.[b] As of 2016, the OTCs had prevailed in eighteen of twenty-five cases nationwide. An exception is a 2014 case in Wyoming in which the state supreme court held that Travelocity, Priceline, Hotwire, Expedia, and Trip Network had to collect and remit sales tax.[c]

---

b. *Travelscape, LLC v. South Carolina Department of Revenue*, 391 S.C. 89, 705 S.E.2d 28 (2011).

c. *Travelocity.com, LP v. Wyoming Dept. of Revenue*, 329 P.3d 131 (2014).

The Market Place Fairness Act

By the time you read this, online sales taxes may have become a reality for every online business that has annual revenues of more than $1 million. For several years now, legislation called the Market Place Fairness Act has been under consideration in the U.S. Senate. The act, if passed, would allow states to collect sales taxes from online retailers for in-state transactions.

A significant problem with such legislation is the complexity of collecting taxes for multiple jurisdictions. The current tax system involves 9,600 taxing jurisdictions. Even one zip code may cover multiple taxing entities, such as different cities and counties. Consider that the Dallas–Fort Worth airport includes six separate taxing jurisdictions. Current software enables retailers to collect and remit sales taxes for different jurisdictions, but the software is extremely costly to install and operate. Overstock.com, for example, spent $1.3 million to add just one state to its sales tax collection system.

- Some argue that if online retailers are required to collect and pay sales taxes in jurisdictions in which they have no physical presence, they have no democratic way to fight high taxes in those places. Is this an instance of taxation without representation? Discuss.

---

a. *Quill Corp. v. North Dakota*, 504 U.S. 298, 112 S.Ct. 1904, 119 L.Ed.2d 91 (1992).

Who Is a Merchant? Article 2 governs the sale of goods in general. It applies to sales transactions between all buyers and sellers. In a limited number of instances, though, the UCC presumes that certain special business standards ought to be imposed because of merchants' relatively high degree of commercial expertise.[3] Such standards do not apply to the casual or inexperienced seller or buyer (consumer).

---

3. The provisions that apply only to merchants deal principally with the Statute of Frauds, firm offers, confirmatory memoranda, warranties, and contract modifications. These special rules reflect expedient business practices commonly known to merchants in the commercial setting. They will be discussed later in this chapter.

Section 2–104 sets out three ways in which merchant status can arise:

1. A merchant is a person who *deals in goods of the kind* involved in the sales contract. Thus, a retailer, a wholesaler, or a manufacturer is a merchant of those goods sold in the business. A merchant for one type of goods is not necessarily a merchant for another type. For instance, a sporting equipment retailer is a merchant when selling tennis rackets but not when selling a used iPad.

2. A merchant is a person who, by occupation, *holds himself or herself out as having special knowledge and skill* related to the practices or goods involved in the transaction. This broad definition may include banks or universities as merchants.

3. A person who *employs a merchant as a broker, agent, or other intermediary* has the status of merchant in that transaction. Hence, if an art collector hires a broker to purchase or sell art for her, the collector is considered a merchant in the transaction.

In summary, a person is a **merchant** when she or he, acting in a mercantile (commercial) capacity, possesses or uses an expertise specifically related to the goods being sold. This basic distinction is not always clear-cut. For instance, state courts appear to be split on whether farmers should be considered merchants.

Should merchants be allowed to use buying patterns to learn personal information about their customers? Whether you shop on the Internet or in stores, most major retailers compile information about you based on what, when, and how you buy. Sometimes, based on your purchases, you will instantly be given printed coupons at the cash register. These customized coupons reflect your preferences based on past behavior. If you regularly use Amazon.com, for instance, you receive customized offers every time you visit that site.

Target Brands, Inc., uses a very sophisticated data collection process that assigns each shopper a unique guest identification code. Over time, a shopper's habits become the source of predictions for future consumer behavior. For example, Target can accurately predict which female shoppers are pregnant based on their recent purchases of vitamin and mineral supplements. When Target's system detects a buying pattern suggesting that a customer is pregnant, it starts offering coupons for baby-related products and services.

A father in Minneapolis, Minnesota, complained to a Target manager that his daughter was receiving such coupons for no reason. In reality, Target's system had accurately discovered his daughter's pregnancy. The father was even more furious when he learned that his daughter had lied to him. Was Target's action legal? Probably, it was. Target had complied with the relevant federal and state privacy laws. Current laws even allow retailers to share their customer data with affiliate companies.

17–1b Article 2A—Leases

Leases of personal property (goods such as automobiles and industrial equipment) have become increasingly common. In this context, a **lease** is a transfer of the right to possess and use goods for a period of time in exchange for payment. Article 2A of the UCC was created to fill the need for uniform guidelines in this area.

Article 2A covers any transaction that creates a lease of goods, as well as subleases of goods [UCC 2A–102, 2A–103(1)(k)]. Article 2A is essentially a repetition of Article 2, except that it applies to leases of goods rather than sales of goods and thus varies to reflect differences between sales and lease transactions. (Note that Article 2A does not apply to leases of real property, such as land or buildings.)

Definition of a Lease Agreement
Article 2A defines a **lease agreement** as the bargain between a lessor and a lessee with respect to the lease of goods, as found in their language and

Merchant Under the UCC, a person who deals in goods of the kind involved in the sales contract or who holds herself or himself out as having skill or knowledge peculiar to the practices or goods being purchased or sold.

ETHICAL ISSUE

Is it ethical for Target Brands to data mine information about what its customers have purchased?

Lease Under Article 2A of the UCC, a transfer of the right to possess and use goods for a period of time in exchange for payment.

Lease Agreement An agreement in which one person (the lessor) agrees to transfer the right to the possession and use of property to another person (the lessee) in exchange for rental payments.

Lessor A person who transfers the right to the possession and use of goods to another in exchange for rental payments.

Lessee A person who acquires the right to the possession and use of another's goods in exchange for rental payments.

as implied by other circumstances, including course of dealing and usage of trade or course of performance [UCC 2A–103(1)(k)]. A **lessor** is one who transfers the right to the possession and use of goods under a lease [UCC 2A–103(1)(p)]. A **lessee** is one who acquires the right to the temporary possession and use of goods under a lease [UCC 2A–103(1)(o)]. In other words, the lessee is the party who is leasing the goods from the lessor.

Article 2A applies to all types of leases of goods, including commercial leases and consumer leases. Special rules apply to certain types of leases, however, including consumer leases.

Consumer Leases Under UCC 2A–103(1)(e), a *consumer lease* involves three elements:

1. A lessor who regularly engages in the business of leasing or selling.

2. A lessee (except an organization) who leases the goods "primarily for a personal, family, or household purpose."

3. Total lease payments that are less than a dollar amount set by state statute.

To ensure special protection for consumers, certain provisions of Article 2A apply only to consumer leases. For instance, one provision states that a consumer may recover attorneys' fees if a court finds that a term in a consumer lease contract is unconscionable [UCC 2A–108(4)(a)].

17-2 The Formation of Sales and Lease Contracts

As mentioned, Article 2 and Article 2A of the UCC modify common law contract rules in several ways. Remember, though, that parties to sales contracts are normally free to establish whatever terms they wish. The UCC comes into play only when the parties have failed to provide in their contract for a contingency that later gives rise to a dispute. The UCC makes this clear time and again by using such phrases as "unless the parties otherwise agree" or "absent a contrary agreement by the parties."

17-2a Offer

In general contract law, the moment a definite offer is met by an unqualified acceptance, a binding contract is formed. In commercial sales transactions, the verbal exchanges, correspondence, and actions of the parties may not reveal exactly when a binding contractual obligation arises. The UCC states that an agreement sufficient to constitute a contract can exist even if the moment of its making is undetermined [UCC 2–204(2), 2A–204(2)].

Open Terms Remember that under the common law of contracts, an offer must be definite enough for the parties (and the courts) to ascertain its essential terms when it is accepted. In contrast, the UCC states that a sales or lease contract will not fail for indefiniteness even if one or more terms are left open as long as *both* of the following are true:

1. The parties intended to make a contract.

2. There is a reasonably certain basis for the court to grant an appropriate remedy [UCC 2–204(3), 2A–204(3)].

KNOW THIS
Under the UCC, it is the actions of the parties that determine whether they intended to form a contract.

The UCC provides numerous *open-term* provisions (discussed next) that can be used to fill the gaps in a contract. Thus, if a dispute occurs, all that is necessary to prove the existence of a contract is an indication (such as a purchase order) that there is a contract. Missing terms can be proved by evidence, or a court can presume that the parties intended whatever is reasonable under the circumstances.

Keep in mind, though, that if too many terms are left open, a court may find that the parties did not intend to form a contract. In addition, the *quantity* of goods involved must be expressly stated in the contract. If the quantity term is left open, the courts will have no basis for determining a remedy.

Open Price Term. If the parties have not agreed on a price, the court will determine a "reasonable price at the time for delivery" [UCC 2–305(1)]. If either the buyer or the seller is to determine the price, the price is to be fixed (set) in good faith [UCC 2–305(2)]. Under the UCC, *good faith* means honesty in fact and the observance of reasonable commercial standards of fair dealing in the trade [UCC 2–103(1)(b)]. The concepts of *good faith* and *commercial reasonableness* permeate the UCC.

Sometimes, the price fails to be fixed through the fault of one of the parties. In that situation, the other party can treat the contract as canceled or fix a reasonable price. **EXAMPLE 17.2** Perez and Merrick enter into a contract for the sale of unfinished doors and agree that Perez will determine the price. Perez refuses to specify the price. Merrick can either treat the contract as canceled or set a reasonable price [UCC 2–305(3)]. ■

Open Payment Term. When parties do not specify payment terms, payment is due at the time and place at which the buyer is to receive the goods [UCC 2–310(a)]. The buyer can tender payment using any commercially normal or acceptable means, such as a check or credit card. If the seller demands payment in cash, the buyer must be given a reasonable time to obtain it [UCC 2–511(2)].

EXAMPLE 17.3 Max Angel agrees to purchase hay from Wagner's farm. Angel leaves his truck and trailer at the farm for the seller to load the hay. Nothing is said about when payment is due, and the parties are unaware of the UCC's rules. Nevertheless, because the parties did not specify when payment was due, UCC 2–310(a) controls, and payment is due at the time Angel picks up the hay. Therefore, Wagner can refuse to release the hay (or the vehicles on which the hay is loaded) to Angel until he pays for it. ■

Open Delivery Term. When no delivery terms are specified, the buyer normally takes delivery at the seller's place of business [UCC 2–308(a)]. If the seller has no place of business, the seller's residence is used. When goods are located in some other place and both parties know it, delivery is made there. If the time for shipment or delivery is not clearly specified in the sales contract, the court will infer a "reasonable" time for performance [UCC 2–309(1)].

Duration of an Ongoing Contract. A single contract might specify successive performances but not indicate how long the parties are required to deal with each other. In this situation, either party may terminate the ongoing contractual relationship. Principles of good faith and sound commercial practice call for reasonable notification before termination, however, to give the other party time to make substitute arrangements [UCC 2–309(2), (3)].

Options and Cooperation Regarding Performance. When the contract contemplates shipment of the goods but does not specify the shipping arrangements, the *seller* has the right to make these arrangements in good faith, using commercial reasonableness in the situation [UCC 2–311].

When a sales contract omits terms relating to the assortment of goods, the *buyer* can specify the assortment. **EXAMPLE 17.4** Petry Drugs, Inc., enters an e-contract to purchase one thousand toothbrushes from Marconi's Dental Supply. The toothbrushes come in a variety of colors, but the contract does not specify color. Petry, the buyer, has the right to take six hundred blue toothbrushes and four hundred green ones if it wishes. Petry, however, must exercise good faith and commercial reasonableness in making its selection [UCC 2–311]. ■

Open Quantity Terms. Normally, if the parties do not specify a quantity, there is no contract, because a court will have no basis for determining a remedy.

"Business, more than any other occupation, is a continual dealing with the future. It is a continual calculation, an instinctive exercise in foresight."

HENRY R. LUCE
1898–1967
(U.S. EDITOR AND PUBLISHER)

If no time for payment for hay is specified in a sales contract, when is payment due?

There is almost no way for a court to determine objectively what is a reasonable quantity of goods for someone to buy (whereas a court can objectively determine a reasonable price for particular goods by looking at the market). Nevertheless, the UCC recognizes two exceptions involving *requirements* and *output contracts* [UCC 2–306(1)].

Requirements Contract
An agreement in which a buyer agrees to purchase and the seller agrees to sell all or up to a stated amount of what the buyer needs or requires.

1. *Requirements Contracts.* In a **requirements contract,** the buyer agrees to purchase and the seller agrees to sell all or up to a stated amount of what the buyer *needs* or *requires*. **EXAMPLE 17.5** Umpqua Cannery forms a contract with Al Garcia. The cannery agrees to purchase from Garcia, and Garcia agrees to sell to the cannery, all of the green beans that the cannery needs or requires during the following summer. There is implicit consideration in this contract because the buyer (the cannery) gives up the right to buy goods (green beans) from any other seller. This forfeited right creates a legal *detriment*—that is, consideration. ■

   Requirements contracts are common in the business world and normally are enforceable. In contrast, if the buyer promises to purchase only if the buyer *wishes* to do so, or if the buyer reserves the right to buy the goods from someone other than the seller, the promise is illusory (without consideration) and unenforceable by either party.

Output Contract An agreement in which a seller agrees to sell and a buyer agrees to buy all or up to a stated amount of what the seller produces.

2. *Output Contracts.* In an **output contract,** the seller agrees to sell and the buyer agrees to buy all or up to a stated amount of what the seller *produces*. **EXAMPLE 17.6** Ruth Sewell has planted two acres of organic tomatoes. Bella Union, a local restaurant, agrees to buy all of the tomatoes that Sewell produces that year to use at the restaurant. ■ Again, because the seller essentially forfeits the right to sell goods to another buyer, there is implicit consideration in an output contract.

The UCC imposes a *good faith limitation* on requirements and output contracts. The quantity under such contracts is the amount of requirements or the amount of output that occurs during a *normal* production year. The actual quantity purchased or sold cannot be unreasonably disproportionate to normal or comparable prior requirements or output [UCC 2–306(1)].

PREVENTING LEGAL DISPUTES

If a business owner leaves certain terms of a sales or lease contract open, the UCC allows a court to supply the missing terms. Although this rule can sometimes be advantageous (to establish that a contract existed, for instance), it can also be a major disadvantage. If a party fails to state a price in the contract offer, for example, a court will impose a reasonable price by looking at the market price of similar goods *at the time of delivery*. Thus, instead of receiving the usual price for the goods, a business will receive what a court considers a reasonable price when the goods are delivered. Therefore, when drafting contracts for the sale or lease of goods, make sure that the contract clearly states any terms that are essential to the bargain, particularly the price. It is generally better to establish the terms of a contract than to leave it up to a court to determine what terms are reasonable after a dispute has arisen.

Merchant's Firm Offer Under regular contract principles, an offer can be revoked at any time before acceptance. The major common law exception is an *option contract,* in which the offeree pays consideration for the offeror's irrevocable promise to keep the offer open for a stated period. The UCC creates a second exception for firm offers made by a merchant to sell, buy, or lease goods.

Firm Offer An offer (by a merchant) that is irrevocable without the necessity of consideration for a stated period of time or, if no definite period is stated, for a reasonable time (neither period to exceed three months).

A **firm offer** arises when a merchant-offeror gives *assurances* in a *signed writing* that the offer will remain open. The offer must be both *written* and *signed* by the offeror.[4] A merchant's firm offer is irrevocable without the necessity of consideration[5] for the stated period or, if no

---

4. *Signed* includes any symbol executed or adopted by a party with a present intention to authenticate a writing [UCC 1–201(39)]. A complete signature is not required. Therefore, initials, a thumbprint, a trade name, or any mark used in lieu of a written signature will suffice, regardless of its location on the document.

5. If the offeree pays consideration, then an option contract (not a merchant's firm offer) is formed.

definite period is stated, a reasonable period (neither period to exceed three months) [UCC 2–205, 2A–205].

EXAMPLE 17.7 Osaka, a used-car dealer, e-mails Saucedo on January 1 stating, "I have a used 2016 Toyota RAV4 on the lot that I'll sell you for $26,000 any time between now and January 31." This e-mail creates a firm offer, and Osaka will be liable for breach if he sells that Toyota RAV4 to someone other than Saucedo before January 31. ■

17–2b Acceptance

Acceptance of an offer to buy, sell, or lease goods generally may be made in any reasonable manner and by any reasonable means. The UCC permits acceptance of an offer to buy goods "either by a prompt *promise* to ship or by the prompt or current shipment of conforming or nonconforming goods" [UCC 2–206(1)(b)]. *Conforming goods* accord with the contract's terms, whereas *nonconforming goods* do not.

Shipment of Nonconforming Goods   The prompt shipment of nonconforming goods constitutes both an acceptance, which creates a contract, and a breach of that contract. This rule does not apply if the seller **seasonably** (within a reasonable amount of time) notifies the buyer that the nonconforming shipment is offered only as an *accommodation,* or a favor. The notice of accommodation must clearly indicate to the buyer that the shipment does not constitute an acceptance and that, therefore, no contract has been formed.

Seasonably Within a specified time period or, if no period is specified, within a reasonable time.

EXAMPLE 17.8 McFarrell Pharmacy orders five cases of Johnson & Johnson 3-by-5-inch gauze pads from H.T. Medical Supply, Inc. If H.T. ships five cases of Xeroform 3-by-5-inch gauze pads instead, the shipment acts as both an acceptance of McFarrell's offer and a *breach* of the resulting contract. McFarrell may sue H.T. for any appropriate damages.

If, however, H.T. notifies McFarrell that the Xeroform gauze pads are being shipped *as an accommodation*—because H.T. has only Xeroform pads in stock—the shipment will constitute a counteroffer, not an acceptance. A contract will be formed only if McFarrell accepts the Xeroform gauze pads. ■

Communication of Acceptance Required   Under the common law, because a unilateral offer invites acceptance by performance, the offeree need not notify the offeror of performance unless the offeror would not otherwise know about it. In other words, a unilateral offer can be accepted by beginning performance.

The UCC is more stringent than the common law in this regard because it requires notification. Under the UCC, if the offeror is not notified within a reasonable time that the offeree has accepted the contract by beginning performance, then the offeror can treat the offer as having lapsed before acceptance [UCC 2–206(2), 2A–206(2)].

Additional Terms   Recall that under the common law, the *mirror image rule* requires that the terms of the acceptance exactly match those of the offer. **EXAMPLE 17.9** Aldrich e-mails an offer to sell twenty Samsung Galaxy Tab S 8.4 tablets to Beale. If Beale accepts the offer but changes it to require Tab S 10.5 tablets, then there is no contract. ■

To avoid these problems, the UCC dispenses with the mirror image rule. Under the UCC, a contract is formed if the offeree's response indicates a *definite* acceptance of the offer, *even if the acceptance includes terms additional to or different from those contained in the offer* [UCC 2–207(1)]. Whether the additional terms become part of the contract depends, in part, on whether the parties are nonmerchants or merchants.

Rules When One Party or Both Parties Are Nonmerchants.   If one (or both) of the parties is a *nonmerchant,* the contract is formed according to the terms of the original offer submitted by the original offeror and not according to the additional terms of the acceptance [UCC 2–207(2)].

iStockPhoto.com/Joe_Potato

If a pharmacy orders 3" x 5" gauze pads, but is shipped 2" x 2" pads, is this an acceptance of the pharmacy's order?

LEARNING OBJECTIVE 2

In a sales contract, if an offeree includes additional or different terms in an acceptance, will a contract result? If so, what happens to these terms?

CASE EXAMPLE 17.10 OfficeSupplyStore.com sells office supplies on the Web. Employees of the Kansas City School District in Missouri ordered $17,642.54 worth of office supplies—without the authority or approval of their employer—from the Web site. The invoices accompanying the goods contained a forum-selection clause that required all disputes to be resolved in California.

When the goods were not paid for, Office Supply filed suit in California. The Kansas City School District objected, arguing that the forum-selection clause was not binding. The court held that the forum-selection clause was not part of the parties' contract. The clause was an additional term included in the invoices delivered to a nonmerchant buyer (the school district) with the purchased goods. Therefore, the clause would have become part of the contract only if the buyer expressly agreed, which did not happen in this case.[6] ▪

Rules When Both Parties Are Merchants. The drafters of the UCC created a special rule for merchants to avoid the "battle of the forms," which occurs when two merchants exchange separate standard forms containing different contract terms. Under UCC 2–207(2), in contracts *between merchants,* the additional terms *automatically* become part of the contract unless one of the following conditions exists:

1. The original offer expressly limited acceptance to its terms.

2. The new or changed terms materially alter the contract.

3. The offeror objects to the new or changed terms within a reasonable period of time.

When determining whether an alteration is material, courts consider several factors. Generally, if the modification does not involve an unreasonable element of surprise or hardship for the offeror, the court will hold that the modification did not materially alter the contract. As shown in the following case, however, what constitutes a material alteration is frequently a question of fact that only a court can decide.

---

6. *OfficeSupplyStore.com v. Kansas City School Board*, 334 S.W.3d 574 (Kan. 2011).

CASE 17.2

C. Mahendra (N.Y.), LLC v. National Gold & Diamond Center, Inc.

New York Supreme Court, Appellate Division, First Department, 125 A.D.3d 454, 3 N.Y.S.3d 27 (2015).

FACTS C. Mahendra (N.Y.), LLC, is a New York wholesaler of loose diamonds. National Gold & Diamond Center, Inc., is a California seller of jewelry. Over a ten-year period, National placed orders, totaling millions of dollars, with Mahendra by phoning and negotiating the terms. Mahendra shipped diamonds "on memorandum" for National to examine. Mahendra then sent invoices for the diamonds that National chose to keep. Both the memoranda and the invoices stated, "You consent to the exclusive jurisdiction of the . . . courts situated in New York County." When two orders totaling $64,000 went unpaid, Mahendra filed a suit in a New York state court against National, alleging breach of contract. National filed a motion to dismiss the complaint for lack of personal jurisdiction, contending that

What happens if one party to an ongoing contract inserts a forum-selection clause without approval?

the forum-selection clause was not binding. The court granted the motion. Mahendra appealed.

ISSUE Did the forum-selection clause materially alter the parties' contracts?

DECISION Yes. A state intermediate appellate court agreed that the forum-selection clause was an additional term that materially altered the parties' contracts and was therefore not binding.

REASON The court explained that UCC 2–207 deals with situations in which parties do business through an exchange of forms, such as purchase orders and invoices. In such forms, a merchant often includes terms that were not negotiated with, or even mentioned to, the other party. Under UCC 2–207(2) "the additional terms are to be construed as proposals for addition to the contract. Between merchants such terms become part of the contract unless . . . they materially alter it."

In this case, through phone calls, the parties negotiated the essential terms to form contracts for purchases of diamonds. The memoranda and invoices that Mahendra sent to National were "merely confirmatory." The forum-selection clause in those documents was not a subject of negotiation or discussion, and National did not sign the forms or otherwise consent to the clause. The court thus ruled that the forum-selection clause was not binding. The court reversed the dismissal of Mahendra's complaint on another ground, however. It found that National's phone calls with Mahendra were sufficient contacts to subject the defendant to personal jurisdiction in New York under the state's long-arm statute.

CRITICAL THINKING—Legal Consideration *What is Mahendra's best argument that the forum-selection clause was, in fact, binding on National? Discuss.*

Prior Dealings Between Merchants.   Courts also consider the parties' prior dealings in contracts between merchants.   **CASE EXAMPLE 17.11**   WPS, Inc., submitted a proposal to manufacture equipment for Expro Americas, LLC, and Surface Production Systems, Inc. (SPS). Expro and SPS then submitted two purchase orders. WPS accepted the first purchase order in part and the second order conditionally. Among other things, WPS's acceptance required that Expro and SPS give their "full release to proceed" and agree to "pay all valid costs associated with any order cancellation." The parties' negotiations continued, and Expro and SPS eventually submitted a third purchase order.

Although the third purchase order did not comply with all of WPS's requirements, it did give WPS full permission to proceed and agreed that Expro and SPS would pay all cancellation costs. With Expro and SPS's knowledge, WPS then began working on that order. Expro and SPS later canceled the order and refused to pay the cancellation costs. When the dispute ended up in court, Expro and SPS claimed that the parties' contract was not enforceable because the additional terms in WPS's acceptance had materially altered the contract. The court found in favor of WPS. Expro and SPS had given a release to proceed that authorized WPS to go forward with manufacturing the equipment. Because "the parties operated as if they had additional time to resolve the outstanding differences," the court reasoned that Expro and SPS were contractually obligated to pay the cancellation costs.[7] ■

Conditioned on Offeror's Assent.   Regardless of merchant status, the UCC provides that the offeree's expression cannot be construed as an acceptance if it contains additional or different terms that are explicitly conditioned on the offeror's assent to those terms [UCC 2–207(1)].   **EXAMPLE 17.12**   Philips offers to sell Hundert 650 pounds of turkey thighs at a specified price and with specified delivery terms. Hundert responds, "I accept your offer for 650 pounds of turkey thighs *on the condition that you give me ninety days to pay for them.*" Hundert's response will be construed not as an acceptance but as a counteroffer, which Philips may or may not accept. ■

Additional Terms May Be Stricken.   The UCC provides yet another option for dealing with conflicting terms in the parties' writings. Section 2–207(3) states that conduct by both parties that recognizes the existence of a contract is sufficient to establish a contract for the sale of goods even though the writings of the parties do not otherwise establish a contract. In this situation, "the terms of the particular contract will consist of those terms on which the writings of the parties agree, together with any supplementary terms incorporated under any other provisions of this Act."

In a dispute over contract terms, this provision allows a court simply to strike from the contract those terms on which the parties do not agree.   **EXAMPLE 17.13**   SMT Marketing orders

If a supplier offers to sell 100 pounds of turkey thighs at a specific price and delivery date, can the buyer accept on the condition that it pay ninety days after delivery?

---

7. *WPS, Inc. v. Expro Americas, LLC*, 369 S.W.3d 384 (Tex.App. 2012).

goods over the phone from Brigg Sales, Inc., which ships the goods with an acknowledgment form (confirming the order) to SMT. SMT accepts and pays for the goods. The parties' writings do not establish a contract, but there is no question that a contract exists. If a dispute arises over the terms, such as the extent of any warranties, UCC 2–207(3) provides the governing rule. ■

As noted previously, the fact that a merchant's acceptance frequently contains terms that add to or even conflict with those of the offer is often referred to as the "battle of the forms." Although the UCC tries to eliminate this battle, the problem of differing contract terms still arises in commercial settings, particularly when standard forms for placing and confirming orders are used.

17–2c Consideration

The common law rule that a contract requires consideration also applies to sales and lease contracts. Unlike the common law, however, the UCC does not require a contract modification to be supported by new consideration. An agreement modifying a contract for the sale or lease of goods "needs no consideration to be binding" [UCC 2–209(1), 2A–208(1)]. Of course, a contract modification must be sought in good faith [UCC 1–304].

In some situations, an agreement to modify a sales or lease contract without consideration must be in writing to be enforceable. If the contract itself prohibits any changes to the contract unless they are in a signed writing, for instance, then only those changes agreed to in a signed writing are enforceable.

If a consumer (nonmerchant buyer) is dealing with a merchant and the merchant supplies the form that contains a clause prohibiting oral modification, the consumer must sign a separate acknowledgment of the clause [UCC 2–209(2), 2A–208(2)]. Also, any modification that brings a sales contract under Article 2's Statute of Frauds provision usually must be in writing to be enforceable.

17–2d The Statute of Frauds

The UCC contains Statute of Frauds provisions covering sales and lease contracts. Under these provisions, sales contracts for goods priced at $500 or more and lease contracts requiring payments of $1,000 or more must be in writing to be enforceable [UCC 2–201(1), 2A–201(1)]. (These low threshold amounts may eventually be raised.)

Sufficiency of the Writing   A writing, including an e-mail or other electronic record, will be sufficient to satisfy the UCC's Statute of Frauds as long as it meets the following requirements:

1. It indicates that the parties intended to form a contract.
2. It is signed by the party (or agent of the party) against whom enforcement is sought. (Remember that a typed name can qualify as a signature.)

The contract normally will not be enforceable beyond the quantity of goods shown in the writing, however. All other terms can be proved in court by oral testimony. For leases, the writing or record must reasonably identify and describe the goods leased and the lease term.

Special Rules for Contracts between Merchants   Once again, the UCC provides a special rule for merchants in sales transactions. (There is no corresponding rule that applies to leases under Article 2A.) Merchants can satisfy the Statute of Frauds if, after the parties have agreed orally, one of the merchants sends a signed written confirmation to the other merchant within a reasonable time.

The communication must indicate the terms of the agreement, and the merchant receiving the confirmation must have reason to know of its contents. Unless the merchant who receives the confirmation gives written notice of objection to its contents within ten days after receipt, the writing or record is sufficient, even though she or he has not signed anything [UCC 2–201(2)].

EXAMPLE 17.14 Alfonso is a merchant-buyer in Cleveland. He contracts over the telephone to purchase $6,000 worth of spare aircraft parts from Goldstein, a merchant-seller in New York City. Two days later, Goldstein e-mails a signed confirmation detailing the terms of the oral contract, and Alfonso receives it. Alfonso does not notify Goldstein in writing of any objection to the contents of the confirmation within ten days of receipt. Therefore, Alfonso cannot raise the Statute of Frauds as a defense against the enforcement of the oral contract. ■

LEARNING OBJECTIVE 3
What exceptions to the writing requirements of the Statute of Frauds are provided in Article 2 and Article 2A of the UCC?

Exceptions In addition to the special rules for merchants, the UCC defines three exceptions to the writing requirements of the Statute of Frauds. An oral contract for the sale of goods priced at $500 or more—or the lease of goods involving total payments of $1,000 or more—will be enforceable despite the absence of a writing in the circumstances described next [UCC 2–201(3), 2A–201(4)].

Specially Manufactured Goods. An oral contract for the sale or lease of custom-made goods will be enforceable if the following conditions exist:

1. The goods are *specially manufactured* for a particular buyer or specially manufactured or obtained for a particular lessee.

2. The goods are *not suitable for resale or lease* to others in the ordinary course of the seller's or lessor's business.

3. The seller or lessor has *substantially started to manufacture* the goods or has made commitments for the manufacture or procurement of the goods.

Under these conditions, once the seller or lessor has taken action, the buyer or lessee cannot repudiate the agreement claiming the Statute of Frauds as a defense. **EXAMPLE 17.15** Womach orders custom window treatments from Hunter Douglas to use at her day spa business. The contract is oral, and the price is $6,000. When Hunter Douglas manufactures the window coverings and tenders delivery to Womach, she refuses to pay for them, even though the job is completed on time. Womach claims that she is not liable because the contract is oral. If the unique style, size, and color of the window treatments make it improbable that Hunter Douglas can find another buyer, Womach is liable to Hunter Douglas. ■

Admissions. An oral contract for the sale or lease of goods is enforceable if the party against whom enforcement of the contract is sought admits in pleadings, testimony, or other court proceedings that a contract for sale or lease was made. In this situation, the contract will be enforceable even though it was oral, but enforceability will be limited to the quantity of goods admitted.

CASE EXAMPLE 17.16 Gerald Lindgren, a farmer, agreed by phone to sell his crops to Glacial Plains Cooperative. The parties reached four oral agreements: two for the delivery of soybeans and two for the delivery of corn. Lindgren made the soybean deliveries and part of the first corn delivery, but he sold the rest of his corn to another dealer. Glacial Plains bought corn elsewhere, paying a higher price, and then sued Lindgren for breach of contract. In papers filed with the court, Lindgren acknowledged his oral agreements with Glacial Plains and admitted that he did not fully perform. The court applied the admissions exception and held that the four agreements were enforceable. [8] ■

Can oral agreements for delivery of corn be enforced if the seller admits that the agreements occurred?

---

8. *Glacial Plains Cooperative v. Lindgren*, 759 N.W.2d 661 (Minn.App. 2009).

"Whatever is not nailed down is mine. Whatever I can pry loose is not nailed down."

COLLIS P. HUNTINGTON
1821–1900
(U.S. RAILROAD BUILDER AND OWNER)

Under what conditions will an oral agreement for renting chairs be enforceable?

Partial Performance. An oral contract for the sale or lease of goods is enforceable if payment has been made and accepted or goods have been received and accepted. This is the "partial performance" exception. The oral contract will be enforced at least to the extent that performance *actually* took place.

EXAMPLE 17.17 Jamal orally contracts to lease to Opus Enterprises a thousand chairs at $2 each to be used during a one-day concert. Before delivery, Opus sends Jamal a check for $1,000, which Jamal cashes. Later, when Jamal attempts to deliver the chairs, Opus refuses delivery, claiming the Statute of Frauds as a defense, and demands the return of its $1,000. Under the UCC's partial performance rule, Jamal can enforce the oral contract by tender of delivery of five hundred chairs for the $1,000 accepted. Similarly, if Opus had made no payment but had accepted the delivery of five hundred chairs from Jamal, the oral contract would have been enforceable against Opus for $1,000, the lease payment due for the five hundred chairs delivered. ■

These exceptions and other ways in which sales law differs from general contract law are summarized in Exhibit 17–2.

17-2e Parol Evidence

Recall that *parol evidence* consists of evidence outside the contract, such as evidence of the parties' prior negotiations, prior agreements, or oral agreements made at the time of contract formation. When a contract completely sets forth all the terms and conditions agreed to by the parties and is intended as a final statement of their agreement, it is considered *fully integrated*. The *parol evidence rule* applies. The terms of a fully integrated contract cannot be contradicted by evidence outside the contract.

If, however, the writing (or record) contains some of the terms the parties agreed on but not others, the contract is *not fully integrated*. In this situation, a court may allow evidence of

Exhibit 17–2 Major Differences between Contract Law and Sales Law

TOPIC	CONTRACT LAW	SALES LAW
Contract Terms	Contract must contain all material terms.	Open terms are acceptable, if parties intended to form a contract, but quantity term normally must be specified, and contract is not enforceable beyond quantity term.
Acceptance	Mirror image rule applies. If additional terms are added in acceptance, counteroffer is created.	Additional terms will not negate acceptance unless acceptance is made expressly conditional on assent to the additional terms.
Contract Modification	Modification requires consideration.	Modification does not require consideration.
Irrevocable Offers	Option contracts (with consideration) are irrevocable.	Merchants' firm offers (without consideration) are irrevocable.
Statute of Frauds Requirements	All material terms must be included in the writing.	Writing is required only for the sale of goods priced at $500 or more, but contract is not enforceable beyond quantity specified. Merchants can satisfy the requirement by a confirmatory memorandum evidencing agreement. *Exceptions:* 1. Specially manufactured goods. 2. Admissions by party against whom enforcement is sought. 3. Partial performance.

iStockPhoto.com/abzee

consistent additional terms to explain or supplement the terms stated in the contract. The court may also allow the parties to submit evidence of *course of dealing, usage of trade,* or *course of performance* [UCC 2–202, 2A–202]. A court will not under any circumstances allow the parties to submit evidence that contradicts the contract's stated terms, however. (This is also the rule under the common law.)

Course of Dealing and Usage of Trade
Under the UCC, the meaning of any agreement, evidenced by the language of the parties and by their actions, must be interpreted in light of commercial practices and other surrounding circumstances. In interpreting a commercial agreement, the court will assume that the course of prior dealing between the parties and the usage of trade were taken into account when the agreement was phrased.

Course of Dealing. A **course of dealing** is a sequence of actions and communications between the parties to a particular transaction that establishes a common basis for their understanding [UCC 1–303(b)]. A course of dealing is restricted to the sequence of conduct between the parties in their transactions prior to the agreement.

Under the UCC, a course of dealing between the parties is relevant in ascertaining the meaning of the parties' agreement. It "may give particular meaning to specific terms of the agreement, and may supplement or qualify the terms of the agreement" [UCC 1–303(d)].

> **Course of Dealing**
> Prior conduct between the parties to a contract that establishes a common basis for their understanding.

Usage of Trade. Any practice or method of dealing that is so regularly observed in a place, vocation, or trade as to justify an expectation by the parties that it will be observed in their transaction is a **usage of trade** [UCC 1–303(c)].

EXAMPLE 17.18 United Loans, Inc., hires Fleet Title Review to search the public records for prior claims on potential borrrowers' assets. Fleet's invoice states, "Liability limited to amount of fee." In the search industry, liability limits are common. After conducting many searches for United, Fleet reports that there are no claims with respect to Main Street Autos. United loans $100,000 to Main, with payment guaranteed by Main's assets.

When Main defaults on the loan, United learns that another lender has priority to Main's assets under a previous claim. If United sues Fleet Title for breach of contract, Fleet's liability will normally be limited to the amount of its fee. The statement in the invoice was part of the contract between United and Title, according to the usage of trade in the industry and the parties' course of dealing. ■

> **Usage of Trade** Any practice or method of dealing that is so regularly observed in a place, vocation, or trade that parties justifiably expect it will be observed in their transaction.

Course of Performance
A **course of performance** is the conduct that occurs under the terms of a particular agreement [UCC 1–303(a)]. Presumably, the parties themselves know best what they meant by their words. Thus, the course of performance actually carried out under their agreement is the best indication of what they meant [UCC 2–208(1), 2A–207(1)].

EXAMPLE 17.19 Janson's Lumber Company contracts with Lopez to sell Lopez a specified number of two-by-fours. The lumber in fact does not measure exactly 2 inches by 4 inches but rather $1^7/_8$ inches by $3^3/_4$ inches. Janson's agrees to deliver the lumber in five deliveries, and Lopez, without objection, accepts the lumber in the first three deliveries. On the fourth delivery, however, Lopez objects that the two-by-fours do not measure 2 inches by 4 inches.

The course of performance in this transaction—that is, Lopez's acceptance of three deliveries without objection under the agreement—is relevant in determining that here the term *two-by-four* actually means "$1^7/_8$ by $3^3/_4$." Janson's can also prove that two-by-fours need not be exactly 2 inches by 4 inches by applying course of prior dealing, usage of trade, or both. Janson's can, for example, show that in previous transactions, Lopez took $1^7/_8$-by-$3^3/_4$-inch lumber without objection. In addition, Janson's can show that in the lumber trade, two-by-fours are commonly $1^7/_8$ inches by $3^3/_4$ inches. ■

> **Course of Performance**
> The conduct that occurs under the terms of a particular agreement, which indicates what the parties to that agreement intended the agreement to mean.

Do two-by-fours actually measure 2 inches by 4 inches?

Rules of Construction
The UCC provides *rules of construction* for interpreting contracts. Express terms, course of performance, course of dealing, and usage of trade are to be construed

to be consistent with each other whenever reasonable. When such a construction is unreasonable, however, the UCC establishes the following order of priority [UCC 1–303(e), 2–208(2), 2A–207(2)]:

1. Express terms.

2. Course of performance.

3. Course of dealing.

4. Usage of trade.

17–2f Unconscionability

As previously discussed, an unconscionable contract is one that is so unfair and one sided that it would be unreasonable to enforce it. The UCC allows the courts to evaluate unconscionability. If a court deems a contract or a clause in a contract to have been unconscionable at the time it was made, the court can do any of the following [UCC 2–302, 2A–108]:

1. Refuse to enforce the contract.

2. Enforce the remainder of the contract without the unconscionable part.

3. Limit the application of the unconscionable term to avoid an unconscionable result.

The following *Classic Case* illustrates an early application of the UCC's unconscionability provisions.

★★★ CLASSIC CASE 17.3 ★★★

Jones v. Star Credit Corp.

Supreme Court of New York, Nassau County, 59 Misc.2d 189, 298 N.Y.S.2d 264 (1969).

FACTS The Joneses, the plaintiffs, agreed to purchase a freezer for $900 as the result of a salesperson's visit to their home. Tax and financing charges raised the total price to $1,234.80. After making payments totaling $619.88, the plaintiffs brought a suit in a New York state court to have the purchase contract declared unconscionable under the UCC. At trial, the freezer was found to have a maximum retail value of approximately $300.

Can a retailer sell a freezer at four times its wholesale price?

ISSUE Could this contract be denied enforcement on the ground of unconscionability?

DECISION Yes. The court held that the contract was not enforceable as it stood, and the contract was reformed so that no further payments were required.

REASON The court relied on UCC 2–302(1), which states that if "the court as a matter of law finds the contract or any clause of the contract to have been unconscionable at the time it was made,

the court may . . . so limit the application of any unconscionable clause as to avoid any unconscionable result." The court then considered the disparity between the $900 purchase price and the $300 retail value, as well as the fact that the credit charges alone exceeded the retail value. These excessive charges were exacted despite the seller's knowledge of the plaintiffs' limited resources. The court reformed the contract so that the plaintiffs' payments, amounting to more than $600, were regarded as payment in full.

CRITICAL THINKING—Legal Consideration *Why would the seller's knowledge of the buyers' limited resources support a finding of unconscionability?*

IMPACT OF THIS CASE ON TODAY'S LAW *This early case illustrates the approach that many courts today take when deciding whether a sales contract is unconscionable—an approach that focuses on excessive price and unequal bargaining power.*

17-3 Title and Risk of Loss

Before the creation of the UCC, *title*—the right of ownership—was the central concept in sales law and controlled all issues of rights and remedies of the parties to a sales contract. In some situations, title is still relevant under the UCC, and the UCC has special rules for determining who has title. (These rules do not apply to leased goods, obviously, because title remains with the lessor, or owner, of the goods.) In most situations, however, the UCC focuses less on title than on the concepts of *identification, risk of loss,* and *insurable interest.*

> "To win, you have to risk loss."
>
> **JEAN-CLAUDE KILLY**
> 1943–PRESENT
> (FRENCH ALPINE SKIER)

17-3a Identification

Before any interest in specific goods can pass from the seller or lessor to the buyer or lessee, the goods must exist and must be identified as the specific goods designated in the contract. **Identification** takes place when specific goods are designated as the subject matter of a sales or lease contract.

Identification allows title to pass from the seller to the buyer. (Remember that title to leased goods does not pass to the lessee.) In addition, it allows risk of loss to pass from the seller or lessor to the buyer or lessee. This is important because it gives the buyer or lessee the right to insure the goods and the right to recover from third parties who damage the goods.

For goods already in existence, the parties can agree in their contract on when identification will take place. If the parties do not so specify, the UCC provisions discussed here determine when identification takes place [UCC 2–501(1), 2A–217].

Identification In a sale of goods, the express designation of the goods provided for in the contract.

Existing Goods If the contract calls for the sale or lease of specific goods that are already in existence, identification takes place at the time the contract is made. **EXAMPLE 17.20** Litco Company contracts to lease a fleet of five cars designated by their vehicle identification numbers (VINs). Because the cars are identified by their VINs, identification has taken place, and Litco acquires an insurable interest in the cars at the time of contracting. ■

Future Goods Any goods that are not in existence at the time of contracting are known as *future goods.* Various rules apply to identification of future goods, depending on the goods.

- If a sale or lease involves unborn animals to be born within twelve months after contracting, identification takes place when the animals are conceived.
- If a sale involves crops that are to be harvested within twelve months (or the next harvest season occurring after contracting, whichever is longer), identification takes place when the crops are planted. Otherwise, identification takes place when the crops begin to grow.
- In a sale or lease of any other future goods, identification occurs when the goods are shipped, marked, or otherwise designated by the seller or lessor as the goods to which the contract refers.

Can identification take place for automobiles by using vehicle identification numbers?

Goods That Are Part of a Larger Mass As a general rule, goods that are part of a larger mass are identified when the goods are marked, shipped, or somehow designated by the seller or lessor as the particular goods that are the subject of the contract. **EXAMPLE 17.21** Carlos orders 10,000 pairs of men's jeans from a lot that contains 90,000 articles of clothing for men, women, and children. Until the seller separates the 10,000 pairs of men's jeans from the other items, title and risk of loss remain with the seller. ■

A common exception to this rule involves fungible goods. **Fungible goods** are goods that are alike naturally, by agreement, or by trade usage. Typical examples include specific grades or types of wheat, petroleum, and cooking oil, which usually are stored in large containers. If

Fungible Goods Goods that are alike by physical nature, agreement, or trade usage.

the owners of these goods hold title as *tenants in common* (owners with undivided shares of the whole), a seller-owner can pass title and risk of loss to the buyer without actually separating the goods. The buyer replaces the seller as an owner in common [UCC 2–105(4)].

17-3b Passage of Title

Once goods are identified, the provisions of UCC 2–401 apply to the passage of title. Parties can expressly agree when and how title will pass. Throughout UCC 2–401, the words "unless otherwise explicitly agreed" appear, meaning that any explicit understanding between the buyer and the seller determines when title passes.

Without an explicit agreement to the contrary, *title passes to the buyer at the time and the place the seller performs by delivering the goods* [UCC 2–401(2)]. For instance, if a person buys cattle at a livestock auction, title will pass to the buyer when the cattle are physically delivered to him or her (unless, of course, the parties agree otherwise).

CASE EXAMPLE 17.22 Timothy Allen contracted with Indy Route 66 Cycles, Inc., to have a motorcycle custom built for him. Indy built the motorcycle and issued a "Certificate of Origin." Two years later, federal law enforcement officers arrested Allen on drug charges and seized his home and other property. The officers also seized the Indy-made motorcycle from the garage of the home of Allen's sister, Tena. Indy filed a claim against the government, arguing that it owned the motorcycle because it still possessed the "Certificate of Origin." The court applied UCC Section 2–401(2) and ruled in favor of the government. Testimony by Indy's former vice president was "inconclusive" but implied that Indy had delivered the motorcycle to Allen. Because Indy had given up possession of the cycle to Allen, this was sufficient to pass title even though Indy had kept a "Certificate of Origin."[9] ■

(In the future, the delivery of goods may sometimes be accomplished by drones. This chapter's *Managerial Strategy* feature discusses the use of drones in commerce.)

Shipment and Destination Contracts
Unless otherwise agreed, delivery arrangements can determine when title passes from the seller to the buyer. In a **shipment contract,** the seller is required or authorized to ship goods by carrier, such as a trucking company. Under a shipment contract, the seller is required only to deliver conforming goods into the hands of a carrier, and title passes to the buyer at the time and place of shipment [UCC 2–401(2)(a)]. Generally, *all contracts are assumed to be shipment contracts if nothing to the contrary is stated in the contract.*

In a **destination contract,** the seller is required to deliver the goods to a particular destination, usually directly to the buyer, but sometimes to another party designated by the buyer. Title passes to the buyer when the goods are *tendered* at that destination [UCC 2–401(2)(b)]. *Tender of delivery* occurs when the seller places or holds conforming goods at the buyer's disposal (with any necessary notice), enabling the buyer to take possession [UCC 2–503(1)].

Delivery without Movement of the Goods
When the sales contract does not call for the seller to ship or deliver the goods (when the buyer is to pick up the goods), the passage of title depends on whether the seller must deliver a **document of title,** such as a bill of lading or a warehouse receipt, to the buyer. A *bill of lading* is a receipt for goods that is signed by a carrier and serves as a contract for the transport of the goods. A *warehouse receipt* is a receipt issued by a warehouser for goods stored in a warehouse.

When a document of title is required, title passes to the buyer *when and where the document is delivered.* Thus, if the goods are stored in a warehouse, title passes to the buyer when the

---

Shipment Contract A contract for the sale of goods in which the seller is required or authorized to ship the goods by carrier. The seller assumes liability for any losses or damage to the goods until they are delivered to the carrier.

When does title pass to the buyer of a motorcycle?

Destination Contract A contract for the sale of goods in which the seller is required or authorized to ship the goods by carrier and tender delivery of the goods at a particular destination. The seller assumes liability for any losses or damage to the goods until they are tendered at the destination specified in the contract.

Document of Title A paper exchanged in the regular course of business that evidences the right to possession of goods (for example, a bill of lading or a warehouse receipt).

---

9. *United States v. 2007 Custom Motorcycle*, 2011 WL 232331 (D.Ariz. 2011).

Management Faces a Legal Issue

The commercial use of drones—small, pilotless aerial vehicles—has, until recently, been on hold in the United States. Possible commercial uses of drones are numerous—railroad track inspection, oil and gas pipeline review, real estate videos for use by brokers, discovery for land boundary disputes, and many others. In addition, businesses have begun making plans to use drones for delivery of goods. Amazon is developing Amazon Prime Air, a drone-based delivery service. Google Project Wing is another drone-based service that is under development.

The problem has been the Federal Aviation Agency (FAA). The FAA claims authority to regulate *all* unmanned aircraft systems (UASs). In 2012, Congress mandated the FAA "to establish a roadmap for getting UASs integrated into the national air space." Not until 2015, however, did the FAA issue its proposed rules on commercial drone use. The rules require operators to apply for a license to use drones commercially. Drone flights are expected to be limited to daylight hours, and drones will not be allowed to go above five hundred feet or faster than one hundred miles per hour. The proposed rules also require that licensed drone operators maintain a continuous visual line of sight with the drones during operation.

The proposed FAA rules are now in a public comment period, and it is expected that final rules will be issued in 2016 or 2017. Thus, it is not yet clear how soon your packages from Amazon.com will be delivered by a commercial drone.

What the Courts Say

In the past, the FAA has attempted to fine other-than-recreational users of drones. One case involved Texas EquuSearch, a group that searches for missing persons. The organization requested an emergency injunction after receiving an e-mail from an FAA employee indicating that its drone use was illegal. The U.S. Court of Appeals for the District of Columbia Circuit refused to act on the suit. The court stated that the e-mail from the FAA did not have legal effect and therefore was not subject to judicial review.[a]

In a case involving an administrative hearing, the FAA assessed a civil penalty against Raphael Pirker for careless and reckless operation of an unmanned aircraft. Pirker flew a drone over the University of Virginia in 2011 while filming a video advertisement for the medical school. Pirker appealed to the National Transportation Safety Board Office of Administrative Law Judges. He prevailed in early 2014.[b] The FAA has appealed the ruling.

In other countries, the commercial drone business is flourishing. In the United States, whether it is worthwhile to create such a business will depend on how strict the final FAA rules on drones are. Delivery by drones via Amazon Prime Air or Google Project Wing may be in jeopardy.

---

a. *Texas EquuSearch Mounted Search and Recovery Team, RP Search Services, Inc., v. Federal Aviation Administration,* 2014 WL 2860332 (C.A.D.C. 2014).

b. *Huerta v. Pirker,* Decisional Order of National Transportation Safety Board Office of Administrative Law Judges, Docket CP-217, March 6, 2014.

---

appropriate documents are delivered to the buyer. The goods never move. In fact, the buyer can choose to leave the goods at the same warehouse for a period of time, and the buyer's title to those goods will be unaffected.

When no documents of title are required and delivery is made without moving the goods, title passes at the time and place the sales contract is made, if the goods have already been identified. If the goods have not been identified, title does not pass until identification occurs [UCC 2–401(3)].

EXAMPLE 17.23 Greg sells lumber to Bodan. They agree that Bodan will pick up the lumber at the lumberyard. If the lumber has been identified (segregated, marked, or in any other way distinguished from all other lumber), title passes to Bodan when the contract is signed. If the lumber is still in large storage bins at the lumberyard, title does not pass to Bodan until the particular pieces of lumber to be sold under this contract are identified. ■

Sales or Leases by Nonowners
Problems occur when a person who acquires goods with *imperfect* title attempts to sell or lease them. Sections 2–402 and 2–403 of the UCC deal with the rights of two parties who lay claim to the same goods, sold with imperfect title. Generally, a buyer acquires at least whatever title the seller has to the goods sold.

Void Title. A buyer may unknowingly purchase goods from a seller who is not the owner of the goods. If the seller is a thief, the seller's title is *void*—legally, no title exists. Thus, the buyer acquires no title, and the real owner can reclaim the goods from the buyer. If the goods were leased, the same result would occur, because the lessor has no leasehold interest to transfer.

EXAMPLE 17.24 If Saki steals diamonds owned by Bruce, Saki has a *void title* to those diamonds. If Saki sells the diamonds to Shannon, Bruce can reclaim them from Shannon even though Shannon acted in good faith and honestly was not aware that the goods were stolen. ■ Article 2A contains similar provisions for leases.

Voidable Title. A seller has *voidable title* if the goods that she or he is selling were (1) obtained by fraud, (2) paid for with a check that is later *dishonored* (returned for insufficient funds), or (3) purchased on credit when the seller was **insolvent.** Under the UCC, insolvency occurs when a person ceases to pay his or her debts in the ordinary course of business, cannot pay debts as they become due, or is insolvent under federal bankruptcy law [UCC 1–201(23)].

In contrast to a seller with *void title,* a seller with *voidable title* has the power to transfer good title to a good faith purchaser for value. A **good faith purchaser** is one who buys without knowledge of circumstances that would make a person of ordinary prudence inquire about the validity of the seller's title to the goods. One who purchases *for value* gives legally sufficient consideration (value) for the goods purchased. The real, or original, owner cannot recover goods from a good faith purchaser for value [UCC 2–403(1)].[10]

If the buyer of the goods is not a good faith purchaser for value, then the actual owner of the goods can reclaim them from the buyer (or from the seller, if the goods are still in the seller's possession). Exhibit 17–3 illustrates these concepts.

The Entrustment Rule. According to Section 2–403(2), when goods are entrusted to a merchant *who deals in goods of that kind,* the merchant has the power to transfer all rights to *a buyer in the ordinary course of business.* This is known as the **entrustment rule.** Entrusted goods include both goods that are turned over to the merchant and purchased goods left with the

---

Insolvent A condition in which a person cannot pay his or her debts as they become due or ceases to pay debts in the ordinary course of business.

Good Faith Purchaser
A purchaser who buys without notice of any circumstance that would cause a person of ordinary prudence to inquire as to whether the seller has valid title to the goods being sold.

Entrustment Rule The rule that entrusting goods to a merchant who deals in goods of that kind gives that merchant the power to transfer those goods and all rights to them to a buyer in the ordinary course of business.

---

10. The real owner could, of course, sue the person who initially obtained voidable title to the goods.

Exhibit 17–3 Void and Voidable Titles

If goods are transferred from their owner to another by theft, the thief acquires no ownership rights. Because the thief's title is *void,* a later buyer can acquire no title, and the owner can recover the goods. If the transfer occurs by fraud, for instance, the transferee acquires a *voidable* title, as shown in this exhibit. A later good faith purchaser for value can acquire good title, and the original owner cannot recover the goods.

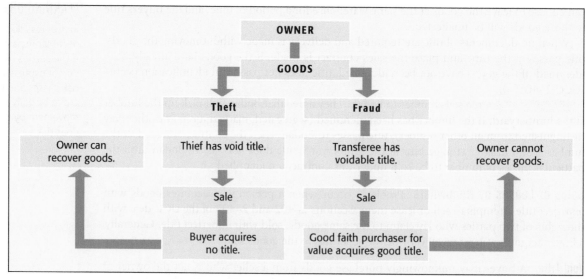

merchant for later delivery or pickup [UCC 2–403(3)]. Article 2A provides a similar rule for leased goods [UCC 2A–305(2)].

Under the UCC, a person is a **buyer in the ordinary course of business** in the following circumstances:

1. She or he buys goods in good faith (honestly).

2. The goods are purchased without knowledge that the sale violates the rights of another person in the goods.

3. The goods are purchased in the ordinary course from a merchant (other than a pawnbroker) in the business of selling goods of that kind.

4. The sale to that person is consistent with the usual or customary practices in the kind of business in which the seller is engaged [UCC 1–201(9)].

The entrustment rule basically allows innocent buyers to obtain legitimate title to goods purchased from merchants even if the merchants do not have good title. **EXAMPLE 17.25** Jan leaves her watch with a jeweler to be repaired. The jeweler sells both new and used watches. The jeweler sells Jan's watch to Kim, a customer, who is unaware that the jeweler has no right to sell it. Kim, as a good faith buyer, gets good title against Jan's claim of ownership.[11] Kim, however, obtains only those rights held by the person entrusting the goods (here, Jan).

Now suppose that Jan stole the watch from Greg and left it with the jeweler to be repaired. The jeweler then sells it to Kim. In this situation, Kim gets good title against Jan, who entrusted the watch to the jeweler, but not against Greg (the real owner), who neither entrusted the watch to Jan nor authorized Jan to entrust it. ■

17–3c **Risk of Loss**

Under the UCC, risk of loss does not necessarily pass with title. When risk of loss passes from a seller or lessor to a buyer or lessee is generally determined by the contract between the parties. Sometimes, the contract states expressly when the risk of loss passes. At other times, it does not, and a court must interpret the performance and delivery terms of the contract to determine whether the risk has passed.

Like risk of loss, the risk of liability that arises from the goods does not necessarily require the passage of title. In addition, as with risk of loss, when this risk passes from a seller to a buyer is generally determined by the contract between the parties. **CASE EXAMPLE 17.26** Tammy Herring contracted to buy a horse named Toby from Stacy and Gregory Bowman, who owned Summit Stables in Washington. The contract required Herring to make monthly payments until she paid $2,200 in total for Toby. Additionally, Herring agreed to pay Toby's monthly boarding fee at Summit Stables until the purchase price balance was paid. The Bowmans were to provide Toby's registration papers to Herring only when she had paid in full.

One day, another stable boarder, Diana Person, was injured when she was thrown from a buggy drawn by Toby and driven by Herring's daughter. Person sued the Bowmans to recover for her injuries, but the court held that Herring (not the Bowmans) owned Toby at the time of the accident. Herring argued that she did not own the horse because she did not yet have its registration papers, but the court found that the contract clearly showed that Herring owned Toby. Therefore, the Bowmans were not liable for the injuries that Toby caused.[12] ■

Delivery with Movement of the Goods—Carrier Cases

When the contract involves movement of the goods through a common carrier but does not specify when risk of loss passes, the courts first look for specific delivery terms in the contract.

Buyer in the Ordinary Course of Business A buyer who, in good faith and without knowledge that the sale violates the ownership rights or security interest of a third party in the goods, purchases goods in the ordinary course of business from a person in the business of selling goods of that kind.

KNOW THIS

The purpose of holding most goods in inventory is to turn those goods into revenues by selling them. That is one of the reasons for the entrustment rule.

---

11. Jan, of course, can sue the jeweler for the tort of trespass to personalty or conversion for the equivalent cash value of the watch.
12. *Person v. Bowman*, 173 Wash.App. 1024 (2013).

When does the risk of loss pass to the buyer in the sale of a horse?

The terms that have traditionally been used in contracts within the United States are listed and defined in Exhibit 17–4. These terms determine which party will pay the costs of delivering the goods and who bears the risk of loss. If the contract does not include these terms, then the courts must decide whether the contract is a shipment or a destination contract.

Shipment Contracts.   In a shipment contract, the seller or lessor is required or authorized to ship goods by carrier, but is not required to deliver them to a particular final destination. The risk of loss in a shipment contract passes to the buyer or lessee when the goods are delivered to the carrier [UCC 2–319(1)(a), 2–509(1)(a), 2A–219(2)(a)].

EXAMPLE 17.27 Pitman, a seller in Texas, sells five hundred cases of grapefruit to a buyer in New York, F.O.B. Houston (free on board in Houston—see Exhibit 17–4). The contract authorizes shipment by carrier. It does not require that the seller tender the grapefruit in New York. Risk passes to the buyer when conforming goods are properly placed in the possession of the carrier in Houston. If the goods are damaged in transit, the loss is the buyer's. (Actually, buyers have recourse against carriers, subject to certain limitations, and buyers usually insure the goods from the time the goods leave the seller.) ■

Destination Contracts.   In a destination contract, the risk of loss passes to the buyer or lessee when the goods are tendered to the buyer or lessee at the specified destination [UCC 2–319(1)(b), 2–509(1)(b), 2A–219(2)(b)]. In *Example 17.27,* if the contract had been F.O.B. New York, the risk of loss during transit to New York would have been the seller's. Risk of loss would not have passed to the buyer until the carrier tendered the grapefruit to the buyer in New York.

Delivery without Movement of the Goods   The UCC also addresses situations in which the contract does not require the goods to be shipped or moved. Frequently, the buyer or lessee is to pick up the goods from the seller or lessor, or the goods are held by a bailee.

A **bailment** is a temporary delivery of personal property, without passage of title, into the care of another, called a *bailee.* Under the UCC, a *bailee* is a party who, by a bill of lading, warehouse receipt, or other document of title, acknowledges possession of goods and/or contracts to deliver them. For instance, a warehousing company or a trucking company may be a bailee.

Goods Held by the Seller.   When the seller keeps the goods for pickup, a document of title usually is not used. If the seller is a merchant, risk of loss to goods held by the seller passes to the buyer when the buyer *actually takes physical possession of the goods* [UCC 2–509(3)]. In

Bailment A situation in which the personal property of one person (a bailor) is entrusted to another (a bailee), who is obligated to return the bailed property to the bailor or dispose of it as directed.

Exhibit 17–4 Contract Terms—Definitions

The contract terms listed and defined in this exhibit help to determine which party will bear the costs of delivery and when risk of loss will pass from the seller to the buyer.

F.O.B. (free on board)—Indicates that the selling price of goods includes transportation costs to the specific F.O.B. place named in the contract. The seller pays the expenses and carries the risk of loss to the F.O.B. place named [UCC 2–319(1)]. If the named place is the place from which the goods are shipped (for example, the seller's city or place of business), the contract is a shipment contract. If the named place is the place to which the goods are to be shipped (for example, the buyer's city or place of business), the contract is a destination contract.

F.A.S. (free alongside ship)—Requires that the seller, at his or her own expense and risk, deliver the goods alongside the carrier before risk passes to the buyer [UCC 2–319(2)]. An F.A.S. contract is essentially an F.O.B. contract for ships.

C.I.F. or **C.&F.** (cost, insurance, and freight, or just cost and freight)—Requires, among other things, that the seller "put the goods in the possession of a carrier" before risk passes to the buyer [UCC 2–320(2)]. (These are basically pricing terms, and the contracts remain shipment contracts, not destination contracts.)

Delivery ex-ship (delivery from the carrying vessel)—Means that risk of loss does not pass to the buyer until the goods are properly unloaded from the ship or other carrier [UCC 2–322].

other words, the merchant bears the risk of loss between the time the contract is formed and the time the buyer picks up the goods.

CASE EXAMPLE 17.28 Henry Ganno purchased a twelve-foot beam at a lumberyard. The lumberyard loaded the beam onto Ganno's truck, but did not tie it down (it was policy not to secure loads for customers). After he drove onto the highway, the beam fell out of Ganno's truck, and he was injured while trying to retrieve it. Ganno sued the lumberyard for negligence, but the court held that Ganno—not the lumberyard—bore the risk of loss and injury after he left the lumberyard's premises. Once the truck was loaded, the risk of loss passed to Ganno under the UCC because he had taken physical possession of the goods.[13]

If the seller is not a merchant, the risk of loss to goods held by the seller passes to the buyer on *tender of delivery* [UCC 2–509(3)]. This means that the seller bears the risk of loss until he or she makes the goods available to the buyer and notifies the buyer that the goods are ready to be picked up.

With respect to leases, similar rules apply. The risk of loss passes to the lessee on the lessee's receipt of the goods if the lessor is a merchant. Otherwise, the risk passes to the lessee on tender of delivery [UCC 2A–219(2)(c)].

Goods Held by a Bailee. When a bailee is holding goods for a person who has contracted to sell them and the goods are to be delivered without being moved, the goods are usually represented by a document of title. The title document may be written, such as a bill of lading or a warehouse receipt, or evidenced by an electronic record.

When goods are held by a bailee, risk of loss passes to the buyer when one of the following occurs:

1. The buyer receives a negotiable document of title for the goods.

2. The bailee acknowledges the buyer's right to possess the goods.

3. The buyer receives a nonnegotiable document of title, *and* the buyer has a *reasonable time* to present the document to the bailee and demand the goods. If the bailee refuses to honor the document, the risk of loss remains with the seller [UCC 2–503(4)(b), 2–509(2)].

With respect to leases, if goods held by a bailee are to be delivered without being moved, the risk of loss passes to the lessee on acknowledgment by the bailee of the lessee's right to possession of the goods [UCC 2A–219(2)(b)].

Risk of Loss When the Contract Is Breached

When a sales or lease contract is breached, the transfer of risk operates differently depending on which party breaches. Generally, the party in breach bears the risk of loss.

When the Seller or Lessor Breaches. If the seller or lessor breaches by supplying goods that are so nonconforming that the buyer has the right to reject them, the risk of loss does not pass to the buyer. **EXAMPLE 17.29** A buyer orders ten stainless steel refrigerators from a seller, F.O.B. the seller's plant. The seller ships white refrigerators instead. The white refrigerators (nonconforming goods) are damaged in transit. The risk of loss falls on the seller. Had the seller shipped stainless steel refrigerators (conforming goods) instead, the risk would have fallen on the buyer [UCC 2–510(1)].

With nonconforming goods, the risk of loss does not pass to the buyer until one of the following occurs:

1. The defects are **cured** (that is, the goods are repaired, replaced, or discounted in price by the seller).

2. The buyer accepts the goods in spite of their defects (thus waiving the right to reject).

Cure The right of a party who tenders nonconforming performance to correct his or her performance within the contract period.

---

13. *Ganno v. Lanoga Corp.*, 119 Wash.App. 310, 80 P.3d 180 (2003).

iStockPhoto.com/cherezoff

When a seller ships nonconforming refrigerators that are damaged in shipment, who incurs the risk of loss?

If a buyer accepts a shipment of goods and later discovers a defect, acceptance can be revoked. Revocation allows the buyer to pass the risk of loss back to the seller, at least to the extent that the buyer's insurance does not cover the loss [UCC 2–510(2)]. Article 2A provides similar rules for leases.

When the Buyer or Lessee Breaches. The general rule is that when a buyer or lessee breaches a contract, the risk of loss immediately shifts to the buyer or lessee. This rule has three important limitations:

1. The seller or lessor must already have identified the contract goods.
2. The buyer or lessee bears the risk for only a commercially reasonable time after the seller or lessor has learned of the breach.
3. The buyer or lessee is liable only to the extent of any deficiency in the seller's insurance coverage [UCC 2–510(3), 2A–220(2)].

17-3d Insurable Interest

Insurable Interest A property interest in goods being sold or leased that is sufficiently substantial to permit a party to insure against damage to the goods.

Parties to sales and lease contracts often obtain insurance coverage to protect against damage, loss, or destruction of goods. Any party purchasing insurance must have a sufficient interest in the insured item to obtain a valid policy. Insurance laws—not the UCC—determine sufficiency. The UCC is helpful, however, because it contains certain rules regarding insurable interests in goods.

Insurable Interest of the Buyer or Lessee A buyer or lessee has an **insurable interest** in *identified* goods. The moment the contract goods are identified by the seller or lessor, the buyer or lessee has a property interest in them. That allows the buyer or lessee to obtain necessary insurance coverage for those goods even before the risk of loss has passed [UCC 2–501(1), 2A–218(1)]. When the parties do not explicitly agree on identification in their contract, then the UCC provisions on identification discussed earlier in this chapter apply.

Insurable Interest of the Seller or Lessor A seller has an insurable interest in goods as long as she or he retains title to the goods. Even after title passes to the buyer, a seller who has a *security interest* in the goods (a right to secure payment) still has an insurable interest [UCC 2–501(2)]. Thus, both a buyer and a seller can have an insurable interest in the same goods at the same time. Of course, the buyer or seller must sustain an actual loss to recover from an insurance company. In regard to leases, the lessor retains an insurable interest in leased goods until the lessee exercises an option to buy and the risk of loss has passed to the lessee [UCC 2A–218(3)].

See the *Business Application* feature at the end of this chapter for a discussion of insurance coverage and other measures that buyers and sellers can take to protect against losses.

17-4 Contracts for the International Sale of Goods

LEARNING OBJECTIVE 5

What law governs contracts for the international sale of goods?

International sales contracts between firms or individuals located in different countries are governed by the 1980 United Nations Convention on Contracts for the International Sale of Goods (CISG). The CISG governs international contracts only if the countries of the parties to the contract have ratified the CISG and if the parties have not agreed that some other law will govern their contract. As of 2015, the CISG had been adopted by seventy-eight countries, including the United States, Canada, some Central and South American countries, China, most European nations, Japan, and Mexico. That means that the CISG is the uniform international sales law of countries that account for more than two-thirds of all global trade.

17-4a Applicability of the CISG

Essentially, the CISG is to international sales contracts what Article 2 of the UCC is to domestic sales contracts. As discussed earlier, in domestic transactions the UCC applies when the parties to a contract for a sale of goods have failed to specify in writing some important term concerning price, delivery, or the like. Similarly, whenever the parties subject to the CISG have failed to specify in writing the precise terms of a contract for the international sale of goods, the CISG will be applied.

Unlike the UCC, *the CISG does not apply to consumer sales.* Neither the UCC nor the CISG applies to contracts for services.

17–4b A Comparison of CISG and UCC Provisions

The provisions of the CISG, although similar for the most part to those of the UCC, differ from them in certain respects. If the CISG and the UCC conflict, the CISG applies (because it is a treaty of the U.S. national government and therefore takes precedence over state laws under the U.S. Constitution). We look here at some differences with respect to contract formation.

The appendix at the end of this chapter—which shows an actual international sales contract used by Starbucks Coffee Company—illustrates many of the special terms and clauses that are typically contained in international contracts for the sale of goods. Annotations in the appendix explain the meaning and significance of specific contract clauses.

Statute of Frauds Unlike the UCC, the CISG does not include any Statute of Frauds provisions. Under Article 11 of the CISG, an international sales contract does not need to be evidenced by a writing or to be in any particular form.

Offers UCC 2–205 provides that a merchant's firm offer is irrevocable, even without consideration, if the merchant gives assurances in a signed writing or record. In contrast, under the CISG, an offer can become irrevocable without a signed writing or record. Article 16(2) of the CISG provides that an offer will be irrevocable in either of the following circumstances:

1. The offeror states orally that the offer is irrevocable.

2. The offeree reasonably relies on the offer as being irrevocable.

In both of these situations, the offer will be irrevocable without a writing or record and without consideration.

Another difference is that, under the UCC, if the price term is left open, the court will determine "a reasonable price at the time for delivery" [UCC 2–305(1)]. Under the CISG, however, the price term must be specified, or at least provisions for its specification must be included in the agreement. Otherwise, normally no contract will exist.

Acceptances Under the UCC, a definite expression of acceptance that contains additional terms can still result in the formation of a contract, unless the additional terms are conditioned on the assent of the offeror. In other words, the UCC does away with the mirror image rule in domestic sales contracts.

Article 19 of the CISG provides that a contract can be formed even though the acceptance contains additional terms, unless the additional terms materially alter the contract. Under the CISG, however, a "material alteration" includes almost any change in the terms. If an additional term relates to payment, quality, quantity, price, time and place of delivery, extent of one party's liability to the other, or the settlement of disputes, the CISG considers the added term a material alteration. In effect, then, the CISG requires that the terms of the acceptance mirror those of the offer.

Additionally, under the UCC, an acceptance is effective on dispatch, so a contract is created when the acceptance is transmitted. Under the CISG, in contrast, a contract is created not at the time the acceptance is transmitted but only on its *receipt* by the offeror. (The offer becomes *irrevocable,* however, when the acceptance is sent.)

Also, in contrast to the UCC, the CISG provides that acceptance by performance does not require that the offeror be notified of the performance.

Reviewing . . . The Formation of Sales and Lease Contracts

Guy Holcomb owns and operates Oasis Goodtime Emporium, an adult entertainment establishment. Holcomb wanted to create an adult Internet system for Oasis that would offer customers adult theme videos and live chat room programs using performers at the club. On May 10, Holcomb signed a work order authorizing Thomas Consulting Group (TCG) "to deliver a working prototype of a customer chat system, demonstrating the integration of live video and chatting in a Web browser." In exchange for creating the prototype, Holcomb agreed to pay TCG $64,697. On May 20, Holcomb signed an additional work order in the amount of $12,943 for TCG to install a customized firewall system. The work orders stated that Holcomb would make monthly installment payments to TCG, and both parties expected the work would be finished by September.

Due to unforeseen problems largely attributable to system configuration and software incompatibility, the project required more time than anticipated. By the end of the summer, the Web site was still not ready, and Holcomb had fallen behind in the payments to TCG. TCG was threatening to cease work and file suit for breach of contract unless the bill was paid. Rather than make further payments, Holcomb wanted to abandon the Web site project. Using the information presented in the chapter, answer the following questions.

1. Would a court be likely to decide that the transaction between Holcomb and TCG was covered by the Uniform Commercial Code (UCC)? Why or why not?

2. Would a court be likely to consider Holcomb a merchant under the UCC? Why or why not?

3. Did the parties have a valid contract under the UCC? Explain.

4. Suppose that Holcomb and TCG meet in October in an attempt to resolve their problems. At that time, the parties reach an oral agreement that TCG will continue to work without demanding full payment of the past-due amounts and Holcomb will pay CCG $5,000 per week. Assuming that the contract falls under the UCC, is the oral agreement enforceable? Why or why not?

DEBATE THIS

- The UCC should require the same degree of definiteness of terms, especially with respect to price and quantity, as general contract law does.

BUSINESS APPLICATION

Who Bears the Risk of Loss— the Seller or the Buyer?*

The shipment of goods is a major aspect of commercial transactions. Many issues arise when an unforeseen event, such as fire

* This *Business Application* is not meant to substitute for the services of an attorney who is licensed to practice law in your state.

or theft, causes damage to goods in transit. At the time of contract negotiation, both the seller and the buyer should determine the importance of the risk of loss. In some circumstances, risk is relatively unimportant (such as when ten boxes of copier paper are being sold), and the delivery terms should simply reflect costs and price. In other circumstances, risk is extremely important (such as when a fragile piece of pharmaceutical testing equipment is being sold), and the parties will need

an express agreement as to the moment risk is to pass so that they can insure the goods accordingly. Risk should always be considered before a loss occurs, not after.

A major consideration relating to risk is when to insure goods against possible losses. Buyers and sellers should determine the point at which risk passes so that they can obtain insurance coverage to protect themselves against loss when they have an insurable interest in the goods.

Checklist to Determine Risk of Loss

The UCC uses a three-part checklist to determine risk of loss:

1. If the contract includes terms allocating the risk of loss, those terms are binding and must be applied.

2. If the contract is silent as to risk and either party breaches the contract, the breaching party is liable for the risk of loss.

3. If the contract makes no reference to risk and the goods are to be shipped or delivered, the risk of loss is borne by the party having control over the goods (delivery terms) if neither party breaches.

If You Are the Seller

If you are a seller of goods to be shipped, realize that as long as you have control over the goods, you are liable for any loss unless the buyer is in breach or the contract contains an explicit agreement to the contrary. When there is no explicit agreement, the delivery terms in your contract can serve as a basis for determining control. Thus, if goods are shipped "F.O.B. buyer's business," risk of loss does not pass to the buyer until there is a tender of delivery at the destination—the buyer's business. Any loss or damage in transit falls on the seller because the seller has control until proper tender has been made.

If You Are the Buyer

If you are a buyer of goods, it is important to remember that most sellers prefer "F.O.B. seller's business" as a delivery term. Under this term, once the goods are delivered to the carrier, the buyer bears the risk of loss. Thus, if conforming goods are completely destroyed or lost in transit, the buyer not only suffers the loss but is obligated to pay the seller the contract price.

CHECKLIST for the Seller or the Buyer:

1. Before entering into a contract, determine the importance of the risk of loss for a given sale.

2. If risk is extremely important, the contract should expressly state the moment the risk of loss will pass from the seller to the buyer. This clause could even provide that risk will not pass until the goods are "delivered, installed, inspected, and tested (or in running order for a period of time)."

3. If an express clause is not included, delivery terms determine the passage of risk of loss.

4. When appropriate, either party or both parties should consider procuring insurance.

Key Terms

bailment 420
buyer in the ordinary course of business 419
course of dealing 413
course of performance 413
cure 421
destination contract 416
document of title 416
entrustment rule 418
firm offer 406

fungible goods 415
good faith purchaser 418
identification 415
insolvent 418
insurable interest 422
intangible property 401
lease 403
lease agreement 403
lessee 404
lessor 404

merchant 403
output contract 406
predominant-factor test 401
requirements contract 406
sale 400
sales contract 399
seasonably 407
shipment contract 416
tangible property 401
usage of trade 413

Chapter Summary: The Formation of Sales and Lease Contracts

The Scope of Articles 2 and 2A	1. *The UCC*—The UCC attempts to provide a consistent, uniform, and integrated framework of rules to deal with all phases ordinarily arising in a commercial sales or lease transaction, including contract formation, passage of title and risk of loss, performance, remedies, payment for goods, warehoused goods, and secured transactions.
	2. *Article 2 (sales)*—Article 2 governs contracts for the sale of goods (tangible, movable personal property). The common law of contracts also applies to sales contracts to the extent that the common law has not been modified by the UCC. If there is a conflict between a common law rule and the UCC, the UCC controls.
	3. *Article 2A (leases)*—Article 2A governs contracts for the lease of goods. Except that it applies to leases, instead of sales, of goods, Article 2A is essentially a repetition of Article 2 and varies only to reflect differences between sales and lease transactions.

Continues

The Formation of Sales and Lease Contracts	1. *Offer*—

The Formation of Sales and Lease Contracts

1. *Offer*—
   a. Not all terms have to be included for a contract to be formed (only the subject matter and quantity term must be specified).
   b. The price does not have to be included for a contract to be formed.
   c. Particulars of performance can be left open.
   d. A written and signed offer by a *merchant,* covering a period of three months or less, is irrevocable without payment of consideration.
2. *Acceptance*—
   a. Acceptance may be made by any reasonable means of communication. It is effective when dispatched.
   b. An offer can be accepted by a promise to ship or by prompt shipment of conforming goods, or by prompt shipment of nonconforming goods if not accompanied by a notice of accommodation.
   c. Acceptance by performance requires notice within a reasonable time. Otherwise, the offer can be treated as lapsed.
   d. A definite expression of acceptance creates a contract even if the terms of the acceptance differ from those of the offer, unless the additional or different terms in the acceptance are expressly conditioned on the offeror's assent to those terms.
3. *Consideration*—A modification of a contract for the sale of goods does not require consideration.
4. *The Statute of Frauds*—
   a. All contracts for the sale of goods priced at $500 or more must be in writing. A writing is sufficient as long as it indicates a contract between the parties and is signed by the party against whom enforcement is sought. A contract is not enforceable beyond the quantity shown in the writing.
   b. When written confirmation of an oral contract *between merchants* is not objected to in writing by the receiver within ten days, the contract is enforceable.
   c. For exceptions to the Statute of Frauds, see Exhibit 17–2.
5. *Parol evidence rule*—
   a. The terms of a clear and complete written contract cannot be contradicted by evidence of prior agreements or contemporaneous oral agreements.
   b. Evidence is admissible to clarify the terms of a writing if the contract terms are ambiguous or if evidence of course of dealing, usage of trade, or course of performance is necessary to learn or to clarify the parties' intentions.
6. *Unconscionability*—An unconscionable contract is one that is so unfair and one sided that it would be unreasonable to enforce it. If the court deems a sales contract to have been unconscionable at the time it was made, the court can (a) refuse to enforce the contract, (b) refuse to enforce the unconscionable clause, or (c) limit the application of any unconscionable clauses to avoid an unconscionable result.

Title and Risk of Loss

1. *Shipment contract*—In the absence of an agreement, title and risk pass on the seller's or lessor's delivery of conforming goods to the carrier [UCC 2–319(1)(a), 2–401(2)(a), 2–509(1)(a), 2A–219(2)(a)].
2. *Destination contract*—In the absence of an agreement, title and risk pass on the seller's or lessor's *tender* of delivery of conforming goods to the buyer or lessee at the point of destination [UCC 2–319(1)(b), 2–401(2)(b), 2–509(1)(b), 2A–219(2)(b)].
3. *Delivery without movement of the goods*—In the absence of an agreement, if the goods are not represented by a document of title, title passes on the formation of the contract, and risk passes on the buyer's or lessee's receipt of the goods if the seller or lessor is a merchant or on the tender of delivery if the seller or lessor is a nonmerchant.
4. *Sales or leases by nonowners*—Between the owner and a good faith purchaser:
   a. Void title—Owner prevails [UCC 2–403(1)].
   b. Voidable title—Buyer prevails [UCC 2–403(1)].
   c. Entrusted to a merchant—Buyer prevails [UCC 2–403(2), (3); 2A–305(2)].
5. *Risk of loss when the contract is breached*—
   a. If the seller or lessor breaches by tendering nonconforming goods that are rejected by the buyer or lessee, the risk of loss does not pass to the buyer or lessee until the defects are cured (unless the buyer or lessee accepts the goods in spite of their defects, thus waiving the right to reject) [UCC 2–510(1), 2A–220(1)].
   b. If the buyer or lessee breaches the contract, the risk of loss immediately shifts to the buyer or lessee for goods that are identified to the contract. The buyer or lessee bears the risk for only a commercially reasonable time after the seller or lessor has learned of the breach [UCC 2–510(3), 2A–220(2)].

Contracts for the International Sale of Goods

International sales contracts are governed by the United Nations Convention on Contracts for the International Sale of Goods (CISG) if the countries of the parties to the contract have ratified the CISG and if the parties have not agreed that some other law will govern their contract. Essentially, the CISG is to international sales contracts what Article 2 of the UCC is to domestic sales contracts. Whenever parties who are subject to the CISG have failed to specify in writing the precise terms of a contract for the international sale of goods, the CISG will be applied.

Issue Spotters

1. E-Design, Inc., orders 150 computer desks. Fav-O-Rite Supplies, Inc., ships 150 printer stands. Is this an acceptance of the offer or a counteroffer? If it is an acceptance, is it a breach of the contract? What if Fav-O-Rite told E-Design it was sending the printer stands as "an accommodation"? (See *The Formation of Sales and Lease Contracts*.)

2. Truck Parts, Inc. (TPI), often sells supplies to United Fix-It Company (UFC), which services trucks. Over the phone, they negotiate for the sale of eighty-four sets of tires. TPI sends a letter to UFC detailing the terms and two weeks later ships the tires. Is there an enforceable contract between them? Why or why not? (See *The Formation of Sales and Lease Contracts*.)

—**Check your answers to the *Issue Spotters* against the answers provided in Appendix D at the end of this text.**

Learning Objectives Check

1. If a contract involves both goods and services, does the UCC apply?

2. In a sales contract, if an offeree includes additional or different terms in an acceptance, will a contract result? If so, what happens to these terms?

3. What exceptions to the writing requirements of the Statute of Frauds are provided in Article 2 and Article 2A of the UCC?

4. Risk of loss does not necessarily pass with title. If the parties to a contract do not expressly agree when risk passes and the goods are to be delivered without movement by the seller, when does risk pass?

5. What law governs contracts for the international sale of goods?

—**Answers to the even-numbered *Learning Objectives Check* questions can be found in Appendix E at the end of this text.**

Business Scenarios and Case Problems

17–1. Additional Terms. Strike offers to sell Bailey one thousand shirts for a stated price. The offer declares that shipment will be made by Dependable Truck Line. Bailey replies, "I accept your offer for one thousand shirts at the price quoted. Delivery to be by Yellow Express Truck Line." Both Strike and Bailey are merchants. Three weeks later, Strike ships the shirts by Dependable Truck Line, and Bailey refuses to accept delivery. Strike sues for breach of contract. Bailey claims that there never was a contract because his reply, which included a modification of carriers, did not constitute an acceptance. Bailey further claims that even if there had been a contract, Strike would have been in breach because Strike shipped the shirts by Dependable, contrary to the contract terms. Discuss fully Bailey's claims. (See *The Formation of Sales and Lease Contracts*.)

17–2. Spotlight on Goods and Services—The Statute of Frauds. Fallsview Glatt Kosher Caterers ran a business that provided travel packages, including food, entertainment, and lectures on religious subjects, to customers during the Passover holiday at a New York resort. Willie Rosenfeld verbally agreed to pay Fallsview $24,050 for the Passover package for himself and his family. Rosenfeld did not appear at the resort and never paid the money owed. Fallsview sued Rosenfeld for breach of contract. Rosenfeld claimed that the contract was unenforceable because it was not in writing and violated the UCC's Statute of Frauds. Is the contract valid? Explain. [*Fallsview Glatt Kosher Caterers, Inc. v. Rosenfeld*, 794 N.Y.S.2d 790 (N.Y. Super. 2005)] (See *The Formation of Sales and Lease Contracts*.)

17–3. Business Case Problem with Sample Answer— Passage of Title. Kenzie Godfrey was a passenger in a taxi when it collided with a car driven by Dawn Altieri. Altieri had originally leased the car from G.E. Capital Auto Lease, Inc. By the time of the accident, she had bought it, but she had not fully paid for it or completed the transfer-of-title paperwork. Godfrey suffered a brain injury and sought to recover damages from the owner of the car that Altieri was driving. Who had title to the car at the time of the accident? Explain. [*Godfrey v. G.E. Capital Auto Lease, Inc.*, 89 A.D.3d 471, 933 N.Y.S.2d 208 (1 Dept. 2011)] (See *Title and Risk of Loss*.)

—**For a sample answer to Problem 17–3, go to Appendix F at the end of this text.**

17–4. Additional Terms. B.S. International, Ltd. (BSI), makes costume jewelry. JMAM, LLC, is a wholesaler of costume jewelry. JMAM sent BSI a letter with the terms for orders, including the necessary procedure for obtaining credit for items that customers rejected. The letter stated, "By signing below, you agree to the terms." Steven Baracsi, BSI's owner, signed the letter and returned it. For six years, BSI made jewelry for JMAM, which resold it. Items rejected by customers were sent back to JMAM, but were never returned to BSI. BSI filed a suit against JMAM, claiming $41,294.21 for the unreturned items. BSI showed the court a copy of JMAM's terms. Across the bottom had been typed a "PS" requiring the return of rejected merchandise. Was this "PS" part of the contract? Discuss. [*B.S. International, Ltd. v. JMAM, LLC*, 13 A.3d 1057 (R.I. 2011)] (See *Formation of Sales and Lease Contracts*.)

17–5. Goods Held by the Seller or Lessor. Douglas Singletary bought a manufactured home from Andy's Mobile Home and Land Sales. The contract stated that the buyer accepted the home "as is where is." Singletary paid the full price, and his crew began to ready the home to relocate it to his property. The night before the home was to be moved, however, it was destroyed by fire. Who suffered the loss? Explain. [*Singletary, III v. P&A Investments, Inc.,* 712 S.E.2d 681 (N.C.App. 2011)] (See *Title and Risk of Loss.*)

17–6. The Statute of Frauds. Kendall Gardner agreed to buy a specially built shaving mill from B&C Shavings. He planned to use the mill to produce wood shavings for poultry processors. B&C faxed an invoice to Gardner reflecting a purchase price of $86,200, with a 30 percent down payment and the "balance due before shipment." Gardner paid the down payment. B&C finished the mill and wrote Gardner a letter telling him to "pay the balance due or you will lose the down payment." By then, Gardner had lost his customers for the wood shavings, could not pay the balance due, and asked for the return of his down payment. Did these parties have an enforceable contract under the Statute of Frauds? Explain. [*Bowen v. Gardner,* 2013 Ark.App. 52, 425 S.W.3d 875 (2013)] (See *The Formation of Sales and Lease Contracts.*)

17–7. Risk of Loss. Ethicon, Inc., a pharmaceutical company, entered into an agreement with UPS Supply Chain Solutions, Inc., to transport pharmaceuticals. The drivers were provided by International Management Services Co. under a contract with a UPS subsidiary, Worldwide Dedicated Services, Inc. During the transport of a shipment from Ethicon's facility in Texas to buyers "F.O.B. Tennessee," one of the trucks collided with a concrete barrier near Little Rock, Arkansas, and caught fire, damaging the goods. Who was liable for the loss? Why? [*Royal & Sun Alliance Insurance, PLC v. International Management Services Co.,* 703 F.3d 604 (2d Cir. 2013)] (See *Title and Risk of Loss.*)

17–8. Goods and Services Combined. Allied Shelving and Equipment, Inc., sells and installs shelving systems. National Deli, LLC, contracted with Allied to provide and install a parallel rack system (a series of large shelves) in National's warehouse. Both parties were dissatisfied with the result. National filed a suit in a Florida state court against Allied, which filed a counterclaim. Each contended that the other had materially breached the contract. The court applied common law contract principles to rule in National's favor on both claims. Allied appealed, arguing that the court should have applied the UCC. When does a court apply common law principles to a contract that involves both goods and services? In this case, why might an appellate court rule that the UCC should be applied instead? Explain. [*Allied Shelving and Equipment, Inc. v. National Deli, LLC,* 40 Fla. L. Weekly D145, 154 So.3d 482 (Dist.App. 2015)] (See *The Scope of Articles 2 and 2A.*)

17–9. A Question of Ethics—Statute of Frauds. Daniel Fox owned Fox & Lamberth Enterprises, Inc., a kitchen remodeling business. Fox leased a building from Carl Hussong. When Fox planned to close his business, Craftsmen Home Improvement, Inc., expressed an interest in buying his assets. Fox set a price of $50,000. Craftsmen's owners agreed and gave Fox a list of the desired items and a "Bill of Sale" that set the terms for payment. Craftsmen expected to negotiate a new lease with Hussong and modified the premises, including removal of some of the displays. When Hussong and Craftsmen could not agree on new terms, Craftsmen told Fox that the deal was off. [*Fox & Lamberth Enterprises, Inc. v. Craftsmen Home Improvement, Inc.,* __ N.E.2d __ (2 Dist. 2006)]

1. In Fox's suit for breach of contract, Craftsmen raised the Statute of Frauds as a defense. What are the requirements of the Statute of Frauds? Did the deal between Fox and Craftsmen meet these requirements? Did it fall under one of the exceptions? Explain. (See *The Formation and of Sales and Lease Contracts.*)

2. Craftsmen also claimed that the "predominant factor" of its agreement with Fox was a lease for Hussong's building. What is the predominant-factor test? Does it apply here? In any event, is it fair to hold a party to a contract to buy a business's assets when the buyer is unable to negotiate a favorable lease of the premises on which the assets are located? Discuss. (See *The Scope of Articles 2 and 2A.*)

Critical Thinking and Writing Assignments

17–10. Business Law Critical Thinking Group Assignment. Mountain Stream Trout Co. agreed to buy "market size" trout from trout grower Lake Farms, LLC. Their five-year contract did not define *market size*. At the time, in the trade, *market size* referred to fish of one-pound live weight. After three years, Mountain Stream began taking fewer, smaller deliveries of larger fish, claiming that *market size* varied according to whatever its customers demanded and that its customers now demanded larger fish. Lake Farms filed a suit for breach of contract. (See *The Formation and of Sales and Lease Contracts.*)

1. The first group will decide whether parol evidence is admissible to explain the terms of this contract. Are there any exceptions that could apply?

2. A second group will determine the impact of course of dealing and usage of trade on the interpretation of contract terms.

3. A third group will discuss how parties to a commercial contract can avoid the possibility that a court will interpret the contract terms in accordance with trade usage.

An Example of a Contract for the International Sale of Coffee

1 OVERLAND COFFEE IMPORT CONTRACT
OF THE
GREEN COFFEE ASSOCIATION
OF
2 NEW YORK CITY, INC.*

Contract Seller's No.: __**504617**__
Buyer's No.: __**P9264**__
Date: __**10/11/17**__

SOLD BY: __**XYZ Co.**__
TO: __**Starbucks**__

3 QUANTITY: __**Five Hundred**__ (**500**) Tons of (Bags) __**Mexican**__ coffee
weighing about __**152.117 lbs.**__ per bag.

PACKAGING: Coffee must be packed in clean sound bags of uniform size made of sisal, henequen, jute, burlap, or similar
4 woven material, without inner lining or outer covering of any material properly sewn by hand and/or machine.
Bulk shipments are allowed if agreed by mutual consent of Buyer and Seller.

DESCRIPTION: __**High grown Mexican Altura**__
5

PRICE: At __**Ten/$10.00 dollars**__ U.S. Currency, per __**lb.**__ net, (U.S. Funds)
Upon delivery in Bonded Public Warehouse at __**Laredo, TX**__
(City and State)

6 PAYMENT: __**Cash against warehouse receipts**__

Bill and tender to DATE when all import requirements and governmental regulations have been satisfied, and
coffee delivered or discharged (as per contract terms). Seller is obliged to give the Buyer two (2) calendar
days free time in Bonded Public Warehouse following but not including date of tender.

7 ARRIVAL: During __**December**__ via __**truck**__
(Period) (Method of Transportation)
from __**Mexico**__ for arrival at __**Laredo, TX, USA**__
(Country of Exportation) (Country of Importation)
Partial shipments permitted.

8 ADVICE OF
ARRIVAL: Advice of arrival with warehouse name and location, together with the quantity, description, marks and place of
entry, must be transmitted directly, or through Seller's Agent/Broker, to the Buyer or his Agent/ Broker. Advice
will be given as soon as known but not later than the fifth business day following arrival at the named warehouse.
Such advice may be given verbally with written confirmation to be sent the same day.

9 WEIGHTS: (1) DELIVERED WEIGHTS: Coffee covered by this contract is to be weighed at location named in tender.
Actual tare to be allowed.
(2) SHIPPING WEIGHTS: Coffee covered by this contract is sold on shipping weights. Any loss in
weight exceeding __**1/2**__ percent at location named in tender is for account of Seller at contract price.
(3) Coffee is to be weighed within fifteen (15) calendar days after tender. Weighing expenses, if any, for
account of __**Seller**__ (Seller or Buyer)

10 MARKINGS: Bags to be branded in English with the name of Country of Origin and otherwise to comply with laws
and regulations of the Country of Importation, in effect at the time of entry, governing marking of import
merchandise. Any expense incurred by failure to comply with these regulations to be borne by
Exporter/Seller.

11 RULINGS: The "Rulings on Coffee Contracts" of the Green Coffee Association of New York City, Inc., in effect on the
date this contract is made, is incorporated for all purposes as a part of this agreement, and together herewith,
constitute the entire contract. No variation or addition hereto shall be valid unless signed by the parties to
the contract.
Seller guarantees that the terms printed on the reverse hereof, which by reference are made a part hereof, are
identical with the terms as printed in By-Laws and Rules of the Green Coffee Association of New
York City, Inc., heretofore adopted.
Exceptions to this guarantee are:

ACCEPTED: COMMISSION TO BE PAID BY:
__**XYZ Co.**__ __**Seller**__
BY ___*Dm*___ Seller
Agent
__**Starbucks**__
BY _____ Buyer
Agent __**ABC Brokerage**__
Broker(s)
12
13 When this contract is executed by a person acting for another, such person hereby represents that he is
fully authorized to commit his principal.

Continues

1 This is a contract for a sale of coffee to be *imported* internationally. If the parties have their principal places of business located in different countries, the contract may be subject to the United Nations Convention on Contracts for the International Sale of Goods (CISG). If the parties' principal places of business are located in the United States, the contract may be subject to the Uniform Commercial Code (UCC).

2 Quantity is one of the most important terms to include in a contract. Without it, a court may not be able to enforce the contract.

3 Weight per unit (bag) can be exactly stated or approximately stated. If it is not so stated, usage of trade in international contracts determines standards of weight.

4 Packaging requirements can be conditions for acceptance and payment. Bulk shipments are not permitted without the consent of the buyer.

5 A description of the coffee and the "Markings" constitute express warranties. International contracts rely more heavily on descriptions and models or samples.

6 Under the UCC, parties may enter into a valid contract even though the price is not set. Under the CISG, a contract must provide for an exact determination of the price.

7 The terms of payment may take one of two forms: credit or cash. Credit terms can be complicated. A cash term can be simple, and payment can be made by any means acceptable in the ordinary course of business (for example, a personal check or a letter of credit). If the seller insists on actual cash, the buyer must be given a reasonable time to get it.

8 *Tender* means the seller has placed goods that conform to the contract at the buyer's disposition. This contract requires that the coffee meet all import regulations and that it be ready for pickup by the buyer at a "Bonded Public Warehouse." (A *bonded warehouse* is a place in which goods can be stored without payment of taxes until the goods are removed.)

9 The delivery date is significant because, if it is not met, the buyer may hold the seller in breach of the contract. Under this contract, the seller is given a "period" within which to deliver the goods, instead of a specific day. The seller is also given some time to rectify goods that do not pass inspection (see the "Guarantee" clause on the second page of the contract).

10 As part of a proper tender, the seller (or its agent) must inform the buyer (or its agent) when the goods have arrived at their destination.

11 In some contracts, delivered and shipping weights can be important. During shipping, some loss can be attributed to the type of goods (spoilage of fresh produce, for example) or to the transportation itself. A seller and buyer can agree on the extent to which either of them will bear such losses.

12 Documents are often incorporated in a contract by reference, because including them word for word can make a contract difficult to read. If the document is later revised, the entire contract might have to be reworked. Documents that are typically incorporated by reference include detailed payment and delivery terms, special provisions, and sets of rules, codes, and standards.

13 In international sales transactions, and for domestic deals involving certain products, brokers are used to form the contracts. When so used, the brokers are entitled to a commission.

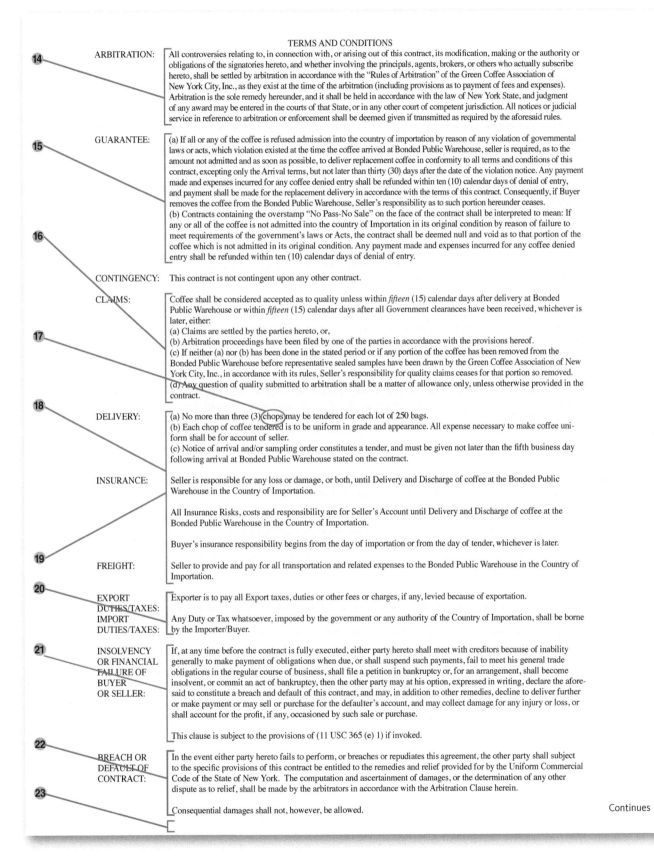

TERMS AND CONDITIONS

14 ARBITRATION: All controversies relating to, in connection with, or arising out of this contract, its modification, making or the authority or obligations of the signatories hereto, and whether involving the principals, agents, brokers, or others who actually subscribe hereto, shall be settled by arbitration in accordance with the "Rules of Arbitration" of the Green Coffee Association of New York City, Inc., as they exist at the time of the arbitration (including provisions as to payment of fees and expenses). Arbitration is the sole remedy hereunder, and it shall be held in accordance with the law of New York State, and judgment of any award may be entered in the courts of that State, or in any other court of competent jurisdiction. All notices or judicial service in reference to arbitration or enforcement shall be deemed given if transmitted as required by the aforesaid rules.

15 GUARANTEE: (a) If all or any of the coffee is refused admission into the country of importation by reason of any violation of governmental laws or acts, which violation existed at the time the coffee arrived at Bonded Public Warehouse, seller is required, as to the amount not admitted and as soon as possible, to deliver replacement coffee in conformity to all terms and conditions of this contract, excepting only the Arrival terms, but not later than thirty (30) days after the date of the violation notice. Any payment made and expenses incurred for any coffee denied entry shall be refunded within ten (10) calendar days of denial of entry, and payment shall be made for the replacement delivery in accordance with the terms of this contract. Consequently, if Buyer removes the coffee from the Bonded Public Warehouse, Seller's responsibility as to such portion hereunder ceases.
(b) Contracts containing the overstamp "No Pass-No Sale" on the face of the contract shall be interpreted to mean: If any or all of the coffee is not admitted into the country of Importation in its original condition by reason of failure to meet requirements of the government's laws or Acts, the contract shall be deemed null and void as to that portion of the coffee which is not admitted in its original condition. Any payment made and expenses incurred for any coffee denied entry shall be refunded within ten (10) calendar days of denial of entry.

16 CONTINGENCY: This contract is not contingent upon any other contract.

17 CLAIMS: Coffee shall be considered accepted as to quality unless within *fifteen* (15) calendar days after delivery at Bonded Public Warehouse or within *fifteen* (15) calendar days after all Government clearances have been received, whichever is later, either:
(a) Claims are settled by the parties hereto, or,
(b) Arbitration proceedings have been filed by one of the parties in accordance with the provisions hereof.
(c) If neither (a) nor (b) has been done in the stated period or if any portion of the coffee has been removed from the Bonded Public Warehouse before representative sealed samples have been drawn by the Green Coffee Association of New York City, Inc., in accordance with its rules, Seller's responsibility for quality claims ceases for that portion so removed.
(d) Any question of quality submitted to arbitration shall be a matter of allowance only, unless otherwise provided in the contract.

18 DELIVERY: (a) No more than three (3) chops may be tendered for each lot of 250 bags.
(b) Each chop of coffee tendered is to be uniform in grade and appearance. All expense necessary to make coffee uniform shall be for account of seller.
(c) Notice of arrival and/or sampling order constitutes a tender, and must be given not later than the fifth business day following arrival at Bonded Public Warehouse stated on the contract.

INSURANCE: Seller is responsible for any loss or damage, or both, until Delivery and Discharge of coffee at the Bonded Public Warehouse in the Country of Importation.

All Insurance Risks, costs and responsibility are for Seller's Account until Delivery and Discharge of coffee at the Bonded Public Warehouse in the Country of Importation.

Buyer's insurance responsibility begins from the day of importation or from the day of tender, whichever is later.

19 FREIGHT: Seller to provide and pay for all transportation and related expenses to the Bonded Public Warehouse in the Country of Importation.

20 EXPORT DUTIES/TAXES: Exporter is to pay all Export taxes, duties or other fees or charges, if any, levied because of exportation.

IMPORT DUTIES/TAXES: Any Duty or Tax whatsoever, imposed by the government or any authority of the Country of Importation, shall be borne by the Importer/Buyer.

21 INSOLVENCY OR FINANCIAL FAILURE OF BUYER OR SELLER: If, at any time before the contract is fully executed, either party hereto shall meet with creditors because of inability generally to make payment of obligations when due, or shall suspend such payments, fail to meet his general trade obligations in the regular course of business, shall file a petition in bankruptcy or, for an arrangement, shall become insolvent, or commit an act of bankruptcy, then the other party may at his option, expressed in writing, declare the aforesaid to constitute a breach and default of this contract, and may, in addition to other remedies, decline to deliver further or make payment or may sell or purchase for the defaulter's account, and may collect damage for any injury or loss, or shall account for the profit, if any, occasioned by such sale or purchase.

This clause is subject to the provisions of (11 USC 365 (e) 1) if invoked.

22 BREACH OR DEFAULT OF CONTRACT: In the event either party hereto fails to perform, or breaches or repudiates this agreement, the other party shall subject to the specific provisions of this contract be entitled to the remedies and relief provided for by the Uniform Commercial Code of the State of New York. The computation and ascertainment of damages, or the determination of any other dispute as to relief, shall be made by the arbitrators in accordance with the Arbitration Clause herein.

23 Consequential damages shall not, however, be allowed.

Continues

14 Arbitration is the settling of a dispute by submitting it to a disinterested party (other than a court), which renders a decision. The procedures and costs can be provided for in an arbitration clause or incorporated through other documents. To enforce an award rendered in an arbitration, the winning party can "enter" (submit) the award in a court "of competent jurisdiction."

15 When goods are imported internationally, they must meet certain import requirements before being released to the buyer. Because of this, buyers frequently want a guaranty clause that covers the goods not admitted into the country and that either requires the seller to replace the goods within a stated time or allows the contract for those goods not admitted to be void.

16 In the "Claims" clause, the parties agree that the buyer has a certain time within which to reject the goods. The right to reject is a right by law and does not need to be stated in a contract. If the buyer does not exercise the right within the time specified in the contract, the goods will be considered accepted.

17 Many international contracts include definitions of terms so that the parties understand what they mean. Some terms are used in a particular industry in a specific way. Here, the word *chop* refers to a unit of like-grade coffee beans. The buyer has a right to inspect ("sample") the coffee. If the coffee does not conform to the contract, the seller must correct the nonconformity.

18 The "Delivery," "Insurance," and "Freight" clauses, with the "Arrival" clause on the first page of the contract, indicate that this is a destination contract. The seller has the obligation to deliver the goods to the destination, not simply deliver them into the hands of a carrier. Under this contract, the destination is a "Bonded Public Warehouse" in a specific location. The seller bears the risk of loss until the goods are delivered at their destination. Typically, the seller will have bought insurance to cover the risk.

19 Delivery terms are commonly placed in all sales contracts. Such terms determine who pays freight and other costs and, in the absence of an agreement specifying otherwise, who bears the risk of loss. International contracts may use these delivery terms, or they may use INCOTERMS, which are published by the International Chamber of Commerce. For example, the INCOTERM DDP (delivered duty paid) requires the seller to arrange shipment, obtain and pay for import or export permits, and get the goods through customs to a named destination.

20 Exported and imported goods are subject to duties, taxes, and other charges imposed by the governments of the countries involved. International contracts spell out who is responsible for these charges.

21 This clause protects a party if the other party should become financially unable to fulfill the obligations under the contract. Thus, if the seller cannot afford to deliver, or the buyer cannot afford to pay, for the stated reasons, the other party can consider the contract breached. This right is subject to "11 USC 365(e)(1)," which refers to a specific provision of the U.S. Bankruptcy Code dealing with executory contracts.

22 In the "Breach or Default of Contract" clause, the parties agree that the remedies under this contract are the remedies (except for consequential damages) provided by the UCC, as in effect in the state of New York. The amount and "ascertainment" of damages, as well as other disputes about relief, are to be determined by arbitration.

23 Three clauses frequently included in international contracts are *omitted* here. There is no choice-of-language clause designating the official language to be used in interpreting the contract terms. There is no choice-of-forum clause designating the place in which disputes will be litigated, except for arbitration (law of New York State). Finally, there is no *force majeure* clause relieving the sellers or buyers from nonperformance due to events beyond their control.

iStockPhoto.com/kupicoo

25

CHAPTER OUTLINE

- Title VII of the Civil Rights Act
- Discrimination Based on Age
- Discrimination Based on Disability
- Defenses to Employment Discrimination
- Affirmative Action

Employment Discrimination

LEARNING OBJECTIVES

The five Learning Objectives *below are designed to help improve your understanding of the chapter. After reading this chapter, you should be able to answer the following questions:*

1. What is required to establish a *prima facie* case of disparate-treatment discrimination?

2. What must an employer do to avoid liability for religious discrimination?

3. What is a constructive discharge? To which employment discrimination claims does the theory of constructive discharge apply?

4. What federal act prohibits discrimination based on age?

5. What are three defenses to claims of employment discrimination?

"Equal rights for all, special privileges for none."

THOMAS JEFFERSON
1743–1826
(THIRD PRESIDENT OF THE UNITED STATES, 1801–1809)

Out of the civil rights movement of the 1960s grew a body of law protecting employees against discrimination in the workplace. Legislation, judicial decisions, and administrative agency actions restrict employers from discriminating against workers on the basis of race, color, religion, national origin, gender, age, or disability. A class of persons defined by one or more of these criteria is known as a **protected class.** The laws designed to protect these individuals embody the sentiment expressed by Thomas Jefferson in the chapter-opening quotation.

The federal statutes discussed in this chapter prohibit *employment discrimination* against members of protected classes. Although this chapter focuses on federal statutes, many states have their own laws that protect employees against discrimination, and some provide more protection to employees than federal laws do.

25-1 Title VII of the Civil Rights Act

The most important statute covering employment discrimination is Title VII of the Civil Rights Act.[1] Title VII prohibits discrimination against employees, applicants, and union members on the basis of race, color, national origin, religion, or gender at any stage of employment.

Title VII applies to employers with fifteen or more employees and labor unions with fifteen or more members. Title VII also applies to labor unions that operate hiring halls (to which

Protected Class A group of persons protected by specific laws because of the group's defining characteristics, including race, color, religion, national origin, gender, age, and disability.

---

1. 42 U.S.C. Sections 2000e–2000e-17.

U.S. Attorney General Robert F. Kennedy met with civil rights leaders in the Rose Garden of the White House in 1964. To what employers does Title VII of the Civil Rights Act apply?

members go regularly to be rationed jobs as they become available), employment agencies, and state and local governing units or agencies. A special section of the act prohibits discrimination in most federal government employment.

25–1a The Equal Employment Opportunity Commission

Compliance with Title VII is monitored by the Equal Employment Opportunity Commission (EEOC). A victim of alleged discrimination must file a claim with the EEOC before bringing a suit against the employer. The EEOC may investigate the dispute and attempt to arrange an out-of-court settlement. If a voluntary agreement cannot be reached, the EEOC may file a suit against the employer on the employee's behalf. If the EEOC decides not to investigate the claim, the EEOC issues a "right to sue" that allows the victim to bring her or his own lawsuit against the employer.

The EEOC does not investigate every claim of employment discrimination, regardless of the merits of the claim. Generally, it investigates only "priority cases," such as cases involving retaliatory discharge (firing an employee in retaliation for submitting a claim to the EEOC) and cases involving types of discrimination that are of particular concern to the EEOC.

25–1b Limitations on Class Actions

The United States Supreme Court issued an important decision in 2011 that limits the rights of employees—as a group, or class—to bring discrimination claims against their employer. **CASE EXAMPLE 25.1** A small group of female employees sued Wal-Mart, the nation's largest private employer, alleging that store managers who had discretion over pay and promotions were biased against women and disproportionately favored men. The employees wished to bring a class action—a lawsuit in which a small number of plaintiffs sue on behalf of a larger group. Lower courts ruled that the employees' class-action suit could proceed, and Wal-Mart appealed. The United States Supreme Court ruled in favor of Wal-Mart, effectively blocking the class action. The Court held that the women could not maintain a class action because they had failed to prove a company-wide policy of discrimination that had a common effect on all women covered by the action.[2]

25–1c Intentional and Unintentional Discrimination

Title VII prohibits both intentional and unintentional discrimination.

Intentional Discrimination   Intentional discrimination by an employer against an employee is known as **disparate-treatment discrimination.** Because intent can be difficult to prove, courts have established certain procedures for resolving disparate-treatment cases.

A plaintiff who sues on the basis of disparate-treatment discrimination in hiring must first make out a *prima facie* **case.** *Prima facie* is Latin for "at first sight." Legally, it refers to a fact that is presumed to be true unless contradicted by evidence.

To establish a *prima facie* case of disparate-treatment discrimination in hiring, a plaintiff must show all of the following:

1. The plaintiff is a member of a protected class.
2. The plaintiff applied and was qualified for the job in question.
3. The plaintiff was rejected by the employer.
4. The employer continued to seek applicants for the position or filled the position with a person not in a protected class.

LEARNING OBJECTIVE 1

What is required to establish a *prima facie* case of disparate-treatment discrimination?

Disparate-Treatment Discrimination A form of employment discrimination that results when an employer intentionally discriminates against employees who are members of protected classes.

***Prima Facie* Case** A case in which the plaintiff has produced sufficient evidence of his or her claim that the case will be decided for the plaintiff unless the defendant produces no evidence to rebut it.

---

2. *Wal-Mart Stores, Inc. v. Dukes,* ___ U.S. ___, 131 S.Ct. 2541, 180 L.Ed.2d 374 (2011).

A plaintiff who can meet these relatively easy requirements has made out a *prima facie* case of illegal discrimination and will win in the absence of a legally acceptable employer defense.

The burden then shifts to the employer-defendant, who must articulate a legal reason for not hiring the plaintiff. If the employer did not have a legal reason for taking the adverse employment action, the plaintiff wins.

If the employer can articulate a legitimate reason for the action, the burden shifts back to the plaintiff. To prevail, the plaintiff must then show that the employer's reason is a *pretext* (not the true reason) and that the employer's decision was actually motivated by discriminatory intent.

Unintentional Discrimination Employers often use interviews and tests to choose from among a large number of applicants for job openings. Minimum educational requirements are also common. These practices and procedures may have an unintended discriminatory impact on a protected class. **Disparate-impact discrimination** occurs when a protected group is adversely affected by an employer's practices, procedures, or tests, even though they do not appear to be discriminatory. (For tips on how human resources managers can prevent these types of discrimination claims, see the *Linking Business Law to Corporate Management* feature at the end of this chapter.)

Disparate-Impact Discrimination Discrimination that results from certain employer practices or procedures that, although not discriminatory on their face, have a discriminatory effect.

In a disparate-impact discrimination case, the complaining party must first show statistically that the employer's practices, procedures, or tests are discriminatory in effect. Once the plaintiff has made out a *prima facie* case, the burden of proof shifts to the employer to show that the practices or procedures in question were justified.

There are two ways of proving that disparate-impact discrimination exists, as discussed next.

Pool of Applicants. A plaintiff can prove a disparate impact by comparing the employer's workforce with the pool of qualified individuals available in the local labor market. The plaintiff must show that (1) as a result of educational or other job requirements or hiring procedures, (2) the percentage of nonwhites, women, or members of other protected classes in the employer's workforce (3) does not reflect the percentage of that group in the pool of qualified applicants. If the plaintiff can show a connection between the practice and the disparity, he or she has made out a *prima facie* case and need not provide evidence of discriminatory intent.

Rate of Hiring. A plaintiff can also prove disparate-impact discrimination by comparing the employer's selection rates of members and nonmembers of a protected class (for instance, whites and nonwhites). When a job requirement or hiring procedure excludes members of a protected class from an employer's workforce at a substantially higher rate than nonmembers, discrimination occurs, regardless of the balance in the employer's workforce.

The EEOC has devised a test, called the "four-fifths rule," to determine whether an employment selection procedure is discriminatory on its face. Under this rule, a selection rate for protected classes that is less than four-fifths, or 80 percent, of the rate for the group with the highest rate will generally be regarded as evidence of disparate impact.

EXAMPLE 25.2 Shady Cove District Fire Department administers an exam to applicants for the position of firefighter. At the exam session, one hundred white applicants take the test, and fifty pass and are hired. At the same exam session, sixty minority applicants take the test, but only twelve pass and are hired. Because twelve is less than four-fifths (80 percent) of fifty, the test will be considered discriminatory under the EEOC guidelines. ■

25-1d Discrimination Based on Race, Color, and National Origin

Title VII prohibits employers from discriminating against employees or job applicants on the basis of race, color, or national origin. If an employer's standards for selecting or promoting employees have a discriminatory effect on job applicants or employees in these protected

How might the "four-fifths rule" apply to the results of a fire department's entrance exam?

classes, then a presumption of illegal discrimination arises. To avoid liability, the employer must then show that its standards have a substantial, demonstrable relationship to realistic qualifications for the job in question.

CASE EXAMPLE 25.3 Jiann Min Chang was an instructor at Alabama Agricultural and Mechanical University (AAMU). When AAMU terminated his employment, Chang filed a lawsuit claiming discrimination based on national origin. Chang established a *prima facie* case because he (1) was a member of a protected class, (2) was qualified for the job, (3) suffered an adverse employment action, and (4) was replaced by someone outside his protected class (a non-Asian instructor).

AAMU, however, showed that Chang had argued with a university vice president and refused to comply with her instructions. The court ruled that the university had not renewed Chang's contract for a legitimate reason—insubordination—and therefore was not liable for unlawful discrimination.[3]

Reverse Discrimination   Note that discrimination based on race can also take the form of *reverse discrimination,* or discrimination against "majority" individuals, such as white males. **EXAMPLE 25.4** An African American woman fires four white men from their management positions at a school district. The men file a lawsuit for reverse discrimination. They argue that the woman was trying to eliminate white males from the district administration in violation of Title VII. The woman claims that the terminations were part of a reorganization plan to cut costs. If the judge (or jury in a jury trial) agrees with the men that they were fired for racially discriminatory reasons, then they will be entitled to damages. If, however, the school district can show that the real reason for the terminations was a legitimate cost-cutting measure, then normally their case will be dismissed. ■

Potential Section 1981 Claims   Victims of racial or ethnic discrimination may also have a cause of action under 42 U.S.C. Section 1981. This section, which was enacted in 1866 to protect the rights of freed slaves, prohibits discrimination on the basis of race or ethnicity in the formation or enforcement of contracts. Because employment is often a contractual relationship, Section 1981 can provide an alternative basis for a plaintiff's action and is potentially advantageous because it does not place a cap on damages.

25–1e Discrimination Based on Religion

Title VII also prohibits government employers, private employers, and unions from discriminating against persons because of their religion. (This chapter's *Adapting the Law to the Online Environment* feature discusses how employers who examine prospective employees' social media posts, including posts concerning religion, might engage in unlawful discrimination.)

Employers cannot treat their employees more or less favorably based on the employees' religious beliefs or practices and cannot require employees to participate in any religious activity (or forbid them from participating in one). **EXAMPLE 25.5** Jason Sewell, a salesperson for TC Chevy, does not attend the weekly prayer meetings of dealership employees for several months. Then he is discharged by his employer. If he can show that the dealership required its employees to attend prayer gatherings and fired him for not attending, he has a valid claim of religious discrimination. ■

Reasonable Accommodation   An employer must "reasonably accommodate" the religious practices of its employees, unless to do so would cause undue hardship to the employer's business. Reasonable accommodation is required even if the employee's belief is not based on the doctrines of a traditionally recognized religion, such as Christianity or Judaism, or a

If this salesperson refuses to attend weekly Christian prayer meetings at the company headquarters, what might happen if he is fired as a consequence?

---

3. *Jiann Min Chang v. Alabama Agricultural and Mechanical University*, 2009 WL 3403180 (11th Cir. 2009).

particular denomination, such as Baptist. The only requirement is that the belief be sincerely held by the employee.

Undue Hardship If an employee's religion prohibits him or her from working on a certain day of the week, for instance, the employer must make a reasonable attempt to accommodate this requirement. The employer is not required to permanently give the employee the requested day off, however, if to do so would cause the employer undue hardship.

CASE EXAMPLE 25.6 Miguel Sánchez-Rodríguez sold cell phones in shopping malls for AT&T. After six years, Sánchez informed his supervisors that he had become a Seventh Day

ADAPTING THE LAW TO THE **ONLINE** ENVIRONMENT
Hiring Discrimination
Based on Social Media Posts

Human resource officers in most companies routinely check job candidates' social media posts when deciding whom to hire. Certainly, every young person is warned not to post photos that they might later regret having made available to potential employers. But a more serious issue involves standard reviewing of job candidates' social media information. Specifically, do employers discriminate based on such information?

An Experiment in Hiring Discrimination via Online Social Networks

Two researchers at Carnegie-Mellon University conducted an experiment to determine whether social media information posted by prospective employees influences employers' hiring decisions.[a] The researchers created false résumés and social media profiles. They submitted job applications on behalf of the fictional "candidates" to about four thousand U.S. employers. They then compared employers' responses to different groups— for example, to Muslim candidates versus Christian candidates.

The researchers found that candidates whose public profiles indicated that they

were Muslim were less likely to be called for interviews than Christian applicants. The difference was particularly pronounced in parts of the country with more conservative residents. In those locations, Muslims received callbacks only 2 percent of the time, compared with 17 percent for Christian applicants. According to the authors of the study, "Hiring discrimination via online searches of candidates may not be widespread, but online disclosures of personal traits can significantly influence the hiring decisions of a self-selected set of employers."

Job Candidates' Perception of the Hiring Process

In another study, researchers at North Carolina State University looked at how job applicants view prospective employers' use of their social media profiles during the hiring process.[b] Job candidates appear to view the hiring process as unfair when they know that their social media profiles have been used in the selection process. This perception, according to the researchers, makes litigation more likely.

The EEOC Speaks Up

Since 2014, the Equal Employment Opportunity Commission (EEOC) has investigated how prospective employers can use social media to engage in discrimination in the hiring process. Given that the Society for Human Resource Management estimates that more than three-fourths of its members use social media in their employment screening process, the EEOC is interested in regulating this procedure. Social media sites, examined closely, can provide information to a prospective employer on the applicant's race, color, national origin, disability, religion, and other protected characteristics. The EEOC has reminded employers that such information—whether it comes from social media postings or other sources—may not legally be used to make employment decisions on prohibited bases, such as race, gender, and religion.

■ Can you think of a way a company could use information from an applicant's social media posts without running the risk of being accused of hiring discrimination?

a. A. Acquisti and C. N. Fong, "An Experiment in Hiring Discrimination Via Online Social Networks," *Social Service Research Network*, October 26, 2014.

b. J. W. Stoughton, L. F. Thompson, and A. W. Meade, "Examining Applicant Reactions to the Use of Social Networking Websites in Pre-Employment Screening," *Journal of Business and Psychology*, November 2013, DOI: 10.1007/s10869-013-9333-6.

Adventist and could no longer work on Saturdays for religious reasons. AT&T responded that his inability to work on Saturdays would cause it hardship.

As a reasonable accommodation, the company suggested that Sánchez swap schedules with others and offered him two other positions that did not require work on Saturdays. Sánchez could not find workers to swap shifts with him, however, and he declined the other jobs because they would result in less income. He began missing work on Saturdays. After a time, AT&T indicated that it would discipline him for any additional Saturdays that he missed. Eventually, he was placed on active disciplinary status. Sánchez resigned and filed a religious discrimination lawsuit against AT&T. The court found in favor of AT&T, and a federal appellate court affirmed. The company had made adequate efforts at accommodation.[4] ■

25-1f Discrimination Based on Gender

Under Title VII, as well as other federal acts, employers are forbidden from discriminating against employees on the basis of gender. Employers are prohibited from classifying jobs as male or female and from advertising positions as male or female unless they can prove that the gender of the applicant is essential to the job. In addition, employers cannot have separate male and female seniority lists and cannot refuse to promote employees based on gender.

Gender Must Be a Determining Factor Generally, to succeed in a suit for gender discrimination, a plaintiff must demonstrate that gender was a determining factor in the employer's decision to fire or refuse to hire or promote her or him. Typically, this involves looking at all of the surrounding circumstances.

CASE EXAMPLE 25.7 Wanda Collier worked for Turner Industries Group, LLC, in the maintenance department. She complained to her supervisor that Jack Daniell, the head of the department, treated her unfairly. Her supervisor told her that Daniell had a problem with her gender and was harder on women. The supervisor talked to Daniell but did not take any disciplinary action.

A month later, Daniell confronted Collier, pushing her up against a wall and berating her. After this incident, Collier filed a formal complaint and kept a male co-worker with her at all times. A month later, she was fired. She subsequently filed a lawsuit alleging gender discrimination. The court concluded that there was enough evidence that gender was a determining factor in Daniell's conduct to allow Collier's claims to go to a jury.[5] ■

Pregnancy Discrimination The Pregnancy Discrimination Act[6] expanded Title VII's definition of gender discrimination to include discrimination based on pregnancy. Women affected by pregnancy, childbirth, or related medical conditions must be treated the same as other persons not so affected but similar in ability to work. For instance, an employer cannot discriminate against a pregnant woman by withholding benefits available to others under employee benefit programs.

In the following case, an employer accommodated many of its employees who had lifting restrictions due to disabilities. The employer refused to accommodate a pregnant employee with a similar restriction. Did this refusal constitute a violation of the Pregnancy Discrimination Act?

> "A sign that says 'men only' looks very different on a bathroom door than a courthouse door."
>
> **THURGOOD MARSHALL**
> 1908–1993
> (ASSOCIATE JUSTICE OF THE UNITED STATES SUPREME COURT, 1967–1991)

4. *Sánchez-Rodríguez v. AT&T Mobility Puerto Rico, Inc.*, 673 F.3d 1 (1st Cir. 2012).
5. *Collier v. Turner Industries Group, LLC*, 797 F.Supp.2d 1029 (D. Idaho 2011).
6. 42 U.S.C. Section 2000e(k).

CASE 25.1

Young v. United Parcel Service, Inc.

United States Supreme Court, __ U.S. __, 135 S.Ct. 1338, __ L.Ed.2d __ (2015).

FACTS Peggy Young was a driver for United Parcel Service, Inc. (UPS). When she became pregnant, her doctor advised her not to lift more than twenty pounds. UPS required drivers to lift up to seventy pounds and told Young that she could not work under a lifting restriction. She filed a suit in a federal district court against UPS, claiming an unlawful refusal to accommodate her pregnancy-related lifting restriction. She alleged that UPS had multiple light-duty-for-injury categories to accommodate individuals whose non-pregnancy-related

Is UPS required to offer a pregnant employee a less physically demanding job?

disabilities created work restrictions similar to hers. UPS responded that, because Young did not fall into any of those categories, it had not discriminated against her. The court issued a summary judgment in UPS's favor. The U.S. Court of Appeals of the Fourth Circuit affirmed the judgment. Young appealed to the United States Supreme Court.

ISSUE Did Young create a genuine dispute as to whether UPS provided more favorable treatment to employees whose situation could not reasonably be distinguished from hers?

DECISION Yes. The United States Supreme Court vacated the judgment of the U.S. Court of Appeals for the Fourth Circuit and remanded the case for further proceedings. On remand, the court must also determine whether Young created a genuine issue of material fact as

to whether UPS's stated reasons for treating Young less favorably were a pretext.

REASON In an action under the Pregnancy Discrimination Act, a plaintiff creates a genuine issue of material fact as to whether an employer's policies impose a significant burden on pregnant employees by providing evidence that the employer accommodates non-pregnant workers while failing to accommodate pregnant workers. In this case, if Young's allegations are true, she can show that UPS accommodates non-pregnant employees with lifting restrictions and does not accommodate pregnant employees with similar limitations. This showing would establish a *prima facie* case of disparate treatment. In response to UPS's defense, Young can point out the fact that the employer has multiple policies to accommodate non-pregnant employees with lifting restrictions. This fact might suggest that UPS's reasons for not accommodating pregnant employees with lifting restrictions are weak—"to the point that a jury could find that its reasons for failing to accommodate pregnant employees give rise to an inference of intentional discrimination."

CRITICAL THINKING—Legal Consideration *Could UPS have succeeded in this case if it had claimed simply that it would be more expensive or less convenient to include pregnant women among those whom it accommodates? Explain.*

Wage Discrimination

The Equal Pay Act of 1963 requires equal pay for male and female employees doing similar work at the same establishment. To determine whether the Equal Pay Act has been violated, a court will look to the primary duties of the two jobs—the job content rather than the job description controls. If the wage differential is due to "any factor other than gender," such as a seniority or merit system, then it does not violate the Equal Pay Act.

In 2009, Congress enacted the Lilly Ledbetter Fair Pay Act,[7] which made discriminatory wages actionable under federal law regardless of when the discrimination began. This act overturned a previous decision by the United States Supreme Court that had limited plaintiffs' time period for filing a wage discrimination complaint to 180 days after the employer's decision.[8] Today, if a plaintiff continues to work for the employer while receiving discriminatory wages, the time period for filing a complaint is basically unlimited.

How did the Lilly Ledbetter Fair Pay Act, signed by President Obama, change the time period for filing a claim of wage discrimination?

---

7. Pub. L. No. 111-2, 123 Stat. 5 (January 5, 2009), amending 42 U.S.C. Section 2000e-5[e].
8. *Ledbetter v. Goodyear Tire Co.*, 550 U.S. 618, 127 S.Ct. 2162, 167 L.Ed.2d 982 (2007).

ETHICAL ISSUE

Should corporations be forced to publicize the ratio of CEO-to-worker pay? As part of wide-ranging changes in U.S. financial regulation, the Dodd-Frank Wall Street Reform and Consumer Protection Act[9] set forth new rules intended to hold corporate executives more accountable for their companies' performance. The Securities and Exchange Commission (SEC) was tasked with creating a regulation that forces certain companies not only to disclose how much the chief executive officer (CEO) makes, but also to establish a ratio of that pay to the median pay of the workforce. For example, if the median employee makes $45,790 and the CEO makes $12,260,000, then the pay ratio is 1 to 268. Otherwise stated, the CEO's total compensation is 268 times that of the median annual compensation for all employees.

In announcing this rule, the SEC indicated that it was unsure what potential economic benefits, "if any," would be realized from making this information public. The SEC estimates that the regulation will cost companies, in total, almost 550,000 annual paperwork hours, plus about $75 million per year to hire outside professionals. Supporters of the new regulation, however, argue that it will help investors evaluate the relative value a CEO creates. In other words, pay ratio information is supposed to act as a check against insiders paying themselves "too much."

LEARNING OBJECTIVE 3

What is a constructive discharge? To which employment discrimination claims does the theory of constructive discharge apply?

Constructive Discharge
A termination of employment brought about by making the employee's working conditions so intolerable that the employee reasonably feels compelled to leave.

25–1g Constructive Discharge

The majority of Title VII complaints involve unlawful discrimination in decisions to hire or fire employees. In some situations, however, employees who leave their jobs voluntarily can claim that they were "constructively discharged" by the employer. **Constructive discharge** occurs when the employer causes the employee's working conditions to be so intolerable that a reasonable person in the employee's position would feel compelled to quit.

Proving Constructive Discharge To prove constructive discharge, an employee must present objective proof of intolerable working conditions. The employee must also show that the employer knew or had reason to know about the conditions yet failed to correct them within a reasonable period. In addition, courts generally require the employee to show causation—that the employer's unlawful discrimination caused the working conditions to be intolerable. Put in a different way, the employee's resignation must be a foreseeable result of the employer's discriminatory action.

Although courts weigh the facts on a case-by-case basis, employee demotion is one of the most frequently cited reasons for a finding of constructive discharge, particularly when the employee was subjected to humiliation. **EXAMPLE 25.8** Khalil's employer humiliates him in front of his co-workers by informing him that he is being demoted to an inferior position. Khalil's co-workers continually insult and harass him about his national origin (he is from Iran). The employer is aware of this discriminatory treatment but does nothing to remedy the situation, despite repeated complaints from Khalil. After several months, Khalil quits his job and files a Title VII claim. In this situation, Khalil would likely have sufficient evidence to maintain an action for constructive discharge in violation of Title VII. ■

Applies to All Title VII Discrimination Note that constructive discharge is a theory that plaintiffs can use to establish any type of discrimination claims under Title VII, including race, color, national origin, religion, gender, pregnancy, and sexual harassment. Constructive discharge has also been successfully used in situations involving discrimination based on age or disability, although it is most commonly asserted in sexual harassment cases.

When constructive discharge is claimed, the employee can pursue damages for loss of income, including back pay. These damages ordinarily are not available to an employee who left a job voluntarily.

---

9. Pub. L. No. 111-203, 124 Stat. 1376, 2010 H.R. 4173.

25-1h Sexual Harassment

Title VII also protects employees against **sexual harassment** in the workplace. Sexual harassment can take two forms: *quid pro quo* harassment and hostile-environment harassment.

Quid pro quo is a Latin phrase that is often translated to mean "something in exchange for something else." *Quid pro quo* harassment occurs when sexual favors are demanded in return for job opportunities, promotions, salary increases, and the like.

Hostile-environment harassment occurs when a pattern of sexually offensive conduct permeates the workplace and is sufficiently severe or pervasive to alter the conditions of employment and create an abusive working environment. Some sexual behavior may be acceptable in certain contexts, but unacceptable in others. Therefore, the courts evaluate hostile environment claims on a case-by-case basis.

A court considers a number of factors in assessing the severity and pervasiveness of the alleged sexual harassment. As the following case shows, these factors include the nature and frequency of the conduct and whether it unreasonably interfered with the victim's work performance.

Sexual Harassment
The demanding of sexual favors in return for job promotions or other benefits, or language or conduct that is so sexually offensive that it creates a hostile working environment.

"Sexual harassment at work: Is it a problem for the self-employed?"

VICTORIA WOOD
1953–PRESENT
(ENGLISH COMEDIAN AND ACTOR)

CASE 25.2

Roberts v. Mike's Trucking, Ltd.
Court of Appeals of Ohio, Twelfth District, 9 N.E.3d 483 (2014).

FACTS Teresa Roberts worked for Mike's Trucking, Ltd., in Columbus, Ohio. Her supervisor was the company's owner, Mike Culbertson. According to Roberts, Culbertson called her his "sexretary" and constantly talked about his sex life. He often invited her to sit on "Big Daddy's" lap, rubbed against her, trapped her at the door and asked her for hugs or kisses, and inquired if she needed help in the restroom. Roberts asked him to stop this conduct, but he did not. She became less productive and began to suffer anxiety attacks and high blood pressure. Roberts filed a suit in an Ohio state court against Mike's, alleging a hostile work environment through sexual harassment in violation of Title VII. A jury decided in Roberts's favor, and Mike's appealed.

ISSUE Was Culbertson's conduct sufficiently severe or pervasive to create a hostile work environment through sexual harassment in violation of Title VII?

DECISION Yes. A state intermediate appellate court affirmed the lower court's judgment in Roberts's favor. "There was sufficient and substantial evidence to support the jury's finding that a reasonable person would find Culbertson's conduct created a hostile environment and Roberts found the conduct to be sufficiently severe or pervasive to affect her employment."

Can the constant sexual banter by the owner of a trucking company create a hostile work environment for employees?

REASON To conclude that conduct is severe or pervasive enough to create a hostile or abusive work environment requires a determination that (1) a reasonable person would find the environment objectively hostile and (2) the plaintiff did subjectively find the conduct severe or pervasive.

In this case, the testimony of other company employees and Roberts's fiancé corroborated her account. The witnesses confirmed that Culbertson frequently engaged in conduct ranging from inappropriate discussions to groping women. He talked about his sex life. He asked Roberts and other female employees if they needed help in the restroom. He asked them to sit in "Big Daddy's" lap. The witnesses also confirmed that Culbertson's behavior became worse over time. Additionally, Roberts's testimony that she did not want to go to work anymore, became less productive, and suffered anxiety attacks established that Culbertson's conduct unreasonably interfered with her work performance. Her fiancé confirmed that she had lost confidence in her ability to perform her job.

CRITICAL THINKING—Ethical Consideration *Was Culbertson's conduct at any point unethical? Discuss.*

Tangible Employment Action A significant change in employment status or benefits, such as occurs when an employee is fired, refused a promotion, or reassigned to a lesser position.

Harassment by Supervisors

For an employer to be held liable for a supervisor's sexual harassment, the supervisor normally must have taken a *tangible employment action* against the employee. A **tangible employment action** is a significant change in employment status or benefits, such as when an employee is fired, refused a promotion, demoted, or reassigned to a position with significantly different responsibilities. Only a supervisor, or another person acting with the authority of the employer, can cause this sort of injury. A constructive discharge also qualifies as a tangible employment action.

The United States Supreme Court has issued several important rulings in cases alleging sexual harassment by supervisors that established what is known as the "*Ellerth/Faragher* affirmative defense."[10] The defense has two elements:

1. That the employer has taken reasonable care to prevent and promptly correct any sexually harassing behavior (by establishing effective antiharassment policies and complaint procedures, for example).

2. That the plaintiff-employee unreasonably failed to take advantage of any preventive or corrective opportunities provided by the employer to avoid harm.

An employer that can prove both elements will not be liable for a supervisor's harassment.

PREVENTING LEGAL DISPUTES

To avoid sexual-harassment complaints, you should be proactive in preventing sexual harassment in the workplace. Establish written policies, distribute them to employees, and review them annually. Make it clear that the policies prohibiting harassment and discrimination apply to everyone at all levels of your organization. Provide training. Assure employees that no one will be punished for making a complaint. If you receive complaints, always take them seriously and investigate—no matter how trivial they might seem.

Prompt remedial action is key, but normally it must not include any adverse action against the complainant (such as immediate termination). Also, never discourage employees from seeking the assistance of government agencies (such as the EEOC) or threaten or punish them for doing so. It is generally best to obtain the advice of counsel when you receive a sexual-harassment complaint.

Why is a tangible employment action required for a company to be held liable for harassment by supervisors?

Retaliation by Employers

Employers sometimes retaliate against employees who complain about sexual harassment or other Title VII violations. Retaliation can take many forms. An employer might demote or fire the person, or otherwise change the terms, conditions, and benefits of employment. Title VII prohibits retaliation, and employees can sue their employers on that basis.

In a *retaliation claim,* an individual asserts that she or he has suffered a harm as a result of making a charge, testifying, or participating in a Title VII investigation or proceeding. Plaintiffs do not have to prove that the challenged action adversely affected their workplace or employment. Instead, to prove retaliation, plaintiffs must show that the challenged action was one that would likely have dissuaded a reasonable worker from making or supporting a charge of discrimination.

Title VII's retaliation protection has been extended to an employee who spoke out about discrimination during an employer's internal investigation of another employee's complaint.[11] The retaliation provision has also protected an employee who was fired after his fiancée filed a gender discrimination claim against their employer.[12]

---

10. *Burlington Industries, Inc. v. Ellerth*, 524 U.S. 742, 118 S.Ct. 2257, 141 L.Ed.2d 633 (1998); and *Faragher v. City of Boca Raton*, 524 U.S. 775, 118 S.Ct. 2275, 141 L.Ed.2d 662 (1998).
11. See *Crawford v. Metropolitan Government of Nashville and Davidson County, Tennessee*, 555 U.S. 271, 129 S.Ct. 846, 172 L.Ed.2d 650 (2009).
12. See *Thompson v. North American Stainless, LP*, 562 U.S. 170, 131 S.Ct. 863, 178 L.Ed.2d 694 (2011).

In the following case, a female law professor lost her job after she complained about comments made by her dean and colleagues. The court had to decide whether her employer had retaliated against her for engaging in protected conduct.

CASE 25.3

Morales-Cruz v. University of Puerto Rico

United States Court of Appeals, First Circuit, 676 F.3d 220 (2012).

FACTS In 2003, Myrta Morales-Cruz began a tenure-track teaching position at the University of Puerto Rico School of Law. During her five-year probationary period, one of her colleagues in a law school clinic had an affair with one of their students that resulted in a pregnancy. Morales-Cruz did not report the affair, but no university rule required her to do so.

In 2008, Morales-Cruz asked the university's administrative committee to approve a one-year extension for her tenure review. The law school's dean criticized Morales-Cruz for failing to report her colleague's affair. He later recommended granting the extension but called Morales-Cruz "insecure," "immature," and "fragile." Similarly, a law school committee recommended granting the extension, but a dissenting professor commented that Morales-Cruz had shown poor judgment, had "personality flaws," and had trouble with "complex and sensitive" situations.

Morales-Cruz soon learned about the negative comments and complained in writing to the university's chancellor. The dean then recommended denying the one-year extension, and the administrative committee ultimately did so. When her employment was terminated, Morales-Cruz sued the university under Title VII. Among other things, she asserted that the dean had retaliated against her for complaining to the chancellor. A federal district court found that Morales-Cruz had not stated a proper retaliation claim under Title VII, and she appealed.

When a university does not renew an instructor's employment contract after she complains about a supervisor's criticisms of her, can she sue for retaliation?

ISSUE Can Morales-Cruz bring a retaliation claim under Title VII because the law school's dean retaliated against her for complaining to the university's chancellor?

DECISION No. The appellate court affirmed the district court's judgment for the University of Puerto Rico.

REASON Under Title VII, an employer may not retaliate against an employee because he or she has opposed a practice prohibited by Title VII. In this case, Morales-Cruz argued that the dean had recommended not granting the one-year extension because she had complained about "discriminatory" comments. The court found that Morales-Cruz did not allege any facts that could be construed as gender-based discrimination. While the comments were hardly flattering, they were entirely gender-neutral. After all, the dean and the dissenting professor had said only that Morales-Cruz had showed poor judgment, had personality flaws, and was fragile, insecure, and immature. Thus, even if the dean had retaliated against Morales-Cruz, it was not for engaging in conduct protected by Title VII.

CRITICAL THINKING—Ethical Consideration *Could the dean have had legitimate reasons for changing his mind about the one-year extension? If so, what were they?*

Harassment by Co-Workers and Nonemployees

When the harassment of co-workers, rather than supervisors, creates a hostile working environment, an employee may still have a cause of action against the employer. Normally, though, the employer will be held liable only if the employer knew, or should have known, about the harassment and failed to take immediate remedial action.

Occasionally, a court may also hold an employer liable for harassment by *nonemployees* if the employer knew about the harassment and failed to take corrective action. **EXAMPLE 25.9** Gordon, who owns and manages a Great Bites restaurant, knows that one of his regular customers, Dean, repeatedly harasses Sharon, a waitress. If Gordon does nothing and permits the harassment to continue, he may be liable under Title VII even though Dean is not an employee of the restaurant. ■

Same-Gender Harassment In *Oncale v. Sundowner Offshore Services, Inc.,*[13] the United States Supreme Court held that Title VII protection extends to individuals who are sexually harassed by members of the same gender. Proving that the harassment in same-gender cases is "based on sex" can be difficult, though. It is usually easier to establish a case of same-gender harassment when the harasser is homosexual.

Sexual Orientation Harassment Although federal law (Title VII) does not prohibit discrimination or harassment based on a person's sexual orientation, a growing number of states have enacted laws that prohibit sexual orientation discrimination in private employment. Some states, such as Michigan, explicitly prohibit discrimination based on a person's gender identity or expression. Also, many companies have voluntarily established nondiscrimination policies that include sexual orientation.

Workers in the United States often have more protection against sexual harassment in the workplace than workers in other countries, as this chapter's *Beyond Our Borders* feature explains.

25–1i Online Harassment

Employees' online activities can create a hostile working environment in many ways. Racial jokes, ethnic slurs, or other comments contained in e-mail, text or instant messages, or social media or blog posts can become the basis for a claim of hostile-environment harassment or other forms of discrimination. Similarly, a worker who regularly sees sexually explicit and offensive images on a co-worker's computer screen or tablet device may claim that they create a hostile working environment.

Nevertheless, employers may be able to avoid liability for online harassment if they take prompt remedial action. **EXAMPLE 25.10** While working at TriCom, Shonda Dean receives racially harassing e-mailed jokes from another employee. Shortly afterward, the company issues a warning to the offending employee about the proper use of the e-mail system and holds two meetings to discuss company policy on the use of the system. If Dean sues TriCom

---

13. 523 U.S. 75, 118 S.Ct. 998, 140 L.Ed.2d 207 (1998).

BEYOND OUR BORDERS Sexual Harassment in Other Nations

The problem of sexual harassment in the workplace is not confined to the United States. Indeed, it is a worldwide problem for female workers.

In Argentina, Brazil, Egypt, Turkey, and many other countries, there is no legal protection against any form of employment discrimination. Even in countries that do have laws prohibiting discriminatory employment practices, including gender-based discrimination, those laws often do not specifically include sexual harassment as a discriminatory practice.

Several countries have attempted to remedy this omission by passing new laws or amending others to specifically prohibit sexual harassment in the workplace. Japan, for example, has amended its Equal Employment Opportunity Law to include a provision making sexual harassment illegal. Thailand has also passed a sexual-harassment law. The European Union has adopted a directive that specifically identifies sexual harassment as a form of discrimination.

Nevertheless, women's groups throughout Europe contend that corporations in European countries tend to view sexual harassment with "quiet tolerance." They contrast this attitude with that of most U.S. corporations, which have implemented specific procedures to deal with harassment claims.

CRITICAL THINKING

■ Why do you think U.S. corporations are more aggressive than European companies in taking steps to prevent sexual harassment in the workplace?

for racial discrimination, a court may find that because the employer took prompt remedial action, TriCom should not be held liable for its employee's racially harassing e-mails. ■

25–1j Remedies under Title VII

Employer liability under Title VII may be extensive. If the plaintiff successfully proves that unlawful discrimination occurred, he or she may be awarded reinstatement, back pay, retroactive promotions, and damages. Compensatory damages are available only in cases of intentional discrimination. Punitive damages may be recovered against a private employer only if the employer acted with malice or reckless indifference to an individual's rights.

The statute limits the total amount of compensatory and punitive damages that the plaintiff can recover from specific employers, depending on the size of the employer. The cap ranges from $50,000 for employers with one hundred or fewer employees to $300,000 for employers with more than five hundred employees.

iStockPhoto.com/sturti

If this employee receives racially harassing e-mail jokes from another employee, why might she not prevail in a lawsuit for racial discrimination?

25–2 Discrimination Based on Age

LEARNING OBJECTIVE 4
What federal act prohibits discrimination based on age?

Age discrimination is potentially the most widespread form of discrimination, because anyone—regardless of race, color, national origin, or gender—could eventually be a victim. The Age Discrimination in Employment Act (ADEA)[14] prohibits employment discrimination on the basis of age against individuals forty years of age or older. The act also prohibits mandatory retirement for nonmanagerial workers.

For the act to apply, an employer must have twenty or more employees, and the employer's business activities must affect interstate commerce. The EEOC administers the ADEA, but the act also permits private causes of action against employers for age discrimination.

The ADEA includes a provision that extends protections against age discrimination to federal government employees.[15] This provision encompasses not only claims of age discrimination, but also claims of retaliation for complaining about age discrimination, which are not specifically mentioned in the statute.[16] Thus, the ADEA protects federal and private-sector employees from retaliation based on age-related complaints.

25–2a Procedures under the ADEA

The burden-shifting procedure under the ADEA differs from the procedure under Title VII as a result of a United States Supreme Court decision that dramatically changed the burden of proof in age discrimination cases.[17] As explained earlier, if the plaintiff in a Title VII case can show that the employer was motivated, at least in part, by unlawful discrimination, the burden of proof shifts to the employer to articulate a legitimate nondiscriminatory reason. Thus, in cases in which the employer has a "mixed motive" for discharging an employee, the employer has the burden of proving its reason was legitimate.

Under the ADEA, in contrast, a plaintiff must show that the unlawful discrimination was not just a reason but *the* reason for the adverse employment action. In other words, the employee has the burden of establishing "but for" causation—but for the plaintiff's age, the adverse action would not have happened.

---

14. 29 U.S.C. Sections 621–634.
15. See 29 U.S.C. Section 632(a) (2000 ed., Supp. V).
16. *Gomez-Perez v. Potter*, 553 U.S. 474, 128 S.Ct. 1931, 170 L.Ed.2d 887 (2008).
17. *Gross v. FBL Financial Services*, 557 U.S. 167, 129 S.Ct. 2343, 174 L.Ed.2d 119 (2009).

Prima Facie **Age Discrimination Case**   To establish a *prima facie* case, the plaintiff must show that he or she was the following:

1. A member of the protected age group.

2. Qualified for the position from which he or she was discharged.

3. Discharged because of age discrimination.

Then the burden shifts to the employer to give a legitimate nondiscriminatory reason for the adverse action.

Pretext   If the employer offers a legitimate reason for its action, then the plaintiff must show that the stated reason is only a pretext and that the plaintiff's age was the real reason for the employer's decision.

> "Growing old is like being increasingly penalized for a crime you have not committed."
>
> **ANTHONY POWELL**
> 1905–2000
> (ENGLISH NOVELIST)

CASE EXAMPLE 25.11 Josephine Mora, a fund-raiser for Jackson Memorial Foundation, Inc., was sixty-two years old when the foundation's chief executive officer (CEO) fired her. Mora filed an age discrimination suit against the foundation. She asserted that when she was fired, the CEO told her, "I need someone younger I can pay less." A witness heard that statement and also heard the CEO say that Mora was "too old to be working here anyway." The CEO denied making these statements, and the foundation claimed that Mora was terminated for poor job performance.

A district court granted a summary judgment in the foundation's favor, and Mora appealed. A federal appellate court reversed, concluding that the lower court's analysis of causation was incorrect. The court held that a reasonable juror could have accepted that the CEO had made discriminatory remarks and could have found that these remarks were sufficient evidence of a discriminatory motive. If so, that could show that Mora was fired because of her age. The court therefore remanded the case back to the lower court for a trial.[18] ▨

25–2b State Employees Not Covered by the ADEA

When is firing an older worker considered age discrimination?

Generally, the states are immune from lawsuits brought by private individuals in federal court, unless a state consents to the suit. This immunity stems from the United States Supreme Court's interpretation of the Eleventh Amendment (the text of this amendment is included in Appendix B of this text).

State immunity under the Eleventh Amendment is not absolute, however. In some situations, such as when fundamental rights are at stake, Congress has the power to abrogate (revoke) state immunity to private suits through legislation that unequivocally shows Congress's intent to subject states to private suits.[19]

Generally, state employers are immune from private suits brought by employees under the ADEA (for age discrimination), the Americans with Disabilities Act (for disability discrimination), and the Fair Labor Standards Act (which relates to wages and hours). In contrast, states are not immune from the requirements of the Family and Medical Leave Act.

25–3 Discrimination Based on Disability

The Americans with Disabilities Act (ADA)[20] prohibits disability-based discrimination in workplaces with fifteen or more workers (with the exception of state government employers, who are generally immune under the Eleventh Amendment, as just discussed). Basically, the

---

18. *Mora v. Jackson Memorial Foundation, Inc.*, 597 F.3d 1201 (2010).
19. *Tennessee v. Lane*, 541 U.S. 509, 124 S.Ct. 1978, 158 L.Ed.2d 820 (2004).
20. 42 U.S.C. Sections 12102–12118.

ADA requires that employers reasonably accommodate the needs of persons with disabilities unless to do so would cause undue hardship. The ADA Amendments Act broadened the ADA's coverage.[21]

25-3a Procedures under the ADA

To prevail on a claim under the ADA, a plaintiff must show all of the following:

1. The plaintiff has a disability.

2. The plaintiff is otherwise qualified for the employment in question.

3. The plaintiff was excluded from the employment solely because of the disability.

As in Title VII cases, a plaintiff must pursue her or his claim through the EEOC before filing an action in court for a violation of the ADA.

The EEOC may decide to investigate and perhaps even sue the employer on behalf of the employee. If the EEOC decides not to sue, then the employee is entitled to sue in court. The EEOC can bring a suit against an employer for disability-based discrimination even though the employee previously agreed to submit any job-related disputes to arbitration.

Plaintiffs in lawsuits brought under the ADA may obtain many of the same remedies available under Title VII. These include reinstatement, back pay, a limited amount of compensatory and punitive damages (for intentional discrimination), and certain other forms of relief. Repeat violators may be ordered to pay fines of up to $100,000.

25-3b What Is a Disability?

The ADA is broadly drafted to cover persons with a wide range of disabilities. Specifically, the ADA defines *disability* to include any of the following:

1. A physical or mental impairment that substantially limits one or more of an individual's major life activities.

2. A record of such impairment.

3. Being regarded as having such an impairment.

Health conditions that have been considered disabilities under the federal law include alcoholism, acquired immune deficiency syndrome (AIDS), blindness, cancer, cerebral palsy, diabetes, heart disease, muscular dystrophy, and paraplegia. Testing positive for the human immunodeficiency virus (HIV) and morbid obesity (defined as existing when an individual's weight is two times the normal weight for his or her height) have also qualified as disabilities.

Association with Disabled Persons A separate provision in the ADA prevents employers from taking adverse employment actions based on stereotypes or assumptions about individuals who associate with people who have disabilities.[22] **EXAMPLE 25.12** Joan, an employer, refuses to hire Edward, who has a daughter with a physical disability. She bases her decision on the assumption that because of his daughter's disability, Edward will miss work too often or be unreliable. Edward can sue Joan for violating the ADA's provisions. ■

Mitigating Measures At one time, the courts focused on whether a person was disabled *after* the use of corrective devices or medication. Then Congress amended the ADA to strengthen its protections and prohibit employers from considering mitigating measures, such as medications, when determining if an individual has a disability.

"Jobs are physically easier, but the worker now takes home worries instead of an aching back."

HOMER BIGART
1907–1991
(AMERICAN JOURNALIST)

---

21. 42 U.S.C. Sections 12103 and 12205a.
22. 42 U.S.C. Section 12112(b)(4)

Disability is now determined on a case-by-case basis. A condition may fit the definition of disability in one set of circumstances, but not in another. **CASE EXAMPLE 25.13** Larry Rohr, a welding specialist for a power district in Arizona, was diagnosed with type 2 diabetes. If he fails to follow a complex regimen of daily insulin injections and blood tests, as well as a strict diet, his blood sugar will rise to a level that aggravates his disease. Therefore, Rohr's physician forbade him from taking work assignments that involved overnight, out-of-town travel, which were common in his job.

Because of these limitations, the power district asked him to transfer, apply for disability, or take early retirement. Rohr sued for disability discrimination. The lower court granted summary judgment for the employer. Rohr appealed. A federal appellate court reversed. The court held that under the amended ADA, diabetes is a disability if it significantly restricts an individual's eating (a major life activity), as it did for Rohr. Therefore, Rohr was entitled to a trial on his discrimination claim.[23] ▨

This welding specialist suffers from type 2 diabetes and therefore can't travel overnight because of his need for injections, blood tests, and a strict diet. Can his employer force him to take early retirement?

Disclosure of Confidential Medical Information ADA provisions also require employers to keep their employees' medical information confidential.[24] An employee who discovers that an employer has disclosed his or her confidential medical information has a right to sue the employer—even if the employee was not technically disabled.

Employers can expect lawsuits if an employee makes a Facebook post about an injury sustained by someone else in the company. **CASE EXAMPLE 25.14** George Shoun was working at his job at Best Formed Plastics, Inc., when he fell and injured his shoulder. Another Best Formed employee, Jane Stewart, prepared an accident report for the incident and processed Shoun's workers' compensation claim. As a result of the injury, Shoun had to take several months off work and received workers' compensation.

Stewart posted on her Facebook page a statement about how Shoun's shoulder injury "kept him away from work for 11 months and now he is trying to sue us." Shoun sued Best Formed under the ADA for wrongfully disclosing confidential information about his medical condition to other people via Facebook. He claimed the action resulted in loss of employment and impairment of his earning capacity. The court allowed Shoun's claim to go forward to trial.[25] ▨

25-3c Reasonable Accommodation

The ADA does not require that employers accommodate the needs of job applicants or employees with disabilities who are not otherwise qualified for the work. If a job applicant or an employee with a disability can perform essential job functions with a reasonable accommodation, however, the employer must make the accommodation.

Required modifications may include installing ramps for a wheelchair, establishing more flexible working hours, creating or modifying job assignments, and creating or improving training materials and procedures. Generally, employers should give primary consideration to employees' preferences in deciding what accommodations should be made.

Undue Hardship Employers who do not accommodate the needs of persons with disabilities must demonstrate that the accommodations will cause "undue hardship" in terms of being significantly difficult or expensive for the employer. Usually, the courts decide whether an accommodation constitutes an undue hardship on a case-by-case basis by looking at the employer's resources in relation to the specific accommodation.

---

23. *Rohr v. Salt River Project Agricultural Improvement and Power District*, 555 F.3d 850 (9th Cir. 2009).
24. 42 U.S.C. Sections 12112(d)(3)(B), (C), and 12112(d)(4)(C).
25. *Shoun v. Best Formed Plastics, Inc.*, 28 F.Supp.3d 786 (N.D.Ind. 2014).

EXAMPLE 25.15 Bryan Lockhart, who uses a wheelchair, works for a cell phone company that provides parking for its employees. Lockhart informs company supervisors that the parking spaces are so narrow that he is unable to extend the ramp that allows him to get in and out of his van. Lockhart requests that the company reasonably accommodate his needs by paying a monthly fee for him to use a larger parking space in an adjacent lot. In this situation, a court would likely find that it would not be an undue hardship for the employer to pay for additional parking for Lockhart. ■

Job Applications and Preemployment Physical Exams Employers must modify their job-application process so that those with disabilities can compete for jobs with those who do not have disabilities. For instance, a job announcement might be modified to allow job applicants to respond by e-mail or letter, as well as by telephone, so that it does not discriminate against potential applicants with hearing impairments.

Employers are restricted in the kinds of questions they may ask on job-application forms and during preemployment interviews. Furthermore, they cannot require persons with disabilities to submit to preemployment physicals unless such exams are required of all other applicants. Employers can condition an offer of employment on the applicant's successfully passing a medical examination, but can disqualify the applicant only if the medical problems discovered would render the applicant unable to perform the job.

Substance Abuse Drug addiction is a disability under the ADA because drug addiction is a substantially limiting impairment. Those who are actually using illegal drugs are not protected by the act, however. The ADA protects only persons with *former* drug addictions—those who have completed or are now in a supervised drug-rehabilitation program. Individuals who have used drugs casually in the past are not protected under the act. They are not considered addicts and therefore do not have a disability (addiction).

People suffering from alcoholism are protected by the ADA. Employers cannot legally discriminate against employees simply because they are suffering from alcoholism. Of course, employers have the right to prohibit the use of alcohol in the workplace and can require that employees not be under the influence of alcohol while working. Employers can also fire or refuse to hire a person who is an alcoholic if he or she poses a substantial risk of harm either to himself or herself or to others and the risk cannot be reduced by reasonable accommodation.

Exhibit 25–1 illustrates the coverage of the employment discrimination laws discussed in this chapter.

Health-Insurance Plans Workers with disabilities must be given equal access to any health insurance provided to other employees and cannot be excluded from coverage for preexisting

KNOW THIS
Preemployment screening procedures must be applied equally in regard to all job applicants.

Exhibit 25–1 Coverage of Employment Discrimination Laws

TITLE VII OF THE CIVIL RIGHTS ACT	AGE DISCRIMINATION IN EMPLOYMENT ACT	AMERICANS WITH DISABILITIES ACT (AS AMENDED)
Prohibits discrimination based on race, color, national origin, religion, gender (including wage discrimination), and pregnancy; prohibits sexual harassment.	Prohibits discrimination against persons over 40.	Prohibits discrimination against persons with a mental or physical impairment that substantially limits a major life activity now or in the past, or who are regarded as having such an impairment, or who are associated with a disabled person.
Applies to employers with 15 or more employees.	Applies to employers with 20 or more employees.	Applies to employers with 15 or more employees.

health conditions. An employer can put a limit, or cap, on health-care payments under its group health policy, but such caps must be "applied equally to all insured employees" and must not "discriminate on the basis of disability." Whenever a group health-care plan makes a disability-based distinction in its benefits, the plan violates the ADA (unless the employer can justify its actions under the business necessity defense, discussed shortly).

LEARNING OBJECTIVE 5
What are three defenses to claims of employment discrimination?

25-4 Defenses to Employment Discrimination

The first line of defense for an employer charged with employment discrimination is to assert that the plaintiff has failed to meet his or her initial burden of proving that discrimination occurred. Once a plaintiff succeeds in proving discrimination, the burden shifts to the employer to justify the discriminatory practice.

Possible justifications include that the discrimination was the result of a business necessity, a bona fide occupational qualification, or a seniority system. In addition, as noted earlier, an effective antiharassment policy and prompt remedial action when harassment occurs can sometimes shield employers from liability for sexual harassment under Title VII.

25-4a Business Necessity

Business Necessity A defense to an allegation of employment discrimination in which the employer demonstrates that an employment practice that discriminates against members of a protected class is related to job performance.

An employer may defend against a claim of disparate-impact (unintentional) discrimination by asserting that a practice that has a discriminatory effect is a **business necessity. EXAMPLE 25.16** EarthFix, Inc., an international consulting agency, requires its applicants to be fluent in at least one foreign language. If requiring a foreign language is shown to have a discriminatory effect, EarthFix can argue that a foreign language is necessary for its workers to perform the job at a required level of competence. If EarthFix can demonstrate a definite connection between foreign language fluency and job performance, it normally will succeed in this business necessity defense. ■

25-4b Bona Fide Occupational Qualification

Bona Fide Occupational Qualification (BFOQ)
An identifiable characteristic reasonably necessary to the normal operation of a particular business. Such characteristics can include gender, national origin, and religion, but not race.

Another defense applies when discrimination against a protected class is essential to a job—that is, when a particular trait is a **bona fide occupational qualification (BFOQ).** Race, however, can never be a BFOQ.

Generally, courts have restricted the BFOQ defense to instances in which the employee's gender is essential to the job. For instance, a women's clothing store might legitimately hire only female sales attendants if part of an attendant's job involves assisting clients in the store's dressing rooms. Similarly, the Federal Aviation Administration can legitimately impose age limits for airline pilots—but an airline cannot impose weight limits only on female flight attendants.

25-4c Seniority Systems

Seniority System A system in which those who have worked longest for an employer are first in line for promotions, salary increases, and other benefits, and are last to be laid off if the workforce must be reduced.

An employer with a history of discrimination may have no members of protected classes in upper-level positions. Nevertheless, the employer may have a defense against a discrimination suit if promotions or other job benefits have been distributed according to a fair *seniority system.* In a **seniority system,** workers with more years of service are promoted first or laid off last.

CASE EXAMPLE 25.17 Cathalene Johnson, an African American woman, was a senior service agent for Federal Express Corporation (FedEx) for more than seventeen years. She resigned in 2014 and filed suit against FedEx for discrimination based on race and gender, as well as for violation of the Equal Pay Act. Johnson claimed that FedEx had paid a white male coworker about two dollars more per hour than she received for basically the same position. FedEx argued that the man had seniority. He had worked for FedEx for seven years longer, was the most senior employee at the station where Johnson worked, and had been a courier in addition to being a service agent. The court ruled that FedEx's seniority system was fair and provided a defense to Johnson's claims.[26]

25-4d After-Acquired Evidence of Employee Misconduct

In some situations, employers have attempted to avoid liability for employment discrimination on the basis of *after-acquired evidence* of an employee's misconduct—that is, evidence that the employer discovered after the employee had filed a lawsuit. **EXAMPLE 25.18** Pratt Legal Services fires Lucy, who then sues Pratt for employment discrimination. During pretrial investigation, Pratt discovers that Lucy made material misrepresentations on her job application. Had Pratt known of these misrepresentations, it would have had grounds to fire Lucy. ■

After-acquired evidence of wrongdoing cannot shield an employer entirely from liability for discrimination. It may, however, be used to limit the amount of damages for which the employer is liable.

Affirmative Action
Job-hiring policies that give special consideration to members of protected classes in an effort to overcome present effects of past discrimination.

25-5 Affirmative Action

Federal statutes and regulations providing for equal opportunity in the workplace were designed to reduce or eliminate discriminatory practices with respect to hiring, retaining, and promoting employees. **Affirmative action** programs go further and attempt to "make up" for past patterns of discrimination by giving members of protected classes preferential treatment in hiring or promotion. During the 1960s, all federal and state government agencies, private companies that contracted to do business with the federal government, and institutions that received federal funding were required to implement affirmative action policies.

Title VII of the Civil Rights Act neither requires nor prohibits affirmative action. Thus, most private firms have not been required to implement affirmative action policies, though many have voluntarily done so. Affirmative action programs have been controversial, however, particularly when they have resulted in reverse discrimination.

If this job candidate makes material misrepresentations on her application and is hired, can her employer use after-acquired evidence to shield itself from a discrimination lawsuit?

25-5a Equal Protection Issues

Because of their inherently discriminatory nature, affirmative action programs may violate the equal protection clause of the Fourteenth Amendment to the U.S. Constitution. Any federal, state, or local affirmative action program that uses racial or ethnic classifications as the basis for making decisions is subject to strict scrutiny (the highest standard to meet) by the courts.

Today, an affirmative action program normally is constitutional only if it attempts to remedy past discrimination and does not make use of quotas or preferences. Furthermore, once such a program has succeeded in the goal of remedying past discrimination, it must be changed or eliminated.

25-5b State Laws Prohibiting Affirmative Action Programs

Some states, including California, Maryland, Michigan, New Hampshire, Oklahoma, Virginia, and Washington, have enacted laws that prohibit affirmative action programs at public institutions (colleges, universities, and state agencies) within their borders. The United

KNOW THIS
The Fourteenth Amendment prohibits any state from denying any person "the equal protection of the laws." This prohibition applies to the federal government through the due process clause of the Fifth Amendment.

---

26. *Johnson v. Federal Exp. Corp.,* 996 F.Supp.2d 302 (M.D. Pa. 2014).

States Supreme Court recognized that states have the power to enact such bans in 2014. **CASE EXAMPLE 25.19** Michigan voters passed an initiative to amend the state's constitution to prohibit publically funded colleges from granting preferential treatment to any group on the basis of race, sex, color, ethnicity, or national origin. The law also prohibited Michigan from considering race and gender in public hiring and contracting decisions.

A group that supports affirmative action programs in education sued the state's attorney general and others, claiming that the initiative deprived minorities of equal protection and violated the U.S. Constitution. A federal appellate court agreed that the law violated the equal protection clause, but the United States Supreme Court reversed. The Court ruled that a state has the inherent power to ban affirmative action within that state, but it did not rule on the constitutionality of any specific affirmative action program.[27] ■

---

27. *Schuette v. Coalition to Defend Affirmative Action, Integration and Immigrant Rights,* __ U.S. __, 134 S.Ct. 1623, 188 L.Ed.2d 613 (2014).

Reviewing . . . Employment Discrimination

Amaani Lyle, an African American woman, took a job as a scriptwriters' assistant at Warner Brothers Television Productions. She worked for the writers of *Friends,* a popular, adult-oriented television series. One of her essential job duties was to type detailed notes for the scriptwriters during brainstorming sessions in which they discussed jokes, dialogue, and story lines. The writers then combed through Lyle's notes after the meetings for script material.

During the meetings, the three male scriptwriters told lewd and vulgar jokes and made sexually explicit comments and gestures. They often talked about their personal sexual experiences and fantasies, and some of these conversations were later used in episodes of *Friends.* During the meetings, Lyle never complained that she found the writers' conduct offensive.

After four months, Lyle was fired because she could not type fast enough to keep up with the writers' conversations during the meetings. She filed a suit against Warner Brothers alleging sexual harassment and claiming that her termination was based on racial discrimination. Using the information presented in the chapter, answer the following questions.

1. Would Lyle's claim of racial discrimination be for intentional (disparate-treatment) or unintentional (disparate-impact) discrimination? Explain.

2. Can Lyle establish a *prima facie* case of racial discrimination? Why or why not?

3. When she was hired, Lyle was told that typing speed was extremely important to her position. At the time, she maintained that she could type eighty words per minute, so she was not given a typing test. It later turned out that Lyle could type only fifty words per minute. What impact might typing speed have on Lyle's lawsuit?

4. Lyle's sexual-harassment claim is based on the hostile work environment created by the writers' sexually offensive conduct at meetings that she was required to attend. The writers, however, argue that their behavior was essential to the "creative process" of writing *Friends,* a show that routinely contained sexual innuendos and adult humor. Which defense discussed in the chapter might Warner Brothers assert using this argument?

DEBATE THIS

■ Members of minority groups and women have made enough economic progress in the last several decades that they no longer need special legislation to protect them.

LINKING BUSINESS LAW TO CORPORATE MANAGEMENT
Human Resource Management

Your career may lead to running a small business, managing a small part of a larger business, or making decisions for the operations of a big business. In any context, you may be responsible for employment decisions. As this chapter has suggested, an ill-conceived hiring or firing process can lead to a lawsuit. As a manager, you must also ensure that employees do not practice discrimination on the job. Enter the human resource management specialist.

What Is Human Resource Management?
Human resource management (HRM) is concerned with the acquisition, maintenance, and development of an organization's employees. All managers need to be skilled in HRM. Some firms require managers to play an active role in recruiting and selecting personnel, as well as in developing training programs. Anyone engaging in these practices should be aware of the issues outlined in this chapter. That is especially true of those who work in an organization's human resources department.

The Acquisition Phase of HRM
Acquiring talented employees is the first step in an HRM system. All recruitment must be done without violating any of the laws and regulations outlined in this chapter. Obviously, recruitment must be colorblind, as well as indifferent to gender, religion, national origin, and age. Recruitment methods must not have even the slightest hint of discriminatory basis. Recruitment methods must also give an equal chance to people with disabilities. Only the applicant's qualifications can be considered, not his or her disability. If a candidate with a disability is rejected, the employer should make sure to document that the rejection is based solely on the applicant's lack of training or ability.

On-the-Job HRM Issues
In addition, the HRM professional must monitor the working environment. Sexual harassment is a major concern. It may be necessary to work closely with an employment law specialist to develop antiharassment rules and policies. The company must publish these rules and policies and provide training to ensure that all employees are familiar with them. In addition, the company should create and supervise a grievance system so that any harassment can be stopped before it becomes actionable.

HRM Issues Concerning Employee Termination
Even in employment-at-will jurisdictions, lawsuits can arise for improper termination. The company should develop a system to protect itself from lawsuits, such as procedures for documenting an employee's misconduct and the employer's warnings and other disciplinary actions. The company should have an established policy for dealing with improper or incompetent behavior. It should also clearly establish the amount of severance pay that terminated employees will receive. Sometimes, it is better to err on the side of generosity to maintain the goodwill of terminated employees.

CRITICAL THINKING

- What are some types of actions that an HRM professional can take to reduce the probability of harassment lawsuits against her or his company?

Key Terms

affirmative action 647

bona fide occupational qualification (BFOQ) 646

business necessity 646

constructive discharge 636

disparate-impact discrimination 631

disparate-treatment discrimination 630

prima facie case 630

protected class 629

seniority system 646

sexual harassment 637

tangible employment action 638

Chapter Summary: Employment Discrimination

Title VII of the Civil Rights Act	Title VII prohibits employment discrimination based on race, color, national origin, religion, or gender.
	1. *Procedures*—Employees must file a claim with the Equal Employment Opportunity Commission (EEOC). The EEOC may sue the employer on the employee's behalf. If it does not, the employee may sue the employer directly.
	2. *Types of discrimination*—Title VII prohibits both intentional (disparate-treatment) and unintentional (disparate-impact) discrimination. Disparate-impact discrimination occurs when an employer's practices or procedures, such as requiring a certain level of education, have the effect of discriminating against a protected class. Title VII extends to discriminatory practices, such as various forms of harassment, in the online environment.
	3. *Remedies for discrimination under Title VII*—Remedies include reinstatement, back pay, and retroactive promotions. Damages (both compensatory and punitive) may be awarded for intentional discrimination.
Discrimination Based on Age	The Age Discrimination in Employment Act (ADEA) prohibits employment discrimination on the basis of age against individuals forty years of age or older. Procedures for bringing a case under the ADEA are similar to those for bringing a case under Title VII.
Discrimination Based on Disability	The Americans with Disabilities Act (ADA) prohibits employment discrimination against persons with disabilities who are otherwise qualified to perform the essential functions of the jobs for which they apply.
	1. *Procedures and remedies*—To prevail on a claim, the plaintiff must show that she or he has a disability, is otherwise qualified for the employment in question, and was excluded from it solely because of the disability. Procedures and remedies under the ADA are similar to those in Title VII cases.
	2. *Definition of disability*—The ADA defines the term *disability* as a physical or mental impairment that substantially limits one or more of an individual's major life activities, a record of such impairment, or being regarded as having such an impairment.
	3. *Reasonable accommodation*—Employers are required to reasonably accommodate the needs of qualified persons with disabilities through such measures as modifying the physical work environment and permitting more flexible work schedules.
Defenses to Employment Discrimination	As defenses to claims of employment discrimination, employers may assert that the discrimination was required for reasons of business necessity, to meet a bona fide occupational qualification, or to maintain a legitimate seniority system. Evidence of prior employee misconduct acquired after the employee has been fired is not a defense to discrimination.
Affirmative Action	Affirmative action programs attempt to "make up" for past patterns of discrimination by giving members of protected classes preferential treatment in hiring or promotion. Such programs are subject to strict scrutiny by the courts and are often struck down for violating the Fourteenth Amendment.

Issue Spotters

1. Ruth is a supervisor for a Subs & Suds restaurant. Tim is a Subs & Suds employee. The owner announces that some employees will be discharged. Ruth tells Tim that if he has sex with her, he can keep his job. Is this sexual harassment? Why or why not? (See *Title VII of the Civil Rights Act*.)

2. Koko, a person with a disability, applies for a job at Lively Sales Corporation for which she is well qualified, but she is rejected. Lively continues to seek applicants and eventually fills the position with a person who does not have a disability. Could Koko succeed in a suit against Lively for discrimination? Explain. (See *Discrimination Based on Disability*.)

—**Check your answers to the *Issue Spotters* against the answers provided in Appendix D at the end of this text.**

Learning Objectives Check

1. What is required to establish a *prima facie* case of disparate-treatment discrimination?

2. What must an employer do to avoid liability for religious discrimination?

3. What is a constructive discharge? To which employment discrimination claims does the theory of constructive discharge apply?

4. What federal act prohibits discrimination based on age?

5. What are three defenses to claims of employment discrimination?

—**Answers to the even-numbered *Learning Objectives Check* questions can be found in Appendix E at the end of this text.**

Business Scenarios and Case Problems

25–1. Title VII Violations. Discuss fully whether either of the following actions would constitute a violation of Title VII of the Civil Rights Act.

1. Tennington, Inc., is a consulting firm with ten employees. These employees travel on consulting jobs in seven states. Tennington has an employment record of hiring only white males. (See *Title VII of the Civil Rights Act*.)

2. Novo Films, Inc., is making a film about Africa and needs to employ approximately one hundred extras for this picture. To hire these extras, Novo advertises in all major newspapers in Southern California. The ad states that only African Americans need apply. (See *Defenses to Employment Discrimination*.)

25–2. Religious Discrimination. Gina Gomez, a devout Roman Catholic, worked for Sam's Department Stores, Inc., in Phoenix, Arizona. Sam's considered Gomez a productive employee because her sales exceeded $200,000 per year. The store gave its managers the discretion to grant unpaid leave to employees but prohibited vacations or leave during the holiday season—October through December. Gomez felt that she had a "calling" to go on a "pilgrimage" in October to a location in Bosnia where some persons claimed to have had visions of the Virgin Mary. The Catholic Church had not designated the site an official pilgrimage site, the visions were not expected to be stronger in October, and tours were available at other times. The store managers denied Gomez's request for leave, but she had a nonrefundable ticket and left anyway. Sam's terminated her employment, and she could not find another job. Can Gomez establish a *prima facie* case of religious discrimination? Explain. (See *Title VII of the Civil Rights Act*.)

25–3. Spotlight on Dress Code Policies—Discrimination Based on Gender. Burlington Coat Factory Warehouse, Inc., had a dress code that required male sales clerks to wear business attire consisting of slacks, shirt, and necktie. Female salesclerks, by contrast, were required to wear a smock so that customers could readily identify them. Karen O'Donnell and other female employees refused to wear the smock. Instead they reported to work in business attire and were suspended. After numerous suspensions, the female employees were fired for violating Burlington's dress code policy. All other conditions of employment, including salary, hours, and benefits, were the same for female and male employees. Was the dress code policy discriminatory? Why or why not? [*O'Donnell v. Burlington Coat Factory Warehouse, Inc.,* 656 F.Supp. 263 (S.D. Ohio 1987)] (See *Title VII of the Civil Rights Act*.)

25–4. Sexual Harassment by Co-Worker. Billie Bradford worked for the Kentucky Department of Community Based Services (DCBS). One of Bradford's co-workers, Lisa Stander, routinely engaged in extreme sexual behavior (such as touching herself and making crude comments) in Bradford's presence. Bradford and others regularly complained about Stander's conduct to their supervisor, Angie Taylor. Rather than resolve the problem, Taylor nonchalantly told Stander to stop, encouraged Bradford to talk to Stander, and suggested that Stander was just having fun. Assuming that Bradford was subjected to a hostile-work environment, could DCBS be liable? Why or why not? [*Bradford v. Department of Community Based Services,* 2012 WL 360032 (E.D.Ky. 2012)] (See *Title VII of the Civil Rights Act*.)

25–5. Business Case Problem with Sample Answer—Age Discrimination. Beginning in 1986, Paul Rangel was a sales professional for pharmaceutical company Sanofi-Aventis U.S., LLC (S-A). Rangel had satisfactory performance reviews until 2006, when S-A issued new expectations guidelines with sales call quotas and other standards that he failed to meet. After two years of negative performance reviews, Rangel—who was then more than forty years old—was terminated as part of a nationwide reduction of sales professionals who had not met the expectations guidelines. This sales force reduction also included younger workers. Did S-A engage in age discrimination? Discuss. [*Rangel v. Sanofi Aventis U.S. LLC,* 507 Fed.Appx. 782 (10th Cir. 2013)] (See *Discrimination Based on Age*.)

—For a sample answer to Problem 25–5, go to Appendix F at the end of this text.

25–6. Discrimination Based on Disability. Cynthia Horn worked for Knight Facilities Management–GM, Inc., in Detroit, Michigan, as a janitor. When Horn developed a sensitivity to cleaning products, her physician gave her a "no exposure to cleaning solutions" restriction. Knight discussed possible accommodations with Horn. She suggested that restrooms be eliminated from her cleaning route or that she be provided with a respirator. Knight explained that she would be exposed to cleaning solutions in any situation and concluded that there was no work available within her physician's restriction. Has Knight violated the Americans with Disabilities Act by failing to provide Horn with the requested accommodations? Explain. [*Horn v. Knight Facilities Management–GM, Inc.,* 556 Fed.Appx. 452 (6th Cir. 2014)] (See *Discrimination Based on Disability*.)

25–7. Sexual Harassment. Jamel Blanton, a male employee at a Pizza Hut restaurant operated by Newton Associates, Inc., in San Antonio, Texas, was subjected to sexual and racial harassment by the general manager, who was female. Newton had a clear, straightforward antidiscrimination policy and complaint procedure. The policy provided that in such a situation, an employee should complain to the harasser's supervisor. Blanton alerted a shift leader and an assistant manager about the harassment, but they were subordinate to the general manager and did not report the harassment to higher-level management. When Blanton finally complained to a manager with authority over the general manager, the employer investigated and fired the general manager within four days. Blanton filed a suit in a federal district court against Newton, seeking to impose liability on the employer for the general manager's actions. What is Newton's best defense? Discuss. [*Blanton v. Newton Associates, Inc.*, 593 Fed.Appx. 389 (5th Cir. 2015)] (See *Title VII of the Civil Rights Act.*)

25–8. A Question of Ethics—Retaliation by Employers. Shane Dawson, a male homosexual, worked for Entek International. Some of Dawson's co-workers, including his supervisor, made derogatory comments about his sexual orientation. Dawson's work deteriorated. He filed a complaint with Entek's human resources department. Two days later, he was fired. State law made it unlawful for an employer to discriminate against an individual based on sexual orientation. [*Dawson v. Entek International*, 630 F.3d 928 (9th Cir. 2011)] (See *Title VII of the Civil Rights Act.*)

1. Could Dawson establish a claim for retaliation? Explain.

2. Should homosexuals be a protected class under Title VII of the Civil Rights Act? Discuss the arguments for and against amending federal law to prohibit employment discrimination based on sexual orientation.

Critical Thinking and Writing Assignments

25–9. Critical Legal Thinking. Why has the federal government limited the application of the statutes discussed in this chapter to firms with a specified number of employees, such as fifteen or twenty? Should these laws apply to all employers, regardless of size? Why or why not? (See *Title VII of the Civil Rights Act.*)

25–10. Case Analysis Question. Go to Appendix G at the end of this text and examine the excerpt of Case No. 4, *Dees v. United Rentals North America, Inc.* Review and then brief the case, making sure that your brief answers the following questions. (See *Title VII of the Civil Rights Act.*)

1. **Issue:** What conduct on the part of the plaintiff, and what action on the part of the defendant, were at the center of the dispute in this case?

2. **Rule of Law:** Once a *prima facie* case of employment discrimination has been established, who must prove what as the case moves forward, and who must respond with what evidence?

3. **Applying the Rule of Law:** What was the court's evaluation of the parties' allegations and evidence in this case?

4. **Conclusion:** In whose favor did the court rule? Why?

25–11. Business Law Critical Thinking Group Assignment. Two African American plaintiffs sued the producers of the reality television series *The Bachelor* and *The Bachelorette* for racial discrimination. The plaintiffs claimed that the shows had never featured a person of color in the lead role. Plaintiffs also alleged that the producers had failed to provide people of color who auditioned for lead roles with the same opportunities to compete as white people who auditioned. (See *Title VII of the Civil Rights Act.*)

1. The first group will assess whether the plaintiffs can establish a *prima facie* case of disparate-treatment discrimination.

2. The second group will consider what the plaintiffs would have to show to establish disparate-impact discrimination.

3. The third group will assume that the plaintiffs established a *prima facie* case and that the burden has shifted to the employer to articulate a legal reason for not hiring the plaintiffs. What legitimate reasons might the employer assert for not hiring the plaintiffs in this situation? Should the law require television producers to hire persons of color for lead roles in reality television shows? Explain your answer.

Unit Four—Business Case Study with Dissenting Opinion

EEOC v. Greater Baltimore Medical Center, Inc.

The Americans with Disabilities Act (ADA) prohibits employment discrimination based on disability. Although an employer is often required to reasonably accommodate the needs of an employee with a disability, the ADA does not protect an employee who cannot perform the essential functions of a job even when given a reasonable accommodation.

In this *Business Case Study with Dissenting Opinion,* we review *EEOC v. Greater Baltimore Medical Center, Inc.*[1] In this case, the Equal Employment Opportunity Commission (EEOC) filed an enforcement action on behalf of a disabled employee who was receiving Social Security Disability Income benefits. To receive the benefits, the employee had to state that he was incapable of working. The issue for the court was whether, despite the employee's representations, the EEOC could show that he was capable of performing the job's essential functions.

Can an employee claim protection under the Americans with Disabilities Act while simultaneously receiving Social Security Disability Income benefits?

CASE BACKGROUND

Michael Turner worked as a secretary for Greater Baltimore Medical Center (GBMC). Beginning in January 2005, Turner was hospitalized for five months because of a life-threatening condition called necrotizing fasciitis. Turner returned to work in November 2005 with his doctor's permission, but he soon suffered a stroke and was hospitalized again until late December.

On December 29, 2005, with his mother's help, Turner applied to the Social Security Administration (SSA) for Social Security Disability Income (SSDI) benefits. The application stated, "I became unable to work because of my disabling condition on January 15, 2005. I am still disabled." The application also said that Turner would tell the SSA if his condition improved to the point that he could work. A few days later, Turner's mother also submitted a report stating that Turner could not work because of his disabilities. Turner began receiving SSDI benefits in January 2006.

That same month, Turner told GBMC that he wanted to return to work as a part-time secretary. Turner submitted a form from his physician, but GBMC concluded that his conditions prevented him from performing his old job. As a result, GBMC said that it was not obligated to give Turner a position. By May 2006, Turner's condition had improved, and his doctor found that he could work full-time without any restrictions. But GBMC disagreed, and it terminated Turner in June 2006, when his leave expired. Afterward, Turner did more than 1,100 hours of volunteer work for GBMC. All the while, he continued to receive SSDI benefits.

In February 2007, Turner filed a discrimination charge with the EEOC. In September 2009, the EEOC filed an enforcement action in federal court on Turner's behalf. The district court granted summary judgment for GBMC because it found that, given Turner's SSDI benefits, the EEOC could not show that Turner could perform his old job's essential functions. The EEOC appealed.

MAJORITY OPINION

O'GRADY, District Judge:

* * * *

The ADA prohibits a covered employer from discriminating "against a qualified individual with a disability because of the disability of such individual." *Among other things, EEOC must show that Mr. Turner is a "qualified individual with a disability," that is, "an individual with a disability who, with or without reasonable accommodation, can perform the essential functions of the employment position * * * ."* [Emphasis added.]

Many persons who experience disabling medical problems become eligible for programs like SSDI, at least temporarily, during medical leave. If such a person seeks SSDI benefits and attempts to bring a claim under the ADA, he may assert disability in an application for SSDI benefits while simultaneously asserting that he is a "qualified individual" under the ADA, that is, he is able to work with or without reasonable accommodation. A conflict of this sort may appear to bar the claimant from receiving both disability benefits and ADA coverage.

* * * *

* * * There can be little doubt that the conflict between Mr. Turner's SSDI application and his ability to work with or without reasonable accommodation is genuine. Mr. Turner's SSDI application, submitted on December 29, 2005, states, "I became unable to work because of my disabling condition on January 15, 2005," and, "I am

---

1. 2012 WL 1302604 (4th Cir. 2012).

Continues

still disabled." Moreover, "I [Mr. Turner] agree to notify the Social Security Administration * * * [i]f my medical condition improves so that I would be able to work, even though I have not yet returned to work." The record indicates without contradiction that Mr. Turner was unable to work after he left the hospital on December 27, 2005. Mrs. Turner later submitted a form called a "Function Report" * * * in which she described Mr. Turner's symptoms and impairment. She noted severe disability in his left arm or hand, use of a bedside commode with hand rails, left-sided weakness requiring assistance, leg bracing, inability to drive, inability to lift more than 2–3 pounds, severely limited ability to stand, bend over and back, and walk. * * * Taken together, the SSDI application and documentation reasonably communicated that Mr. Turner was and would continue to be [unable to work].

Consistent with the application, the SSA awarded benefits to Mr. Turner on January 22, 2006. Mr. Turner continued to receive SSDI benefits at the time of the district court's decision. Mr. Turner did not revise his statements to SSDI, and apparently never notified the SSA about a change in his condition.

These reported disabilities conflict with the multiple work releases provided by [Turner's doctor] * * * . They all indicated that Mr. Turner could have returned to work, directly contradicting the assertion in his SSDI application that he was and continued to be unable to work. * * * If Mr. Turner told GBMC in good faith that he could return to work, then he had no reason to believe that his earlier representations of disability were still accurate.

* * * *

* * * We in no way condone GBMC's refusal to reinstate Mr. Turner. Quite the contrary. We are deeply concerned about GBMC's attempts to prevent a partially disabled former employee from returning to work after he was cleared to return without restriction. Our result is nonetheless mandated by the plain language of the ADA and the relevant case law. The district court's judgment is therefore affirmed.

DISSENTING OPINION
GREGORY, Circuit Judge, dissenting:

* * * *

This case * * * involves two different parties' context-related legal representations—*Turner's* assertion in the proceedings before the SSA and the *EEOC's* assertion in this action. While it is true that the EEOC is seeking relief on Turner's behalf, it cannot be said that the EEOC made a prior inconsistent statement in Turner's SSDI application. Its action should not be barred through the happenstance of an unemployed victim having applied for and received SSDI benefits. Moreover, the Supreme Court has repeatedly recognized that "the EEOC is not merely a proxy" for the individuals for whom it seeks relief. Rather, the Court has observed, "[w]hen the EEOC acts, albeit at the behest of and for the benefit of specific individuals, it acts also to vindicate the public interest in preventing employment discrimination." [Emphasis in original.]

Barring EEOC enforcement actions based on a charging party's legal assertions of disability in SSA proceedings * * * is also contrary to public policy. The EEOC's enforcement actions typically seek not only victim-specific relief but also injunctive relief such as training, posting of notices, and reporting requirements. As discussed above, these enforcement actions not only benefit the individuals on whose behalf the agency sues, but also benefit the public, which has an interest in the eradication of employment discrimination.

* * * *

QUESTIONS FOR ANALYSIS

1. *Law.* What was the majority's decision in this case? What were the reasons for its decision?

2. *Law.* Why did the dissent disagree with the majority? If the court had adopted the dissent's position, how would this have affected the result?

3. *Ethics.* Does the majority express any ethical reservations about its decision? If so, what are they? Do you have any ethical concerns about the majority's decision?

4. *Economic Dimensions.* Based on this case, what do you think is the purpose of SSDI benefits? Did Turner need them?

5. *Implications for the Businessperson.* What does the majority's ruling mean for employers who have disabled employees? Does the ruling tend to make the repercussions of disability discrimination more or less serious? Explain your answer.

iStockPhoto.com/KLH49

Unit Four—Business Scenario

Two brothers, Ray and Paul Ashford, start a business—Ashford Brothers, Inc.—manufacturing a new type of battery system for hybrid automobiles. The batteries hit the market at the perfect time and are in great demand.

1. **Agency.** Loren, one of Ashford's salespersons, anxious to make a sale, intentionally quotes a price to a customer that

is $500 lower than Ashford has authorized for the product. The customer purchases the product at the quoted price. When Ashford learns of the deal, it claims that it is not legally bound to the sales contract because it has not authorized Loren to sell the product at that price. Is Ashford bound to the contract? Discuss fully.

2. **Workers' Compensation.** One day, Gina, an Ashford employee, suffered a serious burn when she accidentally spilled some acid on her hand. The accident occurred because another employee, who was suspected of using illegal drugs, carelessly bumped into her. Gina's hand required a series of skin grafts before it healed sufficiently to allow her to return to work. Gina wants to obtain compensation for her lost wages and medical expenses. Can she do that? If so, how?

3. **Drug Testing.** After Gina's injury, Ashford decides to conduct random drug tests on all of its employees. Several employees claim that the testing violates their privacy rights and bring a lawsuit. What factors will the court consider in deciding whether the random drug testing is legally permissible?

4. **COBRA.** Ashford provides health insurance for its two hundred employees, including Dan. For personal medical reasons, Dan takes twelve weeks' leave. During this period, can Dan continue his coverage under Ashford's health-insurance plan? After Dan returns to work, Ashford closes Dan's division and terminates the employees, including Dan. Can Dan continue his coverage under Ashford's health-insurance plan after the termination? Explain.

5. **Sexual Harassment.** Aretha, another employee at Ashford, is disgusted by the sexually offensive behavior of several male employees. She has complained to her supervisor on several occasions about the behavior, but the supervisor merely laughs at her concerns. Aretha decides to bring a legal action against the company for sexual harassment. Does Aretha's complaint concern *quid pro quo* harassment or hostile-environment harassment? What federal statute protects employees from sexual harassment? What remedies are available under that statute? What procedures must Aretha follow in pursuing her legal action?

Unit Four—Group Project

iStockPhoto.com/AndreyPopov

Cerebral palsy limits Eli's use of his legs, but with support, he can get on and off a stool. Eli applied for a cashier position at Mars Market. The job description required "no experience or qualifications." Eli's application was rejected. According to Ravenna, the market's human resources manager, her decision was based on the threat that Eli posed to his safety and the safety of others. Eli claimed that Mars Market had refused to hire him because of his disability.

1. One group will outline the requirements to prove a *prima facie* case of disability discrimination and decide whether Eli can meet these requirements.

2. A second group will decide what reasonable accommodations Mars Market could make in this situation.

3. A third group will discuss whether Eli poses a safety threat to himself and others in the store or whether this reason was just a pretext. It will also determine if Mars Market can establish a defense to employment discrimination.

32

iStockPhoto.com/Christophe Testi

Consumer and Environmental Law

LEARNING OBJECTIVES

The five Learning Objectives *below are designed to help improve your understanding of the chapter. After reading this chapter, you should be able to answer the following questions:*

1. When will advertising be deemed deceptive?

2. What law protects consumers against contaminated and misbranded foods and drugs?

3. What does Regulation Z require, and how does it relate to the Truth-in-Lending Act?

4. What is contained in an environmental impact statement, and who must file one?

5. What are three main goals of the Clean Water Act?

Congress has enacted a substantial amount of legislation to protect "the good of the people," to borrow Cicero's phrase from the chapter-opening quotation. All statutes, agency rules, and common law judicial decisions that attempt to protect the interests of consumers are classified as *consumer law.*

"The good of the people is the greatest law."

MARCUS TULLIUS CICERO
106–43 B.C.E.
(ROMAN POLITICIAN AND ORATOR)

Sources of consumer protection exist at all levels of government. At the federal level, laws have been passed to define the duties of sellers and the rights of consumers. Exhibit 32–1 indicates some of the areas of consumer law that are regulated by statutes. In recent years, a renewed interest in protecting consumers from credit-card companies, financial institutions, and insurance companies has led to enactment of federal credit-card regulations, financial reforms, and health-care reforms.

In the first part of this chapter, we examine some of the major laws and regulations protecting consumers. We then turn to a discussion of environmental law, which consists of all of the laws and regulations designed to protect and preserve the environment.

32–1 Advertising, Marketing, and Sales

Federal administrative agencies, such as the Federal Trade Commission (FTC), provide an important source of consumer protection. Nearly every agency and department of the federal government has an office of consumer affairs. Most states have one or more such offices, including the offices of state attorneys general, to assist consumers. Many of the complaints received by these offices involve consumers who say they were misled by sellers' advertising, marketing, and sales tactics.

32–1a Deceptive Advertising

One of the most important federal consumer protection laws is the Federal Trade Commission Act.[1] The act created the FTC to carry out the broadly stated goal of preventing unfair and deceptive trade practices, including deceptive advertising.

Generally, **deceptive advertising** involves a claim that would mislead a reasonable consumer. Vague generalities and obvious exaggerations (that a reasonable person would not believe to be true) are permissible. These claims are known as *puffery*. When a claim has the appearance of authenticity, however, it may create problems.

Claims that Appear to Be Based on Factual Evidence   Advertising that *appears* to be based on factual evidence but that in fact cannot be scientifically supported will be deemed deceptive. **CASE EXAMPLE 32.1** MedLab, Inc., advertised that its weight-loss supplement ("The New Skinny Pill") would cause users to lose substantial amounts of weight rapidly. The ads claimed that "clinical studies prove" that people who take the pill lose "as much as 15 to 18 pounds per week and as much as 50 percent of all excess weight in just 14 days, without dieting or exercising."

The FTC sued MedLab for deceptive advertising. An expert hired by the FTC to evaluate the claim testified that to lose this much weight, "a 200-pound individual would need to run between 57 and 68 miles every day"—the equivalent of more than two marathons per day. The court concluded that the advertisement was false and misleading, granted the FTC a summary judgment, and issued a permanent injunction to stop MedLab from running the ads.[2] ■

The following case involved an advertising claim based on limited scientific evidence.

LEARNING OBJECTIVE 1
When will advertising be deemed deceptive?

Deceptive Advertising
Advertising that misleads consumers, either by making unjustified claims about a product's performance or by omitting a material fact concerning the product's composition or performance.

---

1. 15 U.S.C. Sections 41–58.
2. *Federal Trade Commission v. MedLab, Inc,* 615 F.Supp.2d 1068 (N.D.Cal. 2009).

Exhibit 32–1 Selected Areas of Consumer Law Regulated by Statutes

CASE 32.1

POM Wonderful, LLC v. Federal Trade Commission

United States Court of Appeals, District of Columbia Circuit, 777 F.3d 478 (2015).

FACTS POM Wonderful, LLC makes and sells pomegranate-based products. In ads, POM touted medical studies claiming to show that daily consumption of its products could treat, prevent, or reduce the risk of heart disease, prostate cancer, and erectile dysfunction. These ads mischaracterized the scientific evidence.

The Federal Trade Commission (FTC) charged POM with, and held POM liable for, making false, misleading, and unsubstantiated representations in violation of the FTC Act. POM was barred from running future ads asserting that its products treat or prevent any disease unless "randomized, controlled, human clinical trials" (RCTs, for "randomized controlled trials") demonstrated statistically significant results. POM petitioned the U.S. Court of Appeals for the District of Columbia Circuit to review this injunctive order.

ISSUE Can an advertising claim based on limited scientific evidence be deemed deceptive?

DECISION Yes. The U.S. Court of Appeals for the District of Columbia Circuit enforced the FTC's order. "An advertiser who makes express representations about the level of support for a particular claim must possess the level of proof claimed in the ad and must convey that information to consumers in a non-misleading way."

REASON POM's ads conveyed the impression that clinical studies had established the ability of its products to treat, prevent, or reduce

What kinds of health claims about pomegranate juice can its producer make?

iStockPhoto.com/gresei

the risk of serious disease. To establish such a relationship, however, requires RCTs. The FTC examined the studies that POM cited and concluded that the studies did not qualify as RCTs that would adequately substantiate POM's claims.

Experts in cardiology and urology require "randomized, double-blinded, placebo-controlled clinical trials to substantiate any claim that a product treats, prevents, or reduces the risk of disease." Investigators can use an RCT's control group to distinguish the real effects of a tested product from other changes, such as those due to the act of being treated (the placebo effect). The random assignment of a subject to a treatment or control group increases the likelihood that the groups are similar, so that any difference in the outcome between the groups can be attributed to the treatment. When a study is double-blinded, the participants and the investigators do not know who is in which group, making bias less likely to affect the results.

CRITICAL THINKING—Ethical Consideration *POM argued that it is unethical to require RCTs to substantiate disease-related claims about food products because "doctors cannot . . . ethically deprive a control group of patients of all Vitamin C for a decade to determine whether Vitamin C helps prevent cancer." Is this a valid argument? Why or why not?*

> "Ads are the cave art of the twentieth century."
>
> **MARSHALL MCLUHAN**
> 1911–1980
> (CANADIAN ACADEMIC AND COMMENTATOR)

Claims Based on Half-Truths Some advertisements contain "half-truths," meaning that the information is true but incomplete and, therefore, leads consumers to a false conclusion. **EXAMPLE 32.2** The maker of Campbell's soups advertised that "most" Campbell's soups were low in fat and cholesterol and thus were helpful in fighting heart disease. What the ad did not say was that Campbell's soups were also high in sodium and that high-sodium diets may increase the risk of heart disease. Hence, the FTC ruled that the company's claims were deceptive. ■ In addition, advertising featuring an endorsement by a celebrity may be deemed deceptive if the celebrity does not actually use the product.

Bait-and-Switch Advertising The FTC has issued rules that govern specific advertising techniques.[3] Some retailers systematically advertise merchandise at low prices to get customers into their stores and then fail to have that merchandise and encourage customers to purchase a more expensive item instead. This practice, known as **bait-and-switch advertising,** is a form of deceptive advertising.

Bait-and-Switch Advertising Advertising a product at an attractive price and then telling the consumer that the advertised product is not available or is of poor quality and encouraging her or him to purchase a more expensive item.

---

3. 16 C.F.R. Section 288.

The low price is the "bait" to lure the consumer into the store. The salesperson is instructed to "switch" the consumer to a different, more expensive item. According to the FTC, bait-and-switch advertising occurs if the seller refuses to show the advertised item, fails to have reasonable quantities of it available, fails to promise to deliver the advertised item within a reasonable time, or discourages employees from selling the item.

Online Deceptive Advertising Deceptive advertising occurs in the online environment as well. The FTC actively monitors online advertising and has identified numerous Web sites that have made false or deceptive claims for products and services. Some online ads include fake reviews of products and services—see this chapter's *Adapting the Law to the Online Environment* feature for a discussion of this issue.

The FTC issues guidelines to help online businesses comply with the laws prohibiting deceptive advertising. Current guidelines include the following basic requirements:

1. All advertisements—both online and offline—must be truthful and not misleading.

2. The claims made in an ad must be substantiated—that is, advertisers must have evidence to back up their claims.

3. Ads cannot be unfair, which the FTC defines as "likely to cause substantial consumer injury that consumers could not reasonably avoid and that is not outweighed by the benefit to consumers or competition."

4. Ads must disclose relevant limitations and qualifying information underlying the claims.

5. Required disclosures must be "clear and conspicuous." Because consumers may not read an entire Web page, an online disclosure should be placed as close as possible to the claim being qualified. Generally, hyperlinks to a disclosure are recommended only for lengthy disclosures. If hyperlinks are used, they should be obvious and should be placed as close as possible to the information they qualify.

Federal Trade Commission Actions The FTC receives complaints from many sources, including competitors of alleged violators, consumers, trade associations, Better Business Bureaus, and government organizations and officials. When the agency receives numerous and widespread complaints about a particular problem, it will investigate.

Formal Complaint. If the FTC concludes that a given advertisement is unfair or deceptive, it sends a formal complaint to the alleged offender. The company may agree to settle the complaint without further proceedings. If not, the FTC can conduct a hearing before an administrative law judge in which the company can present its defense.

FTC Orders and Remedies. If the FTC succeeds in proving that an advertisement is unfair or deceptive, it usually issues a **cease-and-desist order** requiring the company to stop the challenged advertising. In some circumstances, the FTC may also require **counteradvertising,** in which the company advertises anew—in print, on the Internet, on radio, or on television—to inform the public about the earlier misinformation. The FTC sometimes institutes a **multiple product order,** which requires a firm to cease and desist from false advertising in regard to all of its products, not just the product that was the subject of the action.

Damages When Consumers Are Injured. When a company's deceptive ad involves wrongful charges to consumers, the FTC may seek other remedies, including restitution. **CASE EXAMPLE 32.3** The FTC sued Bronson Partners, LLC, for deceptively advertising two products—Chinese Diet Tea and Bio-Slim Patch. Bronson's ads claimed that the diet tea "eliminates 91 percent of absorbed sugars," "prevents 83 percent of fat absorption," and "doubles your metabolic rate to burn calories fast." The Bio-Slim Patch ads promised consumers that "ugly fatty tissue will disappear at a spectacular rate" when they wore the patch and carried on their normal lifestyle.

Can Campbell's advertise that its soups help fight heart disease even if they are high in sodium?

iStockPhoto.com/LauriPatterson

KNOW THIS
Changes in technology often require changes in the law.

Cease-and-Desist Order
An administrative or judicial order prohibiting a person or business firm from conducting activities that an agency or court has deemed illegal.

Counteradvertising New advertising that is undertaken to correct earlier false claims that were made about a product.

Multiple Product Order
An order requiring a firm that has engaged in deceptive advertising to cease and desist from false advertising in regard to all the firm's products.

ADAPTING THE LAW TO THE **ONLINE** ENVIRONMENT
The FTC's Guideline Regulating Astroturfing

Astroturfing is a term that was first used in politics. Long before the Internet existed, the preferred way of influencing legislation was to "write your congressperson." Groups opposed to or in favor of particular legislation would send out a call for letters to be sent to members of Congress. In that way, it appeared that there was a "grass roots" campaign to initiate, approve, or oppose the legislation. AstroTurf is artificial grass. Hence the term *astroturfing*.

Today, the term also refers to posting fake reviews of products and services online in return for payment. Some have argued that Microsoft is one of hundreds of companies that engage in astroturfing to promote their products.

Astroturfing may take the form of tweets, blog posts, Facebook comments, and Amazon.com reviews, among others. This modern-day version of word-of-mouth advertising is popular because consumers tend to trust reviews written by other consumers. An estimated 60 percent of consumers read online reviews before making a purchase.[a]

Astroturfing Is Everywhere
It has been estimated that from 20 to 40 percent of all online reviews are fake. Indeed, among social media reviews alone, more than 15 percent are undercover promotions, according to the technology research and advisory company Gartner.

A plethora of online reviewing companies pay their reviewers. These reviewers may use a company-written review, which is then posted on several online forums under the writers' own user names or e-mail addresses. It is certainly legal to write such reviews, but failing to disclose the connection between the writer and the employer is illegal.[b]

The FTC Steps In
The act that created the Federal Trade Commission (FTC) states, "Unfair methods of competition and dissemination of false advertisements are illegal."[c] Nonetheless, the FTC did not at first actively pursue online astroturfers. State attorneys general, however, began to sue companies that created fake reviews. One of the first cases occurred in New York in 2009 when that state's

attorney general sued Lifestyle Lift, a cosmetic surgery company. Its employees were posting fake consumer reviews online.

Finally, for the first time in over twenty-nine years, the FTC amended its guidelines in an effort to crack down on false reviews posted online. By the time you read this, these guidelines will be in effect. They require full disclosure of all payments to bloggers and consumer reviewers. For instance, anyone who is on a company's payroll must disclose that information when posting online comments, testimonials, or reviews about the company's products or services.

Consumer advocates believe that the new guidelines include blogs by average consumers. If a consumer blogger has received free product samples, the blogger must disclose this fact when reviewing the product. The FTC also can now require proof to support claims about a product. Many companies will have to revise their marketing strategies to ensure compliance with the new FTC rules.

CRITICAL THINKING

■ In the long run, is astroturfing likely to benefit a company that is selling an inferior product? Why or why not?

---

a. Graham Charlton, "e-Commerce Consumer Reviews: Why You Need Them and How to Use Them," *Econsultancy*, March 21, 2012.

b. 16 C.F.R. Section 255.5 (2012).
c. 15 U.S.C. Sections 45, 52 (2012).

What remedies can the FTC seek when a company advertises that its tea eliminates almost all absorbed sugars?

Eventually, Bronson conceded that it had engaged in deceptive advertising, and the FTC sought damages. The court awarded the FTC $1,942,325, which was the amount of Bronson's unjust gains and consumer losses from the two products.[4] ■

32–1b False Advertising Claims under the Lanham Act

The Lanham Act protects trademarks, as discussed earlier in this text. The act also covers false advertising claims. To state a successful claim for false advertising under this act, a business must establish each of the following elements:

1. An injury to a commercial interest in reputation or sales.

2. Direct causation of the injury by false or deceptive advertising.

3. A loss of business from buyers who were deceived by the advertising.

---

4. *Federal Trade Commission v. Bronson Partners, LLC*, 654 F.3d 359 (2d Cir. 2011).

The dispute between the parties in the following case focused initially on a mimicked microchip. When the case reached the United States Supreme Court, the question was whether Static Control Components, Inc., could sue Lexmark International, Inc., for false advertising under the Lanham Act.

CASE 32.2

Lexmark International, Inc. v. Static Control Components, Inc.

United States Supreme Court, __ U.S. __, 134 S.Ct. 1377, 188 L.Ed.2d 392 (2014).

FACTS Lexmark International, Inc., sells the only style of toner cartridges that work with the company's laser printers. Other businesses—known as remanufacturers—acquire and refurbish used Lexmark cartridges to sell in competition with the cartridges sold by Lexmark. To deter remanufacturing, Lexmark introduced a program that gave customers a 20-percent discount on new toner cartridges if they agreed to return the empty cartridges to Lexmark. Static Control Components, Inc., makes and sells components for the remanufactured cartridges, including microchips that mimic the chips in Lexmark's cartridges.

Lexmark released ads that claimed Static Control's microchips illegally infringed Lexmark's patents. Lexmark then filed a suit in a federal district court against Static Control, alleging violations of intellectual property law. Static Control counterclaimed, alleging that Lexmark engaged in false advertising in violation of the Lanham Act. The court dismissed the counterclaim. On Static Control's appeal, the U.S. Court of Appeals for the Sixth Circuit reversed the dismissal. Lexmark appealed to the United States Supreme Court.

ISSUE Did Static Control adequately plead the elements of a cause of action under the Lanham Act for false advertising?

DECISION Yes. The United States Supreme Court affirmed the lower court's ruling. The Supreme Court's decision clarified that businesses

Can a manufacturer's packaging of its toner cartridges lead to false advertising claims?

iStockPhoto.com/JoKMedia

do not need to be direct competitors to bring an action for false advertising under the act.

REASON A cause of action for false advertising under the Lanham Act extends to plaintiffs whose interests "fall within the zone of interests protected by the law." To establish a claim, a plaintiff must allege an injury to a commercial interest in reputation or sales. The injury must have been proximately caused by a violation of the statute, which can be shown by a loss in business reputation or sales that directly flows from the defendant's false advertising. Under these principles, Static Control fell within the class of plaintiffs who can sue under the Lanham Act.

Static Control alleged injuries consisting of lost sales and damage to its business reputation by Lexmark's advertising. Static Control also alleged that the injuries were proximately caused by the ads. The misrepresentations included Lexmark's assertion that Static Control's business was illegal. And because Static Control's microchips were necessary for, and had no other use than, refurbishing Lexmark's cartridges, any false advertising that reduced the remanufacturers' business also injured Static Control.

WHAT IF THE FACTS WERE DIFFERENT? *Suppose that Lexmark had issued a retraction of its ad claims before this case reached the Supreme Court. Would the outcome have been different? Discuss.*

32–1c Marketing

In addition to regulating advertising practices, Congress has passed several laws to protect consumers against other marketing practices.

Telephone Solicitation The Telephone Consumer Protection Act (TCPA)[5] prohibits telephone solicitation using an automatic telephone dialing system or a prerecorded voice. In addition, most states have statutes regulating telephone solicitation. The TCPA also makes it illegal to transmit ads via fax without first obtaining the recipient's permission.

The Federal Communications Commission (FCC) enforces the TCPA. The FCC imposes substantial fines ($11,000 each day) on companies that violate the junk fax provisions of the

---

5. 47 U.S.C. Sections 227 *et seq.*

act. The TCPA also gives consumers a right to sue and recover either $500 for each violation of the act or the actual monetary losses resulting from a violation, whichever is greater. If a court finds that a defendant willfully or knowingly violated the act, the court has the discretion to treble (triple) the amount of damages awarded.

Fraudulent Telemarketing   The Telemarketing and Consumer Fraud and Abuse Prevention Act[6] directed the FTC to establish rules governing telemarketing and to bring actions against fraudulent telemarketers.

The FTC's Telemarketing Sales Rule (TSR)[7] requires a telemarketer to identify the seller's name, describe the product being sold, and disclose all material facts related to the sale (such as the total cost of the goods being sold). The TSR makes it illegal for telemarketers to misrepresent information or facts about their goods or services. A telemarketer must also remove a consumer's name from its list of potential contacts if the customer so requests.

An amendment to the TSR established the national Do Not Call Registry. Telemarketers must refrain from calling consumers who have placed their names on the list. Significantly, the TSR applies to any offer made to consumers in the United States—even if the offer comes from a foreign firm. Thus, the TSR helps to protect consumers from illegal cross-border telemarketing operations.

32-1d Sales

A number of statutes protect consumers by requiring the disclosure of certain terms in sales transactions. The FTC has regulatory authority in this area, as do some other federal agencies.

Many states and the FTC have **"cooling-off" laws** that permit the buyers of goods sold in certain transactions to cancel their contracts within three business days. The FTC rule also requires that consumers be notified in Spanish of this right if the oral negotiations for the sale were in that language.

The contracts that fall under these cancellation rules include trade show sales contracts, contracts for home equity loans, Internet purchase contracts, and home (door-to-door) sales contracts. In addition, certain states have passed laws allowing consumers to cancel contracts for things like dating services, gym memberships, and weight loss programs.

The FTC's Mail or Telephone Order Merchandise Rule[8] protects consumers who purchase goods via mail, Internet, phone, or fax. Merchants are required to ship orders within the time promised in their advertisements and to notify consumers when orders cannot be shipped on time. If the seller does not give an estimated shipping time, it must ship within thirty days. Merchants must also issue a refund within a specified period of time when a consumer cancels an order.

32-2 Labeling and Packaging

In general, labels must be accurate, and they must use words that are understood by the ordinary consumer. In some instances, labels must specify the raw materials used in the product, such as the percentage of cotton, nylon, or other fibers used in a garment. In other instances, the product must carry a warning, such as those required on cigarette packages and advertising.[9]

---

6. 15 U.S.C. Sections 6101–6108.
7. 16 C.F.R. Sections 310.1–310.8.
8. 16 C.F.R. Sections 435.1–435.2.
9. 15 U.S.C. Sections 1331 *et seq.*

"Cooling-Off" Laws Laws that allow buyers of goods sold in certain transactions to cancel their contracts within three business days.

32–2a Automobile Fuel Economy Labels

The Energy Policy and Conservation Act (EPCA)[10] requires automakers to attach an information label to every new car. This label must include the Environmental Protection Agency's fuel economy estimate for the vehicle. **CASE EXAMPLE 32.4** Gaetano Paduano bought a new Honda Civic Hybrid in California. The information label on the car included the fuel economy estimate from the Environmental Protection Agency (EPA). Honda's sales brochure added, "Just drive the Hybrid like you would a conventional car and save on fuel bills."

When Paduano discovered that the car's fuel economy was less than half of the EPA's estimate, he sued Honda for deceptive advertising. The automaker claimed that the federal law (the EPCA) preempted the state's deceptive advertising law, but the court held in Paduano's favor, finding that the federal statute did not preempt a claim for deceptive advertising made under state law.[11] ▪

32–2b Food Labeling

Because the quality and safety of food are so important to consumers, several statutes deal specifically with food labeling. The Fair Packaging and Labeling Act requires that food product labels identify (1) the product, (2) the net quantity of the contents, (3) the manufacturer, and (4) the packager or distributor.[12] The act includes additional requirements concerning descriptions on packages, savings claims, components of nonfood products, and standards for the partial filling of packages.

Gobob/ShutterStock.com

Can a buyer of a hybrid car sue in state court for deceptive advertising about the car's fuel economy?

Nutritional Content Food products must bear labels detailing the food's nutritional content, including the number of calories and the amounts of various nutrients. The Nutrition Labeling and Education Act requires food labels to provide standard nutrition facts and regulates the use of such terms as *fresh* and *low fat*.

The U.S. Food and Drug Administration (FDA) and the U.S. Department of Agriculture (USDA) are the primary agencies that issue regulations on food labeling. These rules are published in the *Federal Register* and updated annually. For instance, current rules require labels on fresh meats, vegetables, and fruits to indicate where the food originated so that consumers can know if their food was imported.

Caloric Content of Restaurant Foods The health-care reform bill enacted in 2010 (the Affordable Care Act) included provisions aimed at combating the problem of obesity in the United States. All restaurant chains with twenty or more locations are now required to post the caloric content of the foods on their menus so that customers will know how many calories the foods contain.[13] Foods offered through vending machines must also be labeled so that their caloric content is visible to would-be purchasers.

In addition, restaurants must post guidelines on the number of calories that an average person requires daily so that customers can determine what portion of a day's calories a particular food will provide. The hope is that consumers, armed with this information, will consider the number of calories when they make their food choices. The federal law on menu labeling supersedes all state and local laws already in existence.

> "A consumer is a shopper who is sore about something."
>
> **HAROLD COFFIN**
> 1905–1981
> (AMERICAN HUMORIST)

---

10. 49 U.S.C. Section 32908(b)(1).
11. *Paduano v. American Honda Motor Co.*, 169 Cal.App. 4th 1453, 88 Cal.Rptr.3d 90 (2009).
12. 15 U.S.C. Sections 4401–4408.
13. See Section 4205 of the Patient Protection and Affordable Care Act, Pub. L. No.111-148, March 23, 2010, 124 Stat. 119.

32–3 Protection of Health and Safety

Although labeling and packaging laws promote consumer health and safety, there is a significant distinction between regulating the information dispensed about a product and regulating the actual content of the product. The classic example is tobacco products. Producers of tobacco products are required to warn consumers about the hazards associated with the use of their products, but the sale of tobacco products has not been subjected to significant restrictions or banned outright despite the obvious dangers to health. We now examine various laws that regulate the actual products made available to consumers.

32–3a Food and Drugs

The most important legislation regulating food and drugs is the Federal Food, Drug, and Cosmetic Act (FDCA).[14] The act protects consumers against adulterated (contaminated) and misbranded foods and drugs.

The FDCA establishes food standards, specifies safe levels of potentially hazardous food additives, and provides guidelines for advertising and labeling food products. The FDCA also creates a reportable food registry, establishes record-keeping requirements, requires the registration of all food facilities, and provides for inspections. Most of these statutory requirements are monitored and enforced by the FDA. (Some foods considered safe in the United States are prohibited in Europe, as discussed in this chapter's *Beyond Our Borders* feature.)

---

14. 21 U.S.C. Section 301.

BEYOND OUR BORDERS   Europe Bans Foods That Americans Eat

Many Americans believe that the foods sold in our country are some of the safest foods on earth. The Food and Drug Administration (FDA) and other government agencies regulate much of what we eat. Nonetheless, the European Union (EU) and a number of other countries, such as Canada, have banned many common processed foods that the FDA assumes to be safe for human consumption.

Internationally Banned Ingredients
The following ingredients are banned throughout Europe and in some other places.

- Olestra/Olean.
- Brominated vegetable oil.

- Potassium bromate.
- Azodicarbonamide.
- BHA and BHT.

Consequently, any processed foods made in the United States that have these ingredients are banned in the EU and elsewhere. These foods include some soft drinks, such as Mountain Dew, numerous breakfast cereals, and some reconstituted potato chips. Many sports drinks, such as Gatorade, contain brominated vegetable oil. They are therefore banned in the EU. The chemical azodicarbonamide may be found in bagels, bread, and tortillas (as well as flip-flops and yoga mats). Such foods are banned in the EU if they contain this substance.

Banned Colorings
Many countries also ban the use of certain food colorings, such as Blue #1, Blue #2,

Blue #3, Yellow #5, Yellow #6, and Red 40. Therefore, some countries, particularly in Europe, have banned Nutri-Grain bars because they contain Blue #1 food coloring. Austria and Norway have banned Yellow #5. Therefore, you will find no Kraft Macaroni & Cheese in those nations. M&Ms in Europe do not have Blue #2 coloring, as they do in the United States.

CRITICAL THINKING

- One chemist claims that the list of "dangerous" chemicals is an example of "chemophobia." What do you think he meant?

Tainted Foods In the last several years, many people in the United States have contracted food poisoning from eating foods that were contaminated—often with salmonella or *E. coli* bacteria. In response, Congress enacted the Food Safety Modernization Act (FSMA)[15] in 2010, which provides greater government control over the U.S. food safety system.

The goal of the modernization act was to shift the focus of federal regulators from responding to incidents of contamination to preventing them. The act also gives the FDA authority to directly recall any food products that it suspects are tainted, rather than relying on the producers to recall items.

The FSMA requires any party that manufactures, processes, packs, distributes, receives, holds, or imports food products to pay a fee and register with the U.S. Department of Health and Human Services. (There are some exceptions for small farmers.) Owners and operators of such facilities are required to analyze and identify food safety hazards, implement preventive controls, monitor effectiveness, and take corrective actions. The act also places more restrictions on importers of food and requires them to verify that imported foods meet U.S. safety standards.

Drugs and Medical Devices The FDA is also responsible under the FDCA for ensuring that drugs are safe and effective before they are marketed to the public. It is the responsibility of the company seeking to market a drug to test it and submit evidence that it is safe and effective. The FDA has established extensive procedures that drug manufacturers must follow. The FDA also has the authority to regulate medical devices, such as pacemakers, and to withdraw from the market any such device that is mislabeled.[16]

Because the FDA must ensure the safety of new medications, there is always a delay before drugs are available to the public, and this sometimes leads to controversy. **CASE EXAMPLE 32.5** A group of citizens petitioned the FDA to allow everyone access to "Plan B"—the morning-after birth control pill—without a prescription. The FDA denied the petition and continued to require women under the age of seventeen to obtain a prescription. The group appealed to a federal district court, claiming that the prescription requirement can delay access to the pill. The pill should be taken as soon as possible after sexual intercourse, preferably within twenty-four hours. The court ruled in favor of the plaintiffs and ordered the FDA to make the morning-after pill available to people of any age without a prescription.[17] ▪

32–3b Consumer Product Safety

The Consumer Product Safety Act[18] created a comprehensive regulatory scheme over consumer safety matters and established the Consumer Product Safety Commission (CPSC).

The CPSC's Authority The CPSC conducts research on the safety of individual products and maintains a clearinghouse on the risks associated with various products. The Consumer Product Safety Act authorizes the CPSC to do the following:

1. Set safety standards for consumer products.

2. Ban the manufacture and sale of any product that the commission believes poses an "unreasonable risk" to consumers. (Products banned by the CPSC have included various types of fireworks, cribs, and toys, as well as many products containing asbestos or vinyl chloride.)

3. Remove from the market any products it believes to be imminently hazardous. The CPSC frequently works with manufacturers to voluntarily recall defective products from

---

15. Pub. L. No. 111-353, 124 Stat. 3885 (January 4, 2011). This statute affected numerous parts of Title 21 of the U.S.C.

16. 21 U.S.C. Sections 352(o), 360(j), 360(k), and 360c–360k.

17. *Tummino v. Hamburg*, 936 F.Supp.2d 162 (E.D.N.Y. 2013).

18. 15 U.S.C. Section 2051.

stores. **EXAMPLE 32.6** In cooperation with the CPSC, the Scandinavian company IKEA recalled three million baby bed canopies and thirty million wall-mounted children's lamps because they posed a strangulation risk to children. ■

4. Require manufacturers to report any products already sold or intended for sale that have proved to be hazardous.

5. Administer other product-safety legislation, including the Child Protection and Toy Safety Act[19] and the Federal Hazardous Substances Act.[20]

Why would IKEA want to cooperate with the Consumer Product Safety Commission?

Notification Requirements The Consumer Product Safety Act imposes notification requirements on distributors of consumer products. Distributors must immediately notify the CPSC when they receive information that a product "contains a defect which . . . creates a substantial risk to the public" or "an unreasonable risk of serious injury or death."

32-3c Health-Care Reforms

The health-care reforms (Obamacare) enacted in 2010 gave Americans new rights and benefits with regard to health care.[21] These laws prohibit certain insurance company practices, such as denial of coverage for preexisting conditions.

Expanded Coverage for Children and Seniors The reforms enabled more children to obtain health-insurance coverage and allowed young adults (under age twenty-six) to remain covered by their parents' health-insurance policies. The legislation also ended lifetime limits and most annual limits on care, and gave patients access to recommended preventive services (such as cancer screenings, vaccinations, and well-baby checks) without cost. Medicare recipients receive a 50 percent discount on name-brand drugs, and a gap that exists in Medicare's prescription drug coverage will be eliminated by 2020.

Controlling Costs of Health Insurance In an attempt to control the rising costs of health insurance, the laws placed restrictions on insurance companies. Insurance companies must spend at least 85 percent of all premium dollars collected from large employers (80 percent of premiums collected from individuals and small employers) on benefits and quality improvement. If insurance companies do not meet these goals, they must provide rebates to consumers. Additionally, states can require insurance companies to justify their premium increases to be eligible to participate in the new health-insurance exchanges mandated by the law.

32-4 Credit Protection

Credit protection is one of the most important aspects of consumer protection legislation. Nearly 80 percent of U.S. consumers have credit cards, and most carry a balance on these cards, which amounts to about $3.4 trillion of debt nationwide. The Consumer Financial Protection Bureau oversees the credit practices of banks, mortgage lenders, and credit-card companies.

---

19. 15 U.S.C. Section 1262(e).
20. 15 U.S.C. Sections 1261–1273.
21. Patient Protection and Affordable Health Care Act of 2010, Pub. L. No.111-148, March 23, 2010, 124 Stat. 119; and Health Care and Education Reconciliation Act of 2010, Pub. L. No. 111-152, March 30, 2010, 124 Stat. 1029.

32–4a Truth-in-Lending Act

A key statute regulating the credit and credit-card industries is the Truth-in-Lending Act (TILA), the name commonly given to Title 1 of the Consumer Credit Protection Act (CCPA), as amended.[22] The TILA is basically a *disclosure law.* It is administered by the Federal Reserve Board and requires sellers and lenders to disclose credit terms or loan terms (such as the annual percentage rate, or APR, and any finance charges) so that individuals can shop around for the best financing arrangements.

Application TILA requirements apply only to persons who, in the ordinary course of business, lend funds, sell on credit, or arrange for the extension of credit. Thus, sales or loans made between two consumers do not come under the act. Additionally, this law protects only debtors who are *natural* persons (as opposed to the artificial "person" of a corporation) and does not extend to other legal entities.

Disclosure The TILA's disclosure requirements are found in **Regulation Z,** issued by the Federal Reserve Board of Governors. If the contracting parties are subject to the TILA, the requirements of Regulation Z apply to any transaction involving an installment sales contract that calls for payment to be made in more than four installments. Transactions subject to Regulation Z typically include installment loans, retail installment sales, car loans, home-improvement loans, and certain real estate loans, if the amount of financing is less than $25,000.

Equal Credit Opportunity The Equal Credit Opportunity Act (ECOA) amended the TILA. The ECOA prohibits the denial of credit solely on the basis of race, religion, national origin, color, gender, marital status, or age. The act also prohibits credit discrimination on the basis of whether an individual receives certain forms of income, such as public-assistance benefits.

A creditor may not require the signature of an applicant's spouse or a cosigner on a credit instrument if the applicant qualifies under the creditor's standards of creditworthiness for the amount requested. **CASE EXAMPLE 32.7** T.R. Hughes, Inc., and Summit Pointe, LLC, obtained financing from Frontenac Bank to construct two real estate developments near St. Louis, Missouri. The bank also required the builder, Thomas R. Hughes, and his wife, Carolyn Hughes, to sign personal guaranty agreements for the loans.

When the borrowers failed to make the loan payments, the bank sued the two companies and Thomas and Carolyn Hughes personally, and foreclosed on the properties. Carolyn claimed that personal guaranty contracts that she signed were obtained in violation of the ECOA. The court held that because the applicant, Thomas R. Hughes, was creditworthy, the personal guarantees of Carolyn Hughes were obtained in violation of the ECOA and were therefore unenforceable.[23] ■

Credit-Card Rules The TILA also contains provisions regarding credit cards. One provision limits the liability of a cardholder to $50 per card for unauthorized charges made before the creditor was notified that the card was lost. If a consumer received an *unsolicited* credit card in the mail that was later stolen, the company that issued the card cannot charge the consumer for any unauthorized charges.

Another provision requires credit-card companies to disclose the balance computation method that is used to determine the outstanding balance and to state when finance charges begin to accrue. Other provisions set forth procedures for resolving billing disputes with the credit-card company. These procedures may be used if, for instance, a cardholder wishes to withhold payment for a faulty product purchased with a credit card.

---

22. 15 U.S.C. Sections 1601–1693r. The TILA was amended in 1980 by the Truth-in-Lending Simplification and Reform Act and again in 2009 by the Credit Card Accountability Responsibility and Disclosure Act.
23. *Frontenac Bank v. T.R. Hughes, Inc.,* 404 S.W.3d 272 (Mo.App. 2012).

LEARNING OBJECTIVE 3

What does Regulation Z require, and how does it relate to the Truth-in-Lending Act?

Regulation Z A set of rules issued by the Federal Reserve Board of Governors to implement the provisions of the Truth-in-Lending Act.

KNOW THIS

The Federal Reserve Board is part of the Federal Reserve System, which influences the lending and investing activities of commercial banks and the cost and availability of credit.

Amendments to Credit-Card Rules
Amendments to TILA's credit-card rules added the following protections:

1. A company may not retroactively increase the interest rates on existing card balances unless the account is sixty days delinquent.

2. A company must provide forty-five days' advance notice to consumers before changing its credit-card terms.

3. Monthly bills must be sent to cardholders twenty-one days before the due date.

4. The interest rate charged on a customer's credit-card balance may not be increased except in specific situations, such as when a promotional rate ends.

5. A company may not charge fees for being over the credit card's limit except in specified situations.

6. When the customer has balances at different interest rates, payments in excess of the minimum amount due must be applied first to the balance with the highest rate (for instance, a higher interest rate is commonly charged for cash advances).

7. A company may not compute finance charges based on the previous billing cycle (a practice known as double-cycle billing, which hurts consumers because they are charged interest for the previous cycle even if they have paid the bill in full).

ETHICAL ISSUE

Are arbitration clauses in credit-card and checking-account contracts fair? Currently, clauses in most credit-card and checking-account contracts require consumers to resolve disputes through arbitration. These disputes may involve checking-account fees, for example, or credit-card charges. The arbitration clauses typically prevent individuals from joining group (class-action) litigation concerning such issues.

According to Consumer Financial Protection Bureau (CFPB) director Richard Cordray, the bureau has "found that these arbitration clauses restrict consumer relief in disputes with financial companies by limiting class actions that provide millions of dollars in redress each year." In response, the financial-services industry has argued that the efficiency and lower cost of arbitration provides benefits not only for the industry in general but also for consumers. Notwithstanding the benefits of arbitration, the CFPB is considering barring lenders from requiring consumers to waive their class-action rights when they sign a contract that includes an arbitration clause.

32–4b Fair Credit Reporting Act

The Fair Credit Reporting Act (FCRA)[24] protects consumers against inaccurate credit reporting and requires that lenders and other creditors report correct, relevant, and up-to-date information. The act provides that consumer credit reporting agencies may issue credit reports to users only for specified purposes. Legitimate purposes include the extension of credit, the issuance of insurance policies, and in response to the consumer's request. (See the *Business Application* feature at the end of this chapter for tips on how businesspersons can use credit reporting services.)

Consumer Notification and Inaccurate Information
Any time a consumer is denied credit or insurance on the basis of his or her credit report, the consumer must be notified of that fact. The same notice must be sent to consumers who are charged more than others ordinarily would be for credit or insurance because of their credit reports.

---

24. 15 U.S.C. Sections 1681 *et seq.*

Under the FCRA, consumers can request the source of any information used by the credit agency, as well as the identity of anyone who has received an agency's report. Consumers are also permitted to have access to the information contained about them in a credit reporting agency's files.

If a consumer discovers that the agency's files contain inaccurate information, he or she should report the problem to the agency. On the consumer's written (or electronic) request, the agency must conduct a systematic examination of its records. Any unverifiable or erroneous information must be deleted within a reasonable period of time.

Which law attempts to protect consumers against inaccurate credit information?

Remedies for Violations A credit reporting agency that fails to comply with the act is liable for actual damages, plus additional damages not to exceed $1,000 and attorneys' fees.[25] Creditors and other companies that use information from credit reporting agencies may also be liable for violations of the FCRA. An insurance company's failure to notify new customers that they are paying higher insurance rates as a result of their credit scores is considered a *willful* violation of the FCRA.[26]

CASE EXAMPLE 32.8 Branch Banking & Trust Company of Virginia (BB&T) gave Rex Saunders an auto loan but failed to give him a payment coupon book and rebuffed his attempts to make payments on the loan. Eventually, BB&T discovered its mistake and demanded full payment, plus interest and penalties. When payment was not immediately forthcoming, BB&T declared that Saunders was in default. It then repossessed the car and forwarded adverse credit information about Saunders to credit reporting agencies without noting that Saunders disputed the information. Saunders filed a lawsuit alleging violations of the FCRA and was awarded $80,000 in punitive damages. An appellate court found that the damages award was reasonable, given BB&T's willful violation.[27]

32–4c Fair and Accurate Credit Transactions Act

Congress passed the Fair and Accurate Credit Transactions (FACT) Act to combat identity theft.[28] The act established a national fraud alert system so that consumers who suspect that they have been or may be victimized by identity theft can place an alert in their credit files. The act also requires the major credit reporting agencies to provide consumers with a free copy of their credit reports every twelve months.

Another provision requires account numbers on credit-card receipts to be truncated (shortened) so that merchants, employees, and others who have access to the receipts cannot obtain a consumer's name and full credit-card number. The act also mandates that financial institutions work with the FTC to identify "red flag" indicators of identity theft and to develop rules for disposing of sensitive credit information.

> "Credit is a system whereby a person who can't pay gets another person who can't pay to guarantee that he can pay."
>
> **CHARLES DICKENS**
> 1812–1870
> (ENGLISH NOVELIST)

32–4d Fair Debt-Collection Practices

The Fair Debt Collection Practices Act (FDCPA)[29] attempts to curb abuses by collection agencies. The act applies only to specialized debt-collection agencies and attorneys who regularly attempt to collect debts on behalf of someone else, usually for a percentage of the amount owed. Creditors attempting to collect debts are not covered by the act unless, by misrepresenting themselves, they cause the debtors to believe that they are collection agencies.

---

25. 15 U.S.C. Section 1681n.
26. This was the holding of the United States Supreme Court in *Safeco Insurance Co. of America v. Burr*, 551 U.S. 47, 127 S.Ct. 2201, 167 L.Ed.2d 1045 (2007).
27. *Saunders v. Branch Banking & Trust Co. of Virginia*, 526 F.3d 142 (4th Cir. 2008).
28. Pub. L. No. 108-159, 117 Stat. 1952 (December 4, 2003).
29. 15 U.S.C. Section 1692.

Requirements of the Act Under the FDCPA, a collection agency may not do any of the following:

1. Contact the debtor at the debtor's place of employment if the debtor's employer objects.
2. Contact the debtor at inconvenient or unusual times (such as three o'clock in the morning), or at any time if the debtor is being represented by an attorney.
3. Contact third parties other than the debtor's parents, spouse, or financial adviser about payment of a debt unless a court authorizes such action.
4. Harass or intimidate the debtor (by using abusive language or threatening violence, for instance) or make false or misleading statements (such as posing as a police officer).
5. Communicate with the debtor at any time after receiving notice that the debtor is refusing to pay the debt, except to advise the debtor of further action to be taken by the collection agency.

The FDCPA also requires a collection agency to include a *validation notice* whenever it initially contacts a debtor for payment of a debt or within five days of that initial contact. The notice must state that the debtor has thirty days in which to dispute the debt and to request a written verification of the debt from the collection agency. The debtor's request for debt validation must be in writing.

Enforcement of the Act The Federal Trade Commission is primarily responsible for enforcing the FDCPA. A debt collector who fails to comply with the act is liable for actual damages, plus additional damages not to exceed $1,000[30] and attorneys' fees.

Debt collectors who violate the act are exempt from liability if they can show that the violation was not intentional and resulted from a bona fide error. The "bona fide error" defense typically has been applied to mistakes of fact or clerical errors. A few courts have gone further and allowed the defense to be used by collection agencies that had left voice mail messages on a debtor's phone that were later accidentally heard by third parties.[31]

32-5 Protecting the Environment

We now turn to a discussion of the various ways in which businesses are regulated by the government in the interest of attempting to protect the environment. Environmental protection is not without a price. For many businesses, the costs of complying with environmental regulations are high, and for some, they may seem too high.

32-5a Federal Regulation

Congress has enacted a number of statutes to control the impact of human activities on the environment. Some of these laws have been passed in an attempt to improve the quality of air and water. Other laws specifically regulate toxic chemicals, including pesticides, herbicides, and hazardous wastes.

Environmental Regulatory Agencies The primary agency regulating environmental law is the Environmental Protection Agency (EPA). Other federal agencies with authority to regulate specific environmental matters include the Department of the Interior, the Department of Defense, the Department of Labor, the Food and Drug Administration, and the Nuclear Regulatory Commission.

State and local agencies also play an important role in enforcing federal environmental legislation. In addition, most federal environmental laws provide that private parties can sue to

---

30. According to the U.S. Court of Appeals for the Sixth Circuit, the $1,000 limit on damages applies to each lawsuit, not to each violation. See *Wright v. Finance Service of Norwalk, Inc.*, 22 F.3d 647 (6th Cir. 1994).
31. See, for example, *Zortman v. J.C. Christensen & Associates, Inc.*, 870 F.Supp.2d 694 (D.Minn. 2012); see also *Mbaku v. Bank of America, N.A.*, 2013 WL 425981 (D.Colo. 2013).

enforce environmental regulations if government agencies fail to do so. Typically, a threshold hurdle in such suits is meeting the requirements for standing to sue.

Environmental Impact Statements

All agencies of the federal government must take environmental factors into consideration when making significant decisions. The National Environmental Policy Act (NEPA)[32] requires that an **environmental impact statement (EIS)** be prepared for every major federal action that significantly affects the quality of the environment (see Exhibit 32–2). An EIS must analyze the following:

1. The impact that the action will have on the environment.

2. Any adverse effects on the environment and alternative actions that might be taken.

3. Irreversible effects the action might generate.

Note that an EIS must be prepared for every major federal action. An action qualifies as "major" if it involves a substantial commitment of resources (monetary or otherwise). An action is "federal" if a federal agency has the power to control it. **EXAMPLE 32.9** Development of a ski resort by a private developer on federal land may require an EIS. Construction or operation of a nuclear plant, which requires a federal permit, or creation of a dam as part of a federal project requires an EIS. ■

If an agency decides that an EIS is unnecessary, it must issue a statement supporting this conclusion. Private individuals, consumer interest groups, businesses, and others who believe that a federal agency's actions threaten the environment often use EISs as a means of challenging those actions.

---

32. 42 U.S.C. Sections 4321–4370d.

LEARNING OBJECTIVE 4

What is contained in an environmental impact statement, and who must file one?

Environmental Impact Statement (EIS) A formal analysis required for any major federal action that will significantly affect the quality of the environment to determine the action's impact and explore alternatives.

Exhibit 32–2 Environmental Impact Statements

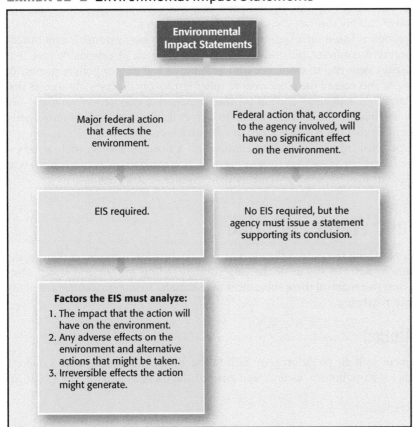

Would any federal agency allow a dam to be built without an environmental impact statement? Why or why not?

Nuisance A common law doctrine under which persons may be held liable for using their property in a manner that unreasonably interferes with others' rights to use or enjoy their own property.

32–5b Common Law Actions

Even before there were statutes and regulations explicitly protecting the environment, the common law recognized that individuals have the right not to have their environment contaminated by others. Common law remedies against environmental pollution originated centuries ago in England. Those responsible for operations that created dirt, smoke, noxious odors, noise, or toxic substances were sometimes held liable under common law theories of nuisance or negligence. Today, individuals who have suffered harm from pollution continue to rely on the common law to obtain damages and injunctions against business polluters.

Nuisance Under the common law doctrine of **nuisance,** persons may be held liable if they use their property in a manner that unreasonably interferes with others' rights to use or enjoy their own property. In these situations, the courts commonly balance the harm caused by the pollution against the costs of stopping it.

Courts have often denied injunctive relief on the ground that the hardships that would be imposed on the polluter and on the community are relatively greater than the hardships suffered by the plaintiff. **EXAMPLE 32.10** Hewitt's Factory causes neighboring landowners to suffer from smoke, soot, and vibrations. If the factory is the core of the local economy, a court may leave it in operation and award monetary damages to the injured parties. Damages may include compensation for any decline in the value of their property caused by Hewitt's operation. ■

To obtain relief from pollution under the nuisance doctrine, a property owner may have to identify a distinct harm (a "private" nuisance) separate from that affecting the general public. Under the common law—which is still followed in some states—individuals must establish a private nuisance to have standing to sue. A public authority (such as a state's attorney general), though, can sue to abate a "public" nuisance.

Negligence and Strict Liability An injured party may sue a business polluter under the negligence and strict liability theories discussed in the torts chapter.

A negligence action is based on a business's alleged failure to use reasonable care toward a party whose injury was foreseeable and was caused by the lack of reasonable care. For instance, employees might sue an employer whose failure to use proper pollution controls contaminated the air and caused the employees to suffer respiratory illnesses. Businesses that engage in ultrahazardous activities—such as the transportation of radioactive materials—are strictly liable for any injuries the activities cause. In a strict liability action, the injured party does not need to prove that the business failed to exercise reasonable care.

Lawsuits for personal injuries caused by exposure to a toxic substance, such as asbestos, radiation, or hazardous waste, have given rise to a growing body of tort law known as **toxic torts.** These torts may be based on a theory of negligence or strict liability.

Toxic Tort A civil wrong arising from exposure to a toxic substance, such as asbestos, radiation, or hazardous waste.

32–6 Air and Water Pollution

The United States has long recognized the need to protect our natural resources. During the industrial revolution, factories began discharging substances into our air and water. Over time, it became clear that many of these substances were harmful to our environment, and the government began regulating.

32–6a Air Pollution

Federal involvement with air pollution goes back to the 1950s and 1960s, when Congress authorized funds for air-pollution research and enacted the Clean Air Act.[33] The Clean Air

---

33. 42 U.S.C. Sections 7401 *et seq.*

Act provides the basis for issuing regulations to control multistate air pollution. It covers both mobile sources of pollution (such as automobiles and other vehicles) and stationary sources of pollution (such as electric utilities and industrial plants).

Mobile Sources of Air Pollution

Regulations governing air pollution from automobiles and other mobile sources specify pollution standards and establish time schedules for meeting the standards. The EPA periodically updates the pollution standards to reduce the amount of emissions allowed in light of new developments and data.

The Obama administration announced a long-term goal of reducing emissions of certain pollutants, including those from automobiles, by 80 percent by 2050. The administration also ordered the EPA to develop national standards regulating fuel economy and emissions for medium- and heavy-duty trucks, starting with 2014 models.

Stationary Sources of Air Pollution

The Clean Air Act authorizes the EPA to establish air-quality standards for stationary sources (such as manufacturing plants). But the act recognizes that the primary responsibility for preventing and controlling air pollution rests with state and local governments. The standards are aimed at controlling hazardous air pollutants—those likely to cause death or a serious, irreversible, or incapacitating condition, such as cancer or neurological or reproductive damage.

The EPA sets primary and secondary levels of ambient standards—that is, the maximum permissible levels of certain pollutants—and the states formulate plans to achieve those standards. Different standards apply depending on whether the sources of pollution are located in clean areas or polluted areas and whether they are existing sources or major new sources.

Hazardous Air Pollutants. The Clean Air Act requires the EPA to list all regulated hazardous air pollutants on a prioritized schedule. In all, nearly two hundred substances, including asbestos, benzene, beryllium, cadmium, and vinyl chloride, have been classified as hazardous. They are emitted from stationary sources by a variety of business activities, including smelting (melting ore to produce metal), dry cleaning, house painting, and commercial baking.

Maximum Achievable Control Technology. Instead of establishing specific emissions standards for each hazardous air pollutant, the Clean Air Act requires major sources of pollutants to use pollution-control equipment that represents the *maximum achievable control technology,* or MACT, to reduce emissions. The EPA issues guidelines as to what equipment meets this standard.[34]

Greenhouse Gases

Although greenhouse gases, such as carbon dioxide (CO_2), are generally thought to contribute to global climate change, the Clean Air Act does not specifically mention CO_2 emissions. Therefore, the EPA did not regulate CO_2 emissions until 2009, after the Supreme Court ruled that it had the authority to do so.

CASE EXAMPLE 32.11 Environmental groups and several states, including Massachusetts, sued the EPA in an effort to force the agency to regulate CO_2 emissions. When the case reached the United States Supreme Court, the EPA argued that the plaintiffs lacked standing. The agency claimed that because climate change has widespread effects, an individual plaintiff cannot show the particularized harm required for standing. The agency also maintained that it did not have authority under the Clean Air Act to address global climate change and regulate CO_2.

The Court, however, ruled that Massachusetts had standing because its coastline, including state-owned lands, faced a threat from the rising sea levels that may result from climate change. The Court also held that the Clean Air Act's broad definition of air pollution gives the EPA authority to regulate CO_2 and requires the EPA to regulate any air pollutants that might "endanger public health or welfare." Accordingly, the Court ordered the EPA to determine

> "There's so much pollution in the air now that if it weren't for our lungs, there'd be no place to put it all."
>
> **ROBERT ORBEN**
> 1927–PRESENT
> (AMERICAN COMEDIAN)

---

34. The EPA has also issued rules to regulate hazardous air pollutants emitted by landfills. See 40 C.F.R. Sections 60.750–60.759.

Does the Environmental Protection Agency have the power to regulate CO_2 emissions from power plants?

whether CO_2 was a pollutant that endangered the public health.[35] ■ The EPA later concluded that greenhouse gases, including CO_2 emissions, do constitute a public danger.

Violations of the Clean Air Act For violations of emission limits under the Clean Air Act, the EPA can assess civil penalties of up to $25,000 per day. Additional fines of up to $5,000 per day can be assessed for other violations, such as failing to maintain the required records. To penalize those who find it more cost-effective to violate the act than to comply with it, the EPA is authorized to obtain a penalty equal to the violator's economic benefits from noncompliance. Persons who provide information about violators may be paid up to $10,000. Private individuals can also sue violators.

Those who knowingly violate the act may be subject to criminal penalties, including fines of up to $1 million and imprisonment for up to two years (for false statements or failures to report violations). Corporate officers are among those who may be subject to these penalties. The phrase "knowingly violate" was at the center of the dispute in an individual's appeal of his conviction for violations of the Clean Air Act.

---

35. *Massachusetts v. EPA*, 549 U.S. 497, 127 S.Ct. 1438, 167 L.Ed.2d 248 (2007).

CASE 32.3

United States v. O'Malley

United States Court of Appeals, Seventh Circuit, 739 F.3d 1001 (2014).

FACTS Duane O'Malley operated Origin Fire Protection. Michael Pinski hired Origin to remove and dispose of 2,200 feet of insulation from a building Pinski owned in Kankakee, Illinois. The insulation contained asbestos, which Pinski, O'Malley, and O'Malley's employees recognized. O'Malley did not have a license to remove the asbestos, and none of his employees were trained in complying with federal asbestos regulations. Nevertheless, Origin removed the debris and disposed of it at various sites, including a vacant lot where it spilled onto the soil, resulting in clean-up costs of nearly $50,000. In a federal district court, a jury convicted O'Malley of removing, transporting, and dumping asbestos in violation of the Clean Air Act. The court sentenced him to 120 months of imprisonment, three years of supervised release, a $15,000 fine, and $47,085.70 in restitution to the Environmental Protection Agency (EPA). O'Malley appealed.

ISSUE Did O'Malley's knowledge that the insulation around the pipes contained asbestos satisfy the "knowingly violate" requirement of the Clean Air Act?

DECISION Yes. The U.S. Court of Appeals for the Seventh Circuit affirmed the lower court's judgment. "The very fact that O'Malley was knowingly working with asbestos-containing material met the *mens rea* [criminal intent] requirement."

Is a license required for asbestos removal?

REASON O'Malley claimed that the government was required to prove he knew the asbestos was one of the six types regulated by the EPA. The court disagreed. When "dangerous . . . materials are involved, . . . the probability of regulation is so great that anyone who is aware that he is in possession of them or dealing with them must be presumed to be aware of the regulation."

Under the Clean Air Act, the EPA regulates the emission of hazardous air pollutants, including asbestos. The handling of asbestos is subject to an EPA work-practice standard—a prescribed method for dealing with the substance. Any person who "knowingly violates" the work-practice standard commits a crime. The standard applies to six types of asbestos-containing material, which includes friable asbestos material—"any material containing more than 1 percent asbestos . . . that, when dry, can be crumbled, pulverized, or reduced to powder by hand pressure." Here, the insulation clearly met the definition of "friable asbestos material."

WHAT IF THE FACTS WERE DIFFERENT? *Suppose that O'Malley had been licensed to remove the asbestos. Would the result have been different? Why or why not?*

32–6b Water Pollution

Water pollution stems mostly from industrial, municipal, and agricultural sources. Pollutants entering streams, lakes, and oceans include organic wastes, heated water, sediments from soil runoff, nutrients (including fertilizers and human and animal wastes), and toxic chemicals and other hazardous substances.

Federal regulations governing the pollution of water can be traced back to the 1899 Rivers and Harbors Appropriations Act.[36] These regulations prohibited ships and manufacturers from discharging or depositing refuse in navigable waterways without a permit. In 1948, Congress passed the Federal Water Pollution Control Act (FWPCA),[37] but its regulatory system and enforcement powers proved to be inadequate.

The Clean Water Act In 1972, amendments to the FWPCA—known as the Clean Water Act (CWA)—established the following goals: (1) make waters safe for swimming, (2) protect fish and wildlife, and (3) eliminate the discharge of pollutants into the water. The amendments set specific time schedules, which were extended by amendment and by the Water Quality Act.[38] Under these schedules, the EPA limits the discharge of various types of pollutants based on the technology available for controlling them.

LEARNING OBJECTIVE 5
What are three main goals of the Clean Water Act?

Permit System for Point-Source Emissions. The CWA established a permit system, called the National Pollutant Discharge Elimination System (NPDES), for regulating discharges from "point sources" of pollution. Point sources include industrial facilities, municipal facilities (such as sewer pipes and sewage treatment plants), and agricultural facilities.[39] Under this system, industrial, municipal, and agricultural polluters must apply for permits before discharging wastes into surface waters.

NPDES permits can be issued by the EPA, authorized state agencies, and Indian tribes, but only if the discharge will not violate water-quality standards (either federal or state standards). Special requirements must be met to discharge toxic chemicals and residue from oil spills. NPDES permits must be renewed every five years.

Standards for Equipment. Regulations generally specify that the *best available control technology,* or BACT, be installed. The EPA issues guidelines as to what equipment meets this standard. Essentially, the guidelines require the most effective pollution-control equipment available.

New sources must install BACT equipment before beginning operations. Existing sources are subject to timetables for the installation of BACT equipment and must immediately install equipment that utilizes the *best practical control technology,* or BPCT. The EPA also issues guidelines as to what equipment meets this standard.

Violations of the Clean Water Act Because point-source water pollution control is based on a permit system, the permits are the key to enforcement. States have primary responsibility for enforcing the permit system, subject to EPA monitoring.

Discharging emissions into navigable waters without a permit, or in violation of pollution limits under a permit, violates the CWA. Violators are subject to a variety of civil and criminal penalties. Depending on the violation, civil penalties range from $10,000 to $25,000 per day, but not more than $25,000 per violation.

Criminal penalties, which apply only if a violation was intentional, range from a fine of $2,500 per day and imprisonment for up to one year to a fine of $1 million and fifteen years' imprisonment. Injunctive relief and damages can also be imposed. The polluting party can be required to clean up the pollution or pay for the cost of doing so.

> "Among the treasures of our land is water—fast becoming our most valuable, most prized, most critical resource."
>
> **DWIGHT D. EISENHOWER**
> 1890–1969
> (THIRTY-FOURTH PRESIDENT OF THE UNITED STATES, 1953–1961)

---

36. 33 U.S.C. Sections 401–418.
37. 33 U.S.C. Sections 1251–1387.
38. This act amended 33 U.S.C. Section 1251.
39. 33 U.S.C. Section 1342.

Drinking Water   The Safe Drinking Water Act[40] requires the EPA to set maximum levels for pollutants in public water systems. Public water system operators must come as close as possible to meeting the EPA's standards by using the best available technology that is economically and technologically feasible.

The act, as amended, also requires each supplier of drinking water to send an annual statement describing the source of its water to every household it supplies. The statement must disclose the level of any contaminants in the water and any possible health concerns associated with the contaminants.

Oil Pollution   When more than 10 million gallons of oil leaked into Alaska's Prince William Sound from the *Exxon Valdez* supertanker in 1989, Congress responded by passing the Oil Pollution Act.[41] (At that time, the *Exxon Valdez* disaster was the worst oil spill in U.S. history, but the British Petroleum oil spill in the Gulf of Mexico in 2010 surpassed it.)

Under this act, any onshore or offshore oil facility, oil shipper, vessel owner, or vessel operator that discharges oil into navigable waters or onto an adjoining shore can be liable for clean-up costs and damages. In addition, the polluter can be ordered to pay for damage to natural resources, private property, and the local economy, including the increased cost of providing public services.

32–7 Toxic Chemicals and Hazardous Waste

Originally, most environmental clean-up efforts were directed toward reducing smog and making water safe for fishing and swimming. Today, the control of toxic chemicals used in agriculture and in industry has become increasingly important.

Some industrial, agricultural, and household wastes pose more serious threats than others. If not properly disposed of, these toxic chemicals may present a substantial danger to human health and the environment. If released into the environment, they may contaminate public drinking water resources.

32–7a Pesticides and Herbicides

The Federal Insecticide, Fungicide, and Rodenticide Act (FIFRA)[42] regulates the use of pesticides and herbicides. These substances must be (1) registered before they can be sold, (2) certified and used only for approved applications, and (3) used in limited quantities when applied to food crops. The act gives the EPA authority to oversee the sale and use of these substances and to determine whether, and at what levels, a substance may be harmful.

It is a violation of FIFRA to sell a pesticide or herbicide that is unregistered or has had its registration canceled or suspended. It is also a violation to sell a pesticide or herbicide with a false or misleading label or to destroy or deface any labeling required under the act.

Penalties for commercial dealers include imprisonment for up to one year and a fine of up to $25,000. Farmers and other private users of pesticides or herbicides who violate the act are subject to a $1,000 fine and incarceration for up to thirty days. Note that a state can also regulate the sale and use of federally registered pesticides.

32–7b Toxic Substances

The Toxic Substances Control Act[43] regulates chemicals and chemical compounds that are known to be toxic, such as asbestos and polychlorinated biphenyls (PCBs). The act also

---

40. 42 U.S.C. Sections 300f to 300j-25.
41. 33 U.S.C. Sections 2701–2761.
42. 7 U.S.C. Sections 135–136y.
43. 15 U.S.C. Sections 2601–2692.

controls the introduction of new chemical compounds by requiring investigation of any possible harmful effects from these substances.

The act authorizes the EPA to require that manufacturers, processors, and other organizations planning to use chemicals first determine their effects on human health and the environment. The EPA can regulate substances that could pose an imminent hazard or an unreasonable risk of injury to health or the environment. The EPA may require special labeling, limit the use of a substance, set production quotas, or prohibit the use of a substance altogether.

32–7c Resource Conservation and Recovery Act

The Resource Conservation and Recovery Act (RCRA)[44] was passed in reaction to concern over the effects of hazardous waste materials on the environment. The RCRA required the EPA to determine which forms of solid waste should be considered hazardous and to establish regulations to monitor and control hazardous waste disposal.

The act authorized the EPA to issue technical requirements for facilities that store and treat hazardous waste. The act also required all producers of hazardous waste materials to label and package properly any hazardous waste to be transported. Amendments to the RCRA decreased the use of land containment in the disposal of hazardous waste and required smaller generators of hazardous waste to comply with the act.

Under the RCRA, a company may be assessed a civil penalty of up to $25,000 for each violation.[45] Penalties are based on the seriousness of the violation, the probability of harm, and the extent to which the violation deviates from RCRA requirements. Criminal penalties include fines of up to $50,000 for each day of violation, imprisonment for up to two years (in most instances), or both.[46] Criminal fines and the period of imprisonment can be doubled for certain repeat offenders.

32–7d Superfund

The Comprehensive Environmental Response, Compensation, and Liability Act (CERCLA),[47] commonly known as Superfund, regulates the clean-up of disposal sites in which hazardous waste is leaking into the environment. CERCLA, as amended, has four primary elements:

1. It established an information-gathering and analysis system that enables the government to identify chemical dump sites and determine the appropriate action.

2. It authorized the EPA to respond to hazardous substance emergencies and to arrange for the clean-up of a leaking site directly if the persons responsible for the problem fail to clean up the site.

3. It created a Hazardous Substance Response Trust Fund (also called Superfund) to pay for the clean-up of hazardous sites using funds obtained through taxes on certain businesses.

4. It allowed the government to recover the cost of clean-up from persons who were (even remotely) responsible for hazardous substance releases.

Potentially Responsible Parties Superfund provides that when a release or a potential release of hazardous chemicals from a site occurs, the following persons may be held responsible for cleaning up the site:

1. The person who generated the wastes disposed of at the site.

2. The person who transported the waste to the site.

---

44. 42 U.S.C. Sections 6901 *et seq.*
45. 42 U.S.C. Section 6928(a).
46. 42 U.S.C. Section 6928(d).
47. 42 U.S.C. Sections 9601–9675.

3. The person who owned or operated the site at the time of the disposal.

4. The current owner or operator of the site.

A person falling within one of these categories is referred to as a **potentially responsible party (PRP)**. If the PRPs do not clean up the site, the EPA can clean up the site and recover the clean-up costs from the PRPs.

Potentially Responsible Party (PRP) A party liable for the costs of cleaning up a hazardous waste disposal site under the Comprehensive Environmental Response, Compensation, and Liability Act.

Strict Liability of PRPs Superfund imposes strict liability on PRPs, and that liability cannot be avoided through transfer of ownership. Thus, selling a site where hazardous wastes were disposed of does not relieve the seller of liability, and the buyer also becomes liable for the clean-up. Liability also extends to businesses that merge with or buy corporations that have violated CERCLA.

Joint and Several Liability Liability under Superfund is usually joint and several—that is, a person who generated *only a fraction of the hazardous waste* disposed of at the site may nevertheless be liable for *all* of the clean-up costs. CERCLA authorizes a party who has incurred clean-up costs to bring a "contribution action" against any other person who is liable or potentially liable for a percentage of the costs.

PREVENTING LEGAL DISPUTES

One way for a business to minimize its potential liability under Superfund is to conduct environmental compliance audits of its own operations regularly to determine whether any environmental hazards exist. The EPA encourages companies to conduct self-audits and promptly detect, disclose, and correct wrongdoing. Companies that do so are subject to lighter penalties (fines may be reduced as much as 75 percent) for violations of environmental laws.

In addition, under EPA guidelines, the EPA will waive all fines if a small company corrects environmental violations within 180 days after being notified of the violations (or 360 days if pollution-prevention techniques are involved). The policy does not apply to criminal violations of environmental laws or to violations that pose a significant threat to public health, safety, or the environment.

Defenses There are a few defenses to liability under CERCLA. The most important is the *innocent landowner defense*.[48] Under this defense, an innocent property owner may be able to avoid liability by showing that he or she had no contractual or employment relationship with the person who released the hazardous substance onto the land. If the party who disposed of the substances transferred the property *by contract* to the current owner, the defense normally will not be available.

The current owner may still be able to assert the defense, however, by showing that at the time the property was acquired, she or he had no reason to know that it had been used for hazardous waste disposal. The owner must show that at the time of the purchase, she or he undertook all appropriate investigation into the previous ownership and uses of the property to determine whether there was reason to be concerned about hazardous substances. In effect, this defense protects only property owners who took precautions and investigated the possibility of environmental hazards at the time they bought the property.

---

48. 42 U.S.C. Section 9601(35)(B).

Reviewing . . . Consumer and Environmental Law

Residents of Lake Caliopa, Minnesota, began noticing an unusually high number of lung ailments among the local population. Several concerned citizens pooled their resources and commissioned a study to compare the frequency of these health conditions in Lake Caliopa with national averages. The study concluded that residents of Lake Caliopa experienced four to seven times the rate of frequency of asthma, bronchitis, and emphysema as the population nationwide.

During the study period, citizens began expressing concerns about the large volume of smog emitted by the Cotton Design apparel manufacturing plant on the outskirts of town. The plant had a production facility two miles east of town beside the Tawakoni River and employed seventy workers. Just downstream on the Tawakoni River, the city of Lake Caliopa operated a public waterworks facility, which supplied all city residents with water.

After conducting its own investigation, the Minnesota Pollution Control Agency ordered Cotton Design to install new equipment to control air and water pollution. Later, citizens brought a lawsuit in a Minnesota state court against Cotton Design for various respiratory ailments allegedly caused or compounded by smog from Cotton Design's factory. Using the information presented in the chapter, answer the following questions.

1. Under the common law, what would each plaintiff be required to identify in order to be given relief by the court?

2. What standard for limiting emissions into the air does Cotton Design's pollution-control equipment have to meet?

3. If Cotton Design's emissions violated the Clean Air Act, how much can the EPA assess in fines per day?

4. What information must the city send to every household that it supplies with water?

DEBATE THIS

- Laws against bait-and-switch advertising should be abolished because no consumer is ever forced to buy anything.

BUSINESS APPLICATION

The Proper Approach to Using Credit Reporting Services*

As explained in the chapter, the Fair Credit Reporting Act (FCRA) protects consumers against inaccurate credit reporting. Many credit reporting agencies provide

much more than just credit reports, however. Increasingly, they are providing employers with employment history, information on educational attainment, and criminal records for current employees and job applicants.

Disclosure Issues When Making Background Checks

If a company uses credit reporting agencies for background checks, it must disclose this

fact to current employees and to applicants. A company that does not conform to the requirements of advance notice, disclosure, and consent may become involved in litigation.

For example, Vitran Express used credit reporting agencies to determine whether prospective employees had criminal records without disclosing this practice to applicants as required by the FCRA. One applicant lost a

* This *Business Application* is not meant to substitute for the services of an attorney who is licensed to practice law in your state.

Continues

job offer because the credit reporting agency forwarded inaccurate information indicating that he had a criminal history when he did not. When he and other job applicants brought a class-action lawsuit against Vitran Express, the company ultimately agreed to pay millions of dollars to settle the case.

Steps That Employers Should Take to Avoid Litigation

To guard against legal problems, all companies must make sure that they comply with federal law when they perform background checks. Employers should certify in writing to each credit reporting agency they hire that they will follow federal rules in this area.

Employers must give advance notice and disclosure and obtain consent to any background check that exceeds a simple credit check. Thus, each employee or applicant should be given a clear disclosure—in a separate document—stating that a background report may be requested from a consumer reporting service. At that time, the employer should obtain the person's written consent.

When a consumer report influences an employer's decision not to hire someone, or to take some other negative employment action, the company should provide the following documents to the individual *before* taking the negative action:

- The Federal Trade Commission document called "A Summary of Your Rights under the Fair Credit Reporting Act."

- A copy of the consumer report on which the company based its negative decision.

CHECKLIST for the Businessperson:

1. You or your in-house counsel should carefully review federal law concerning this matter.

2. Always let employees and job applicants know if you are going to use a consumer reporting service's report in evaluating them.

3. Create a separate document that indicates that you are going to use a consumer reporting service.

Key Terms

bait-and-switch advertising 804
cease-and-desist order 805
"cooling-off" laws 808
counteradvertising 805
deceptive advertising 803

environmental impact statement (EIS) 817
multiple product order 805
nuisance 818

potentially responsible party (PRP) 824
Regulation Z 813
toxic tort 818

Chapter Summary: Consumer and Environmental Law

CONSUMER LAW	

Advertising, Marketing, and Sales	1. *Deceptive advertising*—Generally, an advertising claim will be deemed deceptive if it would mislead a reasonable consumer.
	2. *Bait-and-switch advertising*—Advertising a lower-priced product (the bait) to lure consumers into the store and then telling them the product is unavailable and urging them to buy a higher-priced product (the switch) is prohibited by the FTC.
	3. *Online deceptive advertising*—The FTC has issued guidelines to help online businesses comply with the laws prohibiting deceptive advertising.
	4. *FTC actions against deceptive advertising*—
	  a. Cease-and-desist orders—Requiring the advertiser to stop the challenged advertising.
	  b. Counteradvertising—Requiring the advertiser to advertise to correct the earlier misinformation.
	5. *Marketing*—Telemarketers are prohibited from using automatic dialing systems and prerecorded voices and cannot fax ads without the recipient's permission. Telemarketers must identify the seller, describe the product being sold, and disclose all material facts related to the sale.
	6. *Sales*—"Cooling-off" laws permit buyers of goods sold in certain sales transactions (such as trade shows and door-to-door sales) to cancel their contracts within three business days.

Labeling and Packaging	Manufacturers must comply with the labeling and packaging requirements for their specific products. In general, all labels must be accurate and not misleading.
Protection of Health and Safety	1. *Food and drugs*—The Federal Food, Drug, and Cosmetic Act protects consumers against adulterated and misbranded foods and drugs. The act establishes food standards, specifies safe levels of potentially hazardous food additives, and sets classifications of food and food advertising. 2. *Consumer product safety*—The Consumer Product Safety Act seeks to protect consumers from injury from hazardous products. The Consumer Product Safety Commission has the power to remove products that are deemed imminently hazardous from the market and to ban the manufacture and sale of hazardous products.

Credit Protection	1. *Consumer Credit Protection Act, Title I (Truth-in-Lending Act, or TILA)*—A disclosure law that requires sellers and lenders to disclose credit terms or loan terms in certain transactions, including retail installment sales and loans, car loans, home-improvement loans, and certain real estate loans. Additionally, the TILA provides for the following:
	    a. Equal credit opportunity—Creditors are prohibited from discriminating on the basis of race, religion, marital status, gender, national origin, color, or age.
	    b. Credit-card protection—Liability of cardholders for unauthorized charges is limited to $50, providing notice requirements are met. Consumers are not liable for unauthorized charges made on unsolicited credit cards. The act also sets out procedures to be used in settling disputes between credit-card companies and their cardholders.
	2. *Fair Credit Reporting Act*—Entitles consumers to request verification of the accuracy of a credit report and to have unverified or false information removed from their files.
	3. *Fair and Accurate Credit Transaction Act*—Combats identity theft by establishing a national fraud alert system. Requires account numbers to be truncated and credit reporting agencies to provide one free credit report per year to consumers.
	4. *Fair Debt Collection Practices Act*—Prohibits debt collectors from using unfair debt-collection practices, such as contacting the debtor at his or her place of employment if the employer objects or at unreasonable times, contacting third parties about the debt, and harassing the debtor.

ENVIRONMENTAL LAW	
Protecting the Environment	1. *Environmental protection agencies*—The primary agency regulating environmental law is the federal Environmental Protection Agency (EPA), which administers most federal environmental policies and statutes. 2. *Assessing environmental impact*—The National Environmental Policy Act requires the preparation of an environmental impact statement (EIS) for every major federal action. An EIS must analyze the action's impact on the environment, its adverse effects and possible alternatives, and its irreversible effects on environmental quality. 3. *Nuisance*—A common law doctrine under which persons may be held liable if their use of their property unreasonably interferes with others' rights to use their own property. 4. *Negligence and strict liability*—Parties may recover damages for injuries sustained as a result of a firm's pollution-causing activities if they can demonstrate that the harm was a foreseeable result of the firm's failure to exercise reasonable care (negligence). Businesses engaging in ultrahazardous activities are liable for whatever injuries the activities cause, regardless of whether the firms exercise reasonable care.
Air and Water Pollution	1. *Air pollution*—Regulated under the authority of the Clean Air Act and its amendments. 2. *Water pollution*—Regulated under the authority of the Rivers and Harbors Appropriations Act and the Federal Water Pollution Control Act, as amended by the Clean Water Act.
Toxic Chemicals and Hazardous Waste	Pesticides and herbicides, toxic substances, and hazardous waste are regulated under the authority of the Federal Insecticide, Fungicide, and Rodenticide Act; the Toxic Substances Control Act; and the Resource Conservation and Recovery Act, respectively. The Comprehensive Environmental Response, Compensation, and Liability Act (CERCLA), or Superfund, regulates the clean-up of hazardous waste disposal sites.

Issue Spotters

1. United Pharmaceuticals, Inc., has developed a new drug that it believes will be effective in the treatment of patients with AIDS. The drug has had only limited testing, but United wants to make the drug widely available as soon as possible. To market the drug, what must United prove to the U.S. Food and Drug Administration? (See *Protection of Health and Safety.*)

2. ChemCorp generates hazardous wastes from its operations. Disposal Trucking Company transports those wastes to Eliminators, Inc., which owns a site for hazardous waste disposal. Eliminators sells the property on which the disposal site is located to Fluid Properties, Inc. If the Environmental Protection Agency cleans up the site, from whom can it recover the cost? (See *Toxic Chemicals and Hazardous Waste.*)

—**Check your answers to the *Issue Spotters* against the answers provided in Appendix D at the end of this text.**

Learning Objectives Check

1. When will advertising be deemed deceptive?
2. What law protects consumers against contaminated and misbranded foods and drugs?
3. What does Regulation Z require, and how does it relate to the Truth-in-Lending Act?
4. What is contained in an environmental impact statement, and who must file one?
5. What are three main goals of the Clean Water Act?

—**Answers to the even-numbered *Learning Objectives Check* questions can be found in Appendix E at the end of this text.**

Business Scenarios and Case Problems

32–1. Environmental Laws. Fruitade, Inc., is a processor of a soft drink called Freshen Up. Fruitade uses returnable bottles, which it cleans with a special acid to allow for further beverage processing. The acid is diluted with water and then allowed to pass into a navigable stream. Fruitade crushes its broken bottles and throws the crushed glass into the stream. Discuss fully any environmental laws that Fruitade may have violated. (See *Air and Water Pollution*.)

32–2. Credit Protection. Maria Ochoa receives two new credit cards on May 1. She has solicited one of them from Midtown Department Store, and the other arrives unsolicited from High-Flying Airlines. During the month of May, Ochoa makes numerous credit-card purchases from Midtown Department Store, but she does not use the High-Flying Airlines card. On May 31, a burglar breaks into Ochoa's home and steals both credit cards, along with other items.

Ochoa notifies Midtown Department Store of the theft on June 2, but she fails to notify High-Flying Airlines. Using the Midtown credit card, the burglar makes a $500 purchase on June 1 and a $200 purchase on June 3. The burglar then charges a vacation flight on the High-Flying Airlines card for $1,000 on June 5. Ochoa receives the bills for these charges and refuses to pay them. Discuss Ochoa's liability in these situations. (See *Credit Protection*.)

32–3. Spotlight on McDonald's—Food Labeling. A McDonald's Happy Meal® consists of an entrée, a small order of French fries, a small drink, and a toy. In the early 1990s, McDonald's Corp. began to aim its Happy Meal marketing at children aged one to three. In 1995, McDonald's began making nutritional information for its food products available in documents known as "McDonald's Nutrition Facts." Each document lists the food items that the restaurant serves and provides a nutritional breakdown, but the Happy Meal is not included.

Marc Cohen filed a suit in an Illinois state court against McDonald's. Cohen alleged, among other things, that McDonald's had violated a state law prohibiting consumer fraud and deceptive business practices by failing to follow the Nutrition Labeling and Education Act (NLEA) of 1990. The NLEA sets out different, less detailed requirements for products specifically intended for children under the age of four. Does it make sense to have different requirements for children of this age? Why or why not? Should a state court impose regulations where the NLEA has not done so? Explain. [*Cohen v. McDonald's Corp.*, 347 Ill.App.3d 627, 808 N.E.2d 1, 283 Ill.Dec. 451 (1 Dist. 2004)] (See *Labeling and Packaging*.)

32–4. Business Case Problem with Sample Answer—Fair Debt-Collection Practices. Bank of America hired Atlantic Resource Management, LLC, to collect a debt from Michael Engler. Atlantic called Engler's employer and asked his supervisor about the company's policy concerning the execution of warrants. The caller then told the supervisor that, to stop process of the warrant, Engler needed to call Atlantic about "Case Number 37291 NY0969" during the first three hours of Engler's next shift. When Engler's supervisor told him about the call, Engler feared that he might be arrested, and he experienced discomfort, embarrassment, and emotional distress at work. Can Engler recover under the Fair Debt Collection Practices Act? Why or why not? [*Engler v. Atlantic Resource Management, LLC*, 2012 WL 464728 (W.D.N.Y. 2012)] (See *Credit Protection*.)

—**For a sample answer to Problem 32–4, go to Appendix F at the end of this text.**

32–5. Superfund. A by-product of phosphate fertilizer production is pyrite waste, which contains arsenic and lead. From 1884 to 1906, seven phosphate fertilizer plants operated on a forty-three-acre site in Charleston, South Carolina. Planters Fertilizer & Phosphate Co. bought the site in 1906 and continued to make fertilizer. In 1966, Planters sold the site to Columbia Nitrogen Corp. (CNC), which also operated the fertilizer plants. In 1985, CNC sold the site to James Holcombe and J. Henry Fair. Holcombe and Fair subdivided and sold the site to Allwaste Tank Cleaning, Inc., Robin Hood Container Express, the city of Charleston, and Ashley II of Charleston, Inc. Ashley spent almost $200,000 cleaning up the contaminated soil. Who can be held liable for the cost? Why? [*PCS Nitrogen Inc. v. Ashley II of Charleston LLC*, 714 F.3d 161 (4th Cir. 2013)] (See *Toxic Chemicals and Hazardous Waste*.)

32–6. Environmental Impact Statements. The U.S. Forest Service (USFS) proposed a travel management plan (TMP) for the Beartooth Ranger District in the Pryor and Absaroka Mountains in the Custer National Forest of southern Montana. The TMP would convert unauthorized user-created routes within the wilderness to routes authorized for motor vehicle use. It would also permit off-road "dispersed vehicle camping" within 300 feet of the routes, with some seasonal restrictions. The TMP would ban cross-country motorized travel outside the designated routes. Is an environmental impact statement required before the USFS implements the TMP? If so, what aspects of the environment should the USFS consider in preparing it? Discuss. [*Pryors Coalition v. Weldon*, 551 Fed.Appx. 426 (9th Cir. 2014)] (See *Protecting the Environment*.)

32–7. Deceptive Advertising. Innovative Marketing, Inc. (IMI), sold "scareware"—computer security software. IMI's Internet ads redirected consumers to sites where they were told that a scan of their computers had detected dangerous files—viruses, spyware, and "illegal" pornography. In fact, no scans were conducted. Kristy Ross, an IMI cofounder and vice president, reviewed and edited the ads, and was aware of the many complaints that consumers had made about them. An individual can be held liable under the Federal Trade Commission Act's prohibition of deceptive acts or practices if the person (1) participated directly in the deceptive practices or had the authority to control them and (2) had or should have had knowledge of them. Were IMI's ads deceptive? If so, can Ross be held liable? Explain. [*Federal Trade Commission v. Ross,* 743 F.3d 886 (4th Cir. 2014)] (See *Advertising, Marketing, and Sales.*)

32–8. The Clean Water Act. ICG Hazard, LLC, operates the Thunder Ridge surface coal mine in Leslie County, Kentucky, under a National Pollutant Discharge Elimination System permit issued by the Kentucky Division of Water (KDOW). As part of the operation, ICG discharges selenium into the surrounding water. Selenium is a naturally occurring element that endangers aquatic life once it reaches a certain concentration. KDOW knew when it issued the permit that mines in the area could produce selenium but did not specify discharge limits for the element in ICG's permit. Instead, the agency imposed a one-time monitoring requirement, which ICG met. Does ICG's discharge of selenium violate the Clean Water Act? Explain. [*Sierra Club v. ICG Hazard, LLC,* 781 F.3d 281 (6th Cir. 2015)] (See *Air and Water Pollution.*)

32–9. A Question of Ethics—Clean Air Act. In the Clean Air Act, Congress allowed California, which has particular problems with clean air, to adopt its own standard for emissions from cars and trucks. The standard was subject to the approval of the Environmental Protection Agency (EPA), and other states were allowed to adopt the standard after the EPA's approval.

In 2004, in an effort to address climate change, the California Air Resources Board amended the state's standard to attain "the maximum feasible and cost-effective reduction of GHG [greenhouse gas] emissions from motor vehicles." The regulation, which applied to new passenger vehicles and light-duty trucks for 2009 and later, imposed decreasing limits on emissions of carbon dioxide through 2016. While EPA approval was pending, Vermont and other states adopted similar standards. Green Mountain Chrysler Plymouth Dodge Jeep and other auto dealers, automakers, and associations of automakers filed a suit in a federal district court against George Crombie (secretary of the Vermont Agency of Natural Resources) and others, seeking relief from the state regulations. [*Green Mountain Chrysler Plymouth Dodge Jeep v. Crombie,* 508 F.Supp.2d 295 (D.Vt. 2007)] (See *Air and Water Pollution.*)

1. Under the Energy Policy and Conservation Act (EPCA), the National Highway Traffic Safety Administration sets fuel economy standards for new cars. The plaintiffs argued, among other things, that the EPCA, which prohibits states from adopting separate fuel economy standards, preempts Vermont's GHG regulation. Can the GHG rules be treated as equivalent to the fuel economy standards? Discuss.

2. Do Vermont's rules tread on the efforts of the federal government to address climate change internationally? Who should regulate GHG emissions? The federal government? The state governments? Both? Neither? Why?

3. The plaintiffs claimed that they would go bankrupt if they were forced to adhere to the state's GHG standards. Should they be granted relief on this basis? Does history support their claim? Explain.

Critical Thinking and Writing Assignments

32–10. Business Law Critical Thinking Group Assignment.
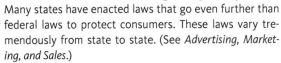
Many states have enacted laws that go even further than federal laws to protect consumers. These laws vary tremendously from state to state. (See *Advertising, Marketing, and Sales.*)

1. The first group will decide whether having different laws is fair to sellers, who may be prohibited from engaging in a practice in one state that is legal in another.

2. The second group will consider how these different laws might affect a business.

3. A third group will determine whether it is fair that residents of one state have more protection than residents of another.

Appendix A

How to Brief Cases and Analyze Case Problems

How to Brief Cases

To fully understand the law with respect to business, you need to be able to read and understand court decisions. To make this task easier, you can use a method of case analysis that is called *briefing*. There is a fairly standard procedure that you can follow when you "brief" any court case. You must first read the case opinion carefully. When you feel you understand the case, you can prepare a brief of it.

Although the format of the brief may vary, typically it will present the essentials of the case under headings such as those listed below.

1. **Citation.** Give the full citation for the case, including the name of the case, the date it was decided, and the court that decided it.

2. **Facts.** Briefly indicate (a) the reasons for the lawsuit; (b) the identity and arguments of the plaintiff(s) and defendant(s), respectively; and (c) the lower court's decision—if appropriate.

3. **Issue.** Concisely phrase, in the form of a question, the essential issue before the court. (If more than one issue is involved, you may have two—or even more—questions here.)

4. **Decision.** Indicate here—with a "yes" or "no," if possible—the court's answer to the question (or questions) in the Issue section above.

5. **Reason.** Summarize as briefly as possible the reasons given by the court for its decision (or decisions) and the case or statutory law relied on by the court in arriving at its decision.

For a case-specific example of what should be included under each of the above headings when briefing a case, see the review of the sample court case presented in the appendix to Chapter 1 of this text.

Analyzing Case Problems

In addition to learning how to brief cases, students of business law and the legal environment also find it helpful to know how to analyze case problems. Part of the study of business law and the legal environment usually involves analyzing case problems, such as those included in this text at the end of each chapter.

For each case problem in this book, we provide the relevant background and facts of the lawsuit and the issue before the court.

When you are assigned one of these problems, your job will be to determine how the court should decide the issue, and why. In other words, you will need to engage in legal analysis and reasoning. Here, we offer some suggestions on how to make this task less daunting. We begin by presenting a sample case problem:

> While Janet Lawson, a famous pianist, was shopping in Quality Market, she slipped and fell on a wet floor in one of the aisles. The floor had recently been mopped by one of the store's employees, but there were no signs warning customers that the floor in that area was wet. As a result of the fall, Lawson injured her right arm and was unable to perform piano concerts for the next six months. Had she been able to perform the scheduled concerts, she would have earned approximately $60,000 over that period of time. Lawson sued Quality Market for this amount, plus another $10,000 in medical expenses. She claimed that the store's failure to warn customers of the wet floor constituted negligence and therefore the market was liable for her injuries. Will the court agree with Lawson? Discuss.

Understand the Facts

This may sound obvious, but before you can analyze or apply the relevant law to a specific set of facts, you must clearly understand those facts. In other words, you should read through the case problem carefully—more than once, if necessary—to make sure you understand the identity of the plaintiff(s) and defendant(s) in the case and the progression of events that led to the lawsuit.

In the sample case problem just given, the identity of the parties is fairly obvious. Janet Lawson is the one bringing the suit; therefore, she is the plaintiff. Lawson is bringing the suit against Quality Market, so it is the defendant. Some of the case problems you may work on have multiple plaintiffs or defendants. Often, it is helpful to use abbreviations for the parties. To indicate a reference to a plaintiff, for example, the *pi* symbol—π—is often used, and a defendant is denoted by a *delta*—Δ—a triangle.

The events leading to the lawsuit are also fairly straightforward. Lawson slipped and fell on a wet floor, and she contends that Quality Market should be liable for her injuries because it was negligent in not posting a sign warning customers of the wet floor.

When you are working on case problems, realize that the facts should be accepted as they are given. For instance, in our sample

A-1

problem, it should be accepted that the floor was wet and that there was no sign. In other words, avoid making conjectures, such as "Maybe the floor wasn't too wet," or "Maybe an employee was getting a sign to put up," or "Maybe someone stole the sign." Questioning the facts as they are presented only adds confusion to your analysis.

Legal Analysis and Reasoning

Once you understand the facts given in the case problem, you can begin to analyze the case. The **IRAC method** is a helpful tool to use in the legal analysis and reasoning process. IRAC is an acronym for **I**ssue, **R**ule, **A**pplication, **C**onclusion. Applying this method to our sample problem would involve the following steps:

1. First, you need to decide what legal **issue** is involved in the case. In our sample case, the basic issue is whether Quality Market's failure to warn customers of the wet floor constituted negligence. Negligence is a *tort*—a civil wrong. In a tort lawsuit, the plaintiff seeks to be compensated for another's wrongful act. A defendant will be deemed negligent if he or she breached a duty of care owed to the plaintiff and the breach of that duty caused the plaintiff to suffer harm.

2. Once you have identified the issue, the next step is to determine what **rule of law** applies to the issue. To make this determination, you will want to carefully review the text discussion relating to the issue involved in the problem. Our sample case problem involves the tort of negligence. The applicable rule of law is the tort law principle that business owners owe a duty to exercise reasonable care to protect their customers (*business invitees*). Reasonable care, in this context, includes either removing—or warning customers of—*foreseeable* risks about which the owner *knew* or *should have known*. Business owners need not warn customers of "open and obvious" risks, however. If a business owner breaches this duty of care (fails to exercise the appropriate degree of care toward customers), and the breach of duty causes a customer to be injured, the business owner will be liable to the customer for the customer's injuries.

3. The next—and usually the most difficult—step in analyzing case problems is the **application** of the relevant rule of law to the specific facts of the case you are studying. In our sample problem, applying the tort law principle just discussed presents few difficulties. An employee of the store had mopped the floor in the aisle where Lawson slipped and fell, but no sign was present indicating that the floor was wet. That a customer might fall on a wet floor is clearly a foreseeable risk. Therefore, the failure to warn customers about the wet floor was a breach of the duty of care owed by the business owner to the store's customers.

4. Once you have completed Step 3 in the IRAC method, you should be ready to draw your **conclusion.** In our sample problem, Quality Market is liable to Lawson for her injuries because the market's breach of its duty of care caused Lawson's injuries.

The fact patterns in the case problems presented in this text are not always as simple as those presented in our sample problem. Often, a case has more than one plaintiff or defendant. A case may also involve more than one issue and have more than one applicable rule of law. Furthermore, in some case problems the facts may indicate that the general rule of law should not apply. Suppose that a store employee told Lawson about the wet floor and advised her not to walk in that aisle, but Lawson decided to walk there anyway. This fact could alter the outcome of the case because the store could then raise the defense of *assumption of risk*. Nonetheless, a careful review of the chapter should always provide you with the knowledge you need to analyze the problem thoroughly and arrive at accurate conclusions.

The Uniform Commercial Code (Excerpts)

(Adopted in fifty-two jurisdictions; all fifty States, although Louisiana has adopted only Articles 1, 3, 4, 7, 8, and 9; the District of Columbia; and the Virgin Islands.)

The Uniform Commercial Code consists of the following articles:

Articles:

1. **General Provisions**
2. **Sales**
2A. **Leases**
3. **Negotiable Instruments**
4. **Bank Deposits and Collections**
4A. **Fund Transfers**
5. **Letters of Credit**
6. **Repealer of Article 6—Bulk Transfers and [Revised] Article 6—Bulk Sales**
7. **Warehouse Receipts, Bills of Lading and Other Documents of Title**
8. **Investment Securities**
9. **Secured Transactions**
10. **Effective Date and Repealer**
11. **Effective Date and Transition Provisions**

Article 1
GENERAL PROVISIONS

Part 1   General Provisions

§ 1–101.   Short Titles.

(a) This [Act] may be cited as Uniform Commercial Code.

(b) This article may be cited as Uniform Commercial Code–Uniform Provisions.

§ 1–102.   Scope of Article.

This article applies to a transaction to the extent that it is governed by another article of [the Uniform Commercial Code].

§ 1–103.   Construction of [Uniform Commercial Code] to Promote Its Purpose and Policies; Applicability of Supplemental Principles of Law.

(a) [The Uniform Commercial Code] must be liberally construed and applied to promote its underlying purposes and policies, which are:

(1) to simplify, clarify, and modernize the law governing commercial transactions;

(2) to permit the continued expansion of commercial practices through custom, usage, and agreement of the parties; and

(3) to make uniform the law among the various jurisdictions.

(b) Unless displaced by the particular provisions of [the Uniform Commercial Code], the principles of law and equity, including the law merchant and the law relative to capacity to contract, principal and agent, estoppel, fraud, misrepresentation, duress, coercion, mistake, bankruptcy, and other validating or invalidating cause, supplement its provisions.

§ 1–104.   Construction Against Implicit Repeal.

This Act being a general act intended as a unified coverage of its subject matter, no part of it shall be deemed to be impliedly repealed by subsequent legislation if such construction can reasonably be avoided.

§ 1–105.   Severability.

If any provision or clause of [the Uniform Commercial Code] or its application to any person or circumstance is held invalid, the invalidity does not affect other provisions or applications of [the Uniform Commercial Code] which can be given effect without the invalid provision or application, and to this end the provisions of [the Uniform Commercial Code] are severable.

§ 1–106.   Use of Singular and Plural; Gender.

In [the Uniform Commercial Code], unless the statutory context otherwise requires:

(1) words in the singular number include the plural, and those in the plural include the singular; and

(2) words of any gender also refer to any other gender.

§ 1–107.   Section Captions.

Section captions are part of [the Uniform Commercial Code].

§ 1–108.   Relation to Electronic Signatures in Global and National Commerce Act.

This article modifies, limits, and supersedes the Federal Electronic Signatures in Global and National Commerce Act, 15 U.S.C. Sections 7001 *et seq.,* except that nothing in this article modifies, limits, or supersedes section 7001(c) of that act or authorizes electronic delivery of any of the notices described in section 7003(b) of that Act.

Part 2   General Definitions and Principles of Interpretation

§ 1–201.   General Definitions.

Subject to additional definitions contained in the subsequent Articles of this Act which are applicable to specific Articles or Parts thereof, and unless the context otherwise requires, in this Act:

(1) "Action", in the sense of a judicial proceeding, includes recoupment, counterclaim, set-off, suit in equity, and any other proceedings in which rights are determined.

(2) "Aggrieved party" means a party entitled to resort to a remedy.

(3) "Agreement", as distinguished from "contract", means the bargain of the parties in fact, as found in their language or by implication from other circumstances, including course of performance, course of dealing, or usage of trade as provided in Section 1–303.

(4) "Bank" means a person engaged in the business of banking and includes a savings bank, savings and loan association, credit union, and trust company.

(5) "Bearer" means a person in control of a negotiable electronic document of title or a person in possession of a negotiable instrument, negotiable tangible document of title, or certificated security that is payable to bearer or indorsed in blank.

(6) "Bill of lading" means a document of title evidencing the receipt of goods for shipment issued by a person engaged in the business of directly or indirectly transporting or forwarding goods. The term does not include a warehouse receipt.

(7) "Branch" includes a separately incorporated foreign branch of a bank.

(8) "Burden of establishing" a fact means the burden of persuading the trier of fact that the existence of the fact is more probable than its nonexistence.

(9) "Buyer in ordinary course of business" means a person that buys goods in good faith, without knowledge that the sale violates the rights of another person in the goods, and in the ordinary course from a person, other than a pawnbroker, in the business of selling goods of that kind. A person buys goods in the ordinary course if the sale to the person comports with the usual or customary practices in the kind of business in which the seller is engaged or with the seller's own usual or customary practices. A person that sells oil, gas, or other minerals at the wellhead or minehead is a person in the business of selling goods of that kind. A buyer in ordinary course of business may buy for cash, by exchange of other property, or on secured or unsecured credit, and may acquire goods or documents of title under a pre-existing contract for sale. Only a buyer that takes possession of the goods or has a right to recover the goods from the seller under Article 2 may be a buyer in ordinary course of business. A person that acquires goods in a transfer in bulk or as security for or in total or partial satisfaction of a money debt is not a buyer in ordinary course of business.

(10) "Conspicuous", with reference to a term, means so written, displayed, or presented that a reasonable person against which it is to operate ought to have noticed it. Whether a term is "conspicuous" or not is a decision for the court. Conspicuous terms include the following:

(A) a heading in capitals equal to or greater in size than the surrounding text, or in contrasting type, font, or color to the surrounding text of the same or lesser size; and

(B) language in the body of a record or display in larger type than the surrounding text, or in contrasting type, font, or color to the surrounding text of the same size, or set off from surrounding text of the same size by symbols or other marks that call attention to the language.

(11) "Consumer" means an individual who enters into a transaction primarily for personal, family, or household purposes.

(12) "Contract", as distinguished from "agreement", means the total legal obligation that results from the parties' agreement as determined by [the Uniform Commercial Code] as supplemented by any other laws.

(13) "Creditor" includes a general creditor, a secured creditor, a lien creditor and any representative of creditors, including an assignee for the benefit of creditors, a trustee in bankruptcy, a receiver in equity and an executor or administrator of an insolvent debtor's or assignor's estate.

(14) "Defendant" includes a person in the position of defendant in a counterclaim, cross-action, or third-party claim.

(15) "Delivery" with respect to an electronic document of title means voluntary transfer of control and with respect to an instrument, a tangible document of title, or chattel paper means voluntary transfer of possession.

(16) "Document of title" means a record (i) that in regular course of business or financing is treated as adequately evidencing that the person in possession or control of the record is entitled to receive, control, hold, and dispose of the record and the goods the record covers and (ii) that purports to be issued by or addressed to a bailee and to cover goods in the bailee's possession which are either identified or are fungible portions of an identified mass. The term includes a bill of lading, transport document, dock warrant, dock receipt, warehouse receipt, and order for delivery of goods. An electronic document of title means a document of title evidenced by a record consisting of information stored in an electronic medium. A tangible document of title means a document of title evidenced by a record consisting of information that is inscribed on a tangible medium.

(17) "Fault" means a default, breach, or wrongful act or omission.

(18) "Fungible goods" means:

(A) goods of which any unit, by nature or usage of trade, is the equivalent of any other like unit; or

(B) goods that by agreement are treated as equivalent.

(19) "Genuine" means free of forgery or counterfeiting.

(20) "Good faith," except as otherwise provided in Article 5, means honesty in fact and the observance of reasonable commercial standards of fair dealing.

(21) "Holder" means:

(A) the person in possession of a negotiable instrument that is payable either to bearer or to an identified person that is the person in possession;

(B) the person in possession of a negotiable tangible document of title if the goods are deliverable either to bearer or to the order of the person in possession; or

(C) the person in control of a negotiable electronic document of title.

(22) "Insolvency proceeding" includes an assignment for the benefit of creditors or other proceeding intended to liquidate or rehabilitate the estate of the person involved.

(23) "Insolvent" means:

(A) having generally ceased to pay debts in the ordinary course of business other than as a result of bona fide dispute;

(B) being unable to pay debts as they become due; or

(C) being insolvent within the meaning of federal bankruptcy law.

(24) "Money" means a medium of exchange currently authorized or adopted by a domestic or foreign government. The term includes a monetary unit of account established by an intergovernmental organization or by agreement between two or more countries.

(25) "Organization" means a person other than an individual.

(26) "Party", as distinguished from "third party", means a person that has engaged in a transaction or made an agreement subject to [the Uniform Commercial Code].

(27) "Person" means an individual, corporation, business trust, estate, trust, partnership, limited liability company, association, joint venture, government, governmental subdivision, agency, or instrumentality, public corporation, or any other legal or commercial entity.

(28) "Present value" means the amount as of a date certain of one or more sums payable in the future, discounted to the date certain by use of either an interest rate specified by the parties if that rate is not manifestly unreasonable at the time the transaction is entered into or, if an interest rate is not so specified, a commercially reasonable rate that takes into account the facts and circumstances at the time the transaction is entered into.

(29) "Purchase" means taking by sale, lease, discount, negotiation, mortgage, pledge, lien, security interest, issue or reissue, gift, or any other voluntary transaction creating an interest in property.

(30) "Purchaser" means a person that takes by purchase.

(31) "Record" means information that is inscribed on a tangible medium or that is stored in an electronic or other medium and is retrievable in perceivable form.

(32) "Remedy" means any remedial right to which an aggrieved party is entitled with or without resort to a tribunal.

(33) "Representative" means a person empowered to act for another, including an agent, an officer of a corporation or association, and a trustee, executor, or administrator of an estate.

(34) "Right" includes remedy.

(35) "Security interest" means an interest in personal property or fixtures which secures payment or performance of an obligation. "Security interest" includes any interest of a consignor and a buyer of accounts, chattel paper, a payment intangible, or a promissory note in a transaction that is subject to Article 9. "Security interest" does not include the special property interest of a buyer of goods on identification of those goods to a contract for sale under Section 2–401, but a buyer may also acquire a "security interest" by complying with Article 9. Except as otherwise provided in Section 2–505, the right of a seller or lessor of goods under Article 2 or 2A to retain or acquire possession of the goods is not a "security interest", but a seller or lessor may also acquire a "security interest" by complying with Article 9. The retention or reservation of title by a seller of goods notwithstanding shipment or delivery to the buyer under Section 2–401 is limited in effect to a reservation of a "security interest." Whether a transaction in the form of a lease creates a "security interest" is determined pursuant to Section 1–203.

(36) "Send" in connection with a writing, record, or notice means:

(A) to deposit in the mail or deliver for transmission by any other usual means of communication with postage or cost of transmission provided for and properly addressed and, in the case of an instrument, to an address specified thereon or otherwise agreed, or if there be none to any address reasonable under the circumstances; or

(B) in any other way to cause to be received any record or notice within the time it would have arrived if properly sent.

(37) "Signed" includes using any symbol executed or adopted with present intention to adopt or accept a writing.

(38) "State" means a State of the United States, the District of Columbia, Puerto Rico, the United States Virgin Islands, or any territory or insular possession subject to the jurisdiction of the United States.

(39) "Surety" includes a guarantor or other secondary obligor.

(40) "Term" means a portion of an agreement that relates to a particular matter.

(41) "Unauthorized signature" means a signature made without actual, implied, or apparent authority. The term includes a forgery.

(42) "Warehouse receipt" means a document of title issued by a person engaged in the business of storing goods for hire.

(43) "Writing" includes printing, typewriting, or any other intentional reduction to tangible form. "Written" has a corresponding meaning.

As amended in 2003.

* * * *

§ 1–205.   Reasonable Time; Seasonableness.

(a) Whether a time for taking an action required by [the Uniform Commercial Code] is reasonable depends on the nature, purpose, and circumstances of the action.

(b) An action is taken seasonably if it is taken at or within the time agreed or, if no time is agreed, at or within a reasonable time.

* * * *

Part 3   Territorial Applicability and General Rules

* * * *

§ 1–303.   Course of Performance, Course of Dealing, and Usage of Trade.

(a) A "course of performance" is a sequence of conduct between the parties to a particular transaction that exists if:

(1) the agreement of the parties with respect to the transaction involves repeated occasions for performance by a party; and

(2) the other party, with knowledge of the nature of the performance and opportunity for objection to it, accepts the performance or acquiesces in it without objection.

(b) A "course of dealing" is a sequence of conduct concerning previous transactions between the parties to a particular transaction that is fairly to be regarded as establishing a common basis of understanding for interpreting their expressions and other conduct.

(c) A "usage of trade" is any practice or method of dealing having such regularity of observance in a place, vocation, or trade as to justify an expectation that it will be observed with respect to the transaction in question. The existence and scope of such a usage must be proved as facts. If it is established that such a usage is embodied in a trade code or similar record, the interpretation of the record is a question of law.

(d) A course of performance or course of dealing between the parties or usage of trade in the vocation or trade in which they are engaged or of which they are or should be aware is relevant in ascertaining the meaning of the parties' agreement, may give particular meaning to specific terms of the agreement, and may supplement or qualify the terms of the agreement. A usage of trade applicable in the place in which part of the performance under the agreement is to occur may be so utilized as to that part of the performance.

(e) Except as otherwise provided in subsection (f), the express terms of an agreement and any applicable course of performance, course of dealing, or usage of trade must be construed whenever reasonable as consistent with each other. If such a construction is unreasonable:

(1) express terms prevail over course of performance, course of dealing, and usage of trade;

(2) course of performance prevails over course of dealing and usage of trade; and

(3) course of dealing prevails over usage of trade.

(f) Subject to Section 2–209 and Section 2A–208, a course of performance is relevant to show a waiver or modification of any term inconsistent with the course of performance.

(g) Evidence of a relevant usage of trade offered by one party is not admissible unless that party has given the other party notice that the court finds sufficient to prevent unfair surprise to the other party.

§ 1–304.   Obligation of Good Faith.

Every contract or duty within [the Uniform Commercial Code] imposes an obligation of good faith in its performance and enforcement.

* * * *

§ 1–309.   Option to Accelerate at Will.

A term providing that one party or that party's successor in interest may accelerate payment or performance or require collateral or additional collateral "at will" or when the party "deems itself insecure," or words of similar import, means that the party has power to do so only if that party in good faith believes that the prospect of payment or performance is impaired. The burden of establishing lack of good faith is on the party against which the power has been exercised.

§ 1–310.   Subordinated Obligations.

An obligation may be issued as subordinated to performance of another obligation of the person obligated, or a creditor may subordinate its right to performance of an obligation by agreement with either the person obligated or another creditor of the person obligated. Subordination does not create a security interest as against either the common debtor or a subordinated creditor.

Article 2
SALES

Part 1   Short Title, General Construction and Subject Matter

§ 2–101.   Short Title.

This Article shall be known and may be cited as Uniform Commercial Code—Sales.

§ 2–102.   Scope; Certain Security and Other Transactions Excluded From This Article.

Unless the context otherwise requires, this Article applies to transactions in goods; it does not apply to any transaction which although in the form of an unconditional contract to sell or present sale is intended to operate only as a security transaction nor does this Article impair or repeal any statute regulating sales to consumers, farmers or other specified classes of buyers.

§ 2–103.   Definitions and Index of Definitions.

(1) In this Article unless the context otherwise requires

(a) "Buyer" means a person who buys or contracts to buy goods.

(b) "Good faith" in the case of a merchant means honesty in fact and the observance of reasonable commercial standards of fair dealing in the trade.

(c) "Receipt" of goods means taking physical possession of them.

(d) "Seller" means a person who sells or contracts to sell goods.

(2) Other definitions applying to this Article or to specified Parts thereof, and the sections in which they appear are:

"Acceptance". Section 2–606.

"Banker's credit". Section 2–325.

"Between merchants". Section 2–104.

"Cancellation". Section 2–106(4).

"Commercial unit". Section 2–105.

"Confirmed credit". Section 2–325.

"Conforming to contract". Section 2–106.

"Contract for sale". Section 2–106.

"Cover". Section 2–712.

"Entrusting". Section 2–403.

"Financing agency". Section 2–104.

"Future goods". Section 2–105.

"Goods". Section 2–105.

"Identification". Section 2–501.

"Installment contract". Section 2–612.

"Letter of Credit". Section 2–325.

"Lot". Section 2–105.

"Merchant". Section 2–104.

"Overseas". Section 2–323.

"Person in position of seller". Section 2–707.

"Present sale". Section 2–106.

"Sale". Section 2–106.

"Sale on approval". Section 2–326.

"Sale or return". Section 2–326.

"Termination". Section 2–106.

(3) The following definitions in other Articles apply to this Article:

"Check". Section 3–104.

"Consignee". Section 7–102.

"Consignor". Section 7–102.

"Consumer goods". Section 9–109.

"Dishonor". Section 3–507.

"Draft". Section 3–104.

(4) In addition Article 1 contains general definitions and principles of construction and interpretation applicable throughout this Article. As amended in 1994 and 1999.

§ 2–104.   Definitions: "Merchant"; "Between Merchants"; "Financing Agency".

(1) "Merchant" means a person who deals in goods of the kind or otherwise by his occupation holds himself out as having knowledge or skill peculiar to the practices or goods involved in the transaction or to whom such knowledge or skill may be attributed by his employment of an agent or broker or other intermediary who by his occupation holds himself out as having such knowledge or skill.

(2) "Financing agency" means a bank, finance company or other person who in the ordinary course of business makes advances against goods or documents of title or who by arrangement with either the seller or the buyer intervenes in ordinary course to make or collect payment due or claimed under the contract for sale, as by purchasing or paying the seller's draft or making advances against it or by merely taking it for collection whether or not documents of title accompany the draft. "Financing agency" includes also a bank or other person who similarly intervenes between persons who are in the position of seller and buyer in respect to the goods (Section 2–707).

(3) "Between merchants" means in any transaction with respect to which both parties are chargeable with the knowledge or skill of merchants.

§ 2–105.   Definitions: Transferability; "Goods"; "Future" Goods; "Lot"; "Commercial Unit".

(1) "Goods" means all things (including specially manufactured goods) which are movable at the time of identification to the contract for sale other than the money in which the price is to be paid, investment securities (Article 8) and things in action. "Goods" also includes the unborn young of animals and growing crops and other identified things attached to realty as described in the section on goods to be severed from realty (Section 2–107).

(2) Goods must be both existing and identified before any interest in them can pass. Goods which are not both existing and identified are "future" goods. A purported present sale of future goods or of any interest therein operates as a contract to sell.

(3) There may be a sale of a part interest in existing identified goods.

(4) An undivided share in an identified bulk of fungible goods is sufficiently identified to be sold although the quantity of the bulk is not determined. Any agreed proportion of such a bulk or any quantity thereof agreed upon by number, weight or other measure may to the extent of the seller's interest in the bulk be sold to the buyer who then becomes an owner in common.

(5) "Lot" means a parcel or a single article which is the subject matter of a separate sale or delivery, whether or not it is sufficient to perform the contract.

(6) "Commercial unit" means such a unit of goods as by commercial usage is a single whole for purposes of sale and division of which materially impairs its character or value on the market or in use. A commercial unit may be a single article (as a machine) or a set of articles (as a suite of furniture or an assortment of sizes) or a quantity (as a bale, gross, or carload) or any other unit treated in use or in the relevant market as a single whole.

§ 2–106.   Definitions: "Contract"; "Agreement"; "Contract for Sale"; "Sale"; "Present Sale"; "Conforming" to Contract; "Termination"; "Cancellation".

(1) In this Article unless the context otherwise requires "contract" and "agreement" are limited to those relating to the present or future sale of goods. "Contract for sale" includes both a present sale of goods and a contract to sell goods at a future time. A "sale" consists in the passing of title from the seller to the buyer for a price (Section 2–401). A "present sale" means a sale which is accomplished by the making of the contract.

(2) Goods or conduct including any part of a performance are "conforming" or conform to the contract when they are in accordance with the obligations under the contract.

(3) "Termination" occurs when either party pursuant to a power created by agreement or law puts an end to the contract otherwise than for its breach. On "termination" all obligations which are still executory on both sides are discharged but any right based on prior breach or performance survives.

(4) "Cancellation" occurs when either party puts an end to the contract for breach by the other and its effect is the same as that of "termination" except that the cancelling party also retains any remedy for breach of the whole contract or any unperformed balance.

§ 2–107.   Goods to Be Severed From Realty: Recording.

(1) A contract for the sale of minerals or the like (including oil and gas) or a structure or its materials to be removed from realty is a contract for the sale of goods within this Article if they are to be severed by the seller but until severance a purported present sale thereof which is not effective as a transfer of an interest in land is effective only as a contract to sell.

(2) A contract for the sale apart from the land of growing crops or other things attached to realty and capable of severance without material harm thereto but not described in subsection (1) or of timber to be cut is a contract for the sale of goods within this Article whether the subject matter is to be severed by the buyer or by the seller even though it forms part of the realty at the time of contracting, and the parties can by identification effect a present sale before severance.

(3) The provisions of this section are subject to any third party rights provided by the law relating to realty records, and the contract for sale may be executed and recorded as a document transferring an interest in land and shall then constitute notice to third parties of the buyer's rights under the contract for sale.

As amended in 1972.

Part 2   Form, Formation and Readjustment of Contract

§ 2–201.   Formal Requirements; Statute of Frauds.

(1) Except as otherwise provided in this section a contract for the sale of goods for the price of $500 or more is not enforceable by way of action or defense unless there is some writing sufficient to indicate that a contract for sale has been made between the parties and signed by the party against whom enforcement is sought or by his authorized agent or broker. A writing is not insufficient because it omits or incorrectly states a term agreed upon but the contract is not enforceable under this paragraph beyond the quantity of goods shown in such writing.

(2) Between merchants if within a reasonable time a writing in confirmation of the contract and sufficient against the sender is received and the party receiving it has reason to know its contents, its satisfies the requirements of subsection (1) against such party unless written notice of objection to its contents is given within ten days after it is received.

(3) A contract which does not satisfy the requirements of subsection (1) but which is valid in other respects is enforceable

   (a) if the goods are to be specially manufactured for the buyer and are not suitable for sale to others in the ordinary course of the seller's business and the seller, before notice of repudiation is received and under circumstances which reasonably indicate that the goods are for the buyer, has made either a substantial beginning of their manufacture or commitments for their procurement; or

   (b) if the party against whom enforcement is sought admits in his pleading, testimony or otherwise in court that a contract for sale was made, but the contract is not enforceable under this provision beyond the quantity of goods admitted; or

   (c) with respect to goods for which payment has been made and accepted or which have been received and accepted (Sec. 2–606).

§ 2–202.   Final Written Expression: Parol or Extrinsic Evidence.

Terms with respect to which the confirmatory memoranda of the parties agree or which are otherwise set forth in a writing intended by the parties as a final expression of their agreement with respect to such terms as are included therein may not be contradicted by evidence of any prior agreement or of a contemporaneous oral agreement but may be explained or supplemented

   (a) by course of dealing or usage of trade (Section 1–205) or by course of performance (Section 2–208); and

   (b) by evidence of consistent additional terms unless the court finds the writing to have been intended also as a complete and exclusive statement of the terms of the agreement.

§ 2–203.   Seals Inoperative.

The affixing of a seal to a writing evidencing a contract for sale or an offer to buy or sell goods does not constitute the writing a sealed instrument and the law with respect to sealed instruments does not apply to such a contract or offer.

§ 2–204.   Formation in General.

(1) A contract for sale of goods may be made in any manner sufficient to show agreement, including conduct by both parties which recognizes the existence of such a contract.

(2) An agreement sufficient to constitute a contract for sale may be found even though the moment of its making is undetermined.

(3) Even though one or more terms are left open a contract for sale does not fail for indefiniteness if the parties have intended to make a contract and there is a reasonably certain basis for giving an appropriate remedy.

§ 2–205.   Firm Offers.

An offer by a merchant to buy or sell goods in a signed writing which by its terms gives assurance that it will be held open is not revocable, for lack of consideration, during the time stated or if no time is stated for a reasonable time, but in no event may such period of irrevocability exceed three months; but any such term of assurance on a form supplied by the offeree must be separately signed by the offeror.

§ 2–206.   Offer and Acceptance in Formation of Contract.

(1) Unless other unambiguously indicated by the language or circumstances

   (a) an offer to make a contract shall be construed as inviting acceptance in any manner and by any medium reasonable in the circumstances;

   (b) an order or other offer to buy goods for prompt or current shipment shall be construed as inviting acceptance either by a prompt promise to ship or by the prompt or current shipment of conforming or nonconforming goods, but such a shipment of non-conforming goods does not constitute an acceptance if the seller seasonably notifies the buyer that the shipment is offered only as an accommodation to the buyer.

(2) Where the beginning of a requested performance is a reasonable mode of acceptance an offeror who is not notified of acceptance within a reasonable time may treat the offer as having lapsed before acceptance.

§ 2-207. Additional Terms in Acceptance or Confirmation.

(1) A definite and seasonable expression of acceptance or a written confirmation which is sent within a reasonable time operates as an acceptance even though it states terms additional to or different from those offered or agreed upon, unless acceptance is expressly made conditional on assent to the additional or different terms.

(2) The additional terms are to be construed as proposals for addition to the contract. Between merchants such terms become part of the contract unless:

(a) the offer expressly limits acceptance to the terms of the offer;

(b) they materially alter it; or

(c) notification of objection to them has already been given or is given within a reasonable time after notice of them is received.

(3) Conduct by both parties which recognizes the existence of a contract is sufficient to establish a contract for sale although the writings of the parties do not otherwise establish a contract. In such case the terms of the particular contract consist of those terms on which the writings of the parties agree, together with any supplementary terms incorporated under any other provisions of this Act.

§ 2-208. Course of Performance or Practical Construction.

(1) Where the contract for sale involves repeated occasions for performance by either party with knowledge of the nature of the performance and opportunity for objection to it by the other, any course of performance accepted or acquiesced in without objection shall be relevant to determine the meaning of the agreement.

(2) The express terms of the agreement and any such course of performance, as well as any course of dealing and usage of trade, shall be construed whenever reasonable as consistent with each other; but when such construction is unreasonable, express terms shall control course of performance and course of performance shall control both course of dealing and usage of trade (Section 1–205).

(3) Subject to the provisions of the next section on modification and waiver, such course of performance shall be relevant to show a waiver or modification of any term inconsistent with such course of performance.

§ 2-209. Modification, Rescission and Waiver.

(1) An agreement modifying a contract within this Article needs no consideration to be binding.

(2) A signed agreement which excludes modification or rescission except by a signed writing cannot be otherwise modified or rescinded, but except as between merchants such a requirement on a form supplied by the merchant must be separately signed by the other party.

(3) The requirements of the statute of frauds section of this Article (Section 2–201) must be satisfied if the contract as modified is within its provisions.

(4) Although an attempt at modification or rescission does not satisfy the requirements of subsection (2) or (3) it can operate as a waiver.

(5) A party who has made a waiver affecting an executory portion of the contract may retract the waiver by reasonable notification received by the other party that strict performance will be required of any term waived, unless the retraction would be unjust in view of a material change of position in reliance on the waiver.

§ 2-210. Delegation of Performance; Assignment of Rights.

(1) A party may perform his duty through a delegate unless otherwise agreed or unless the other party has a substantial interest in having his original promisor perform or control the acts required by the contract. No delegation of performance relieves the party delegating of any duty to perform or any liability for breach.

(2) Except as otherwise provided in Section 9–406, unless otherwise agreed, all rights of either seller or buyer can be assigned except where the assignment would materially change the duty of the other party, or increase materially the burden or risk imposed on him by his contract, or impair materially his chance of obtaining return performance. A right to damages for breach of the whole contract or a right arising out of the assignor's due performance of his entire obligation can be assigned despite agreement otherwise.

(3) The creation, attachment, perfection, or enforcement of a security interest in the seller's interest under a contract is not a transfer that materially changes the duty of or increases materially the burden or risk imposed on the buyer or impairs materially the buyer's chance of obtaining return performance within the purview of subsection (2) unless, and then only to the extent that, enforcement actually results in a delegation of material performance of the seller. Even in that event, the creation, attachment, perfection, and enforcement of the security interest remain effective, but (i) the seller is liable to the buyer for damages caused by the delegation to the extent that the damages could not reasonably by prevented by the buyer, and (ii) a court having jurisdiction may grant other appropriate relief, including cancellation of the contract for sale or an injunction against enforcement of the security interest or consummation of the enforcement.

(4) Unless the circumstances indicate the contrary a prohibition of assignment of "the contract" is to be construed as barring only the delegation to the assignee of the assignor's performance.

(5) An assignment of "the contract" or of "all my rights under the contract" or an assignment in similar general terms is an assignment of rights and unless the language or the circumstances (as in an assignment for security) indicate the contrary, it is a delegation of performance of the duties of the assignor and its acceptance by the assignee constitutes a promise by him to perform those duties. This promise is enforceable by either the assignor or the other party to the original contract.

(6) The other party may treat any assignment which delegates performance as creating reasonable grounds for insecurity and may

without prejudice to his rights against the assignor demand assurances from the assignee (Section 2–609).

As amended in 1999.

Part 3   General Obligation and Construction of Contract

§ 2–301.   General Obligations of Parties.

The obligation of the seller is to transfer and deliver and that of the buyer is to accept and pay in accordance with the contract.

§ 2–302.   Unconscionable Contract or Clause.

(1) If the court as a matter of law finds the contract or any clause of the contract to have been unconscionable at the time it was made the court may refuse to enforce the contract, or it may enforce the remainder of the contract without the unconscionable clause, or it may so limit the application of any unconscionable clause as to avoid any unconscionable result.

(2) When it is claimed or appears to the court that the contract or any clause thereof may be unconscionable the parties shall be afforded a reasonable opportunity to present evidence as to its commercial setting, purpose and effect to aid the court in making the determination.

§ 2–303.   Allocations or Division of Risks.

Where this Article allocates a risk or a burden as between the parties "unless otherwise agreed", the agreement may not only shift the allocation but may also divide the risk or burden.

§ 2–304.   Price Payable in Money, Goods, Realty, or Otherwise.

(1) The price can be made payable in money or otherwise. If it is payable in whole or in part in goods each party is a seller of the goods which he is to transfer.

(2) Even though all or part of the price is payable in an interest in realty the transfer of the goods and the seller's obligations with reference to them are subject to this Article, but not the transfer of the interest in realty or the transferor's obligations in connection therewith.

§ 2–305.   Open Price Term.

(1) The parties if they so intend can conclude a contract for sale even though the price is not settled. In such a case the price is a reasonable price at the time for delivery if

(a) nothing is said as to price; or

(b) the price is left to be agreed by the parties and they fail to agree; or

(c) the price is to be fixed in terms of some agreed market or other standard as set or recorded by a third person or agency and it is not so set or recorded.

(2) A price to be fixed by the seller or by the buyer means a price for him to fix in good faith.

(3) When a price left to be fixed otherwise than by agreement of the parties fails to be fixed through fault of one party the other may at his option treat the contract as cancelled or himself fix a reasonable price.

(4) Where, however, the parties intend not to be bound unless the price be fixed or agreed and it is not fixed or agreed there is no contract. In such a case the buyer must return any goods already received or if unable so to do must pay their reasonable value at the time of delivery and the seller must return any portion of the price paid on account.

§ 2–306.   Output, Requirements and Exclusive Dealings.

(1) A term which measures the quantity by the output of the seller or the requirements of the buyer means such actual output or requirements as may occur in good faith, except that no quantity unreasonably disproportionate to any stated estimate or in the absence of a stated estimate to any normal or otherwise comparable prior output or requirements may be tendered or demanded.

(2) A lawful agreement by either the seller or the buyer for exclusive dealing in the kind of goods concerned imposes unless otherwise agreed an obligation by the seller to use best efforts to supply the goods and by the buyer to use best efforts to promote their sale.

§ 2–307.   Delivery in Single Lot or Several Lots.

Unless otherwise agreed all goods called for by a contract for sale must be tendered in a single delivery and payment is due only on such tender but where the circumstances give either party the right to make or demand delivery in lots the price if it can be apportioned may be demanded for each lot.

§ 2–308.   Absence of Specified Place for Delivery.

Unless otherwise agreed

(a) the place for delivery of goods is the seller's place of business or if he has none his residence; but

(b) in a contract for sale of identified goods which to the knowledge of the parties at the time of contracting are in some other place, that place is the place for their delivery; and

(c) documents of title may be delivered through customary banking channels.

§ 2–309.   Absence of Specific Time Provisions; Notice of Termination.

(1) The time for shipment or delivery or any other action under a contract if not provided in this Article or agreed upon shall be a reasonable time.

(2) Where the contract provides for successive performances but is indefinite in duration it is valid for a reasonable time but unless otherwise agreed may be terminated at any time by either party.

(3) Termination of a contract by one party except on the happening of an agreed event requires that reasonable notification be received by the other party and an agreement dispensing with notification is invalid if its operation would be unconscionable.

§ 2–310.   Open Time for Payment or Running of Credit; Authority to Ship Under Reservation.

Unless otherwise agreed

(a) payment is due at the time and place at which the buyer is to receive the goods even though the place of shipment is the place of delivery; and

(b) if the seller is authorized to send the goods he may ship them under reservation, and may tender the documents of title, but the buyer may inspect the goods after their arrival before payment is due unless such inspection is inconsistent with the terms of the contract (Section 2–513); and

(c) if delivery is authorized and made by way of documents of title otherwise than by subsection (b) then payment is due at the time and place at which the buyer is to receive the documents regardless of where the goods are to be received; and

(d) where the seller is required or authorized to ship the goods on credit the credit period runs from the time of shipment but post-dating the invoice or delaying its dispatch will correspondingly delay the starting of the credit period.

§ 2-311.   Options and Cooperation Respecting Performance.

(1) An agreement for sale which is otherwise sufficiently definite (subsection (3) of Section 2-204) to be a contract is not made invalid by the fact that it leaves particulars of performance to be specified by one of the parties. Any such specification must be made in good faith and within limits set by commercial reasonableness.

(2) Unless otherwise agreed specifications relating to assortment of the goods are at the buyer's option and except as otherwise provided in subsections (1)(c) and (3) of Section 2-319 specifications or arrangements relating to shipment are at the seller's option.

(3) Where such specification would materially affect the other party's performance but is not seasonably made or where one party's cooperation is necessary to the agreed performance of the other but is not seasonably forthcoming, the other party in addition to all other remedies

(a) is excused for any resulting delay in his own performance; and

(b) may also either proceed to perform in any reasonable manner or after the time for a material part of his own performance treat the failure to specify or to cooperate as a breach by failure to deliver or accept the goods.

§ 2-312.   Warranty of Title and Against Infringement; Buyer's Obligation Against Infringement.

(1) Subject to subsection (2) there is in a contract for sale a warranty by the seller that

(a) the title conveyed shall be good, and its transfer rightful; and

(b) the goods shall be delivered free from any security interest or other lien or encumbrance of which the buyer at the time of contracting has no knowledge.

(2) A warranty under subsection (1) will be excluded or modified only by specific language or by circumstances which give the buyer reason to know that the person selling does not claim title in himself or that he is purporting to sell only such right or title as he or a third person may have.

(3) Unless otherwise agreed a seller who is a merchant regularly dealing in goods of the kind warrants that the goods shall be delivered free of the rightful claim of any third person by way of infringement or the like but a buyer who furnishes specifications to the seller must hold the seller harmless against any such claim which arises out of compliance with the specifications.

§ 2-313.   Express Warranties by Affirmation, Promise, Description, Sample.

(1) Express warranties by the seller are created as follows:

(a) Any affirmation of fact or promise made by the seller to the buyer which relates to the goods and becomes part of the basis of the bargain creates an express warranty that the goods shall conform to the affirmation or promise.

(b) Any description of the goods which is made part of the basis of the bargain creates an express warranty that the goods shall conform to the description.

(c) Any sample or model which is made part of the basis of the bargain creates an express warranty that the whole of the goods shall conform to the sample or model.

(2) It is not necessary to the creation of an express warranty that the seller use formal words such as "warrant" or "guarantee" or that he have a specific intention to make a warranty, but an affirmation merely of the value of the goods or a statement purporting to be merely the seller's opinion or commendation of the goods does not create a warranty.

§ 2-314.   Implied Warranty: Merchantability; Usage of Trade.

(1) Unless excluded or modified (Section 2-316), a warranty that the goods shall be merchantable is implied in a contract for their sale if the seller is a merchant with respect to goods of that kind. Under this section the serving for value of food or drink to be consumed either on the premises or elsewhere is a sale.

(2) Goods to be merchantable must be at least such as

(a) pass without objection in the trade under the contract description; and

(b) in the case of fungible goods, are of fair average quality within the description; and

(c) are fit for the ordinary purposes for which such goods are used; and

(d) run, within the variations permitted by the agreement, of even kind, quality and quantity within each unit and among all units involved; and

(e) are adequately contained, packaged, and labeled as the agreement may require; and

(f) conform to the promises or affirmations of fact made on the container or label if any.

(3) Unless excluded or modified (Section 2-316) other implied warranties may arise from course of dealing or usage of trade.

§ 2-315.   Implied Warranty: Fitness for Particular Purpose.

Where the seller at the time of contracting has reason to know any particular purpose for which the goods are required and that the buyer is relying on the seller's skill or judgment to select or furnish suitable goods, there is unless excluded or modified under the next section an implied warranty that the goods shall be fit for such purpose.

§ 2-316.   Exclusion or Modification of Warranties.

(1) Words or conduct relevant to the creation of an express warranty and words or conduct tending to negate or limit warranty shall be construed wherever reasonable as consistent with each other; but subject to the provisions of this Article on parol or extrinsic evidence (Section 2-202) negation or limitation is inoperative to the extent that such construction is unreasonable.

(2) Subject to subsection (3), to exclude or modify the implied warranty of merchantability or any part of it the language must

mention merchantability and in case of a writing must be conspicuous, and to exclude or modify any implied warranty of fitness the exclusion must be by a writing and conspicuous. Language to exclude all implied warranties of fitness is sufficient if it states, for example, that "There are no warranties which extend beyond the description on the face hereof."

(3) Notwithstanding subsection (2)

(a) unless the circumstances indicate otherwise, all implied warranties are excluded by expressions like "as is", "with all faults" or other language which in common understanding calls the buyer's attention to the exclusion of warranties and makes plain that there is no implied warranty; and

(b) when the buyer before entering into the contract has examined the goods or the sample or model as fully as he desired or has refused to examine the goods there is no implied warranty with regard to defects which an examination ought in the circumstances to have revealed to him; and

(c) an implied warranty can also be excluded or modified by course of dealing or course of performance or usage of trade.

(4) Remedies for breach of warranty can be limited in accordance with the provisions of this Article on liquidation or limitation of damages and on contractual modification of remedy (Sections 2–718 and 2–719).

§ 2–317.   Cumulation and Conflict of Warranties Express or Implied.

Warranties whether express or implied shall be construed as consistent with each other and as cumulative, but if such construction is unreasonable the intention of the parties shall determine which warranty is dominant. In ascertaining that intention the following rules apply:

(a) Exact or technical specifications displace an inconsistent sample or model or general language of description.

(b) A sample from an existing bulk displaces inconsistent general language of description.

(c) Express warranties displace inconsistent implied warranties other than an implied warranty of fitness for a particular purpose.

§ 2–318.   Third Party Beneficiaries of Warranties Express or Implied.

Note: If this Act is introduced in the Congress of the United States this section should be omitted. (States to select one alternative.)

Alternative A

A seller's warranty whether express or implied extends to any natural person who is in the family or household of his buyer or who is a guest in his home if it is reasonable to expect that such person may use, consume or be affected by the goods and who is injured in person by breach of the warranty. A seller may not exclude or limit the operation of this section.

Alternative B

A seller's warranty whether express or implied extends to any natural person who may reasonably be expected to use, consume or be affected by the goods and who is injured in person by breach of the warranty. A seller may not exclude or limit the operation of this section.

Alternative C

A seller's warranty whether express or implied extends to any person who may reasonably be expected to use, consume or be affected by the goods and who is injured by breach of the warranty. A seller may not exclude or limit the operation of this section with respect to injury to the person of an individual to whom the warranty extends.

As amended 1966.

§ 2–319.   F.O.B. and F.A.S. Terms.

(1) Unless otherwise agreed the term F.O.B. (which means "free on board") at a named place, even though used only in connection with the stated price, is a delivery term under which

(a) when the term is F.O.B. the place of shipment, the seller must at that place ship the goods in the manner provided in this Article (Section 2–504) and bear the expense and risk of putting them into the possession of the carrier; or

(b) when the term is F.O.B. the place of destination, the seller must at his own expense and risk transport the goods to that place and there tender delivery of them in the manner provided in this Article (Section 2–503);

(c) when under either (a) or (b) the term is also F.O.B. vessel, car or other vehicle, the seller must in addition at his own expense and risk load the goods on board. If the term is F.O.B. vessel the buyer must name the vessel and in an appropriate case the seller must comply with the provisions of this Article on the form of bill of lading (Section 2–323).

(2) Unless otherwise agreed the term F.A.S. vessel (which means "free alongside") at a named port, even though used only in connection with the stated price, is a delivery term under which the seller must

(a) at his own expense and risk deliver the goods alongside the vessel in the manner usual in that port or on a dock designated and provided by the buyer; and

(b) obtain and tender a receipt for the goods in exchange for which the carrier is under a duty to issue a bill of lading.

(3) Unless otherwise agreed in any case falling within subsection (1)(a) or (c) or subsection (2) the buyer must seasonably give any needed instructions for making delivery, including when the term is F.A.S. or F.O.B. the loading berth of the vessel and in an appropriate case its name and sailing date. The seller may treat the failure of needed instructions as a failure of cooperation under this Article (Section 2–311). He may also at his option move the goods in any reasonable manner preparatory to delivery or shipment.

(4) Under the term F.O.B. vessel or F.A.S. unless otherwise agreed the buyer must make payment against tender of the required documents and the seller may not tender nor the buyer demand delivery of the goods in substitution for the documents.

§ 2–320.   C.I.F. and C. & F. Terms.

(1) The term C.I.F. means that the price includes in a lump sum the cost of the goods and the insurance and freight to the named destination. The term C. & F. or C.F. means that the price so includes cost and freight to the named destination.

(2) Unless otherwise agreed and even though used only in connection with the stated price and destination, the term C.I.F. destination or its equivalent requires the seller at his own expense and risk to

(a) put the goods into the possession of a carrier at the port for shipment and obtain a negotiable bill or bills of lading covering the entire transportation to the named destination; and

(b) load the goods and obtain a receipt from the carrier (which may be contained in the bill of lading) showing that the freight has been paid or provided for; and

(c) obtain a policy or certificate of insurance, including any war risk insurance, of a kind and on terms then current at the port of shipment in the usual amount, in the currency of the contract, shown to cover the same goods covered by the bill of lading and providing for payment of loss to the order of the buyer or for the account of whom it may concern; but the seller may add to the price the amount of the premium for any such war risk insurance; and

(d) prepare an invoice of the goods and procure any other documents required to effect shipment or to comply with the contract; and

(e) forward and tender with commercial promptness all the documents in due form and with any indorsement necessary to perfect the buyer's rights.

(3) Unless otherwise agreed the term C. & F. or its equivalent has the same effect and imposes upon the seller the same obligations and risks as a C.I.F. term except the obligation as to insurance.

(4) Under the term C.I.F. or C. & F. unless otherwise agreed the buyer must make payment against tender of the required documents and the seller may not tender nor the buyer demand delivery of the goods in substitution for the documents.

§ 2–321.   C.I.F. or C. & F.: "Net Landed Weights"; "Payment on Arrival"; Warranty of Condition on Arrival.

Under a contract containing a term C.I.F. or C. & F.

(1) Where the price is based on or is to be adjusted according to "net landed weights", "delivered weights", "out turn" quantity or quality or the like, unless otherwise agreed the seller must reasonably estimate the price. The payment due on tender of the documents called for by the contract is the amount so estimated, but after final adjustment of the price a settlement must be made with commercial promptness.

(2) An agreement described in subsection (1) or any warranty of quality or condition of the goods on arrival places upon the seller the risk of ordinary deterioration, shrinkage and the like in transportation but has no effect on the place or time of identification to the contract for sale or delivery or on the passing of the risk of loss.

(3) Unless otherwise agreed where the contract provides for payment on or after arrival of the goods the seller must before payment allow such preliminary inspection as is feasible; but if the goods are lost delivery of the documents and payment are due when the goods should have arrived.

§ 2–322.   Delivery "Ex-Ship".

(1) Unless otherwise agreed a term for delivery of goods "ex-ship" (which means from the carrying vessel) or in equivalent language is not restricted to a particular ship and requires delivery from a ship which has reached a place at the named port of destination where goods of the kind are usually discharged.

(2) Under such a term unless otherwise agreed

(a) the seller must discharge all liens arising out of the carriage and furnish the buyer with a direction which puts the carrier under a duty to deliver the goods; and

(b) the risk of loss does not pass to the buyer until the goods leave the ship's tackle or are otherwise properly unloaded.

§ 2–323.   Form of Bill of Lading Required in Overseas Shipment; "Overseas".

(1) Where the contract contemplates overseas shipment and contains a term C.I.F. or C. & F. or F.O.B. vessel, the seller unless otherwise agreed must obtain a negotiable bill of lading stating that the goods have been loaded on board or, in the case of a term C.I.F. or C. & F., received for shipment.

(2) Where in a case within subsection (1) a bill of lading has been issued in a set of parts, unless otherwise agreed if the documents are not to be sent from abroad the buyer may demand tender of the full set; otherwise only one part of the bill of lading need be tendered. Even if the agreement expressly requires a full set

(a) due tender of a single part is acceptable within the provisions of this Article on cure of improper delivery (subsection (1) of Section 2–508); and

(b) even though the full set is demanded, if the documents are sent from abroad the person tendering an incomplete set may nevertheless require payment upon furnishing an indemnity which the buyer in good faith deems adequate.

(3) A shipment by water or by air or a contract contemplating such shipment is "overseas" insofar as by usage of trade or agreement it is subject to the commercial, financing or shipping practices characteristic of international deep water commerce.

§ 2–324.   "No Arrival, No Sale" Term.

Under a term "no arrival, no sale" or terms of like meaning, unless otherwise agreed,

(a) the seller must properly ship conforming goods and if they arrive by any means he must tender them on arrival but he assumes no obligation that the goods will arrive unless he has caused the non-arrival; and

(b) where without fault of the seller the goods are in part lost or have so deteriorated as no longer to conform to the contract or arrive after the contract time, the buyer may proceed as if there had been casualty to identified goods (Section 2–613).

§ 2–325.   "Letter of Credit" Term; "Confirmed Credit".

(1) Failure of the buyer seasonably to furnish an agreed letter of credit is a breach of the contract for sale.

(2) The delivery to seller of a proper letter of credit suspends the buyer's obligation to pay. If the letter of credit is dishonored, the

seller may on seasonable notification to the buyer require payment directly from him.

(3) Unless otherwise agreed the term "letter of credit" or "banker's credit" in a contract for sale means an irrevocable credit issued by a financing agency of good repute and, where the shipment is overseas, of good international repute. The term "confirmed credit" means that the credit must also carry the direct obligation of such an agency which does business in the seller's financial market.

§ 2-326.   Sale on Approval and Sale or Return; Rights of Creditors.

(1) Unless otherwise agreed, if delivered goods may be returned by the buyer even though they conform to the contract, the transaction is

(a) a "sale on approval" if the goods are delivered primarily for use, and

(b) a "sale or return" if the goods are delivered primarily for resale.

(2) Goods held on approval are not subject to the claims of the buyer's creditors until acceptance; goods held on sale or return are subject to such claims while in the buyer's possession.

(3) Any "or return" term of a contract for sale is to be treated as a separate contract for sale within the statute of frauds section of this Article (Section 2-201) and as contradicting the sale aspect of the contract within the provisions of this Article or on parol or extrinsic evidence (Section 2-202).

As amended in 1999.

§ 2-327.   Special Incidents of Sale on Approval and Sale or Return.

(1) Under a sale on approval unless otherwise agreed

(a) although the goods are identified to the contract the risk of loss and the title do not pass to the buyer until acceptance; and

(b) use of the goods consistent with the purpose of trial is not acceptance but failure seasonably to notify the seller of election to return the goods is acceptance, and if the goods conform to the contract acceptance of any part is acceptance of the whole; and

(c) after due notification of election to return, the return is at the seller's risk and expense but a merchant buyer must follow any reasonable instructions.

(2) Under a sale or return unless otherwise agreed

(a) the option to return extends to the whole or any commercial unit of the goods while in substantially their original condition, but must be exercised seasonably; and

(b) the return is at the buyer's risk and expense.

§ 2-328.   Sale by Auction.

(1) In a sale by auction if goods are put up in lots each lot is the subject of a separate sale.

(2) A sale by auction is complete when the auctioneer so announces by the fall of the hammer or in other customary manner. Where a bid is made while the hammer is falling in acceptance of a prior bid the auctioneer may in his discretion reopen the bidding or declare the goods sold under the bid on which the hammer was falling.

(3) Such a sale is with reserve unless the goods are in explicit terms put up without reserve. In an auction with reserve the auctioneer may withdraw the goods at any time until he announces completion of the sale. In an auction without reserve, after the auctioneer calls for bids on an article or lot, that article or lot cannot be withdrawn unless no bid is made within a reasonable time. In either case a bidder may retract his bid until the auctioneer's announcement of completion of the sale, but a bidder's retraction does not revive any previous bid.

(4) If the auctioneer knowingly receives a bid on the seller's behalf or the seller makes or procures such as bid, and notice has not been given that liberty for such bidding is reserved, the buyer may at his option avoid the sale or take the goods at the price of the last good faith bid prior to the completion of the sale. This subsection shall not apply to any bid at a forced sale.

Part 4   Title, Creditors and Good Faith Purchasers

§ 2-401.   Passing of Title; Reservation for Security; Limited Application of This Section.

Each provision of this Article with regard to the rights, obligations and remedies of the seller, the buyer, purchasers or other third parties applies irrespective of title to the goods except where the provision refers to such title. Insofar as situations are not covered by the other provisions of this Article and matters concerning title became material the following rules apply:

(1) Title to goods cannot pass under a contract for sale prior to their identification to the contract (Section 2-501), and unless otherwise explicitly agreed the buyer acquires by their identification a special property as limited by this Act. Any retention or reservation by the seller of the title (property) in goods shipped or delivered to the buyer is limited in effect to a reservation of a security interest. Subject to these provisions and to the provisions of the Article on Secured Transactions (Article 9), title to goods passes from the seller to the buyer in any manner and on any conditions explicitly agreed on by the parties.

(2) Unless otherwise explicitly agreed title passes to the buyer at the time and place at which the seller completes his performance with reference to the physical delivery of the goods, despite any reservation of a security interest and even though a document of title is to be delivered at a different time or place; and in particular and despite any reservation of a security interest by the bill of lading

(a) if the contract requires or authorizes the seller to send the goods to the buyer but does not require him to deliver them at destination, title passes to the buyer at the time and place of shipment; but

(b) if the contract requires delivery at destination, title passes on tender there.

(3) Unless otherwise explicitly agreed where delivery is to be made without moving the goods,

(a) if the seller is to deliver a document of title, title passes at the time when and the place where he delivers such documents; or

(b) if the goods are at the time of contracting already identified and no documents are to be delivered, title passes at the time and place of contracting.

(4) A rejection or other refusal by the buyer to receive or retain the goods, whether or not justified, or a justified revocation of acceptance revests title to the goods in the seller. Such revesting occurs by operation of law and is not a "sale".

§ 2–402.   Rights of Seller's Creditors Against Sold Goods.

(1) Except as provided in subsections (2) and (3), rights of unsecured creditors of the seller with respect to goods which have been identified to a contract for sale are subject to the buyer's rights to recover the goods under this Article (Sections 2–502 and 2–716).

(2) A creditor of the seller may treat a sale or an identification of goods to a contract for sale as void if as against him a retention of possession by the seller is fraudulent under any rule of law of the state where the goods are situated, except that retention of possession in good faith and current course of trade by a merchant-seller for a commercially reasonable time after a sale or identification is not fraudulent.

(3) Nothing in this Article shall be deemed to impair the rights of creditors of the seller

(a) under the provisions of the Article on Secured Transactions (Article 9); or

(b) where identification to the contract or delivery is made not in current course of trade but in satisfaction of or as security for a pre-existing claim for money, security or the like and is made under circumstances which under any rule of law of the state where the goods are situated would apart from this Article constitute the transaction a fraudulent transfer or voidable preference.

§ 2–403.   Power to Transfer; Good Faith Purchase of Goods; "Entrusting".

(1) A purchaser of goods acquires all title which his transferor had or had power to transfer except that a purchaser of a limited interest acquires rights only to the extent of the interest purchased. A person with voidable title has power to transfer a good title to a good faith purchaser for value. When goods have been delivered under a transaction of purchase the purchaser has such power even though

(a) the transferor was deceived as to the identity of the purchaser, or

(b) the delivery was in exchange for a check which is later dishonored, or

(c) it was agreed that the transaction was to be a "cash sale", or

(d) the delivery was procured through fraud punishable as larcenous under the criminal law.

(2) Any entrusting of possession of goods to a merchant who deals in goods of that kind gives him power to transfer all rights of the entruster to a buyer in ordinary course of business.

(3) "Entrusting" includes any delivery and any acquiescence in retention of possession regardless of any condition expressed between the parties to the delivery or acquiescence and regardless of whether the procurement of the entrusting or the possessor's disposition of the goods have been such as to be larcenous under the criminal law.

(4) The rights of other purchasers of goods and of lien creditors are governed by the Articles on Secured Transactions (Article 9), Bulk Transfers (Article 6) and Documents of Title (Article 7).

As amended in 1988.

Part 5   Performance

§ 2–501.   Insurable Interest in Goods; Manner of Identification of Goods.

(1) The buyer obtains a special property and an insurable interest in goods by identification of existing goods as goods to which the contract refers even though the goods so identified are non-conforming and he has an option to return or reject them. Such identification can be made at any time and in any manner explicitly agreed to by the parties. In the absence of explicit agreement identification occurs

(a) when the contract is made if it is for the sale of goods already existing and identified;

(b) if the contract is for the sale of future goods other than those described in paragraph (c), when goods are shipped, marked or otherwise designated by the seller as goods to which the contract refers;

(c) when the crops are planted or otherwise become growing crops or the young are conceived if the contract is for the sale of unborn young to be born within twelve months after contracting or for the sale of crops to be harvested within twelve months or the next normal harvest season after contracting whichever is longer.

(2) The seller retains an insurable interest in goods so long as title to or any security interest in the goods remains in him and where the identification is by the seller alone he may until default or insolvency or notification to the buyer that the identification is final substitute other goods for those identified.

(3) Nothing in this section impairs any insurable interest recognized under any other statute or rule of law.

§ 2–502.   Buyer's Right to Goods on Seller's Insolvency.

(1) Subject to subsections (2) and (3) and even though the goods have not been shipped a buyer who has paid a part or all of the price of goods in which he has a special property under the provisions of the immediately preceding section may on making and keeping good a tender of any unpaid portion of their price recover them from the seller if:

(a) in the case of goods bought for personal, family, or household purposes, the seller repudiates or fails to deliver as required by the contract; or

(b) in all cases, the seller becomes insolvent within ten days after receipt of the first installment on their price.

(2) The buyer's right to recover the goods under subsection (1)(a) vests upon acquisition of a special property, even if the seller had not then repudiated or failed to deliver.

(3) If the identification creating his special property has been made by the buyer he acquires the right to recover the goods only if they conform to the contract for sale.

As amended in 1999.

§ 2–503.   Manner of Seller's Tender of Delivery.

(1) Tender of delivery requires that the seller put and hold conforming goods at the buyer's disposition and give the buyer any notification reasonably necessary to enable him to take delivery. The manner, time and place for tender are determined by the agreement and this Article, and in particular

(a) tender must be at a reasonable hour, and if it is of goods they must be kept available for the period reasonably necessary to enable the buyer to take possession; but

(b) unless otherwise agreed the buyer must furnish facilities reasonably suited to the receipt of the goods.

(2) Where the case is within the next section respecting shipment tender requires that the seller comply with its provisions.

(3) Where the seller is required to deliver at a particular destination tender requires that he comply with subsection (1) and also in any appropriate case tender documents as described in subsections (4) and (5) of this section.

(4) Where goods are in the possession of a bailee and are to be delivered without being moved

(a) tender requires that the seller either tender a negotiable document of title covering such goods or procure acknowledgment by the bailee of the buyer's right to possession of the goods; but

(b) tender to the buyer of a non-negotiable document of title or of a written direction to the bailee to deliver is sufficient tender unless the buyer seasonably objects, and receipt by the bailee of notification of the buyer's rights fixes those rights as against the bailee and all third persons; but risk of loss of the goods and of any failure by the bailee to honor the non-negotiable document of title or to obey the direction remains on the seller until the buyer has had a reasonable time to present the document or direction, and a refusal by the bailee to honor the document or to obey the direction defeats the tender.

(5) Where the contract requires the seller to deliver documents

(a) he must tender all such documents in correct form, except as provided in this Article with respect to bills of lading in a set (subsection (2) of Section 2–323); and

(b) tender through customary banking channels is sufficient and dishonor of a draft accompanying the documents constitutes non-acceptance or rejection.

§ 2–504.   Shipment by Seller.

Where the seller is required or authorized to send the goods to the buyer and the contract does not require him to deliver them at a particular destination, then unless otherwise agreed he must

(a) put the goods in the possession of such a carrier and make such a contract for their transportation as may be reasonable having regard to the nature of the goods and other circumstances of the case; and

(b) obtain and promptly deliver or tender in due form any document necessary to enable the buyer to obtain possession of the goods or otherwise required by the agreement or by usage of trade; and

(c) promptly notify the buyer of the shipment.

Failure to notify the buyer under paragraph (c) or to make a proper contract under paragraph (a) is a ground for rejection only if material delay or loss ensues.

§ 2–505.   Seller's Shipment under Reservation.

(1) Where the seller has identified goods to the contract by or before shipment:

(a) his procurement of a negotiable bill of lading to his own order or otherwise reserves in him a security interest in the goods. His procurement of the bill to the order of a financing agency or of the buyer indicates in addition only the seller's expectation of transferring that interest to the person named.

(b) a non-negotiable bill of lading to himself or his nominee reserves possession of the goods as security but except in a case of conditional delivery (subsection (2) of Section 2–507) a non-negotiable bill of lading naming the buyer as consignee reserves no security interest even though the seller retains possession of the bill of lading.

(2) When shipment by the seller with reservation of a security interest is in violation of the contract for sale it constitutes an improper contract for transportation within the preceding section but impairs neither the rights given to the buyer by shipment and identification of the goods to the contract nor the seller's powers as a holder of a negotiable document.

§ 2–506.   Rights of Financing Agency.

(1) A financing agency by paying or purchasing for value a draft which relates to a shipment of goods acquires to the extent of the payment or purchase and in addition to its own rights under the draft and any document of title securing it any rights of the shipper in the goods including the right to stop delivery and the shipper's right to have the draft honored by the buyer.

(2) The right to reimbursement of a financing agency which has in good faith honored or purchased the draft under commitment to or authority from the buyer is not impaired by subsequent discovery of defects with reference to any relevant document which was apparently regular on its face.

§ 2–507.   Effect of Seller's Tender; Delivery on Condition.

(1) Tender of delivery is a condition to the buyer's duty to accept the goods and, unless otherwise agreed, to his duty to pay for them. Tender entitles the seller to acceptance of the goods and to payment according to the contract.

(2) Where payment is due and demanded on the delivery to the buyer of goods or documents of title, his right as against the seller to retain or dispose of them is conditional upon his making the payment due.

§ 2–508.   Cure by Seller of Improper Tender or Delivery; Replacement.

(1) Where any tender or delivery by the seller is rejected because non-conforming and the time for performance has not yet expired,

the seller may seasonally notify the buyer of his intention to cure and may then within the contract time make a conforming delivery.

(2) Where the buyer rejects a non-conforming tender which the seller had reasonable grounds to believe would be acceptable with or without money allowance the seller may if he seasonably notifies the buyer have a further reasonable time to substitute a conforming tender.

§ 2–509.   Risk of Loss in the Absence of Breach.

(1) Where the contract requires or authorizes the seller to ship the goods by carrier

(a) if it does not require him to deliver them at a particular destination, the risk of loss passes to the buyer when the goods are duly delivered to the carrier even though the shipment is under reservation (Section 2–505); but

(b) if it does require him to deliver them at a particular destination and the goods are there duly tendered while in the possession of the carrier, the risk of loss passes to the buyer when the goods are there duly so tendered as to enable the buyer to take delivery.

(2) Where the goods are held by a bailee to be delivered without being moved, the risk of loss passes to the buyer

(a) on his receipt of a negotiable document of title covering the goods; or

(b) on acknowledgment by the bailee of the buyer's right to possession of the goods; or

(c) after his receipt of a non-negotiable document of title or other written direction to deliver, as provided in subsection (4)(b) of Section 2–503.

(3) In any case not within subsection (1) or (2), the risk of loss passes to the buyer on his receipt of the goods if the seller is a merchant; otherwise the risk passes to the buyer on tender of delivery.

(4) The provisions of this section are subject to contrary agreement of the parties and to the provisions of this Article on sale on approval (Section 2–327) and on effect of breach on risk of loss (Section 2–510).

§ 2–510.   Effect of Breach on Risk of Loss.

(1) Where a tender or delivery of goods so fails to conform to the contract as to give a right of rejection the risk of their loss remains on the seller until cure or acceptance.

(2) Where the buyer rightfully revokes acceptance he may to the extent of any deficiency in his effective insurance coverage treat the risk of loss as having rested on the seller from the beginning.

(3) Where the buyer as to conforming goods already identified to the contract for sale repudiates or is otherwise in breach before risk of their loss has passed to him, the seller may to the extent of any deficiency in his effective insurance coverage treat the risk of loss as resting on the buyer for a commercially reasonable time.

§ 2–511.   Tender of Payment by Buyer; Payment by Check.

(1) Unless otherwise agreed tender of payment is a condition to the seller's duty to tender and complete any delivery.

(2) Tender of payment is sufficient when made by any means or in any manner current in the ordinary course of business unless the seller demands payment in legal tender and gives any extension of time reasonably necessary to procure it.

(3) Subject to the provisions of this Act on the effect of an instrument on an obligation (Section 3–310), payment by check is conditional and is defeated as between the parties by dishonor of the check on due presentment.

As amended in 1994.

§ 2–512.   Payment by Buyer Before Inspection.

(1) Where the contract requires payment before inspection non-conformity of the goods does not excuse the buyer from so making payment unless

(a) the non-conformity appears without inspection; or

(b) despite tender of the required documents the circumstances would justify injunction against honor under this Act (Section 5–109(b)).

(2) Payment pursuant to subsection (1) does not constitute an acceptance of goods or impair the buyer's right to inspect or any of his remedies.

As amended in 1995.

§ 2–513.   Buyer's Right to Inspection of Goods.

(1) Unless otherwise agreed and subject to subsection (3), where goods are tendered or delivered or identified to the contract for sale, the buyer has a right before payment or acceptance to inspect them at any reasonable place and time and in any reasonable manner. When the seller is required or authorized to send the goods to the buyer, the inspection may be after their arrival.

(2) Expenses of inspection must be borne by the buyer but may be recovered from the seller if the goods do not conform and are rejected.

(3) Unless otherwise agreed and subject to the provisions of this Article on C.I.F. contracts (subsection (3) of Section 2–321), the buyer is not entitled to inspect the goods before payment of the price when the contract provides

(a) for delivery "C.O.D." or on other like terms; or

(b) for payment against documents of title, except where such payment is due only after the goods are to become available for inspection.

(4) A place or method of inspection fixed by the parties is presumed to be exclusive but unless otherwise expressly agreed it does not postpone identification or shift the place for delivery or for passing the risk of loss. If compliance becomes impossible, inspection shall be as provided in this section unless the place or method fixed was clearly intended as an indispensable condition failure of which avoids the contract.

§ 2–514.   When Documents Deliverable on Acceptance; When on Payment.

Unless otherwise agreed documents against which a draft is drawn are to be delivered to the drawee on acceptance of the draft if it is payable more than three days after presentment; otherwise, only on payment.

§ 2–515.   Preserving Evidence of Goods in Dispute.

In furtherance of the adjustment of any claim or dispute

(a) either party on reasonable notification to the other and for the purpose of ascertaining the facts and preserving evidence has the right to inspect, test and sample the goods including such of them as may be in the possession or control of the other; and

(b) the parties may agree to a third party inspection or survey to determine the conformity or condition of the goods and may agree that the findings shall be binding upon them in any subsequent litigation or adjustment.

Part 6   Breach, Repudiation and Excuse

§ 2–601.   Buyer's Rights on Improper Delivery.

Subject to the provisions of this Article on breach in installment contracts (Section 2–612) and unless otherwise agreed under the sections on contractual limitations of remedy (Sections 2–718 and 2–719), if the goods or the tender of delivery fail in any respect to conform to the contract, the buyer may

(a) reject the whole; or

(b) accept the whole; or

(c) accept any commercial unit or units and reject the rest.

§ 2–602.   Manner and Effect of Rightful Rejection.

(1) Rejection of goods must be within a reasonable time after their delivery or tender. It is ineffective unless the buyer seasonably notifies the seller.

(2) Subject to the provisions of the two following sections on rejected goods (Sections 2–603 and 2–604),

(a) after rejection any exercise of ownership by the buyer with respect to any commercial unit is wrongful as against the seller; and

(b) if the buyer has before rejection taken physical possession of goods in which he does not have a security interest under the provisions of this Article (subsection (3) of Section 2–711), he is under a duty after rejection to hold them with reasonable care at the seller's disposition for a time sufficient to permit the seller to remove them; but

(c) the buyer has no further obligations with regard to goods rightfully rejected.

(3) The seller's rights with respect to goods wrongfully rejected are governed by the provisions of this Article on Seller's remedies in general (Section 2–703).

§ 2–603.   Merchant Buyer's Duties as to Rightfully Rejected Goods.

(1) Subject to any security interest in the buyer (subsection (3) of Section 2–711), when the seller has no agent or place of business at the market of rejection a merchant buyer is under a duty after rejection of goods in his possession or control to follow any reasonable instructions received from the seller with respect to the goods and in the absence of such instructions to make reasonable efforts to sell them for the seller's account if they are perishable or threaten to decline in value speedily. Instructions are not reasonable if on demand indemnity for expenses is not forthcoming.

(2) When the buyer sells goods under subsection (1), he is entitled to reimbursement from the seller or out of the proceeds for reasonable expenses of caring for and selling them, and if the expenses include no selling commission then to such commission as is usual

in the trade or if there is none to a reasonable sum not exceeding ten per cent on the gross proceeds.

(3) In complying with this section the buyer is held only to good faith and good faith conduct hereunder is neither acceptance nor conversion nor the basis of an action for damages.

§ 2–604.   Buyer's Options as to Salvage of Rightfully Rejected Goods.

Subject to the provisions of the immediately preceding section on perishables if the seller gives no instructions within a reasonable time after notification of rejection the buyer may store the rejected goods for the seller's account or reship them to him or resell them for the seller's account with reimbursement as provided in the preceding section. Such action is not acceptance or conversion.

§ 2–605.   Waiver of Buyer's Objections by Failure to Particularize.

(1) The buyer's failure to state in connection with rejection a particular defect which is ascertainable by reasonable inspection precludes him from relying on the unstated defect to justify rejection or to establish breach

(a) where the seller could have cured it if stated seasonably; or

(b) between merchants when the seller has after rejection made a request in writing for a full and final written statement of all defects on which the buyer proposes to rely.

(2) Payment against documents made without reservation of rights precludes recovery of the payment for defects apparent on the face of the documents.

§ 2–606.   What Constitutes Acceptance of Goods.

(1) Acceptance of goods occurs when the buyer

(a) after a reasonable opportunity to inspect the goods signifies to the seller that the goods are conforming or that he will take or retain them in spite of their nonconformity; or

(b) fails to make an effective rejection (subsection (1) of Section 2–602), but such acceptance does not occur until the buyer has had a reasonable opportunity to inspect them; or

(c) does any act inconsistent with the seller's ownership; but if such act is wrongful as against the seller it is an acceptance only if ratified by him.

(2) Acceptance of a part of any commercial unit is acceptance of that entire unit.

§ 2–607.   Effect of Acceptance; Notice of Breach; Burden of Establishing Breach After Acceptance; Notice of Claim or Litigation to Person Answerable Over.

(1) The buyer must pay at the contract rate for any goods accepted.

(2) Acceptance of goods by the buyer precludes rejection of the goods accepted and if made with knowledge of a non-conformity cannot be revoked because of it unless the acceptance was on the reasonable assumption that the non-conformity would be seasonably cured but acceptance does not of itself impair any other remedy provided by this Article for non-conformity.

(3) Where a tender has been accepted

(a) the buyer must within a reasonable time after he discovers or should have discovered any breach notify the seller of breach or be barred from any remedy; and

(b) if the claim is one for infringement or the like (subsection (3) of Section 2–312) and the buyer is sued as a result of such a breach he must so notify the seller within a reasonable time after he receives notice of the litigation or be barred from any remedy over for liability established by the litigation.

(4) The burden is on the buyer to establish any breach with respect to the goods accepted.

(5) Where the buyer is sued for breach of a warranty or other obligation for which his seller is answerable over

(a) he may give his seller written notice of the litigation. If the notice states that the seller may come in and defend and that if the seller does not do so he will be bound in any action against him by his buyer by any determination of fact common to the two litigations, then unless the seller after seasonable receipt of the notice does come in and defend he is so bound.

(b) if the claim is one for infringement or the like (subsection (3) of Section 2–312) the original seller may demand in writing that his buyer turn over to him control of the litigation including settlement or else be barred from any remedy over and if he also agrees to bear all expense and to satisfy any adverse judgment, then unless the buyer after seasonable receipt of the demand does turn over control the buyer is so barred.

(6) The provisions of subsections (3), (4) and (5) apply to any obligation of a buyer to hold the seller harmless against infringement or the like (subsection (3) of Section 2–312).

§ 2–608. Revocation of Acceptance in Whole or in Part.

(1) The buyer may revoke his acceptance of a lot or commercial unit whose non-conformity substantially impairs its value to him if he has accepted it

(a) on the reasonable assumption that its nonconformity would be cured and it has not been seasonably cured; or

(b) without discovery of such non-conformity if his acceptance was reasonably induced either by the difficulty of discovery before acceptance or by the seller's assurances.

(2) Revocation of acceptance must occur within a reasonable time after the buyer discovers or should have discovered the ground for it and before any substantial change in condition of the goods which is not caused by their own defects. It is not effective until the buyer notifies the seller of it.

(3) A buyer who so revokes has the same rights and duties with regard to the goods involved as if he had rejected them.

§ 2–609. Right to Adequate Assurance of Performance.

(1) A contract for sale imposes an obligation on each party that the other's expectation of receiving due performance will not be impaired. When reasonable grounds for insecurity arise with respect to the performance of either party the other may in writing demand adequate assurance of due performance and until he receives such assurance may if commercially reasonable suspend any performance for which he has not already received the agreed return.

(2) Between merchants the reasonableness of grounds for insecurity and the adequacy of any assurance offered shall be determined according to commercial standards.

(3) Acceptance of any improper delivery or payment does not prejudice the party's right to demand adequate assurance of future performance.

(4) After receipt of a justified demand failure to provide within a reasonable time not exceeding thirty days such assurance of due performance as is adequate under the circumstances of the particular case is a repudiation of the contract.

§ 2–610. Anticipatory Repudiation.

When either party repudiates the contract with respect to a performance not yet due the loss of which will substantially impair the value of the contract to the other, the aggrieved party may

(a) for a commercially reasonable time await performance by the repudiating party; or

(b) resort to any remedy for breach (Section 2–703 or Section 2–711), even though he has notified the repudiating party that he would await the latter's performance and has urged retraction; and

(c) in either case suspend his own performance or proceed in accordance with the provisions of this Article on the seller's right to identify goods to the contract notwithstanding breach or to salvage unfinished goods (Section 2–704).

§ 2–611. Retraction of Anticipatory Repudiation.

(1) Until the repudiating party's next performance is due he can retract his repudiation unless the aggrieved party has since the repudiation cancelled or materially changed his position or otherwise indicated that he considers the repudiation final.

(2) Retraction may be by any method which clearly indicates to the aggrieved party that the repudiating party intends to perform, but must include any assurance justifiably demanded under the provisions of this Article (Section 2–609).

(3) Retraction reinstates the repudiating party's rights under the contract with due excuse and allowance to the aggrieved party for any delay occasioned by the repudiation.

§ 2–612. "Installment Contract"; Breach.

(1) An "installment contract" is one which requires or authorizes the delivery of goods in separate lots to be separately accepted, even though the contract contains a clause "each delivery is a separate contract" or its equivalent.

(2) The buyer may reject any installment which is non-conforming if the non-conformity substantially impairs the value of that installment and cannot be cured or if the non-conformity is a defect in the required documents; but if the non-conformity does not fall within subsection (3) and the seller gives adequate assurance of its cure the buyer must accept that installment.

(3) Whenever non-conformity or default with respect to one or more installments substantially impairs the value of the whole contract there is a breach of the whole. But the aggrieved party reinstates the contract if he accepts a non-conforming installment without seasonably notifying of cancellation or if he brings an action with respect only to past installments or demands performance as to future installments.

§ 2–613.   Casualty to Identified Goods.

Where the contract requires for its performance goods identified when the contract is made, and the goods suffer casualty without fault of either party before the risk of loss passes to the buyer, or in a proper case under a "no arrival, no sale" term (Section 2–324) then

(a) if the loss is total the contract is avoided; and

(b) if the loss is partial or the goods have so deteriorated as no longer to conform to the contract the buyer may nevertheless demand inspection and at his option either treat the contract as voided or accept the goods with due allowance from the contract price for the deterioration or the deficiency in quantity but without further right against the seller.

§ 2–614.   Substituted Performance.

(1) Where without fault of either party the agreed berthing, loading, or unloading facilities fail or an agreed type of carrier becomes unavailable or the agreed manner of delivery otherwise becomes commercially impracticable but a commercially reasonable substitute is available, such substitute performance must be tendered and accepted.

(2) If the agreed means or manner of payment fails because of domestic or foreign governmental regulation, the seller may withhold or stop delivery unless the buyer provides a means or manner of payment which is commercially a substantial equivalent. If delivery has already been taken, payment by the means or in the manner provided by the regulation discharges the buyer's obligation unless the regulation is discriminatory, oppressive or predatory.

§ 2–615.   Excuse by Failure of Presupposed Conditions.

Except so far as a seller may have assumed a greater obligation and subject to the preceding section on substituted performance:

(a) Delay in delivery or non-delivery in whole or in part by a seller who complies with paragraphs (b) and (c) is not a breach of his duty under a contract for sale if performance as agreed has been made impracticable by the occurrence of a contingency the nonoccurrence of which was a basic assumption on which the contract was made or by compliance in good faith with any applicable foreign or domestic governmental regulation or order whether or not it later proves to be invalid.

(b) Where the causes mentioned in paragraph (a) affect only a part of the seller's capacity to perform, he must allocate production and deliveries among his customers but may at his option include regular customers not then under contract as well as his own requirements for further manufacture. He may so allocate in any manner which is fair and reasonable.

(c) The seller must notify the buyer seasonably that there will be delay or non-delivery and, when allocation is required under paragraph (b), of the estimated quota thus made available for the buyer.

§ 2–616.   Procedure on Notice Claiming Excuse.

(1) Where the buyer receives notification of a material or indefinite delay or an allocation justified under the preceding section he may by written notification to the seller as to any delivery concerned, and where the prospective deficiency substantially impairs the value of the whole contract under the provisions of this Article relating to breach of installment contracts (Section 2–612), then also as to the whole,

(a) terminate and thereby discharge any unexecuted portion of the contract; or

(b) modify the contract by agreeing to take his available quota in substitution.

(2) If after receipt of such notification from the seller the buyer fails so to modify the contract within a reasonable time not exceeding thirty days the contract lapses with respect to any deliveries affected.

(3) The provisions of this section may not be negated by agreement except in so far as the seller has assumed a greater obligation under the preceding section.

Part 7   Remedies

§ 2–701.   Remedies for Breach of Collateral Contracts Not Impaired.

Remedies for breach of any obligation or promise collateral or ancillary to a contract for sale are not impaired by the provisions of this Article.

§ 2–702.   Seller's Remedies on Discovery of Buyer's Insolvency.

(1) Where the seller discovers the buyer to be insolvent he may refuse delivery except for cash including payment for all goods theretofore delivered under the contract, and stop delivery under this Article (Section 2–705).

(2) Where the seller discovers that the buyer has received goods on credit while insolvent he may reclaim the goods upon demand made within ten days after the receipt, but if misrepresentation of solvency has been made to the particular seller in writing within three months before delivery the ten day limitation does not apply. Except as provided in this subsection the seller may not base a right to reclaim goods on the buyer's fraudulent or innocent misrepresentation of solvency or of intent to pay.

(3) The seller's right to reclaim under subsection (2) is subject to the rights of a buyer in ordinary course or other good faith purchaser under this Article (Section 2–403). Successful reclamation of goods excludes all other remedies with respect to them.

§ 2–703.   Seller's Remedies in General.

Where the buyer wrongfully rejects or revokes acceptance of goods or fails to make a payment due on or before delivery or repudiates with respect to a part or the whole, then with respect to any goods directly affected and, if the breach is of the whole contract (Section 2–612), then also with respect to the whole undelivered balance, the aggrieved seller may

(a) withhold delivery of such goods;

(b) stop delivery by any bailee as hereafter provided (Section 2–705);

(c) proceed under the next section respecting goods still unidentified to the contract;

(d) resell and recover damages as hereafter provided (Section 2–706);

(e) recover damages for non-acceptance (Section 2–708) or in a proper case the price (Section 2–709);

(f) cancel.

§ 2–704.   Seller's Right to Identify Goods to the Contract Notwithstanding Breach or to Salvage Unfinished Goods.

(1) An aggrieved seller under the preceding section may

(a) identify to the contract conforming goods not already identified if at the time he learned of the breach they are in his possession or control;

(b) treat as the subject of resale goods which have demonstrably been intended for the particular contract even though those goods are unfinished.

(2) Where the goods are unfinished an aggrieved seller may in the exercise of reasonable commercial judgment for the purposes of avoiding loss and of effective realization either complete the manufacture and wholly identify the goods to the contract or cease manufacture and resell for scrap or salvage value or proceed in any other reasonable manner.

§ 2–705.   Seller's Stoppage of Delivery in Transit or Otherwise.

(1) The seller may stop delivery of goods in the possession of a carrier or other bailee when he discovers the buyer to be insolvent (Section 2–702) and may stop delivery of carload, truckload, planeload or larger shipments of express or freight when the buyer repudiates or fails to make a payment due before delivery or if for any other reason the seller has a right to withhold or reclaim the goods.

(2) As against such buyer the seller may stop delivery until

(a) receipt of the goods by the buyer; or

(b) acknowledgment to the buyer by any bailee of the goods except a carrier that the bailee holds the goods for the buyer; or

(c) such acknowledgment to the buyer by a carrier by reshipment or as warehouseman; or

(d) negotiation to the buyer of any negotiable document of title covering the goods.

(3) (a) To stop delivery the seller must so notify as to enable the bailee by reasonable diligence to prevent delivery of the goods.

(b) After such notification the bailee must hold and deliver the goods according to the directions of the seller but the seller is liable to the bailee for any ensuing charges or damages.

(c) If a negotiable document of title has been issued for goods the bailee is not obliged to obey a notification to stop until surrender of the document.

(d) A carrier who has issued a non-negotiable bill of lading is not obliged to obey a notification to stop received from a person other than the consignor.

§ 2–706.   Seller's Resale Including Contract for Resale.

(1) Under the conditions stated in Section 2–703 on seller's remedies, the seller may resell the goods concerned or the undelivered balance thereof. Where the resale is made in good faith and in a commercially reasonable manner the seller may recover the difference between the resale price and the contract price together with any incidental damages allowed under the provisions of this Article (Section 2–710), but less expenses saved in consequence of the buyer's breach.

(2) Except as otherwise provided in subsection (3) or unless otherwise agreed resale may be at public or private sale including sale by way of one or more contracts to sell or of identification to an existing contract of the seller. Sale may be as a unit or in parcels and at any time and place and on any terms but every aspect of the sale including the method, manner, time, place and terms must be commercially reasonable. The resale must be reasonably identified as referring to the broken contract, but it is not necessary that the goods be in existence or that any or all of them have been identified to the contract before the breach.

(3) Where the resale is at private sale the seller must give the buyer reasonable notification of his intention to resell.

(4) Where the resale is at public sale

(a) only identified goods can be sold except where there is a recognized market for a public sale of futures in goods of the kind; and

(b) it must be made at a usual place or market for public sale if one is reasonably available and except in the case of goods which are perishable or threaten to decline in value speedily the seller must give the buyer reasonable notice of the time and place of the resale; and

(c) if the goods are not to be within the view of those attending the sale the notification of sale must state the place where the goods are located and provide for their reasonable inspection by prospective bidders; and

(d) the seller may buy.

(5) A purchaser who buys in good faith at a resale takes the goods free of any rights of the original buyer even though the seller fails to comply with one or more of the requirements of this section.

(6) The seller is not accountable to the buyer for any profit made on any resale. A person in the position of a seller (Section 2–707) or a buyer who has rightfully rejected or justifiably revoked acceptance must account for any excess over the amount of his security interest, as hereinafter defined (subsection (3) of Section 2–711).

§ 2–707.   "Person in the Position of a Seller".

(1) A "person in the position of a seller" includes as against a principal an agent who has paid or become responsible for the price of goods on behalf of his principal or anyone who otherwise holds a security interest or other right in goods similar to that of a seller.

(2) A person in the position of a seller may as provided in this Article withhold or stop delivery (Section 2–705) and resell (Section 2–706) and recover incidental damages (Section 2–710).

§ 2–708.   Seller's Damages for Non-Acceptance or Repudiation.

(1) Subject to subsection (2) and to the provisions of this Article with respect to proof of market price (Section 2–723), the measure of damages for non-acceptance or repudiation by the buyer is the difference between the market price at the time and place for tender and the unpaid contract price together with any incidental damages provided in this Article (Section 2–710), but less expenses saved in consequence of the buyer's breach.

(2) If the measure of damages provided in subsection (1) is inadequate to put the seller in as good a position as performance would have

done then the measure of damages is the profit (including reasonable overhead) which the seller would have made from full performance by the buyer, together with any incidental damages provided in this Article (Section 2–710), due allowance for costs reasonably incurred and due credit for payments or proceeds of resale.

§ 2–709.   Action for the Price.

(1) When the buyer fails to pay the price as it becomes due the seller may recover, together with any incidental damages under the next section, the price

(a) of goods accepted or of conforming goods lost or damaged within a commercially reasonable time after risk of their loss has passed to the buyer; and

(b) of goods identified to the contract if the seller is unable after reasonable effort to resell them at a reasonable price or the circumstances reasonably indicate that such effort will be unavailing.

(2) Where the seller sues for the price he must hold for the buyer any goods which have been identified to the contract and are still in his control except that if resale becomes possible he may resell them at any time prior to the collection of the judgment. The net proceeds of any such resale must be credited to the buyer and payment of the judgment entitles him to any goods not resold.

(3) After the buyer has wrongfully rejected or revoked acceptance of the goods or has failed to make a payment due or has repudiated (Section 2–610), a seller who is held not entitled to the price under this section shall nevertheless be awarded damages for nonacceptance under the preceding section.

§ 2–710.   Seller's Incidental Damages.

Incidental damages to an aggrieved seller include any commercially reasonable charges, expenses or commissions incurred in stopping delivery, in the transportation, care and custody of goods after the buyer's breach, in connection with return or resale of the goods or otherwise resulting from the breach.

§ 2–711.   Buyer's Remedies in General;
Buyer's Security Interest in Rejected Goods.

(1) Where the seller fails to make delivery or repudiates or the buyer rightfully rejects or justifiably revokes acceptance then with respect to any goods involved, and with respect to the whole if the breach goes to the whole contract (Section 2–612), the buyer may cancel and whether or not he has done so may in addition to recovering so much of the price as has been paid

(a) "cover" and have damages under the next section as to all the goods affected whether or not they have been identified to the contract; or

(b) recover damages for non-delivery as provided in this Article (Section 2–713).

(2) Where the seller fails to deliver or repudiates the buyer may also

(a) if the goods have been identified recover them as provided in this Article (Section 2–502); or

(b) in a proper case obtain specific performance or replevy the goods as provided in this Article (Section 2–716).

(3) On rightful rejection or justifiable revocation of acceptance a buyer has a security interest in goods in his possession or control

for any payments made on their price and any expenses reasonably incurred in their inspection, receipt, transportation, care and custody and may hold such goods and resell them in like manner as an aggrieved seller (Section 2–706).

§ 2–712.   "Cover"; Buyer's Procurement of Substitute Goods.

(1) After a breach within the preceding section the buyer may "cover" by making in good faith and without unreasonable delay any reasonable purchase of or contract to purchase goods in substitution for those due from the seller.

(2) The buyer may recover from the seller as damages the difference between the cost of cover and the contract price together with any incidental or consequential damages as hereinafter defined (Section 2–715), but less expenses saved in consequence of the seller's breach.

(3) Failure of the buyer to effect cover within this section does not bar him from any other remedy.

§ 2–713.   Buyer's Damages for Non-Delivery or Repudiation.

(1) Subject to the provisions of this Article with respect to proof of market price (Section 2–723), the measure of damages for non-delivery or repudiation by the seller is the difference between the market price at the time when the buyer learned of the breach and the contract price together with any incidental and consequential damages provided in this Article (Section 2–715), but less expenses saved in consequence of the seller's breach.

(2) Market price is to be determined as of the place for tender or, in cases of rejection after arrival or revocation of acceptance, as of the place of arrival.

§ 2–714.   Buyer's Damages for Breach in Regard to Accepted Goods.

(1) Where the buyer has accepted goods and given notification (subsection (3) of Section 2–607) he may recover as damages for any non-conformity of tender the loss resulting in the ordinary course of events from the seller's breach as determined in any manner which is reasonable.

(2) The measure of damages for breach of warranty is the difference at the time and place of acceptance between the value of the goods accepted and the value they would have had if they had been as warranted, unless special circumstances show proximate damages of a different amount.

(3) In a proper case any incidental and consequential damages under the next section may also be recovered.

§ 2–715.   Buyer's Incidental and Consequential Damages.

(1) Incidental damages resulting from the seller's breach include expenses reasonably incurred in inspection, receipt, transportation and care and custody of goods rightfully rejected, any commercially reasonable charges, expenses or commissions in connection with effecting cover and any other reasonable expense incident to the delay or other breach.

(2) Consequential damages resulting from the seller's breach include

(a) any loss resulting from general or particular requirements and needs of which the seller at the time of contracting had reason to know and which could not reasonably be prevented by cover or otherwise; and

(b) injury to person or property proximately resulting from any breach of warranty.

§ 2–716.   Buyer's Right to Specific Performance or Replevin.

(1) Specific performance may be decreed where the goods are unique or in other proper circumstances.

(2) The decree for specific performance may include such terms and conditions as to payment of the price, damages, or other relief as the court may deem just.

(3) The buyer has a right of replevin for goods identified to the contract if after reasonable effort he is unable to effect cover for such goods or the circumstances reasonably indicate that such effort will be unavailing or if the goods have been shipped under reservation and satisfaction of the security interest in them has been made or tendered. In the case of goods bought for personal, family, or household purposes, the buyer's right of replevin vests upon acquisition of a special property, even if the seller had not then repudiated or failed to deliver.

As amended in 1999.

§ 2–717.   Deduction of Damages From the Price.

The buyer on notifying the seller of his intention to do so may deduct all or any part of the damages resulting from any breach of the contract from any part of the price still due under the same contract.

§ 2–718.   Liquidation or Limitation of Damages; Deposits.

(1) Damages for breach by either party may be liquidated in the agreement but only at an amount which is reasonable in the light of the anticipated or actual harm caused by the breach, the difficulties of proof of loss, and the inconvenience or nonfeasibility of otherwise obtaining an adequate remedy. A term fixing unreasonably large liquidated damages is void as a penalty.

(2) Where the seller justifiably withholds delivery of goods because of the buyer's breach, the buyer is entitled to restitution of any amount by which the sum of his payments exceeds

(a) the amount to which the seller is entitled by virtue of terms liquidating the seller's damages in accordance with subsection (1), or

(b) in the absence of such terms, twenty per cent of the value of the total performance for which the buyer is obligated under the contract or $500, whichever is smaller.

(3) The buyer's right to restitution under subsection (2) is subject to offset to the extent that the seller establishes

(a) a right to recover damages under the provisions of this Article other than subsection (1), and

(b) the amount or value of any benefits received by the buyer directly or indirectly by reason of the contract.

(4) Where a seller has received payment in goods their reasonable value or the proceeds of their resale shall be treated as payments for the purposes of subsection (2); but if the seller has notice of the buyer's breach before reselling goods received in part performance, his resale is subject to the conditions laid down in this Article on resale by an aggrieved seller (Section 2–706).

§ 2–719.   Contractual Modification or Limitation of Remedy.

(1) Subject to the provisions of subsections (2) and (3) of this section and of the preceding section on liquidation and limitation of damages,

(a) the agreement may provide for remedies in addition to or in substitution for those provided in this Article and may limit or alter the measure of damages recoverable under this Article, as by limiting the buyer's remedies to return of the goods and repayment of the price or to repair and replacement of nonconforming goods or parts; and

(b) resort to a remedy as provided is optional unless the remedy is expressly agreed to be exclusive, in which case it is the sole remedy.

(2) Where circumstances cause an exclusive or limited remedy to fail of its essential purpose, remedy may be had as provided in this Act.

(3) Consequential damages may be limited or excluded unless the limitation or exclusion is unconscionable. Limitation of consequential damages for injury to the person in the case of consumer goods is prima facie unconscionable but limitation of damages where the loss is commercial is not.

§ 2–720.   Effect of "Cancellation" or "Rescission" on Claims for Antecedent Breach.

Unless the contrary intention clearly appears, expressions of "cancellation" or "rescission" of the contract or the like shall not be construed as a renunciation or discharge of any claim in damages for an antecedent breach.

§ 2–721.   Remedies for Fraud.

Remedies for material misrepresentation or fraud include all remedies available under this Article for non-fraudulent breach. Neither rescission or a claim for rescission of the contract for sale nor rejection or return of the goods shall bar or be deemed inconsistent with a claim for damages or other remedy.

§ 2–722.   Who Can Sue Third Parties for Injury to Goods.

Where a third party so deals with goods which have been identified to a contract for sale as to cause actionable injury to a party to that contract

(a) a right of action against the third party is in either party to the contract for sale who has title to or a security interest or a special property or an insurable interest in the goods; and if the goods have been destroyed or converted a right of action is also in the party who either bore the risk of loss under the contract for sale or has since the injury assumed that risk as against the other;

(b) if at the time of the injury the party plaintiff did not bear the risk of loss as against the other party to the contract for sale and there is no arrangement between them for disposition of the recovery, his suit or settlement is, subject to his own interest, as a fiduciary for the other party to the contract;

(c) either party may with the consent of the other sue for the benefit of whom it may concern.

§ 2–723.   Proof of Market Price: Time and Place.

(1) If an action based on anticipatory repudiation comes to trial before the time for performance with respect to some or all of the goods, any damages based on market price (Section 2–708 or Section 2–713) shall be determined according to the price of such goods prevailing at the time when the aggrieved party learned of the repudiation.

(2) If evidence of a price prevailing at the times or places described in this Article is not readily available the price prevailing within any reasonable time before or after the time described or at any other

place which in commercial judgment or under usage of trade would serve as a reasonable substitute for the one described may be used, making any proper allowance for the cost of transporting the goods to or from such other place.

(3) Evidence of a relevant price prevailing at a time or place other than the one described in this Article offered by one party is not admissible unless and until he has given the other party such notice as the court finds sufficient to prevent unfair surprise.

§ 2–724.   Admissibility of Market Quotations.

Whenever the prevailing price or value of any goods regularly bought and sold in any established commodity market is in issue, reports in official publications or trade journals or in newspapers or periodicals of general circulation published as the reports of such market shall be admissible in evidence. The circumstances of the preparation of such a report may be shown to affect its weight but not its admissibility.

§ 2–725.   Statute of Limitations in Contracts for Sale.

(1) An action for breach of any contract for sale must be commenced within four years after the cause of action has accrued. By the original agreement the parties may reduce the period of limitation to not less than one year but may not extend it.

(2) A cause of action accrues when the breach occurs, regardless of the aggrieved party's lack of knowledge of the breach. A breach of warranty occurs when tender of delivery is made, except that where a warranty explicitly extends to future performance of the goods and discovery of the breach must await the time of such performance the cause of action accrues when the breach is or should have been discovered.

(3) Where an action commenced within the time limited by subsection (1) is so terminated as to leave available a remedy by another action for the same breach such other action may be commenced after the expiration of the time limited and within six months after the termination of the first action unless the termination resulted from voluntary discontinuance or from dismissal for failure or neglect to prosecute.

(4) This section does not alter the law on tolling of the statute of limitations nor does it apply to causes of action which have accrued before this Act becomes effective.

Appendix D

Answers to *Issue Spotters*

Chapter 1

1. No. The U.S. Constitution is the supreme law of the land and applies to all jurisdictions. A law in violation of the Constitution (in this question, the First Amendment to the Constitution) will be declared unconstitutional.

2. Yes. Administrative rulemaking starts with the publication of a notice of the rulemaking in the *Federal Register*. Among other details, this notice states where and when the proceedings, such as a public hearing, will be held. Proponents and opponents can offer their comments and concerns regarding the pending rule. After reviewing all the comments from the proceedings, the agency's decision makers consider what was presented and draft the final rule.

Chapter 2

1. No. Even if commercial speech is not related to illegal activities or misleading, it may be restricted if a state has a substantial government interest that cannot be achieved by less restrictive means. In this case, the interest in energy conservation is substantial, but it could be achieved by less restrictive means. That would be the utilities' defense against the enforcement of this state law.

2. Yes. The tax would limit the liberty of some persons, such as out-of-state businesses, so it is subject to a review under the equal protection clause. Protecting local businesses from out-of-state competition is not a legitimate government objective. Thus, such a tax would violate the equal protection clause.

Chapter 3

1. Tom could file a motion for a directed verdict. This motion asks the judge to direct a verdict for Tom on the ground that Sue presented no evidence that would justify granting her relief. The judge grants the motion if there is insufficient evidence to raise an issue of fact.

2. Yes. Submission of the dispute to mediation or nonbinding arbitration is mandatory, but compliance with the decision of the mediator or arbitrator is voluntary.

Chapter 4

1. Probably. To recover on the basis of negligence, the injured party as a plaintiff must show that the truck's owner owed the plaintiff a duty of care, that the owner breached that duty, that the plaintiff was injured, and that the breach caused the injury. In this problem, the owner's actions breached the duty of reasonable care. The billboard falling on the plaintiff was the direct cause of the injury, not the plaintiff's own negligence. Thus, liability turns on whether the plaintiff can connect the breach of duty to the injury. This involves the test of proximate cause—the question of foreseeability. The consequences to the injured party must have been a foreseeable result of the owner's carelessness.

2. The company might defend against this electrician's claim by asserting that the electrician should have known of the risk and, therefore, the company had no duty to warn. According to the problem, the danger is common knowledge in the electrician's field and should have been apparent to this electrician, given his years of training and experience. In other words, the company most likely had no need to warn the electrician of the risk.

   The firm could also raise comparative negligence. Both parties' negligence, if any, could be weighed and the liability distributed proportionally. The defendant could furthermore assert assumption of risk, claiming that the electrician voluntarily entered into a dangerous situation, knowing the risk involved.

Chapter 5

1. Yes. The manufacturer is liable for the injuries to the user of the product. A manufacturer is liable for its failure to exercise due care to any person who sustains an injury proximately caused by a negligently made (defective) product. In this scenario, the failure to inspect is a failure to use due care. Thus, Rim Corporation is liable to the injured buyer, Uri. Of course, the maker of the component part may also be liable.

2. Bensing can assert the defense of preemption. An injured party may not be able to sue the manufacturer of defective products that are subject to comprehensive federal regulatory schemes (such as medical devices and vaccinations). In this situation, it is likely that a court would conclude that the federal regulations pertaining to drug labeling preempt Ohio's common law rules. Therefore, Bensing would not be liable to Rothfus for defective labeling if it complied with federal law.

Chapter 6

1. Yes, Roslyn has committed theft of trade secrets. Lists of suppliers and customers cannot be patented, copyrighted, or trademarked, but the information they contain is protected against appropriation by others as trade secrets. And most likely, Roslyn signed a contract, agreeing not to use this information outside her employment by Organic. But even without this contract, Organic could have made a convincing case against its ex-employee for a theft of trade secrets.

2. This is patent infringement. A software maker in this situation might best protect its product, save litigation costs, and profit from its patent by the use of a license. In the context of this problem, a license would grant permission to sell a patented item. (A license can be limited to certain purposes and to the licensee only.)

Chapter 7

1. Karl may have committed trademark infringement. Search engines compile their results by looking through Web sites' keyword fields. Key words, or meta tags, increase the likelihood that a site will be included in search engine results, even if the words have no connection to the site.

A site that appropriates the key words of other sites with more frequent hits will appear in the same search engine results as the more popular sites. But using another's trademark as a key word without the owner's permission normally constitutes trademark infringement. Of course, some uses of another's trademark as a meta tag may be permissible if the use is reasonably necessary and does not suggest that the owner authorized or sponsored the use.

2. Yes. This may be an instance of trademark dilution. Dilution occurs when a trademark is used, without permission, in a way that diminishes the distinctive quality of the mark. Dilution does not require proof that consumers are likely to be confused by the use of the unauthorized mark. The products involved do not have to be similar. Dilution does require, however, that a mark be famous when the dilution occurs.

Chapter 8

1. Yes. With respect to the gas station, Daisy has obtained goods by false pretenses. She might also be charged with the crimes of larceny and forgery, and most states have special statutes covering illegal use of credit cards.

2. Yes. The Counterfeit Access Device and Computer Fraud and Abuse Act provides that a person who accesses a computer online, without permission, to obtain classified data—such as consumer

credit files in a credit agency's database—is subject to criminal prosecution. The crime has two elements: accessing the computer without permission and taking data. It is a felony if done for private financial gain. Penalties include fines and imprisonment for up to twenty years. The victim of the theft can also bring a civil suit against the criminal to obtain damages and other relief.

Chapter 9

1. When a corporation decides to respond to what it sees as a moral obligation to correct for past discrimination by adjusting pay differences among its employees, an ethical conflict is raised between the firm and its employees and between the firm and its shareholders. This dilemma arises directly out of the effect such a decision has on the firm's profits. If satisfying this obligation increases profitability, then the dilemma is easily resolved in favor of "doing the right thing."

2. Maybe. On the one hand, it is not the company's "fault" when a product is misused. Also, keeping the product on the market is not a violation of the law, and stopping sales would hurt profits. On the other hand, suspending sales could reduce suffering and could prevent negative publicity that might occur if sales continued.

Chapter 10

1. Under the objective theory of contracts, if a reasonable person would have thought that Joli had accepted Kerin's offer when she signed and returned the letter, then a contract was made, and Joli is obligated to buy the book. This depends, in part, on what was said in the letter and what was said in response. For instance, did the letter contain a valid offer, and did the response constitute a valid acceptance? Under any circumstances, the issue is not whether either party subjectively believed that they did, or did not, have a contract.

2. No. This contract, although not fully executed, is for an illegal purpose and therefore is void. A void contract gives rise to no legal obligation on the part of any party. A contract that is void is no contract. There is nothing to enforce.

Chapter 11

1. No. Revocation of an offer may be implied by conduct inconsistent with the offer. When Fidelity Corporation rehired Monica, and Ron learned of the hiring, the offer was revoked. His acceptance was too late.

2. First, it might be noted that the Uniform Electronic Transactions Act (UETA) does not apply unless the parties to a contract agree to use e-commerce in their transaction. In this deal, of course, the parties used e-commerce. The UETA removes barriers to e-commerce by giving the same legal effect to e-records and e-signatures as to paper documents and signatures. The UETA itself does not include rules for e-commerce transactions, however.

Chapter 12

1. Yes. The original contract was executory—that is, not yet performed by both parties. The parties rescinded the original contract and agreed to a new contract.

2. No. Generally, an exculpatory clause (a clause attempting to absolve a party of negligence or other wrongs) is not enforced if the party seeking its enforcement is involved in a business that is important to the public as a matter of practical necessity, such as an airline. Because of the essential nature of such services, the party would have an advantage in bargaining strength and could insist that anyone contracting for its services agree not to hold it liable.

Chapter 13

1. Yes. Rescission may be granted on the basis of fraudulent misrepresentation. The elements of fraudulent misrepresentation include intent to deceive, or *scienter*. *Scienter* exists if a party makes a statement recklessly, without regard to whether it is true or false, or if a party says or implies that a statement is made on some basis such as personal knowledge or personal investigation when it is not.

2. No. This memo is not a sufficient writing to enforce the contract against Nu! Sales, because it does not include Nu!'s signature. If My-T had been the party refusing to complete the deal, however, the memo would be considered a sufficient writing to enforce the contract against it. Letterhead stationery can constitute a signature. If the memo names the parties, the subject matter, the consideration, and the quantity involved in the transaction, it may be sufficient to be enforced against the party whose letterhead appears on it.

Chapter 14

1. Yes. Generally, if a contract clearly states that a right is not assignable, no assignment will be effective, but there are exceptions. Assignment of the right to receive monetary payment cannot be prohibited.

2. Contracts that are executory on both sides—contracts on which neither party has performed—can be rescinded solely by agreement. Contracts that are executed on one side—contracts on which one party has performed—can be rescinded only if the party who has performed receives consideration for the promise to call off the deal.

Chapter 15

1. A nonbreaching party is entitled to her or his benefit of the bargain under the contract. Here, the innocent party is entitled to be put in the position she would have been in if the contract had been fully performed. The measure of the benefit is the cost to complete the work ($500). These are compensatory damages.

2. No. To recover damages that flow from the consequences of a breach but that are caused by circumstances beyond the contract (consequential damages), the breaching party must know, or have reason to know, that special circumstances will cause the non-breaching party to suffer the additional loss. That was not the circumstance in this problem.

Chapter 16

1. Under the principle of comity, a U.S court would defer and give effect to foreign laws and judicial decrees that are consistent with U.S. law and public policy.

2. The practice described in this problem is known as dumping, which is regarded as an unfair international trade practice. Dumping is the sale of imported goods at "less than fair value." Based on the price of those goods in the exporting country, an extra tariff—known as an antidumping duty—can be imposed on the imports.

Chapter 17

1. A shipment of nonconforming goods constitutes an acceptance and a breach, unless the seller seasonably notifies the buyer that the nonconforming shipment does not constitute an acceptance and is offered only as an accommodation. Thus, since there was no notification in this problem, the shipment was both an acceptance and a breach.

2. Yes. In a transaction between merchants, the requirement of a writing is satisfied if one of them sends to the other a signed written confirmation that indicates the terms of the agreement, and the merchant receiving it has reason to know of its contents. If the merchant who receives the confirmation does not object in writing within ten days after receipt, the writing will be enforceable against him or her even though he or she has not signed anything.

Chapter 18

1. Yes. A seller is obligated to deliver goods in conformity with a contract in every detail. This is the perfect tender rule. The exception of the seller's right to cure does not apply here because the seller delivered too little too late to take advantage of this exception.

2. Yes. When anticipatory repudiation occurs, a buyer (or lessee) can resort to any remedy for breach even if the buyer tells the seller (the repudiating party in this problem) that the buyer will wait for the seller's performance.

Chapter 19

1. A statement that "I.O.U." money (or anything else) or an instruction to a bank stating, "I wish you would pay," would render any instrument nonnegotiable. To be negotiable, an instrument must contain an express promise to pay. An I.O.U. is only an acknowledgment of indebtedness. An order stating, "I wish you would pay," is not sufficiently precise.

2. No. When a drawer's employee provides the drawer with the name of a fictitious payee (a payee whom the drawer does not actually intend to have any interest in an instrument), a forgery of the payee's name is effective to pass good title to subsequent transferees.

Chapter 20

1. Yes, to both questions. In a civil suit, a drawer (Lyn) is liable to a payee (Nan) or to a holder of a check that is not honored. If intent to defraud can be proved, the drawer (Lyn) can also be subject to criminal prosecution for writing a bad check.

2. The drawer is entitled to $6,300—the amount to which the check was altered ($7,000) less the amount that the drawer ordered the bank to pay ($700). The bank may recover this amount from the party who presented the altered check for payment.

Chapter 21

1. When collateral consists of consumer goods, and the debtor has paid less than 60 percent of the debt or the purchase price, the creditor has the option of disposing of the collateral in a commercially reasonable manner. This generally requires notice to the debtor of the place, time, and manner of sale. A debtor can waive the right to notice, but only after default. Before the disposal, a debtor can redeem the collateral by tendering performance of all of the obligations secured by the collateral and by paying the creditor's reasonable expenses in retaking and maintaining the collateral.

2. Each of the parties can place a mechanic's lien on the debtor's property. If the debtor does not pay what is owed, the property can be sold to satisfy the debt. The only requirements are that the lien be filed within a specific time from the time of the work, depending on the state statute, and that notice of the foreclosure and sale be given to the debtor in advance.

Chapter 22

1. No. Besides the claims listed in this problem, the debts that cannot be discharged in bankruptcy include amounts borrowed to pay back taxes, goods obtained by fraud, debts that were not listed in the petition, domestic support obligations, certain cash advances, and others.

2. Yes. A debtor's payment to a creditor made for a preexisting debt, within ninety days (one year in the case of an insider or fraud) of a bankruptcy filing, can be recovered if it gives a creditor more than he or she would have received in the bankruptcy proceedings. A trustee can recover this preference using his or her specific avoidance powers.

Chapter 23

1. No. Nadine, as an agent, is prohibited from taking advantage of the agency relationship to obtain property that the principal (Dimka Corporation) wants to purchase. This is the *duty of loyalty* that arises with every agency relationship.

2. Yes. A principal has a duty to indemnify (reimburse) an agent for liabilities incurred because of authorized and lawful acts and transactions and for losses suffered because of the principal's failure to perform his or her duties.

Chapter 24

1. Workers' compensation laws establish a procedure for compensating workers who are injured on the job. Instead of suing to collect benefits, an injured worker notifies the employer of the injury and files a claim with the appropriate state agency. The right to recover is normally determined without regard to negligence or fault, but intentionally inflicted injuries are not covered. Unlike the potential for recovery in a lawsuit based on negligence or fault, recovery under a workers' compensation statute is limited to the specific amount designated in the statute for the employee's injury.

2. No. A closed shop (a company that requires union membership as a condition of employment) is illegal. A union shop (a company that does not require union membership as a condition of employment but requires workers to join the union after a certain time on the job) is illegal in a state with a right-to-work law, which makes it illegal to require union membership for continued employment.

Chapter 25

1. Yes. One type of sexual harassment occurs when a request for sexual favors is a condition of employment, and the person making the request is a supervisor or acts with the authority of the employer. A tangible employment action, such as continued employment, may also lead to the employer's liability for the supervisor's conduct. That the injured employee is a male and the supervisor a female, instead of the other way around, would not affect the outcome. Same-gender harassment is also actionable.

2. Yes, Koko could succeed in a discrimination suit if she can show that she was not hired solely because of her disability. The other elements for a discrimination suit based on a disability are that the plaintiff (1) has a disability and (2) is otherwise qualified for the job. Both of these elements appear to be satisfied in this scenario.

Chapter 26

1. When a business is relatively small and is not diversified, employs relatively few people, has modest profits, and is not likely to expand significantly or require extensive financing in the immediate future, the most appropriate form for doing business may be a sole proprietorship.

2. Yes. Failing to meet a specified sales quota can constitute a breach of a franchise agreement. If the franchisor is acting in good faith, "cause" may also include the death or disability of the franchisee, the insolvency of the franchisee, and a breach of another term of the franchise agreement.

Chapter 27

1. No. A widow (or widower) has no right to take a dead partner's place. A partner's death causes dissociation after which the partnership must purchase the dissociated partner's partnership interest. Therefore, the surviving partners must pay the decedent's estate (for his widow) the value of the deceased partner's interest in the partnership.

2. No. Under the partners' fiduciary duty, a partner must account to the partnership for any personal profits or benefits derived without the consent of all the partners in connection with the use of any partnership property. Here, the leasing partner may not keep the funds.

Chapter 28

1. The members of a limited liability company (LLC) may designate a group to run their firm. In that situation, the firm would be a manager-managed LLC. The group may include only members, only nonmembers, or members and nonmembers. If, instead, all members participate in management, the firm would be a member-managed LLC. In fact, unless the members agree otherwise, all members are considered to participate in the management of the firm.

2. Although there are differences, all of these forms of business organizations resemble corporations. A joint stock company, for example, features ownership by shares of stock, it is managed by directors and officers, and it has perpetual existence. A business trust, like a corporation, distributes profits to persons who are not personally responsible for the debts of the organization, and management of the business is in the hands of trustees, just as the management of a corporation is in the hands of directors and officers. An incorporated cooperative, which is subject to state laws covering nonprofit corporations, distributes profits to its owners.

Chapter 29

1. Yes. Small businesses that meet certain requirements can qualify as S corporations, created specifically to permit small businesses to avoid double taxation. The six requirements of an S corporation are (1) the firm must be a domestic corporation; (2) the firm must not be a member of an affiliated group of corporations; (3) the firm must have fewer than a certain number of shareholders; (4) the shareholders must be individuals, estates, or qualified trusts (or corporations in some cases); (5) there can be only one class of stock; and (6) no shareholder can be a nonresident alien.

2. Yes. A shareholder can bring a derivative suit on behalf of a corporation if some wrong is done to the corporation. Normally, any damages recovered go into the corporate treasury.

Chapter 30

1. The average investor is not concerned with minor inaccuracies but with facts that if disclosed would tend to deter him or her from buying the securities. These would include material facts that have an important bearing on the condition of the issuer and its business—such as liabilities, loans to officers and directors, customer delinquencies, and pending lawsuits.

2. No. The Securities Exchange Act of 1934 extends liability to officers and directors in their personal transactions for taking advantage of inside information when they know it is unavailable to the persons with whom they are dealing.

Chapter 31

1. Size alone does not determine whether a firm is a monopoly—size in relation to the market is what matters. A small store in a small, isolated town is a monopolist if it is the only store serving that market. Monopoly involves the power to affect prices and output. If a firm has sufficient market power to control prices and exclude competition, that firm has monopoly power. Monopoly power in itself is not a violation of Section 2 of the Sherman Act. The offense also requires an intent to acquire or maintain that power through anticompetitive means.

2. This agreement is a tying arrangement. The legality of a tying arrangement depends on the purpose of the agreement, the agreement's likely effect on competition in the relevant markets (the market for the tying product and the market for the tied product), and other factors. Tying arrangements for commodities are subject to Section 3 of the Clayton Act. Tying arrangements for services can be agreements in restraint of trade in violation of Section 1 of the Sherman Act.

Chapter 32

1. Under an extensive set of procedures established by the U.S. Food and Drug Administration, which administers the federal Food, Drug, and Cosmetic Act, drugs must be shown to be effective as well as safe before they may be marketed to the public. In general, manufacturers are responsible for ensuring that the drugs they offer for sale are free of any substances that could injure consumers.

2. The Comprehensive Environmental Response, Compensation, and Liability Act (CERCLA) regulates the cleanup of hazardous waste disposal sites. Any potentially responsible party can be charged with the entire cost of cleaning up a site. Potentially responsible parties include the person that generated the waste (ChemCorp), the person that transported the waste to the site (Disposal), the person that owned or operated the site at the time of the disposal (Eliminators), and the current owner or operator of the site (Fluid). A party held responsible for the entire cost may be able to recoup some of it in a lawsuit against other potentially responsible parties.

Chapter 33

1. Yes. In these circumstances, when the accountant knows that the bank will use the statement, the bank is a foreseeable user. A foreseeable user is a third party within the class of parties to whom an accountant may be liable for negligence.

2. No. In the circumstances described, the accountant will not be held liable to a purchaser of the securities. Although an accountant may be liable under securities laws for including untrue statements or omitting material facts from financial statements, due diligence is a defense to liability. Due diligence requires an accountant to conduct a reasonable investigation and have reason to believe that the financial statements were true at the time. The facts say that the misstatement of material fact in Omega's financial statement was not attributable to any fraud or negligence on Nora's part. Therefore, Nora can show that she used due diligence and will not be held liable to Pat.

Chapter 34

1. The ring is classified as lost property because it was discovered under circumstances indicating that the owner had not placed the property there voluntarily. The general rule is that the finder of the lost property has the right to possession (and eventual title) over all others *except* the true owner of the lost property. Therefore, Martin, as the true owner of the ring, is entitled to repossess the ring from Hunter.

2. Rosa de la Mar Corporation, the shipper, suffers the loss. A common carrier is liable for damage caused by the willful acts of third persons or by an accident. Other losses must be borne by the shipper (or the recipient, depending on the terms of their contract). In this situation, this shipment was lost due to an act of God.

Chapter 35

1. This is a breach of the warranty deed's covenant of quiet enjoyment. Consuela can sue Bernie and recover the purchase price of the house, plus any damages.

2. Yes. An owner of a fee simple has the most rights possible—he or she can give the property away, sell it, transfer it by will, use it for almost any purpose, possess it to the exclusion of all the world, or, as in this case, transfer possession for any period of time. The party to whom possession is transferred can also transfer her or his interest (usually only with the owner's permission) for any lesser period of time.

Chapter 36

1. No. To have testamentary capacity, a testator must be of legal age and sound mind *at the time the will is made*. Generally, the testator must (1) know the nature of the act, (2) comprehend and remember the "natural objects of his or her bounty," (3) know the nature and extent of her or his property, and (4) understand the distribution of assets called for by the will. In this situation, Sheila had testamentary capacity at the time she made the will. The fact that she was ruled mentally incompetent two years after making the will does not provide sufficient grounds to revoke it.

2. The estate will pass according to the state's intestacy laws. Intestacy laws set out how property is distributed when a person dies without a will. Their purpose is to carry out the likely intent of the decedent. The laws determine which of the deceased's natural heirs (including, in this order, the surviving spouse, lineal descendants, parents, and collateral heirs) inherit his or her property.

Appendix E

Answers to Even-Numbered *Learning Objectives Check* Questions

Chapter 1

2. What is the common law tradition?

Because of our colonial heritage, much of American law is based on the English legal system. After the Norman Conquest of England in 1066, the king's courts sought to establish a uniform set of rules for the entire country. What evolved in these courts was the common law—a body of general legal principles that applied throughout the entire English realm. Courts developed the common law rules from the principles underlying judges' decisions in actual legal controversies.

4. What is the difference between remedies at law and remedies in equity?

An award of compensation in either money or property, including land, is a remedy at law. Remedies in equity include the following:

1. A decree for specific performance—that is, an order to perform what was promised.

2. An injunction, which is an order directing a party to do or refrain from doing a particular act.

3. A rescission, or cancellation, of a contract and a return of the parties to the positions that they held before the contract's formation.

As a rule, courts will grant an equitable remedy only when the remedy at law (monetary damages) is inadequate. Remedies in equity on the whole are more flexible than remedies at law.

Chapter 2

2. What constitutional clause gives the federal government the power to regulate commercial activities among the various states?

To prevent states from establishing laws and regulations that would interfere with trade and commerce among the states, the Constitution expressly delegated to the national government the power to regulate interstate commerce. The commerce clause—Article I, Section 8, of the U.S. Constitution—expressly permits Congress "to regulate Commerce with foreign Nations, and among the several States, and with the Indian Tribes."

4. What is the Bill of Rights? What freedoms does the First Amendment guarantee?

The Bill of Rights consists of the first ten amendments to the U.S. Constitution. Adopted in 1791, the Bill of Rights embodies protections for individuals against interference by the federal government. Some of the protections also apply to business entities. The First Amendment guarantees the freedoms of religion, speech, and the press, and the rights to assemble peaceably and to petition the government.

Chapter 3

2. How are the courts applying traditional jurisdictional concepts to cases involving Internet transactions?

To hear a case, a court must have jurisdiction over the person against whom the suit is brought or over the property involved in the suit. The court must also have jurisdiction over the subject matter. Generally, courts apply a "sliding-scale" standard to determine when it is proper to exercise jurisdiction over a defendant whose only connection with the jurisdiction is the Internet.

4. What is discovery, and how does electronic discovery differ from traditional discovery?

Discovery is the process of obtaining information and evidence about a case from the other party or third parties. Discovery entails gaining access to witnesses, documents, records, and other types of evidence. Electronic discovery differs in its subject—that is, e-media, such as e-mail or text messages, rather than traditional sources of information, such as paper documents.

Chapter 4

2. What are two basic categories of torts?

Generally, the purpose of tort law is to provide remedies for the invasion of legally recognized and protected interests, such as personal safety, freedom of movement, property, and some intangibles, including privacy and reputation. The two broad categories of torts are intentional and unintentional.

4. Identify the four elements of negligence.

The four elements of negligence are as follows:

1. A duty of care owed by the defendant to the plaintiff.
2. The defendant's breach of that duty.
3. The plaintiff's suffering a legally recognizable injury.
4. The in-fact and proximate cause of that injury by the defendant's breach.

Chapter 5

2. What public policy assumptions underlie strict product liability?

The law imposes strict product liability as a matter of public policy. This public policy rests on the threefold assumption that:

1. Consumers should be protected against unsafe products.
2. Manufacturers and distributors should not escape liability for faulty products simply because they are not in privity of contract with the ultimate user of those products.
3. Manufacturers, sellers, and lessors of products are generally in a better position than consumers to bear the costs associated with injuries caused by their products—costs that they can ultimately pass on to all consumers in the form of higher prices.

4. What are three types of product defects?

The three types of product defects traditionally recognized in product liability law are manufacturing defects, design defects, and defective (inadequate) warnings.

A manufacturing defect is a departure from a product unit's design specifications that results in products that are physically flawed, damaged, or incorrectly assembled.

A product with a design defect is made in conformity with the manufacturer's design specifications, but it nevertheless results in injury to the user because the design itself is flawed.

A product may also be deemed defective because of inadequate instructions or warnings about foreseeable risks. The seller or other distributor must include comprehensible warnings if the product will not be reasonably safe without them. The seller must also warn consumers about foreseeable misuses of the product.

Chapter 6

2. Why is the protection of trademarks important?

Article I, Section 8, of the U.S. Constitution authorizes Congress "to promote the Progress of Science and useful Arts, by securing for limited Times to Authors and Inventors the exclusive Right to their respective Writings and Discoveries." Laws protecting trademarks—and patents and copyrights as well—are designed to protect and reward inventive and artistic creativity.

4. What laws protect authors' rights in the works they create?

Copyright law protects the rights of the authors of certain literary or artistic productions. The Copyright Act of 1976, as amended, covers these rights.

Chapter 7

2. What steps have been taken to protect intellectual property rights in the digital age?

The steps that have been taken to protect intellectual property in today's digital age include the application of traditional and existing law in the cyber context. For example, the passage of such federal laws as the Digital Millennium Copyright Act and the drafting of such state laws as the Uniform Electronic Transactions Act (UETA) are major steps in protecting intellectual property rights. Additionally, the signing of such treaties as the Trade-Related Aspects of Intellectual Property Rights (TRIPS) agreement and the World Intellectual Property Organization (WIPO) Copyright Treaty add protection on a global level.

4. What law governs whether Internet service providers are liable for online defamatory statements made by users?

The Communications Decency Act (CDA) sets out the liability of Internet service providers (ISPs) for online defamatory statements made by users.

Under the CDA, "No provider or user of an interactive computer service shall be treated as the publisher or speaker of any information provided by another information content provider." Thus, an ISP is usually not liable for the publication of a user's defamatory statement. This is a broad shield, and some courts have established some limits. For example, an ISP that prompts its users to make such statements would likely not be permitted to avoid liability for the statements.

Chapter 8

2. What are five broad categories of crimes? What is white-collar crime?

Traditionally, crimes have been grouped into the following categories: violent crime (crimes against persons), property crime, public order crime, white-collar crime, and organized crime.

White-collar crime is an illegal act or series of acts committed by an individual or business entity using some nonviolent means, usually in the course of a legitimate occupation.

4. What constitutional safeguards exist to protect persons accused of crimes?

Under the Fourth Amendment, before searching or seizing private property, law enforcement officers must obtain a search warrant, which requires probable cause.

Under the Fifth Amendment, no one can be deprived of "life, liberty, or property without due process of law." The Fifth Amendment also protects persons against double jeopardy and self-incrimination.

The Sixth Amendment guarantees the right to a speedy trial, the right to a jury trial, the right to a public trial, the right to confront witnesses, and the right to counsel. Individuals who are arrested must be informed of certain constitutional rights, including their Fifth Amendment right to remain silent and their Sixth Amendment right to counsel. All evidence obtained in violation of the Fourth, Fifth, and Sixth Amendments, as well as all evidence derived from the illegally obtained evidence, must be excluded from the trial.

The Eighth Amendment prohibits excessive bail and fines, and cruel and unusual punishment.

Chapter 9

2. How do duty-based ethical standards differ from outcome-based ethical standards?

Duty-based ethical standards are derived from religious precepts or philosophical principles. Outcome-based ethics focus on the consequences of an action, not on the nature of the action or on a set of pre-established moral values or religious beliefs.

4. How can business leaders encourage their companies to act ethically?

Ethical leadership is important to create and maintain an ethical workplace. Managers can set standards and then apply those standards to themselves and their firm's employees.

Chapter 10

2. What are the four basic elements necessary to the formation of a valid contract?

The basic elements for the formation of a valid contract are an agreement, consideration, contractual capacity, and legality.

4. How does a void contract differ from a voidable contract? What is an unenforceable contract?

A void contract is not a valid contract—it is not a contract at all. A voidable contract is a valid contract, but one that can be avoided at the option of one or both of the parties.

An unenforceable contract is one that cannot be enforced because of certain legal defenses against it.

Chapter 11

2. In what circumstances will an offer be irrevocable?

An offeror may not effectively revoke an offer if the offeree has changed position in justifiable reliance on the offer. Also, an option contract takes away the offeror's power to revoke an offer for the period of time specified in the option (or, if unspecified, for a reasonable time).

4. How do shrink-wrap and click-on agreements differ from other contracts? How have traditional laws been applied to these agreements?

With a shrink-wrap agreement, the terms are expressed inside the box in which the goods are packaged. A click-on agreement arises when a buyer, completing a transaction on a computer, is required to indicate assent to the terms by clicking on a button that says, for example, "I agree."

Generally, courts have enforced the terms of these agreements the same as the terms of other contracts, applying the traditional common law of contracts. Article 2 of the Uniform Commercial Code provides that acceptance can be made by conduct. The *Restatement (Second) of Contracts* has a similar provision. Under these provisions, a binding contract can be created by conduct, including conduct accepting the terms in a shrink-wrap or click-on agreement.

Chapter 12

2. In what circumstances might a promise be enforced despite a lack of consideration?

Under the doctrine of promissory estoppel (or detrimental reliance), a promisor (the offeror) is estopped, or prevented, from revoking a promise even in the absence of consideration. There are three required elements:

1. A clear and definite promise.
2. The promisee's justifiable reliance on the promise.
3. Reliance of a substantial and definite character.

4. Under what circumstances will a covenant not to compete be enforced? When will such covenants not be enforced?

A covenant not to compete can be enforced:

1. If it is ancillary (secondary) to an agreement to sell an ongoing business, thus enabling the seller to sell, and the purchaser to buy, the goodwill and reputation of the business.
2. If it is contained in an employment contract and is reasonable in terms of time and geographic area.

A covenant not to compete will be unenforceable if it does not protect a legitimate business interest or is broader than necessary to protect a legitimate interest. This is because such a covenant would unreasonably restrain trade and be contrary to public policy.

Chapter 13

2. What is the difference between a unilateral mistake and a bilateral mistake?

A unilateral mistake occurs when only one party is mistaken as to a material fact underlying the contract. Normally, the contract is enforceable even if one party made a mistake, unless an exception applies. A bilateral, or mutual, mistake occurs when both parties are mistaken about the same material fact. When the mistake is mutual, the contract can be rescinded, or canceled, by either party.

4. What contracts must be in writing to be enforceable?

Contracts that are normally required to be in writing or evidenced by a written memorandum include:

- Contracts involving interests in land.
- Contracts that cannot by their terms be performed within one year from the day after the date of formation.
- Collateral contracts, such as promises to answer for the debt or duty of another.

- Promises made in consideration of marriage.
- Contracts for the sale of goods priced at $500 or more.

Chapter 14

2. In what situations is the delegation of duties prohibited?

Delegation of duties is prohibited in the following situations:

1. When the performance depends on the personal skill or talents of the obligor.
2. When special trust has been placed in the obligor.
3. When performance by a third party will vary materially from that expected by the obligee under the contract.
4. When the contract expressly prohibits delegation.

4. How are most contracts discharged?

The most common way to discharge, or terminate, a contract is by the performance of contractual duties.

Chapter 15

2. What is the difference between compensatory damages and consequential damages? What are nominal damages, and when do courts award nominal damages?

Compensatory damages compensate an injured party for injuries or damages. Foreseeable damages that result from a party's breach of contract are consequential damages. Consequential damages differ from compensatory damages in that they are caused by special circumstances beyond the contract.

Nominal damages are awarded to an innocent party when no actual damage has been suffered. Nominal damages might be awarded as a matter of principle to establish fault or wrongful behavior.

4. When do courts grant specific performance as a remedy?

Specific performance might be granted as a remedy when damages offer an inadequate remedy and the subject matter of the contract is unique.

Chapter 16

2. What is the act of state doctrine? In what circumstances is this doctrine applied?

The act of state doctrine is a judicially created doctrine that provides that the judicial branch of one country will not examine the validity of public acts committed by a recognized foreign government within its own territory. This doctrine is often employed in cases involving expropriation or confiscation.

4. What are some clauses commonly included in international business contracts?

Choice-of-language, forum-selection, choice-of-law, and *force majeure* clauses are commonly used in international business contracts.

Chapter 17

2. In a sales contract, if an offeree includes additional or different terms in an acceptance, will a contract result? If so, what happens to these terms?

Under the Uniform Commercial Code, a contract can be formed even if the offeree's acceptance includes additional or different terms. If one of the parties is a nonmerchant, the contract does not include the additional terms. If both parties are merchants, the additional terms automatically become part of the contract unless one of the following occurs:

1. The original offer expressly limits acceptance to the terms of the offer.
2. The new or changed terms materially alter the contract.
3. The offeror objects to the new or changed terms within a reasonable period of time.

(If the additional terms expressly require the offeror's assent, the offeree's response is not an acceptance, but a counteroffer.) Under some circumstances, a court might strike the additional terms.

4. Risk of loss does not necessarily pass with title. If the parties to a contract do not expressly agree when risk passes and the goods are to be delivered without movement by the seller, when does risk pass?

If the seller holds the goods and is a merchant, the risk of loss passes to the buyer when the buyer takes physical possession of the goods. If the seller holds the goods and is not a merchant, the risk of loss passes to the buyer on tender of delivery. When a bailee is holding the goods, the risk of loss passes to the buyer when (1) the buyer receives a negotiable document of title for the goods, (2) the bailee acknowledges the buyer's right to possess the goods, or (3) the buyer receives a nonnegotiable document of title and has had a reasonable time to present the document to the bailee and demand the goods.

Chapter 18

2. What is the perfect tender rule? What are some important exceptions to this rule that apply to sales and lease contracts?

Under the perfect tender rule, the seller or lessor has an obligation to ship or tender conforming goods. If the goods or tender of delivery fails in any respect, the buyer or lessee has the right to accept the goods, reject the entire shipment, or accept part and reject part. Exceptions to the rule may be established by agreement.

When goods are rejected because they are nonconforming and the time for performance has not expired, the seller or lessor can notify the buyer or lessee promptly of the intention to cure and then do so within the contract time for performance. If the time for performance has expired, the seller or lessor can still cure within a reasonable time if, at the time of delivery, he or she had reasonable grounds to believe that the nonconforming tender would be acceptable. When an agreed-on manner of delivery becomes impracticable or unavailable through no fault of either party, a seller may choose a commercially reasonable substitute.

4. What remedies are available to a seller or lessor when the buyer or lessee breaches the contract?

Depending on the circumstances at the time of a buyer's or lessee's breach, a seller or lessor may have the right to cancel the contract, withhold delivery, or resell or dispose of the goods subject to the contract. In addition, a seller or lessor may have the right to recover the purchase price (or lease payments), recover damages, stop delivery in transit, or reclaim the goods.

Chapter 19

2. What is the advantage of transferring an instrument by negotiation? How does the negotiation of order instruments differ from the negotiation of bearer instruments?

Negotiation is the only way to transfer an instrument that allows the party receiving the instrument to obtain the rights of a holder. Unlike a transfer by assignment, a transfer by negotiation can make it possible for a holder to receive more rights in the instrument than the prior possessor had [UCC 3–202(b), 3–305, 3–306].

Negotiating order instruments requires both delivery and indorsement. In contrast, negotiating bearer instruments is accomplished by delivery alone (without the need for indorsement).

4. What is the difference between signature liability and warranty liability?

The key to liability on a negotiable instrument is a signature. Every party, except a qualified indorser, who signs a negotiable instrument is primarily or secondarily liable for payment of that instrument when it comes due.

Signature liability arises from indorsing an instrument. Warranty liability arises from transferring an instrument, whether or not the transferor also indorses it.

Chapter 20

2. When may a bank properly dishonor a customer's check without being liable to the customer?

A bank may dishonor a customer's check without liability to the customer when the customer's account contains insufficient funds to pay the check, providing the bank did not agree to cover overdrafts. A bank may also properly dishonor a stale check, a timely check subject to a valid stop-payment order, a check drawn after the customer's death, and forged or altered checks.

4. What is electronic check presentment, and how does it differ from the traditional check-clearing process?

With electronic check presentment, items are encoded with information (such as the amount of the check) that is read and processed by other banks' computers. A check may sometimes be retained at its place of deposit, and then only its image or description is presented for payment. A bank that encodes information on an item warrants to any subsequent bank or payor that the encoded information is correct.

This differs from the traditional check-clearing process because employees of each bank in the collection chain no longer have to physically handle each check that passes through the bank for collection or payment. Therefore, obtaining payment is much quicker. Whereas manual check processing can take days, electronic check presentment can be done on the day of deposit.

Chapter 21

2. How is a purchase-money security interest in consumer goods created and perfected?

A purchase-money security interest (PMSI) in consumer goods is created when a person buys goods and the seller or lender agrees to extend credit for part or all of the purchase price of the goods. The entity that extends the credit and obtains the PMSI can be either the seller (a store, for example) or a financial institution that lends the buyer the funds with which to purchase the goods [UCC 9–102(a)(2)].

A PMSI in consumer goods is perfected automatically at the time of a credit sale—that is, at the time the PMSI is created. The seller in this situation does not need to do anything more to perfect her or his interest.

4. How does a mechanic's lien assist creditors?

When a creditor follows the individual state's procedure to create a mechanic's lien, the debtor's real estate becomes security for the debt. If the debtor continues not to pay the underlying debt, the creditor can foreclose on the debtor's real property to collect the amount due.

Chapter 22

2. In a Chapter 7 bankruptcy, what happens if a court finds that there was "substantial abuse"? How is the means test used?

If a court concludes there was substantial abuse, the court can dismiss a petition or convert it from a Chapter 7 to a Chapter 11 or Chapter 13 case. In the means test, the debtor's average monthly income in recent months is compared with the median income in the geographic area in which the person lives. If the debtor's income is below the median income, the debtor usually is allowed to file for Chapter 7 bankruptcy. If the debtor's income is above the median income, then further calculations are necessary to determine if there is substantial abuse. The goal is to determine whether the person will have sufficient disposable income in the future to repay at least some of his or her unsecured debts.

4. In a Chapter 11 reorganization, what is the role of the debtor in possession?

Under Chapter 11, a debtor in possession (DIP) is allowed to continue to operate his or her business while the bankruptcy proceeds. The DIP's role is similar to that of a trustee in a liquidation, or Chapter 7, proceeding. Like a trustee, the DIP has certain powers and can avoid preferential transfers and cancel unperformed contracts and unexpired leases.

Chapter 23

2. How do agency relationships arise?

Agency relationships normally are consensual—that is, they arise by voluntary consent and agreement between the parties.

4. When is a principal liable for the agent's actions with respect to third parties? When is the agent liable?

A disclosed or partially disclosed principal is liable to a third party for a contract made by an agent who was acting within the scope of her or his authority. If the agent exceeds the scope of authority and the principal fails to ratify the contract, the agent may be liable (and the principal may not).

When neither the fact of agency nor the identity of the principal is disclosed, the agent is liable, and if the agent has acted within the scope of his or her authority, the undisclosed principal is also liable. Each party is liable for his or her own torts and crimes. A principal may also be liable for an agent's torts committed within the course or scope of employment. A principal is liable for an agent's crime if the principal participated by conspiracy or other action.

Chapter 24

2. What federal statute governs working hours and wages?

The Fair Labor Standards Act is the most significant federal statute governing working hours and wages.

4. What are the two most important federal statutes governing immigration and employment today?

The most important federal statutes governing immigration and the employment of noncitizens are the Immigration Reform and Control Act (IRCA) and the Immigration Act.

Chapter 25

2. What must an employer do to avoid liability for religious discrimination?

Employers cannot treat their employees more or less favorably based on their religious beliefs or practices. Employers also cannot require employees to participate in any religious activity (or forbid them from participating in one). An employer must reasonably accommodate the religious practices of its employees, unless to do so would cause undue hardship to the employer's business.

4. What federal act prohibits discrimination based on age?

The Age Discrimination in Employment Act prohibits discrimination on the basis of age.

Chapter 26

2. What are the most common types of franchises?

The majority of franchises are distributorships, chain-style business operations, or manufacturing or processing-plant arrangements.

4. How are franchises normally terminated? When will a court decide that a franchisor has wrongfully terminated a franchise?

Franchise agreements are usually terminated through provisions in the franchise contract, which often specify that the termination must be "for cause." Cause might include, for instance, the death or disability of the franchisee, insolvency of the franchisee, breach of the franchise agreement, or failure to meet specified sales quotas.

Usually, notice of the termination must be given to the franchisee. The franchisee may be given a chance to cure a breach of the contract within a specific period of time.

If a franchisor has acted arbitrarily or unfairly terminated a franchise (i.e., not in good faith) a court may decide that the termination was wrongful and provide a remedy to the franchisee. Courts look at the good faith and fair dealing of the parties in the franchise relationship when deciding whether the termination was wrongful.

Chapter 27

2. What are the rights and duties of partners in an ordinary partnership?

The rights and duties of partners may be whatever the partners declare them to be. In the absence of partners' agreements to the contrary, the law imposes certain rights and duties. These include:

- A sharing of profits and losses in equal measure.
- The ability to assign a partnership interest.
- Equal rights in managing the firm (subject to majority rule).
- Access to all of the firm's books and records.
- An accounting of assets and profits.
- A sharing of the firm's property.

The duties include fiduciary duties, being bound to third parties through contracts entered into with other partners, and liability for the firm's debts and liabilities.

4. What advantages do limited liability partnerships offer to businesspersons that are not offered by general partnerships?

An advantage of a limited liability partnership over a general partnership is that, depending on the applicable state statute, the liability of the partners for partnership and partners' debts and torts can be limited to the amount of the partners' investments. Another advantage is that partners in a limited liability partnership generally are not liable for other partners' malpractice.

Chapter 28

2. What advantages do limited liability companies offer to businesspersons that are not offered by sole proprietorships or partnerships?

An important advantage of limited liability companies (LLCs) is that the liability of the members is limited to the amount of their investments. Another advantage of LLCs is the flexibility they offer in regard to taxation and management.

4. What is a joint venture? How is it similar to a partnership? How is it different?

A joint venture is an enterprise in which two or more persons or business entities combine their efforts or their property for a single transaction or project, or a related series of transactions or projects.

Generally, partnership law applies to joint ventures, although joint venturers have less implied and apparent authority than partners because they have less power to bind the members of their organization.

Chapter 29

2. What four steps are involved in bringing a corporation into existence?

The four basic steps to bring a corporation into existence include (1) selecting the state of incorporation, (2) securing the corporate name, (3) preparing the articles of incorporation, and (4) filing those articles with the state.

4. What are the duties of corporate directors and officers?

Directors and officers are fiduciaries of the corporation. The fiduciary duties of the directors and officers include the duty of care and the duty of loyalty.

Chapter 30

2. What are the two major statutes regulating the securities industry?

The major statutes regulating the securities industry are the Securities Act of 1933 and the Securities Exchange Act of 1934, which created the Securities and Exchange Commission.

4. What are some of the features of state securities laws?

Typically, state laws have disclosure requirements and anti-fraud provisions patterned after Section 10(b) of the Securities Exchange Act of 1934 and SEC Rule 10b-5. State laws provide for the registration or qualification of securities offered or issued for sale within the state with the appropriate state official. Also, most state securities laws regulate securities brokers and dealers.

Chapter 31

2. What rule do courts apply to price-fixing agreements, and why?

Courts apply the *per se* rule to price-fixing agreements. Because agreements to fix prices are so blatantly and substantially anticompetitive, they are deemed *per se* illegal. That is, even if the parties had good reasons for entering the agreement, if the agreement restricts output or artificially fixes prices, it violates Section 1 of the Sherman Act.

4. What are the four major provisions of the Clayton Act, and what types of activities do these provisions prohibit?

Section 2 of the Clayton Act prohibits price discrimination. Section 3 prohibits two types of vertical agreements involving exclusionary practices: exclusive-dealing contracts and tying arrangements. Section 7 prohibits mergers or acquisitions that result in monopoly power or a substantial lessening of competition in the marketplace. Section 8 prohibits a person from being a director in two or more competing corporations at the same time if either of the corporations has capital, surplus, or undivided profits aggregating more than a specified amount or competitive sales of a certain amount or more (the dollar limits are changed periodically by Congress).

Chapter 32

2. What law protects consumers against contaminated and misbranded foods and drugs?

The Federal Food, Drug, and Cosmetic Act (FDCA) protects consumers against adulterated and misbranded foods and drugs. The FDCA establishes food standards, specifies safe levels of potentially hazardous food additives, and provides classifications of foods and food advertising.

4. What is contained in an environmental impact statement, and who must file one?

An environmental impact statement (EIS) analyzes the following:

1. The impact on the environment that an action will have.
2. Any adverse effects on the environment and alternative actions that might be taken.
3. Irreversible effects the action might generate.

An EIS must be prepared for every major federal action that significantly affects the quality of the environment. An action is "major" if it involves a substantial commitment of resources (monetary or otherwise). An action is "federal" if a federal agency has the power to control it.

Chapter 33

2. What are the rules concerning an auditor's liability to third parties?

An auditor may be liable to a third party on the ground of negligence, when the auditor knew or should have known that the third party would benefit from the auditor's work. Depending on the jurisdiction, liability may be imposed only if one of the following occurs:

1. The auditor is in privity, or near privity, with the third party.
2. The third party's reliance on the auditor's work was foreseen, or the third party was within a class of known or foreseeable users.
3. The third party's use of the auditor's work was reasonably foreseeable.

4. What crimes might an accountant commit under the Internal Revenue Code?

Crimes under the Internal Revenue Code include the following:

1. Aiding or assisting in the preparation of a false tax return.
2. Aiding or abetting an individual's understatement of tax liability.
3. Negligently or willfully understating a client's tax liability, or recklessly or intentionally disregarding Internal Revenue Code rules or regulations.
4. Failing to provide a taxpayer with a copy of a tax return, failing to sign the return, or failing to furnish the appropriate tax identification numbers.

Chapter 34

2. What are the three necessary elements for an effective gift?

To make an effective gift, the donor must intend to make the gift, the gift must be delivered to the donee, and the donee must accept the gift.

4. What are the basic duties of a bailee?

The bailee has two basic responsibilities: (1) to take appropriate care of the property and (2) to surrender the property at the end of the bailment. The appropriate degree of care required for the bailor's property depends on whether the bailment is for the benefit of the bailor, the benefit of the bailee, or for their mutual benefit.

Chapter 35

2. What is the difference between a joint tenancy and a tenancy in common?

A tenancy in common is a form of co-ownership in which each of two or more persons owns an undivided interest in the whole property. On the death of a tenant in common, that tenant's interest passes to his or her heirs. In a joint tenancy, each of two or more persons owns an undivided interest in the property, and a deceased joint tenant's interest passes to the surviving joint tenant or tenants. This right distinguishes the joint tenancy from the tenancy in common.

4. What are the requirements for acquiring property by adverse possession?

The adverse possessor's possession must be (1) actual and exclusive, (2) open, visible, and notorious, not secret or clandestine, (3) continuous and peaceable for the statutory period of time, and (4) hostile and adverse.

Chapter 36

2. How do courts interpret ambiguities in an insurance policy?

The courts will interpret the words used in an insurance contract according to their ordinary meanings in light of the nature of the coverage involved. When there is an ambiguity in the policy, the provision generally is interpreted *against the insurance company*.

4. What is the difference between a *per stirpes* distribution and a *per capita* distribution of an estate to the grandchildren of the deceased?

Per stirpes distribution dictates that grandchildren share the part of the estate that their deceased parent (and descendant of the deceased grandparent) would have been entitled to inherit.

Per capita distribution dictates that each grandchild takes an equal share of the estate.

Appendix F

Sample Answers for *Business Case Problems with Sample Answer*

1–6. Sample Answer—Law around the World.

The common law system spread throughout medieval England after the Norman Conquest in 1066. Courts developed the common law rules from the principles behind the decisions in actual legal controversies. Judges attempted to be consistent. When possible, they based their decisions on the principles suggested by earlier cases. They sought to decide similar cases in a similar way and considered new cases with care because they knew that their decisions would make new law. Each interpretation became part of the law on the subject and served as a legal precedent. Later cases that involved similar legal principles or facts could be decided with reference to that precedent.

The practice of deciding new cases with reference to former decisions, or precedents, eventually became a cornerstone of the English and American judicial systems. It forms a doctrine called stare decisis. Under this doctrine, judges are obligated to follow the precedents established within their jurisdictions. Generally, those countries that were once colonies of Great Britain retained their English common law heritage after they achieved their independence. Today, common law systems exist in Australia, Canada, India, Ireland, and New Zealand, as well as the United States.

Most of the other European nations base their legal systems on Roman civil law. Civil law is codified law—an ordered grouping of legal principles enacted into law by a legislature or governing body. In a civil law system, the primary source of law is a statutory code, and case precedents are not judicially binding as they are in a common law system. Nonetheless, judges in such systems commonly refer to previous decisions as sources of legal guidance. The difference is that judges in a civil law system are not bound by precedent—in other words, the doctrine of *stare decisis* does not apply.

2–3. Sample Answer—Establishment Clause.

The establishment clause prohibits the government from passing laws or taking actions that promote religion or show a preference for one religion over another. In assessing a government action, the courts look at the predominant purpose for the action and ask whether the action has the effect of endorsing religion.

Although DeWeese claimed to have a nonreligious purpose for displaying the poster of the Ten Commandments in a courtroom, his own statements showed a religious purpose. These statements reflected his views about "warring" legal philosophies and his belief that "our legal system is based on moral absolutes from divine law handed down by God through the Ten Commandments." This plainly constitutes a religious purpose that violates the establishment clause because it has the effect of endorsing Judaism or Christianity over other religions. In the case on which this problem is based, the court ruled in favor of the American Civil Liberties Union.

3–6. Sample Answer—Discovery.

Yes, the items that were deleted from a Facebook page can be recovered. Normally, a party must hire an expert to recover material in an electronic format, and this can be time consuming and expensive.

Electronic evidence, or e-evidence, consists of all computer-generated or electronically recorded information, such as posts on Facebook and other social media sites. The effect that e-evidence can have in a case depends on its relevance and what it reveals. In the facts presented in this problem, Isaiah should be sanctioned—he should be required to cover Allied's cost to hire the recovery expert and attorney's fees to confront the misconduct. In a jury trial, the court might also instruct the jury to presume that any missing items are harmful to Isaiah's case. If all of the material is retrieved and presented at the trial, any prejudice (disadvantage) to Allied's case might thereby be mitigated (lessened). If not, of course, the court might go so far as to order a new trial.

In the actual case on which this problem is based, Allied hired an expert, who determined that Isaiah had in fact removed some photos and other items from his Facebook page. After the expert testified about the missing material, Isaiah provided Allied with all of it, including the photos that he had deleted. Allied sought a retrial, but the court instead reduced the amount of Isaiah's damages by the amount that it cost Allied to address his "misconduct."

4–5. Sample Answer—Negligence.

Negligence requires proof that (a) the defendant owed a duty of care to the plaintiff, (b) the defendant breached that duty, (c) the defendant's breach caused the plaintiff's injury, and (d) the plaintiff suffered a legally recognizable injury. With respect to the duty of care, a business owner has a duty to use reasonable care to protect business invitees. This duty includes an obligation to discover and correct or warn of unreasonably dangerous conditions that the owner of the premises should reasonably foresee might endanger an invitee. Some risks are so obvious that an owner need not warn of them. But even if a risk is obvious, a business owner may not be excused from the duty to protect the business's customers from foreseeable harm.

Because Lucario was the Weatherford's business invitee, the hotel owed her a duty of reasonable care to make its premises safe for her use. The balcony ran nearly the entire width of the window in Lucario's room. She could have reasonably believed that the window was a means of access to the balcony. The window/balcony configuration was dangerous, however, because the window opened wide enough for an adult to climb out, but the twelve-inch gap between one side of the window and the balcony was unprotected. This unprotected gap opened to a drop of more than three stories to a concrete surface below.

Should the hotel have anticipated the potential harm to a guest opening the window in Room 59 and attempting to access the balcony? The hotel encouraged guests to "step out onto the balcony" to smoke. The dangerous window/balcony configuration could have been remedied at a minimal cost. These circumstances could be perceived as creating an "unreasonably dangerous" condition. And it could be concluded that the hotel created or knew of the condition and failed to take reasonable steps to warn of it or correct it. Of course, the Weatherford might argue that the window/balcony configuration was so obvious that the hotel was not liable for Lucario's fall.

In the actual case on which this problem is based, the court concluded that the Weatherford did not breach its duty of care to Lucario. On McMurtry's appeal, a state intermediate appellate court held that this conclusion was in error, vacated the lower court's judgment in favor of the hotel on this issue, and remanded the case.

5–7. Sample Answer—Product Liability.

The accident in this case was caused by Jett's inattention, not by the texting device in the cab of his truck. In a product-liability case based on a design defect, the plaintiff has to prove that the product was defective at the time it left the hands of the seller or lessor. The plaintiff must also show that this defective condition made it "unreasonably dangerous" to the user or consumer. If the product was delivered in a safe condition and subsequent mishandling made it harmful to the user, the seller or lessor normally is not liable. To successfully assert a design defect, a plaintiff has to show that a reasonable alternative design was available and that the defendant failed to use it.

The plaintiffs could argue that the defendant manufacturer of the texting device owed them a duty of care because injuries to vehicle drivers, passengers, and others on the roads were reasonably foreseeable. They could claim that the product's design (1) required the driver to divert his eyes from the road to view an incoming text, and (2) permitted the receipt of texts while the vehicle was moving.

But manufacturers are not required to design a product incapable of distracting a driver. The duty owed by a manufacturer to the user or consumer of a product does not require guarding against hazards that are commonly known or obvious. Nor does a manufacturer's duty extend to protecting against injuries that result from a user's careless conduct, such as Jett's carelessness in this situation.

6–6. Sample Answer—Patents.

One ground on which the denial of the patent application in this problem could be reversed on appeal is that the design of Raymond Gianelli's "Rowing Machine" is *not obvious* in light of the design of the "Chest Press Apparatus for Exercising Regions of the Upper Body."

To obtain a patent, an applicant must demonstrate to the satisfaction of the U.S. Patent and Trademark Office (PTO) that the invention, discovery, process, or design is novel, useful, and not obvious in light of current technology. In this problem, the PTO denied Gianelli's application for a patent for his "Rowing Machine"—an exercise machine on which a user *pulls* on handles to perform a rowing motion against a selected resistance to strengthen the back muscles. The PTO considered the device obvious in light of a patented "Chest Press Apparatus for Exercising Regions of the Upper Body"—a chest press exercise machine on which a user *pushes* on handles to overcome a selected resistance. But it can be easily argued that it is *not* obvious to modify a machine with handles designed to be *pushed* into one with handles designed to be *pulled*. In fact, anyone who has used exercise machines knows that a way to cause injury is to use a machine in a manner not intended by the manufacturer.

In the actual case on which this problem is based, the U.S. Court of Appeals for the Federal Circuit reversed the PTO's denial of Gianelli's application for a patent, based on the reasoning stated above.

7–5. Sample Answer—Privacy.

No, Rolfe did not have a privacy interest in the information obtained by the subpoenas issued to Midcontinent Communications. The courts have held that the right to privacy is guaranteed by the U.S. Constitution's Bill of Rights, and some state constitutions contain an explicit guarantee of the right. A person must have a reasonable expectation of privacy, though, to maintain a suit or to assert a successful defense for an invasion of privacy.

People clearly have a reasonable expectation of privacy when they enter their personal banking or credit-card information online. They also have a reasonable expectation that online companies will follow their own privacy policies. But people do not have a reasonable expectation of privacy in statements made on Twitter and other data that they publicly disseminate. In other words, there is no violation of a subscriber's right to privacy when a third party Internet service provider receives a subpoena and discloses the subscriber's information.

Here, Rolfe supplied his e-mail address and other personal information, including his Internet protocol address, to Midcontinent. In other words, Rolfe publicly disseminated this information. Law enforcement officers obtained this information from Midcontinent through the subpoenas issued by the South Dakota state court. Rolfe provided his information to Midcontinent—he has no legitimate expectation of privacy in that information.

In the actual case on which this problem is based, Rolfe was charged with, and convicted of, possessing, manufacturing, and distributing child pornography, as well as other crimes. As part of the proceedings, the court found that Rolfe had no expectation of privacy in the information that he made available to Midcontinent. On appeal, the South Dakota Supreme Court upheld the conviction.

8–5. Sample Answer—Criminal Liability.

Yes, Green exhibited the required mental state to establish criminal liability. A wrongful mental state (*mens rea*) is one of the elements typically required to establish criminal liability. The required mental state, or intent, is indicated in an applicable statute or law. For example, for murder, the required mental state is the intent to take another's life. A court can also find that the required mental state is present when a defendant's acts are reckless or criminally negligent. A defendant is criminally reckless if he or she consciously disregards a substantial and unjustifiable risk.

In this problem, Green was clearly aware of the danger to which he was exposing people on the street below, but he did not indicate that he specifically intended to harm anyone. The risk of death created by his conduct, however, was obvious. He must have known what was likely to happen if a bottle or plate thrown from the height of twenty-six stories hit a pedestrian or the windshield of an occupied motor vehicle on the street below. Despite his claim that he was intoxicated, he was sufficiently aware to stop throwing things from the balcony when he saw police in the area, and he later recalled what he had done and what had happened.

In the actual case on which this problem is based, after a jury trial, Green was convicted of reckless endangerment. On appeal, a state intermediate appellate court affirmed the conviction, based in part on the reasoning just stated.

9–4. Sample Answer—Online Privacy.

Facebook created a program that makes decisions for users. Many believe that privacy is an extremely important right that should be fiercely protected. Thus, using duty-based ethics, any program that has a default setting of giving out information is unethical. Facebook should create the program as an opt-in program.

In addition, under the Kantian categorical imperative, if every company used opt-out programs that allowed the disclosure of potentially personal information, privacy might become merely theoretical. If privacy were reduced or eliminated, the world might not be a better place. From a utilitarian or outcome-based approach, an opt-out program might offer the benefits of being easy to created and start, as well as making it easy to recruit partner programs. On the negative side, the program would eliminate users' ability to chose whether to disclose information about themselves. An opt-in program would maintain that user control but might entail higher start-up costs because it would require more marketing to users up front to persuade them to opt in.

10–6. Sample Answer—Quasi Contract.

Gutkowski does not have a valid claim for payment, nor should he recover on the basis of a quasi contract. Quasi contracts are imposed by courts on parties in the interest of fairness and justice. Usually, a quasi contract is imposed to avoid the unjust enrichment of one party at the expense of another. Gutkowski was compensated as a consultant. For him to establish a claim that he is due more compensation based on unjust enrichment, he must have proof. As it is, he has only his claim that there were discussions

about him being a part owner of YES. Discussions and negotiations are not a basis for recovery on a quasi contract.

In the actual case on which this problem is based, the court dismissed Gutkowski's claim for payment.

11–4. Sample Answer—Online Acceptances.

No. A shrink-wrap agreement is an agreement whose terms are expressed inside the box in which the goods are packaged. The party who opens the box may be informed that he or she agrees to the terms by keeping whatever is in the box. In many cases, the courts have enforced the terms of shrink-wrap agreements just as they enforce the terms of other contracts.

But not all of the terms presented in shrink-wrap agreements have been enforced by the courts. One important consideration is whether the buyer had adequate notice of the terms. A click-on agreement is formed when a buyer, completing a transaction on a computer, is required to indicate his or her assent to be bound by the terms of an offer by clicking on a button that says, for example, "I agree."

In Reasonover's situation, the confirmation e-mail sent by Clearwire was not adequate notice of its "Terms of Service" (TOS). The e-mail did not contain a direct link to the terms—accessing them required clicks on further links through the firm's homepage. The written, shrink-wrap materials accompanying the modem did not provide adequate notice of the TOS. There was only a reference to Clearwire's Web site in small print at the bottom of one page.

Similarly, Reasonover's access to an "I accept terms" box did not establish notice of the terms. She did not click on the box but quit the page. Even if any of these references were sufficient notice, Reasonover kept the modem only because Clearwire told her that she could not return it. In the actual case on which this problem is based, the court refused to compel arbitration on the basis of the clause in Clearwire's TOS.

12–3. Sample Answer—Unconscionable Contracts or Clauses.

In this case, the agreement that restricted the buyer's options for resolution of a dispute to arbitration and limited the amount of damages was both procedurally and substantively unconscionable. Procedural unconscionability concerns the manner in which the parties enter into a contract. Substantive unconscionability can occur when a contract leaves one party to the agreement without a remedy for the nonperformance of the other.

Here, GeoEx told customers that the arbitration terms in its release form were nonnegotiable and that climbers would encounter the same requirements with any other travel company. This amounted to procedural unconscionability, underscoring the customers' lack of bargaining power. The imbalance resulted in oppressive terms, with no real negotiation and an absence of meaningful choice. Furthermore, the restriction on forum (San Francisco) and the limitation on damages (the cost of the trip)—with no limitation on GeoEx's damages—amounted to substantive unconscionability.

In the actual case on which this problem is based, the court ruled that the agreement was unconscionable.

13–7. Sample Answer—Fraudulent Misrepresentation.

Yes, the facts in this problem evidence fraud. There are three elements to fraud: (1) the misrepresentation of a material fact, (2) an intent to deceive, and (3) an innocent party's justifiable reliance on the misrepresentation. To collect damages, the innocent party must suffer an injury.

Here, Pervis represented to Pauley that no further commission would be paid by Osbrink. This representation was false—despite Pervis's statement to the contrary, Osbrink continued to send payments to Pervis. Pervis knew the representation was false, as shown by the fact that she made it more than once during the time that she was continuing to receive payments from Osbrink. Each time Pauley asked about commissions, Pervis replied that she was not receiving any. Pauley's reliance on her business associate's statements was justified and reasonable. And for the purpose of recovering damages, Pauley suffered an injury in the amount of her share of the commissions that Pervis received as a result of the fraud.

In the actual case on which this problem is based, Pauley filed a suit in a Georgia state court against Pervis, who filed for bankruptcy in a federal bankruptcy court to stay the state action. The federal court held Pervis liable on the ground of fraud for the amount of the commissions that were not paid to Pauley, and denied Pervis a discharge of the debt.

14–5. Sample Answer—Material Breach.

Yes, STR breached the contract with NTI. A breach of contract is the nonperformance of a contractual duty. A breach is *material* when performance is not at least substantial. On a material breach, the nonbreaching party is excused from performance. If a breach is *minor,* the nonbreaching party's duty to perform can sometimes be suspended until the breach has been remedied, but the duty to perform is not entirely excused. Once a minor breach has been cured, the nonbreaching party must resume performance. Any breach—material or minor—entitles the nonbreaching party to sue for damages.

In this problem, NTI had to redo its work constantly because STR permitted its employees and the employees of other subcontractors to walk over and damage the newly installed tile. Furthermore, despite NTI's requests for payment, STR remitted only half the amount due under their contract. Thus, NTI was deprived of at least half of the money it was owed under the contract. And STR terminated the contract, apparently wrongfully and without cause. The tile work would have been completed satisfactorily if STR had not allowed other workers to trample the newly installed tile before it had cured.

In the actual case on which this problem is based, when STR refused to pay NTI and then terminated their contract, the subcontractor filed a suit in a Texas state court to recover. From a jury verdict in NTI's favor, STR appealed. A state intermediate appellate court affirmed. "The evidence presented was legally sufficient for the jury to conclude that STR materially breached the contract."

15–6. Sample Answer—Consequential Damages.

Simard is liable only for the losses and expenses related to the first resale. Simard could reasonably anticipate that his breach would require another sale and that the sales price might be less than what he agreed to pay. Therefore, he should be liable for the difference between his sales price and the first resale price ($29,000), plus any expenses arising from the first resale.

Simard is not liable, however, for any expenses and losses related to the second resale. After all, Simard did not cause the second purchaser's default, and he could not reasonably foresee that default as a probable result of his breach.

16–6. Sample Answer—Import Controls.

Yes, an antidumping duty can be assessed retrospectively (retroactively). But it does not seem likely that such a duty should be assessed here.

In this problem, the Wind Tower Trade Coalition (an association of domestic manufacturers of utility scale wind towers) filed a suit in the U.S. Court of International Trade against the U.S. Department of Commerce. Wind Tower challenged the Commerce Department's decision to impose only *prospective* antidumping duties on imports of utility scale wind towers from China and Vietnam. The Commerce Department had found that the domestic industry had not suffered any "material injury" or "threat of material injury," and that it would be protected by a prospective assessment. Because there was no previously cognizable injury—and any retrospective duties collected would not be payable to the members of the domestic industry—it does not seem likely that retroactive duties should be imposed.

In the actual case on which this problem is based, the court denied the plaintiff's request for an injunction. On appeal, the U.S. Court of Appeals for the Federal Circuit affirmed the denial, holding that the lower court acted within its discretion in determining that retrospective duties were not appropriate.

17–3. Sample Answer—Passage of Title.

Altieri held title to the car that she was driving at the time of the accident in which Godfrey was injured. Once goods exist and are identified, title can be determined. Under the UCC, any explicit understanding between the buyer and the seller determines when title passes. If there is no such agreement, title passes to the buyer at the time and place that the seller physically delivers the goods.

In lease contracts, title to the goods is retained by the lessor-owner of the goods. The UCC's provisions relating to passage to title do not apply to leased goods. Here, Altieri originally leased the car from G.E. Capital Auto Lease, Inc., but by the time of the accident she had bought it. Even though she had not fully paid for the car or completed the transfer-of-title paperwork, she owned it. Title to the car passed to Altieri when she bought it and took delivery of it. Thus, Altieri, not G.E., was the owner of the car at the time of the accident.

In the actual case on which this problem is based, the court concluded that G.E. was not the owner of the vehicle when Godfrey was injured.

18–5. Sample Answer—Nonconforming Goods.

Padma notified Universal Exports about its breach, so Padma has two ways to recover even though it accepted the goods. Padma's first option is to argue that it revoked its acceptance, giving it the right to reject the goods. To revoke acceptance, Padma would have to show that:

1. The nonconformity substantially impaired the value of the shipment.

2. It predicated its acceptance on a reasonable assumption that Universal Exports would cure the nonconformity.

3. Universal Exports did not cure the nonconformity within a reasonable time.

Padma's second option is to keep the goods and recover for the damages caused by Universal Exports' breach. Under this option, Padma could recover at least the difference between the value of the goods as promised and their value as accepted.

19–5. Sample Answer—Negotiation.

A negotiable instrument can be transferred by assignment or by negotiation. An assignment is a transfer of rights by contract. A transfer by assignment to an assignee gives the assignee only those rights that the assignor possessed. Any defenses that can be raised against the assignor can be raised against the assignee. When an instrument is transferred by negotiation, the transferee becomes a holder. A holder receives at least the rights of the previous possessor.

Unlike an assignment, a transfer by negotiation can make it possible for the holder to receive more rights in the instrument than the prior possessor had. A holder who receives greater rights is a holder in due course (HDC) and takes the instrument free of any claims to it and defenses against its payment. Negotiating order instruments requires delivery and indorsement. If a party to whom a negotiable note is made payable signs it and delivers it to a bank, the transfer is a negotiation, and the bank becomes a holder. If the party does not sign it, however, the transfer would be treated as an assignment, and the bank would become an assignee instead of a holder.

In this problem, Argent was the payee of the note and its holder. Argent transferred the note to Wells Fargo without an indorsement. Thus, the transfer was not a negotiation but an assignment. Wells Fargo did not then become a holder of the note but an assignee. As an assignee, the bank acquired only those rights that the lender possessed before the assignment. And any defenses—including fraud in connection with the note—that Ford could assert against the lender could also be asserted by the borrower against the bank. If Argent indorsed the note to Wells Fargo now, after the defendant's response to the complaint, the bank could become a holder of the note, but it could not become an HDC. One of the requirements for HDC status is that a holder must take an instrument without notice of defenses against payment. The bank could not do this, because it is now aware of the borrower's defenses.

In the actual case on which this problem is based, the court issued a judgment in Wells Fargo's favor, and Ford appealed. A state intermediate appellate court reversed the judgment and remanded the case for trial, finding that the bank had failed to prove that it was a holder, an assignee, or even a transferee of the note.

20–4. Sample Answer—Honoring Checks.

Wells Fargo is liable to W Financial for the amount of the check. A bank that pays a customer's check bearing a forged indorsement must recredit the customer's account or be liable to the customer-drawer for breach of contract. The bank must recredit the account because it failed to carry out the drawer's order to

pay to the order of the named party. Eventually, the loss falls on the first party to take the instrument bearing the forged indorsement because a forged indorsement does not transfer title. Thus, whoever takes an instrument with a forged indorsement cannot become a holder.

Under these rules, Wells Fargo is liable to W Financial for the amount of the check. The bank had an obligation to ensure that the check was properly indorsed. The bank did not pay the check to the order of Lateef, the named payee, but accepted the check for deposit into the account of CA Houston without Lateef's indorsement. The bank did not obtain title to the instrument and could not become a holder, nor was it entitled to enforce the instrument on behalf of any other party who was entitled to enforce it.

In the actual case on which this problem is based, the court held the bank liable to pay the amount of the check to W Financial.

21–4. Sample Answer—Perfecting a Security Interest.

Yes, these financing statements were sufficient to perfect the bank's security interests in Tille's equipment. In most situations, perfection is accomplished by filing a financing statement with the appropriate official. To effectively perfect a security interest, a financing statement must contain (1) the debtor's signature, (2) the debtor's and creditor's addresses, and (3) a description of the collateral by type or item.

In this case, all of Union's financing statements were sufficient to perfect security interests. They each provided the name and address of the debtor (Tille), the name and address of the secured party (Union Bank), and a description of the collateral covered by the financing statement. One loan covered all of Tille's equipment, including after-acquired property; another loan covered the truck crane; and the third loan was for a Bobcat mini excavator. These descriptions were clearly sufficient to put a prospective creditor on notice that the collateral was the subject of a security interest.

In the actual case on which this problem is based, the court concluded that all of the statements created perfected security interests.

22–4. Sample Answer—Automatic Stay.

Gholston can recover damages because EZ Auto willfully violated the automatic stay. EZ Auto repossessed the car even though it received notice of the automatic stay from the bankruptcy court. Moreover, EZ Auto retained the car even after it was reminded of the stay by Gholston's attorney. Thus, EZ Auto knew about the automatic stay and violated it intentionally. Because Gholston suffered direct damages as a result, she can recover from EZ Auto.

23–7. Sample Answer—Determining Employee Status.

No, Cox is not liable to Cayer for the injuries or damage that she sustained in the accident with Ovalles. Generally, an employer is not liable for physical harm caused to a third person by the negligent act of an independent contractor in the performance of a contract. This is because the employer does not have the right to control the details of the performance. In determining whether a worker has the status of an independent contractor, how much control the employer can exercise over the details of the work is the most important factor weighed by the courts.

In this problem, Ovalles worked as a cable installer for Cox under an agreement with M&M. The agreement disavowed any employer-employee relationship between Cox and M&M's installers. Ovalles was required to designate his affiliation with Cox on his van, clothing, and an I.D. badge. But Cox had minimal contact with Ovalles and limited power to control the manner in which he performed his work. Cox supplied cable wire and other equipment, but these items were delivered to M&M, not Ovalles. These facts indicate that Ovalles was an independent contractor, not an employee. Thus, Cox was not liable to Cayer for the harm caused to her by Ovalles when his van rear-ended Cayer's car.

In the actual case on which this problem is based, the court issued a judgment in Cox's favor. The Rhode Island Supreme Court affirmed, applying the principles stated above to arrive at the same conclusion.

24–7. Sample Answer—Unemployment Compensation.

Yes, Ramirez qualifies for unemployment compensation. Generally, to be eligible for unemployment compensation, a worker must be willing and able to work. Workers who have been fired for misconduct or who have voluntarily left their jobs are not eligible for benefits. In the facts of this problem, the applicable state statute disqualifies an employee from receiving benefits if he or she voluntarily leaves work without "good cause."

The issue is whether Ramirez left her job for "good cause." When her father in the Dominican Republic had a stroke, she asked her employer for time off to be with him. Her employer refused the request. But Ramirez left to be with her father and called to inform her employer. It seems likely that this family emergency would constitute "good cause," and Ramirez's call and return to work after her father's death indicated that she did not disregard her employer's interests.

In the actual case on which this problem is based, the state of Florida denied Ramirez unemployment compensation. On Ramirez's appeal, a state intermediate appellate court reversed, on the reasoning stated above.

25–7. Sample Answer—Age Discrimination.

No, Sanofi-Aventis U.S. LLC (S-A) does not appear to have engaged in age discrimination. The Age Discrimination in Employment Act (ADEA) prohibits employment discrimination on the basis of age against individuals forty years of age or older. For the act to apply, an employer must have twenty or more employees, and the employer's business activities must affect interstate commerce.

To establish a *prima facie* case, a plaintiff must show that he or she was (1) a member of the protected age group, (2) qualified for the position from which he or she was discharged, and (3) discharged because of age discrimination. If the employer offers a legitimate reason for its action, the plaintiff must show that the stated reason is only a pretext.

In this problem, Rangel was over forty years old. But he also had negative sales performance reviews for more than two years before he was terminated as part of S-A's nationwide reduction in force of all sales professionals who had not met the "Expectations" guidelines, including younger workers. The facts do not indicate that a person younger than Rangel replaced him or that S-A intended to discriminate against him on the basis of age. Based on these facts, Rangel could not establish a *prima facie* case of age discrimination on the part of S-A.

In the actual case on which this problem is based, in Rangel's suit against S-A under the ADEA, alleging age discrimination, a federal district court issued a judgment in S-A's favor. On Rangel's appeal, the U.S. Court of Appeals for the Tenth Circuit affirmed, according to the reasoning stated above.

26–5. Sample Answer—Wrongful Termination of a Franchise.

Oshana and GTO have stated a claim for wrongful termination of their franchise. A franchisor must act in good faith when terminating a franchise agreement. If the termination is arbitrary or unfair, a franchisee may have a claim for wrongful termination.

In this case, Oshana and GTO have alleged that Buchanan acted in bad faith. Their failure to pay rent would ordinarily be a valid basis for termination, but not if it was entirely precipitated by Buchanan. Thus, Oshana and GTO may recover if they can prove that their allegations are true.

27–6. Sample Answer—Partnerships.

Yes, Sacco is entitled to 50 percent of the profits of Pierce Paxton Collections, PPDS, and KPD. The requirements for establishing a partnership are (1) a sharing of profits and losses, (2) a joint ownership of the business, and (3) an equal right to be involved in the management of the business.

The effort and time that Sacco expended in the business constituted a sharing of losses. His proprietary interest in the assets of the partnership consisted of his share of the profits, which he had expressly left in the business to "grow the company" and "build sweat equity" for the future. He was involved in every aspect of the business. Although he was not paid a salary, he was reimbursed for business expenses charged to his personal credit card, which Paxton also used. These facts arguably meet the requirements for establishing a partnership.

In the actual case on which this problem is based, Sacco filed a suit in a Louisiana state court against Paxton, and the court awarded Sacco 50 percent of the profits. A state intermediate appellate court affirmed, based generally on the reasoning stated above.

28–6. Sample Answer—LLC Operation.

No. One Bluewater member could not unilaterally "fire" another member without providing a reason. Part of the attractiveness of an LLC as a form of business enterprise is its flexibility. The members can decide how to operate the business through an operating agreement. For example, the agreement can set forth procedures for choosing or removing members or managers.

Here, the Bluewater operating agreement provided for a "super majority" vote to remove a member under circumstances that would jeopardize the firm's contractor status. Thus, one Bluewater member could not unilaterally "fire" another member without providing a reason. In fact, a majority of the members could not terminate the other's interest in the firm without providing a reason. Moreover, the only acceptable reason would be a circumstance that undercut the firm's status as a contractor.

The flexibility of the LLC business form relates to its framework, not to its members' capacity to violate its operating agreement. In the actual case on which this problem is based, Smith attempted to "fire" Williford without providing a reason. In Williford's suit, the court issued a judgment in his favor.

29–6. Sample Answer—Duty of Loyalty.

Dweck breached the fiduciary duty of loyalty that a director and officer owes to his or her corporation—in this case, Kids. The essence of the duty of loyalty is the subordination of self-interest to the interest of the entity to which the duty is owed. The duty presumes constant loyalty to the corporation on the part of the directors and officers. The duty prohibits directors from using corporate funds or confidential corporate information for their personal advantage.

Here, Dweck breached her duty of loyalty to Kids by establishing a competing company that usurped Kids' business opportunities and converted Kids' resources—employees, office space, credit, and customer relationships—to conduct the competing firm's operations. The "administrative fee" was most likely insufficient compensation. Dweck would be liable to Kids for the damages caused by this breach of duty.

In the actual case on which this problem is based, the court held that Dweck breached her duty of loyalty to Kids and awarded as damages the lost profits that Kids would have generated from the business diverted to Success.

30–3. Sample Answer—Violations of the 1934 Act.

An omission or misrepresentation of a material fact in connection with the purchase or sale of a security may violate Section 10(b) of the Securities Exchange Act of 1934 and SEC Rule 10b-5. The key question is whether the omitted or misrepresented information is material. A fact, by itself, is not automatically material. A fact will be regarded as material only if it is significant enough that it would likely affect an investor's decision as to whether to buy or sell the company's securities. For example, a company's potential liability in a product liability suit and the financial consequences to the firm are material facts that must be disclosed because they are significant enough to affect an investor's decision as to whether to buy stock in the company.

In this case, the plaintiffs' claim should not be dismissed. To prevail on their claim that the defendants made material omissions in violation of Section 10(b) and SEC Rule 10-5, the plaintiffs must prove that the omission was material. Their complaint alleged the omission of information linking Zicam and anosmia (a loss of the sense of smell) and plausibly suggested that reasonable investors would have viewed this information as material. Zicam products account for 70 percent of Matrixx's sales. Matrixx received reports of consumers who suffered anosia after using Zicam Cold Remedy.

In public statements discussing revenues and product safety, Matrixx did not disclose this information. But the information was significant enough to likely affect a consumer's decision to use the product, and this would affect revenue and ultimately the commercial viability of the product. The information was therefore significant enough to likely affect an investor's decision whether to buy or sell Matrixx's stock, and this would affect the stock price.

Thus, the plaintiffs' allegations were sufficient. Contrary to the defendants' assertion, statistical sampling is not required to show materiality—reasonable investors could view reports of adverse events as material even if the reports did not provide statistically significant evidence.

31–5. Sample Answer—Price Discrimination.

Spa Steel satisfies most of the requirements for a price discrimination claim under Section 2 of the Clayton Act. Dayton Superior is engaged in interstate commerce, and it sells goods of like grade and quality to at least three purchasers. Moreover, Spa Steel can show that, because it sells Dayton Superior's products at a higher price, it lost business and thus suffered an injury. To recover, however, Spa Steel will also need to prove that Dayton Superior charged Spa Steel's competitors a lower price for the same product. Spa Steel cannot recover if its prices were higher for reasons related to its own business, such as having higher overhead or seeking a larger profit.

32–4. Sample Answer—Fair Debt Collection Practices.

Engler may recover under the Fair Debt Collection Practices Act (FDCPA). Atlantic is subject to the FDCPA because it is a debt-collection agency and it was attempting to collect a debt on behalf of Bank of America. Atlantic also used offensive tactics to collect from Engler. After all, Atlantic gave Engler's employer the false impression that Engler was a criminal, had a pending case, and was about to be arrested. Finally, Engler suffered harm because he experienced discomfort, embarrassment, and distress as a result of Atlantic's abusive conduct. Engler may recover actual damages, statutory damages, and attorneys' fees from Atlantic.

33–7. Sample Answer—Potential Liability to Third Parties.

KPMG is potentially liable to the hedge funds' partners under the *Restatement (Third) of Torts*. Under Section 552 of the *Restatement*, an auditor owes a duty to "persons for whose benefit and guidance the accountant intends to supply . . . information."

In this case, KPMG prepared annual reports on the hedge funds and addressed them to the funds' "Partners." Additionally, KPMG knew who the partners were because it prepared individual tax forms for them each year. Thus, KPMG's annual reports were for the partners' benefit and guidance. The partners relied on the reports, including their representations that they complied with generally accepted accounting principles.

As a result, they lost millions of dollars, which exposes KPMG to possible liability under Section 552.

34–6. Sample Answer—Bailment Obligation.

Moreland should be awarded damages, and Gray should take nothing. The bailee must exercise reasonable care in preserving the bailed property. What constitutes reasonable care in a bailment situation normally depends on the nature and specific circumstances of the bailment. If the bailed property has been lost or is returned damaged, a court will presume that the bailee was negligent.

In the circumstances of this problem, when the bailor (Moreland, the owner of the aircraft) entrusted the plane to the bailee's (Gray's) repair shop for painting, the work was not properly performed. This violated the bailee's duty to exercise reasonable care and breached the bailment contract. Because the plane was returned damaged, this may also constitute negligence. In the event of a breach, the bailor may sue for damages. The measure of damages is the difference between the value of the bailed property in its present condition and what it would have been worth if the work had been properly performed.

Thus, Gray is liable to Moreland for failing to properly paint the plane. In the actual case on which this problem is based, the court upheld a jury award to Moreland of damages and attorneys' fees.

35–5. Sample Answer—Adverse Possession.

The McKeags satisfied the first three requirements for adverse possession:

1. Their possession was actual and exclusive because they used the beach and prevented others from doing so, including the Finleys.

2. Their possession was open, visible, and notorious because they made improvements to the beach and regularly kept their belongings there.

3. Their possession was continuous and peaceable for the required ten years. They possessed the property for more than four decades, and they even kept a large float there during the winter months.

Nevertheless, the McKeags' possession was *not* hostile and adverse, which is the fourth requirement. The Finleys had substantial evidence that they gave the McKeags permission to use the beach. Rather than reject the Finleys' permission as unnecessary, the McKeags sometimes said nothing and other times seemingly affirmed that the property belonged to the Finleys. Thus, because the McKeags did not satisfy all four requirements, they cannot establish adverse possession.

36–5. Sample Answer—Undue Influence.

No, undue influence does not appear to have occurred in this problem. To invalidate a will on the basis of undue influence, a plaintiff must show that the decedent's plan of distribution was the result of improper pressure brought by another person. Undue influence may be inferred if the testator ignores blood relatives and names as a beneficiary a nonrelative who is in constant close contact and in a position to influence the making of the will.

In this problem, although Tommy's ex-wife lived with Susie Walker and was thus in a position to influence Susie's will, she was not a beneficiary under it, so there is no inference of undue influence. Moreover, neither of the wills that Walker executed left any property to her son, so there was no indication that she had been influenced to change her mind regarding the distribution of her estate. Additionally, she expressly disinherited her son, and several witnesses testified that she was mentally competent at the time she made the will.

In the actual case on which this problem is based, the court presumed that Walker's will was valid.

Appendix G

Case Excerpts for *Case Analysis Questions*

Case No. 1 for Chapter 6

Winstead v. Jackson
United States Court of Appeals, Third Circuit, 2013 WL 139622 (2013).

PER CURIAM. [By the Whole Court]

* * * *

* * * Winstead filed his * * * complaint in the United States District Court for the District of New Jersey, claiming that Jackson's album/CD and film derived their contents from, and infringed the copyright of, his book.

* * * *

* * * The District Court dismissed Winstead's * * * complaint * * * , concluding that Jackson * * * did not improperly copy protected aspects of Winstead's book.

* * * *

Winstead appeals.

* * * *

Here, it is not disputed that Winstead is the owner of the copyrighted property * * *. However, *not all copying is copyright infringement, so even if actual copying is proven, the court must decide, by comparing the allegedly infringing work with the original work, whether the copying was unlawful. Copying may be proved inferentially by showing that the allegedly infringing work is substantially similar to the copyrighted work.* A court compares the allegedly infringing work with the original work, and considers whether a "lay-observer" would believe that the copying was of protectable aspects of the copyrighted work. The inquiry involves distinguishing between the author's expression and the idea or theme that he or she seeks to convey or explore, because the former is protected and the latter is not. The court must determine whether the allegedly infringing work is similar because it appropriates the unique expressions of the original work, or merely because it contains elements that would be expected when two works express the same idea or explore the same theme. [Emphasis added.]

* * * A lay observer would not believe that Jackson's album/CD and film copied protectable aspects of Winstead's book. Jackson's album/CD is comprised of 16 individual songs, which explore drug-dealing, guns and money, vengeance, and other similar clichés of hip hop gangsterism. Jackson's fictional film is the story of a young man who turns to violence when his mother is killed in a

drive-by shooting. The young man takes revenge by killing the man who killed his mother, and then gets rich by becoming an "enforcer" for a powerful criminal. He takes up with a woman who eventually betrays him, and is shot to death by her boyfriend, who has just been released from prison. The movie ends with his younger brother vowing to seek vengeance. Winstead's book purports to be autobiographical and tells the story of a young man whose beloved father was a Bishop in the church. The protagonist was angry as a child because his stepmother abused him, but he found acceptance and self-esteem on the streets of Newark because he was physically powerful. He earned money robbing and beating people, went to jail, returned to crime upon his release, and then made even more money. The protagonist discusses his time at Rahway State Prison in great and compelling detail. The story ends when the protagonist learns that his father has passed away; he conveys his belief that this tragedy has led to his redemption, and he hopes that others might learn from his mistakes.

* * * Although Winstead's book and Jackson's works share similar themes and setting, the story of an angry and wronged protagonist who turns to a life of violence and crime has long been a part of the public domain [and is therefore not protected by copyright law]. Winstead argues * * * that a protagonist asking for God's help when his father dies, cutting drugs with mixing agents to maximize profits, and complaining about relatives who are addicts and steal the product, are protectable, but these things are not unique. To the extent that Jackson's works contain these elements, they are to be expected when two works express the same idea about "the streets" or explore the same theme. Winstead argues that not every protagonist whose story concerns guns, drugs, and violence in an urban setting winds up in prison or loses a parent, but this argument only serves to illustrate an important difference between his book and Jackson's film. Jackson's protagonist never spends any time in prison, whereas Winstead's protagonist devotes a considerable part of his story to his incarcerations.

In addition, Winstead's book and Jackson's works are different with respect to character, plot, mood, and sequence of events. Winstead's protagonist embarks on a life of crime at a very young age, but is redeemed by the death of his beloved father. Jackson's protagonist turns to crime when he is much older and only after his mother is murdered. He winds up dead at a young age, unredeemed. Winstead's book is hopeful; Jackson's film is characterized * * * by moral apathy. It is true that both works involve the loss of a parent and the protagonist's recognition of the parent's importance in his life, but nowhere does Jackson appropriate anything unique about Winstead's expression of this generic topic.

Winstead contends that direct phrases from his book appear in Jackson's film. * * * He emphasizes these phrases: "Yo, where is my money at," "I would never have done no shit like that to you," "my father, my strength was gone," "he was everything to me," and "I did not know what to do," but, like the phrases "putting the work in," "get the dope, cut the dope," "let's keep it popping," and "the strong take from the weak but the smart take from everybody," they are either common in general or common with respect to hip hop culture, and do not enjoy copyright protection. *The average person reading or listening to these phrases in the context of an overall story or song would not regard them as unique and protectable.* Moreover, words and short phrases do not enjoy copyright protection. The similarity between Winstead's book and the lyrics to Jackson's songs on the album/CD is even more tenuous. "Stretching the dope" and "bloodshot red eyes" are common phrases that do not enjoy copyright protection. *A side-by-side comparison of Winstead's book and the lyrics from Jackson's album/CD do not support a claim of copyright infringement.* [Emphasis added.]

For the foregoing reasons, we will affirm the order of the District Court dismissing [Winstead's] complaint.

Case No. 2 for Chapter 11

Gyabaah v. Rivlab Transportation Corp.
New York Supreme Court, Appellate Division, First Department, 102 A.D.3d 451, 958 N.Y.S.2d 109 (2013).

TOM, J.P. [Judge Presiding], *ANDRIAS, RENWICK, DEGRASSE, ABDUS-SALAAM*, JJ. [Judges]
* * * *

[Adwoa Gyabaah was hit by a bus owned by Rivlab Transportation Corporation. She retained attorney Jeffrey Aronsky to represent her in negotiations with Rivlab, its insurer National Casualty Company, and their attorneys. Gyabaah agreed to pay Aronsky a contingency fee of one-third of the amount of her recovery. Aronsky] commenced this personal injury action on plaintiff's behalf on August 25, 2010 [against Rivlab]. By letter to Aronsky dated October 1, 2010, defendant's carrier tendered its $1 million policy limits for purposes of settlement. Aronsky explained the proposal to plaintiff who, at that time, chose to accept the settlement. Accordingly, plaintiff executed a general release on October 5, 2010 * * *. Aronsky advised plaintiff that he would hold the release pending receipt of * * * advice from plaintiff as to whether she preferred to have the settlement structured [paid over a period of time rather than in one lump sum].

By December 9, 2010, plaintiff had retained new counsel, Kenneth A. Wilhelm, Esq. [Esquire, or lawyer]. On that date, Wilhelm advised Aronsky that plaintiff did not wish to settle the case or have the release sent to defendant. Aronsky moved the court below for an order enforcing what he contended was a $1 million settlement and setting his firm's contingency fee at one-third of the recovery pursuant to plaintiff's retainer agreement. In making his motion, Aronsky did not allege that acceptance of the offer was ever communicated to defendant or its carrier. This omission is fatal to Aronsky's claim of a settlement for reasons that follow. Aronsky maintained that "plaintiff's signing of the General Release constituted a binding legal contract." The court denied the motion and vacated the release in what it perceived to be the interest of justice.

* * * The application of contract law * * * required the denial of Aronsky's motion. A general release is governed by principles of contract law. * * * *It is essential in any bilateral contract that the fact of acceptance be communicated to the offeror. Therefore, this action was not settled because the executed release was never forwarded to defendant nor was acceptance of the offer otherwise communicated to defendant or its carrier.* This record does not contain a single affidavit by anyone asserting that either occurred. * * * We do not share the * * * view that an October 6, 2010 letter from defendant's counsel to Aronsky "evidenced" an agreement to settle. Defense counsel's statement in the letter that he was "advised" of a settlement does not suffice as evidence that such a settlement was effected. * * * Because there has been no settlement, the amount of Aronsky's fee should be determined upon the disposition of this action [as a percentage of the fee recovered by the Wilhelm firm based on the *pro rata* share of the work the two attorneys performed in obtaining the recovery]. [Emphasis added.]

* * * We see no need for a hearing to determine whether Aronsky was discharged for cause. The record discloses that plaintiff has not made a *prima facie* showing of any cause for Aronsky's discharge. Plaintiff stated in her affidavit that she signed the release * * * because she felt "pressured" to do so. Plaintiff made no mention of what the pressure consisted of or, more importantly, what professional misconduct, if any, brought it about. To be sure, a hearing was not warranted by plaintiff's untenable [indefensible] argument that Aronsky disobeyed her instructions by making the instant motion albeit [although] after he had already been discharged as her attorney.

[The order of the lower court denying Aronsky's motion insofar as it sought to enforce a purported settlement and set Aronsky's fee accordingly is affirmed.]

Case No. 3 for Chapter 19

Mills v. Chauvin
Supreme Court of New York, Appellate Division, Third Department, 103 A.D.3d 1041, 962 N.Y.S.2d 412 (2013).

PER CURIAM. [By the Whole Court]
* * * *

Plaintiff, Gregory Mills, and defendant, Robert Chauvin, are two experienced attorneys who shared both a friendship and a professional/business relationship. Those longstanding relationships deteriorated and gave rise to this action.
* * * *

* * * The parties formed a partnership and took ownership of a commercial office building located on Crescent Road in the Town of Clifton Park, Saratoga County. * * * After Chauvin decided, for a

variety of reasons, that he no longer wished to maintain his ownership of the Crescent Road property, the parties agreed that Mills would purchase Chauvin's one-half interest in such property and they executed a purchase and sale agreement establishing a purchase price of $261,176.67 and a closing date.

* * * *

Chauvin was an investor in the Amelia Village [real estate development] project [in Virginia]. Over a course of time, Mills made multiple monetary payments to Chauvin—totaling $395,750—which Chauvin claims were investments in the project and Mills claims were loans. Ultimately, Mills requested that Chauvin return the payments he had advanced. In connection therewith, Chauvin executed a promissory note * * * that obligated him to pay Mills $395,750. However, Chauvin later challenged the validity of the promissory note and claimed that Mills was not entitled to a return of his investments.

* * * *

Mills subsequently filed [a] complaint [in a New York state court against Chauvin] to recover the payments Mills had made with respect to the Amelia Village project, based upon claims of breach of contract and unjust enrichment, respectively.

* * * *

The action proceeded to a nonjury trial * * *. At the conclusion thereof, Supreme Court [the trial court] found * * * that the promissory note was valid and enforceable and that Mills was entitled to recover pursuant to its terms. Chauvin now appeals from the judgment entered upon that decision.

* * * *

* * * Initially, we reject Chauvin's claim that Supreme Court erred in concluding that the * * * promissory note was enforceable. Chauvin does not dispute that Mills had previously paid him $395,750 in connection with the Amelia Village project, that he signed the promissory note promising to repay that amount to Mills, or that he tendered the note to Mills for the purpose of providing documentation to Mills' lending institution in support of Mills' application for financing of the purchase of the Crescent Road property. Instead, Chauvin claims that the promissory note was not enforceable because it was not given to secure a debt and, therefore, lacked consideration.

In this regard, Mills testified that * * * the parties * * * agreed that Chauvin would repay Mills all of the money that Mills had contributed to the Amelia Village project and that the promissory note confirmed their agreement. On the other hand, Chauvin claims that the payments that Mills made to the Amelia Village project were investments that could not be returned when Mills withdrew from that project, and that the promissory note was not intended to be a promise of repayment.

* * * *

The record amply supports Supreme Court's finding that the consideration for the promissory note was the $395,750 that Mills had provided to Chauvin in connection with the Amelia Village project and that the promissory note represented security for Chauvin's antecedent obligation to repay such funds. *The note itself—which was drafted by Chauvin, signed by him, notarized and transmitted to Mills clearly states that it was executed in return for a loan received by Chauvin and contained an unconditional promise*

or order to pay a sum certain in money. In addition, Mills took the note as a holder in due course. Based upon our independent evaluation of the evidence and, giving due deference to the trial court's credibility determinations concerning witnesses, we conclude that Supreme Court's determination that Chauvin failed to establish a bona fide defense of lack of consideration is supported by the record. [Emphasis added.]

* * * *

ORDERED that the order and judgments are affirmed, with costs to plaintiff.

Case No. 4 for Chapter 25

Dees v. United Rentals North America, Inc.

United States Court of Appeals, Ninth Circuit, 505 Fed.Appx. 302 (2013).

PER CURIAM:

* * * *

In * * * 2006 [Ellis Dees, an African American, applied] to United Rentals for employment at its Gulfport, Mississippi location, and was offered a service technician position in St. Rose, Louisiana. Branch Manager Mike Sauve made the decision to make the offer, which Dees accepted.

Although the first two years of Dees' employment in St. Rose went smoothly, United Rentals contends that his attitude and work performance deteriorated beginning in 2009. Specifically, it alleges that he began, with increasing frequency, to mark equipment as fit to be rented even though it was not in working order. Dees' managers—Sauve and Lee Vincent—coached him when these incidents occurred, and noted them in his 2009 mid-year and full-year performance reviews. Dees was also given written warnings in August 2009, October 2009, February 2010, and March 2010. Dees was given a "final written warning" on March 4, 2010, advising him that "the next incident will result in immediate termination." Following a further incident six days later, Sauve and Vincent told Dees that he was fired. Dees was sixty-two years old at the time.

Dees filed a charge with the Equal Employment Opportunity Commission, alleging employment discrimination based on his race and age [in violation of Title VII of the Civil Rights Act and the Age Discrimination in Employment Act (ADEA)]. After receiving a "right to sue" notice, he filed suit in [a federal district court]. United Rentals filed a motion for summary judgment, which the district court granted * * *. Dees timely appealed.

* * * *

* * * [Under Title VII or the ADEA] Dees first must make a *prima facie* case of discrimination based on age or race. To establish a *prima facie* case, Dees must show that he: (1) was a member of a protected group; (2) qualified for the position in question; (3) was subjected to an adverse employment action; and (4) received less favorable treatment due to his membership in the protected class than did other similarly situated employees who were not members of the protected class, under nearly identical circumstances.

If Dees makes a prima facie *case, the burden then shifts to United Rentals to articulate a legitimate, non-discriminatory reason for firing him.* If it does so, Dees must, as to his Title VII claim, offer sufficient evidence to create a genuine issue of material fact either (1) that United Rentals' reason is not true, but is instead a pretext for discrimination * * *; or (2) that United Rentals' reason, while true, is only one of the reasons for its conduct, and another motivating factor is Dees' protected characteristic. [Emphasis added.]

* * * *

The district court assumed, without deciding, that Dees established a *prima facie* case of discrimination under Title VII and the ADEA. The district court * * * determined that United Rentals had provided extensive evidence of a legitimate, non-discriminatory reason for Dees' termination—namely, unsatisfactory job performance. * * * The burden shifted back to Dees to produce evidence that United Rentals' reason was a pretext for discrimination. The district court concluded that Dees had only made conclusory [conclusive] allegations that he was discriminated against.

* * * *

His termination notice states that he was terminated for failing to follow United Rentals' policy of ensuring that the batteries in rental equipment were in good working order prior to delivery of the equipment.

* * * Dees has presented nothing to tie United Rentals' final termination decision to a discriminatory motive. * * * Dees himself describes United Rentals as motivated by an "I ain't missing no rents" philosophy that encouraged renting out equipment regardless of its readiness. No evidence shows that United Rentals' philosophy also included discriminating against African Americans or senior workers. Similarly, no evidence demonstrates that United Rentals' decision to discharge Dees was motivated by his race or age. * * * Dees' subjective belief that United Rentals discriminated against him is clearly insufficient to demonstrate pretext.

* * * *

For the reasons set forth above, we AFFIRM the district court's grant of summary judgment in United Rentals' favor.

Case No. 5 for Chapter 30

City of Livonia Employees' Retirement System and Local 295/Local 851 v. Boeing Co.
United States Court of Appeals, Seventh Circuit, 711 F.3d 754 (2013).

POSNER, Circuit Judge.

* * * *

* * * On April 21 [2009] Boeing [Company] performed a stress test on the wings of its new 787-8 Dreamliner, a plane that had not yet flown. The wings failed the test * * *. Yet Boeing announced on May 3 that "all structural tests required on the static airframe prior to first flight are complete" and that "the initial results of the test are positive" * * *. The implication was that the plane was on track for its "First Flight," which had been scheduled for June 30.

In mid-May, after making some changes in the design * * *, Boeing conducted another test. Although the plane failed that test too, [Boeing's chief executive officer James] McNerney stated publicly that he thought the plane would fly in June. Later [the head of Boeing's commercial aircraft division Scott] Carson told [the media] that the Dreamliner "definitely will fly" this month (June).

* * * Yet on June 23, * * * Boeing announced that the First Flight of the Dreamliner had been canceled because, Carson explained, of an "anomaly" revealed by the * * * tests. He said that Boeing had hoped to be able to solve the problem in time for a First Flight in June, but had been unable to do so. In fact the First Flight did not take place until December 2009.

When Boeing announced the cancellation of the First Flight, it also announced that the cancellation would cause a delay of unspecified length in the delivery of the Dreamliner, which many airlines had already ordered. In the two days after these announcements, Boeing's stock price dropped by more than 10 percent. * * * Persons who bought Boeing stock between the tests and the announcements of the cancellation and of the delay in delivery and who therefore lost money when the price dropped [filed a suit in a federal district court against Boeing and its officers, alleging violations of Section 10(b) and Rule 10b-5].

The district judge dismissed the * * * complaint. [The plaintiffs appealed.]

There is no securities fraud by hindsight. The law does not require public disclosure of mere risks of failure. No prediction—even a prediction that the sun will rise tomorrow—has a 100 percent probability of being correct. The future is shrouded in uncertainty. If a mistaken prediction is deemed a fraud, there will be few predictions, including ones that are well grounded, as no one wants to be held hostage to an unknown future. [Emphasis added.]

Any sophisticated purchaser of a product that is still on the drawing boards knows, moreover, that its market debut may be delayed, or indeed that the project may be abandoned before it yields salable product. The purchasers of the Dreamliner protected themselves against the possibility of delay in delivery by reserving the right to cancel their orders; there are no allegations regarding cancellation penalties, or for that matter penalties imposed on Boeing for delivery delays. And therefore * * * the defendants * * * had, so far as appears, little incentive to delay the announcement of the postponement.

Without a motive to commit securities fraud, businessmen are unlikely to commit it. A more plausible inference than that of fraud is that the defendants, unsure whether they could fix the problem by the end of June, were reluctant to tell the world "we have a problem and maybe it will cause us to delay the First Flight and maybe not, but we're working on the problem and we hope we can fix it in time to prevent any significant delay, but we can't be sure, so stay tuned." There is a difference * * * between a duty of truthfulness and a duty of candor, or between a lie and reticence [uncommunicativeness]. There is no duty of total corporate transparency—no rule that every hitch or glitch, every pratfall [embarrassing mistake], in a company's operations must be disclosed in real time, forming a running commentary, a baring of the corporate innards, day and night. [Emphasis added.]

* * * *

* * * The * * * complaint alleged [that] what McNerney and Carson knew about the likely postponement of the First Flight * * * was confirmed by "internal e-mails" of Boeing. The reference to internal e-mails implied that someone inside Boeing was aiding the plaintiffs. But as no such person was identified, the judge could not determine whether such e-mails * * * existed.

Allegations * * * merely implying unnamed confidential sources of damaging information require a heavy discount. The sources may be ill-informed, may be acting from spite rather than knowledge, may be misrepresented, may even be nonexistent * * *. The district judge therefore rightly refused to give any weight to the "internal e-mails" to which the complaint referred.

* * * *

The judgment dismissing the suit is affirmed.

Case No. 6 for Chapter 31

Leegin Creative Leather Products, Inc. v. PSKS, Inc.
Supreme Court of the United States, 551 U.S. 877, 127 S.Ct. 2705, 168 L.Ed.2d 623 (2007).

Justice *KENNEDY* delivered the opinion of the Court.

* * * *

Petitioner, Leegin Creative Leather Products, Inc. (Leegin), designs, manufactures, and distributes leather goods and accessories. In 1991, Leegin began to sell [products] under the brand name "Brighton."

Respondent, PSKS, Inc. (PSKS), operates Kay's Kloset, a women's apparel store in Lewisville, Texas. * * * It first started purchasing Brighton goods from Leegin in 1995.

* * * *

In December 2002, Leegin discovered Kay's Kloset had been marking down Brighton's entire line by 20 percent. * * * Leegin stopped selling [Brighton products] to the store.

PSKS sued Leegin in the United States District Court for the Eastern District of Texas. It alleged, among other claims, that Leegin had violated the antitrust laws by "enter[ing] into agreements with retailers to charge only those prices fixed by Leegin." * * * [The court] entered judgment against Leegin in the amount of $3,975,000.80.

The [U.S.] Court of Appeals for the Fifth Circuit affirmed. * * * We granted *certiorari* * * *.

* * * *

The rule of reason is the accepted standard for testing whether a practice restrains trade in violation of [Section] 1 [of the Sherman Act].

* * * *

Resort to per se *rules is confined to restraints * * * that would always or almost always tend to restrict competition and decrease output. To justify a* per se *prohibition a restraint must have manifestly anticompetitive effects, and lack * * * any redeeming virtue.* [Emphasis added.]

As a consequence, the *per se* rule is appropriate only after courts have had considerable experience with the type of restraint at issue, and only if courts can predict with confidence that it would be invalidated in all or almost all instances under the rule of reason.

* * * *

The reasoning of the Court's more recent jurisprudence has rejected the rationales on which [the application of the *per se* rule to minimum resale price maintenance agreements] was based. * * * [These rationales were] based on formalistic legal doctrine rather than demonstrable economic effect. * * *

* * * Furthermore [the Court] treated vertical agreements a manufacturer makes with its distributors as analogous to a horizontal combination among competing distributors. * * * Our recent cases formulate antitrust principles in accordance with the appreciated differences in economic effect between vertical and horizontal agreements * * *.

* * * *

The justifications for vertical price restraints are similar to those for other vertical restraints. *Minimum resale price maintenance can stimulate interbrand competition * * * by reducing intrabrand competition * * *.* The promotion of interbrand competition is important because the primary purpose of the antitrust laws is to protect this type of competition. * * * *Resale price maintenance also has the potential to give consumers more options so that they can choose among low-price, low-service brands; high-price, high-service brands; and brands that fall in between.* [Emphasis added.]

* * * *

While vertical agreements setting minimum resale prices can have procompetitive justifications, they may have anticompetitive effects in other cases; and unlawful price fixing, designed solely to obtain monopoly profits, is an ever present temptation.

* * * *

Notwithstanding the risks of unlawful conduct, it cannot be stated with any degree of confidence that resale price maintenance always or almost always tends to restrict competition and decrease output. Vertical agreements establishing minimum resale prices can have either procompetitive or anticompetitive effects, depending upon the circumstances in which they are formed. * * * As the [*per se*] rule would proscribe a significant amount of procompetitive conduct, these agreements appear ill suited for *per se* condemnation.

* * * *

The judgment of the Court of Appeals is reversed, and the case is remanded for proceedings consistent with this opinion.

Case No. 7 for Chapter 35

Town of Midland v. Morris
Court of Appeals of North Carolina, 704 S.E.2d 329 (2011).

STEPHENS, Judge.

The Transcontinental Pipeline transports and distributes natural gas from the Gulf of Mexico to the northeastern United States. In April 2002, the City of Monroe, North Carolina, decided to supply the citizens of Monroe and the surrounding area with natural gas by a direct connection between its natural gas distribution system and the Transcontinental Pipeline. To directly connect to the Transcontinental Pipeline, Monroe needed to acquire the rights to property through which to run a pipeline along the forty-two miles between Monroe and the direct connection on the Transcontinental Pipeline located in Iredell County.

To facilitate the acquisition of land for the construction of the new pipeline ("Pipeline"), Monroe, located in Union County, entered into interlocal agreements with the Town of Mooresville, located in Iredell County, and the Town of Midland, located in Cabarrus County.

The relevant terms of the interlocal agreement between Midland and Monroe * * * provide as follows:

4. Midland shall be responsible for obtaining either by acquisition or by the power of eminent domain and holding in its name for the benefit of the parties and this Interlocal Agreement all easements (both permanent and temporary construction), rights of way, and real property required for the project in Cabarrus County.
* * * *

20. * * * Midland shall retain a perpetual right to locate and install one (1) tap in the pipeline within the corporate limits of Midland from which to operate and supply its own natural gas distribution utility for the benefit of Midland's utility customers in Cabarrus County only. The one tap for Midland's use shall be subject to a right of first refusal granted to a private natural gas provider to serve customers that would otherwise be served by Midland. . . .

* * * *

In 2008 Midland began the process of acquiring the property necessary for the construction of the Pipeline. When negotiations for voluntary acquisitions for the rights of way failed, Midland exercised its eminent domain authority to condemn the needed property.

The present controversy stems from fifteen condemnation actions filed by the Town of Midland in Cabarrus County Superior Court. In those fifteen actions, the opposing parties (hereinafter "Property Owners") filed defenses and counterclaims, challenging Midland's power to condemn the properties in question * * *.
* * * *

Property Owners first argue that because Midland neither currently provides natural gas services to its citizens, nor currently has any plans to provide natural gas to its citizens in the future, the condemnations were undertaken in violation of the statutes governing eminent domain. We disagree.
* * * *

* * * *We find it manifest [obvious] that Midland may acquire property by condemnation to establish a gas transmission and distribution system, even in the absence of a concrete, immediate plan to furnish gas services to its citizens. [Emphasis added.]*

While we acknowledge the existence of the requirement that the public enterprise be established and conducted for the city and its citizens, we conclude that this requirement is satisfied by Midland's placement of a tap on the Pipeline and by Midland's acquisition of the right to low-cost natural gas. Further, * * * *there is nothing in the record to indicate that Midland will never offer natural gas services to its citizens. In fact, Midland's contracted-for right to install a tap on the Pipeline "from which to operate and supply its own natural gas distribution utility for the benefit of Midland's utility customers" indicates just the opposite*: that Midland will, eventually, furnish natural gas services to its citizens. [Emphasis added.]

* * * *

Property Owners further argue that Midland's condemnations violate [the state's statute] because the condemnations are not "for the public use or benefit."
* * * *

It is clear from the statutory language that establishing a gas transmission and distribution system is an appropriate purpose for the condemnation of property under [the relevant provisions].

Despite the disjunctive language of this statutory requirement, our courts have determined the propriety of a condemnation under [the statute] based on the condemnation's satisfaction of both a "public use test" and a "public benefit test."

The first approach—the public use test—asks whether the public has a right to a definite use of the condemned property. The second approach—the public benefit test—asks whether some benefit accrues to the public as a result of the desired condemnation.

Under the public use test, "the principal and dispositive determination is whether the general public has a right to a definite use of the property sought to be condemned." * * * Applying this test to the present case in the appropriate context, there is nothing to indicate that gas services—were they to be provided by Midland— would be available to anything less than the entire population. Accordingly, there can be no doubt that the Midland condemnations would pass the public use test * * *.
* * * *

Under the public benefit test, "*a given condemnor's desired use of the condemned property in question is for 'the public use or benefit' if that use would contribute to the general welfare and prosperity of the public at large.*" In this case, we must take care in defining Midland's "desired use" of the property. Midland is condemning the property to run the Pipeline and to control a tap on the Pipeline, not to immediately provide gas to the citizens of Midland. Accordingly, it is the *availability* of natural gas that must contribute to the general welfare and prosperity of the public at large. [Emphasis added.]

As noted by our Courts, the construction and extension of public utilities, and especially the concomitant commercial and residential growth, provide a clear public benefit to local citizens. * * * Midland's tap on the Pipeline, and its potential to provide natural gas service, likely will spur growth, as well as provide Midland with an advantage in industrial recruitment. These opportunities must be seen as public benefits accruing to the citizens of Midland, such that Midland's condemnations are for the public benefit.
* * * *

Accordingly, we conclude that the Midland condemnations were not undertaken to provide a solely private benefit.
* * * *

We hold that Midland lawfully exercised its eminent domain power.

Glossary

A

Abandoned Property Property that has been discarded by the owner, who has no intention of reclaiming it.

Acceleration Clause A clause that allows a payee or other holder of a time instrument to demand payment of the entire amount due, with interest, if a certain event occurs, such as a default in the payment of an installment when due.

Acceptance The act of voluntarily agreeing, through words or conduct, to the terms of an offer, thereby creating a contract. In negotiable instruments law, a drawee's signed agreement to pay a draft when it is presented.

Acceptor A drawee that accepts, or promises to pay, an instrument when it is presented later for payment.

Accession The addition of value to personal property by the use of labor or materials.

Accord and Satisfaction A common means of settling a disputed claim, whereby a debtor offers to pay a lesser amount than the creditor purports to be owed.

Accredited Investor In the context of securities offerings, sophisticated investors, such as banks, insurance companies, investment companies, the issuer's executive officers and directors, and persons whose income or net worth exceeds certain limits.

Act of State Doctrine A doctrine providing that the judicial branch of one country will not examine the validity of public acts committed by a recognized foreign government within its own territory.

Actionable Capable of serving as the basis of a lawsuit. An actionable claim can be pursued in a lawsuit or other court action.

Actual Malice The deliberate intent to cause harm that exists when a person makes a statement with either knowledge of its falsity or reckless disregard of the truth. Actual malice is required to establish defamation against public figures.

Actus Reus A guilty (prohibited) act; one of the two essential elements required to establish criminal liability.

Adhesion Contract A standard-form contract in which the stronger party dictates the terms.

Adjudicate To render a judicial decision. Adjudication is the trial-like proceeding in which an administrative law judge hears and resolves disputes involving an administrative agency's regulations.

Administrative Agency A federal or state government agency created by the legislature to perform a specific function, such as to make and enforce rules pertaining to the environment.

Administrative Law The body of law created by administrative agencies in order to carry out their duties and responsibilities.

Administrative Law Judge (ALJ) One who presides over an administrative agency hearing and has the power to administer oaths, take testimony, rule on questions of evidence, and make determinations of fact.

Administrative Process The procedure used by administrative agencies in administering the law.

Administrator One who is appointed by a court to administer a person's estate if the decedent died without a valid will or if the executor named in the will cannot serve.

Adverse Possession The acquisition of title to real property through open occupation, without the consent of the owner, for a period of time specified by a state statute. The occupation must be actual, exclusive, open, continuous, and in opposition to all others, including the owner.

Affirmative Action Job-hiring policies that give special consideration to members of protected classes in an effort to overcome present effects of past discrimination.

After-Acquired Property Property that is acquired by the debtor after the execution of a security agreement.

Age of Majority The age (eighteen in most states) at which a person, formerly a minor, is recognized by law as an adult and is legally responsible for his or her actions.

Agency A relationship between two parties in which one party (the agent) agrees to represent or act for the other (the principal).

Agency Coupled with an Interest An agency, created for the benefit of the agent, in which the agent has some legal right (interest) in the property that is the subject of the agency.

Agreement A mutual understanding or meeting of the minds between two or more individuals regarding the terms of a contract.

Alien Corporation A corporation formed in another country but doing business in the United States.

Alienation The transfer of title to real property (which "alienates" the real property from the former owner).

Alternative Dispute Resolution (ADR) The resolution of disputes in ways other than those involved in the traditional judicial process, such as negotiation, mediation, and arbitration.

Answer Procedurally, a defendant's response to the plaintiff's complaint.

Anticipatory Repudiation An assertion or action by a party indicating that he or she will not perform a contractual obligation.

Antitrust Law Laws protecting commerce from unlawful restraints and anticompetitive practices.

Apparent Authority Authority that is only apparent, not real. An agent's apparent authority arises when the principal causes a third party to believe that the agent has authority, even though she or he does not.

Appropriation In tort law, the use by one person of another person's name, likeness, or other identifying characteristic without permission and for the benefit of the user.

Arbitration The settling of a dispute by submitting it to a disinterested third party (other than a court), who renders a decision.

Arbitration Clause A clause in a contract that provides that, in the event of a dispute, the parties will submit the dispute to arbitration rather than litigate the dispute in court.

Arson The intentional burning of a building.

Articles of Incorporation The document that is filed with the appropriate state official, usually the secretary of state, when a business is incorporated and that contains basic information about the corporation

Articles of Organization The document filed with a designated state official by which a limited liability company is formed.

Articles of Partnership A written agreement that sets forth each partner's rights and obligations with respect to the partnership.

Artisan's Lien A possessory lien held by a party who has made improvements and added value to the personal property of another party as security for payment for services performed.

Assault Any word or action intended to make another person fearful of immediate physical harm—a reasonably believable threat.

Assignee A party to whom the rights under a contract are transferred, or assigned.

Assignment The transfer to another of all or part of one's rights arising under a contract.

Assignor A party who transfers (assigns) his or her rights under a contract to another party (the *assignee*).

Assumption of Risk A defense to negligence that bars a plaintiff from recovering for injuries or damage suffered as a result of risks he or she knew of and voluntarily assumed.

Attachment In a secured transaction, the process by which a secured creditor's interest "attaches" to the collateral and the creditor's security interest becomes enforceable. In the context of judicial liens, a court-ordered seizure of property before a judgment is secured for a past-due debt.

Attempted Monopolization An action by a firm that involves anticompetitive conduct, the intent to gain monopoly power, and a "dangerous probability" of success in achieving monopoly power.

Auditor An accountant qualified to perform audits (systematic inspections) of a business's financial records.

Authorization Card A card signed by an employee that gives a union permission to act on his or her behalf in negotiations with management.

Automatic Stay In bankruptcy proceedings, the suspension of almost all litigation and other action by creditors against the debtor or the debtor's property. The stay is effective the moment the debtor files a petition in bankruptcy.

Award The monetary compensation given to a party at the end of a trial or other proceeding.

B

Bailee One to whom goods are entrusted by a bailor.

Bailee's Lien A possessory (artisan's) lien that a bailee entitled to compensation can place on the bailed property to ensure that he or she will be paid for the services provided.

Bailment A situation in which the personal property of one person (a bailor) is entrusted to another (a bailee), who is obligated to return the bailed property to the bailor or dispose of it as directed.

Bailor One who entrusts goods to a bailee.

Bait-and-Switch Advertising Advertising a product at an attractive price and then telling the consumer that the advertised product is not available or is of poor quality and encouraging her or him to purchase a more expensive item.

Bankruptcy Court A federal court of limited jurisdiction that handles only bankruptcy proceedings, which are governed by federal bankruptcy law.

Bankruptcy Trustee A person appointed by the court to manage the debtor's funds.

Battery Physical contact with another that is unexcused, harmful or offensive, and intentionally performed.

Bearer A person in possession of an instrument payable to bearer or indorsed in blank.

Bearer Instrument Any instrument that is not payable to a specific person, including instruments payable to the bearer or to "cash."

Benefit Corporation A for-profit corporation that seeks to have a material positive impact on society and the environment. It is available by statute in a number of states.

Bequest A gift of personal property by will (from the verb *to bequeath*).

Beyond a Reasonable Doubt The standard of proof used in criminal cases.

Bilateral Contract A type of contract that arises when a promise is given in exchange for a return promise.

Bilateral Mistake A mistake that occurs when both parties to a contract are mistaken about the same material fact.

Bill of Rights The first ten amendments to the U.S. Constitution.

Binder A written, temporary insurance policy.

Binding Authority Any source of law that a court *must* follow when deciding a case.

Blank Indorsement An indorsement on an instrument that specifies no indorsee. An order instrument that is indorsed in blank becomes a bearer instrument.

Bona Fide Occupational Qualification (BFOQ) An identifiable characteristic reasonably necessary to the normal operation of a particular business. Such characteristics can include gender, national origin, and religion, but not race.

Bond A security that evidences a corporate (or government) debt.

Botnet A network of compromised computers connected to the Internet that can be used to generate spam, relay viruses, or cause servers to fail.

Breach of Contract The failure, without legal excuse, of a promisor to perform the obligations of a contract.

Brief A written summary or statement prepared by one side in a lawsuit to explain its case to the judge.

Browse-Wrap Term A term or condition of use that is presented when an online buyer downloads a product but to which the buyer does not have to agree before installing or using the product.

Burglary The unlawful entry or breaking into a building with the intent to commit a felony.

Business Ethics The application of moral and ethical principles in a business context.

Business Invitee A person, such as a customer or a client, who is invited onto business premises by the owner of those premises for business purposes.

Business Judgment Rule A rule under which courts will not hold corporate officers and directors liable for honest mistakes of judgment and bad business decisions that were made in good faith.

Business Necessity A defense to an allegation of employment discrimination in which the employer demonstrates that an employment practice that discriminates against members of a protected class is related to job performance.

Business Tort Wrongful interference with another's business rights and relationships.

Business Trust A form of business organization, created by a written trust agreement, that resembles a corporation. Legal ownership and management of the trust's property stay with the trustees, and the profits are distributed to the beneficiaries, who have limited liability.

Buyer in the Ordinary Course of Business A buyer who, in good faith and without knowledge that the sale violates the ownership rights or security interest of a third party in the goods, purchases goods in the ordinary course of business from a person in the business of selling goods of that kind.

Buyout Price The amount payable to a partner on his or her dissociation from a partnership, based on the amount distributable to that partner if the firm were wound up on that date, and offset by any damages for wrongful dissociation.

Bylaws The internal rules of management adopted by a corporation at its first organizational meeting.

C

Case Law The rules of law announced in court decisions. Case law interprets statutes, regulations, constitutional provisions, and other case law.

Cashier's Check A check drawn by a bank on itself.

Categorical Imperative An ethical guideline developed by Immanuel Kant under which an action is evaluated in terms of what would happen if everybody else in the same situation, or category, acted the same way.

Causation in Fact An act or omission without which an event would not have occurred.

Cease-and-Desist Order An administrative or judicial order prohibiting a person or business firm from conducting activities that an agency or court has deemed illegal.

Certificate of Deposit (CD) A note issued by a bank in which the bank acknowledges the receipt of funds from a party and promises to repay that amount, with interest, to the party on a certain date.

Certificate of Limited Partnership The document that must be filed with a designated state official to form a limited partnership.

Certification Mark A mark used by one or more persons, other than the owner, to certify the region, materials, mode of manufacture, quality, or other characteristic of specific goods or services.

Certified Check A check that has been accepted in writing by the bank on which it is drawn. By certifying (accepting) the check, the bank promises to pay the check at the time it is presented.

Charging Order In partnership law, an order granted by a court to a judgment creditor that entitles the creditor to attach a partner's interest in the partnership.

Charitable Trust A trust in which the property held by the trustee must be used for a charitable purpose, such as the advancement of health, education, or religion.

Chattel Personal property.

Check A draft drawn by a drawer ordering the drawee bank or financial institution to pay a certain amount of funds to the payee on demand.

Checks and Balances The principle under which the powers of the national government are divided among three separate branches— the executive, legislative, and judicial branches—each of which exercises a check on the actions of the others.

Choice-of-Language Clause A clause in a contract designating the official language by which the contract will be interpreted in the event of a disagreement over the contract's terms.

Choice-of-Law Clause A clause in a contract designating the law (such as the law of a particular state or nation) that will govern the contract.

Citation A reference to a publication in which a legal authority—such as a statute or a court decision—or other source can be found.

Civil Law The branch of law dealing with the definition and enforcement of all private or public rights, as opposed to criminal matters.

Civil Law System A system of law derived from Roman law that is based on codified laws (rather than on case precedents).

Clearinghouse A system or place where banks exchange checks and drafts drawn on each other and settle daily balances.

Click-On Agreement An agreement that arises when an online buyer clicks on "I agree" or otherwise indicates her or his assent to be bound by the terms of an offer.

Close Corporation A corporation whose shareholders are limited to a small group of persons, often family members.

Closed Shop A firm that requires union membership by its workers as a condition of employment.

Cloud Computing The delivery to users of on-demand services from third-party servers over a network.

Codicil A written supplement or modification to a will. A codicil must be executed with the same formalities as a will.

Collateral Under Article 9 of the UCC, the property subject to a security interest.

Collateral Promise A secondary promise to a primary transaction, such as a promise made by one person to pay the debts of another if the latter fails to perform. A collateral promise normally must be in writing to be enforceable.

Collecting Bank Any bank handling an item for collection, except the payor bank.

Collective Bargaining The process by which labor and management negotiate the terms and conditions of employment, including working hours and workplace conditions.

Collective Mark A mark used by members of a cooperative, association, union, or other organization to certify the region, materials, mode of manufacture, quality, or other characteristic of specific goods or services.

Comity The principle by which one nation defers to and gives effect to the laws and judicial decrees of another nation. This recognition is based primarily on respect.

Commerce Clause The provision in Article I, Section 8, of the U.S. Constitution that gives Congress the power to regulate interstate commerce.

Commercial Impracticability A doctrine that may excuse the duty to perform a contract when performance becomes much more difficult or costly due to forces that neither party could control or foresee at the time the contract was formed.

Commingle To put funds or goods together into one mass so that they are mixed to such a degree that they no longer have separate identities.

Common Law The body of law developed from custom or judicial decisions in English and U.S. courts, not attributable to a legislature.

Common Stock Shares of ownership in a corporation that give the owner a proportionate interest in the corporation with regard to control, earnings, and net assets. Common stock is lowest in priority with respect to payment of dividends and distribution of the corporation's assets on dissolution.

Community Property A form of concurrent property ownership in which each spouse owns an undivided one-half interest in property acquired during the marriage.

Comparative Negligence A rule in tort law, used in the majority of states, that reduces the plaintiff's recovery in proportion to the plaintiff's degree of fault, rather than barring recovery completely.

Compelling Government Interest A test of constitutionality that requires the government to have convincing reasons for passing any law that restricts fundamental rights, such as free speech, or distinguishes between people based on a suspect trait.

Compensatory Damages A monetary award equivalent to the actual value of injuries or damage sustained by the aggrieved party.

Complaint The pleading made by a plaintiff alleging wrongdoing on the part of the defendant. When filed with a court, the complaint initiates a lawsuit.

Computer Crime Any violation of criminal law that involves knowledge of computer technology for its perpetration, investigation, or prosecution.

Concentrated Industry An industry in which a single firm or a small number of firms control a large percentage of market sales.

Concurrent Conditions Conditions that must occur or be performed at the same time— they are mutually dependent. No obligations arise until these conditions are simultaneously performed.

Concurrent Jurisdiction Jurisdiction that exists when two different courts have the power to hear a case.

Concurrent Ownership Joint ownership.

Concurring Opinion A court opinion by one or more judges or justices who agree with the majority but want to make or emphasize a point that was not made or emphasized in the majority's opinion.

Condemnation Proceedings The judicial procedure by which the government exercises its power of eminent domain. It generally involves two phases: a taking and a determination of fair value.

Condition A qualification, provision, or clause in a contractual agreement, the occurrence or nonoccurrence of which creates, suspends, or terminates the obligations of the contracting parties.

Condition Precedent A condition in a contract that must be met before a party's promise becomes absolute.

Condition Subsequent A condition in a contract that, if it occurs, operates to terminate a party's absolute promise to perform.

Confiscation A government's taking of a privately owned business or personal property without a proper public purpose or an award of just compensation.

Conforming Goods Goods that conform to contract specifications.

Confusion The mixing together of goods belonging to two or more owners to such an extent that the separately owned goods cannot be identified.

Consequential Damages Foreseeable damages that result from a party's breach of contract but are caused by special circumstances beyond the contract itself.

Consideration The value given in return for a promise or performance in a contractual agreement.

Constitutional Law The body of law derived from the U.S. Constitution and the constitutions of the various states.

Constructive Delivery A symbolic delivery of property that cannot be physically delivered.

Constructive Discharge A termination of employment brought about by making the employee's working conditions so intolerable that the employee reasonably feels compelled to leave.

Constructive Eviction A form of eviction that occurs when a landlord fails to perform adequately any of the duties required by the lease, thereby making the tenant's further use and enjoyment of the property exceedingly difficult or impossible.

Constructive Fraud Conduct that is treated as fraud under the law even when there is no proof of intent to defraud, usually because of the existence of a special relationship or fiduciary duty.

Constructive Trust An equitable trust that is imposed in the interests of fairness and justice when someone wrongfully holds legal title to property.

Consumer-Debtor One whose debts result primarily from the purchases of goods for personal, family, or household use.

Continuation Statement A statement that, if filed within six months prior to the expiration date of the original financing statement, continues the perfection of the security interest for another five years.

Contract A set of promises constituting an agreement between parties, giving each a legal duty to the other and the right to seek a remedy for the breach of the promises or duties.

Contractual Capacity The capacity required by the law for a party who enters into a contract to be bound by that contract.

Contributory Negligence A rule in tort law, used in only a few states, that completely bars the plaintiff from recovering any damages if the damage suffered is partly the plaintiff's own fault.

Conversion Wrongfully taking or retaining possession of an individual's personal property and placing it in the service of another.

Conveyance The transfer of title to real property from one person to another by deed or other document.

Cookie A small file sent from a Web site and stored in a user's Web browser to track the user's Web browsing activities.

"Cooling-Off" Laws Laws that allow buyers of goods sold in certain transactions to cancel their contracts within three business days.

Cooperative An association, which may or may not be incorporated, that is organized to provide an economic service to its members. Unincorporated cooperatives are often treated like partnerships for tax and other legal purposes.

Copyright The exclusive right of an author or originator of a literary or artistic production to publish, print, sell, or otherwise use that production for a statutory period of time.

Corporate Governance A set of policies specifying the rights and responsibilities of the various participants in a corporation and spelling out the rules and procedures for making corporate decisions.

Corporate Social Responsibility (CSR) The idea that corporations can and should act ethically and be accountable to society for their actions.

Corporation A legal entity formed in compliance with statutory requirements that is distinct from its shareholder-owners.

Correspondent Bank A bank that acts on behalf of another bank for the purpose of facilitating fund transfers.

Cost-Benefit Analysis A decision-making technique that involves weighing the costs of a given action against the benefits of that action.

Co-Surety A joint surety; a party who assumes liability jointly with another surety for the payment of a debtor's obligation under a suretyship arrangement.

Counteradvertising New advertising that is undertaken to correct earlier false claims that were made about a product.

Counterclaim A claim made by a defendant in a civil lawsuit against the plaintiff. In effect, the defendant is suing the plaintiff.

Counteroffer An offeree's response to an offer in which the offeree rejects the original offer and at the same time makes a new offer.

Course of Dealing Prior conduct between the parties to a contract that establishes a common basis for their understanding.

Course of Performance The conduct that occurs under the terms of a particular agreement, which indicates what the parties to that agreement intended the agreement to mean.

Covenant Not to Compete A contractual promise of one party to refrain from conducting business similar to that of another party for a certain period of time and within a specified geographical area.

Covenant Not to Sue An agreement to substitute a contractual obligation for some other type of legal action based on a valid claim.

Cover A remedy that allows the buyer or lessee, on the seller's or lessor's breach, to obtain substitute goods from another seller or lessor.

Cram-Down Provision A provision of the Bankruptcy Code that allows a court to confirm a debtor's Chapter 11 reorganization plan even though only one class of creditors has accepted it.

Creditors' Composition Agreement A contract between a debtor and his or her creditors in which the creditors agree to discharge the debts on the debtor's payment of a sum less than the amount actually owed.

Crime A wrong against society proclaimed in a statute and, if committed, punishable by society through fines, imprisonment, or death.

Criminal Law The branch of law that defines and punishes wrongful actions committed against the public.

Cross-Collateralization The use of an asset that is not the subject of a loan to collateralize that loan.

Crowdfunding A cooperative activity in which people network and pool funds and other resources via the Internet to assist a cause (such as disaster relief) or invest in a venture (business).

Cure The right of a party who tenders nonconforming performance to correct his or her performance within the contract period.

Cyber Crime A crime that occurs in the online environment.

Cyber Fraud Any misrepresentation knowingly made over the Internet with the intention of deceiving another for the purpose of obtaining property or funds.

Cyberlaw An informal term used to refer to all laws governing electronic communications and transactions, particularly those conducted via the Internet.

Cybersquatting The act of registering a domain name that is the same as, or confusingly similar to, the trademark of another and then offering to sell that domain name back to the trademark owner.

Cyber Tort A tort committed via the Internet.

D

Damages A monetary award sought as a remedy for a breach of contract or a tortious action.

Debtor Under Article 9 of the UCC, any party who owes payment or performance of a secured obligation.

Debtor in Possession (DIP) In Chapter 11 bankruptcy proceedings, a debtor who is allowed to continue in possession of the estate in property (the business) and to continue business operations.

Deceptive Advertising Advertising that misleads consumers, either by making unjustified claims about a product's performance or by omitting a material fact concerning the product's composition or performance.

Deed A document by which title to real property is passed.

Defalcation Embezzlement or misappropriation of funds.

Defamation Anything published or publicly spoken that causes injury to another's good name, reputation, or character.

Default Failure to pay a debt when it is due.

Default Judgment A judgment entered by a court against a defendant who has failed to appear in court to answer or defend against the plaintiff's claim.

Defendant One against whom a lawsuit is brought or the accused person in a criminal proceeding.

Defense A reason offered by a defendant in an action or lawsuit as to why the plaintiff should not recover or establish what she or he seeks.

Deficiency Judgment A judgment against a debtor for the amount of a debt remaining unpaid after the collateral has been repossessed and sold.

Delegatee A party to whom contractual obligations are transferred, or delegated.

Delegation of Duties The transfer to another of a contractual duty.

Delegator A party who transfers (delegates) her or his obligations under a contract to another party (the *delegatee*).

Depositary Bank The first bank to receive a check for payment.

Deposition The testimony of a party to a lawsuit or a witness taken under oath before a trial.

Destination Contract A contract for the sale of goods in which the seller is required or authorized to ship the goods by carrier and tender delivery of the goods at a particular destination. The seller assumes liability for any losses or damage to the goods until they are tendered at the destination specified in the contract.

Devise A gift of real property by will, or the act of giving real property by will.

Devisee One designated in a will to receive a gift of real property.

Digital Cash Prepaid funds stored on microchips in laptops, smartphones, tablets, and other devices.

Disaffirmance The legal avoidance, or setting aside, of a contractual obligation.

Discharge The termination of an obligation, such as occurs when the parties to a contract have fully performed their contractual obligations. The termination of a bankruptcy debtor's obligation to pay debts.

Disclosed Principal A principal whose identity is known to a third party at the time the agent makes a contract with the third party.

Discovery A method by which the opposing parties obtain information from each other to prepare for trial.

Dishonor To refuse to pay or to accept a negotiable instrument that has been presented in a timely and proper manner.

Disparagement of Property An economically injurious falsehood about another's product or property.

Disparate-Impact Discrimination Discrimination that results from certain employer practices or procedures that, although not discriminatory on their face, have a discriminatory effect.

Disparate-Treatment Discrimination A form of employment discrimination that results when an employer intentionally discriminates against employees who are members of protected classes.

Dissenting Opinion A court opinion that presents the views of one or more judges or justices who disagree with the majority's decision.

Dissociation The severance of the relationship between a partner and a partnership.

Dissolution The formal disbanding of a partnership or a corporation. Partnerships can be dissolved by acts of the partners, by operation of law, or by judicial decree.

Distributed Network A network that can be used by persons located (distributed) around the country or the globe to share computer files.

Distribution Agreement A contract between a seller and a distributor of the seller's products setting out the terms and conditions of the distributorship.

Diversity of Citizenship A basis for federal court jurisdiction over a lawsuit between citizens of different states or a lawsuit involving a U.S. citizen and a citizen of a different country.

Divestiture A company's sale of one or more of its divisions' operating functions under court order as part of the enforcement of the antitrust laws.

Dividend A distribution of corporate profits to the corporation's shareholders in proportion to the number of shares held.

Docket The list of cases entered on a court's calendar and thus scheduled to be heard by the court.

Document of Title A paper exchanged in the regular course of business that evidences the right to possession of goods (for example, a bill of lading or a warehouse receipt).

Domain Name Part of an Internet address, such as "cengage.com." The series of letters and symbols used to identify a site operator on the Internet; an Internet "address."

Domestic Corporation In a given state, a corporation that is organized under the law of that state.

Dominion Ownership rights in property, including the right to possess and control the property.

Double Jeopardy The Fifth Amendment requirement that prohibits a person from being tried twice for the same criminal offense.

Down Payment An initial cash payment made when an expensive item, such as a house, is purchased. The payment represents a percentage of the purchase price, and the remainder is financed.

Draft Any instrument drawn on a drawee that orders the drawee to pay a certain amount of funds, usually to a third party (the payee), on demand or at a definite future time.

Dram Shop Act A state statute that imposes liability on the owners of bars and taverns, as well as those who serve alcoholic drinks to the public, for injuries resulting from accidents caused by intoxicated persons when the sellers or servers of alcoholic drinks contributed to the intoxication.

Drawee The party that is ordered to pay a draft or check. With a check, a bank or a financial institution is always the drawee.

Drawer The party that initiates a draft (such as a check), thereby ordering the drawee to pay.

Due Diligence A required standard of care that certain professionals, such as accountants, must meet to avoid liability for securities violations.

Due Process Clause The provisions in the Fifth and Fourteenth Amendments that guarantee that no person shall be deprived of life, liberty, or property without due process of law. State constitutions often include similar clauses.

Dumping The sale of goods in a foreign country at a price below the price charged for the same goods in the domestic market.

Duress Unlawful pressure brought to bear on a person, causing the person to perform an act that she or he would not otherwise perform.

Duty-based Ethics An ethical philosophy rooted in the idea that every person has certain duties to others, including both humans and the planet. Those duties may be derived from religious principles or from other philosophical reasoning.

Duty of Care The duty of all persons, as established by tort law, to exercise a reasonable amount of care in their dealings with others. Failure to exercise due care, which is normally determined by the reasonable person standard, constitutes the tort of negligence.

E

Easement A nonpossessory right, established by express or implied agreement, to make limited use of another's property without removing anything from the property.

E-Contract A contract that is formed electronically.

E-Evidence A type of evidence that consists of computer-generated or electronically recorded information.

Electronic Fund Transfer (EFT) A transfer of funds through the use of an electronic terminal, a telephone, a computer, or magnetic tape.

Emancipation In regard to minors, the act of being freed from parental control.

Embezzlement The fraudulent appropriation of funds or other property by a person who was entrusted with the funds or property.

Eminent Domain The power of a government to take land from private citizens for public use on the payment of just compensation.

E-Money Prepaid funds stored on microchips in laptops, smartphones, tablets, and other devices.

Employment at Will A common law doctrine under which either party may terminate an employment relationship at any time for any reason, unless a contract specifies otherwise.

Employment Contract A contract between an employer and an employee in which the terms and conditions of employment are stated.

Enabling Legislation A statute enacted by Congress that authorizes the creation of an administrative agency and specifies the name, composition, purpose, and powers of the agency being created.

Entrapment A defense in which a defendant claims that he or she was induced by a public official to commit a crime that he or she would otherwise not have committed.

Entrepreneur One who initiates and assumes the financial risk of a new business enterprise and undertakes to provide or control its management.

Entrustment Rule The rule that entrusting goods to a merchant who deals in goods of that kind gives that merchant the power to transfer those goods and all rights to them to a buyer in the ordinary course of business.

Environmental Impact Statement (EIS) A formal analysis required for any major federal action that will significantly affect the quality of the environment to determine the action's impact and explore alternatives.

Equal Dignity Rule A rule requiring that an agent's authority be in writing if the contract to be made on behalf of the principal must be in writing.

Equal Protection Clause The provision in the Fourteenth Amendment that requires state governments to treat similarly situated individuals in a similar manner.

Equitable Principles and Maxims General propositions or principles of law that have to do with fairness (equity).

Equitable Right of Redemption The right of a mortgagor who has breached the mortgage agreement to redeem or purchase the mortgaged property prior to foreclosure proceedings.

E-Signature An electronic sound, symbol, or process attached to or logically associated with a record and adopted by a person with the intent to sign the record.

Establishment Clause The provision in the First Amendment that prohibits the government from establishing any state-sponsored religion or enacting any law that promotes religion or favors one religion over another.

Estate in Bankruptcy All of the property owned by a person, including real estate and personal property.

Estopped Barred, impeded, or precluded.

Estray Statute A statute defining finders' rights in property when the true owners are unknown.

Ethical Reasoning A reasoning process in which an individual links his or her moral convictions or ethical standards to the situation at hand.

Ethics Moral principles and values applied to social behavior.

Eviction A landlord's act of depriving a tenant of possession of the leased premises.

Exclusionary Rule A rule that prevents evidence that is obtained illegally or without a proper search warrant from being admissible in court.

Exclusive-Dealing Contract An agreement under which a seller forbids a buyer to purchase products from the seller's competitors.

Exclusive Jurisdiction Jurisdiction that exists when a case can be heard only in a particular court or type of court.

Exculpatory Clause A clause that releases a contractual party from liability in the event of monetary or physical injury, no matter who is at fault.

Executed Contract A contract that has been fully performed by both parties.

Execution The implementation of a court's decree or judgment.

Executor A person appointed by a testator in a will to administer her or his estate.

Executory Contract A contract that has not yet been fully performed.

Export The sale of goods and services by domestic firms to buyers located in other countries.

Express Contract A contract in which the terms of the agreement are stated in words, oral or written.

Express Warranty A seller's or lessor's promise as to the quality, condition, description, or performance of the goods being sold or leased.

Expropriation A government's seizure of a privately owned business or personal property for a proper public purpose and with just compensation.

Extension Clause A clause in a time instrument that allows the instrument's date of maturity to be extended into the future.

Extrinsic Evidence Any evidence not contained in the contract itself, which may include the testimony of the parties, additional agreements or communications, or other information relevant to determining the parties' intent.

F

Federal Form of Government A system of government in which the states form a union and the sovereign power is divided between the central government and the member states.

Federal Question A question that pertains to the U.S. Constitution, an act of Congress, or a treaty and provides a basis for federal jurisdiction in a case.

Federal Reserve System A network of twelve district banks and related branches located around the country and headed by the

Federal Reserve Board of Governors. Most banks in the United States have Federal Reserve accounts.

Fee Simple An ownership interest in land in which the owner has the greatest possible aggregation of rights, privileges, and power.

Felony A crime—such as arson, murder, rape, or robbery—that carries the most severe sanctions, ranging from more than one year in a state or federal prison to the death penalty.

Fictitious Payee A payee on a negotiable instrument whom the maker or drawer did not intend to have an interest in the instrument. Indorsements by fictitious payees are treated as authorized indorsements under UCC Article 3.

Fiduciary As a noun, a person having a duty created by his or her undertaking to act primarily for another's benefit in matters connected with the undertaking. As an adjective, a relationship founded on trust and confidence.

Filtering Software A computer program that is designed to block access to certain Web sites, based on their content. The software blocks the retrieval of a site whose URL or key words are on a list within the program.

Financing Statement A document filed by a secured creditor with the appropriate official to give notice to the public of the creditor's security interest in collateral belonging to the debtor named in the statement.

Firm Offer An offer (by a merchant) that is irrevocable without the necessity of consideration for a stated period of time or, if no definite period is stated, for a reasonable time (neither period to exceed three months).

Fixed-Term Tenancy A type of tenancy under which property is leased for a specified period of time, such as a month, a year, or a period of years; also called a *tenancy for years*.

Fixture An item of personal property that has become so closely associated with real property that it is legally regarded as part of that real property.

Floating Lien A security interest in proceeds, after-acquired property, or collateral subject to future advances by the secured party (or all three). The security interest is retained even when the collateral changes in character, classification, or location.

Forbearance A postponement of part or all of the payments on a loan for a limited time. The act of refraining from an action that one has a legal right to undertake.

Force Majeure Clause A provision in a contract stipulating that certain unforeseen events—such as war, political upheavals, or acts of God—will excuse a party from liability for nonperformance of contractual obligations.

Foreclosure The legal process by which a lender repossesses and disposes of property that has secured a loan.

Foreign Corporation In a given state, a corporation that does business in that state but is not incorporated there.

Foreign Exchange Market A worldwide system in which foreign currencies are bought and sold.

Forgery The fraudulent making or altering of any writing in a way that changes the legal rights and liabilities of another.

Formal Contract An agreement that by law requires a specific form for its validity.

Forum-Selection Clause A provision in a contract designating the court, jurisdiction, or tribunal that will decide any disputes arising under the contract.

Franchise Any arrangement in which the owner of a trademark, trade name, or copyright licenses another to use that trademark, trade name, or copyright in the selling of goods or services.

Franchisee One receiving a license to use another's (the franchisor's) trademark, trade name, or copyright in the sale of goods and services.

Franchisor One licensing another (the franchisee) to use the owner's trademark, trade name, or copyright in the selling of goods or services.

Fraudulent Misrepresentation Any misrepresentation, either by misstatement or by omission of a material fact, knowingly made with the intention of deceiving another and on which a reasonable person would and does rely to his or her detriment.

Free Exercise Clause The provision in the First Amendment that prohibits the government from interfering with people's religious practices or forms of worship.

Free-Writing Prospectus A written, electronic, or graphic communication associated with the offer to sell a security and used during the waiting period to supplement other information about the security.

Frustration of Purpose A court-created doctrine under which a party to a contract will be relieved of her or his duty to perform when the objective purpose for performance no longer exists due to reasons beyond that party's control.

Fungible Goods Goods that are alike by physical nature, agreement, or trade usage.

G

Garnishment A legal process whereby a creditor collects a debt by seizing property of the debtor that is in the hands of a third party.

General Damages In a tort case, an amount awarded to compensate individuals for the nonmonetary aspects of the harm suffered, such as pain and suffering. Not available to companies.

Generally Accepted Accounting Principles (GAAP) The conventions, rules, and procedures developed by the Financial Accounting Standards Board to define accepted accounting practices at a particular time.

Generally Accepted Auditing Standards (GAAS) Standards established by the American Institute of Certified Public Accountants to define the professional qualities and judgment that should be exercised by an auditor in performing an audit.

General Partner In a limited partnership, a partner who assumes responsibility for the management of the partnership and has full liability for all partnership debts.

Gift A voluntary transfer of property made without consideration, past or present.

Gift *Causa Mortis* A gift made in contemplation of imminent death. The gift is revoked if the donor does not die as contemplated.

Gift *Inter Vivos* A gift made during one's lifetime and not in contemplation of imminent death, in contrast to a gift *causa mortis*.

Good Faith Purchaser A purchaser who buys without notice of any circumstance that would cause a person of ordinary prudence to inquire as to whether the seller has valid title to the goods being sold.

Good Samaritan Statute A state statute stipulating that persons who provide emergency services to, or rescue, someone in peril cannot be sued for negligence unless they act recklessly and cause further harm.

Goodwill In the business context, the valuable reputation of a business viewed as an intangible asset.

Grand Jury A group of citizens who decide, after hearing the state's evidence, whether a reasonable basis (probable cause) exists for believing that a crime has been committed and that a trial ought to be held.

Group Boycott An agreement by two or more sellers to refuse to deal with a particular person or firm.

Guarantor A third party who promises to be responsible for a debtor's obligation under a guaranty arrangement.

H

Hacker A person who uses computers to gain unauthorized access to data.

Historical School A school of legal thought that looks to the past to determine what the principles of contemporary law should be.

Holder Any person in possession of an instrument drawn, issued, or indorsed to him or her, to his or her order, to bearer, or in blank.

Holder in Due Course (HDC) A holder who acquires a negotiable instrument for value, in good faith, and without notice that the instrument is defective.

Holographic Will A will written entirely in the testator's handwriting.

Homeowner's Insurance A form of property insurance that protects the holder against damage or loss to the holder's home.

Homestead Exemption A law permitting a debtor to retain the family home, either in its entirety or up to a specified dollar amount, free from the claims of unsecured creditors or trustees in bankruptcy.

Horizontal Merger A merger between two firms that are competing in the same market.

Horizontal Restraint Any agreement that restrains competition between rival firms competing in the same market.

Hot-Cargo Agreement An illegal agreement in which employers voluntarily agree with unions not to handle, use, or deal in the nonunion-produced goods of other employers.

I

I-551 Alien Registration Receipt A document, known as a "green card," that shows that a foreign-born individual can legally work in the United States.

I-9 Verification The process of verifying the employment eligibility and identity of a new worker. It must be completed within three days after the worker commences employment.

Identification In a sale of goods, the express designation of the goods provided for in the contract.

Identity Theft The illegal use of someone else's personal information to access the victim's financial resources.

Implied Contract A contract formed in whole or in part from the conduct of the parties.

Implied Warranty A warranty that arises by law because of the circumstances of a sale and not from the seller's express promise.

Implied Warranty of Fitness for a Particular Purpose A warranty that goods sold or leased are fit for the particular purpose for which the buyer or lessee will use the goods.

Implied Warranty of Habitability An implied promise by a seller of a new house that the house is fit for human habitation. Also, the implied promise by a landlord that rented residential premises are habitable.

Implied Warranty of Merchantability A warranty that goods being sold or leased are reasonably fit for the general purpose for which they are sold or leased, are properly packaged and labeled, and are of proper quality.

Impossibility of Performance A doctrine under which a party to a contract is relieved of his or her duty to perform when performance becomes objectively impossible or totally impracticable.

Imposter One who induces a maker or drawer to issue a negotiable instrument in the name of an impersonated payee. Indorsements by imposters are treated as authorized indorsements under UCC Article 3.

Incidental Beneficiary A third party who benefits from a contract even though the contract was not formed for that purpose. An incidental beneficiary has no rights in the contract and cannot sue to have it enforced.

Incidental Damages Damages that compensate for expenses directly incurred because of a breach of contract, such as those incurred to obtain performance from another source.

Incontestability Clause A clause in a policy for life or health insurance stating that after the policy has been in force for a specified length of time (usually two or three years), the insurer cannot contest statements made in the policyholder's application.

Independent Contractor One who works for, and receives payment from, an employer but whose working conditions and methods are not controlled by the employer. An independent contractor is not an employee but may be an agent.

Indictment A formal charge by a grand jury that there is probable cause to believe that a named person has committed a crime.

Indorsement A signature placed on an instrument for the purpose of transferring ownership rights in the instrument.

Informal Contract A contract that does not require a specific form or method of creation to be valid.

Information A formal accusation or complaint (without an indictment) issued in certain types of actions (usually criminal actions involving lesser crimes) by a government prosecutor.

Information Return A tax return submitted by a partnership that reports the business's income and losses. The partnership itself does not pay taxes on the income, but each partner's share of the profit (whether distributed or not) is taxed as individual income to that partner.

Innocent Misrepresentation A misrepresentation that occurs when a person makes a false statement of fact that he or she believes is true.

Inside Director A person on the board of directors who is also an officer of the corporation.

Insider Trading The purchase or sale of securities on the basis of information that has not been made available to the public.

Insolvent A condition in which a person cannot pay his or her debts as they become due or ceases to pay debts in the ordinary course of business.

Installment Contract A contract that requires or authorizes delivery in two or more separate lots to be accepted and paid for separately.

Insurable Interest A property interest in goods being sold or leased that is sufficiently substantial to permit a party to insure against damage to the goods. An interest that exists when a person benefits from the preservation of the health or life of the insured or the property to be insured.

Insurance A contract by which the insurer promises to reimburse the insured or a beneficiary in the event that the insured is injured, dies, or sustains damage to property as a result of particular, stated contingencies.

Intangible Property Property that cannot be seen or touched but exists only conceptually, such as corporate stocks. Such property is not governed by Article 2 of the UCC.

Integrated Contract A written contract that constitutes the final expression of the parties' agreement. Evidence extraneous to the contract that contradicts or alters the meaning of the contract in any way is inadmissible.

Intellectual Property Property resulting from intellectual and creative processes.

Intended Beneficiary A third party for whose benefit a contract is formed. An intended beneficiary can sue the promisor if the contract is breached.

Intentional Tort A wrongful act knowingly committed.

Intermediary Bank Any bank to which an item is transferred in the course of collection, except the depositary or payor bank.

International Financial Reporting Standards (IFRS) A set of global accounting standards that are being phased in by companies in the United States.

International Law The law that governs relations among nations.

International Organization An organization composed mainly of member nations and usually established by treaty—for example, the United Nations. More broadly, the term also includes nongovernmental organizations (NGOs) such as the Red Cross.

Internet Service Provider (ISP) A business or organization that offers users access to the Internet and related services.

Interpretive Rule A nonbinding rule or policy statement issued by an administrative agency that explains how it interprets and intends to apply the statutes it enforces.

Interrogatories A series of written questions for which written answers are prepared by a party to a lawsuit, usually with the assistance of the party's attorney, and then signed under oath.

Intestacy Laws State statutes that specify how property will be distributed when a person dies intestate (without a valid will).

Intestate As a noun, one who has died without having created a valid will. As an adjective, the state of having died without a will.

Investment Company A company that acts on the behalf of many smaller shareholders-owners by buying a large portfolio of securities and professionally managing that portfolio.

Investment Contract In securities law, a transaction in which a person invests in a common enterprise reasonably expecting profits that are derived primarily from the efforts of others.

J

Joint and Several Liability In partnership law, a doctrine under which a plaintiff may sue, and collect a judgment from, all of the partners together (jointly) or one or more of the partners separately (severally, or individually). A partner can be held liable even if she or he did not participate in, ratify, or know about the conduct that gave rise to the lawsuit.

Joint Liability In partnership law, the partners' shared liability for partnership obligations and debts. A third party must sue all of the partners as a group, but each partner can be held liable for the full amount.

Joint Stock Company A hybrid form of business organization that combines characteristics of a corporation and a partnership. Usually, a joint stock company is regarded as a partnership for tax and other legal purposes.

Joint Tenancy Joint ownership of property by two or more co-owners in which each co-owner owns an undivided portion of the property. On the death of one of the joint tenants, his or her interest automatically passes to the surviving joint tenant(s).

Joint Venture A joint undertaking by two or more persons or business entities to combine their efforts or their property for a single transaction or project or for a related series of transactions or projects. A joint venture is generally treated like a partnership for tax and other legal purposes.

Judicial Review The process by which a court decides on the constitutionality of legislative enactments and actions of the executive branch.

Jurisdiction The authority of a court to hear and decide a specific case.

Jurisprudence The science or philosophy of law.

Justiciable Controversy A controversy that is not hypothetical or academic but real and substantial; a requirement that must be satisfied before a court will hear a case.

L

Larceny The wrongful taking and carrying away of another person's personal property with the intent to permanently deprive the owner of the property.

Latent Defect A defect that is not obvious or cannot readily be ascertained.

Law A body of enforceable rules governing relationships among individuals and between individuals and their society.

Lease Under Article 2A of the UCC, a transfer of the right to possess and use goods for a period of time in exchange for payment.

Lease Agreement An agreement in which one person (the lessor) agrees to transfer the right to the possession and use of property to another person (the lessee) in exchange for rental payments.

Leasehold Estate An interest in real property that gives a tenant a qualified right to possess and/or use the property for a limited time under a lease.

Legacy A gift of personal property under a will.

Legal Positivism A school of legal thought centered on the assumption that there is no law higher than the laws created by a national government. Laws must be obeyed, even if they are unjust, to prevent anarchy.

Legal Realism A school of legal thought that holds that the law is only one factor to be considered when deciding cases and that social and economic circumstances should also be taken into account.

Legatee One designated in a will to receive a gift of personal property.

Legislative Rule An administrative agency rule that carries the same weight as a congressionally enacted statute.

Lessee A person who acquires the right to the possession and use of another's goods in exchange for rental payments.

Lessor A person who transfers the right to the possession and use of goods to another in exchange for rental payments.

Letter of Credit A written document in which the issuer (usually a bank) promises to honor drafts or other demands for payment by third persons in accordance with the terms of the instrument.

Levy The legal process of obtaining funds through the seizure and sale of nonexempt property, usually done after a writ of execution has been issued.

Liability The state of being legally responsible (liable) for something, such as a debt or obligation.

Libel Defamation in writing or another permanent form (such as a digital recording).

License An agreement by the owner of intellectual property to permit another to use a trademark, copyright, patent, or trade secret for certain limited purposes. In the context of real property, a revocable right or privilege to enter onto another person's land.

Lien An encumbrance on a property to satisfy a debt or protect a claim for payment of a debt.

Life Estate An interest in land that exists only for the duration of the life of a specified individual, usually the holder of the estate.

Limited Liability Company (LLC) A hybrid form of business enterprise that offers the limited liability of a corporation and the tax advantages of a partnership.

Limited Liability Partnership (LLP) A hybrid form of business organization that is used mainly by professionals who normally do business in a partnership. An LLP is a pass-through entity for tax purposes, but a partner's personal liability for the malpractice of other partners is limited.

Limited Partner In a limited partnership, a partner who contributes capital to the partnership but has no right to participate in its management and has no liability for partnership debts beyond the amount of her or his investment.

Limited Partnership (LP) A partnership consisting of one or more general partners and one or more limited partners.

Liquidated Damages An amount, stipulated in a contract, that the parties to the contract believe to be a reasonable estimation of the damages that will occur in the event of a breach.

Liquidated Debt A debt whose amount has been ascertained, fixed, agreed on, settled, or exactly determined.

Liquidation The sale of the nonexempt assets of a debtor and the distribution of the funds received to creditors.

Litigation The process of resolving a dispute through the court system.

Living (Inter Vivos) Trust A trust created by the grantor (settlor) and effective during his or her lifetime.

Lockout An action in which an employer shuts down to prevent employees from working, typically because it cannot reach a collective bargaining agreement with the employees' union.

Long Arm Statute A state statute that permits a state to exercise jurisdiction over nonresident defendants.

Lost Property Property that the owner has involuntarily by the owner.

M

Mailbox Rule A common law rule that acceptance takes effect, and thus completes formation of the contract, at the time the offeree sends or delivers the acceptance via the communication mode expressly or impliedly authorized by the offeror.

Majority Opinion A court opinion that represents the views of the majority (more than half) of the judges or justices deciding the case.

Maker One who promises to pay a fixed amount of funds to the holder of a promissory note or a certificate of deposit (CD).

Malpractice Professional misconduct or the lack of the requisite degree of skill as a professional. Professional negligence, or failure to exercise reasonable care and professional judgment, that results in injury, loss, or damage to those relying on the professional.

Malware Malicious software programs, such as viruses and worms, that are designed to cause harm to a computer, network, or other device.

Market Concentration The degree to which a small number of firms control a large percentage of a relevant market.

Market Power The power of a firm to control the market price of its product. A monopoly has the greatest degree of market power.

Market-Share Liability A theory under which liability is shared among all firms that manufactured and distributed a particular product during a certain period of time. This form of liability sharing is used only when the specific source of the harmful product is unidentifiable.

Mechanic's Lien A nonpossessory, filed lien on an owner's real estate for labor, services, or materials furnished for making improvements on the realty.

Mediation A method of settling disputes outside the courts by using the services of a neutral third party, who acts as a communicating agent between the parties and assists them in negotiating a settlement.

Member A person who has an ownership interest in a limited liability company.

Mens Rea A wrongful mental state ("guilty mind"), or intent; one of the two essential elements required to establish criminal liability.

Merchant Under the UCC, a person who deals in goods of the kind involved in the sales contract or who holds herself or himself out as having skill or knowledge peculiar to the practices or goods being purchased or sold.

Metadata Data that are automatically recorded by electronic devices and provide information about who created a file and when, and who accessed, modified, or transmitted the file on their hard drives. Can be described as data about data.

Meta Tag A key word in a document that can serve as an index reference to the document. On the Web, search engines return results based, in part, on the tags in Web documents.

Minimum Wage The lowest wage, either by government regulation or union contract, that an employer may pay an hourly worker.

Mirror Image Rule A common law rule that requires that the terms of the offeree's acceptance adhere exactly to the terms of the offeror's offer for a valid contract to be formed.

Misdemeanor A lesser crime than a felony, punishable by a fine or incarceration in jail for up to one year.

Mislaid Property Property that the owner has voluntarily parted with and then has inadvertently forgotten.

Mitigation of Damages The requirement that a plaintiff do whatever is reasonable to minimize the damages caused by the defendant's breach of contract.

Money Laundering Engaging in financial transactions to conceal the identity, source, or destination of illegally gained funds.

Monopolization The possession of monopoly power in the relevant market and the willful acquisition or maintenance of that power, as distinguished from growth or development as a consequence of a superior product, business acumen, or historic accident.

Monopoly A market in which there is a single seller or a very limited number of sellers.

Monopoly Power The ability of a monopoly to dictate what takes place in a given market.

Moral Minimum The minimum level of ethical behavior expected by society, which is usually defined as compliance with the law.

Mortgage A written instrument that gives a creditor an interest in, or lien on, a debtor's real property as security for a debt.

Motion for a Directed Verdict A motion for the judge to take the decision out of the hands of the jury and to direct a verdict for the party making the motion on the ground that the other party has not produced sufficient evidence to support her or his claim.

Motion for a New Trial A motion asserting that the trial was so fundamentally flawed (because of error, newly discovered evidence, prejudice, or another reason) that a new trial is necessary to prevent a miscarriage of justice.

Motion for Judgment *n.o.v.* A motion requesting the court to grant judgment in favor of the party making the motion on the ground that the jury's verdict against him or her was unreasonable and erroneous.

Motion for Judgment on the Pleadings A motion by either party to a lawsuit at the close of the pleadings requesting the court to decide the issue solely on the pleadings without proceeding to trial. The motion will be granted only if no facts are in dispute.

Motion for Summary Judgment A motion requesting the court to enter a judgment without proceeding to trial. The motion can be based on evidence outside the pleadings and will be granted only if no facts are in dispute.

Motion to Dismiss A pleading in which a defendant admits the facts as alleged by the plaintiff but asserts that the plaintiff's claim to state a cause of action has no basis in law.

Multiple Product Order An order requiring a firm that has engaged in deceptive advertising to cease and desist from false advertising in regard to all the firm's products.

Mutual Fund A specific type of investment company that continually buys or sells to investors shares of ownership in a portfolio.

N

National Law Law that pertains to a particular nation (as opposed to international law).

Natural Law The oldest school of legal thought, based on the belief that the legal system should reflect universal ("higher") moral and ethical principles that are inherent in human nature.

Necessaries Necessities required for life, such as food, shelter, clothing, and medical attention.

Negligence The failure to exercise the standard of care that a reasonable person would exercise in similar circumstances.

Negligence *Per Se* An action or failure to act in violation of a statutory requirement.

Negligent Misrepresentation A misrepresentation that occurs when a person makes a false statement of fact because he or she did not exercise reasonable care or use the skill and competence required by her or his business or profession.

Negotiable Instrument A signed writing (record) that contains an unconditional promise or order to pay an exact sum on demand or at a specified future time to a specific person or order, or to bearer.

Negotiation A process in which parties attempt to settle their dispute informally, with or without attorneys to represent them. In the context of negotiable instruments, the transfer of an instrument in such form that the transferee (the person to whom the instrument is transferred) becomes a holder.

Nominal Damages A small monetary award (often one dollar) granted to a plaintiff when no actual damage was suffered.

Nonpossessory Interest In the context of real property, an interest that involves the right to use land but not the right to possess it.

Normal Trade Relations (NTR) Status A legal trade status granted to member countries of the World Trade Organization.

Notary Public A public official authorized to attest to the authenticity of signatures.

Novation The substitution, by agreement, of a new contract for an old one, with the rights under the old one being terminated.

Nuisance A common law doctrine under which persons may be held liable for using their property in a manner that unreasonably interferes with others' rights to use or enjoy their own property.

Nuncupative Will An oral will (often called a *deathbed will*) made before witnesses. Usually, such wills are limited to transfers of personal property.

O

Objective Theory of Contracts The view that contracting parties shall only be bound by terms that can be objectively inferred from promises made.

Obligee One to whom an obligation is owed.

Obligor One who owes an obligation to another.

Offer A promise or commitment to perform or refrain from performing some specified act in the future.

Offeree A person to whom an offer is made.

Offeror A person who makes an offer.

Online Dispute Resolution (ODR) The resolution of disputes with the assistance of organizations that offer dispute-resolution services via the Internet.

Operating Agreement An agreement in which the members of a limited liability company set forth the details of how the business will be managed and operated.

Option Contract A contract under which the offeror cannot revoke the offer for a stipulated time period (because the offeree has given consideration for the offer to remain open).

Order for Relief A court's grant of assistance to a complainant. In bankruptcy proceedings, the order relieves the debtor of the immediate obligation to pay the debts listed in the bankruptcy petition.

Order Instrument A negotiable instrument that is payable "to the order of an identified person" or "to an identified person or order."

Ordinance A regulation enacted by a city or county legislative body that becomes part of that state's statutory law.

Outcome-based Ethics An ethical philosophy that focuses on the impacts of a decision on society or on key stakeholders.

Output Contract An agreement in which a seller agrees to sell and a buyer agrees to buy all or up to a stated amount of what the seller produces.

Outside Director A person on the board of directors who does not hold a management position at the corporation.

Overdraft A check that is paid by a bank when the checking account on which the check is written contains insufficient funds to cover the check.

P

Parol Evidence Rule A rule of contracts under which a court will not receive into evidence prior or contemporaneous external agreements that contradict the terms of the parties' written contract.

Partially Disclosed Principal A principal whose identity is unknown by a third party, but the third party knows that the agent is or may be acting for a principal at the time the agent and the third party form a contract.

Partnering Agreement An agreement between a seller and a buyer who frequently do business with each other concerning the terms and conditions that will apply to all subsequently formed electronic contracts.

Partnership An agreement by two or more persons to carry on, as co-owners, a business for profit.

Partnership by Estoppel A partnership imposed by a court when nonpartners have held themselves out to be partners, or have allowed themselves to be held out as partners, and others have detrimentally relied on their misrepresentations.

Pass-Through Entity A business entity that has no tax liability. The entity's income is passed through to the owners, and they pay taxes on the income.

Past Consideration An act that takes place before a contract is made and that ordinarily, by itself, cannot later be consideration with respect to that contract.

Patent A property right granted by the federal government that gives an inventor an exclusive right to make, use, sell, or offer to sell an invention in the United States for a limited time.

Payee A person to whom an instrument is made payable.

Payor Bank The bank on which a check is drawn (the drawee bank).

Peer-to-Peer (P2P) Networking The sharing of resources (such as files, hard drives, and processing styles) among multiple computers without the requirement of a central network server.

Penalty A contract clause that specifies a certain amount to be paid in the event of a default or breach of contract but is unenforceable because it is designed to punish the breaching party rather than to provide a reasonable estimate of damages.

Per Capita A method of distributing an intestate's estate so that each heir in a certain class (such as grandchildren) receives an equal share.

***Per Curiam* Opinion** A court opinion that does not indicate which judge or justice authored the opinion.

Perfection The legal process by which secured parties protect themselves against the claims of third parties who may wish to have their debts satisfied out of the same collateral. It is usually accomplished by filing a financing statement with the appropriate government official.

Performance The fulfillment of one's duties under a contract—the normal way of discharging one's contractual obligations.

Periodic Tenancy A lease interest in land for an indefinite period involving payment of rent at fixed intervals, such as week to week, month to month, or year to year.

***Per Se* Violation** A restraint of trade that is so anticompetitive that it is deemed inherently (*per se*) illegal.

Personal Defense A defense that can be used to avoid payment to an ordinary holder of a negotiable instrument but not a holder in due course (HDC) or a holder with the rights of an HDC.

Personal Property Property that is movable. Any property that is not real property.

Per Stirpes A method of distributing an intestate's estate so that each heir in a certain class (such as grandchildren) takes the share to which her or his deceased ancestor (such as a mother or father) would have been entitled.

Persuasive Authority Any legal authority or source of law that a court may look to for guidance but need not follow when making its decision.

Petition in Bankruptcy The document that is filed with a bankruptcy court to initiate bankruptcy proceedings.

Petty Offense The least serious kind of criminal offense, such as a traffic or building-code violation.

Phishing A form of identity theft in which the perpetrator sends e-mails purporting to be from legitimate businesses to induce recipients to reveal their personal financial data, passwords, or other information.

Piercing the Corporate Veil The action of a court to disregard the corporate entity and hold the shareholders personally liable for corporate debts and obligations.

Plaintiff One who initiates a lawsuit.

Plea Bargaining The process by which a criminal defendant and the prosecutor work out an agreement to dispose of the criminal case, subject to court approval.

Pleadings Statements by the plaintiff and the defendant that detail the facts, charges, and defenses of a case.

Pledge A security device in which personal property is transferred into the possession of the creditor as security for the payment of a debt and retained by the creditor until the debt is paid.

Plurality Opinion A court opinion that is joined by the largest number of the judges or justices hearing the case, but less than half of the total number.

Police Powers Powers possessed by the states as part of their inherent sovereignty. These powers may be exercised to protect or promote the public order, health, safety, morals, and general welfare.

Policy In insurance law, the contract between the insurer and the insured.

Potentially Responsible Party (PRP) A party liable for the costs of cleaning up a hazardous waste disposal site under the Comprehensive Environmental Response, Compensation, and Liability Act.

Power of Attorney Authorization for another to act as one's agent or attorney either in specified circumstances (special) or in all situations (general).

Precedent A court decision that furnishes an example or authority for deciding subsequent cases involving identical or similar facts.

Predatory Pricing The pricing of a product below cost with the intent to drive competitors out of the market.

Predominant-Factor Test A test courts use to determine whether a contract is primarily for the sale of goods or for the sale of services.

Preemption A doctrine under which certain federal laws preempt, or take precedence over, conflicting state or local laws.

Preemptive Rights The right of a shareholder in a corporation to have the first opportunity to purchase a new issue of that corporation's stock in proportion to the amount of stock already owned by the shareholder.

Preference In bankruptcy proceedings, a property transfer or payment made by the debtor that favors one creditor over others.

Preferred Creditor In the context of bankruptcy, a creditor who has received a preferential transfer from a debtor.

Preferred Stock Stock that has priority over common stock as to payment of dividends and distribution of assets on the corporation's dissolution.

Premium In insurance law, the price paid by the insured for insurance protection for a specified period of time.

Prenuptial Agreement An agreement made before marriage that defines each partner's ownership rights in the other partner's property. Prenuptial agreements must be in writing to be enforceable.

Prepayment Penalty Clause A mortgage provision requiring the borrower to pay a penalty if the mortgage is repaid in full within a certain period.

Presentment The act of presenting an instrument to the party liable on the instrument in order to collect payment. Presentment also occurs when a person presents an instrument to a drawee for a required acceptance.

Presentment Warranty A person who presents an instrument for payment or acceptance impliedly makes three warranties relating to good title, no alterations, and no unauthorized signatures.

Price Discrimination A seller's act of charging competing buyers different prices for identical products or services.

Price-Fixing Agreement An agreement between competitors to fix the prices of products or services at a certain level.

Prima Facie Case A case in which the plaintiff has produced sufficient evidence of his or her claim that the case will be decided for the plaintiff unless the defendant produces no evidence to rebut it.

Primary Source of Law A document that establishes the law on a particular issue, such as a constitution, a statute, an administrative rule, or a court decision.

Principle of Rights The belief that human beings have certain fundamental rights. Whether an action or decision is ethical depends on how it affects the rights of various groups, such as owners, employees, consumers, suppliers, the community, and society.

Private Equity Capital Funds invested by a private equity firm in an existing corporation, usually to purchase and reorganize it.

Privilege A special right, advantage, or immunity that enables a person or a class of persons to avoid liability for defamation.

Privity of Contract The relationship that exists between the promisor and the promisee of a contract.

Probable Cause Reasonable grounds for believing that a search should be conducted or that a person should be arrested.

Probate The process of proving and validating a will and settling all matters pertaining to an estate.

Probate Court A state court of limited jurisdiction that conducts proceedings relating to the settlement of a deceased person's estate.

Procedural Law Law that establishes the methods of enforcing the rights established by substantive law.

Proceeds Under Article 9 of the UCC, whatever is received when collateral is sold or disposed of in some other way.

Product Liability The legal liability of manufacturers, sellers, and lessors of goods for injuries or damage caused by the goods to consumers, users, or bystanders.

Profit In real property law, the right to enter onto another's property and remove something of value from that property.

Promise A declaration that binds a person who makes it (the promisor) to do or not to do a certain act.

Promisee A person to whom a promise is made.

Promisor A person who makes a promise.

Promissory Estoppel A doctrine that can be used to enforce a promise when the promisee has justifiably relied on the promise and when justice will be better served by enforcing the promise.

Promissory Note A written promise made by one person (the maker) to pay a fixed amount of funds to another person (the payee or a subsequent holder) on demand or on a specified date.

Prospectus A written document required by securities laws when a security is being sold. The prospectus describes the security, the financial operations of the issuing corporation, and the risk attaching to the security.

Protected Class A group of persons protected by specific laws because of the group's defining characteristics, including race, color, religion, national origin, gender, age, and disability.

Proximate Cause Legal cause. It exists when the connection between an act and an injury is strong enough to justify imposing liability.

Proxy When a shareholder formally authorizes another to serve as his or her agent and vote his or her shares in a certain manner.

Publicly Held Corporation A corporation whose shares are publicly traded in securities markets, such as the New York Stock Exchange or the NASDAQ.

Puffery A salesperson's exaggerated claims concerning the quality of property offered for sale. Such claims involve opinions rather than facts and are not legally binding promises or warranties.

Punitive Damages Monetary damages that may be awarded to a plaintiff to punish the defendant and deter similar conduct in the future.

Purchase-Money Security Interest (PMSI) A security interest that arises when a seller or lender extends credit for part or all of the purchase price of goods purchased by a buyer.

Q

Qualified Indorsement An indorsement on a negotiable instrument in which the indorser disclaims any contract liability on the instrument. The notation "without recourse" is commonly used to create a qualified indorsement.

Quantum Meruit A Latin phrase meaning "as much as he or she deserves." The expression describes the extent of compensation owed under a quasi contract.

Quasi Contract An obligation or contract imposed by law (a court), in the absence of an agreement, to prevent the unjust enrichment of one party.

Question of Fact In a lawsuit, an issue that involves only disputed facts, and not what the law is on a given point.

Question of Law In a lawsuit, an issue involving the application or interpretation of a law.

Quitclaim Deed A deed that conveys only whatever interest the grantor had in the property and therefore offers the least amount of protection against defects of title.

Quorum The number of members of a decision-making body that must be present before business may be transacted.

Quota A set limit on the amount of goods that can be imported.

R

Ratification The acceptance or confirmation of an act or agreement that gives legal force to an obligation that previously was not enforceable.

Reaffirmation Agreement An agreement between a debtor and a creditor in which the debtor voluntarily agrees to pay a debt dischargeable in bankruptcy.

Real Property Land and everything attached to it, such as trees and buildings.

Reasonable Person Standard The standard of behavior expected of a hypothetical "reasonable person." It is the standard against which negligence is measured and that must be observed to avoid liability for negligence.

Receiver In a corporate dissolution, a court-appointed person who winds up corporate affairs and liquidates corporate assets.

Record Information that is either inscribed on a tangible medium or stored in an electronic or other medium and is retrievable.

Recording Statute A statute that allow deeds, mortgages, and other real property transactions to be recorded so as to provide notice to future purchasers or creditors of an existing claim on the property.

Reformation A court-ordered correction of a written contract so that it reflects the true intentions of the parties.

Regulation E A set of rules issued by the Federal Reserve System's Board of Governors to protect users of electronic fund transfer systems.

Regulation Z A set of rules issued by the Federal Reserve Board of Governors to implement the provisions of the Truth-in-Lending Act.

Release An agreement in which one party gives up the right to pursue a legal claim against another party.

Remedy The relief given to an innocent party to enforce a right or compensate for the violation of a right.

Replevin An action that can be used by a buyer or lessee to recover identified goods from a third party, such as a bailee, who is wrongfully withholding them.

Reply Procedurally, a plaintiff's response to a defendant's answer.

Requirements Contract An agreement in which a buyer agrees to purchase and the seller agrees to sell all or up to a stated amount of what the buyer needs or requires.

Resale Price Maintenance Agreement An agreement between a manufacturer and a retailer in which the manufacturer specifies what the retail prices of its products must be.

Rescission A remedy whereby a contract is canceled and the parties are returned to the positions they occupied before the contract was made.

Res Ipsa Loquitur A doctrine under which negligence may be inferred simply because an event occurred, if it is the type of event that would not occur in the absence of negligence. Literally, the term means "the facts speak for themselves."

Respondeat Superior A doctrine under which a principal or an employer is held liable for the wrongful acts committed by agents or employees while acting within the course and scope of their agency or employment.

Restitution An equitable remedy under which a person is restored to his or her original position prior to loss or injury, or placed in the position he or she would have been in had the breach not occurred.

Restrictive Indorsement An indorsement on a negotiable instrument that requires the indorsee to comply with certain instructions regarding the funds involved.

Resulting Trust An implied trust that arises when one party holds the legal title to another's property only for that other's benefit.

Retained Earnings The portion of a corporation's profits that has not been paid out as dividends to shareholders.

Revocation The withdrawal of a contract offer by the offeror. Unless an offer is irrevocable, it can be revoked at any time prior to acceptance without liability.

Right of Contribution The right of a co-surety who pays more than his or her proportionate share on a debtor's default to recover the excess paid from other co-sureties.

Right of Reimbursement The right of a party to be repaid for costs, expenses, or losses incurred on behalf of another.

Right of Subrogation The right of a party to stand in the place of another, giving the substituted party the same legal rights that the original party had.

Right-to-Work Law A state law providing that employees may not be required to join a union as a condition of retaining employment.

Risk A prediction concerning potential loss based on known and unknown factors.

Risk Management In the context of insurance, the transfer of certain risks from the insured to the insurance company by contractual agreement.

Robbery The act of forcefully and unlawfully taking personal property of any value from another.

Rulemaking The process by which an administrative agency formally adopts a new regulation or amends an old one.

Rule of Four A rule of the United States Supreme Court under which the Court will not issue a writ of *certiorari* unless at least four justices approve of the decision to issue the writ.

Rule of Reason A test used to determine whether an anticompetitive agreement constitutes a reasonable restraint on trade. Courts consider such factors as the purpose of the agreement, its effect on competition, and whether less restrictive means could have been used.

S

Sale The passing of title to property from the seller to the buyer for a price.

Sales Contract A contract for the sale of goods.

Scienter Knowledge on the part of a misrepresenting party that material facts have been falsely represented or omitted with an intent to deceive.

S Corporation A close business corporation that has most corporate attributes, including limited liability, but qualifies under the Internal Revenue Code to be taxed as a partnership.

Search Warrant An order granted by a public authority, such as a judge, that authorizes law enforcement personnel to search particular premises or property.

Seasonably Within a specified time period or, if no period is specified, within a reasonable time.

Secondary Source of Law A publication that summarizes or interprets the law, such as a legal encyclopedia, a legal treatise, or an article in a law review.

SEC Rule 10b-5 A rule of the Securities and Exchange Commission that prohibits the commission of fraud in connection with the purchase or sale of any security.

Secured Party A creditor who has a security interest in the debtor's collateral, including a seller, lender, cosigner, or buyer of accounts or chattel paper.

Secured Transaction Any transaction in which the payment of a debt is guaranteed, or secured, by personal property owned by the debtor or in which the debtor has a legal interest.

Securities Generally, stocks, bonds, or other items that represent an ownership interest in a corporation or a promise of repayment of debt by a corporation.

Security Agreement An agreement that creates or provides for a security interest between the debtor and a secured party.

Security Interest Any interest in personal property or fixtures that secures payment or performance of an obligation.

Self-Defense The legally recognized privilege to do what is reasonably necessary to protect oneself, one's property, or someone else against injury by another.

Self-Incrimination Giving testimony in a trial or other legal proceeding that could expose the person testifying to criminal prosecution.

Seniority System A system in which those who have worked longest for an employer are first in line for promotions, salary increases, and other benefits, and are last to be laid off if the workforce must be reduced.

Service Mark A trademark that is used to distinguish the services (rather than the products) of one person or company from those of another.

Service of Process The delivery of the complaint and summons to a defendant.

Sexual Harassment The demanding of sexual favors in return for job promotions or other benefits, or language or conduct that is so sexually offensive that it creates a hostile working environment.

Shareholder's Derivative Suit A suit brought by a shareholder to enforce a corporate cause of action against a third person.

Shelter Principle The principle that the holder of a negotiable instrument who cannot qualify as a holder in due course (HDC), but who derives his or her title through an HDC, acquires the rights of an HDC.

Shipment Contract A contract for the sale of goods in which the seller is required or authorized to ship the goods by carrier. The seller assumes liability for any losses or damage to the goods until they are delivered to the carrier.

Short Sale A sale of mortgaged property for less than the balance due on the mortgage loan.

Short-Swing Profits Profits earned by a purchase and sale, or sale and purchase, of the same security within a six-month period.

Shrink-Wrap Agreement An agreement whose terms are expressed in a document located inside a box in which goods (usually software) are packaged.

Slander Defamation in oral form.

Slander of Quality (Trade Libel) The publication of false information about another's product, alleging that it is not what its seller claims.

Slander of Title The publication of a statement that denies or casts doubt on another's legal ownership of property, causing financial loss to that property's owner.

Small Claims Court A special court in which parties can litigate small claims without an attorney.

Smart Card A card containing a microprocessor and typically used for financial transactions, personal identification, and other purposes.

Social Media Forms of communication through which users create and share information, ideas, messages, and other content via the Internet.

Sole Proprietorship The simplest form of business organization, in which the owner is the business. The owner reports business income on his or her personal income tax return and is legally responsible for all debts and obligations incurred by the business.

Sovereign Immunity A doctrine that immunizes foreign nations from the jurisdiction of U.S. courts when certain conditions are satisfied.

Spam Bulk, unsolicited (junk) e-mail.

Special Damages In a tort case, an amount awarded to compensate the plaintiff for quantifiable monetary losses, such as medical expenses, property damage, and lost wages and benefits (now and in the future).

Special Indorsement An indorsement on an instrument that identifies the specific person to whom the indorser intends to make the instrument payable.

Special Warranty Deed A deed that warrants only that the grantor held good title during his or her ownership of the property and does not warrant that there were no defects of title when the property was held by previous owners.

Specific Performance An equitable remedy in which a court orders the parties to perform as promised in the contract. This remedy normally is granted only when the legal remedy (monetary damages) is inadequate.

Spendthrift Trust A trust created to protect the beneficiary from spending all the funds to which she or he is entitled. Only a certain portion of the total amount is given to the beneficiary at any one time, and most states prohibit creditors from attaching assets of the trust.

Stakeholders Groups that are affected by corporate decisions. Stakeholders include employees, customers, creditors, suppliers, and the community in which the corporation operates.

Stale Check A check, other than a certified check, that is presented for payment more than six months after its date.

Standing to Sue The legal requirement that an individual must have a sufficient stake in a controversy before he or she can bring a lawsuit.

Stare Decisis A common law doctrine under which judges are obligated to follow the precedents established in prior decisions.

Statute of Frauds A state statute that requires certain types of contracts to be in writing to be enforceable.

Statute of Repose A statute that places outer time limits on product liability actions. Such statutes cut off absolutely the right to bring an action after a specified period of time following some event (often the product's manufacture or purchase) other than the occurrence of an injury.

Statutory Law The body of law enacted by legislative bodies (as opposed to constitutional law, administrative law, or case law).

Statutory Right of Redemption A right provided by statute in some states under which mortgagors can redeem or purchase their property after a judicial foreclosure for a limited time period, such as one year.

Stock An ownership (equity) interest in a corporation, measured in units of shares.

Stock Certificate A certificate issued by a corporation evidencing the ownership of a specified number of shares in the corporation.

Stock Option A right to buy a given number of shares of stock at a set price, usually within a specified time period.

Stop-Payment Order An order by a bank customer to his or her bank not to pay or certify a certain check.

Stored-Value Card A card bearing a magnetic strip that holds magnetically encoded data providing access to stored funds.

Strict Liability Liability regardless of fault, which is imposed on those engaged in abnormally dangerous activities, on persons who keep dangerous animals, and on manufacturers or sellers that introduce into commerce defective and unreasonably dangerous goods.

Strike An action undertaken by unionized workers when collective bargaining fails. The workers leave their jobs, refuse to work, and (typically) picket the employer's workplace.

Sublease A tenant's transfer of all or part of the leased premises to a third person for a period shorter than the lease term.

Substantive Law Law that defines, describes, regulates, and creates legal rights and obligations.

Summary Jury Trial (SJT) A method of settling disputes by holding a trial in which the jury's verdict is not binding but instead guides the parties toward reaching an agreement during the mandatory negotiations that immediately follow.

Summons A document informing a defendant that a legal action has been commenced against her or him and that the defendant must appear in court on a certain date to answer the plaintiff's complaint.

Supremacy Clause The provision in Article VI of the U.S. Constitution that the Constitution, laws, and treaties of the United States are "the supreme Law of the Land."

Surety A third party who promises to be responsible for a debtor's obligation under a suretyship arrangement.

Suretyship A promise made by a third party to be responsible for a debtor's obligation.

Symbolic Speech Nonverbal expressions of beliefs. Symbolic speech, which includes gestures, movements, and articles of clothing, is given substantial protection by the courts.

Syndicate A group of individuals or firms that join together to finance a project. A syndicate is also called an *investment group*.

T

Taking The taking of private property by the government for public use through the power of eminent domain.

Tangible Employment Action A significant change in employment status or benefits, such as occurs when an employee is fired, refused a promotion, or reassigned to a lesser position.

Tangible Property Property that has physical existence and can be distinguished by the senses of touch and sight.

Tariff A tax on imported goods.

Tenancy at Sufferance A tenancy that arises when a tenant wrongfully continues to occupy leased property after the lease has terminated.

Tenancy at Will A type of tenancy that either the landlord or the tenant can terminate without notice.

Tenancy by the Entirety Joint ownership of property by a married couple in which neither spouse can transfer his or her interest in the property without the consent of the other.

Tenancy in Common Joint ownership of property in which each party owns an undivided interest that passes to his or her heirs at death.

Tender An unconditional offer to perform an obligation by a person who is ready, willing, and able to do so.

Tender of Delivery A seller's or lessor's act of placing conforming goods at the disposal of the buyer or lessee and providing whatever notification is reasonably necessary to enable the buyer or lessee to take delivery.

Testamentary Trust A trust that is created by will and therefore does not take effect until the death of the testator.

Testate Having left a will at death.

Testator One who makes and executes a will.

Third Party Beneficiary One who is not a party to the contract but who stands to benefit from the contract's performance.

Tippee A person who receives inside information.

Tolling Temporary suspension of the running of a prescribed time period, such as a statute of limitations.

Tort A wrongful act (other than a breach of contract) that results in harm or injury to another and leads to civil liability.

Tortfeasor One who commits a tort.

Totten Trust A trust created when a person deposits funds in his or her own name for a specific beneficiary, who will receive the funds on the depositor's death. The trust is revocable at will until the depositor dies or completes the gift.

Toxic Tort A civil wrong arising from exposure to a toxic substance, such as asbestos, radiation, or hazardous waste.

Trade Dress The image and overall appearance of a product.

Trademark A distinctive word, symbol, or design that identifies the manufacturer as the source of particular goods and distinguishes its products from those made or sold by others.

Trademark Dilution The unauthorized use of a distinctive and famous mark in a way that impairs the mark's distinctiveness or harms its reputation.

Trade Name A name that a business uses to identify itself and its brand. A trade name is directly related to a business's reputation and goodwill and is protected under trademark law.

Trade Secret A formula, device, idea, process, or other information used in a business that gives the owner a competitive advantage in the marketplace.

Transferred Intent A legal principle under which a person who intends to harm one individual, but unintentionally harms a different individual, can be liable to the second victim for an intentional tort.

Transfer Warranty A person who transfers an instrument for consideration impliedly makes five warranties—relating to good title, authentic signatures, no alterations, defenses, or insolvencies—to all subsequent transferees.

Traveler's Check A check that is payable on demand, drawn on or payable through a financial institution, and designated as a traveler's check.

Treaty A formal international agreement negotiated between two nations or among several nations.

Treble Damages Damages that, by statute, are three times the amount of actual damages suffered.

Trespass to Land Entry onto, above, or below the surface of land owned by another without the owner's permission or legal authorization.

Trespass to Personal Property Wrongfully taking or harming the personal property of another or otherwise interfering with the lawful owner's possession of personal property.

Triple Bottom Line A measure that includes a corporation's profits, its impact on people, and its impact on the planet.

Trust An arrangement in which title to property is held by one person (a trustee) for the benefit of another (a beneficiary).

Trust Indorsement An indorsement to a person who is to hold or use funds for the benefit of the indorser or a third person. It is also known as an *agency indorsement*.

Tying Arrangement A seller's act of conditioning the sale of a product or service on the buyer's agreement to purchase another product or service from the seller.

Typosquatting A form of cybersquatting that relies on mistakes, such as typographical errors, made by Internet users when inputting information into a Web browser.

U

Ultra Vires Acts Acts of a corporation that are beyond its express and implied powers to undertake (the Latin phrase means "beyond the powers").

Unconscionable (Contract or Clause) A contract or clause that is void on the basis of public policy because one party was forced to accept terms that are unfairly burdensome and that unfairly benefit the other party.

Underwriter In insurance law, the insurer, or the one assuming a risk in return for the payment of a premium.

Undisclosed Principal A principal whose identity is unknown by a third party, and that person has no knowledge that the agent is acting for a principal at the time the agent and the third party form a contract.

Undue Influence Persuasion that is less than actual force but more than advice and that induces a person to act according to the will or purposes of the dominating party.

Unenforceable Contract A valid contract rendered unenforceable by some statute or law.

Uniform Law A model law developed by the National Conference of Commissioners on Uniform State Laws for the states to consider enacting into statute.

Unilateral Contract A type of contract that results when an offer can be accepted only by the offeree's performance.

Unilateral Mistake A mistake that occurs when one party to a contract is mistaken as to a material fact.

Union Shop A firm that requires all workers, once employed, to become union members within a specified period of time as a condition of their continued employment.

Universal Defense A defense that can be used to avoid payment to all holders of a negotiable instrument, including a holder in due course (HDC) or a holder with the rights of an HDC. Also called a *real defense*.

Unliquidated Debt A debt that is uncertain in amount.

Unreasonably Dangerous Product A product that is so defective that it is dangerous beyond the expectation of an ordinary consumer or a product for which a less dangerous alternative was feasible but the manufacturer failed to produce it.

Usage of Trade Any practice or method of dealing that is so regularly observed in a place, vocation, or trade that parties justifiably expect it will be observed in their transaction.

Usury Charging an illegal rate of interest.

Utilitarianism An approach to ethical reasoning in which an action is evaluated in terms of its consequences for those whom it will affect. A "good" action is one that results in the greatest good for the greatest number of people.

V

Valid Contract A contract that results when the elements necessary for contract formation (agreement, consideration, capacity, and legality) are present.

Venture Capital Financing provided by professional, outside investors (venture capitalists) to new business ventures.

Venue The geographic district in which a legal action is tried and from which the jury is selected.

Vertically Integrated Firm A firm that carries out two or more functional phases (manufacturing, distribution, and retailing, for example) of the chain of production.

Vertical Merger The acquisition by a company at one stage of production of a company at a higher or lower stage of production (such as a company merging with one of its suppliers or retailers).

Vertical Restraint A restraint of trade created by an agreement between firms at different levels in the manufacturing and distribution process.

Vesting The creation of an absolute or unconditional right or power.

Vicarious Liability Indirect liability imposed on a supervisory party (such as an employer) for the actions of a subordinate (such as an employee) because of the relationship between the two parties.

Virus A software program that can replicate itself over a network and spread from one device to another, altering files and interfering with normal operations.

Voidable Contract A contract that may be legally avoided at the option of one or both of the parties.

Void Contract A contract having no legal force or binding effect.

Voir Dire An important part of the jury selection process in which the attorneys question prospective jurors about their backgrounds, attitudes, and biases to ascertain whether they can be impartial jurors.

W

Warranty Deed A deed that provides the greatest amount of protection for the grantee. The grantor promises that she or he has title to the property conveyed in the deed, that there are no undisclosed encumbrances on the property, and that the grantee will enjoy quiet possession of the property.

Waste The use of real property in a manner that damages or destroys its value.

Whistleblowing An employee's disclosure to government authorities, upper-level managers, or the media that the employer is engaged in unsafe or illegal activities.

White-Collar Crime Nonviolent crime committed by individuals or corporations to obtain a personal or business advantage.

Will An instrument made by a testator directing what is to be done with her or his property after death.

Will Substitutes Various instruments, such as living trusts and life insurance plans, that may be used to avoid the formal probate process.

Winding Up The second of two stages in the termination of a partnership or corporation, in which the firm's assets are collected, liquidated, and distributed, and liabilities are discharged.

Workers' Compensation Laws State statutes that establish an administrative process for compensating workers for injuries that arise in the course of their employment, regardless of fault.

Working Papers The documents used and developed by an accountant during an audit, such as notes, computations, and memoranda.

Workout Agreement A contract that describes the respective rights and responsibilities of a borrower and a lender as they try to resolve the borrower's default.

Worm A software program that automatically replicates itself over a network but does not alter files and is usually invisible to the user until it has consumed system resources.

Writ of Attachment A court order to seize a debtor's nonexempt property prior to a court's final determination of a creditor's rights to the property.

Writ of Certiorari A writ from a higher court asking a lower court for the record of a case.

Writ of Execution A court order directing the sheriff to seize (levy) and sell a debtor's nonexempt real or personal property to satisfy a court's judgment in the creditor's favor.

Wrongful Discharge An employer's termination of an employee's employment in violation of the law or an employment contract.

Additional Cases

TABLE OF CASES

Case 4-1

In addition to showing that the tortfeasor engaged in negligent conduct (duty and breach), the victim of negligence must show that the breach was the proximate cause of harm to him. This case examines the issue of proximate cause.

Palsgraf v. Long Island Railroad Co.
Court of Appeals of New York, 1928
248 N.Y. 339; 162 N.E. 99

CARDOZO, C.J.

Plaintiff was standing on a platform of defendant's railroad after buying a ticket to go to Rockaway Beach. A train stopped at the station, bound for another place. Two men ran forward to catch it. One of the men reached the platform of the car without mishap, though the train was already moving. The other man, carrying a package, jumped aboard the car, but seemed unsteady as if about to fall. A guard on the car, who had held the door open, reached forward to help him in, and another guard on the platform pushed him from behind. In this act, the package was dislodged, and fell upon the rails. It was a package of small size, about fifteen inches long, and was covered by a newspaper. In fact it contained fireworks, but there was nothing in its appearance to give notice of its contents. The fireworks when they fell exploded. The shock of the explosion threw down some scales at the other end of the platform, many feet away. The scales struck the plaintiff, causing injuries for which she sues.

The conduct of the defendant's guard, if a wrong in its relation to the holder of the package, was not a wrong in its relation to the plaintiff, standing far away. Relatively to her it was not negligence at all. Nothing in the situation gave notice that the falling package had in it the potency of peril to persons thus removed. Negligence is not actionable unless it involves the invasion of a legally protected interest, the violation of a right. "Proof of negligence in the air, so to speak, will not do" [Citations] "Negligence is the absence of care, according to the circumstances." [Citations]

* * *

If no hazard was apparent to the eye of ordinary vigilance, an act innocent and harmless, at least to outward seeming, with reference to her, did not take to itself the quality of a tort because it happened to be a wrong, though apparently not one involving the risk of bodily insecurity, with reference to someone else. "In every instance, before negligence can be predicated of a given act, back of the act must be sought and found a duty to the individual complaining, the observance of which would have averted or avoided the injury." [Citation].

* * *

A different conclusion will involve us, and swiftly too, in a maze of contradictions. A guard stumbles over a package which has been left upon a platform. It seems to be a bundle of newspapers. It turns out to be a can of dynamite. To the eye of ordinary vigilance, the bundle is abandoned waste, which may be kicked or trod on with impunity. Is a passenger at the other end of the platform protected by the law against the unsuspected hazard concealed beneath the waste? If not, is the result to be any different, so far as the distant passenger is concerned, when the guard stumbles over a valise which a truckman or a porter has left upon the walk? The passenger far away, if the victim of a wrong at all, has a cause of action, not derivative, but original and primary. His claim to be protected against invasion of his bodily security is neither greater nor less because the act resulting in the invasion is a wrong to another far removed. In this case, the rights that are said to have been violated, the interests said to have been invaded, are not even of the same order. The man was not injured in his person nor even put in danger. The purpose of the act, as well as its effect, was to make his person safe. If there was a wrong to him at all, which may very well be doubted, it was a wrong to a property interest only, the safety of his package. Out of this wrong to property, which threatened injury to nothing else, there has passed, we are told, to the plaintiff by derivation or succession a right of action for the invasion of an interest of another order, the right to bodily security. The diversity of interests emphasizes the futility of the effort to build the plaintiff's right upon the basis of a wrong to someone else. . . . One who jostles one's neighbor in a crowd does not invade the rights of others standing at the outer fringe when the unintended contact casts a bomb upon the ground. The wrongdoer as to them is the man who carries the bomb, not the one who explodes it without suspicion of the danger. Life will have to be made over, and human nature transformed, before prevision so extravagant can be accepted as the norm of conduct, the customary standard to which behavior must conform.

The argument for the plaintiff is built upon the shifting meanings of such words as "wrong" and "wrongful," and shares their instability. What the plaintiff must show is "a wrong" to herself, *i. e.,* a violation of her own right, and not merely a wrong to someone else, nor conduct "wrongful" because unsocial, but not "a wrong" to anyone. We are told that one who drives at reckless speed through a crowded city street is guilty of a negligent act and, therefore, of a wrongful one irrespective of the consequences. Negligent the act is, and wrongful in the sense that it is unsocial, but wrongful and unsocial in relation to other travelers, only because the eye of vigilance perceives the risk of damage. If the same act were to be committed on a speedway or a race course, it would lose its wrongful quality. The risk reasonably to be perceived defines the duty to be obeyed, and risk imports relation; it is risk to another or to others within the range of apprehension. [Citations] This does not mean, of course, that one who launches a destructive force is always relieved of liability if the force, though known to be destructive, pursues an unexpected path. "It was not necessary that the defendant should have had notice of the particular method in which an accident would occur, if the possibility of an accident was clear to the ordinarily prudent eye." [Citations] Some acts, such as shooting, are so imminently dangerous to anyone who may come within reach of the missile, however unexpectedly, as to impose a duty of prevision not far from that of an insurer. Even today, and much oftener in earlier stages of the law, one acts sometimes at one's peril. [Citation] Under this head, it may be, fall certain cases of what is known as transferred intent, an act willfully dangerous to A resulting by misadventure in injury to B. [Citation] These cases aside, wrong is defined in terms of the natural or probable, at least when unintentional. [Citation] The range of reasonable apprehension is at times a question for the court, and at times, if varying inferences are possible, a question for the jury. Here, by concession, there was nothing in the situation to suggest to the most cautious mind that the parcel wrapped in newspaper would spread wreckage through the station. If the guard had thrown it down knowingly and willfully, he would not have threatened the plaintiff's safety, so far as appearances could warn him. His conduct would not have involved, even then, an unreasonable probability of invasion of her bodily security. Liability can be no greater where the act is inadvertent.

* * *

The judgment of the Appellate Division and that of the Trial Term should be reversed, and the complaint dismissed, with costs in all courts.

CASE 10-1

An implied in fact contract may be formed by the conduct of the parties, rather than by their words. This case illustrates how a court determines whether such a contract was formed, and if so, what its terms are.

WATTS v. COLUMBIA ARTISTS MANAGEMENT INC.
Appellate Division, New York (3rd Dept.), 1992
188 A.D.2d 799, 591 N.Y.S.2d 234

CASEY, Justice. Appeal (transferred to this court by order of the Appellate Division, Second Department) from a judgment of the Supreme Court (Weiner, J.), entered May 17, 1991 in Rockland County, upon a decision of the court in favor of defendant.

Plaintiff, a concert pianist, commenced this declaratory judgment action seeking, *inter alia,* a determination of his liability to defendant, which provides managerial services to performing artists, for services performed by defendant prior to September 1, 1988. Defendant began to provide its services to plaintiff in 1983 when it entered into a contract with Andre Watts Performances Inc. (hereinafter the Corporation), which provided that defendant would act as plaintiff's exclusive agent and that defendant would be compensated for its services by receiving, *inter alia,* 15% of plaintiff's earnings for American concerts, but defendant would be entitled to no fee if plaintiff was not paid for an engagement. Although the Corporation dissolved in August 1985 and the term of the contract expired September 1, 1986, defendant continued to provide services to plaintiff and plaintiff continued to pay for those services in the manner provided for in the expired contract between defendant and the Corporation. Plaintiff notified defendant in writing on August 9, 1988 that he wished to terminate his relationship with defendant effective September 1, 1988.

When the parties' relationship was terminated, defendant had scheduled a total of 82 engagements for plaintiff for the next two concert seasons. Contracts had been executed as of September 1, 1988 for 48 of the 82 scheduled engagements, and plaintiff performed and was paid for 46 of those 48 engagements. Of the remaining 34 scheduled engagements, for which no contract had been executed as of September 1, 1988, plaintiff performed 33 of them and was paid for 32 of the performances. Defendant claims entitlement to its 15% commission for all 78 of the engagements performed by plaintiff for which he was paid. Plaintiff contends that defendant is entitled to no commission on the 32 engagements for which no contract had been executed prior to September 1, 1988. As to the remaining 46 engagements, plaintiff contends that defendant is entitled only to one half of its usual 15% commission because additional managerial services, including travel arrangements, rehearsal schedules, piano delivery and tuning, receptions, master classes and other details, were required after September 1, 1988. According to plaintiff, the additional services were performed by another manager retained by plaintiff after September 1, 1988.

At the nonjury trial, plaintiff, an officer of defendant and other witnesses testified. Much of the testimony concerned the managerial services provided to plaintiff in particular and the industry practice in general. Supreme Court found that a contract implied in fact existed between the parties with the same terms and conditions as the expired written contract between the Corporation and defendant, and that defendant was entitled to full commissions for all 78 engagements at issue. Plaintiff appeals from the judgment entered on Supreme Court's decision.

According to plaintiff, Supreme Court erred in "piercing the corporate veil" to bind plaintiff to the terms and conditions of a contract to which he was not a party. Although Supreme Court's decision is not entirely clear on the issue, we read it as finding a separate and distinct contractual relationship between plaintiff and defendant, implied in fact, which arose out of the parties' continued relationship after the Corporation was dissolved and the written contract expired. A contract implied in fact rests upon the conduct of the parties and not their verbal or written words [Citation]. Thus, the theories of express contract and of contract implied in fact are mutually exclusive [Citation] Whether an implied-in-fact contract was formed and, if so, the extent of its terms involve factual issues regarding the intent of the parties and the surrounding circumstances [Citation]. We are of the view that the parties' conduct after the expiration of the written contract, including defendant's continued rendition of services, plaintiff's acceptance of those services and plaintiff's payment of commissions in accordance with the terms of the written contract, clearly establish a contract implied in fact with substantially the same terms and conditions as embodied in the expired written contract between defendant and the Corporation [Citations]. The mere fact that plaintiff was not a party to the written contract does not preclude the formation of a new contract, implied in fact, between plaintiff and defendant, with terms and conditions similar to those contained in the written contract.

The remaining question is whether defendant was entitled to full commissions on all 78 engagements booked by defendant prior to September 1, 1988 for which plaintiff was ultimately paid, as found by Supreme Court, or whether defendant was limited to the recovery of one half of its regular commission on only those 46 engagements for which a contract had been executed prior to September 1, 1988, as plaintiff contends. The evidence establishes that an engagement was booked by defendant when it arranged the date, time and fee for a performance, informed plaintiff of the engagement and was informed by plaintiff that he accepted the engagement. Plaintiff offered evidence that additional management services prior to the execution of a contract are necessary to assure a meeting of the minds between the presenter and plaintiff on the essential terms of the engagement. Defendant offered evidence that the essential terms of date, time and fee were arranged with the booking and that the execution of a contract was largely a formality, involving ministerial details. That plaintiff actually performed 33 of the 34 engagements booked by defendant for which no contract was executed prior to September 1, 1988 tends to support defendant's position. In any event, the terms of the written contract, which were continued by the parties in their new contract implied in fact formed after the expiration of the written contract, contains no reference to the execution of a formal contract with the presenter. Rather, defendant's commission is dependent upon the scheduling of the engagement during the term of the contract and plaintiff's receipt of payment for the engagement. We conclude, therefore, that Supreme Court correctly found plaintiff liable for commissions on all 78 bookings, regardless of whether a contract had been executed prior to September 1, 1988.

We also agree with Supreme Court that defendant is entitled to the full commission on each of the engagements. As previously noted, defendant earned its commission when the engagement was booked and plaintiff received payment for his performance, and it is undisputed that defendant remained ready, willing and able to provide the additional management services which plaintiff contends were necessary before he actually performed the engagements booked by defendant. That plaintiff elected to have those services performed by another manager does not, in the facts and circumstances revealed by the evidence in the record, preclude defendant from receiving the full amount of its commissions. Supreme Court's judgment should, therefore, be affirmed.

ORDERED that the judgment is affirmed, with costs.

CASE 10-2

Here a court applies the doctrine of promissory estoppel to an entertainer's promise to appear in a musical production although no contract had yet been agreed to.

ELVIN ASSOCIATES V. ARETHA FRANKLIN
United States District Court, S.D. New York, 1990
735 F. Supp. 1171

Whitman Knapp, District Judge.

* * *

In early 1984 Ashton Springer, the principal of plaintiff Elvin Associates, began efforts to mount a Broadway musical production about the life and music of Mahalia Jackson, and wrote to defendant Aretha Franklin seeking her agreement to appear in the title role. Franklin called Springer and expressed her strong interest in the production, and told Springer to contact her agents at the William Morris Agency. Springer spoke with Phil Citron and Katy Rothacker of that agency and in several conversations with the latter discussed the basic financial terms of Franklin's engagement to appear. Several proposals and counter-proposals were exchanged, in each instance relayed by Rothacker to Franklin and then back to Springer. Near the end of February 1984, Rothacker called Springer and informed him that his final proposal was acceptable.

In the interim, Springer had already set about making the necessary arrangements to get the production going. He was in frequent consultation with Franklin concerning artistic and production matters, although he negotiated the financial terms of the agreement strictly through her agents. During a conversation about rehearsal and performance dates, Franklin indicated to Springer that there were no other conflicting engagements on her schedule, stating: "This is what I am doing."

After consulting with Franklin, Springer hired George Faison as director-choreographer. In the second week of March, Springer and Faison flew to Detroit to meet with Franklin to discuss various aspects of the production, including rehearsal and performance dates. Franklin agreed on a tentative schedule that called for rehearsals to begin in April and performances to begin in May.

After returning to New York, Springer began negotiating limited partnership agreements with various investors to finance the "Mahalia" production. He also began calling promoters and theaters in various cities in an effort to reserve dates for performances. During discussions with several promoters he learned for the first time that Franklin had recently cancelled several performances, purportedly due to a newly acquired fear of flying. Springer spoke with Citron at William Morris regarding these incidents, and the latter stated that the cancellations resulted from commitments made by prior agents for Franklin without her approval, and reassured Springer that there was no such problem here. Springer also spoke with Franklin, who reassured him that she wanted to do the show and that she would fly as necessary. Springer offered to make alternative arrangements for transportation to the various performance sites, and to alter the performance schedule to accommodate slower forms of transportation. Franklin told Springer that she was uncomfortable traveling more than 200 miles per day by ground transportation, but strongly assured him that she would overcome her fear of flying.

Springer had also in the interim contacted Jay Kramer, his attorney, about the proposed production and the terms he had discussed with Franklin's representatives. Kramer set up a meeting for March 23, 1984 with Franklin's representatives for the purpose of finalizing the agreement.

* * *

A final draft of the contract was ready for signature as of June 7, the date that Franklin was scheduled to come to New York to begin rehearsals for the show.

Springer had in the intervening weeks made all of the arrangements necessary for rehearsals to begin. He had hired set, lighting and costume designers, stage and technical crew, and had reserved dance studios. Springer was in frequent communication with Franklin during this period, as were Faison and other members of the production staff, concerning such varied matters as the compositions to be performed, the costumes she would wear, and the hiring of her own regular backup singers to be in the chorus. At one point, Franklin sang one of the production songs to Springer over the telephone. At some point during this period, Faison made final determinations as to the compositions to be performed and as to the cast and chorus.

As planned, rehearsals actually began on June 4 without Franklin, and continued for several days. Franklin did not arrive in New York on June 7 and, indeed, never came to New York for the rehearsals. Kramer immediately sought an explanation from Franklin's representatives and was informed that she would not fly. Springer paid the cast through the end of that week, but then suspended the production. He attempted to secure some other well-known performer to fill the title role, but none of the performers whom he contacted would agree to step into the role at that juncture.

On July 18, after having positive discussions with Les Matthews, a Texas financier who purported to be interested in backing the production, Springer wrote to Franklin with a proposal to revive it, whereby rehearsals and opening performances would take place in Detroit, with Franklin covering the excess expense caused by such an arrangement. The terms of Franklin's profit-sharing would be altered to account for the losses and additional costs caused by the suspended production. In August Franklin agreed to sign a draft agreement (doing so only on behalf of Crown Productions) so that Springer could regain some of his lost credibility with potential investors. Franklin's attorney held the signed draft in escrow, release from which was expressly conditioned on Springer's finalization of a performance schedule.

A final performance schedule was never arranged. One of the difficulties Springer encountered was that, due to the collapse of the earlier production, theaters and concert halls were now requiring substantial deposits to reserve particular dates. Springer lacked the capital to make those deposits. Matthews failed to appear for the scheduled closing of the investment agreement in early September, and Springer was unable to obtain any other financing for the production. He ultimately abandoned this second attempt at mounting the "Mahalia" production.

This lawsuit ensued, with Springer (suing in the name of Elvin Associates) alleging breach of the original agreement to appear in "Mahalia," and Franklin counter-claiming for breach of the second agreement concerning the proposed Detroit-based production. In his pre-trial memorandum, Springer asserted an alternative right to recover on a theory of promissory estoppel.

DISCUSSION

The central issue pertaining to plaintiff's claim for breach of contract is whether or not the parties to that proposed contract, i.e. Springer, Crown Productions, Inc., and Franklin in her capacity as guarantor of Crown's performance, evinced an intent not to be formally bound before execution of a written, integrated contract. Language inserted in a draft of the agreement referring to its validity upon execution has generally been found to be strong (though not conclusive) evidence of intent *not* to be bound prior to execution. . . . Although we based our tentative findings largely on the fact that all of the incidental terms had been worked out by the final draft, and that the understanding was that Franklin would sign the agreement when she came to New York, there remains the obstacle of the preamble that Kramer drafted and that remained in every draft, namely: "This letter, when countersigned by you, shall constitute our understanding until a more formal agreement is prepared." After reviewing the above cited authorities and the post-trial submissions, we are constrained to find that such language indicates that Crown Productions, Inc. was not to be contractually bound to Springer until the draft agreement was executed. . . . The cause of action for breach of contract must therefore be dismissed as against both defendants . . .

That, however, does not end the case. As above noted, plaintiff has asserted, in the alternative, a right to recover on a theory of promissory estoppel. The elements of a claim for promissory estoppel are: "[A] clear and unambiguous promise; a reasonable and foreseeable reliance by the party to whom the promise is made; and an injury sustained by the party asserting the estoppel by reason of his reliance." The " 'circumstances [must be] such as to render it *unconscionable* to deny' the promise upon which plaintiff has relied." [Citations omitted.]

It is difficult to imagine a more fitting case for applying the above-described doctrine. Although for her own business purposes Franklin insisted that the formal contract be with the corporate entity through which her services were to be "furnished," in the real world the agreement was with her, and we find that she had unequivocally and intentionally committed herself to appear in the production long before day on which it was intended that the finalized agreement with her corporation would be signed.

First, it is clear from the testimony of all of the witnesses that Franklin was enthusiastic about appearing in the production and that at all times during the relevant period gave it the highest professional priority. She early on stated to Springer: "This is what I am doing." Combined with her oral agreement, through her agents, to the basic financial terms of her engagement, her continued expression of this enthusiasm to Springer more than amply afforded Springer a reasonable basis for beginning to make the various arrangements and expenditures necessary to bring the production to fruition.

Second, Franklin could not possibly have assumed that Springer could have performed his obligations to her-which, among other things, included arranging a complicated schedule of performances to commence shortly after her arrival in New York-without committing himself to and actually spending considerable sums prior to her affixing her signature to the contract on the date of such arrival. Throughout the time that he was making those commitments and advancing the necessary sums, she accepted his performance without any disclaimer of her prior promises to him. Indeed, she actively participated in many aspects of the necessary arrangements.

Third, Franklin's expression to Springer of her fear of flying did not, as she has contended, make her promise conditional or coat it with a patina of ambiguity that should have alerted Springer to suspend his efforts to mount the production. Although Franklin rejected Springer's offer to make alternative ground transportation arrangements, her primary reason for doing so was that she was determined to overcome her fear of flying, and it was reasonable for Springer to rely on her reassurances that she would be able to fly. Moreover, it was also entirely reasonable for him to assume that if she could not overcome her fear she would travel to New York by other means, even if it meant spreading the trip over several days. In short, Franklin's fear of flying provides no basis whatsoever for avoiding liability for failing to fulfill her promise, reiterated on several occasions, to appear in "Mahalia." If she could not bring herself to fly, she should have traveled by way of ground transportation. It has not been established that she was otherwise unable to come to New York to meet her obligations.

We conclude that under the circumstances as we have outlined them it would be unconscionable not to compensate Springer for the losses he incurred through his entirely justified reliance on Franklin's oral promises. A determination of the exact amount to be awarded has been reserved for a later trial on damages.

CASE 11-1

The following case involves the question of whether an advertisement constitutes an offer.

Lefkowitz v. Great Minneapolis Surplus Store Inc.

Minn. Sup. Ct. 1957
251 Minn. 188, 86 N.W.2d 689

Murphy, J.

This is an appeal from an order of the municipal court of Minneapolis denying the motion of the defendant for amended findings of fact, or, in the alternative, for a new trial. The order for judgment awarded the plaintiff the sum of $138.50 as damages for breach of contract.

This case grows out of the alleged refusal of the defendant to sell to the plaintiff a certain fur piece which it had offered for sale in a newspaper advertisement. It appears from the record that on April 6, 1956, the defendant published the following advertisement in a Minneapolis newspaper:

'Saturday 9 A.M. sharp 3 brand new fur coats worth to $100.00

First come first served $1 each'

On April 13, the defendant again published an advertisement in the same

Newspaper as follows: 'Saturday 9 A.M. 2 brand new pastel mink 3-skin scarfs selling for $89.50

Out they go Saturday. Each ... $1.00

1 black lapin stole beautiful, worth $139.50 ... $1.00

First come first served'

The record supports the findings of the court that on each of the Saturdays following the publication of the above-described ads the plaintiff was the first to present himself at the appropriate counter in the defendant's store and on each occasion demanded the coat and the stole so advertised and indicated his readiness to pay the sale price of $1. On both occasions, the defendant refused to sell the merchandise to the plaintiff, stating on the first occasion that by a 'house rule' the offer was intended for women only and sales would not be made to men, and on the second visit that plaintiff knew defendant's house rules.

* * *

The defendant contends that a newspaper advertisement offering items of merchandise for sale at a named price is a 'unilateral offer' which may be withdrawn without notice. He relies upon authorities which hold that, where an advertiser publishes in a newspaper that he has a certain quantity or quality of goods which he wants to dispose of at certain prices and on certain terms, such advertisements are not offers which become contracts as soon as any person to whose notice they may come signifies his acceptance by notifying the other that he will take a certain quantity of them. Such advertisements have been construed as an invitation for an offer of sale on the terms stated, which offer, when received, may be accepted or rejected and which therefore does not become a contract of sale until accepted by the seller; and until a contract has been so made, the seller [Citations]

* * *

. . . . On the facts before us we are concerned with whether the advertisement constituted an offer, and, if so, whether the plaintiff's conduct constituted an acceptance.

There are numerous authorities which hold that a particular advertisement in a newspaper or circular letter relating to a sale of articles may be construed by the court as constituting an offer, acceptance of which would complete a contract. [Citations]

The test of whether a binding obligation may originate in advertisements addressed to the general public is 'whether the facts show that some performance was promised in positive terms in return for something requested.' [Citation]

Whether in any individual instance a newspaper advertisement is an offer rather than an invitation to make an offer depends on the legal intention of the parties and the surrounding circumstances. [Citations] We are of the view on the facts before us that the offer by the defendant of the sale of the lapin fur was clear, definite, and explicit, and left nothing open for negotiation. The plaintiff having successfully managed to be the first one to appear at the seller's place of business to be served, as requested by the advertisement, and having offered the stated purchase price of the article, he was entitled to performance on the part of the defendant. We think the trial court was correct in holding that there was in the conduct of the parties a sufficient mutuality of obligation to constitute a contract of sale.

* * *

Affirmed.

CASE 11-2

This case concerns the need for definiteness and certainty in the terms of a contract.

DOMBROWSKI v. SOMERS
Court of Appeals of New York, 1977
41 N.Y.2d 858, 393 N.Y.2d 706

MEMORANDUM. By this action plaintiff seeks compensation for housekeeping chores rendered pursuant to an alleged oral agreement between herself and the decedent, Edward Vogel, whose household she was sharing.

Three witnesses testified that they heard Vogel say he would "take care of" plaintiff. None recalled any reference to a specific date. The claim itself was not filed until 18 months after the decedent's death.

The words to "take care of", in the context of this record, are too vague to spell out a meaningful promise.

Even if they were not, standing alone, they would be legally insufficient to support a finding that there was a contract to compensate plaintiff during her lifetime rather than one to do so by bequest. In the latter case, an enforceable agreement would be required to be in writing.... In short, plaintiff has not met her burden of proof as a matter of law....

Accordingly, the order of the Appellate Division is reversed and the complaint dismissed.

CASE 11-3

In the following case, the court applies the rules regarding definiteness and certainty of contractual terms to an interesting set of facts.

TRIMMER v. VAN BOMEL
Supreme Court of New York (N.Y. Co.), 1980
107 Misc.2d 201, 434 N.Y.S.2d 82

GREENFIELD, Judge. The complex and varied relationships between men and women, when they come to an end, oft leave a bitter residue and a smoldering irritation for which the salve, often the only soothing balm, is cash. It is a poor substitute for love, affection or attention, but for many its satisfactions are longer lasting. "Ordinarily, alimony is the end product of the fission of matrimony by acrimony." More recently, the termination of informal "live-in" relationships has given rise to claims for "palimony". Now, in this case, a man who claims to have been the constant companion of an elderly wealthy widow, who changed her life style from genteel poverty to luxury at her behest, sues at the breakup of their relationship for what may be called, for want of a better term, "companiomony".

Plaintiff is a 67-year-old gentleman, who was earning a modest but respectable living as a travel tour operator, when a person on one of his tours, the defendant, Mrs. Catherine Bryer Van Bomel, a wealthy widow with assets stated to be in excess of $40,000,000, began making demands on his time, and allegedly agreed to support him in luxurious fashion, if he would devote all his time and attention to her. He gave up his business career, in which he admits he was earning no more than $8,900 a year and became the ever-present companion of Mrs. Von Bomel. He moved to larger quarters and modified his wardrobe to suit her tastes. He accompanied her to lunch and dinner, escorted her to the theatre and parties, and traveled with her on her trips to Europe. All this was at the lady's expense, of course. He also acted as her confidante and her friends became his friends.

For five years his life was constantly dominated by the needs, whims and desires of Mrs. Van Bomel. She spent money lavishly on him. Apart from taking care of his rent and his travel expenses, she had his suits hand tailored in Italy and in London, presented him with two Pontiacs and a Jaguar and gave him a monthly stipend. All in all, she expended well over $300,000 for his personal needs. Then, suddenly, it all came to an end. Accustomed to a life of luxury, and now without the means to attain it, plaintiff sues his former benefactress for $1,500,000.

In the first cause of action, plaintiff seeks recovery on an alleged express oral agreement, pursuant to which he agreed to give up his business and render services to the defendant, in return for which defendant would pay and provide (a) all his costs and expenses incurred in connection with the performance of his services, (b) all his costs and expenses for sumptuous living during the time the services were rendered, and (c) to pay "within a reasonable time" an amount sufficient to pay for all his costs and expenses for sumptuous living for the rest of his life. The plaintiff further alleges that he fully performed the agreement on his part and that the defendant, in part performance, paid all his costs and expenses during the period of rendition of services, but has failed and refused to provide plaintiff with a sum sufficient to maintain him on a standard of "sumptuous living" for the remainder of his life, which sum plaintiff contends would be $1,500,000.

In his second cause of action, which sounds in quantum meruit, plaintiff alleges that he performed the various services for defendant for a five-year period and gave up pursuit of his separate business career. For the agreed and reasonable value of his services on the second cause of action, he seeks $1,500,000.

Defendant has moved for summary judgment...contending that the action is without merit and that the purported agreement is too vague and indefinite to be enforceable; that defendant's obligations under the alleged agreement are illusory; that the agreement is void for lack of consideration and that plaintiff has already been paid far in excess of the value of any purported services.

Defendant had previously moved for summary judgment...and a denial of the motion at that time was affirmed by the Appellate Division. Plaintiff misconstrues the nature of that prior order, since, in clarification, the Appellate Division specifically held that

its affirmance of the denial of summary judgment was "without prejudice to renewal thereof after the conclusion of pretrial procedures herein." The Appellate Division specifically noted: "We do not pass upon the merits of plaintiff's claims or defendant's position with respect thereto at this time". Depositions having been concluded, defendant has moved again for summary judgment. That right to renew in these circumstances is predicated not upon the allegation of new or additional material, but upon the completion of discovery. There is now a complete record before the court containing the entire recollections of both plaintiff and defendant, the only parties to the alleged agreement.

While there have been a number of cases dealing with lawsuits by one partner in a nonmarital relationship seeking to recover against the other on the basis of an express or implied agreement the court in this case is not confronted with the public policy considerations which compel the judiciary to uphold the institution of marriage and to distinguish its consequences from less formal and less permanent living arrangements. No meretricious relationship appears to be here involved. At best, plaintiff may be regarded as a companion and paid escort, and not as a substitute mate. These cases are instructive, however, as to which type of agreements may be enforceable and whether recovery is to be permitted on a theory of implied contract or quantum meruit.

In this State, cases of unmarried persons living together who thereafter seek financial recovery frequently run afoul of the theory that a contract founded upon an agreement to live together as man and wife will not be enforced. While one may not claim compensation for having been a paramour, if there are services rendered which are nonsexual in nature and do not arise directly from such a relationship, then such services may be deemed separable, and form the basis for compensation....

The extramatrimonial case involving a claim for the value of services rendered which has received the most publicity to date is *Marvin v Marvin*. In that case the California Supreme Court had reversed the dismissal of Michelle Marvin's complaint as a de facto spouse, and remanded the matter for trial to determine whether or not she was entitled to recovery on an express or implied contract. It was not the holding of the California court that a mistress was entitled to "palimony". At Trial Term, the court found that the allegations that there had been an explicit contract to compensate the plaintiff were not borne out by the facts. Nevertheless, the court, exercising its equitable powers, decided to award the sum of $1,000 per week for a two-year period to enable the plaintiff, who had allegedly given up her budding career, to rehabilitate herself. Interestingly, on the same day that Michelle Marvin was awarded "severance pay" by the California trial court, in

New York the female companion of rock star Peter Frampton was cut off without compensation....

The most recent case in this State dealing with extramarital contracts is *Morone v Morone*. In that case, as here, two causes of action were alleged -- the first based upon implied contract and the second alleging an explicit oral "partnership agreement". The concept of an implied contract to compensate for services was declared by the court "to be conceptually so amorphous as practically to defy equitable enforcement". Nevertheless, the court concluded that the allegations of an express contract that the woman would furnish domestic services and the man was to have full charge of business transactions and that the "net profits" from the partnership were to be shared equally, set forth an enforceable cause of action. Evidently, "housewifely" services are to be distinguished from such other services as may be rendered during the course of a living-together relationship. When the "tainted" consideration for such contracts is removed, the claim for recovery in extramarital cases stands in precisely the same posture as in this case.

In this case, the services for which plaintiff seeks compensation on a quantum meruit basis, like those in a quasimarital relationship, arise out of the nature of the relationship of the parties to one another. The services involved -- to devote time and attention to the defendant, to allow her wishes to prevail concerning his deportment, habits and associations and to act as companion, to accompany defendant to restaurants, to travel with her, to accept gifts and jewelry, clothing and motor cars from her are of a nature which would ordinarily be exchanged without expectation of pay. As Judge Meyer noted in *Morone v Morone*: "As a matter of human experience personal services will frequently be rendered by two people...because they value each other's company or because they find it a convenient or rewarding thing to do.... For courts to attempt through hindsight to sort out the intentions of the parties and affix jural significance to conduct carried out within an essentially private and generally noncontractual relationship runs too great a risk of error. Absent an express agreement, there is no frame of reference against which to compare the testimony presented and the character of the evidence that can be presented becomes more evanescent. There is, therefore, substantially greater risk of emotion-laden afterthought, not to mention fraud, in attempting to ascertain by implication what services, if any, were rendered gratuitously and what compensation, if any, the parties intended to be paid."

As to personal services between unmarried persons living together or unmarried persons whose actions flow out of mutual friendship and reciprocal regard, there is very little difference. An implied contract to compensate for those things which are ordinarily done by one person for another as a matter of regard and affection should not, under these well-established principles, be recognized in this State. Plaintiff has already received $300,000 from the defendant during the course of their relationship. What further "obligation" can be implied?

The claims of friendship, like the claims of kinship, may be many and varied. To imply an obligation by a wealthy friend to compensate a less wealthy companion for being together, dining together, talking together and accepting tokens of regard stretches the bond of friendship to the breaking point. The implied obligation to compensate arises from those things which, in normal society, we expect to pay for. An obligation to pay for friendship is not ordinarily to be implied -- it is too crass. Friendship, like virtue, must be its own reward.

Accordingly, the second cause of action, founded in implied contract, must be dismissed.

The first cause of action, however, alleges an express agreement to pay the plaintiff. For the purposes of this motion for summary judgment, the court must accept as true plaintiff's allegation that defendant agreed to set up a fund which would permit plaintiff to live for the remainder of his life in the sumptuous style to which he had become accustomed. While defendant denies that there were specific conversations about setting up a fund, she does admit having discussions from time to time about making finances available to the plaintiff. She denies, however, and the plaintiff's testimony in his deposition confirms, that no specific dollar amounts were ever specified, no time for performance was ever set and no conditions as to the manner of payment were given, nor was anything ever said about what would happen if the relationship between the parties terminated. Thus, the principal issue presented is whether such an agreement as alleged in the complaint, and as expanded upon in plaintiff's deposition, can be regarded as enforceable. While there is no public policy bar to such an agreement, as an alleged express oral contract, its validity must be tested exactly the same as other contracts. Such a contract is not conceptually invalid....

All courts would agree with the doctrine, although not necessarily the application, that as a basic premise of contract law "'It is a necessary requirement in the nature of things that an agreement in order to be binding must be sufficiently definite to enable a court to give it an exact meaning' (1 Williston, Contracts [3d ed], § 37)." In *Dombrowski v Somers*, a unanimous Court of Appeals found that an alleged oral agreement, pursuant to which the decedent said that in return for plaintiff's services he would "take care of" the plaintiff, was too vague to spell out a meaningful promise.

The question in this case is whether an alleged agreement by defendant to pay an amount sufficient to take care of all of plaintiff's "costs and expenses for sumptuous living and maintenance for the remainder of his life" as amplified by plaintiff's testimony, will enable the court to award plaintiff a judgment in a specific sum of dollars. It is clear from the pretrial depositions of both parties, that no specific dollar amount, or approximate dollar amount, of any alleged fund was ever discussed. No facts are presented which would tend to establish a meeting of minds as to the definition of "sumptuous living". In his 237-page bill of particulars, plaintiff asserted that the defendant had agreed "to provide and set up for him a fund, either by giving him a block of stock or cash, or both, which would take care of all his living expenses in the same expensive style for the rest of his life." Plaintiff is alleging, in essence, a contract of employment, but as reference to his own testimony indicates, there was no specification as to the length of the term, the amount of the compensation, the terms of the payment, the nature of the duties, the manner in which the employment could be terminated and the method of computing "severance pay". Plaintiff's deposition indicates that there was no specific time at which the alleged agreement was worked out, but rather that it developed as part of numerous conversations over an extended period of time, and it is clear that he commenced his "employment" long before any such agreement to take care of him for the rest of his life was discussed.

With respect to the alleged promise of the defendant to set up a "fund" to take care of his needs for "sumptuous living", no specifics were ever discussed....

Nor, admittedly, was there ever any discussion about what was necessary for the plaintiff's living expenses either at that time or at some point off in the future....

What we are talking about, then, at best is "a fund" in some unspecified amount to be set up on some unspecified date in some unspecified manner, and that it was wholly in the discretion of the defendant. The agreement boils down to these words, "She would do it in some way."

Plaintiff has attempted to overcome the inherent vagueness of this "agreement" by trying to spell out, after the fact, what amounts he deems to be required for "sumptuous living". What is "sumptuous" to one person may be merely adequate to another, of course.

"Sumptuous" is defined as involving great expense; costly, lavish, magnificent (Webster's Dictionary, p 1825,...)

Moreover, sumptuous living "cannot be computed from anything that was said by the parties or by reference to any document, paper or other transaction" nor would it be provable by evidence of custom. Nor, for that matter, could defendant be required to account since no partnership agreement is alleged and additionally, defendant's vast holdings were accumulated before she had ever met plaintiff. Essentially, then the amount was left subject to the will of the defendant or for further negotiation. Courts cannot aid parties who have not specified the terms of their own agreements....

Plaintiff calculates that since he was given an average of $71,672 (tax free) by Mrs. Van Bomel during their five-year relationship, that this is the sum he should be given for the rest of his life. That is how he comes to the $1,500,000 set forth in the ad damnum. One million five hundred dollars in six-month certificates would give him $180,000 a year and that same sum in tax-free municipals would produce well over $100,000 per year, in which case the principal would be left intact. It appears clear that we are dealing with an alleged agreement which is too vague in any of its material terms to be deemed enforceable. No amount being specified, no time having been set forth, no mechanics for the payments having been spelled out and there being no specification as to what had to be done to qualify or disqualify the plaintiff for the payments, what we have, at best, is some vague but legally unenforceable reassurance that plaintiff "would be taken care of".

Since plaintiff alleges an express agreement which is to be governed by the law applicable to all contracts, it is instructive to compare the kind of agreement upon which plaintiff relies with other, more detailed contracts which the courts have nevertheless found to be unenforceable. Thus, in *Brause v Goldman*, where negotiations had progressed to a point of much greater detail than what was involved here, the court found that many of the essentials of an agreement were lacking. In that case, the court declared: "When the wording...exchanged between the parties reveal no present intent to form a binding contract, but rather to continue negotiations with the possible ultimate meeting of minds deferred until some future time, either party may withdraw with impunity prior to that time...."

Further, "The absence of any of the essential elements of an agreement is a bar to its enforcibility." The court found that even though there were memoranda of agreement prepared after oral negotiations, there was no indication as to the date on which the arrangement was to be commenced nor as to the method of payment, nor as to the rights of the parties in the event of various contingencies coming to pass. The Appellate Division declared, "It is not for the court to dictate such terms to the parties, for its function is to enforce agreements only if they exist, and not to create them by the imposition of such terms as it considers reasonable."

In essence, if the relationship between the plaintiff and defendant was that of employer and employee rather than that of friends or benefactress and protege, then clearly it was an employment relationship terminable at will. Plaintiff recognized that he would be rendering services at the pleasure of Mrs. Van Bomel, and that could be for months, for years or on into the indefinite future. Plaintiff testified, "The discussion was that I was to start doing this for her. There was no time limit put on it... I knew that if she decided that she would like to terminate my employment with her, she could do that. She had a perfect right to do that." Would a defendant be bound by a committment to put up a fund of $1,500,000 for someone who rendered "services" to her for a matter of months by accompanying her to restaurants such as Lutece and the Palm Court? Plaintiff would accompany the defendant to lunch two or three times weekly. He agreed that the defendant never imposed any restrictions upon his activities. For these companionable social activities, it cannot be said that defendant, or her estate, is to be bound for the rest of plaintiff's life.

In an agreement terminable at will, and with no clear bounds and parameters set forth, an alleged obligation which would continue and survive beyond the termination of employment must appear with specificity. What if the relationship had been terminated for "cause"? Suppose plaintiff had been disloyal or discourteous or had secretly embezzled some of defendant's funds, would the agreement to take care of him for life continue nevertheless? Since this relationship was terminable at will, and the relationship had come to an end, this court can see no legal basis upon which the defendant can be compelled to continue lavishing her favors and her bounty upon the plaintiff. There are no guarantees in life, and good fortune, to be enjoyed while it lasts, does not invariably bring with it a life-long annuity. It was defendant who decided to get plaintiff tickets for the Royal Enclosure at Ascot, to buy him fabrics in London to be tailored in Rome. It was defendant who took pleasure in seeing that plaintiff's shoes came from Gucci and his accessories from Saks. When the relationship is terminated, the law does not compel... the dead relationship to continue.

Accordingly, defendant is entitled to summary judgment on the first cause of action as well as the second. The complaint should be dismissed.

CASE 11-4

In the following case, the court determines whether the parties have reached agreement on all material terms and thus have an enforceable contract.

ANSORGE v. KANE
Court of Appeals of New York, 1927
244 N.Y. 395

POUND, Judge. The main point is simply stated. Defendant owned real property in Flushing, New York. Plaintiff desired to purchase it. Through her agent the parties came together March 25, 1925, and made a memorandum of purchase and sale which describes the property and acknowledges the receipt of $500 as binder thereon and then provides:

"The price is $32,625; payable $12,625 cash; balance of $20,000 to remain on 1st mortgage for five years. The sum to be paid on signing of contract on March 26th, 1925, to be agreed on. The balance of cash payment on passing of title on May 26th, 1925."

The parties never agreed on the sum to be paid on signing the contract. When the owner refused to sign a contract or execute a deed the court below ordered specific performance at the suit of the purchaser. That

the parties had not agreed was held immaterial. It was said that the agreement in substance was that the balance of the cash payment would be payable when title passed unless the parties in the interim agreed otherwise....

Appellant contends that the scheme or plan of the parties was left incomplete by the failure to name the sum to be paid when the contract was signed; and that until the sum was named the contract was unenforceable.... The memorandum states the price to be paid but it does not state all the terms of payment.... The fundamental question here presented is whether there was any contract; any actual meeting of minds on all the material elements of the agreement.

If a material element of a contemplated contract is left for future negotiations, there is no enforceable contract.... The price is a material element of any contract of sale and an agreement to agree thereon in the future is too indefinite to be enforceable....

The terms of payment may be no less material. Is this memorandum in effect an agreement to convey the property described if the parties can agree upon the amount to be paid on the signing of the contract but for no sale if they do not agree? Or is the agreement on the sum to be paid on signing the contract a minor and non-essential detail of the transaction? That is the question before us.... The memorandum was on its face a mere binder. The formal contract was to be prepared and executed on the next day. As a part of the agreement was left to future negotiations, the contract was embryonic. It never reached full time. It was not for nothing that the parties provided that a sum should be agreed on to be paid on the signing of the contract; nor was it a minor matter for the owner whether nothing should be paid when the contract was signed and she should wait two months for her money, or whether she should receive a substantial sum, the stronger to bind the agreement, on which she also might receive interest, or even a greater increment, if she had her hands on it. In this connection we observe that the broker demanded that his full commission of ten per cent be paid on the signing of the contract which further suggests that the down payment had more than theoretical importance to the vendor.

The parties had decided to purchase and sell. They had agreed on the purchase price. They had not agreed on the terms of payment. The law implies nothing as to such terms as it does in cases where the rate of interest and date of maturity of a mortgage are not stated...or where it appears that an agreement is to take effect and be acted upon before the details reserved for future agreement, such as time of delivery, are settled, when an implication may arise that, in the event of a failure to agree, the terms shall be such as are reasonable or customary.... The amount to be paid on the signing of the contract was an important element of the complete contract. It was left open. The contract was never completed. The transaction was destitute of legal effect. Specific performance is, therefore, impossible....

The judgment of the Appellate Division and that of the Special Term should be reversed and the complaint dismissed.

CASE 11-5

If the duration of an offer is not specified, it expires in a "reasonable time." The following case illustrates that a court will consider the particular circumstances in determining whether acceptance has been made in a reasonable time.

22 WEST MAIN STREET, INC. v. BOGUSZEWSKI
Appellate Division, New York (4th Dept.), 1970
34 A.D. 2d 358, 311 N.Y.S.2d 565

DEL VECCHIO, Justice. Plaintiff appeals from an order of Special Term denying its motion for summary judgment in an action to compel specific performance of a real estate contract.

There is no dispute about the events which preceded this action.

On February 21, 1968 defendant executed an offer to purchase approximately 4.9 acres of land in the Village of Fredonia for $7,000. The offer stated that the closing was to be held at the offices of the attorneys for the defendant 'on or before March 22, 1968 or as soon thereafter as abstracts can be brought to date'. There was no acceptance by plaintiff until March 26, 1968 (four days after the closing date specified in the offer), when the seller crossed out the closing date of March 22, 1968, inserted the date 'April 10, 1968' and signed the acceptance portion of the offer. On April 2, 1968 the seller's attorneys wrote to defendant's attorney enclosing the executed purchase offer, the abstract of title, a copy of a proposed deed and other papers relating to the premises. Receiving no reply, plaintiff's attorneys wrote on five subsequent occasions requesting that a closing date for the transfer be set. Defendant's counsel did not respond directly to any of these letters but did send plaintiff's attorneys a copy of a letter sent to defendant by his attorney on July 5 in which the latter advised that since the client was unwilling to close the transaction he was no longer representing him in the matter and enclosing a bill for his services. He also advised that the abstract of title and the proposed deed description were being returned to the seller's attorneys. By letter to defendant dated July 26 plaintiff tendered a deed and set August 5 as a date for closing. When the tender was not accepted plaintiff commenced this action for specific performance.

After service of the pleadings which put in issue the making of the contract plaintiff served on defendant a notice to admit the execution by him of the purchase offer, the genuineness of his signature thereon and the fact that the offer was not withdrawn prior to acceptance. When no response to the notice was served plaintiff moved for summary judgment on the basis of the notice and an affidavit and supporting papers setting forth the facts recited above.

It is plaintiff's contention that its execution of the acceptance of defendant's purchase offer on March 26, 1968 created a binding contract between the parties which it is now entitled to enforce. Defendant takes the position that the acceptance on March 26 was not an acceptance of a viable offer but was merely a counter offer which was never accepted by the buyer. . . .

Upon the undisputed facts there was never a contract entered into by the parties. The act of the plaintiff in signing the acceptance of the purchase offer on March 26 was too late to constitute an acceptance of defendant's offer to buy made one month and five days prior thereto.

The offer executed on February 21 did not contain any express time limit on its duration. In that circumstance the offer remained open for a reasonable time. 'Where an offer specifies the time of its duration, it must of course by accepted within the time limited; where, however, no time is specified for the offer's duration, it is the general rule that it must be accepted within a reasonable time.' . . . . The circumstances surrounding the offer, or usage or custom of trade, may also raise an implied limitation on the offer. (9 N.Y.Jur., Contracts §24.) Here, the original offer to buy contained a proposed closing date one month

after the offer. The inclusion of the closing date of March 22 is compelling evidence that acceptance of the offer, if it were to occur, must happen before that date, else the closing date would be an impossibility. A similar case is *Hamilton v. Patrick*, . . . in which the court said:

'The proposal itself implies the necessity of acceptance on or before that day. It is therein proposed that the deed should be executed and delivered to the plaintiff 'on or before March 1, 1885, at which date said money shall be paid.' Acceptance must precede any obligation to perform, and of necessity must be made so as to admit of performance as proposed. Any subsequent acceptance would imply a contract different from the terms proposed.' . . .

The reasonable time for duration of the offer was not longer than the one month within which the offeror hoped to complete the transaction. An acceptance which occurred four days after the proposed closing date and one month and five days after the tender of the offer is clearly beyond a reasonable period of duration. The late acceptance was merely a counter offer which must in turn be accepted by the original offeror to create a contract. (1 Williston on Contracts, 3d ed. §§ 92, 93; Restatement, Law of Contracts, § 73; . . ..) Since there was never any acceptance by defendant of plaintiff's counter proposal, there was no contract between the parties to be enforced.

The order should be modified to grant summary judgment to defendant dismissing the complaint.

CASE 11-6

This case illustrates the operation of the three month limitation on the irrevocability of firm offers under UCC §2-205 and also how revocation may occur by conduct.

NORCA CORPORATION v. TOKHEIM CORPORATION
Appellate Division, New York (2d Dept.), 1996
227 A.D.2d 458, 643 N.Y.S.2d 139

MEMORANDUM BY THE COURT. In an action, *inter alia,* to recover damages for breach of contract, the plaintiff appeals from an order and judgment (one paper) of the Supreme Court, Nassau County (Alpert, J.), entered April 11, 1995, which, *inter alia,* granted the respective motions of the defendants for summary judgment dismissing the complaint.
ORDERED that the order and judgment is affirmed, with costs.

If a firm offer is made for a specified period which is in excess of three months, the offer is subject to revocation at the expiration of the three month period (*see,* Uniform Commercial Code § 2-205, Official Comment 3; [Citations]). An offer may be terminated by indirect revocation . . . . An offeror need not say "revoke" to effectuate a revocation . . . . Where an offeror takes "definite action inconsistent with an intention to enter into the proposed contract", such action is considered a valid revocation (Restatement [Second] of Contracts § 43; *see also,* 1 Farnsworth, Contracts § 3.17, at 250 [1990]).

In the instant case, the defendant Saint Switch, Inc. (hereinafter Saint Switch), agreed to purchase the assets of the manufacturing pump division of the defendant Tokheim Corporation. On April 14, 1993, Saint Switch offered, on Tokheim Corporation letterhead, to sell fuel pumps to the appellant. The offer was firm until July 31, 1994. On August 18, 1993, more than three months after the original offer was made, Saint Switch forwarded to the appellant a new offer stating different price terms for the fuel pumps. On November 4, 1993, the appellant attempted to accept the original offer made on April 14, 1993.

We find that the offer made by Saint Switch on August 18, 1993, revoked its earlier offer made on April 14, 1993. The offer made on August 18, 1993, was inconsistent with the original offer in that it had a different price term . . . . In addition, it was made prior to any effective acceptance on the part of the appellant . . . . Accordingly, the Supreme Court properly granted the respective motions of the defendants for summary judgment.

The appellant's remaining contentions are without merit.

CASE 11-7

The following case deals with the reasonableness of the means of acceptance used by the offeror.

DEFEO v. AMFARMS ASSOCIATES
Appellate Division, New York (3rd Dept.), 1990
161 A.D.2d 904, 557 N.Y.S.2d 469

WEISS, Justice. Appeal from an order of the Supreme Court (Rose, J.), entered July 14, 1989 in Tioga County, which, *inter alia,* granted defendant's motion for summary judgment dismissing the complaint.

In 1986 defendant listed its farm located in the Town of Candor, Tioga County, for sale with W.D. Seeley Real Estate. On September 5, 1987 defendant received an offer from plaintiffs submitted through the broker. It rejected the offer on September 7, 1987 and submitted a counteroffer in which the sale price was increased and certain conditions which defendant found objectionable were deleted. This counteroffer was made through the broker with instructions that the sale would have to proceed promptly. A month later, on October 5, 1987, plaintiffs submitted another offer with an acceptable price, but again included the objectionable conditions. On October 9, 1987 defendant rejected this offer and, using the same form, countered by deleting and initialing the objectionable conditions. In this final counteroffer, a new additional term appeared in handwriting: "13. Offer valid to Oct. 17, 1987 at 1700 hours." Peculiarly, the parties claim to be unaware who inserted the clause. This counteroffer was forwarded directly by defendant's attorney . . . to plaintiffs' attorney by Federal Express overnight delivery. Thereafter, plaintiffs' attorney contacted defendant's attorney by telephone on October 13, 1987 and another of defendant's partners on October 15, 1987. The parties dispute the contents of these communications. In the meantime, on October 13, 1987, defendant received a purchase offer with a higher price from third parties through a different real estate broker which it accepted on October 16, 1987. On that very same day, plaintiffs accepted the October 9, 1987 counteroffer and sent it to Seeley Real Estate by certified mail, which Seeley received on October 19, 1987. Defendant denied the effectiveness of acceptance. Supreme Court granted summary judgment dismissing the complaint seeking specific performance, holding that since the offer had been transmitted to plaintiffs' attorney by Federal Express, acceptance sent by mail to the listing real estate broker was unauthorized and ineffective to accept the offer. The court found that since plaintiffs failed to timely communicate acceptance before the offer expired, no binding contract was formed and plaintiffs were not entitled to specific performance. This appeal followed.

The reasonableness of the manner in which an offer is accepted must be viewed under the circumstances in which the offer had been made, with speed and reliability being relevant factors (Restatement [Second] of Contracts § 65; *see,* 1 Williston, Contracts § 83, at 273 [Jaeger 3d ed.]).

Here, the transmission using Federal Express overnight delivery invited acceptance by similar dispatch . . . and plaintiffs' acceptance by mail, particularly to an agent who had been uninvolved in the negotiations of the moment and who had lost contact with the parties, was not invited especially in view of defendant's expressed concern with time. The receipt of the acceptance by the broker two days after the appointed day was not operative (Restatement [Second] of Contracts § 67).

Order affirmed, with costs.

CASE 11-8

The following case concerns whether an effective acceptance was made before revocation of the offer.

TENCZA v. HYLAND
Appellate Division, New York (4th Dept.), 1991
171 A.D.2d 1057, 569 N.Y.S.2d 242

MEMORANDUM: Supreme Court erred in finding that there was a binding contract between the parties and granting plaintiffs' request for specific performance. On or about April 15, 1987, plaintiffs submitted to defendants an offer to purchase a mobile home park in New Hartford, New York. Defendants responded by inserting four modifications to the purchase offer and advised plaintiffs' counsel that, if the changes were acceptable, plaintiffs should initial them and return the signed purchase offer. One of the modifications was that plaintiff corporation's three principal shareholders would be required to sign, individually, a $160,000 note to secure payment of the purchase price. Another modification made defendants responsible only for commencing eviction proceedings against all tenants in arrears more than 30 days, rather than for evicting those tenants before closing. Defendants' material alterations of plaintiffs' offer to purchase constituted a counteroffer that required plaintiffs' acceptance to form a binding contract . . . . Plaintiffs signed the counteroffer, but their agreement was never communicated by their counsel to defendants. Counsel instead attempted to negotiate changes in the contract that were beneficial to his clients. On May 12, 1987 defendants' counsel advised plaintiffs' counsel by letter that his clients were no longer interested in selling the property and returned plaintiffs' $5,000 deposit. Because the signed counteroffer was never delivered to defendants and defendants were never advised of plaintiffs' acceptance of the counteroffer prior to their revocation, no contract was entered into between the parties . . . .

Order and judgment unanimously reversed on the law with costs and complaint dismissed; motion for stay denied as moot.

CASE 11-9

MURRAY v. THE CUNARD STEAMSHIP COMPANY, LTD.
Court of Appeals of New York, 1923
235 N.Y. 162, 139 N.E. 226

CARDOZO, J.
The plaintiff left New York on April 24, 1920, as a second cabin passenger on the defendant's steamship Mauretania. On April 28 he broke his knee cap by a fall upon the deck. His statement is that he caught his foot in a rope attached to a canvas curtain, which had been left unfastened so that it was blown by the wind. The defendant says that he was injured in jumping over ropes which separated the deck for one class of passengers from the deck for another. The vessel reached Southampton on May 2, 1920. The plaintiff went ashore with the aid of a crutch, and was taken by train to London. From London he went to Dublin, where he was for six weeks in Dublin Hospital. Leaving the hospital, he spent a week or two in his home in Strokstown, Roscommon county. As the result of trouble which developed in his knee, he went to Roscommon Hospital and was there for several

months. He then spent another fortnight in his home; and, dissatisfied with his progress, returned to Dublin Hospital, where he submitted to an operation involving the removal of pieces of bone. His final discharge from the hospital was about the middle of November. After remaining some weeks in Ireland, he sailed for New York on January 8, 1921. On February 24, 1921, without preliminary notice, this action was begun.

The plaintiff's ticket, issued to him some days before the departure of the vessel, is described in large type as a 'cabin passage contract ticket.' It provides, again in large type, that 'this contract ticket is issued by the company and accepted by the passenger on the following terms and conditions.' One of the terms and conditions is that no action shall be maintained either for injury to property or for personal injury to the passenger unless commenced within one year after the termination of the voyage. That requirement was obeyed. Another term or condition is that no action shall be maintained for injury to property unless written notice of the claim be delivered to the company within twenty days after debarkation, and that no action shall be maintained for injury to the passenger unless written notice of the claim be delivered to the company within forty days after debarkation. That requirement was not obeyed. At the top of the ticket is printed a notice: 'The attention of passengers is specially directed to the terms and conditions of this contract.'

We assume, without intending to decide, that the plaintiff's narrative, if accepted, would sustain a finding by the jury that the defendant had been negligent. We assume also that a contract exonerating the defendant altogether from liability for negligent injury to a passenger would be ineffective and void because opposed to public policy . . . . Exoneration, however, is not to be confused with regulation. 'A stipulation for written notice within a reasonable time stands on a different footing, and of this there is no doubt.' . . . There is no evidence that this plaintiff was physically or mentally unable to give notice of the injury. Even if we were to assume in his favor that there was incapacity for a time, with a resulting extension of the period for notice, he did not make a move within forty days thereafter. Limitations of this kind have their justification in the need of some safeguard to protect the carrier against fraud. Passengers on steamships scatter in all directions when the voyage is at an end. If claims may be presented at any time within the term of years permitted by the Statute of Limitations, the opportunity for investigation will often be lost beyond recall. 'The practice of fraud is too common to be ignored'.

The plaintiff argues that he is not bound by the conditions of the ticket because he did not read them.

The omission does not help his case. The law is settled in this state that a ticket in this form, issued by a steamship company for a voyage across the ocean, is more than a mere token or voucher. It is a contract, creating the obligation and defining the terms of carriage. [Citations omitted] The ruling is in accord with judgments in other jurisdictions. [Citations omitted] This is not a case of a mere notice on the back of a ticket, separate either in substance or in form from the body of the contract. . . . Here the condition is wrought into the tissue, the two inseparably integrated. This ticket, to the most casual observer, is as plainly a contract, burdened with all kinds of conditions, as if it were a bill of lading or a policy of insurance. 'No one who could read could glance at it without seeing that it undertook to prescribe the particulars which should govern the conduct of the parties until the passenger reached the port of destination'. In such circumstances, the act of acceptance gives rise to an implication of assent . . . . The passenger who omits to read takes the risk of the omission.

The plaintiff is not helped by his surrender of the ticket when he went aboard the ship, after he had then held it several days with ample time to read it. A contract valid and reasonable in its inception does not become invalid and unreasonable thereafter, because the passenger who has assented, is unable, when the voyage is over, to recall the terms of the assent. If some aid to memory is required, his business is to make for himself a note of the conditions, or to procure from the carrier a copy, which doubtless would be given for the asking. There is little ground for the belief that this plaintiff would have examined his ticket within the period of forty days, though he had taken it ashore on the termination of the voyage. If we accept his own testimony, he paid no heed to the conditions, and the thought of any need to refer to them did not enter his mind. He had abundant opportunity both on the ship and later to inquire about the terms of carriage, if he supposed them to be important. We should indulge in the merest speculation if we were to say that the surrender of the ticket was the cause of the omission of the notice. Whether it was or not, his contract remained the same. He is charged as if he had signed . . . . The obligation of one who signs is not defeated by proof that the document has been lost or that its contents have been forgotten.

* * *

The judgment of the Appellate Division and that of the Trial Term should be reversed, and the complaint dismissed, with costs in all courts.

CASE 11-10

WARD v. CROSS SOUND FERRY
U. S. Ct. of Appeals, 2d Circuit (2001)
273 F.3d 520

Walker, Chief Judge.

Plaintiff-appellant Debra Ward, a resident of New York, appeals from the March 29, 2001 judgment of the United States District Court for the Eastern District of New York (Denis R. Hurley, *District Judge*) granting summary judgment to defendant-appellee Cross Sound Ferry ("CSF"), a Connecticut company, and dismissing Ward's complaint as time-barred.

On June 23, 1997, Ward fell and injured herself on a gangway while boarding a CSF ferry in New London, Conn., bound for Orient Point, N.Y. Although Ward's counsel sent a claim letter to CSF within a month of the injuries, no suit was filed until November 1999, some two-and-a-half years after the accident.

After removing the case from state court to federal court on the basis of diversity and admiralty jurisdiction, CSF moved in the district court for summary judgment on the ground that the suit was time-barred. Although a statutory limitations period of three years would otherwise apply to the case , . . CSF sought to enforce a contractual time limitation appearing on the back of the passage ticket that required suits to be filed within one year of an injury. A ticket identical to the one received by plaintiff was submitted with CSF's motion. The front of that ticket, which measures about two inches by three-and-a-half inches, reads as follows:

Cross Sound Ferry

Ticket Good on Date of Issue Only
Contract: Subject to Terms on Reverse Side

"Cross Sound Ferry" at the top appears to be in fifteen-point bold Times New Roman type and "Ticket Good on Date of Issue Only / Contract: Subject to Terms on Reverse Side" on the bottom appears to be in twelve-point bold Times New Roman type. The writing on the reverse side of the ticket appears to be in seven-point Arial type and reads as follows:

> Terms of Passage Contract Between the Ferry, its Owners and their Employees and Concessionaires ("The Carrier") and passenger: (1) By accepting this contract passenger agrees to its terms. (2) Contract not transferable and valid and refundable only on day issued. (3) Carrier's liability for loss or damage to vehicles or personalty is limited to $500. (4) Carrier is not liable for loss of or damage to vehicles or personalty, or for personal injuries, illnesses or death, unless written notice is given to Owners within six months of the date of the occurrence, and suits on all such claims shall not be maintainable unless commenced within 1 year after the occurrence. (5) All disputes in any way connected with this contract must be litigated in a State Court of New London County, or in the U.S. District Court of Connecticut, Ticketed Vehicles must remain in staging area until boarding. Ferry passage may be denied at the discretion of the "Carrier".

It is undisputed that plaintiff's husband obtained both her ticket and his just two to three minutes before boarding the ferry. Plaintiff, after falling on the gangway, was carried on board by her husband, who simultaneously handed the tickets for both husband and wife to the ticket collector. CSF does not dispute that it typically issues tickets just prior to boarding and collects them upon boarding, and that plaintiff's possession of the tickets for a total of only two to three minutes is not unusual.

Following oral argument on the motion, the district court issued its decision from the bench. Relying on various cases, the district court reasoned that plaintiff had ample time to read the ticket's terms before handing it to the ticket collector while boarding, and that she had ample opportunity to obtain a duplicate ticket after the injury if she had not read the ticket or could not remember its contractual terms. Concluding that Ward's attorney "presumably dropped the ball" in failing to get a duplicate copy of the ticket, the district court upheld the contractual limitation, granted summary judgment for CSF, and dismissed plaintiff's complaint. This appeal followed.

DISCUSSION

We review the district court's grant of summary judgment *de novo,* including the issue of whether a passage ticket "reasonably communicated" contractual limitations imposed by the sea carrier, which is a question of law for the court. [Citation omitted.] Jurisdiction in the district court was properly based on admiralty. [Citations omitted.]

The issue of whether time limitations appearing on a passenger ticket are enforceable is one that arises with surprising regularity, although the particular facts of this case-namely, possession of the ticket for only a few minutes-are seemingly unique. Title 46 U.S.C.App. § 183b(a) permits a sea carrier to contractually limit the time period in which a suit for injuries may be filed by passengers, provided that time period is at least one year. . . . The only restriction to enforcement of such limitations is that the carrier "reasonably communicate" the existence and importance of the limitation to the passenger. [Citation omitted.] The "reasonably communicate" standard devolved from Judge Friendly's seminal opinion in *Silvestri v. Italia Societa Per Azioni Di Navigazione,* 388 F.2d 11, 17 (2d Cir.1968), in which he found, based on his review of the case law, that a contractual limitation would not be enforceable unless the carrier satisfied its burden of showing that it "had done all it reasonably could to warn the passenger that the terms and conditions were important matters of contract affecting his legal rights." Most circuits, including ours, have since construed *Silvestri* as requiring that "sea carriers reasonably communicate any limitations period to their passengers." [Citation omitted.]

In applying this standard, several circuits have adopted a two-part test: (1) whether the physical characteristics of the ticket itself "reasonably communicate[d] to the passenger the existence therein of important terms and conditions" that affected the passenger's legal rights,

and (2) whether "the circumstances surrounding the passenger's purchase and subsequent retention of the ticket/contract" permitted the passenger "to become meaningfully informed of the contractual terms at stake." [Citations omitted] [G]iven the likelihood that a passenger will not read the fine print upon purchase or during a pleasure cruise, the surrounding circumstances examined in the second part of the test "may be of equal importance as the prominence of warnings and clarity of conditions [examined in the first part] in deciding whether a provision should be held to bind a particular passenger," since "the same passenger might very well be expected to consult the multifarious terms and conditions of the ticket/contract in the event of an accident resulting in a loss or injury.".

The Second Circuit has never discussed, much less adopted, the two-part test, perhaps because the second part has never been at issue. . . . In the instant case, however, plaintiff conceded that there was no dispute with respect to the first part of the test because the physical characteristics of the passenger ticket reasonably communicated the existence and importance of the contractual terms of passage. Thus, plaintiff's success depends entirely on whether we adopt the second part of the test and apply it in her favor.

Several district courts in this circuit have employed the two-part test, reasoning that it is used widely among other circuits and is not inconsistent with our circuit's approach. . . . The district court below also applied the two-part test, finding that it could be "harmonized" with the test applied by the Second Circuit. We believe the two-part test to be useful in analyzing the reasonably communicated standard and to be a satisfactory refinement of Judge Friendly's holding in *Silvestri,* and therefore, take this opportunity to expressly adopt it.

Applying the test's second part to the facts of this case, we must decide whether a carrier gives reasonable notice of contractual limitations when it issues a ticket bearing the terms of the limitations to the passenger just minutes before she boards the ship and then collects the entire ticket at boarding, thereby leaving her with no written notice of the terms or even that such terms exist.

As the district court below noted, in the majority of cases in which a time limitation contained on a passenger ticket has been upheld, the court's decision rested in part on the fact that the passenger or the passenger's agent received the ticket several days in advance of the trip and was allowed to retain the ticket (or at least that portion of the ticket containing the contract terms and conditions) either permanently or for a substantial period of time after boarding the ship. . . .

In some cases it is unclear whether the passenger was allowed to retain the ticket, while in others the passenger specifically sought to avoid the terms because the ticket was collected upon boarding. In each of these cases, however, enforcement of the ticket's terms was upheld in part because the passenger had received the ticket several days in advance of boarding and thus had ample time to read it. . . . . Notably, in each of these cases, the amount of time the passenger had to examine the ticket was critical to the decision to uphold the contractual limitation.

No case cited by the parties or the district court involved the rare situation presented in this case: one in which the passenger's possession of the ticket is limited to two to three minutes as a result of the carrier's own practices. The district court, nevertheless, held that the clause here was enforceable because it took less than a minute to read and, therefore, Ward-or her husband acting as her agent-had adequate time to read it before boarding the ferry. The district court went on to state that, even if Ward had not read the ticket before boarding, she had ample opportunity to obtain a duplicate ticket after the accident and her attorney "presumably dropped the ball" by failing to do so.

In our view, the district court's reasoning is flawed because it confuses the significant question of whether CSF reasonably communicated to passengers that the ticket contained important terms and conditions, given the amount of time CSF allowed passengers to possess the tickets, with the less important question of whether it was possible to read the ticket in the amount of time provided..

We find that possession of the ticket for such a short period of time was insufficient to give Ward reasonable notice that the ticket contained important contractual limitations. Indeed, the fact that CSF collected the tickets so quickly after providing them to the passenger tended to negate the idea that the tickets were important contractual documents. . . . .

[M]oreover, the second part of the test "focuses on the subjective circumstances attending a particular plaintiff's opportunity to review the ticket terms before embarkation. Such factors include 'the passenger's

familiarity with the ticket, the time and incentive under the circumstances to study the provisions of the ticket, and any other notice the passenger received outside of the ticket.' [Citations omitted.] In this case, the circumstances surrounding Ward's purchase and subsequent retention of the ticket are that her husband entered the terminal building and purchased the ticket two to three minutes prior to boarding, then proceeded across the parking lot to board the ferry with Ward. Ward fell on the gangway while boarding and had to be carried on board by her husband, who handed the tickets to the ticket collector in the process. Under these circumstances, even if Ward or her husband might otherwise have had ample opportunity and incentive to inspect the tickets, both she and her husband would certainly have been distracted from studying the ticket's provisions. . . .

The district court relied on several cases for the proposition that Ward had ample opportunity to obtain a duplicate ticket after the trip. We find those cases to be distinguishable because in each of them the passengers had received their original tickets well in advance of the trip, and thus the carrier had satisfied its burden of providing reasonable notice.

* * *

In light of the rationale employed in these other cases, we do not think that giving a passenger a ticket that is collected two to three minutes later sufficiently notifies the passenger that the ticket contains important contractual terms such that the passenger, or her lawyer, would be expected to obtain a duplicate ticket in the event of an injury. The district court's reasoning that the lawyer "presumably dropped the ball" improperly shifted the burden to Ward to learn if notice had been given, rather than determining whether CSF had given reasonable notice in the first place.

As a practical matter, moreover, denying enforcement of the contractual limitation here does not place an unreasonable burden on CSF. No reason has been advanced why, for example, CSF could not give passengers a two-part ticket and then collect only the part that does not contain the contract terms.

Accordingly, we reverse the district court's grant of summary judgment for defendants and remand for further proceedings not inconsistent with this opinion.

CASE 12-1

The common law rule requires that consideration be given by each party to the other in order for the contract to be binding. This leading case addresses the question of whether consideration is given when a party incurs a legal detriment by giving up a legal right if the other party receives no benefit.

HAMER v. SIDWAY
Court of Appeals of New York, 1891
124 N.Y. 538

PARKER, Judge. The question which provoked the most discussion by counsel on this appeal, and which lies at the foundation of plaintiff's asserted right of recovery, is whether by virtue of a contract defendant's testator William E. Story became indebted to his nephew William E. Story, 2d, on his twenty-first birthday in the sum of five thousand dollars. The trial court found as a fact that "on the 20th day of March, 1869, William E. Story agreed to and with William E. Story, 2d, that if he would refrain from drinking liquor, using tobacco, swearing, and playing cards or billiards for money until he should become 21 years of age then he, the said William E. Story, would at that time pay him, the said William E. Story, 2d, the sum of $5,000 for such refraining, to which the said William E. Story, 2d, agreed," and that he "in all things fully performed his part of said agreement."

The defendant contends that the contract was without consideration to support it, and, therefore, invalid. He asserts that the promisee by refraining from the use of liquor and tobacco was not harmed but benefited; that that which he did was best for him to do independently of his uncle's promise, and insists that it follows that unless the promisor was benefited, the contract was without consideration. A contention, which if well founded, would seem to leave open for controversy in many cases whether that which the promisee did or omitted to do was, in fact, of such benefit to him as to leave no consideration to support the enforcement of the promisor's agreement. Such a rule could not be tolerated, and is without foundation in the law. The Exchequer Chamber, in 1875, defined consideration as follows: "A valuable consideration in the sense of the law may consist either in some right, interest, profit or benefit accruing to the one party, or some forbearance, detriment, loss or responsibility given, suffered or undertaken by the other." Courts "will not ask whether the thing which forms the consideration does in fact benefit the promisee or a third party, or is of any substantial value to anyone. It is enough that something is promised, done, forborne or suffered by the party to whom the promise is made as consideration for the promise made to him."

"In general a waiver of any legal right at the request of another party is a sufficient consideration for a promise."

"Any damage, or suspension, or forbearance of a right will be sufficient to sustain a promise."

Pollock, in his work on contracts, page 166, after citing the definition given by the Exchequer Chamber already quoted, says: "The second branch of this judicial description is really the most important one. Consideration means not so much that one party is profiting as that the other abandons some legal right in the present or limits his legal freedom of action in the future as an inducement for the promise of the first."

Now, applying this rule to the facts before us, the promisee used tobacco, occasionally drank liquor, and he had a legal right to do so. That right he abandoned for a period of years upon the strength of the promise of the testator that for such forbearance he would give him $5,000. We need not speculate on the effort which may have been required to give up the use of those stimulants. It is sufficient that he restricted his lawful freedom of action within certain prescribed limits upon the faith of his uncle's agreement, and now having fully performed the conditions imposed, it is of no moment whether such performance actually proved a benefit to the promisor, and the court will not inquire into it, but were it a proper subject of inquiry, we see nothing in this record that would permit a determination that the uncle was not benefited in a legal sense.

The cases cited by the defendant on this question are not in point.

B24

CASE 12-2

Often good faith disputes arise between a creditor and debtor as to whether any money is owed or how much money is owed. In such cases, a debtor may tender a check to the creditor for a smaller amount and may write words such as "paid in full" on the check or indicate such facts in a letter. May the creditor cash the check and still sue to collect the balance he claims is due? The following case illustrates the common law rules as to whether a debt is unliquidated and whether an accord and satisfaction discharging the debt has occurred.

SCHNELL v. PERLMON
Court of Appeals of New York, 1924
238 N.Y. 362; 144 N.E. 641

CRANE, Judge. This action is brought to recover an alleged balance due for goods, wares and merchandise sold by the plaintiffs to the defendant. Defendant pleaded an accord and satisfaction. The trial court directed a verdict for the plaintiffs for the full amount claimed, and the judgment entered thereon has been unanimously affirmed by the Appellate Division. That court, however, granted leave to appeal to this court, certifying that in its opinion there is a question of law involved which ought to be reviewed by us.

The question of law referred to arises through the payment by the defendant of an amount less than the agreed price in full payment and satisfaction of the claimed debt. As in all like cases the result depends very much upon the facts of each case, it is, therefore, necessary at the outset to state fully the transaction between these parties. The plaintiffs, trading under the firm name of H. Schnell & Co., sold to Sol Perlmon, the defendant, trading under the firm name of Detroit Celery & Produce Co., ten cars of Spanish onions, pursuant to the terms of a written contract dated November 14, 1921. These ten carloads were to consist of 2,500 crates to be shipped by the Michigan Central Railroad from New York to Detroit; all goods sold F. O. B. New York, delivery to the common carrier being delivery to the purchaser. When the onions arrived in Detroit some of them were found to be in a defective condition due to decay consisting of fusarean rot, slimy soft rot, and a bacteria heart rot involving the greater portion of the onions. The defendant had the onions inspected by the Food Products Inspector of the United States Department of Agriculture, who gave five separate certificates certifying to this condition of the onions examined by him and stating that the decay amounted in some of the containers from ten per cent to thirty-five per cent, in others from fifteen to twenty-five per cent of the contents. The percentage varied in these certificates, running as high, however, as fifty per cent and as low

as three per cent. The defendant notified the plaintiffs by letter regarding this condition, and sent them copies of the government official's report. On December 13, 1921, the defendant sent to the plaintiffs five checks in payment of five of the cars shipped and deducted a total of $425 for a percentage of the decay as covered by the government reports. Accompanying these checks was a letter in which an explanation of the deduction was made in the following words: "These deductions are made to cover the percentage of decay on each car. We mailed you, some time ago, the inspection reports covering each of these cars in order that you might satisfy yourself that we are making only reasonable deductions." Each of the checks was marked in full payment of the car number for which payment was remitted.

On December 16th the plaintiffs acknowledged receipt of checks totaling $4,575, which they stated they had placed to the credit of the defendant, but insisted that there was still a balance due of $425 for which they demanded payment. In other words, they accepted the checks but rejected the proposed deduction.

On February 11, 1922, the defendant, who was still indebted to the plaintiffs for five cars, sent to them a check for $2,000 and a promissory note for $2,328.70 with interest payable in thirty days. On the back of this note there was this notation: "Payment in full of balance owing you on the following cars of Onions:" (giving numbers of cars). A letter also accompanied this note showing the reasons for the deductions mentioned therein, reading as follows: "We have already advised you the percentage of decay on cars NYC-138745 and NYC-138762 and have deducted off the first car Two Hundred and Eight Dollars ($208.00), representing twenty per cent of the invoice which the Government inspection shows as running from ten to thirty-five per cent decay and an average of fifteen to twenty-five per cent. You know that decay of this particular kind Slimy Soft Rot, hurts the sale of the entire shipment as the onions that are sound lose in value after being sorted over as they are never so bright and clean as when shipment is sound.

Car NYC-138762 also shows the same kind of decay and we have deducted fifteen per cent from the invoice and this in no way represents what we should have deducted as the bad onions affected the sale and condition of the others."

The plaintiffs replied to this letter crediting these amounts on the account of the defendant and demanding all the balance due, $801.29, the amount sued for in this action....

The facts, briefly stated, therefore, are: The plaintiffs sold to the defendant onions for an agreed price. The shipment in part was rotten and decayed. The defendant notified the plaintiffs of the fact sending to them the government reports made by the Food Products Inspector. The defendant paid for the goods which were in good condition, deducting $801.29 for those which he claimed to have been decayed. The payment was made by checks and notes and accompanying letters notifying the plaintiffs that if accepted by them they would be in full payment of the amount due, and the balance, $801.29, the amount of the deduction, would thus be paid by agreement or by accord and satisfaction (to use the legal terms). The claim put forth by the defendant for deduction was apparently made in good faith, and in view of the government reports seems to be reasonable and fair. The percentage of the deduction made by the defendant was not as large as the percentage of decay reported by the government reports sent to the plaintiffs and might be less than the amount which the defendant could have recovered if he had sued the plaintiffs for damages or upon their warranty. Under these circumstances, was the trial judge justified in holding as a matter of law that there had been no accord and satisfaction and that the plaintiffs were entitled to the balance claimed?

The general rule is that a liquidated claim, that is, a claim which is not disputed, but admitted to be due, cannot be discharged by any payment of a less amount. In *Jackson v. Volkening* we find the following language used: "The rule of law is well established, undoubtedly, that where a liquidated sum is due, the payment of part only, although accepted in satisfaction, is not, for want of consideration, a discharge of the entire indebtedness, but this rule is not looked upon with favor and is confined strictly to cases falling within it." In *Fuller v. Kemp* it was said: "Where the demand is liquidated, and the liability of the debtor is not in good faith disputed, a different rule has been applied. In such cases the acceptance of a less sum than is the

creditor's due, will not of itself discharge the debt, even if a receipt in full is given." And in *Simons v. Supreme Council American Legion of Honor* the point was stated in these words: "Now it is the settled law of this state that if a debt or claim be disputed or contingent at the time of payment, the payment, when accepted, of a part of the whole debt is a good satisfaction and it matters not that there was no solid foundation for the dispute." And in *Eames Vacuum Brake Co. v. Prosser* this court said: "It is only in cases where a dispute has arisen between the parties as to the amount due and a check is tendered on one side in full satisfaction of the matter in controversy that the other party will be deemed to have acquiesced in the amount offered by an acceptance and a retention of the check." The term "liquidated," therefore, when used in connection with the subject of accord and satisfaction has reference to a claim which the debtor does not dispute; a claim which he admits to be due but attempts to satisfy by the payment of a smaller amount. Thus in *Nassoiy v. Tomlinson* this court said: "A demand is not liquidated, even if it appears that something is due, unless it appears how much is due; and when it is admitted that one of two specific sums is due, but there is a genuine dispute as to which is the proper amount, the demand is regarded as unliquidated, within the meaning of that term as applied to the subject of accord and satisfaction."

In this case before us, the full amount claimed by the plaintiffs was not admittedly due. The fact that the contract called for a stated amount or an amount which could be easily figured according to deliveries did not make the claim liquidated within this meaning of the law as applied to accord and satisfaction. The term "liquidated" has an entirely different meaning in this connection than it has when used to determine whether or not interest is payable upon a recovery. The amount claimed by the plaintiffs and specified in the contract was repudiated by the defendant. He denied that he owed the money. He disputed the plaintiffs' demand. The contract had not been fulfilled and completed. Deliveries had not been made as called for. The goods were rotten and decayed, and not as warranted. For the purpose of this subject, to my mind, it makes no difference whether the defendant had a claim for breach of warranty or whether he had a right to reject or claimed a right to reject the imperfect goods. The fact still exists that he insisted with the plaintiffs that he should not be obliged to pay for articles he had not purchased. It is a statement inconsistent with the fact to say that the plaintiffs' claim was liquidated in the sense that it was admitted and acknowledged to be due by the defendant. He disputed it at every step, and sent to the plaintiffs written evidence to justify the honesty and good faith of his statements. Thus there was a difference between these parties over the amount due on this contract. If the plaintiffs had sued the defendant for the full amount, the latter could have defended. There was some evidence at least to indicate that the onions were rotten at the heart when delivered to the railroad. Thus, there never had been a complete delivery and the defendant might have defended, or if there had been acceptance and no rejection within a reasonable time, then the defendant having given notice, could have counterclaimed on his warranty. However we look at it there was relief at law in some form for the defendant. He was not obliged to pay for rotten onions.

Thus within all the cases the claim of the plaintiffs was not liquidated within the meaning of that term as used in this connection. It was a disputed claim. The plaintiffs knew it was disputed. They knew also that the checks and notes which they received and cashed were received in full payment of their disputed claim. They could not under these circumstances keep the money and reject the conditions attached to payment. Having accepted payment the conditions attached and the balance of $801.29 has been satisfied.

Therefore, the judgments below must be reversed and judgment directed for the defendant dismissing the complaint....

CASE 12-3

The following case explains how and why the Uniform Commercial Code has changed common law rules regarding accord and satisfaction in New York. The changes allow a creditor who complies with UCC § 1-207 (now UCC §1-308) to cash a debtor's "full satisfaction" check but avoid an accord and satisfaction and reserve its rights against the debtor for the balance the creditor claims is due.

HORN WATERPROOFING CORP. v. BUSHWICK IRON & STEEL CO.
Court of Appeals of New York, 1985
66 N.Y.2d 321; 497 N.Y.S.2d 310

JASEN, Judge. This appeal presents an issue of first impression: whether the common-law doctrine of accord and satisfaction has been superseded by operation of Uniform Commercial Code § 1-207 in situations involving the tender of a negotiable instrument as full payment of a disputed claim.

The relevant facts are uncomplicated. The parties entered into an oral agreement whereby plaintiff was to repair the leaking roof on defendant's building. After two days work, plaintiff concluded that a new roof was needed and submitted a bill for work already done. Defendant disputed the amount charged and plaintiff revised the bill downward from $1,241 to $1,080. Defendant remained unsatisfied with the charges and sent plaintiff a check for only $500. The check bore the following notation affixed on the reverse side: "This check is accepted in full payment, settlement, satisfaction, release and discharge of any and all claims and/or demands of whatsoever kind and nature." Directly thereunder, plaintiff printed the words "Under Protest", indorsed the check with its stamp, and deposited the $500 into its account.

Plaintiff then commenced this action in Civil Court seeking $580 as the balance due on its revised bill.

Defendant moved for summary judgment on the ground that plaintiff's acceptance and negotiation of the check constituted an accord and satisfaction. The motion was denied and the Appellate Term affirmed. The court held that the Uniform Commercial Code (the Code) was applicable to the type of commercial transaction in which the parties were involved and that, under the provisions of § 1-207, plaintiff was entitled to reserve its right to demand the balance due.

On appeal by leave of the Appellate Term, the Appellate Division reversed, granted defendant's motion, and dismissed the complaint. The majority of that court held that the parties' agreement, being a contract for the performance of services, fell outside the scope of the Code. It was, therefore, concluded that the common law applied and that the doctrine of accord and satisfaction precluded plaintiff's recovery. In dissent, Justice Weinstein argued that application of the common-law doctrine to the facts of this case is inequitable and needlessly constricts the modernizing effect of the Code. We now reverse and hold that, under § 1-207 of the Code, a creditor may preserve his right to the balance of a disputed claim, by explicit reservation in his indorsement of a check tendered by the debtor as full payment.

The effect of Code § 1-207 upon the common-law doctrine of accord and satisfaction has been much debated. Indeed, the courts that have addressed the issue in this State have rendered conflicting decisions, and our sister state courts are likewise divided. In our view, applying § 1-207 to a "full payment" check situation, to permit a creditor to reserve his rights and, thereby, preclude an accord and satisfaction, more nearly comports with the content and context of the statutory provision and with the legislative history and underlying purposes of the Code as well, and is a fairer policy in debtor-creditor transactions.

It has long been the general rule in this State that "if a debt or claim be disputed or contingent at the time of payment, the payment, when accepted, of a part of the whole debt is a good satisfaction and it matters not that there was no solid foundation for the dispute. The test in such cases is, Was the dispute honest or fraudulent? If honest, it affords the basis for an accord between the parties, which the law favors, the execution of which is the satisfaction."

The theory underlying this common-law rule of accord and satisfaction is that the parties have thus entered into a new contract displacing all or part of their original one. Although the creditor might have been confronted with an "embarrassing... choice" upon the debtor's presentment to him of partial payment, such as in the case of a "full payment" or "conditional" check, nevertheless, the rule of accord and satisfaction has generally been accepted as a legitimate and expeditious means of settling contract disputes. As this court stated more than 70 years ago: "The law wisely favors settlements, and where there is a real and genuine contest between the parties and a settlement is had without fraud or misrepresentation for an amount determined upon as a compromise between the conflicting claims such settlement should be upheld, although such amount is materially less than the amount claimed by the person to whom it is paid."

Still, where the creditor is presented with partial payment as satisfaction in full, but, nevertheless, wishes to preserve his claim to the balance left unpaid, it cannot be gainsaid that conflicting considerations of policy and fairness are implicated. This is particularly so in the case of a full payment check. On the one hand, the debtor, as the master of his offer, has reason to expect that his offer will either be accepted or his check returned. At the same time, however, the creditor has good cause to believe that he is fully entitled to retain the partial payment that is rightfully his and presently in his possession, without having to forfeit entitlement to whatever else is his due.

In dismissing these latter considerations with specific regard to the applicability of Code § 1-207 to a check tendered as "full payment", one commentary argued that: "Besides operating as an unnecessary destruction of a valuable common law doctrine, the expansive interpretation of U.C.C. § 1-207 conflicts with another basic principle of the Uniform Commercial Code, the duty of good faith imposed by § 1-203, certainly the more fundamental concept.... It is unfair to the party who writes the check thinking that he will be spending his money only if the whole dispute will be over, to allow the other party, knowing of that reasonable expectation, to weasel around the deal by putting his own markings on the other person's checks. There is no reason why § 1-207 should be interpreted as being an exception to the basic duty of good faith, when it is possible to interpret the two sections consistently. The academic writers who support this result offer no analysis, to the current knowledge of this treatise, which would justify licensing the recipient of the check to so deceive the drawer."

However, an entirely different conclusion is reached in another commentary which explains that:

"Offering a check for less than the contract amount, but 'in full settlement' inflicts an exquisite form of commercial torture on the payee. If the offer is reasonable it creates a marvelous anxiety in some recipients: 'Shall I risk the loss of $9,000 for the additional $1,000 that the bloke really owes me?' In general the law has authorized such drawer behavior by regarding such a check as an offer of accord and satisfaction which the payee accepts if he cashes the check. Traditionally the payee could write all manner of disclaimers over his indorsement without avail; by cashing the check he was held to have accepted the offer on the drawer's terms. Even if he scratched out the drawer's notation or indorsed it under protest he was deemed to have accepted subject to the conditions under which the drawer offered it.
* * * *

"However, we believe... that 1-207 authorizes the payee to indorse under protest and accept the amount of the check without entering an accord and satisfaction or otherwise forsaking his claim to any additional sum allegedly due him."

We concur with the latter view. Indeed, the common-law doctrine of accord and satisfaction creates a cruel dilemma for the good-faith creditor in possession of a full payment check. Under that rule, the creditor would have no other choice but to surrender the partial payment or forfeit his right to the remainder. We are persuaded, however, that the common law was changed with the adoption of § 1-207 pursuant to which a fairer rule now prevails.

§ 1-207 provides: "A party who with explicit reservation of rights performs or promises performance or assents to performance in a manner demanded or offered by the other party does not thereby prejudice the rights reserved. Such words as 'without prejudice', 'under protest' or the like are sufficient." The plain language of the provision, "without much stretching", would seem applicable to a full payment check. A fortiori, if liberally construed, as the Code's provisions are explicitly intended to be, it seems clear that the reach of § 1-207 is sufficiently extensive to alter the doctrine of accord and satisfaction by permitting a creditor to reserve his rights though accepting the debtor's check.

The Comment prepared by the National Conference of Commissioners on Uniform State Laws and the American Law Institute is fairly subject to a variety of interpretations as to the purpose of § 1-207. It simply does not, however, specifically address the law of accord and satisfaction and how it might have been altered. By contrast, the Report of the State of New York Commission on Uniform State Laws quite clearly took the position that the common-law doctrine would be changed. With specific reference to § 1-207, the report stated:

"This section permits a party involved in a Code-covered transaction to accept whatever he can get by way of payment, performance, etc., without losing his rights to demand the remainder of the goods, to set-off a failure of quality, or to sue for the balance of the payment, so long as he explicitly reserves his rights.

"In *Nassoiy v. Tomlinson*, the debtor paid no more than the exact amount he claimed was due. The court held that the conditional payment was payment of an unliquidated claim if any part was disputed, and that the acceptance of the payment discharged the entire debt. The Code rule would permit, in Code-covered transactions, the acceptance of a part performance or payment tendered in full settlement without requiring the acceptor to gamble with his legal right to demand the balance of the performance or payment." (Report of Comm. on Uniform State Laws to Legislature, at 19-20 [1961].)

This interpretive analysis, which was submitted to the Legislature together with the Commission's recommendation for enactment of the Code, unmistakeably addresses the common-law doctrine and notes that the section permits a reservation of rights upon acceptance of partial payment where an accord and satisfaction might otherwise have resulted.

Particularly significant is the reference to *Nassoiy v Tomlinson*, a seminal decision in this State applying the doctrine of accord and satisfaction under facts involving a full payment check. This commentary clearly apprised the Legislature that § 1-207 would change the rule upheld in that case. Moreover, it is notable that the analysis explicitly speaks of the acceptance of part "payment tendered in full settlement." The section was clearly not deemed restricted to situations involving the acceptance of goods or such other "performance" in part.

This view derives further support from the very context of § 1-207 within the Code. The provision is set forth in the introductory article 1, among the general provisions of the Code dealing with such matters as its title, underlying purposes, general definitions, and principles of interpretation. Presumably, § 1-207, as with other provisions in the introductory article, is to apply to any commercial transaction within the reach of one of the substantive articles -- i.e., to any "Code-covered" transaction, as denominated in the New York Annotations. There is simply no language in § 1-207 expressing or intimating a more restrictive intention to limit its application to specific kinds of transactions particular to one of the articles, or sections, of the Code such as the purchase and acceptance of goods (art 2), investment securities (art 8) or chattel paper (art 9). Rather, the nonlimiting language of § 1-207 and its placement in the Code with the other generally applicable provisions of article 1 is persuasive that the section is, indeed, applicable to all commercial transactions fairly considered to be "Code-covered".

Hence, the payment of a contract debt by check or other commercial paper and its acceptance by the creditor fall within the reach of § 1-207. Whether the underlying contract between the parties be for the purchase of goods, chattel paper or personal services, the use of a negotiable instrument for the purpose of payment or attempted satisfaction of a contract debt is explicitly and specifically regulated by the provisions of article 3 and, therefore, undeniably a Code-covered transaction. Consequently, a debtor's tender of a full payment check is an article 3 transaction which is governed by § 1-207, regardless of the nature of the contract underlying the parties' commercial relationship.

Indeed, Dean Rosenthal, who otherwise contended that § 1-207 was not originally intended by the drafters to alter the doctrine of accord and satisfaction by full payment checks, observed that:

"Article three ('Commercial Paper'), however, is a special case. Does the fact that a check is used as the device to effect a settlement in itself bring the transaction within the Code (and therefore make § 1-207 arguably applicable) even if the underlying transaction was one not otherwise covered by the Code? Article three contains no scope provision analogous to the "transactions in goods' language in [article 2].

* * * *

"[I]t seems fairly clear that if such a check is tendered in settlement, the transaction must be regarded as being within article three, and if § 1-207 is otherwise relevant its application cannot be avoided by showing either that article one was not meant to be applied to non-Code transactions or that the underlying obligation did not arise out of one of the other substantive articles of the Code." (Rosenthal, *Discord and Dissatisfaction: § 1-207 of the Uniform Commercial Code*, 78 Colum L Rev 48, 70.)

Finally, . . . such a reading of § 1-207 would seem to promote the underlying policies and purposes of the Code. . . . By construing the section to permit a reservation of rights whenever a negotiable instrument is used to make payment on an existing debt, regardless of the nature of the underlying obligation between the parties, the commercial law of negotiable instruments is rendered more simple, clear and uniform. Moreover, the policy embodied in § 1-207, to favor a preservation of rights despite acceptance of partial satisfaction of the underlying obligation, is thus

extended to reach all commercial transactions in which the Code is implicated by reason of payment by an article 3 instrument. As a consequence, such a reading of § 1-207 serves to liberalize, or "de-technicalize", that important branch of commercial law governing the full payment check.

Application of the foregoing to the facts of this case is evident. Defendant presented a "full payment" check for $500 in satisfaction of a debt in the amount of $1,080. Plaintiff indorsed the check below its notation, "Under Protest", thereby indicating its intent to preserve all rights to the $580 balance. Such an explicit reservation of rights, falling squarely within § 1-207 as we construe that provision today, was an effective means of precluding an accord and satisfaction or any other prejudice to the rights thus reserved. Regardless of whether the underlying transaction between the parties was a contract for the performance of services rather than for the sale of goods, defendant's tender of a check to plaintiff brought the attempted full payment or satisfaction of the underlying obligation within the scope of article 3, thereby rendering it a "Code-covered" transaction to which the provisions of § 1-207 are applicable.

Accordingly, the order of the Appellate Division should be reversed, with costs, and defendant's motion to dismiss denied.

CASE 12-4

The following case interprets what is required under UCC § 1-207 (now UCC 1-308) for a creditor to make an "explicit reservation" of rights to avoid an accord and satisfaction when cashing a "full satisfaction" check.

SULLIVAN v. CONANT VALLEY ASSOCIATES
Supreme Court of New York, Westchester County, 1990
148 Misc. 2d 483; 560 N.Y.S.2d 617

DONOVAN, Judge. Plaintiff... has sued the two first-named defendants in contract for a balance of moneys allegedly due him for performing plumbing work and providing certain materials improving defendants' property.

By motion, the main defendants... seek summary judgment dismissing the complaint upon ground of payment or accord and satisfaction....

The central issue presented is whether plaintiff's scratching out of "complete and final payment" verbiage placed by defendants at the top of the endorsement blocks, followed by his depositing of the checks for collection, sufficiently reserved his rights so as to permit the subsequent suit here for the higher claimed amount.

The court concedes that a close and novel question of law is presented.

The rule at common law is that acceptance and cashing of a final check even with explicit words of reservation of rights by the payee as to further claims constitute in all events an accord and satisfaction. This rule was, however, substantially changed upon the passage of Uniform Commercial Code § 1-207 which allows for such reservation by the payee. That section reads in full as follows: "A party who with explicit reservation of rights performs or promises performance or assents to performance in a manner demanded or offered by the other party does not thereby prejudice the rights reserved. Such words as 'without prejudice', 'under protest' or the like are sufficient."

While much case law has construed the section, it has primarily dealt with the types of transactions and situations covered by the provision. Research by the court has not disclosed any precedent examining what verbiage short of the type indicated in the statute would still be "explicit". The common thread, however, running between both the near cases examined and the statute itself is the necessity for "explicit" verbiage reserving further rights despite endorsement and cashing (see, "Horn Waterproofing Corp."). Here, in addition to the defendants' "full payment" conditions appearing over the endorsement blocks on the checks themselves, letters accompanying the checks from the defendants indicated the existence of the dispute and tender of the checks as a "complete amount and final payment" and "should you elect not to accept this final payment then all documents and backcharges are withdrawn".

On strength of general case authority, the statute itself which must be narrowly interpreted since in derogation of the common law and under the particular facts here, the court must conclude that standing alone, mere scratching out of final payment conditions on a check followed by endorsement and cashing is not the explicit and unambiguous reservation of rights required; further added words clearly bespeaking reservation are necessary.

CASE 12-5

The following case deals with a claim by a debtor that a creditor's acceptance of a "full satisfaction" check resulted in an accord and satisfaction that discharged the debtor's liquidated debt.

CENTURY 21 KAATERSKILL REALTY v. GRASSO
Appellate Division, New York (3rd Dept.), 1986
124 A.D.2d 316; 508 N.Y.S.2d 99

MIKOLL, Judge. Appeal from an order of the Supreme Court at Special Term (Williams, J.), entered August 8, 1985 in Sullivan County, which denied defendants' motion to dismiss the complaint.

Plaintiff sued defendants seeking judgment in the sum of $2,200 claimed to be the balance due and owing for a real estate broker's commission for the sale of real property belonging to defendant Michele Grasso (hereinafter Grasso). Defendants moved to dismiss the complaint on the grounds of discharge and failure to state a cause of action.

Plaintiff was retained to sell land owned by Grasso, who agreed pursuant to a written contract to pay brokerage fees of 10% of the purchase price. The property was sold for $82,000 and title was transferred on May 11, 1984. Plaintiff demanded payment of $8,200. Grasso's attorney sent plaintiff a check for $6,000 which bore the legend:

"In full accord and satisfaction for any real estate commission claimed by Centruy 21 against Michele Grasso."

The check was indorsed by Rubin J. Katz, an officer of plaintiff, and deposited in plaintiff's account. Defendants contend that the $2,200 sought in plaintiff's complaint was discharged by plaintiff's acceptance without protest of the check tendered on Grasso's behalf in full satisfaction of the debt owed. Special Term held that defendants were not entitled to a dismissal of the complaint based on an accord and satisfaction in that the submissions failed to evidence the existence of a dispute which would make viable the accord and satisfaction defense.

Defendants contend that plaintiff's failure to protest the partial payment as to conform to UCC 1-207 entitles defendants to a dismissal of the complaint. . . . We concur with Special Term's interpretation that UCC 1-207 is not implicated absent a pending dispute as to delivery, acceptance or payment. Defendants never disputed the amount owed before the check was sent to plaintiff. Accord and satisfaction pursuant to UCC 1-207 pertains only to a method of procedure where one party is claiming as of right something which the other feels is unwarranted.

Order affirmed, with costs.

CASE 12-6

This case considers whether endorsement of a full payment check constitutes a written signed promise to discharge a debt under GOL 5-1103.

KING METAL PRODUCTS, INC. v. WORKMEN'S COMPENSATION BD.
Appellate Division, New York (2d Dept.), 1963
20 A.D.2d 565, 245 N.Y.S.2d 882

Memorandum. In our opinion, respondent's retention and deposit of a check in the sum of $250, drawn by petitioner's attorney to its order and bearing legends on the face and back thereof indicating that it was in full satisfaction and settlement of the judgment, did not constitute an accord and satisfaction. On the record presented, the general rule applies that a liquidated and undisputed claim cannot be discharged by the payment of a lesser amount.

We are also of the opinion that the endorsement of the check did not constitute an agreement which was enforceable under section [5-1103 of the General Obligations Law].

CASE 12-7

Unless prohibited by statute, courts may enforce contracts in which parties agree to waive claims arising from another party's negligence. The following case illustrates how the courts view such exculpatory clauses in general and what tests must be met before a court will enforce an exculpatory clause and deny recovery to an injured party. Not surprisingly, these issues have arisen in the context of recreational parachute jumping.

GROSS v. SWEET
Court of Appeals of New York, 1979
49 N.Y.2d 102, 424 N.Y.S.2d 365

FUCHSBERG, Judge. We hold that, in the circumstances of this case, a release signed by the plaintiff as a precondition for his enrollment in defendant's parachute jumping course does not bar him from suing for personal injuries he allegedly incurred as a result of defendant's negligence.

Plaintiff Bruce Gross, wishing to learn how to parachute, enrolled in the Stormville Parachute Center Training School, a facility owned and operated by the defendant William Sweet for the purpose of offering instruction in the sport. The ensuing events are essentially undisputed. As a prerequisite for admission into the course, Gross had to pay a fee and sign a form entitled "Responsibility Release". He was then given the standard introductory lesson, which consisted of approximately one hour of on-land training, including oral instruction as well as several jumps off a two and a half foot table. Plaintiff then was equipped with a parachute and flown to an altitude of 2,800 feet for his first practice jump. Upon coming in contact with the ground on his descent, plaintiff suffered serious personal injuries.

The suit is grounded on negligence, breach of warranty and gross negligence. In the main, plaintiff claims that defendant failed to provide adequate training and safe equipment, violated certain rules and procedures promulgated by the Federal Aviation Administration governing the conduct of parachute jumping schools and failed to warn him sufficiently of the attendant dangers.

Defendant pleaded the release plaintiff had signed and moved for summary judgment, contending that the terms of the release exculpated the defendant from any liability. Plaintiff, in turn, cross-moved to strike this affirmative defense contending, primarily, that the terms of the release did not specifically bar a suit for personal injuries negligently caused by the defendant. He also urged that, as a matter of policy, the release should not be enforceable as between a student and his teacher, a relationship in which one of the parties holds himself out as qualified and responsible to provide training in a skill and the other party relies on this expertise, particularly in the context of an activity in which the degree of training necessary for safe participation is much greater than might be apparent to a novice. Alternatively, plaintiff argues that the release in any event does not excuse defendant's violation of the Federal Aviation Administration's regulations governing parachute jumping schools and student parachutists, one of which allegedly required that a medical certificate be furnished as a prerequisite to enrollment in a parachute jumping course. Defendant's failure to request one, plaintiff asserts, bore critically on his situation because, despite his having informed defendant that several years earlier an orthopedic pin had been inserted in his leg, he was accepted as a student though, as the school must have known, landing in a parachute puts special stress on one's legs.

However, Special Term granted defendant's motion, denied plaintiff's cross motion and dismissed the complaint. On plaintiff's appeal from that order, a divided Appellate Division reversed, reinstated the complaint and granted plaintiff's motion to dismiss the affirmative defense. The appeal is now before us on a certified question: "Was the order of this Court, which reinstated the complaint and granted plaintiff's motion to dismiss the affirmative defense of release, correct as a matter of law?" Our answer is that it was.

We begin with the proposition, too well settled to invoke any dispute, that the law frowns upon contracts intended to exculpate a party from the consequences of his own negligence and though, with certain exceptions, they are enforceable, such agreements are subject to close judicial scrutiny.... To the extent that agreements purport to grant exemption for liability for willful or grossly negligent acts they have been viewed as wholly void.... And so, here, so much of plaintiff's complaint as contains allegations that defendant was grossly negligent, may not be barred by the release in any event. But we need not explore further this possibility for we conclude the complaint in its entirety withstands the exculpatory agreement.

Nor need we consider plaintiff's request that we ignore the release on the grounds that the special relationship of the parties and the public interest involved forbids its enforcement. While we have, for example, had occasion to invalidate such provisions when they were contained in the contract between a passenger and a common carrier... or in a contract between a customer and a public utility under a duty to furnish telephone service... or when imposed by an employer as a condition of employment... the circumstances here do not fit within any of these relationships. And, though we note that a recent statute renders void agreements purporting to exempt from liability for negligence those engaged in a variety of businesses that serve the public (e.g., landlords (General Obligations Law, § 5-321); caterers (§ 5-322);

building service or maintenance contractors (§ 5-323); those who maintain garages or parking garages (§ 5-325); or pools, gymnasiums or places of public amusement or recreation (§ 5-326)), defendant's occupation does not fall within any of these classes either. We also decline, at this point, plaintiff's invitation that we proceed further to consider what effect, if any, the alleged contravention of Federal regulations may have on the relationship of the parties or the public interest involved. Such questions need not be reached in view of our holding that the wording of the exculpatory agreement does not preclude plaintiff's suit for negligence.

As the cases make clear, the law's reluctance to enforce exculpatory provisions of this nature has resulted in the development of an exacting standard by which courts measure their validity. So, it has been repeatedly emphasized that unless the intention of the parties is expressed in unmistakable language, an exculpatory clause will not be deemed to insulate a party from liability for his own negligent acts.... Put another way, it must appear plainly and precisely that the "limitation of liability extends to negligence or other fault of the party attempting to shed his ordinary responsibility"....

Not only does this stringent standard require that the drafter of such an agreement make its terms unambiguous, but it mandates that the terms be understandable as well. Thus, a provision that would exempt its drafter from any liability occasioned by his fault should not compel resort to a magnifying glass and lexicon.... Of course, this does not imply that only simple or monosyllabic language can be used in such clauses. Rather, what the law demands is that such provisions be clear and coherent....

By and large, if such is the intention of the parties, the fairest course is to provide explicitly that claims based on negligence are included.... That does not mean that the word "negligence" must be employed for courts to give effect to an exculpatory agreement; however, words conveying a similar import must appear....

We are, of course, cognizant of the fact that the general rule of strict judicial construction has been somewhat liberalized in its application to exoneration clauses in indemnification agreements, which are usually "negotiated at arm's length between... sophisticated business entities" and which can be viewed as merely "allocating the risk of liability to third parties between themselves, essentially through the employment of insurance". In such cases, the law, reflecting the economic realities, will recognize an agreement to relieve one party from the consequences of his negligence on the strength of a broadly worded clause framed in less precise language than would normally be required, though even then it must evince the "unmistakable intent of the parties".

The case before us today obviously does not fit within this exception to the strict legal standard generally employed by the courts of this State under which exculpatory provisions drawn in broad and sweeping language have not been given effect. For example, agreements to release from "any and all responsibility or liability of any nature whatsoever for any loss of property or personal injury occurring on this trip"... or to "waive claim for any loss to personal property, or for any personal injury while a member of (a) club"... have not barred claims based on negligence.... Moreover, in *Boll v Sharp & Dohme*... we held not sufficiently unambiguous a release form in which a blood donor was required to agree that defendants were not "in any way responsible for any consequences... resulting from the giving of such blood or from any of the tests, examinations or procedures incident thereto", and further "release(d) and discharge(d) (defendants) from all claims and demands whatsoever against them or any of them by reason of any matter relative or incident to such donation of blood".... The donor was thus allowed to sue in negligence for injuries he sustained when, on the completion of the blood donation, he fainted and fell to the floor.

With all this as background, the language of the "Responsibility Release" in the case before us, must be viewed as no more explicit than that in *Boll*. In its entirety, it reads:

> "I, the undersigned, hereby, and by these covenants, do waive any and all claims that I, my heirs, and/or assignees may have against Nathaniel Sweet, the Stormville Parachute Center, the Jumpmaster and the Pilot who shall operate the aircraft when used for the purpose of parachute jumping for any personal injuries or property damage that I may sustain or which may arise out of my learning, practicing or actually jumping from an aircraft. I also assume full responsibility for any damage that I may do or cause while participating in this sport".

Assuming that this language alerted the plaintiff to the dangers inherent in parachute jumping and that he entered into the sport with apprehension of the risks, it does not follow that he was aware of, much less intended to accept, any enhanced exposure to injury occasioned by the carelessness of the very persons on which he depended for his safety. Specifically, the release nowhere expresses any intention to exempt the defendant from liability for injury or property damages which may result from his failure to use due care either in his training methods or in his furnishing safe equipment. Thus, whether on a running reading or a careful analysis, the agreement could most reasonably be taken merely as driving home the fact that the defendant was not to bear any responsibility for injuries that ordinarily and inevitably would occur, without any fault of the defendant, to those who participate in such a physically demanding sport.

In short, instead of specifying to prospective students that they would have to abide any consequences attributable to the instructor's own carelessness, the defendant seems to have preferred the use of opaque terminology rather than suffer the possibility of lower enrollment. But, while, with exceptions not pertinent to this case, the law grudgingly accepts the proposition that men may contract away their liability for negligently caused injuries, they may do so only on the condition that their intention be expressed clearly and in "unequivocal terms".

Accordingly, the certified question is answered in the affirmative, and the order of the Appellate Division reversing the grant of summary judgment, reinstating the complaint and dismissing the defense based on the release should be affirmed.

CASE 12-8

Courts are reluctant to enforce contracts exculpating professionals from acts of negligence. In the following case, a New York court addressed the enforceability of a contract that attempted to release dentists from liability for malpractice.

DEVITO v. N.Y.U. COLLEGE OF DENTISTRY
Supreme Court of New York (N.Y. Co.), 1989
145 Misc. 2d 144, 544 N.Y.S.2d 109

PREMINGER, Judge. Defendants move for summary judgment dismissing this dental malpractice action on the ground that a release executed by plaintiff precludes the action.

Defendant New York University College of Dentistry (NYU) operates a dental clinic where, in exchange for reduced fees, patients agree to be treated by students working under faculty supervision. Plaintiff was treated at the clinic for approximately one year beginning in December 1982 by various students including defendants Wisun and Chiha.

Prior to any treatment plaintiff executed a release which reads, in relevant part: "In consideration of the reduced rates given to me by New York University, I hereby release and agree to save harmless New York University, its doctors, and students, from any and all liability arising out of, or in connection with, any injuries or damages which I may sustain while on its premises, or as a result of any treatment in its infirmaries."

Defendants contend that this release bars plaintiff's claims against them for malpractice. Plaintiff argues that the release was not intended to relieve defendants from responsibility for their negligent acts, and that to give the release such effect would be against public policy.

The very release involved here has been examined by several New York courts with disparate results.
* * * *

... [t]his court will reexamine the legal principles governing the validity and effect of contracts which attempt to release a doctor or hospital from liability to a patient.

In general, the law frowns upon contracts which seek to exculpate persons from their own negligence, and to the extent such contracts bar suits against willful or gross negligence, they are void. However, where, as here, the claim sought to be foreclosed is one grounded in ordinary negligence, the contract may generally be enforced, but only after being subjected to intense judicial scrutiny on a variety of issues.

The threshold consideration is whether the parties have a special relationship which would make enforcement of an exculpatory clause between them against the public interest. This occurs where the party seeking exculpation is in a business or profession which is either publicly regulated or providing an essential service to members of the public. Examples include common carriers and their passengers; public utilities and their customers; employers who impose the clause as a condition of employment and a host of statutorily created prohibited persons, such as landlords, caterers, and those who maintain parking lots, gymnasiums, and other public places. (See, GOL § 5-321 et seq.)

In these relationships, the consumer's need for the service creates an inequality in bargaining strength which enables the purveyor to insist upon a release, generally on its own prepared form, as a condition to providing the service. As in any adhesion contract a true and voluntary meeting of the minds on the terms of the agreement is unlikely.
* * * *

The courts of this State have not conclusively determined whether it would be against the public interest to allow physicians to insulate themselves from liability for negligence. However, other jurisdictions have held that the physician-patient relationship precludes the enforcement of such exculpatory agreements.

Thus, in *Olson v Molzen* the Supreme Court of Tennessee declared that the "general rule [that] a party may contract against his or her own negligence... do[es] not afford a satisfactory solution in a case involving a professional person operating in an area of public interest and pursuing a profession subject to licensure by the state. The rules that govern tradesmen in the marketplace are of little relevancy in dealing with professional persons who hold themselves out as experts and whose practice is regulated by the state." To the same effect are *Meiman v Rehabilitation Center* (Kentucky), *Tunkl v Regents of Univ. of Cal.* and *Smith v Hospital Auth.* (Georgia).

Assuming that the status of the parties withstands scrutiny, it next becomes necessary to examine the actual wording of the agreement. One must determine whether its terms are so clear, explicit and unambiguous that it appears certain that the limitation of liability is intended to cover negligent, as well as ordinary, acts of the party seeking to shed responsibility....

Although the word "negligent" need not actually be used, the Court of Appeals has indicated that such would be the "fairest course." In those instances where releases from liability which do not contain the word "negligence" have been construed to include negligent behavior, the words used have referred to the concept of fault in specific and unambiguous terms.

All-encompassing or open-ended phrases such as "any and all claims" or "any and all responsibility or liability of any nature whatsoever" and "all claims and demands whatsoever" are considered insufficient to indicate an intention to waive injury occasioned by fault.

Even if a clause is found to be clear and unambiguous, it must be examined further to determine whether it would be understandable to a layman, which, while not requiring "only... monosyllabic language", does compel that the language used be "clear and coherent".

The NYU release cannot survive the close scrutiny mandated by the concepts discussed above. It fails, in all particulars, to meet the established standards. Even if the status of the parties is removed from consideration, the contract cannot be construed to include exemption from negligent acts. There is no reference, either explicitly or implicitly, by "words... [of] similar import" to the concept of negligence or fault. No layman perusing this release would find it immediately understandable that the signatory had contracted to accept not only injuries that might ordinarily and inevitably occur, but also any and all consequences of defendants' carelessness.

Although the law grudgingly accepts the proposition that men may contract away their liability for negligently caused injuries it may not do so here. The circumstances of this case and the wording of the release militate against such a result. The parties' status is, at the very least, suspect, the contract is ambiguous, and the language used is far from instantly coherent to a layman.

For all of the foregoing reasons, defendants' motion for summary judgment is denied. Although no cross motion was brought by plaintiff the court searches the record (CPLR 3212 [b]) and awards summary judgment dismissing defendants' affirmative defense based on the release.

CASE 12-9

The types of legitimate employer interests that might support enforcement of a restrictive covenant are noted in this case.

1 MODEL MANAGEMENT, LLC, v. KAVOUSSI
NY App. Div. 1st Dept., 2011
82 A.D. 3d 502, 918 N.Y.S. 2d 431

Plaintiff 1 Model Management (1MM), a model agency, seeks damages and injunctive relief against Ali Kavoussi, a former 1MM model agent employed pursuant to a May 2004 contract. In May 2008, Kavoussi terminated the contract, left 1MM, and began working for another model agency, Men Women N.Y. Model Management Inc. d/b/a Women Management (Men Women). During the next eight months, three models whom 1MM had been representing when Kavoussi terminated the contract also left 1MM for Men Women.

* * *

The contract also provided that, for the one-year period after his termination, which has now passed, Kavoussi could not "be employed by ... any entity which ... represents ... any model managed by 1MM at the time of Employee's termination or at any time during the 90–day period preceding such termination." Such a restrictive covenant is enforceable only to the extent, among other things, that it is reasonable and necessary to protect the employer's legitimate interest and does not impose undue hardship on the employee. [Citation]

An employer's legitimate interest can include preventing an employee from misappropriating trade secrets or confidential customer lists or keeping an employee with unique or extraordinary skills from joining a competitor to the employer's detriment. [Citations] Here, 1MM failed to establish that its customer lists and model contact information are confidential, since it has not shown that the information is not readily available to others in the modeling industry. [Citation] But 1MM has raised a viable issue of fact as to whether Kavoussi's services were "special, unique or extraordinary," given that he had cultivated personal relationships with 1MM's models while working for 1MM and using its resources. [Citation]

Kavoussi argues that enforcing the restrictive covenant as written would prevent him from working in the modeling industry, but a triable issue has been raised concerning whether the restriction against working for agencies representing former 1MM models was unreasonably burdensome.

[Breach of contract claim reinstated]

CASE 12-10

In this case the court considers whether the employer demonstrated a sufficient legitimate interest to justify restraining a former employee from working for a competitor.

NATURAL ORGANICS, INC. v. KIRKENDALL
N.Y. App. Div. 2d Dept., 2008
52 A.D. 2d 488, 860 N.Y.S.2d 142

The defendant James A. Kirkendall worked for the plaintiff for approximately nine years selling vitamins and dietary supplements to specialized health food stores under the plaintiff's national brand name. When he was hired for the position, Kirkendall signed a nondisclosure and noncompetition agreement for employees (hereinafter the noncompete agreement), which prohibited employment with a competitor of the plaintiff for a period of 18 months from the date of termination of employment, and where the employee is a sales person, for an additional 18 months within 300 miles of the boundaries of his or her territory. Kirkendall resigned from his position with the plaintiff and began working for the defendant Reliance Vitamin Company, Inc. (hereinafter Reliance), which sold "private label" vitamins and dietary supplements to vitamin stores, health food stores, and others, who wanted to market the items to customers under their own name. The plaintiff commenced the instant action against Kirkendall and Reliance (hereinafter collectively the defendants) seeking, *inter alia*, injunctive relief and monetary damages for breach of the noncompete agreement.

In BDO Seidman v. Hirshberg, [Citation] the Court of Appeals set forth the "modern, prevailing common-law standard of reasonableness" for the enforceability of employee noncompete agreements [Citation]. "A restraint is reasonable only if it: (1) is no greater than is required for the protection of the legitimate interest of the employer, (2) does not impose undue hardship on the employee, and (3) is not injurious to the public" [Citation]. A noncompete agreement must also be reasonably limited temporally and geographically. [Citation]

Here, the defendants met their prima facie burden of establishing their entitlement to judgment as a matter of law by demonstrating that the noncompete agreement does not serve to protect a legitimate employer interest. The evidence demonstrated that Kirkendall, after leaving the plaintiff's employ, did not physically appropriate, copy, or intentionally memorize any purported confidential business information. [Citations]

In opposition, the plaintiff failed to raise a triable issue of fact. Although the plaintiff submitted evidence that Kirkendall was privy to reports containing detailed sales information concerning the plaintiff's customers, "an employee's recollection of information pertaining to specific needs and business habits of particular customers is not confidential." [Citations] Furthermore, the plaintiff failed to show that enforcement of the noncompete agreement was necessary to protect the goodwill of its clients. . . [Citation] or that Kirkendall used or threatened to use any protected trade lists or confidential customer lists. [Citation]

Since there is no legitimate employer interest to protect, the noncompete agreement is unenforceable and the issue of partial enforcement does not arise. [Citations] Accordingly, the Supreme Court properly granted the defendants' motion for summary judgment dismissing the complaint.

Case 13-1

The following case deals with the question of whether a party has a claim for fraud based on an affirmative misrepresentation of a material fact, when the party has been put on notice of material facts that have not been documented, but nevertheless goes forward with the transaction.

RODAS v. MANITARAS
Appellate Division, New York (1st Dept.), 1990
159 A.D.2d 341; 552 N.Y.S.2d 618

MEMORANDUM.

Pursuant to a contract of sale dated November 6, 1987, plaintiffs purchased a restaurant business from defendant Oyster House, Inc. Plaintiffs later signed a lease agreement for the premises dated March 9, 1988 with defendant Manitaras. Plaintiffs brought this action seeking rescission of the sale and lease agreements on the ground that defendants' false representations that the income of the business was $20,000 a week fraudulently induced them to enter into said agreements.

Paragraph 20 of the contract of sale contains a general merger clause and specifically recites that the business, its equipment, fixtures, chattels and furnishings are purchased in the exercise of plaintiffs' business judgment "and not upon any representations made by the seller, or by anyone acting in his behalf, as to the character, condition or quality of said chattels, fixtures, equipment and furnishings or as to the past, present or prospective income or profits of the said business, other than those contained in this agreement." While a general merger clause will not operate to bar parol evidence of fraud in the inducement where the parties expressly disclaim reliance on the representations alleged to be fraudulent, parol evidence as to those representations will not be admitted. Plaintiffs, however, allege that a specific disclaimer clause cannot bar the introduction of parol evidence of prior misrepresentations where the facts misrepresented were peculiarly within the knowledge of the defendant.

The defect in plaintiffs' reasoning lies not in the statement of the rule, but in their perception of its application. A classic example is provided by *Tahini Invs. v Bobrowsky*, in which the purchaser of land discovered 15 or more drums containing a hazardous material buried on the property. Although the contract contained specific language that the purchaser was not relying on representations as to the physical condition of the property, the court ruled that questions of fact were presented as to (1) whether the seller knew of the existence of the dumping site and (2) whether the purchaser, with reasonable diligence, could have ascertained the site's existence. The case illustrates that a party seeking to avoid a specific disclaimer clause must demonstrate that the facts alleged to have been fraudulently concealed could not be discovered through the exercise of reasonable diligence.

In the matter under review, by contrast, plaintiffs specifically requested examination of the records of the business and were refused. It is apparent that they were aware that the income of the business was a material fact in which they had received no documentation. In entering into the contract, with the assistance of counsel and without conducting an examination of the books and records, plaintiffs clearly assumed the risk that the documentation might not support the $20,000 weekly income that was represented to them.

Plaintiffs could have easily protected themselves by insisting on an examination of the books as a condition of closing. Alternatively, the contract could have included a condition subsequent that the sale would be rescinded if the actual sales experienced were significantly less than the represented figure. The standard which a party claiming fraud must meet in order to overcome a specific disclaimer clause is set forth in *Danann Realty Corp. v Harris*, relied upon by plaintiffs. It quotes *Schumaker v Mather*, which states that "if the facts represented are not matters peculiarly within the party's knowledge, and the other party has the means available to him of knowing, by the exercise of ordinary intelligence, the truth or the real quality of the subject of the representation, he must make use of those means, or he will not be heard to complain that he was induced to enter into the transaction by misrepresentations."

Where a party has no knowledge of a latent condition and no way of discovering the existence of that condition in the exercise of reasonable diligence then, as in *Tahini Invs. v Bobrowsky*, he may overcome a specific disclaimer clause and introduce parol evidence of fraudulent inducement. But where, as here, a party has been put on notice of the existence of material facts which have not been documented and he nevertheless proceeds with a transaction without securing the available documentation or inserting appropriate language in the agreement for his protection, he may truly be said to have willingly assumed the business risk that the facts may not be as represented. Succinctly put, a party will not be heard to complain that he has been defrauded when it is his own evident lack of due care which is responsible for his predicament.

CASE 13-2

A statement of opinion generally may not be the basis of a claim for fraud. This case discusses when a statement of opinion may be regarded and as statement of fact and thus may be actionable as fraud.

VOKES v. ARTHUR MURRAY, INC.
Fla. Dist. Ct. of Appeal of Florida, Sec. Dist., 1968
212 So.2d 906

PIERCE, J.

This is an appeal by Audrey E. Vokes, plaintiff below, from a final order dismissing with prejudice, for failure to state a cause of action, . . . plaintiff's complaint.

Defendant Arthur Murray, Inc., a corporation, authorizes the operation throughout the nation of dancing schools under the name of 'Arthur Murray School of Dancing' through local franchised operators, one of whom was defendant J. P. Davenport whose dancing establishment was in Clearwater.

Plaintiff Mrs. Audrey E. Vokes, a widow of 51 years and without family, had a yen to be 'an accomplished dancer' with the hopes of finding 'new interest in life'. So, on February 10, 1961, a dubious fate, with the assist of a motivated acquaintance, procured her to attend a 'dance party' at Davenport's 'School of Dancing' where she whiled away the pleasant hours, sometimes in a private room, absorbing his accomplished sales technique, during which her grace and poise were elaborated upon and her rosy future as 'an excellent dancer' was painted for her in vivid and glowing colors. As an incident to this interlude, he sold her eight 1/2-hour dance lessons to be utilized within one calendar month therefrom, for the sum of $14.50 cash in hand paid, obviously a baited 'comeon'.

Thus she embarked upon an almost endless pursuit of the terpsichorean art during which, over a period of less than sixteen months, she was sold fourteen 'dance courses' totalling in the aggregate 2302 hours of dancing lessons for a total cash outlay of $31,090.45, all at Davenport's dance emporium. . . . .

These dance lesson contracts and the monetary consideration therefor of over $31,000 were procured from her by means and methods of Davenport and his associates which went beyond the unsavory, yet legally permissible, perimeter of 'sales puffing' and intruded well into the forbidden area of undue influence, the suggestion of falsehood, the suppression of truth, and the free exercise of rational judgment, if what plaintiff alleged in her complaint was true. From the time of her first contact with the dancing school in February, 1961, she was influenced unwittingly by a constant and continuous barrage of flattery, false praise, excessive compliments, and panegyric encomiums, to such extent that it would be not only inequitable, but unconscionable, for a Court exercising inherent chancery power to allow such contracts to stand.

She was incessantly subjected to overreaching blandishment and cajolery. She was assured she had 'grace and poise'; that she was 'rapidly improving and developing in her dancing skill'; that the additional lessons would 'make her a beautiful dancer, capable of dancing with the most accomplished dancers'; that she was 'rapidly progressing in the development of her dancing skill and gracefulness', etc., etc. She was given 'dance aptitude tests' for the ostensible purpose of 'determining' the number of remaining hours of instructions needed by her from time to time.

At one point she was sold 545 additional hours of dancing lessons to be entitled to award of the 'Bronze Medal' signifying that she had reached 'the Bronze Standard', a supposed designation of dance achievement by students of Arthur Murray, Inc.
Later she was sold an additional 926 hours in order to gain the 'Silver Medal', indicating she had reached 'the Silver Standard', at a cost of $12,501.35.
At one point, while she still had to her credit about 900 unused hours of instructions, she was induced to purchase an additional 24 hours of lessons to participate in a trip to Miami at her own expense, where she would be 'given the opportunity to dance with members of the Miami Studio'.

She was induced at another point to purchase an additional 123 hours of lessons in order to be not only eligible for the Miami trip but also to become 'a life member of the Arthur Murray Studio', carrying with it certain dubious emoluments, at a further cost of $1,752.30.

At another point, while she still had over 1,000 unused hours of instruction she was induced to buy 151 additional hours at a cost of $2,049.00 to be eligible for a 'Student Trip to Trinidad', at her own expense as she later learned.

Also, when she still had 1100 unused hours to her credit, she was prevailed upon to purchase an additional 347 hours at a cost of $4,235.74, to qualify her to receive a 'Gold Medal' for achievement, indicating she had advanced to 'the Gold Standard'.
On another occasion, while she still had over 1200 unused hours, she was induced to buy an additional 175 hours of instruction at a cost of $2,472.75 to be eligible 'to take a trip to Mexico'.

Finally, sandwiched in between other lesser sales promotions, she was influenced to buy an additional 481 hours of instruction at a cost of $6,523.81 in order to 'be classified as a Gold Bar Member, the ultimate achievement of the dancing studio'.

All the foregoing sales promotions, illustrative of the entire fourteen separate contracts, were procured by defendant Davenport and Arthur Murray, Inc., by false representations to her that she was improving in her dancing ability, that she had excellent potential, that she was responding to instructions in dancing grace, and that they were developing her into a beautiful dancer, whereas in truth and in fact she did not develop in her dancing ability, she had no 'dance aptitude', and in fact had difficulty in 'hearing that musical beat'. The complaint alleged that such representations to her 'were in fact false and known by the defendant to be false and contrary to the plaintiff's true ability, the truth of plaintiff's ability being fully known to the defendants, but withheld from the plaintiff for the sole and specific intent to deceive and defraud the plaintiff and to induce her in the purchasing of additional hours of dance lessons'. It was averred that the lessons were sold to her 'in total disregard to the true physical, rhythm, and mental ability of the plaintiff'. In other words, while she first exulted that she was entering the 'spring of her life', she finally was awakened to the fact there was 'spring' neither in her life nor in her feet.

* * *

. . . . Defendants contend that contracts can only be rescinded for fraud or misrepresentation when the alleged misrepresentation is as to a material fact, rather than an opinion, prediction or expectation, and that the statements and representations set forth at length in the complaint were in the category of 'trade puffing', within its legal orbit.

It is true that 'generally a misrepresentation, to be actionable, must be one of fact rather than of opinion'. [Citations] But this rule has significant qualifications, applicable here. . . . As stated by Judge Allen of this Court in [Citation]:

'* * * A statement of a party having * * * superior knowledge may be regarded as a statement of fact although it would be considered as opinion if the parties were dealing on equal terms.'

It could be reasonably supposed here that defendants had 'superior knowledge' as to whether plaintiff had 'dance potential' and as to whether she was noticeably improving in the art of terpsichore. And it would be a reasonable inference from the undenied averments of the complaint that the flowery eulogiums heaped upon her by defendants as a prelude to her contracting for 1944 additional hours of instruction in order to attain the rank of the Bronze Standard, thence to the bracket of the Silver Standard, thence to the class of the Gold Bar Standard, and finally to the crowning plateau of a Life Member of the Studio, proceeded as much or more from the urge to 'ring the cash register' as from any honest or realistic appraisal of her dancing prowess or a factual representation of her progress.

Even in contractual situations where a party to a transaction owes no duty to disclose facts within his knowledge or to answer inquiries respecting such facts, the law is if he undertakes to do so he must disclose the whole truth. [Citations] From the face of the complaint, it should have been reasonably apparent to defendants that her vast outlay of cash for the many hundreds of additional hours of instruction was not justified by her slow and awkward progress, which she would have been made well aware of if they had spoken the 'whole truth'.

* * *

It accordingly follows that the order dismissing plaintiff's last amended complaint with prejudice should be and is reversed.

CASE 13-3

The following case demonstrates the type of circumstances a party must show to be entitled to rescission of a contract on the grounds of economic duress.

AUSTIN INSTRUMENT, INC. v. LORAL CORPORATION
Court of Appeals of New York, 1971
29 N.Y.2d 124, 324 N.Y.S.2d 22

FULD, Chief Judge. The defendant, Loral Corporation, seeks to recover payment for goods delivered under a contract which it had with plaintiff Austin Instrument, Inc., on the ground that the evidence establishes, as a matter of law, that it was forced to agree to an increase in price on the items in question under circumstances amounting to economic duress.

In July of 1965, Loral was awarded a $6,000,000 contract by the Navy for the production of radar sets. The contract contained a schedule of deliveries, a liquidated damages clause applying to late deliveries and a cancellation clause in case of default by Loral. The latter thereupon solicited bids for some 40 precision gear components needed to produce the radar sets, and awarded Austin a subcontract to supply 23 such parts. That party commenced delivery in early 1966.

In May 1966, Loral was awarded a second Navy contract for the production of more radar sets and again went about soliciting bids. Austin bid on all 40 gear components but, on July 15, a representative from Loral informed Austin's president, Mr. Krauss, that his company would be awarded the subcontract only for those items on which it was low bidder. The Austin officer refused to accept an order for less than all 40 of the gear parts and on the next day he told Loral that Austin would cease deliveries of the parts due under the existing subcontract unless Loral consented to substantial increases in the prices provided for by that agreement -- both retroactively for parts already delivered and prospectively on those not yet shipped -- and placed with Austin the order for all 40 parts needed under Loral's second Navy contract. Shortly thereafter, Austin did, indeed, stop delivery. After contacting 10 manufacturers of precision gears and finding none who could produce the parts in time to meet its commitments to the Navy, Loral acceded to Austin's demands; in a letter dated July 22, Loral wrote to Austin that "We have feverishly surveyed other sources of supply and find that because of the prevailing military exigencies, were they to start from scratch as would have to be the case, they could not even remotely begin to deliver on time.... Accordingly, we are left with no choice or alternative but to meet your conditions."

Loral thereupon consented to the price increases insisted upon by Austin under the first subcontract and the latter was awarded a second subcontract making it the supplier of all 40 gear parts for Loral's second contract with the Navy. Although Austin was granted until September to resume deliveries, Loral did, in fact, receive parts in August and was able to produce the radar sets in time to meet its commitments to the Navy on both contracts. After Austin's last delivery under the second subcontract in July, 1967, Loral notified it of its intention to seek recovery of the price increases.

On September 15, 1967, Austin instituted this action against Loral to recover an amount in excess of $17,750 which was still due on the second subcontract. On the same day, Loral commenced an action against Austin claiming damages of some $22,250 -- the aggregate of the price increases under the first subcontract -- on the ground of economic duress. The two actions were consolidated and, following a trial, Austin was awarded the sum it requested and Loral's complaint against Austin was dismissed on the ground that it was not shown that "it could not have obtained the items in question from other sources in time to meet its commitment to the Navy under the first contract." A closely divided Appellate Division affirmed.... There was no material disagreement concerning the facts; as Justice STEUER stated in the course of his dissent below, "the facts are virtually undisputed, nor is there any serious question of law. The difficulty lies in the application of the law to these facts."...

The applicable law is clear and, indeed, is not disputed by the parties. A contract is voidable on the ground of duress when it is established that the party making the claim was forced to agree to it by means of a wrongful threat precluding the exercise of his free will.... The existence of economic duress or business compulsion is demonstrated by proof that "immediate possession of needful goods is threatened"... or, more particularly, in cases such as the one before us, by proof that one party to a contract has threatened to breach the agreement by withholding goods unless the other party agrees to some further demand.... However, a mere threat by one party to breach the contract by not delivering the required items, though wrongful, does not in itself constitute economic duress. It must also appear that the threatened party could not obtain the goods from another source of supply and that the ordinary remedy of an action for breach of contract would not be adequate.

We find without any support in the record the conclusion reached by the courts below that Loral failed to establish that it was the victim of economic duress. On the contrary, the evidence makes out a classic case, as a matter of law, of such duress.

It must be remembered that Loral was producing a needed item of military hardware. Moreover, there is authority for Loral's position that nonperformance by a subcontractor is not an excuse for default in the main contract.... In light of all this, Loral's claim should not be held insufficiently supported because it did not request an extension from the Government.

Loral, as indicated above, also had the burden of demonstrating that it could not obtain the parts elsewhere within a reasonable time, and there can be no doubt that it met this burden. The 10 manufacturers whom Loral contacted comprised its entire list of "approved vendors" for precision gears, and none was able to commence delivery soon enough. As Loral was producing a highly sophisticated item of military machinery requiring parts made to the strictest engineering standards, it would be unreasonable to hold that Loral should have gone to other vendors, with whom it was either unfamiliar or dissatisfied, to procure the needed parts. As Justice STEUER noted in his dissent, Loral "contacted all the manufacturers whom it believed capable of making these parts", and this was all the law requires.

It is hardly necessary to add that Loral's normal legal remedy of accepting Austin's breach of the contract and then suing for damages would have been inadequate under the circumstances, as Loral would still have had to obtain the gears elsewhere with all the concomitant consequences mentioned above. In other words, Loral actually had no choice, when the prices were raised by Austin, except to take the gears at the "coerced" prices and then sue to get the excess back.

Austin's final argument is that Loral, even if it did enter into the contract under duress, lost any rights it had to a refund of money by waiting until July, 1967, long after the termination date of the contract, to disaffirm it. It is true that one who would recover moneys allegedly paid under duress must act promptly to make his claim known.... In this case, Loral delayed making its demand for a refund until three days after Austin's last delivery on the second subcontract. Loral's reason -- for waiting until that time -- is that it feared another stoppage of deliveries which would again put it in an untenable situation. Considering Austin's conduct in the past, this was perfectly reasonable, as the possibility of an application by Austin of further business compulsion still existed until all of the parts were delivered.

In sum, the record before us demonstrates that Loral agreed to the price increases in consequence of the economic duress employed by Austin. Accordingly, the matter should be remanded to the trial court for a computation of its damages.

CASE 13-4

In the following case, the court discusses the circumstances under which a party may be entitled to relief from a contract on the grounds of a unilateral mistake.

BALABAN-GORDON CO., INC. v. BRIGHTON SEW. DIST.

Appellate Division, New York (4th Dept.), 1973
41 A.D.2d 246; 342 N.Y.S.2d 435

SIMONS, Judge. This appeal questions the right of a contractor to withdraw its bid on a public construction contract because of a unilateral mistake in interpreting the engineers' specifications concerning equipment to be included in the bid price.

A bid is a binding offer to make a contract. It may be withdrawn in the case of unilateral mistake by the bidder where the mistake is known to the other party to the transaction and (1) the bid is of such consequence that enforcement would be unconscionable, (2) the mistake is material, (3) the mistake occurred despite the exercise of ordinary care by the bidder and (4) it is possible to place the other party in status quo....

In 1967 the appellant Brighton Sewer District No. 2 advertised for bids to construct two sewage treatment plants. Bids were received for the general construction, plumbing, heating and electrical work for each facility and bidders could bid each contract separately or in combination. Respondent Balaban-Gordon Company, Inc. was the lowest bidder on the general construction contract for both plants. Its total bid for the work was $2,249,700, $530,300 below the second bidder. It also bid on the plumbing contract. It was the high bidder for that job, its bid being $376,230 higher than the low bid of $687,770. The respondent's representatives, upon learning of the difference in the bids, checked with the appellant's engineers and re-examined their worksheets. They determined that they had incorrectly interpreted the specifications and had included the cost of several pieces of mechanical equipment in the bid for the plumbing contract which should have been in the bid for the general construction. The trial court has found this mistake was due to the bidder's negligence. The respondent explained the error in detail at a conference with appellant's representatives and asked that its bid be withdrawn. The appellant insisted that the bid could not be withdrawn under General Municipal Law (§ 105) and demanded that respondent execute the contracts for general construction. When the respondent refused to do so, the appellant readvertised for bids and declared the respondent's bid bond forfeited. This action to rescind the bid and to cancel the bond followed. The trial court granted judgment for respondent, holding that it was entitled to rescind its mistaken bid notwithstanding its negligence.

If the bid may be rescinded, then the bid bond must be canceled because the municipality may not retain the proceeds either as a penalty or liquidated damages. If there is no legal obligation on the part of the contractor to fulfill its bid, it may not be held on the bid bond for its failure to do so....

It is apparent from the facts that there was a material mistake of serious consequence to the bidder from which it should be relieved if the appellant can be placed in status quo and if respondent's mistake is excusable. The mistake in computing the bid was "palpable", i.e., known to the other party because of the disparity in the bids and because of the prompt actual notice to appellant once the bids were opened and before the contract was awarded. Furthermore, the appellant's position has not been damaged. It could have awarded the contract to the second bidder. The election to rebid the job was its own and not required by any act of respondent. Appellant lost the bargain but that is not a compensable loss if the bid may be rescinded, because it was a bargain to which the appellant was never entitled. The case turns on whether this is the type of a mistake which justifies relief by rescission. Mistakes by definition reflect oversight or some lack of care and so the requirement that the mistake occur in the exercise of ordinary care may not be interpreted narrowly. The question is whether the mistake is of the variety considered excusable, and each case must be considered on its own facts....

The parties are in agreement that relief is available where the mistake is clerical or arithmetical.... In such a case, the mistaken bid does not express the true intention of the bidder. If he were to recompute the bid or if another person were to do so, the obvious error would be discovered and corrected. Its existence may be objectively determined. In those circumstances, there is said to be no meeting of the minds because the bid was one which the bidder never intended to make.

On the other hand, it is commonly recognized that a bidder will not be relieved from an error in a value judgment in estimating the requirements or costs necessary to fulfill a contract. Mistakes of this type are inherent business risks assumed by contractors in all bidding situations. If the specifics of the job were recalculated by the bidder, his bid would be the same, for these estimates do not involve oversights. They represent subjective judgments deliberately made with respect to the requirements of the job. Another person calculating the bid might or might not make the same "mistake", depending upon his mental evaluation of the work to be performed, but in any event, the minds of the bidder and the offeree meet because the bid is precisely what the bidder intends even though his judgment later proves faulty.

The appellant claims that the error must be considered one of these two types, either clerical and arithmetical, or an error of judgment, relief by rescission being available in the former case but not in the latter. Since the incorrect interpretation of the specifications was not clerical or arithmetical appellant claims that respondent should be held to the bid and liable for liquidated damages under its bid bond. Unfortunately, not all mistakes made by contractors are categorized so easily. Applying the reasoning of the two types of mistakes to the facts of this case illustrates the difficulty. If respondent's representatives were to recompute its bid, they doubtless would interpret the specifications the same way. In that sense, the bid accurately represented the contract respondent was willing to make and there was a meeting of the minds. Nevertheless, the error was objectively discoverable. Another contractor computing the bid would not, and in fact no others did, make the same mistake in interpretation and in that sense the bid did not represent the bid intended because respondent was working under a misapprehension with respect to the particulars called for by the specifications. Reasonable care probably dictated that respondent should have asked the engineers to clarify the meaning of the ambiguous specifications (at least one other bidder did so), but respondent's failure to investigate should not prevent it from obtaining relief.

The case fits squarely within the factual pattern of *President & Council of Mount St. Mary's Coll. v. Aetna Cas. & Sur. Co.* There, the court granted relief by rescission to a bidder who, because of an error in interpreting the specifications, failed to include the cost of certain equipment in his bid. Although the error was the result of negligence by the bidder in not asking the architect for an interpretation of the specifications, relief was granted because the bidder's negligence was not "culpable". Similar analyses of the degree of the bidder's mistake, i.e., whether the bidder is "more" or "less" negligent, have been made in other cases.... When an effort is made to apply these tests, they are found to be elusive to say the least. The decisive factual question is whether the mistake is one the courts will excuse. Then, if the mistake concerns a material matter in an executory contract under circumstances where relief to the bidder results in no damage to the municipality but enforcement results in serious harm to the bidder, rescission will be granted. Manifestly, rescission may be allowed more readily for a mistake made by a bidder which is objectively established and which does not evolve from an inherent risk of business. Even though the mistake is the product of negligence on the part of the bidder, relief should be granted because the assurance exists from the objective proof that the transaction is free from mischief. This satisfies a fundamental purpose of the public bidding statutes.

The error in this case did not pertain to an evaluation of risks or estimation of requirements or costs by the bidder and the effect of the mistake was verifiable in much the same way as a clerical error, the impossibility of performance or an arithmetical error. That being the case, it should be excused and rescission granted. In these days of multi-million dollar construction contracts, the public interest requires stability in bidding of public contracts under rules that protect against chicane and overreaching. Nevertheless, little is to be gained if a contractor is forced to perform a contract at an extravagant loss or the risk of possible bankruptcy. If a mistake has been made under circumstances justifying relief, the municipality should not be allowed to enforce the bargain. Its remedy to avoid loss is to award the contract to the next bidder or assume the responsibility of rebidding.

The judgment granting respondent rescission of its bid and canceling the bond should therefore be affirmed.

Judgment unanimously affirmed, with costs.

CASE 13-5

The New York Statute of Frauds provides that the Statute of Frauds may be satisfied by a "note or memorandum" of the contract that is signed by the party against whom enforcement of the contract is sought. The following case answers several significant questions about what the note or memorandum must contain and whether it may be "pieced together" from several different documents.

CRABTREE v. ELIZABETH ARDEN SALES CORP.

Court of Appeals of New York, 1953
305 N.Y. 48

FULD, Judge. In September of 1947, Nate Crabtree entered into preliminary negotiations with Elizabeth Arden Sales Corporation, manufacturers and sellers of cosmetics, looking toward his employment as sales manager. Interviewed on September 26th, by Robert P. Johns, executive vice-president and general manager of the corporation, who had apprised him of the possible opening, Crabtree requested a three-year contract at $25,000 a year. Explaining that he would be giving up a secure well-paying job to take a position in an entirely new field of endeavor - which he believed would take him some years to master - he insisted upon an agreement for a definite term. And he repeated his desire for a contract for three years to Miss Elizabeth Arden, the corporation's president. When Miss Arden finally indicated that she was prepared to offer a two-year contract, based on an annual salary of $20,000 for the first six months, $25,000 for the second six months and $30,000 for the second year, plus expenses of $5,000 a year for each of those years, Crabtree replied that that offer was "interesting". Miss Arden thereupon had her personal secretary make this memorandum on a telephone order blank that happened to be at hand:

"EMPLOYMENT AGREEMENT WITH
NATE CRABTREE Date Sept 26-1947
At 681 - 5th Ave   6: PM
          * * *
Begin $20,000.
6 months $25,000.
6 months $30,000.
$5,000. - per year
Expense money
2 years to make good

Arrangement with Mr. Crabtree
By Miss Arden

Present Miss Arden
Mr. John
Mr. Crabtree
Miss OLeary"

A few days later, Crabtree 'phoned Mr. Johns and telegraphed Miss Arden; he accepted the "invitation to join the Arden organization", and Miss Arden wired back her "welcome". When he reported for work, a "pay-roll change" card was made up and initialed by Mr. Johns, and then forwarded to the payroll department. Reciting that it was prepared on September 30, 1947, and was to be effective as of October 22d, it specified the names of the parties, Crabtree's "Job Classification" and, in addition, contained the notation that "This employee is to be paid as follows:

"First six months of employment $20,000. per annum
Next six months of employment 25,000. per annum
After one year of employment 30,000. per annum
Approved by RPJ [initialed]"

After six months of employment, Crabtree received the scheduled increase from $20,000 to $25,000, but the further specified increase at the end of the year was not paid. Both Mr. Johns and the comptroller of the corporation, Mr. Carstens, told Crabtree that they would attempt to straighten out the matter with Miss Arden, and, with that in mind, the comptroller prepared another "pay-roll change" card, to which his signature is appended, noting that there was to be a "Salary increase" from $25,000 to $30,000 a year, "per contractual arrangements with Miss Arden". The latter, however, refused to approve the increase and, after further fruitless discussion, plaintiff left defendant's employ and commenced this action for breach of contract.

At the ensuing trial, defendant denied the existence of any agreement to employ plaintiff for two years, and further contended that, even if one had been made, the statute of frauds barred its enforcement. The trial court found against defendant on both issues and awarded plaintiff damages of about $14,000, and the Appellate Division, two justices dissenting, affirmed. Since the contract relied upon was not to be performed within a year, the primary question for decision is whether there was a memorandum of its terms, subscribed by defendant, to satisfy the statute of frauds....

Each of the two payroll cards - the one initialed by defendant's general manager, the other signed by its comptroller - unquestionably constitutes a memorandum under the statute. That they were not prepared or signed with the intention of evidencing the contract, or that they came into existence subsequent to its execution, is of no consequence...; it is enough, to meet the statute's demands, that they were signed with intent to authenticate the information contained therein and that such information does evidence the terms of the contract. Those two writings contain all of the essential terms of the contract - the parties to it, the position that plaintiff was to assume, the salary that he was to receive - except that relating to the duration of plaintiff's employment. Accordingly, we must consider whether that item, the length of the contract, may be supplied by reference to the earlier unsigned office memorandum, and, if so, whether its notation, "2 years to make good", sufficiently designates a period of employment.

The statute of frauds does not require the "memorandum to be in one document. It may be pieced together out of separate writings, connected with one another either expressly or by the internal evidence of subject matter and occasion". Where each of the separate writings has been subscribed by the party to be charged, little if any difficulty is encountered. Where, however, some writings have been signed, and others have not - as in the case before us - there is basic disagreement as to what constitutes a sufficient connection permitting the unsigned papers to be considered as part of the statutory memorandum. The courts of some jurisdictions insist that there be a reference, of varying degrees of specificity, in the signed writing to that unsigned, and, if there is no such reference, they refuse to permit consideration of the latter in determining whether the memorandum satisfies the statute. That conclusion is based upon a construction of the statute which requires that the connection between the writings and defendant's acknowledgment of the one not subscribed, appear from examination of the papers alone, without the aid of parol evidence. The other position - which has gained increasing support over the years - is that a sufficient connection between the papers

is established simply by a reference in them to the same subject matter or transaction. The statute is not pressed "to the extreme of a literal and rigid logic"... and oral testimony is admitted to show the connection between the documents and to establish the acquiescence, of the party to be charged, to the contents of the one unsigned.

The view last expressed impresses us as the more sound, and we now definitively adopt it, permitting the signed and unsigned writings to be read together, provided that they clearly refer to the same subject matter or transaction.

The language of the statute - "Every agreement... is void, unless... some note or memorandum thereof be in writing, and subscribed by the party to be charged", does not impose the requirement that the signed acknowledgment of the contract must appear from the writings alone, unaided by oral testimony. The danger of fraud and perjury, generally attendant upon the admission of parol evidence, is at a minimum in a case such as this. None of the terms of the contract are supplied by parol. All of them must be set out in the various writings presented to the court, and at least one writing, the one establishing a contractual relationship between the parties, must bear the signature of the party to be charged, while the unsigned document must on its face refer to the same transaction as that set forth in the one that was signed. Parol evidence to portray the circumstances surrounding the making of the memorandum - serves only to connect the separate documents and to show that there was assent, by the party to be charged, to the contents of the one unsigned. If that testimony does not convincingly connect the papers, or does not show assent to the unsigned paper, it is within the province of the judge to conclude, as a matter of law, that the statute has not been satisfied. True, the possibility still remains that, by fraud or perjury, an agreement never in fact made may occasionally be enforced under the subject matter or transaction test. It is better to run that risk, though, than to deny enforcement to all agreements, merely because the signed document made no specific mention of the unsigned writing. As the United States Supreme Court declared, in sanctioning the admission of parol evidence to establish the connection between the signed and unsigned writings. "There may be cases in which it would be a violation of reason and common sense to ignore a reference which derives its significance from such [parol] proof. If there is ground for any doubt in the matter, the general rule should be enforced. But where there is no ground for doubt, its enforcement would aid, instead of discouraging, fraud."...

Turning to the writings in the case before us - the unsigned office memo, the payroll change form initialed by the general manager Johns, and the paper signed by the comptroller Carstens - it is apparent, and most patently, that all three refer on their face to the same transaction. The parties, the position to be filled by plaintiff, the salary to be paid him, are all identically set forth; it is hardly possible that such detailed information could refer to another or a different agreement. Even more, the card signed by Carstens notes that it was prepared for the purpose of a "Salary increase per contractual arrangements with Miss Arden". That certainly constitutes a reference of sorts to a more comprehensive "arrangement," and parol is permissible to furnish the explanation.

The corroborative evidence of defendant's assent to the contents of the unsigned office memorandum is also convincing. Prepared by defendant's agent, Miss Arden's personal secretary, there is little likelihood that that paper was fraudulently manufactured or that defendant had not assented to its contents. Furthermore, the evidence as to the conduct of the parties at the time it was prepared persuasively demonstrates defendant's assent to its terms. Under such circumstances, the courts below were fully justified in finding that the three papers constituted the "memorandum" of their agreement within the meaning of the statute.

Nor can there be any doubt that the memorandum contains all of the essential terms of the contract. Only one term, the length of the employment, is in dispute. The September 26th office memorandum contains the notation, "2 years to make good". What purpose, other than to denote the length of the contract term, such a notation could have, is hard to imagine. Without it, the employment would be at will... and its inclusion may not be treated as meaningless or purposeless. Quite obviously, as the courts below decided, the phrase signifies that the parties agreed to a term, a certain and definite term, of two years, after which, if plaintiff did not "make good", he would be subject to discharge. And examination of other parts of the memorandum supports that construction. Throughout the writings, a scale of wages, increasing plaintiff's salary periodically, is set out; that type of arrangement is hardly consistent with the hypothesis that the employment was meant to be at will. The most that may be argued from defendant's standpoint is that "2 years to make good", is a cryptic and ambiguous statement. But, in such a case, parol evidence is admissible to explain its meaning. Having in mind the relations of the parties, the course of the negotiations and plaintiff's insistence upon security of employment, the purpose of the phrase - or so the trier of the facts was warranted in finding - was to grant plaintiff the tenure he desired.

CASE 13-6

The Statute of Frauds may be satisfied by a written a note or memorandum of the contract that is signed by the party against whom enforcement of the contract is sought. The following case considers whether the buyer's deposit check, which the seller endorsed and deposited, is sufficient to satisfy the Statute of Frauds for a contract for the sale of real property.

H. ROTHVOSS & SONS, INC. v. ESTATE OF NEER
Supreme Court of New York, Appellate Division, Third Department, 1988
139 A.D.2d 37; 530 N.Y.S.2d 331

MERCURE, Judge. Plaintiff seeks specific performance and money damages resulting from the alleged breach of a contract for the sale of real property by S. Hollis Neer, defendants' decedent and predecessor in title, to plaintiff. The complaint alleges the terms of the purported contract, that "[a]s evidence of plaintiff's good faith and intentions to carry out the contract" plaintiff's officer executed and delivered to Neer a check in the amount of $500 dated July 24, 1984, which check was endorsed and deposited by Neer, and that Neer died on October 30, 1985, prior to completion of the contract of sale. Annexed to the complaint is a detailed and unsigned contract for the sale of real property.

Defendants moved to dismiss the complaint on grounds that it failed to state a cause of action and was barred by the Statute of Frauds. In opposition thereto, plaintiff submitted the affidavit of its vice-president, Henry F. Rothvoss, Jr., in which he stated that the terms of the oral contract of sale with Neer were embodied in the unexecuted contract, that the contract was prepared by Neer's attorney, and that, as evidence of his good faith and "to insure that the contract would be carried out", he handed the $500 check to Neer. The check, annexed to the affidavit, contains the purported endorsement of Neer. The memo portion thereof contains the words "land on Rt 22" and "down payment". There is no dispute that the land in question is located on State Route 22 in the Town of Ancram, Columbia County.

Supreme Court denied the motion, finding that the canceled check, endorsed and thereby subscribed by Neer, together with the unexecuted contract, satisfied the Statute of Frauds and the provision that a "contract for * * * the sale, of any real property, or an interest therein, is void unless the contract or some note or memorandum thereof, expressing the consideration, is in writing, subscribed by the party to be charged" (General Obligations Law § 5-703 [2]). Defendants appeal.

We reverse. The action is barred by the Statute of Frauds, and the motion to dismiss should have been granted on that basis. Although the requisite memorandum may be pieced together out of several writings, some signed and others unsigned, and parol evidence may be resorted to in aid thereof, it is essential that the separate writings sought to be so employed clearly refer to the same subject matter or transaction. Additionally, in such case the signed writing must establish a contractual relationship between the parties. Here, the signed writing, the check, does not establish such a contractual relationship. Moreover, it does not contain even a general description of the land to be conveyed and fails to state the purchase price and other essential terms of sale, such as financing.

In *Mulford v Borg-Warner Acceptance Corp.*, this court rejected the contention that an endorsed check could establish the necessary contractual relationship. We conclude that just as the check notation "(new lease)" was insufficient to establish a tenancy involving all the provisions of a proposed unsigned lease, including the term, the words "land on Rt 22" and "down payment" noted on the check herein are insufficient to establish an agreement involving all the terms of a proposed unsigned contract of sale including the purchase price, terms of payment and description of property to be conveyed. Further, although plaintiff is the drawer of the check, the purchasers under the formal written contract of sale are plaintiff and two other individuals, August F. Corsini and Laura M. Corsini, thereby creating uncertainty as to the identity of the parties to the purported contract. Additionally, the $500 actually paid is not reflected in and bears no relationship to the claimed contract, which provides for a $15,000 down payment upon execution.

Nor would treatment of the $500 as partial payment of the purchase price remove the contract from the Statute of Frauds. "With respect to land contracts, part payment of the purchase price, or even full payment thereof, is not considered part performance of the contract, standing alone; such payment, to be sufficient, must be accompanied by other acts, such as possession, or possession and improvements." Clearly, the $500 check was nothing more than earnest money to show plaintiff's good intentions and was not intended to evidence a completed contract. Where, as here, the parties contemplate a formal, binding, written contract, which is never executed, there is no mutual assent and no contract.

Order reversed, on the law, with costs, motion granted and complaint dismissed.

Case 13-7

The following case illustrates the type of circumstances that may constitute "part performance" sufficient to satisfy the real property provision of the New York Statute of Frauds.

Schafer v. Albro
Appellate Division, New York (4th Dept.), 1996
233 A.D.2d 900, 649 N.Y.S.2d 260

Memorandum: Supreme Court properly denied that part of defendant's motion seeking partial summary judgment dismissing the cause of action alleging breach of a real estate contract between the parties. Although the alleged contract is not in writing or subscribed by plaintiffs (see, General Obligations Law § 5-703 [2]), plaintiffs allege in their verified complaint that they had possession of the property; made part payment of the purchase price to defendant and her husband; made extensive improvements to the property at a total cost of over $ 20,000; paid off the second mortgage in the amount of $ 25,733.76; and, from November 1, 1988 to February 1991, made the payments on the first mortgage. Plaintiffs have thereby raised an issue of fact whether they are entitled to specific performance of the contract based upon part performance (see, General Obligations Law § 5-703 [4] [Citations]).

* * *

CASE 14-1

This case involves an employment contract pursuant to which the employee must perform to the employer's satisfaction. The court discusses how satisfaction must be defined or measured.

APPELGATE v. MACFADDEN NEWSPAPER CORP.

Appellate Division, New York (1st Dept.), 1925
214 A.D. 221, 212 N.Y.S. 67

MERRELL, Judge. The action was brought to recover the sum of $12,000 damages alleged to have been sustained by the plaintiff by reason of his wrongful discharge by the defendant from its employ. The contract between the parties whereby the plaintiff was employed by the defendant was in writing. The defendant is a newspaper publishing corporation and employed the plaintiff "as Editor of the Saturday feature section and to have charge of the Rotogravure section" of the defendant's newspaper. The contract, a copy of which is annexed to the complaint, recites that "Whereas, Mr. Appelgate is an editor possessing unique and original ability," and the employer desired to secure his exclusive services, the said Appelgate desiring to secure and accept employment with the defendant, "First. The Employer does hereby employ the Employee to render his services as Editor of the Saturday feature section and to have charge of the Rotogravure Section of the newspaper to be published by the MacFadden Newspaper Publishing Corporation exclusively...." It is further provided "that the Employee will work for and devote his entire time, skill, attention and energy to the Employer exclusively," and that "it being conceded by the Employee that his services are special, unique and extraordinary." In the 4th paragraph of the contract it is provided: "Fourth. The Employee shall faithfully execute to the satisfaction of the Employer all instructions in respect to his duties given by his Employer."

The plaintiff alleges that the contract in question was entered into between the parties on July 28, 1924, and that pursuant thereto and on or about August 4, 1924, the plaintiff entered upon his duties as editor of the Saturday feature section and took charge of the rotogravure section of the newspaper published by the defendant, and continued to perform such duties until on or about November 7, 1924, and duly performed all the terms and conditions on the part of the plaintiff to be performed under the said agreement; that on or about said last-mentioned date the defendant wrongfully and without just cause therefor discharged the plaintiff to plaintiff's damage in the sum of $12,000.

A perusal of the contract discloses that the parties regarded the services of the plaintiff for which the defendant contracted as of the character commonly known as unique. The contract itself recites that "Mr. Appelgate is an editor possessing unique and original ability" Plaintiff was hired as "Editor of the Saturday feature section and to have charge of the Rotogravure Section" of the defendant's newspaper. There can be no doubt that the parties understood that the plaintiff was to render services involving "art, taste, fancy and judgment".

In a contract for services involving fancy, taste and judgment, the question whether the fancy, taste or judgment of the employer is arbitrary or unreasonable does not arise, the question being whether the claimed dissatisfaction was feigned or genuine.

In *Crawford v. Mail & Express Publishing Co.* the plaintiff was employed as an editor to write at least two columns a week on the progress of the world or other appropriate subjects for publication in The *Mail and Express*, and in his contract with the defendant agreed that his services would be satisfactory to the defendant, and that in case they were not he should receive one week's notice. In discussing the absence of limitation upon the exercise by the employer of its judgment as to what was satisfactory to it, the Court of Appeals said "But, on the part of the publishers of The *Mail & Express*, it is very clear that they did not intend to be bound for a period longer than his services proved satisfactory, and that they expressly reserved the right to discharge him upon a week's notice. It is also apparent from a reading of the contract that the employment was not intended to be that of an ordinary servant to perform work, labor and services of an ordinary business or of a commercial nature. He was not called upon to perform the work of an ordinary reporter, writing up the general news of the day, but contracted to prepare articles on the progress of the world or other appropriate subjects in the line of the policy of the paper for the purpose, as expressed, of promoting the general interests of the paper, of aiding in its circulation and the obtaining of advertisements, by improving the quality of its contents. The evident design was that the articles should be interesting and attractive, involving art, taste, fancy and judgment. There is no provision in the contract in any manner limiting the publishers in the exercise of their judgment as to what is satisfactory, but if his services are unsatisfactory for any reason they are given the right to terminate the employment upon a week's notice, at any time they so elect."

In *Diamond v. Mendelsohn* the contract required the employee to "perform the duties of foreman competently and energetically to the best of his abilities and complete satisfaction of his employers." Mr. Justice CLARKE of this court, now its presiding justice, in writing in that case said: "There is no doubt that under the terms of this written contract it lay within the power of the defendants to discharge the plaintiff because he did not perform his duties to their complete satisfaction

and that it would not be proper to submit to a jury the question whether they ought to have been satisfied."

It, therefore, seems very clear to me that the only question to be determined upon the trial was as to whether the dissatisfaction pleaded by the defendant as ground for the discharge of the plaintiff was real or feigned. If the dissatisfaction was a mere whim of the employer, then, of course, it was not justified in terminating the contract, but if, in fact, the defendant was dissatisfied with the special and unique services rendered by the plaintiff as editor, then the defendant was justified in discharging him. The contract with the plaintiff clearly involved personal taste, fancy and judgment, and when the employer became dissatisfied with the services of the character specified which its employee was to render, it had the right to discharge him and was not called upon to give reasons therefor.

The order appealed from should be reversed.

CASE 15-1

This case distinguishes between *material* and *trivial* breaches of contract and discusses the appropriate measure of damage for each kind of breach.

JACOB & YOUNG v. KENT
Court of Appeals of New York, 1921
230 N.Y. 239

CARDOZO, Judge. The plaintiff built a country residence for the defendant at a cost of upwards of $77,000, and now sues to recover a balance of $3,483.46, remaining unpaid. The work of construction ceased in June, 1914, and the defendant then began to occupy the dwelling. There was no complaint of defective performance until March, 1915. One of the specifications for the plumbing work provides that "all wrought iron pipe must be well galvanized, lap welded pipe of the grade known as 'standard pipe' of Reading manufacture." The defendant learned in March, 1915, that some of the pipe, instead of being made in Reading, was the product of other factories. The plaintiff was accordingly directed by the architect to do the work anew. The plumbing was then encased within the walls except in a few places where it had to be exposed. Obedience to the order meant more than the substitution of other pipe. It meant the demolition at great expense of substantial parts of the completed structure. The plaintiff left the work untouched, and asked for a certificate that the final payment was due. Refusal of the certificate was followed by this suit.

The evidence sustains a finding that the omission of the prescribed brand of pipe was neither fraudulent

nor willful. It was the result of the oversight and inattention of the plaintiff's subcontractor. Reading pipe is distinguished from Cohoes pipe and other brands only by the name of the manufacturer stamped upon it at intervals of between six and seven feet. Even the defendant's architect, though he inspected the pipe upon arrival, failed to notice the discrepancy. The plaintiff tried to show that the brands installed, though made by other manufacturers, were the same in quality, in appearance, in market value and in cost as the brand stated in the contract -- that they were, indeed, the same thing, though manufactured in another place. The evidence was excluded, and a verdict directed for the defendant. The Appellate Division reversed, and granted a new trial.

We think the evidence, if admitted, would have supplied some basis for the inference that the defect was insignificant in its relation to the project. The courts never say that one who makes a contract fills the measure of his duty by less than full performance. They do say, however, that an omission, both trivial and innocent, will sometimes be atoned for by allowance of the resulting damage, and will not always be the breach of a condition to be followed by a forfeiture. The decisions in this state commit us to the liberal view, which is making its way, nowadays, in jurisdictions slow to welcome it. Where the line is to be drawn between the important and the trivial cannot be settled by a formula. "In the nature of the case precise boundaries are impossible" (2 Williston on Contracts, sec. 841). The same omission may take on one aspect or another according to its setting. Substitution of equivalents may not have the same significance in fields of art on the one side and in those of mere utility on the other. Nowhere will change be tolerated, however, if it is so dominant or pervasive as in any real or substantial measure to frustrate the purpose of the contract. There is no general license to install whatever, in the builder's judgment, may be regarded as "just as good". The question is one of degree, to be answered, if there is doubt, by the triers of the facts and, if the inferences are certain, by the judges of the law. We must weigh the purpose to be served, the desire to be gratified, the excuse for deviation from the letter, the cruelty of enforced adherence. Then only can we tell whether literal fulfillment is to be implied by law as a condition. This is not to say that the parties are not free by apt and certain words to effectuate a purpose that performance of every term shall be a condition of recovery. That question is not here. This is merely to say that the law will be slow to impute the purpose, in the silence of the parties, where the significance of the default is grievously out of proportion to the oppression of the forfeiture. The willful transgressor must accept the penalty of his transgression. For him there is no occasion to mitigate the rigor of implied conditions. The transgressor whose default is unintentional and trivial may hope for mercy if he will offer atonement for his wrong.

In the circumstances of this case, we think the measure of the allowance is not the cost of replacement, which would be great, but the difference in value, which would be either nominal or nothing. Some of the exposed sections might perhaps have been replaced at moderate expense. The defendant did not limit his demand to them, but treated the plumbing as a unit to be corrected from cellar to roof. In point of fact, the plaintiff never reached the stage at which evidence of the extent of the allowance became necessary. The trial court had excluded evidence that the defect was unsubstantial, and in view of that ruling there was no occasion for the plaintiff to go farther with an offer of proof. We think, however, that the offer, if it had been made, would not of necessity have been defective because directed to difference in value. It is true that in most cases the cost of replacement is the measure. The owner is entitled to the money which will permit him to complete, unless the cost of completion is grossly and unfairly out of proportion to the good to be attained. When that is true, the measure is the difference in value. Specifications call, let us say, for a foundation built of granite quarried in Vermont. On the completion of the building, the owner learns that through the blunder of a subcontractor part of the foundation has been built of granite of the same quality quarried in New Hampshire. The measure of allowance is not the cost of reconstruction. "There may be omissions of that which could not afterwards be supplied exactly as called for by the contract without taking down the building to its foundations, and at the same time the omission may not affect the value of the building for use or otherwise, except so slightly as to be hardly appreciable." The rule that gives a remedy in cases of substantial performance with compensation for defects of trivial or inappreciable importance, has been developed by the courts as an instrument of justice. The measure of the allowance must be shaped to the same end.

Case 15-2

A party seeking to recover damages for breach of contract must prove the existence and amount of such damages with reasonable certainty. The following case illustrates the difficulties faced by a plaintiff who seeks to recover damages for lost profits

SCHONFELD v. HILLIARD
U.S. Ct. App. 2d Cir., 2000
218 F.3d 164

McLAUGHLIN, C. J.

This case involves a closely-held cable television corporation that imploded just as it was about to launch its flagship channel. In 1988, brothers Russ and Les Hilliard formed International News Network, Inc. ("INN") to distribute a British news and information channel in the United States (the "Channel"). Prior to this ambitious venture, the Hilliard brothers owned small mid-western cable television companies with an aggregate of only 66,000 subscribers.

To secure large-scale expertise and prestige, INN brought in Reese Schonfeld, a founder and former President of Cable News Network ("CNN")-initially as a consultant, and later as a shareholder-to help INN negotiate with the British Broadcasting Corporation (the "BBC") for a programming license. INN also retained Daniels & Associates ("Daniels"), the nation's leading financial services company for the cable industry, to prepare a business plan and to drum up investors.

In February 1994, the Hilliards and Schonfeld executed a written Shareholders' Agreement whereby each became a one-third shareholder in INN in return for a $10,000 capital contribution. In addition, the Hilliards, who had each already lent $300,000 to INN, agreed to lend up to another $350,000 to INN if necessary to meet its obligations to the BBC. In lieu of a further cash contribution, Schonfeld agreed to invest his time and effort.

The Shareholders' Agreement confirmed the parties' understanding that INN itself would not operate the Channel. Instead, INN would invest in a yet-to-be-formed operating entity. INN's shareholders, if they chose, could increase their personal stakes in the Channel by making additional cash investments in the separate operating entity. The agreement said nothing about the percentage of profits that INN, or any other equity investor, would receive from the Channel's operation.

Although the Shareholders' Agreement provided for a two-member board of directors (one chosen by Schonfeld, the other by the Hilliards), no board members were formally designated. It appears, however, that Schonfeld assumed the three roles of director, President and CEO of INN. Russ Hilliard acted as the other director. Les Hilliard apparently played no role in INN, other than investor.

The final piece of the puzzle fell into place on March 4, 1994, when the BBC granted INN a 20-year exclusive license to distribute its news and information programming in a 24-hour format, commencing not later than February 1995 (the "March Supply Agreement"). The agreement provided for INN's assignment of the benefits and privileges of the agreement to the yet-to-be-formed operating entity upon written consent of the BBC, whose consent would not be unreasonably withheld. The BBC retained its right, however, to withhold consent to any delegation of INN's duties under the contract.

* * *

In October 1994, the FCC promulgated a new rule allowing cable operators to charge an increased per-channel monthly rate for up to six new channels as of January 1, 1995. To take advantage of this window of opportunity, INN asked the BBC to accelerate the launch date of the Channel.

INN and the BBC signed an "Interim Agreement," effective December 14, 1994, in which the BBC agreed to provide provisional programming as early as possible, and to develop an "Americanized" programming format to become available to INN no later than December 31, 1995 under a revised 20-year supply agreement (the "December Supply Agreement"). In consideration for the interim programming feed, INN agreed to pay the BBC approximately $20 million in installments beginning January 3, 1995. The BBC retained the right to terminate the Interim Agreement if, by January 31, 1995, INN had failed to get letters indicating an intent to carry the Channel from cable systems with an aggregate of at least 500,000 subscribers. The December Supply Agreement also: (1) capped INN's initial capital contribution to the operating entity at 15%; and (2) gave the BBC a non-dilutable 20% equity interest in the operating entity.

According to three witnesses-Richard Blumenthal (INN's attorney), Schonfeld and Mark Young (a representative of the BBC)-Russ Hilliard repeatedly promised orally that he and his brother would personally fund the Interim Agreement. These promises were allegedly made to induce Schonfeld and the BBC to abandon the March Supply Agreement and enter into the Interim and December Supply Agreements despite the fact that INN did not yet have the cash available to make the necessary payments to the BBC. Schonfeld and Blumenthal testified in depositions that the Hilliards said they planned to invest up to $20 million in the operating entity as financing for the BBC payments. However, there is no oral or written agreement memorializing the precise amount promised, or defining the liabilities and remedies of the parties in the event of the Hilliards' failure to fund.

By mid-January 1995, the Hilliards had provided none of the promised funding and INN was in default under the Interim Agreement. In February 1995, the parties met in New York to discuss the situation. Russ Hilliard did not deny that he and his brother had promised to fund the Interim Agreement. He claimed, however, that funding had been withheld because INN was having difficulty obtaining cable operator support. Rather than suing the Hilliards and INN for breach of contract, the BBC offered a chivalrous solution: in exchange for the dissolution of both the Interim and December Supply Agreements, the BBC agreed to release the Hilliards and INN from any and all claims arising out of their breach of the oral agreement and Interim Supply Agreement.

Schonfeld alleges that the Hilliards never really intended to fund the Interim Agreement themselves. He claims that, all along, they had been unsuccessfully attempting to get the money from William Bresnan, the CEO of Bresnan Communications (which is 80% owned by TCI Cable). Russ Hilliard has admitted in deposition testimony that: (1) the funds he had promised were supposed to come from Bresnan or TCI, not from himself and his brother; and (2) he knew the BBC would never have signed the Interim Agreement had it known the truth (i.e., would never have agreed to make the Interim Agreement contingent on funding from Bresnan or TCI).

In April 1995, Schonfeld commenced this diversity action in the United States District Court for the Southern District of New York . . . . Schonfeld alleged derivative claims on behalf of INN for: . . . breach of contract . . . .

In a nutshell, Schonfeld alleged that the Hilliards induced him and INN to abandon the March Supply Agreement and enter into the Interim and December

Supply Agreements by falsely representing their intention to personally fund the Interim Agreement. He alleged that the Hilliards' breach of this oral agreement to fund led directly to INN's breach of the Interim Agreement and subsequent loss of the December Supply Agreement.

* * *

To establish lost profit damages, Schonfeld relied on: (1) INN's Business Plan; . . . (3) the BBC's, the Hilliards' and Schonfeld's "belief" that the proposed operating entity would be profitable; and (4) the reports and deposition testimony of two damage experts-Donald Curtis and William Grimes.

* * *

. . . [T]he district court held that Schonfeld could not prove, with reasonable certainty, the existence or amount of damages for lost profits.

* * *

Finding Schonfeld's claims for lost asset damages to be nothing more than a "back door" attempt to recover lost profits, . . . the district court held that Schonfeld could not establish lost asset damages with reasonable certainty because the value of the supply agreements also depended on their ability to generate profits. In addition, the district court held that Schonfeld had failed to establish that the supply agreements were "recoverable assets." All expert testimony proffered to establish their market value was, therefore, excluded as irrelevant.

Finally, the court ruled that, as a matter of law, Schonfeld was not entitled to punitive damages.

Accordingly, the district court granted summary judgment . . . .

Plaintiff, Schonfeld, now appeals . . . .

* * *

DISCUSSION

* * *

I. Lost Profits

* * *

In an action for breach of contract, a plaintiff is entitled to recover lost profits only if he can establish both the existence and amount of such damages with reasonable certainty. [Citation] "[T]he damages may not be merely speculative, possible or imaginary." Although lost profits need not be proven with "mathematical precision," they must be "capable of measurement based upon known reliable factors without undue speculation." [Citations] Therefore, evidence of lost profits from a new business venture receives greater scrutiny because there is no track record upon which to base an estimate. [Citation] Projections of future profits based upon "a multitude of assumptions" that require "speculation and conjecture" and few known factors do not provide the requisite certainty. [Citation]

The plaintiff faces an additional hurdle: he must prove that lost profit damages were within the contemplation of the parties when the contract was made. [Citation] "The party breaching the contract is liable for those risks foreseen or which should have been foreseen at the time the contract was made." Where the contract is silent on the subject, the court must take a "common sense" approach, and determine what the parties intended by considering "the nature, purpose and particular circumstances of the contract known by the parties ... as well as what liability the defendant fairly may be supposed to have assumed consciously." [Citations]

Here, the district court concluded that the Channel was a new entertainment venture . . . . The operating entity's profits, the court noted, "were purely hypothetical, stemming from the sale of untested programming to a hypothetical subscriber base, sold to advertisers at a hypothetical price and supported by hypothetical investors and carriers." [Citation] After reviewing the seemingly endless list of assumptions upon which Schonfeld's expert relied in determining lost profits, the court held that Schonfeld could establish neither the existence nor the amount of lost profits with reasonable certainty. The court also concluded that lost profits were not within the contemplation of the parties. We fully agree with the district court's analysis.

* * *

Subject as they are to the changing whims and artistic tastes of the general public, claims for profits lost in unsuccessful entertainment ventures have received a chilly reception in the New York courts. [Citations] Curtis believes he adjusted his profit figures to take such factors into account by providing for a 25% variance on the projected cash flows of the operating entity. In his deposition, he stated that he chose the 25% variance based on his experience with the cable industry. However, Curtis failed to establish that this variance would adequately account for any inaccuracies in the revenue and expense assumptions discussed above as well as any changes in consumer demand for British-style news reporting.

Indeed, Curtis failed to account for the effects of any general market risks on the Channel's probability of success. These risks include: (1) the entry of competitors; (2) technological developments; (3) regulatory changes; or (4) general market movements. As the district court correctly noted, "[f]ailure to control for adverse market conditions allows the false inference that plaintiff's venture was an assured success." [Citation] Therefore, the court properly held that Schonfeld failed to establish a foundation for the existence of lost profits.

C. The Contemplation of the Parties

Finally, Schonfeld maintains that he adduced sufficient evidence to establish that liability for lost profits was within the parties' contemplation at the time the Hilliards promised to fund the Interim Agreement.

* * *

. . . Schonfeld is not seeking profits that would have accrued under the alleged oral agreement to fund, or even under the Interim Agreement. Rather, Schonfeld wants to recover lost profits that INN or a non-existent operating entity might have received from the operation of the Channel. Further, the profitability of the Channel was highly uncertain when the Hilliards promised to fund the Interim Agreement. Nor did they exercise "near exclusive control" over the profitability of the venture. In light of "the nature, purpose and particular circumstances of the contract known by the parties," by orally promising to provide up to $20 million to fund the Interim Agreement, the Hilliards cannot "be supposed to have assumed" liability for approximately $269 million in lost profits that might have been garnered in the future by a non-existent operating entity. [Citation].

* * *

For all the foregoing reasons, we affirm the district court's grant of summary judgment dismissing all claims insofar as they seek damages for lost profits.

Case 15-3

A plaintiff must demonstrate that she has mitigated her damages. This case illustrates some of the principles determining whether a plaintiff has mitigated her damages.

SHIRLEY MACLAINE PARKER, v.TWENTIETH CENTURY-FOX FILM CORP.
Sup. Ct. Cal. 1970
3 Cal.3d 176, 474 P.2d 689, 89 Cal.Rptr. 737

BURKE, J.

Defendant Twentieth Century-Fox Film Corporation appeals from a summary judgment granting to plaintiff the recovery of agreed compensation under a written contract for her services as an actress in a motion picture. As will appear, we have concluded that the trial court correctly ruled in plaintiff's favor and that the judgment should be affirmed.

Plaintiff is well known as an actress, and in the contract between plaintiff and defendant is sometimes referred to as the "Artist." Under the contract, dated August 6, 1965, plaintiff was to play the female lead in defendant's contemplated production of a motion picture entitled "Bloomer Girl." The contract provided that defendant would pay plaintiff a minimum "guaranteed compensation" of $53,571.42 per week for 14 weeks commencing May 23, 1966, for a total of $750,000. Prior to May 1966 defendant decided not to produce the picture and by a letter dated April 4, 1966, it notified plaintiff of that decision and that it would not "comply with our obligations to you under" the written contract.

By the same letter and with the professed purpose "to avoid any damage to you," defendant instead offered to employ plaintiff as the leading actress in another film tentatively entitled "Big Country, Big Man" (hereinafter, "Big Country"). The compensation offered was identical, as were 31 of the 34 numbered provisions or articles of the original contract.[1] Unlike "Bloomer Girl," however, which was to have been a musical production, "Big Country" was a dramatic "western type" movie. "Bloomer Girl" was to have been filmed in California; "Big Country" was to be produced in Australia. Also, certain terms in the proffered contract varied from those of the original.[2] Plaintiff was given one week within which to accept; she did not and the offer lapsed. Plaintiff then commenced this action seeking recovery of the agreed guaranteed compensation.

The complaint sets forth two causes of action. The first is for money due under the contract; the second, based upon the same allegations as the first, is for damages resulting from defendant's breach of contract. Defendant in its answer admits the existence and validity of the contract, that plaintiff complied with all the conditions, covenants and promises and stood ready to complete the performance, and that defendant breached and "anticipatorily repudiated" the contract. It denies, however, that any money is due to plaintiff either under the contract or as a result of its breach, and pleads as an affirmative defense to both causes of action plaintiff's allegedly deliberate failure to mitigate damages, asserting that she unreasonably refused to accept its offer of the leading role in "Big Country."

Plaintiff moved for summary judgment ..., the motion was granted, and summary judgment for $750,000 plus interest was entered in plaintiff's favor. This appeal by defendant followed.

The familiar rules are that the matter to be determined by the trial court on a motion for summary judgment is whether facts have been presented which give rise to a triable factual issue.

* * *

As stated, defendant's sole defense to this action which resulted from its deliberate breach of contract is that in rejecting defendant's substitute offer of employment plaintiff unreasonably refused to mitigate damages.

The general rule is that the measure of recovery by a wrongfully discharged employee is the amount of salary agreed upon for the period of service, less the amount which the employer affirmatively proves the employee has earned or with reasonable effort might have earned from other employment. . . . However, before projected earnings from other employment opportunities not sought or accepted by the discharged employee can be applied in mitigation, the employer must show that the other employment was comparable, or substantially similar, to that of which the employee has been deprived; the employee's rejection of or failure to seek other available employment of a different or inferior kind may not be resorted to in order to mitigate damages.

In the present case defendant has raised no issue of *reasonableness of efforts* by plaintiffs to obtain other employment; the sole issue is whether plaintiff's refusal of defendant's substitute offer of "Big Country" may be used in mitigation. Nor, if the "Big Country" offer was of employment different or inferior when compared with the original "Bloomer Girl" employment, is there an issue as to whether or not plaintiff acted reasonably in refusing the substitute offer. Despite defendant's arguments to the contrary, no case cited or which our research has discovered holds or suggests that reasonableness is an element of a wrongfully discharged employee's option to reject, or fail to seek, different or inferior employment lest the possible earnings therefrom be charged against him in mitigation of damages.[5]

Applying the foregoing rules to the record in the present case, with all intendments in favor of the party opposing the summary judgment motion-here, defendant-it is clear that the trial court correctly ruled that plaintiff's failure to accept defendant's tendered substitute employment could not be applied in mitigation of damages because the offer of the "Big Country" lead was of employment both different and inferior, and that no factual dispute was presented on that issue. The mere circumstance that "Bloomer Girl" was to be a musical review calling upon plaintiff's talents as a dancer as well as an actress, and was to be produced in the City of Los Angeles, whereas "Big Country" was a straight dramatic role in a "Western Type" story taking place in an opal mine in Australia, demonstrates the difference in kind between the two employments; the female lead as a dramatic actress in a western style motion picture can by no stretch of imagination be considered the equivalent of or substantially similar to the lead in a song-and-dance production.

Additionally, the substitute "Big Country" offer proposed to eliminate or impair the director and screenplay approvals accorded to plaintiff under the original "Bloomer Girl" contract (see fn. 2, *ante*), and thus constituted an offer of inferior employment. No expertise or judicial notice is required in order to hold that the deprivation or infringement of an employee's rights held under an original employment contract converts the available "other employment" relied upon by the employer to mitigate damages, into inferior employment which the employee need not seek or accept.

Statements found in affidavits submitted by defendant in opposition to plaintiff's summary judgment motion, to the effect that the "Big County" offer was not of employment different from or inferior to that under the "Bloomer Girl" contract, merely repeat the allegations of defendant's answer to the complaint in this action, constitute only conclusionary assertions with respect to undisputed facts, and do not give rise to a triable factual issue so as to defeat the motion for summary judgment.

In view of the determination that defendant failed to present any facts showing the existence of a factual issue with respect to its sole defense-plaintiff's rejection of its substitute employment offer in mitigation of damages-we need not consider plaintiff's further contention that for various reasons, including the provisions of the original contract set forth in footnote 1, *ante*, plaintiff was excused from attempting to mitigate damages.

The judgment is affirmed.

Case 15-4

This case discusses the requirements for awarding the remedy of specific performance for a breach of contract and applies them to a failure to give screen credit for making a motion picture.

TAMARIND LITHOGRAPHY WORKSHOP, INC. v. SANDERS
Cal. Ct. App. Sec. Dist., 1983
143 Cal. App. 3d 571, 193 Cal. Rptr. 409

STEPHENS, J.

The essence of this appeal concerns the question of whether an award of damages is an adequate remedy at law in lieu of specific performance for the breach of an agreement to give screen credits. Our saga traces its origin to March of 1969, at which time appellant, and cross-complainant below, Terry Sanders (hereinafter "Sanders" or "appellant"), agreed in writing to write, direct and produce a motion picture on the subject of lithography for respondent, Tamarind Lithography Workshop, Inc. (hereinafter referred to as "Tamarind" or "respondent").

Pursuant to the terms of the agreement, the film was shot during the summer of 1969, wherein Sanders directed the film according to an outline/treatment of his authorship, and acted as production manager by personally hiring and supervising personnel comprising the film crew. Additionally, Sanders exercised both artistic control over the mixing of the sound track and overall editing of the picture.

After completion, the film, now titled the "Four Stones for Kanemitsu," was screened by Tamarind at its tenth anniversary celebration on April 28, 1970. Thereafter, a dispute arose between the parties concerning their respective rights and obligations under the original 1969 agreement. Litigation ensued and in January 1973 the matter went to trial. Prior to the entry of judgment, the parties entered into a written settlement agreement, which became the premise for the instant action. Specifically, this April 30, 1973, agreement provided that Sanders would be entitled to a screen credit entitled "A Film by Terry Sanders."

Tamarind did not comply with its expressed obligation pursuant to that agreement, in that it failed to include Sanders' screen credits in the prints it distributed. As a result a situation developed wherein Tamarind and co-defendant Wayne filed suit for declaratory relief, damages due to breach of contract, emotional distress, defamation and fraud.

Sanders cross-complained, seeking damages for Tamarind's breach of contract, declaratory relief, specific performance of the contract to give Sanders screen credits, and defamation. Both causes were consolidated and brought to trial on May 31, 1977. A jury was impaneled for purposes of determining damage issues and decided that Tamarind had breached the agreement and awarded Sanders $25,000 in damages.

The remaining claims for declaratory and injunctive relief were tried by the court. The court made findings that Tamarind had sole ownership rights in the film, that "both June Wayne and Terry Sanders were each creative producers of the film, that Sanders shall have the right to modify the prints in his personal possession to include his credits." All other prayers for relief were denied.

It is from the denial of appellant's request for specific performance upon which appellant predicates this appeal.

* * *

The availability of the remedy of specific performance is premised upon well established requisites. These requisites include: A showing by plaintiff of (1) the inadequacy of his legal remedy; (2) an underlying contract that is both reasonable and supported by adequate consideration; (3) the existence of a mutuality of remedies; (4) contractual terms which are sufficiently definite to enable the court to know what it is to enforce; and (5) a substantial similarity of the requested performance to that promised in the contract. [Citation]

It is manifest that the legal remedies available to Sanders for harm resulting from the future exhibition of the film are inadequate as a matter of law. The primary reasons are twofold: (1) that an accurate assessment of damages would be far too difficult and require much speculation, and (2) that any future exhibitions might be deemed to be a continuous breach of contract and thereby create the danger of an untold number of lawsuits.

There is no doubt that the exhibition of a film, which is favorably received by its critics and the public at large, can result in valuable advertising or publicity for the artists responsible for that film's making. Likewise, it is unquestionable that the non-appearance of an artist's name or likeness in the form of screen credit on a successful film can result in a loss of that valuable publicity. However, whether that loss of publicity is measurable dollar wise is quite another matter.

By its very nature, public acclaim is unique and very difficult, if not sometimes impossible, to quantify in monetary terms.

* * *

We return to the remaining requisites for Sanders' entitlement to specific performance. The need for our finding the contract to be reasonable and supported by adequate consideration is obviated by the jury's determination of respondent's breach of that contract. The requisite of mutuality of remedy has been satisfied in that Sanders had fully performed his obligations

pursuant to the agreement (i.e., release of all claims of copyright to the film and dismissal of his then pending action against respondents). [Citation] Similarly, we find the terms of the agreement sufficiently definite to permit enforcement of the respondent's performance as promised.

In conclusion, the record shows that the appellant is entitled to relief consisting of the damages recovered, and an injunction against future injury.

CASE 25-1

Courts in a number of states have allowed at-will employees to bring claims for "wrongful discharge" under tort or contract theories. In the following case, the New York Court of Appeals considers – and rejects – a plaintiff's arguments that New York should recognize such causes of action.

Murphy v. American Home Products Corporation
Court of Appeals of New York, 1983
58 N.Y. 2d 293, 461 N.Y.S.2d 232, 448 N.E.2d 86

Jones, J. This court has not and does not now recognize a cause of action in tort for abusive or wrongful discharge of an employee; such recognition must await action of the Legislature. Nor does the complaint here state a cause of action for intentional infliction of emotional distress, for prima facie tort, or for breach of contract. These causes of action were, therefore, properly dismissed. . . .

Plaintiff, Joseph Murphy, was first employed by defendant, American Home Products Corp., in 1957. He thereafter served in various accounting positions, eventually attaining the office of assistant treasurer, but he never had a formal contract of employment. On April 18, 1980, when he was 59 years old, he was discharged.

Plaintiff claims that he was fired for two reasons: because of his disclosure to top management of alleged accounting improprieties on the part of corporate personnel and because of his age. As to the first ground, plaintiff asserts that his firing was in retaliation for his revelation to officers and directors of defendant corporation that he had uncovered at least $50 million in illegal account manipulations of secret pension reserves which improperly inflated the company's growth in income and allowed high-ranking officers to reap unwarranted bonuses from a management

incentive plan, as well as in retaliation for his own refusal to engage in the alleged accounting improprieties. He contends that the company's internal regulations required him to make the disclosure that he did. He also alleges that his termination was carried out in a humiliating manner.

* * *

The complaint set up four causes of action. As his first cause of action, plaintiff alleged that his discharge "was wrongful, malicious and in bad faith" and that defendant was bound "not to dismiss its employees for reasons that are contrary to public policy". In his second cause of action, plaintiff claimed that his dismissal "was intended to and did cause plaintiff severe mental and emotional distress thereby damaging plaintiff". His third claim was based on an allegation that the manner of his termination "was deliberately and viciously insulting, was designed to and did embarrass and humiliate plaintiff and was intended to and did cause plaintiff severe mental and emotional distress thereby damaging plaintiff". In his fourth cause of action, plaintiff asserted that, although his employment contract was of indefinite duration, the law imposes in every employment contract "the requirement that an employer shall deal with each employee fairly and in good faith". On that predicate he alleged that defendant's conduct in stalling his advancement and ultimately firing him for his disclosures "breached the terms of its contract requiring good faith and fair dealing toward plaintiff and damaged plaintiff thereby". Plaintiff demanded compensatory and punitive damages.

[D]efendant moved on July 27, 1981 to dismiss the complaint on the grounds that it failed to state a cause of action and that the fourth cause of action was barred by the Statute of Frauds. Defendant contended that plaintiff was an at-will employee subject to discharge at any time, that New York does not recognize a tort action for abusive or wrongful discharge, and that the prima facie tort and intentional infliction of emotional distress claims were unavailable and insufficient.

On October 16, 1981, plaintiff served an amended complaint with his opposing papers on the motion. The amended complaint, among other things, added a fifth cause of action, alleging that plaintiff was denied advancement due to his age which constituted "illegal employment discrimination on the basis of age in violation of New York Executive Law § 296. "

Special Term denied defendant's motion to dismiss the wrongful discharge tort claim but granted the motion as to the causes of action for breach of contract, prima facie tort, intentional infliction of emotional distress, and age discrimination. Although the court noted that New York had not yet adopted the doctrine of abusive discharge, it declined to put plaintiff out of court before he had had opportunity by means of disclosure procedures to elicit evidence which might put his claim on firmer footing. Special Term held the cause of action for breach of contract barred by the Statute of Frauds. As to the second and third causes of action the court ruled that plaintiff's allegations as to the manner of his dismissal were not sufficient to support causes of action for intentional infliction of emotional distress or for prima facie tort. . . .

On cross appeals, the Appellate Division, modified, to the extent of granting the motion to dismiss the first cause of action, and otherwise affirmed the order of Special Term. The court noted that it does not appear that New York recognizes a cause of action for abusive discharge and that, in any event, plaintiff had failed to show the type of violation of penal law or public policy that has been held sufficient in other jurisdictions to support a cause of action for abusive discharge. According to the appellate court, plaintiff's charge that the corporation's records were not kept in accordance with generally accepted accounting principles appeared to involve a dispute over a matter of judgment as to the proper accounting treatment to be given the terms involved and not a dispute over false book entries. As to the other causes of action, the court ruled that

Special Term had properly dismissed them either for failure to state a cause of action [and] failure to comply with the Statute of Frauds or, regarding the age discrimination claim, failure to assert it within the statutory time period . . . We modify the order of the Appellate Division from which plaintiff appeals by reinstating the fifth cause of action for age discrimination and otherwise affirm. [*The age discrimination claim was reinstated because the court below had applied the wrong statute of limitations.*]

With respect to his first cause of action, plaintiff urges that the time has come when the courts of New York should recognize the tort of abusive or wrongful discharge of an at-will employee. To do so would alter our long- settled rule that where an employment is for an indefinite term it is presumed to be a hiring at will which may be freely terminated by either party at any time for any reason or even for no reason . . . . Plaintiff argues that a trend has emerged in the courts of other States to temper what is perceived as the unfairness of the traditional rule by allowing a cause of action in tort to redress abusive discharges. He accurately points out that this tort has elsewhere been recognized to hold employers liable for dismissal of employees in retaliation for employee conduct that is protected by public policy. Thus, the abusive discharge doctrine has been applied to impose liability on employers where employees have been discharged for disclosing illegal activities on the part of their employers . . . , where employees have been terminated due to their service on jury duty . . . , and where employees have been dismissed because they have filed workers' compensation . . . . Plaintiff would have this court adopt this emerging view. We decline his invitation, being of the opinion that such a significant change in our law is best left to the Legislature.

Those jurisdictions that have modified the traditional at-will rule appear to have been motivated by conclusions that the freedom of contract underpinnings of the rule have become outdated, that individual employees in the modern work force do not have the bargaining power to negotiate security for the jobs on which they have grown to rely, and that the rule yields harsh results for those employees who do not enjoy the benefits of express contractual limitations on the power of dismissal. Whether these conclusions are supportable or whether for other compelling reasons employers should, as a matter of policy, be held liable to at-will employees discharged in circumstances for which no liability has existed at common law, are issues better left to resolution at the hands of the Legislature. In addition to the fundamental question whether such liability should be recognized in New York, of no less practical importance is the definition of its configuration if it is to be recognized.

Both of these aspects of the issue, involving perception and declaration of relevant public policy (the underlying determinative consideration with respect to tort liability in general, . . . are best and more appropriately explored and resolved by the legislative branch of our government. The Legislature has infinitely greater resources and procedural means to discern the public will, to examine the variety of pertinent considerations, to elicit the views of the various segments of the community that would be directly affected and in any event critically interested, and to investigate and anticipate the impact of imposition of such liability. Standards should doubtless be established applicable to the multifarious types of employment and the various circumstances of discharge. If the rule of nonliability for termination of at-will employment is to be tempered, it should be accomplished through a principled statutory scheme, adopted after opportunity for public ventilation, rather than in consequence of judicial resolution of the partisan arguments of individual adversarial litigants.

Additionally, if the rights and obligations under a relationship forged, perhaps some time ago, between employer and employee in reliance on existing legal principles are to be significantly altered, a fitting accommodation of the competing interests to be affected may well dictate that any change should be given prospective effect only, or at least so the Legislature might conclude.

For all the reasons stated, we conclude that recognition in New York State of tort liability for what has become known as abusive or wrongful discharge should await legislative action.

Plaintiff's second cause of action is framed in terms of a claim for intentional infliction of emotional distress. To survive a motion to dismiss, plaintiff's allegations must satisfy the rule set out in Restatement of Torts, Second, which we adopted in *Fischer v Maloney* . . ., that: "One who by extreme and outrageous conduct intentionally or recklessly causes severe emotional distress to another is subject to liability for such emotional distress" (§ 46, subd [1]). Comment *d* to that section notes that: "Liability has been found only where the conduct has been so outrageous in character, and so extreme in degree, as to go beyond all possible bounds of decency, and to be regarded as atrocious, and utterly intolerable in a civilized community". The facts alleged by plaintiff regarding the manner of his termination fall far short of this strict standard. Further, in light of our holding above that there is now no cause of action in tort in New York

for abusive or wrongful discharge of an at-will employee, plaintiff should not be allowed to evade that conclusion or to subvert the traditional at-will contract rule by casting his cause of action in terms of a tort of intentional infliction of emotional distress . . . .

Plaintiff's third cause of action was also properly dismissed. If considered, as plaintiff would have us, as intended to allege a prima facie tort it is deficient inasmuch as there is no allegation that his, discharge was without economic or social justification . . . . Moreover, we held in *James v Board of Educ.* . . ., which also involved the exercise of an unrestricted right to discharge an employee, that: "Plaintiff cannot, by the device of an allegation that the sole reason for the termination of his employment by these public officials acting within the ambit of their authority was to harm him without justification (a contention which could be advanced with respect to almost any such termination), bootstrap himself around a motion addressed to the pleadings". Nor does the conclusory allegation of malice by plaintiff here supply the deficiency. As with the intentional infliction of emotional distress claim, this cause of action cannot be allowed in circumvention of the unavailability of a tort claim for wrongful discharge or the contract rule against liability for discharge of an at-will employee.

Plaintiff's fourth cause of action is for breach of contract. Although he concedes in his complaint that his employment contract was of indefinite duration (inferentially recognizing that, were there no more, under traditional principles his employer might have discharged him at any time), he asserts that in all employment contracts the law implies an obligation on the part of the employer to deal with his employees fairly and in good faith and that a discharge in violation of that implied obligation exposes the employer to liability for breach of contract. Seeking then to apply this proposition to the present case, plaintiff argues in substance that he was required by the terms of his employment to disclose accounting improprieties and that defendant's discharge of him for having done so constituted a failure by the employer to act in good faith and thus a breach of the contract of employment.

No New York case upholding any such broad proposition is cited to us by plaintiff (or identified by our dissenting colleague), and we know of none. New York does recognize that in appropriate circumstances an obligation of good faith and fair dealing on the part of a party to a contract may be implied and, if implied will be enforced . . . . In such instances the implied obligation is in aid and furtherance of other terms of the agreement of the parties. No obligation can be implied, however, which would be inconsistent with other terms of the contractual relationship. Thus, in the case now before us, plaintiff's employment was at will, a relationship in which the law accords the employer an unfettered right to terminate the employment at any time. In the context of such an employment it would be incongruous to say that an inference may be drawn that the employer impliedly agreed to a provision which would be destructive of his right of termination. The parties may by express agreement limit or restrict the employer's right of discharge, but to imply such a limitation from the existence of an unrestricted right would be internally inconsistent. In sum, under New York law as it now stands, absent a constitutionally impermissible purpose, a statutory proscription, or an express limitation in the individual contract of employment, an employer's right at any time to terminate an employment at will remains unimpaired.

* * *

Accordingly, the fourth cause of action should have been dismissed for failure to state a cause of action. [*The Court notes that the courts below appear to have erred in dismissing this cause of action under the Statute of Frauds because the contract of employment was not one which, by its terms, could not have been performed within one year.*]

* * *

For the reasons stated, the order of the Appellate Division should be modified, with costs, to reinstate plaintiff's fifth cause of action for age discrimination.

Selected New York Statutes

SELECTED NEW YORK STATE STATUTES

NEW YORK GENERAL OBLIGATIONS LAW

§ 1-202. Definition

As used in this chapter, the term "infant" or "minor" means a person who has not attained the age of eighteen years. (eff. Sept. 1, 1974)

§ 3-101. When contracts may not be disaffirmed on ground of infancy

1. A contract made on or after September first, nineteen hundred seventy-four by a person after he has attained the age of eighteen years may not be disaffirmed by him on the ground of infancy.

* * *

3. A husband and wife, with respect only to real property they occupy or which they affirm they are about to occupy as a home, regardless of the minority of either or both and without limitation of the powers of any such person who is of full age, shall each have power (a) to enter into and contract for a loan or loans with a bank, trust company, ... savings bank or savings and loan association whose home office is located in this state, with any insurance company authorized to do business in this state, with the United States government and its agencies, with respect to such real property and take any other action and execute any other document or instrument to the extent necessary or appropriate to effect any such loan, provide security therefor, carry out or modify the terms thereof, and effect any compromise or settlement of any such loan or of any claim with respect thereto; (b) to receive, hold and dispose of such real property, make and execute contracts, notes, deeds, mortgages, agreements and other instruments necessary and appropriate to acquire such property; and (c) to dispose of such real property so acquired, and make and execute contracts, deeds, agreements and other instruments necessary and appropriate to dispose of such property.

Notwithstanding any contrary provision or rule of law, no such husband or wife shall have the power to disaffirm, because of minority, any act or transaction which he or she is hereinabove empowered to perform or engage in, nor shall any defense based upon minority be interposed in any action or proceeding arising out of any such act or transaction.

****

§ 3-102. Obligations of certain minors for hospital, medical and surgical treatment and care

An obligation incurred by a married minor for hospital, medical and surgical treatment and care for such minor or such minor's children shall not be voidable because of minority. For the purpose of this section only, subsequent judgment of divorce or annulment shall not alter the obligation previously incurred.

§ 3-112. Liability of parents and legal guardians having custody of an infant for certain damages caused by such infant

1. The parent or legal guardian, other than the state, a local social services department or a foster parent, of an infant over ten and less than eighteen years of age, shall be liable to any public officer, organization or authority, having by law the care and/or custody of any public property of the state or of any political subdivision thereof, or to any private individual or organization having by law the care, custody and/or ownership of any private property, for damages caused by such infant, where such infant has willfully, maliciously, or unlawfully damaged, defaced or destroyed such public or private property, whether real or personal, or, where such infant, with intent to deprive the owner and/or custodian of such property or to appropriate the same to himself or herself or to a third person, has knowingly entered or remained in a building and has wrongfully taken, obtained or withheld such public or private personal property from such building which personal property is owned or maintained by the state or any political subdivision thereof or which is owned or maintained by any individual, organization or authority, or where such infant has falsely reported an incident or placed a false bomb . . . . Such public officer, organization or authority, or private individual or organization, as the case may be, may bring an action for civil damages in a court of competent jurisdiction for a judgment to recover such damages from such parent or legal guardian other than the state or a local social services department or a foster parent. For the purposes of this subdivision, damages for falsely reporting an incident or placing a false bomb shall mean the funds reasonably expended by a victim in responding to such false report . . . . In no event shall such damages portion of a judgment authorized by this section, as described in

this subdivision, exceed the sum of five thousand dollars.

2. Notwithstanding the provisions of subdivision one of this section, prior to the entering of a judgment under this section in the sum total of five hundred dollars or more, the court shall provide such parent or legal guardian of such infant with an opportunity to make an application to the court based upon such parent's or legal guardian's financial inability to pay any portion or all of the amount of such sum total which is in excess of five hundred dollars . . .

3. It shall be a defense to an action brought under this section that restitution has been paid . . . . It shall also be a defense to an action brought under this section that such infant had voluntarily and without good cause abandoned the home of the parent or guardian and without good cause refused to submit to the guidance and control of the parent or guardian prior to and at the time of the occurrence of such damages or destruction. In no event shall it be a defense that the parent or legal guardian has exercised due diligent supervision over the activities of such infant, provided, however, that in the interests of justice, the court may consider mitigating circumstances that bear directly upon the actions of the parent or legal guardian in supervising such unemancipated infant.

§ 5-325. Garages and parking places

1. No person who conducts or maintains for hire or other consideration a garage, parking lot or other similar place which has the capacity for the housing, storage, parking, repair or servicing of four or more motor vehicles, as defined by the vehicle and traffic law, may exempt himself from liability for damages for injury to person or property resulting from the negligence of such person, his agents or employees, in the operation of any such vehicle, or in its housing, storage, parking, repair or servicing, or in the conduct or maintenance of such garage, parking lot or other similar place, and, except as hereinafter provided, any agreement so exempting such person shall be void.

2. Damages for loss or injury to property may be limited by a provision in the storage agreement limiting the liability in case of loss or damage by theft, fire or explosion and setting forth a specific liability per vehicle, which shall in no event be less than twenty-five thousand dollars, beyond which the person owning or operating such garage or lot shall not be liable; provided, however, that such liability may on request of the person delivering such vehicle be increased, in which event increased rates may be charged based on such increased liability.

§ 5-326. Agreements exempting pools, gymnasiums, places of public amusement or recreation and similar establishments from liability for negligence void and unenforceable

Every covenant, agreement or understanding in or in connection with, or collateral to, any contract, membership application, ticket of admission or similar writing, entered into between the owner or operator of any pool, gymnasium, place of amusement or recreation, or similar establishment and the user of such facilities, pursuant to which such owner or operator receives a fee or other compensation for the use of such facilities, which exempts the said owner or operator from liability for damages caused by or resulting from the negligence of the owner, operator or person in charge of such establishment, or their agents, servants or employees, shall be deemed to be void as against public policy and wholly unenforceable.

§ 5-332. Unsolicited and voluntarily sent merchandise deemed unconditional gift

1. No person, firm, partnership, association or corporation, or agent or employee thereof, shall, in any manner, or by any means, offer for sale goods, wares, or merchandise, where the offer includes the voluntary and unsolicited sending of such goods, wares, or merchandise not actually ordered or requested by the recipient, either orally or in writing. The receipt of any such goods, wares, or merchandise shall for all purposes be deemed an unconditional gift to the recipient who may use or dispose of such goods, wares, or merchandise in any manner he sees fit without any obligation on his part to the sender.
If after any such receipt deemed to be an unconditional gift under this section, the sender continues to send bill statements or requests for payment with respect thereto, an action may be brought by the recipient to enjoin such conduct, in which action there may also be awarded reasonable attorney's fees and costs to the prevailing party.

* * *

§ 5-401. Illegal wagers, bets and stakes

All wagers, bets or stakes, made to depend upon any race, or upon any gaming by lot or chance, or upon any lot, chance, casualty, or unknown or contingent event whatever, shall be unlawful.

§ 5-411. Contracts on account of money or property wagered, bet or staked are void

All contracts for or on account of any money or property, or thing in action wagered, bet or staked, as provided in section 5-401, shall be void.

§ 5-501. Rate of interest; usury forbidden

1. The rate of interest, as computed pursuant to this title, upon the loan or forbearance of any money, goods, or things in action, except as provided in subdivisions five and six of this section or as otherwise provided by law, shall be six per centum per annum unless a different rate is prescribed in section fourteen-a of the banking law. . . . [See below.]

§ 5-511. Usurious contracts void

1. All bonds, bills, notes, assurances, conveyances, all other contracts or securities whatsoever, . . . and all deposits of goods or other things whatsoever, whereupon or whereby there shall be reserved or taken, or secured or agreed to be reserved or taken, any greater sum, or greater value, for the loan or forbearance of any money, goods or other things in action, than is prescribed in section 5-501, shall be void, except that the knowingly taking, receiving, reserving or charging such a greater sum or greater value by a savings bank, a savings and loan association or a federal savings and loan association shall only be held and adjudged a forfeiture of the entire interest which the loan or obligation carries with it or which has been agreed to be paid thereon. If a greater sum or greater value has been paid, the person paying the same or his legal representative may recover from the savings bank, the savings and loan association or the federal savings and loan association twice the entire amount of the interest thus paid.

2. Except as provided in subdivision one, whenever it shall satisfactorily appear by the admissions of the defendant, or by proof, that any bond, bill, note, assurance, pledge, conveyance, contract, security or any evidence of debt, has been taken or received in violation of the foregoing provisions, the court shall declare the same to be void, and enjoin any prosecution thereon, and order the same to be surrendered and cancelled.

§ 5-513. Recovery of excess

Every person who, for any such loan or forbearance, shall pay or deliver any greater sum or value than is allowed to be received pursuant to section 5-501, and his personal representatives, may recover in an action against the person who shall have taken or received the same, and his personal representatives, the amount of the money so paid or value delivered, above the rate aforesaid.

§ 5-515. Borrower bringing an action need not offer to repay

Whenever any borrower of money, goods or things in action, shall begin an action for the recovery of the money, goods or things in action taken in violation of the foregoing provisions of this title, it shall not be necessary for him to pay or offer to pay any interest or principal on the sum or thing loaned; nor shall any court require or compel the payment or deposit of the principal sum or interest, or any portion thereof, as a condition of granting relief to the borrower in any case of usurious loans forbidden by the foregoing provisions of this title.

§ 5-521. Corporations prohibited from interposing defense of usury

1. No corporation shall hereafter interpose the defense of usury in any action . . . .

2. The provisions of subdivision one of this section shall not apply to a corporation, the principal asset of which shall be the ownership of a one or two family dwelling, where it appears either that the said corporation was organized and created, or that the controlling interest therein was acquired, within a period of six months prior to the execution, by said corporation of a bond or note evidencing indebtedness, and a mortgage creating a lien for said indebtedness on the said one or two family dwelling; . . . .

Any provision of any contract, or any separate written instrument executed prior to, simultaneously with or within sixty days after the delivery of any moneys to any borrower in connection with such indebtedness, whereby the defense of usury is waived or any such corporation is estopped from asserting it, is hereby declared to be contrary to public policy and absolutely void. . . .

§ 5-701. Agreements required to be in writing

a. Every agreement, promise or undertaking is void, unless it or some note or memorandum thereof be in writing, and subscribed by the party to be charged therewith, or by his lawful agent, if such agreement, promise or undertaking:

1. By its terms is not to be performed within one year from the making thereof or the performance of which is not to be completed before the end of a lifetime;

2. Is a special promise to answer for the debt, default or miscarriage of another person;

3. Is made in consideration of marriage, except mutual promises to marry;

* * *

§ 5-703. Conveyances and contracts concerning real property required to be in writing

1. An estate or interest in real property, other than a lease for a term not exceeding one year, or any trust or power, over or concerning real property, or in any manner relating thereto, cannot be created, granted, assigned, surrendered or declared, unless by act or operation of law, or by a deed or conveyance in writing, subscribed by the person creating, granting, assigning, surrendering or declaring the same, or by his lawful agent, thereunto authorized by writing. But this subdivision does not affect the power of a testator in the disposition of his real property by will; nor prevent any trust from arising or being extinguished by implication or operation of law, nor any declaration of trust from being proved by a writing subscribed by the person declaring the same.

2. A contract for the leasing for a longer period than one year, or for the sale, of any real property, or an interest therein, is void unless the contract or some note

or memorandum thereof, expressing the consideration, is in writing, subscribed by the party to be charged, or by his lawful agent thereunto authorized by writing.

3. A contract to devise real property or establish a trust of real property, or any interest therein or right with reference thereto, is void unless the contract or some note or memorandum thereof is in writing and subscribed by the party to be charged therewith, or by his lawfully authorized agent.

4. Nothing contained in this section abridges the powers of courts of equity to compel the specific performance of agreements in cases of part performance.

§ 5-1103. Written agreement for modification or discharge

An agreement, promise or undertaking to change or modify, or to discharge in whole or in part, any contract, obligation, or lease, or any mortgage or other security interest in personal or real property, shall not be invalid because of the absence of consideration, provided that the agreement, promise or undertaking changing, modifying, or discharging such contract, obligation, lease, mortgage or security interest, shall be in writing and signed by the party against whom it is sought to enforce the change, modification or discharge, or by his agent.

§ 5-1105. Written promise expressing past consideration

A promise in writing and signed by the promisor or by his agent shall not be denied effect as a valid contractual obligation on the ground that consideration for the promise is past or executed, if the consideration is expressed in the writing and is proved to have been given or performed and would be a valid consideration but for the time when it was given or performed.

§ 5-1107. Written assignment

An assignment shall not be denied the effect of irrevocably transferring the assignor's rights because of the absence of consideration, if such assignment is in writing and signed by the assignor, or by his agent.

§ 5-1109. Written irrevocable offer

Except as otherwise provided in section 2-205 of the uniform commercial code with respect to an offer by a merchant to buy or sell goods, when an offer to enter into a contract is made in a writing signed by the offeror, or by his agent, which states that the offer is irrevocable during a period set forth or until a time fixed, the offer shall not be revocable during such period or until such time because of the absence of consideration for the assurance of irrevocability. When such a writing states that the offer is irrevocable but does not state any period or time of irrevocability, it shall be construed to state that the offer is irrevocable for a reasonable time.

§ 5-1113. Written or published promise or reward

A promise to pay a reward for return of lost or mislaid property is not unenforceable because of absence of consideration if the promise was made in writing or the promisor caused it to be published.

§ 15-303. Release in writing without consideration or seal

A written instrument which purports to be a total or partial release of all claims, debts, demands or obligations, or a total or partial release of any particular claim, debt, demand or obligation, or a release or discharge in whole or in part of a mortgage, lien, security interest or charge upon personal or real property, shall not be invalid because of the absence of consideration or of a seal.

§ 15-501. Executory accord

1. Executory accord as used in this section means an agreement embodying a promise express or implied to accept at some future time a stipulated performance in satisfaction or discharge in whole or in part of any present claim, cause of action, contract, obligation, or lease, or any mortgage or other security interest in personal or real property, and a promise express or implied to render such performance in satisfaction or in discharge of such claim, cause of action, contract, obligation, lease, mortgage or security interest.

2. An executory accord shall not be denied effect as a defense or as the basis of an action or counterclaim by reason of the fact that the satisfaction or discharge of the claim, cause of action, contract, obligation, lease, mortgage or other security interest which is the subject of the accord was to occur at a time after the making of the accord, provided the promise of the party against whom it is sought to enforce the accord is in writing and signed by such party or by his agent. If executed by an agent, any promise required by this section to be in writing which affects or relates to real property or an interest therein as defined in section 5-101 in any manner stated in subdivisions one or two of section 5-703 of this chapter shall be void unless such agent was thereunto authorized in writing.

3. If an executory accord is not performed according to its terms by one party, the other party shall be entitled either to assert his rights under the claim, cause of action, contract, obligation, lease, mortgage or other security interest which is the subject of the accord, or to assert his right under the accord.

§ 15-503. Offer of accord followed by tender

1. An offer in writing, signed by the offeror or by his agent, to accept a performance therein designated in satisfaction or discharge in whole or in part of any claim, cause of action, contract, obligation, or lease, or any mortgage or other security interest in personal or real property, followed by tender of such performance by the offeree or by his agent before revocation of the offer, shall not be denied effect as a defense or as the basis of an action or counterclaim by reason of the fact that such tender was not accepted by the offeror or by his agent.

2. If executed by an agent, any offer required by this section to be in writing which affects or relates to real property or an interest therein as defined in section 5-101 in any manner stated in subdivisions one or two of section 5-703 of this chapter shall be void unless such agent was thereunto authorized in writing.

§ 17-103. Agreements waiving the statute of limitation

1. A promise to waive, to extend, or not to plead the statute of limitation applicable to an action arising out of a contract express or implied in fact or in law, if made after the accrual of the cause of action and made, either with or without consideration, in a writing signed by the promisor or his agent is effective, according to its terms, to prevent interposition of the defense of the statute of limitation in an action or proceeding commenced within the time that would be applicable if the cause of action had arisen at the date of the promise, or within such shorter time as may be provided in the promise.

2. A promise to waive, to extend, or not to plead the statute of limitation may be enforced as provided in this section by the person to whom the promise is made or for whose benefit it is expressed to be made or by any person who, after the making of the promise, succeeds or is subrogated to the interest of either of them.

3. A promise to waive, to extend, or not to plead the statute of limitation has no effect to extend the time limited by statute for commencement of an action or proceeding for any greater time or in any other manner than that provided in this section, or unless made as provided in this section.

4. This section

   a. does not change the requirements or the effect with respect to the statute of limitation, of an acknowledgment or promise to pay, or a payment or part payment of principal or interest, or a stipulation made in an action or proceeding;

   b. does not affect the power of the court to find that by reason of conduct of the party to be charged it is inequitable to permit him to interpose the defense of the statute of limitation; and

   c. does not apply in any respect to a cause of action to foreclose a mortgage of real property or a mortgage of a lease of real property, or to a cause of action to recover a judgment affecting the title to or the possession, use or enjoyment of real property, or a promise or waiver with respect to any statute of limitation applicable thereto.

NEW YORK BANKING LAW

§ 14-a. Rate of interest; banking board to adopt regulations

1. The maximum rate of interest provided for in section 5-501 of the general obligations law shall be sixteen per centum per annum.

2. The rate of interest as so prescribed under this section shall include as interest any and all amounts paid or payable, directly or indirectly, by any person, to or for the account of the lender in consideration for the making of a loan or forbearance as defined by the banking board pursuant to subdivision three of this section.

NEW YORK CIVIL PRACTICE LAW AND RULES (C.P.L.R.)

§ 1411. Damages recoverable when contributory negligence or assumption of risk is established

In any action to recover damages for personal injury, injury to property, or wrongful death, the culpable conduct attributable to the claimant or to the decedent, including contributory negligence or assumption of risk, shall not bar recovery, but the amount of damages otherwise recoverable shall be diminished in the proportion which the culpable conduct attributable to the claimant or decedent bears to the culpable conduct which caused the damages.

§ 3002. Actions and relief not barred for inconsistency

* * *

(d) *Action on contract and to reform.* A judgment denying recovery in an action upon an agreement in writing shall not be deemed to bar an action to reform such agreement and to enforce it as reformed.

(e) *Claim for damages and rescission.* A claim for damages sustained as a result of fraud or misrepresentation in the inducement of a contract or other transaction, shall not be deemed inconsistent with a claim for rescission or based upon rescission. In an action for rescission or based upon rescission the aggrieved party shall be allowed to obtain complete relief in one action, including rescission, restitution of the benefits, if any, conferred by him as a result of the transaction, and damages to which he is entitled because of such fraud or misrepresentation; but such complete relief shall not include duplication of items of recovery.

§ 3004. Where restoration of benefits before judgment unnecessary

A party who has received benefits by reason of a transaction that is void or voidable because of fraud, misrepresentation, mistake, duress, infancy or incompetency, and who, in an action or by way of defense or counterclaim, seeks rescission, restitution, a declaration or judgment that such transaction is void, or other relief, whether formerly denominated legal or equitable, dependent upon a determination that such transaction was void or voidable, shall not be denied relief because of a failure to tender before judgment restoration of such benefits; but the court may make a tender of restoration a condition of its judgment, and may otherwise in its judgment so adjust the equities between the parties that unjust enrichment is avoided.

§ 7501. Effect of arbitration agreement

A written agreement to submit any controversy thereafter arising or any existing controversy to arbitration is enforceable without regard to the justiciable character of the controversy and confers jurisdiction on the courts of the state to enforce it and to enter judgment on an award. In determining any matter arising under this article, the court shall not consider whether the claim with respect to which arbitration is sought is tenable, or otherwise pass upon the merits of the dispute.

NEW YORK EDUCATION LAW

§ 281. Loans and extensions of credit to infants

A contract hereafter made by an infant after he has attained the age of sixteen years in relation to obtaining a loan or extension of credit from an institution of the university of the state of New York in connection with such infant's attendance upon a course of instruction offered by such institution, or from a bank, trust company, industrial bank or national bank whose principal office is in this state for the purpose of defraying all or a portion of the expenses of such infant's attendance upon a course of instruction in an institution of the university of the state of New York or any other institution for higher education without this state which is a member of or accredited by an accrediting agency recognized by the department, may not be disaffirmed by him on the ground of infancy.

§ 6501. Admission to a profession (licensing)

Admission to practice of a profession in this state is accomplished by a license being issued to a qualified applicant by the education department. To qualify for a license an applicant shall meet the requirements prescribed in the article for the particular profession . . . .

§ 6503. Practice of a profession

Admission to the practice of a profession (1) entitles the licensee to practice the profession as defined in the article for the particular profession, (2) entitles the individual licensee to use the professional title as provided in the article for the particular profession, and (3) subjects the licensee to the procedures and penalties for professional misconduct as prescribed in this article . . . .

§ 6512. Unauthorized practice a crime

1. Anyone not authorized to practice under this title who practices or offers to practice or holds himself out as being able to practice in any profession in which a license is a prerequisite to the practice of the acts, or who practices any profession as an exempt person during the time when his professional license is suspended, revoked or annulled, or who aids or abets an unlicensed person to practice a profession, or who fraudulently sells, files, furnishes, obtains, or who attempts fraudulently to sell, file, furnish or obtain any diploma, license, record or permit purporting to authorize the practice of a profession, shall be guilty of a class E felony. . . .

§ 6513. Unauthorized use of a professional title a crime

1. Anyone not authorized to use a professional title regulated by this title, and who uses such professional title, shall be guilty of a class A misdemeanor. . . .

NEW YORK PENAL LAW

§ 180.00 Commercial bribing in the second degree

A person is guilty of commercial bribing in the second degree when he confers, or offers or agrees to confer, any benefit upon any employee, agent or fiduciary without the consent of the latter's employer or principal, with intent to influence his conduct in relation to his employer's or principal's affairs.

Commercial bribing in the second degree is a class A misdemeanor.

§ 180.03 Commercial bribing in the first degree

A person is guilty of commercial bribing in the first degree when he confers, or offers or agrees to confer, any benefit upon any employee, agent or fiduciary without the consent of the latter's employer or principal, with intent to influence his conduct in relation to his employer's or principal's affairs, and when the value of the benefit conferred or offered or agreed to be conferred exceeds one thousand dollars and causes economic harm to the employer or principal in an amount exceeding two hundred fifty dollars.

Commercial bribing in the first degree is a class E felony.

§ 180.08 Commercial bribe receiving in the first degree

An employee, agent or fiduciary is guilty of commercial bribe receiving in the first degree when, without the consent of his employer or principal, he solicits, accepts or agrees to accept any benefit from another person upon an agreement or understanding that such benefit will influence his conduct in relation to his employer's or principal's affairs, and when the value of the benefit solicited, accepted or agreed to be accepted exceeds one thousand dollars and causes economic harm to the employer or principal in an amount exceeding two hundred fifty dollars.

Commercial bribe receiving in the first degree is a class E felony.

§ 190.40 Criminal usury in the second degree

A person is guilty of criminal usury in the second degree when, not being authorized or permitted by law to do so, he knowingly charges, takes or receives any money or other property as interest on the loan or forbearance of any money or other property, at a rate exceeding twenty-five per centum per annum or the equivalent rate for a longer or shorter period.

Criminal usury in the second degree is a class E felony.

NEW YORK ARTS AND CULTURAL AFFAIRS LAW

§ 35.03. Judicial approval of certain contracts for services of infants; . . . .

1. A contract made by an infant or made by a parent or guardian of an infant, or a contract proposed to be so made, under which (a) the infant is to perform or render services as an actor, actress, dancer, musician, vocalist or other performing artist, or as a participant or player in professional sports, or (b) a person is employed to render services to the infant in connection with such services of the infant or in connection with contracts therefor, may be approved by the supreme court or the surrogate's court as provided in this section where the infant is a resident of this state or the services of the infant are to be performed or rendered in this state. If the contract is so approved the infant may not, either during his minority or upon reaching his majority, disaffirm the contract on the ground of infancy or assert that the parent or guardian lacked authority to make the contract. A contract modified, amended or assigned after its approval under this section shall be deemed a new contract.

2. (a) Approval of the contract pursuant to this section shall not exempt any person from any other law with respect to licenses, consents or authorizations required for any conduct, employment, use or exhibition of the infant in this state, nor limit in any manner the discretion of the licensing authority or other persons charged with the administration of such requirements, nor dispense with any other requirement of law relating to the infant.

(b) No contract shall be approved which provides for an employment, use or exhibition of the infant, within or without the state, which is prohibited by law and could not be licensed to take place in this state.

(c) No contract shall be approved unless (i) the written acquiescence to such contract of the parent or parents having custody, or other person having custody of the infant, is filed in the proceeding or (ii) the court shall find that the infant is emancipated.

(d) No contract shall be approved if the term during which the infant is to perform or render services or during which a person is employed to render services to the infant, including any extensions thereof by option or otherwise, extends for a period of more than three years from the date of approval of the contract . . . .

NEW YORK CIVIL SERVICE LAW

§ 75-b. Retaliatory action by public employers
* * *

2. (a) A public employer shall not dismiss or take other disciplinary or other adverse personnel action against a public employee regarding the employee's employment because the employee discloses to a governmental body information: (i) regarding a violation of a law, rule or regulation which violation creates and presents a substantial and specific danger to the public health or safety; or (ii) which the employee reasonably believes to be true and reasonably believes constitutes an improper governmental action. "Improper governmental action" shall mean any action by a public employer or employee, or an agent of such employer or employee, which is undertaken in the performance of such agent's official duties, whether or not such action is within the scope of his employment, and which is in violation of any federal, state or local law, rule or regulation.

* * *

NEW YORK LABOR LAW

§ 201-d. Discrimination against the engagement in certain activities

1. Definitions. As used in this section:

a. "Political activities" shall mean (i) running for public office, (ii) campaigning for a candidate for public office, or (iii) participating in fund-raising activities for the benefit of a candidate, political party or political advocacy group;

b. "Recreational activities" shall mean any lawful, leisure-time activity, for which the employee receives no compensation and which is generally engaged in for recreational purposes, including but not limited to sports, games, hobbies, exercise, reading and the viewing of television, movies and similar material;
* * *

2. Unless otherwise provided by law, it shall be unlawful for any employer or employment agency to refuse to hire, employ or license, or to discharge from employment or otherwise discriminate against an individual in compensation, promotion or terms, conditions or privileges of employment because of:

a. an individual's political activities outside of working hours, off of the employer's premises and without use of the employer's equipment or other property, if such activities are legal, provided, however, that this paragraph shall not apply to persons whose employment is defined in paragraph six of subdivision (a) of section seventy-nine-h of the civil rights law, and provided further that this paragraph shall not apply to persons who would otherwise be prohibited from engaging in political activity pursuant to chapter 15 of title 5 and subchapter III of chapter 73 of title 5 of the USCA;

b. an individual's legal use of consumable products prior to the beginning or after the conclusion of the employee's work hours, and off of the employer's premises and without use of the employer's equipment or other property;

c. an individual's legal recreational activities outside work hours, off of the employer's premises and without use of the employer's equipment or other property; or

d. an individual's membership in a union or any exercise of rights granted under Title 29, USCA, Chapter 7 or under article fourteen of the civil service law.

§ 740. Retaliatory personnel action by employers; prohibition
* * *

2. Prohibitions. An employer shall not take any retaliatory personnel action against an employee because such employee does any of the following:
    (a) discloses, or threatens to disclose to a supervisor or to a public body an activity, policy or practice of the employer that is in violation of law, rule or regulation which violation creates and presents a substantial and specific danger to the public health or safety or which constitutes health care fraud;
    (b) provides information to, or testifies before, any public body conducting an investigation, hearing or inquiry into any such violation of a law, rule or regulation by such employer; or
    (c) objects to, or refuses to participate in any such activity, policy or practice in violation of a law, rule or regulation.

3. Application. The protection against retaliatory personnel action provided by paragraph (a) of subdivision two of this section pertaining to disclosure to a public body shall not apply to an employee who makes such disclosure to a public body unless the employee has brought the activity, policy or practice in violation of law, rule or regulation to the attention of a supervisor of the employer and has afforded such employer a reasonable opportunity to correct such activity, policy or practice.

4. Violation; remedy. (a) An employee who has been the subject of a retaliatory personnel action in violation of this section may institute a civil action in a court of competent jurisdiction for relief as set forth in subdivision

five of this section within one year after the alleged retaliatory personnel action was taken.

* * *

5. Relief. In any action brought pursuant to subdivision four of this section, the court may order relief as follows:

(a) an injunction to restrain continued violation of this section;

(b) the reinstatement of the employee to the same position held before the retaliatory personnel action, or to an equivalent position;

(c) the reinstatement of full fringe benefits and seniority rights;

(d) the compensation for lost wages, benefits and other remuneration; and

(e) the payment by the employer of reasonable costs, disbursements, and attorney's fees.

6. Employer relief. A court, in its discretion, may also order that reasonable attorneys' fees and court costs and disbursements be awarded to an employer if the court determines that an action brought by an employee under this section was without basis in law or in fact.

* * *

741 Prohibition; health care employer who penalizes employees because of complaints of employer violations.

2. Retaliatory action prohibited. Notwithstanding any other provision of law, no employer shall take retaliatory action against any employee because the employee does any of the following:

(a) discloses or threatens to disclose to a supervisor, or to a public body an activity, policy or practice of the employer or agent that the employee, in good faith, reasonably believes constitutes improper quality of patient care; or

(b) objects to, or refuses to participate in any activity, policy or practice of the employer or agent that the employee, in good faith, reasonably believes constitutes improper quality of patient care.

3. Application. The protection against retaliatory personnel action provided by subdivision two of this section shall not apply unless the employee has brought the improper quality of patient care to the attention of a supervisor and has afforded the employer a reasonable opportunity to correct such activity, policy or practice. This subdivision shall not apply to an action or failure to act described in paragraph (a) of subdivision two of this section where the improper quality of patient care described therein presents an imminent threat to public health or safety or to the health of a specific patient and the employee reasonably believes in good faith that reporting to a supervisor would not result in corrective action.

NEW YORK UNIFORM COMMERCIAL CODE

Section 1-308. Performance or Acceptance Under Reservation of Rights.

A party who with explicit reservation of rights performs or promises performance or assents to performance in a manner demanded or offered by the other party does not thereby prejudice the rights reserved. Such words as "without prejudice," "under protest" or the like are sufficient.

Additional Problems

Chapter 4 - Tort Law

1. Don Juan is so busy trying to get the attention of a young woman that he walks into a light pole and is knocked unconscious. Driver happens to be driving down the road and sees Don Juan's unfortunate incident. Driver is so amused by the incident that he takes his eyes off the road for a moment and nearly slams into the car ahead of him. Veering off the road to avoid an accident, Driver drives into a restaurant, breaking a large window. Noodle, who was enjoying a bowl of soup at that moment, is burned by the hot soup, which is knocked off the table and into Noodle's lap. Noodle sues the restaurant, Driver and Don Juan for negligence. As to each claim, what result? Explain.

Chapter 11 - Agreement

1. Danforth Corporation entered into a written employment agreement with Eva on September 1, which provided in part that employment would commence on the following January 1 and "will continue for a period of time to be mutually agreed upon". One month before January 1, Danforth Corporation notified Eva that it had changed its mind and would not employ Eva. In Eva's action against Danforth for breach of contract, Danforth contends that there is no contract. Judgment for whom? Explain.

2. On April 15, Ramon wrote to Ivana offering to sell a piece of land that Ramon owned for $50,000. The letter, which was signed by Ramon, stated that the offer would expire on July 30.

On April 20, Ramon received a better offer from Lou. Ramon called Ivana and told her that he was withdrawing his offer to Ivana.

On April 25, Ivana called Ramon and told him that she was accepting Ramon's offer of April 15. Ramon said that it was too late to accept the offer.

In an action by Ivana against Ramon for breach of contract, judgment for whom? Explain.

3. On May 1, Esther, a retail wine seller, sent a letter to Samuel offering to buy 50 cases of Chateau Le Pew wine at $100 a case. The letter, which was signed by Esther, stated that it was a firm offer for 30 days. Samuel received the offer on May 2.

By May 10, however, the price of wine was dropping and Esther wrote to Samuel saying, "I am sorry but I hereby withdraw the offer." Samuel received this letter on May 12.

On May 15, Samuel called Esther and told her that he accepted Esther's offer of May 1. Esther claimed that the offer had been withdrawn and refused to accept delivery of the wine.

In an action by Samuel against Esther for breach of contract, judgment for whom? Explain.

4. On July 1, Stan, a steel manufacturer, telephoned Byron and offered to sell Byron six carloads of steel at $600 a ton. Byron said, "That's a lot of steel! Would you promise to keep your offer open for 10 days so that I can think about whether I can use that much?" Stan replied, "Sure. I promise to keep the offer open for 10 days."

On July 6, Stan sent a letter to Byron that stated, "I hereby revoke my offer of July 1." Byron received this letter on July 7.

On July 7, Byron called Stan and said that he was accepting Stan's offer of July 1. Stan refused to deliver the steel, claiming that he had validly revoked the offer.

In an action by Byron against Stan for breach of contract, judgment for whom. Explain?

5. Mira offered to sell Peter a parking lot for $75,000. The offer was in writing and signed by Mira and provided that any acceptance by Peter must be within 5 days. On the fourth day, Mira accepted a better offer from Dean and transferred the parking lot to Dean on that day. Unaware of this sale, Peter telephoned Mira on the fifth day and accepted Mira's offer. In an action by Peter against Mira for breach of contract, judgment for whom?

6. Ty, a merchant, wrote to Marcus: "August 1, I offer to sell you one Model A Desktop Computer system, price $1,000. This is a firm offer for 30 days from the above date. (*Signed*) Ty."
(a) On August 10, Marcus received a letter from Ty: "I hereby revoke my offer of August 1."

On August 17, Marcus wrote to Ty: "I hereby accept your offer of August 1."

Is there a contract? Explain.

(b) Assume that Ty's offer stated that it was a firm offer for four months, and that on November 15, Marcus mailed an acceptance. Is there a contract? Explain.

(c) Assume that Ty's offer stated that it was a firm offer for four months, and that on November 14, Marcus received a letter from Ty, dated November 12: "I hereby revoke my offer of August 1." On November 15, Marcus mailed an acceptance. Is there a contract? Explain.

7. On March 1, Irina wrote a signed letter to Benito and offered to sell the piano in her home to Benito for $400, and stated that she would keep her offer open for 4 months. On April 1, Irina sold the piano to Tonya, her cousin, for $500, without informing Benito that she did so. On June 10, Benito wrote Irina stating that he accepted Irina's offer. Irina immediately notified Benito that she could not sell him the piano because she had already sold it to Tonya. Benito sues Irina for breach of contract. Judgment for whom? Explain.

8. On September 15, Preet wrote to Lila as follows: "I offer to sell you my farm, Blackacre, for $300,000, all cash, closing on November 1. Please advise as soon as possible. (Signed) Preet."

On October 1, Lila mailed her acceptance to Preet, unaware that Preet had died on September 30 When Lila learned of Preet's death on October 5, Lila insisted that the Estate of Preet nevertheless deliver the deed to Blackacre in exchange for Lila's certified check for $300,000. Xavier, the Executor of Preet's Estate, refused to do so.

(a) In an action by Lila against the Estate of Preet for breach of contract, judgment for whom? Explain.

(b) If Preet's offer was a valid irrevocable offer for 30 days, would your answer to (a) be different? Explain.

9. On October 1, Tsering received the following letter from Shoshanna: "I understand that you are interested in buying a pick-up truck, I will sell you mine for $10,000 all cash, and will have it ready for delivery to you on November 15. *(Signed)* Shoshanna."

Later that day Tsering telephoned Shoshanna and inquired: "Can I have 20 days to think over your offer?" Shoshanna replied: "O.K., you have an irrevocable option for 20 days. Write to me when you decide."

On October 6, Tsering wrote Shoshanna: "I am still very much interested in your offer. I'm a little short of cash at the moment and would like to know if you would consider taking $5,000 cash and my 30-day note for the other $5,000? (Signed) Tsering." Shoshanna did not reply.

On October 10, without Tsering's knowledge, Shoshanna sold and delivered the truck to Mario for $11,000 cash.

On October 15, Tsering wrote Shoshanna: "I have decided to accept your offer and will pay you $10,000 in cash when I pick up the truck on Nov.15. (Signed) Tsering." Shoshanna wrote back: "The truck is sold." Tsering sued Shoshanna for damages for breach of contract. Judgment for whom? Explain.

10. On May 1, Kodzo, a textile manufacturer, mailed to Bonnie, a merchant, a written and signed offer to sell 1,000 bolts of blue denim at $40 per bolt. Each bolt would contain 25 square yards. The offer stated that "it would remain open for 10 days from the above date (May 1) and that it would not be withdrawn prior to that date."

Two days later, Kodzo, noting a sudden increase in the price of blue denim, changed his mind. After making great personal efforts to contact Bonnie, Kodzo sent Bonnie a letter revoking the offer of May 1. The letter was mailed on May 4 and received by Bonnie on May 5. Bonnie chose to disregard the letter of May 4. Instead, she continued to watch the price of blue denim rise.

On May 9, Bonnie mailed a letter accepting the original offer. The letter was sent by mail and was properly addressed and contained the correct postage. However, it was not received by Kodzo until May 12, due to a delay in the mail. Bonnie demanded delivery of the goods according to the terms of the offer of May 1, but Kodzo has refused, claiming there is no contract

(a) Is there a contract? Explain.

(b) If Kodzo was not a merchant, would there be a contract? Explain.

11. Sara, a wholesale fruit dealer, sent the following letter to Bud, a fruit merchant: "Feb. 1, offer 1,000 boxes of Los Angeles, San Gabriel oranges, at $10.60 per box, F.O.B. Los Angeles: March delivery. Unless I receive your acceptance by 2 P.M. on Feb. 4, I will dispose of them elsewhere. (Signed Sara)." Sara's letter was received by Bud on Feb. 2, at 3 P.M.

At 1 P.M. on Feb. 2, Sara mailed Bud the following letter. "I regret to inform you that I am compelled to withdraw my offer dated Feb. 1." Sara's second letter was not received by Bud until Feb. 3.

Meanwhile at 5 P.M. on Feb. 2, Bud mailed the following letter to Sara: "I accept your offer dated Feb. 1. (Signed Bud)." Because of a severe snowstorm, which disrupted all means of communication, Bud's letter was not delivered to Sara until 4 P.M. on Feb. 4.

(a) Is there a contract between Sara and Bud? Explain.

(b) Assume that the words "Unless I receive your acceptance by 2 P.M. on Feb 4, I will dispose of them elsewhere" were not included in Sara's Feb. 1 letter to Bud. Is there a contract between Sara and Bud? Explain.

12. Mel offered to sell to Sue a ten-acre tract of commercial property for $750,000. Mel's signed letter indicated the offer would expire on March 1 at 3:00 P.M. and that any acceptance must be received in his office by that time.

On February 28, Sue decided to accept the offer and mailed an acceptance at 4:00 P.M. Sue indicated in her letter that in the event the acceptance did not arrive on time, she would assume there was a contract if she did not hear anything from Mel by March 10. The letter arrived on March 2. Mel never responded to Sue's letter.

In an action by Sue against Mel for breach of contract, judgment for whom? Explain.

13. On March 10, Lev sent a signed written offer to Boris to sell 3,000 tons of steel rails on certain specified terms. Boris received this letter on March 11. On March 25, Boris faxed his acceptance, which reached Lev at 3 P.M. on that day. On the same day, March 25, at 2 PM., Lev mailed Boris a revocation of his March 10 offer, which Boris received the following day. Is there a contract? Explain.

14. Seth, a manufacturer, sent to Belkys, a retail merchant, an offer to sell 100 television sets for $30,000, terms C.O.D. Belkys wrote to Seth: "I accept your offer, and will pay you 30 days after delivery. (Signed Belkys)." Seth tendered delivery of the TV sets to Belkys and demanded cash on delivery. Belkys refused to pay on delivery, and Seth withheld delivery. Seth then sued to recover damages for breach of contract.
(a) Judgment for whom? Explain.
(b) Assume that Belkys's letter read as follows: "I accept your offer provided that you agree that payment is due 30 days after delivery." Is there a contract if Seth made no reply? Explain.

Chapter 12 - Consideration, Capacity and Legality

1. The chairman of the board of directors of Xerxes Corp. wrote a signed letter to Pablo, the president, who is 68 years old and planned to retire at the end of the year. "The corporation will pay you a pension of $100,000 a year for life if you retire as planned, and agree not to take another job in this industry." Pablo replied, "I promise to do as you wish." Two years later, Xerxes Corp. stopped the pension payments. Pablo sues Xerxes Corp. for the current installment.
(a) May he recover? Explain.
(b) Instead of the above letter, assume that at Pablo's retirement dinner, the chairman of the board of directors of Xerxes Corp., in his speech, said "In view of the fact that you have been faithful to Xerxes Corp. for 30 years and have resisted efforts of our competitors to hire you away from us, the corporation promises to pay you a pension of $100,000 a year for life." Pablo stood up and said, "I accept your pension promise with gratitude." Is Xerxes Corp.'s promise enforceable by Pablo and if not, what would be necessary to make it enforceable? Explain.

2. Alfalfa, a novice rock climber, decided to go on a very difficult climb. Half way up, he found himself in trouble. Darla, a more experienced climber, at great peril to herself, rescued Alfalfa from almost certain serious injury, if not death. Alfalfa was so grateful for what Darla had done that he promised to send her a check for $1,000. Alfalfa failed to send the check and Darla sues him for breach of contract. Judgment for whom? Explain.

3. Debbie owed Carlos $50,000 on a contract for the purchase of 200 air-conditioners on credit, the terms of payment stating "Payment due 60 days after delivery." Delivery was made on January 2. On March 10, Debbie met Carlos and told him, "I'm sorry I missed out on paying you what I owe you. Collections have been slow. If you give me until May 1, I'll pay you what I owe plus interest at 9%." Carlos said, "O.K. I'll give you until May 1." On March 15, Carlos changed his mind and sued Debbie for $50,000. Debbie contends that the debt is not due until May 1. Is Debbie's contention valid? Explain.

4. Benito borrowed $1,000 from Leslie at 5% interest and gave Leslie a promissory note for $1,050 payable in one year. The year having elapsed, Benito tendered a check for $900 with these words written on the back above the space where Leslie would endorse it: "I (Leslie) hereby accept the face amount of this check in complete satisfaction of the debt owed by Benito." Leslie cashed the check and now seeks to recover the balance from Benito. Is the entire debt discharged? Explain.

5. Aldo shipped 10 refrigerators to Rafael pursuant to a sales contract under which title to the goods and risk of loss would pass to Rafael upon delivery to Fleet Railroad. The agreed price was $5,000. When the refrigerators were delivered to Rafael, he found they were damaged. An estimate for repairing them showed it would cost up to $1,000, and an expert opinion was to the effect that they were defective when shipped. Rafael put in a claim to Aldo, which Aldo rejected. Rafael then wrote to

Aldo, "I don't like to get into a dispute of this nature. I am enclosing my check for $4,000 in full payment of the shipment." Aldo did not reply, but he cashed the check and then sued Rafael for the $1,000 balance. May he recover? Explain.

6. In the previous problem, assume that there was no damage to the refrigerators and no dispute, but that Rafael did not pay. One month after payment was due, Rafael wrote to Aldo, "I'll pay you $4,000 if you will accept it in full payment." Aldo wrote back, "Since I have despaired of getting any more out of you, I'll take the $4,000 in full payment." Rafael paid the $4,000 and later, Aldo sued Rafael for the $1,000 balance. May he recover? Explain.

7. Eva and Maria entered into a written contract pursuant to which Eva was to render decorating services for Maria for a total price of $75,000. After the services had been performed, a good faith dispute arose between Eva and Maria over whether all of the services had been properly performed. Eva claimed that the full amount was due, but Maria argued that only $50,000 worth of services had been performed. After several weeks of argument, Maria sent a check for $60,000 to Eva on which Maria had written "payment in full for decorating services."
  (a) Eva endorsed the check, without making any further notations on it, deposited it and sued Maria for the remaining $15,000 she claims is due. Judgment for whom? Explain.
  (b) Instead of the facts in (a) assume that Eva wrote "under protest" on the check when she endorsed it and, after depositing it, sues Maria for $15,000. What result? Explain.
  (c) Instead of the facts in (a) and (b), assume that Eva and Maria had a telephone conversation in which Eva agreed to take $60,000 in full satisfaction of Maria's obligation under the contract. Maria then sent the check, with a letter referencing the telephone conversation. Eva wrote "under protest" on the check, endorsed and deposited it, and then sued Maria for $15,000. What result? Explain.

8. Digna owed Cecelia $10,000 under a valid loan agreement. Payment was due on September 1. Digna informed Cecelia that she was unable to pay on September 1.
(a) Assume that on September 5, Cecelia orally agreed to accept $8,000 plus the transfer of Digna's stamp collection (which Cecelia admired) as payment in full, if Digna would do so by September 10. Digna did pay the $8,000 and transferred the stamp collection to Cecelia

on September 8. The stamp collection had a market value of $1,000. On September 15, Cecelia sued Digna for the $1,000 balance Cecelia claims is due. How much, if anything, will Cecelia recover from Digna? Explain.
(b) Instead of the assumption in (a), assume that on September 5, Cecelia orally agreed to accept $9,000 in full payment of Digna's debt if Digna paid before September 10. Digna paid Cecelia $9,000 on September 8. On September 15, Cecelia sued Digna for $1,000. How much, if anything, will Cecelia recover from Digna? Explain.
(c) Would your answer to (b) be different if Cecelia agreed in a signed writing to accept $9,000 in full payment of Digna's debt? Explain.

9. Camila, a building contractor, entered into a written agreement with Owen, the owner of 27 Y Street, to build a new wing on Owen's house for $90,000. After the work was one-half done, Camila complained about the rising cost of materials and stopped work. Owen said to Camila: "If you go ahead and finish the job, I'll pay you a bonus of $10,000." Camila agreed and finished the job. Camila then demanded payment of $100,000, but Owen refused to pay more than $90,000.
(a) How much may Camila collect from Owen? Explain.
(b) Assume that Camila wrote on the bottom of the written contract, "The agreed price for the above work is $100,000" and said to Owen: "I'll go ahead if you sign that," which Owen did. How much may Camila collect from Owen? Explain.

10. Armand was hired to work as the chef for the restaurant at Scallop's seaside resort for 3 months during the summer, under a written contract that provided that Armand would receive compensation of $50,000. During the first month, the guests were wildly enthusiastic about the quality of the food and Scallop's reservations for the resort and restaurant doubled. Noticing this, Armand felt he was entitled to share in Scallop's increased profits. During a conversation, Scallop promised to pay Armand a $20,000 bonus at the end of the summer if he continued to work under his contract. At the end of the three months, Scallop paid Armand $50,000 and refused to pay the $20,000 bonus he had promised. Armand sued Scallop for breach of contract. Judgment for whom? Explain.

11. In May, Mike, a 17-year-old college student, was introduced to Dover, the operator of a summer camp, through Excel Employment Agency. Mike and Dover entered into a written agreement whereby Dover hired Mike as a camp counselor during the summer vacation period at a salary of $2,000 per month. Mike also agreed in writing to pay Excel Employment Agency a certain commission for their services. In June, Mike discovered that he had failed one of his final exams, and decided that, instead of working, he would attend college during the summer session. Mike disaffirmed both contracts.

(a) What rights, if any, do Dover and Excel Employment Agency have against Mike? Explain.

(b) Would your answer to (a) be the same if, when he entered into the contracts, Mike had fraudulently misrepresented his age as 18? Explain.

12. The father of a 17-year-old daughter, Alicia, sent his daughter away to college, and paid Alicia's expenses for board, clothing and tuition.

(a) Assume that Alicia decided to occupy her spare time, and accordingly contracted to take a two-year correspondence course in computer repair with Careers Correspondence School. After Alicia became 18, she continued to receive the course materials for 6 months, did the correspondence lessons, used the books sent to her, and made six monthly payments. Then she notified Careers Correspondence School that she disaffirmed any further obligation under the contract. In an action by Careers Correspondence School against Alicia to recover the balance due under the contract, judgment for whom? Explain.

(b) Assume that while Alicia was 17, her father suffered financial reverses and Alicia and her father agreed that thereafter Alicia was on her own. In order to return to college, Alicia borrowed $25,000 from the college's Student Aid Fund to cover her expenses for the next year. The loan was payable at the end of 3 years. When Alicia became 18, she immediately notified the college that she disaffirmed the loan agreement. May the college enforce the loan agreement against Alicia? Explain.

13. On his 17th birthday, Alex received a deed to Blackacre, a tract of farmland, as a gift from his uncle. Alex cut down a number of trees suitable for making railroad ties. Alex sold Blackacre to Bertha for $100,000 and the felled timber to Carmen for $3,000. He spent the money and, immediately after his 18th birthday, notified Bertha and Carmen that he disaffirmed the respective contracts. In the meantime, however, Bertha had sold Blackacre to Marvin and Carmen had sold the timber to Ned. Is Alex entitled to recover:

(a) Blackacre from Marvin? Explain.

(b) the timber from Ned? Explain.

14. Bob, who was 17 years old, bought a used sports car for $12,000 from Ace Motors on the installment plan. He had already paid $3,000 on the car when he disaffirmed the contract on his 18th birthday. He offered to return the car and demanded the return of the $3,000 he had paid. The car is now worth only $8,000. What are the rights of the parties? Explain.

15. Ad and Bookem, an accounting firm operating nationally over a long period of years, with branch offices in all major cities and coverage of all major industrial areas in the United States, acquired the entire practice and goodwill of Sub and Div. another accounting firm operating nationally, with branch offices in all major cities. The price was to be paid in ten annual installments. The agreement contained a provision that provided that the five major partners of Sub and Div, both individually and as members of the accounting firm, were not to engage in practice anywhere in the United States for three years.

(a) Is the provision enforceable? Explain.

(b) Assuming the provision is enforceable, what remedies does Ad and Bookem have against any of the partners who breach the contract provision? Explain.

16. On February 1, Brad purchased the assets of Smalls, a small management-consulting firm based in Manhattan. Under their written agreement, Brad agreed to pay $80,000 a year for five years. The agreement required Smalls to transfer all of his assets and goodwill to Brad. Further, the agreement required Smalls not to compete with Brad for a period of five years within Manhattan, where the majority of Small's clients were located. Other clients of Smalls were located throughout New York State. Three months later, on May 1, Brad learned that Smalls had opened a management consulting firm three blocks from where Smalls' office had been located on February 1. What rights, if any, does Brad have against Smalls?

17. Dr. Livingston was the only oral dental surgeon in the village of Briarcliff Manor, New York, which has a population of 10,000. The nearest oral dental surgeon to Briarcliff Manor was 15 miles away. Dr. Livingston, who intended to retire that year, learned that Dr. Stanley, a recently licensed oral dental surgeon, intended to open her dental office in Briarcliff Manor within the next two months. Dr. Livingston persuaded Dr. Stanley to execute a contract with Dr. Livingston, which provided that Dr.

Livingston would pay Dr. Stanley $50,000 if she would not open her dental office in Briarcliff Manor during the next six months. Seven months later, Dr. Livingston retired and Dr. Stanley immediately thereafter opened her dental office in Briarcliff Manor When Dr. Livingston refused to pay Dr. Stanley $50,000, she sued him for breach of contract. Judgment for whom? Explain.

18. OmniHealth, a national biotechnology firm, executed a three-year written employment contract with Edgar, who was to be in charge of the research and development division responsible for developing new drugs, at an annual salary of $350,000. At that time, OmniHealth was working on several different highly experimental drugs, trying to bring them to market. OmniHealth was anxious to protect its trade secrets and Edgar agreed in his employment contract that he would not work for any of OmniHealth's competitors anywhere in the United States for a period of one year after his employment terminated. At the end of the second year of Edgar's employment, Edgar resigned and promptly went to work for Technology, Inc. Technology, Inc. had known of Edgar's contract with OmniHealth, but persuaded Edgar to breach that contract and to become an employee of Technology, Inc.
(a) What rights, if any, does OmniHealth have against Edgar? Explain.
(b) What rights, if any, does OmniHealth have against Technology, Inc.? Explain.

For problems 19 to 21, assume that the legal rate of interest in New York is 16%.

19. For each of the following transactions, explain whether the transaction is usurious and how much, if anything, the lender may recover.
(a) Jack lends Bobby $1,000 and Bobby signs a promissory note for $1,160, payable in one year.
(b) Jack lends Bobby $1,000 and Bobby signs a promissory note for $1,160, payable in three months.
(c) Barry agrees to sell Lisa his valuable oil painting for $50,000 and to buy it back from her in three months for $75,000.

20. Devin had been down on his luck for years. Unable to pay his bills, Devin approached his best friend Craig for a loan. On January 1, 2009, Craig and Devin agreed in a signed writing that Craig would lend Devin $10,000. The terms of the loan agreement called for Devin to repay the loan, along with $3,250 in interest, on January 1, 2010.
On December 31, 2009, Devin called Craig and advised that he would not repay the above loan.
(a) In an action by Craig against Devin for money damages, judgment for whom?
(b) In an action by Craig against Devin for equitable relief, judgment for whom?

21. Caleb and Dexter entered into a loan agreement on February 1. The agreement called for Caleb to lend Dexter $5,000, and in return Dexter was to pay off the loan in monthly installments of $900 for a period of six (6) months. In addition, the agreement also called for Dexter to pay Caleb a monthly $3.00 service fee on the loan. In fact, this fee did not relate to any services performed by Caleb either in connection with the loan, or in connection with the processing of Dexter's loan repayment checks.
After making the first two monthly installment payments, Dexter made no further payments to Caleb.
In an action by Caleb against Dexter, judgment for whom?

Chapter 13 - Defenses to Contract Enforceability

1. Smith owned five acres of land in Wilton, New York, on which were two springs of mineral water and machinery to bottle the mineral water. Smith sold the real property to Brown for $300,000, representing that the water was natural mineral water and could be bottled or sold as it flowed from the ground. Smith also represented to Brown that the daily natural flow of water from the two springs was 4,200 gallons. Brown entered into possession and purchased and installed modern machinery for the bottling and distribution of the mineral water. He soon discovered that the water was not natural mineral water, but fresh water to which certain chemicals had been added. He also discovered that the daily flow did not exceed 160 gallons. By the time he discovered these facts, Brown had expended $75,000 for the installation of new machinery.
(a) Did Smith commit fraud? Explain.
(b) What remedy or remedies, if any, are available to Brown? Explain.

2. On April 1, Santos, a dealer in mining stocks, sold to Burns, 10,000 shares of Alaska Uranium, Inc., at $5 per share, knowingly misrepresenting that Alaska Uranium, Inc. had proven uranium deposits in its Alaska properties. Burns paid Santos for the stock on April 1.

On April 15, on the advice of friends, Burns had the corporation investigated and found that it had never had any prospects of uranium, but that it had just discovered a copper vein on its property and was putting it into production. During the following February, Burns received and deposited a $100 check from Alaska Uranium, Inc. for its one cent per share dividend. One month later, Burns regretted his purchase.

(a) In an action by Burns against Santos to disaffirm the contract on the grounds of fraud, judgment for whom? Explain.

(b) In an action by Burns against Santos to recover damages based on fraud, judgment for whom? Explain.

(c) In an action by Burns against Alaska Uranium, Inc. to recover damages based on fraud, judgment for whom? Explain.

3. On February 13, Mario purchased an engagement ring from John, a jeweler, for $5,000, relying upon John's representation that the ring was set with a genuine diamond. The next morning, Mario had the ring appraised by a gemologist and learned to his amazement that the center stone was not a genuine diamond, but rather a zircon, a cheap imitation that looked like a diamond but was worth only $50, and that the entire value of the ring was $200. Nevertheless, the next day, Mario gave the engagement ring to Gina, his fiancée, on Valentine's Day, as he had promised. One month later, Gina terminated her engagement to Mario and returned the ring to him. The following day, Mario decided to rescind his contract with John and to sue John for damages.

(a) Does Mario have the right to rescind his contract with John? Explain.

(b) Does Mario have the right to recover damages, from John and if so, how would the damages be computed? Explain.

4. Max Corporation, a well-known television manufacturer, had several odd lots of discontinued models, which it desired to clear out. Max, the president, invited Dharun, the owner of Dharun Discount Chain, to come in and examine the different models and make Max an offer for the entire lot. The sets were segregated from the regular inventory. Fifteen televisions that were not discontinued models were accidentally included in this segregated group by one of Max's employees. Dharun was unaware that Max did not intend to include the fifteen televisions in the group. Dharun made Max an offer of $10,000 for the entire lot. Unaware of his employee's error, Max accepted the offer. Max would not have accepted Dharun's offer if Max had known the fifteen current models had been included. Upon learning of the error, Max Corporation refused to perform and alleged mistake as a defense. Dharun Discount Chain sued Max Corporation for breach of contract. Judgment for whom? Explain.

5. Cynthia was bequeathed an oil painting by her childless aunt. Cynthia was not favorably disposed toward the painting because it reminded her that her aunt had left her entire estate (except the painting) to the Society for the Prevention of Cruelty to Animals. When Cynthia's best friend, Beatrice, admired the painting, Cynthia offered to sell it to her for $10. Beatrice accepted, paid the $10 and took the painting. The painting was clearly an original and bore the signature, "Ad Schreyer," but neither Cynthia nor Beatrice had ever heard of the painter.

Several weeks later, Beatrice informed Cynthia that she had inquired about the artist and had learned that the painting was worth $15,000. On hearing this, Cynthia tendered $10 to Beatrice and demanded the return of the painting. Beatrice refused and Cynthia brought suit against Beatrice to recover the painting.

(a) Judgment for whom? Explain.

(b) Would your answer to (a) be the same if Beatrice had known, at the time she bought the painting, that Ad Schreyer was a famous artist and that the painting was far more valuable than Cynthia realized? Explain.

(c) Would your answer to (a) be the same if Beatrice had told Cynthia that Ad Schreyer was an amateur painter when Beatrice knew that Shreyer was a famous painter? Explain

6. Jorge is the owner of a 20-story office building undergoing renovation. A flooring contractor, Mikhail, came to the building to measure the job in preparation for making an offer. Mikhail mistakenly failed to include one of the floors, and his offer was thus 5% lower than it otherwise would have been. Jorge, who did not know of Mikhail's error, accepted Mikhail's offer. When Mikhail's workers came to start the job, they noticed the error. Mikhail now wants to avoid the contract. Will he be successful? Explain.

7. Aldo, an adult college student, went to Brentwood Department store to buy clothes. He selected two new suits and a coat for $950 and asked to open up a charge account. The credit manager was willing to open account but was concerned about payment. Aldo told the credit manager to call Franco, his father. On the telephone, Franco told the credit manager. "Go ahead, open the account for him. It will teach him to stand on his own feet if he has to pay his own bills. But don't worry, if Aldo doesn't pay you, I will." The clothes were given to Aldo and billed to Aldo. Aldo failed to pay. The store sues Franco who pleads the Statute of Frauds as a defense. Judgment for whom? Explain.

8. Assume in the previous question that the credit manager refused to open the account for Aldo, that he called Franco on the telephone, and Franco said. "I have an account with your store, give Aldo the clothes and charge them to my account. "The clothes were given to Aldo. Is Franco liable for payment if he pleads the Statute of Frauds as a defense? Explain.

9. Bo was the owner of Lot No. 1 on which he had built his home. Sadia owned the adjoining Lots No. 2 and 3, which were undeveloped, along with Lot No. 4 on which Sadia's home was located. Bo wished to acquire Lot No. 2 in order to protect his home site from crowding if Lot No. 2 should be sold to a stranger.

Meeting Sadia on the street on January 2, Bo explained his wish to acquire Lot No. 2 and offered to buy it from Sadia for $75,000 cash. Sadia agreed and promised to deliver a deed to Lot No. 2 in 4 weeks. Bo paid Sadia $1,000 as a deposit or down payment towards the purchase price of $75.000.

On February 1, Sadia told Bo that she had changed her mind. Bo demands that Sadia perform the contract. Sadia contends that if there is any contract, it is unenforceable.

(a) Was there an offer and acceptance sufficient to constitute a contract between Sadia and Bo? Explain.

(b) In an action by Bo against Sadia for breach of contract, judgment for whom? Explain.

(c) Assume that on January 10, Bo sent to Sadia his check for $1,000 bearing the notation "On account of purchase price of Lot No. 2" and that Sadia cashed the check, but later refused to convey Lot No. 2. Would Bo's payment constitute sufficient part performance to enable Bo to enforce the contract against Sadia? Explain.

(d) If the contract is not enforceable, may Bo recover his $1,000? Explain.

(e) Assume that in addition to the payment, Bo, with Sadia's knowledge and consent, entered on Lot No. 2 and had it cleared of brush on January 20 at a cost of $150,

but Sadia still refused to convey. Would Bo be entitled to obtain a decree of specific performance to compel Sadia to deliver a deed to Lot No. 2 to Bo upon paying to Sadia the balance of $74,000? Explain.

(f) Would Bo be entitled to recover his $1,000 payment plus the $150 cost of clearing the land? Explain.

(g) Assume that on March 1. Bo instituted a suit for specific performance and that Sadia denied she had agreed to sell. At the trial, the court decided that Bo was telling the truth and ordered Sadia to execute and deliver to Bo a deed to Lot. No. 2 upon Bo paying the balance of $74,000. Is Sadia entitled to have the decision reversed on appeal, if on the appeal Sadia raises for the first time the defense that her agreement was not in a writing signed by the party to be charged? Explain.

10. Assume that in the preceding problem Sadia had sent to Bo a receipt for the $1,000 reading as follows: "January 11. Received from Bo $1,000 on account of $75,000 purchase price of Lot No. 2 at 27 Y Street. Albans, NY Closing in 4 weeks. (Signed) Sadia."
(a) Would Bo be entitled to a decree of specific performance against Sadia? Explain.
(b) Assume that Sadia is willing to perform, but that Bo refuses. Would Sadia be entitled to damages against Bo? Explain.

11. On September 15, Lubov agreed orally with Tim to lease a store to Tim in Manhattan at $5,000 per month for one year starting the following January 1.
(a) Is the oral agreement enforceable? Explain.

Assume that the oral lease was for three years, that Tim moved in on January 1, and paid the monthly rent for six months, and that Lubov then notified Tim to vacate.
(b) Is the oral agreement enforceable by Tim for the balance of the three-year term? Explain.
(c) Is the oral agreement enforceable by Tim for an additional six months? Explain.

12. On December 15, Lisa, a landlord, entered into an oral agreement with Tom to lease apartment 5W to Tom for one year starting on January 1, at a rental of $2,000 per month. On the same day Lisa hired Jarvis as superintendent of the building for a period of one year starting January 1 at a salary of $5,000 per month. On December 20, Lisa changed her mind and notified Tom and Jarvis that she would not rent to Tom or employ Jarvis.

(a) In an action by Tom against Lisa, judgment for whom if Lisa pleads the Statute of Frauds as a defense? Explain.

(b) In an action by Jarvis against Lisa judgment for whom if Lisa pleads the Statute of Frauds as a defense? Explain.

13. (a) On December 5, Alvin entered into an oral agreement with Courtney to perform certain advisory services for Courtney for a fee of $15,000 per month. The services were to commence on the following February 15, and to end on December 15. Is the agreement enforceable? Explain.

(b) Also on December 5, Alvin entered into an oral agreement with Francine for Francine to do some remodeling and rewiring of Alvin's offices. The agreement provided that Francine was to be paid $20,000 and was to complete all work no later than December 15 of the following year. Is the agreement enforceable? Explain.

14. Bonnie, wishing to start her own business, borrowed $15,000 from Laura. Bonnie orally agreed to repay the loan in two years. Bonnie refused to pay when the loan became due. Laura sued Bonnie for breach of contract. Bonnie asserts the oral contract is unenforceable according to the Statue of Frauds. Judgment for whom? Explain.

15. Sven and Brent entered into an oral agreement under which Sven agreed to sell to Brent 8 used air-conditioners at $200 each, delivery at Brent's place of business ten days later; payment C.O.D. Brent refused to complete the purchase. Assume that Brent pleads the Statute of Frauds.

(a) If Sven sues Brent for breach of contract, judgment for whom? Explain.

(b) Would Sven be entitled to judgment if Sven can prove that Brent made a down payment of $200? Explain.

(c) Would Sven be entitled to judgment if Sven can prove that Brent took 4 air-conditioners at the time the agreement was made? Explain.

16. During the examination of the financial statements of the Wilbur Watch Company, the following problem was discovered. On January 16, Corey, one of Wilbur's salesmen, called upon Percy, the vice president of purchasing for Xenon Department Stores. He showed Percy the new line of plastic watches with large, bright-colored faces. Percy ordered 150 watches from $5 to $20 each at a total cost of $1,475. Delivery was to be made not later than March 15. Corey wrote the orders in his order book as Percy orally indicated the quantity of each watch he desired. Neither party signed anything.

Corey promptly submitted the Xenon Department Stores' order to the sales department of Wilbur Watch Company. The next day the order was recorded and a memorandum was sent to Xenon Department Stores, in care of Percy. The memorandum described the transaction, indicated the number and prices of the watches purchased and was signed by S.A. Williams, vice president of marketing. However, the total price and delivery terms were erroneously omitted.

Percy received the memo on January 20. He read it and placed it in his goods-on-order file.

On February 20, the market for plastic watches collapsed. Percy promptly notified Wilbur Watch Company by phone that Xenon Department Stores was not interested in the plastic watches and would refuse delivery. Wilbur Watch Company Store sued Xenon Department Stores to recover damages for breach of contract. Xenon Department Stores contends (1) there is no contract and (2) if there was a contract it is unenforceable under the Statute of Frauds Will Wilbur Watch Company prevail in its action against Xenon Department Stores? Explain.

17. On May 1, Study and Burrow, two college professors, entered into an oral contract under which Study agreed to sell his computer to Burrow for $1,300, with delivery and payment on May 15. On May 2, Study sent Burrow a signed letter confirming all the terms of their oral contract. Burrow received Study's letter on May 3 but never responded. On May 15, Study tendered delivery of the computer to Burrow, but Burrow refused to accept or pay for it, stating that he had changed his mind and did not need Study's computer. Study sues Burrow for breach of contract. Burrow pleads the Statute of Frauds as a defense.

(a) Judgment for whom? Explain.

(b) If Study and Burrow were merchants who sold computers, judgment for whom? Explain.

Chapter 14 - Third Party Rights and Discharge

1. Salvador, who owned a retail shoe store, decided to sell the business. The assets of the business consisted of a one story building worth $100,000, merchandise worth $50,000, accounts receivable of $10,000, fixtures worth $30,000 and goodwill estimated at $50,000. He owed various wholesalers a total of $20,000 for shoes bought by him on credit.

Salvador offered to sell all of these assets to Byron for $220,000 cash, provided that Byron would also agree to assume payment of the $20,000 owed for merchandise. Byron agreed, and a written contract was executed by both parties. Upon payment of $220,000 by Byron, Salvador signed a deed and bill of sale for all the assets listed.

Charles, who is one of the wholesalers to whom Salvador owed $5,000, demanded that Salvador pay the $5,000 owed. Salvador informed him that Byron was to pay. Charles sued Salvador and Byron for payment.

(a) Byron defended on the ground that he had made no contract with Charles. Is the defense valid? Explain.

(b) Salvador defended on the ground that Byron had agreed to pay. Is the defense valid? Explain.

Assume that the court entered judgment against Salvador and Byron for $5,000 as a joint liability.

(c) If Salvador paid $2,500 and Byron paid $2,500, has either any claim against the other? Explain.

(d) Would your answer to (a) be the same if Byron had paid $240,000 for the assets but had not agreed to pay the $20,000 owed to Salvador's creditors. Explain.

2. In the previous question, assume that Salvador wished to make a present to his wife, Wilma, of one half of the sales value of the business, and that Byron agreed to pay for the business in two installments. Accordingly, the contract between Salvador and Byron provided that Byron would "pay $110,000 to Salvador upon taking over the store, and $110,000 to Wilma two years later." Wilma was not one of the parties to the contract. Two years have elapsed and Byron has not paid Wilma.

(a) Does Wilma have a cause of action against Byron for the $110,000 promised to her? Explain.

(b) Would the one year Statute of Frauds be a defense to Byron if the agreement between Salvador and Byron were oral? Explain.

3. In question 1, assume that Salvador, on closing the contract with Byron, signed a document reading as follows: "May 1. For value received, I hereby transfer to Byron all of my right, title and interest in and to the following accounts receivable owed to me: (1) From Darren, $5,000 due June 1; (2) From Ellen, $2,000 presently due, and (3) From Fatima, $3,000 due July 1."

(a) If Darren paid Salvador $5,000 on June 3, without knowledge of the assignment, what are Byron's rights against Darren and Salvador?

(b) If Byron immediately notified Ellen of the assignment, and then Ellen paid Salvador the $2,000, what are Byron's rights against Ellen and Salvador? Explain.

(c) If Byron notified Ellen of the assignment, but Ellen did not pay because she was insolvent, what are Byron's rights against Salvador?

(d) Assume that Byron notified Fatima of the assignment on June 15 and Fatima failed to pay on the due date. Byron then sued Fatima for $3,000, and Fatima interposed as a defense the fact that the goods sold to her by Salvador (the transaction from which her debt to Salvador arose) were defective, and worth only $1,000. What are Byron's rights against Fatima and Salvador?

(e) Assume that in (d), Fatima instead interposed as a defense the fact that she had paid the $3,000 on June 10 to Xavier, to whom Salvador had assigned the same debt on June 1. What are Byron's rights against Fatima, Xavier and Salvador? Explain

(f) In (c) and (d) above, what steps could Byron have taken to ensure the collectability of the debts. Explain.

4. Tom sold goods to Gerard on 30 days credit for $10,000. The next day, Tom assigned this account receivable to Lou, who promptly notified Gerard in writing of the assignment. One week after receiving notice of the assignment from Lou, Gerard discovered that $2,000 of Tom's goods were defective and were worth only $500. Gerard promptly reported this information to Tom and Lou. Tom acknowledged that the defective goods were his fault but said that he could do nothing about it because he had already assigned the account receivable to Lou. Lou informed Gerard that he should pursue his claim with Tom, but should pay Lou the $10,000 due.

(a) What rights, if any, does Lou have against Gerard to recover the $10,000? Explain.

(b) Assume Lou agrees to accept $8,500 from Gerard, after deducting $1,500 for defective goods. What rights, if any, does Lou have against Tom? Explain.

5. Ed owned a company that cleaned swimming pools. He charged his customers $100 per month and billed them every two months. At the beginning of September, Ed had not yet collected for the months of July and August from his customer, Suzy, whose pool he had cleaned during that period.

On September 5, Ed spoke with Larry who was selling a used mountain bike. Larry said that he would sell the bike to Ed for $250. Ed accepted this offer, gave Larry $50 and a signed writing assigning to Larry the debt owed by Suzy.

The next day, Larry attempted to collect the $200 from Suzy. She refused to pay, telling Larry that she was not prepared to pay anything because Ed had been adding the wrong chemicals to the water, causing her to suffer a severe skin rash. She only discovered the cause, she said, after seeing a doctor in mid-August. Larry sues both Suzy and Ed for $200.

(a) How much if anything, may Larry recover from Suzy?

(b) How much, if anything, may Larry recover from Ed?

6. Abbott enters into a written signed contract with Costello to sell Costello 3,000 reels of comedy films for $60,000. Without the knowledge or consent of Costello, Abbott assigns his right to receive Costello's payment to Edgar, a creditor of Abbott.

Edgar gives notice of the assignment to Costello and demands payment of $60,000. Costello, however, contends that he has no obligation to pay Edgar because: (1) Costello never consented to the assignment and (2) in any event, 2,000 of the film reels are totally defective and, therefore, Costello only owes $20,000.

Assume that Costello's claim of defective reels is proven and that Edgar did not know of the defects at the time the assignment was made. What rights, if any, does Edgar have:

(a) against Costello? Explain.

(b) against Abbott? Explain.

7. On January 10, Simpson sold her business to Bart for $250,000 under an executed contract that provided that Bart would pay Simpson's indebtedness to Homer, which was due on February 10.

On February 10, Simpson refused Homer's demand for payment, explaining that Bart has agreed to pay Homer and that Homer should look to Bart for payment.

The next day, Homer demanded payment from Bart, who refused to pay upon the grounds that: (1) Bart had no contract with Homer requiring Bart to pay Homer

and (2) Homer cannot enforce the contract between Simpson and Bart because Homer gave no consideration.

(a) In an action by Homer against Bart, judgment for whom? Explain.

(b) In an action by Homer against Simpson, judgment for whom? Explain.

8. By contract dated May 1, Rob agreed to sell to Nancy, and Nancy agreed to buy from Rob, a certain house located at 10 Melbourne Road. At the time she signed the contract, Nancy transferred to Rob a deposit equal to 10% of the purchase price. The contract stated that closing and transfer of the property would occur on or before July 15. Nancy's finances were such that she needed to obtain a loan to pay the full purchase price for the house. Pursuant to the terms of the contract, Nancy was to obtain financing for the house in an amount of $180,000. The contract stated that Nancy was to apply for such financing in good faith within 7 days of the signing of the contract. It further stated that if Nancy could not obtain $180,000 in financing from a bank, savings bank, or savings and loan association, then Nancy could cancel the contract and recover her deposit.

(a) On May 5, Nancy applied for the $180,000 loan in good faith, but on July 1, the bank notified her that she would only be allowed a loan of $50,000. Rob demands that Nancy close on the purchase and sale of the house on July 15 and Nancy sues Rob for return of her deposit. Judgment for whom? Explain.

(b) Assume instead that Nancy waits until July 1 to apply for a bank loan, and when she applies, she does not give complete or accurate information to the bank about her income or assets. On July 10, the bank denies Nancy's application for a loan. On July 15, Rob demands that Nancy close on the purchase and sale of the house and she demands return of her deposit. Rob sues Nancy for breach of contract. Judgment for whom?

9. Dacor, a famous interior decorator and music lover, ordered a custom made, state of the art, big screen entertainment center from High Tech Manufacturing. Dacor maintained a lavish apartment that he used as a showcase to impress his wealthy clientele. In making the contract, Dacor insisted that the center meet his personal approval, and the contract guaranteed personal satisfaction. Skilled craftsman worked for months on the center and even competitors of High Tech considered it one of the finest products ever produced. Dacor, however, was not satisfied. He did not like the finish and he did not find the picture and sound quality to be as outstanding as he wished. He therefore refused to accept the entertainment center unless it was refinished and substantial improvements were made in the picture and sound quality. High Tech, stating that the entertainment center was the best that could be made, refused to make the changes and sued Dacor for breach of contract. Judgment for whom? Explain.

10. Saul, a cotton merchant, had 50 bales of cotton in his warehouse. Brown, a prospective buyer, inspected the bales in the warehouse, and entered into a signed written contract with Saul to buy the bales at a price of $1,000 per bale. Delivery was to be made by Saul to Brown's factory in two weeks. Two days before the delivery date, Saul's warehouse and the cotton were destroyed by fire caused by lightning. Brown demanded that Saul deliver another 50 bales of similar grade cotton. Upon Saul's refusal, Brown sued Saul for breach of contract. Judgment for whom? Explain.

11. On May 1, Peters, a concert producer, executed two contracts. The first contract was with Selena, a world renowned singer, which provided that Selena was to perform a concert at Thomas's theater in Manhattan on July 4 for a fee of $200.000. The second contract was with Thomas, the owner of a theater in Manhattan, under which Peters rented Thomas's theater in Manhattan for the July 4 concert for a rental fee of $20,000. Peters sold out in advance all of the tickets for the concert and would have made a net profit on the concert of $100,000, after deducting the rental cost of the theater, Selena's fee and $20,000 for advertising expenses.

On July 2, Thomas' theater burned down due to lightning. Peters immediately notified Selena, canceled the July 4 concert and refunded the full purchase price of the tickets to those who had bought tickets. Selena insisted upon payment of her fee because she was ready, willing and able to perform and the fire was not her fault.
(a) In an action by Selena against Peters to recover her fee, judgment for whom? Explain.
(b) In an action by Peters against Thomas to recover Peters actual expenses or $20,000 for advertising the concert and his lost profits of $100,000, judgment for whom? Explain.
(c) How could the parties protect themselves from financial loss in this situation? Explain.

12. Nissan Corp., wishing to dispose of its surplus warehouse, offered it for sale for $500,000 cash. Belle informed Nissan that she would pay the price asked. A contract of sale was executed by the parties and Belle paid 10% of the price as a down payment to Nissan. The closing was set for 4 weeks later, at which time Belle was to pay the balance by certified check and Nissan was to deliver the deed. The contract provided that Nissan Corp. would retain the down payment as liquidated damages if Belle defaulted. When the time for the closing arrived, Belle told Nissan Corp that her arrangements to borrow the balance of the purchase price had not been completed and she requested an additional two weeks to complete the arrangements, Nissan Corp. refused and stated that it was cancelling the contract and retaining the down payment.
(a) Did Belle's failure to pay on time constitute a material breach of the contract? Explain.
(b) If Belle raises the money in two weeks, is she entitled to a decree of specific performance of the contract against Nissan Corp.? Explain.

Assume that Nissan Corp. granted Belle an additional 6 weeks to raise the money, but notified her that it would grant no further extensions. At the end of 6 weeks, Belle had still been unable to raise the money, and Nissan Corp. notified her that it was cancelling the contract. A month later, Nissan Corp. sold the warehouse to Chin for $550,000.
(c) Is Belle now entitled to recover her $50,000 down payment? Explain.

Assume that when Belle originally negotiated for the purchase, Nissan Corp. had little confidence in Belle's ability to raise the money. Accordingly, the parties agreed to a clause in the contract stating, "Time is of the essence in this contract." At the closing Nissan Corp was unable to tender clear title to Belle because the day before the State Tax Department had notified Nissan that an unpaid franchise tax constituted a lien on the warehouse. Nissan Corp. requested a delay of 3 days to pay the tax and satisfy the lien. Belle, who had reconsidered her bargain, refused any extension, tendered her certified check for the balance, and demanded that Nissan deliver clear title. When Nissan Corp. was unable to comply, Belle said she was cancelling the contract.

(d) Is Belle entitled to the return of her down payment? Explain.
(e) Is Nissan Corp. liable in damages to Belle for Belle's cost of conducting a title search? Explain.

13. Camille, a builder, contracted to build a house for Alan, in accordance with the specifications prepared by Alan's architect, for a total price of $350,000, payable in stages as the work progressed. The final payment of $20,000 was to be made when Camille obtained a completion certificate from Alan's architect certifying that the work had been done according to the detailed specifications. Camille, as was customary in the industry, subcontracted out various parts of the work to sub-contractors who were specialists in excavation, brickwork, electricity, flooring and other trades. When the house was finished, Alan's architect refused to issue a certificate of completion because the flooring was done in maple, instead of oak, as was required by the specifications. The difference in value because of the variation was $3,000. It turned out that Dan, the flooring subcontractor, had deliberately used the maple flooring to reduce the cost of

his contract with Camille and, therefore, to make a larger profit. Camille did not know of or consent to the substitution. Alan refused to make the final payment of $20,000. Camille, who had already paid Dan, refused to replace the floors with oak wood. Camille now sues Alan for $20,000.

(a) Has Camille committed a material breach of the contract? Explain.

(b) Are Alan's damages measured by the cost of removing the maple floors and replacing them with oak floors? Explain.

(c) Is Camille entitled to be paid $20,000 less the damages incurred by Alan? Explain.

(d) Does Camille have a claim for damages against Dan? If so, for how much? Explain.

Chapter 15 - Breach and Remedies

1. On April 1, Conrad and Owen executed a contract under which Conrad agreed to build a specified house on Owen's land for $700,000. The contract provided that Owen was to make periodic payments to Conrad as different phases of construction were completed, with the last payment of $70,000 due 5 days after completion of the house. The contract further provided that the house was to be completed by August 1 and included the following provision: "If Conrad is late in completing the construction of the house, the purchase price is to be reduced by $3,000 for each and every day after August 1." Conrad constructed the house according to the contract, except that it was completed 5 days after August 1. Owen made all scheduled payments except for the final payment of $70,000. Although Owen could not prove any monetary damages caused by Conrad's delay, Owen offered to make a final payment of $55,000 to Conrad, after deducting $15,000 for the 5 day delay. Conrad rejected Owen's offer and sued Owen for $70,000. How much, if anything, will Conrad recover from Owen? Explain.

2. Millie, a famous singer, entered into a contract to perform at Tanya's night club during the month of December. Tanya advertised that Millie would be performing at Tanya's nightclub and obtained many advance reservations from customers for the performance.

In November, Raisa, the owner of another nightclub, convinced Millie to breach her contract with Tanya and to perform at Raisa's nightclub instead during the month of December. On November 15, Millie told Tanya that she would not be available to perform at Tanya's nightclub as planned. When Tanya found out that Millie would be performing at Raisa's nightclub instead, Tanya became furious and immediately called her lawyer.

(a) Tanya sues Millie, demanding specific performance of the contract. Discuss.

(b) Tanya seeks an injunction against Millie, to stop her from performing at Raisa's nightclub during December. Discuss.

(c) Tanya sues Millie for breach of contract and demands damages. What damages, if any, may Tanya recover?

(d) Does Tanya have any action for damages against Raisa? Discuss.

1. Tom, Dick and Jane are employed by Atlantic Motors, a large chain of used car lots with several hundred employees. None of them was hired for a definite period of time and each has an excellent record of sales. On April 15, all of them were fired.

(a)   Tom, who is 50, was told by his manager that he was being fired so that the company could "make room for some young faces on the sales force."

(b)   Dick, who is 49, was fired because, on April 15, he had become frustrated with a prospective customer who was arguing about prices and had punched the customer in the nose.

(c)   Jane was fired because she repeatedly refused invitations from Al, the sole owner of Atlantic, to spend weekends with him at his beach house. Al had warned Jane that she would be fired if she continued to reject his advances.

Discuss, separately, whether Tom, Dick or Jane has any claim against Atlantic Motors.